Physics-Based Animation

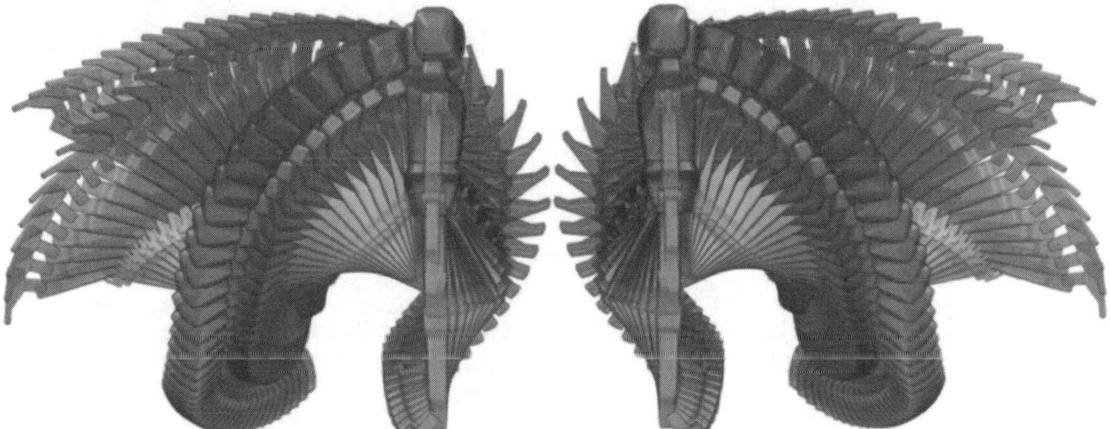

LIMITED WARRANTY AND DISCLAIMER OF LIABILITY

CHARLES RIVER MEDIA, INC. ("CRM") AND/OR ANYONE WHO HAS BEEN INVOLVED IN THE WRITING, CREATION OR PRODUCTION OF THE ACCOMPANYING CODE IN THE TEXTUAL MATERIAL IN THE BOOK, CANNOT AND DO NOT WARRANT THE PERFORMANCE OR RESULTS THAT MAY BE OBTAINED BY USING THE CONTENTS OF THE BOOK. THE AUTHOR AND PUBLISHER HAVE USED THEIR BEST EFFORTS TO ENSURE THE ACCURACY AND FUNCTIONALITY OF THE TEXTUAL MATERIAL AND PROGRAMS DESCRIBED HEREIN. WE HOWEVER, MAKE NO WARRANTY OF ANY KIND, EXPRESS OR IMPLIED, REGARDING THE PERFORMANCE OF THESE PROGRAMS OR CONTENTS. THE BOOK IS SOLD "AS IS" WITHOUT WARRANTY (EXCEPT FOR DEFECTIVE MATERIALS USED IN MANUFACTURING THE BOOK OR DUE TO FAULTY WORKMANSHIP).

THE AUTHOR, THE PUBLISHER, AND ANYONE INVOLVED IN THE PRODUCTION AND MANUFACTURING OF THIS WORK SHALL NOT BE LIABLE FOR DAMAGES OF ANY KIND ARISING OUT OF THE USE OF (OR THE INABILITY TO USE) THE PROGRAMS, SOURCE CODE, OR TEXTUAL MATERIAL CONTAINED IN THIS PUBLICATION. THIS INCLUDES, BUT IS NOT LIMITED TO, LOSS OF REVENUE OR PROFIT, OR OTHER INCIDENTAL OR CONSEQUENTIAL DAMAGES ARISING OUT OF THE USE OF THE PRODUCT.

THE SOLE REMEDY IN THE EVENT OF A CLAIM OF ANY KIND IS EXPRESSLY LIMITED TO REPLACEMENT OF THE BOOK, AND ONLY AT THE DISCRETION OF CRM.

THE USE OF "IMPLIED WARRANTY" AND CERTAIN "EXCLUSIONS" VARIES FROM STATE TO STATE, AND MAY NOT APPLY TO THE PURCHASER OF THIS PRODUCT.

Physics-Based Animation

Kenny Erleben, Jon Sporring, Knud Henriksen, and Henrik Dohlmann

CHARLES RIVER MEDIA, INC.
Hingham, Massachusetts

Publisher: Jenifer Niles
Cover Design: Tyler Creative
Cover Image: Kenny Erleben
Graphical Consultant: André Tischer Poulsen

CHARLES RIVER MEDIA, INC.
10 Downer Avenue
Hingham, Massachusetts 02043
781-740-0400
781-740-8816 (FAX)
info@charlesriver.com
www.charlesriver.com

This book is printed in Canada on acid-free paper.

Kenny Erleben, Jon Sporring, Knud Henriksen, and Henrik Dohlmann. Physics-Based Animation.
ISBN: 1-58450-380-7

Library of Congress Cataloging-in-Publication Data
Physics-based animation / Kenny Erleben . . . [et al.]. — 1st ed.
p. cm.
Includes index.
ISBN 1-58450-380-7 (hardcover : alk. paper)
1. Computer animation. I. Erleben, Kenny, 1974-
TR897.7.P525 2005
006.6'96–dc22

2005017654

05 7 6 5 4 3 2 First Edition

CHARLES RIVER MEDIA titles are available for site license or bulk purchase by institutions, user groups, corporations, etc. For additional information, please contact the Special Sales Department at 781-740-0400.

Contents

Preface

Physics-based animation is becoming increasingly popular due to its use in computer games, for producing special effects in movies, and as part of surgical simulation systems. Over the past decade the field has matured, and today there is a wealth of simulation methods solving many simulation problems. There is a vast amount of examples where physics-based animation is used, e.g., rigid bodies stumbling around (The Hulk®, Grand Turismo®, Medal of Honor®, Half-Life®); skin and muscle deformations (Shrek®, the Nutty Professor®, Jurassic Park®, the Mummy®); water splashing (Shrek®, Titanic®, Finding Nemo®); jelly blobs dancing around (Flopper®); death-like animations (Hitman®); hair blowing in the wind or bending due to motion of a character (Monsters Inc®); cloth moving (Monsters Inc®); and melting robots and cyborg parts of characters (Terminator3®, Treasure Island®), just to mention a few.

There is an ongoing quest for exploiting physics-based animation. While it was a computationally heavy burden 10–20 years ago to kinetically animate a linked character consisting of no more than a handful of limbs [Wellman, 1993], today this is considered a trivial task due to the large increase of computer power. The increase of computer power allows us to simulate increasingly complex scenarios, in an apparently never-ending spiral, and it appears that there will always be a demand for faster methods,with more details, larger scenes, etc. Nevertheless, a major part of such animations will always be a physical model of the world constructed from the laws of physics and solved numerically. A major part of the physical models and their numerical solutions were developed prior to the twentieth century. Clever algorithms for solving geometrically-complex systems are less than 40 years old and still part of a very active research field.

The widespread use of physics-based animation, especially in the entertainment industry, has resulted in a strong demand for education in these topics, both from students and industry. Quite a few books on computer animation such as [Watt et al., 1992, Parent, 2001] and computer games such as [Eberly, 2000, Eberly, 2003b] introduce the reader to physics-based animation, but these books often refrain from covering advanced topics, either because they only consider real-time computations, or because of space limitations. The details of the simulation methods used in big commercial productions are usually not accessible by the general public, since they are kept as business secrets. Most of the advanced literature on these topics is written as scientific papers addressing specific problems e.g., [Baraff et al., 2003a, Osher et al., 2003, Bergen, 2003a], which requires a broad basic education in physics, mathematics, and computer science to read and understand. Finally most "tricks of the trade" are not published in scientific papers, but learned through experience and word of mouth in the graphics community.

These are the reasons that motivated us to write an advanced textbook on physics-based animation with a focus on the theory. We wanted to create an advanced textbook for computer science graduate students, teaching them the basis while at the same time teaching them the thin red line that separates the different simulation methods. Our pedagogical goal is to prepare readers for a commercial or academic career on the subject of physics-based animation, rather than to produce yet another code-hacker for the gaming industry.

Almost all of the methods described in this book have been tested as implementation in the open source project OpenTissue. Major parts of this book and the OpenTissue project have been used in our classes during the last two years, from which we have gotten much feedback, and for which we are very grateful. Special thanks should be given to Andrè Tischer Poulsen, Katrine Hommelhoff Jensen, Anders Holbøll, Micky Kelager Christensen, and Anders Fleron who have served as our student reading committee. Andrè Tischer has also given invaluable help with improving the visual appeal of many of the figures. We would also like to thank our ever-patient publisher Jenifer Niles from Charles River Media, together with her anonymous reviewing panel and technical writers. Finally, we wish to thank our respective families, without whose support, we would not have been able to complete this project.

Kenny Erleben, Jon Sporring, Knud Henriksen, and Henrik Dohlmann.

1st July 2005

1

Introduction

A long-term goal in computer graphics is to increase realism and *believability* in computer generated animations and pictures. Some original work includes [Armstrong et al., 1985, Terzopoulos et al., 1987, Moore et al., 1988, Hahn, 1988, Barzel et al., 1988, Platt et al., 1988, Baraff, 1989, Barsky et al., 1991]. The general belief is that as we get better and better at rendering images, the lack of *physical realism* and believability will be more obvious and therefore more annoying to the common observer. The main argument for achieving the goal of more realism has been to use physics to model the behavior and movement of computer models. Today these efforts have culminated in what is usually referred to as *physics-based animation* or modeling.

Physics-based animation is a highly-interdisciplinary field, which is based on theories from engineering [Zienkiewicz et al., 2000, Stewart et al., 1996, Pfeiffer et al., 1996b, Enright et al., 2002], from physics [Baraff, 2001], and from mathematics. Some of the most noteworthy simulation models are based on robotics [Craig, 1986, Featherstone, 1998] and solid mechanics [House et al., 2000, Teran et al., 2003]. To our knowledge, the field of physics-based animation was first named in a course in the 1987 *ACM SIGGRAPH* (the Association for Computing Machinery's Special Interest Group on Computer Graphics) conference, "Topics in Physically-Based Modeling" organized by Alan H. Barr. In recent years the emphasis in physics-based animation on computationally efficient algorithms has spawned a new field: *plausible simulation* [Barzel et al., 1996].

In a movie production pipeline, it is generally believed that using physics inhibits the creativity and aesthetics of an animator. The reason is quite obvious: it is hard to be true toward a physical model, while at the same time using every aspect of the *Principles of Animation* [Lassiter, 1987, Frank et al., 1995]. While some of the principles focus on implementing the physical reality such as *squash and stretch*, *timing and motion*, and *slow in and out*, most of the principles are about exaggerating motion to entertain an audience and keeping the audience's attention. Hence, animators have a preference for surrealistic movement in lieu of entertainment, and they have no shame in putting their characters in unnatural poses. They often apply a lazy approach to render only what is visible, as long as the motion and the scene conveys an interesting story.

This book is not concerned with the Principles of Animation, nor does it attempt to qualify or quantify believability or plausibility of the presented methods and algorithms. It is not concerned with the rendering process or animation systems. Instead, this book is first devoted to giving the reader a firm and solid foundation for understanding how the mathematical models are derived from physical and mathematical principles, and second, how the mathematical models are solved in an efficient, robust, and stable manner on a computer. As such, the book introduces the reader to physics, mathematics, and numerics, nevertheless this book is not a substitute for text books in these fields.

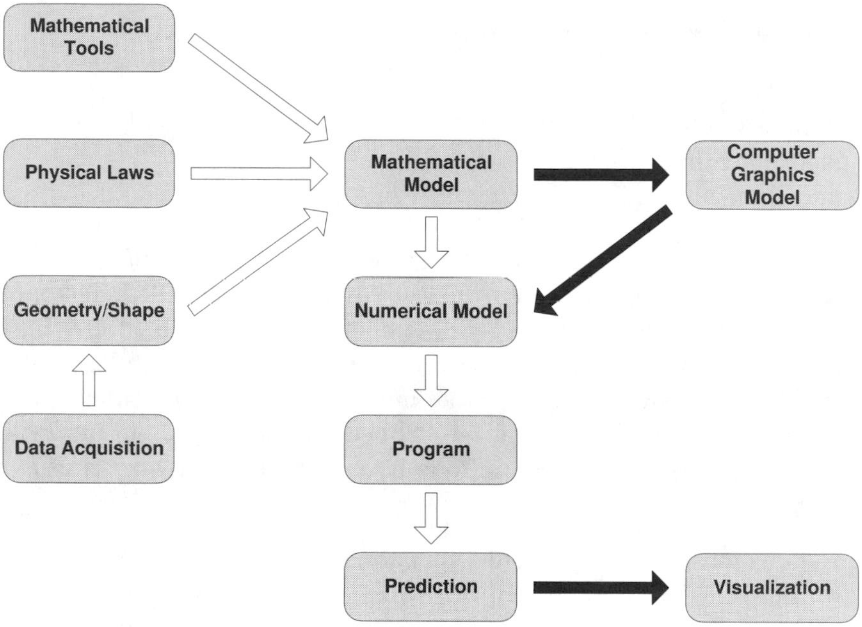

Figure 1.1: Schematic overview of physics-based animation and simulation. The white arrows are typical of the engineering disciplines, whereas the black arrows are typical extra steps taken in computer graphics.

1.1 The Computer Graphics Model

One perspective of physics-based animation is that it consists of many theoretical laws and tools from physics and mathematics with some geometry added to it, and these are all mixed together to obtain a mathematical model of the real world. Once this model is obtained, it can be remodeled into a numerical model, which in turn may be programmed on a computer. The program is then able to make predictions about the real world, and these predictions may be used to estimate where objects are expected to move (forward kinematics and dynamics), or they may be used to calculate how objects should be handled in order to obtain some desired movement (inverse kinematics and dynamics). This view of the world is schematized in Figure 1.1 with the white arrows and is typical of the engineering disciplines. In engineering, the goal is often to make highly accurate predictions about the real world in the long term e.g., to ensure the stability of a bridge or to predict the efficiency of a heating system. Using a surgical simulator as an example, we will describe typical steps covered by Figure 1.1: the initial point is typically some kind of *data acquisition and modeling* step, where a patient is scanned, and the resulting 3-dimensional image is segmented into meaningful anatomical objects and represented as *geometrical shapes*. These objects are then augmented with relevant *physical laws* often in the form of an energy system. To perform a physical simulation, the energy system is analyzed with *mathematical tools* such as calculus of variation, and the system is converted into a set of partial differential equations. The *mathematical model* is often a set of partial differential equations together with a detailed description of geometry acting as boundary conditions. To implement the mathematical model on a computer, the equations are often discretized e.g., using the appropriate finite differences method, which in turn can be programmed in C++ or a similar programming language. Finally, the simulator is able to be run, and be used to make *predictions* about the future, i.e., what will happen if certain structures are changed or removed.

In spite of the impressive accomplishments of physical, mathematical, and engineering disciplines, it is often the case that neither the mathematical model nor the numerical techniques are useful for computer animation. Computer animation favors high visual detail, high performance, and low memory consumption. In contrast, the engineering approach is often not interested in momentary visual details, since its primary goal is often to predict long-term behavior and/or high precision. Hence, computation time and memory consumption is often high, since if the task is to predict whether a bridge will stand for 100 years, then it might easily be justified to have tens or hundreds of computers work on the problem over several days or weeks. In computer animation however, we would rather be able to visualize the crash of a bridge with visual appeal on a laptop computer in real time. Due to these differences between engineering and computer graphics, computer scientists remodel the mathematical models to favor visual details, and choose numerical techniques favoring speed, robustness, and stability over accuracy and convergence. These tradeoffs may be called the *computer graphics model*. To summarize, the goals of physics-based animation is to model the physical world, but in contrast to engineering disciplines, the computer graphical approach favors visual flair and low computational resources.

1.2 The Taxonomy of Physics-Based Animation Methods

At the highest level, the field of physics-based animation and simulation can roughly be subdivided into two large groups:

Kinematics is the study of motion without consideration of mass or forces.

Dynamics is the study of motion taking mass and forces into consideration.

But the story does not end here, because kinematics and dynamics come in two flavors or subgroups:

Inverse is the study of motion knowing the starting and ending points.

Forward is the study of motion solely given the starting point.

In the first subgroup, one typically knows where to go, but needs to figure out how to do it. As an example, one might know the end position of a tool frame of a robot manipulator, without knowing what forces and torques to apply at the actuators in order to get to the final destination. In other words, inverse kinematics and dynamics computes the motion "backwards". Forward kinematics and dynamics work exactly the opposite. Using the same example as before, one typically knows the starting position of the tool frame and the forces and torques acting through the actuators. The goal is then to predict the final destination. The difference between inverse and forward kinematics/dynamics is illustrated in Figure 1.2.

There are numerous techniques and methods in physics-based animation and simulation, and you probably already have heard several buzzwords. In Table 1.1 we have tried to classify some of the most popular techniques and methods according to the four subgroups introduced above.

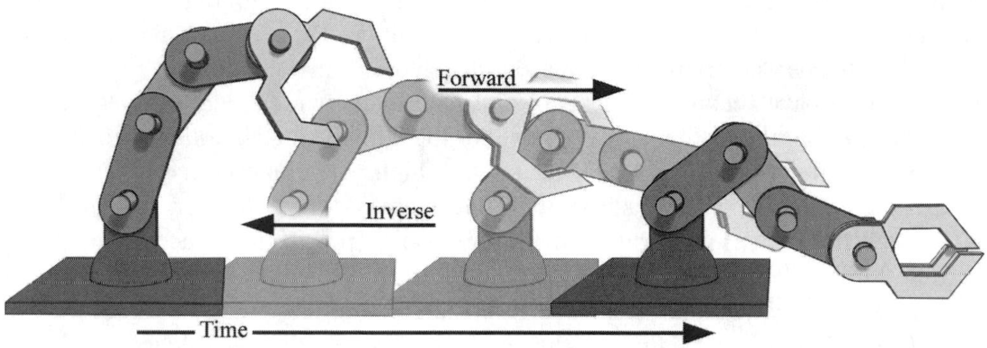

Figure 1.2: Example showing the difference in forward and inverse kinematics and dynamics. In the case of inverse motion, the starting and ending positions of the robot gripping tool is given, whereas in the case of forward motion, only the starting position is given.

	Inverse	Forward
Kinematics	• Cyclic Coordinate Descent • Jacobian Method	• Spline Driven Animation • Key Frame Animation (Interpolation) • Closed-Form Solutions • Free-Form Deformation
Dynamics	• Recursive Newton Euler Method • Optimization Problems	• Featherstone's Method (The Articulated-Body Method) • Composite-Rigid-Body Method • Particle Systems, Mass-Spring Systems • Finite Element Method • Constraint-Based Simulation

Table 1.1: Common methods and their classification into inverse/forward kinematics/dynamics.

1.3 Scientific Computing versus Computer Graphics in Practice

The engineering methods are dominated by the field of *scientific computing*. Looking at some of the applications, it becomes clear that the diversity is large. Examples of current simulators for real projects follow. Since the authors are Danish, most of the examples are Danish, however, we strongly suspect that the range of problems and their computational demands are international.

Numerical wind tunnels at RISOE:
The numerical wind tunnel at RISOE (`www.risoe.dk/vea-aed/numwind`) uses a hyperbolic grid generator for both two-dimensional and three-dimensional domains. Navier-Stokes is solved using EllipSys2D/3D code, which is an incompressible finite volume code. The computation of a stationary windmill rotor takes roughly 50 CPU hours. Using 14 CPUs (3.2GHz Pentium M, 2GB RAM) in a cluster the simulation takes about four hours. Nonstationary computations take three to four times longer [Johansen, 2005].

Deformation of atomic-scale materials:
In atomic-scale materials physics simulations of plastic deformation in nano crystalline copper are done on a cluster (Niflheim, 2.1 Teraflops) of everyday PCs. A simulation involves 100 nodes running in parallel and often takes weeks to complete (`www.dcsc.dk`). In quantum chemistry, problems often involve 10^9 variables and simulations can take up to 10 days or more to complete [Rettrup, 2005].

Computational fluid mechanics
Fluid mechanics involves a wide range of flow problems. Three dimensional nonstationary flows typically require $10 - -100 \times 10^6$ grid nodes and use up to 1000 CPU hours per simulation (`www.dcsc.dk`). Solid mechanics are also simulated (`www.dcsc.sdu.dk`) but often not visualized [Vinter, 2005].

Computational astrophysics:
Computational astrophysics (`www.nbi.ku.dk/side22730.htm`) involves simulating the formation of Galaxy, Star, and Planet. Smoothed Particle Hydrodynamics and Adaptive Mesh Refinement are some of the methods used. Computations often take weeks or months to complete [Nordlund, 2005].

Weather reports:
Weather reports are simulated continuously and saved to disk regularly at DMI (`www.dmi.dk`). Information is saved every three hours. Forty-eight-hour reports are computed on 2.5 grid nodes using time-step size of two minutes. The total number of computations are in the order of 10^{12} and solved on very large supercomputers [Sørensen, 2005].

From this short survey of scientific computing it is evident that the simulations rely on large supercomputers, often in clusters. The amount of data is astronomical and computation times that cover a wide range from minutes to hours, from hours to days, weeks, and even months are not unheard of. Visualization ranges from simple arrows illustration flow fields to quite advanced scientific visualization.

A noteworthy point is that the concept of real time is often not a very useful term in scientific computing. For instance, in chemistry, simulated time is the order of pico seconds but the computation takes days to complete. The main idea of the simulations is often to see a chemical process in slow motion in order to observe what is happening. This is not doable in a laboratory. In contrast, astro and sea simulations are too slow and are therefore simulated at higher rates. In sea-flow simulations a couple of hundred years are simulated per day. In conclusion, turn-around time in scientific computing is often of the order of 24 hours to 30 days [Vinter, 2005].

Looking at physics-based animation from a computer graphical perspective gives a slightly different picture.

Fluid phenomena:

Smoke simulation for large-scale phenomena [Rasmussen et al., 2003] using half a million particles takes 2–10 secs. of simulation time per frame, and rendering time takes 5–10 minutes per frame (2.2 GHz Pentium 4). In [McNamara et al., 2003], key frame control of smoke simulations takes between 2–24 hours to perform on a 2 GHz Pentium 4. Target-driven smoke simulation [Fattal et al., 2004] on a 2.4 GHz Pentium 4 in 2D on a 256^2 grid takes 50 secs. for a 1 second animation in 3D on a 128^3 grid it takes 35 minutes.

Particle systems:

In [Feldman et al., 2003] suspended particle explosions are animated. The simulation time ranges from 4–6 secs. per frame on a 3GHz Pentium 4. With render times included, a simulated second is in order of minutes. Animation of viscoelastic fluids [Goktekin et al., 2004] using a 40^3 grid runs at half an hour per second of animation on a 3 GHz Pentium 4. Animation of two-way interaction between rigid objects and fluid [Carlson et al., 2004] using a $64 \times 68 \times 84$ grid on a 3GHz Pentium 4 with 1 GB RAM takes 401 simulation steps for one second of animation with average CPU time per simulation step of 27.5 secs.

Cloth animation:

Robust cloth simulation without penetration [Bridson et al., 2002] of a 150×150 nodes piece of cloth runs at two minutes per frame on a 1.2 GHz Pentium3. Untangling cloth [Baraff et al., 2003b] for a cloth model with 14 K vertices yields additional cost of 0.5 secs simulation time per frame on a 2 GHz Pentium 4. Changing mesh topology [Molino et al., 2004] during simulation for 1 K triangles runs at 5–20 minutes per frame, 380 K tetrahedra runs at 20 minutes per frame. Stacked rigid body simulation [Guendelman et al., 2003] with simulations of 500–1000 objects takes 3–7 minutes per frame on average.

Computer Games

Game consoles such as Play Station 2 (`www.playstation.com`) has only 32 MB RAM and 6.2 GFLOPS and common home PCs are for the most part inferior to the computers used by computer graphics researchers. This has called for some creative thinking in computer game development to reach the performance requirements. Furthermore, there must be time set aside for other tasks in such applications as computer games. For instance, in *Hitman* from IO-Interactive, only 5–10% of the frame time is used for physics simulation [Jakobsen, 2005]. The future may change these hardware limitations. For instance, recent GPUs do not suffer from latency problems and promise 60

GFLOPS (www.nvidia.com), also PPUs (www.ageia.com) seems to be an emerging technology. Finally cell chips (www.ibm.com/news/us/en/2005/02/2005_02_08.html) are also promising.

From this short literature survey of recent work on physics-based animation in computer graphics, it is evident that frame times ranging from the order of seconds to hours running on single PCs are used. In conclusion, design-work both in computer graphics and scientific computing requires reasonably low turn-around times.

1.4 Future Points of Study

Physics-based animation is a large field, and it is growing rapidly. Every year new techniques are presented for animating new phenomena, and existing methods are improved both in speed, accuracy, and visual detail. Covering everything is not possible in one book, needless to say that keeping up-to-date is an important job of any physics-based animator. A good place to start for industry standards are the Physics Engines, many of which are shown in Table 1.2.

In the following we will briefly mention some topics we find interesting, but will not cover in this book due to space limitations and for pedagogical reasons:

Recursive methods for jointed mechanics.
Recursive methods for jointed mechanics are also called *minimal coordinate methods*, and the theory is extensively covered in the literature, see e.g., [Featherstone, 1998].

Mathematical programming.
Mathematical programming is the study of, among other things, complementarity problems. The field has a history going back to the 1940s. It is a huge field and would justify several textbooks in itself. In this book we recommend using an existing library such as [Path, 2005] during a course or confer with e.g., [Cottle et al., 1992, Murty, 1988].

Deformable objects with *nonlinear anisotropic material properties*.
Nonlinear and large deformations are still very much a problem of ongoing research and not something we feel fits into an introductory textbook.

Cutting and fracture of deformable objects.
Recently there has been published work on fracture, but both cutting and fracture is just on the brim for today's real-time applications.

Particle level set methods and adaptive data structures for water simulation.
We have chosen to focus on the more classical approach, giving the reader a good understanding of the basics. It should not be difficult to proceed with the recent literature after this, see e.g., [Osher et al., 2003].

Control in physical-based animations.
Recently, attempts have been made to include animator control by using inverse dynamics ap-

Name	Notes
DynaMechs	Development started in 1991 by S. McMillan, (dynamechs.sourceforge.net)
Renderware Physics	Business unit of Criterion Software established in 1993, (www.renderware.com/physics.asp)
Havok	Founded in 1998, (www.havok.com)
Meqon	Started as a university project in 1999, company founded in 2002 by D. Gustafsson and M. Lysén, (www.meqon.com)
Ipion	Bought by Havok in June 2000, (www.ipion.com)
Open Dynamics Engine	Seems to have been around somewhere between 2000–2001, started by R. Smith former MathEngine employee, (www.ode.org)
Novodex	Started spring 2002 by A. Moravansky and M. Müller, (www.novodex.com)
Tokamak	D. Lam is the original author of Tokamak, appears to have started in 2003, (www.tokamakphysics.com)
Newton Game Dynamics	Appear to have been around since 2003, (www.physicsengine.com/)
Karma	Developed by MathEngine, which was acquired by Criterion Software in July 2003, (www.mathengine.com)
Vortex	Developed by CMLabs, (www.cm-labs.com)
Free Cloth	Appears to have started around 2002 by D. Pritchard, (sourceforge.net/projects/freecloth)
OpenTissue	Started November 2001 by K. Erleben, H. Dohlmann, J. Sporring and K. Henriksen, (www.opentissue.org)
AGEIA	Company Founded 2002, March 2005 AGEIA announces a new class of physics processing unit (PPU) PhysX, (www.ageia.com)

Table 1.2: A list of commercially and publicly available physics engines.

proaches. We have omitted all theory and methods regarding how to control and manipulate an animation, since we do not regard these as part of a low-level physics engine.

Continuous collision detection.
Tunneling effects and overshooting are some tedious problems in animation. One remedy for these problems is continuous collision detection, which promises better contact point generation and determination of contact areas in dynamic simulations. The field is rather new but very promising. However, in our opinion there is not yet a firmly established standard, and we have therefore omitted this material. Interested readers may refer to [Redon et al., 2002, Redon, 2004a, Redon, 2004b, Redon et al., 2004a].

Simplex methods for collision detection.
Simplex-based methods for collision detection are based on the mathematical concept of an affine linear independent set of variables. It is our experience that these methods are difficult to approach for students and not essential, which is the main reason why we have omitted these methods. Good references are [Bergen, 2003b, Bergen, 2001, Bergen, 1999].

1.5 Readers Guide

Having taught advanced computer graphics and animation for several years we found that we lacked a thorough introduction to physics-based animation. Therefore we started writing notes first on the mathematical tools needed for the simulators, and then notes describing the various animation methods. Hence, the primary recipients of this book are graduate students in a computer science department. The background of our students is typically well-versed in the art of programming, introductory computer graphics, and what we call mathematical maturity. By mathematical maturity we mean that students don't necessarily have a rigorous mathematical training, but that they are eager to learn new mathematical techniques. Our approach is then practical: we strive to teach the students theories such as presented in this book, and we emphasize that they must be able to implement the theories in actual working simulators. We hope the book reflects these goals, e.g., by the numerous pseudocode examples. Almost all algorithms described have been implemented in the accompanying open source project [OpenTissue, 2005].

The book contains five parts reflecting the diversity of the field of physics-based animation. There are therefore several ways to read this book:

Geometry of motion:
For the reader interested in the geometry of motion and kinematics, and those who wish to have total control of motion patterns, we suggest Part I, which describes the design of motion patterns regardless of the physics of the real world.

From particles to rigid bodies:
The most common starting point of physics-based animation is to begin with particle systems (Chapter 8), followed by a study of rigid body animation in Part II, then an advanced investigation into deformable objects in Part III, and ending with a study of Computational Fluid Dynamics in Chapter 11.

Computational fluid dynamics:

Some readers will find that Computational Fluid Dynamics is simple and choose to read Chapter 8, followed by Computational Fluid Dynamics in Chapter 11, and Continuum Models with Finite Differences in Chapter 9. It is our experience that finite element analysis in Chapter 10 poses the biggest challenges for novices.

Collision detection:

Collision detection covered in Part IV is often treated in parallel with any of the above subjects.

Mathematical and physical compendium:

Part V is written as a very extended appendix, which contains much of the physics and mathematics needed for understanding the theories in this book.

Happy reading!

Part I

The Kinematics

Kinematics is the study of the motion of parts without considering mass or forces. Newton's laws, therefore, are neglectable. The main application of kinematical methods is preconfigured animation, where the physical simulation is not required, too complex to bother with, or does not live up to the *Principles of Animation* [Frank et al., 1995, Lassiter, 1987]. Many computer films rely heavily on kinematics for motion; much of the theory may thus be seen as a natural extension to the stop-motion techniques developed by Disney in the early twentieth century. Kinematics are divided into forward kinematics and inverse kinematics, depending on whether the end configuration is given or not.

Forward kinematics is characterized by the motion being prescribed by the user or some function. Therefore, it is often also called direct kinematics. Forward kinematics requires much manual labor; nevertheless, direct kinematics is widely used in movie production. Here animators specify every parameter as a function of time. Often the animators act out the motion of the figures they are about to animate. To reduce production time, a computer vision technique called *motion capture* is often applied.

Motion capture is the process of tracking annotated points on an actor via video, reconstructing the points location in three dimensions, and using the reconstruction as input to direct kinematics. With this tool, animators can create astonishing realistic-looking motion that obeys the laws of physics. Motion capture is a great tool for movie production, where the reconstructed motion is used to specify the parameters for a specific motion. Motion capture may also be used as a tool for creating new motion sequences for computer games. In this case, the motion capture data is seen as a discrete sample of physical motion and the new motion sequence is obtained by fitting a continuous model to the discrete data. One such technique is called *motion blending* or *animation blending*. Blending techniques are often found in game engines such as those listed at `www.devmaster.net/`. There are three basic problems when doing motion blending:

Motion Time-Warping: How to match to motion sequences so they are aligned in time. In other words, one has to figure out what frame in one motion corresponds to what frame in another motion.

Motion Alignment: One motion may be heading left and the other right, so what position should the blending motion have?

Motion Constraint Matching: If we want to blend a running and walking motion, then we should carefully match frames where the corresponding feet touch the ground, in order not to make a sliding or floating motion result.

Motion blending is used in computer games to create motion transitions between motion-captured data and is seen in many third-person shooter games such as Hitman®etc. The techniques are often ad hoc and rely heavily on animators to completely specify motion transitions a priori. Recent research focuses on making the motions blend more naturally by taking the balance of a figure into account.

Parameters for forward kinematics may also be generated using *motion programs* [Barsky et al., 1991]. In motion programs, joint parameters are given as some continuous function of time, such as $\cos(t)$, which generates an oscillating motion. Motion functions have to be carefully designed for the specific motion such as biped gait walking [Parent, 2001, Chapter 6.2] or fish swimming [Terzopoulos et al., 1994].

Inverse kinematics deals with the interpolation of a figure from a specified starting and ending point. This is also often used in animation tools such as Maya®or 3DMax®. Even for simple objects such as the human arm, there will almost always be several solutions, since the elbow is movable even when the hand and the shoulder are fixed. Hence, a central problem in inverse kinematics is to select one out of several possible motions. A solution is often sought that generates a natural looking motion. This is achieved either by augmenting the inverse kinematics with extra constraints or combining with dynamics; for instance, using minimum energy principles.

Finally, forward and inverse kinematics are often combined in real applications. For example, direct kinematics may be used to give natural looking motions for some objects and inverse kinematics for others. Another example is to use motion capture to generate statistics on realistic motions and use this information to select solutions for inverse kinematical problems. Many physics engines further support the mixture of forward and inverse kinematics with physically simulated objects. A typical example in a movie production is to use inverse kinematics or physics-based animation to determine a rough set of parameters for a given motion. Then the animation is computed in detail, where parameters for all objects in each frame are recorded. This is called *baking* [Kačić-Alesić et al., 2003]. After having baked the animated objects, an animator can fine-tune the motions using the direct kinematics method to produce entertaining animations. In conclusion, in real applications, techniques are used interchangeably both in combination, as pre- and postprocessing steps.

In Part I we describe the basics of forward and inverse kinematics of articulated figures in Chapters 2 and 3, and the subject of scripted motion in Chapter 4.

2

Articulated Figures

This chapter describes *articulated figures* and their representation. This representation is used later for animation and simulation of articulated figures. An articulated figure can be thought of as a robot arm or a human arm made of a number of solid rods, which are connected to each other by joints that can move independently. When all the joints move, the overall motion of an articulated figure can be very complex. The goal of this chapter is to present methods that make it easy to describe the kinematics of articulated figures, which will be used later for animation and simulation of articulated figures.

The chapter is divided into three sections. Section 2.1 defines precisely what is meant by an articulated figure, and how it is constructed. The last two sections explain two different methods of describing articulated figures. Section 2.2 presents a general method named *Paired Joint Coordinates*, and Section 2.3 presents a specialized method named *Denavit-Hartenberg*.

2.1 Links and Joints

An *articulated figure* is a construction made of *links* and *joints*. The different links are connected by joints, which have some degree of freedom. A *link* can be thought of as a solid rod, which cannot change its shape nor length. Hence, a link is considered a rigid body that defines the relation between two neighboring joint axes, see Figure 2.1. A joint can be thought of as a connection between two neighboring links. A joint might have several degrees of freedom, i.e., it might rotate around *one*, *two*, or *three* axes, or it might translate along *one*, *two*, or *three* axes.

An example of an articulated figure with one revolute joint is shown in Figure 2.1. One can think of the links and joints as the building blocks which make up an articulated figure. Examples of articulated figures are: industrial robots, construction equipment, and the human skeleton.

Links and joints are numbered from $0, \ldots, N$, and an articulated figure always starts with $joint_0$, which is fixed at some stationary *base coordinate system*. The numbering of the links and joints is very important. A joint inside an articulated figure, say $joint_i$ connects $link_{i-1}$ and $link_i$, where $link_{i-1}$ is closer to the base.

The joint shown in Figure 2.1 is a revolute joint, i.e., it can rotate around *one* axis. Generally, joints are named for what they can do:

***revolute joint*:** A joint that can rotate around *one* or *more* axes. Figure 2.2(a) shows a revolute joint with *one* degree of freedom, but in general a revolute joint can have up to three degrees of freedom, i.e., it can rotate around all three coordinate axes.

***prismatic joint*:** A joint that can translate along *one* or *more* axes. Figure 2.2(b) shows a prismatic joint with *one* degree of freedom, but in general a prismatic joint can have up to three degrees of freedom, i.e., it can translate along all three coordinate axes.

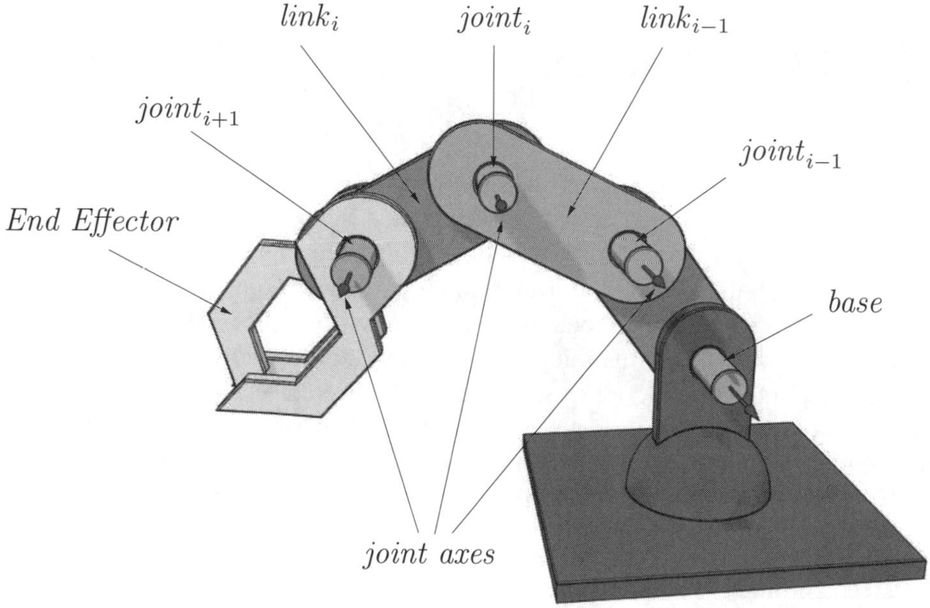

Figure 2.1: An example of an articulated figure with one revolute joint. The revolute joint can rotate around *one* axis. The numbering of the joints is very important, i.e., joint_i connects link_{i-1} and link_i.

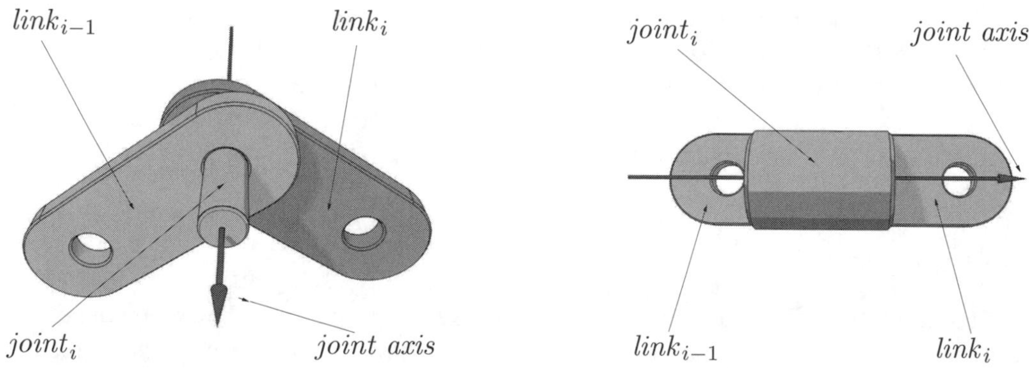

(a) revolute joint (rotation)

(b) prismatic joint (translation)

Figure 2.2: Examples of different joints used to construct articulated figures.

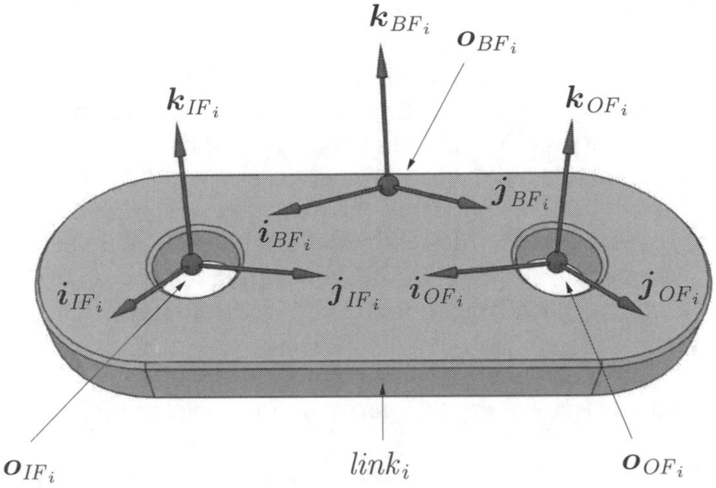

Figure 2.3: The three coordinate systems associated with each $link_i$: BF_i, IF_i, and OF_i. The origins and coordinate axes of the inner-frame IF_i, and the outer-frame OF_i are specified in the body-frame BF_i.

2.2 Paired Joint Coordinates

As mentioned previously, an articulated figure is constructed of links and joints. Because each joint can either rotate or translate, the motion of the individual links and joints can be very complex. This is because the motion of $joint_j$ and $link_j$ affect the motion of $joint_i$ and $link_i$ for $i > j$. An example of this is: if the base joint rotates or translates its motion affects all other joints and links of the articulated figure. Therefore, it is very complicated to describe the motion of an articulated figure in a coordinate system common to all joints and links. This difficulty can be overcome by introducing local coordinate systems for all joints and links, and establishing transformations between the local coordinate systems.

An articulated figure can be described using the *paired joint coordinates* method [Featherstone, 1998]. The method is very general and it is based on associating three predefined coordinate systems with each link. For $link_i$ these coordinate systems are named: *body frame* (BF_i), *inner frame* (IF_i), and *outer frame* (OF_i), and they are all associated with $link_i$. The origins of the inner-frame and outer-frame are located on the respective joint axes. This makes it easy to transform entities between successive links, as we will show later. These coordinate systems are illustrated in Figure 2.3 and explained below.

The Body Frame (BF_i)**:** is a *local* coordinate system that is associated with $link_i$. The geometry of $link_i$ is described in this local coordinate system. Generally, the origin and the axes of this coordinate system can be chosen arbitrarily, but in order to handle articulated figures easily, it is recommended that you choose the origin of BF_i to be the *center of mass* of $link_i$. Also, it is recommended that you choose an orthogonal coordinate system. If $link_i$ has some symmetry axes, it is recommended that you choose some of them as basis axes for the local orthogonal coordinate system. In the following it is assumed that all coordinate systems are orthogonal.

The Inner Frame (IF_i)**:** is a *local* coordinate system that is associated with $link_i$. Usually, this coordinate system is associated with $joint_i$. It has its origin located on the axis of $joint_i$, and has one axis parallel to the direction of motion of the joint. Both the origin and the coordinate axes of this coordinate system are specified in the body frame.

The Outer Frame (OF_i)**:** is a *local* coordinate system that is associated with $link_i$. Usually, this coordinate system is associated with $joint_{i+1}$. It has its origin located on the axis of $joint_{i+1}$, and has one axis parallel to the direction of motion of the joint. Both the origin and the coordinate axes of this coordinate system are specified in the body frame.

The rest of this section contains subsections that derive transformations between the different frames

1. Compute the transformation ${}^{BF_i}\boldsymbol{T}_{IF_i}$ from inner frame to body frame (Section 2.2.1).
2. Compute the transformation ${}^{BF_i}\boldsymbol{T}_{OF_i}$ from outer frame to body frame (Section 2.2.2).
3. Compute the transformation ${}^{OF_{i-1}}\boldsymbol{T}_{IF_i}$ from inner frame of $link_i$ to outer frame of $link_{i-1}$.
4. Compute the transformation ${}^{(i-1)}\boldsymbol{T}_i$ which transforms entities from the body frame of $link_i$ to the body frame of $link_{i-1}$.

The notation ${}^{TO}\boldsymbol{T}_{FROM}$ means that the transformation transforms an entity given in frame $FROM$ coordinates to coordinates in the TO frame.

When all these transformations are derived, it is possible to transform the coordinates of a point $\boldsymbol{p}$ specified in the body frame of $link_i$ to coordinates in any other body frame, e.g., the body frame of $link_j$. This is very general. But it makes it easy to transform the coordinates of a point $\boldsymbol{p}$ specified in any body frame of $link_i$ to the base coordinate frame, the body frame of $link_0$. This makes it possible to transform positions, orientations, velocities, and accelerations of a point $\boldsymbol{p}$, specified in any body frame to the base frame, which can be used as a coordinate system common to all joints and links.

2.2.1 The Transformation ${}^{BF_i}\boldsymbol{T}_{IF_i}$

This section describes how to make a mapping from the inner frame to the body frame. To be more specific, the problem is: given a point $\boldsymbol{p}$ in inner frame coordinates, determine its coordinates in the body frame.

With the definitions from Section 2.2 for $link_i$, let $\boldsymbol{o}_{IF_i}$, $\boldsymbol{i}_{IF_i}$, $\boldsymbol{j}_{IF_i}$, and $\boldsymbol{k}_{IF_i}$ be the origin and the basis vectors of the inner frame expressed in the body frame, see Figure 2.4.
The relation between the inner frame and the body frame is as follows: given a point $\boldsymbol{p} = [x, y, z]^T$ in the inner frame IF_i its coordinates in the body frame, BF_i, can be expressed by an angular rotation φ around some axis $\boldsymbol{u}$ followed by a translation $\boldsymbol{r}_{IF_i}$. This transformation is denoted ${}^{BF_i}\boldsymbol{T}_{IF_i}$, where the subscript IF_i and the superscript BF_i indicate that the coordinates of a point $\boldsymbol{p}$ specified in inner frame coordinates is transformed to body frame coordinates.

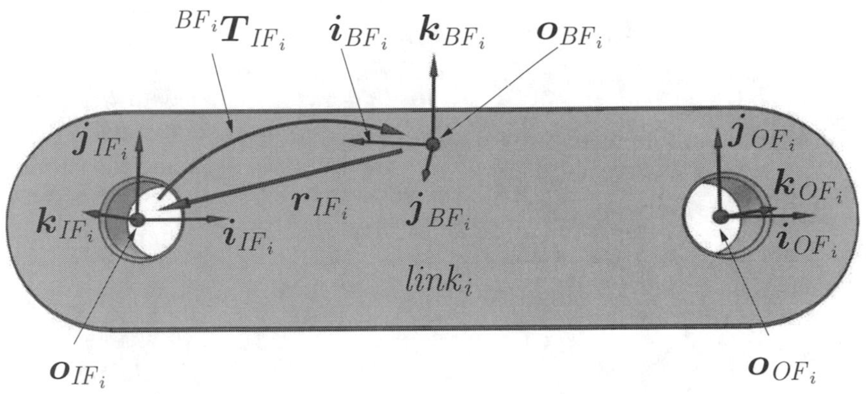

Figure 2.4: The mapping between the inner frame IF_i and the body frame BF_i for $link_i$. The origin and coordinate axes of the inner frame IF_i are specified in the body frame BF_i.

In homogeneous coordinates the transformation from the inner frame to the body frame is given by a matrix

$$^{BF_i}\boldsymbol{T}_{IF_i} = \boldsymbol{T}_{IF_i}(\boldsymbol{r}_{IF_i})\boldsymbol{R}_{IF_i}(\varphi_{IF_i}, \boldsymbol{u}_{IF_i}) \tag{2.1}$$

The translation and rotation matrices are given below

$$\boldsymbol{T}_{IF_i}(\boldsymbol{r}_{IF_i}) = \begin{bmatrix} \mathbf{1} & \boldsymbol{r}_{IF_i} \\ \mathbf{0}^T & 1 \end{bmatrix} \tag{2.2a}$$

$$\boldsymbol{R}_{IF_i}(\varphi_{IF_i}, \boldsymbol{u}_{IF_i}) = \begin{bmatrix} \boldsymbol{i}_{IF_i} & \boldsymbol{j}_{IF_i} & \boldsymbol{k}_{IF_i} & \mathbf{0} \\ 0 & 0 & 0 & 1 \end{bmatrix} \tag{2.2b}$$

where the symbol $\mathbf{1}$ denotes a 3×3 identity matrix, and the vectors $\boldsymbol{i}_{IF_i}, \boldsymbol{j}_{IF_i}, \boldsymbol{k}_{IF_i}$, and $\mathbf{0}$ are 3×1 column vectors. This makes both matrices 4×4. Both the translation matrix and the rotation matrix are constant, depending only on the relative position and orientation of the inner frame and body frame. Therefore, the resulting transformation $^{BF_i}\boldsymbol{T}_{IF_i}$ is also constant.

2.2.2 The Transformation $^{BF_i}\boldsymbol{T}_{OF_i}$

In this section it is described how to make a mapping from the inner frame to the body frame. To be more specific, the problem is: given a point $\boldsymbol{p}$ in outer frame coordinates, determine its coordinates in the body frame.

Recall the definitions from Section 2.2 for $link_i$, and let $\boldsymbol{o}_{OF_i}$, $\boldsymbol{i}_{OF_i}$, $\boldsymbol{j}_{OF_i}$, and $\boldsymbol{k}_{OF_i}$ be the origin and the basis vectors of the outer frame expressed in the body frame, see Figure 2.5. A transformation can be specified between the outer frame OF_i and the body frame, BF_i by defining the origin and the basis vectors of the outer frame in the body frame coordinate system. Let this transformation be denoted $^{BF_i}\boldsymbol{T}_{OF_i}$, where the subscript OF_i and the superscript BF_i indicate that the coordinates of a point $\boldsymbol{p}$ given in outer frame coordinates is transformed to body frame coordinates.

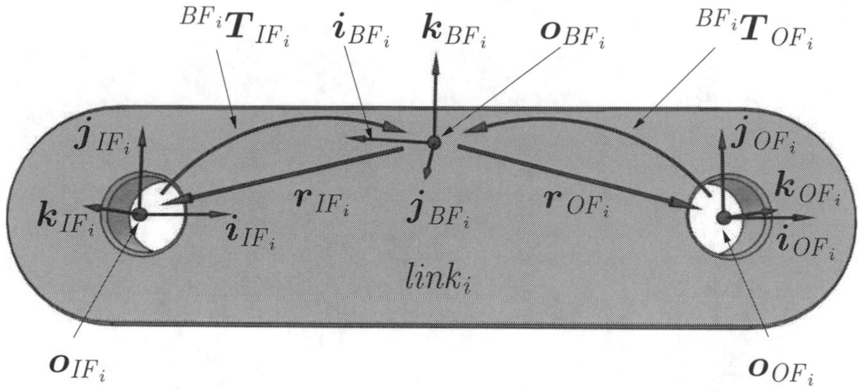

Figure 2.5: The mapping between the outer frame OF_i and the body frame BF_i for $link_i$. The origin and coordinate axes of the outer frame OF_i are specified in the body frame BF_i.

In homogeneous coordinates the transformation from the outer frame to the body frame is given by a matrix

$$^{BF_i}\boldsymbol{T}_{OF_i} = \boldsymbol{T}_{OF_i}(\boldsymbol{r}_{OF_i})\boldsymbol{R}_{OF_i}(\varphi_{OF_i}, \boldsymbol{u}_{OF_i}) \tag{2.3}$$

The translation and rotation matrices are given below

$$\boldsymbol{T}_{OF_i}(\boldsymbol{r}_{OF_i}) = \begin{bmatrix} \mathbf{1} & \boldsymbol{r}_{OF_i} \\ \mathbf{0}^T & 1 \end{bmatrix} \tag{2.4a}$$

$$\boldsymbol{R}_{OF_i}(\varphi_{OF_i}, \boldsymbol{u}_{OF_i}) = \begin{bmatrix} \boldsymbol{i}_{OF_i} & \boldsymbol{j}_{OF_i} & \boldsymbol{k}_{OF_i} & \mathbf{0} \\ 0 & 0 & 0 & 1 \end{bmatrix} \tag{2.4b}$$

where $\mathbf{1}$ is a 3×3 identity matrix, and the vectors $\boldsymbol{i}_{OF_i}, \boldsymbol{j}_{OF_i}, \boldsymbol{k}_{OF_i}$, and $\mathbf{0}$ are 3×1 column vectors, which makes both matrices 4×4. Both the translation matrix and the rotation matrix are constant, depending only on the relative position and orientation of the inner frame and body frame. Therefore, the resulting transformation $^{BF_i}\boldsymbol{T}_{OF_i}$ is also constant.

2.2.3 The Transformation $^{OF_{i-1}}\boldsymbol{T}_{IF_i}(\boldsymbol{d}_i, \varphi_i, \boldsymbol{u}_i)$

In previous sections the link transformations $^{BF_i}\boldsymbol{T}_{IF_i}$ and $^{BF_i}\boldsymbol{T}_{OF_i}$ were derived, see Sections 2.2.1 and 2.2.2. These transformations are local to the link in question, namely $link_i$. In this section a transformation from the inner frame of $link_i$ to the outer frame of $link_{i-1}$ will be derived. Let this transformation be denoted $^{OF_{i-1}}\boldsymbol{T}_{IF_i}$.

The links $link_{i-1}$ and $link_i$ are connected by $joint_i$. The relation between the inner frame of $link_i$ and the outer frame of $link_{i-1}$ is given by a joint-transformation consisting of a rotation $(\varphi_i, \boldsymbol{u}_i)$ and a translation $\boldsymbol{d}_i$

$$^{OF_{i-1}}\boldsymbol{T}_{IF_i}(\boldsymbol{d}_i, \varphi_i, \boldsymbol{u}_i) = \boldsymbol{T}_i(\boldsymbol{d}_i)\boldsymbol{R}_i(\varphi_i, \boldsymbol{u}_i) \tag{2.5}$$

where φ_i is the rotation angle, $\boldsymbol{u}_i$ is the rotation axis, and $\boldsymbol{d}_i$ is the translation vector, see Figure 2.6. To make the notation easier, the index i is omitted in the following two equations. This means that $\varphi_i = \varphi$,

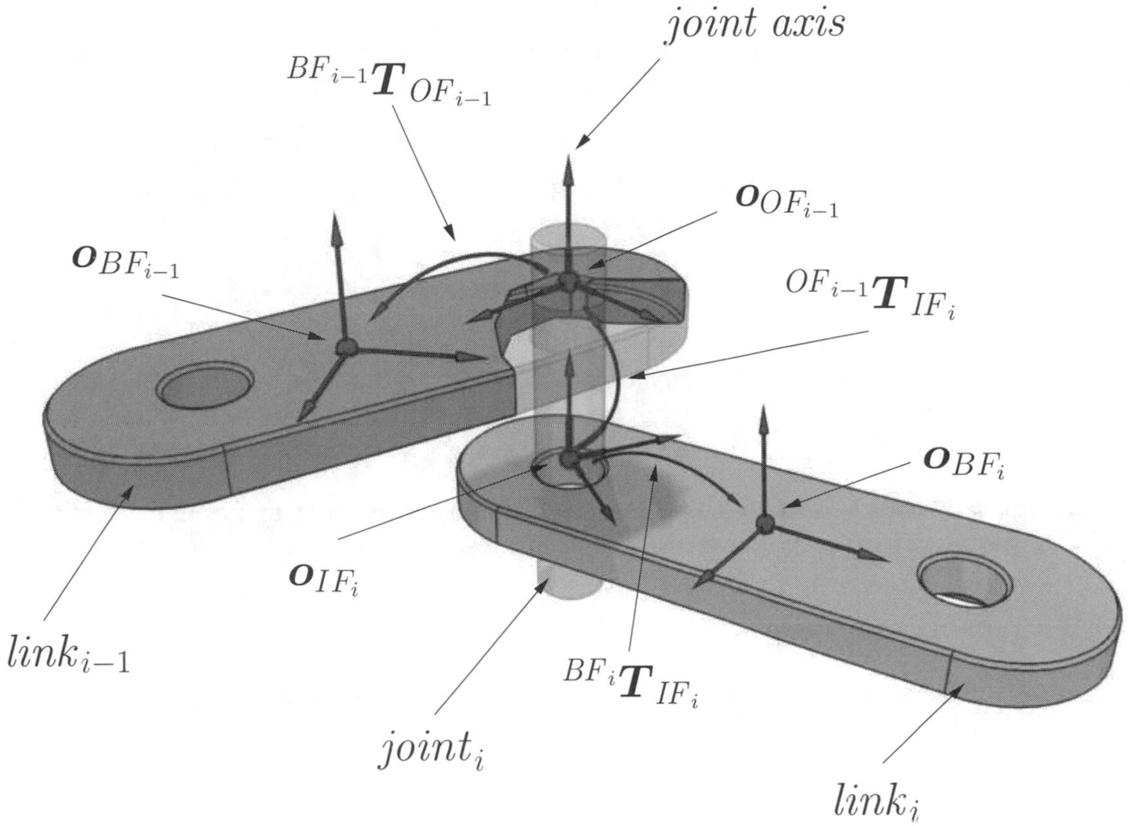

Figure 2.6: $Link_{i-1}$ and $link_i$ are connected by $joint_i$, and an associated joint-transformation ${}^{OF_{i-1}}\boldsymbol{T}_{IF_i}$. The figure shows a revolute joint, but the transformation ${}^{OF_{i-1}}\boldsymbol{T}_{IF_i}$ can be any transformation.

$\boldsymbol{u}_i = [u_x, u_y, u_z]^T$, and $\boldsymbol{d}_i = [d_x, d_y, d_z]^T$. With this notation the translation matrix $\boldsymbol{T}(\boldsymbol{d_i})$ and the rotation matrix $\boldsymbol{R}(\varphi_i, \boldsymbol{u}_i)$ are given by

$$\boldsymbol{T}(\boldsymbol{d_i}) = \begin{bmatrix} 1 & 0 & 0 & d_x \\ 0 & 1 & 0 & d_y \\ 0 & 0 & 1 & d_z \\ 0 & 0 & 0 & 1 \end{bmatrix} \tag{2.6a}$$

$$\boldsymbol{R}(\varphi_i, \boldsymbol{u}_i) = \begin{bmatrix} u_x^2 + (1 - u_x^1)c\varphi & u_z u_y(1 - c\varphi) - u_z s\varphi & u_x u_z(1 - c\varphi) + u_y s\varphi & 0 \\ u_x u_y(1 - c\varphi) + u_z s\varphi & u_y^2 + (1 - u_y^2)c\varphi & u_y u_z(1 - c\varphi) - u_x s\varphi & 0 \\ u_x u_z(1 - c\varphi) - u_y s\varphi & u_y u_z(1 - c\varphi) + u_x s\varphi & u_z^2 + (1 - u_z^2)c\varphi & 0 \\ 0 & 0 & 0 & 1 \end{bmatrix} \tag{2.6b}$$

where $s\varphi$ is shorthand for $\sin\varphi$, and $c\varphi$ for $\cos\varphi$. The parameters $(\boldsymbol{d}_i, \varphi_i, \boldsymbol{u}_i)$ are denoted joint parameters.

2.2.4 The Transformation ${}^{(i-1)}\boldsymbol{T}_i(\boldsymbol{d}_i, \varphi_i, \boldsymbol{u}_i)$

From Figure 2.6 it can be seen that the transformation between the body frame of $link_i$ and the body frame of $link_{i-1}$ is given by

$$ {}^{(i-1)}\boldsymbol{T}_i(\boldsymbol{d}_i, \varphi_i, \boldsymbol{u}_i) = \left({}^{BF_{i-1}}\boldsymbol{T}_{OF_{i-1}}\right)\left({}^{OF_{i-1}}\boldsymbol{T}_{IF_i}(\boldsymbol{d}_i, \varphi_i, \boldsymbol{u}_i)\right)\left({}^{BF_i}\boldsymbol{T}_{IF_i}\right)^{-1} \tag{2.7} $$

By specifying the transformation ${}^{(i-1)}\boldsymbol{T}_i(\boldsymbol{d}_i, \varphi_i, \boldsymbol{u}_i)$ for all links, $i = 1, \ldots, N$ a transformation from link N to the base, $link_0$ can be written

$$ \begin{aligned} {}^0\boldsymbol{T}_N &= {}^0\boldsymbol{T}_N(\boldsymbol{d}_1, \varphi_1, \boldsymbol{u}_1, \ldots, \boldsymbol{d}_N, \varphi_N, \boldsymbol{u}_N) \\ &= {}^0\boldsymbol{T}_1(\boldsymbol{d}_1, \varphi_1, \boldsymbol{u}_1){}^1\boldsymbol{T}_2(\boldsymbol{d}_2, \varphi_2, \boldsymbol{u}_2)\cdots{}^{N-1}\boldsymbol{T}_N(\boldsymbol{d}_N, \varphi_N, \boldsymbol{u}_N) \end{aligned} \tag{2.8} $$

Let $\boldsymbol{\theta}_i$ denote the generalized joint parameters for joint i, i.e., $\boldsymbol{\theta}_i = (\boldsymbol{d}_i, \varphi_i, \boldsymbol{u}_i)$. Then (2.8) may be written in a more compact form

$$ {}^0\boldsymbol{T}_N = {}^0\boldsymbol{T}_N(\boldsymbol{\theta}_1, \ldots, \boldsymbol{\theta}_N) = {}^0\boldsymbol{T}_1(\boldsymbol{\theta}_1){}^1\boldsymbol{T}_2(\boldsymbol{\theta}_2)\cdots{}^{(N-1)}\boldsymbol{T}_N(\boldsymbol{\theta}_N) \tag{2.9} $$

This is a very general approach. It is possible to use it, but it is not very easy to use. In the next section it is shown how the approach can be specialized, so it is much easier to use.

2.3 Denavit-Hartenberg

The *Denavit-Hartenberg notation* [Craig, 1986] is a very specialized description of an articulated figure. It is specialized such that each joint has only one degree of freedom: it can either translate along its z-axis or rotate around its z-axis. If a joint needs more degrees of freedom, several joints with link lengths equal to zero are located on top of each other.

Because each joint has only one degree of freedom, the Denavit-Hartenberg notation is very compact. There are only four parameters to describe a relation between two links. These parameters are the *link length*, *link twist*, *link offset*, and *link rotation*. The parameters are also known as the Denavit-Hartenberg parameters. The Denavit-Hartenberg notation is a specialization of the Paired Joint Coordinates method for describing an articulated figure, see Section 2.2.

Consider an articulated figure as the one shown in Figure 2.7. The Denavit-Hartenberg parameters of this articulated figure are defined below and summarized in Table 2.1. The Denavit-Hartenberg parameters used to describe an articulated figure can be computed by the following steps:

1. Compute the link vector $\boldsymbol{a}_i$ and the link length $a_i = \boldsymbol{a}_i$.
2. Attach coordinate frames to the joint axes.
3. Compute the link twist α_i.
4. Compute the link offset d_i.
5. Compute the joint angle φ_i.
6. Compute the transformation ${}^{(i-1)}\boldsymbol{T}_i$, which transforms entities from $link_i$ to $link_{i-1}$.

The rest of this section contains subsections that describe how to perform each of the steps listed above.

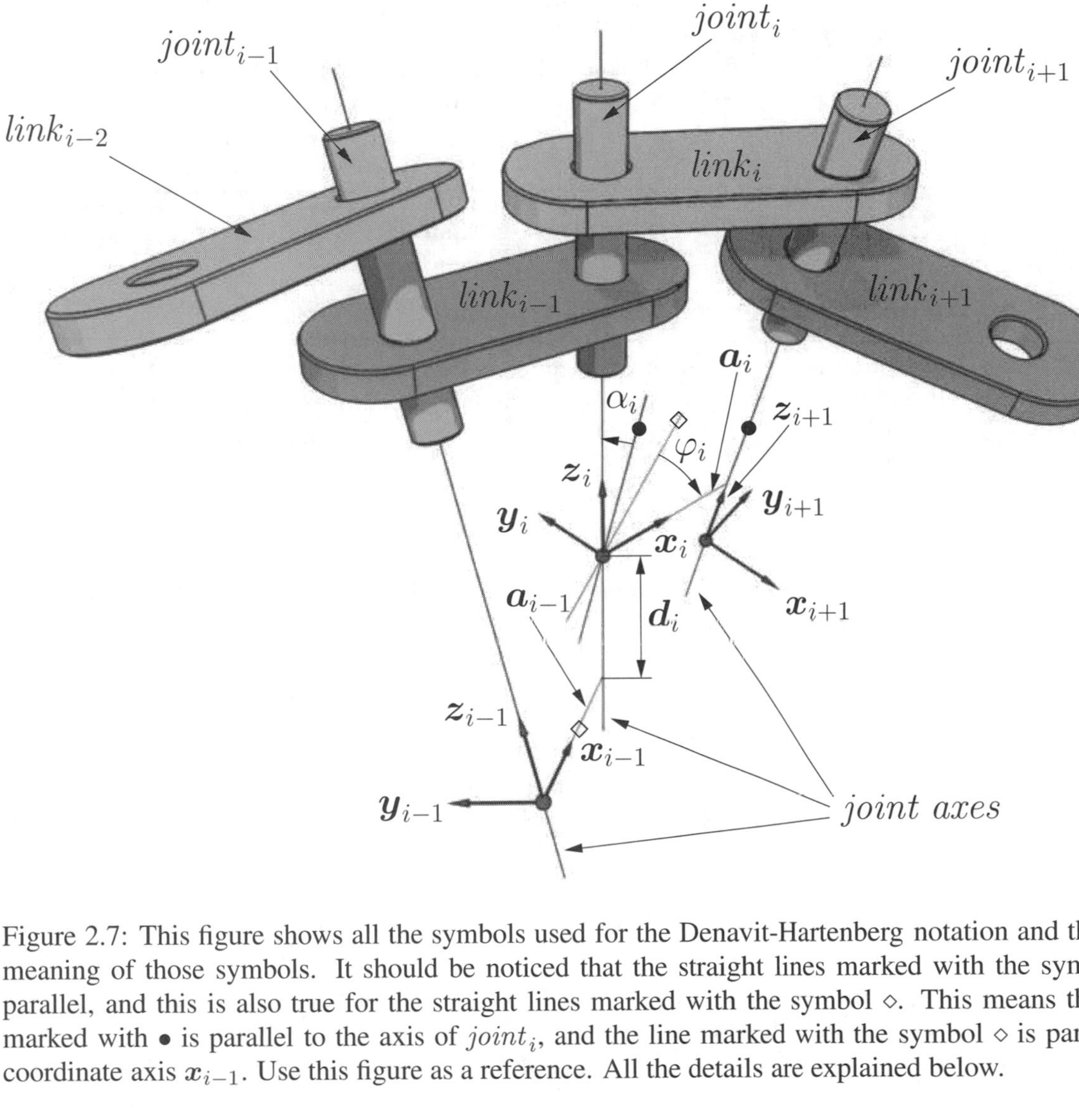

Figure 2.7: This figure shows all the symbols used for the Denavit-Hartenberg notation and the physical meaning of those symbols. It should be noticed that the straight lines marked with the symbols • are parallel, and this is also true for the straight lines marked with the symbol ⋄. This means that the line marked with • is parallel to the axis of $joint_i$, and the line marked with the symbol ⋄ is parallel to the coordinate axis $\boldsymbol{x}_{i-1}$. Use this figure as a reference. All the details are explained below.

link length	a_i	The perpendicular distance between the axes of $joint_i$ and $joint_{i+1}$.
link twist	α_i	The angle between the axes of $joint_i$ and $joint_{i+1}$. The angle α_i is measured around the $\boldsymbol{x}_i$-axis. Positive angles are measured counterclockwise when looking from the tip of vector $\boldsymbol{x}_i$ toward its foot.
link offset	d_i	The distance between the origins of the coordinate frames attached to joint $joint_{i-1}$ and $joint_i$ measured along the axis of $joint_i$. For a prismatic joint this is a joint parameter.
joint angle	φ_i	The angle between the link lengths $\boldsymbol{a}_{i-1}$ and $\boldsymbol{a}_i$. The angle φ_i is measured around the $\boldsymbol{z}_i$-axis. Positive angles are measured counterclockwise when looking from the tip of vector $\boldsymbol{z}_i$ toward its foot. For a revolute joint this is a joint parameter.

Table 2.1: Denavit-Hartenberg parameters.

2.3.1 The Link Vector $\boldsymbol{a}_i$ and the Link Length $a_i = \|\boldsymbol{a}_i\|_2$

Consider the axes of $joint_i$ and $joint_{i+1}$. The link length a_i is the shortest distance between these axes. This can also be formulated as: the link length a_i is the distance between the closest point $\boldsymbol{p}_i$ on the axis of $joint_i$ and $\boldsymbol{p}_{i+1}$ on the axis of $joint_{i+1}$. Let the joint axes be given by the parametric vector equations

$$\boldsymbol{l}_i(s) = \boldsymbol{p}_i + s\boldsymbol{u}_i \tag{2.10a}$$

$$\boldsymbol{l}_{i+1}(t) = \boldsymbol{p}_{i+1} + t\boldsymbol{u}_{i+1} \tag{2.10b}$$

where $\boldsymbol{p}_i$ is a point on axis of $joint_i$, and $\boldsymbol{u}_i$ is a direction vector of that axis. Analogous for $\boldsymbol{p}_{i+1}$ and $\boldsymbol{u}_{i+1}$. This is shown in Figure 2.8. The following three sections describe three different methods for computing the link vector $\boldsymbol{a}_i$.

2.3.1.1 Method 1: The Pseudonaive Approach

The shortest distance, a_i, between the axes of $joint_i$ and $joint_{i+1}$ is given by the length of the vector which connects the axes and which is perpendicular to both of them. That distance can be computed as the dot product between the vector $\boldsymbol{p}_{i+1} - \boldsymbol{p}_i$ and a unit vector in the direction of $\boldsymbol{u}_i \times \boldsymbol{u}_{i+1}$

$$a_i = (\boldsymbol{p}_{i+1} - \boldsymbol{p}_i) \cdot \frac{\boldsymbol{u}_i \times \boldsymbol{u}_{i+1}}{\|\boldsymbol{u}_i \times \boldsymbol{u}_{i+1}\|_2} \tag{2.11}$$

To find the locations of the points $\boldsymbol{o}_i$ and $\boldsymbol{o}_{\boldsymbol{a}_i}$ where this distance exists, one can go some distance s from point $\boldsymbol{p}_i$ along joint axis i, and then the distance a_i along the unit vector $\boldsymbol{u}_i \times \boldsymbol{u}_{i+1} / \|\boldsymbol{u}_i \times \boldsymbol{u}_{i+1}\|_2$, and finally some distance t along joint axis $i+1$ to arrive at point $\boldsymbol{p}_{i+1}$. This results in the following equation

$$\boldsymbol{p}_i + s\boldsymbol{u}_i + a_i \frac{\boldsymbol{u}_i \times \boldsymbol{u}_{i+1}}{\|\boldsymbol{u}_i \times \boldsymbol{u}_{i+1}\|_2} = \boldsymbol{p}_{i+1} + t\boldsymbol{u}_{i+1} \quad \Longrightarrow \tag{2.12a}$$

$$s\boldsymbol{u}_i - t\boldsymbol{u}_{i+1} = \boldsymbol{p}_{i+1} - \boldsymbol{p}_i - a_i \frac{\boldsymbol{u}_i \times \boldsymbol{u}_{i+1}}{\|\boldsymbol{u}_i \times \boldsymbol{u}_{i+1}\|_2} \tag{2.12b}$$

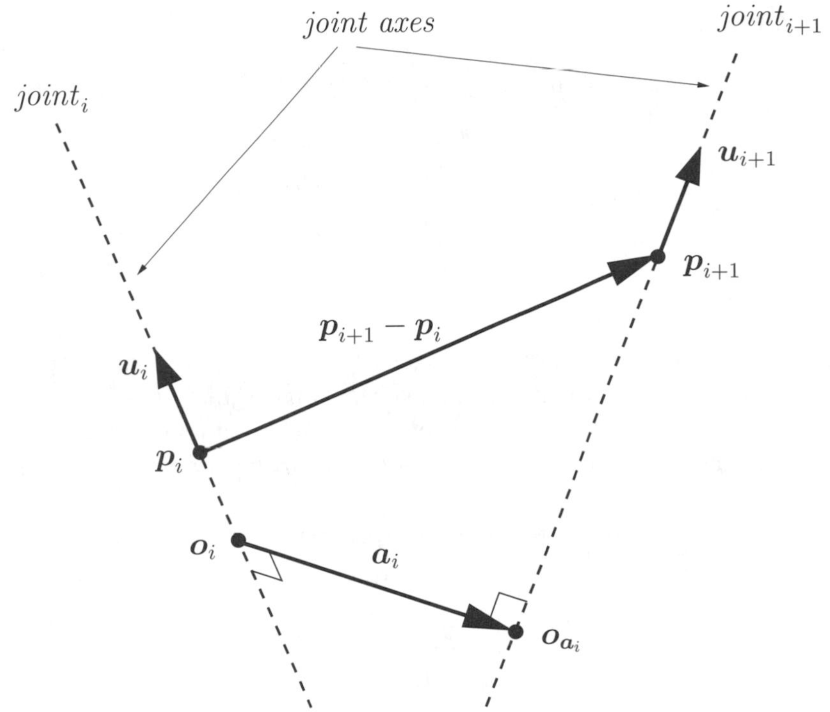

Figure 2.8: The shortest distance between the axes of $joint_i$ and $joint_{i+1}$ is given by the vector $\boldsymbol{a}_i$, which is perpendicular to both joint axes. The length of $\boldsymbol{a}_i$ is denoted the link length.

Computing the dot products of (2.12b) and the vectors $\boldsymbol{u}_i$ and $\boldsymbol{u}_{i+1}$, and recalling that the dot product between $\boldsymbol{u}_i \times \boldsymbol{u}_{i+1}$ and $\boldsymbol{u}_i$ and $\boldsymbol{u}_{i+1}$ vanish, the following equations in the unknowns s, t are obtained.

$$s \left\| \boldsymbol{u}_i \right\|_2^2 - t(\boldsymbol{u}_i \cdot \boldsymbol{u}_{i+1}) = (\boldsymbol{p}_{i+1} - \boldsymbol{p}_i) \cdot \boldsymbol{u}_i \tag{2.13a}$$

$$s(\boldsymbol{u}_i \cdot \boldsymbol{u}_{i+1}) - t \left\| \boldsymbol{u}_{i+1} \right\|_2^2 = (\boldsymbol{p}_{i+1} - \boldsymbol{p}_i) \cdot \boldsymbol{u}_{i+1} \tag{2.13b}$$

The solution s, t of this linear system of equations is given by

$$s = \frac{(\boldsymbol{p}_{i+1} - \boldsymbol{p}_i) \cdot (\boldsymbol{u}_i \left\| \boldsymbol{u}_{i+1} \right\|_2^2 - \boldsymbol{u}_{i+1}(\boldsymbol{u}_i \cdot \boldsymbol{u}_{i+1}))}{\left\| \boldsymbol{u}_i \right\|_2^2 \left\| \boldsymbol{u}_{i+1} \right\|_2^2 - (\boldsymbol{u}_i \cdot \boldsymbol{u}_{i+1})^2} \tag{2.14a}$$

$$t = \frac{(\boldsymbol{p}_{i+1} - \boldsymbol{p}_i) \cdot (\boldsymbol{u}_i(\boldsymbol{u}_i \cdot \boldsymbol{u}_{i+1}) - \boldsymbol{u}_{i+1} \left\| \boldsymbol{u}_i \right\|_2^2)}{\left\| \boldsymbol{u}_i \right\|_2^2 \left\| \boldsymbol{u}_{i+1} \right\|_2^2 - (\boldsymbol{u}_i \cdot \boldsymbol{u}_{i+1})^2} \tag{2.14b}$$

Using (2.10) the points $\boldsymbol{o}_i$ and $\boldsymbol{o}_{\boldsymbol{a}_i}$ can be computed as

$$\boldsymbol{o}_i = \boldsymbol{l}_i(s) = \boldsymbol{p}_i + \frac{(\boldsymbol{p}_{i+1} - \boldsymbol{p}_i) \cdot (\boldsymbol{u}_i \|\boldsymbol{u}_{i+1}\|_2^2 - \boldsymbol{u}_{i+1}(\boldsymbol{u}_i \cdot \boldsymbol{u}_{i+1}))}{\|\boldsymbol{u}_i\|_2^2 \|\boldsymbol{u}_{i+1}\|_2^2 - (\boldsymbol{u}_i \cdot \boldsymbol{u}_{i+1})^2} \boldsymbol{u}_i \tag{2.15a}$$

$$\boldsymbol{o}_{\boldsymbol{a}_i} = \boldsymbol{l}_{i+1}(t) = \boldsymbol{p}_{i+1} + \frac{(\boldsymbol{p}_{i+1} - \boldsymbol{p}_i) \cdot (\boldsymbol{u}_i(\boldsymbol{u}_i \cdot \boldsymbol{u}_{i+1}) - \boldsymbol{u}_{i+1} \|\boldsymbol{u}_i\|_2^2)}{\|\boldsymbol{u}_i\|_2^2 \|\boldsymbol{u}_{i+1}\|_2^2 - (\boldsymbol{u}_i \cdot \boldsymbol{u}_{i+1})^2} \boldsymbol{u}_{i+1} \tag{2.15b}$$

2.3.1.2 Method 2: The Geometric Approach

The vector, which is perpendicular to both joint axes is given by the cross product of the direction vectors $\boldsymbol{u}_i \times \boldsymbol{u}_{i+1}$, but it is not known where this vector is located on the joint axes. To find this location, one can go some distance s from point $\boldsymbol{p}_i$ along the axis of $joint_i$, and then go some distance k along $\boldsymbol{u}_i \times \boldsymbol{u}_{i+1}$, and finally go some distance t along the axis of $joint_{i+1}$ to arrive at point $\boldsymbol{p}_{i+1}$. This can be expressed in the following equation

$$\boldsymbol{p}_i + s\boldsymbol{u}_i + k\boldsymbol{u}_i \times \boldsymbol{u}_{i+1} = \boldsymbol{p}_{i+1} + t\boldsymbol{u}_{i+1} \tag{2.16}$$

This is a vector equation in three unknowns s, t, k. To solve this equation, first eliminate the unknown k by computing the dot product of (2.16) and vector $\boldsymbol{u}_i$.

$$\boldsymbol{p}_i \cdot \boldsymbol{u}_i + s\boldsymbol{u}_i \cdot \boldsymbol{u}_i + k(\boldsymbol{u}_i \times \boldsymbol{u}_{i+1}) \cdot \boldsymbol{u}_i = \boldsymbol{p}_{i+1} \cdot \boldsymbol{u}_i + t\boldsymbol{u}_{i+1} \cdot \boldsymbol{u}_i, \tag{2.17a}$$

$$\boldsymbol{p}_i \cdot \boldsymbol{u}_i + s\boldsymbol{u}_i \cdot \boldsymbol{u}_i = \boldsymbol{p}_{i+1} \cdot \boldsymbol{u}_i + t\boldsymbol{u}_{i+1} \cdot \boldsymbol{u}_i, \tag{2.17b}$$

$$s \|\boldsymbol{u}_i\|_2^2 - t(\boldsymbol{u}_i \cdot \boldsymbol{u}_{i+1}) = (\boldsymbol{p}_{i+1} - \boldsymbol{p}_i) \cdot \boldsymbol{u}_i \tag{2.17c}$$

Second, eliminate the unknown k by computing the dot product of (2.16) and vector $\boldsymbol{u}_{i+1}$.

$$\boldsymbol{p}_i \cdot \boldsymbol{u}_{i+1} + s\boldsymbol{u}_i \cdot \boldsymbol{u}_{i+1} + k(\boldsymbol{u}_i \times \boldsymbol{u}_{i+1}) \cdot \boldsymbol{u}_{i+1} = \boldsymbol{p}_{i+1} \cdot \boldsymbol{u}_{i+1} + t\boldsymbol{u}_{i+1} \cdot \boldsymbol{u}_{i+1}, \tag{2.18a}$$

$$\boldsymbol{p}_i \cdot \boldsymbol{u}_{i+1} + s\boldsymbol{u}_i \cdot \boldsymbol{u}_{i+1} = \boldsymbol{p}_{i+1} \cdot \boldsymbol{u}_{i+1} + t\boldsymbol{u}_{i+1} \cdot \boldsymbol{u}_{i+1}, \tag{2.18b}$$

$$s(\boldsymbol{u}_i \cdot \boldsymbol{u}_{i+1}) - t \|\boldsymbol{u}_{i+1}\|_2^2 = (\boldsymbol{p}_{i+1} - \boldsymbol{p}_i) \cdot \boldsymbol{u}_{i+1} \tag{2.18c}$$

Finally, eliminate the unknowns s, t by computing the dot product of (2.16) and vector $\boldsymbol{u}_i \times \boldsymbol{u}_{i+1}$.

$$\begin{aligned}\boldsymbol{p}_i \cdot (\boldsymbol{u}_i \times \boldsymbol{u}_{i+1}) + s\boldsymbol{u}_i \cdot (\boldsymbol{u}_i \times \boldsymbol{u}_{i+1}) + k(\boldsymbol{u}_i \times \boldsymbol{u}_{i+1}) \cdot (\boldsymbol{u}_i \times \boldsymbol{u}_{i+1})&\\ = \boldsymbol{p}_{i+1} \cdot (\boldsymbol{u}_i \times \boldsymbol{u}_{i+1}) + t\boldsymbol{u}_{i+1} \cdot (\boldsymbol{u}_i \times \boldsymbol{u}_{i+1}),&\end{aligned} \tag{2.19a}$$

$$\boldsymbol{p}_i \cdot (\boldsymbol{u}_i \times \boldsymbol{u}_{i+1}) + k(\boldsymbol{u}_i \times \boldsymbol{u}_{i+1}) \cdot (\boldsymbol{u}_i \times \boldsymbol{u}_{i+1}) = \boldsymbol{p}_{i+1} \cdot (\boldsymbol{u}_i \times \boldsymbol{u}_{i+1}), \tag{2.19b}$$

$$k \|\boldsymbol{u}_i \times \boldsymbol{u}_{i+1}\|_2^2 = (\boldsymbol{p}_{i+1} - \boldsymbol{p}_i) \cdot (\boldsymbol{u}_i \times \boldsymbol{u}_{i+1}) \tag{2.19c}$$

The equations (2.17c), (2.18c) and (2.19a) form a system of three equations in the unknowns s, t, k.

$$s \|\boldsymbol{u}_i\|_2^2 - t(\boldsymbol{u}_i \cdot \boldsymbol{u}_{i+1}) = (\boldsymbol{p}_{i+1} - \boldsymbol{p}_i) \cdot \boldsymbol{u}_i \tag{2.20a}$$

$$s(\boldsymbol{u}_i \cdot \boldsymbol{u}_{i+1}) - t \|\boldsymbol{u}_{i+1}\|_2^2 = (\boldsymbol{p}_{i+1} - \boldsymbol{p}_i) \cdot \boldsymbol{u}_{i+1} \tag{2.20b}$$

$$k \|\boldsymbol{u}_i \times \boldsymbol{u}_{i+1}\|_2^2 = (\boldsymbol{p}_{i+1} - \boldsymbol{p}_i) \cdot (\boldsymbol{u}_i \times \boldsymbol{u}_{i+1}) \tag{2.20c}$$

It can be seen that only (2.20a) and (2.20b) are needed to solve for the unknowns s, t, and (2.20c) yields k directly.

From (2.20c) it can be seen that the shortest distance between the axes of $joint_i$ and $joint_{i+1}$ is given by the vector

$$\boldsymbol{a}_i = \frac{(\boldsymbol{p}_{i+1} - \boldsymbol{p}_i) \cdot (\boldsymbol{u}_i \times \boldsymbol{u}_{i+1})}{\|\boldsymbol{u}_i \times \boldsymbol{u}_{i+1}\|_2^2} (\boldsymbol{u}_i \times \boldsymbol{u}_{i+1}) \tag{2.21a}$$

$$= \frac{(\boldsymbol{p}_{i+1} - \boldsymbol{p}_i) \cdot (\boldsymbol{u}_i \times \boldsymbol{u}_{i+1})}{\|\boldsymbol{u}_i \times \boldsymbol{u}_{i+1}\|_2} \frac{\boldsymbol{u}_i \times \boldsymbol{u}_{i+1}}{\|\boldsymbol{u}_i \times \boldsymbol{u}_{i+1}\|_2} \tag{2.21b}$$

$$= a_i \frac{\boldsymbol{u}_i \times \boldsymbol{u}_{i+1}}{\|\boldsymbol{u}_i \times \boldsymbol{u}_{i+1}\|_2} \tag{2.21c}$$

where the link length a_i is given by

$$a_i = \frac{(\boldsymbol{p}_{i+1} - \boldsymbol{p}_i) \cdot (\boldsymbol{u}_i \times \boldsymbol{u}_{i+1})}{\|\boldsymbol{u}_i \times \boldsymbol{u}_{i+1}\|_2} \tag{2.22a}$$

From (2.20a) and (2.20b) the unknowns s, t can be computed

$$s = \frac{(\boldsymbol{p}_{i+1} - \boldsymbol{p}_i) \cdot (\boldsymbol{u}_i \|\boldsymbol{u}_{i+1}\|_2^2 - \boldsymbol{u}_{i+1}(\boldsymbol{u}_i \cdot \boldsymbol{u}_{i+1}))}{\|\boldsymbol{u}_i\|_2^2 \|\boldsymbol{u}_{i+1}\|_2^2 - (\boldsymbol{u}_i \cdot \boldsymbol{u}_{i+1})^2} \tag{2.23a}$$

$$t = \frac{(\boldsymbol{p}_{i+1} - \boldsymbol{p}_i) \cdot (\boldsymbol{u}_i(\boldsymbol{u}_i \cdot \boldsymbol{u}_{i+1}) - \boldsymbol{u}_{i+1} \|\boldsymbol{u}_i\|_2^2)}{\|\boldsymbol{u}_i\|_2^2 \|\boldsymbol{u}_{i+1}\|_2^2 - (\boldsymbol{u}_i \cdot \boldsymbol{u}_{i+1})^2} \tag{2.23b}$$

Using (2.10) and the solution s, t the points $\boldsymbol{o}_i$ and $\boldsymbol{o}_{\boldsymbol{a}_i}$ can be computed as

$$\boldsymbol{o}_i = \boldsymbol{l}_i(s) = \boldsymbol{p}_i + \frac{(\boldsymbol{p}_{i+1} - \boldsymbol{p}_i) \cdot (\boldsymbol{u}_i \|\boldsymbol{u}_{i+1}\|_2^2 - \boldsymbol{u}_{i+1}(\boldsymbol{u}_i \cdot \boldsymbol{u}_{i+1}))}{\|\boldsymbol{u}_i\|_2^2 \|\boldsymbol{u}_{i+1}\|_2^2 - (\boldsymbol{u}_i \cdot \boldsymbol{u}_{i+1})^2} \boldsymbol{u}_i \tag{2.24a}$$

$$\boldsymbol{o}_{\boldsymbol{a}_i} = \boldsymbol{l}_{i+1}(t) = \boldsymbol{p}_{i+1} + \frac{(\boldsymbol{p}_{i+1} - \boldsymbol{p}_i) \cdot (\boldsymbol{u}_i(\boldsymbol{u}_i \cdot \boldsymbol{u}_{i+1}) - \boldsymbol{u}_{i+1} \|\boldsymbol{u}_i\|_2^2)}{\|\boldsymbol{u}_i\|_2^2 \|\boldsymbol{u}_{i+1}\|_2^2 - (\boldsymbol{u}_i \cdot \boldsymbol{u}_{i+1})^2} \boldsymbol{u}_{i+1} \tag{2.24b}$$

The point $\boldsymbol{o}_i$ is the origin of the coordinate system attached to the axis of $joint_i$, and the point $\boldsymbol{o}_{\boldsymbol{a}_i}$ is the intersection between the axis of $joint_{i+1}$ and the vector $\boldsymbol{a}_i$ when it starts at point $\boldsymbol{o}_i$.

2.3.1.3 Method 3: The Analytic Approach

The distance between two arbitrary points located on the axes of $joint_i$ and $joint_{i+1}$ respectively is given by the expression

$$d(s,t) = \sqrt{(\boldsymbol{l}_{i+1}(t) - \boldsymbol{l}_i(s)) \cdot (\boldsymbol{l}_{i+1}(t) - \boldsymbol{l}_i(s))} \tag{2.25a}$$

$$= \sqrt{(\boldsymbol{p}_{i+1} + t\boldsymbol{u}_{i+1} - \boldsymbol{p}_i - s\boldsymbol{u}_i) \cdot (\boldsymbol{p}_{i+1} + t\boldsymbol{u}_{i+1} - \boldsymbol{p}_i - s\boldsymbol{u}_i)} \tag{2.25b}$$

The link length of $link_i$, a_i, is given as minimum distance between the joint axes. Therefore, a_i is the solution to the minimization problem

$$a_i = \min d(s,t) = \min \sqrt{(\boldsymbol{l}_{i+1}(t) - \boldsymbol{l}_i(s)) \cdot (\boldsymbol{l}_{i+1}(t) - \boldsymbol{l}_i(s))} \tag{2.26a}$$

$$= \min \sqrt{(\boldsymbol{p}_{i+1} + t\boldsymbol{u}_{i+1} - \boldsymbol{p}_i - s\boldsymbol{u}_i) \cdot (\boldsymbol{p}_{i+1} + t\boldsymbol{u}_{i+1} - \boldsymbol{p}_i - s\boldsymbol{u}_i)} \tag{2.26b}$$

A necessary condition for (2.26a) to have an extrema is that it has the stationary points

$$\frac{\partial d(s,t)}{\partial s} = \frac{(\boldsymbol{p}_{i+1} + t\boldsymbol{u}_{i+1} - \boldsymbol{p}_i - s\boldsymbol{u}_i) \cdot \boldsymbol{u}_i}{\sqrt{(\boldsymbol{p}_{i+1} + t\boldsymbol{u}_{i+1} - \boldsymbol{p}_i - s\boldsymbol{u}_i) \cdot (\boldsymbol{p}_{i+1} + t\boldsymbol{u}_{i+1} - \boldsymbol{p}_i - s\boldsymbol{u}_i)}} = 0 \tag{2.27a}$$

$$\frac{\partial d(s,t)}{\partial t} = \frac{(\boldsymbol{p}_{i+1} + t\boldsymbol{u}_{i+1} - \boldsymbol{p}_i - s\boldsymbol{u}_i) \cdot \boldsymbol{u}_{i+1}}{\sqrt{(\boldsymbol{p}_{i+1} + t\boldsymbol{u}_{i+1} - \boldsymbol{p}_i - s\boldsymbol{u}_i) \cdot (\boldsymbol{p}_{i+1} + t\boldsymbol{u}_{i+1} - \boldsymbol{p}_i - s\boldsymbol{u}_i)}} = 0 \tag{2.27b}$$

The requirement that (2.27) vanish is equivalent to their numerators being equal to zero

$$(\boldsymbol{p}_{i+1} + t\boldsymbol{u}_{i+1} - \boldsymbol{p}_i - s\boldsymbol{u}_i) \cdot \boldsymbol{u}_i = 0 \tag{2.28a}$$

$$(\boldsymbol{p}_{i+1} + t\boldsymbol{u}_{i+1} - \boldsymbol{p}_i - s\boldsymbol{u}_i) \cdot \boldsymbol{u}_{i+1} = 0 \tag{2.28b}$$

Rewriting this system of equations yields

$$s \left\|\boldsymbol{u}_i\right\|_2^2 - t(\boldsymbol{u}_i \cdot \boldsymbol{u}_{i+1}) = (\boldsymbol{p}_{i+1} - \boldsymbol{p}_i) \cdot \boldsymbol{u}_i \tag{2.29a}$$

$$s(\boldsymbol{u}_i \cdot \boldsymbol{u}_{i+1}) - t \left\|\boldsymbol{u}_{i+1}\right\|_2^2 = (\boldsymbol{p}_{i+1} - \boldsymbol{p}_i) \cdot \boldsymbol{u}_{i+1} \tag{2.29b}$$

The solution s, t of this linear system of equations is given by

$$s = \frac{(\boldsymbol{p}_{i+1} - \boldsymbol{p}_i) \cdot (\boldsymbol{u}_i \left\|\boldsymbol{u}_{i+1}\right\|_2^2 - \boldsymbol{u}_{i+1}(\boldsymbol{u}_i \cdot \boldsymbol{u}_{i+1}))}{\left\|\boldsymbol{u}_i\right\|_2^2 \left\|\boldsymbol{u}_{i+1}\right\|_2^2 - (\boldsymbol{u}_i \cdot \boldsymbol{u}_{i+1})^2} \tag{2.30a}$$

$$t = \frac{(\boldsymbol{p}_{i+1} - \boldsymbol{p}_i) \cdot (\boldsymbol{u}_i(\boldsymbol{u}_i \cdot \boldsymbol{u}_{i+1}) - \boldsymbol{u}_{i+1} \left\|\boldsymbol{u}_i\right\|_2^2)}{\left\|\boldsymbol{u}_i\right\|_2^2 \left\|\boldsymbol{u}_{i+1}\right\|_2^2 - (\boldsymbol{u}_i \cdot \boldsymbol{u}_{i+1})^2} \tag{2.30b}$$

Using (2.10) and the solution s, t the points $\boldsymbol{o}_i$ and $\boldsymbol{o}_{\boldsymbol{a}_i}$ can be computed as

$$\boldsymbol{o}_i = \boldsymbol{l}_i(s) = \boldsymbol{p}_i + \frac{(\boldsymbol{p}_{i+1} - \boldsymbol{p}_i) \cdot (\boldsymbol{u}_i \left\|\boldsymbol{u}_{i+1}\right\|_2^2 - \boldsymbol{u}_{i+1}(\boldsymbol{u}_i \cdot \boldsymbol{u}_{i+1}))}{\left\|\boldsymbol{u}_i\right\|_2^2 \left\|\boldsymbol{u}_{i+1}\right\|_2^2 - (\boldsymbol{u}_i \cdot \boldsymbol{u}_{i+1})^2} \boldsymbol{u}_i \tag{2.31a}$$

$$\boldsymbol{o}_{\boldsymbol{a}_i} = \boldsymbol{l}_{i+1}(t) = \boldsymbol{p}_{i+1} + \frac{(\boldsymbol{p}_{i+1} - \boldsymbol{p}_i) \cdot (\boldsymbol{u}_i(\boldsymbol{u}_i \cdot \boldsymbol{u}_{i+1}) - \boldsymbol{u}_{i+1} \left\|\boldsymbol{u}_i\right\|_2^2)}{\left\|\boldsymbol{u}_i\right\|_2^2 \left\|\boldsymbol{u}_{i+1}\right\|_2^2 - (\boldsymbol{u}_i \cdot \boldsymbol{u}_{i+1})^2} \boldsymbol{u}_{i+1} \tag{2.31b}$$

These two points are the closest points on the axes of $joint_i$ and $joint_{i+1}$. Therefore, the link vector $\boldsymbol{a}_i$ and the link length a_i are given by

$$\boldsymbol{a}_i = \boldsymbol{o}_{\boldsymbol{a}_i} - \boldsymbol{o}_i \tag{2.32a}$$

$$a_i = \left\|\boldsymbol{a}_i\right\|_2 = \left\|\boldsymbol{o}_{\boldsymbol{a}_i} - \boldsymbol{o}_i\right\|_2 \tag{2.32b}$$

The Link Vector $\boldsymbol{a}_i$

The link vector $\boldsymbol{a}_i$ is the vector that connects the two closest points on the axes of $joint_i$ and $joint_{i+1}$ respectively. Therefore, the link vector $\boldsymbol{a}_i$ is the difference between the points $\boldsymbol{o}_{\boldsymbol{a}_i}$ and $\boldsymbol{o}_i$ from (2.31).

$$\boldsymbol{a}_i = \boldsymbol{o}_{\boldsymbol{a}_i} - \boldsymbol{o}_i \tag{2.33a}$$

$$= \left(\boldsymbol{p}_{i+1} + \frac{(\boldsymbol{p}_{i+1} - \boldsymbol{p}_i) \cdot (\boldsymbol{u}_i(\boldsymbol{u}_i \cdot \boldsymbol{u}_{i+1}) - \boldsymbol{u}_{i+1} \|\boldsymbol{u}_i\|_2^2)}{\|\boldsymbol{u}_i\|_2^2 \|\boldsymbol{u}_{i+1}\|_2^2 - (\boldsymbol{u}_i \cdot \boldsymbol{u}_{i+1})^2} \boldsymbol{u}_{i+1} \right) - \left(\boldsymbol{p}_i + \frac{(\boldsymbol{p}_{i+1} - \boldsymbol{p}_i) \cdot (\boldsymbol{u}_i \|\boldsymbol{u}_{i+1}\|_2^2 - \boldsymbol{u}_{i+1}(\boldsymbol{u}_i \cdot \boldsymbol{u}_{i+1}))}{\|\boldsymbol{u}_i\|_2^2 \|\boldsymbol{u}_{i+1}\|_2^2 - (\boldsymbol{u}_i \cdot \boldsymbol{u}_{i+1})^2} \boldsymbol{u}_i \right) \tag{2.33b}$$

$$= (\boldsymbol{p}_{i+1} - \boldsymbol{p}_i) - \frac{(\boldsymbol{p}_{i+1} - \boldsymbol{p}_i) \cdot (\boldsymbol{u}_i \|\boldsymbol{u}_{i+1}\|_2^2 - \boldsymbol{u}_{i+1}(\boldsymbol{u}_i \cdot \boldsymbol{u}_{i+1}))}{\|\boldsymbol{u}_i\|_2^2 \|\boldsymbol{u}_{i+1}\|_2^2 - (\boldsymbol{u}_i \cdot \boldsymbol{u}_{i+1})^2} \boldsymbol{u}_i + \frac{(\boldsymbol{p}_{i+1} - \boldsymbol{p}_i) \cdot (\boldsymbol{u}_i(\boldsymbol{u}_i \cdot \boldsymbol{u}_{i+1}) - \boldsymbol{u}_{i+1} \|\boldsymbol{u}_i\|_2^2)}{\|\boldsymbol{u}_i\|_2^2 \|\boldsymbol{u}_{i+1}\|_2^2 - (\boldsymbol{u}_i \cdot \boldsymbol{u}_{i+1})^2} \boldsymbol{u}_{i+1} \tag{2.33c}$$

In the next section it will be shown that the link vector $\boldsymbol{a}_i$ is perpendicular to the axes of $joint_i$ and $joint_{i+1}$.

The Dot Products $\boldsymbol{a}_i \cdot \boldsymbol{u}_i$ and $\boldsymbol{a}_i \cdot \boldsymbol{u}_{i+1}$

In this section it is shown that the link vector $\boldsymbol{a}_i$ is perpendicular to both axes of $joint_i$ and $joint_{i+1}$. The dot product between the link vector $\boldsymbol{a}_i$ and the direction vector $\boldsymbol{u}_i$ of the axis of $joint_i$ is equal to

$$\boldsymbol{a}_i \cdot \boldsymbol{u}_i = (\boldsymbol{p}_{i+1} - \boldsymbol{p}_i) \cdot \boldsymbol{u}_i - \frac{(\boldsymbol{p}_{i+1} - \boldsymbol{p}_i) \cdot (\boldsymbol{u}_i \|\boldsymbol{u}_{i+1}\|_2^2 - \boldsymbol{u}_{i+1}(\boldsymbol{u}_i \cdot \boldsymbol{u}_{i+1}))}{\|\boldsymbol{u}_i\|_2^2 \|\boldsymbol{u}_{i+1}\|_2^2 - (\boldsymbol{u}_i \cdot \boldsymbol{u}_{i+1})^2} (\boldsymbol{u}_i \cdot \boldsymbol{u}_i) + \frac{(\boldsymbol{p}_{i+1} - \boldsymbol{p}_i) \cdot (\boldsymbol{u}_i(\boldsymbol{u}_i \cdot \boldsymbol{u}_{i+1}) - \boldsymbol{u}_{i+1} \|\boldsymbol{u}_i\|_2^2)}{\|\boldsymbol{u}_i\|_2^2 \|\boldsymbol{u}_{i+1}\|_2^2 - (\boldsymbol{u}_i \cdot \boldsymbol{u}_{i+1})^2} (\boldsymbol{u}_{i+1} \cdot \boldsymbol{u}_i) \tag{2.34a}$$

$$= (\boldsymbol{p}_{i+1} - \boldsymbol{p}_i) \cdot \boldsymbol{u}_i - \frac{(\boldsymbol{p}_{i+1} - \boldsymbol{p}_i) \cdot (\boldsymbol{u}_i \|\boldsymbol{u}_i\|_2^2 \|\boldsymbol{u}_{i+1}\|_2^2 - \boldsymbol{u}_{i+1} \|\boldsymbol{u}_i\|_2^2 (\boldsymbol{u}_i \cdot \boldsymbol{u}_{i+1}))}{\|\boldsymbol{u}_i\|_2^2 \|\boldsymbol{u}_{i+1}\|_2^2 - (\boldsymbol{u}_i \cdot \boldsymbol{u}_{i+1})^2} + \frac{(\boldsymbol{p}_{i+1} - \boldsymbol{p}_i) \cdot (\boldsymbol{u}_i(\boldsymbol{u}_i \cdot \boldsymbol{u}_{i+1})^2 - \boldsymbol{u}_{i+1} \|\boldsymbol{u}_i\|_2^2 (\boldsymbol{u}_i \cdot \boldsymbol{u}_{i+1}))}{\|\boldsymbol{u}_i\|_2^2 \|\boldsymbol{u}_{i+1}\|_2^2 - (\boldsymbol{u}_i \cdot \boldsymbol{u}_{i+1})^2} \tag{2.34b}$$

$$= (\boldsymbol{p}_{i+1} - \boldsymbol{p}_i) \cdot \boldsymbol{u}_i + (\boldsymbol{p}_{i+1} - \boldsymbol{p}_i) \cdot \boldsymbol{u}_i \left(\frac{-\|\boldsymbol{u}_i\|_2^2 \|\boldsymbol{u}_{i+1}\|_2^2 + (\boldsymbol{u}_i \cdot \boldsymbol{u}_{i+1})^2}{\|\boldsymbol{u}_i\|_2^2 \|\boldsymbol{u}_{i+1}\|_2^2 - (\boldsymbol{u}_i \cdot \boldsymbol{u}_{i+1})^2} \right) \tag{2.34c}$$

$$= (\boldsymbol{p}_{i+1} - \boldsymbol{p}_i) \cdot \boldsymbol{u}_i - (\boldsymbol{p}_{i+1} - \boldsymbol{p}_i) \cdot \boldsymbol{u}_i = 0 \tag{2.34d}$$

Analogously, it can be shown that the dot product between the link vector $\boldsymbol{a}_i$ and the direction vector $\boldsymbol{u}_{i+1}$ of the axis of $joint_{i+1}$ is then equal to 0, i.e., $\boldsymbol{a}_i \cdot \boldsymbol{u}_{i+1} = 0$.

$$\begin{aligned}
\boldsymbol{a}_i \cdot \boldsymbol{u}_{i+1} &= (\boldsymbol{p}_{i+1} - \boldsymbol{p}_i) \cdot \boldsymbol{u}_{i+1} - \frac{(\boldsymbol{p}_{i+1} - \boldsymbol{p}_i) \cdot (\boldsymbol{u}_i \left\|\boldsymbol{u}_{i+1}\right\|_2^2 - \boldsymbol{u}_{i+1}(\boldsymbol{u}_i \cdot \boldsymbol{u}_{i+1}))}{\left\|\boldsymbol{u}_i\right\|_2^2 \left\|\boldsymbol{u}_{i+1}\right\|_2^2 - (\boldsymbol{u}_i \cdot \boldsymbol{u}_{i+1})^2}(\boldsymbol{u}_i \cdot \boldsymbol{u}_{i+1}) \\
&\quad + \frac{(\boldsymbol{p}_{i+1} - \boldsymbol{p}_i) \cdot (\boldsymbol{u}_i(\boldsymbol{u}_i \cdot \boldsymbol{u}_{i+1}) - \boldsymbol{u}_{i+1} \left\|\boldsymbol{u}_i\right\|_2^2)}{\left\|\boldsymbol{u}_i\right\|_2^2 \left\|\boldsymbol{u}_{i+1}\right\|_2^2 - (\boldsymbol{u}_i \cdot \boldsymbol{u}_{i+1})^2}(\boldsymbol{u}_{i+1} \cdot \boldsymbol{u}_{i+1}) && \text{(2.35a)} \\
&= (\boldsymbol{p}_{i+1} - \boldsymbol{p}_i) \cdot \boldsymbol{u}_{i+1} - \frac{(\boldsymbol{p}_{i+1} - \boldsymbol{p}_i) \cdot (\boldsymbol{u}_i \left\|\boldsymbol{u}_{i+1}\right\|_2^2 (\boldsymbol{u}_i \cdot \boldsymbol{u}_{i+1}) - \boldsymbol{u}_{i+1}(\boldsymbol{u}_i \cdot \boldsymbol{u}_{i+1})^2)}{\left\|\boldsymbol{u}_i\right\|_2^2 \left\|\boldsymbol{u}_{i+1}\right\|_2^2 - (\boldsymbol{u}_i \cdot \boldsymbol{u}_{i+1})^2} \\
&\quad + \frac{(\boldsymbol{p}_{i+1} - \boldsymbol{p}_i) \cdot (\boldsymbol{u}_i \left\|\boldsymbol{u}_{i+1}\right\|_2^2 (\boldsymbol{u}_i \cdot \boldsymbol{u}_{i+1}) - \boldsymbol{u}_{i+1} \left\|\boldsymbol{u}_i\right\|_2^2 \left\|\boldsymbol{u}_{i+1}\right\|_2^2)}{\left\|\boldsymbol{u}_i\right\|_2^2 \left\|\boldsymbol{u}_{i+1}\right\|_2^2 - (\boldsymbol{u}_i \cdot \boldsymbol{u}_{i+1})^2} && \text{(2.35b)} \\
&= (\boldsymbol{p}_{i+1} - \boldsymbol{p}_i) \cdot \boldsymbol{u}_{i+1} + (\boldsymbol{p}_{i+1} - \boldsymbol{p}_i) \cdot \boldsymbol{u}_{i+1}\left(\frac{-\left\|\boldsymbol{u}_i\right\|_2^2 \left\|\boldsymbol{u}_{i+1}\right\|_2^2 + (\boldsymbol{u}_i \cdot \boldsymbol{u}_{i+1})^2}{\left\|\boldsymbol{u}_i\right\|_2^2 \left\|\boldsymbol{u}_{i+1}\right\|_2^2 - (\boldsymbol{u}_i \cdot \boldsymbol{u}_{i+1})^2}\right) && \text{(2.35c)} \\
&= (\boldsymbol{p}_{i+1} - \boldsymbol{p}_i) \cdot \boldsymbol{u}_{i+1} - (\boldsymbol{p}_{i+1} - \boldsymbol{p}_i) \cdot \boldsymbol{u}_{i+1} = 0 && \text{(2.35d)}
\end{aligned}$$

Thus, the link vector $\boldsymbol{a}_i$ is perpendicular to both axes of joints $joint_i$ and $joint_{i+1}$. This means that there exists a plane π_i with normal vector $\boldsymbol{a}_i$ which contains the axis of $joint_i$. Also, there exists a plane π_{i+1} with the same normal vector $\boldsymbol{a}_i$ which contains the axis of $joint_{i+1}$, see Figure 2.9.

2.3.1.4 The Easy Way to Compute $\boldsymbol{a}_i$ and $\left\|\boldsymbol{a}_i\right\|_2$

The link vector $\boldsymbol{a}_i$ is perpendicular to both of the axes of $joint_i$ and $joint_{i+1}$ as shown in (2.34) and (2.35) and in Figure 2.9. The unit vector $\boldsymbol{c}_i$ given by the cross product between the direction vectors $\boldsymbol{u}_i$ and of the $\boldsymbol{u}_{i+1}$ of the joint axes

$$\boldsymbol{c}_i = \frac{\boldsymbol{u}_i \times \boldsymbol{u}_{i+1}}{\left\|\boldsymbol{u}_i \times \boldsymbol{u}_{i+1}\right\|_2} \tag{2.36}$$

is parallel to the link vector $\boldsymbol{a}_i$.

Given two points $\boldsymbol{p}_i$ and $\boldsymbol{p}_i$ on the axes of $joint_i$ and $joint_i$ respectively, the link length can be computed as

$$\left\|\boldsymbol{a}_i\right\|_2 = \left\|(\boldsymbol{p}_{i+1} - \boldsymbol{p}_i) \cdot \boldsymbol{c}_i\right\|_2 = \left|(\boldsymbol{p}_{i+1} - \boldsymbol{p}_i) \cdot \frac{\boldsymbol{u}_i \times \boldsymbol{u}_{i+1}}{\left\|\boldsymbol{u}_i \times \boldsymbol{u}_{i+1}\right\|_2}\right| \tag{2.37}$$

and the link vector $\boldsymbol{a}_i$ can be computed as

$$\boldsymbol{a}_i = ((\boldsymbol{p}_{i+1} - \boldsymbol{p}_i) \cdot \boldsymbol{c}_i)\boldsymbol{c}_i = \left((\boldsymbol{p}_{i+1} - \boldsymbol{p}_i) \cdot \frac{\boldsymbol{u}_i \times \boldsymbol{u}_{i+1}}{\left\|\boldsymbol{u}_i \times \boldsymbol{u}_{i+1}\right\|_2}\right)\frac{\boldsymbol{u}_i \times \boldsymbol{u}_{i+1}}{\left\|\boldsymbol{u}_i \times \boldsymbol{u}_{i+1}\right\|_2} \tag{2.38}$$

These computations are illustrated in Figure 2.10. It can be shown by simple but very many algebraic manipulations that the link vectors computed by (2.33) and (2.38) are identical.

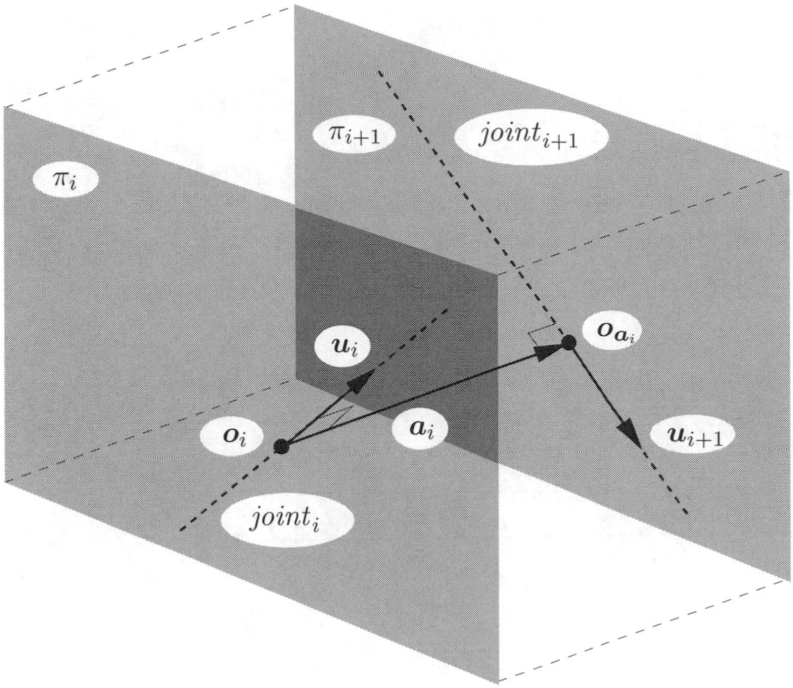

Figure 2.9: The axes of $joint_i$ and $joint_{i+1}$ are contained in two parallel planes π_i and π_{i+1} respectively. The perpendicular distance between the planes π_i and π_{i+1} is equal to $\|\boldsymbol{a}_i\|_2$.

The vector $\boldsymbol{c}_i = \boldsymbol{u}_i \times \boldsymbol{u}_{i+1} / \|\boldsymbol{u}_i \times \boldsymbol{u}_{i+1}\|_2$ can either point from the axis of $joint_i$ to the axis of $joint_{i+1}$ or in the opposite direction depending on the orientations of the vectors $\boldsymbol{u}_i$ and $\boldsymbol{u}_{i+1}$. If the vector $\boldsymbol{c}_i$ points from the axis of $joint_{i+1}$ to the axis of $joint_i$, the dot product $(\boldsymbol{p}_{i+1} - \boldsymbol{p}_i) \cdot \boldsymbol{c}_i$ is negative, and the link vector $\boldsymbol{a}_i$ will get the right orientation.

In the other case where the vector $\boldsymbol{c}_i$ points from the axis of $joint_i$ to the axis of $joint_{i+1}$, the one shown in Figure 2.10, the orientation will obviously be right.

2.3.1.5 Special Case: The Joint Axes Intersect

If the axes of $joint_i$ and $joint_{i+i}$ intersect then the shortest distance between the axes, a_i is equal to zero, and the link vector is the null vector, which has any direction. In this case, choose the link length, $a_i = 0$ and the link vector to be equal to the cross product between the direction vectors, $\boldsymbol{u}_i$ and $\boldsymbol{u}_{i+1}$ between the axes of $joint_i$ and $joint_{i+1}$. That is, choose

$$\boldsymbol{a}_i = \frac{\boldsymbol{u}_i \times \boldsymbol{u}_{i+1}}{\|\boldsymbol{u}_i \times \boldsymbol{u}_{i+1}\|_2} \tag{2.39a}$$

$$a_i = 0 \tag{2.39b}$$

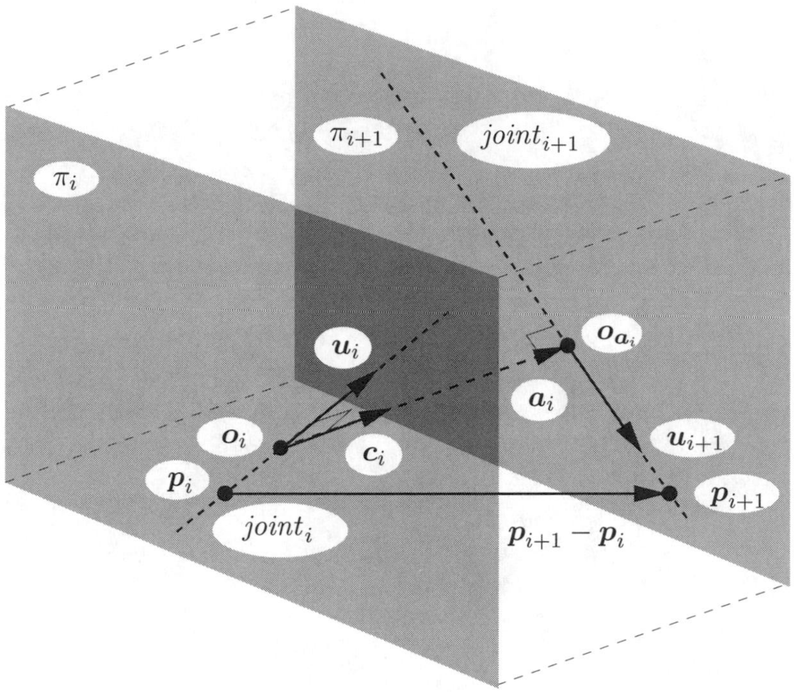

Figure 2.10: An easy way of computing the link length a_i. Let the vector $\boldsymbol{c}$ be equal to the unit cross product between the direction vectors of the axes, i.e., the vector $\boldsymbol{c}_i$ is given as $\boldsymbol{c}_i = \frac{\boldsymbol{u}_i \times \boldsymbol{u}_{i+1}}{\|\boldsymbol{u}_i \times \boldsymbol{u}_{i+1}\|_2}$, and let the points $\boldsymbol{p}_i$ and $\boldsymbol{p}_{i+1}$ be arbitrary points on the axes, e.g., the points given in (2.10). Then the link length is equal to the dot product between the vector $\boldsymbol{c}_i$ and the vector $(\boldsymbol{p}_{i+1} - \boldsymbol{p}_i)$. That is $a_i = (\boldsymbol{p}_{i+1} - \boldsymbol{p}_i) \cdot \boldsymbol{c}_i$.

For this special case it is convenient to choose such a strange link vector that does not conform to (2.38), because the link length a_i is a Denavit-Hartenberg parameter, and the link vector $\boldsymbol{a}_i$ is used to attach the coordinate frame, the $\boldsymbol{x}_i$-axis of $link_i$. Furthermore, the origin $\boldsymbol{o}_i$ and the point $\boldsymbol{o}_{\boldsymbol{a}_i}$ are uniquely defined as the intersection point.

2.3.1.6 Special Case: The Joint Axes are Parallel

If the axes of $joint_i$ and $joint_{i+i}$ are parallel, there is no unique shortest distance between the axes, see Figure 2.11. In this case, compute the link vector and the link length as follows

$$\boldsymbol{a}_i = (\boldsymbol{p}_{i+1} - \boldsymbol{p}_i) - \left((\boldsymbol{p}_{i+1} - \boldsymbol{p}_i) \cdot \frac{\boldsymbol{u}_i}{\|\boldsymbol{u}_i\|_2} \right) \frac{\boldsymbol{u}_i}{\|\boldsymbol{u}_i\|_2} \tag{2.40a}$$

$$a_i = \|\boldsymbol{a}_i\|_2 \tag{2.40b}$$

where $\boldsymbol{p}_i$ and $\boldsymbol{p}_{i+1}$ are known points, and $\boldsymbol{u}_i$ and $\boldsymbol{u}_{i+1}$ are known direction vectors of the axes of $joint_i$ and $joint_{i+1}$, see (2.10). The origin $\boldsymbol{o}_i$ can be chosen arbitrarily, and the point $\boldsymbol{o}_{\boldsymbol{a}_i}$ is obviously given by

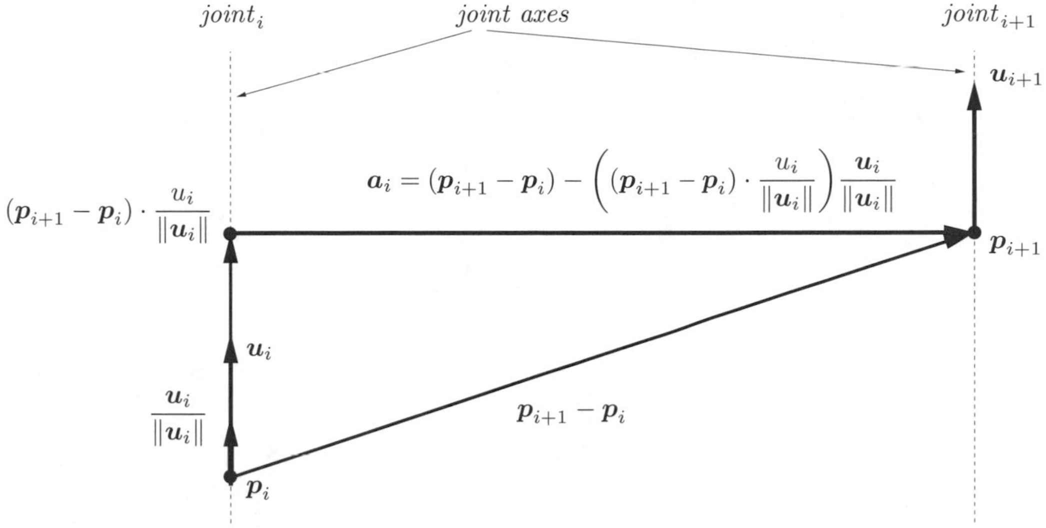

Figure 2.11: The joint axes are parallel, so there is no unique shortest distance between them.

$\boldsymbol{o}_i$ and $\boldsymbol{a}_i$. Since the origin $\boldsymbol{o}_i$ can be chosen arbitrarily, it might be clever to choose it such that most of the Denavit-Hartenberg parameters will be equal to zero.

2.3.1.7 Special Case: The First Joint

An articulated figure must start at some place, and therefore there is a problem with the very first joint, because there is no link preceding it. Therefore, a *base link* is introduced, denoted $link_0$. The link frame for $link_0$ can be chosen arbitrarily, but it is clever to let it coincide with the link frame of $link_1$ when the articulated figure is in its rest position. Then most of the Denavit-Hartenberg parameters will be equal to zero.

2.3.1.8 Special Case: The Last Joint

An articulated figure must stop at some place, and therefore there is a problem with the very last joint, because there is no link following it. Generally, the coordinate frame of the last link can be chosen arbitrarily, because there is no physical link, i.e., the articulated figure stops at the axis of $joint_N$, so there is no link vector $\boldsymbol{a}_N$. The only thing that is given is the axis of $joint_N$ which becomes the $\boldsymbol{z}_N$-axis. But it is clever to choose the origin $\boldsymbol{o}_N$, the link vector $\boldsymbol{a}_N$ (the $\boldsymbol{x}_N$-axis), the link offset d_N, and the link twist α_N so that most of the Denavit-Hartenberg parameters are equal to zero.

2.3.2 Coordinate-Frame Attachment

Given an articulated figure, the first thing to do is to attach one coordinate system to each link. These coordinate systems are called link frames. The procedure for attaching the link frames is as follows:

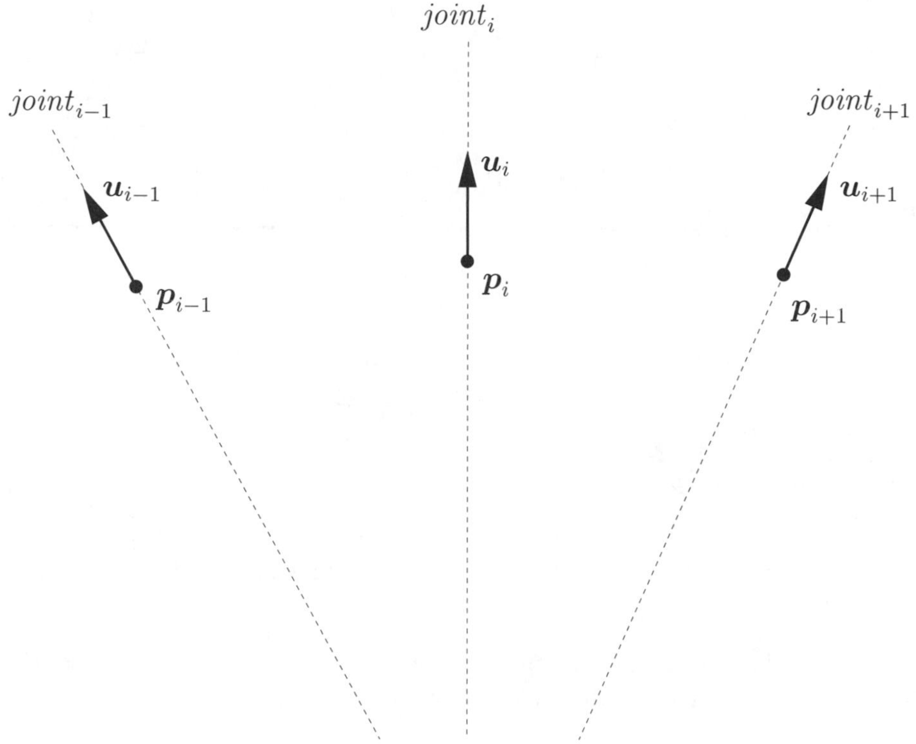

Figure 2.12: The joint axes of an articulated figure. The axes are given by the parametric equations $\boldsymbol{l}_i(s) = \boldsymbol{p}_i + s\boldsymbol{u}_i$. Think of the joint axes as the vectors $\boldsymbol{u}_i$.

1. Identify the joint axes.
2. Identify the common perpendiculars of successive joint axes.
3. Attach coordinate frames to each joint axis.

In the following will each of the above steps be performed.

First, identify the joint axes of the articulated figure (see Figure 2.12). The axis of $joint_i$ is given by (2.10a), and repeated here for convenience.

$$\boldsymbol{l}_i(s) = \boldsymbol{p}_i + s\boldsymbol{u}_i \tag{2.41}$$

Next, identify the common perpendicular between neighboring joint axes. That is, identify the common perpendicular $\boldsymbol{a}_i$ between the axes of $joint_i$ and $joint_{i+1}$. Also, identify the point $\boldsymbol{o}_i$ where the common perpendicular intersects the axis of $joint_i$. This is illustrated in Figure 2.13.

In Section 2.3.1.3 we showed how to compute the shortest distance a_i between the axes of $joint_i$ and $joint_{i+1}$. We also showed that the shortest distance is along the common perpendicular between the axes of $joint_i$ and $joint_{i+1}$. Finally, we showed how to compute the location of the shortest distance $\boldsymbol{o}_i$ on the

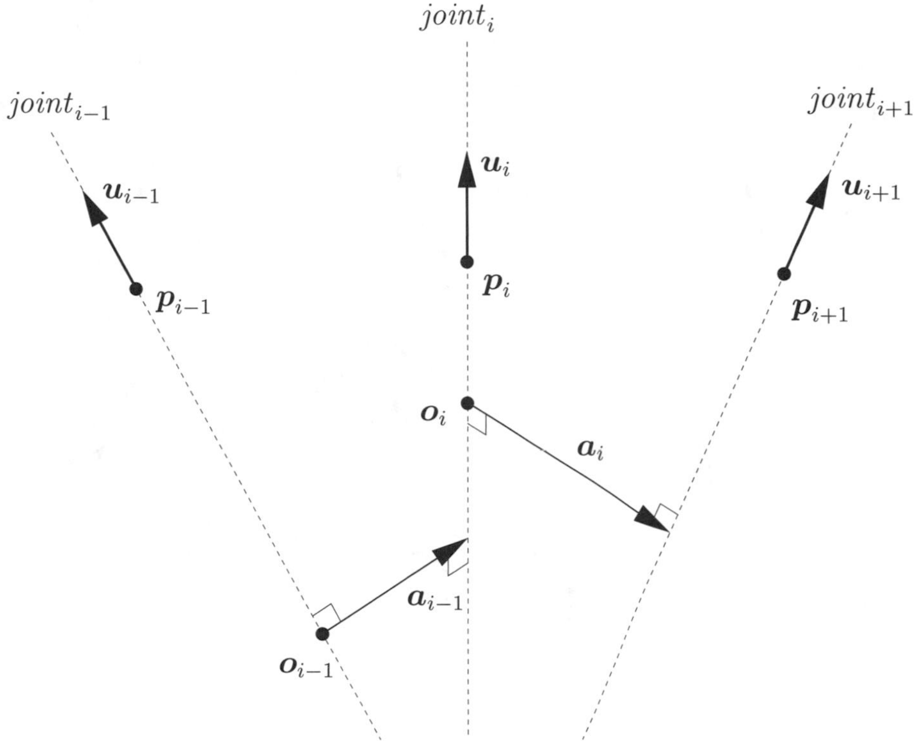

Figure 2.13: The link vectors $\boldsymbol{a}_i$ and the origins $\boldsymbol{o}_i$.

axis of $joint_i$. What is needed here is the link vector $\boldsymbol{a}_i$ and its intersection $\boldsymbol{o}_i$ with the axis of $joint_i$, see (2.31) and (2.32a) in Section 2.3.1.3.

Finally, the ith link frame, shown in Figure 2.14, can be constructed in as follows:

1. **The Origin:** Let the origin of the ith link frame be at the point $\boldsymbol{o}_i$ on the axis of $joint_i$.

2. **The $\boldsymbol{z}_i$-axis:** Let the $\boldsymbol{z}_i$-axis be along the ith joint axis. That is, let the $\boldsymbol{z}_i$ be parallel to vector $\boldsymbol{u}_i$ from (2.41)
$$\boldsymbol{z}_i = \frac{\boldsymbol{u}_i}{\|\boldsymbol{u}_i\|_2} \tag{2.42}$$

3. **The $\boldsymbol{x}_i$-axis:** Let the $\boldsymbol{x}_i$-axis be along the link vector $\boldsymbol{a}_i$ from (2.32a)
$$\boldsymbol{x}_i = \frac{\boldsymbol{a}_i}{\|\boldsymbol{a}_i\|_2} \tag{2.43}$$

4. **The $\boldsymbol{y}_i$-axis:** Let the $\boldsymbol{x}_i$-axis be such that the vectors $\boldsymbol{x}_i, \boldsymbol{y}_i, \boldsymbol{z}_i$ form a right-handed orthogonal coordinate system. That is, let $\boldsymbol{y}_i$ be given as
$$\boldsymbol{y}_i = \frac{\boldsymbol{z}_i \times \boldsymbol{x}_i}{\|\boldsymbol{z}_i \times \boldsymbol{x}_i\|_2} \tag{2.44}$$

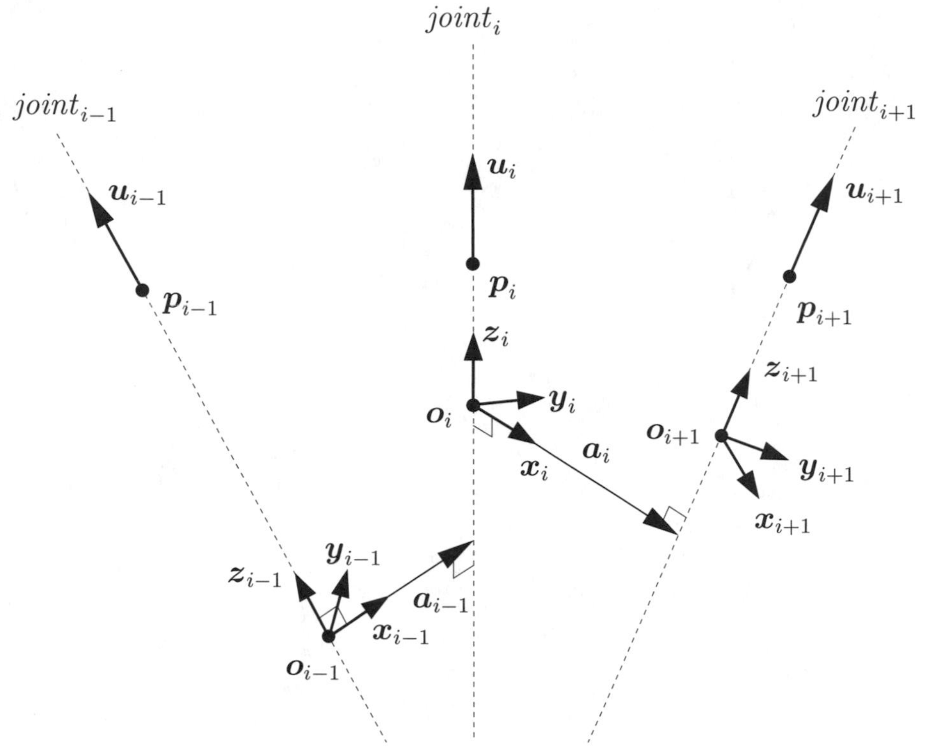

Figure 2.14: The articulated figure and its link frames $\boldsymbol{o}_i, \boldsymbol{x}_i, \boldsymbol{y}_i, \boldsymbol{z}_i$.

2.3.3 The Link Twist α_i

The link twist is the angle α_i between axes of $joint_i$ and $joint_{i+1}$. The angle α_i is measured around the $\boldsymbol{x}_i$-axis. Positive angles are measured counterclockwise when looking from the tip of vector $\boldsymbol{x}_i$ toward its foot, see Figure 2.15. More specifically, the link twist α_i is the angle between the direction vectors of the joint axes $\boldsymbol{u}_i$ and $\boldsymbol{u}_{i+1}$ measured around the link vector $\boldsymbol{a}_i$.

Recall some properties of the scalar and vector products.

$$\boldsymbol{u}_i \cdot \boldsymbol{u}_{i+1} = \|\boldsymbol{u}_i\|_2 \|\boldsymbol{u}_{i+1}\|_2 \cos\alpha_i \qquad 0 \le \alpha_i \le \pi \tag{2.45a}$$

$$\|\boldsymbol{u}_i \times \boldsymbol{u}_{i+1}\|_2 = \|\boldsymbol{u}_i\|_2 \|\boldsymbol{u}_{i+1}\|_2 \sin\alpha_i \qquad 0 \le \alpha_i \le \pi \tag{2.45b}$$

which is equivalent to

$$\cos\alpha_i = \frac{\boldsymbol{u}_i \cdot \boldsymbol{u}_{i+1}}{\|\boldsymbol{u}_i\|_2 \|\boldsymbol{u}_{i+1}\|_2} \qquad 0 \le \alpha_i \le \pi \tag{2.46a}$$

$$\sin\alpha_i = \frac{\|\boldsymbol{u}_i \times \boldsymbol{u}_{i+1}\|_2}{\|\boldsymbol{u}_i\|_2 \|\boldsymbol{u}_{i+1}\|_2} \qquad 0 \le \alpha_i \le \pi \tag{2.46b}$$

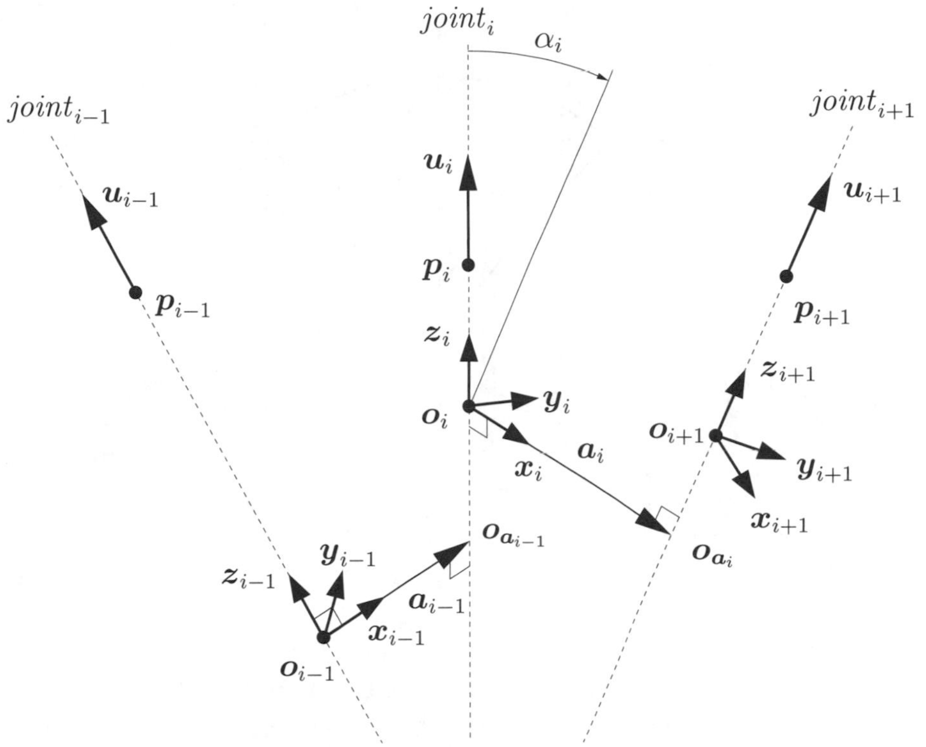

Figure 2.15: The link frames and link twist α_i. In the figure, the link twist α_i is negative.

Notice, since $0 \leq \sin\alpha_i \leq 1$ while $-1 \leq \cos\alpha_i \leq 1$, the angle α_i will always be in the interval $0 \leq \alpha_i \leq \pi$, see Figure 2.16. In the following we show how to compute the link twist α_i correctly.

Recall that the mathematical function $\arctan : \mathbb{R} \longrightarrow \mathbb{R}$ returns a value in the interval $[-\pi, \pi]$. Let the function $\text{arctan2} : \mathbb{R}^2 \longrightarrow \mathbb{R}$ be defined as

$$\text{arctan2}(n,d) = \begin{cases} \arctan\left(\dfrac{n}{d}\right) & \text{if} \quad n > 0 \wedge d > 0 \\ \arctan\left(\dfrac{n}{d}\right) & \text{if} \quad n < 0 \wedge d > 0 \\ \arctan\left(\dfrac{n}{d}\right) + \pi & \text{if} \quad n > 0 \wedge d < 0 \\ \arctan\left(\dfrac{n}{d}\right) - \pi & \text{if} \quad n < 0 \wedge d < 0 \end{cases} \tag{2.47}$$

That is, if the link twist α_i is naively computed as

$$\alpha_i = \text{arctan2}\left(\frac{\|\boldsymbol{u}_i \times \boldsymbol{u}_{i+1}\|_2}{\|\boldsymbol{u}_i\|_2 \, \|\boldsymbol{u}_{i+1}\|_2}, \frac{\boldsymbol{u}_i \cdot \boldsymbol{u}_{i+1}}{\|\boldsymbol{u}_i\|_2 \, \|\boldsymbol{u}_{i+1}\|_2} \right) \tag{2.48}$$

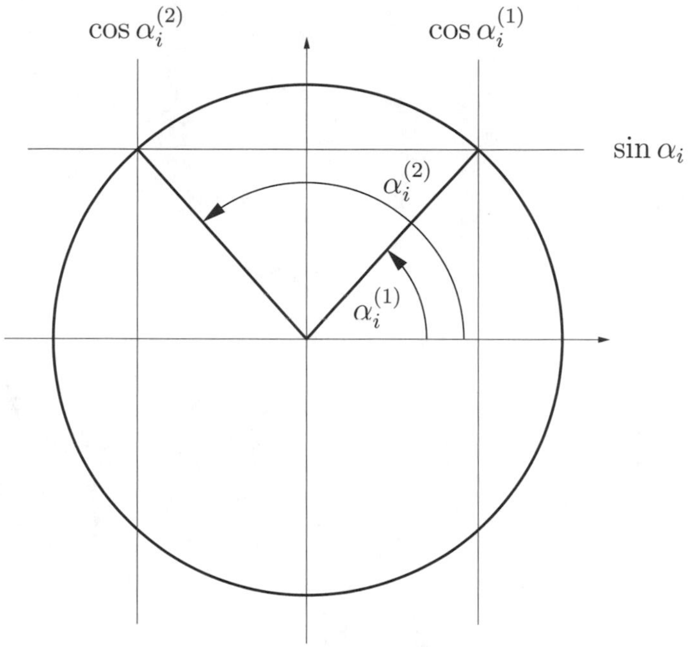

Figure 2.16: The twist angle α_i is always positive and in the interval $0 \le \alpha_i \le \pi$. Since $0 \le \sin\alpha_i \le 1$ and $-1 \le \cos\alpha_i \le 1$ there are two possible angles $\alpha_i^{(1)}$ and $\alpha_i^{(2)}$ depending on the sign of $\cos\alpha_i$.

the result will sometimes be wrong, because $\sin\alpha_i$ from (2.46b) is always positive. That means, the angle α_i will always be one of the two positive angles $\alpha_i^{(1)}$ or $\alpha_i^{(2)}$ shown in Figure 2.16, i.e., α_i will always be positive.

The angle α_i in the cross product, (2.46b), is measured around the axis $\boldsymbol{u}_i \times \boldsymbol{u}_{i+1}$. If the vector $\boldsymbol{u}_i \times \boldsymbol{u}_{i+1}$ has the same direction as the link vector $\boldsymbol{a}_i$ then the angle α_i in (2.48) is correct, see Figure 2.17 If the vector $\boldsymbol{u}_i \times \boldsymbol{u}_{i+1}$ has the opposite direction as the link vector $\boldsymbol{a}_i$ then the angle α_i in (2.48) is not correct. The correct angle α_i is the negative of the angle in (2.48), see Figure 2.18.

To distinguish between the two cases where the vectors $\boldsymbol{u}_i \times \boldsymbol{u}_{i+1}$ and $\boldsymbol{a}_i$ have the same or opposite directions, it suffices to check the sign of their dot product $(\boldsymbol{u}_i \times \boldsymbol{u}_{i+1}) \cdot \boldsymbol{a}_i$. That can be expressed in the following equation

$$\alpha_i = \begin{cases} +\operatorname{arctan2}\left(\dfrac{\|\boldsymbol{u}_i \times \boldsymbol{u}_{i+1}\|_2}{\|\boldsymbol{u}_i\|_2 \, \|\boldsymbol{u}_{i+1}\|_2}, \dfrac{\boldsymbol{u}_i \cdot \boldsymbol{u}_{i+1}}{\|\boldsymbol{u}_i\|_2 \, \|\boldsymbol{u}_{i+1}\|_2} \right) & \text{if} \quad (\boldsymbol{u}_i \times \boldsymbol{u}_{i+1}) \cdot \boldsymbol{a}_i \ge 0 \\ -\operatorname{arctan2}\left(\dfrac{\|\boldsymbol{u}_i \times \boldsymbol{u}_{i+1}\|_2}{\|\boldsymbol{u}_i\|_2 \, \|\boldsymbol{u}_{i+1}\|_2}, \dfrac{\boldsymbol{u}_i \cdot \boldsymbol{u}_{i+1}}{\|\boldsymbol{u}_i\|_2 \, \|\boldsymbol{u}_{i+1}\|_2} \right) & \text{if} \quad (\boldsymbol{u}_i \times \boldsymbol{u}_{i+1}) \cdot \boldsymbol{a}_i < 0 \end{cases} \tag{2.49}$$

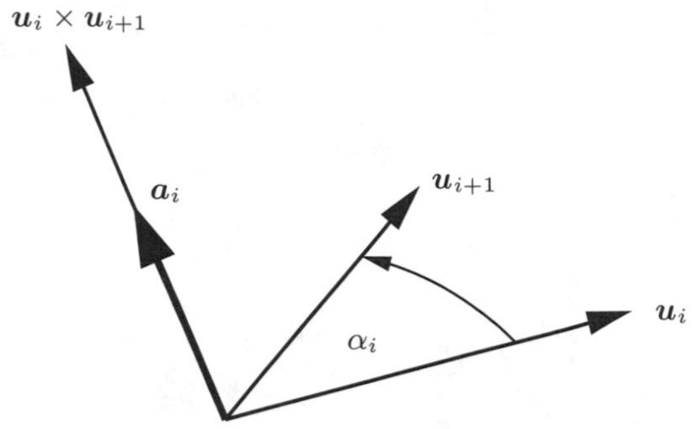

Figure 2.17: The twist angle is positive because the direction of the vector $\boldsymbol{u}_i \times \boldsymbol{u}_{i+1}$ has the same direction as the link vector $\boldsymbol{a}_i$.

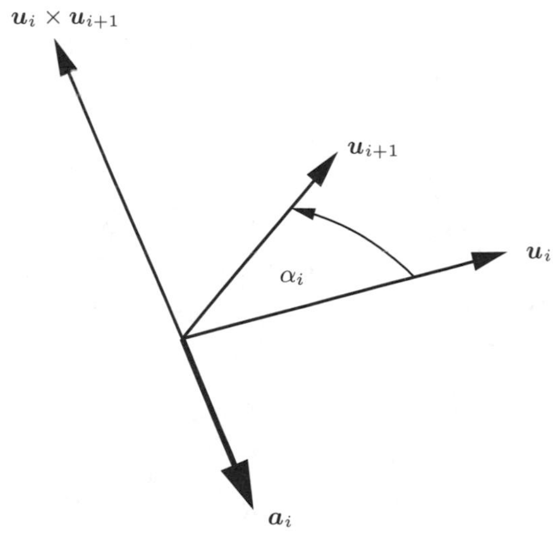

Figure 2.18: The twist angle α_i is negative because the direction of the vector $\boldsymbol{u}_i \times \boldsymbol{u}_{i+1}$ has the opposite direction of the link vector $\boldsymbol{a}_i$.

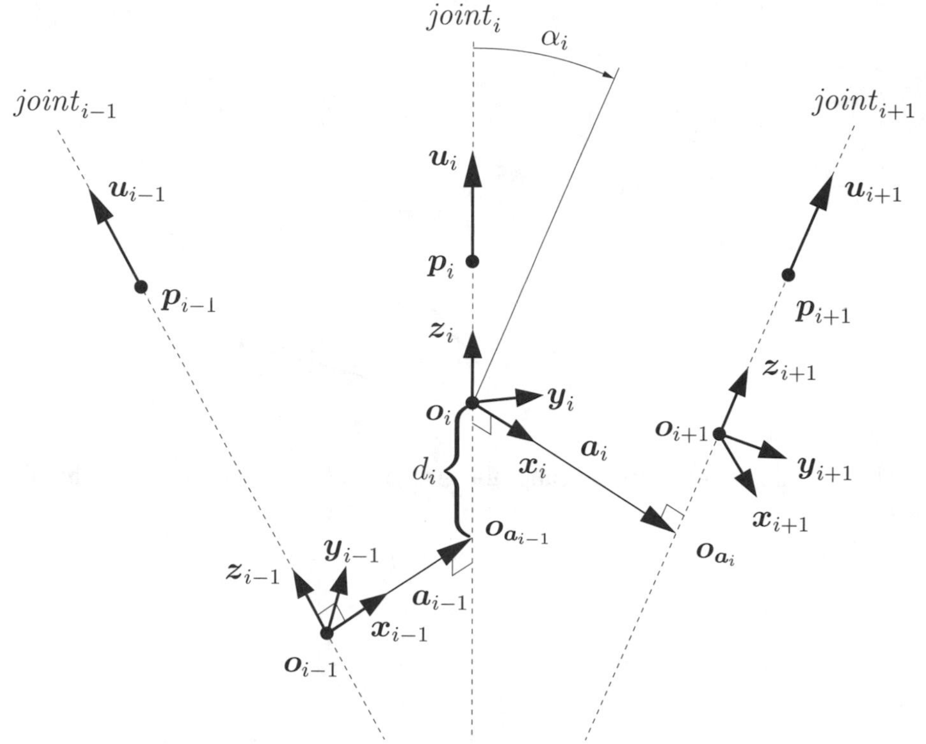

Figure 2.19: The link offset is the distance between the origins of the coordinate frames attached to joint $joint_{i-1}$ and $joint_i$ measured along the axis of $joint_i$.

2.3.4 The Link Offset d_i

The link offset is the distance between the origins of the coordinate frames attached to joint $joint_{i-1}$ and $joint_i$ measured along the axis of $joint_i$. More specific, it is the distance between the point $\boldsymbol{o}_{\boldsymbol{a}_{i-1}}$ where the $\boldsymbol{x}_{i-1}$-axis intersects the axis of $joint_i$ and the origin $\boldsymbol{o}_i$ of the link frame of $link_i$, see Figure 2.19. The points $\boldsymbol{o}_i$ and $\boldsymbol{o}_{\boldsymbol{a}_i}$ are given by (2.31) for any i. That is

$$d_i = \begin{cases} +\left\|\boldsymbol{o}_i - \boldsymbol{o}_{\boldsymbol{a}_{i-1}}\right\|_2 & \text{if} \quad (\boldsymbol{o}_i - \boldsymbol{o}_{\boldsymbol{a}_{i-1}}) \cdot \boldsymbol{u}_i \geq 0 \\ -\left\|\boldsymbol{o}_i - \boldsymbol{o}_{\boldsymbol{a}_{i-1}}\right\|_2 & \text{if} \quad (\boldsymbol{o}_i - \boldsymbol{o}_{\boldsymbol{a}_{i-1}}) \cdot \boldsymbol{u}_i < 0 \end{cases} \tag{2.50}$$

2.3.5 The Joint Angle φ_i

The joint angle φ_i is the angle between the link vectors $\boldsymbol{a}_{i-1}$ and $\boldsymbol{a}_i$. The angle φ_i is measured around the $\boldsymbol{z}_i$-axis. Positive angles are measured counterclockwise when looking from the tip of vector $\boldsymbol{z}_i$ toward its foot, see Figure 2.20. The joint angle φ_i is computed the same way as the link twist α_i, which was described in Section 2.3.3. The difference between the computations are the vectors which are involved.

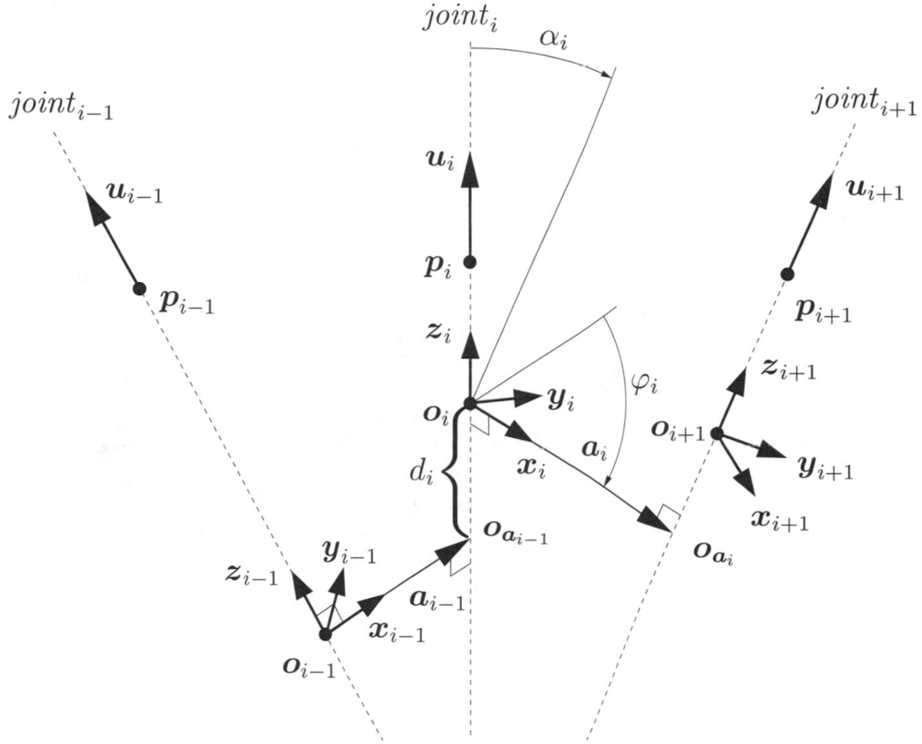

Figure 2.20: The coordinate frames of the links and the joint angle. In the figure, the joint angle φ_i is negative.

The joint angle φ_i is the angle between the link vectors $\boldsymbol{a}_{i-1}$ and $\boldsymbol{a}_i$ measured around the axis $\boldsymbol{z}_i$ which is parallel to the joint axis $\boldsymbol{u}_i$. Using the same arguments as in Section 2.3.3 the joint angle is computed as follows

$$\varphi_i = \begin{cases} +\operatorname{arctan2}\left(\dfrac{\|\boldsymbol{a}_{i-1}\times\boldsymbol{a}_i\|_2}{\|\boldsymbol{a}_{i-1}\|_2\,\|\boldsymbol{a}_i\|_2}, \dfrac{\boldsymbol{a}_{i-1}\cdot\boldsymbol{a}_i}{\|\boldsymbol{a}_{i-1}\|_2\,\|\boldsymbol{a}_i\|_2}\right) & \text{if} \quad (\boldsymbol{a}_{i-1}\times\boldsymbol{a}_i)\cdot\boldsymbol{z}_i \geq 0 \\ -\operatorname{arctan2}\left(\dfrac{\|\boldsymbol{a}_{i-1}\times\boldsymbol{a}_i\|_2}{\|\boldsymbol{a}_{i-1}\|_2\,\|\boldsymbol{a}_i\|_2}, \dfrac{\boldsymbol{a}_{i-1}\cdot\boldsymbol{a}_i}{\|\boldsymbol{a}_{i-1}\|_2\,\|\boldsymbol{a}_i\|_2}\right) & \text{if} \quad (\boldsymbol{a}_{i-1}\times\boldsymbol{a}_i)\cdot\boldsymbol{z}_i < 0 \end{cases} \tag{2.51}$$

2.3.6 The Link Transformation ${}^{(i-1)}\boldsymbol{T}_i$

The transformation ${}^{(i-1)}\boldsymbol{T}_i$ transforms entities from one frame to the preceding frame. This can be explained as follows. Given the coordinates of a point $\boldsymbol{p}_i$ specified in *linkframe*$_i$, the transformation ${}^{(i-1)}\boldsymbol{T}_i$ transforms point $\boldsymbol{p}_i$ such that its coordinates are specified in *linkframe*$_{i-1}$.

The idea is to transform the point $\boldsymbol{p}_i$ with coordinates in *linkframe*$_i$ with a transformation that makes *linkframe*$_{i-1}$ coincide with *linkframe*$_i$. The transformation of the coordinates of point $\boldsymbol{p}_i$ from

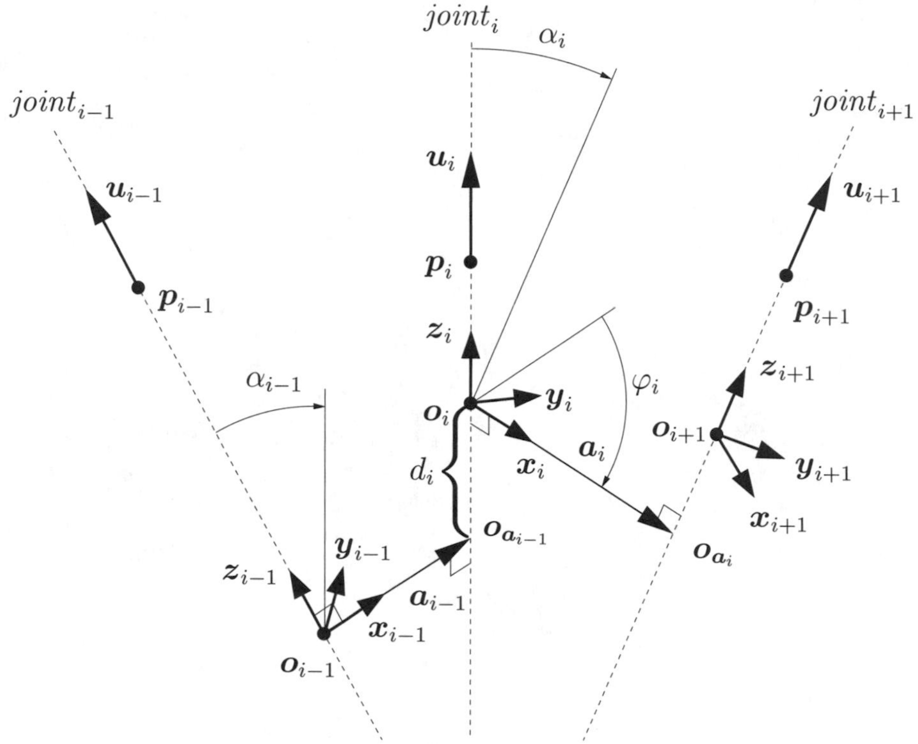

Figure 2.21: The coordinate frames of the links and the joint angle.

$linkframe_i$ to $linkframe_{i-1}$ is done in several steps:

1. Rotate the joint angle φ_i around the axis $\boldsymbol{z}_i$.
2. Translate the link offset d_i along the axis $\boldsymbol{z}_i$.
3. Translate the link length a_{i-1} along the axis $\boldsymbol{x}_i$.
4. Rotate the link twist angle α_{i-1} around the axis $\boldsymbol{x}_i$.

That is, the transformation ${}^{(i-1)}\boldsymbol{T}_i$ has the form

$$ {}^{(i-1)}\boldsymbol{T}_i(\varphi_i, d_i, a_{i-1}, \alpha_{i-1}) = \boldsymbol{R}_{\boldsymbol{x}_i}(\alpha_{i-1})\boldsymbol{T}_{\boldsymbol{x}_i}(a_{i-1})\boldsymbol{T}_{\boldsymbol{z}_i}(d_i)\boldsymbol{R}_{\boldsymbol{z}_i}(\varphi_i) \tag{2.52} $$

A detailed description of the transformations $\boldsymbol{R}_{\boldsymbol{x}_i}(\alpha_{i-1}), \boldsymbol{T}_{\boldsymbol{x}_i}(a_{i-1}), \boldsymbol{T}_{\boldsymbol{z}_i}(d_i), \boldsymbol{R}_{\boldsymbol{z}_i}(\varphi_i)$ is given in the following sections.

2.3.6.1 The Transformation $\boldsymbol{R}_{\boldsymbol{z}_i}(\varphi_i)$

Consider Figure 2.21. The angle between the $\boldsymbol{x}_i$ and $\boldsymbol{x}_{i-1}$ is equal to φ_i measured around the axis $\boldsymbol{z}_i$. So, by rotating the angle φ_i around the axis $\boldsymbol{z}_i$ we make the coordinate axes $\boldsymbol{x}_i$ and $\boldsymbol{x}_{i-1}$ parallel. The actual transformation is given as

$$R_{z_i}(\varphi_i) = \begin{bmatrix} \cos\varphi_i & -\sin\varphi_i & 0 & 0 \\ \sin\varphi_i & \cos\varphi_i & 0 & 0 \\ 0 & 0 & 1 & 0 \\ 0 & 0 & 0 & 1 \end{bmatrix} \tag{2.53}$$

After this transformation, the axes $\boldsymbol{x}_i$ and $\boldsymbol{x}_{i-1}$ are parallel, i.e., $\boldsymbol{x}_i \parallel \boldsymbol{x}_{i-1}$.

2.3.6.2 The Transformation $\boldsymbol{T}_{\boldsymbol{z}_i}(d_i)$

Still consider Figure 2.21, but remember that the axis $\boldsymbol{x}_i$ has been rotated such that it is parallel to the axis $\boldsymbol{x}_{i-1}$. By translating the distance d_i along the $\boldsymbol{z}_i$-axis the axes $\boldsymbol{x}_i$ and $\boldsymbol{x}_{i-1}$ will not only be parallel, they will lie on the same line. The actual transformation is given as

$$\boldsymbol{T}_{\boldsymbol{z}_i}(d_i) = \begin{bmatrix} 1 & 0 & 0 & 0 \\ 0 & 1 & 0 & 0 \\ 0 & 0 & 1 & d_i \\ 0 & 0 & 0 & 1 \end{bmatrix} \tag{2.54}$$

After this transformation, the axes $\boldsymbol{x}_i$ and $\boldsymbol{x}_{i-1}$ are not only parallel, but they are located on the same line i.e., $\boldsymbol{x}_i = \lambda\boldsymbol{x}_{i-1}$.

2.3.6.3 The Transformation $\boldsymbol{T}_{\boldsymbol{x}_i}(a_{i-1})$

Still consider Figure 2.21, but remember that after the previous transformations the axes $\boldsymbol{x}_i$ and $\boldsymbol{x}_{i-1}$ are now on the same line. By translating the distance a_{i-1} along the $\boldsymbol{x}_i$-axis, the origins $\boldsymbol{o_i}$ and $\boldsymbol{o}_{i-1}$ will coincide. The actual transformation is given as

$$\boldsymbol{T}_{\boldsymbol{x}_i}(a_{i-1}) = \begin{bmatrix} 1 & 0 & 0 & a_{i-1} \\ 0 & 1 & 0 & 0 \\ 0 & 0 & 1 & 0 \\ 0 & 0 & 0 & 1 \end{bmatrix} \tag{2.55}$$

After this transformation, the axes $\boldsymbol{x}_i$ and $\boldsymbol{x}_{i-1}$ are on the same line, and the origins $\boldsymbol{o_i}$ and $\boldsymbol{o}_{i-1}$ coincide, i.e., $\boldsymbol{o}_i = \boldsymbol{o}_{i-1}$

2.3.6.4 The Transformation $\boldsymbol{R}_{\boldsymbol{x}_i}(\alpha_i)$

Still consider Figure 2.21, but remember that the axes $\boldsymbol{x}_i$ and $\boldsymbol{x}_{i-1}$ are now on the same line and that the origins $\boldsymbol{o_i}$ and $\boldsymbol{o}_{i-1}$ are coincident. The only thing that needs to be taken care of is to transform the $\boldsymbol{z}_{i-1}$-axis into the $\boldsymbol{z}_i$-axis. This is done by rotating the angle α_{i-i} around the axis $\boldsymbol{x}_i \equiv \boldsymbol{x}_{i-1}$. The actual transformation is given as

$$\boldsymbol{R}_{\boldsymbol{x}_i}(\alpha_{i-1}) = \begin{bmatrix} 1 & 0 & 0 & 0 \\ 0 & \cos\alpha_{i-1} & -\sin\alpha_{i-1} & 0 \\ 0 & \sin\alpha_{i-1} & \cos\alpha_{i-1} & 0 \\ 0 & 0 & 0 & 1 \end{bmatrix} \tag{2.56}$$

After these transformations the two coordinate systems coincide and the final transformation ${}^{(i-i)}\boldsymbol{T}_i$ from $linkframe_i$ to $linkframe_{i-1}$ is established.

2.3.6.5 The Transformation ${}^{(i-1)}\boldsymbol{T}_i(d_i, \varphi_i)$

As shown in the previous sections, the transformation ${}^{(i-1)}\boldsymbol{T}_i$ is given as

$$ {}^{(i-1)}\boldsymbol{T}_i(d_i, \varphi_i, a_{i-1}, \alpha_{i-1}) = \boldsymbol{R}_{\boldsymbol{x}_i}(\alpha_{i-1})\boldsymbol{T}_{\boldsymbol{x}_i}(a_{i-1})\boldsymbol{T}_{\boldsymbol{z}_i}(d_i)\boldsymbol{R}_{\boldsymbol{z}_i}(\varphi_i) \tag{2.57} $$

Usually, the link parameters a_{i-i} and α_{i-1} are constant for a given articulated figure, so the transformation ${}^{(i-1)}\boldsymbol{T}_i$ is really only a function of the two parameters d_i and φ_i. Multiplying the matrices yields the following expression for the transformation ${}^{(i-1)}\boldsymbol{T}_i$

$$ {}^{(i-1)}\boldsymbol{T}_i(d_i, \varphi_i) = \begin{bmatrix} \cos\varphi_i & -\sin\varphi_i & 0 & a_{i-1} \\ \cos\alpha_{i-1}\sin\varphi_i & \cos\alpha_{i-1}\cos\varphi_i & -\sin\alpha_{i-1} & -d_i\sin\alpha_{i-1} \\ \sin\alpha_{i-1}\sin\varphi_i & \sin\alpha_{i-1}\cos\varphi_i & \cos\alpha_{i-1} & d_i\cos\alpha_{i-1} \\ 0 & 0 & 0 & 1 \end{bmatrix} \tag{2.58} $$

In some literature, it is often seen that the transformation ${}^{(i-1)}\boldsymbol{T}_i$ is written in a different way. Omitting the parameters, the transformation has the form

$$ {}^{(i-1)}\boldsymbol{T}_i = \boldsymbol{R}_{\boldsymbol{x}_i}\boldsymbol{T}_{\boldsymbol{x}_i}\boldsymbol{T}_{\boldsymbol{z}_i}\boldsymbol{R}_{\boldsymbol{z}_i} \tag{2.59} $$

from which it can be seen that there are only translation and rotation matrices. Furthermore, it can be seen that they can be written in two groups

$$ {}^{(i-1)}\boldsymbol{T}_i = (\boldsymbol{R}_{\boldsymbol{x}_i}\boldsymbol{T}_{\boldsymbol{x}_i})(\boldsymbol{T}_{\boldsymbol{z}_i}\boldsymbol{R}_{\boldsymbol{z}_i}) \tag{2.60} $$

By inspection, it can be seen that this special matrix product commutes

$$ \boldsymbol{R}_{\boldsymbol{x}_i}\boldsymbol{T}_{\boldsymbol{x}_i} = \boldsymbol{T}_{\boldsymbol{x}_i}\boldsymbol{R}_{\boldsymbol{x}_i} \tag{2.61} $$

and that is because the matrix $\boldsymbol{T}_{\boldsymbol{x}_i}$ does only change the x-coordinate, and the matrix $\boldsymbol{R}_{\boldsymbol{x}_i}$ does not change the x-coordinate.

By specifying the transformation ${}^{i-1}\boldsymbol{T}_i(d_i, \varphi_i)$ for all links, $i = 1, \ldots, N$ a transformation from link N to the base, $link_0$ can be written

$$ {}^{0}\boldsymbol{T}_N = {}^{0}\boldsymbol{T}_N(d_1, \varphi_1, \ldots, d_N, \varphi_N) = {}^{0}\boldsymbol{T}_1(d_1, \varphi_1){}^{1}\boldsymbol{T}_2(d_2, \varphi_2)\cdots{}^{N-1}\boldsymbol{T}_N(d_N, \varphi_N) \tag{2.62} $$

Let $\boldsymbol{\theta}_i$ denote the generalized joint parameters for joint i, i.e., $\boldsymbol{\theta}_i = (d_i, \varphi_i)$. Then (2.8) may be written

$$ {}^{0}\boldsymbol{T}_N = {}^{0}\boldsymbol{T}_N(\boldsymbol{\theta}_1, \ldots, \boldsymbol{\theta}_N) = {}^{0}\boldsymbol{T}_1(\boldsymbol{\theta}_1){}^{1}\boldsymbol{T}_2(\boldsymbol{\theta}_2)\cdots{}^{(N-1)}\boldsymbol{T}_N(\boldsymbol{\theta}_N) \tag{2.63} $$

When using the Denavit-Hartenberg description of an articulated figure, usually each joint is restricted to having only one degree of freedom. That is, each joint has only a translatory parameter d_i along its $\boldsymbol{z}$-axis if it is a prismatic joint, or it has one rotational parameter φ_i around its $\boldsymbol{z}$-axis if it is a revolute joint. If a joint needs more degrees of freedom, several joints with link lengths equal to zero are located on top of each other.

This means that the generalized parameter vector $\boldsymbol{\theta}_i = (\varphi_i, d_i)^T$ becomes an ordinary parameter, i.e., the generalized parameter $\boldsymbol{\theta}_i$ becomes d_i for a prismatic joint, and it becomes φ_i for a revolute joint.

3

Forward and Inverse Kinematics

Kinematics is the study of the motion of rigid bodies without consideration of Newtonian laws. This and the following chapter describe methods of how to manipulate an articulated figure. Recall from Chapter 2 the definition of an articulated figure, its notation, and how to navigate the structure.

Forward kinematics , Section 3.2, is the most basic way to animate an articulated figure. All the *joint parameters* are set manually and the result is the placement of all the links and joints in the whole figure. This method is not very practical if one wants to have the end-point of the articulated figure touching some specific point; for example, if a character in a computer game is to grab the door handle when opening the door. It is almost impossible to calculate the parameters of each joint in order to get the arm and hand in the position where they align with the door handle.

An easier way is to use *inverse kinematics*, Section 3.3. This method, as the name suggests, starts with the end-point of an articulated figure and uses that to calculate each joint parameter. So an animator only has to worry about this end-point. In forward kinematics, one specifies each joint variable and the result is the end-point. In inverse kinematics the end-point is specified and the result is the joint variable. The end-point is most often called the end effector. This chapter starts by giving a description of the properties of this end effector.

3.1 End Effector

The *end effector* is defined to be the last coordinate system of an *articulated figure*. Notice that a complicated structure like a hand will have end effectors at the tip of each finger.

In the notation in Chapter 2, the end effector is located in joint N. Usually, an animator is interested in the position and orientation of the end effector specified in base coordinates for easy use.

Sections 2.2 and 2.3 derived two expressions (2.9) and (2.63) for the transformation ${}^{0}\boldsymbol{T}_N$, which transforms the Nth link frame to the base coordinate frame. The transformation is given by a 4×4 matrix, which is parameterized by the *generalized joint parameters* $\boldsymbol{\theta}_i$. This transformation is repeated here for convenience.

$$
{}^{0}\boldsymbol{T}_N = {}^{0}\boldsymbol{T}_N(\boldsymbol{\theta}_1, \ldots, \boldsymbol{\theta}_N) = {}^{0}\boldsymbol{T}_1(\boldsymbol{\theta}_1)\,{}^{1}\boldsymbol{T}_2(\boldsymbol{\theta}_2) \cdots {}^{(N-1)}\boldsymbol{T}_N(\boldsymbol{\theta}_N) \tag{3.1a}
$$

$$
= \begin{bmatrix} m_{11}(\boldsymbol{\theta}_1, \ldots, \boldsymbol{\theta}_N) & m_{12}(\boldsymbol{\theta}_1, \ldots, \boldsymbol{\theta}_N) & m_{13}(\boldsymbol{\theta}_1, \ldots, \boldsymbol{\theta}_N) & m_{14}(\boldsymbol{\theta}_1, \ldots, \boldsymbol{\theta}_N) \\ m_{21}(\boldsymbol{\theta}_1, \ldots, \boldsymbol{\theta}_N) & m_{22}(\boldsymbol{\theta}_1, \ldots, \boldsymbol{\theta}_N) & m_{23}(\boldsymbol{\theta}_1, \ldots, \boldsymbol{\theta}_N) & m_{24}(\boldsymbol{\theta}_1, \ldots, \boldsymbol{\theta}_N) \\ m_{31}(\boldsymbol{\theta}_1, \ldots, \boldsymbol{\theta}_N) & m_{32}(\boldsymbol{\theta}_1, \ldots, \boldsymbol{\theta}_N) & m_{33}(\boldsymbol{\theta}_1, \ldots, \boldsymbol{\theta}_N) & m_{34}(\boldsymbol{\theta}_1, \ldots, \boldsymbol{\theta}_N) \\ 0 & 0 & 0 & 1 \end{bmatrix}. \tag{3.1b}
$$

The location and orientation of the Nth link frame might also be expressed relative to the base coordinate frame as three rotations, one around each of the coordinate axes followed by a translation. This results in

First:	Yaw	Ψ	Rotate the angle Ψ around the x-axis
Second:	Pitch	Θ	Rotate the angle Θ around the y-axis
Third:	Roll	Φ	Rotate the angle Φ around the z-axis

Table 3.1: Order, name, and definition of the rotations.

an alternative expression for the transformation ${}^0\boldsymbol{T}_N$

$$ {}^0\boldsymbol{T}_N = {}^0\boldsymbol{T}_N(\boldsymbol{p}, \Phi, \Theta, \Psi) = \boldsymbol{T}(\boldsymbol{p})\boldsymbol{R}_z(\Phi)\boldsymbol{R}_y(\Theta)\boldsymbol{R}_x(\Psi) \tag{3.2} $$

where $\boldsymbol{T}(\boldsymbol{p})$ is a translation matrix, and $\boldsymbol{R}_z(\Phi), \boldsymbol{R}_y(\Theta), \boldsymbol{R}_x(\Psi)$ are rotation matrices. This expression is a 4×4 matrix, where the elements are functions of the translation vector $\boldsymbol{p}$ and the *Euler angles* Φ, Θ, and Ψ.

The following sections will compute the transformation $\boldsymbol{T}(\boldsymbol{p})\boldsymbol{R}_z(\Phi)\boldsymbol{R}_y(\Theta)\boldsymbol{R}_x(\Psi)$ and establish the relations to the transformation ${}^0\boldsymbol{T}_N(\boldsymbol{\theta}_1, \ldots, \boldsymbol{\theta}_N)$ given by (3.1). Finally, the notion of a *state vector* is defined. The state vector relates the position $\boldsymbol{p}$ and orientation Φ, Θ, Ψ of the end effector to the generalized joint parameters $\boldsymbol{\theta}_1, \ldots, \boldsymbol{\theta}_N$.

3.1.1 Location of the End Effector $\boldsymbol{T}(\boldsymbol{p})$

The origin of the coordinate frame relative to some base coordinate frame can be specified by a translation by a vector $\boldsymbol{p} = \begin{bmatrix} p_x & p_y & p_z \end{bmatrix}^T$. Using *homogeneous coordinates*, the corresponding transformation matrix $\boldsymbol{T}(\boldsymbol{p})$ is given by

$$ \boldsymbol{T}(\boldsymbol{p}) = \begin{bmatrix} 1 & 0 & 0 & p_x \\ 0 & 1 & 0 & p_y \\ 0 & 0 & 1 & p_z \\ 0 & 0 & 0 & 1 \end{bmatrix}. \tag{3.3} $$

3.1.2 Orientation of the End Effector—Roll, Pitch, and Yaw

Any 3D orientation relative to some base coordinate frame can be specified by three rotations, one around each of the coordinate axes. These rotations are named *roll*, *pitch*, and *yaw* respectively, and are shown in Figure 3.1.

The order in which these rotations are performed must be fixed. In the following, the order is: first rotate around the x-axis, second rotate around the y-axis, and finally rotate around the z-axis. The order and names of these rotations are summarized in Table 3.1, and described in the following sections.

3.1.2.1 The Yaw Transformation $\boldsymbol{Y}(\Psi) = \boldsymbol{R}_x(\Psi)$

The Yaw transformation is a rotation by the angle Ψ around the x-axis, and it can be expressed as

$$ \boldsymbol{Y}(\Psi) = \boldsymbol{R}_x(\Psi) = \begin{bmatrix} 1 & 0 & 0 & 0 \\ 0 & \cos\Psi & -\sin\Psi & 0 \\ 0 & \sin\Psi & \cos\Psi & 0 \\ 0 & 0 & 0 & 1 \end{bmatrix}. \tag{3.4} $$

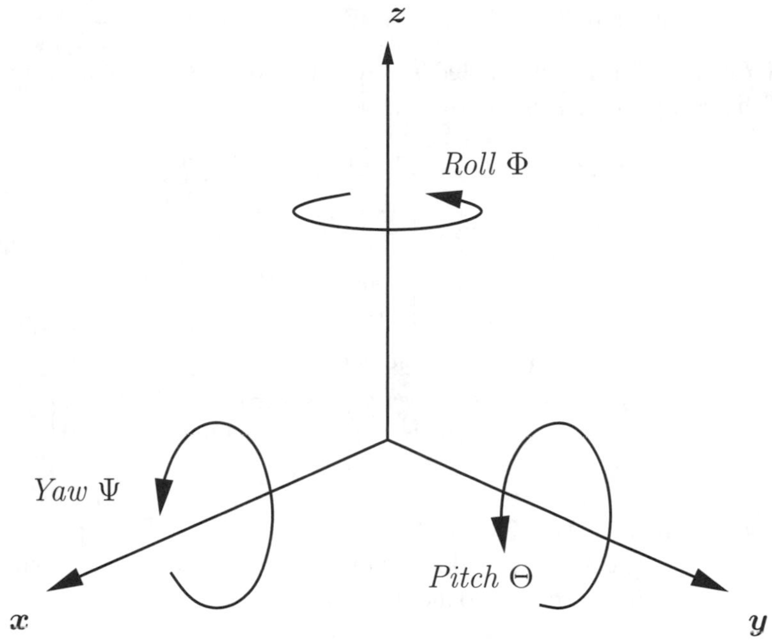

Figure 3.1: Any orientation can be specified by three rotations, the *Roll*, *Pitch*, and *Yaw* around the $\boldsymbol{x}$, $\boldsymbol{y}$, and $\boldsymbol{z}$ axes respectively. The order of rotations are: rotate around the axis $\boldsymbol{x}, \boldsymbol{y}, \boldsymbol{z}$.

3.1.2.2 The Pitch Transformation $\boldsymbol{P}(\Theta) = \boldsymbol{R}_{\boldsymbol{y}}(\Theta)$

The Pitch transformation is a rotation by the angle Θ around the $\boldsymbol{y}$-axis, and it can be expressed as

$$\boldsymbol{P}(\Theta) = \boldsymbol{R}_y(\Theta) = \begin{bmatrix} \cos\Theta & 0 & \sin\Theta & 0 \\ 0 & 1 & 0 & 0 \\ -\sin\Theta & 0 & \cos\Theta & 0 \\ 0 & 0 & 0 & 1 \end{bmatrix}. \tag{3.5}$$

3.1.2.3 The Roll Transformation $\boldsymbol{R}(\Phi) = \boldsymbol{R}_{\boldsymbol{z}}(\Phi)$

The Roll transformation is a rotation by the angle Φ around the $\boldsymbol{z}$-axis, and it can be expressed as

$$\boldsymbol{R}(\Phi) = \boldsymbol{R}_z(\Phi) = \begin{bmatrix} \cos\Phi & -\sin\Phi & 0 & 0 \\ \sin\Phi & \cos\Phi & 0 & 0 \\ 0 & 0 & 1 & 0 \\ 0 & 0 & 0 & 1 \end{bmatrix}. \tag{3.6}$$

3.1.2.4 The Roll, Pitch, and Yaw Transformation $\boldsymbol{T}_{RPY}(\Phi, \Theta, \Psi)$

The Roll, Pitch, and Yaw transformation denoted $\boldsymbol{T}_{RPY}$ is the composition of the three rotations described above. The order of the composition is as follows

$$\boldsymbol{T}_{RPY}(\Phi, \Theta, \Psi) = \boldsymbol{R}(\Phi)\boldsymbol{P}(\Theta)\boldsymbol{Y}(\Psi) = \boldsymbol{R}_z(\Phi)\boldsymbol{R}_y(\Theta)\boldsymbol{R}_x(\Psi) \tag{3.7a}$$

$$= \begin{bmatrix} c\Phi & -s\Phi & 0 & 0 \\ s\Phi & c\Phi & 0 & 0 \\ 0 & 0 & 1 & 0 \\ 0 & 0 & 0 & 1 \end{bmatrix} \begin{bmatrix} c\Theta & 0 & s\Theta & 0 \\ 0 & 1 & 0 & 0 \\ -s\Theta & 0 & c\Theta & 0 \\ 0 & 0 & 0 & 1 \end{bmatrix} \begin{bmatrix} 1 & 0 & 0 & 0 \\ 0 & c\Psi & -s\Psi & 0 \\ 0 & s\Psi & c\Psi & 0 \\ 0 & 0 & 0 & 1 \end{bmatrix} \tag{3.7b}$$

$$= \begin{bmatrix} c\Phi c\Theta & c\Phi s\Theta s\Psi - s\Phi c\Psi & c\Phi s\Theta c\Psi + s\Phi s\Psi & 0 \\ s\Phi c\Theta & s\Phi s\Theta s\Psi + c\Phi c\Psi & s\Phi s\Theta c\Psi - c\Phi s\Psi & 0 \\ -s\Theta & c\Theta s\Psi & c\Theta c\Psi & 0 \\ 0 & 0 & 0 & 1 \end{bmatrix} \tag{3.7c}$$

where $s\Phi$ is shorthand for $\sin\Phi$, and $c\Phi$ for $\cos\Phi$, etc.

The order of the rotations is essential: reading from right to left, first rotate around the $\boldsymbol{x}$-axis, second rotate around the $\boldsymbol{y}$-axis, and finally rotate around the $\boldsymbol{z}$-axis.

3.1.3 The Transformation of the End Effector ${}^0\boldsymbol{T}_N(\boldsymbol{p}, \Phi, \Theta, \Psi)$

As outlined in the previous sections the 3D location and orientation of the end effector in some coordinate frame can be expressed as three rotations and a translation. Specifically, the coordinate frame of the end effector can be expressed in the base coordinate frame of the articulated figure as

$${}^0\boldsymbol{T}_N = {}^0\boldsymbol{T}_N(\boldsymbol{p}, \Phi, \Theta, \Psi) = \boldsymbol{T}(\boldsymbol{p})\boldsymbol{T}_{RPY}(\Phi, \Theta, \Psi) \tag{3.8a}$$

$$= \begin{bmatrix} 1 & 0 & 0 & p_x \\ 0 & 1 & 0 & p_y \\ 0 & 0 & 1 & p_z \\ 0 & 0 & 0 & 1 \end{bmatrix} \begin{bmatrix} c\Phi c\Theta & c\Phi s\Theta s\Psi - s\Phi c\Psi & c\Phi s\Theta c\Psi + s\Phi s\Psi & 0 \\ s\Phi c\Theta & s\Phi s\Theta s\Psi + c\Phi c\Psi & s\Phi s\Theta c\Psi - c\Phi s\Psi & 0 \\ -s\Theta & c\Theta s\Psi & c\Theta c\Psi & 0 \\ 0 & 0 & 0 & 1 \end{bmatrix} \tag{3.8b}$$

$$= \begin{bmatrix} c\Phi c\Theta & c\Phi s\Theta s\Psi - s\Phi c\Psi & c\Phi s\Theta c\Psi + s\Phi s\Psi & p_x \\ s\Phi c\Theta & s\Phi s\Theta s\Psi + c\Phi c\Psi & s\Phi s\Theta c\Psi - c\Phi s\Psi & p_y \\ -s\Theta & c\Theta s\Psi & c\Theta c\Psi & p_z \\ 0 & 0 & 0 & 1 \end{bmatrix} \tag{3.8c}$$

where $s\Phi$ is shorthand for $\sin\Phi$, and $c\Phi$ for $\cos\Phi$, etc.

3.1.4 Computation of the Parameters $\boldsymbol{p}, \Phi, \Theta, \Psi$

This section describes the relation between the general transformations ${}^0\boldsymbol{T}_N$ given by (2.9) or (2.58) in Sections 2.2.4 and 2.58 respectively, and the transformation (3.8c) from the previous section.

More specifically, it describes how to compute the parameters, $\boldsymbol{p}, \Phi, \Theta, \Psi$, of the Roll, Pitch, and Yaw model described in Section 3.1.3, given an arbitrary transformation matrix ${}^0\boldsymbol{T}_N$ which is a composition of translations and rotations. Such a transformation matrix could be obtained as described in Sections 2.2.4 and 2.3.6.5.

A transformation ${}^{0}\boldsymbol{T}_N$, which transforms points in the end effector's coordinate frame to the base coordinate frame of the articulated figure (see (2.9) or (2.58)), can be represented as a 4×4 matrix, where the elements of the matrix m_{ij} are functions of the joint parameters $\theta_1, \ldots, \theta_N$. Omitting the joint parameters θ_i for readability, the matrix has the form

$$
{}^{0}\boldsymbol{T}_N = \begin{bmatrix} m_{11} & m_{12} & m_{13} & m_{14} \\ m_{21} & m_{22} & m_{23} & m_{24} \\ m_{31} & m_{32} & m_{33} & m_{34} \\ 0 & 0 & 0 & 1 \end{bmatrix}. \tag{3.9}
$$

The reason why the last row in this matrix is equal to $\begin{bmatrix} 0 & 0 & 0 & 1 \end{bmatrix}$ is that the computations are done in homogeneous coordinates and that translations and rotations are isomorphisms. Therefore, there are no perspective effects of this transformation.

The matrix (3.9) and the matrix resulting from the Roll, Pitch, and Yaw model (3.8c) do the same thing. They transform entities specified in the coordinate system of the end effector to the coordinate system of the base of the articulated figure. Therefore, these matrices must be identical

$$
\begin{bmatrix} m_{11} & m_{12} & m_{13} & m_{14} \\ m_{21} & m_{22} & m_{23} & m_{24} \\ m_{31} & m_{32} & m_{33} & m_{34} \\ 0 & 0 & 0 & 1 \end{bmatrix} = \begin{bmatrix} c\Phi c\Theta & c\Phi s\Theta s\Psi - s\Phi c\Psi & c\Phi s\Theta c\Psi + s\Phi s\Psi & p_x \\ s\Phi c\Theta & s\Phi s\Theta s\Psi + c\Phi c\Psi & s\Phi s\Theta c\Psi - c\Phi s\Psi & p_y \\ -s\Theta & c\Theta s\Psi & c\Theta c\Psi & p_z \\ 0 & 0 & 0 & 1 \end{bmatrix}. \tag{3.10}
$$

By observation several relations can be found. The following sections show how to express the parameters $\boldsymbol{p}, \Phi, \Theta$, and Ψ as functions of the matrix elements $\{m_{ij} \mid i, j = 1, \ldots, 4\}$.

3.1.4.1 The Translation $\boldsymbol{p}$

From (3.10) it can be seen directly that the translation vector $\boldsymbol{p} = \begin{bmatrix} p_x & p_y & p_z \end{bmatrix}^T$ is given by

$$
\boldsymbol{p} = \begin{bmatrix} p_x \\ p_y \\ p_z \end{bmatrix} = \begin{bmatrix} m_{14} \\ m_{24} \\ m_{34} \end{bmatrix} \tag{3.11}
$$

3.1.4.2 The Yaw Angle Ψ

The angle Ψ can be computed as follows by inspection of (3.10)

$$
\Psi = \arctan\left(\frac{m_{32}}{m_{33}}\right). \tag{3.12}
$$

This is possible because the following relations hold

$$
\Psi = \arctan\left(\frac{m_{32}}{m_{33}}\right) = \arctan\left(\frac{\cos\Theta \sin\Psi}{\cos\Theta \cos\Psi}\right) = \arctan\left(\frac{\sin\Psi}{\cos\Psi}\right) \tag{3.13}
$$

The function $\tan$ has a period of π which might cause problems. In order to get the angle right, it is better to use the function arctan2 given by (2.47). The result then becomes

$$\Psi = \arctan2(m_{32}, m_{33}). \tag{3.14}$$

3.1.4.3 The Pitch Angle Θ

At this point, the angle Ψ is known, and it can by used for further computations. By inspection of (3.10), and the knowledge of the value of the angle Ψ, the angle Θ can be computed as follows:

$$\Theta = \arctan\left(\frac{-m_{31}}{m_{32}\sin\Psi + m_{33}\cos\Psi}\right). \tag{3.15}$$

This can be seen because the following relations hold

$$\Theta = \arctan\left(\frac{-m_{31}}{m_{32}\sin\Psi + m_{33}\cos\Psi}\right) = \arctan\left(\frac{\sin\Theta}{\cos\Theta\sin^2\Psi + \cos\Theta\cos^2\Psi}\right) \tag{3.16a}$$

$$= \arctan\left(\frac{\sin\Theta}{\cos\Theta(\sin^2\Psi + \cos^2\Psi)}\right) = \arctan\left(\frac{\sin\Theta}{\cos\Theta}\right). \tag{3.16b}$$

The function $\tan$ has a period of π, so in order to get the angle right it is better to use the function arctan2 given by (2.47). The result is

$$\Theta = \arctan2(-m_{31}, m_{32}\sin\Psi + m_{33}\cos\Psi) \tag{3.17}$$

3.1.4.4 The Roll Angle Φ

The angle Ψ can be computed as follows by inspection of (3.10)

$$\Phi = \arctan\left(\frac{m_{21}}{m_{11}}\right). \tag{3.18}$$

This can be done because the following relations hold

$$\Phi = \arctan\left(\frac{m_{21}}{m_{11}}\right) = \arctan\left(\frac{\sin\Phi\cos\Theta}{\cos\Phi\cos\Theta}\right) = \arctan\left(\frac{\sin\Phi}{\cos\Phi}\right). \tag{3.19}$$

The function $\tan$ has a period of π. This might cause problems in some cases, so in order to get the angle right, it's better to use the function arctan2 given by (2.47)

$$\Phi = \arctan2(m_{21}, m_{11}) \tag{3.20}$$

3.1.5 The State Vector

Let the *state vector* $\boldsymbol{s}$ be defined as follows:

$$\boldsymbol{s} = \begin{bmatrix} Xposition \\ Yposition \\ Zposition \\ Yaw \\ Pitch \\ Roll \end{bmatrix} = \begin{bmatrix} p_x \\ p_y \\ p_z \\ \Psi \\ \Theta \\ \Phi \end{bmatrix} \tag{3.21}$$

where the vector $\boldsymbol{p} = \begin{bmatrix} p_x & p_y & p_z \end{bmatrix}^T$ is given by (3.11), and the angles Ψ, Θ, and Φ are given by (3.12), (3.15), and (3.18).

As shown previously, the elements of the state vector $\boldsymbol{s}$ are computed from the elements of the transformation matrix ${}^0\boldsymbol{T}_N$ given by (3.9), and the transformation matrix is a function of the joint parameters $\boldsymbol{\theta}_1, \ldots, \boldsymbol{\theta}_N$

$$\begin{aligned} {}^0\boldsymbol{T}_N(\boldsymbol{\theta}_1, \ldots, \boldsymbol{\theta}_N) &= {}^0\boldsymbol{T}_1(\boldsymbol{\theta}_1) \cdots {}^{(i-1)}\boldsymbol{T}_i(\boldsymbol{\theta}_i) \cdots {}^{(N-1)}\boldsymbol{T}_N(\boldsymbol{\theta}_N) = \\ &\begin{bmatrix} m_{11}(\boldsymbol{\theta}_1, \ldots, \boldsymbol{\theta}_N) & m_{12}(\boldsymbol{\theta}_1, \ldots, \boldsymbol{\theta}_N) & m_{13}(\boldsymbol{\theta}_1, \ldots, \boldsymbol{\theta}_N) & m_{14}(\boldsymbol{\theta}_1, \ldots, \boldsymbol{\theta}_N) \\ m_{21}(\boldsymbol{\theta}_1, \ldots, \boldsymbol{\theta}_N) & m_{22}(\boldsymbol{\theta}_1, \ldots, \boldsymbol{\theta}_N) & m_{23}(\boldsymbol{\theta}_1, \ldots, \boldsymbol{\theta}_N) & m_{24}(\boldsymbol{\theta}_1, \ldots, \boldsymbol{\theta}_N) \\ m_{31}(\boldsymbol{\theta}_1, \ldots, \boldsymbol{\theta}_N) & m_{32}(\boldsymbol{\theta}_1, \ldots, \boldsymbol{\theta}_N) & m_{33}(\boldsymbol{\theta}_1, \ldots, \boldsymbol{\theta}_N) & m_{34}(\boldsymbol{\theta}_1, \ldots, \boldsymbol{\theta}_N) \\ 0 & 0 & 0 & 1 \end{bmatrix}. \end{aligned} \tag{3.22}$$

Because all the elements of the state vector $\boldsymbol{s}$ are computed from the elements of this matrix, the state vector $\boldsymbol{s}$ is also a function of the joint parameters $\boldsymbol{\theta}_i, \ldots, \boldsymbol{\theta}_N$, which yields

$$\boldsymbol{s}(\boldsymbol{\theta}_1, \ldots, \boldsymbol{\theta}_N) = \begin{bmatrix} p_x(\boldsymbol{\theta}_1, \ldots, \boldsymbol{\theta}_N) \\ p_y(\boldsymbol{\theta}_1, \ldots, \boldsymbol{\theta}_N) \\ p_z(\boldsymbol{\theta}_1, \ldots, \boldsymbol{\theta}_N) \\ \Psi(\boldsymbol{\theta}_1, \ldots, \boldsymbol{\theta}_N) \\ \Theta(\boldsymbol{\theta}_1, \ldots, \boldsymbol{\theta}_N) \\ \Phi(\boldsymbol{\theta}_1, \ldots, \boldsymbol{\theta}_N) \end{bmatrix}. \tag{3.23}$$

3.2 Forward Kinematics

Forward kinematics can be explained as follows: given all the link and joint parameters of an articulated body, determine the 3D position and orientation of the link farthest away from the base, the end effector.

The assumption is that the link and joint parameters are known. Therefore, the generalized joint parameters $\boldsymbol{\theta}_1, \ldots, \boldsymbol{\theta}_N$ are known, and the transformation from the end effector to the base of the articulated figure ${}^0\boldsymbol{T}_N(\boldsymbol{\theta}_1, \ldots, \boldsymbol{\theta}_N)$ can be computed as

$$
{}^0\boldsymbol{T}_N(\boldsymbol{\theta}_1, \ldots, \boldsymbol{\theta}_N) = {}^0\boldsymbol{T}_1(\boldsymbol{\theta}_1) \cdots {}^{(i-1)}\boldsymbol{T}_i(\boldsymbol{\theta}_i) \cdots {}^{(N-1)}\boldsymbol{T}_N(\boldsymbol{\theta}_N) =
\begin{bmatrix}
m_{11}(\boldsymbol{\theta}_1, \ldots, \boldsymbol{\theta}_N) & m_{12}(\boldsymbol{\theta}_1, \ldots, \boldsymbol{\theta}_N) & m_{13}(\boldsymbol{\theta}_1, \ldots, \boldsymbol{\theta}_N) & m_{14}(\boldsymbol{\theta}_1, \ldots, \boldsymbol{\theta}_N) \\
m_{21}(\boldsymbol{\theta}_1, \ldots, \boldsymbol{\theta}_N) & m_{22}(\boldsymbol{\theta}_1, \ldots, \boldsymbol{\theta}_N) & m_{23}(\boldsymbol{\theta}_1, \ldots, \boldsymbol{\theta}_N) & m_{24}(\boldsymbol{\theta}_1, \ldots, \boldsymbol{\theta}_N) \\
m_{31}(\boldsymbol{\theta}_1, \ldots, \boldsymbol{\theta}_N) & m_{32}(\boldsymbol{\theta}_1, \ldots, \boldsymbol{\theta}_N) & m_{33}(\boldsymbol{\theta}_1, \ldots, \boldsymbol{\theta}_N) & m_{34}(\boldsymbol{\theta}_1, \ldots, \boldsymbol{\theta}_N) \\
0 & 0 & 0 & 1
\end{bmatrix}. \tag{3.24}
$$

The elements of the matrix $\{m_{ij}(\boldsymbol{\theta}_1, \ldots, \boldsymbol{\theta}_N)\} \mid i, j = 1, \ldots, 4\}$ can be computed as described in Sections 2.2 and 2.3. From the transformation ${}^0\boldsymbol{T}_N(\boldsymbol{\theta}_1, \ldots, \boldsymbol{\theta}_N)$, the state vector $\boldsymbol{s}(\boldsymbol{\theta}_1, \ldots, \boldsymbol{\theta}_N)$ can be computed as

$$
\boldsymbol{s}(\boldsymbol{\theta}_1, \ldots, \boldsymbol{\theta}_N) =
\begin{bmatrix}
p_x(\boldsymbol{\theta}_1, \ldots, \boldsymbol{\theta}_N) \\
p_y(\boldsymbol{\theta}_1, \ldots, \boldsymbol{\theta}_N) \\
p_z(\boldsymbol{\theta}_1, \ldots, \boldsymbol{\theta}_N) \\
\Psi(\boldsymbol{\theta}_1, \ldots, \boldsymbol{\theta}_N) \\
\Theta(\boldsymbol{\theta}_1, \ldots, \boldsymbol{\theta}_N) \\
\Phi(\boldsymbol{\theta}_1, \ldots, \boldsymbol{\theta}_N)
\end{bmatrix}. \tag{3.25}
$$

The elements of the state vector are functions of the matrix elements $m_{ij}(\boldsymbol{\theta}_1, \ldots, \boldsymbol{\theta}_N)$ and therefore also of the generalized joint parameters $\boldsymbol{\theta}_1, \ldots, \boldsymbol{\theta}_N$. The individual elements of the state vector $\boldsymbol{s}$ are computed as described in Section 3.1.4.

Hence, by specifying all the generalized joint parameters $\boldsymbol{\theta}_i$ the position $\boldsymbol{p}$ and orientation Ψ, Θ, Φ of the end effector can be computed by computing the state vector $\boldsymbol{s}$.

3.3 Inverse Kinematics

Inverse kinematics can be explained as follows: given a 3D position and orientation of the link furthest away from the base, the end effector determines the parameters of the individual links and joints.

In forward kinematics, all parameters are given, and the only real work is to fill in all the values and calculate the state vector. In contrast, inverse kinematics is more challenging. Given an end effector position, there can be numerous valid solutions for the state of the remaining states of the articulated figure. This can be verified by a simple test: place your index finger on a hard surface and move your elbow. All positions the elbow passes through presents valid solutions of the articulated system (the whole arm).

The first part of this section describes the theory, shows how to set up an equation system, and how to reach valid solutions. Finally, a complete walk through is given using the Denavit-Hartenberg notation.

3.3.1 Computation of the Joint Parameters $\boldsymbol{\theta}_i$

Assume that one wants to locate the end effector at some goal position $\boldsymbol{p}_g$ with some goal orientation Φ_g, Θ_g, Ψ_g. This results in a goal state vector $\boldsymbol{s}_g$ which the end effector should move to. The problem is now how to compute the joint parameters $\boldsymbol{\theta}_i, \quad i = 1, \ldots, N$ such that the end effector reaches its goal. Stated mathematically, it means: determine a vector $\left[\boldsymbol{\theta}_1, \ldots, \boldsymbol{\theta}_N\right]^T$ such that the function

$$\boldsymbol{f}(\boldsymbol{\theta}_1, \ldots, \boldsymbol{\theta}_N) = \boldsymbol{s}(\boldsymbol{\theta}_1, \ldots, \boldsymbol{\theta}_N) - \boldsymbol{s}_g = 0. \tag{3.26}$$

We will now study the *Taylor expansion* of $\boldsymbol{s} - \boldsymbol{s}_g$, but for convenience this will be done using the function $\boldsymbol{f}$. The Taylor series is discussed in detail in Chapter 20. The following sections describes a method that uses an iterative process that slowly crawls toward the goal where $\boldsymbol{f}$ is sufficiently close to zero.

At each step in the iteration scheme presented, one has to calculate a new guess for the joint parameters. This is done via a Taylor expansion and the derivative of the state vector seeded with the old joint parameter values. These values are then fed to the next iteration.

In this section, we present the Taylor expansion together with the step equation. The following three sections present three special cases for computing the new guess for the joint parameters. Finally, we walk through how to compute the derivative matrix of the state vector.

The Taylor expansion of the function $\boldsymbol{f}$ is equal to

$$\begin{aligned} \boldsymbol{f}\big((\boldsymbol{\theta}_1, \ldots, \boldsymbol{\theta}_N) + &\Delta(\boldsymbol{\theta}_1, \ldots, \boldsymbol{\theta}_N)\big) = \\ &\boldsymbol{f}(\boldsymbol{\theta}_1, \ldots, \boldsymbol{\theta}_N) + \frac{\partial \boldsymbol{f}(\boldsymbol{\theta}_1, \ldots, \boldsymbol{\theta}_N)}{\partial(\boldsymbol{\theta}_1, \ldots, \boldsymbol{\theta}_N)} \Delta(\boldsymbol{\theta}_1, \ldots, \boldsymbol{\theta}_N) + \\ &\boldsymbol{o}(\|\Delta(\boldsymbol{\theta}_1, \ldots, \boldsymbol{\theta}_N)\|_2^2). \end{aligned} \tag{3.27}$$

Considering only the first two terms yields

$$\boldsymbol{f}\big((\boldsymbol{\theta}_1, \ldots, \boldsymbol{\theta}_N) + \Delta(\boldsymbol{\theta}_1, \ldots, \boldsymbol{\theta}_N)\big) \approx \boldsymbol{f}(\boldsymbol{\theta}_1, \ldots, \boldsymbol{\theta}_N) + \frac{\partial \boldsymbol{f}(\boldsymbol{\theta}_1, \ldots, \boldsymbol{\theta}_N)}{\partial(\boldsymbol{\theta}_1, \ldots, \boldsymbol{\theta}_N)} \Delta(\boldsymbol{\theta}_1, \ldots, \boldsymbol{\theta}_N). \tag{3.28}$$

The goal is that for some $\Delta(\boldsymbol{\theta}_1, \ldots, \boldsymbol{\theta}_N)$ the result should be zero, in which case the end effector is at the right position and has the right orientation. Therefore, let the new value of $\boldsymbol{f}$ be equal to zero

$$\boldsymbol{f}\big((\boldsymbol{\theta}_1, \ldots, \boldsymbol{\theta}_N) + \Delta(\boldsymbol{\theta}_1, \ldots, \boldsymbol{\theta}_N)\big) = 0. \tag{3.29}$$

Substituting this into (3.28) yields the following equation

$$\boldsymbol{0} \approx \boldsymbol{f}(\boldsymbol{\theta}_1, \ldots, \boldsymbol{\theta}_N) + \frac{\partial \boldsymbol{f}(\boldsymbol{\theta}_1, \ldots, \boldsymbol{\theta}_N)}{\partial(\boldsymbol{\theta}_1, \ldots, \boldsymbol{\theta}_N)} \Delta(\boldsymbol{\theta}_1, \ldots, \boldsymbol{\theta}_N) \tag{3.30}$$

which can also be written

$$\boldsymbol{f}(\boldsymbol{\theta}_1, \ldots, \boldsymbol{\theta}_N) \approx -\frac{\partial \boldsymbol{f}(\boldsymbol{\theta}_1, \ldots, \boldsymbol{\theta}_N)}{\partial(\boldsymbol{\theta}_1, \ldots, \boldsymbol{\theta}_N)} \Delta(\boldsymbol{\theta}_1, \ldots, \boldsymbol{\theta}_N). \tag{3.31}$$

The function $\boldsymbol{f}$ only differs from the function $\boldsymbol{s}$ by a constant $\boldsymbol{s}_g$. Differentiating a constant yields zero, so the *Jacobian matrix* is equal to

$$\frac{\partial \boldsymbol{f}(\boldsymbol{\theta}_1, \ldots, \boldsymbol{\theta}_N)}{\partial(\boldsymbol{\theta}_1, \ldots, \boldsymbol{\theta}_N)} = \frac{\partial \boldsymbol{s}(\boldsymbol{\theta}_1, \ldots, \boldsymbol{\theta}_N)}{\partial(\boldsymbol{\theta}_1, \ldots, \boldsymbol{\theta}_N)} \tag{3.32}$$

where

$$\frac{\partial \boldsymbol{s}(\boldsymbol{\theta}_1,\dots,\boldsymbol{\theta}_N)}{\partial(\boldsymbol{\theta}_1,\dots,\boldsymbol{\theta}_N)} = \begin{bmatrix} \frac{\partial p_x}{\partial \boldsymbol{\theta}_1}(\boldsymbol{\theta}_1,\dots,\boldsymbol{\theta}_N) & \dots & \frac{\partial p_x}{\partial \boldsymbol{\theta}_N}(\boldsymbol{\theta}_1,\dots,\boldsymbol{\theta}_N) \\ \frac{\partial p_y}{\partial \boldsymbol{\theta}_1}(\boldsymbol{\theta}_1,\dots,\boldsymbol{\theta}_N) & \dots & \frac{\partial p_y}{\partial \boldsymbol{\theta}_N}(\boldsymbol{\theta}_1,\dots,\boldsymbol{\theta}_N) \\ \frac{\partial p_z}{\partial \boldsymbol{\theta}_1}(\boldsymbol{\theta}_1,\dots,\boldsymbol{\theta}_N) & \dots & \frac{\partial p_z}{\partial \boldsymbol{\theta}_N}(\boldsymbol{\theta}_1,\dots,\boldsymbol{\theta}_N) \\ \frac{\partial \Psi}{\partial \boldsymbol{\theta}_1}(\boldsymbol{\theta}_1,\dots,\boldsymbol{\theta}_N) & \dots & \frac{\partial \Psi}{\partial \boldsymbol{\theta}_N}(\boldsymbol{\theta}_1,\dots,\boldsymbol{\theta}_N) \\ \frac{\partial \Theta}{\partial \boldsymbol{\theta}_1}(\boldsymbol{\theta}_1,\dots,\boldsymbol{\theta}_N) & \dots & \frac{\partial \Theta}{\partial \boldsymbol{\theta}_N}(\boldsymbol{\theta}_1,\dots,\boldsymbol{\theta}_N) \\ \frac{\partial \Phi}{\partial \boldsymbol{\theta}_1}(\boldsymbol{\theta}_1,\dots,\boldsymbol{\theta}_N) & \dots & \frac{\partial \Phi}{\partial \boldsymbol{\theta}_N}(\boldsymbol{\theta}_1,\dots,\boldsymbol{\theta}_N) \end{bmatrix}. \tag{3.33}$$

Therefore (3.31) can now be written

$$\boldsymbol{s}(\boldsymbol{\theta}_1,\dots,\boldsymbol{\theta}_N) - \boldsymbol{s}_g \approx -\frac{\partial \boldsymbol{s}(\boldsymbol{\theta}_1,\dots,\boldsymbol{\theta}_N)}{\partial(\boldsymbol{\theta}_1,\dots,\boldsymbol{\theta}_N)} \Delta(\boldsymbol{\theta}_1,\dots,\boldsymbol{\theta}_N). \tag{3.34}$$

The difference joint parameters vector $\Delta(\boldsymbol{\theta}_1,\dots,\boldsymbol{\theta}_N)$ is equal to

$$\Delta(\boldsymbol{\theta}_1,\dots,\boldsymbol{\theta}_N) = \begin{bmatrix} \Delta\boldsymbol{\theta}_1 \\ \vdots \\ \Delta\boldsymbol{\theta}_N \end{bmatrix} = \begin{bmatrix} \boldsymbol{\theta}_1^{new} - \boldsymbol{\theta}_1 \\ \vdots \\ \boldsymbol{\theta}_N^{new} - \boldsymbol{\theta}_N \end{bmatrix} = \begin{bmatrix} \boldsymbol{\theta}_1 \\ \vdots \\ \boldsymbol{\theta}_N \end{bmatrix}_{new} - \begin{bmatrix} \boldsymbol{\theta}_1 \\ \vdots \\ \boldsymbol{\theta}_N \end{bmatrix} \tag{3.35}$$

and we conclude that

$$\boldsymbol{s}(\boldsymbol{\theta}_1,\dots,\boldsymbol{\theta}_N) - \boldsymbol{s}_g \approx -\frac{\partial \boldsymbol{s}(\boldsymbol{\theta}_1,\dots,\boldsymbol{\theta}_N)}{\partial(\boldsymbol{\theta}_1,\dots,\boldsymbol{\theta}_N)} \left(\begin{bmatrix} \boldsymbol{\theta}_1 \\ \vdots \\ \boldsymbol{\theta}_N \end{bmatrix}_{new} - \begin{bmatrix} \boldsymbol{\theta}_1 \\ \vdots \\ \boldsymbol{\theta}_N \end{bmatrix}. \right) \tag{3.36}$$

This equation is derived using only the two first terms of the Taylor expansion of $\boldsymbol{s}$, and it forms the basis of the following derivations. It is only an approximation, but it can be used as an iteration scheme; see Section 19, to obtain the desired solution. This will be shown in the following sections.

3.3.2 The Regular Case

If the Jacoby matrix $\partial \boldsymbol{s}(\boldsymbol{\theta}_1,\dots,\boldsymbol{\theta}_N)/\partial(\boldsymbol{\theta}_1,\dots,\boldsymbol{\theta}_N)$ of the vector function $\boldsymbol{s}$ is invertible, the matrix

$$\left(\frac{\partial \boldsymbol{s}(\boldsymbol{\theta}_1,\dots,\boldsymbol{\theta}_N)}{\partial(\boldsymbol{\theta}_1,\dots,\boldsymbol{\theta}_N)} \right)^{-1} \tag{3.37}$$

exists, and (3.36) can be rewritten

$$\begin{bmatrix} \boldsymbol{\theta}_1 \\ \vdots \\ \boldsymbol{\theta}_N \end{bmatrix}_{new} = \begin{bmatrix} \boldsymbol{\theta}_1 \\ \vdots \\ \boldsymbol{\theta}_N \end{bmatrix} - \left(\frac{\partial \boldsymbol{s}(\boldsymbol{\theta}_1,\dots,\boldsymbol{\theta}_N)}{\partial(\boldsymbol{\theta}_1,\dots,\boldsymbol{\theta}_N)} \right)^{-1} (\boldsymbol{s}(\boldsymbol{\theta}_1,\dots,\boldsymbol{\theta}_N) - \boldsymbol{s}_g) \tag{3.38}$$

Because the matrix $\partial \boldsymbol{s}(\boldsymbol{\theta}_1,\ldots,\boldsymbol{\theta}_N)/\partial(\boldsymbol{\theta}_1,\ldots,\boldsymbol{\theta}_N)$ is a function of $(\boldsymbol{\theta}_1,\ldots,\boldsymbol{\theta}_N)$, it must be inverted and evaluated at each iteration.

3.3.3 The Over-Determined Case

If the Jacoby matrix $\partial \boldsymbol{s}(\boldsymbol{\theta}_1,\ldots,\boldsymbol{\theta}_N)/\partial(\boldsymbol{\theta}_1,\ldots,\boldsymbol{\theta}_N)$ is over-determined, then it has more rows than columns, and it can not be inverted. In this case the pseudoinverse can be used to obtain a least-squares solution. To make the notation readable, let

$$\boldsymbol{J} = \frac{\partial \boldsymbol{s}(\boldsymbol{\theta}_1,\ldots,\boldsymbol{\theta}_N)}{\partial(\boldsymbol{\theta}_1,\ldots,\boldsymbol{\theta}_N)}. \tag{3.39}$$

In the over-determined case, the pseudoinverse has the form (see Chapter 19.4)

$$\boldsymbol{J}^+ = \left(\boldsymbol{J}^T\boldsymbol{J}\right)^{-1}\boldsymbol{J}^T. \tag{3.40}$$

Insert $\boldsymbol{J}^+$ instead of $(\partial \boldsymbol{s}(\boldsymbol{\theta}_1,\ldots,\boldsymbol{\theta}_N)/\partial(\boldsymbol{\theta}_1,\ldots,\boldsymbol{\theta}_N))^{-1}$ in (3.38) yielding

$$\begin{bmatrix}\boldsymbol{\theta}_1\\ \vdots\\ \boldsymbol{\theta}_N\end{bmatrix}_{new} = \begin{bmatrix}\boldsymbol{\theta}_1\\ \vdots\\ \boldsymbol{\theta}_N\end{bmatrix} - \boldsymbol{J}^+\left(\boldsymbol{s}(\boldsymbol{\theta}_1,\ldots,\boldsymbol{\theta}_N) - \boldsymbol{s}_g\right). \tag{3.41}$$

The matrix $\boldsymbol{T}+$ is a function of $(\boldsymbol{\theta}_1,\ldots,\boldsymbol{\theta}_N)$. Therefore, it must be evaluated at each iteration.

3.3.4 The Under-Determined Case

If the Jacoby matrix $\partial \boldsymbol{s}(\boldsymbol{\theta}_1,\ldots,\boldsymbol{\theta}_N)/\partial(\boldsymbol{\theta}_1,\ldots,\boldsymbol{\theta}_N)$ is under-determined, it has more columns than rows, and is not be invertible. In this case the *pseudoinverse* can be used to obtain the least-squares solution, which has the smallest norm. To make the notation more readable, let

$$\boldsymbol{J} = \frac{\partial \boldsymbol{s}(\boldsymbol{\theta}_1,\ldots,\boldsymbol{\theta}_N)}{\partial(\boldsymbol{\theta}_1,\ldots,\boldsymbol{\theta}_N)}. \tag{3.42}$$

In the under-determined case, the pseudoinverse has the form

$$\boldsymbol{J}^+ = \boldsymbol{J}^T\left(\boldsymbol{J}\boldsymbol{J}^T\right)^{-1}. \tag{3.43}$$

Inserting $\boldsymbol{J}^+$ instead of $(\partial \boldsymbol{s}(\boldsymbol{\theta}_1,\ldots,\boldsymbol{\theta}_N)/\partial(\boldsymbol{\theta}_1,\ldots,\boldsymbol{\theta}_N))^{-1}$ in (3.38) results in the following equation

$$\begin{bmatrix}\boldsymbol{\theta}_1\\ \vdots\\ \boldsymbol{\theta}_N\end{bmatrix}_{new} = \begin{bmatrix}\boldsymbol{\theta}_1\\ \vdots\\ \boldsymbol{\theta}_N\end{bmatrix} - \boldsymbol{J}^+\left(\boldsymbol{s}(\boldsymbol{\theta}_1,\ldots,\boldsymbol{\theta}_N) - \boldsymbol{s}_g\right). \tag{3.44}$$

Because the matrix $\boldsymbol{J}+$ is a function of $(\boldsymbol{\theta}_1,\ldots,\boldsymbol{\theta}_N)$, it must be evaluated at each iteration.

3.3.5 Computing the Jacobian of the State Vector

In Section 3.3.1 we showed generally how to set up an iteration scheme (see Section 19), to compute the joint parameters $\boldsymbol{\theta}_1, \ldots, \boldsymbol{\theta}_N$. The only thing that is missing is how to compute the Jacoby matrix of the state vector $\boldsymbol{s}$. The Jacobian of $\boldsymbol{s}$ is equal to

$$\frac{\partial \boldsymbol{s}(\boldsymbol{\theta}_1, \ldots, \boldsymbol{\theta}_N)}{\partial(\boldsymbol{\theta}_1, \ldots, \boldsymbol{\theta}_N)} = \begin{bmatrix} \frac{\partial p_x}{\partial \boldsymbol{\theta}_1}(\boldsymbol{\theta}_1, \ldots, \boldsymbol{\theta}_N) & \cdots & \frac{\partial p_x}{\partial \boldsymbol{\theta}_N}(\boldsymbol{\theta}_1, \ldots, \boldsymbol{\theta}_N) \\ \frac{\partial p_y}{\partial \boldsymbol{\theta}_1}(\boldsymbol{\theta}_1, \ldots, \boldsymbol{\theta}_N) & \cdots & \frac{\partial p_y}{\partial \boldsymbol{\theta}_N}(\boldsymbol{\theta}_1, \ldots, \boldsymbol{\theta}_N) \\ \frac{\partial p_z}{\partial \boldsymbol{\theta}_1}(\boldsymbol{\theta}_1, \ldots, \boldsymbol{\theta}_N) & \cdots & \frac{\partial p_z}{\partial \boldsymbol{\theta}_N}(\boldsymbol{\theta}_1, \ldots, \boldsymbol{\theta}_N) \\ \frac{\partial \Psi}{\partial \boldsymbol{\theta}_1}(\boldsymbol{\theta}_1, \ldots, \boldsymbol{\theta}_N) & \cdots & \frac{\partial \Psi}{\partial \boldsymbol{\theta}_N}(\boldsymbol{\theta}_1, \ldots, \boldsymbol{\theta}_N) \\ \frac{\partial \Theta}{\partial \boldsymbol{\theta}_1}(\boldsymbol{\theta}_1, \ldots, \boldsymbol{\theta}_N) & \cdots & \frac{\partial \Theta}{\partial \boldsymbol{\theta}_N}(\boldsymbol{\theta}_1, \ldots, \boldsymbol{\theta}_N) \\ \frac{\partial \Phi}{\partial \boldsymbol{\theta}_1}(\boldsymbol{\theta}_1, \ldots, \boldsymbol{\theta}_N) & \cdots & \frac{\partial \Phi}{\partial \boldsymbol{\theta}_N}(\boldsymbol{\theta}_1, \ldots, \boldsymbol{\theta}_N) \end{bmatrix}. \tag{3.45}$$

From (3.22) it can be seen that the transformation ${}^0\boldsymbol{T}_N$ has a special form

$$\begin{aligned} &{}^0\boldsymbol{T}_N(\boldsymbol{\theta}_1, \ldots, \boldsymbol{\theta}_N) \\ &\quad = {}^0\boldsymbol{T}_1(\boldsymbol{\theta}_1) \cdots {}^{(i-2)}\boldsymbol{T}_{(i-1)}(\boldsymbol{\theta}_{(i-1)}) {}^{(i-1)}\boldsymbol{T}_i(\boldsymbol{\theta}_i) {}^i\boldsymbol{T}_{(i+1)}(\boldsymbol{\theta}_{(i+1)}) \cdots {}^{(N-1)}\boldsymbol{T}_N(\boldsymbol{\theta}_N). \end{aligned} \tag{3.46}$$

When computing the partial derivative of the transformation ${}^0\boldsymbol{T}_N(\boldsymbol{\theta}_1, \ldots, \boldsymbol{\theta}_N)$ with respect to some variable $\boldsymbol{\theta}_i$, only one matrix ${}^{(i-1)}\boldsymbol{T}_i$ depends on the variable $\boldsymbol{\theta}_i$. This observation will be used in the following to compute the elements of the Jacoby matrix of the state vector.

Considering partial differentiation with respect to the joint variable $\boldsymbol{\theta}_i$, let the matrices $\boldsymbol{P}$ and $\boldsymbol{C}$ be given as

$$\boldsymbol{P} = {}^0\boldsymbol{T}_{(i-1)}(\boldsymbol{\theta}_1, \ldots, \boldsymbol{\theta}_{i-1}) = {}^0\boldsymbol{T}_1(\boldsymbol{\theta}_1) \cdots {}^{(i-2)}\boldsymbol{T}_i(\boldsymbol{\theta}_{i-1}) \tag{3.47a}$$

$$\boldsymbol{C} = {}^i\boldsymbol{T}_N(\boldsymbol{\theta}_{(i+1)}, \ldots, \boldsymbol{\theta}_N) = {}^i\boldsymbol{T}_{(i+1)}(\boldsymbol{\theta}_{(i+1)}) \cdots {}^{(N-1)}\boldsymbol{T}_N(\boldsymbol{\theta}_N). \tag{3.47b}$$

The choice of name $\boldsymbol{P}$ indicates that the matrix contains the transformations of all the links that are *parents* to $link_i$, and the name $\boldsymbol{C}$ indicates that the matrix contains the transformations of the links that are *children* of $link_i$.

It can be seen that the matrices $\boldsymbol{P}$ and $\boldsymbol{C}$ are constant with respect to the variable $\boldsymbol{\theta}_i$. Therefore, partial differentiation of the matrices with respect to the variable $\boldsymbol{\theta}_i$ yields zero. With these assumptions, the transformation ${}^0\boldsymbol{T}_N$ can be written

$${}^0\boldsymbol{T}_N(\boldsymbol{\theta}_i) = \boldsymbol{P}\left({}^{(i-1)}\boldsymbol{T}_i(\boldsymbol{\theta}_i)\right)\boldsymbol{C} \tag{3.48}$$

which is a product of three matrices where only the one matrix $\{m_{ij} \mid i,j = 1,\dots,4\}$ is a function of joint variable $\boldsymbol{\theta}_i$

$$\begin{bmatrix} p_{11} & p_{12} & p_{13} & p_{14} \\ p_{21} & p_{22} & p_{23} & p_{24} \\ p_{31} & p_{32} & p_{33} & p_{34} \\ 0 & 0 & 0 & 1 \end{bmatrix} \begin{bmatrix} m_{11}(\boldsymbol{\theta_i}) & m_{12}(\boldsymbol{\theta_i}) & m_{13}(\boldsymbol{\theta_i}) & m_{14}(\boldsymbol{\theta_i}) \\ m_{21}(\boldsymbol{\theta_i}) & m_{22}(\boldsymbol{\theta_i}) & m_{23}(\boldsymbol{\theta_i}) & m_{24}(\boldsymbol{\theta_i}) \\ m_{31}(\boldsymbol{\theta_i}) & m_{32}(\boldsymbol{\theta_i}) & m_{33}(\boldsymbol{\theta_i}) & m_{34}(\boldsymbol{\theta_i}) \\ 0 & 0 & 0 & 1 \end{bmatrix} \begin{bmatrix} c_{11} & c_{12} & c_{13} & c_{14} \\ c_{21} & c_{22} & c_{23} & c_{24} \\ c_{31} & c_{32} & c_{33} & c_{34} \\ 0 & 0 & 0 & 1 \end{bmatrix}. \tag{3.49}$$

Under these assumptions, the $(kj)^{\text{th}}$ element of the matrix ${}^0\boldsymbol{T}_N$, denoted $\left({}^0\boldsymbol{T}_N\right)_{kj}$, can be written

$${}^0\boldsymbol{T}_N(\boldsymbol{\theta}_i)_{kj} = \sum_{l=1}^{4}\sum_{h=1}^{4} p_{kh} m_{hl}(\boldsymbol{\theta}_i) c_{lj} \tag{3.50}$$

and its partial derivative with respect to $\boldsymbol{\theta}_i$ is equal to

$$\frac{\partial\left({}^0\boldsymbol{T}_N(\boldsymbol{\theta}_i)_{kj}\right)}{\partial\boldsymbol{\theta}_i} = \sum_{l=1}^{l=4}\sum_{h=1}^{h=4} p_{kh}\left(\frac{\partial m_{hl}(\boldsymbol{\theta}_i)}{\partial\boldsymbol{\theta}_i}\right) c_{lj} \tag{3.51}$$

which is equivalent to

$$\frac{\partial\left({}^0\boldsymbol{T}_N(\boldsymbol{\theta}_i)_{kj}\right)}{\partial\boldsymbol{\theta}_i} = \boldsymbol{P}_{k*}\left(\frac{\partial\left({}^{(i-1)}\boldsymbol{T}_i(\boldsymbol{\theta}_i)\right)}{\partial\boldsymbol{\theta}_i}\right)\boldsymbol{C}_{*j} \tag{3.52}$$

where $\boldsymbol{P}_{k*}$ denotes the kth row of matrix $\boldsymbol{P}$, and $\boldsymbol{C}_{*j}$ denotes the jth column of matrix $\boldsymbol{C}$, and

$$\frac{\partial\left({}^{(i-1)}\boldsymbol{T}_i(\boldsymbol{\theta}_i)\right)}{\partial\boldsymbol{\theta}_i} = \begin{bmatrix} \frac{\partial m_{11}(\boldsymbol{\theta}_i)}{\partial\boldsymbol{\theta}_i} & \frac{\partial m_{12}(\boldsymbol{\theta}_i)}{\partial\boldsymbol{\theta}_i} & \frac{\partial m_{13}(\boldsymbol{\theta}_i)}{\partial\boldsymbol{\theta}_i} & \frac{\partial m_{14}(\boldsymbol{\theta}_i)}{\partial\boldsymbol{\theta}_i} \\ \frac{\partial m_{21}(\boldsymbol{\theta}_i)}{\partial\boldsymbol{\theta}_i} & \frac{\partial m_{22}(\boldsymbol{\theta}_i)}{\partial\boldsymbol{\theta}_i} & \frac{\partial m_{23}(\boldsymbol{\theta}_i)}{\partial\boldsymbol{\theta}_i} & \frac{\partial m_{24}(\boldsymbol{\theta}_i)}{\partial\boldsymbol{\theta}_i} \\ \frac{\partial m_{31}(\boldsymbol{\theta}_i)}{\partial\boldsymbol{\theta}_i} & \frac{\partial m_{32}(\boldsymbol{\theta}_i)}{\partial\boldsymbol{\theta}_i} & \frac{\partial m_{33}(\boldsymbol{\theta}_i)}{\partial\boldsymbol{\theta}_i} & \frac{\partial m_{34}(\boldsymbol{\theta}_i)}{\partial\boldsymbol{\theta}_i} \\ \frac{\partial m_{41}(\boldsymbol{\theta}_i)}{\partial\boldsymbol{\theta}_i} & \frac{\partial m_{42}(\boldsymbol{\theta}_i)}{\partial\boldsymbol{\theta}_i} & \frac{\partial m_{43}(\boldsymbol{\theta}_i)}{\partial\boldsymbol{\theta}_i} & \frac{\partial m_{44}(\boldsymbol{\theta}_i)}{\partial\boldsymbol{\theta}_i} \end{bmatrix}. \tag{3.53}$$

With (3.53) and either (3.38), (3.41), or (3.44), we can now solve the iterative scheme of (3.36).

When using the *Denavit-Hartenberg* description of an articulated figure, each joint is restricted to have only one degree of freedom: it has either a translatory parameter d_i along its z-axis if it is a *prismatic joint*, or it has one rotational parameter φ_i around its z-axis if it is a *revolute joint*. If a joint needs more degrees of freedom, several joints with link lengths equal to zero are located on top of each other. This means that the generalized parameter vector $\boldsymbol{\theta}_i = (\varphi_i, d_i)^T$ becomes an ordinary parameter. For a prismatic joint, the generalized parameter $\boldsymbol{\theta}_i$ becomes d_i, and for a revolute joint it becomes φ_i.

The following sections show examples of how to compute the Jacoby matrix of a prismatic and a revolute joint.

3.3.6 Example Using Denavit-Hartenberg

Recall that the state vector $\boldsymbol{s}$ is given by

$$\begin{bmatrix} p_x(\boldsymbol{\theta}_i) \\ p_y(\boldsymbol{\theta}_i) \\ p_z(\boldsymbol{\theta}_i) \\ \Psi(\boldsymbol{\theta}_i) \\ \Theta(\boldsymbol{\theta}_i) \\ \Phi(\boldsymbol{\theta}_i) \end{bmatrix} = \begin{bmatrix} m_{14}(\boldsymbol{\theta}_i) \\ m_{24}(\boldsymbol{\theta}_i) \\ m_{34}(\boldsymbol{\theta}_i) \\ \arctan\left(\dfrac{m_{32}(\boldsymbol{\theta}_i)}{m_{33}(\boldsymbol{\theta}_i)}\right) \\ \arctan\left(\dfrac{-m_{31}(\boldsymbol{\theta}_i)}{m_{32}(\boldsymbol{\theta}_i)\sin\Psi(\boldsymbol{\theta}_i) + m_{33}(\boldsymbol{\theta}_i)\cos\Psi(\boldsymbol{\theta}_i)}\right) \\ \arctan\left(\dfrac{m_{21}(\boldsymbol{\theta}_i)}{m_{11}(\boldsymbol{\theta}_i)}\right) \end{bmatrix}, \tag{3.54}$$

where $m_{kj}(\boldsymbol{\theta}_i)$ is the kj^{th} element of the matrix given by (3.48). The matrix is repeated here for convenience

$$^{0}\boldsymbol{T}_N(\boldsymbol{\theta}_i) = \boldsymbol{P}\left({}^{(i-1)}\boldsymbol{T}_i(\boldsymbol{\theta}_i)\right)\boldsymbol{C} \tag{3.55}$$

where the matrices $\boldsymbol{P}$ and $\boldsymbol{C}$ are given by (3.47).

When using the Denavit-Hartenberg notation, the generalized parameter is equal to $\boldsymbol{\theta}_i = \begin{bmatrix}\varphi_i & d_i\end{bmatrix}^T$, and the transformation matrix ${}^{(i-1)}\boldsymbol{T}_i(\boldsymbol{\theta}_i)$ is given as

$${}^{(i-1)}\boldsymbol{T}_i(d_i, \varphi_i) = \begin{bmatrix} \cos\varphi_i & -\sin\varphi_i & 0 & a_{i-1} \\ \cos\alpha_{i-1}\sin\varphi_i & \cos\alpha_{i-1}\cos\varphi_i & -\sin\alpha_{i-1} & -d_i\sin\alpha_{i-1} \\ \sin\alpha_{i-1}\sin\varphi_i & \sin\alpha_{i-1}\cos\varphi_i & \cos\alpha_{i-1} & d_i\cos\alpha_{i-1} \\ 0 & 0 & 0 & 1 \end{bmatrix}. \tag{3.56}$$

The Jacobian of the state vector $\boldsymbol{s}$ is given as

$$\frac{\partial\boldsymbol{s}(\boldsymbol{\theta}_1,\ldots,\boldsymbol{\theta}_N)}{\partial(\boldsymbol{\theta}_1,\ldots,\boldsymbol{\theta}_N)} = \begin{bmatrix} \frac{\partial p_x}{\partial\boldsymbol{\theta}_1}(\boldsymbol{\theta}_1,\ldots,\boldsymbol{\theta}_N) & \cdots & \frac{\partial p_x}{\partial\boldsymbol{\theta}_N}(\boldsymbol{\theta}_1,\ldots,\boldsymbol{\theta}_N) \\ \frac{\partial p_y}{\partial\boldsymbol{\theta}_1}(\boldsymbol{\theta}_1,\ldots,\boldsymbol{\theta}_N) & \cdots & \frac{\partial p_y}{\partial\boldsymbol{\theta}_N}(\boldsymbol{\theta}_1,\ldots,\boldsymbol{\theta}_N) \\ \frac{\partial p_z}{\partial\boldsymbol{\theta}_1}(\boldsymbol{\theta}_1,\ldots,\boldsymbol{\theta}_N) & \cdots & \frac{\partial p_z}{\partial\boldsymbol{\theta}_N}(\boldsymbol{\theta}_1,\ldots,\boldsymbol{\theta}_N) \\ \frac{\partial\Psi}{\partial\boldsymbol{\theta}_1}(\boldsymbol{\theta}_1,\ldots,\boldsymbol{\theta}_N) & \cdots & \frac{\partial\Psi}{\partial\boldsymbol{\theta}_N}(\boldsymbol{\theta}_1,\ldots,\boldsymbol{\theta}_N) \\ \frac{\partial\Theta}{\partial\boldsymbol{\theta}_1}(\boldsymbol{\theta}_1,\ldots,\boldsymbol{\theta}_N) & \cdots & \frac{\partial\Theta}{\partial\boldsymbol{\theta}_N}(\boldsymbol{\theta}_1,\ldots,\boldsymbol{\theta}_N) \\ \frac{\partial\Phi}{\partial\boldsymbol{\theta}_1}(\boldsymbol{\theta}_1,\ldots,\boldsymbol{\theta}_N) & \cdots & \frac{\partial\Phi}{\partial\boldsymbol{\theta}_N}(\boldsymbol{\theta}_1,\ldots,\boldsymbol{\theta}_N) \end{bmatrix} \tag{3.57}$$

where the kj^{th} entry is the partial derivative with respect to the variable $\boldsymbol{\theta}_k$

$$\frac{\partial\left({}^{0}\boldsymbol{T}_N(\boldsymbol{\theta}_i)\right)_{kj}}{\partial\boldsymbol{\theta}_i} = \boldsymbol{P}_{k*}\left(\frac{\partial\left({}^{(i-1)}\boldsymbol{T}_i(\boldsymbol{\theta}_i)\right)}{\partial\boldsymbol{\theta}_i}\right)\boldsymbol{C}_{*j} \tag{3.58}$$

The matrices $\boldsymbol{P}$ and $\boldsymbol{C}$ are given by (3.47).

In the following sections, the matrix $\partial\left({}^{(i-1)}\boldsymbol{T}_i(\boldsymbol{\theta}_i)\right)/\partial\boldsymbol{\theta}_i$ is computed for both a prismatic and a revolute joint.

3.3.6.1 A Prismatic Joint

The general transformation matrix ${}^{(i-1)}\boldsymbol{T}_i$ is given by (3.56). For a prismatic joint, the generalized joint parameter $\boldsymbol{\theta}_i$ is equal to $\boldsymbol{\theta}_i = d_i$. Therefore, the partial derivative of ${}^{(i-1)}\boldsymbol{T}_i$ given by the matrix (3.56) reduces to

$$\frac{\partial\left({}^{(i-1)}\boldsymbol{T}_i(\boldsymbol{\theta}_i)\right)}{\partial d_i} = \begin{bmatrix} 0 & 0 & 0 & 0 \\ 0 & 0 & 0 & -\sin\alpha_{i-1} \\ 0 & 0 & 0 & \cos\alpha_{i-1} \\ 0 & 0 & 0 & 0 \end{bmatrix}. \tag{3.59}$$

The State Variable $\mathbf{p}(d_i)$ The *state variable* $\mathbf{p}$ is given by (3.11) as

$$\mathbf{p}(d_i) = \begin{bmatrix} p_x \\ p_y \\ p_z \end{bmatrix} = \begin{bmatrix} m_{14} \\ m_{24} \\ m_{34} \end{bmatrix} = \begin{bmatrix} \left({}^{0}\boldsymbol{T}_N(d_i)\right)_{14} \\ \left({}^{0}\boldsymbol{T}_N(d_i)\right)_{24} \\ \left({}^{0}\boldsymbol{T}_N(d_i)\right)_{34} \end{bmatrix}. \tag{3.60}$$

Computing the transformation matrix ${}^{0}\boldsymbol{T}_N(d_i)$ using (3.55) and (3.56) yields the following expression for the location vector $\boldsymbol{p}$

$$\begin{aligned} p_x(d_i) &= a_{i-1}p_{11} + p_{14} - p_{12}c_{34}\sin\alpha_{i-1} - d_i p_{12}\sin\alpha_{i-1} \\ &\quad + \left(p_{11}c_{14} + p_{13}c_{24}\sin\alpha_{i-1}\right)\cos\varphi_i - p_{11}c_{24}\sin\varphi_i + p_{13}c_{14}\sin\alpha_{i-1}\sin\varphi_i \\ &\quad + \left(p_{13}\left(c_{34} + d_i\right) + p_{12}c_{24}\cos\varphi_i + p_{12}c_{14}\sin\varphi_i\right)\cos\alpha_{i-1} \end{aligned} \tag{3.61a}$$

$$\begin{aligned} p_y(d_i) &= a_{i-1}p_{21} + p_{24} - p_{22}c_{34}\sin\alpha_{i-1} - d_i p_{22}\sin\alpha_{i-1} \\ &\quad + \left(p_{21}c_{14} + p_{23}c_{24}\sin\alpha_{i-1}\right)\cos\varphi_i - p_{21}c_{24}\sin\varphi_i + p_{23}c_{14}\sin\alpha_{i-1}\sin\varphi_i \\ &\quad + \left(p_{23}\left(c_{34} + d_i\right) + p_{22}c_{24}\cos\varphi_i + p_{22}c_{14}\sin\varphi_i\right)\cos\alpha_{i-1} \end{aligned} \tag{3.61b}$$

$$\begin{aligned} p_z(d_i) &= a_{i-1}p_{31} + p_{34} - p_{32}c_{34}\sin\alpha_{i-1} - d_i p_{32}\sin\alpha_{i-1} \\ &\quad + \left(p_{31}c_{14} + p_{33}c_{24}\sin\alpha_{i-1}\right)\cos\varphi_i - p_{31}c_{24}\sin\varphi_i + p_{33}c_{14}\sin\alpha_{i-1}\sin\varphi_i \\ &\quad + \left(p_{33}\left(c_{34} + d_i\right) + p_{32}c_{24}\cos\varphi_i + p_{32}c_{14}\sin\varphi_i\right)\cos\alpha_{i-1}. \end{aligned} \tag{3.61c}$$

The partial derivative of the location $\boldsymbol{p}$ with respect to the variable d_i is equal to

$$\frac{\partial\mathbf{p}(d_i)}{\partial d_i} = \begin{bmatrix} \frac{\partial p_x(d_i)}{\partial d_i} \\ \frac{\partial p_y(d_i)}{\partial d_i} \\ \frac{\partial p_z(d_i)}{\partial d_i} \end{bmatrix} = \begin{bmatrix} \frac{\partial\left({}^{0}\boldsymbol{T}_N(d_i)\right)_{14}}{\partial d_i} \\ \frac{\partial\left({}^{0}\boldsymbol{T}_N(d_i)\right)_{24}}{\partial d_i} \\ \frac{\partial\left({}^{0}\boldsymbol{T}_N(d_i)\right)_{34}}{\partial d_i} \end{bmatrix} = \begin{bmatrix} \boldsymbol{P}_{1*}\left(\frac{\partial\left({}^{(i-1)}\boldsymbol{T}_i(d_i)\right)}{\partial d_i}\right)\boldsymbol{C}_{*4} \\ \boldsymbol{P}_{2*}\left(\frac{\partial\left({}^{(i-1)}\boldsymbol{T}_i(d_i)\right)}{\partial d_i}\right)\boldsymbol{C}_{*4} \\ \boldsymbol{P}_{3*}\left(\frac{\partial\left({}^{(i-1)}\boldsymbol{T}_i(d_i)\right)}{\partial d_i}\right)\boldsymbol{C}_{*4} \end{bmatrix} \tag{3.62}$$

where the matrices $\boldsymbol{P}$ and $\boldsymbol{C}$ are given by (3.47), and the matrix $\partial\left({}^{(i-1)}\boldsymbol{T}_i(d_i)\right)/\partial d_i$ is given by (3.59). Multiplying the matrices yields the following expressions for the partial derivative $\partial \boldsymbol{p}/\partial d_i$ of the state variable $\boldsymbol{p}$ with respect to the joint parameter d_i

$$\frac{\partial p_x(d_i)}{\partial d_i} = p_{13}\cos\alpha_{i-1} - p_{12}\sin\alpha_{i-1} \tag{3.63a}$$

$$\frac{\partial p_y(d_i)}{\partial d_i} = p_{23}\cos\alpha_{i-1} - p_{22}\sin\alpha_{i-1} \tag{3.63b}$$

$$\frac{\partial p_z(d_i)}{\partial d_i} = p_{33}\cos\alpha_{i-1} - p_{32}\sin\alpha_{i-1}. \tag{3.63c}$$

The Yaw Angle $\Psi(d_i)$ The state variable Ψ is given by (3.12) as

$$\Psi(d_i) = \arctan\left(\frac{m_{32}(d_i)}{m_{33}(d_i)}\right) \tag{3.64}$$

and its partial derivative with respect to the variable d_i is equal to

$$\frac{\partial\Psi(d_i)}{\partial d_i} = \frac{\partial}{\partial d_i}\arctan\left(\frac{m_{32}(d_i)}{m_{33}(d_i)}\right) \tag{3.65a}$$

$$= \frac{1}{1+\left(\frac{m_{32}(d_i)}{m_{33}(d_i)}\right)^2}\frac{\partial}{\partial d_i}\left(\frac{m_{32}(d_i)}{m_{33}(d_i)}\right) \tag{3.65b}$$

$$= \frac{1}{1+\left(\frac{m_{32}(d_i)}{m_{33}(d_i)}\right)^2}\frac{m_{33}(d_i)\frac{\partial m_{32}(d_i)}{\partial d_i} - m_{32}(d_i)\frac{\partial m_{33}(d_i)}{\partial d_i}}{m_{33}(d_i)^2} \tag{3.65c}$$

$$= \frac{1}{1+\left(\frac{m_{32}(d_i)}{m_{33}(d_i)}\right)^2}\left(\frac{1}{m_{33}(d_i)}\frac{\partial m_{32}(d_i)}{\partial d_i} - \frac{m_{32}(d_i)}{m_{33}(d_i)^2}\frac{\partial m_{33}(d_i)}{\partial d_i}\right) = 0 \tag{3.65d}$$

The elements $m_{kj}(d_i)$ are elements of the matrix ${}^0\boldsymbol{T}_N$, which are given by (3.55) and (3.56). Computing ${}^0\boldsymbol{T}_N$ yields the following expressions for the elements $m_{32}(d_i)$ and $m_{33}(d_i)$

$$\begin{aligned} m_{32}(d_i) = &-p_{32}c_{32}\sin\alpha_{i-1} + (p_{31}c_{12} + p_{33}c_{22}\sin\alpha_{i-1})\cos\varphi_i \\ &- p_{31}c_{22}\sin\varphi_i + p_{33}c_{12}\sin\alpha_{i-1}\sin\varphi_i \\ &+ (p_{33}c_{32} + p_{32}c_{22}\cos\varphi_i + p_{32}c_{12}\sin\varphi_i)\cos\alpha_{i-1} \end{aligned} \tag{3.66a}$$

$$\begin{aligned} m_{33}(d_i) = &-p_{32}c_{33}\sin\alpha_{i-1} + (p_{31}c_{13} + p_{33}c_{23}\sin\alpha_{i-1})\cos\varphi_i \\ &- p_{31}c_{23}\sin\varphi_i + p_{33}c_{13}\sin\alpha_{i-1}\sin\varphi_i \\ &+ (p_{33}c_{33} + p_{32}c_{23}\cos\varphi_i + p_{32}c_{13}\sin\varphi_i)\cos\alpha_{i-1} \end{aligned} \tag{3.66b}$$

The elements $\partial m_{kj}(d_i)/\partial d_i$ are given by

$$\frac{\partial m_{kj}}{\partial d_i} = \boldsymbol{P}_{k*}\left(\frac{\partial\left({}^{(i-1)}\boldsymbol{T}_i(d_i)\right)}{\partial d_i}\right)\boldsymbol{C}_{*j} \tag{3.67}$$

where the matrices $\boldsymbol{P}$ and $\boldsymbol{C}$ are given by (3.47), and the matrix $\partial\left({}^{(i-1)}\boldsymbol{T}_i(d_i)\right)/\partial d_i$ is given by (3.59). This yields

$$\frac{\partial m_{32}(d_i)}{\partial d_i} = \boldsymbol{P}_{3*}\left(\frac{\partial\left({}^{(i-1)}\boldsymbol{T}_i(d_i)\right)}{\partial d_i}\right)\boldsymbol{C}_{*2} = 0 \tag{3.68a}$$

$$\frac{\partial m_{33}(d_i)}{\partial d_i} = \boldsymbol{P}_{3*}\left(\frac{\partial\left({}^{(i-1)}\boldsymbol{T}_i(d_i)\right)}{\partial d_i}\right)\boldsymbol{C}_{*3} = 0 \tag{3.68b}$$

from which it can be seen that (3.65d) is equal to zero

$$\frac{\partial \Psi(d_i)}{\partial d_i} = 0 \tag{3.69}$$

The Pitch Angle $\Theta(d_i)$ The state variable Θ is given by (3.15) as

$$\Theta(d_i) = \arctan\left(\frac{-m_{31}(d_i)}{m_{32}(d_i)\sin\Psi(d_i) + m_{33}(d_i)\cos\Psi(d_i)}\right). \tag{3.70}$$

The expression for Θ has the form

$$\Theta(d_i) = \arctan\left(\frac{N(d_i)}{D(d_i)}\right) \tag{3.71}$$

where the numerator N and the denominator D are equal to

$$N(d_i) = -m_{31}(d_i) \tag{3.72a}$$

$$D(d_i) = \quad m_{32}(d_i)\sin\Psi(d_i) + m_{33}(d_i)\cos\Psi(d_i) \tag{3.72b}$$

where the angle Ψ is given by (3.64) and (3.66).

The elements $m_{kj}(d_i)$ are elements of the matrix ${}^0\boldsymbol{T}_N$, which are given by (3.55) and (3.56). Computing ${}^0\boldsymbol{T}_N$ yields the following expressions for the elements $m_{31}(d_i)$, $m_{32}(d_i)$, and $m_{33}(d_i)$

$$\begin{aligned} m_{31}(d_i) = &-p_{32}c_{31}\sin\alpha_{i-1} + (p_{31}c_{11} + p_{33}c_{21}\sin\alpha_{i-1})\cos\varphi_i \\ &- p_{31}c_{21}\sin\varphi_i + p_{33}c_{11}\sin\alpha_{i-1}\sin\varphi_i \\ &+ (p_{33}c_{31} + p_{32}c_{21}\cos\varphi_i + p_{32}c_{11}\sin\varphi_i)\cos\alpha_{i-1} \end{aligned} \tag{3.73a}$$

$$\begin{aligned} m_{32}(d_i) = &-p_{32}c_{32}\sin\alpha_{i-1} + (p_{31}c_{12} + p_{33}c_{22}\sin\alpha_{i-1})\cos\varphi_i \\ &- p_{31}c_{22}\sin\varphi_i + p_{33}c_{12}\sin\alpha_{i-1}\sin\varphi_i \\ &+ (p_{33}c_{32} + p_{32}c_{22}\cos\varphi_i + p_{32}c_{12}\sin\varphi_i)\cos\alpha_{i-1} \end{aligned} \tag{3.73b}$$

$$\begin{aligned} m_{33}(d_i) = &-p_{32}c_{33}\sin\alpha_{i-1} + (p_{31}c_{13} + p_{33}c_{23}\sin\alpha_{i-1})\cos\varphi_i \\ &- p_{31}c_{23}\sin\varphi_i + p_{33}c_{13}\sin\alpha_{i-1}\sin\varphi_i \\ &+ (p_{33}c_{33} + p_{32}c_{23}\cos\varphi_i + p_{32}c_{13}\sin\varphi_i)\cos\alpha_{i-1} \end{aligned} \tag{3.73c}$$

Using this simplified notation, the partial derivative of Θ with respect to the joint variable d_i can be written

$$\frac{\partial\Theta(d_i)}{\partial d_i} = \frac{1}{1+\left(\frac{N(d_i)}{D(d_i)}\right)^2}\frac{\partial}{\partial d_i}\left(\frac{N(d_i)}{D(d_i)}\right) \tag{3.74a}$$

$$= \frac{1}{1+\left(\frac{N(d_i)}{D(d_i)}\right)^2}\frac{D(d_i)\frac{\partial N(d_i)}{\partial d_i} - N(d_i)\frac{\partial D(d_i)}{\partial d_i}}{D(d_i)^2} \tag{3.74b}$$

$$= \frac{1}{1+\left(\frac{N(d_i)}{D(d_i)}\right)^2}\left(\frac{1}{D(d_i)}\frac{\partial N(d_i)}{\partial d_i} - \frac{N(d_i)}{D(d_i)^2}\frac{\partial D(d_i)}{\partial d_i}\right) \tag{3.74c}$$

where expressions for N and D have already been derived in (3.72). Expressions for $\partial N(d_i)/\partial d_i$ and $\partial D(d_i)/\partial d_i$ will be derived in the following

$$\frac{\partial N(d_i)}{\partial d_i} = -\frac{\partial m_{31}(d_i)}{\partial d_i} \tag{3.75a}$$

$$\frac{\partial D(d_i)}{\partial d_i} = m_{32}(d_i)\sin\Psi(d_i) + m_{33}(d_i)\cos\Psi(d_i) \tag{3.75b}$$

$$= \frac{\partial m_{32}(d_i)}{\partial d_i}\sin\Psi(d_i) + m_{32}(d_i)\cos\Psi(d_i)\frac{\partial\Psi(d_i)}{\partial d_i} \tag{3.75c}$$

$$+ \frac{\partial m_{33}(d_i)}{\partial d_i}\cos\Psi(d_i) - m_{33}(d_i)\sin\Psi(d_i)\frac{\partial\Psi(d_i)}{\partial d_i} \tag{3.75d}$$

The elements $\partial m_{kj}(d_i)/\partial d_i$ are given by

$$\frac{\partial m_{kj}}{\partial d_i} = \boldsymbol{P}_{k*}\left(\frac{\partial\left({}^{(i-1)}\boldsymbol{T}_i(d_i)\right)}{\partial d_i}\right)\boldsymbol{C}_{*j} \tag{3.76}$$

where the matrices $\boldsymbol{P}$ and $\boldsymbol{C}$ are given by (3.47), and the matrix $\partial\left({}^{(i-1)}\boldsymbol{T}_i(d_i)\right)/\partial d_i$ is given by (3.59). This yields

$$\frac{\partial m_{31}(d_i)}{\partial d_i} = \boldsymbol{P}_{3*}\left(\frac{\partial\left({}^{(i-1)}\boldsymbol{T}_i(d_i)\right)}{\partial d_i}\right)\boldsymbol{C}_{*1} = 0 \tag{3.77}$$

from which it follows that the partial derivative of the numerator $\partial N(d_i)/\partial d_i$ is equal to zero. In (3.65d) it was shown that the partial derivative $\partial\Psi(d_i)/\partial d_i$ is equal to zero, and (3.68) shows that the partial derivatives $\partial m_{32}/\partial d_i$ and $\partial m_{33}/\partial d_i$ are also equal to zero. Therefore, the partial derivative $\partial D(d_i)/\partial d_i$ is equal to zero

$$\frac{\partial m_{31}(d_i)}{\partial d_i} = \frac{\partial m_{32}(d_i)}{\partial d_i} = \frac{\partial m_{33}(d_i)}{\partial d_i} = \frac{\partial\Psi(d_i)}{\partial d_i} = 0 \quad\Longrightarrow\quad \frac{\partial N(d_i)}{\partial d_i} = \frac{\partial D(d_i)}{\partial d_i} = 0 \tag{3.78}$$

from which it can be seen that (3.74c) is equal to zero

$$\frac{\partial N(d_i)}{\partial d_i} = \frac{\partial D(d_i)}{\partial d_i} = 0 \quad \Longrightarrow \quad \frac{\partial \Theta(d_i)}{\partial d_i} = 0 \tag{3.79}$$

The Roll Angle $\Phi(d_i)$ The state variable Φ is given by (3.18) as

$$\Phi(d_i) = \arctan\left(\frac{m_{21}(d_i)}{m_{11}(d_i)}\right) \tag{3.80}$$

and its partial derivative with respect to the variable φ_i is equal to

$$\frac{\partial \Phi(d_i)}{\partial d_i} = \frac{\partial}{\partial d_i} \arctan\left(\frac{m_{21}(d_i)}{m_{11}(d_i)}\right) \tag{3.81a}$$

$$= \frac{1}{1 + \left(\frac{m_{21}(d_i)}{m_{11}(d_i)}\right)^2} \frac{\partial}{\partial d_i}\left(\frac{m_{21}(d_i)}{m_{11}(d_i)}\right) \tag{3.81b}$$

$$= \frac{1}{1 + \left(\frac{m_{21}(d_i)}{m_{11}(d_i)}\right)^2} \frac{m_{11}(d_i)\frac{\partial m_{21}(d_i)}{\partial d_i} - m_{21}(d_i)\frac{\partial m_{11}(d_i)}{\partial d_i}}{m_{11}(d_i)^2} \tag{3.81c}$$

$$= \frac{1}{1 + \left(\frac{m_{21}(d_i)}{m_{11}(d_i)}\right)^2} \left(\frac{1}{m_{11}(d_i)} \frac{\partial m_{21}(d_i)}{\partial d_i} - \frac{m_{21}(d_i)}{m_{11}(d_i)^2} \frac{\partial m_{11}(d_i)}{\partial d_i}\right) = 0. \tag{3.81d}$$

The elements $m_{kj}(d_i)$ are elements of the matrix ${}^0\boldsymbol{T}_N$, which are given by (3.55) and (3.56). Computing ${}^0\boldsymbol{T}_N$ yields the following expressions for the elements $m_{21}(d_i)$ and $m_{11}(d_i)$

$$\begin{aligned} m_{11}(d_i) = &-p_{12}c_{31}\sin\alpha_{i-1} + (p_{11}c_{11} + p_{13}c_{21}\sin\alpha_{i-1})\cos\varphi_i \\ &- p_{11}c_{21}\sin\varphi_i + p_{13}c_{11}\sin\alpha_{i-1}\sin\varphi_i \\ &+ (p_{13}c_{31} + p_{12}c_{21}\cos\varphi_i + p_{12}c_{11}\sin\varphi_i)\cos\alpha_{i-1} \end{aligned} \tag{3.82a}$$

$$\begin{aligned} m_{21}(d_i) = &-p_{22}c_{31}\sin\alpha_{i-1} + (p_{21}c_{11} + p_{23}c_{21}\sin\alpha_{i-1})\cos\varphi_i \\ &- p_{21}c_{21}\sin\varphi_i + p_{23}c_{11}\sin\alpha_{i-1}\sin\varphi_i \\ &+ (p_{23}c_{31} + p_{22}c_{21}\cos\varphi_i + p_{22}c_{11}\sin\varphi_i)\cos\alpha_{i-1} \end{aligned} \tag{3.82b}$$

The elements $\partial m_{kj}(d_i)/\partial d_i$ are given by

$$\frac{\partial m_{kj}}{\partial d_i} = \boldsymbol{P}_{k*}\left(\frac{\partial\left({}^{(i-1)}\boldsymbol{T}_i(d_i)\right)}{\partial d_i}\right)\boldsymbol{C}_{*j} \tag{3.83}$$

where the matrices $\boldsymbol{P}$ and $\boldsymbol{C}$ are given by (3.47), and the matrix $\partial\left({}^{(i-1)}\boldsymbol{T}_i(d_i)\right)/\partial d_i$ is given by (3.86). This yields

$$\frac{\partial m_{11}(d_i)}{\partial d_i} = \boldsymbol{P}_{1*}\left(\frac{\partial\left({}^{(i-1)}\boldsymbol{T}_i(d_i)\right)}{\partial d_i}\right)\boldsymbol{C}_{*1} = 0 \tag{3.84a}$$

$$\frac{\partial m_{21}(d_i)}{\partial d_i} = \boldsymbol{P}_{2*}\left(\frac{\partial\left({}^{(i-1)}\boldsymbol{T}_i(d_i)\right)}{\partial d_i}\right)\boldsymbol{C}_{*1} = 0 \tag{3.84b}$$

from which it can be seen that (3.81d) is equal to zero

$$\frac{\partial \Phi(d_i)}{\partial d_i} = 0 \tag{3.85}$$

3.3.6.2 A Revolute Joint

The general transformation matrix ${}^{(i-1)}\boldsymbol{T}_i$ is given by (3.56). For a revolute joint, the generalized joint parameter $\boldsymbol{\theta}_i$ is equal to $\boldsymbol{\theta}_i = \varphi_i$. Therefore, the partial derivative of ${}^{(i-1)}\boldsymbol{T}_i$ given by the matrix (3.56) reduces to

$$\frac{\partial\left({}^{(i-1)}\boldsymbol{T}_i(\boldsymbol{\theta}_i)\right)}{\partial d_i} = \begin{bmatrix} -\sin\varphi_i & -\cos\varphi_i & 0 & 0 \\ \cos\alpha_{i-1}\cos\varphi_i & -\cos\alpha_{i-1}\sin\varphi_i & 0 & 0 \\ \sin\alpha_{i-1}\cos\varphi_i & -\sin\alpha_{i-1}\sin\varphi_i & 0 & 0 \\ 0 & 0 & 0 & 0 \end{bmatrix}. \tag{3.86}$$

The State Variable $\boldsymbol{p}(d_i)$ The state variable $\boldsymbol{p}$ is given by (3.11) as

$$\boldsymbol{p}(\varphi_i) = \begin{bmatrix} p_x \\ p_y \\ p_z \end{bmatrix} = \begin{bmatrix} m_{14} \\ m_{24} \\ m_{34} \end{bmatrix} = \begin{bmatrix} \left({}^0\boldsymbol{T}_N(\varphi_i)\right)_{14} \\ \left({}^0\boldsymbol{T}_N(\varphi_i)\right)_{24} \\ \left({}^0\boldsymbol{T}_N(\varphi_i)\right)_{34} \end{bmatrix} \tag{3.87}$$

Computing the transformation matrix ${}^0\boldsymbol{T}_N(\varphi_i)$ using (3.55) and (3.56) yields the following expression for the location vector $\boldsymbol{p}$

$$\begin{aligned} p_x(\varphi_i) = {} & a_{i-1}p_{11} + p_{14} - p_{12}c_{34}\sin\alpha_{i-1} - d_i p_{12}\sin\alpha_{i-1} \\ & + (p_{11}c_{14} + p_{13}c_{24}\sin\alpha_{i-1})\cos\varphi_i - p_{11}c_{24}\sin\varphi_i + p_{13}c_{14}\sin\alpha_{i-1}\sin\varphi_i \\ & + (p_{13}(c_{34} + d_i) + p_{12}c_{24}\cos\varphi_i + p_{12}c_{14}\sin\varphi_i)\cos\alpha_{i-1} \end{aligned} \tag{3.88a}$$

$$\begin{aligned} p_y(\varphi_i) = {} & a_{i-1}p_{21} + p_{24} - p_{22}c_{34}\sin\alpha_{i-1} - d_i p_{22}\sin\alpha_{i-1} \\ & + (p_{21}c_{14} + p_{23}c_{24}\sin\alpha_{i-1})\cos\varphi_i - p_{21}c_{24}\sin\varphi_i + p_{23}c_{14}\sin\alpha_{i-1}\sin\varphi_i \\ & + (p_{23}(c_{34} + d_i) + p_{22}c_{24}\cos\varphi_i + p_{22}c_{14}\sin\varphi_i)\cos\alpha_{i-1} \end{aligned} \tag{3.88b}$$

$$\begin{aligned} p_z(\varphi_i) = {} & a_{i-1}p_{31} + p_{34} - p_{32}c_{34}\sin\alpha_{i-1} - d_i p_{32}\sin\alpha_{i-1} \\ & + (p_{31}c_{14} + p_{33}c_{24}\sin\alpha_{i-1})\cos\varphi_i - p_{31}c_{24}\sin\varphi_i + p_{33}c_{14}\sin\alpha_{i-1}\sin\varphi_i \\ & + (p_{33}(c_{34} + d_i) + p_{32}c_{24}\cos\varphi_i + p_{32}c_{14}\sin\varphi_i)\cos\alpha_{i-1} \end{aligned} \tag{3.88c}$$

The partial derivative of the location $\boldsymbol{p}$ with respect to the variable φ_i is equal to

$$\frac{\partial \boldsymbol{p}(\varphi_i)}{\partial \varphi_i} = \begin{bmatrix} \frac{\partial p_x(\varphi_i)}{\partial \varphi_i} \\ \frac{\partial p_y(\varphi_i)}{\partial \varphi_i} \\ \frac{\partial p_z(\varphi_i)}{\partial \varphi_i} \end{bmatrix} = \begin{bmatrix} \frac{\partial \left({}^0\boldsymbol{T}_N(\varphi_i)\right)_{14}}{\partial d_i} \\ \frac{\partial \left({}^0\boldsymbol{T}_N(\varphi_i)\right)_{24}}{\partial d_i} \\ \frac{\partial \left({}^0\boldsymbol{T}_N(\varphi_i)\right)_{34}}{\partial d_i} \end{bmatrix} = \begin{bmatrix} \boldsymbol{P}_{1*}\left(\frac{\partial\left({}^{(i-1)}\boldsymbol{T}_i(\varphi_i)\right)}{\partial \varphi_i}\right)\boldsymbol{C}_{*4} \\ \boldsymbol{P}_{2*}\left(\frac{\partial\left({}^{(i-1)}\boldsymbol{T}_i(\varphi_i)\right)}{\partial \varphi_i}\right)\boldsymbol{C}_{*4} \\ \boldsymbol{P}_{3*}\left(\frac{\partial\left({}^{(i-1)}\boldsymbol{T}_i(\varphi_i)\right)}{\partial \varphi_i}\right)\boldsymbol{C}_{*4} \end{bmatrix} \tag{3.89}$$

where the matrices $\boldsymbol{P}$ and $\boldsymbol{C}$ are given by (3.47), and the matrix $\partial\left({}^{(i-1)}\boldsymbol{T}_i(\varphi_i)\right)/\partial\varphi_i$ is given by (3.86). Multiplying the matrices yields the following expressions for the partial derivative $\partial \boldsymbol{p}/\partial \varphi_i$ of the state variable $\boldsymbol{p}$ with respect to the joint parameter φ_i

$$\begin{aligned} \frac{\partial p_x(\varphi_i)}{\partial \varphi_i} &= \left(-p_{11}c_{24} + p_{12}c_{14}\cos\alpha_{i-1} + p_{13}c_{14}\sin\alpha_{i-1}\right)\cos\varphi_i \\ &\quad - \left(p_{11}c_{14} + p_{12}c_{24}\cos\alpha_{i-1} + p_{13}c_{24}\sin\alpha_{i-1}\right)\sin\varphi_i \end{aligned} \tag{3.90a}$$

$$\begin{aligned} \frac{\partial p_y(\varphi_i)}{\partial \varphi_i} &= \left(-p_{21}c_{24} + p_{22}c_{14}\cos\alpha_{i-1} + p_{23}c_{14}\sin\alpha_{i-1}\right)\cos\varphi_i \\ &\quad - \left(p_{21}c_{14} + p_{22}c_{24}\cos\alpha_{i-1} + p_{23}c_{24}\sin\alpha_{i-1}\right)\sin\varphi_i \end{aligned} \tag{3.90b}$$

$$\begin{aligned} \frac{\partial p_z(\varphi_i)}{\partial \varphi_i} &= \left(-p_{31}c_{24} + p_{32}c_{14}\cos\alpha_{i-1} + p_{33}c_{14}\sin\alpha_{i-1}\right)\cos\varphi_i \\ &\quad - \left(p_{31}c_{14} + p_{32}c_{24}\cos\alpha_{i-1} + p_{33}c_{24}\sin\alpha_{i-1}\right)\sin\varphi_i \end{aligned} \tag{3.90c}$$

The Yaw Angle $\Psi(\varphi_i)$ The state variable Ψ is given by (3.12) as

$$\Psi(\varphi_i) = \arctan\left(\frac{m_{32}(\varphi_i)}{m_{33}(\varphi_i)}\right) \tag{3.91}$$

and its partial derivative with respect to the variable φ_i is equal to

$$\frac{\partial \Psi(\varphi_i)}{\partial \varphi_i} = \frac{\partial}{\partial \varphi_i} \arctan\left(\frac{m_{32}(\varphi_i)}{m_{33}(\varphi_i)}\right) \tag{3.92a}$$

$$= \frac{1}{1+\left(\frac{m_{32}(\varphi_i)}{m_{33}(\varphi_i)}\right)^2} \frac{\partial}{\partial \varphi_i}\left(\frac{m_{32}(\varphi_i)}{m_{33}(\varphi_i)}\right) \tag{3.92b}$$

$$= \frac{1}{1+\left(\frac{m_{32}(\varphi_i)}{m_{33}(\varphi_i)}\right)^2} \frac{m_{33}(\varphi_i)\frac{\partial m_{32}(\varphi_i)}{\partial \varphi_i} - m_{32}(\varphi_i)\frac{\partial m_{33}(\varphi_i)}{\partial \varphi_i}}{m_{33}(\varphi_i)^2} \tag{3.92c}$$

$$= \frac{1}{1+\left(\frac{m_{32}(\varphi_i)}{m_{33}(\varphi_i)}\right)^2} \left(\frac{1}{m_{33}(\varphi_i)}\frac{\partial m_{32}(\varphi_i)}{\partial \varphi_i} - \frac{m_{32}(\varphi_i)}{m_{33}(\varphi_i)^2}\frac{\partial m_{33}(\varphi_i)}{\partial \varphi_i}\right) \tag{3.92d}$$

The elements $m_{kj}(\varphi_i)$ are elements of the matrix ${}^0\boldsymbol{T}_N$, which are given by (3.55) and (3.56). Computing ${}^0\boldsymbol{T}_N$ yields the following expressions for the elements $m_{32}(\varphi_i)$ and $m_{33}(\varphi_i)$

$$\begin{aligned} m_{32}(\varphi_i) = & -p_{32}c_{32}\sin\alpha_{i-1} + (p_{31}c_{12} + p_{33}c_{22}\sin\alpha_{i-1})\cos\varphi_i \\ & - p_{31}c_{22}\sin\varphi_i + p_{33}c_{12}\sin\alpha_{i-1}\sin\varphi_i \\ & + (p_{33}c_{32} + p_{32}c_{22}\cos\varphi_i + p_{32}c_{12}\sin\varphi_i)\cos\alpha_{i-1} \end{aligned} \tag{3.93a}$$

$$\begin{aligned} m_{33}(\varphi_i) = & -p_{32}c_{33}\sin\alpha_{i-1} + (p_{31}c_{13} + p_{33}c_{23}\sin\alpha_{i-1})\cos\varphi_i \\ & - p_{31}c_{23}\sin\varphi_i + p_{33}c_{13}\sin\alpha_{i-1}\sin\varphi_i \\ & + (p_{33}c_{33} + p_{32}c_{23}\cos\varphi_i + p_{32}c_{13}\sin\varphi_i)\cos\alpha_{i-1} \end{aligned} \tag{3.93b}$$

The elements $\partial m_{kj}(\varphi_i)/\partial \varphi_i$ are given by

$$\frac{\partial m_{kj}}{\partial \varphi_i} = \boldsymbol{P}_{k*}\left(\frac{\partial\left({}^{(i-1)}\boldsymbol{T}_i(\varphi_i)\right)}{\partial \varphi_i}\right)\boldsymbol{C}_{*j} \tag{3.94}$$

where the matrices $\boldsymbol{P}$ and $\boldsymbol{C}$ are given by (3.47), and the matrix $\partial\left({}^{(i-1)}\boldsymbol{T}_i(\varphi_i)\right)/\partial \varphi_i$ is given by (3.86). This yields

$$\frac{\partial m_{32}(\varphi_i)}{\partial \varphi_i} = \boldsymbol{P}_{3*}\left(\frac{\partial\left({}^{(i-1)}\boldsymbol{T}_i(\varphi_i)\right)}{\partial \varphi_i}\right)\boldsymbol{C}_{*2} \tag{3.95a}$$

$$\begin{aligned} = & (-p_{31}c_{22} + p_{32}c_{12}\cos\alpha_{i-1} + p_{33}c_{12}\sin\alpha_{i-1})\cos\varphi_i \\ & - (p_{31}c_{12} + p_{32}c_{22}\cos\alpha_{i-1} + p_{33}c_{22}\sin\alpha_{i-1})\sin\varphi_i \end{aligned} \tag{3.95b}$$

$$\frac{\partial m_{33}(\varphi_i)}{\partial \varphi_i} = \boldsymbol{P}_{3*}\left(\frac{\partial\left({}^{(i-1)}\boldsymbol{T}_i(\varphi_i)\right)}{\partial \varphi_i}\right)\boldsymbol{C}_{*3} \tag{3.95c}$$

$$\begin{aligned} = & (-p_{31}c_{23} + p_{32}c_{13}\cos\alpha_{i-1} + p_{33}c_{13}\sin\alpha_{i-1})\cos\varphi_i \\ & - (p_{31}c_{13} + p_{32}c_{23}\cos\alpha_{i-1} + p_{33}c_{23}\sin\alpha_{i-1})\sin\varphi_i \end{aligned} \tag{3.95d}$$

The Pitch Angle $\Theta(\varphi_i)$ The state variable Θ is given by (3.15) as

$$\Theta(\varphi_i) = \arctan\left(\frac{-m_{31}(\varphi_i)}{m_{32}(\varphi_i)\sin\Psi(\varphi_i) + m_{33}(\varphi_i)\cos\Psi(\varphi_i)}\right) \tag{3.96}$$

The expression for Θ has the form

$$\Theta(\varphi_i) = \arctan\left(\frac{N(\varphi_i)}{D(\varphi_i)}\right) \tag{3.97}$$

where the numerator N and the denominator D are equal to

$$N(\varphi_i) = -m_{31}(\varphi_i) \tag{3.98a}$$
$$D(\varphi_i) = \quad m_{32}(\varphi_i)\sin\Psi(\varphi_i) + m_{33}(\varphi_i)\cos\Psi(\varphi_i) \tag{3.98b}$$

where the angle Ψ is given by (3.91) and (3.93).

The elements $m_{kj}(\varphi_i)$ are elements of the matrix ${}^0\boldsymbol{T}_N$, which are given by (3.55) and (3.56). Computing ${}^0\boldsymbol{T}_N$ yields the following expressions for the elements $m_{31}(\varphi_i)$, $m_{32}(\varphi_i)$, and $m_{33}(\varphi_i)$

$$\begin{aligned} m_{31}(\varphi_i) = {} & -p_{32}c_{31}\sin\alpha_{i-1} + (p_{31}c_{11} + p_{33}c_{21}\sin\alpha_{i-1})\cos\varphi_i \\ & - p_{31}c_{21}\sin\varphi_i + p_{33}c_{11}\sin\alpha_{i-1}\sin\varphi_i \\ & + (p_{33}c_{31} + p_{32}c_{21}\cos\varphi_i + p_{32}c_{11}\sin\varphi_i)\cos\alpha_{i-1} \end{aligned} \tag{3.99a}$$

$$\begin{aligned} m_{32}(\varphi_i) = {} & -p_{32}c_{32}\sin\alpha_{i-1} + (p_{31}c_{12} + p_{33}c_{22}\sin\alpha_{i-1})\cos\varphi_i \\ & - p_{31}c_{22}\sin\varphi_i + p_{33}c_{12}\sin\alpha_{i-1}\sin\varphi_i \\ & + (p_{33}c_{32} + p_{32}c_{22}\cos\varphi_i + p_{32}c_{12}\sin\varphi_i)\cos\alpha_{i-1} \end{aligned} \tag{3.99b}$$

$$\begin{aligned} m_{33}(\varphi_i) = {} & -p_{32}c_{33}\sin\alpha_{i-1} + (p_{31}c_{13} + p_{33}c_{23}\sin\alpha_{i-1})\cos\varphi_i \\ & - p_{31}c_{23}\sin\varphi_i + p_{33}c_{13}\sin\alpha_{i-1}\sin\varphi_i \\ & + (p_{33}c_{33} + p_{32}c_{23}\cos\varphi_i + p_{32}c_{13}\sin\varphi_i)\cos\alpha_{i-1} \end{aligned} \tag{3.99c}$$

Using this simplified notation, the partial derivative of Θ with respect to the joint variable φ_i can be written

$$\frac{\partial\Theta(\varphi_i)}{\partial\varphi_i} = \frac{1}{1 + \left(\frac{N(\varphi_i)}{D(\varphi_i)}\right)^2} \frac{\partial}{\partial\varphi_i}\left(\frac{N(\varphi_i)}{D(\varphi_i)}\right) \tag{3.100a}$$

$$= \frac{1}{1 + \left(\frac{N(\varphi_i)}{D(\varphi_i)}\right)^2} \frac{D(\varphi_i)\frac{\partial N(\varphi_i)}{\partial\varphi_i} - N(\varphi_i)\frac{\partial D(\varphi_i)}{\partial\varphi_i}}{D(\varphi_i)^2} \tag{3.100b}$$

$$= \frac{1}{1 + \left(\frac{N(\varphi_i)}{D(\varphi_i)}\right)^2} \left(\frac{1}{D(\varphi_i)}\frac{\partial N(\varphi_i)}{\partial\varphi_i} - \frac{N(\varphi_i)}{D(\varphi_i)^2}\frac{\partial D(\varphi_i)}{\partial\varphi_i}\right) \tag{3.100c}$$

where expressions for N and D have already been derived in (3.98). Expressions for $\partial N(\varphi_i)/\partial\varphi_i$ and $\partial D(\varphi_i)/\partial\varphi_i$ will be derived in the following

$$\frac{\partial N(\varphi_i)}{\partial\varphi_i} = -\frac{\partial m_{31}(\varphi_i)}{\partial\varphi_i} \tag{3.101a}$$

$$\frac{\partial D(\varphi_i)}{\partial\varphi_i} = m_{32}(\varphi_i)\sin\Psi(\varphi_i) + m_{33}(\varphi_i)\cos\Psi(\varphi_i) \tag{3.101b}$$

$$= \frac{\partial m_{32}(\varphi_i)}{\partial\varphi_i}\sin\Psi(\varphi_i) + m_{32}(\varphi_i)\cos\Psi(\varphi_i)\frac{\partial\Psi(\varphi_i)}{\partial\varphi_i} \tag{3.101c}$$

$$+ \frac{\partial m_{33}(\varphi_i)}{\partial\varphi_i}\cos\Psi(\varphi_i) - m_{33}(\varphi_i)\sin\Psi(\varphi_i)\frac{\partial\Psi(\varphi_i)}{\partial\varphi_i} \tag{3.101d}$$

The elements $\partial m_{kj}(\varphi_i)/\partial\varphi_i$ are given by

$$\frac{\partial m_{kj}}{\partial\varphi_i} = \boldsymbol{P}_{k*}\left(\frac{\partial\left({}^{(i-1)}\boldsymbol{T}_i(\varphi_i)\right)}{\partial\varphi_i}\right)\boldsymbol{C}_{*j} \tag{3.102}$$

where the matrices $\boldsymbol{P}$ and $\boldsymbol{C}$ are given by (3.47), and the matrix $\partial\left({}^{(i-1)}\boldsymbol{T}_i(\varphi_i)\right)/\partial\varphi_i$ is given by (3.86). This yields

$$\frac{\partial m_{31}(\varphi_i)}{\partial\varphi_i} = \boldsymbol{P}_{3*}\left(\frac{\partial\left({}^{(i-1)}\boldsymbol{T}_i(\varphi_i)\right)}{\partial\varphi_i}\right)\boldsymbol{C}_{*1} \tag{3.103a}$$

$$\begin{aligned} &= (-p_{31}c_{21} + p_{32}c_{11}\cos\alpha_{i-1} + p_{33}c_{11}\sin\alpha_{i-1})\cos\varphi_i \\ &\quad - (p_{31}c_{11} + p_{32}c_{21}\cos\alpha_{i-1} + p_{33}c_{21}\sin\alpha_{i-1})\sin\varphi_i \end{aligned} \tag{3.103b}$$

$$\frac{\partial m_{32}(\varphi_i)}{\partial\varphi_i} = \boldsymbol{P}_{3*}\left(\frac{\partial\left({}^{(i-1)}\boldsymbol{T}_i(\varphi_i)\right)}{\partial\varphi_i}\right)\boldsymbol{C}_{*2} \tag{3.103c}$$

$$\begin{aligned} &= (-p_{31}c_{22} + p_{32}c_{12}\cos\alpha_{i-1} + p_{33}c_{12}\sin\alpha_{i-1})\cos\varphi_i \\ &\quad - (p_{31}c_{12} + p_{32}c_{22}\cos\alpha_{i-1} + p_{33}c_{22}\sin\alpha_{i-1})\sin\varphi_i \end{aligned} \tag{3.103d}$$

$$\frac{\partial m_{33}(\varphi_i)}{\partial\varphi_i} = \boldsymbol{P}_{3*}\left(\frac{\partial\left({}^{(i-1)}\boldsymbol{T}_i(\varphi_i)\right)}{\partial\varphi_i}\right)\boldsymbol{C}_{*3} \tag{3.103e}$$

$$\begin{aligned} &= (-p_{31}c_{23} + p_{32}c_{13}\cos\alpha_{i-1} + p_{33}c_{13}\sin\alpha_{i-1})\cos\varphi_i \\ &\quad - (p_{31}c_{13} + p_{32}c_{23}\cos\alpha_{i-1} + p_{33}c_{23}\sin\alpha_{i-1})\sin\varphi_i \end{aligned} \tag{3.103f}$$

The Roll Angle $\Phi(\varphi_i)$ The state variable Φ is given by (3.18) as

$$\Phi(\varphi_i) = \arctan\left(\frac{m_{21}(\varphi_i)}{m_{11}(\varphi_i)}\right) \tag{3.104}$$

and its partial derivative with respect to the variable d_i is equal to

$$\frac{\partial \Phi(\varphi_i)}{\partial \varphi_i} = \frac{\partial}{\partial \varphi_i} \arctan\left(\frac{m_{21}(\varphi_i)}{m_{11}(\varphi_i)}\right) \tag{3.105a}$$

$$= \frac{1}{1+\left(\frac{m_{21}(\varphi_i)}{m_{11}(\varphi_i)}\right)^2} \frac{\partial}{\partial \varphi_i}\left(\frac{m_{21}(\varphi_i)}{m_{11}(\varphi_i)}\right) \tag{3.105b}$$

$$= \frac{1}{1+\left(\frac{m_{21}(\varphi_i)}{m_{11}(\varphi_i)}\right)^2} \frac{m_{11}(\varphi_i)\frac{\partial m_{21}(\varphi_i)}{\partial \varphi_i} - m_{21}(\varphi_i)\frac{\partial m_{11}(\varphi_i)}{\partial \varphi_i}}{m_{11}(\varphi_i)^2} \tag{3.105c}$$

$$= \frac{1}{1+\left(\frac{m_{21}(\varphi_i)}{m_{11}(\varphi_i)}\right)^2} \left(\frac{1}{m_{11}(\varphi_i)}\frac{\partial m_{21}(\varphi_i)}{\partial \varphi_i} - \frac{m_{21}(\varphi_i)}{m_{11}(\varphi_i)^2}\frac{\partial m_{11}(\varphi_i)}{\partial \varphi_i}\right) \tag{3.105d}$$

The elements $m_{kj}(\varphi_i)$ are elements of the matrix ${}^0\boldsymbol{T}_N$, which are given by (3.55) and (3.56). Computing ${}^0\boldsymbol{T}_N$ yields the following expressions for the elements $m_{21}(\varphi_i)$ and $m_{11}(\varphi_i)$

$$\begin{aligned} m_{11}(\varphi_i) = & -p_{12}c_{31}\sin\alpha_{i-1} + (p_{11}c_{11} + p_{13}c_{21}\sin\alpha_{i-1})\cos\varphi_i \\ & - p_{11}c_{21}\sin\varphi_i + p_{13}c_{11}\sin\alpha_{i-1}\sin\varphi_i \\ & + (p_{13}c_{31} + p_{12}c_{21}\cos\varphi_i + p_{12}c_{11}\sin\varphi_i)\cos\alpha_{i-1} \end{aligned} \tag{3.106a}$$

$$\begin{aligned} m_{21}(\varphi_i) = & -p_{22}c_{31}\sin\alpha_{i-1} + (p_{21}c_{11} + p_{23}c_{21}\sin\alpha_{i-1})\cos\varphi_i \\ & - p_{21}c_{21}\sin\varphi_i + p_{23}c_{11}\sin\alpha_{i-1}\sin\varphi_i \\ & + (p_{23}c_{31} + p_{22}c_{21}\cos\varphi_i + p_{22}c_{11}\sin\varphi_i)\cos\alpha_{i-1} \end{aligned} \tag{3.106b}$$

The elements $\partial m_{kj}(\varphi_i)/\partial \varphi_i$ are given by

$$\frac{\partial m_{kj}}{\partial \varphi_i} = \boldsymbol{P}_{k*}\left(\frac{\partial\left({}^{(i-1)}\boldsymbol{T}_i(\varphi_i)\right)}{\partial \varphi_i}\right)\boldsymbol{C}_{*j} \tag{3.107}$$

where the matrices $\boldsymbol{P}$ and $\boldsymbol{C}$ are given by (3.47), and the matrix $\partial\left({}^{(i-1)}\boldsymbol{T}_i(\varphi_i)\right)/\partial\varphi_i$ is given by (3.86). This yields

$$\frac{\partial m_{11}(\varphi_i)}{\partial \varphi_i} = \boldsymbol{P}_{1*}\left(\frac{\partial\left({}^{(i-1)}\boldsymbol{T}_i(\varphi_i)\right)}{\partial \varphi_i}\right)\boldsymbol{C}_{*1} \tag{3.108a}$$

$$\begin{aligned} = & (-p_{11}c_{21} + p_{12}c_{11}\cos\alpha_{i-1} + p_{13}c_{11}\sin\alpha_{i-1})\, cos\varphi_i \\ & - (p_{11}c_{11} + p_{12}c_{21}\cos\alpha_{i-1} + p_{13}c_{21}\sin\alpha_{i-1})\sin\varphi_i \end{aligned} \tag{3.108b}$$

$$\frac{\partial m_{21}(\varphi_i)}{\partial \varphi_i} = \boldsymbol{P}_{2*}\left(\frac{\partial\left({}^{(i-1)}\boldsymbol{T}_i(\varphi_i)\right)}{\partial \varphi_i}\right)\boldsymbol{C}_{*1} \tag{3.108c}$$

$$\begin{aligned} = & (-p_{21}c_{21} + p_{22}c_{11}\cos\alpha_{i-1} + p_{23}c_{11}\sin\alpha_{i-1})\cos\varphi_i \\ & - (p_{21}c_{11} + p_{22}c_{21}\cos\alpha_{i-1} + p_{23}c_{21}\sin\alpha_{i-1})\sin\varphi_i \end{aligned} \tag{3.108d}$$

3.3.6.3 Summary

From the above it can be seen that, for a prismatic joint, the partial derivatives of the state variables Ψ, Θ, Φ with respect to the joint parameter d_i all vanish, that is,

$$\frac{\partial \Psi}{\partial d_i} = \frac{\partial \Theta}{\partial d_i} = \frac{\partial \Phi}{\partial d_i} = 0 \tag{3.109}$$

This should come as no surprise, because the state variables Ψ, Θ, Φ describe the orientation of the end effector. A prismatic joint performs only translation, and a translation can only change the position of the end effector, but it can not change its orientation.

4

Motion Interpolation

An animation can be defined as "a motion picture made by photographing successive positions of inanimate objects (as puppets or mechanical parts)." The first animations were drawn by hand and then photographed onto a film strip. In this way, Walt Disney made Mickey Mouse come to life. It is a very time-consuming task to draw all the frames by hand, and in the beginning of this industry, cartoon films only had twelve frames per second as opposed to the 25–30 frames per second of modern films. A time and money saver was the use of in-betweeners. An in-betweener was a less-known artist whose job was to fill in the blanks left by the famous artists. So the expensive artist would draw up Donald Duck in the meaningful poses (key frames), and the in-betweeners would draw all the in-between less important frames, thereby making sure that Donald Duck was animated from key-frame to key-frame.

Today computers are the in-betweeners. The animation artist places the character or object in the key positions and tells the system when the model should be in a specific position. Then the computer calculates the positions of the model at each frame, renders it, and saves it.

In the previous chapters, we showed how to model a complex model and how to help the computer calculate specific positions for each object in the model. That is just one example of an automated calculation. One could also use a simulator to estimate the position and shape of the model. The most basic way to animate is to use forward kinematics and no automation, just like the old Disney animators did. The focus of this chapter is how to calculate the frames without a simulator or an automated system—although they are often used in conjunction with each other.

The most basic way to calculate the in-between frames is to interpolate the storytelling poses, the key-frames. Simple linear interpolation results in a jerky result. The character will walk like a stiff robot, or if one is animating a color, it will flicker.

The first part of this chapter explores how to use higher-order splines instead of simple linear interpolation so as to preserve the continuity over the key-frames and hide the key-frames. The parameter of the interpolating curve has no physical meaning. This can present some difficulty to the animator. A more intuitive way to think about the interpolating parameter is by using time or traveled distance along the spline. The latter part of this chapter shows how to reparameterize the splines so they become a motion function of time instead of the spline parameter and have some sort of physical meaning.

4.1 Key-Framing

In this section we will show how *forward kinematics* can be used to animate articulated bodies. It has just been shown how the state vector $\boldsymbol{s}$ specifies the position and orientation of the end effector given values for the generalized joint parameters $\boldsymbol{\theta}_1, \ldots, \boldsymbol{\theta}_N$. By varying the joint parameters, the articulated figure will move. So, by letting the joint parameters be functions of time t, that is, $\boldsymbol{\theta}_1(t), \ldots, \boldsymbol{\theta}_N(t)$, the state vector will also be a function of time, $\boldsymbol{s}(t)$, and the articulated figure can be animated by stepping the time parameter t, and computing the state vector $\boldsymbol{s}(t)$.

4.1.1 Key-Frames

In practice, it is not easy for an animator to specify all the joint parameters as functions of time, that is, $\boldsymbol{\theta}_1, \ldots, \boldsymbol{\theta}_N$. A helpful tool is to specify the joint parameters by using what is known as *key-frames* or *the storytelling poses*. The animator only has to specify the most important configurations of the articulated figure and also at what time t_i they occur, see Figure 4.1. Having specified the key-frames, that is, the joint parameters $\boldsymbol{\theta}_i$ at some discrete times t_i, the joint parameters at the key-frames can be plotted on a timeline, see Figure 4.2. The idea behind using key-frames is that the animator should *not* specify a huge number of joint parameters, but only the ones that are important for the animation. The joint parameters that are *in between* the key-frames should be calculated automatically such that the animation looks like the animator imagined when he specified the key-frames.

The only thing that is known is the joint parameters at the key-frames, but the joint parameters *between* the key-frames are not known, so this suggests an interpolation between the joint parameters at the key-frames.

4.1.2 Linear Interpolation

The first idea that comes to mind is *linear interpolation*. If linear interpolation is used, the functions that represent the joint parameters will look like the ones shown in Figure 4.3. As it can be seen from the figure, the joint parameters make some very abrupt changes at some of the key-frames. The functions for the joint parameters are continuous, but not differentiable. Especially, it can be seen for joint parameter θ_0 at the key-frame at time t_1. The joint parameter θ_0 varies linearly from $45\,^\circ$ to $90\,^\circ$, and then it abruptly changes and returns to $45\,^\circ$. The same can be seen at time t_2 where the joint parameter θ_0 varies linearly from $90\,^\circ$ to $45\,^\circ$ and then it stops immediately.

At the key-frames, the function is continuous but *not* differentiable, and that might look unnatural to the beholder of the animation. Worse, if the joint parameter functions of the animation was to be used for an actual industrial robot, the forces at time t_1 might be so big that the robot would break.

4.1.3 Spline Interpolation

As it was discussed in Section 4.1.2 linear interpolation is neither adequate for animation nor for simulation of industrial robots. The reason is that the functions representing the joint parameters must be differentiable. Otherwise, the animation will look unnatural or the industrial robot will break.

The idea is now to make a continuous differentiable curve, which passes through the joint parameters at the key-frames, that is, the curve must be continuously differentiable and also pass through the points specified by the joint parameters at the key-frames.

To do this job there is a family of curves named *interpolating splines*. So, in order to get a smooth function for the joint parameters, we use the parameters at the key-frames as points that must be interpolated and use a spline to interpolate them. A result of such a spline-interpolation is shown in Figure 4.4. At first, it seems strange that the curves of the joint parameters have some strange bends. They are necessary because the curves must be continuously differentiable. How much the spline bends and wiggles depends on which type of spline and how many control points are used for controlling the spline, see Figure 4.5, where there are used as extra control points for the spline. Given access to an interactive tool

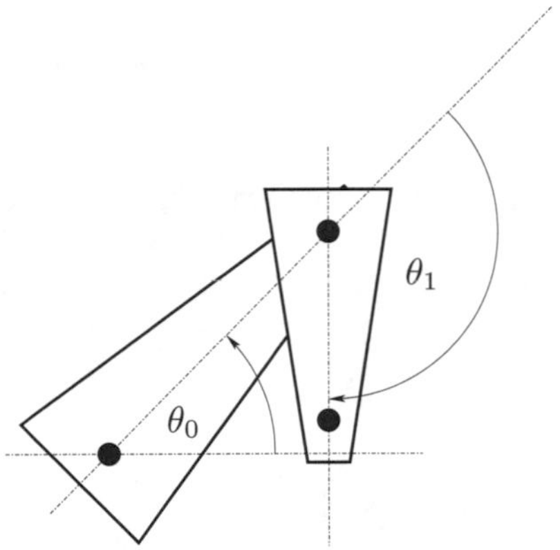

(a) $t_0 : \theta_0 = 45°, \theta_1 = -135°$

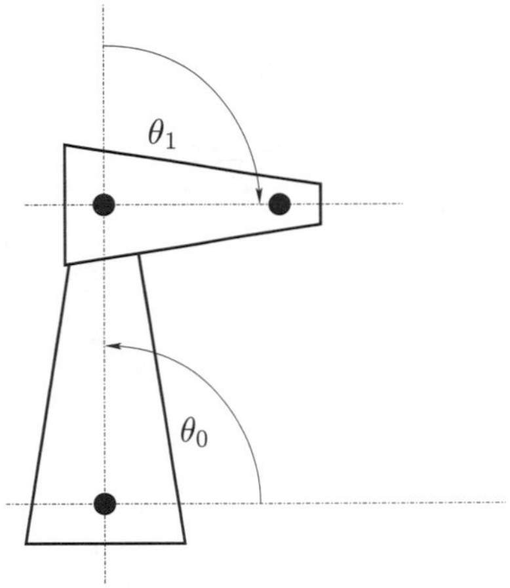

(b) $t_1 : \theta_0 = 90°, \theta_1 = -90°$

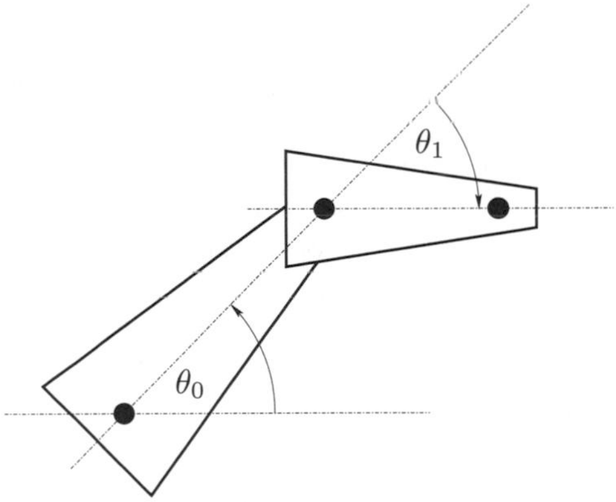

(c) $t_2 : \theta_0 = 45°, \theta_1 = -45°$

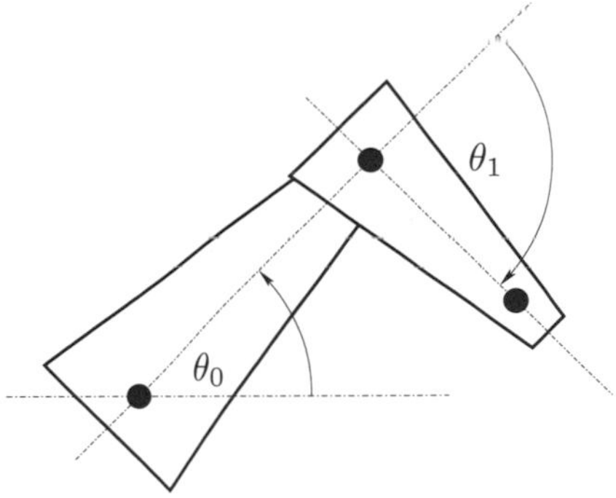

(d) $t_3 : \theta_0 = 45°, \theta_1 = -90°$

Figure 4.1: The configuration of an articulated figure at times $t_0, \ldots, t_3$.

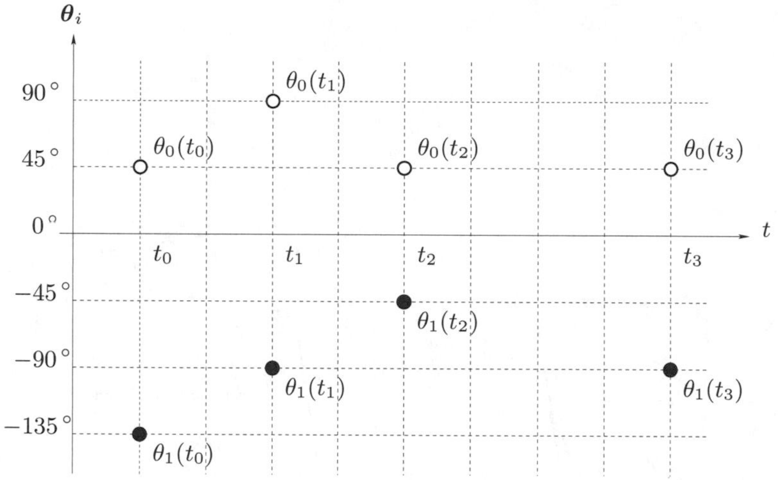

Figure 4.2: The joint parameters at the key-frames plotted against time.

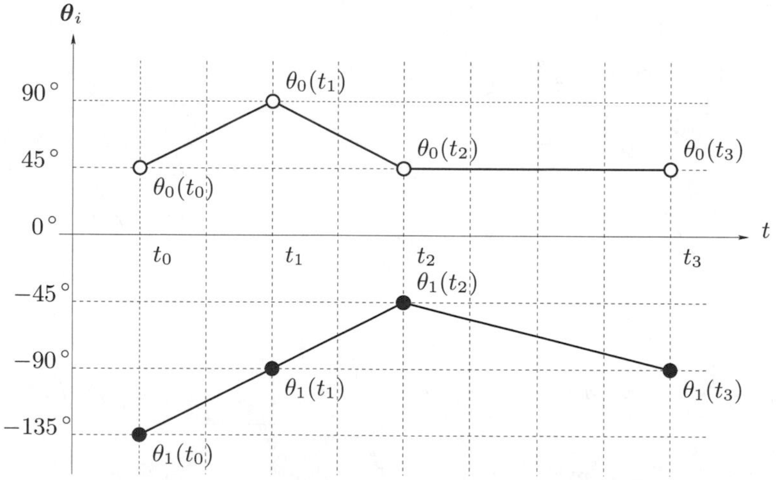

Figure 4.3: The functions of the joint parameters if linear interpolation is used between the joint parameters at the key-frames.

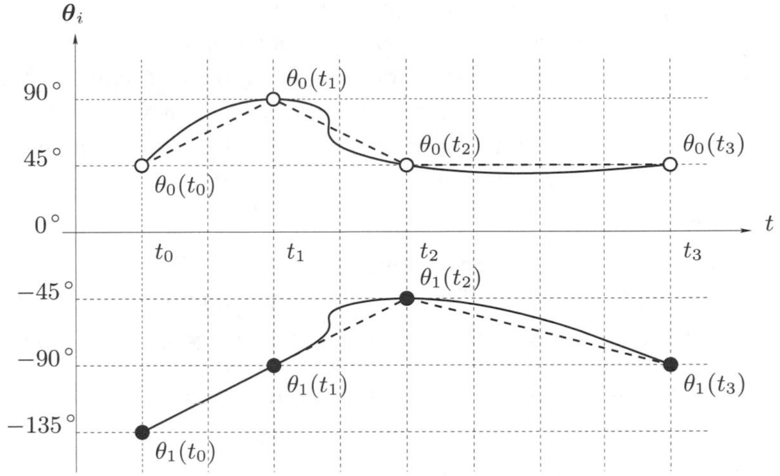

Figure 4.4: The functions of the joint parameters are interpolated between the joint parameters at the key-frames by a smooth interpolating spline. The control polygons used are those from the linear interpolation shown in Figure 4.3, i.e., just the known joint parameters at the key-frames. The control polygons are shown as dashed lines.

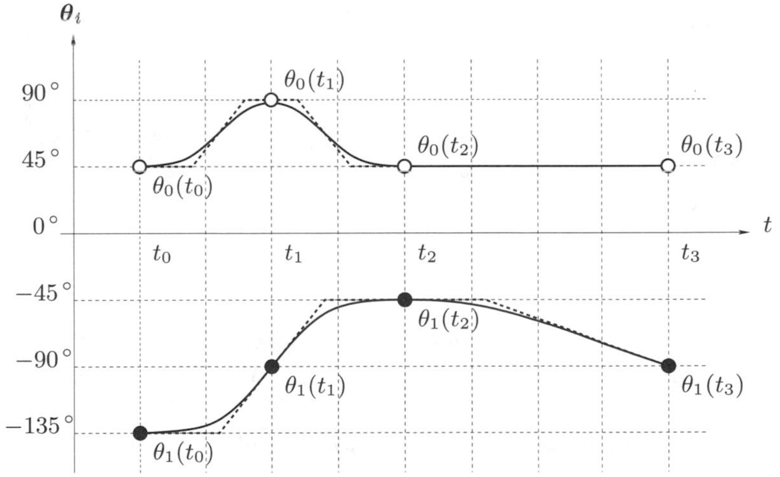

Figure 4.5: The functions of the joint parameters are interpolated between the joint parameters at the key-frames by a smooth interpolating spline. Here, extra control points are used to control the spline, which gives a more smooth curve without wiggles. The control polygons are shown as dashed lines.

where it is possible to choose the type of interpolating spline and to adjust the chosen splines parameters, an experienced animator might obtain very visually pleasing results.

However, using spline interpolation introduces a little inconvenience for the animator. Looking at Figures 4.4 and 4.5 the curves for the joint parameters θ_1 and θ_2 look as if they are functions of time t, but they are not. The curves are given as a vector function $(t(u), \theta_i(u))^T$, where the coordinate functions are functions of the spline parameter u, which is not necessarily intuitive for an animator.

That means if the animator wants to compute the value of a joint parameter θ_i at some given time $\hat{t}$, this must be done in two steps:

1. Compute the spline parameter $\hat{u}$ corresponding to the time $\hat{t}$. This can be done numerically as a root-finding problem, and because the function $t(u)$ is a monotone increasing function, there is a unique solution. That is, find $\hat{u}$ such that $\left\|t(\hat{u}) - \hat{t}\right\|_2 < \epsilon$ using any root-finding algorithm.

2. Compute the joint parameter θ_i corresponding to the spline parameter $\hat{u}$, i.e., $\theta_i(\hat{u})$.

4.2 Scripted Motion Using Splines

Imagine the following scenario: an elevator is riding up and down between the first and fifth floor in a house. Inside the elevator is a person who throws a ping-pong ball against the elevator floor and catches it when it pops back up. When the ping-pong ball and the elevator floor collide, the ball is affected very much by the collision, but the elevator is not. The elevator will continue to move as if the ball had not hit the floor.

To animate such a scenario on a computer, it would be a waste of computer power to animate both the elevator and the ping-pong ball as physically correct. Only the ping-pong ball should be animated physically correct. The motion of the elevator could be modeled by a 3D curve, e.g., a spline, describing the location of the elevator during the animation.

A rigid body whose motion is described this way is called a *scripted body*. Modeling a scripted body as described above might be done by key-frames analogous to the description in Section 4.1. Specify some 3D positions the scripted body must pass through, and then compute an interpolating spline to describe the trajectory of the scripted body.

4.2.1 The Basic Idea

The trajectory is a 3D curve $\boldsymbol{C}(u) = \begin{bmatrix} x(u) & y(u) & z(u) \end{bmatrix}^T$ parameterized by the spline parameter u, and it has the same inconveniences as described in Section 4.1.3. The spline is parameterized by u and not time t.

Animation is about how a point $\boldsymbol{p}$ moves in time. More specifically, it can be stated:

1. What is the location of point $\boldsymbol{p}$ at time t?

2. What is the velocity $\boldsymbol{v}$ of point $\boldsymbol{p}$ at time t?

3. What is the acceleration $\boldsymbol{a}$ of point $\boldsymbol{p}$ at time t?

In order to make it easier for an animator to control the scripted body, the spline $\boldsymbol{C}$ can be reparameterized such that it becomes a function of time t.

This reparameterization can be done in two steps. First, express the spline $\boldsymbol{C}$ as a function of the arc length s, and then express the arc length s as a function of time t.

1. Express the spline $\boldsymbol{C}$ as a function the arc length s. That is, construct a function $U : \mathbb{R} \longrightarrow \mathbb{R}$ which maps the arc length to the corresponding spline parameter u.

2. Express the arc length s as a function of time t. That is, construct a function $S : \mathbb{R} \longrightarrow \mathbb{R}$ which maps time t to arc length s.

Using the above reparameterizing, the original spline $\boldsymbol{C}(u)$ can be expressed as a function of time t

$$\boldsymbol{C}(U(S(t))) \longmapsto \boldsymbol{p} = \begin{bmatrix} x(U(S(t))) \\ y(U(S(t))) \\ z(U(S(t))) \end{bmatrix} \tag{4.1}$$

This means that an animator can control the position $\boldsymbol{p}$, the velocity $\boldsymbol{v}$, and the acceleration $\boldsymbol{a}$ as shown below

$$\boldsymbol{p}(t) = \boldsymbol{C}(U(S(t))) \tag{4.2a}$$

$$\boldsymbol{v}(t) = \frac{d\boldsymbol{p}(t)}{dt} = \frac{d}{dt}(\boldsymbol{C}(U(S(t)))) = \frac{d\boldsymbol{C}}{du}\frac{dU}{ds}\frac{dS}{dt} \tag{4.2b}$$

$$\boldsymbol{a}(t) = \frac{d^2\boldsymbol{p}(t)}{dt^2} = \frac{d^2}{dt^2}(\boldsymbol{C}(U(S(t)))) = \frac{d}{dt}\left(\frac{d\boldsymbol{C}}{du}\frac{dU}{ds}\frac{dS}{dt}\right) \tag{4.2c}$$

$$= \frac{d^2\boldsymbol{C}}{du^2}\left(\frac{dU}{ds}\right)^2\left(\frac{dS}{dt}\right)^2 + \frac{d\boldsymbol{C}}{du}\frac{dU}{ds}\frac{d^2S}{dt^2} + \frac{d\boldsymbol{C}}{du}\frac{d^2U}{ds^2}\left(\frac{dS}{dt}\right)^2. \tag{4.2d}$$

Some of the derivatives

$$\frac{d\boldsymbol{C}}{du} \quad \text{and} \quad \frac{d^2\boldsymbol{C}}{du^2} \tag{4.3}$$

are easy to compute, because they are given directly by the definition of the original spline $\boldsymbol{C}$. The symbol $d\boldsymbol{C}/du$ means the spline $\boldsymbol{C}$ differentiated with respect to the original spline parameter u, analogous to the symbol $d^2\boldsymbol{C}/du^2$. The other derivatives

$$\frac{dU}{ds} \quad \frac{d^2U}{ds^2} \quad \frac{dS}{dt} \quad \text{and} \quad \frac{d^2S}{dt^2} \tag{4.4}$$

are difficult to compute because the functions $U(s)$ and $S(t)$ can not be expressed analytically, but must be computed numerically.

The following sections will describe how to reparameterize the spline $\boldsymbol{C}$ with the arc length s, how to reparameterize the arc length with time t, and how to compute the derivatives in (4.4).

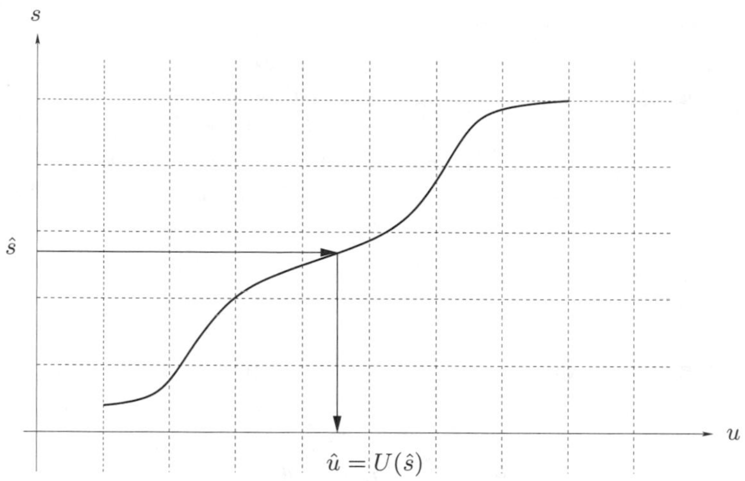

Figure 4.6: The arc length s as a function of the spline parameter u.

4.2.2 Reparameterizing with Arc Length

Let the trajectory of some point $\boldsymbol{p} = \begin{bmatrix} x & y & z \end{bmatrix}^T$ be given by a space-spline $\boldsymbol{C} : \mathbb{R} \longrightarrow \mathbb{R}^3$, and let the spline be parameterized by a global parameter u

$$\boldsymbol{C}(u) \longmapsto \boldsymbol{p}(u) = \begin{bmatrix} x(u) & y(u) & z(u) \end{bmatrix}^T \tag{4.5}$$

However, the parameter u is not intuitive to use for humans. It is quite difficult for a human to predict exactly which point on the spline corresponds to a given value of the parameter u. Humans are much better at thinking in terms of the arc length s of the spline $\boldsymbol{C}$. The arc length s of the spline $\boldsymbol{C}$ can also be explained as the distance traveled along the spline. The arc length s of $\boldsymbol{C}$ is given as the integral

$$s(u) = \int_0^u \left\| \frac{\boldsymbol{C}(u)}{du} \right\|_2 du \tag{4.6}$$

where $\|\boldsymbol{C}(u)/du\|_2$ is the length of the derivative of $\boldsymbol{C}$ with respect to the parameter u.

In order to reparameterize the spline $\boldsymbol{C}$ with the arc length s a function $U : \mathbb{R} \longrightarrow \mathbb{R}$ was introduced in Section 4.2.1. The function $U(s)$ maps the arc length s to the corresponding spline parameter u. This means that the function U is really the inverse of the arc length function from (4.6).

As we will show later, the arc length function (4.6) can not be computed analytically for a spline curve. Therefore, it is not possible to obtain an analytical expression for the inverse function U. The arc length (4.6) is a monotone function as shown in Figure 4.6, so the value $u = U(s)$ can be computed numerically as follows:

1. For some specified arc length $\hat{s}$ find the corresponding parameter value $\hat{u}$ such that $s(\hat{u}) = \hat{s}$.

2. Given $\hat{s}$ compute $\hat{u}$ such that $\|s(\hat{u}) - \hat{s}\|_2 < \epsilon$ using a root-finding algorithm and (4.6).

3. Having computed the value $\hat{u}$, compute $\boldsymbol{C}(\hat{u})$. Using this procedure, points on the spline $\boldsymbol{C}$ can be computed using the arc length s as parameter.

This corresponds to expressing the spline parameter u as a function of the arc length s

$$u = U(s) \tag{4.7}$$

and use it to compute a point $\boldsymbol{p}$ on the spline $\boldsymbol{p}(s) = \boldsymbol{C}(U(s))$.

This reparameterization makes it easier to predict how the scripted body moves along the spline, because the spline parameter used is the arc length, which is the traveled distance along the spline.

4.2.2.1 The Arc Length Integrand

Let $\boldsymbol{C}(u)$ be a cubic spline in 3-dimensional space

$$\boldsymbol{C}(u) = \begin{bmatrix} x(u) \\ y(u) \\ z(u) \end{bmatrix} = \begin{bmatrix} a_x u^3 + b_x u^2 + c_x u + d_x \\ a_y u^3 + b_y u^2 + c_y u + d_y \\ a_z u^3 + b_z u^2 + c_z u + d_z \end{bmatrix}. \tag{4.8}$$

Alternatively in matrix notation

$$\boldsymbol{C}(u) = \begin{bmatrix} a_x & b_x & c_x & d_x \\ a_y & b_y & c_y & d_y \\ a_z & b_z & c_z & d_z \end{bmatrix} \begin{bmatrix} u^3 \\ u^2 \\ u \\ 1 \end{bmatrix} \tag{4.9}$$

The arc length function (4.6) of the cubic curve then becomes

$$s(u) = \int_0^u \left\| \frac{d\boldsymbol{C}(u)}{du} \right\|_2 du \tag{4.10a}$$

$$= \int_0^u \sqrt{Au^4 + Bu^3 + Cu^4 + Du + E du} \tag{4.10b}$$

where

$$A = 9(a_x^2 + a_y^2 + a_z^2) \tag{4.11a}$$

$$B = 12(a_x b_x + a_y b_y + a_z b_z) \tag{4.11b}$$

$$C = 6(a_x c_x + a_y c_y + a_z c_z) + 4(b_x^2 + b_y^2 + b_z^2) \tag{4.11c}$$

$$D = 4(b_x c_x + b_y c_y + b_z c_z) \tag{4.11d}$$

$$E = (c_x^2 + c_y^2 + c_z^2) \tag{4.11e}$$

Unfortunately, it is not possible to find an analytical expression for this integral, so it is necessary to do a *numerical integration* in order to find the value of $s(u)$ for a given a value of u. The function

$$\left\| \frac{d\boldsymbol{C}(u)}{du} \right\|_2 = \sqrt{Au^4 + Bu^3 + Cu^2 + Du + E} \tag{4.12}$$

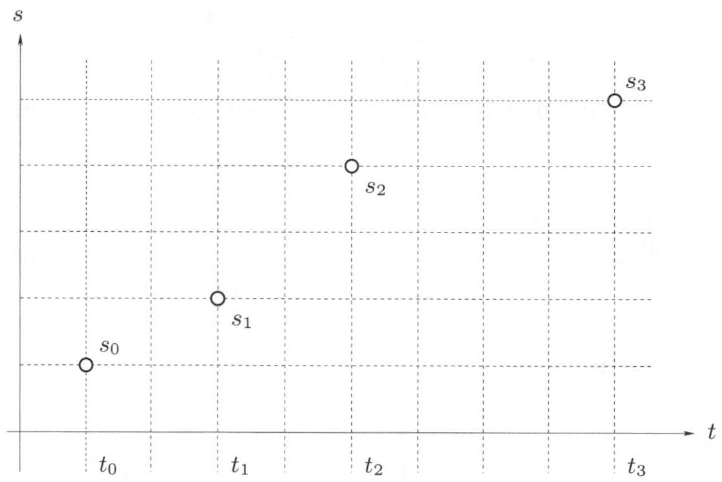

Figure 4.7: The traveled distance s plotted against time t as a number of discrete (t_i, s_i) pairs.

is the arc length integrand. By applying Horner's rule for factoring polynomials (4.12) can be rewritten to a more computationally friendly form

$$\left\| \frac{d\boldsymbol{C}(u)}{du} \right\|_2 = \sqrt{(((Au + B)u + C)u + D)u + E}. \tag{4.13}$$

With the theory developed so far, one can pick any numerical integration method, which fulfills the requirements to performance and accuracy and then apply it in order to compute the arc length $s(u)$.

4.2.3 Reparameterizing with Time

To obtain an even better feeling of how the scripted body moves let $S : \mathbb{R} \longrightarrow \mathbb{R}$ be the arc length expressed as a function of time t.

An animator knows how a point $\boldsymbol{p}$ should move over time, so the function S can be specified by a number of time-distance pairs (t_i, s_i) at discrete points in time as shown in Figure 4.7. The discrete (t_i, s_i) pairs might be interpolated by a spline $V : \mathbb{R} \longrightarrow \mathbb{R}^2$ whose coordinates are functions of the spline parameter v as shown in Figure 4.8.

$$\boldsymbol{V}(v) = \begin{bmatrix} t(v) & s(v) \end{bmatrix}^T \tag{4.14}$$

Now, the arc length function $S(t)$ can be computed as a function of t as follows:

1. Given a value $\hat{t}$ find the corresponding value $\hat{v}$ such that $\left\| t(\hat{v}) - \hat{t} \right\|_2 < \epsilon$, using a root-finding algorithm. Time t is a monotone increasing function, so a unique solution exists.

2. Compute the second coordinate function $s(\hat{v})$ of $\boldsymbol{V}$.

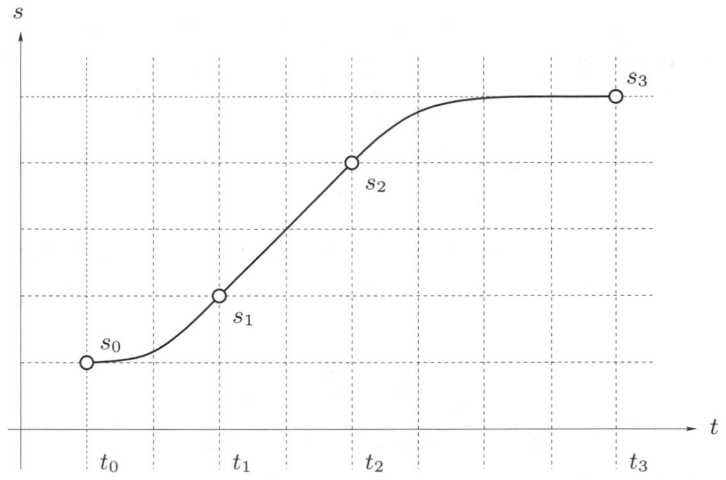

Figure 4.8: The discrete (t_i, s_i) pairs are interpolated by a spline $V : \mathbb{R} \longrightarrow \mathbb{R}^2$ yielding a continuous function $(t(v), s(v))^T$ which can be used to compute the traveled distance $S(t)$ as a function of time t. The slope of the spline is equal to the velocity of the point traveling along the curve.

This corresponds to expressing the spline parameter v as a function of t, and use it to compute the arc length $s = s(v(t)) = S(t)$. This arc length can now be used to compute the parameter u for the spline $\boldsymbol{C}(u)$ as described previously. What has been obtained is the computation $\boldsymbol{C}(U(S(t)))$, which computes points on the trajectory of the scripted body using time t as parameter.

An articulated figure might be animated using scripted motion as follows. Consider the end effector of an articulated figure as a scripted body, and let its trajectory be specified by a space-spline $\boldsymbol{C}(t)$ as explained previously.

Then, by incrementing the time parameter t with small time steps Δt, the corresponding points on the space-spline $\boldsymbol{C}(t)$ might be computed as described above. Finally, the actual joint parameters can be computed using inverse kinematics. This way, it is possible to animate the articulated figure as a scripted body.

4.2.4 Computing the Derivatives

From (4.3) and (4.4) it is seen that the following values need to be computed

$$\frac{d\boldsymbol{C}}{du} \quad \frac{d^2\boldsymbol{C}}{du^2} \quad \frac{dU}{ds} \quad \frac{d^2U}{ds^2} \quad \frac{dS}{dt} \quad \text{and} \quad \frac{d^2S}{dt^2} \tag{4.15}$$

The derivatives $d\boldsymbol{C}/du$ and $d^2\boldsymbol{C}/du^2$ are easily computed from the analytic expression of the spline $\boldsymbol{C}(u)$. This leaves the remaining four derivatives

$$\frac{dU}{ds} \quad \frac{d^2U}{ds^2} \quad \frac{dS}{dt} \quad \text{and} \quad \frac{d^2S}{dt^2} \tag{4.16}$$

Analytic expressions for the functions S and U are not available, but fortunately this is not the case for their derivatives, which can be computed analytically.

Starting with (4.6) the integrand can be rewritten as the dot product of the derivative of the space-spline

$$s(u) = \int_0^u \left\| \frac{\boldsymbol{C}(u)}{du} \right\|_2 du = \int_0^u \sqrt{\frac{d\boldsymbol{C}(u)}{du} \cdot \frac{d\boldsymbol{C}(u)}{du}} du, \tag{4.17}$$

which is a more convenient form. Differentiating the arc length function $s(u)$ with respect to the parameter u, is the same as differentiating the integral as a function of its limits. This yields

$$\frac{ds(u)}{du} = \sqrt{\frac{d\boldsymbol{C}(u)}{du} \cdot \frac{d\boldsymbol{C}(u)}{du}} \tag{4.18}$$

Recall, the function $U(s)$ is the inverse of the arc length function $s(u)$ given in (4.17). Therefore, the derivative of $U(s)$ with respect to the arc length s is equal to

$$\frac{dU(s)}{ds} = \frac{1}{\frac{ds}{du}(U(s))} = \frac{1}{\sqrt{\frac{d\boldsymbol{C}(U(s))}{du} \cdot \frac{d\boldsymbol{C}(U(s))}{du}}} \tag{4.19}$$

From the above, it can be seen that although the function $U(s)$ can only be computed numerically, it is possible to compute its derivative, because $d\boldsymbol{C}/du$ is given by an analytic expression, and $U(s)$ can be computed numerically. Differentiating this derivative with respect to s yields

$$\frac{d^2U(s)}{ds^2} = \frac{d}{ds}\left(\frac{1}{\sqrt{\frac{d\boldsymbol{C}(U(s))}{du} \cdot \frac{d\boldsymbol{C}(U(s))}{du}}}\right) \tag{4.20a}$$

$$= -\frac{\frac{d}{ds}\left(\frac{d\boldsymbol{C}(U(s))}{du} \cdot \frac{d\boldsymbol{C}(U(s))}{du}\right)}{2\left(\frac{d\boldsymbol{C}(U(s))}{du} \cdot \frac{d\boldsymbol{C}(U(s))}{du}\right)^{3/2}} \tag{4.20b}$$

$$= -\frac{\left(\frac{d^2\boldsymbol{C}(U(s))}{du^2} \cdot \frac{d\boldsymbol{C}(U(s))}{du} + \frac{d\boldsymbol{C}(U(s))}{du} \cdot \frac{d^2\boldsymbol{C}(U(s))}{du^2}\right)\frac{dU(s)}{ds}}{2\left(\frac{d\boldsymbol{C}(U(s))}{du} \cdot \frac{d\boldsymbol{C}(U(s))}{du}\right)^{3/2}} \tag{4.20c}$$

After some rearranging of terms it is found that

$$\frac{d^2U(s)}{ds^2} = -\frac{\frac{d\boldsymbol{C}(U(s))}{du} \cdot \frac{d^2\boldsymbol{C}(U(s))}{du^2}}{\left(\frac{d\boldsymbol{C}(U(s))}{du} \cdot \frac{d\boldsymbol{C}(U(s))}{du}\right)^2} \tag{4.21}$$

The derivatives dC/du and d^2C/du^2 are given by analytic expressions and $U(s)$ can be computed numerically, so the derivative $d^2U(s)/ds^2$ can also be computed.

Recall that the reparameterization of the arc length with the time $S(t)$ was done using a spline V given by (4.14) and repeated here for convenience

$$\boldsymbol{V}(v) = \begin{bmatrix} t(v) & s(v) \end{bmatrix}^T \tag{4.22}$$

Since the function $\boldsymbol{V}$ is a spline, so is each of its coordinate functions. This implies that analytic expressions for

$$\frac{dt(v)}{dv} \quad \text{and} \quad \frac{ds(v)}{dv} \tag{4.23}$$

can be found by straight forward computations. In fact, these would be second-order polynomials when $\boldsymbol{V}$ is a cubic spline.

Recall that given a value of t the corresponding value of the spline parameter v could be found numerically by a root search. This corresponds to expressing the spline parameter v as a function of time t. Denote this function $v(t)$. With this notation the arc length can be expressed as a function of time $S(t) = s(v(t))$. The derivatives of S with respect to time is then given by

$$\frac{dS(t)}{dt} = \frac{ds(v(t))}{dt} = \frac{ds(v(t))}{dv}\frac{dv(t)}{dt} \tag{4.24}$$

Looking at the last term, it can be seen that this is in fact the inverse mapping of (4.23). Therefore, the above expression can be written

$$\frac{dS(t)}{dt} = \frac{ds(v(t))}{dv}\frac{1}{\frac{dt}{dv}(v(t))} \tag{4.25}$$

The value of $v(t)$ is already known. It was found by the root search that was performed in the time reparameterization phase of the space-spline.

The second derivative of the function S with respect to t can be computed as follows. From (4.25) it is found that

$$\frac{d^2S(t)}{dt^2} = \frac{d^2s(v(t))}{dt^2} \tag{4.26a}$$

$$= \frac{d^2s(v(t))}{dv^2}\frac{dv(t)}{dt}\frac{1}{\frac{dt(v(t))}{dv}} + \frac{ds(v(t))}{dv}\frac{-1}{\left(\frac{dt(v(t))}{dv}\right)^2}\frac{d}{dt}\left(\frac{dt(v(t))}{dv}\right) \tag{4.26b}$$

$$= \frac{\frac{d^2s(v(t))}{dv^2}}{\left(\frac{dt(v(t))}{dv}\right)^2} - \frac{\frac{ds(v(t))}{dv}}{\left(\frac{dt(v(t))}{dv}\right)^2}\frac{d^2t(v(t))}{dv^2}\frac{dv(t)}{dt} \tag{4.26c}$$

$$= \frac{\frac{d^2s(v(t))}{dv^2}}{\left(\frac{dt(v(t))}{dv}\right)^2} - \frac{\frac{ds(v(t))}{dv}\frac{d^2t(v(t))}{dv^2}}{\left(\frac{dt(v(t))}{dv}\right)^3} \tag{4.26d}$$

The value $v(t)$ is known so the above expression is an analytic expression evaluated at $v(t)$.

Looking at all the equations for the derivatives, it is realized that whenever

$$\frac{d\boldsymbol{C}(U(s))}{du} = 0, \quad \text{or} \quad \frac{dt(v(t))}{dv} = 0, \tag{4.27}$$

might cause problems. However, it turns out these degenerate cases do not cause any problems in practice.

Part II

Multibody Animation

Simulation of multibody dynamics deals with simulating the motion of multiple rigid bodies, possibly connected to each other through joints. The various fields concerned with multibody dynamics have developed slightly different language usages. The computer graphics literature often uses the term *rigid body simulation* and the applied mathematical and engineering literature uses the term *multibody dynamics*. Therefore, it is appropriate to begin our discussion on multibody dynamics with a clarification of the terms we have decided to use in this book: *multibody* simply means multiple bodies. *Multibody Dynamics* is the physics of multiple bodies all in mutual contact with each other or possibly connected to each other by joints. By simulation of the multibody dynamics we get a *Multibody Animation*.

The terms *articulated figure*, *articulated body*, or *jointed mechanism* are often used for rigid bodies connected by joints. Sometimes the term rigid body simulation is used for those simulators that do not handle jointed mechanisms. Thus, multibody animation is the most general term covering every topic and scenario you can think of concerning rigid bodies.

Particles and rigid bodies are often the first concepts introduced in physics, and they are regarded as the basic theoretical building blocks. The same view is also often applied in physics-based animation: rigid body simulation is considered the basic starting point for many practitioners.

Many consider multibody dynamics to be simpler to simulate than chaotic and turbulent natural phenomena such as water, smoke, or fire. In our opinion this is a misconception, and although the free motion of a single rigid body floating in empty space is embarrassingly simple to simulate, rigid bodies are ideal real-world models. However, in the real world everything deforms. For rigid bodies, this idealization results in difficult discontinuities, causing the numerics to become ill-conditioned and sometimes even unsolvable.

The dynamics and mathematics of rigid bodies have been known since Newton. Nevertheless, nearly 400 years later it is still a topic of active interest and scientific publication. Since the 80s there have been papers on rigid body simulation in every ACM SIGGRAPH Proceedings. The explanation is that even though the physics and mathematics is well established, it is not easily solved on a computer. Furthermore, there is a continuous demand to simulate more and more rigid bodies faster and faster. Finally, in animation we often want to simulate unreal things that should appear plausible. Hence methods are needed that are incredibly fast, stable, robust, and tolerant for faulty configurations, none of which is the main focus in classical mechanics.

The traditional approach for analyzing systems in classical mechanics often deals with *systems in equilibrium*. This is of little interest in animation, where we want to see objects in motion and colliding with each other. At equilibrium, the animation is usually over. In contrast, robotics has a long tradition of simulating mechanics; an equilibrium state is often the goal. Further problems are more concerned with kinematics of a single mechanism, controlling, planning, or computing the motion trajectory in a known and controlled environment. In animation, nothing is known about what should happen, and often only animation of several mechanisms is interesting. Besides, robotics tends to be aimed at only simulating the joints of a mechanism, not contact forces with the environment or other mechanisms.

The quest for bigger and faster simulators seems endless and is mainly driven forward by the computer gaming industry and the movie industry. Rigid bodies are attractive in computer games, since they fit in nicely with the level of realism, and they are fairly easy to use to plan game events and build game levels. Basically, the industry knows how to use rigid bodies to create interesting game effects. The movie industry has moved beyond multibody animation to deformable objects, natural phenomena, humans, etc.

This part is a thorough introduction to multibody animation. The theory and methods we present are highly biased toward our own work in the field, and readers should not expect a complete, in-depth, and detailed walk-through of every method and paradigm.

Our contribution on multibody animation in this book begins with the simplest possible approach to model multibody dynamics: the so-called penalty-based methods. Penalty-based methods were among the first to appear and are still in use today. Then we will turn our attention toward the impulse-based methods, which are considered easy to implement compared to other methods. Impulse-based methods are characterized by the fact that they represent every interaction between bodies in the world through collisions; even a cup resting on a table is modeled by a series of highly-frequent collisions. Constraint-based methods are probably the kind of method that resembles a physicist's view of the world. Constraint-based methods set up the motion of equations, and solve explicitly for the contact and constraint forces, considering that Newton's second law can be integrated to calculate the complete motion of the objects.

After we have introduced the reader to the three traditional "main-stream" methods for simulating rigid bodies, we will describe a formal, conceptual module design. The module design is used to explain many details of rigid body simulators, such as interaction with the collision detection engine or the time-stepping strategies. Finally we will present contact graphs, a convenient data structure to store information about contact points.

Our aim with the multibody dynamics theory presented in this book is to equip the reader with the skills for building stable and robust multibody simulators capable of simulating large configurations without breaking down or giving up on unexpected errors or faulty starting conditions. We have focused on high performance, but it's more from an algorithmic point of view, and not our most important concern.

5

Penalty-Based Multibody Animation

Rigid bodies in the real world do not penetrate each other, and the penetration is impossible due to the contact forces between rigid bodies. In penalty-based multibody animation, a *spring-damper system* is used for penalizing penetrations. A spring-damper system behaves like a *harmonic oscillator* in classical mechanics, which will be reviewed here. For full detail see Section 22.4.

Penalty methods have a lot in common with mass-spring systems, because all effects are modeled by springs and dampers, see for instance [Provot, 1995], and they are generally applicable to both deformable and rigid objects. Spring-damper models are even found in biomechanical muscle models such as Hill's muscle model and Zajac's force model, see [Chen et al., 1992].

This chapter covers rigid bodies, but the theory is generally applicable. We strongly encourage readers new to the subject of classical mechanics to examine Section 22.1 for basic theory of the motion of rigid bodies.

5.1 The Basics

The motion of a single rigid body is described in the *Newton-Euler equations*. These are derived in full detail in Section 22.1. Here, we will briefly review the notation and equations.

The center of mass is given by $\boldsymbol{r}$, the orientation is given by the quaternion q and the linear and angular velocities are given by $\boldsymbol{v}$ and $\boldsymbol{\omega}$

$$\frac{d}{dt}\begin{bmatrix} \boldsymbol{r} \\ q \\ \boldsymbol{v} \\ \boldsymbol{\omega} \end{bmatrix} = \begin{bmatrix} \boldsymbol{v} \\ \frac{1}{2}\boldsymbol{\omega} q \\ \boldsymbol{a} \\ \boldsymbol{\alpha} \end{bmatrix}, \tag{5.1}$$

where $\boldsymbol{a}$ and $\boldsymbol{\alpha}$ are the linear and angular acceleration, and can be found by

$$\boldsymbol{a} = \frac{\boldsymbol{F}}{m} \qquad \text{and} \qquad \boldsymbol{\alpha} = \boldsymbol{I}^{-1}\left(\boldsymbol{\tau} + \boldsymbol{\omega} \times \boldsymbol{I}\boldsymbol{\omega}\right). \tag{5.2}$$

Here m is the total mass and $\boldsymbol{I}$ is the inertia tensor. Furthermore, $\boldsymbol{F}$ is the total linear force acting on the center of mass and $\boldsymbol{\tau}$ is the torque w.r.t./ the center of mass. The *ordinary differential equation* (ODE) in (5.1) is called a *Lagrangian formulation*. Given initial conditions, one can use a numerical integrator to integrate the motion of the rigid body. See Chapter 23 for details about *numerical integration*.

The *Hamiltonian formulation* of the motion of the rigid body is an alternative to the Lagrangian formulation and is given by

$$\frac{d}{dt}\begin{bmatrix} \boldsymbol{r} \\ q \\ \boldsymbol{P} \\ \boldsymbol{L} \end{bmatrix} = \begin{bmatrix} \boldsymbol{v} \\ \frac{1}{2}\boldsymbol{\omega} q \\ \boldsymbol{F} \\ \boldsymbol{\tau} \end{bmatrix}, \tag{5.3}$$

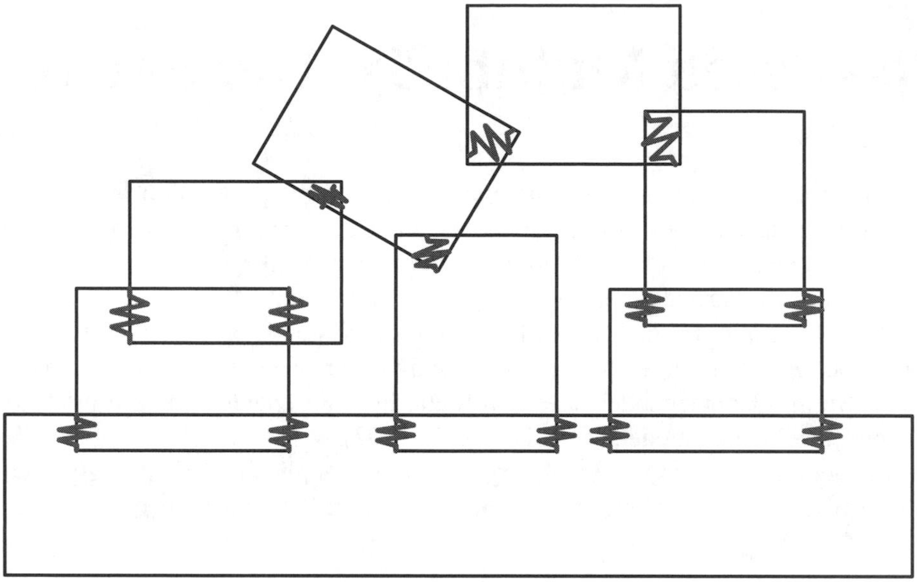

Figure 5.1: Penalizing penetration by insertion of springs.

where $\boldsymbol{P}$ and $\boldsymbol{L}$ are the linear and angular momentum respectively. In the Hamiltonian formulation $\boldsymbol{v}$ and $\boldsymbol{\omega}$ is found by

$$\boldsymbol{v} = \frac{\boldsymbol{P}}{m} \quad \text{and} \quad \boldsymbol{\omega} = \boldsymbol{I}^{-1}\boldsymbol{L} \tag{5.4}$$

As with the Lagrangian formulation the Hamiltonian formulation can also be numerically integrated.

Regardless of the chosen formulation, one needs to find the values of the force $\boldsymbol{F}$ and torque $\boldsymbol{\tau}$ at a given instant in time in order to perform the numerical integration. These values would include contributions from external forces, such as gravity, and contact forces stemming from contact with other rigid bodies.

In order to compute, the contact forces springs with rest-length zero are inserted at all penetrations as shown in Figure 5.1. The springs will try to remove the penetrations, which is why they are called *penalty forces*. Furthermore, larger penetrations means larger spring forces. That is, springs penalize penetrations, hence the name penalty method. The contact force from each point of contact is thus computed as a spring force. Call the external contributions $\boldsymbol{f}_{\text{ext}}$ and $\boldsymbol{\tau}_{\text{ext}}$ and the i'th spring force $\boldsymbol{f}_{\text{spring}_i}$ and $\boldsymbol{\tau}_{\text{spring}_i}$. Now the total force and torque are computed as

$$\boldsymbol{F} = \boldsymbol{f}_{\text{ext}} + \sum_i \boldsymbol{f}_{\text{spring}_i} \tag{5.5}$$

$$\boldsymbol{\tau} = \boldsymbol{\tau}_{\text{ext}} + \sum_i \boldsymbol{\tau}_{\text{spring}_i} \tag{5.6}$$

In case of gravity being the only external force, we have

$$\boldsymbol{f}_{\text{ext}} = m\boldsymbol{g} \tag{5.7}$$
$$\boldsymbol{\tau}_{\text{ext}} = \boldsymbol{0} \tag{5.8}$$

where $\boldsymbol{g} = [0, -9.81, 0]^T$ is the *gravitational acceleration*.

In its most pure form the *simulation loop* of the penalty method can be summarized as

- Detect contact points (run collision detection)
- Compute and accumulate spring forces
- Integrate equations of motion forward in time

This is the pure form of the penalty method. In practice, it is combined with several other techniques, some of these are surveyed in Section 5.9.

Now we'll turn our attention toward the actual computation of the penalty forces in a general simulator. Let the k'th *contact point* between the two bodies i and j with center of mass at $\boldsymbol{r}_i$ and $\boldsymbol{r}_j$ respectively be at position $\boldsymbol{p}_k$ given in 3D world coordinates. The k'th contact point has the contact normal, $\boldsymbol{n}_k$, also in 3D world space, pointing from body i toward body j, and a measure of penetration depth, d_k. Then the penalty force acting on body j is given by

$$\boldsymbol{F}_j = (-kd_k - b\boldsymbol{u}_k \cdot \boldsymbol{n}_k)\,\boldsymbol{n}_k, \tag{5.9}$$

where $\boldsymbol{u}_k$ denotes the relative contact velocity at the k'th contact point, i.e.,

$$\boldsymbol{u}_k = (\boldsymbol{v}_i + \boldsymbol{\omega}_i \times \boldsymbol{r}_{ki}) - (\boldsymbol{v}_j + \omega_j \times \boldsymbol{r}_{kj})\,, \tag{5.10}$$

where $\boldsymbol{r}_{ki} = \boldsymbol{p}_k - \boldsymbol{r}_i$ and $\boldsymbol{r}_{kj} = \boldsymbol{p}_k - \boldsymbol{r}_j$. For $\boldsymbol{u}_k \cdot \boldsymbol{n}_k < 0$ objects are approaching each other, $\boldsymbol{u}_k \cdot \boldsymbol{n}_k = 0$ there is no relative movement, and if $\boldsymbol{u}_k \cdot \boldsymbol{n}_k > 0$ objects are moving away from each other. Notice how carefully the viscosity is modeled only to work in the direction of the contact normal. It was pointed out in [Baraff et al., 2003a], that damping should only work in the constraint direction. The force acting on body i is by Newton's third law,

$$\boldsymbol{F}_i = -\boldsymbol{F}_j. \tag{5.11}$$

Besides the linear force terms arising from the penalty force, there are also some torque terms which must be taken into account.

$$\boldsymbol{T}_j = \boldsymbol{r}_{kj} \times \boldsymbol{F}_j \tag{5.12a}$$
$$\boldsymbol{T}_i = \boldsymbol{r}_{ki} \times \boldsymbol{F}_i. \tag{5.12b}$$

So far we have derived what can be termed the simple or classical penalty method. There are, however, several difficulties associated with it.

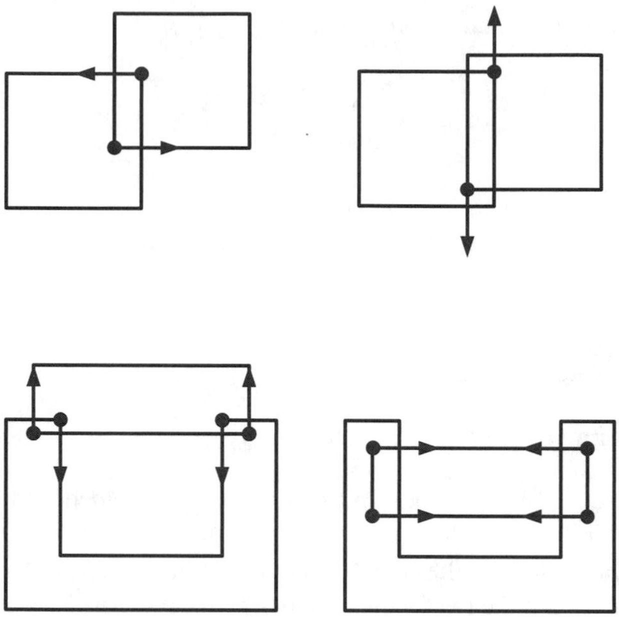

Figure 5.2: Figure illustrating that it is not always easy to determine penetration depths and contact normals based on local information only.

- First of all it is not trivial to compute satisfactory contact normals or penetration depths. This is illustrated by Figure 5.2. Distance fields are ideal for these computations, but they lack global knowledge about the entire state.

  The problem of determining meaningful contact normals and penetration depths is mostly caused by the use of local computations as shown in the figure. If a global computation [Kim et al., 2002] is used instead, these problems can be resolved.

- Some contact points like the face-face case appearing in a box stack is difficult to handle by applying a penalty force at the contact point of deepest penetration [Hasegawa et al., 2003], as illustrated in Figure 5.3. To alleviate this problem, researchers have tried to sample the entire contact region with contact points as shown in Figure 5.4. There also exist methods, that integrate over the intersection area and/or volume.

- Figure 5.2 illustrates another problem with contact normals, in the left column a "healthy" state is shown, the right column shows a slightly more displaced state. Observe that from the left to the right state, the contact normals make a discontinuous change; the problem is treated in detail by [Hirota, 2002, Hirota et al., 2001].

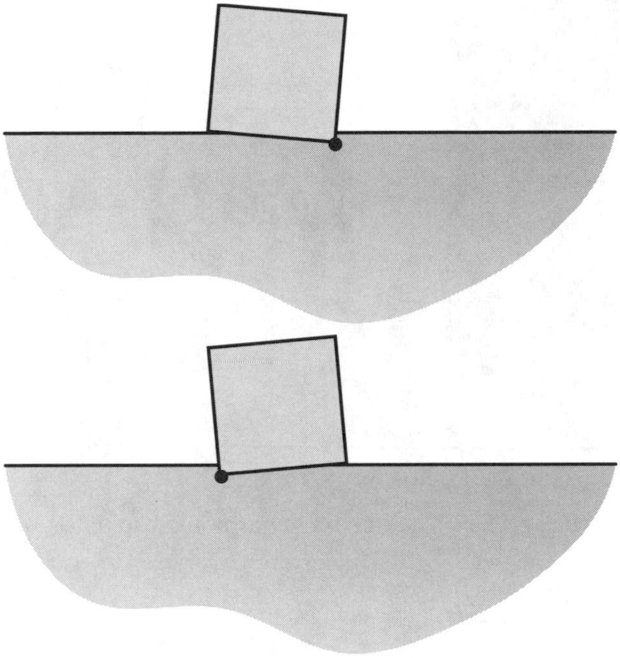

Figure 5.3: Figure illustrating a resting box, undergoing an unwanted and endless wiggling.

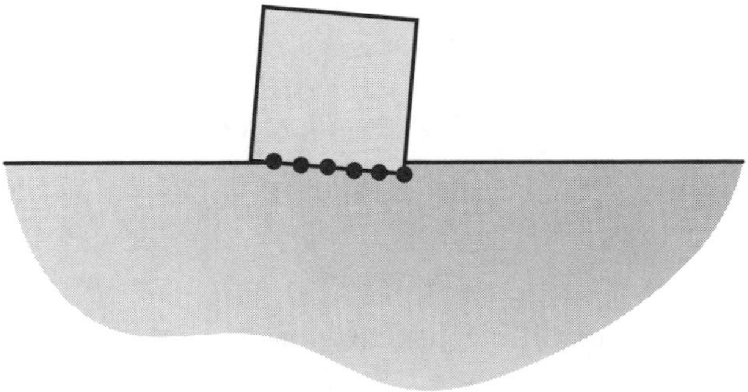

Figure 5.4: Figure illustrating the idea of oversampling to alleviate the wiggling problem.

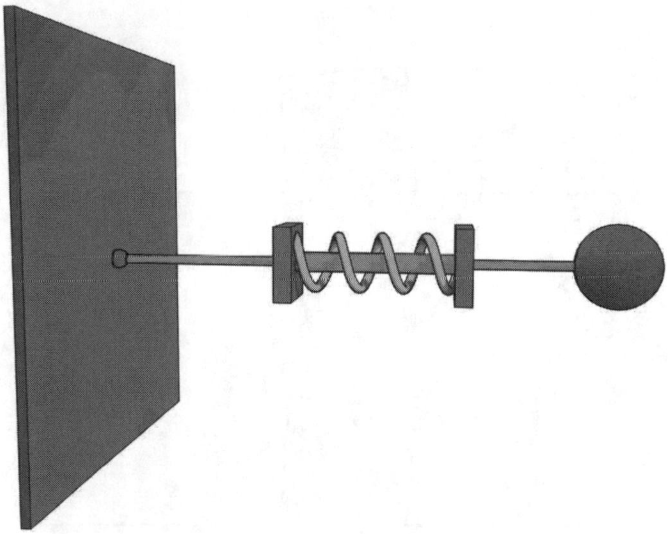

Figure 5.5: The one mass harmonic oscillator.

5.2 The Harmonic Oscillator

In Section 5.1 we showed how penetrations were penalized with spring-damper systems. A spring-damper system is equivalent to a *damped harmonic oscillator*. In order to study the behavior of the penalty method we should study the behavior of the harmonic oscillator.

In this section we will briefly review the harmonic oscillator. The reader is referred to Section 22.4 for more detailed treatment.

5.2.1 The One Object Harmonic Oscillator

Consider a particle attached to a wall of infinite mass with a spring as shown in Figure 5.5. The spring force given by

$$F_{\text{spring}} = -kx, \tag{5.13}$$

is called *Hooke's Spring Law*, and $k > 0$ is called the *spring coefficient*. Newton's second law of motion, dictates the motion of the particle as,

$$m\ddot{x} = -kx, \tag{5.14}$$

which yields the second-order ordinary differential equation

$$m\ddot{x} + kx = 0. \tag{5.15}$$

An analytical solution to this equation exists and can be shown to be

$$x = B\sin(\omega_0 t) + C\cos(\omega_0 t), \tag{5.16}$$

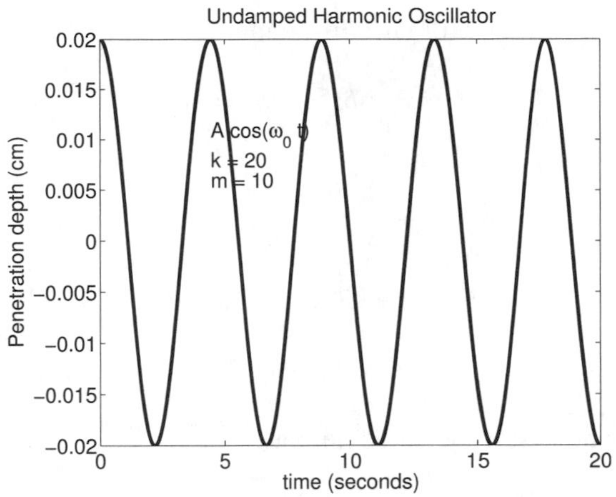

Figure 5.6: An undamped harmonic oscillator

where

$$\omega_0 = \sqrt{\frac{k}{m}} \tag{5.17}$$

is known as the *natural frequency*. The constants B and C can be evaluated from the initial position and velocity of the particle. The analytical solution (5.16) can be rewritten as a single cosine function,

$$x = A\cos\left(\omega_0 t + \phi\right), \tag{5.18}$$

The particle follows a cosine motion with *amplitude* A, *frequency* ω_0, and phase ϕ. The motion is consequently repetitive with a period T,

$$T = \frac{2\pi}{\omega_0}, \tag{5.19a}$$

$$= \frac{2\pi}{\sqrt{\frac{k}{m}}}. \tag{5.19b}$$

Figure 5.6 shows an example of a harmonic oscillator. The idealized harmonic oscillator assumes that there is no loss in energy over time. This is physically unrealistic, and practically not as useful as a damped harmonic oscillator. A typical *damping force* is given by

$$F_{\text{damping}} = -b\dot{x}, \tag{5.20}$$

which is commonly referred to as a linear viscosity force, and the coefficient $b > 0$ is called the *damping* or *viscosity coefficient*. From Newton's second law of motion, the motion of the damped particle must obey,

$$m\ddot{x} = -kx - b\dot{x}, \tag{5.21}$$

which is equivalent to the second-order ordinary differential equation

$$m\ddot{x} + bx' + kx = 0, \tag{5.22}$$

or

$$\ddot{x} + \frac{b}{m}\dot{x} + \frac{k}{m}x = 0. \tag{5.23}$$

Using the natural frequency $\omega_0^2 = \frac{k}{m}$ and introducing $\gamma = \frac{b}{m}$, this may be written as,

$$\ddot{x} + \gamma\dot{x} + \omega_0^2 x = 0. \tag{5.24}$$

An analytical solution exists and is simply stated here as,

$$x = A\exp\left(-\frac{\gamma}{2}t\right)\cos\left(\omega_1 t + \phi\right), \tag{5.25}$$

where A and ϕ are constants determined from initial conditions, and

$$\omega_1 = \sqrt{\omega_0^2 - \frac{\gamma^2}{4}} \tag{5.26}$$

is the frequency. The frequency ω_1 has real solutions when

$$\omega_0^2 - \frac{\gamma^2}{4} \geq 0 \tag{5.27a}$$

$$\Rightarrow \frac{k}{m} - \frac{b^2}{4m^2} \geq 0 \tag{5.27b}$$

$$\Rightarrow 4km - b^2 \geq 0 \tag{5.27c}$$

Comparing the damped harmonic oscillator (5.25) with the undamped harmonic oscillator (5.18) it is seen that the amplitude of the damped oscillator is exponentially decaying and that the frequency ω_1 of the damped oscillator is less than the frequency, ω_0, of the undamped oscillator.

The zero-crossings of the damped harmonic oscillator naturally occurs at equal time intervals by the period

$$T = \frac{2\pi}{\omega_1}. \tag{5.28}$$

Surprisingly, the peaks of the motion do not lie halfway between the zero-crossings as illustrated in Figure 5.7. The damped motion may be described qualitatively by examining the value of $b^2 - 4mk$ and the ratio of

$$\frac{\gamma}{\omega_1}. \tag{5.29}$$

The motion is:

Overdamped, when $b^2 - 4mk > 0$. Two cases of over-damping can be distinguished:

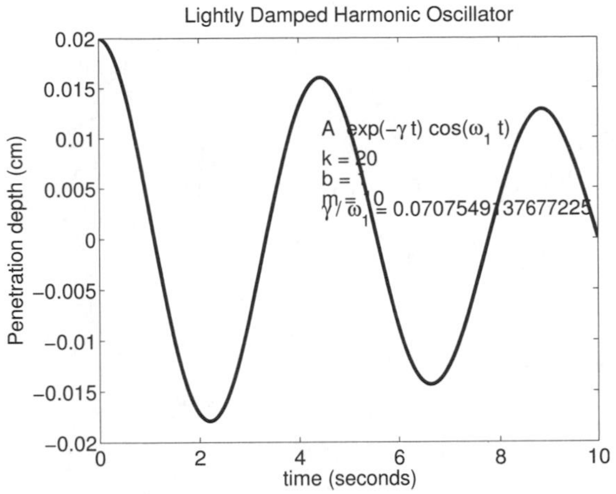

Figure 5.7: A lightly damped harmonic oscillator

Lightly damped, if $\frac{\gamma}{\omega_1} \ll 1$ then $A(t)$ decays very little during the time the cosine makes many zero-crossings.

Heavy damped, if $\frac{\gamma}{\omega_1}$ is large then $A(t)$ rapidly goes to zero while the cosine makes only a few oscillations.

Critical damped, when $b^2 - 4mk = 0$. In this case the amplitude tends most rapidly to zero (without crossing zero) and flattens out.

Underdamped, when $b^2 - 4mk < 0$. In this case the amplitude decays even faster than in the case of critical damping, but the amplitude will cross zero and increase again before flattering out.

Examples of the four categories are illustrated in Figure 5.8. Using a harmonic oscillator for a mass-spring system to model penalty forces, reasonable motion is obtained for heavily damped or at best critical damped, since oscillating forces such as oscillating contact forces are often undesirable. Furthermore, it is often desirable to require that the amplitude should decay to zero within a time-step, since this will make objects appear rigid.

5.2.2 The Two Object Harmonic Oscillator

Consider a two-body system, as shown in Figure 5.9, where two particles are connected with a spring. Hooke's law for this system is given as the following two equations,

$$m_i \ddot{x}_i = k\left(x_j - x_i\right), \tag{5.30a}$$

$$m_j \ddot{x}_j = -k\left(x_j - x_i\right). \tag{5.30b}$$

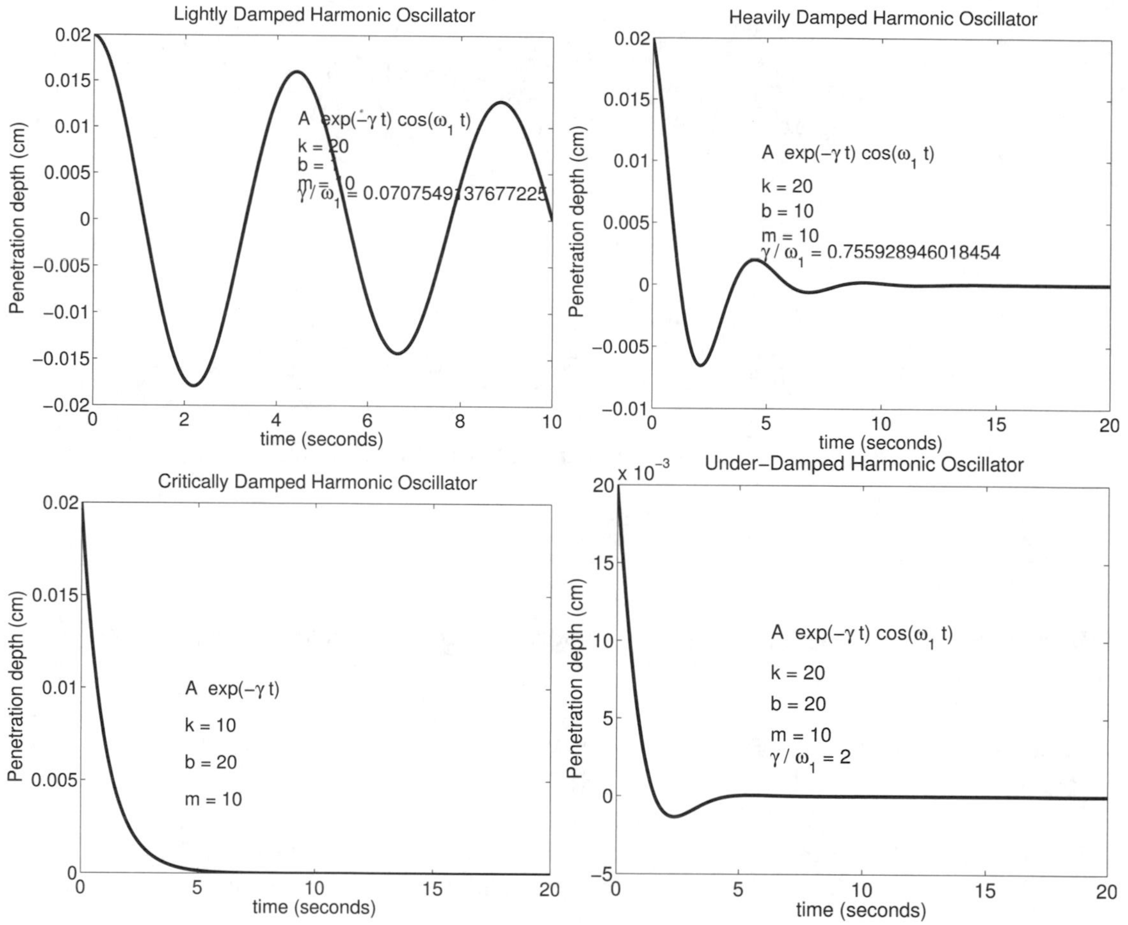

Figure 5.8: A qualitative analysis of a damped harmonic oscillator.

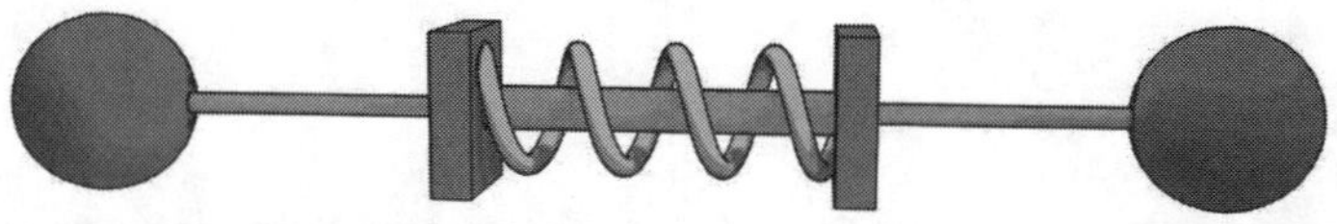

Figure 5.9: The two-mass harmonic oscillator.

Dividing the first equation by m_i and the second by m_j, yields

$$\ddot{x}_i = k\frac{1}{m_i}(x_j - x_i), \tag{5.31a}$$

$$\ddot{x}_j = -k\frac{1}{m_j}(x_j - x_i), \tag{5.31b}$$

and subtracting the first from the second, yields

$$\ddot{x}_j - \ddot{x}_i = -k\frac{1}{m_j}(x_j - x_i) - k\frac{1}{m_i}(x_j - x_i) \tag{5.32a}$$

$$= -k\left(\frac{1}{m_j} + \frac{1}{m_i}\right)(x_j - x_i). \tag{5.32b}$$

The two-object harmonic oscillator has the same motion as the one-object harmonic oscillator. This may be seen by setting, $x = x_j - x_i$, in (5.32b), such that

$$\ddot{x} = -k\left(\frac{1}{m_j} + \frac{1}{m_i}\right)x \tag{5.33}$$

Introducing the reduced mass as,

$$\mu = \frac{m_i m_j}{m_i + m_j} \tag{5.34}$$

it is discovered that

$$\mu\ddot{x} = -kx. \tag{5.35}$$

We conclude that the two-object harmonic oscillator behaves as a one-object system of mass μ.

5.3 Picking Parameter Values

Using a harmonic oscillator to model penalty forces, reasonable motion is obtained in case of a heavily damped or critical damped harmonic oscillator, since oscillating forces such as oscillating contact forces are undesirable. Furthermore, it is desirable to require that the amplitude should decay to zero within a single frame computation, since this will make objects appear rigid and ensure that an observer will not notice any oscillating behavior.

Thus we need a method for picking the values of the spring and damping coefficients, so that we can control the behavior of the harmonic oscillator to achieve the desired motion. That is, we want to pick parameter values such that we are not able to see the springiness of the corresponding mass-spring system.

The oscillation cycle of a harmonic oscillator, i.e., the time period (5.28), is given by

$$T = \frac{2\pi}{\omega_1}. \tag{5.36}$$

To avoid temporal aliasing the time-step Δt between two frames must be smaller than $\frac{1}{2}T$ according to Nyquist sampling theory [McClellan et al., 1998]. That is

$$\Delta t \leq \frac{T}{2}. \tag{5.37}$$

This knowledge can, for instance, be used to determine a suitable spring coefficient k, that will allow us to use the maximum frame time-step without temporal aliasing. That is

$$\Delta t = \frac{T}{2} = \frac{\pi}{\omega_1} = \frac{\pi}{\sqrt{\omega_0^2 - \frac{\gamma^2}{4}}} \tag{5.38}$$

Rearranging, we find that

$$\Delta t \sqrt{\omega_0^2 - \frac{\gamma^2}{4}} = \pi. \tag{5.39}$$

Squaring both sides and isolating ω_0^2 we get,

$$\Delta t^2 \left(\omega_0^2 - \frac{\gamma^2}{4} \right) = \pi^2. \tag{5.40}$$

Using $\omega_0^2 = \frac{k}{m}$ and $\gamma = \frac{b}{m}$ we find that

$$\frac{k}{m} = \frac{\pi^2}{\Delta t^2} + \frac{b^2}{4m^2}. \tag{5.41}$$

It is thus concluded that

$$k = \frac{m\pi^2}{\Delta t^2} + \frac{b^2}{4m}. \tag{5.42}$$

This approach is used in [Hasegawa et al., 2003], but it does not provide us with any means for picking the coefficient of damping b, i.e., it is impossible to control the rate of the decay.

In order to get a method that also allows control of the coefficient of damping, we will start by deriving the conditions for a highly damped oscillator. For such an oscillator we must have that the ratio in (5.29) goes to infinity,

$$\frac{\gamma}{\omega_1} = c \rightarrow \infty. \tag{5.43}$$

Substituting $\gamma = \frac{b}{m}$ and (5.26) we derive

$$\frac{b}{m} = c\sqrt{\omega_0^2 - \frac{b^2}{4m^2}}. \tag{5.44}$$

Squaring yields

$$\left(\frac{b}{m} \right)^2 = c^2\omega_0^2 - c^2\frac{b^2}{4m^2}. \tag{5.45}$$

Substituting (5.17) and collecting terms gives

$$\left(1+\frac{c^2}{4}\right)\left(\frac{b}{m}\right)^2 = c^2\frac{k}{m} \tag{5.46a}$$

$$\Rightarrow \left(\frac{1}{c^2}+\frac{1}{4}\right)\left(\frac{b}{m}\right)^2 = \frac{k}{m}. \tag{5.46b}$$

Taking the limit for c going to infinity, gives

$$k = \frac{b^2}{4m}. \tag{5.47}$$

Observe that this is in fact a *critically damped oscillator*, because we have $b^2 - 4mk = 0$, so we have shown that the limiting case of the *heavily damped oscillator* is in fact the critical damped oscillator, as expected.

We'll investigate the critical damped harmonic oscillator further by looking at the frequency of it

$$\omega_1 = \sqrt{\omega_0^2 - \frac{\gamma^2}{4}} \tag{5.48a}$$

$$= \sqrt{\frac{k}{m} - \frac{b^2}{4m^2}} \tag{5.48b}$$

$$= \frac{1}{2m}\sqrt{4mk - b^2} \tag{5.48c}$$

$$= 0. \tag{5.48d}$$

This means that the frequency vanishes, and there is no oscillation. Observe that this indicates an infinite long period, since

$$\lim_{\omega_1 \to 0} T = \lim_{\omega_1 \to 0} \frac{2\pi}{\omega_1} = \infty. \tag{5.49}$$

Using these facts about the critical damped harmonic oscillator, we see that the equation describing the motion of the harmonic oscillator (5.25) reduces to a simple exponential decay:

$$x = A\exp\left(-\frac{\gamma}{2}t\right)\cos\left(\omega_1 t + \phi\right). \tag{5.50}$$

In our case $\omega_1 = 0$, and the phase shift is zero since at time $t = 0$ the spring will have maximum amplitude equal to the penetration depth between two rigid bodies. Thus we conclude that

$$x = A\exp\left(-\frac{\gamma}{2}t\right). \tag{5.51}$$

Exponential decay is often characterized by the time τ required for the amplitude of the signal to drop to $e^{-1} \approx 0.37$ of its initial value. That is

$$\exp(-1) = \exp\left(-\frac{\gamma}{2}\tau\right) \tag{5.52}$$

This time is called the *characteristic time* or the *damping time* [Kleppner et al., 1978]. For our purpose τ becomes a parameter for controlling the rate by which the signal tends to zero. For the moment we will let the value of τ be a user-specified parameter. By the definition of τ in (5.52) we derive

$$-1 = -\frac{\gamma}{2}\tau, \tag{5.53a}$$

$$\Rightarrow \gamma = \frac{2}{\tau}, \tag{5.53b}$$

which yields a formula for selecting the value of the viscosity coefficient

$$b = \frac{2m}{\tau}. \tag{5.54}$$

Knowing that we want critical damping, indicating that $b^2 - 4mk = 0$, we can derive a formula for selecting the value of the spring coefficient

$$k = \frac{m}{\tau^2}. \tag{5.55}$$

Although our derivations differ from the ones given in [Barzel et al., 1988], the approaches are identical. The problem that remains is a method for picking the value of τ. We will derive such a method in the following.

We want the amplitude to drop to a fraction $0 < \varepsilon < 1$ within a single frame computation. Thus we need to determine how many steps n of τ are needed before the amplitude decays to a fraction below ε,

$$\exp\left(-\frac{\gamma}{2}n\tau\right) = \left(e^{-1}\right)^n \leq \varepsilon, \tag{5.56}$$

from this we derive

$$\left(e^{-1}\right)^n \leq \varepsilon \tag{5.57a}$$

$$\Downarrow$$

$$n \ln\left(e^{-1}\right) \leq \ln \varepsilon \tag{5.57b}$$

$$\Downarrow$$

$$n \geq -\ln \varepsilon \tag{5.57c}$$

In conclusion, we see that we must pick $n = \lceil -\ln \varepsilon \rceil$. Given the time-step Δt between two frames we can compute τ as

$$\tau = \frac{\Delta t}{n} \tag{5.58}$$

This completes the derivation for our method of picking parameter values. Pseudocode is listed in Figure 5.10. In Figure 5.11 is shown a piece of Matlab code, illustrating how parameters could be picked, such that the amplitude drops to below one percent of its initial value within a single simulation time-step. In Figure 5.12 is shown the output from the Matlab code from Figure 5.11. Note the values of the coeffi-

```
Algorithm pick-parameter-values( Δt, ε, m )
  n = ⌈− ln ε⌉
  τ = Δt/n
  b = 2m/τ
  k = m/τ^2
End algorithm
```

Figure 5.10: Pseudocode for picking parameter values of a spring. The time-step between two frames is given by Δt, the decay fraction of the amplitude is given by ε and the mass is given by m. In general m would be the reduced mass (see Section 5.2.2).

```
dt = 0.01;              % Time-step size
tau = dt/6;             % Damping time
A = 0.02;               % Initial Amplitude
m = 10;                 % Mass
gamma = 2/tau;
delta = 1/tau^2;
b = 2*m/tau;            % Damping Coefficient
k = m/tau^2;            % Spring Coefficient
omega_0 = sqrt(delta);                      % Natrual Frequency
omega_1 = sqrt(omega_0^2 - gamma^2/4);      % Frequency
t = 0:tau/100:6*tau;
x = A * exp(-(gamma * t)/2).*cos(omega_1*t);  % Signal of harmonic oscillator
plot(t,x);
title('Critical Damped Harmonic Oscillator');
xlabel('time (seconds)');
ylabel('Penetration depth (cm)');
text(tau,0.5*A,textlabel( 'A *exp(-gamma*t)*cos(omega_1*t)') );
text(tau,0.4*A,['k = '  mat2str(k)] );
text(tau,0.3*A,['b = '  mat2str(b)] );
```

Figure 5.11: Matlab code for picking spring- and damper-parameter values of a critical damped oscillator with a controlled decay.

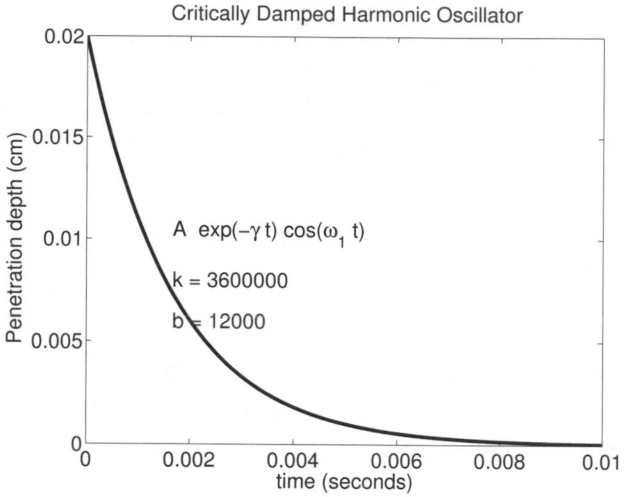

Figure 5.12: Plot showing the amplitude of the critical damped harmonic oscillator from Figure 5.11. Notice that the amplitude, i.e., the penetration depth, drops to almost zero within a single time-step $\Delta t = 0.01$ seconds.

cients, k and b. The *half-life time* is an alternative time constant, which is defined as the value τ for which the signal has dropped to one half of its initial value, that is

$$\exp\left(-\frac{\gamma}{2}\tau\right) = \frac{1}{2}. \tag{5.59}$$

If preferred, one could use the half-life time instead of the damping time, to derive formulas for picking the values of k and b.

5.4 Solving Harmonic Oscillators Numerically

In the previous section we worked directly with the analytical solution to the damped harmonic oscillator. This is seldom possible in a simulator, which must rely on numerical methods. This section is devoted to the task of applying a numerical method to a spring-damper system. Two methods are essentially studied: the explicit Euler method and the implicit Euler method. The interested reader is referred to Chapter 23.1 for more details.

According to (5.51) we have $x(t) = A\exp\left(-\frac{\gamma}{2}t\right)$. Differentiating w.r.t. time yields

$$\dot{x}(t) = -\frac{\gamma}{2}x(t), \tag{5.60}$$

which is the ordinary differential equation we will try to solve numerically.

For the *explicit first-order Euler scheme*, the numerical approximation, x_{i+1}, at time $t_{i+1} = t_i + h$ to the analytical solution $x(t_{i+1})$ is given by

$$x_{i+1} = x_i + h\frac{-\gamma}{2}x_i \tag{5.61a}$$

$$= \left(1 + h\frac{-\gamma}{2}\right) x_i. \tag{5.61b}$$

Initially $x_0 = A$, from which we get

$$x_{i+1} = \left(1 + h\frac{-\gamma}{2}\right)^{i+1} x_0 = A\left(1 - h\frac{\gamma}{2}\right)^{i+1}. \tag{5.62}$$

Since the exact solution is $x(t) = A\exp\left(-\frac{\gamma}{2}t\right)$ then the absolute error is given by

$$|x(t_i) - x_i| = \left|A\exp\left(-\frac{\gamma}{2}ih\right) - A\left(1 - h\frac{\gamma}{2}\right)^i\right| \tag{5.63a}$$

$$= |A|\left|\exp\left(-\frac{\gamma}{2}h\right)^i - \left(1 - h\frac{\gamma}{2}\right)^i\right|, \tag{5.63b}$$

from which we see that the accuracy of the numerical solution is determined by how well $1 - h\frac{\gamma}{2}$ approximates $\exp\left(-\frac{\gamma}{2}h\right)$. Furthermore, the numerical solution will only converge to the analytical solution if

$$\left|1 - h\frac{\gamma}{2}\right| < 1, \tag{5.64}$$

see Chapter 23.1 for more details. This effectively restricts the time step h for the numerical method: since $h, \gamma > 0$ then there are two cases to consider. First, if $h\gamma < 1$, then numerical convergence may only occur, when $1 - h\frac{\gamma}{2} < 1$, hence

$$0 < h\gamma < 2. \tag{5.65}$$

Second, if $h\gamma > 1$, then numerical convergence may only occur, when $1 - h\frac{\gamma}{2} > -1$, hence

$$2 < h\gamma < 4. \tag{5.66}$$

Notice, if in the first case $h > \frac{2}{\gamma}$ then we are in second case. Thus from $\left|1 - h\frac{\gamma}{2}\right| < 1$ and $h, \gamma > 0$ we have

$$h < \frac{4}{\gamma} = \frac{4\mu}{b}, \tag{5.67}$$

where μ is the reduced mass of a two object harmonic oscillator as described in Section 5.2.2. From (5.67) two things become clear:

- The greater mass ratios there are present in the system, i.e., $m_i \ll m_j$, the smaller time-step is required.

- More damping requires less time-step size as well.

An alternative to the explicit Euler is the *implicit first-order Euler scheme* in more depth. It is defined as

$$x_{i+1} = x_i + h\dot{x}_{i+1}. \tag{5.68}$$

Since we know the analytical solution to the problem $x(t) = A\exp(-\frac{\gamma}{2}t)$, this is easily evaluated to

$$x_{i+1} = x_i - h\frac{\gamma}{2}x_{i+1}. \tag{5.69}$$

A little mathematical manipulation yields

$$\left(1 + h\frac{\gamma}{2}\right) x_{i+1} = x_i, \tag{5.70a}$$

$$\Rightarrow x_{i+1} = \frac{x_i}{1 + h\frac{\gamma}{2}}. \tag{5.70b}$$

Remembering that the analytical solution has $x(t) \to 0$ for $t \to \infty$, but in contrast to the explicit method, the implicit method converges even as $h \to \infty$:

$$\lim_{h\to\infty} \left(\frac{x_i}{1 + h\frac{\gamma}{2}}\right) = 0. \tag{5.71}$$

This effectively means that the stability requirements do not require a bound on the time-step of the implicit method. We say that the implicit method is *unconditionally stable*.

Comparing the explicit with the implicit methods for a spring-damper system, the implicit method is obviously superior, since it will always converge to the correct solution regardless of the chosen time-step. Figure 5.13 compares the implicit and explicit method for different values of the time-step. However, while the implicit method always converges to the correct solution, it does so at a slower rate than the exact solution. The explicit method gets into more and more trouble the closer h gets to $\frac{4}{\gamma}$; when h passes this value the numerics simply explode. Furthermore for those time-step sizes where the explicit method is stable, it will converge to zero even faster than the analytical solution.

5.5 Using the Penalty Method in Practice

The previous section appears to supply bulletproof values for the coefficients of the spring-damper system, nevertheless practitioners report that massive amounts of parameter tuning is needed for mass-spring systems. Surprisingly enough, they are still widely used and very popular—soft bodies in tools such as Maya or 3DMax clearly illustrate this. We believe this popularity is mainly due to the simplicity of mass-spring systems; they seem easy to understand and implement. However, there is also a computational justification for using penalty methods. If a configuration has k contact points, the *collision response* only takes $O(k)$ time and has very low time constants. In comparison, a *constraint-based simulation* to be discussed in Chapter 7 has at least $O(k^3)$ expected average time for an exact solution, and with quite high time-constants and some constraint-based methods, only guarantees expected polynomial time, that is $O(k^n)$ for some $n \gg 1$. Although recent research in iterative numerical methods for constraint-based

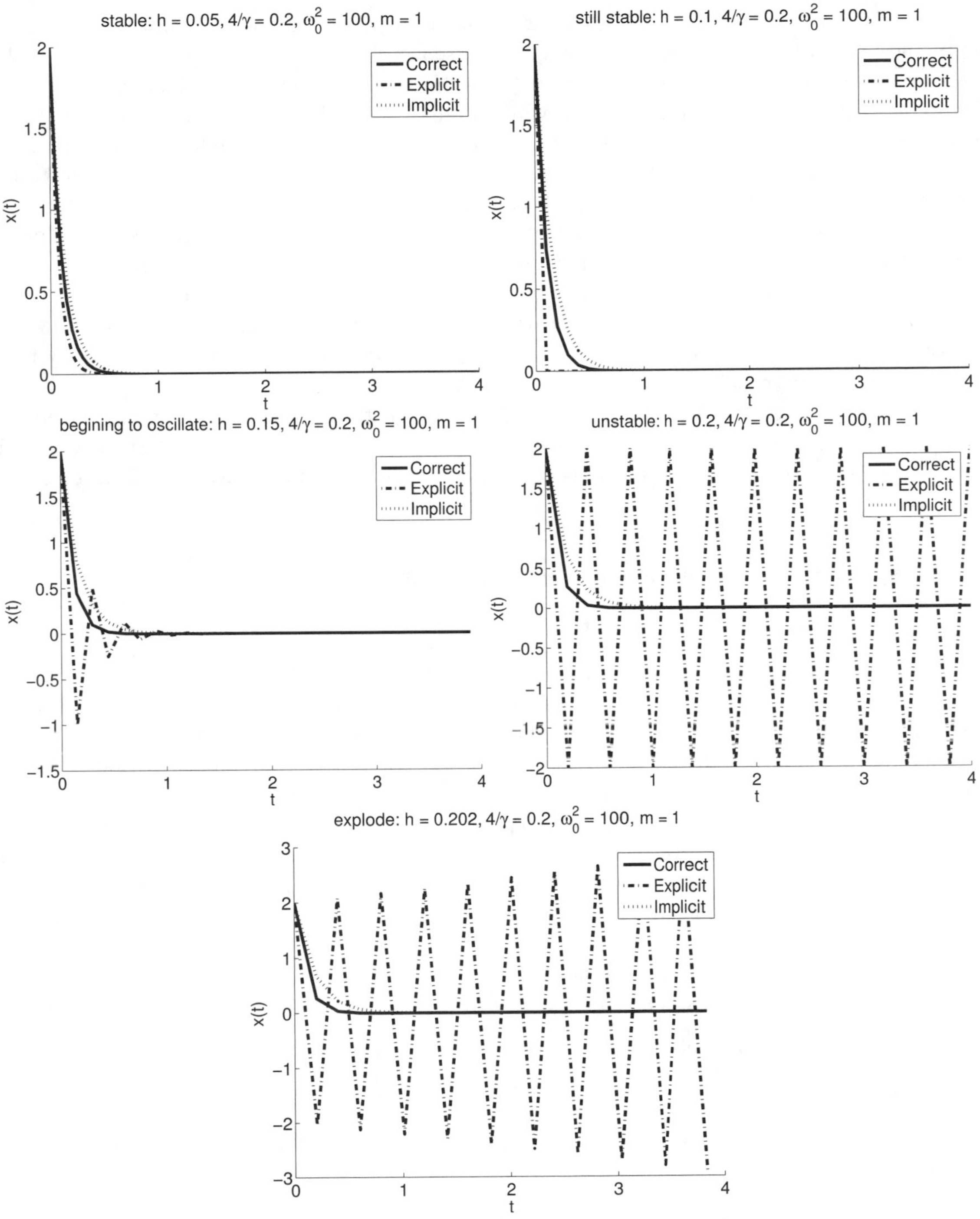

Figure 5.13: Comparison of explicit and implicit Euler method, and exact solution of $x(t) = A\exp\left(-\frac{\gamma}{2}t\right)$.

methods yields much better results [Erleben, 2005], the penalty-based approach is still a computationally cheap method. *Impulse-based simulation*, to be discussed in Section 6, is in some cases comparable to the $O(k)$ running time of the penalty-based method. However, in some cases it is possible to design configurations that have $O(\infty)$ running time with an impulse-based simulator. With some tricks of the trade it is possible to enforce a $O(ck)$ running time for an impulse-based simulator with some constant $c \gg 1$. Other simulation methods solve QP optimization problems. For instance, optimization-based animation [Schmidl, 2002], which is an NP-hard problem. So in short, there is a performance benefit from using penalty-based methods, because even though the other methods have worse time complexities, they can be numerically more pleasant, allowing them to take larger time-steps. Penalty methods are known to produce stiff, ordinary differential equations, which requires small time-steps to satisfactory solve the equation numerically, whereas, for instance, a velocity-based complementarity formulation, as described in Section 7, can take extremely large time-steps in order of thousands times that of the penalty method, without ever becoming unstable.

It is not just the problem of stiff ordinary differential equations that can make penalty methods intractable, they can also suffer from a *secondary oscillations*. These are *resonance effects*, which occur in forced and possibly damped harmonic oscillators, i.e., where some external time dependent force, $F(t)$ is affecting the system,

$$\ddot{x} + \gamma\dot{x} + \omega_0^2 x = F(t). \tag{5.72}$$

In classical mechanics the behavior of this system is often studied with

$$F(t) = F_0 \cos(\omega t). \tag{5.73}$$

Here F_0 is some constant, and ω is the driving frequency. $F(t)$ is called the driving force. Secondary oscillation is seen when ω is close to the frequency of the oscillator i.e., ω_0 for undamped and ω_1 for damped. The effect is seen as an increase in amplitude. For the undamped oscillator the amplitude goes to infinity as $\omega \rightarrow \omega_0$, physically this is not a problem, since no real-world systems are undamped, but in a simulator this might occur, since we are working on an ideal world. In the damped case, the amplitude cannot go to infinity, but is limited by γ, see [Kleppner et al., 1978, pp. 427]. In other words, secondary oscillation can amplify the penalty force in a simulator, such that the amplification can kick objects away from surfaces. One way to combat this is to make γ as large as possible, and one way to detect such a phenomena is to track the total energy of the system—if it suddenly increases, this might be hint of such problems.

The observant reader might at this point claim that it is very unlikely that there is a driving force in form of (5.25), and in most cases, we will often only have to deal with three kinds of driving forces:

Imprecision: In cases of imprecision, ϵ, the equation of motion becomes

$$\ddot{x} + \gamma\dot{x} + \omega_0^2 x = \epsilon. \tag{5.74}$$

We have no way to predict what kind of function ϵ is, we only know it is very small valued, and unlikely to be periodic.

Gravity: Gravity is another force acting on the system, so the equations of motion become

$$\ddot{x} + \gamma\dot{x} + \omega_0^2 x = \epsilon + mg. \tag{5.75}$$

This is a constant force and should not prove to be a problem.

Contact: There is also the contact forces from all other objects, such as in a box stack. This is equivalent to a serial connection of springs as can be seen in Figure 5.14. Looking at the equation of motion for a single spring in such a system gives

$$\ddot{x} + \gamma\dot{x} + \omega_0^2 x = \epsilon + mg + F_{\text{contact}}. \tag{5.76}$$

Since all other contact forces are also modeled by spring-damper systems, these forces will act as a damped driving force. There might be more than one object in contact, which means that the driving force might contain many different frequencies. Multiple contacts might even cause a damped driving frequency close to the oscillators frequency, in which case an effect similar to secondary oscillation can be expected to occur.

Looking at all the spring-damper systems as a whole system, the energy is shifted from one spring-damper system to another, and the damping will dissipate energy over time and the system will eventually settle in *equilibrium*. Thus, from this viewpoint, there is no secondary oscillation effect, instead a wobbly elastic effect may be seen.

In conclusion, we do not know if numerical issues might cause secondary oscillation, nor whether multiple contact formations are likely to cause a local effect for each spring similar to secondary oscillation. It is therefore likely to expect problems similar to secondary oscillation the more complex the configuration gets. These secondary oscillations are another source for parameter tuning, generally speaking, increasing the value of γ should help alleviate the problem. Increasing γ can only be done by increasing b, which means that the system is likely to become over-damped instead of critical damped.

5.6 Secondary Oscillations

A secondary oscillation is a resonance phenomena. To gain more insight into the significance of the secondary oscillation in the penalty method, we will study the case of a idealized box stacking as shown in Figure 5.14. We have three boxes denoted by the numbers 1, 2, and 3. Each box is described by three positions, x_1, x_2, and x_3. Horizontal movement is ignored. The contact forces between the boxes are modeled by a critical damped spring system, that is two springs, a and b, are inserted between the boxes as shown in the figure. The springs and damping coefficients are determined as outlined in Section 5.3. The boxes are given a size of 1 meter, and initially they are displaced such that there is 1 cm empty space between them. The bottommost box is fixed, meaning it has infinite mass and therefore is immovable. Damped springs are inserted between two neighboring boxes whenever they penetrate each other. As soon as neighboring boxes are touching or separated, the springs are removed.

Figure 5.15 shows a Matlab implementation of a box stack simulation. In Figure 5.16(a) the simulation result of the stack of 3 boxes is shown. The simulation is done perfectly, in Figure 5.16(a) no oscillation can be seen, and as verified in Figure 5.16(b) the deviation from *equilibrium position* is small and boxes quickly come to rest. Notice however, that when the upper box comes in contact with the box beneath it, then it is thrown upward. This indicates a small energy gain. The damped secondary oscillation that was previously discussed is not seen in Figure 5.16. However, let us increase the complexity of the

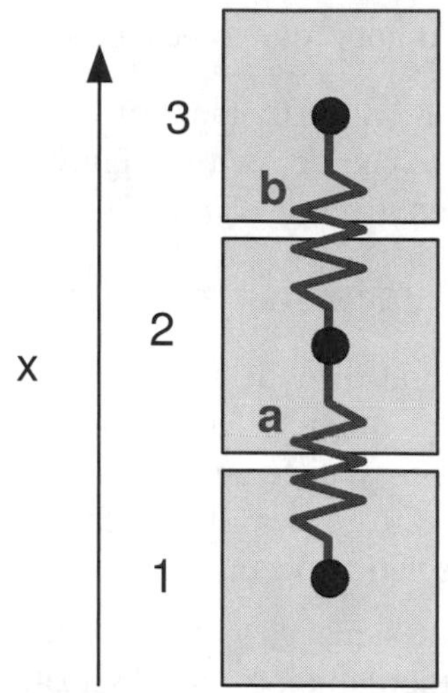

Figure 5.14: Idealized box-stack example, used for analyzing secondary oscillations. Notice that penalty springs are a serial connection of a mass-spring system.

configuration by increasing the stack height. Simulation results are shown in Figures 5.17 and 5.18 for box stacks of 5, 10, 20, and 40 boxes. For a stack of 5 boxes we see nearly the same results as we did for a stack of 3 boxes, however some small jittering is slowly becoming noticeable. It takes roughly 0.2 seconds before the jittering vanishes, which corresponds to 20 frames of the animation. The jittering becomes worse and longer as the box stack is increased. For 20 and 40 boxes it has become so clear that it will catch the eye of an observer. If we look at the deviation from the equilibrium positions, the damped secondary oscillation is clearly seen as we increase the height of the box stack, starting to be noticeable around a stack of 10 boxes. Notice also that the oscillations are orders of magnitude larger than the simulation time. For stack heights of 20 and 40 another effect of the penalty method becomes evident: when the system reaches equilibrium there are still errors in the simulation. Notice that for a box of 40 objects the topmost box deviates from its expected equilibrium position by 5 cm, i.e., 5% error. Of course this an accumulated error, due to the errors in the positions of the 39 boxes below the topmost box. The deviations for the stack height of 40 boxes also shows that within the first second of simulation, we will see a single oscillation of the topmost box with an amplitude of 10 cm. This will definitely be noticeable by an observer.

Another interesting effect of a penalty-based method is seen if the initial conditions of the box stack is changed slightly, such that the boxes are initially penetrating by 1 cm instead of being separated. Figure 5.19 shows the simulation results of a box stack with seven initial penetrating boxes. Notice how objects are being thrown up in the air. The initial penetrations make the springs work like a spring gun on the boxes. Even a small penetration as the one in the example can make the topmost box fly up in the air at a height of the same order as the size of the box itself.

In our simulations shown in Figures 5.16, 5.17, 5.18, and 5.19, the mass properties of the boxes were chosen in a favorable way, the masses were all equal and small in magnitude. If a box stack has large

```
function x_plot = boxstack(N)
  x_equilibrium = 0:1.:N;             %--- Equilibrium of N boxes width of 1 m.
  x = 1.01*x_goal;                    %--- Setup initial positions, 1 cm space.
  v = zeros(size(x));                 %--- initial velocity of boxes
  m = ones(size(x));                  %--- masses of boxes
  m(1) = realmax;                     %--- First box is fixed
  mu = (m(1:end-1).*m(2:end))./(m(1:end-1)+m(2:end)); %--- Reduced masses
  timestep = 0.01;                    %--- Simulation time-step
  tau = timestep/6;                   %--- Damping time
  kc = mu/(tau*tau);                  %--- Spring coefficients
  bc = 2*mu/tau;                      %--- Viscosity coefficients
  h = min( mu./bc);                   %--- Integration time-step (<4 mu/b)
  i = 0;                              %--- Iteration counter
  F     = zeros(size(x));             %--- Total external force
  x_plot = x';                        %--- Results
  while ( i<maxsteps )
    dx = x(2:end) - x(1:end-1) - 1;
    dv = v(2:end) - v(1:end-1);
    S = zeros(size(dx));
    if max(dx<0)
      S(dx<0) = S(dx<0) - kc(dx<0).*dx(dx<0) - bc(dx<0).*dv(dx<0);
    end
    F(2:end) = -m(2:end)*9.81;  %--- Gravity
    F(2:end) = F(2:end) + S(1:end);
    F(2:end-1) = F(2:end-1) - S(2:end);
    F(1) = 0;   %--- First box is fixed
    x = x + h*v;
    v = v + (h * (F./m));
    i = i +1;
    if ( mod(i,20)==0 )
      x_plot = [x_plot,x'];
    end
  end
```

Figure 5.15: Matlab code for resonance phenomena analysis of box stack.

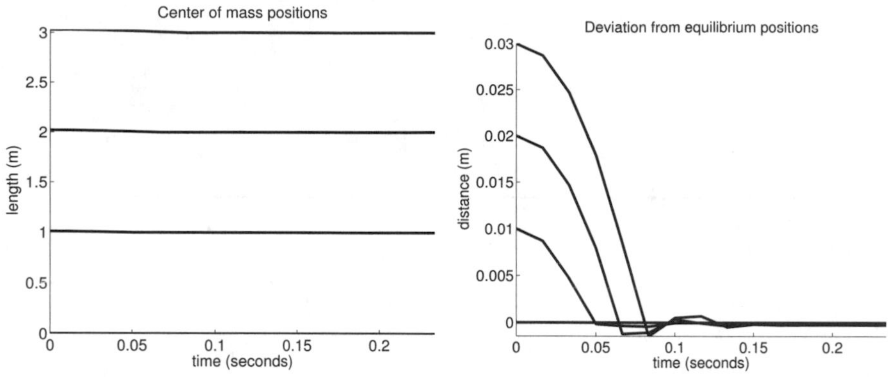

(a) (b)

Figure 5.16: Simulation result for stack of 3 boxes.

ratios in masses, the same effects as we have shown can appear for even small box stacks of height 2 or 3. Besides the large mass ratios will make the ordinary differential equations describing the box motions become even stiffer.

5.7 Inverse Dynamics Approach

In this section we will embark upon a quite different approach originally presented in [Barzel et al., 1988]. The approach taken here does not suffer from the secondary oscillation problems described earlier. The general idea is to set up the desired motion, by using the critical damped spring system, and then solve for the penalty forces required for this desired motion to occur, this is called inverse dynamics. After having solved for the penalty forces, the total force acting on each object can be computed and the equations of motion can be integrated forward in time (forward dynamics). We devote this section to outline the system of equations that needs to be solved for the inverse dynamics problem.

Consider a total of n rigid bodies and K contacts, and assign a unique number k to each contact. Then assign a unique index for each object in our scene, and let i_k and j_k denote the indices of the two incident bodies in contact k. We use the convention that $i_k < j_k$. We also have a contact normal $\boldsymbol{n}_k$ and a contact point $\boldsymbol{p}_{ki}$ with respect to body i_k (similar for body j_k). Both contact normal and points are given in the world coordinate system, and with the convention that the contact normal points from the body with the smallest index to the body with the largest index. This is illustrated in Figure 5.20. Note that we can never have $i_k = j_k$. For each contact we can compute a vector from the center of mass, $\boldsymbol{r}_i$, of an incident body with index i, to the point of contact $\boldsymbol{p}_{ki}$, that is

$$\boldsymbol{r}_{ki} = \boldsymbol{p}_{ki} - \boldsymbol{r}_i \tag{5.77}$$

From classical mechanics we have the Newton-Euler equations (see Section 22.1 for details) describing the motion for all bodies. For the i'th body, the mass of body i is given by m_i and the inertia tensor by I_i,

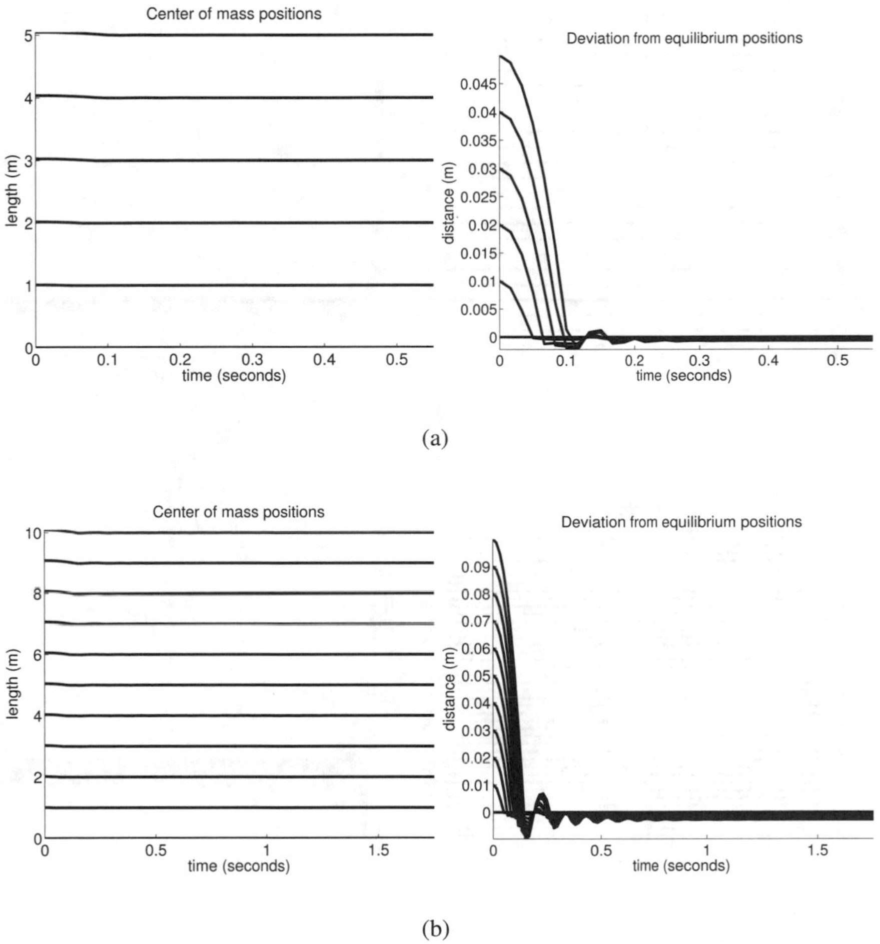

Figure 5.17: Simulation results for box stacks of (a) 5 and (b) 10 boxes.

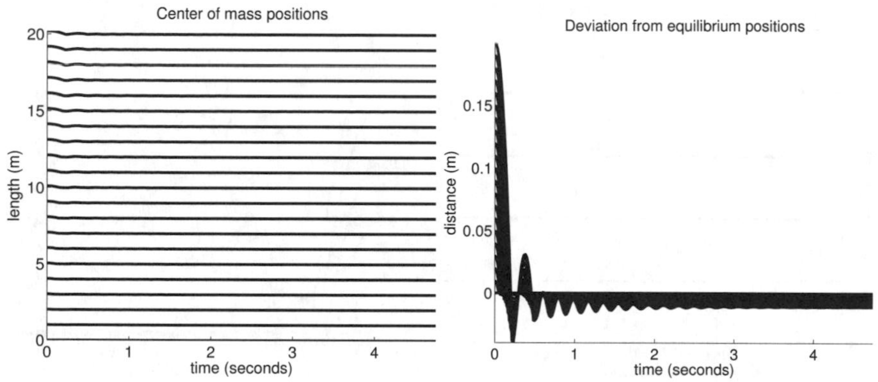

(a)

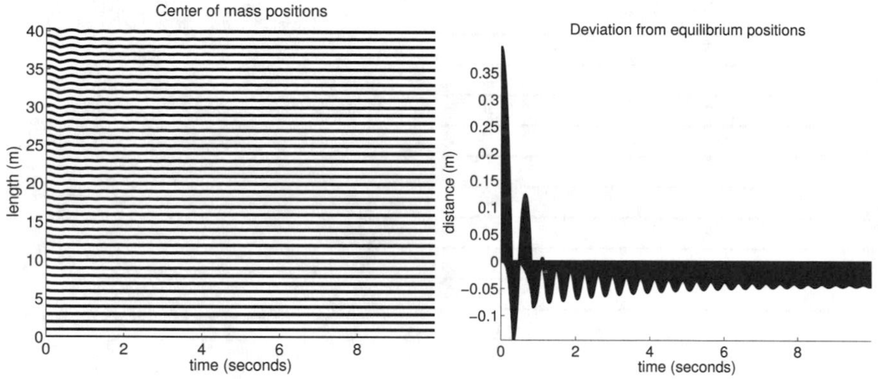

(b)

Figure 5.18: Simulation results for box stacks of (a) 20 and (b) 40 boxes.

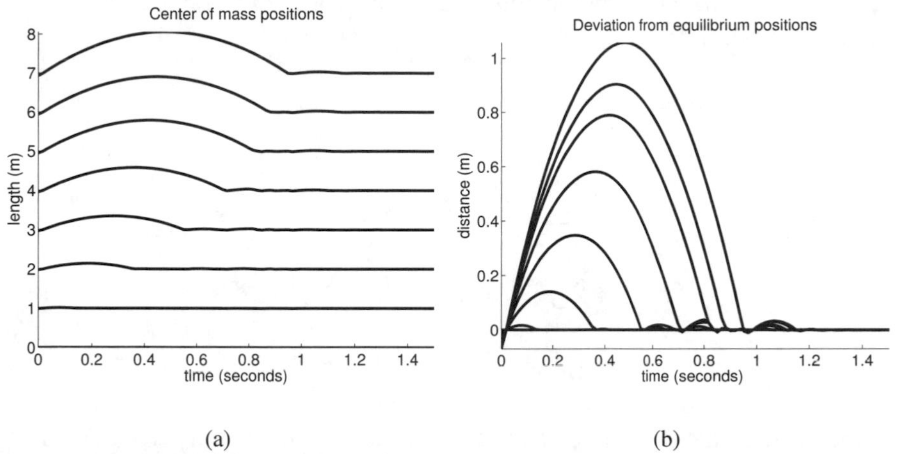

Figure 5.19: Simulation results for stack of seven boxes with initial penetration of 1 cm.

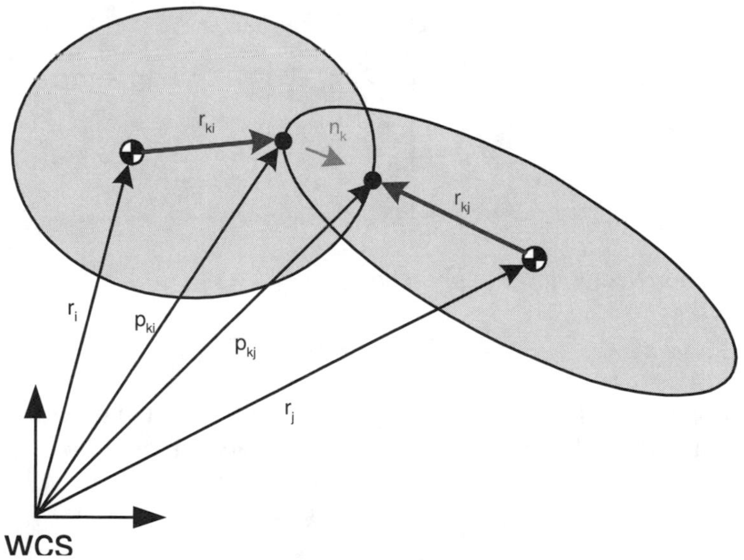

Figure 5.20: Notation for the k'th contact point.

the position is given by $\boldsymbol{r}_i$ and the velocity of the center of mass as $\boldsymbol{v}_i$, the orientation is represented by the quaternion q_i and the angular velocity by $\boldsymbol{\omega}_i$. The acceleration of the center of mass is denoted by $\boldsymbol{a}_i$ and the angular acceleration by $\boldsymbol{\alpha}_i$. The Newton-Euler equations for the i'th body look like this (summations are taken over all contact points):

$$\dot{\boldsymbol{r}}_i = \boldsymbol{v}_i \tag{5.78a}$$

$$\dot{q}_i = \frac{1}{2}\boldsymbol{\omega}_i q_i \tag{5.78b}$$

$$\dot{v}_i = m_i^{-1} \sum_{j_k=i} \boldsymbol{f}_k - m_i^{-1} \sum_{i_k=i} \boldsymbol{f}_k + m_i^{-1} \boldsymbol{f}_i^{\text{ext}} \tag{5.78c}$$

$$\dot{\boldsymbol{\omega}}_i = I_i^{-1} \sum_{j_k=i} \boldsymbol{r}_{kj} \times \boldsymbol{f}_k - I_i^{-1} \sum_{i_k=i} \boldsymbol{r}_{ki} \times \boldsymbol{f}_k \tag{5.78d}$$

$$- I_i^{-1} \boldsymbol{\omega}_i \times I_i \boldsymbol{\omega}_i + I_i^{-1} \boldsymbol{\tau}_i^{\text{ext}} \tag{5.78e}$$

The dot notation means the time derivative $\frac{d}{dt}$, and is used to ease readability. Observe that $\boldsymbol{f}_k$ denotes the contact force at the k'th contact. The effect of all external forces on the center of mass is given by $\boldsymbol{f}_i^{\text{ext}}$ and the total torque from external forces are given by $\boldsymbol{\tau}_i^{\text{ext}}$.

We will start with defining two position vectors,

$$\boldsymbol{p}_j = \begin{bmatrix} \boldsymbol{r}_{j_1} + \boldsymbol{r}_{1j} \\ \boldsymbol{r}_{j_2} + \boldsymbol{r}_{2j} \\ \vdots \\ \boldsymbol{r}_{j_K} + \boldsymbol{r}_{Kj} \end{bmatrix} \tag{5.79}$$

$$\boldsymbol{p}_i = \begin{bmatrix} \boldsymbol{r}_{i_1} + \boldsymbol{r}_{1i} \\ \boldsymbol{r}_{i_2} + \boldsymbol{r}_{2i} \\ \vdots \\ \boldsymbol{r}_{i_K} + \boldsymbol{r}_{Ki} \end{bmatrix}. \tag{5.80}$$

The concatenated separation vector now simply reads

$$\boldsymbol{d} = \boldsymbol{p}_j - \boldsymbol{p}_i. \tag{5.81}$$

In practice, the separation vector is more easily computed by concatenating the contact normals multiplied by the corresponding penetration depths. Introducing the "contact" matrix $\boldsymbol{C} \in \mathbb{R}^{6n \times 3K}$ defined as,

$$\boldsymbol{C}_{hk} = \begin{cases} -\boldsymbol{1} & \text{for } h = 2i_k - 1 \\ -\boldsymbol{r}_{ki}^{\times} & \text{for } h = 2i_k \\ \boldsymbol{1} & \text{for } h = 2j_k - 1 \\ \boldsymbol{r}_{kj}^{\times} & \text{for } h = 2j_k \\ \boldsymbol{0} & \text{otherwise} \end{cases} \tag{5.82}$$

where $\boldsymbol{a}^{\times}$ is the cross product matrix (see Theorem 18.4) and the generalized velocity vector $\boldsymbol{u} \in \mathbb{R}^{6n}$ as

$$\boldsymbol{u} = [\boldsymbol{v}_1, \boldsymbol{\omega}_1, \boldsymbol{v}_2, \boldsymbol{\omega}_2, \cdots, \boldsymbol{v}_n, \boldsymbol{\omega}_n]^T. \tag{5.83}$$

Then the derivative of the separation vector is simply written as

$$\dot{\boldsymbol{d}} = \boldsymbol{C}^T \boldsymbol{u}. \tag{5.84}$$

By the product rule we find the second derivative to be

$$\ddot{\boldsymbol{d}} = \dot{\boldsymbol{C}}^T \boldsymbol{u} + \boldsymbol{C}^T \dot{\boldsymbol{u}}, \tag{5.85}$$

where

$$\dot{\boldsymbol{C}}_{hk} = \begin{cases} -(\boldsymbol{\omega}_{\boldsymbol{i_k}})^{\times} \boldsymbol{r}_{ki}^{\times} & \text{for } h = 2i_k \\ (\boldsymbol{\omega}_{\boldsymbol{j_k}})^{\times} \boldsymbol{r}_{kj}^{\times} & \text{for } h = 2j_k \\ \boldsymbol{0} & \text{otherwise} \end{cases}. \tag{5.86}$$

Now using the generalized mass matrix $\boldsymbol{M} \in \mathbb{R}^{6n \times 6n}$,

$$\boldsymbol{M} = \begin{bmatrix} m_1 \boldsymbol{1} & & & & \boldsymbol{0} \\ & \boldsymbol{I}_1 & & & \\ & & \ddots & & \\ & & & m_n \boldsymbol{1} & \\ \boldsymbol{0} & & & & \boldsymbol{I}_n \end{bmatrix}, \tag{5.87}$$

and the external forces, torques, and velocity dependent forces, $\boldsymbol{f}_{\text{ext}} \in \mathbb{R}^{6n}$,

$$\boldsymbol{f}_{\text{ext}} = \left[\boldsymbol{f}_1^{\text{ext}}, \boldsymbol{\tau}_1^{\text{ext}} - \boldsymbol{\omega}_1 \times I_1 \boldsymbol{\omega}_1, \cdots, \boldsymbol{f}_n^{\text{ext}}, \boldsymbol{\tau}_n^{\text{ext}} - \boldsymbol{\omega}_n \times I_n \boldsymbol{\omega}_n\right]^T. \tag{5.88}$$

The Newton-Euler equation reads,

$$\dot{\boldsymbol{u}} = \boldsymbol{M}^{-1} \left(\boldsymbol{C} \boldsymbol{f}_{\text{penalty}} + \boldsymbol{f}_{\text{ext}}\right). \tag{5.89}$$

Here $\boldsymbol{f}_{\text{penalty}} \in \mathbb{R}^{3K}$ is the concatenation of all the contact forces $\boldsymbol{f}_h$, using this in our derivative formula results in

$$\ddot{\boldsymbol{d}} = \dot{\boldsymbol{C}}^T \boldsymbol{u} + \boldsymbol{C}^T \boldsymbol{M}^{-1} \left(\boldsymbol{C} \boldsymbol{f}_{\text{penalty}} + \boldsymbol{f}_{\text{ext}}\right), \tag{5.90}$$

which is rewritten into,

$$\ddot{\boldsymbol{d}} = \dot{\boldsymbol{C}}^T \boldsymbol{u} + \boldsymbol{C}^T \boldsymbol{M}^{-1} \boldsymbol{C} \boldsymbol{f}_{\text{penalty}} + \boldsymbol{C}^T \boldsymbol{M}^{-1} \boldsymbol{f}_{\text{ext}}. \tag{5.91}$$

Requiring all contacts to be critical damped results in the simultaneous vector equation,

$$\ddot{\boldsymbol{d}} + \frac{2}{\tau} \dot{\boldsymbol{d}} + \frac{1}{\tau^2} \boldsymbol{d} = 0. \tag{5.92}$$

Substitution of our past results yields the matrix equation,

$$\left(\dot{\boldsymbol{C}}^T\boldsymbol{u} + \boldsymbol{C}^T\boldsymbol{M}^{-1}\boldsymbol{C}\boldsymbol{f}_{\text{penalty}} + \boldsymbol{C}^T\boldsymbol{M}^{-1}\boldsymbol{f}_{\text{ext}}\right) + \frac{2}{\tau}\boldsymbol{C}^T\boldsymbol{u} + \frac{1}{\tau^2}\boldsymbol{d} = 0. \tag{5.93}$$

Rearranging a little yields,

$$\underbrace{\boldsymbol{C}^T\boldsymbol{M}^{-1}\boldsymbol{C}}_{\boldsymbol{A}}\boldsymbol{f}_{\text{penalty}} + \underbrace{\dot{\boldsymbol{C}}^T\boldsymbol{u} + \boldsymbol{C}^T\boldsymbol{M}^{-1}\boldsymbol{f}_{\text{ext}} + \frac{2}{\tau}\boldsymbol{C}^T\boldsymbol{u} + \frac{1}{\tau^2}\boldsymbol{d}}_{\boldsymbol{b}} = 0 \tag{5.94}$$

$$\boldsymbol{A}\boldsymbol{f}_{\text{penalty}} - \boldsymbol{b} = 0. \tag{5.95}$$

This is a linear system, which can be solved for the penalty forces. Observe that $\boldsymbol{A}$ might not be invertible; multiple contact points will result in linearly dependent rows. Multiple solutions can exist; a method like singular value decomposition (SVD) can therefore be applied to solve for the penalty forces. Given the generalized position and orientation vector, $\boldsymbol{s} \in \mathbb{R}^{7n}$:

$$\boldsymbol{s} = \left[\boldsymbol{r}_1, q_1, \boldsymbol{r}_2, q_2, \cdots, \boldsymbol{r}_n, q_n\right]^T, \tag{5.96}$$

and the matrix $\boldsymbol{S} \in \mathbb{R}^{7n\times 6n}$,

$$\boldsymbol{S} = \begin{bmatrix} \boldsymbol{1} & & & & \boldsymbol{0} \\ & \boldsymbol{Q}_1 & & & \\ & & \ddots & & \\ & & & \boldsymbol{1} & \\ \boldsymbol{0} & & & & \boldsymbol{Q}_n \end{bmatrix}, \tag{5.97}$$

where $q_i = [s_i, x_i, y_i, z_i]^T \in \mathbb{R}^4$ and $\boldsymbol{Q}_i \in \mathbb{R}^{4\times 3}$:

$$\boldsymbol{Q}_i = \frac{1}{2}\begin{bmatrix} -x_i & -y_i & -z_i \\ s_i & z_i & -y_i \\ -z_i & s_i & x_i \\ y_i & -x_i & s_i \end{bmatrix}. \tag{5.98}$$

The matrix $\boldsymbol{Q}_i$ is derived from the relation $\frac{1}{2}\omega_i q_i = \boldsymbol{Q}_i\boldsymbol{\omega}_i$, as shown in Theorem 18.47. The Newton-Euler equations, see Section 22.1, can now be written as

$$\dot{\boldsymbol{s}} = \boldsymbol{S}\boldsymbol{u} \tag{5.99}$$

$$\dot{\boldsymbol{u}} = \boldsymbol{M}^{-1}\left(\boldsymbol{C}\boldsymbol{f}_{\text{penalty}} + \boldsymbol{f}_{\text{ext}}\right). \tag{5.100}$$

Now all that remains is to solve these *ordinary differential equations* with a suitable *numerical integration* method, see Section 23.1.

If we restrict the penalty forces to work only in the normal direction, that is

$$\boldsymbol{f}_h = \boldsymbol{n}_h f_h, \tag{5.101}$$

and by introducing the matrix of contact normals $\boldsymbol{N} \in \mathbb{R}^{3K \times K}$,

$$\boldsymbol{N} = \begin{bmatrix} \boldsymbol{n}_1 & & & \boldsymbol{0} \\ & \boldsymbol{n}_2 & & \\ & & \ddots & \\ \boldsymbol{0} & & & \boldsymbol{n}_K \end{bmatrix}, \tag{5.102}$$

this is simply written for all contact points as the matrix equation

$$\boldsymbol{f}_{\text{penalty}} = \boldsymbol{N} \begin{bmatrix} f_1 \\ f_2 \\ \vdots \\ f_K \end{bmatrix} = \boldsymbol{N}\boldsymbol{f}. \tag{5.103}$$

Now (5.81) changes slightly, and instead we will have,

$$\boldsymbol{d} = \boldsymbol{N}^T \left(\boldsymbol{p}_j - \boldsymbol{p}_i\right). \tag{5.104}$$

The vector $\boldsymbol{d}$ is now simply a vector of penetration depths measured along the contact normals. Performing the double differentiation again, this time remembering that the newly added term $\boldsymbol{N}$ is also time dependent, yields

$$\dot{\boldsymbol{d}} = \dot{\boldsymbol{N}}^T \left(\boldsymbol{p}_j - \boldsymbol{p}_i\right) + \boldsymbol{N}^T \boldsymbol{C}^T \boldsymbol{u}, \tag{5.105a}$$

$$\ddot{\boldsymbol{d}} = \ddot{\boldsymbol{N}}^T \left(\boldsymbol{p}_j - \boldsymbol{p}_i\right) + \dot{\boldsymbol{N}}^T \boldsymbol{C}^T \boldsymbol{u} + \dot{\boldsymbol{N}}^T \boldsymbol{C}^T \boldsymbol{u} + \boldsymbol{N}^T \dot{\boldsymbol{C}}^T \boldsymbol{u} + \boldsymbol{N}^T \boldsymbol{C}^T \dot{\boldsymbol{u}} \tag{5.105b}$$

$$= \ddot{\boldsymbol{N}}^T \left(\boldsymbol{p}_j - \boldsymbol{p}_i\right) + 2\dot{\boldsymbol{N}}^T \boldsymbol{C}^T \boldsymbol{u} + \boldsymbol{N}^T \dot{\boldsymbol{C}}^T \boldsymbol{u} + \boldsymbol{N}^T \boldsymbol{C}^T \dot{\boldsymbol{u}}. \tag{5.105c}$$

Using $\ddot{\boldsymbol{d}} + \frac{2}{\tau}\dot{\boldsymbol{d}} + \frac{1}{\tau^2}\boldsymbol{d} = 0$ and $\dot{\boldsymbol{u}} = \boldsymbol{M}^{-1}\left(\boldsymbol{C}\boldsymbol{N}\boldsymbol{f} + \boldsymbol{f}_{\text{ext}}\right)$ together with some mathematical manipulation yields the linear system,

$$\boldsymbol{A}\boldsymbol{f} + \boldsymbol{b} = 0, \tag{5.106}$$

where

$$\boldsymbol{A} = \boldsymbol{N}^T \boldsymbol{C}^T \boldsymbol{M}^{-1} \boldsymbol{C} \boldsymbol{N}, \tag{5.107}$$

and

$$\begin{aligned} \boldsymbol{b} = {} & \boldsymbol{N}^T \boldsymbol{C}^T \boldsymbol{M}^{-1} \boldsymbol{f}_{\text{ext}} + \ddot{\boldsymbol{N}}^T \left(\boldsymbol{p}_j - \boldsymbol{p}_i\right) + 2\dot{\boldsymbol{N}}^T \boldsymbol{C}^T \boldsymbol{u} + \boldsymbol{N}^T \dot{\boldsymbol{C}}^T \boldsymbol{u} \\ & + \frac{2}{\tau}\left(\dot{\boldsymbol{N}}^T \left(\boldsymbol{p}_j - \boldsymbol{p}_i\right) + \boldsymbol{N}^T \boldsymbol{C}^T \boldsymbol{u}\right) + \frac{2}{\tau^2}\left(\boldsymbol{N}^T \left(\boldsymbol{p}_j - \boldsymbol{p}_i\right)\right). \end{aligned} \tag{5.108}$$

The only difficult things to handle in (5.108) are the terms $\dot{\boldsymbol{N}}$ and $\ddot{\boldsymbol{N}}$. However, since their elements are vectors each describing only a direction, we can compute these matrices by taking the cross product of the individual elements with the respective angular velocities. That is,

$$\dot{\boldsymbol{N}} = \begin{bmatrix} \boldsymbol{\omega}_{i_1} \times \boldsymbol{n}_1 & & & \boldsymbol{0} \\ & \boldsymbol{\omega}_{i_1} \times \boldsymbol{n}_2 & & \\ & & \ddots & \\ \boldsymbol{0} & & & \boldsymbol{\omega}_{i_K} \times \boldsymbol{n}_K \end{bmatrix}, \tag{5.109}$$

where $\boldsymbol{\omega}_{i_k}$ denotes the angular velocity of body i at the k'th contact point. By differentiation w.r.t. time we have

$$\ddot{\boldsymbol{N}} = \begin{bmatrix} \boldsymbol{\alpha}_{i_1} \times \boldsymbol{n}_1 + \boldsymbol{\omega}_{i_1} \times (\boldsymbol{\omega}_{i_1} \times \boldsymbol{n}_1) & & \boldsymbol{0} \\ & \ddots & \\ \boldsymbol{0} & & \boldsymbol{\alpha}_{i_K} \times \boldsymbol{n}_K + \boldsymbol{\omega}_{i_K} \times (\boldsymbol{\omega}_{i_K} \times \boldsymbol{n}_K) \end{bmatrix}, \tag{5.110}$$

where $\boldsymbol{\alpha}_{i_k}$ denotes the angular acceleration of body i at the k'th contact point. Having solved for $\boldsymbol{f}$, we can write the equations of motion as

$$\dot{\boldsymbol{u}} = \boldsymbol{M}^{-1} \left(\boldsymbol{C} \boldsymbol{N} \boldsymbol{f} + \boldsymbol{f}_{\text{ext}} \right), \tag{5.111}$$

and the forward dynamics problem can be solved by integration of (5.111).

5.8 Modeling Friction

Previously we have only been concerned with normal forces, that is forces that should prevent penetration of the rigid bodies, however another important contact force is friction. *Coulomb's friction law* as described in Section 22.2 is a popular choice. It consists of two kinds of friction *static friction* and *dynamic friction*. The latter occurs in the case when objects are relatively sliding.

Friction is very important for the motion to seem physically plausible for a human observer. The reason is that friction is an important part of our everyday life. In fact we are so used to friction that we often don't even think about it. How should one go about modeling friction in a penalty-based simulator? It seems reasonable to use a spring-damper system for the *friction force* as well [Hasegawa et al., 2003, Pedersen et al., 2004]. This is done by tracking the contact points.

At first point of contact, an *anchor point*, $\boldsymbol{a}$, is saved. This is an unmovable point in the world coordinate system. Subsequently the friction is determined by the spring force stemming from the zero-length spring with spring coefficient k between the anchor point and the current position $\boldsymbol{p}$ of the contact point that caused the creation of the anchor point.

$$\boldsymbol{F}_{\text{friction}} = k \left(\boldsymbol{a} - \boldsymbol{p} \right). \tag{5.112}$$

During the simulation we keep an eye on whether the following condition holds

$$\left\| \boldsymbol{F}_{\text{friction}} \right\| \leq \mu \left\| \boldsymbol{F}_{\text{normal}} \right\|. \tag{5.113}$$

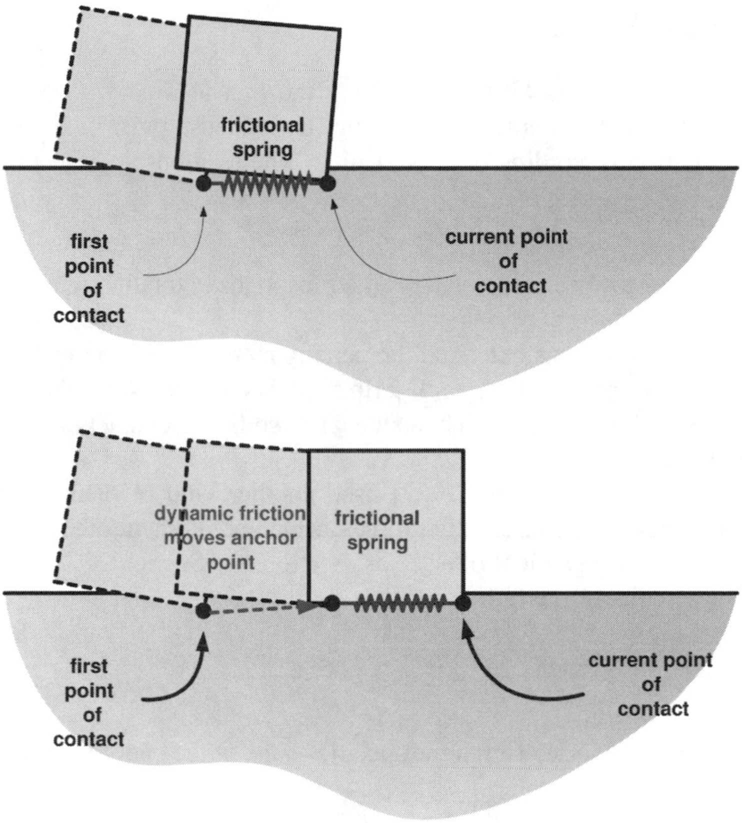

Figure 5.21: Figure illustrating the idea of frictional springs.

Here μ is the *coefficient of friction*, and $\boldsymbol{F}_{\text{normal}}$ is the normal force, where the penalty force often may be used as the normal force. If the condition is fulfilled we say that we have *static friction* and we do nothing, if, on the other hand, the condition is broken we say that we have *dynamic friction*, and the anchor point is moved such that the following condition holds,

$$\|\boldsymbol{F}_{\text{friction}}\| = \mu \|\boldsymbol{F}_{\text{normal}}\| . \tag{5.114}$$

The general idea is illustrated in Figure 5.21. The frictional spring force model can be physical justified as a crude model of the external shear stresses acting between two bodies [Lautrup, 2005]. Since it is the external shear stresses that we experience as friction in our everyday life. As such, the friction model adds an element of compliance to the rigid bodies.

Another approach to model friction is simply to use (5.114) as used in [McKenna et al., 1990], i.e.,

$$\boldsymbol{F}_{\text{friction}} = -\mu \|\boldsymbol{F}_{\text{penalty}}\| \frac{\boldsymbol{u}_t}{\|\boldsymbol{u}_t\|}, \tag{5.115}$$

where $\boldsymbol{u}_t$ is the tangential relative sliding velocity. This approach only models dynamic friction, thus static friction is ignored.

5.9 Survey on Past Work

Moore and Wilhelms [Moore et al., 1988] were among the first to model contact forces by springs in computer animation. They used a simple linear spring, but added a twist of letting the spring constant depend on whether the motion is receding or approaching. The relationship is as follows

$$k_{\text{recede}} = \varepsilon k_{\text{approach}}, \tag{5.116}$$

where ε describes the elasticity of the collision, $\varepsilon = 0$ corresponds to totally inelastic collisions, and $\varepsilon = 1$ to perfectly elastic collisions.

Furthermore, Moore and Wilhelms extended the penalty method with an algebraic collision resolving method, similar to Newton's collision law, as described in Section 6.1.4.1. The main idea is to handle colliding contacts before applying springs. This is because colliding contacts requires very stiff springs, which are numerically intractable.

Terzopoulos, *et al.* [Terzopoulos et al., 1987] used another kind of penalty force. The main idea behind their derivation comes from conservative forces, which are known to be the negative gradient of a energy potential, i.e., the negative gradient of a scalar function, see Section 22.3. A scalar energy function is then designed, which penalizes penetration:

$$E = c \exp\left(\frac{d_{\text{depth}}}{\varepsilon}\right), \tag{5.117}$$

where c and ε are constants used to determine the specific shape of the energy potential. The penalty force is then

$$\boldsymbol{F} = -\left(\frac{\nabla E}{\varepsilon} \exp\left(\frac{-d_{\text{depth}}}{\varepsilon}\right) \cdot \boldsymbol{n}\right) \boldsymbol{n}, \tag{5.118}$$

where $\boldsymbol{n}$ is the unit contact normal. Such penalty forces are called *exponential springs.* Exponential springs are stiffer for large displacement than linear springs. However, for small displacements exponential springs are less stiff than linear springs [McKenna et al., 1990].

Barzel and Barr [Barzel et al., 1988] used a constraint force equation,

$$\ddot{D} + \frac{2}{\tau}\dot{D} + \frac{1}{\tau^2}D = 0, \tag{5.119}$$

where D is a function measuring the constraint deviation, i.e., the penetration depth, τ is a specified time constant, used for controlling the rate of constraint satisfaction. Comparing with our damped harmonic oscillator, we see that

$$\gamma = \frac{2}{\tau} = \frac{b}{m} \tag{5.120a}$$

$$\omega_0^2 = \frac{1}{\tau^2} = \frac{k}{m}. \tag{5.120b}$$

The criteria for critical damping is,

$$b^2 - 4mk = 0. \tag{5.121}$$

Dividing by m^2 gives,

$$\frac{b^2}{m^2} - 4\frac{k}{m} = 0 \tag{5.122a}$$

$$\gamma^2 - 4\omega_0^2 = 0. \tag{5.122b}$$

Substituting the $\gamma = \frac{2}{\tau}$, and $\omega_0^2 = \frac{1}{\tau^2}$ we see that the model used by Barzel and Barr is critical damped. Furthermore the paper [Barzel et al., 1988] formulates an inverse dynamics problem which handles simultaneous constraints.

In [McKenna et al., 1990], a twist on penalty forces is introduced to model collisions, inspired by Newton's impact law, described in Section 6.1.4.1, which relates pre- and postvelocities through a coefficient of restitution, ε, where a value of zero corresponds to completely inelastic collisions and a value of 1 corresponds to fully elastic collisions. For interpenetrating contacts, moving away from each other, the penalty force is multiplied by ε.

```
if d_depth < 0 and u · n > 0 then
  F_penalty = ε F_penalty
end if
```

In Hirota *et al.* [Hirota et al., 2001, Hirota, 2002] a penalty force is integrated over the intersecting polygon and combined with an implicit finite element method.

In Jansson and Vergeest [Jansson et al., 2002a], a mass-spring model is used for modeling both rigid and deformable objects, here simple springs are created when particles move within a nominal distance, and springs are deleted again when their incident particles move further away than a given fracture distance. The spring force is simply modeled as

$$\boldsymbol{F} = -k(\|\boldsymbol{x}_i - \boldsymbol{x}_j\| - l)\frac{\boldsymbol{x}_i - \boldsymbol{x}_j}{\|\boldsymbol{x}_i - \boldsymbol{x}_j\|}, \tag{5.123}$$

where k, is the spring constant, $\boldsymbol{x}_i$ and $\boldsymbol{x}_j$ are the particle positions, and l is the nominal distance. Details for determining nominal and fracture distances can be found in [Jansson et al., 2002b].

6

Impulse-Based Multibody Animation

Impulse-based simulators [Hahn, 1988, Mirtich, 1996, Guendelman et al., 2003] simulates all physical interactions between the objects in the configuration by *collision impulses*. *Static contacts* such as one object resting on another are modeled as a series of collision impulses occurring at a very high frequency. Except for static contacts, impulse-based simulators are computationally effective for systems having many objects moving at high speeds.

Constraint-based simulators, as described in Chapter 7, solve for the *time-integral impulse* in order to determine the final velocities of objects. This is not to be confused with the impulse-based paradigm described in this chapter, which uses collision impulses to model physics. To make the distinction clear, we refer to these constraint-based simulators as *velocity-based simulators*, and simulators using collision impulses as impulse-based simulators.

In an impulse-based simulator a one-sided-approach to advance the simulation time is typically used together with a *sequential collision resolving method* based on some *incremental collision law*. In this chapter, we will introduce the reader to these concepts and their theories.

It is worth noting that impulses often need only to be applied at the closest points between two objects. The contact determination or *spatial-temporal coherence analysis* [Erleben, 2005], therefore may often be completely omitted from the collision detection pipeline. This greatly simplifies the implementation of an impulse-based simulator compared to a constraint-based simulator, as described in Chapter 7.

We will start by studying the physics and mathematics behind a single point of collision, followed by an explanation of how general-purpose simulators can be built using only single-point collisions to model all physical interactions.

6.1 Single-Point Collision

A *single-point collision* means that if we have two objects, A and B, then they touch each other at exactly one point. We call this point $\boldsymbol{p}$. We will assume that we have some method for computing a unique normal vector, $\boldsymbol{n}$, at the point $\boldsymbol{p}$. This is explained in detail in Chapter 14. We call this vector the *contact normal*. For objects with continuous smooth surfaces, the contact normal is parallel to the surface normals of the two objects at the point $\boldsymbol{p}$. Note that under this condition, the two surface normals of the two objects are parallel but pointing in opposite directions. In the following, we will use the convention that the normal $\boldsymbol{n}$ always points from B toward A. The contact normal $\boldsymbol{n}$ and the contact point $\boldsymbol{p}$ define a contact plane consisting of all points that fulfill the equation

$$\forall \boldsymbol{x} \in \mathbb{R}^3 \qquad \text{where} \qquad \boldsymbol{n} \cdot \boldsymbol{x} - \boldsymbol{n} \cdot \boldsymbol{p} = 0. \tag{6.1}$$

Alternatively, we can represent this contact plane by two orthogonal unit vectors $\boldsymbol{t}_1$ and $\boldsymbol{t}_2$, both lying in the contact plane and both orthogonal to the contact normal. We will use the convention that these vectors

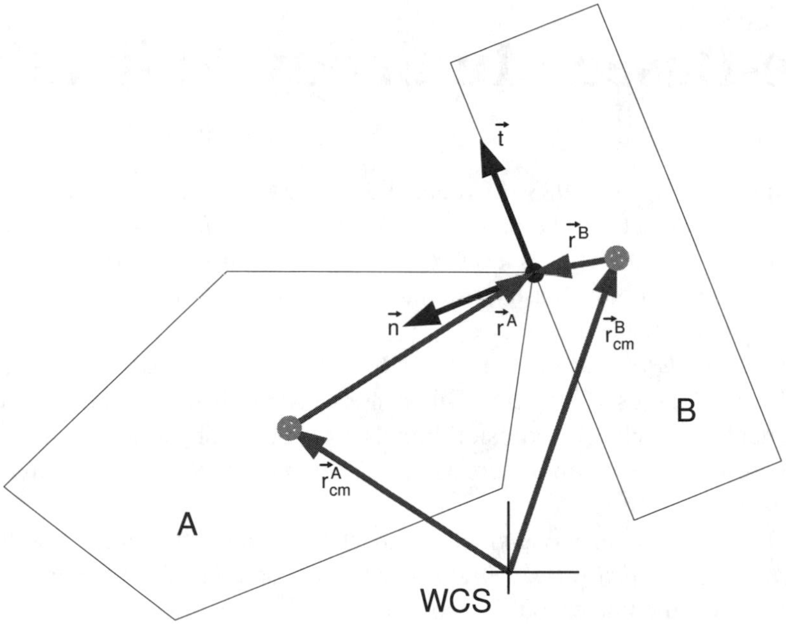

Figure 6.1: An example of a single-point collision with the origin of the World Coordinate System (WCS) indicated.

form a right-hand coordinate system with the contact normal. That is

$$\boldsymbol{n} = \boldsymbol{t}_1 \times \boldsymbol{t}_2. \tag{6.2}$$

For 2D, we will simply drop the subscript on the tangent vectors and use $\boldsymbol{t}$. Knowing the position and orientation of object A and B, we can compute the contact points w.r.t. for either one of these objects, that is,

$$\boldsymbol{p}^{A} = \boldsymbol{r}^{A} + \boldsymbol{r}_{\text{cm}}^{A}, \tag{6.3a}$$

$$\boldsymbol{p}^{B} = \boldsymbol{r}^{B} + \boldsymbol{r}_{\text{cm}}^{B}, \tag{6.3b}$$

$$\boldsymbol{p}^{A} = \boldsymbol{p}^{B}. \tag{6.3c}$$

The superscript refers to the object, $\boldsymbol{r}_{\text{cm}}$ is the position of the *center of mass*, and $\boldsymbol{r}$ is a vector from the center of mass to the contact position. The notation is illustrated in Figure 6.1. We'll look at the contact point on body X, this is given by

$$\boldsymbol{p}^{X} = \boldsymbol{r}^{X} + \boldsymbol{r}_{\text{cm}}^{X}, \tag{6.4}$$

using the *body frame* BF_X, as described in Section 22.1.4, we can rewrite $\boldsymbol{r}^{X}$ as

$$\boldsymbol{r}^{X} = \boldsymbol{R}^{X} \left[\boldsymbol{r}^{X}\right]_{\text{BF}_X}, \tag{6.5}$$

where $\boldsymbol{R}^X$ is the orientation of the body frame of object X represented as a rotation matrix. Now using (6.5) in (6.4) we have

$$\boldsymbol{p}^{X} = \boldsymbol{R}^X \left[\boldsymbol{r}^{X}\right]_{\text{BF}_X} + \boldsymbol{r}_{\text{cm}}^{X}. \tag{6.6}$$

If we differentiate (6.6) with respect to time, we get the *contact velocity* of the contact point on body X, that is,

$$\dot{\boldsymbol{p}}^{X} = \dot{\boldsymbol{R}}^X \left[\boldsymbol{r}^{X}\right]_{\text{BF}_X} + \dot{\boldsymbol{r}}_{\text{cm}}^{X}. \tag{6.7}$$

The columns of $\boldsymbol{R}^X$ are unit vectors along the axes of BF_X. These are body-fixed vectors. So using what we know from (22.27) we can write the time derivative of a body-fixed vector as the cross product of the angular velocity and the body-fixed vector, that is (6.6) is rewritten as

$$\dot{\boldsymbol{p}}^{X} = \dot{\boldsymbol{R}}^X \left[\boldsymbol{r}^{X}\right]_{\text{BF}_X} + \boldsymbol{v}_{\text{cm}}^{X}, \tag{6.8a}$$

$$\dot{\boldsymbol{p}}^{X} = \left[\ \boldsymbol{\omega}^{X} \times \boldsymbol{R}_x^X \ \middle| \ \boldsymbol{\omega}^{X} \times \boldsymbol{R}_y^X \ \middle| \ \boldsymbol{\omega}^{X} \times \boldsymbol{R}_z^X \ \right] \left[\boldsymbol{r}^{X}\right]_{\text{BF}_X} + \boldsymbol{v}_{\text{cm}}^{X}, \tag{6.8b}$$

$$\dot{\boldsymbol{p}}^{X} = \boldsymbol{\omega}^{X} \times \left(\boldsymbol{R}^X \left[\boldsymbol{r}^{X}\right]_{\text{BF}_X}\right) + \boldsymbol{v}_{\text{cm}}^{X}, \tag{6.8c}$$

where we have introduced the notation $\dot{\boldsymbol{r}}_{\text{cm}}^{X} = \boldsymbol{v}_{\text{cm}}^{X}$ for the *linear velocity* of the center of mass. Now we do a mathematical trick of adding zero to (6.8c) and obtain

$$\dot{\boldsymbol{p}}^{X} = \boldsymbol{\omega}^{X} \times \left(\underbrace{\boldsymbol{R}^X \left[\boldsymbol{r}^{X}\right]_{\text{BF}_X} + \boldsymbol{r}_{\text{cm}}^{X}}_{\boldsymbol{p}^{X}} - \boldsymbol{r}_{\text{cm}}^{X} \right) + \boldsymbol{v}_{\text{cm}}^{X}. \tag{6.9}$$

We recognize the (6.6) and reduce (6.9) to

$$\dot{\boldsymbol{p}}^{X} = \boldsymbol{\omega}^{X} \times \left(\boldsymbol{p}^{X} - \boldsymbol{r}_{\text{cm}}^{X}\right) + \boldsymbol{v}_{\text{cm}}, \tag{6.10}$$

using (6.4) we have

$$\boldsymbol{r}^{X} = \boldsymbol{p}^{X} - \boldsymbol{r}_{\text{cm}}^{X}, \tag{6.11}$$

substituting into (6.10), we have

$$\dot{\boldsymbol{p}}^{X} = \boldsymbol{\omega}^{X} \times \boldsymbol{r}^{X} + \boldsymbol{v}_{\text{cm}}^{X}. \tag{6.12}$$

We can now write a formula for the relative contact velocity, $\boldsymbol{u}$, between the two objects A and B.

$$\boldsymbol{u} = \dot{\boldsymbol{p}}^{A} - \dot{\boldsymbol{p}}^{B}. \tag{6.13}$$

The relative contact velocity tells us something about how the two objects are moving relative to each other. For instance, if we look at the relative contact velocity in the normal direction,

$$u_n = \boldsymbol{n}^T \left(\dot{\boldsymbol{p}}^{A} - \dot{\boldsymbol{p}}^{B}\right), \tag{6.14}$$

then we know that

$$\text{relative contact} = \begin{cases} \text{Separating} & \text{if } u_n > 0 \\ \text{Resting} & \text{if } u_n = 0 \\ \text{Colliding} & \text{if } u_n < 0 \end{cases}. \tag{6.15}$$

A *separating contact* means that in the future, no matter how small a time-step we look forward, the objects will no longer be touching at the contact point $\boldsymbol{p}$. *Resting contact* means that the contact point $\boldsymbol{p}$ will persist in the future regardless of how small a time-step we take. *Colliding contact* means that if we do not take any counter action, such as applying a collision impulse at the contact point, then the two objects will penetrate in the future no matter how small a time-step we look ahead.

We are interested in the colliding case, thus we have derived an equation telling us when we need to apply a collision impulse to a single point of contact in order to avoid *penetration*.

Theorem 6.1 (The Collision Test)
Two bodies A and B are colliding, if, and only if,

$$u_n = \boldsymbol{n}^T \left(\left(\boldsymbol{\omega}^A \times \boldsymbol{r}^A + \boldsymbol{v}_{cm}^A \right) - \left(\boldsymbol{\omega}^B \times \boldsymbol{r}^B + \boldsymbol{v}_{cm}^B \right) \right) < 0. \tag{6.16}$$

In the real world, a collision will not happen at a single point of contact, but it will occur over a small area. Actually, what happens is that when real objects come into contact, they deform slightly to accommodate each other's shape. During this deformation the *kinetic energy* of the objects is transformed into internal *elastic energy* in the objects and some of the energy is dissipated as *heat*. When the kinetic energy reaches a minimum, the objects will have come to a stop relative to each other. We say that we have reached the point of maximum compression between the two objects. Now the buildup elastic energy is converted to kinetic energy. While doing so, the objects will begin to move away from each other and the deformation will reverse. This real-world model of a collision is depicted in Figure 6.2. The above description is still a very simplified view about what is going on in the real world. We have neglected many small details, such as plasticity of the deformation, fracture, and chemical and thermo-dynamical effects going on in the materials. However, for our purpose of computer animation, it suffices to understand the real world just a little better.

In particular, we should note two things: first, the collision occurs over a small time duration; it starts at time t_i and ends at time t_f. Somewhere in between we have the time of maximum compression t_{mc}. In particular, we know that for these times, we have

$$t = \begin{cases} t_i & \Rightarrow u_n = \boldsymbol{n}^T \left(\dot{\boldsymbol{p}}^A - \dot{\boldsymbol{p}}^B \right) < 0 \\ t_{\text{mc}} & \Rightarrow u_n = \boldsymbol{n}^T \left(\dot{\boldsymbol{p}}^A - \dot{\boldsymbol{p}}^B \right) = 0 \\ t_f & \Rightarrow u_n = \boldsymbol{n}^T \left(\dot{\boldsymbol{p}}^A - \dot{\boldsymbol{p}}^B \right) > 0 \end{cases}. \tag{6.17}$$

Second, two phases take place, a *compression phase* where energy is built up in objects, then a *restitution phase* where internal energy is released back as kinetic energy. As we will see later, most physical laws describe this process by a *coefficient of restitution*, which indicates the amount of energy that is transformed into kinetic energy during the restitution phase.

From our everyday experience, we do not usually notice the deformation process taking place in what we understand as a rigid body collision. This is because the time-duration of the collision becomes

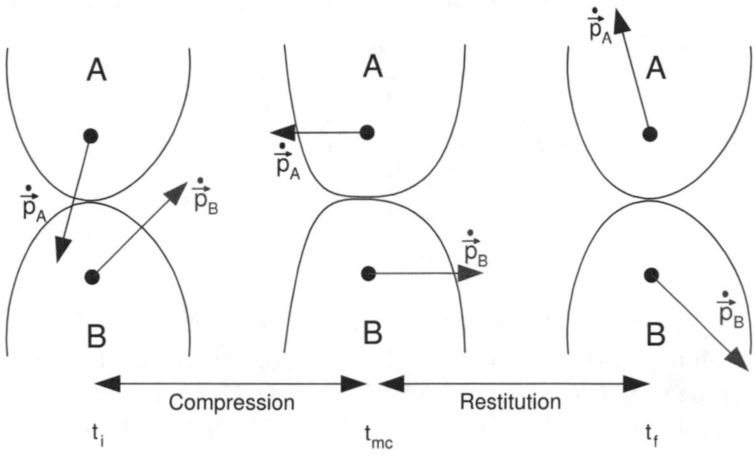

Figure 6.2: A real-world collision consisting of two phases: a compression and a restitution phase.

smaller and smaller the more rigid an object is. In the limiting case of an infinitely rigid object, we have a mathematical model of a rigid body. This model is often referred to as the *rigid body assumptions*. To make it perfectly clear, when those of us in physics, simulation or animation use the term rigid body, we assume the rigid body. There do not exist any such objects in the real world that actually behave according to these assumptions; however, the approximated behavior of many objects can be explained by them.

Definition 6.1 (The Rigid Body Assumptions)
During a collision, the following four assumptions apply to rigid bodies:

- *The duration of the collision is zero, that is* $t_f - t_i \rightarrow 0$.
- *Only impulsive forces must be used to avoid penetration.*
- *Positions and orientations are the same before and after the collision.*
- *Non impulsive forces have no effect during the collision.*

Definition 6.1 has many consequences. In practice it implies that there are no wave "effects" in the collision, such as the deformation. We can ignore gravity and velocity-dependent forces such as *Coriolis forces* etc.

Impulse is defined as the time integral of force. Given the net force, $\boldsymbol{F}$, acting under a collision, the *collision impulse* is therefore

$$\boldsymbol{J} = \int_{t_i}^{t_f} \boldsymbol{F} dt. \tag{6.18}$$

Note that the collision impulse has units of force$\times$time. From Newton's second law we have

$$F = \frac{dP}{dt}, \tag{6.19a}$$

$$\int_{t_i}^{t_f} F dt = \int_{t_i}^{t_f} dP, \tag{6.19b}$$

$$J = P(t_f) - P(t_i), \tag{6.19c}$$

$$J = \Delta P. \tag{6.19d}$$

In the above, we have only considered linear motion, but it is clear that the collision impulse corresponds to a change in the momentum of a rigid body. Since $P = m v_{\text{cm}}$, we see that the impulse is equivalent to a change in the velocity of the rigid body, when the mass of the rigid body is considered to be constant. The exact relationship between impulse and change in rigid body velocities is derived in Theorem 6.2. From Newton's third law it follows

$$J_A = -J_B. \tag{6.20}$$

Mathematically it is difficult to work with (6.18), when $t_f - t_i \rightarrow 0$. In order to circumvent this problem, a reparameterization is used when deriving equations. Any legal parameter γ must by monotonically strictly increasing, that is,

$$\frac{d\gamma}{dt} > 0. \tag{6.21}$$

This requirement comes from the equivalent real-world model, where time always runs forward, never pauses, or stops. If we have a γ parameter with the same property, then there is a one-to-one correspondence between the γ-parameter and the time-parameter. Therefore, it does not matter with which one we choose to parameterize our motion. Looking at a real-world collision, we know that the impulse in the normal direction has

$$\frac{dJ_n}{dt} > 0. \tag{6.22}$$

This means for any legal parameter γ the following condition must also hold

$$\frac{d\gamma}{dJ_n} > 0. \tag{6.23}$$

This follows from the same argumentation that we used to explain the requirement in (6.21).

In order to compute an impulse, we need a method called a *Collision Law*. There are basically four different kinds of Collision Laws:

- *Algebraic Collision Laws*
- *Incremental Collision Laws*
- *Full Deformation Collision Laws*
- *Compliant Contact Model Collision Laws*

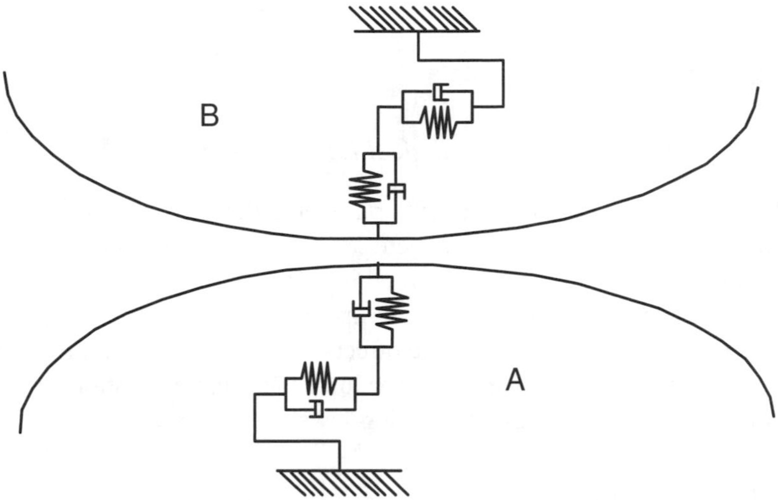

Figure 6.3: A Simple Compliant Contact Model.

Algebraic laws are characterized by the fact that they consist of an algebraic equation. Given the initial conditions of a collision, we immediately know the collision impulse by evaluating an algebraic equation. Therefore, algebraic laws are computational inexpensive and for the same reason, they are attractive in computer games and computer animation. They do, however, lack some realism, which is captured by the three alternative collision laws.

Incremental laws, are characterized by having some microscopic contact model, described as an ordinary differential equation. The resulting impulse is then computed by *integration* over the compression and restitution phases. Incremental laws are computationally more expensive than algebraic laws, but they produce more realistic results. For an example of an incremental law we refer the reader to [Mirtich, 1996].

Full-deformation laws are properly the computationally most expensive of all the four kinds of collision laws. Full-deformation laws are based on continuum mechanics equations for the complete body, such as linear elasto-dynamic equations. Here a partial differential equation is solved using appropriate material properties. Full-deformation laws are not really usable in computer animation for two reasons: first they are too computationally expensive and second, it is impossible to determine the initial conditions for the multitude of material properties that need to be specified. Thus, algebraic laws are prevalent and incremental laws are used to some extent. See [Chatterjee et al., 1998] for references about full-deformation laws.

Finally, there are compliant contact model laws, which we mention for completeness only. These collision laws can be thought of as a kind of spring-damper system, which describes the deformation process that takes place during a real-world collision, similar to the penalty-based methods described in Chapter 5. One has to determine stiffness and damping terms for this kind of collision law. Figure 6.3 illustrates a compliant contact model. We refer the interested reader to [Kraus et al., 1997] for more details. The theme of this book is animation, therefore we will limit ourselves to treat only algebraic collision laws. The general recipe for a collision law consists of combining a contact model with one or more physical laws.

Definition 6.2 (Collision Law)
A collision law is

$$\text{Collision Law} \Leftarrow \text{Physical Law} + \text{Contact Model} \tag{6.24}$$

Physical laws are often used in one of two ways: either as stop criteria in an incremental law or to eliminate unknown variables in an algebraic law. Usually there are also some assumptions, such as the impulse is only pointing in the contact normal direction or something similar.

In computer animation we are interested in: how fast can we compute an impulse? How difficult is it to set up the collision law? How realistic are the effects a collision law can give? In the following, we will derive theory and tools that can help the reader evaluate these three questions, and finally we will end with some examples on typical used algebraic collision laws.

6.1.1 Impact and Friction Laws

Four physical laws are often encountered in collision laws: Newton's impact law, Poisson's hypothesis, Stronge's hypothesis, and Coulomb's friction law.

Newton's impact law defines a simple linear relation between the initial *relative contact normal velocity*, $u_n(\gamma_i)$, and the final relative contact normal velocity, $u_n(\gamma_f)$,

$$u_n(\gamma_f) = -e u_n(\gamma_i), \tag{6.25}$$

where e is the normal restitution coefficient with values limited to the interval

$$0 \leq e \leq 1. \tag{6.26}$$

The restitution coefficient can be thought of as a measure of bounce. A value of one corresponds to a complete elastic collision. That is, if a ball is released over a table, the ball will bounce back from the table and jump back to the same height it was released from, before falling back down toward the table. This bouncing up and down will continue forever. If the value is set to zero, then the ball will hit the table in a perfect inelastic collision, that is, the ball will hit the table bluntly and just stop moving upon impact. This is perhaps best described as a dead ball.

In practice, neither setting the coefficient of restitution to zero nor one yields very realistic behavior. However, some algorithms use these extreme cases to model certain aspects. Also these two extreme cases are very useful when testing a simulator.

Newton's impact law is considered the most simple physical law that describes the effect of a rigid body collision. It is commonly used in computer games, but when combined with friction it suffers from serious problems, such as a breakdown of energy conservation, That is, adding frictional impulses according to Coulomb's friction law could result in energy gain.

Poisson's hypothesis describes a linear relationship between the normal compression impulse $J_n(\gamma_{\text{mc}})$ and the normal restitution impulse $J_n(\gamma_f) - J_n(\gamma_{\text{mc}})$

$$J_n(\gamma_f) - J_n(\gamma_{\text{mc}}) = e J_n(\gamma_{\text{mc}}), \tag{6.27}$$

where e is the normal restitution coefficient with values limited to the interval

$$0 \leq e \leq 1. \tag{6.28}$$

By the normal impulse, we mean the size of the projection of the impulse onto the contact normal. That is, $J_n(\gamma) = \boldsymbol{n} \cdot \boldsymbol{J}(\gamma)$. Poisson's hypothesis is a little more advanced than Newton's impact law, however it suffers from the same problem. Energy conservation breaks down when friction is added.

Stronge's hypothesis describes a quadratic relationship between the work done by the normal impulse during the compression phase $W_n(\gamma_{\text{mc}})$ and the work done by normal impulse during the restitution phase $W_n(\gamma_f) - W_n(\gamma_{\text{mc}})$

$$W_n(\gamma_f) - W_n(\gamma_{mc}) = -e^2 W_n(\gamma_{mc}), \tag{6.29}$$

where e is the normal restitution coefficient with values limited to the interval

$$0 \leq e \leq 1. \tag{6.30}$$

The work done by the collision force $\boldsymbol{F}$ over the duration of a real-world collision is by definition work (see Section 22.3):

$$W = \int_{t_i}^{t_f} \boldsymbol{F}(t) \cdot \dot{\boldsymbol{x}}(t) dt. \tag{6.31}$$

Reparameterization gives us a workable model applicable under the rigid body assumptions

$$W = \int_{\gamma_i}^{\gamma_f} \boldsymbol{F}(\gamma) \cdot \dot{\boldsymbol{x}}(\gamma) \left(\frac{dt}{d\gamma} \right) dt. \tag{6.32}$$

According to Newton's second law $\boldsymbol{F}(\gamma) = \frac{d}{dt}\boldsymbol{J}(\gamma)$, and without loss of generality, we assume $\gamma_i = 0$. Furthermore, $\dot{\boldsymbol{x}}(\gamma)$ is the velocity of the contact point, thus with respect to body A we have $\dot{\boldsymbol{x}}(\gamma) = \boldsymbol{u}_A(\gamma)$. Therefore the work done on object A is

$$W_A = \int_0^{\gamma_f} \boldsymbol{u}_A(\gamma) \cdot \frac{d}{d\gamma} \boldsymbol{J}(\gamma) d\gamma. \tag{6.33}$$

Similarly, the work done on object B is

$$W_B = -\int_0^{\gamma_f} \boldsymbol{u}_B(\gamma) \cdot \frac{d}{d\gamma} \boldsymbol{J}(\gamma) d\gamma. \tag{6.34}$$

Since $\boldsymbol{u} = \boldsymbol{u}_A - \boldsymbol{u}_B$, we end up with the total work

$$W = \int_0^{\gamma_f} \boldsymbol{u}(\gamma) \cdot \frac{d}{d\gamma} \boldsymbol{J}(\gamma) d\gamma. \tag{6.35}$$

Taking the dot product $\boldsymbol{n} \cdot \boldsymbol{J}(\gamma)$ gives the amount of work done in the normal direction. When we have derived the *Impulse-Momentum Law* in Section 6.1.2 the work (6.35) can be written in terms of the relative contact velocity only.

To our knowledge, Stronge's hypothesis is considered the most accurate physical law describing a rigid body collision today. The major benefit of Stronge's hypothesis is that energy conservation holds when friction is added. This means in terms of physics, it is superior to both Newton's impact law and Poisson's hypothesis.

Coulomb's friction law describes a relationship between the frictional force and the magnitude of the normal force. A more detailed description of Coulomb's friction law can be found in Chapter 22.2. If we know the force of the normal direction, $\boldsymbol{F}_n$, and the relative velocity in the contact plane $\boldsymbol{u}_t$ is nonzero, then we have *dynamic friction*, also called *sliding friction*. In this case the *friction force* $\boldsymbol{F}_t$ is given by

$$\boldsymbol{F}_t = -\mu \frac{\boldsymbol{u}_t}{\|\boldsymbol{u}_t\|} \|\boldsymbol{F}_n\|, \tag{6.36}$$

where μ is the coefficient of friction. If the relative velocity in the contact plane is zero then we have *static friction*; also called dry friction. We distinguish between two cases of static friction: stable and unstable. If the time derivative of the contact velocity in the contact plane is zero, that is

$$\dot{\boldsymbol{u}}_t = 0, \tag{6.37}$$

then we have stable static friction and the magnitude of the friction force is given as

$$\|\boldsymbol{F}_t\| \leq \mu \|\boldsymbol{F}_n\|. \tag{6.38}$$

However, unlike dynamic friction, we cannot say anything about the direction. If, on the other hand, $\dot{\boldsymbol{u}}_t \neq 0$, then we have unstable static friction and the friction force is given by

$$\|\boldsymbol{F}_t\| = \mu \|\boldsymbol{F}_n\| \quad \text{and} \quad \boldsymbol{F}_t \cdot \dot{\boldsymbol{u}}_t \leq 0. \tag{6.39}$$

Thus, in this case, we know that the friction force obtains its maximum magnitude and that it opposes the relative acceleration in the contact plane. However, the friction force is still not uniquely determined. The name "unstable" means that a transition can occur either to dynamic or stable static friction.

It should be mentioned that the coefficient of friction often has different values under static and dynamic friction. In computer animation, this is often overlooked and the same value is used for both the static and the dynamic case.

6.1.2 Contact Model

From Newton's second law we have

$$\boldsymbol{F}^A(\gamma) = m_A \boldsymbol{a}^A_{\text{cm}}(\gamma), \tag{6.40}$$

and from Euler's equation we have

$$\boldsymbol{\tau}^A(\gamma) = \boldsymbol{r}^A \times \boldsymbol{F}^A(\gamma) = \boldsymbol{I}_A \boldsymbol{\alpha}^A(\gamma) + \boldsymbol{\omega}^A(\gamma) \times \boldsymbol{I}_A \boldsymbol{\omega}^A(\gamma). \tag{6.41}$$

The term $\boldsymbol{\omega}^{A}(\gamma) \times \boldsymbol{I}_A \boldsymbol{\omega}^{A}(\gamma)$ can be ignored during collision, since it is only dependent on velocity terms. So we have the more simple equations

$$\boldsymbol{F}^{A}(\gamma) = m_A \boldsymbol{a}_{\text{cm}}^{A}(\gamma), \tag{6.42a}$$

$$\boldsymbol{r}^{A} \times \boldsymbol{F}^{A}(\gamma) = \boldsymbol{I}_A \boldsymbol{\alpha}^{A}(\gamma). \tag{6.42b}$$

Integrating from γ_i to $\gamma \leq \gamma_f$, we have

$$\int_{\gamma_i}^{\gamma} \boldsymbol{F}^{A}(\gamma) d\gamma = \int_{\gamma_i}^{\gamma} m_A \boldsymbol{a}_{\text{cm}}^{A}(\gamma) d\gamma, \tag{6.43a}$$

$$\int_{\gamma_i}^{\gamma} \boldsymbol{r}^{A} \times \boldsymbol{F}^{A}(\gamma) d\gamma = \int_{\gamma_i}^{\gamma} \boldsymbol{I}_A \boldsymbol{\alpha}^{A}(\gamma) d\gamma. \tag{6.43b}$$

Using the definition of impulse (6.18) on the left-hand side and noticing that mass terms on the right-hand side are constant, we have

$$\boldsymbol{J}^{A}(\gamma) = m_A \underbrace{\left(\boldsymbol{v}_{\text{cm}}^{A}(\gamma) - \boldsymbol{v}_{\text{cm}}^{A}(\gamma_i)\right)}_{\Delta \boldsymbol{v}_{\text{cm}}^{A}(\gamma)}, \tag{6.44a}$$

$$\boldsymbol{r}^{A} \times \boldsymbol{J}^{A}(\gamma) = \boldsymbol{I}_A \underbrace{\left(\boldsymbol{\omega}^{A}(\gamma) - \boldsymbol{\omega}^{A}(\gamma_i)\right)}_{\Delta \boldsymbol{\omega}^{A}(\gamma)}. \tag{6.44b}$$

By the rigid body assumptions, we can disregard any integration constants. These will be finite and thus insignificant during a infinitesimal time duration. Now we have a simple relation between the collision impulse and the changes in linear and angular velocities

$$\boldsymbol{J}^{A}(\gamma) = m_A \Delta \boldsymbol{v}_{\text{cm}}^{A}(\gamma), \tag{6.45a}$$

$$\boldsymbol{r}^{A} \times \boldsymbol{J}^{A}(\gamma) = \boldsymbol{I}_A \Delta \boldsymbol{\omega}^{A}(\gamma). \tag{6.45b}$$

Rewriting, we end up with a couple of equations telling us how to compute the effect of an impulse on a rigid body.

Theorem 6.2 (Applying Impulse to a Rigid Body)
Applying impulse $\boldsymbol{J}$ to a rigid body changes the linear velocity $\boldsymbol{v}$ and the angular velocity $\boldsymbol{\omega}$, with the amounts:

$$\Delta \boldsymbol{v} = \frac{\boldsymbol{J}}{m}, \tag{6.46a}$$

$$\Delta \boldsymbol{\omega} = \boldsymbol{I}^{-1} \left(\boldsymbol{r} \times \boldsymbol{J}\right). \tag{6.46b}$$

We have omitted the γ-parameter and A-object label in Theorem 6.2 to make it more readable.

Previously from (6.12), we know how to compute the contact-point velocity on object A

$$\dot{\boldsymbol{p}}^{A}(\gamma) = \boldsymbol{\omega}^{A}(\gamma) \times \boldsymbol{r}^{A} + \boldsymbol{v}_{\text{cm}}^{A}(\gamma). \tag{6.47}$$

Therefore, the change in contact-point velocity must be

$$\Delta \dot{\boldsymbol{p}}^{\,A}(\gamma) = \Delta \boldsymbol{\omega}^{\,A}(\gamma) \times \boldsymbol{r}^{\,A} + \Delta \boldsymbol{v}_{\text{cm}}^{A}(\gamma), \tag{6.48}$$

substituting (6.46) for $\Delta \boldsymbol{\omega}^{\,A}$ and $\Delta \boldsymbol{v}_{\text{cm}}^{A}$, we have

$$\Delta \dot{\boldsymbol{p}}^{\,A}(\gamma) = \left(\boldsymbol{I}_A^{-1} \left(\boldsymbol{r}^{\,A} \times \boldsymbol{J}^{\,A}(\gamma) \right) \right) \times \boldsymbol{r}^{\,A} + \frac{\boldsymbol{J}^{\,A}(\gamma)}{m_A}, \tag{6.49}$$

using the cross product matrix (18.65) and letting $\mathbf{1}$ be the identify matrix, we have

$$\Delta \dot{\boldsymbol{p}}^{\,A}(\gamma) = \left(\frac{1}{m_A} \mathbf{1} - \left(\boldsymbol{r}^{\boldsymbol{A}}\right)^{\times} \boldsymbol{I}_A^{-1} \left(\boldsymbol{r}^{\boldsymbol{A}}\right)^{\times} \right) \boldsymbol{J}^{\,A}(\gamma). \tag{6.50}$$

If we do the same thing for object B, then we have

$$\Delta \dot{\boldsymbol{p}}^{\,B}(\gamma) = \left(\frac{1}{m_B} \mathbf{1} - \left(\boldsymbol{r}^{\boldsymbol{B}}\right)^{\times} \boldsymbol{I}_B^{-1} \left(\boldsymbol{r}^{\boldsymbol{B}}\right)^{\times} \right) \boldsymbol{J}^{\,B}(\gamma). \tag{6.51}$$

Recall that $\boldsymbol{J}^B = -\boldsymbol{J}^A$ so

$$\Delta \dot{\boldsymbol{p}}^{\,B}(\gamma) = -\left(\frac{1}{m_B} \mathbf{1} + \left(\boldsymbol{r}^{\boldsymbol{B}}\right)^{\times} \boldsymbol{I}_B^{-1} \left(\boldsymbol{r}^{\boldsymbol{B}}\right)^{\times} \right) \boldsymbol{J}^{\,A}(\gamma). \tag{6.52}$$

Using (6.13), we can write the change in relative contact velocity as

$$\Delta \boldsymbol{u}(\gamma) = \Delta \dot{\boldsymbol{p}}^{\,A}(\gamma) - \Delta \dot{\boldsymbol{p}}^{\,B}(\gamma), \tag{6.53}$$

substitution of (6.50) and (6.52) into (6.53), we have

$$\Delta \boldsymbol{u}(\gamma) = \underbrace{\left(\left(\frac{1}{m_A} + \frac{1}{m_B} \right) \mathbf{1} - \left(\left(\boldsymbol{r}^{\boldsymbol{A}}\right)^{\times} \boldsymbol{I}_A^{-1} \left(\boldsymbol{r}^{\boldsymbol{A}}\right)^{\times} + \left(\boldsymbol{r}^{\boldsymbol{B}}\right)^{\times} \boldsymbol{I}_B^{-1} \left(\boldsymbol{r}^{\boldsymbol{B}}\right)^{\times} \right) \right)}_{\boldsymbol{K}} \boldsymbol{J}^{\,A}(\gamma). \tag{6.54}$$

We have derived the algebraic form of the impulse-momentum relation.

Theorem 6.3 (The Impulse-Momentum Relation)
The change in relative contact velocity between two rigid bodies is given by

$$\Delta \boldsymbol{u}(\gamma) = \boldsymbol{K}\boldsymbol{J}(\gamma), \tag{6.55}$$

where $\boldsymbol{K}$ *is the collision matrix and is given by*

$$\boldsymbol{K} = \left(\frac{1}{m_A} + \frac{1}{m_B} \right) \mathbf{1} - \left(\left(\boldsymbol{r}^{\boldsymbol{A}}\right)^{\times} \boldsymbol{I}_A^{-1} \left(\boldsymbol{r}^{\boldsymbol{A}}\right)^{\times} + \left(\boldsymbol{r}^{\boldsymbol{B}}\right)^{\times} \boldsymbol{I}_B^{-1} \left(\boldsymbol{r}^{\boldsymbol{B}}\right)^{\times} \right). \tag{6.56}$$

In this form the impulse-momentum relation is often used as the contact model for algebraic collision laws.

Theorem 6.4 (Properties of the Collision Matrix)
The collision matrix $\boldsymbol{K}$ is

- *constant*
- *symmetric*
- *positive definite*
- *invertible*

Properties of the Collision Matrix:
Looking at (6.56) we see that the collision matrix is constant because all terms in this equation are constant before, during, and after a collision according to the rigid body assumptions in Definition 6.1.

Looking closely at (6.56) we see that it consists of the summation of three kinds of matrices, that is, we can write the collision matrix as

$$\boldsymbol{K} = \boldsymbol{M} + \boldsymbol{A}_A + \boldsymbol{A}_B, \tag{6.57}$$

where

$$\boldsymbol{M} = \left(\frac{1}{m_A} + \frac{1}{m_B}\right)\boldsymbol{1}, \tag{6.58a}$$
$$\boldsymbol{A}_A = -\left(\boldsymbol{r}^{\boldsymbol{A}}\right)^{\times} \boldsymbol{I}_A^{-1} \left(\boldsymbol{r}^{\boldsymbol{A}}\right)^{\times}, \tag{6.58b}$$
$$\boldsymbol{A}_B = -\left(\boldsymbol{r}^{\boldsymbol{B}}\right)^{\times} \boldsymbol{I}_B^{-1} \left(\boldsymbol{r}^{\boldsymbol{B}}\right)^{\times}. \tag{6.58c}$$

Looking closely at the types (6.58b) and (6.58c), we see that the transpose of $\boldsymbol{A}_X$ is

$$\boldsymbol{A}_X^T = -\left(\left(\boldsymbol{r}^{\boldsymbol{X}}\right)^{\times} \boldsymbol{I}_X^{-1} \left(\boldsymbol{r}^{\boldsymbol{X}}\right)^{\times}\right)^T, \tag{6.59a}$$
$$= -\left(\left(\boldsymbol{r}^{\boldsymbol{X}}\right)^{\times}\right)^T \left(\boldsymbol{I}_X^{-1}\right)^T \left(\left(\boldsymbol{r}^{\boldsymbol{X}}\right)^{\times}\right)^T, \tag{6.59b}$$
$$= -\left(\boldsymbol{r}^{\boldsymbol{X}}\right)^{\times} \boldsymbol{I}_X^{-1} \left(\boldsymbol{r}^{\boldsymbol{X}}\right)^{\times}, \tag{6.59c}$$
$$= \boldsymbol{A}_X. \tag{6.59d}$$

The last step in the derivation follows from the fact that the inertia tensor is a symmetric matrix and the cross product matrix is skew symmetric. In conclusion, the $\boldsymbol{A}_X$-matrices are symmetric. The $\boldsymbol{K}$-matrix consists of the sum of three symmetric matrices and is therefore itself symmetric.

Now we will show that $\boldsymbol{A}_X$-matrices are positive semidefinite. Given any $\boldsymbol{v} \neq \boldsymbol{0}$, we have

$$\boldsymbol{v}^T \boldsymbol{A}_X \boldsymbol{v} = \boldsymbol{v}^T \left(-(\boldsymbol{r}^{\boldsymbol{X}})^\times \boldsymbol{I}_X^{-1} (\boldsymbol{r}^{\boldsymbol{X}})^\times \right) \boldsymbol{v}, \tag{6.60a}$$

$$= -\boldsymbol{v}^T (\boldsymbol{r}^{\boldsymbol{X}})^\times \boldsymbol{I}_X^{-1} (\boldsymbol{r}^{\boldsymbol{X}})^\times \boldsymbol{v}, \tag{6.60b}$$

$$= \left(\underbrace{(\boldsymbol{r}^{\boldsymbol{X}})^\times \boldsymbol{v}}_{\boldsymbol{w}} \right)^T \boldsymbol{I}_X^{-1} \left(\underbrace{(\boldsymbol{r}^{\boldsymbol{X}})^\times \boldsymbol{v}}_{\boldsymbol{w}} \right), \tag{6.60c}$$

$$= \boldsymbol{w}^T \boldsymbol{I}_X^{-1} \boldsymbol{w} \geq 0. \tag{6.60d}$$

The inertia tensor is known to be positive definite, that means for any vector $\boldsymbol{w} \neq \boldsymbol{0}$, we have $\boldsymbol{w}^T \boldsymbol{I}_X^{-1} \boldsymbol{w} > 0$, if $\boldsymbol{w} = \boldsymbol{0}$, then obviously $\boldsymbol{w}^T \boldsymbol{I}_X^{-1} \boldsymbol{w} = 0$. Thus, we realize that

$$\boldsymbol{v}^T \boldsymbol{A}_X \boldsymbol{v} = \boldsymbol{w}^T \boldsymbol{I}_X^{-1} \boldsymbol{w} \geq 0, \tag{6.61}$$

which is the definition of a positive semidefinite matrix. In conclusion, the $\boldsymbol{A}_X$-matrix is positive semidefinite.

This means that $\boldsymbol{K}$-matrix is the sum of a positive definite matrix $\boldsymbol{M}$-matrix and two positive semidefinite matrices $\boldsymbol{A}_A$ and $\boldsymbol{A}_B$, from which we conclude that the $\boldsymbol{K}$-matrix is positive definite. And since $\boldsymbol{K}$ is positive definite it is also invertible. □

From (6.55), we have

$$\Delta \boldsymbol{u}(\gamma) = \boldsymbol{K}\boldsymbol{J}(\gamma), \tag{6.62a}$$

$$\boldsymbol{u}(\gamma) - \boldsymbol{u}(\gamma_i) = \boldsymbol{K}\boldsymbol{J}(\gamma). \tag{6.62b}$$

If we differentiate with respect to γ, then we get

$$\frac{d}{d\gamma}\boldsymbol{u}(\gamma) - \frac{d}{d\gamma}\boldsymbol{u}(\gamma_i) = \boldsymbol{K}\frac{d}{d\gamma}\boldsymbol{J}(\gamma), \tag{6.63a}$$

$$\frac{d}{d\gamma}\boldsymbol{u}(\gamma) = \boldsymbol{K}\frac{d}{d\gamma}\boldsymbol{J}(\gamma), \tag{6.63b}$$

because $\boldsymbol{u}(\gamma_i)$ and $\boldsymbol{K}$ are constants. Since $\boldsymbol{K}$ is invertible, we have

$$\frac{d}{d\gamma}\boldsymbol{J}(\gamma) = \boldsymbol{K}^{-1}\frac{d}{d\gamma}\boldsymbol{u}(\gamma). \tag{6.64}$$

These are the differential forms of the impulse-momentum relation.

Theorem 6.5 (Differential Form of Impulse-Momentum Relation)
Given two objects, the impulse-momentum relation can be written in differential form as either of the equations

$$\frac{d}{d\gamma}\boldsymbol{u}(\gamma) = \boldsymbol{K}\frac{d}{d\gamma}\boldsymbol{J}(\gamma), \tag{6.65}$$

$$\frac{d}{d\gamma}\boldsymbol{J}(\gamma) = \boldsymbol{K}^{-1}\frac{d}{d\gamma}\boldsymbol{u}(\gamma). \tag{6.66}$$

This form is often used as the contact model in incremental laws. Note that substitution of (6.66) into (6.35) yields

$$W = \int_0^{\gamma_f} \boldsymbol{u}(\gamma) \cdot \boldsymbol{K}^{-1} \frac{d}{d\gamma} \boldsymbol{u}(\gamma) d\gamma, \tag{6.67}$$

thus it becomes an integral only in the variable $\boldsymbol{u}(\gamma)$.

6.1.3 The Permissible Region in Impulse Space

Now we will start to describe the region in *impulse space*, where collision impulses yield physically plausible results. For this we will need two reference impulses and a definition of *kinetic contact energy*. Before doing so, we will introduce the shorthand notation $\boldsymbol{u}_i = \boldsymbol{u}(\gamma_i)$ and $\boldsymbol{u}_f = \boldsymbol{u}(\gamma_f)$.

Theorem 6.6 (Plastic Sliding Impulse)
A perfect plastic sliding impulse is given by

$$\boldsymbol{J}_I = -\left(\frac{\boldsymbol{n}^T \boldsymbol{u}_i}{\boldsymbol{n}^T \boldsymbol{K} \boldsymbol{n}}\right) \boldsymbol{n}. \tag{6.68}$$

The relative normal contact velocity is zero and tangential contact velocity *is unchanged when this impulse is applied.*

Plastic Sliding Impulse:
Substitution of (6.68) into (6.55) yields

$$\boldsymbol{u}_f = \boldsymbol{K} \boldsymbol{J}_I + \boldsymbol{u}_i, \tag{6.69a}$$

$$= \boldsymbol{K} \left(\frac{-\boldsymbol{n}^T \boldsymbol{u}_i}{\boldsymbol{n}^T \boldsymbol{K} \boldsymbol{n}}\right) \boldsymbol{n} + \boldsymbol{u}_i. \tag{6.69b}$$

We'll take the dot product with $\boldsymbol{n}$, that is

$$\boldsymbol{u}_f \cdot \boldsymbol{n} = \left(\boldsymbol{K} \left(\frac{-\boldsymbol{n}^T \boldsymbol{u}_i}{\boldsymbol{n}^T \boldsymbol{K} \boldsymbol{n}}\right) \boldsymbol{n}\right) \cdot \boldsymbol{n} + \boldsymbol{u}_i \cdot \boldsymbol{n}, \tag{6.70a}$$

$$= -\boldsymbol{n}^T \boldsymbol{u}_i \frac{(\boldsymbol{K}\boldsymbol{n})^T \boldsymbol{n}}{\boldsymbol{n}^T \boldsymbol{K} \boldsymbol{n}} + \boldsymbol{u}_i \cdot \boldsymbol{n}, \tag{6.70b}$$

$$= -\boldsymbol{n}^T \boldsymbol{u}_i \frac{\boldsymbol{n}^T \boldsymbol{K} \boldsymbol{n}}{\boldsymbol{n}^T \boldsymbol{K} \boldsymbol{n}} + \boldsymbol{u}_i \cdot \boldsymbol{n} = 0. \tag{6.70c}$$

In the last step we used that $\boldsymbol{K}$-matrix is symmetric. From the above, we see that the $\boldsymbol{J}_I$ impulse results in a final zero relative contact normal velocity as wanted. Now we'll take the dot product with a contact plane tangent vector, $\boldsymbol{t}$

$$\boldsymbol{u}_f \cdot \boldsymbol{t} = \left(\boldsymbol{K} \frac{-\boldsymbol{n}^T \boldsymbol{u}_i}{\boldsymbol{n}^T \boldsymbol{K} \boldsymbol{n}}\right) \underbrace{\boldsymbol{n} \cdot \boldsymbol{t}}_{0} + \boldsymbol{u}_i \cdot \boldsymbol{t}, \tag{6.71a}$$

$$= \boldsymbol{u}_i \cdot \boldsymbol{t}. \tag{6.71b}$$

We see that the relative contact velocity in the contact plane is unchanged by the impulse $\boldsymbol{J}_I$. □

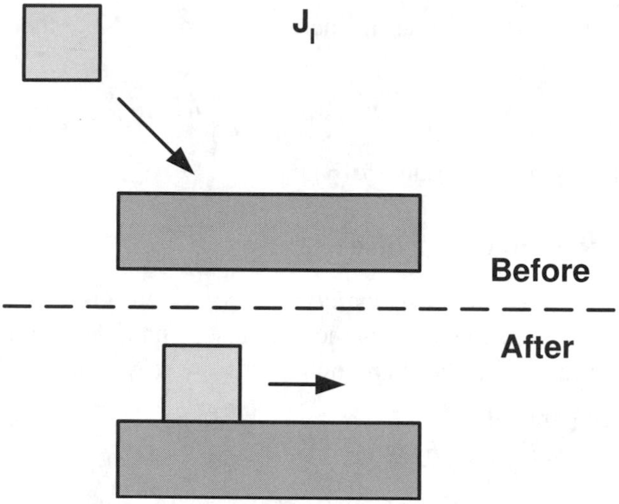

Figure 6.4: Perfect plastic sliding impulse makes normal relative contact velocity, but leaves tangential relative contact velocity unchanged.

A perfectly plastic sliding impulse is illustrated in Figure 6.4.

Theorem 6.7 (Plastic Sticking Impulse)
A perfect plastic sticking impulse is given by

$$\boldsymbol{J}_{II} = -\boldsymbol{K}^{-1}\boldsymbol{u}_i. \tag{6.72}$$

The relative normal contact velocity is zero and so is the tangential contact velocity after applying this impulse.

Plastic Sticking Impulse:
Substitution of (6.72) into (6.55) yields

$$\boldsymbol{u}_f = \boldsymbol{K}\boldsymbol{J}_{\mathrm{II}} + \boldsymbol{u}_i, \tag{6.73a}$$
$$= \boldsymbol{K}\left(-\boldsymbol{K}^{-1}\boldsymbol{u}_i\right) + \boldsymbol{u}_i, \tag{6.73b}$$
$$= -\boldsymbol{K}\boldsymbol{K}^{-1}\boldsymbol{u}_i + \boldsymbol{u}_i, \tag{6.73c}$$
$$= -\boldsymbol{u}_i + \boldsymbol{u}_i = \boldsymbol{0}. \tag{6.73d}$$

That is, the final relative contact velocity is zero, which is what we wanted to show. □

A perfectly plastic sticking impulse is illustrated in Figure 6.5. We can define a quantity called the kinetic contact energy as follows.

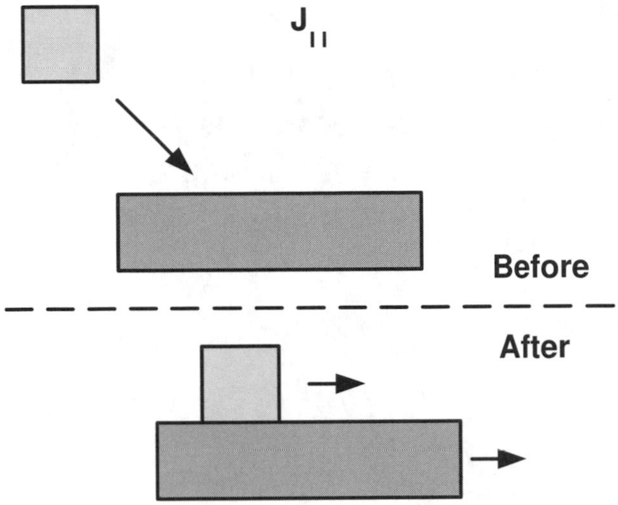

Figure 6.5: Perfect plastic sticking impulse makes relative contact velocity zero.

Definition 6.3 (The Kinetic Contact Energy)
Given the relative contact velocity $\boldsymbol{u}$ and the collision matrix $\boldsymbol{K}$, the kinetic contact energy E_c, is defined as

$$E_c \equiv \frac{1}{2}\boldsymbol{u}_f^T \boldsymbol{K}^{-1}\boldsymbol{u}_f. \tag{6.74}$$

The kinetic contact energy looks nothing like the kinetic energy, as described in Section 22.3, which is

$$E_{\text{kin}} = \frac{1}{2}m_A \boldsymbol{v}_{\text{cm}}^A \cdot \boldsymbol{v}_{\text{cm}}^A + \frac{1}{2}\left(\boldsymbol{\omega}^A\right)^T \boldsymbol{I}_A \boldsymbol{\omega}^A + \frac{1}{2}m_B \boldsymbol{v}_{\text{cm}}^B \cdot \boldsymbol{v}_{\text{cm}}^B + \frac{1}{2}\left(\boldsymbol{\omega}^B\right)^T \boldsymbol{I}_B \boldsymbol{\omega}^B. \tag{6.75}$$

In fact, it is quite trivial that $E_c \neq E_{\text{kin}}$, however, we are interested in measuring changes in energy, not absolute values. It turns out that a change in the kinetic contact energy is equal to a change in the kinetic energy. Thus, the two types of energy are equivalent except for a constant offset.

Theorem 6.8 (Change in E_{kin} is equal to change in E_c)
If the change in relative contact velocity is Δu, then the change in kinetic contact energy

$$\Delta E_c = \frac{1}{2}\Delta u^T \boldsymbol{K}^{-1}\Delta u, \tag{6.76}$$

and the change in kinetic energy ΔE_{kin} are equal, that is,

$$\Delta E_{kin} = \Delta E_c, \tag{6.77}$$

as mentioned in [Chatterjee et al., 1998].

From the impulse-momentum relation (6.55), we have

$$J = K^{-1}(u - u_i), \tag{6.78a}$$
$$J = K^{-1}u - K^{-1}u_i, \tag{6.78b}$$
$$J = K^{-1}u + J_{\text{II}}, \tag{6.78c}$$
$$J - J_{II} = K^{-1}u, \tag{6.78d}$$
$$u = K(J - J_{\text{II}}). \tag{6.78e}$$

Inserting (6.78e) into (6.76) yields

$$E_c = \frac{1}{2}(K(J - J_{II}))^T K^{-1}(K(J - J_{II})), \tag{6.79a}$$
$$E_c = \frac{1}{2}(J - J_{II})^T K(J - J_{II}). \tag{6.79b}$$

Now we have an expression for the kinetic contact energy, E_c, in impulse space.

Theorem 6.9 (The Kinetic Contact Energy in Impulse Space)
Given the collision impulse J between two objects, the kinetic contact energy is given by

$$E_c = \frac{1}{2}(J - J_{II})^T K(J - J_{II}). \tag{6.80}$$

The impulse J_{II} works as a reference point for kinetic contact energy.

Image $J = 0$, then inserting into (6.80) gives

$$E_c = \frac{1}{2}J_{\text{II}}^T K J_{\text{II}}, \tag{6.81a}$$
$$= \frac{1}{2}\left(K^1 u_i\right)^T K K^1 u_i, \tag{6.81b}$$
$$= \frac{1}{2}u_i^T K^1 u_i = E_i. \tag{6.81c}$$

We have discovered the initial kinetic contact energy E_i, that is, the available amount of energy. It would be very unphysical if E_c ever were larger than E_i, since it would indicate an energy gain coming from nowhere.

Theorem 6.10 (The initial Kinetic Contact Energy)
The initial kinetic contact energy, E_i, is given by

$$E_i = \frac{1}{2}u_i^T K^1 u_i. \tag{6.82}$$

If we keep a fixed value of energy E, and try to find all vectors J yielding that energy, we will find an elliptical surface in impulse space. This follows from the fact that K-matrix is positive definite, as was proven in Theorem 6.4, and Proposition 18.11.

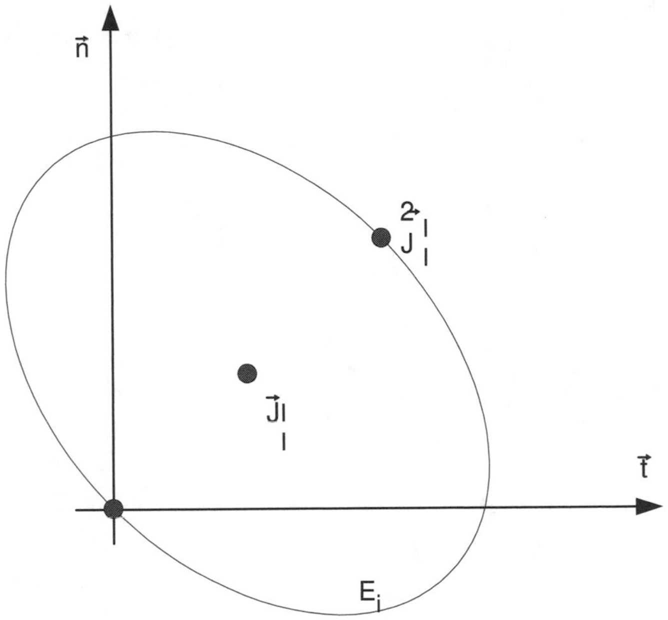

Figure 6.6: Elliptic level set surface corresponding to the initial kinetic contact energy.

Theorem 6.11 (Elliptical Kinetic Contact Energy Level Set Surface)
Given a fixed value of kinetic energy E, all impulse vectors $\boldsymbol{J}$ yielding this energy lie on an elliptical surface in impulse space.

The fact that a given energy level is an ellipsoid is very useful for a geometric interpretation of a collision. We can simply draw elliptic level set surfaces for fixed values of E. In particular, E_i is interesting because if it has an impulse outside this initial energy ellipsoid, it indicates an energy gain, which is unphysical. Figure 6.6 illustrates the initial energy ellipsoid in two dimensions. Notice that the impulse $\boldsymbol{J} = \boldsymbol{0}$ lies on the level set surface of E_i and the impulse J_{II} lies at the center of the ellipsoid. It is easily verified that the impulse $2\boldsymbol{J}_{\text{II}}$ also lies on E_i

$$E_c = \frac{1}{2}\left(2\boldsymbol{J}_{\text{II}} - \boldsymbol{J}_{\text{II}}\right)^T \boldsymbol{K}\left(2\boldsymbol{J}_{\text{II}} - \boldsymbol{J}_{\text{II}}\right), \tag{6.83a}$$

$$= \frac{1}{2}\boldsymbol{J}_{\text{II}}^T \boldsymbol{K} \boldsymbol{J}_{\text{II}}, \tag{6.83b}$$

$$= \frac{1}{2}\left(\boldsymbol{K}^1 \boldsymbol{u}_i\right)^T \boldsymbol{K}\boldsymbol{K}^1 \boldsymbol{u}_i, \tag{6.83c}$$

$$= \frac{1}{2}\boldsymbol{u}_i^T \boldsymbol{K}^1 \boldsymbol{u}_i = E_i. \tag{6.83d}$$

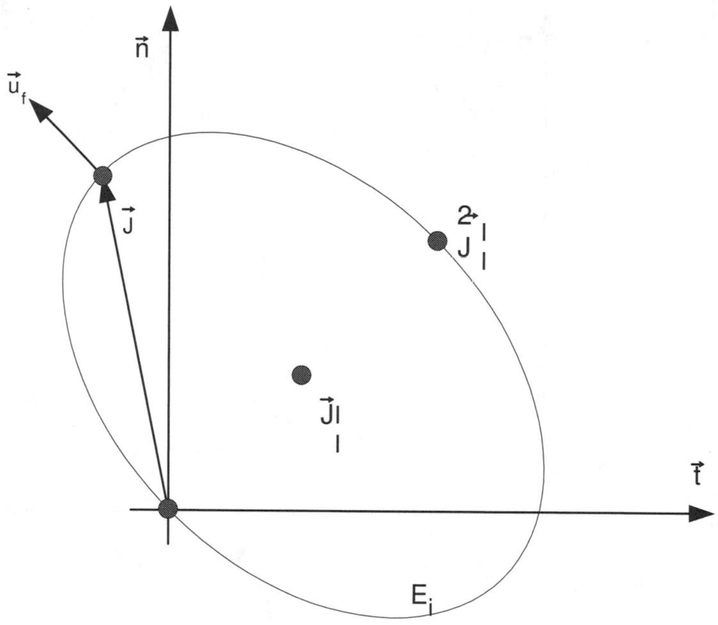

Figure 6.7: Given impulse $\boldsymbol{J}$, resulting relative contact velocity from applying that impulse is equal to normal of energy level set surface.

Given any collision matrix $\boldsymbol{K}$, one can easily draw the initial energy ellipsoid by computing $\boldsymbol{J}_{\mathrm{II}}$, then perform an eigenvalue decomposition on $\boldsymbol{K}$. The eigenvectors will yield the orientation of the axes of the ellipsoid, and the eigenvalues the scalings along these axes (see Theorem 18.12). This implies that one draws a unit sphere, scales it by the eigenvalues of the $\boldsymbol{K}$-matrix, uses the eigenvectors of the $\boldsymbol{K}$-matrix as columns in a rotation matrix, applies the rotation to the sphere, and finally performs a translation by the impulse $\boldsymbol{J}_{\mathrm{II}}$.

We'll try to compute the normal of an energy level set surface E_c,

$$\nabla E_c = \boldsymbol{K}\left(\boldsymbol{J} - \boldsymbol{J}_{\mathrm{II}}\right), \tag{6.84a}$$

$$\nabla E_c = \boldsymbol{K}\boldsymbol{K}^{-1}\boldsymbol{u}, \tag{6.84b}$$

$$\nabla E_c = \boldsymbol{u}. \tag{6.84c}$$

So given an impulse $\boldsymbol{J}$ we can find the resulting relative contact velocity by looking at the normal at the point of the level set surface where $\boldsymbol{J}$ touches. This is illustrated in Figure 6.7.

Theorem 6.12 (The Normal of the Elliptical Kinetic Contact Energy Surface)
Given an impulse $\boldsymbol{J}$, resulting in the kinetic contact energy E_c, the resulting relative contact velocity is given by the normal to the elliptical surface corresponding to E_c at the point where $\boldsymbol{J}$ touches the level

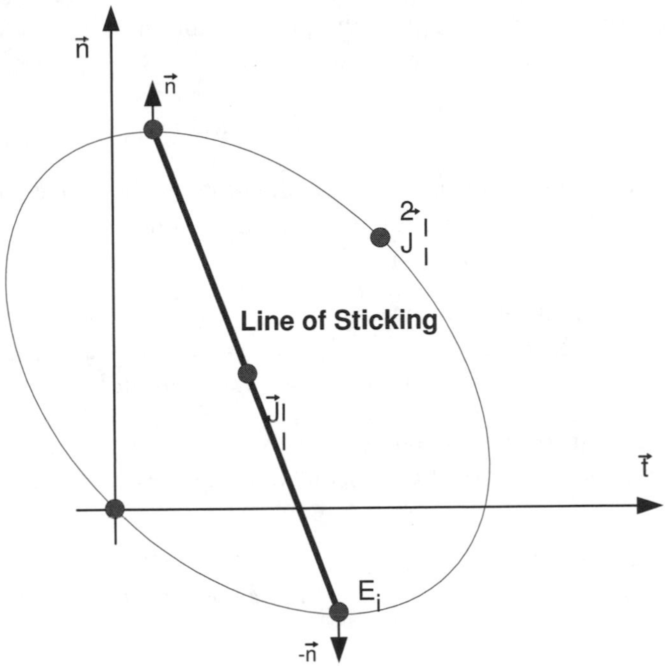

Figure 6.8: Line of sticking, corresponding to impulses that results in zero final relative tangential contact velocity.

set surface. That is

$$\boldsymbol{u} = \nabla E_c. \tag{6.85}$$

Theorem 6.12 gives us another powerful tool for interpreting the effect of certain impulses by geometric constructs. In the following, we will apply this tool to find a line of sticking and a plane of maximum compression.

We define a line running through the point $\boldsymbol{J}_{\text{II}}$ in impulse space and crossing all the kinetic energy level set surfaces at the two points where their normals are parallel to the contact normal. Every impulse that lies on this line yields a resulting final relative contact velocity with no components in the contact plane. This implies that the two objects will not move relatively in the tangent plane after the collision. In other words, they are sticking. We therefore call the line: line of Sticking.

Theorem 6.13 (Line of Sticking)
The line of sticking runs through the point $\boldsymbol{J}_{II}$ and cuts the energy level set surfaces where their normal is parallel with the contact normal.

The line of sticking is illustrated in Figure 6.8. Observe that on the line of sticking we always have $\boldsymbol{u}_f \parallel \boldsymbol{n}$.

In similar fashion to the line of sticking, we define a plane in impulse space. The plane has the point $\boldsymbol{J}_{\text{II}}$ lying on it, and every point belonging to the plane results in final relative contact velocity that is orthogonal to the contact normal. We can write this as

$$\boldsymbol{n}^T \boldsymbol{u} = \boldsymbol{n}^T \left(\boldsymbol{K}\boldsymbol{J} + \boldsymbol{u}_i \right) = 0. \tag{6.86}$$

Looking at a specific energy level set surface in 3D, all points on the surface having a normal orthogonal to the contact normal lie on an elliptical circle and the circle is planar. According to (6.15), we call this plane the Plane of Maximum Compression.

Theorem 6.14 (Plane of Maximum Compression)
The plane of maximum compression is given by all points in impulse space where the normal of the kinetic contact energy level set surfaces are orthogonal to the contact normal.

Note that in 2D, the plane of maximum compression is a line and not a plane. Another property of the plane of maximum compression is that it corresponds to impulses where the coefficient of restitution is zero.

Theorem 6.15 (Zero Restitution)
For all points $\boldsymbol{J}$ on a plane of maximum compression, the coefficient of restitution e, has the value

$$e = 0. \tag{6.87}$$

The plane of maximum compression is illustrated in 2D in Figure 6.9. The impulse $\boldsymbol{J}_I$ must lie on the $\boldsymbol{n}$-axis and it also must lie in the plane of maximum compression, so we can draw $\boldsymbol{J}_I$ where the $\boldsymbol{n}$-axis intersects the plane of maximum compression. The impulse $2\boldsymbol{J}_I$ also lies on the $\boldsymbol{n}$-axis and it conserves energy, so we can draw it where the $\boldsymbol{n}$-axis crosses the initial kinetic contact energy level set surface, E_i. Note the coefficient of restitution is one for $2\boldsymbol{J}_I$. The two impulses $\boldsymbol{J}_I$ and $2\boldsymbol{J}_I$ are shown in Figure 6.10 Observe that both $\boldsymbol{J}_I$ and $\boldsymbol{J}_{\text{II}}$ lie in the plane of maximum compression.

Finally, we will interpret the physical laws in terms of geometry in the impulse space. First there should not be any energy gain, this is equivalent to

$$E_c \leq E_i \tag{6.88}$$

and implies that any resulting collision impulse must lie inside or on the ellipse given by E_i. Second, collision impulses cannot attract objects to each other; they must be repulsive. This implies that the collision impulse must not point in the opposite direction of the contact normal, that is

$$\boldsymbol{n}^T \boldsymbol{J} \geq 0. \tag{6.89}$$

Geometrically, this means that collision impulses are restricted to lie above or on the contact plane. Third, the collision impulse should result in a final relative contact velocity, such that the two objects will not penetrate, that is, we require nonpenetration, which means that

$$\boldsymbol{n}^T \boldsymbol{u}_f \geq 0. \tag{6.90}$$

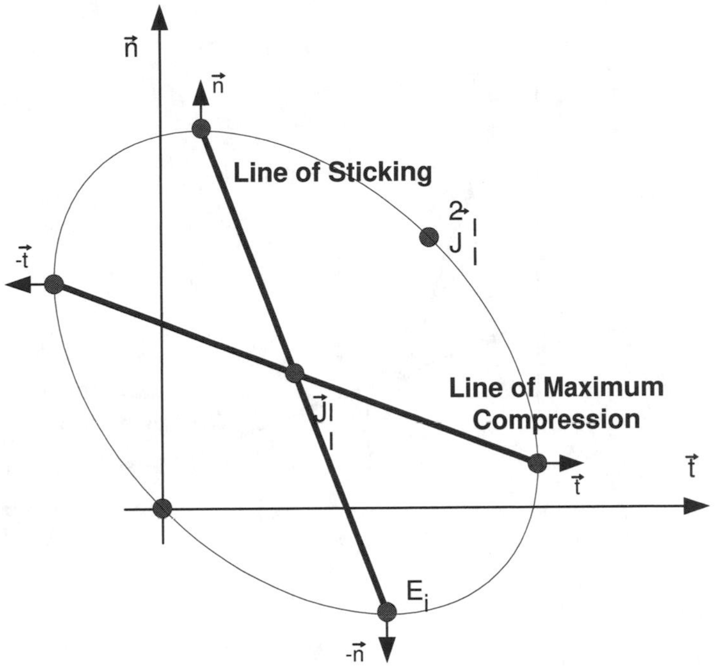

Figure 6.9: Plane of Maximum Compression. This corresponds to zero restitution.

This implies that the impulse must lie on or above the plane of maximum compression. Finally, Coulomb's friction law dictates that the impulse should be inside or on the cone defined by

$$\|\boldsymbol{J} - (\boldsymbol{n} \cdot \boldsymbol{J}) \cdot \boldsymbol{n}\| \leq \mu (\boldsymbol{n} \cdot \boldsymbol{J}) . \tag{6.91}$$

That is, the cone with apex at the origin and sides with slope equal to $\frac{1}{\mu}$. This cone is called the *friction cone*. Applying these four conditions, we end up with a region in impulse space. The region describes the set of all impulses, which make physical sense to apply in a single-point collision. This *permissible region in impulse space* is illustrated in Figure 6.11. We can learn several things from the permissible region of impulse space; first it is a closed 3D space, in fact it is a spherical bounded cone, intersected by the contact plane and the plane of maximum compression. To parameterize the permissible region requires three parameters. This is remarkable because most collision laws in use only have one or two parameters, which means that they cannot reach the full domain of the permissible region. Often they are limited to a line or plane in the permissible region.

Another observation is that it is possible to have a restitution value larger than one, without being in conflict with the physics. This is shown in Figure 6.11, the impulses $2\boldsymbol{J}_I$ and $2\boldsymbol{J}_{\text{II}}$ have $e = 1$. In fact, all impulses lying on the line between $2\boldsymbol{J}_I$ and $2\boldsymbol{J}_{\text{II}}$ have $e = 1$. This means that impulses lying above this line have $e > 1$. It is assumed that coefficient of restitution is a measure of how much the relative normal

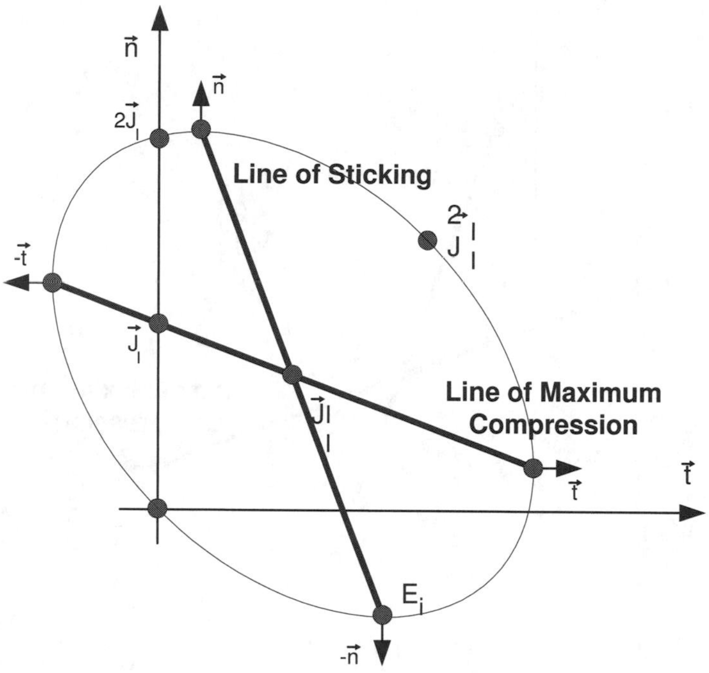

Figure 6.10: The two impulses $\boldsymbol{J}_I$ and $2\boldsymbol{J}_I$.

contact velocity is reversed after the collision.

The geometrical interpretation of physically valid impulses can be used to correct physical invalid collision impulses, simply by projecting these back onto the closest point on the permissible region.

6.1.4 Examples of Algebraic Laws

Now we will derive three examples of simple algebraic collision laws: Newton's collision law, a two-parameter frictional law, and a frictional version of Newton's collision law.

6.1.4.1 Newton's Collision Law

We assume that the collision impulse is parallel with the $\boldsymbol{n}$-axis, that is

$$\boldsymbol{J} = j\boldsymbol{n}, \tag{6.92}$$

where j is the magnitude of the collision impulse. We will also assume that only the relative contact velocity in the normal direction changes. From Newton's impact law we have

$$u_n(\gamma_f) = -eu_n(\gamma_i). \tag{6.93}$$

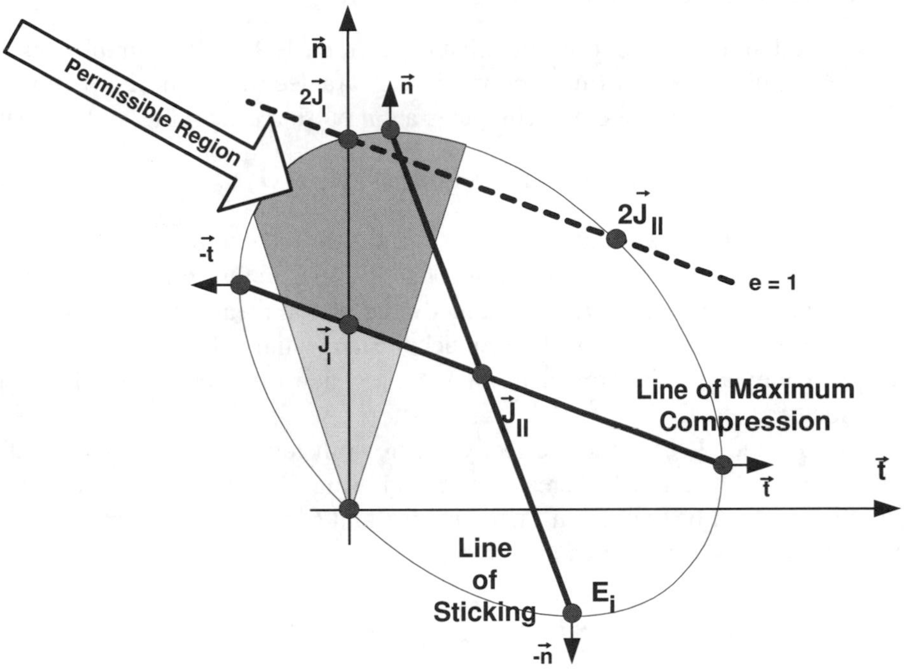

Figure 6.11: The permissible region in impulse space.

So the change in relative contact velocity in the normal direction can be written as

$$\Delta \boldsymbol{u} \cdot \boldsymbol{n} = u_n(\gamma_f) - u_n(\gamma_i), \tag{6.94a}$$

$$\Delta \boldsymbol{u} \cdot \boldsymbol{n} = -e u_n(\gamma_i) - u_n(\gamma_i), \tag{6.94b}$$

$$\Delta \boldsymbol{u} \cdot \boldsymbol{n} = -(1+e)\boldsymbol{u}_i \cdot \boldsymbol{n}. \tag{6.94c}$$

Looking at the impulse momentum relation we have

$$\Delta \boldsymbol{u} = \boldsymbol{K} j \boldsymbol{n}. \tag{6.95}$$

We are only interested in the normal direction, so we take the dot product with the contact normal

$$\Delta \boldsymbol{u} \cdot \boldsymbol{n} = (\boldsymbol{K} j \boldsymbol{n}) \cdot \boldsymbol{n}, \tag{6.96a}$$

$$\Delta \boldsymbol{u} \cdot \boldsymbol{n} = \boldsymbol{n}^T \boldsymbol{K} \boldsymbol{n} j, \tag{6.96b}$$

isolating j we get Newton's collision law

$$j = \frac{-(1+e)\boldsymbol{u}_i \cdot \boldsymbol{n}}{\boldsymbol{n}^T \boldsymbol{K} \boldsymbol{n}}. \tag{6.97}$$

After we compute j by (6.97) we insert into (6.92) to find the resulting impulse $\boldsymbol{J}$.

6.1.4.2 A Two-Parameter Frictional and Energy Conserving Law

Now we will look at collision law proposed in [Chatterjee et al., 1998]. It is simple, fast, and includes friction as well as reversible impacts. Furthermore, it is guaranteed to be in the permissible region of impulse space. In the Collision Law, one first computes an impulse $\boldsymbol{J}$ according to the equation

$$\boldsymbol{J} = (1 + e_n)\,\boldsymbol{J}_I + (1 + e_t)\,(\boldsymbol{J}_{\text{II}} - \boldsymbol{J}_I)\,, \tag{6.98}$$

the coefficient e_n is the coefficient of normal restitution and e_t is the coefficient of tangential restitution. The normal restitution coefficient tells us something about how elastic the collision is in the normal direction. A value of zero means completely inelastic and a value of one means totally elastic. The tangential restitution coefficient tells us something about how much the tangential velocity is reversed. A value of -1 will completely remove any tangential effects, turning $\boldsymbol{J}$ into a newton impulse. A value of 1 corresponds to full tangential velocity reversal.

Here the impulse $\boldsymbol{J}_I$ and $\boldsymbol{J}_{\text{II}}$ are both perfectly elastic collisions in the normal direction. The first does not affect the tangential direction, whereas the second brings the two bodies into sticking contact in the tangential direction, as can be seen from Theorems 6.6 and 6.7. For convenience, we will repeat the equations for the impulses. $\boldsymbol{J}_I$ is computed as follows

$$\boldsymbol{J}_I = -\left(\frac{\boldsymbol{n} \cdot \boldsymbol{u}}{\boldsymbol{n}^T K \boldsymbol{n}}\right)\boldsymbol{n}, \tag{6.99}$$

and $\boldsymbol{J}_{\text{II}}$ as

$$\boldsymbol{J}_{\text{II}} = -\boldsymbol{K}^{-1}\boldsymbol{u}. \tag{6.100}$$

As a final step in the Collision Law, it is tested if the impulse $\boldsymbol{J}$ lies outside the friction cone. This can be done with the following test:

$$\|\boldsymbol{J} - (\boldsymbol{n} \cdot \boldsymbol{J})\,\boldsymbol{n}\| > \mu \boldsymbol{n} \cdot \boldsymbol{J}. \tag{6.101}$$

If the impulse lies outside, then it is projected back onto the friction cone by computing κ,

$$\kappa = \frac{\mu\,(1 + e_n)\,\boldsymbol{n} \cdot \boldsymbol{J}_I}{\|\boldsymbol{J}_{II} - (\boldsymbol{n} \cdot \boldsymbol{J}_{II})\,\boldsymbol{n}\| - \mu \boldsymbol{n} \cdot (\boldsymbol{J}_{II} - \boldsymbol{J}_I)}, \tag{6.102}$$

and finally the impulse $\boldsymbol{J}$ is computed according to

$$\boldsymbol{J} = (1 + e_n)\,\boldsymbol{J}_I + \kappa\,(\boldsymbol{J}_{II} - \boldsymbol{J}_I)\,. \tag{6.103}$$

6.1.4.3 Newton's Collision Law with Friction

The next algebraic law we will describe is based on [Guendelman et al., 2003]. First we will assume sticking, that means for the final tangential relative contact velocity $\boldsymbol{u}_{t_f} = \boldsymbol{u}_t(\gamma_f)$ and the normal contact velocity $u_{n_f} = u_n(\gamma_f)$, we require that

$$\boldsymbol{u}_{t_f} = 0, \tag{6.104a}$$

$$\boldsymbol{u}_{n_f} = -e u_n(\gamma_i)\boldsymbol{n}. \tag{6.104b}$$

Now we can compute the change in relative contact velocity $\Delta u = \boldsymbol{u}_f - \boldsymbol{u}_i$, and from impulse-momentum relation (6.55), we have

$$\boldsymbol{J} = \boldsymbol{K}^{-1}(\boldsymbol{u}_f - \boldsymbol{u}_i). \tag{6.105}$$

Now we compute the normal and tangent components of the impulse, that is

$$\boldsymbol{J}_n = (\boldsymbol{J} \cdot \boldsymbol{n})\,\boldsymbol{n}, \tag{6.106a}$$
$$\boldsymbol{J}_t = \boldsymbol{J} - \boldsymbol{J}_n. \tag{6.106b}$$

If

$$\|\boldsymbol{J}_t\| \leq \|\boldsymbol{J}_n\|, \tag{6.107}$$

then the impulse $\boldsymbol{J}$ is in the friction cone and we can use it. Otherwise we need to consider sliding friction. To consider sliding friction, we first determine the direction of sliding, that is, first we compute the tangential component of the initial relative contact velocity

$$\boldsymbol{u}_{n_i} = (\boldsymbol{u}_i \cdot \boldsymbol{n})\,\boldsymbol{n}, \tag{6.108a}$$
$$\boldsymbol{u}_{t_i} = \boldsymbol{u}_i - \boldsymbol{u}_{n_i}. \tag{6.108b}$$

Now the direction of sliding can be computed as the unit vector

$$\boldsymbol{t} = \frac{\boldsymbol{u}_{t_i}}{\|\boldsymbol{u}_{t_i}\|}, \tag{6.109}$$

and we define an impulse as

$$\boldsymbol{J} = j\boldsymbol{n} - \mu j\boldsymbol{t}, \tag{6.110}$$

where j is the magnitude of the normal impulse. If we take dot product of the impulse-momentum relation and the contact normal we get

$$\boldsymbol{u}_{n_f} = \boldsymbol{u}_{n_i} + \boldsymbol{n}^T\boldsymbol{K}\boldsymbol{J}. \tag{6.111}$$

Using Newton's impact law

$$-e\boldsymbol{u}_{n_i} = \boldsymbol{u}_{n_i} + \boldsymbol{n}^T\boldsymbol{K}\boldsymbol{J}, \tag{6.112}$$

substitution of (6.110) yields

$$-e\boldsymbol{u}_{n_i} = \boldsymbol{u}_{n_i} + \boldsymbol{n}^T\boldsymbol{K}(j\boldsymbol{n} - \mu j\boldsymbol{t}). \tag{6.113}$$

Finally, we can solve for j

$$-(1+e)\,\boldsymbol{u}_{n_i} = \boldsymbol{n}^T\boldsymbol{K}(j\boldsymbol{n} - \mu j\boldsymbol{t}), \tag{6.114a}$$
$$-(1+e)\,\boldsymbol{u}_{n_i} = \boldsymbol{n}^T\boldsymbol{K}\boldsymbol{n}j - \boldsymbol{n}^T\boldsymbol{K}\boldsymbol{t}\mu j, \tag{6.114b}$$
$$-(1+e)\,\boldsymbol{u}_{n_i} = \boldsymbol{n}^T\boldsymbol{K}(\boldsymbol{n} - \boldsymbol{t}\mu)\,j, \tag{6.114c}$$
$$j = \frac{-(1+e)\,\boldsymbol{u}_{n_i}}{\boldsymbol{n}^T\boldsymbol{K}(\boldsymbol{n} - \mu\boldsymbol{t})}. \tag{6.114d}$$

Knowing j, we can insert it into (6.110) and compute the impulse $\boldsymbol{J}$.

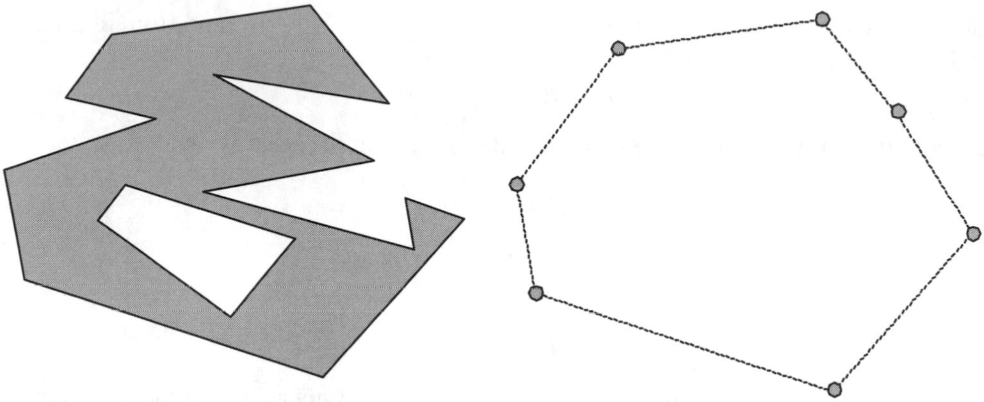

Figure 6.12: The contact force or impulse equivalence principle. The contact region on the left is replaced by a discrete finite set of points, consisting only of vertices lying on the convex hull of the contact region.

6.2 Multiple Points of Collision

The most interesting simulations in computer animation involve pairs of objects that touch each other at more than a single collision point. Even a simple cube falling flat onto a table top, has infinitely many points of contact on the face touching the table during impact. It seems that all the theories we have from single-point collisions are useless.

To avoid the problem of having infinitely many contact points, we can use the contact force/impulse equivalence principle.

Lemma 6.16 (Contact Force and Impulse Equivalence Principle)
Equivalent forces or impulses exist such that when they are applied to the convex hull of the contact region the same resulting motion is obtained, which would have resulted from integrating the true contact force or impulse over the entire contact region.

The principle is illustrated in Figure 6.12. This is a very useful principle, especially in computer animation, where contact regions often are polygonal areas. With this principle we have reduced our problem of infinitely handling many contact points to having to handle a finite discrete set of contact points only.

In a simulator there are generally two basic types of methods for handling multiple points of collisions:

- *Sequential Collisions*
- *Simultaneous Collisions*

The names may be a little misleading. There is no concept of time propagation, as there is in compliant contact models [Kraus et al., 1997]. The names reflect how impulses are computed or propagated at a single instance in time. The sequential collision approach is sometimes referred to in the literature as *propagating impulses*. The task of computing equivalent contact impulses and applying them to the rigid bodies is called collision resolving.

```
algorithm simple-sequential(C : Contacts)
  while collision
    collision = false
    for each c ∈ C
      if c is colliding then
        Resolve collision at c
        collision = true
      end if
    next c
  end while
end algorithm
```

Figure 6.13: Pseudocode of simple sequential collision resolver.

We cannot really talk about one method being more correct or better than the other because it is possible to set up physical configurations of colliding rigid bodies where one of the methods computes the wanted motion and the other does not and vice versa [Mosterman, 2001].

Most simultaneous collision methods are based on complementarity conditions at the velocity level, however it has been found that *complementarity conditions* at the velocity level have no fundamental physical basis for collisions of even extremely stiff objects [Chatterjee, 1999]. We will only treat simultaneous collisions superficially, since Chapter 7 is devoted to velocity-based complementarity formulations.

The sequential collision method is based on the idea of treating multiple concurrent single-point collisions as a series of single-point collisions. One can just continue to iterate over the single-point collisions and resolve them one by one using a suitable collision law until none of them is colliding [Baraff, 1989]. A simple sequential collision resolving algorithm is shown in Figure 6.13. The sequential collisions method suffers from some difficulties:

- Different simulation results can occur if collisions are treated in a different order
- Infinite calculations

Recent research on sequential collision resolving [Chatterjee et al., 1998, Mosterman, 2001] is concerned with the order in which the collisions are resolved and how to avoid infinite calculations. In Section 6.2.4, we present our own solution to the problem. In [Mosterman, 2001] it is shown that there is a relationship between the values of coefficient of restitution e and whether simultaneous or sequential collision resolving produces the physical expected results.

Many consider the simultaneous collision resolving to be more physical, but there is no justification for it, except perhaps that it mimics the way a physicist would solve the problem: determine the degrees of freedom, analyze forces from a free body diagram, set up equations of motion, and solve for the motion.

However, in comparison with the sequential collision resolving, the simultaneous collision resolving always produces the same global solution to a given problem. Whether the solution results in the physical expected motion is another question. The sequential collision resolving, on the other hand, solves the problem through a series of local solutions, thus there is a risk that it will never converge a global solution of the system. The sequential collision resolving is often beneficial over the simultaneous approach in

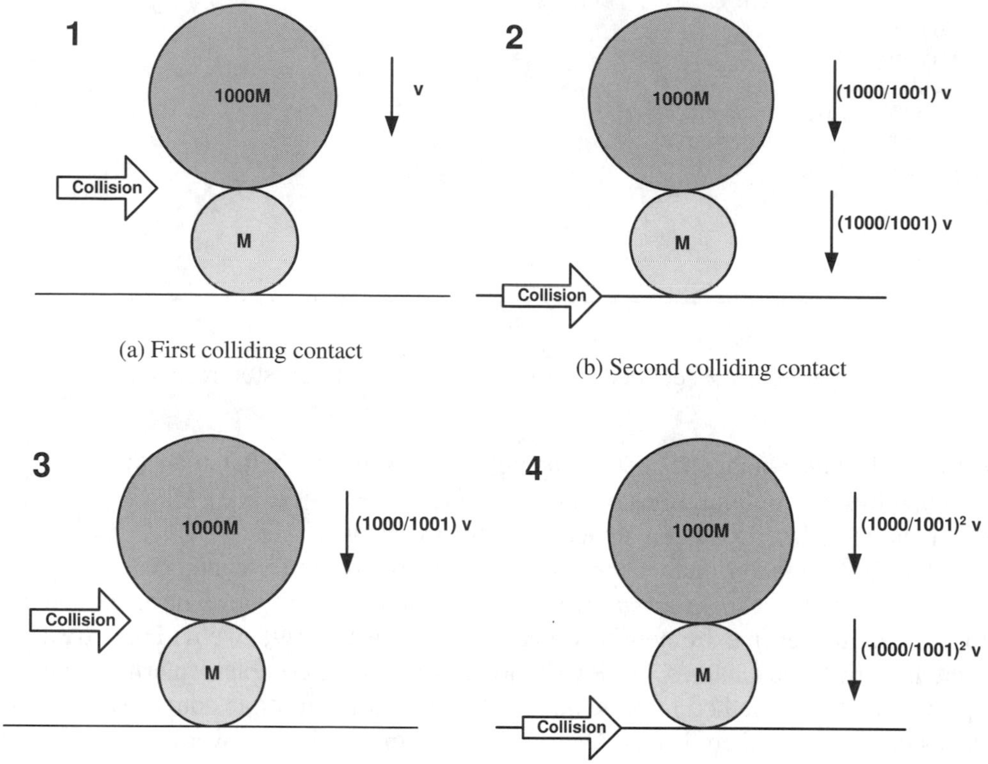

(a) First colliding contact

(b) Second colliding contact

(c) Third colliding contact

(d) Fourth colliding contact

Figure 6.14: Two balls on table, causing sequential collision solver to enter an infinite loop.

terms of computational expense. It is also capable of modeling propagation of forces/impulses through the mechanical system; the simultaneous approach totally lacks this capability.

We'll study the problems of sequential collision resolving through some simple examples.

6.2.1 Nontermination of Sequential Collision Resolving

A small ball is resting upon a fixed plane, the coefficient of restitution between the small ball and the plane is zero. A large ball is resting on top of the small ball; the density of the larger ball is 1,000 times larger than the small ball. The coefficient of restitution between the small and large ball is zero. The large ball is initially given a downward velocity of v. There is no friction in the configuration. The example configuration is illustrated in Figure 6.14. The example is completely one-dimensional, and the balls interact through central frictionless collisions, which mean that we can safely ignore any rotational motion. We have two contact points, the first contact point is between the table and the small ball, the second contact point is between the two balls.

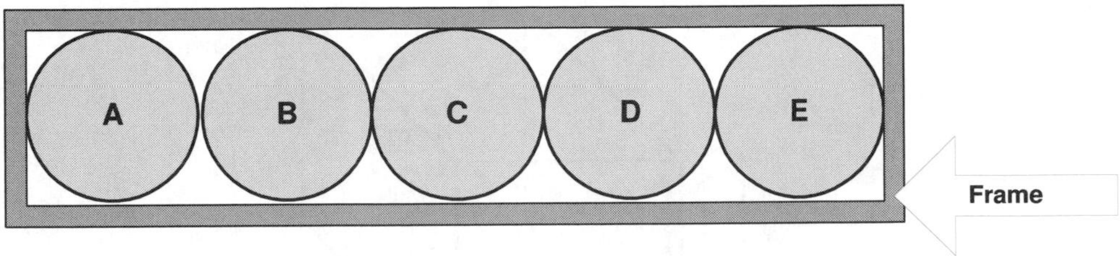

Figure 6.15: Billiard balls wrapped by a frame. Initially ball E is moving to the right with speed v.

The first colliding contact point is the second contact point between the two balls. Since we have a completely inelastic collision, from conservation of momentum we have

$$1000v = 1000v_{\text{after}} + v_{\text{after}}, \tag{6.115a}$$

$$v_{\text{after}} = \frac{1000}{1001}v, \tag{6.115b}$$

where we have used $v = \|\boldsymbol{v}\|$, after having resolved the collision both balls move downward with the same speed of $\frac{1000}{1001}v$. This means that the next colliding contact point is the first contact point.

The plane has infinite mass, which means that after the collision resolving the small ball and the plane move downward with zero velocity. The next colliding contact point is now the second contact point. As before, from conservation of momentum we get

$$1000\frac{1000}{1001}v = 1000v_{\text{after}} + v_{\text{after}}, \tag{6.116a}$$

$$v_{\text{after}} = \left(\frac{1000}{1001}\right)v. \tag{6.116b}$$

Now the two balls move downward with a speed of $\left(\frac{1000}{1001}\right)^2$. The pattern repeats itself, and it is easily seen that after n passes over the two contact points the speed of the large ball will have decreased to $\left(\frac{1000}{1001}\right)^n$.

From the example, it is also clear that the speed of the larger ball will never become zero, thus we will loop infinitely over the two contact points. Of course, in a computer simulation, we will at some point after a lot of computation time, encounter an underflow error and the computations will blow up in our face.

As another example, imagine a series of small billiard balls, with a frame wrapped around them. The balls all have the same mass and the frame has the same mass as a single billiard ball. Furthermore, the coefficient of restitution is one between all objects and there is no friction. The configuration is shown in Figure 6.15. Initially, the rightmost ball E is given a speed v to the right. The ball will collide with the frame in a completely elastic collision, thus after the collision, the ball will have zero speed and the frame will move to the right with speed v. Now the frame is colliding with ball A in a completely elastic collision, meaning that afterward the frame will have zero speed and ball A will move to the right with speed v, ball A will now collide with ball B, and so on until ball D collides with ball E. We are now back where we started. The pattern can thus repeat itself forever without ever changing.

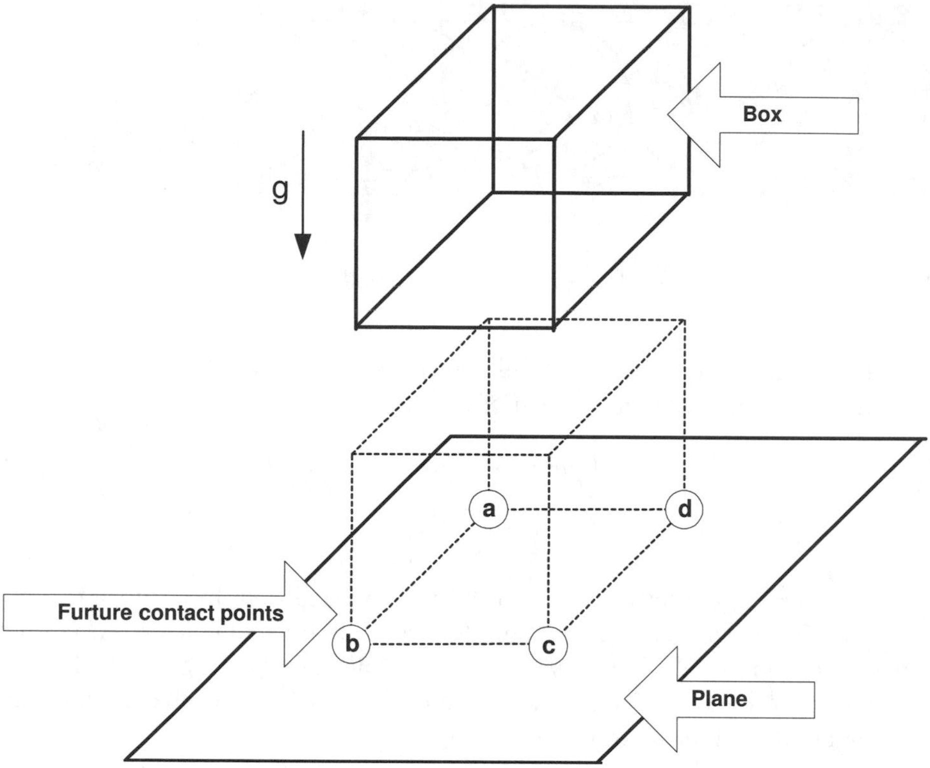

Figure 6.16: Box falling onto plane, making completely elastic impacts at the four contact points a, b, c, and d.

If the experiment is performed in the real world, one sees that the linear momentum will distribute itself equally over all objects, implying that they will all move to the right with the speed of $\frac{1}{6}v$. This is actually the solution a simultaneous method will compute.

6.2.2 Indeterminacy of Sequential Collision Resolving

Another issue with sequential collision resolving is that different results can be obtained depending on the order in which collisions are resolved.

As an example, imagine a box falling with one face flat against a fixed plane. For simplicity we will assume that there is no friction and that the coefficient of restitution is one between the box and the plane. Therefore, we expect the box to bounce back upward again without changing its orientation. In fact, if the simulation is run for long enough time, we expect to see the box jumping up and down on the plane without every changing its orientation. The configuration is shown in Figure 6.16. Upon impact we will have four contact points. We'll label these a, b, c, and d. When the box touches the plane all contact points will collide; therefore we have to choose one contact point. Let's pick a. Applying a normal impulse at a will make the box rotate with its axis going in the direction of b and d.

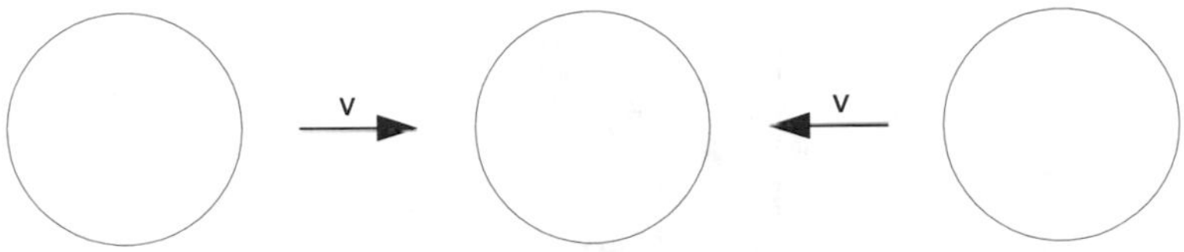

Figure 6.17: Three balls colliding in a completely symmetrical fashion.

By symmetry, two things can happen next, either we choose the contact point c as the next colliding contact point to treat or we choice one of the b and d contact points. Picking the c contact point will correct some of the rotational motion that was caused by the normal impulse at a. It is very likely that none of the contact points will be colliding after having picked c, and the box will bounce upward almost with unaffected rotational motion. On the other hand, if we choose contact point b, the rotational motion will become even worse, and we may end up with a rotating box bouncing back from the plane. The point to be made here is that different things can happen dependent on the order we choose to resolve the contact points a, b, d, and e in.

Heuristics for picking a deterministic and correct order are available [Chatterjee et al., 1998]. These heuristics require that one examines the colliding contact points and sorts them according to some physical measure. This causes the sequential collision resolving to be more computationally expensive.

However, it is possible to come up with configurations that exhibit special geometries, where no heuristic can be applied to resolve the problem of picking an order. Imagine, for instance, a ball at rest with a identical ball on its left side moving to the right and another identical ball on the right side moving to the left. The two balls on the sides are mirror images of each other implying they will hit the center ball at the exact same time. At the time of impact we will have two completely identical contact points. There is no preference for choosing the left contact point over the right or vice versa. The configuration is shown in Figure 6.17. Another commonly encountered case exhibiting special symmetry is a billiard ball hitting a corner. At the time of impact, the ball touches the corner walls at two different contact points, but there is no way of favoring which contact point to resolve first.

Notice that in both of the examples of special symmetry, picking one order over the other would lead to different simulation results. It is important to understand that the cause of this indeterminacy is not due to our lack of ability to find a good heuristic for picking an order. It is a basic physical problem. In [Chatterjee et al., 1998] it is suggested that a random ordering is the best way to deal with special symmetries.

6.2.3 Simple Simultaneous Collision Resolving

As an example of a simultaneous collision resolver we will derive the method proposed in [Baraff, 1989]. It is a simple method in the sense that it only considers normal impulses and normal contact velocities, and there is no friction. We refer the reader to Chapter 7 for more advanced modeling.

If i is the index of a contact point then the collision impulse $\boldsymbol{J}_i$ at that contact is

$$\boldsymbol{J}_i = j_i \boldsymbol{n}_i, \tag{6.117}$$

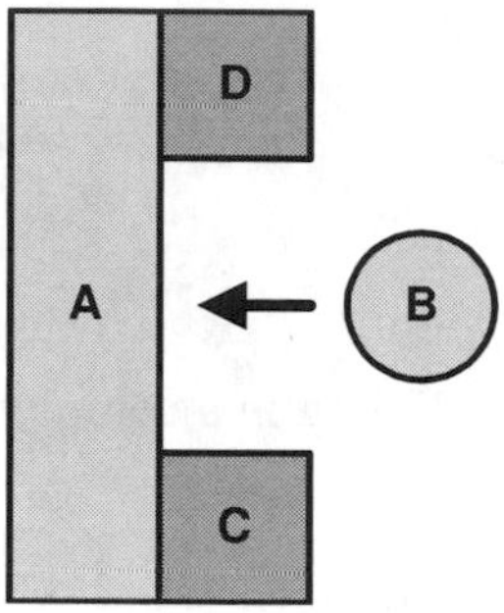

Figure 6.18: Simultaneous Contact. Showing how object B resolves collision between object A, and objects C and D.

where $\boldsymbol{n}_i$ is the contact normal of the i'th contact point. Since impulses are required to be repulsive, we have

$$j_i \geq 0. \tag{6.118}$$

We restate Newton's impact law as described in Section 6.1.1 for multiple contact points, let u_{i_i} be the initial relative contact velocity in the normal direction of the i'th contact point, and similarly u_{i_f} is the final relative normal contact velocity, then

$$u_{i_f} \geq -eu_{i_i}, \tag{6.119a}$$

$$u_{i_f} + eu_{i_i} \geq 0. \tag{6.119b}$$

The $\geq$ is needed because more than one object can be pushing on a single object. To make sure we do not get too much impulse we will require

$$u_{i_f} > -eu_{i_i} \Rightarrow j_i = 0. \tag{6.120}$$

To gain some intuition, it can be helpful to study a small example, as shown in Figure 6.18. Here object B pushes object A away from object C and object D, so there is no need for impulses between objects A and C and objects A and D. We can rewrite (6.120) into a complementary condition,

$$j_i \left(u_{i_f} + eu_{i_i}\right) = 0. \tag{6.121}$$

Knowing that u_{i_f} is a linear function of all the impulses, $\boldsymbol{j} = [j_0 \cdots j_i \cdots]^T$, that is, $u_{i_f}(\boldsymbol{j})$ to be shown shortly, we can write a *linear complementarity problem*, for all i we require

$$j_i \geq 0, \tag{6.122a}$$

$$u_{i_f}(\boldsymbol{j}) + eu_{i_i} \geq 0, \tag{6.122b}$$

$$j_i \left(u_{i_f}(\boldsymbol{j}) + eu_{i_i}\right) = 0. \tag{6.122c}$$

Now we will look at how much the i'th impulse changes the contact velocity at the j'th contact point on X. The situation is depicted in Figure 6.19. The change of contact velocity at the j'th contact point w.r.t.

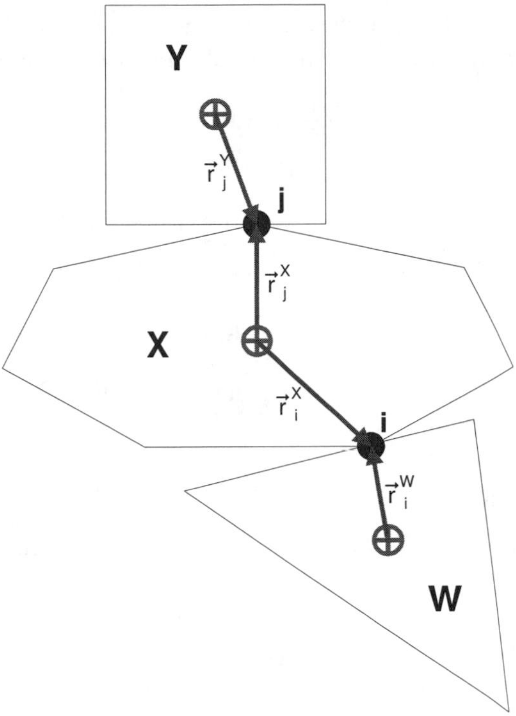

Figure 6.19: Multiple contact points. The change in relative contact velocity at the j'th contact point depends on impulses at both j'th and i'th contact points.

to object X due to the impulse at the i'th contact is

$$\Delta \boldsymbol{u}_{ji}^X = \Delta \boldsymbol{v}_i^X + \Delta \boldsymbol{\omega}_i^X \times \boldsymbol{r}_j^X, \tag{6.123}$$

where $\Delta \boldsymbol{v}_i^X = \pm \frac{\boldsymbol{n}_i}{m_X} j_i$ and $\Delta \boldsymbol{\omega}_i^X = \pm \boldsymbol{I}_X^{-1} \left(\boldsymbol{r}_i^X \times \boldsymbol{n}_i \right) j_i$, where the sign depends on the direction of the contact normal. Substituting for $\Delta \boldsymbol{v}_i^X$ and $\Delta \boldsymbol{\omega}_i^X$ and assuming X plays the role of B at the i'th contact, we have

$$\Delta \boldsymbol{u}_{ji}^X = \frac{-\boldsymbol{n}_i}{m_X} j_i + \left(\boldsymbol{I}_X^{-1} \left(\boldsymbol{r}_i^X \times -\boldsymbol{n}_i \right) j_i \right) \times \boldsymbol{r}_j^X, \tag{6.124}$$

cleaning up

$$\Delta \boldsymbol{u}_{ji}^X = \left(\frac{\boldsymbol{n}_i}{m_X} + \left(\boldsymbol{I}_X^{-1} \left(\boldsymbol{r}_i^X \times \boldsymbol{n}_i \right) \right) \times \boldsymbol{r}_j^X \right) j_i. \tag{6.125}$$

That is,

$$\Delta \boldsymbol{u}_{ji}^X = \boldsymbol{s}_{ji}^X j_i, \tag{6.126}$$

where

$$\boldsymbol{s}_{ji}^X = \left(\frac{-\boldsymbol{n}_i}{m_X} + \left(\boldsymbol{I}_X^{-1} \left(\boldsymbol{r}_i^X \times -\boldsymbol{n}_i \right) \right) \times \boldsymbol{r}_j^X \right). \tag{6.127}$$

If X played the role of A then we should have used $\boldsymbol{n}_i$ instead of $-\boldsymbol{n}_i$. To find the total change of the contact velocity at the j'th contact point we must sum over all the contact points in contact with X,

$$\Delta \boldsymbol{u}_j^X = \Delta \boldsymbol{u}_{j0}^X + \cdots + \Delta \boldsymbol{u}_{ji}^X + \cdots + \Delta \boldsymbol{u}_{jn}^X, \tag{6.128}$$

with our new notation

$$\Delta \boldsymbol{u}_j^X = \boldsymbol{s}_{j0}^X j_0 + \cdots + \boldsymbol{s}_{ji}^X j_i + \cdots + \boldsymbol{s}_{jn}^X j_n. \tag{6.129}$$

Now we must also find the change of contact velocity w.r.t. object Y, similar derivation will lead to

$$\Delta \boldsymbol{u}_j^Y = \boldsymbol{s}_{j0}^Y j_0 + \cdots + \boldsymbol{s}_{ji}^Y j_i + \cdots + \boldsymbol{s}_{jn}^Y j_n. \tag{6.130}$$

Now assume X played the role of A at the j'th contact point, then Y must be B at the j'th contact point, so the change in relative contact velocity is

$$\Delta \boldsymbol{u}_j^X - \Delta \boldsymbol{u}_j^Y = (\boldsymbol{s}_{j0}^X - \boldsymbol{s}_{j0}^Y) j_0 + \cdots + (\boldsymbol{s}_{ji}^X - \boldsymbol{s}_{ji}^Y) j_i + \cdots + (\boldsymbol{s}_{jn}^X - \boldsymbol{s}_{jn}^Y) j_n. \tag{6.131}$$

We are only interested in the normal direction, so we can simplify our derivation by taking the dot product with the contact normal, that is

$$u_{j_f} = \boldsymbol{A}_{j0} j_0 + \cdots + \boldsymbol{A}_{ji} j_i + \cdots + \boldsymbol{A}_{jn} j_n + u_{j_i}, \tag{6.132}$$

where

$$\boldsymbol{A}_{ji} = \left(\boldsymbol{s}_{ji}^X - \boldsymbol{s}_{ji}^Y\right) \cdot \boldsymbol{n}_j. \tag{6.133}$$

Writing up the linear system for all contact points results in

$$\boldsymbol{A}\boldsymbol{j} + \boldsymbol{b} \geq 0 \qquad \text{compl.} \qquad \boldsymbol{j} \geq 0. \tag{6.134}$$

Figure 6.20 illustrates pseudocode for setting up the $\boldsymbol{A}$-matrix and the $\boldsymbol{b}$-vector.

6.2.4 Robust and Stable Sequential Collision Resolving

In this section we give the technical details for an efficient stable and robust implementation of a sequential collision resolver. It overcomes some of the problems with infinite looping at the price of physical realism. The method still yields plausible results. The method is based on the ideas in [Chatterjee et al., 1998].

The method described will need a collision law, which has a coefficient of normal restitution, e. Otherwise any collision law can be used. During initialization all single point collisions, i.e., the contact points, are inserted into a heap data structure S. The contact points are sorted based on their relative normal contact velocity, u_n, computed as in (6.14). If $u_n < 0$, then the objects are colliding at the contact point and we need to apply an impulse $\boldsymbol{J}$ to the objects.

As suggested in [Chatterjee et al., 1998], the contact point with the smallest relative normal contact velocity is obtained from the heap S. This contact point is called the minimum contact point. Getting the minimum contact point is a constant time operation, as the minimum element in a heap often is the first element. If the minimum contact point is colliding, an impulse is applied to resolve the collision. If on the other hand, the minimum contact point is noncolliding, then by the heap property of S, there cannot

```
A = new (n × n)-matrix
b = new n-vector
C = set of all contacts
for each j in C
  b[j] = (1+e)u_{j_i}
  for each i in C
    A[j][i] = 0
    if one of the bodies of i is body A of j
       let X be the body of i that is body A of j
       A[j][i] += s^X_{ji} · n_j
    if one of the bodies of i is body B of j
       let Y be the body of i that is body B of j
       A[j][i] -= s^Y_{ji} · n_j
```

Figure 6.20: Pseudocode for setting up linear complementarity problem for simple simultaneous collision resolving.

be any other contact points with a relative normal contact velocity less than the minimum contact point. Therefore, there cannot be any more colliding contact points and the algorithm can terminate. If a collision impulse is applied, then the relative normal contact velocity is recomputed, for all contact points having at least one object in common with the minimum contact point. These contact points are said to be affected by or dependent on the minimum contact point, since their relative contact velocity depends on the two incident objects at the minimum contact point. After having updated all the dependent contact points, the heap S needs to be updated, in order for the heap property to be fulfilled. Hereafter, the algorithm obtains the minimum contact point from the heap S, and repeats the above steps until termination. A pseudocode version of the algorithm is shown in Figure 6.21. If an implementation is made precisely as the pseudocode outlines, it will quickly cause trouble in practice. A test like $u_n \geq 0$ is difficult to apply due to precision errors. One solution to the problem is to use a threshold value, $\varepsilon > 0$, such that the test becomes

$$u_n \geq -\varepsilon. \tag{6.135}$$

The threshold value ε should be a small positive number indicating the accuracy of the floating-point operations. In practice, the test works excellently, especially in combination with a collision envelope, which it magnitudes greater than the precision.

The problem with the pseudocode algorithm is due to the physics. As explained in Section 6.2.1 there are configurations causing an infinite sequence of collisions. The important thing to notice is that if $e < 1$, then the relative contact velocities are always monotonically decreasing. In [Chatterjee et al., 1998] it is therefore suggested that when infinite loops happen, a truncation or extrapolation can be used to obtain an answer.

However, it's not easy to determine when an infinite sequence of collisions occurs. An ad hoc solution to the problem is to test whether the current value of the relative normal contact velocity has decreased in absolute value to some specified fraction of the initial smallest relative normal contact velocity. A fraction of $1/1000$ usually works well in practice. A smaller fraction means that the collision resolving will take more computation time, and a larger fraction means less correct simulation results. Notice that the test for

```
Algorithm sequential1(C:Contacts)
  Heap S
  for each c ∈ C do
    compute u_n for c
    put (u_n, c) into S
  next c
  while forever
    (u_n, c) = min(S)
    if u_n ≥ 0 then
      return
    end if
    compute J for c
    apply J to objects in c
    for ∀c' ∈ C, c' sharing object with c do
      compute u_n for c'
      update heap with (u_n, c')
    next c'
  end while
End algorithm
```

Figure 6.21: Sequential collision resolving based on minimum relative normal contact velocity.

an infinite loop is based on a global threshold value and a local test for each contact point. The local test is performed each time the minimum contact point is obtained from the heap S.

However, the infinite loop test will only detect infinite loops in configurations where truncation could resolve the problems, such as the two balls on a table configuration, as shown in Figure 6.14. Configurations such as the framed billiard balls in Figure 6.15 will not be detected. To circumvent this problem, a simple counter test is introduced; each contact point keeps track of the number of times it has been resolved. When the minimum contact point is obtained from the heap, its counter is incremented by one, afterward it is tested if the counter exceeds a user-specified maximum count. Care must be taken not to set the maximum count too high or else an excessive amount of computation time can be wasted. If set too low the collision resolver may detect perfectly solvable configurations as containing infinite sequences of colliding contact points. Usually values in the range of 20–100 works well for computer animation purposes. Initially, the resolving counter is set to zero for all contact points.

Figure 6.22 illustrates the modifications to the pseudocode in Figure 6.21. When an infinite sequence of colliding contact points is detected, an evasive action has to be performed or else there is a risk for a never-ending computation. If $e < 1$, then it seems sensible that kinetic contact energy will continue to dissipate a little for each an every collision that is resolved, until there is no more kinetic energy left. The limit at which there is no more kinetic energy corresponds to the relative normal contact velocity being zero, that is, $u_n = 0$. We know from theory that setting the coefficient of restitution to zero, $e = 0$, will make $u_n = 0$ when resolving one contact point. Therefore, an evasive action is simply to set $e = 0$ when computing the impulse for a contact point, which has passed the infinite loop test. Setting e is called truncation and the computed impulse is called a truncated impulse.

Theoretically, setting $e = 0$ should give $u_n = 0$. In practice however, numerical precision often causes

```
Algorithm sequential2(C:Contacts)
  Heap S
  for each c ∈ C do
    compute u_n for c
    counter(c) = 0
    put (u_n, c) into S
  next c
  (u_n, c) = min(S)
  ε_fraction = (1/1000)u_n
  N_max = 20
  while forever
    (u_n, c) = min(S)
    ifu_n ≥ 0 then
      return
    endif
    counter(c) = counter(c) + 1
    if u_n > ε_fraction or counter(c) > N_max then
       ...handle infnitite loop...
    else
      ...compute impulse as usual...
    end if
    ...
  end while
End algorithm
```

Figure 6.22: Modification of sequential collision resolver to detect infinite sequences of colliding contacts.

u_n to be slightly nonzero. During the update of contact points in the heap, it is better simply to set $u_n = 0$ when updating a contact point that has just been resolved with a truncated impulse. A Boolean flag is needed on each contact point, so a contact point can be marked as having been resolved by a truncated impulse or not.

If instead, u_n is recomputed by (6.14) when a contact point has been truncated it might occur that the value is slightly lower than the precision threshold limit. This will cause the algorithm to do several series of truncations on the same contact point before the single-point collision has been resolved. The result is more iterations and slower simulation.

To counter artifacts from numerical precision it is often also advantageous to truncate the post collision velocities of the objects from a contact point where a truncation impulse has been applied. Pseudocode for the velocity truncation is shown in Figure 6.23. The final pseudocode version of sequential collision resolver algorithm is shown in Figure 6.24.

The sequential collision resolver algorithm in Figure 6.24 will be able to to detect an infinite loop in configurations like the two balls on the table and the framed billiard balls. It should be noted that truncation impulses are not the whole answer to making a bulletproof evasive action on an infinite loop. Notice that the coefficient of restitution is zero for all contact points in the two balls on a table configuration, and this results in an infinite loop.

The algorithm will not always return the physical expected result. If detection of infinite loops is

```
algorithm truncate(v,ω)
  If |v_x| < ε Then
    v_x = 0
  End If
  If |v_y| < ε Then
    v_y = 0
  End If
  If |v_z| < ε Then
    v_z = 0
  End If
  If |ω_x| < ε Then
    ω_x = 0
  End If
  If |ω_y| < ε Then
    ω_y = 0
  End If
  If |ω_z| < ε Then
    ω_z = 0
  End If
end algorithm
```

Figure 6.23: Pseudocode for postvelocity truncation to counter numerical precision artifacts.

over-eager, then the algorithm will have an effect of artificially decreasing the coefficient of restitution. Typical large values $\varepsilon > \frac{1}{2}$ returns plausible results, whereas values $\varepsilon < \frac{1}{5}$ seem to be clamped to zero, and values in between seem artificially damped. These value ranges are typical for the values listed for the fraction-test and maximum resolve count test. Other values for these constants would result in different behavior.

The algorithm is excellent for use in computer games or computer animation, since it is robust and stable, and can be made to run very fast if one is willing to sacrifice physical realism. It should be noted that a good heap data structure is crucial for good performance.

It is possible to make variations of the algorithm. For instance, contact points could be sorted in the heap data structure based on penetration depth or some other physical or geometric quantity. Also, other evasive actions could be taken in case an infinite loop is detected. For instance, one could switch to a simultaneous collision resolving method.

The algorithm can have a serious impact on configurations with $e = 1$; if an infinite loop is detected it will simply set $e = 0$. In a configuration like the one shown in Figure 6.15, all objects will come to a halt, which is not the wanted simulation result. To circumvent this problem one could add an extra test on the value of the coefficient of restitution to detect what kind of infinite loop that has been detected. If $e < 1$ it is safe to apply a truncation impulse, if $e = 1$, another solution method could be applied.

```
Algorithm sequential3(C:Contacts)
  Heap S
  for each c ∈ C do
    compute u_n for c
    counter(c) = 0
    truncated(c) =false
    put (u_n, c) into S
  next c
  (u_n, c) = min(S)
  ε_fraction = (1/1000)u_n
  N_max = 20
  while forever
    (u_n, c) = min(S)
    counter(c) = counter(c) + 1
    if u_n ≥ 0 then
      return
    endif
    if u_n > ε_fraction or counter(c) > N_max then
      set e = 0
      compute J for c
      apply J to objects in c
      truncated(c) =true
    else
      ...compute impulse as usual...
    end if
    for ∀c' ∈ C, c' sharing object withc do
      if truncated(c') then
        u_n = 0
        truncate(v_A, ω_A)
        truncate(v_B, ω_B)
        truncated(c') =false
      else
        compute u_n for c'
      end if
      update heap with (u_n, c')
    next c'
  end while
End algorithm
```

Figure 6.24: Final pseudocode version of sequential collision resolver.

6.3 Conservative Advancement

In the work [Mirtich et al., 1994, Mirtich et al., 1995, Mirtich, 1996] a new simulation paradigm emerged building on the early ideas of [Hahn, 1988]. The paradigm was named impulse-based simulation. Later, the work was extended to hybrid simulation [Mirtich, 1995], a paradigm combining constraint-based and impulse-based simulation. The main focus here is the *time-stepping method* presented in [Mirtich, 1996].

Looking at rigid bodies at a microscopic level, all kinds of contact can be modeled by collision impulses, even something like a cup at rest on a table. This type of contact is called static contact. Static contact is modeled as a series of highly-frequent collision impulses occurring between the two objects in static contact. The frequency of the collision impulses is so high that it is nearly impossible to distinguish the individual collision impulses. The limiting case with infinite frequency will be equivalent to computing the time-integral of the contact forces (6.18) over a finite time-step Δt. The force time-integral is confusingly called impulse, but it is not a collision impulse.

In practice, we do not have the computational resources to compute an infinite series of collision impulses, therefore we use a *collision envelope* around each object. The collision envelope can be thought of as a thick surface of an object. It is a model of the atomic layer of an object that comes into contact with the atomic layer of another object. Thus, it is the atoms in these layers that are bouncing against each other during static contact. It is important to realize that objects are defined as touching when they are within each other's collision envelopes. An actual distance of zero between the geometries of two objects is never seen.

Frequent collisions occurring during static contact is now modeled by applying an impulse only at the closest point between two objects. The closest point will lie inside the collision envelopes of the objects. After having applied the collision impulse, the velocities of the objects will have changed, such that if we advance the time of the simulation by integrating the free-moving body state function (22.81) of the two objects, the objects will move away from each other at the closest point, regardless of how small a time-step we integrate forward. This will mean that at some point in the future a new closest point within the collision envelopes will be found. Thus, static contact is modeled as an object that vibrates on top of another object. If the collision envelope is small enough the vibration will occur at a frequency where a human observer will not notice it. Figure 6.25 illustrates the idea using an exaggerated collision envelope. In [Mirtich et al., 1994, Mirtich et al., 1995, Mirtich, 1996] a time-stepping method is presented that computes an estimate for a time-step, that can be used to integrate the rigid body state functions describing the free motion of the objects without causing penetration or zero distance of the object geometries. The time-step is found by computing a conservative lower bound for the *Time of Impact* (*TOI*) between all potential colliding object pairs.

A TOI value should be easy and fast to compute, since it is expected to be recomputed many times. In fact, it must be recomputed every time two objects collide or whenever the time-stepping has reached the time of a TOI. Thus due to performance considerations, it is crucial that a TOI value is computationally inexpensive to compute. A TOI value should always be a lower limit to the true time of impact and the lower limit should converge toward the true time of impact the closer the objects are. This is what we mean by a conservative TOI. Computing TOI values in this way will ensure that a collision is never missed, and that it is safe to integrate forward in time to the minimum TOI value.

Figure 6.26 illustrates the basic idea behind the TOI time-stepping method. Notice that the stepping

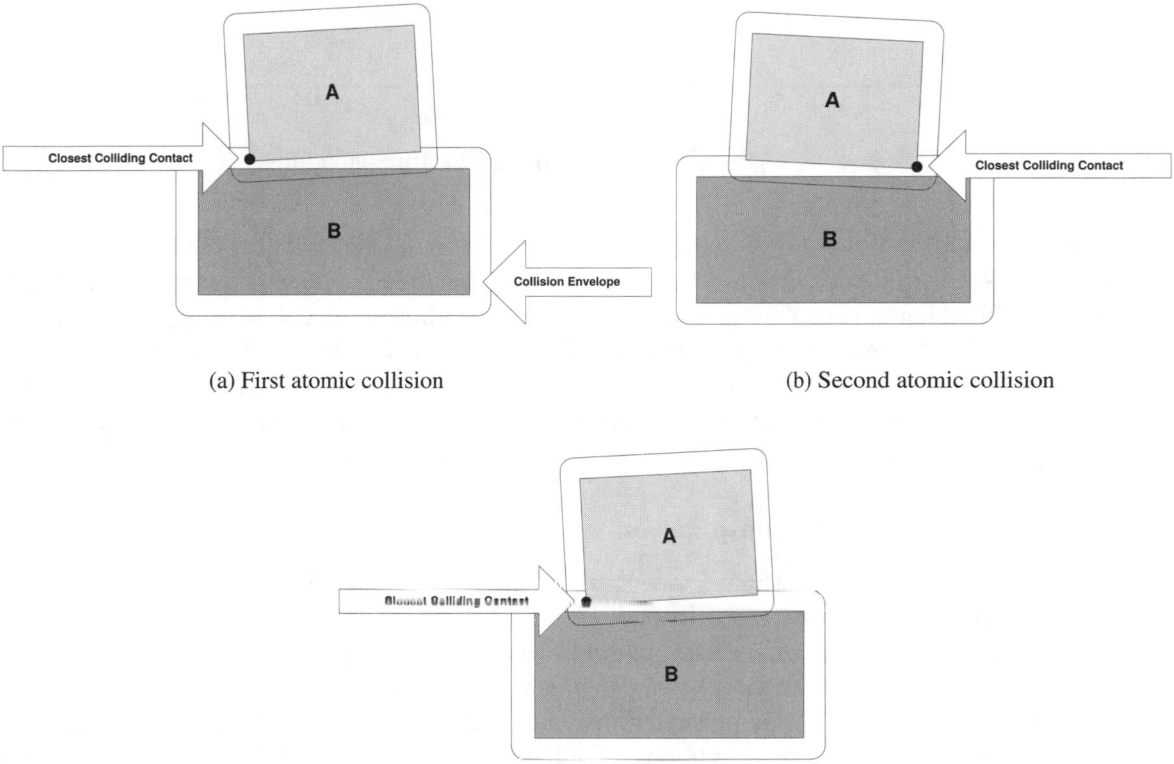

(a) First atomic collision

(b) Second atomic collision

(c) Third atomic collision

Figure 6.25: The collision impulse model of static contact. A box A is resting on top of a fixed box B. The static contact is modeled as a series of collisions occurring between the closest point between A and B. Thus, box A is in fact vibrating on top of box B. The smaller the collision envelope, the higher the vibration frequency, and an end user will not notice the vibration.

```
algorithm run(t, Δt)
  t_final = t + Δt
  do
    do collision detection
    resolve colliding contact points
    t_toi = min(compute toi's for all object pairs)
    Δt = min(t_final − t_toi, t_final − t)
    integrate forward by Δt
    t = t + Δt
  while t < t_final
end algorithm
```

Figure 6.26: Pseudocode for simple TOI time-stepping.

method is invoked with a wanted time-step size, which indicates the end-time for the next frame of the simulation. That is the simulation time for the next frame that should be rendered in an animation. The TOI time-stepping method belongs to a group of time-stepping algorithms termed *Conservative Advancement* because time only runs forward, unlike in Retroactive Detection, where time is rewound when a simulation goes bad. There are two major problems with the time-stepping method outlined in Figure 6.26. First, how should a TOI value be computed? Second, recomputing TOI values between all pairs of objects takes quadratic time, which is computationally intractable in large-scale simulations.

6.3.1 Time of Impact (TOI) Computation

Assume that the narrow-phase collision detection algorithm (see Chapter 13) returns the closest points between two rigid bodies. Unfortunately, these two points do not provide enough information themselves for estimating the position of an actual future impact between the two objects because the objects may be moving away from each other at the closest points, which indicates that some other points on the objects are moving toward each other. This is illustrated in Figure 6.27. However, if we assume that the objects are convex, the closest points can be used to give us some information. If the objects are convex then any future colliding points must at least travel the distance between the closest points before they can collide. This is shown in Figure 6.28. If we let the function $d_A(\cdot)$ be the distance traveled by the colliding point $\boldsymbol{x}_A$ as a function of time, and similar $d_B(\cdot)$ is the traveling distance for $\boldsymbol{x}_B$, then the distance traveled by both the colliding points, $d(\cdot)$, at the true time of impact t_c is

$$d(t_c) = d_A(t_c) + d_B(t_c) \geq \|\boldsymbol{d}\|, \tag{6.136}$$

where $\boldsymbol{d} = \boldsymbol{p}_A - \boldsymbol{p}_B$. If (6.136) is solved for the time t yielding equality, then the solution will be a lower bound for the true time of impact t_c. As objects come closer, the colliding points will end up being the closest points just before the actual impact. Thus, the lower bound becomes a better and better estimate for the time of impact the closer the objects come.

Unfortunately, the functions $d_A(\cdot)$ and $d_B(\cdot)$ are unknown, because the colliding points $\boldsymbol{x}_A$ and $\boldsymbol{x}_B$ are not yet known, only the closest points $\boldsymbol{p}_A$ and $\boldsymbol{p}_B$ are known. To get around the problem, the functions $d_A(\cdot)$ and $d_B(\cdot)$ are approximated by two other functions giving a conservative upper limit for the traveling

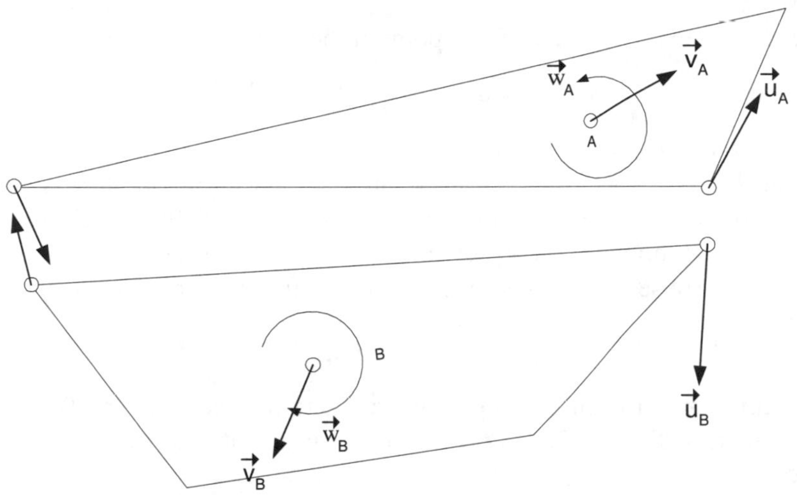

Figure 6.27: A bad case for TOI computation, two closest points are moving away from each other. However, there exist two other points moving toward each other.

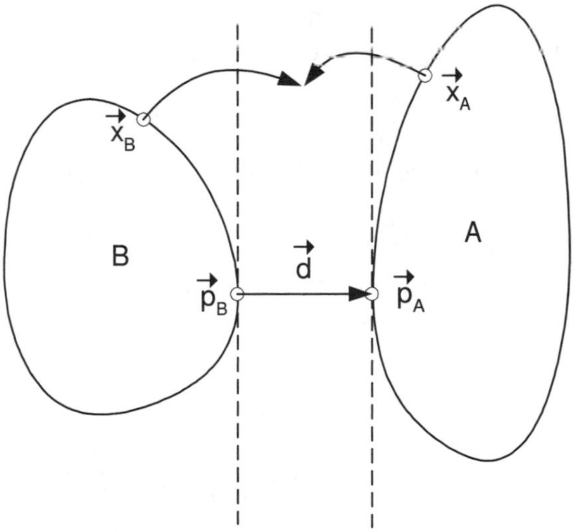

Figure 6.28: The actual colliding points $\boldsymbol{x}_A$ and $\boldsymbol{x}_B$ must at least travel the distance, $\boldsymbol{d}$, given by the closest points $\boldsymbol{p}_A$ and $\boldsymbol{p}_B$ before they can collide.

distance. Notice that it is important that the traveling distance is an upper bound in order for the time estimate to be a lower bound.

From (6.12) we can write the velocity of any point of the surface of an object X, as

$$\boldsymbol{u}_X(t) = \boldsymbol{\omega}^X(t) \times \boldsymbol{r}^X + \boldsymbol{v}_{\text{cm}}^X(t), \tag{6.137}$$

where $\boldsymbol{r}^X$ is the body-fixed vector of the surface point.

If we assume that the forces acting on an object are constant during the time-step Δt and that there is no torque acting on the object, then the object will move along a ballistic trajectory. This may sound prohibitive, but it is the same motion as an object moving freely under gravity, thus, it is a good assumption for computer animation purpose. Under this assumption the linear velocity of the center of mass is given as

$$\boldsymbol{v}_{\text{cm}}(t) = \boldsymbol{v}_{\text{cm}}(t_{\text{cur}}) + \boldsymbol{g}\left[t - t_{\text{cur}}\right], \tag{6.138}$$

where t_{cur} is the current simulation time, and $\boldsymbol{g}$ is the gravitational acceleration. The speed of any surface point on object B in the direction of $\boldsymbol{d}$ can now be found by substituting (6.138) into (6.137) and taking the dot product with $\boldsymbol{d}$,

$$\boldsymbol{u}_B(t) \cdot \boldsymbol{d} = \left(\boldsymbol{\omega}^B(t) \times \boldsymbol{r}^B\right) \cdot \boldsymbol{d} + \boldsymbol{v}_{\text{cm}}^B(t_{\text{cur}}) \cdot \boldsymbol{d} + \boldsymbol{g} \cdot \boldsymbol{d}\left[t - t_{\text{cur}}\right]. \tag{6.139}$$

The surface velocity of any point on object A is almost identical except that $-\boldsymbol{d}$ should be used. Since the actual collision points are unknown, $\boldsymbol{r}^A$ and $\boldsymbol{r}^B$ are unknown. However, since an upper bound is wanted, any surface point can be used, which maximizes the term $\left(\boldsymbol{\omega}^X(t) \times \boldsymbol{r}^X\right) \cdot (\pm\boldsymbol{d})$.

The surface point fulfilling this requirement must be the point lying farthest away from the center of mass. Let the distance of this surface point be given by r_{max}^X, which can easily be precomputed before the simulation starts. The motion of the object is assumed to be torque free, therefore, it's possible to compute an upper bound on the magnitude of the angular velocity, ω_{max}^X, derived in (6.149). Combining these two facts yields

$$\left(\boldsymbol{\omega}^X(t) \times \boldsymbol{r}^X\right) \cdot (\pm\boldsymbol{d}) \le \omega_{\text{max}}^X r_{\text{max}}^X. \tag{6.140}$$

Using (6.140) in (6.139) gives the upper bound on the surface point velocity,

$$\boldsymbol{u}_B(t) \cdot \boldsymbol{d} \le \omega_{\text{max}}^B r_{\text{max}}^B + \boldsymbol{v}_{\text{cm}}^B(t_{\text{cur}}) \cdot \boldsymbol{d} + \boldsymbol{g} \cdot \boldsymbol{d}\left[t - t_{\text{cur}}\right], \tag{6.141}$$

thus integrating (6.141) from t_{cur} to t, yields an upper bound on the distance traveled by any surface point on B, that is,

$$\int_{t_{\text{cur}}}^{t} \left(\boldsymbol{u}(\tau)^X \cdot \boldsymbol{d}\right) d\tau \le \int_{t_{\text{cur}}}^{t} \left(\left(\boldsymbol{v}_{\text{cm}}^X(t_{\text{cur}}) + \boldsymbol{g}\left[t - t_{\text{cur}}\right]\right) \cdot (\pm\boldsymbol{d}) + \omega_{\text{max}}^X r_{\text{max}}^X\right) d\tau, \tag{6.142a}$$

$$= \frac{1}{2}\boldsymbol{g} \cdot (\pm\boldsymbol{d})\left[t - t_{\text{cur}}\right]^2 + \left(\boldsymbol{v}_{\text{cm}}^X(t_{\text{cur}}) \cdot (\pm\boldsymbol{d}) + \omega_{\text{max}}^X r_{\text{max}}^X\right)\left[t - t_{\text{cur}}\right]. \tag{6.142b}$$

Introducing the constants,

$$A_X = \frac{1}{2}\boldsymbol{g} \cdot (\pm\boldsymbol{d}), \tag{6.143a}$$

$$B_X = \boldsymbol{v}_{\text{cm}}^X(t_{\text{cur}}) \cdot (\pm\boldsymbol{d}) + \omega_{\text{max}}^X r_{\text{max}}^X, \tag{6.143b}$$

where "+" is used, if $X = A$, and "−" otherwise, the approximation to (6.136) is

$$(A_A + A_B)\left[t - t_{\text{cur}}\right]^2 + (B_A + B_B)\left[t - t_{\text{cur}}\right] = \|\boldsymbol{d}\|. \quad (6.144)$$

This is a second-order polynomial that is easily solved. The TOI value is now given as the smallest positive root of (6.144) plus the current simulation time. If no such roots exist then the objects cannot collide and the TOI value can be set to infinity.

Note that if the distance between the two objects ever becomes zero, then $\boldsymbol{d} = 0$, the trivial solution to (6.144) is $t = 0$, causing the algorithm in Figure 6.26 to enter an infinite loop, since the smallest TOI value will always be the same as the current simulation time.

Computing the value of ω^X_{max} can be done by noting that the rotational kinetic energy of the object must be conserved, since there is no torque acting on the object. The rotational kinetic energy, E, computed in the body frame of the object is given by

$$E = \frac{1}{2}\boldsymbol{\omega}(t)^T \boldsymbol{I}_{\text{body}}\boldsymbol{\omega}(t), \quad (6.145)$$

for convenience the body label X has been omitted. The term $\boldsymbol{I}_{\text{body}}$ is the inertia tensor w.r.t. body frame. It is thus diagonal and constant. Writing (6.145) element-wise yields

$$E = \frac{1}{2}\begin{bmatrix}\omega_x(t) & \omega_y(t) & \omega_z(t)\end{bmatrix}\begin{bmatrix} I_x & 0 & 0 \\ 0 & I_y & 0 \\ 0 & 0 & I_z \end{bmatrix}\begin{bmatrix}\omega_x(t) \\ \omega_y(t) \\ \omega_z(t)\end{bmatrix}, \quad (6.146)$$

which can be reduced to

$$2E = I_x\omega_x(t)^2 + I_y\omega_y(t)^2 + I_z\omega_z(t)^2, \quad (6.147)$$

this is easily rewritten into the equation of an elliptical level set surface

$$\frac{\omega_x(t)^2}{\frac{2E}{I_x}} + \frac{\omega_y(t)^2}{\frac{2E}{I_y}} + \frac{\omega_z(t)^2}{\frac{2E}{I_z}} = 1. \quad (6.148)$$

This level set surface defines all possible $\boldsymbol{\omega}(t)$, picking the $\boldsymbol{\omega}(t)$ with the largest magnitude will yield a value for $\boldsymbol{\omega}_{\text{max}}$. From geometry it is clear that $\|\boldsymbol{\omega}(t)\|$ is largest along the major axis of the ellipse, which means

$$\boldsymbol{\omega}_{\text{max}} = \sqrt{\frac{2E}{\min\left\{I_x, I_y, I_z\right\}}}. \quad (6.149)$$

6.3.2 Time of Impact Heap

The second problem of the algorithm in Figure 6.26 is that it is computationally intractable to compute TOI values between all pairs of objects. Fortunately, it turns out that this is not necessary.

If a heap data structure is used to store object pairs sorted on their TOI value, then the minimum TOI value can easily be accessed in constant time. Only the TOI value between the object pairs corresponding to the minimum TOI needs to be recomputed, as well as all other TOIs having at least one object in common with the minimum TOI object pair. All other TOI values are known to be larger than the minimum TOI value and the rigid body states of their object pairs are unaffected by a possible collision taking place at the contact point corresponding to the minimum TOI. Thus, their future collisions are unaffected and the TOI values are still valid lower bounds. After having updated the TOI values of all affected object pairs, the TOI heap needs to be updated in order for the heap property to be fulfilled.

Initially, it is a bad idea to compute TOI values for all object pairs in order to initialize the heap. Instead, only TOI values for objects that are in close proximity are kept in the heap. If sweeping volumes are used in the broad-phase collision detection algorithm as described in Section 12.5, then the results from the broad-phase collision detection algorithm yield object pairs that may collide in the near future. Whenever an object pair is reported by the broad-phase collision detection algorithm, which is not already in the heap, it is inserted into the heap.

To keep the storage requirements for the heap from accumulating to quadratic size, it is beneficial to remove object pairs from the heap when they are far from each other. First intuition might suggest simply to remove object pairs when they are no longer reported by the broad-phase collision detection algorithm. However, this can have fatal side-effects. Imagine a ball bouncing up and down on a fixed plane. The TOI value between the plane and the ball will constantly be added and then removed from the heap, thus yielding a substantial overhead in maintaining the heap data structure. A better solution is to approach the removal of heap elements in a lazy manner. That is, TOI values are only removed from the heap if the object pair of the minimum TOI is no longer close to each other.

Figure 6.29 illustrates how the TOI heap works and Figure 6.30 shows a pseudocode version of the algorithm.

In most cases, the TOI heap time-stepping method is extremely fast, especially in cases with many fast-moving objects. It is beneficial in computer games such as flight simulators, where there is almost no static contact. However, the algorithm will have difficulties with rotating objects that have large aspect ratios. For instance, a see-saw configuration can exhibit slow convergence for the TOIs corresponding to impact with the ground. This is because r_{max} is very large, and $\boldsymbol{d}$, is small.

The same behavior of slow convergence of the TOIs, can be seen when objects are in static contact. Here, $\boldsymbol{d}$ becomes very small causing the computed TOI-values to be very small. Stacking of objects can cause a simulator to come to a halt, due to the computations involved in updating the TOI values and taking time-steps close to zero.

Note that the entire algorithm actually only needs to resolve a single-point collision between any two objects. There is no need for sequential or simultaneous collision resolving.

6.4 Fixed Stepping with Separation of Collision and Contacts

Besides the convergence problems of the time-stepping approach described in Section 6.3, it has other serious flaws. It turns out that these flaws stem from the basic nature of doing time-integrating of the free motion of the rigid bodies and then resolving collisions. Any time-stepping method taking this approach to impulse-based simulation will thus suffer from the same flaws. In [Guendelman et al., 2003], the basic nature and cause of these flaws was explained and a new *time-integration* method was proposed as a

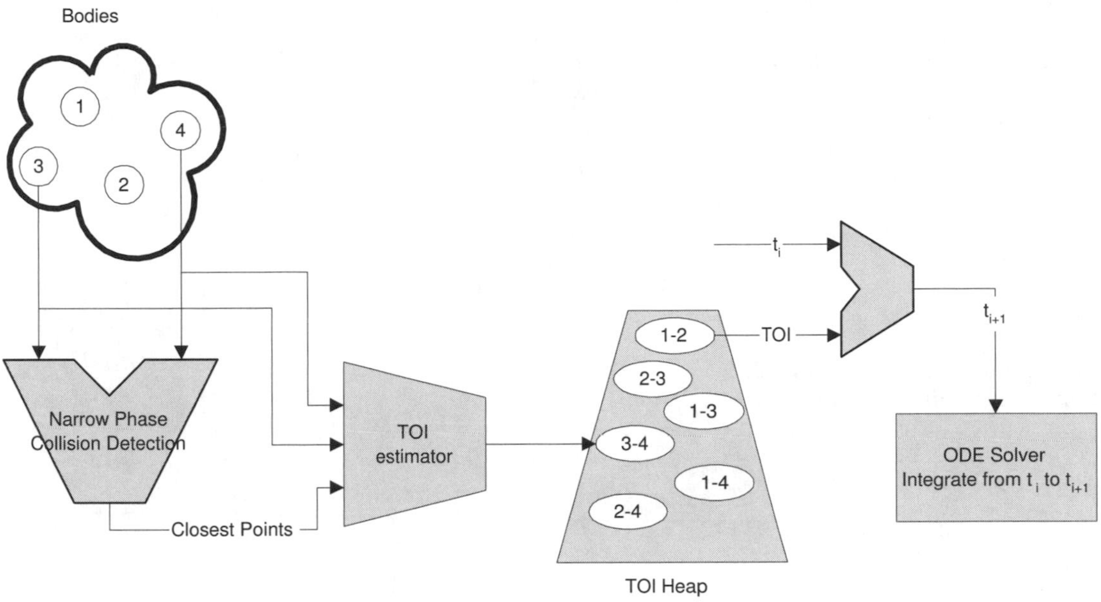

Figure 6.29: Conceptual drawing of how the TOI heap works to control the time-stepping.

solution. This new time-stepping method is the subject of this section. We will discuss the problems of implementing an efficient and robust simulator based on this time-stepping method.

In a traditional *time stepping method*, the equations of motion (22.81) are integrated. That is, the first-order coupled differential equations

$$\frac{d}{dt}\boldsymbol{r}_{\text{cm}} = \boldsymbol{v}_{\text{cm}} \qquad \frac{d}{dt}q = \frac{1}{2}\left[0, \boldsymbol{\omega}\right] q, \tag{6.150a}$$

$$\frac{d}{dt}\boldsymbol{v}_{\text{cm}} = \frac{\boldsymbol{F}}{m} \qquad \frac{d}{dt}\boldsymbol{L}_{\text{cm}} = \boldsymbol{\tau}_{\text{cm}}, \tag{6.150b}$$

are numerically integrated. Here, $\boldsymbol{r}_{\text{cm}}$ is the position of the center of mass, $\boldsymbol{v}_{\text{cm}}$ is the linear velocity of the center of mass, and $\boldsymbol{F}$ is the total force acting on the center of mass, $\boldsymbol{L}_{\text{cm}} = \boldsymbol{I}\boldsymbol{\omega}$ is the angular momentum w.r.t. center of mass, $\boldsymbol{I}$ is the inertia tensor, and $\boldsymbol{\omega}$ is the angular velocity. $\boldsymbol{\tau}_{\text{cm}}$ is the torque. q is the orientation represented as a quaternion after the numerical integration collision resolving is performed. In Figure 6.31 an example simulation of a box on an inclined plane using the traditional time-stepping strategy is shown. In the example, the coefficient of restitution is one, and the coefficient of friction is large enough to prevent the box from sliding down the plane. Initially the box is at rest, however, after having performed the first integration the box will have gained linear velocity, due to gravity acting on the box. During collision resolving a collision impulse is applied to the box and the collision impulse will change the linear velocity of the box, so it no longer will be colliding with the plane. However, since the coefficient of restitution is one, the linear velocity after collision resolving is pointing in the normal direction of the plane. This means when integration is performed again, the box will fly up in the air,

```
algorithm toi-heap-time-stepping()
  while TOI(b,b') at top of heap=t_cur
    narrow-collision(b,b')
    contacts = contact-determination(b,b')
    collision-resolve(contacts)
    recompute all TOI's where b is part of
    recompute all TOI's where b' is part of
    if b and b' no longer close
      remove TOI(b,b') from heap
    end if
  end while
  t_next = TOI at top of heap
  Δt = t_next - t_cur
  overlaps = broad-phase(Δt)
  for each overlap(b,b') in overlaps
    if not TOI(b,b') exist
      compute TOI(b,b')
      insert TOI(b,b') in heap
    end if
  next overlap(b,b')
  t_next = TOI at top of heap

  integrate forward by t_next - t_cur
end algorithm
```

Figure 6.30: Pseudocode illustrating how to use the TOI heap for time-stepping. The pseudocode replaces the body of the while-loop in Figure 6.26.

gravity will then work on the box, and eventually the box will fall down on the plane again, but it will hit the plane at a lower position. Thus, the box seems to bounce downward on the plane. The same artifact causes objects resting on the ground to vibrate, making it impossible to create high stacks of objects.

The novelty of the work in [Guendelman et al., 2003] is to split the numerical integration of (6.150) into two separate phases causing a separation of the collision resolving from the contact handling to give the following simulation loop:

1. Collision resolving
2. Advance the velocities using (6.150b)
3. Contact handling
4. Advance the positions using (6.150a)

The step given by (6.150b) is termed the velocity update and the step by (6.150a) the position update. They are both handled by a single explicit Euler step.

In [Guendelman et al., 2003] a different approach is taken to collision resolving: a fixed number of iterations are performed over all the contact points. Thus, after having performed the collision resolving, there might still be colliding contacts.

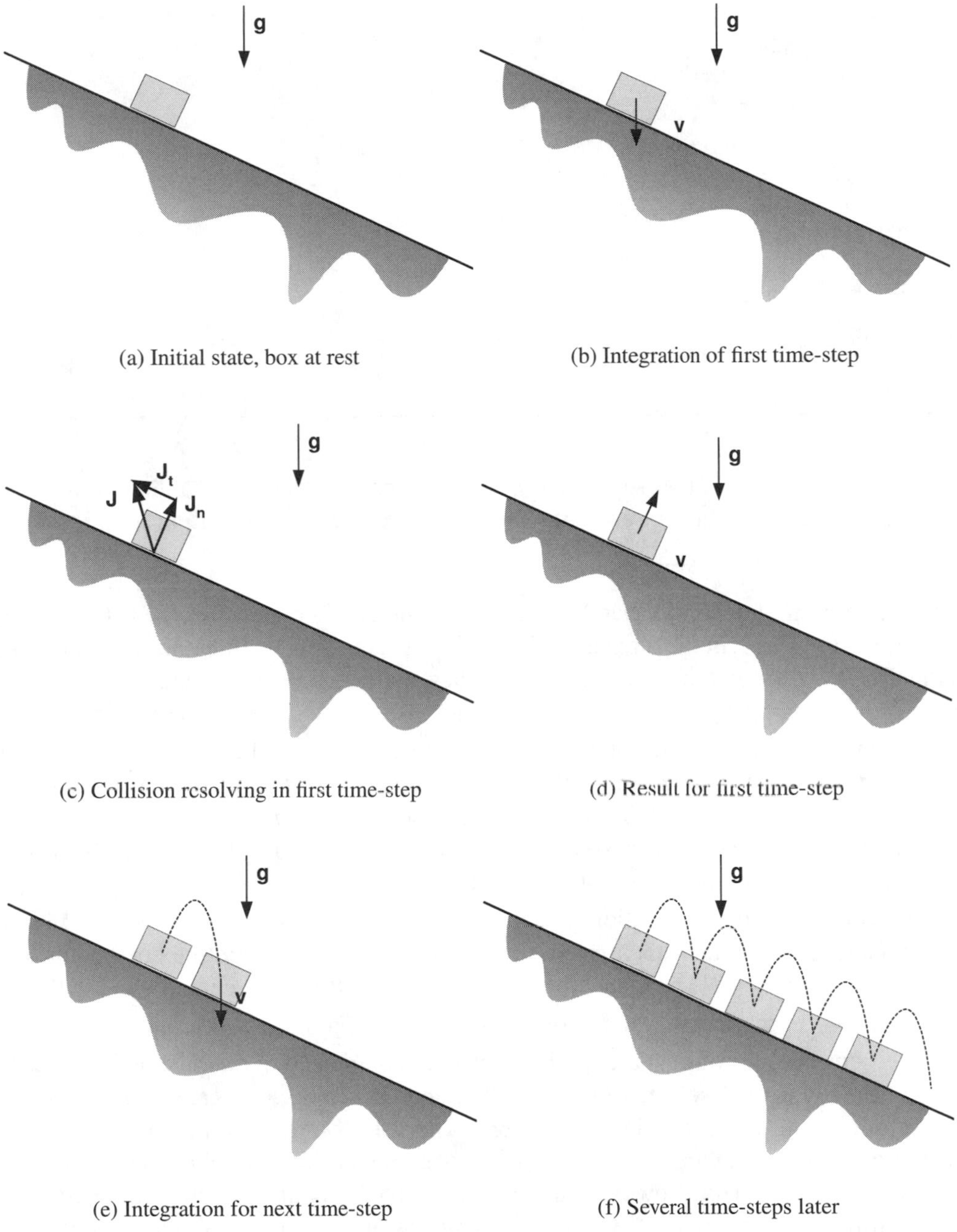

(a) Initial state, box at rest

(b) Integration of first time-step

(c) Collision resolving in first time-step

(d) Result for first time-step

(e) Integration for next time-step

(f) Several time-steps later

Figure 6.31: Box at rest on inclined plane, coefficient of restitution is one, friction is large enough to keep box from sliding. However, due to the nature of the time-stepping method, box starts to bounce down inclined plane.

```
algorithm time-step(Δt)
  for 5 iterations
    collision resolving
  next iteration
  velocity-update
  tmp = epsilon
  epsilon = -1
  for 10 iterations
    epsilon += 1/10
    contact-handling
  next iteration
  shock-propagation
  epsilon = tmp
  position-update
  t_cur = t_cur + Δt
end algorithm
```

Figure 6.32: Pseudocode of the separated collision and contact time integration method. In [Guendelman et al., 2003] 5 collision resolving iterations and 10 contact handling iterations are used.

Similarly, when doing the contact handling, a fixed number of iterations is used. Contact handling is different from collision resolving in several aspects. For instance, the coefficient of restitution is set to 1 and incrementally raised so that in the last iteration it has value zero. This has the effect of slowing down objects before they are stopped. Also, more iterations are used than in the collision resolving.

Shock propagation is done immediately after the last contact handling iteration. Shock propagation also uses a restitution coefficient of zero. Furthermore, objects in a stack are cleverly fixated and unfixated while iterating over the contact points. Together, this has the effect of propagating a shock through a stack of objects, correcting faulty behavior. Note that contact handling is needed before shock propagation, otherwise objects will not feel the weight of each other.

As with the collision resolving, colliding contact points are not guaranteed to be completely resolved after the last contact handling and shock propagation iterations, even though the coefficient of restitution is zero in these cases. This should be clear from the two balls on the plane example in Section 6.2.1.

Figure 6.32 shows a pseudocode version of the new time-stepping method.

The predicted positions of objects are used for the collision detection queries. This means that before each iteration of the collision resolver, contact handler, and the shock propagation, the predicted position is computed before doing a collision detection query. The collision detection query will therefore return future expected colliding contact points. These contact points are used to change the current velocities such that penetration is avoided. However, having altered the velocities, one must update the predicted positions in the following iteration. The predicted positions are computed taking a single explicit Euler step on (6.150a).

Figure 6.33 shows pseudocode of the collision resolving. Contact handling is similar to collision resolving. Shock propagation is similar to the contact handling, however there are some significant differences. A contact graph is built and contact points are processed in an order corresponding to their

```
algorithm collision-resolve
  move all bodies to predicted locations
  collision detection
  order contact points by penetration depth
  for each contact point apply collision law
end algorithm
```

Figure 6.33: Collision resolving consists of a single iteration over all contacts.

```
algorithm shock-propagation-handling
  move all bodies to predicted locations
  collision detection
  compute contact graph
  for each stack layer bottom up order
    order contact points in layer by penetration depth
    for each contact point apply collision law
  next layer
end algorithm
```

Figure 6.34: Shock propagation. This is similar to collision resolving except that contacts are processed in a bottom-to-top stack layer fashion.

placement in the contact graph. The contact graph is used to analyze if objects are stacked on top of each other. Afterward, contact points are organized into disjoint sets representing the *stack layers* in a stack. These layers are processed in a bottom-to-top fashion using a coefficient of restitution equal to zero, and setting lower bodies to be fixed. That is, they have infinite mass for this computation. Figure 6.34 shows a pseudocode version of shock propagation.

Taking large fixed time-steps is an advantage from a computational viewpoint, and thus very attractive for large-scale simulations. However, if time-steps are too large, tunneling or overshooting can easily occur. To reduce the chance of this simulation artifact, the time-step can be limited; for instance, by making sure that the fastest moving object does not move further than some specified fraction of the smallest bounding box width of the smallest object. This can definitely be incorrect, but seems to work well in practice.

In [Guendelman et al., 2003] after having applied an impulse to a contact point, the collision results are reevaluated between the object pairs for that contact point. That is, the object pairs' predicted positions are updated and the narrow-phase collision detection query is repeated. This is done in the hope that resolving a colliding contact point may change the predicted positions, such that the object pair will no longer be colliding. The method outlined here corresponds to the optimized method in [Guendelman et al., 2003].

There are a few publicly available implementations of the method using an even more optimized approach, in the sense that fewer collision detection queries are performed. For instance, one can reduce the number of iterations to just one for both the collision resolving and contact handling. Furthermore, a single collision detection query could be run and the same contact points can be reused for the collision

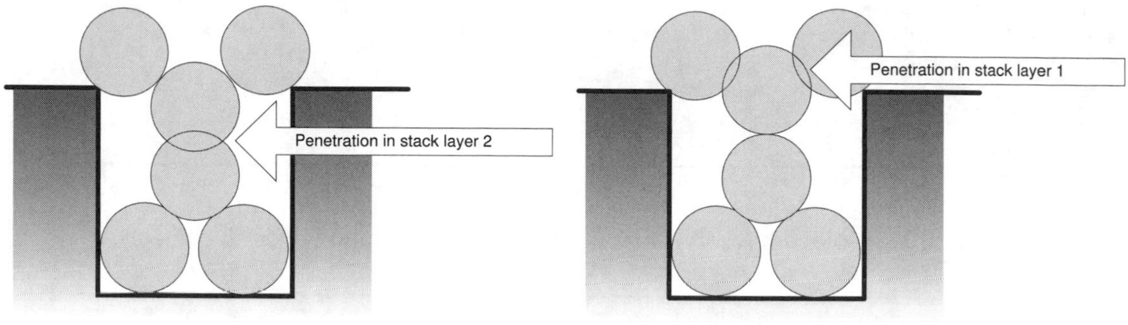

(a) Shock propagation results in Figure 6.35(b)

(b) Shock propagation results in Figure 6.35(a)

Figure 6.35: Errors cannot be corrected by shock propagation if there are cyclic dependencies.

resolving, the contact handling, and the shock propagation. This, of course, will increase the chance of artifacts such as penetrations, tunneling, and overshooting. On the other hand, it will yield a speed-up of a factor of 10–16 depending on the number of iterations and the kind of collision detection algorithms one chooses to use.

Finally, the purpose of shock propagation is to fix simulation errors. Therefore it can be replaced by other *error-correcting methods*, such as the *projection error-correction* explained in Section 7.10 and Section 7.14. These have the advantage of being able to completely fix penetration errors. Note that the propagation that occurs from the bottommost layer of a stack to the top, has trouble fixing errors for cyclic configurations as illustrated in Figure 6.35.

6.4.1 Computing Stack Layers

Contact graphs are easily computed [Erleben, 2005], a contact group is a subset of objects in the configuration, all in mutual contact with each other. Edges are created between objects if they are in contact and contact points are stored directly in these edges. Thus, we want to analyze a contact group for its stack structure and if possible, compute *stack layers* of the contact group.

A stack is defined as a set of objects being supported by one or more fixed objects. A cup on top of a table is a stack. The table is the fixed body and the cup is supported by the table. Objects in a stack can be assigned a number indicating how far away they are from the fixed object supporting them. This number is an indication of the height of the object in the stack. Thus, all fixed objects in a configuration have a stack height of zero. Nonfixed objects in direct contact with the fixed objects have a stack height of one. Nonfixed objects in direct contact with objects with stack height one, but not in contact with any fixed objects, have a stack height of two. A simple example is shown in Figure 6.36. This definition of stack height does not give a unique sense of an up-and-down direction as is commonly known from the real world. This is illustrated in Figure 6.37. Notice the position of the object with the largest stack height. An object is said to be closer to the bottom of the stack compared to another object if the stack height of the object is lower than the other object. Similarly, the bottommost objects are those having the lowest

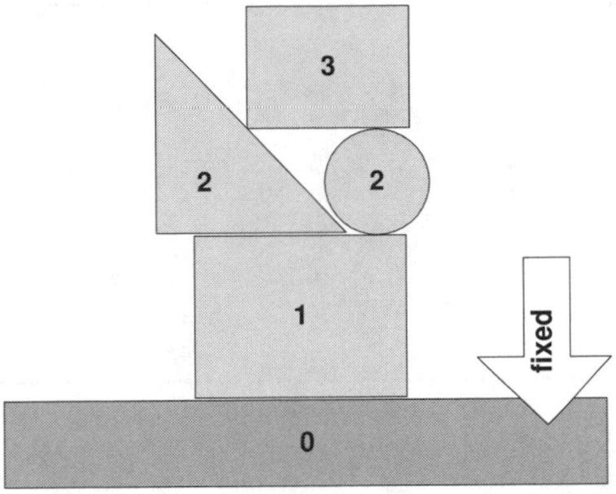

Figure 6.36: Simple stacked objects annotated with stack height.

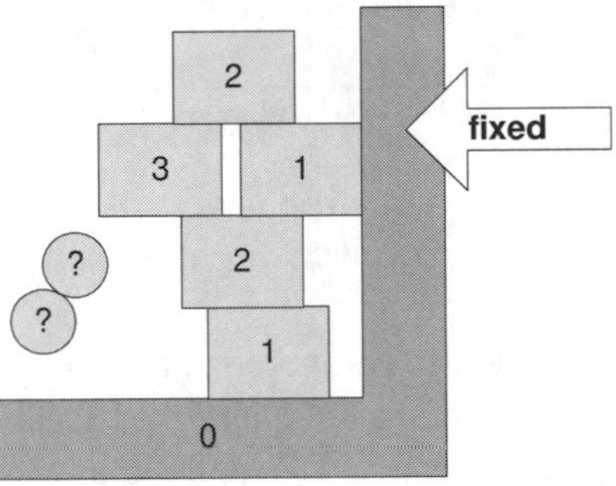

Figure 6.37: Nonsimple stacked objects annotated with stack height. Free-floating objects are marked with a question mark.

stack height, that is the fixed objects.

A free-floating object is special, since it is not in contact with any other objects; however, one may even have an entire group of bodies, all in mutual contact with each other, but none in contact with a fixed object. In these cases, it does not make sense to talk about assigning a stack height to the objects. Instead, the convention can be used to assign these kinds of objects an infinite stack height to distinguish them from objects that are part of a stack. A negative value could also be used, but is not an efficient choice for the algorithm presented in this section.

The stack height of objects is easily computed by doing a *breadth-first traversal* on each contact group. Initially, the stack height of all objects is set to infinity unless they are fixed objects, in which case their stack height is set to zero. Also, all fixed objects are pushed onto a queue. This queue is used by the breadth-first traversal. The initialization steps are shown in Figure 6.38.

After the initialization, the breadth-first traversal will pop an object, A, from the queue and iterate over all incident contact graph edges to object A. For each edge it is tested to determine if the object, B, at the other end of the edge has been visited by the traversal before. If not, this object is pushed onto the

```
Queue Q
for each body in Group do
  if body is fixed then
    height(body)=0
    Q.push(body)
    visit(body) = true
  else
    height(body) = infinity
    visit(body) = false
next body
```

Figure 6.38: Initialization of stack analysis algorithm. All bodies in a contact group are traversed; fixed bodies are identified and added to a queue for further processing.

queue. The height h_B of the object B is also computed as

$$h_B \leftarrow \min(h_B, h_A + 1). \tag{6.151}$$

That is, either a shorter path to object B is already known, in which case h_B is left unchanged, or it is shorter to get to B, by going from A. The cost of taking this part is one more than the cost of getting to object A.

During the traversal a stack layer index is computed for the edges as they are being visited. A stack layer is defined by two succeeding stack heights, such as 0 and 1. These two stack heights define a subset of objects in the contact group. That is, stack layer 0 is defined as all objects with stack height 0 and stack height 1, and all edges between these objects. Stack layer 1 is defined by all objects with stack height 1 and stack height 2, and all edges between these objects, and so on. This means that an edge between an object with height i and another object with height $i + 1$ is given stack layer index i.

Note that there is some subtlety with edges between objects with the same object height. As an example, for stack layer i, if we have an edge between two objects both with stack height $i + 1$, then the edge belongs to stack layer i. Ideally an edge between two objects with height i should also be added to stack layer i. However, this is not done because the stack layers are processed in a bottom-up fashion, thus contact points belonging to the edge between objects at height i were taken care of when stack layer $i - 1$ was processed.

Figure 6.39 shows pseudocode for assigning stack heights to objects and stack layer indices to edges.

After having assigned stack heights to objects and stack layer indices to edges, it is a simple matter to traverse these and assign them to the respective layers they belong to.

Objects are a little special. Given an object, A at stack height i, one must traverse the edges and examine the stack heights of the objects at the other end. If an object B with stack height $i - 1$ is found, then object A is safely added to stack layer $i - 1$; if an object C is found with stack height $i + 1$, then object A is added to stack layer i. Object A can only belong to stack layer $i - 1$ and i; this means as soon as two other objects have been found indicating that object A should be in these two stack layers, one can stop traversing the remaining incident edges of object A.

Figure 6.40 shows the pseudocode for building the stack layers.

```
List edges
timestamp = timestamp + 1
height = 0;
while Q not empty
  A = pop(Q)
  for each edge on A do
    B = body on edge that is not A
    if not visit(B) then
      Q.push(B)
      visit(B) = true
    end if
    height(B) = min( height(B), height(A) + 1 )
    if height(B) = height(A) and height(B) not 0 then
      layer(edge) = height(B) -1
   else
      layer(edge) = min( height(B), height(A) )
   height = max(height,layer(edge))
   if not timestamp(edge) = timestamp then
     timestamp(edge) = timestamp
     edges.push(edge)
   end if
  next edge
end while
```

Figure 6.39: A breadth-first traversal is performed, assigning a stack height to each body, equal to the number of edges on the minimum path to any fixed body. Edges of the contact group are collected into a list for further processing.

```
Group layers[height +1]
for each edge in edges do
   idx  = layer(edge)
   add contacts(edge) to layers(idx)
next edge

for each body A in Group do
  if height(A)=infinity then
    continue
  end if
  in_lower = false
  in_upper = false
  for each edge on A do
    B = other body on edge
    if height(B) > height(A) then
      in_upper = true
    end if
    if height(B) < height(A) then
      in_lower = true
    end if
    if in_upper and in_lower then
      break
  next edge
  if in_upper then
    layers[height(A)].push(body)
  end if
  if in_lower then
    layers[height(A) - 1].push(body)
  end if
next body
return layers
```

Figure 6.40: Building stack layers by processing all edges and bodies examining their stack height and layer indices.

7

Constraint-Based Multibody Animation

Constraint-based simulation is usually grouped in four formulations: force-based, velocity-based, kinetic energy-based, and motion-space based. This chapter will discuss the force- and velocity-based methods. We refer the reader to [Milenkovic et al., 2001, Schmidl, 2002] for the kinetic energy-method and to [Redon et al., 2003] for the motion-space method.

In *force-based formulations*, the exact contact force at a given time is found and then used in an ordinary differential equation describing the motion of the bodies in the scene. In a sense, a force-based formulation sees the instantaneous picture of the configuration, while a *velocity-based formulation* on the other hand, sees the effect of the dynamics over an entire time interval. Imagine that the true physical *contact force*, $\boldsymbol{f}_{\text{true}}(t)$, is somehow known. The *impulse* $\boldsymbol{J}$ in the time interval Δt is then given as

$$\boldsymbol{J} = \int_0^{\Delta t} \boldsymbol{f}_{\text{true}}(t) dt. \tag{7.1}$$

and with Newton's second law of motion one can solve for the velocity, $\boldsymbol{v}_{\Delta t}$, as follows

$$\int_0^{\Delta t} m \frac{d\boldsymbol{v}}{dt} dt = \int_0^{\Delta t} \boldsymbol{f}_{\text{true}}(t) \tag{7.2a}$$

$$m \left(\boldsymbol{v}_{\Delta t} - \boldsymbol{v}_0 \right) = \boldsymbol{J} \tag{7.2b}$$

A new position can now be found by integrating the velocity. The "force," $\boldsymbol{f}$, which we try to solve for in a velocity-based formulation can be interpreted as

$$\boldsymbol{J} = \Delta t \boldsymbol{f}, \tag{7.3}$$

which numerically will produce the same movement as if we had known the true contact force and computed the time integral. Since velocity-based formulations solve for impulses, they are also called impulse-based formulations, not to be mistaken with impulse-based simulation, which is an entirely different simulation paradigm, as discussed in Chapter 6.

A force-based formulation on the other hand, tries to compute the force, $\boldsymbol{f}_{\text{true}}(t)$, then it will use the force to solve for the acceleration of the motion, which is then integrated once to yield velocities and twice to yield a new position.

Force-based formulations cannot handle collisions, and we must switch to an impulse-momentum law at the point of collision [Baraff, 1989, Anitescu et al., 1996, Pfeiffer et al., 1996b, Chatterjee et al., 1998]. Force-based formulations also suffer from indeterminacy and inconsistency [Baraff, 1991, Stewart, 2000]. The velocity-based formulation suffers from none of these drawbacks. Another advantage of the impulse-based formulation is that it does not suffer from the small time-step problem in the same extent as the force-based formulation, meaning that larger time-steps can be taken during the simulation. The small time-step problem is described by Milenkovic and Schmild [Milenkovic et al., 2001, Schmidl, 2002].

Velocity-based formulations in constraint-based methods are widely popular and used, e.g., Open Dynamics Engine [ODE, 2005], Karma from MathEngine [Karma, 2005], and Vortex from Critical Mass Labs [Vortex, 2005]. In the following, we will present the classical velocity-based constraint formulation [Stewart et al., 1996, Stewart et al., 2000], give a possible object-oriented implementation design, and discuss various practical issues. Furthermore, we will discuss work presented [Anitescu et al., 1997, Sauer et al., 1998, ODE, 2005].

Many papers and books written on velocity-based formulations use a rather high and abstract level of mathematical notation together with a great amount of "long forgotten" analytical mechanics. There is a widespread notation and many small variations.

7.1 Equations of Motion

From classical mechanics, we have the *Newton-Euler equations* (see Section 22.1 for details), describing the motion for all bodies. For the i'th body, the mass of body i is given by m_i and the inertia tensor by $\boldsymbol{I}_i$, the position is given by $\boldsymbol{r}_i$ and the velocity of the center of mass as $\boldsymbol{v}_i$, the orientation is represented by the quaternion q_i and the angular velocity by $\boldsymbol{\omega}_i$. The Newton-Euler equations for the i'th body look like this (summations are taken over all contact points):

$$\dot{\boldsymbol{r}}_i = \boldsymbol{v}_i \tag{7.4a}$$

$$\dot{q}_i = \frac{1}{2}\boldsymbol{\omega}_i q_i \tag{7.4b}$$

$$\dot{v}_i = m_i^{-1} \sum_{j_k=i} \boldsymbol{f}_k - m_i^{-1} \sum_{i_k=i} \boldsymbol{f}_k + m_i^{-1} \boldsymbol{f}_i^{\text{ ext}} \tag{7.4c}$$

$$\dot{\boldsymbol{\omega}}_i = I_i^{-1} \sum_{j_k=i} \boldsymbol{r}_{kj} \times \boldsymbol{f}_k - I_i^{-1} \sum_{i_k=i} \boldsymbol{r}_{ki} \times \boldsymbol{f}_k \tag{7.4d}$$

$$- I_i^{-1}\boldsymbol{\omega}_i \times I_i \boldsymbol{\omega}_i + I_i^{-1} \boldsymbol{\tau}_i^{\text{ ext}} \tag{7.4e}$$

The dot-notation means the total time derivative $\frac{d}{dt}$ and is used to ease readability. Observe that $\boldsymbol{f}_k$ denotes the contact force at the k'th contact. For the time being, we will ignore joints and motors. The effect of all external forces on the center of mass is given by $\boldsymbol{f}_i^{\text{ ext}}$ and the total torque from external forces is given by $\boldsymbol{\tau}_i^{\text{ ext}}$.

For notational convenience, we introduce a contact table. Consider a total of K contacts, and assign a unique number k to each contact. For each contact, we know the indices i_k and j_k of the two incident bodies. We use the convention that $i_k < j_k$. We also have a contact normal $\boldsymbol{n}_k$ and a contact point $\boldsymbol{p}_k$ both specified in the world coordinate system, and with the convention that the contact normal points from the body with the smallest index to the body with the largest index. This is illustrated in Figure 7.1. Note that we can never have $i_k = j_k$. For each contact we can compute a vector from the center of mass, $\boldsymbol{r}_i$, of an incident body with index i, to the point of contact $\boldsymbol{p}_k$, that is,

$$\boldsymbol{r}_{ki} = \boldsymbol{p}_k - \boldsymbol{r}_i \tag{7.5}$$

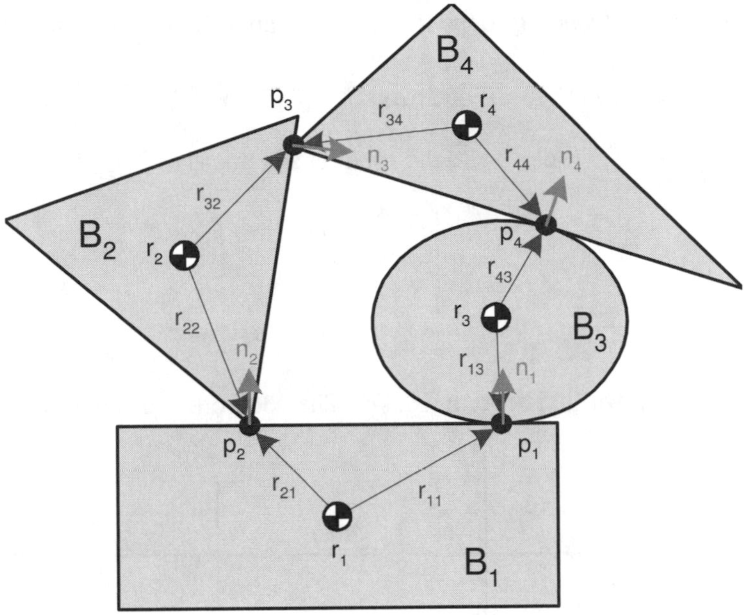

Figure 7.1: The contact normal convention and notation.

The Newton-Euler equations can now be written as

$$\dot{\boldsymbol{s}} = \boldsymbol{S}\boldsymbol{u} \tag{7.6a}$$

$$\dot{\boldsymbol{u}} = \boldsymbol{M}^{-1}\left(\boldsymbol{C}\boldsymbol{N}\boldsymbol{f} + \boldsymbol{f}_{ext}\right). \tag{7.6b}$$

Now we will introduce some matrix notation, which will allow us to write the Newton-Euler equations for all bodies in a single equation. The position and orientation of n bodies may be concatenated into a single *generalized position* and *orientation* vector, $\boldsymbol{s} \in \mathbb{R}^{7n}$:

$$\boldsymbol{s} = \left[\boldsymbol{r}_1, q_1, \boldsymbol{r}_2, q_2, \cdots, \boldsymbol{r}_n, q_n\right]^T. \tag{7.7}$$

Similarly, we can write the *generalized velocity* vector $\boldsymbol{u} \in \mathbb{R}^{6n}$ as

$$\boldsymbol{u} = \left[\boldsymbol{v}_1, \boldsymbol{\omega}_1, \boldsymbol{v}_2, \boldsymbol{\omega}_2, \cdots, \boldsymbol{v}_n, \boldsymbol{\omega}_n\right]^T. \tag{7.8}$$

For the time being, the frictional effects will be ignored, implying that the contact force can be written as

$$\boldsymbol{f}_k = f_k \boldsymbol{n}_k. \tag{7.9}$$

This means that we only need to remember the magnitude, f_k, of the normal force, and these can now be concatenated into a single vector $\boldsymbol{f} \in \mathbb{R}^K$

$$\boldsymbol{f} = \left[f_1, f_2, \cdots, f_K\right]^T. \tag{7.10}$$

The external forces, torques, and velocity-dependent forces can also be concatenated into a vector, $\boldsymbol{f}_{\text{ext}} \in \mathbb{R}^{6n}$,

$$\boldsymbol{f}_{ext} = \left[\boldsymbol{f}_1{}^{\text{ext}}, \boldsymbol{\tau}_1{}^{\text{ext}} - \boldsymbol{\omega}_1 \times I_1\boldsymbol{\omega}_1, \cdots, \boldsymbol{f}_n{}^{\text{ext}}, \boldsymbol{\tau}_n{}^{\text{ext}} - \boldsymbol{\omega}_n \times I_n\boldsymbol{\omega}_n\right]^T. \tag{7.11}$$

Given $q_i = [s_i, x_i, y_i, z_i]^T \in \mathbb{R}^4$, we can write the rotation as a matrix $\boldsymbol{Q}_i \in \mathbb{R}^{4\times 3}$ as:

$$\boldsymbol{Q}_i = \frac{1}{2}\begin{bmatrix} -x_i & -y_i & -z_i \\ s_i & z_i & -y_i \\ -z_i & s_i & x_i \\ y_i & -x_i & s_i \end{bmatrix}. \tag{7.12}$$

where $\frac{1}{2}\boldsymbol{\omega}_i q_i = \boldsymbol{Q}_i\boldsymbol{\omega}_i$, as shown in Theorem 18.47. The rotations can now be concatenated into a matrix $\boldsymbol{S} \in \mathbb{R}^{7n\times 6n}$,

$$\boldsymbol{S} = \begin{bmatrix} \mathbf{1} & & & & \mathbf{0} \\ & \boldsymbol{Q}_1 & & & \\ & & \ddots & & \\ & & & \mathbf{1} & \\ \mathbf{0} & & & & \boldsymbol{Q}_n \end{bmatrix}, \tag{7.13}$$

Matrix $\boldsymbol{S}$ is also illustrated in Figure 7.2. The generalized mass matrix $\boldsymbol{M} \in \mathbb{R}^{6n\times 6n}$ is

$$\boldsymbol{M} = \begin{bmatrix} m_1\mathbf{1} & & & & \mathbf{0} \\ & \boldsymbol{I}_1 & & & \\ & & \vdots & & \\ & & & m_n\mathbf{1} & \\ \mathbf{0} & & & & \boldsymbol{I}_n \end{bmatrix} \tag{7.14}$$

where $\mathbf{1}$ is the identity matrix. The layout of the mass matrix is illustrated in Figure 7.3. The matrix of contact normals $\boldsymbol{N} \in \mathbb{R}^{3K\times K}$ is

$$\boldsymbol{N} = \begin{bmatrix} \boldsymbol{n}_1 & & & \mathbf{0} \\ & \boldsymbol{n}_2 & & \\ & & \ddots & \\ \mathbf{0} & & & \boldsymbol{n}_k \end{bmatrix}, \tag{7.15}$$

as shown in Figure 7.4, and the matrix of contact conditions $\boldsymbol{C} \in \mathbb{R}^{6n\times 3K}$ is

$$\boldsymbol{C}_{lk} = \begin{cases} -\mathbf{1} & \text{for } l = 2i_k - 1 \\ -\boldsymbol{r}_{ki_k}^{\times} & \text{for } l = 2i_k \\ \mathbf{1} & \text{for } l = 2j_k - 1 \\ \boldsymbol{r}_{kj_k}^{\times} & \text{for } l = 2j_k \\ \mathbf{0} & \text{otherwise} \end{cases}. \tag{7.16}$$

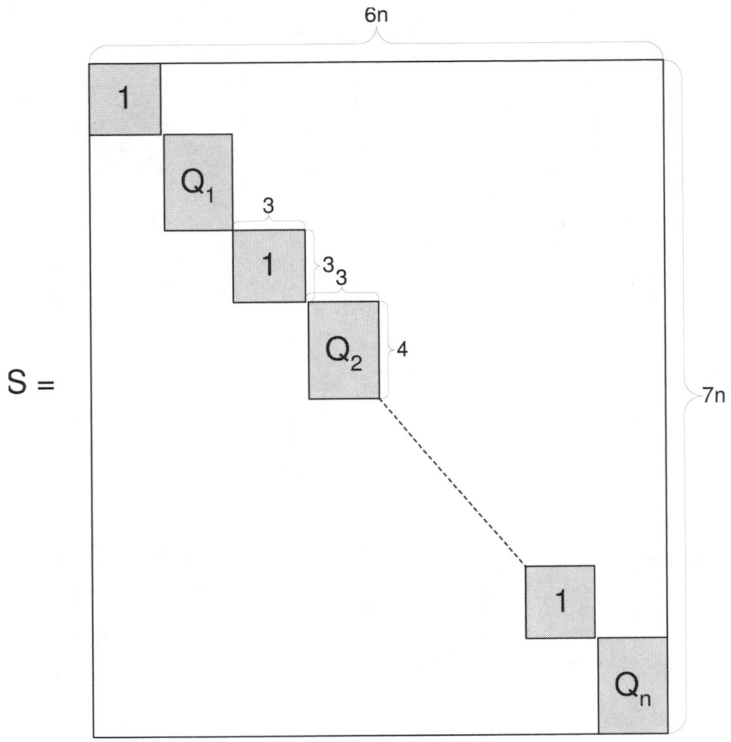

Figure 7.2: The $\boldsymbol{S}$ matrix layout.

Here $\boldsymbol{r}^{\times} \in \mathbb{R}^{3\times 3}$ is the skew-symmetric matrix given by

$$\boldsymbol{r}^{\times} = \begin{bmatrix} 0 & -r_3 & r_2 \\ r_3 & 0 & -r_1 \\ -r_2 & r_1 & 0 \end{bmatrix}. \tag{7.17}$$

It is easy to show that $\boldsymbol{r}^{\times}\boldsymbol{a} = \boldsymbol{r} \times \boldsymbol{a}$ (see Chapter 18). Every column of $\boldsymbol{C}$ corresponds to a single contact and every row to a single body (see Figure 7.5).

Using an *Euler scheme* as described in Chapter 23, we can write the discretized equations of motion as follows,

$$\boldsymbol{s}^{t+\Delta t} = \boldsymbol{s}^t + \Delta t \boldsymbol{S}\boldsymbol{u}^{t+\Delta t}, \tag{7.18a}$$

$$\boldsymbol{u}^{t+\Delta t} = \boldsymbol{u}^t + \Delta t \boldsymbol{M}^{-1}\left(\boldsymbol{C}\boldsymbol{N}\boldsymbol{f}^{t+\Delta t} + \boldsymbol{f}_{ext}\right). \tag{7.18b}$$

Here, superscript denotes the time at which a quantity is computed. Note that the matrices depend on time through $\boldsymbol{u}$ and $\boldsymbol{s}$. If they are evaluated at time t, then we have a semi-implicit method, and if they are evaluated at time $t + \Delta t$, then we have an implicit method.

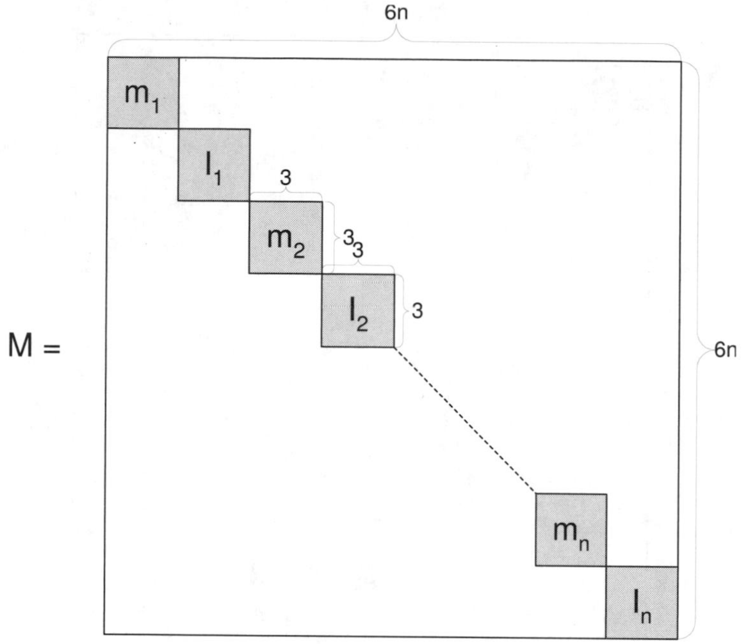

Figure 7.3: The M matrix layout.

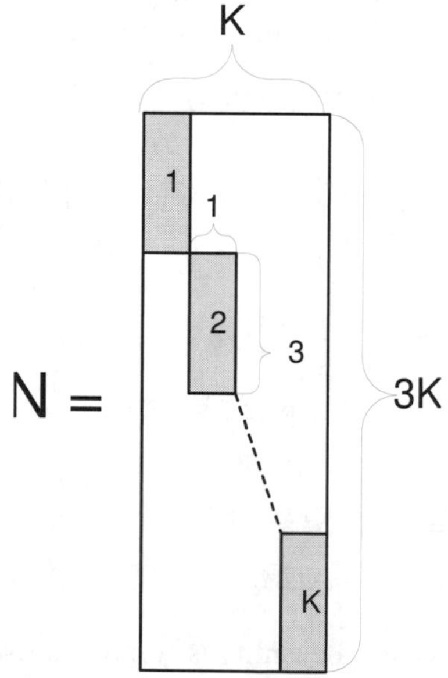

Figure 7.4: The N matrix layout.

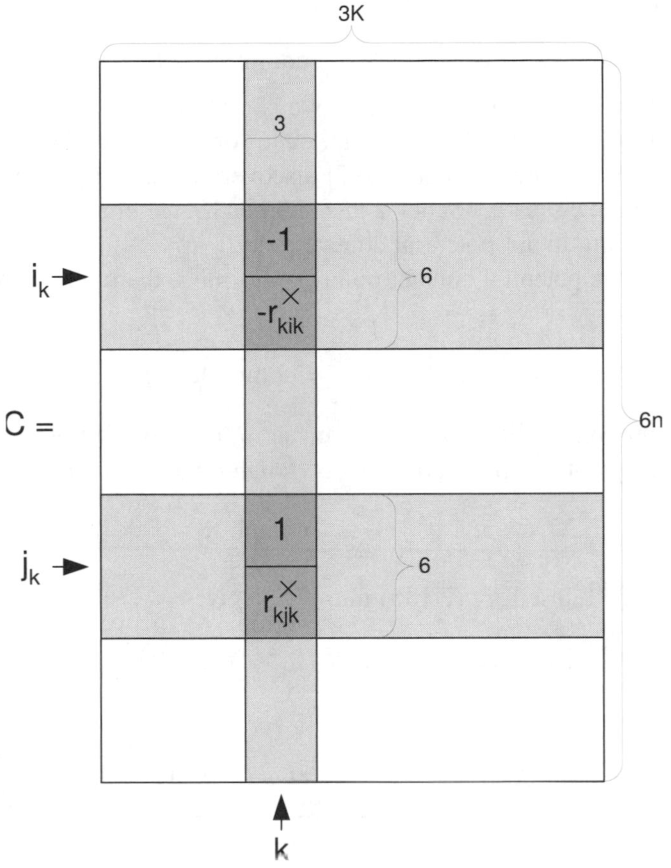

Figure 7.5: The $\boldsymbol{C}$ matrix layout.

7.2 The Contact Condition

The projection matrix, $\boldsymbol{P}_k \in \mathbb{R}^{3K\times 3}$ will be needed for further analysis of the k'th contact point. Its transpose is defined as

$$\boldsymbol{P}_k^T = \left[\left[\begin{matrix} 0 & 0 & 0 \\ 0 & 0 & 0 \\ 0 & 0 & 0 \end{matrix}\right] \middle| \ldots \middle| \left[\begin{matrix} 0 & 0 & 0 \\ 0 & 0 & 0 \\ 0 & 0 & 0 \end{matrix}\right] \middle| \left[\begin{matrix} 1 & 0 & 0 \\ 0 & 1 & 0 \\ 0 & 0 & 1 \end{matrix}\right] \middle| \left[\begin{matrix} 0 & 0 & 0 \\ 0 & 0 & 0 \\ 0 & 0 & 0 \end{matrix}\right] \middle| \ldots \middle| \left[\begin{matrix} 0 & 0 & 0 \\ 0 & 0 & 0 \\ 0 & 0 & 0 \end{matrix}\right] \right]. \tag{7.19}$$

That is, the k'th 3×3 submatrix is set to the identity matrix. The normal component of the relative contact velocity of the k'th contact point is given by

$$\boldsymbol{n}_k^T \boldsymbol{P}_k^T \boldsymbol{C}^T \boldsymbol{u} = \boldsymbol{n}_k^T \left(\boldsymbol{v}_{j_k} + \boldsymbol{\omega}_{j_k} \times \boldsymbol{r}_{kj_k} \right) - \boldsymbol{n}_k^T \left(\boldsymbol{v}_{i_k} + \boldsymbol{\omega}_{i_k} \times \boldsymbol{r}_{ki_k} \right). \tag{7.20}$$

Notice that multiplying by the projection matrix will mask out the k'th contact conditions. If body B_{i_k} and B_{j_k} touch at contact point $\boldsymbol{p}_k$ at time t, then the *complementarity condition* for the velocities must hold

$$n_k^T P_k^T C^T u^{t+\Delta t} \geq 0 \quad \text{compl. to} \quad f_k \geq 0. \tag{7.21}$$

A complementarity condition means that if we have two conditions, then one is nonzero and the other is zero or vice versa. Stewart and Trinkle [Stewart et al., 1996] originally used a complementarity condition on position. Anitscu and Potra [Anitescu et al., 1997] discovered that using the velocity complementarity problem guarantees solution existence. Sauer and Schömer [Sauer et al., 1998] expanded the velocity formulation further by handling future potential contact points.

If there is no contact at the potential contact point p_k at time t, then the following linearized complementarity condition holds:

$$n_k^T P_k^T C^T u^{t+\Delta t} \geq \frac{\nu_k}{\Delta t} \quad \text{compl. to} \quad f_k \geq 0. \tag{7.22}$$

Later we will go into details on the linearizing. If we use $\nu_k = 0$ for all touching contacts, then we can formulate a complementarity condition for all contacts (touching and potential ones) as

$$N^T C^T u^{t+\Delta t} \geq \frac{\nu}{\Delta t} \quad \text{compl. to} \quad f \geq 0, \tag{7.23}$$

with $\nu = [\nu_1, \ldots, \nu_K]^T \in \mathbb{R}^K$. Inserting (7.18b) into (7.23) gives

$$N^T C^T \left(u^t + \Delta t M^{-1} \left(C N f^{t+\Delta t} + f_{ext} \right) \right) - \frac{\nu}{\Delta t} \geq 0. \tag{7.24}$$

Rearranging yields

$$\underbrace{N^T C^T M^{-1} C N}_{A} \underbrace{\Delta t f^{t+\Delta t}}_{x} + \underbrace{N^T C^T \left(u^t + \Delta t M^{-1} f_{ext} \right) - \frac{\nu}{\Delta t}}_{b} \geq 0, \tag{7.25}$$

which results in a *linear complementarity problem* (*LCP*) (see Section 19.10) of the form

$$Ax + b \geq 0 \quad \text{compl. to} \quad x \geq 0, \tag{7.26}$$

where $A \in \mathbb{R}^{K \times K}$ and $x, b \in \mathbb{R}^K$. Entry l, k of A is

$$\begin{aligned} A_{lk} = {} & \delta_{i_l i_k} n_l^T \left(\frac{1}{m_{i_k}} \mathbf{1} - r_{l i_l}^{\times} I_{i_k}^{-1} r_{k i_k}^{\times} \right) n_k \\ & - \delta_{i_l j_k} n_l^T \left(\frac{1}{m_{j_k}} \mathbf{1} - r_{l i_l}^{\times} I_{j_k}^{-1} r_{k j_k}^{\times} \right) n_k \\ & - \delta_{j_l i_k} n_l^T \left(\frac{1}{m_{i_k}} \mathbf{1} - r_{l j_l}^{\times} I_{i_k}^{-1} r_{k i_k}^{\times} \right) n_k \\ & + \delta_{j_l j_k} n_l^T \left(\frac{1}{m_{j_k}} \mathbf{1} - r_{l j_l}^{\times} I_{j_k}^{-1} r_{k j_k}^{\times} \right) n_k, \end{aligned} \tag{7.27}$$

with the *Kronecker symbol* being

$$\delta_{ij} = \begin{cases} 1 & \text{for } i = j, \\ 0 & \text{for } i \neq j. \end{cases} \tag{7.28}$$

7.3 Linearizing

Sauer and Schömer [Sauer et al., 1998] use a linearized contact condition in (7.23). In the following, we will derive the linearized contact condition. The linearization serves as a measure of when a potential contact constraint should be switched on. This allows bigger time-steps to be taken while keeping the error low. Taking the same time-step size without the linearization will imply a larger approximation error.

The k'th potential contact point may be represented by the closest points $\boldsymbol{p}_{i_k}$ and $\boldsymbol{p}_{j_k}$ between two bodies, B_{i_k} and B_{j_k}, which eventually meet and form the k'th contact point. The closest points depend on the position and orientation of the bodies. If we let the vector $\boldsymbol{s}_k \in \mathbb{R}^{14}$ be the generalized position vector of the two bodies, where $\boldsymbol{s}_k$'s function dependency of time has been omitted for readability,

$$\boldsymbol{s}_k = \left[\boldsymbol{r}_{i_k}, q_{i_k}, \boldsymbol{r}_{j_k}, q_{j_k}\right], \tag{7.29}$$

the minimal distance between the two bodies, $d_k(\boldsymbol{s}_k)$, is

$$d_k(\boldsymbol{s}_k) = \boldsymbol{n}_k^T(\boldsymbol{s}_k)\left(\boldsymbol{p}_{j_k} - \boldsymbol{p}_{i_k}\right) \geq 0, \tag{7.30}$$

where $\boldsymbol{n}_k$ is a unit vector pointing from $\boldsymbol{p}_{i_k}$ to $\boldsymbol{p}_{j_k}$. A first-order Taylor-expansion of $d_k(\boldsymbol{s}_k)$ at $\boldsymbol{s}_k{}'$ is

$$d_k(\boldsymbol{s}_k) = d_k(\boldsymbol{s}_k{}') + \left(\nabla_{\boldsymbol{s}_k} d_k(\boldsymbol{s}_k{}')\right)^T \left(\boldsymbol{s}_k - \boldsymbol{s}_k{}'\right) + O(\Delta t^2). \tag{7.31}$$

Notice that $\nabla_{\boldsymbol{s}_k}$ is the functional derivative introduced in Section 18.4. If we look at the backward difference of the time derivative of the generalized position vector, we find

$$\frac{d}{dt}\left(\boldsymbol{s}_k{}^{t+\Delta t}\right) = \frac{\boldsymbol{s}_k{}^{t+\Delta t} - \boldsymbol{s}_k{}^{t}}{\Delta t} + O(\Delta t). \tag{7.32}$$

Rearranging yields

$$\boldsymbol{s}_k{}^{t+\Delta t} = \boldsymbol{s}_k{}^{t} + \frac{d}{dt}\left(\boldsymbol{s}_k{}^{t+\Delta t}\right)\Delta t + O(\Delta t^2) \tag{7.33}$$

Again, we approximate $\nabla_{\boldsymbol{s}_k} d_k(\boldsymbol{s}_k{}')$ at $\boldsymbol{s}_k{}^{t+\Delta t}$ using Taylor's Theorem by taking the zeroth order expansion to get

$$\nabla_{\boldsymbol{s}_k} d_k(\boldsymbol{s}_k{}') = \nabla_{\boldsymbol{s}_k} d_k(\boldsymbol{s}_k{}^{t+\Delta t}) + O(\Delta t). \tag{7.34}$$

Substituting (7.33) for $\boldsymbol{s}_k$ in (7.31) gives

$$d_k(\boldsymbol{s}_k{}^{t+\Delta t}) \approx d_k(\boldsymbol{s}_k{}') + \left(\nabla_{\boldsymbol{s}_k} d_k(\boldsymbol{s}_k{}')\right)^T \left(\boldsymbol{s}_k{}^{t} + \frac{d}{dt}\left(\boldsymbol{s}_k{}^{t+\Delta t}\right)\Delta t - \boldsymbol{s}_k{}'\right) \tag{7.35}$$

$$= d_k(\boldsymbol{s}_k{}') + \left(\nabla_{\boldsymbol{s}_k} d_k(\boldsymbol{s}_k{}')\right)^T \left(\boldsymbol{s}_k{}^{t} - \boldsymbol{s}_k{}'\right)$$

$$+ \Delta t \left(\nabla_{\boldsymbol{s}_k} d_k(\boldsymbol{s}_k{}')\right)^T \frac{d}{dt}\left(\boldsymbol{s}_k{}^{t+\Delta t}\right). \tag{7.36}$$

Now we insert (7.34) in the last term and get

$$\begin{aligned} d_k({\boldsymbol{s}_k}^{t+\Delta t}) &\approx d_k({\boldsymbol{s}_k}') + \left(\nabla_{\boldsymbol{s}_k} d_k({\boldsymbol{s}_k}')\right)^T \left({\boldsymbol{s}_k}^t - {\boldsymbol{s}_k}'\right) \\ &\quad + \Delta t \left(\nabla_{\boldsymbol{s}_k} d_k({\boldsymbol{s}_k}^{t+\Delta t})\right)^T \frac{d}{dt} \left({\boldsymbol{s}_k}^{t+\Delta t}\right). \end{aligned} \tag{7.37}$$

Recall that the distance function is actually a function of time, $d_k(\boldsymbol{s}_k(t))$, so by the chain rule we have

$$\frac{d}{dt}\left(d_k(\boldsymbol{s}_k^{t+\Delta t})\right) = \left(\nabla d_k(\boldsymbol{s}_k^{t+\Delta t})\right)^T \frac{d}{dt}\left(\boldsymbol{s}_k^{t+\Delta t}\right). \tag{7.38}$$

Inserting (7.38) into (7.37) yields

$$\begin{aligned} d_k({\boldsymbol{s}_k}^{t+\Delta t}) &\approx d_k({\boldsymbol{s}_k}') + \left(\nabla_{\boldsymbol{s}_k} d_k({\boldsymbol{s}_k}')\right)^T \left({\boldsymbol{s}_k}^t - {\boldsymbol{s}_k}'\right) \\ &\quad + \Delta t \frac{d}{dt}\left(d_k({\boldsymbol{s}_k}^{t+\Delta t})\right). \end{aligned} \tag{7.39}$$

From past work such as [Baraff, 2001, Baraff, 1994], we know

$$\frac{d}{dt}\left(d_k(t)\right) = \boldsymbol{n}_k^T \left((\boldsymbol{v}_{j_k} + \boldsymbol{\omega}_{j_k} \times \boldsymbol{r}_{j_k}) - (\boldsymbol{v}_{i_k} + \boldsymbol{\omega}_{i_k} \times \boldsymbol{r}_{i_k})\right). \tag{7.40}$$

Using this in (7.39) together with (7.30), we derive

$$\begin{aligned} & d_k({\boldsymbol{s}_k}') + \left(\nabla_{\boldsymbol{s}_k} d_k({\boldsymbol{s}_k}')\right)^T \left({\boldsymbol{s}_k}^t - {\boldsymbol{s}_k}'\right) \\ &\quad + \Delta t \boldsymbol{n}_k^T \left(\left({\boldsymbol{v}_{j_k}}^{t+\Delta t} + {\boldsymbol{\omega}_{j_k}}^{t+\Delta t} \times {\boldsymbol{r}_{j_k}}^{t+\Delta t}\right)\right. \\ &\quad \left. - \left({\boldsymbol{v}_{i_k}}^{t+\Delta t} + {\boldsymbol{\omega}_{i_k}}^{t+\Delta t} \times {\boldsymbol{r}_{i_k}}^{t+\Delta t}\right)\right) \geq 0. \end{aligned} \tag{7.41}$$

Rearranging, we have

$$\begin{aligned} & \boldsymbol{n}_k^T \left(\left({\boldsymbol{v}_{j_k}}^{t+\Delta t} + {\boldsymbol{\omega}_{j_k}}^{t+\Delta t} \times {\boldsymbol{r}_{j_k}}^{t+\Delta t}\right) - \left({\boldsymbol{v}_{i_k}}^{t+\Delta t} + {\boldsymbol{\omega}_{i_k}}^{t+\Delta t} \times {\boldsymbol{r}_{i_k}}^{t+\Delta t}\right)\right) \\ &\quad \geq -\frac{1}{\Delta t}\left(d_k({\boldsymbol{s}_k}') + \left(\nabla_{\boldsymbol{s}_k} d_k({\boldsymbol{s}_k}')\right)^T \left({\boldsymbol{s}_k}^t - {\boldsymbol{s}_k}'\right)\right). \end{aligned} \tag{7.42}$$

Recall that the left side of this equation is in fact $\boldsymbol{n}_k^T \boldsymbol{P}_k^T \boldsymbol{C}^T \boldsymbol{u}^{\ t+\Delta t}$. It now follows that

$$\boldsymbol{n}_k^T \boldsymbol{P}_k^T \boldsymbol{C}^T \boldsymbol{u}^{\ t+\Delta t} \geq -\frac{1}{\Delta t}\left(d_k({\boldsymbol{s}_k}') + \left(\nabla_{\boldsymbol{s}_k} d_k({\boldsymbol{s}_k}')\right)^T \left({\boldsymbol{s}_k}^t - {\boldsymbol{s}_k}'\right)\right). \tag{7.43}$$

Comparing with (7.22), we write

$$\nu_k = -\left(d_k({\boldsymbol{s}_k}') + \left(\nabla_{\boldsymbol{s}_k} d_k({\boldsymbol{s}_k}')\right)^T \left({\boldsymbol{s}_k}^t - {\boldsymbol{s}_k}'\right)\right). \tag{7.44}$$

All curvature information is lost with the linearized constraints, which implies that a step of length $O(\Delta t)$ introduces errors of $O(\Delta t^2)$. Hence the approach of Sauer and Schömer prevents the penetration of increasing to more than $O(h^2)$.

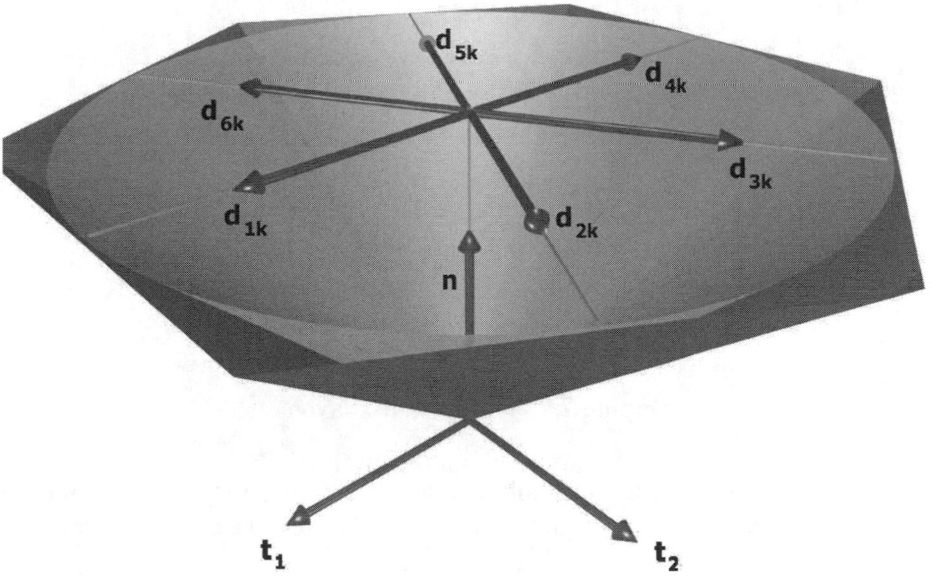

Figure 7.6: The friction pyramid approximation. We have chosen $\eta = 6$; observe that the $\boldsymbol{d}_{h_k}$'s positively span the friction pyramid.

7.4 The Frictional Case

In this section we will expand the formulation given in (7.26) to include *friction*. For each contact, we use two orthogonal unit vectors $\boldsymbol{t}_{1_k}$ and $\boldsymbol{t}_{2_k}$, which span the tangential plane at the k'th contact. Together with the normal vector $\boldsymbol{n}_k$, the three vectors form an orthogonal coordinate system (see Definition 18.6). The *friction cone* at the k'th contact is approximated by a discretized version having η direction vectors $\boldsymbol{d}_{h_k}$ with $h = 1, \ldots, \eta$, where $\eta = 2i$ for all $i \in N$ and $i \geq 2$. The direction vectors are concatenated into a matrix $\boldsymbol{D}_k \in \mathbb{R}^{3\times\eta}$

$$\boldsymbol{D}_k = [\boldsymbol{d}_{1_k}, \ldots, \boldsymbol{d}_{\eta_k}], \tag{7.45}$$

where

$$\boldsymbol{d}_{h_k} = \cos\left(\frac{2(h-1)\pi}{\eta}\right)\boldsymbol{t}_{1_k} + \sin\left(\frac{2(h-1)\pi}{\eta}\right)\boldsymbol{t}_{2_k}. \tag{7.46}$$

We have transformed the spatial cone limiting the *friction force* due to *Coulomb's friction law* and called the friction cone into a *friction pyramid* with η facets, as illustrated in Figure 7.6. For each direction vector we will use β_{h_k} for the magnitude of the component of friction force in the direction of $\boldsymbol{d}_{h_k}$. As before, we can build up a vector of all friction components $\boldsymbol{\beta}_k \in \mathbb{R}^\eta$,

$$\boldsymbol{\beta}_k = [\beta_{1_k}, \ldots, \beta_{\eta_k}]^T. \tag{7.47}$$

The modification of the equations of motion (7.6) is the definition of contact force $\boldsymbol{f}_k$ from (7.9), which we now write as

$$\boldsymbol{f}_k = f_k\boldsymbol{n}_k + \boldsymbol{D}_k\boldsymbol{\beta}_k. \tag{7.48}$$

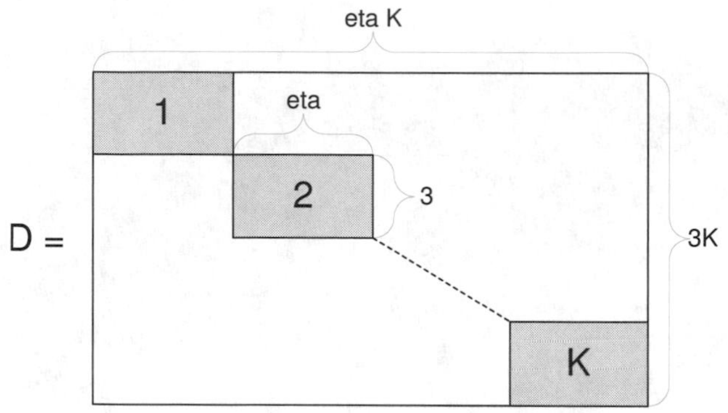

Figure 7.7: The $\boldsymbol{D}$ matrix layout.

As before, we use matrix notation, which will allow us to write the equations of motion in a single matrix equation. The generalized acceleration is again described by the Newton-Euler equations

$$\dot{\boldsymbol{u}} = \boldsymbol{M}^{-1} \left(\boldsymbol{C} \left(\boldsymbol{N} \boldsymbol{f} + \boldsymbol{D} \boldsymbol{\beta} \right) + \boldsymbol{f}_{ext} \right). \tag{7.49}$$

We need a vector, $\boldsymbol{\beta} \in \mathbb{R}^{\eta K}$

$$\boldsymbol{\beta} = \left[\boldsymbol{\beta}_1^T, \ldots, \boldsymbol{\beta}_K^T, \right]^T \tag{7.50}$$

That is the concatenation of the $\boldsymbol{\beta}_k$-vectors; we also need the matrix $\boldsymbol{D} \in \mathbb{R}^{3K \times \eta K}$

$$\boldsymbol{D} = \begin{bmatrix} \boldsymbol{D}_1 & & \boldsymbol{0} \\ & \boldsymbol{D}_2 & \\ & & \vdots \\ \boldsymbol{0} & & \boldsymbol{D}_K \end{bmatrix} \tag{7.51}$$

Figure 7.7 illustrates the $\boldsymbol{D}$ matrix layout. Using an *Euler scheme* gives us the discretized approximation

$$\boldsymbol{u}^{\,t+\Delta t} = \boldsymbol{u}^{\,t} + \Delta t \boldsymbol{M}^{-1} \left(\boldsymbol{C} \left(\boldsymbol{N} \boldsymbol{f} + \boldsymbol{D} \boldsymbol{\beta} \right) + \boldsymbol{f}_{ext} \right). \tag{7.52}$$

In order to model the relationship between the normal force and the friction, known as Coulomb's friction law, we need to add two complementarity conditions for the friction forces in addition to the previous complementarity condition for the normal force. We have a total of three complementarity conditions for the k'th contact:

$$\lambda_k \boldsymbol{e}_k + \boldsymbol{D}_k^T \boldsymbol{P}_k^T \boldsymbol{C}^T \boldsymbol{u}^{\,t+\Delta t} \geq 0 \qquad \text{compl. to} \quad \boldsymbol{\beta}_k \geq 0, \tag{7.53a}$$

$$\mu_k f_k - \boldsymbol{e}_k^T \boldsymbol{\beta}_k \geq 0 \qquad \text{compl. to} \quad \lambda_k \geq 0, \tag{7.53b}$$

$$\boldsymbol{n}_k^T \boldsymbol{P}_k^T \boldsymbol{C}^T \boldsymbol{u}^{\,t+\Delta t} - \frac{\nu_k}{\Delta t} \geq 0 \qquad \text{compl. to} \quad f_k \geq 0. \tag{7.53c}$$

where μ_k is the friction coefficient at the k'th contact point and $\boldsymbol{e}_k = [1, \ldots, 1]^T \in \mathbb{R}^\eta$. The symbol λ_k is a Lagrange multiplier with no real physical meaning, but it is an approximation to the magnitude of the relative tangential contact velocity. Possible contact states modeled by (7.53) are:

Separation: In this case, $\boldsymbol{n}_k^T \boldsymbol{P}_k^T \boldsymbol{C}^T \boldsymbol{u}^{\,t+\Delta t} - \frac{\nu_k}{\Delta t} > 0$, and (7.53c) implies that $f_k = 0$. Substitution of this into (7.53b), implies that $\boldsymbol{\beta}_k = 0$, i.e. there is no friction force. From (7.53a) we see that λ_k can take on any value without violating the conditions.

Sliding: For sliding, $\boldsymbol{D}_k^T \boldsymbol{P}_k^T \boldsymbol{C}^T \boldsymbol{u}^{\,t+\Delta t}$ is nonzero, since the columns of $\boldsymbol{D}_k$ positively span the entire contact plane. There must be at least one direction vector such that $\boldsymbol{d}_{h_k}^T \boldsymbol{P}_k^T \boldsymbol{C}^T \boldsymbol{u}^{\,t+\Delta t} < 0$, and since the corresponding $\beta_{h_k} > 0$, we must have $\lambda_k > 0$ for (7.53a) to hold, and (7.53b) implies that $\beta_{h_k} = \mu_k f_k$.

Rolling: In this case, $\boldsymbol{D}_k^T \boldsymbol{P}_k^T \boldsymbol{C}^T \boldsymbol{u}^{\,t+\Delta t}$ is zero, and (7.53a) implies that $\lambda_k \geq 0$. There are two interesting cases:

Case 1: Choosing $\lambda_k = 0$ (7.53a) implies that $\boldsymbol{\beta}_k \geq 0$. This means that the contact impulse can range over the interior and the surface of discretized friction cone.

Case 2: Choosing $\lambda_k > 0$ (7.53a) implies that $\boldsymbol{\beta}_k = 0$, (7.53b) will only be fulfilled if $\mu_k f_k = 0$. This is a nongeneric case that occurs by chance in the absence of a *frictional impulse*, that is, when $\mu_k = 0$.

We can now proceed analogously to the frictionless case and try to insert (7.52) into (7.53a) and (7.53c):

$$\lambda_k \boldsymbol{e}_k + \boldsymbol{D}_k^T \boldsymbol{P}_k^T \boldsymbol{C}^T \left(\boldsymbol{u}^{\,t} + \Delta t \boldsymbol{M}^{-1} \left(\boldsymbol{C}\left(\boldsymbol{N}\boldsymbol{f} + \boldsymbol{D}\boldsymbol{\beta}\right) + \boldsymbol{f}_{\text{ext}}\right)\right) \geq 0 \quad \text{compl. to} \quad \boldsymbol{\beta}_k \geq 0, \tag{7.54a}$$

$$\boldsymbol{n}_k^T \boldsymbol{P}_k^T \boldsymbol{C}^T \left(\boldsymbol{u}^{\,t} + \Delta t \boldsymbol{M}^{-1} \left(\boldsymbol{C}\left(\boldsymbol{N}\boldsymbol{f} + \boldsymbol{D}\boldsymbol{\beta}\right) + \boldsymbol{f}_{\text{ext}}\right)\right) - \frac{\nu_k}{\Delta t} \geq 0 \quad \text{compl. to} \quad \boldsymbol{f}_k \geq 0. \tag{7.54b}$$

Rearranging provides us with two new complementarity conditions, which replace those in (7.53a) and (7.53c):

$$\begin{aligned}\Delta t \boldsymbol{D}_k^T \boldsymbol{P}_k^T \boldsymbol{C}^T \boldsymbol{M}^{-1} \boldsymbol{C}\boldsymbol{N}\boldsymbol{f} + \Delta t \boldsymbol{D}_k^T \boldsymbol{P}_k^T \boldsymbol{C}^T \boldsymbol{M}^{-1} \boldsymbol{C}\boldsymbol{D}\boldsymbol{\beta} \\ + \lambda_k \boldsymbol{e}_k + \boldsymbol{D}_k^T \boldsymbol{P}_k^T \boldsymbol{C}^T \boldsymbol{u}^{\,t} + \Delta t \boldsymbol{D}_k^T \boldsymbol{P}_k^T \boldsymbol{C}^T \boldsymbol{M}^{-1} \boldsymbol{f}_{\text{ext}} \geq 0 \\ \text{compl. to} \quad \boldsymbol{\beta}_k \geq 0,\end{aligned} \tag{7.55a}$$

$$\begin{aligned}\Delta t \boldsymbol{n}_k^T \boldsymbol{P}_k^T \boldsymbol{C}^T \boldsymbol{M}^{-1} \boldsymbol{C}\boldsymbol{N}\boldsymbol{f} + \Delta t \boldsymbol{n}_k^T \boldsymbol{P}_k^T \boldsymbol{C}^T \boldsymbol{M}^{-1} \boldsymbol{C}\boldsymbol{D}\boldsymbol{\beta} \\ + \boldsymbol{n}_k^T \boldsymbol{P}_k^T \boldsymbol{C}^T \boldsymbol{u}^{\,t} + \Delta t \boldsymbol{n}_k^T \boldsymbol{P}_k^T \boldsymbol{C}^T \boldsymbol{M}^{-1} \boldsymbol{f}_{\text{ext}} - \frac{\nu_k}{\Delta t} \geq 0 \\ \text{compl. to} \quad \boldsymbol{f}_k \geq 0.\end{aligned} \tag{7.55b}$$

By rearranging the complementarity conditions (7.53b), (7.55a), and (7.55b), we can formulate the LCP-formulation (see Section 19.10) on matrix from as

$$\begin{bmatrix} \boldsymbol{D}^T\boldsymbol{C}^T\boldsymbol{M}^{-1}\boldsymbol{C}\boldsymbol{D} & \boldsymbol{D}^T\boldsymbol{C}^T\boldsymbol{M}^{-1}\boldsymbol{C}\boldsymbol{N} & \boldsymbol{E} \\ \boldsymbol{N}^T\boldsymbol{C}^T\boldsymbol{M}^{-1}\boldsymbol{C}\boldsymbol{D} & \boldsymbol{N}^T\boldsymbol{C}^T\boldsymbol{M}^{-1}\boldsymbol{C}\boldsymbol{N} & \boldsymbol{0} \\ -\boldsymbol{E}^T & \boldsymbol{\mu} & \boldsymbol{0} \end{bmatrix} \cdot \begin{bmatrix} \Delta t\boldsymbol{\beta} \\ \Delta t\boldsymbol{f} \\ \boldsymbol{\lambda}_{\text{aux}} \end{bmatrix}$$

$$+ \begin{bmatrix} \boldsymbol{D}^T\boldsymbol{C}^T\left(\boldsymbol{u}^{\,t} + \Delta t\boldsymbol{M}^{-1}\boldsymbol{f}_{\text{ext}}\right) \\ \boldsymbol{N}^T\boldsymbol{C}^T\left(\boldsymbol{u}^{\,t} + \Delta t\boldsymbol{M}^{-1}\boldsymbol{f}_{\text{ext}}\right) - \frac{\boldsymbol{\nu}}{\Delta t} \\ 0 \end{bmatrix} \geq 0$$

$$\text{compl. to} \quad \begin{bmatrix} \Delta t\boldsymbol{\beta} \\ \Delta t\boldsymbol{f} \\ \boldsymbol{\lambda}_{\text{aux}} \end{bmatrix} \geq 0, \tag{7.56}$$

where the diagonal matrix $\boldsymbol{\mu} \in \mathbb{R}^{K \times K}$ is given as

$$\boldsymbol{\mu} = \begin{bmatrix} \mu_1 & & & 0 \\ & \mu_2 & & \\ & & \vdots & \\ 0 & & & \mu_K \end{bmatrix}, \tag{7.57}$$

and the matrix $\boldsymbol{e} \in \mathbb{R}^{\eta K \times K}$ is given by

$$\boldsymbol{E} = \begin{bmatrix} \boldsymbol{e}_1 & & & 0 \\ & \boldsymbol{e}_2 & & \\ & & \vdots & \\ 0 & & & \boldsymbol{e}_K \end{bmatrix}. \tag{7.58}$$

That is, $\boldsymbol{E}$ consist of $\mathbb{R}^{\eta}$ dimensional submatrices. All submatrices on the diagonal consist of ones and of diagonal submatrices that are 0 (see Figure 7.8). Finally, the vector $\boldsymbol{\lambda}_{\text{aux}} \in \mathbb{R}^K$ is given as

$$\boldsymbol{\lambda}_{\text{aux}} = \left[\lambda_1, \ldots, \lambda_K\right]^T. \tag{7.59}$$

Let the matrix $\boldsymbol{A} \in \mathbb{R}^{(\eta+2)K \times (\eta+2)K}$ be defined as

$$\boldsymbol{A} = \begin{bmatrix} \boldsymbol{D}^T\boldsymbol{C}^T\boldsymbol{M}^{-1}\boldsymbol{C}\boldsymbol{D} & \boldsymbol{D}^T\boldsymbol{C}^T\boldsymbol{M}^{-1}\boldsymbol{C}\boldsymbol{N} & \boldsymbol{E} \\ \boldsymbol{N}^T\boldsymbol{C}^T\boldsymbol{M}^{-1}\boldsymbol{C}\boldsymbol{D} & \boldsymbol{N}^T\boldsymbol{C}^T\boldsymbol{M}^{-1}\boldsymbol{C}\boldsymbol{N} & \boldsymbol{0} \\ -\boldsymbol{E}^T & \boldsymbol{\mu} & \boldsymbol{0} \end{bmatrix}, \tag{7.60}$$

and the vector $\boldsymbol{x} \in \mathbb{R}^{(\eta+2)K}$ as

$$\boldsymbol{x} = \begin{bmatrix} \Delta t\boldsymbol{\beta} \\ \Delta t\boldsymbol{f} \\ \boldsymbol{\lambda}_{\text{aux}} \end{bmatrix}, \tag{7.61}$$

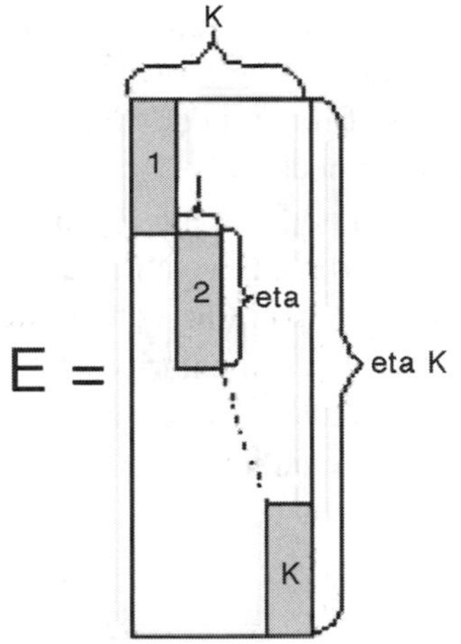

Figure 7.8: The $\boldsymbol{E}$ matrix layout.

and the vector $b \in \mathbb{R}^{(\eta+2)K}$ as

$$\boldsymbol{b} = \begin{bmatrix} \boldsymbol{D}^T \boldsymbol{C}^T \left(\boldsymbol{u}^{\,t} + \Delta t \boldsymbol{M}^{-1} \boldsymbol{f}_{\text{ext}}\right) \\ \boldsymbol{N}^T \boldsymbol{C}^T \left(\boldsymbol{u}^{\,t} + \Delta t \boldsymbol{M}^{-1} \boldsymbol{f}_{\text{ext}}\right) - \frac{\boldsymbol{\nu}}{\Delta t} \\ 0 \end{bmatrix} \tag{7.62}$$

then we see that we have a typical LCP formulation (see Section 19.10) of the form

$$\boldsymbol{A}\boldsymbol{x} + \boldsymbol{b} \geq 0 \quad \text{compl. to} \quad \boldsymbol{x} \geq 0. \tag{7.63}$$

The above formulation can further be extended to include *torsional friction* [Trinkle et al., 2001].

Because of real-time demands, a scalable friction model for time-critical computing is important; the constraint-based method is easily adopted to a scalable friction model by controlling the number of facets, η, used in the friction pyramid approximation.

Several methods could be used for setting the value of η; a global control could be used based on the amount of computation time or the total number of variables in the LCP problem (see Section 19.10). If either of these exceed some given limits, η is decreased correspondingly.

However, local control could also be used. Often only visualization is important; accurate friction is therefore only needed for objects seen by a user. In such cases, it is reasonable to use a low η for all objects outside the view-frustum, and for those objects inside the view-frustum a higher η value is used.

7.5 Joints

In the previous sections we have treated the problem of contact mechanics using classical mechanics taught in first-year undergraduate physics and linear algebra. The approach is straightforward and easy to understand even though there are many symbols and much notation. Until now we have treated what is called *unilateral contacts*, where unilateral refers to the "$\geq$"-constraints on the contact forces. In this section, we will try to generalize our formulation and include *bilateral constraints*. Here bilateral refers to a "="-constraint on the constraint forces. Bilateral constraints are used for modeling joints between the bodies, such as hinges and ball-in-socket connections.

In this section, we will show how we can go from the formulation based on classical mechanics into a formulation based on analytical mechanics. To achieve a more abstract and general formulation, we need to introduce concepts of holonomic and non-holonomic constraints and Jacobians.

The analytical mechanics approach for complementarity problems has been studied amply in the literature, [Pfeiffer et al., 1996b, Anitescu et al., 1996, Anitescu et al., 1997, Anitescu et al., 2002]. A useful reference for further reading on analytical mechanics is [Goldstein et al., 2002].

7.5.1 Holonomic Constraints

Working with constraints, we are particularly interested in the number of degrees of freedom (DOF), that is, the minimum set of parameters needed to describe the motion in our system. For instance, a free-moving body has six DOFs because we need at least three parameters to describe its position and at least three parameters to describe its orientation. For two free-floating rigid bodies we have 12 DOFs, from which we conclude that the smallest possible generalized position vector we can find will have 12 entries.

Following the conventions from previous sections, the spatial position vector $\boldsymbol{s}_l =\in \mathbb{R}^{14}$ for the l'th joint between the two bodies B_{i_l} and B_{j_l} can be written as

$$\boldsymbol{s}_l = \left[\boldsymbol{r}_{i_l}, q_{i_l}, \boldsymbol{r}_{j_l}, q_{j_l}\right]^T. \tag{7.64}$$

To facilitate notation we will not bother to write the subscript indicating the joint number or the contact number in the following sections, so we simply write

$$\boldsymbol{s} = \left[\boldsymbol{r}_i, q_i, \boldsymbol{r}_j, q_j\right]^T. \tag{7.65}$$

The position vector $\boldsymbol{s}$ is not the minimum set of parameters, since we use quaternions for the representation of the orientations, and thus use four parameters instead of the minimal three for each orientation. For describing velocities and accelerations we could use time derivatives of the quaternions, but this is tedious, since the physics laws use angular velocities $\boldsymbol{\omega}$. Instead, we need a transformation like the one we introduced in Section 7.1

$$\dot{\boldsymbol{s}} = \boldsymbol{S}\boldsymbol{u}, \tag{7.66}$$

where

$$\boldsymbol{u} = \left[\boldsymbol{v}_i, \boldsymbol{\omega}_i, \boldsymbol{v}_j, \boldsymbol{\omega}_j\right]^T, \tag{7.67}$$

and

$$\boldsymbol{S} = \begin{bmatrix} \mathbf{1} & & & \mathbf{0} \\ & \boldsymbol{Q}_i & & \\ & & \mathbf{1} & \\ \mathbf{0} & & & \boldsymbol{Q}_j \end{bmatrix}. \tag{7.68}$$

We write the position vector $\boldsymbol{r} \in \mathbb{R}^{12}$ associated with the integrals of $\boldsymbol{u}$ as

$$\boldsymbol{r} = [\boldsymbol{r}_i, \boldsymbol{\theta}_i, \boldsymbol{r}_j, \boldsymbol{\theta}_j]^T, \tag{7.69a}$$

$$= [x_i, y_i, z_i, \alpha_i, \beta_i, \gamma_i, x_j, y_j, z_j, \alpha_j, \beta_j, \gamma_j]^T. \tag{7.69b}$$

Here $\boldsymbol{\theta}_i$ is the integral quantities of $\boldsymbol{\omega}_i$, that is,

$$\boldsymbol{u} = \frac{d}{dt}\boldsymbol{r}. \tag{7.70}$$

In general, the quantities $\boldsymbol{\theta}_i$ and $\boldsymbol{\theta}_j$ in $\boldsymbol{r}$ do not give meaning as finite quantities, and in plain computer graphics language you cannot use them like Euler angles to make a rotation matrix. Nevertheless, $\boldsymbol{r}$ is a minimum spatial position vector.

When we link two rigid bodies together by a joint, then we are removing DOFs from the system, and we can therefore find an even smaller generalized position vector. For instance, if we make a rigid connection between the two free-floating bodies, then we can remove six DOFs because we only need to describe the movement of one of the bodies, and the movement of the other body will follow immediately from the movement of the first body. This means that the smallest possible generalized position vector has six entries. From the example we see that we can at most remove six DOFs from any joint.

By definition, a holonomic constraint between two bodies B_i and B_j can be written as a function Φ of time and spatial position vector $\boldsymbol{s} =\in \mathbb{R}^{14}$, such that we always have

$$\Phi(t, \boldsymbol{s}) = 0. \tag{7.71}$$

All joint types presented by us can be modeled by time-independent holonomic constraints, meaning that for the l'th joint we have m holonomic constraints

$$\Phi_1(\boldsymbol{s}) = 0, \tag{7.72a}$$

$$\Phi_2(\boldsymbol{s}) = 0, \tag{7.72b}$$

$$\vdots$$

$$\Phi_m(\boldsymbol{s}) = 0, \tag{7.72c}$$

where m is the number of degrees of freedom removed by the constraints. This type of holonomic constraint is called a *scleronomous constraint*.

Assume that the l'th joint is a *ball-in-socket joint* between the two bodies B_i and B_j. A ball-in-socket joint is characterized by the fact that two points, one from each body, are always connected to each other, meaning that we have one constraint saying the x-coordinates of the two points must be equal, another constraint requiring equality of the y-coordinates, and a third one for equality of the z-coordinates. That is, if we let the two points be specified by two fixed vectors $\boldsymbol{r}^i_{\text{anc}}$ and $\boldsymbol{r}^j_{\text{anc}}$ in the respective body frames of

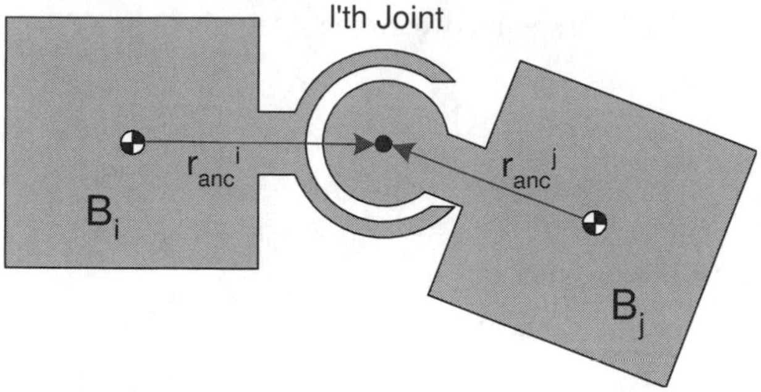

Figure 7.9: A ball in a socket joint in 2D.

the two bodies as shown in Figure 7.9, then we can formulate the geometric constraint as follows

$$\underbrace{\left[\left(\boldsymbol{r}_i + \boldsymbol{R}(q_i)\boldsymbol{r}^i_{\text{anc}}\right) - \left(\boldsymbol{r}_j + \boldsymbol{R}(q_j)\boldsymbol{r}^j_{\text{anc}}\right)\right]_x}_{\Phi_1} = 0, \tag{7.73a}$$

$$\underbrace{\left[\left(\boldsymbol{r}_i + \boldsymbol{R}(q_i)\boldsymbol{r}^i_{\text{anc}}\right) - \left(\boldsymbol{r}_j + \boldsymbol{R}(q_j)\boldsymbol{r}^j_{\text{anc}}\right)\right]_y}_{\Phi_2} = 0, \tag{7.73b}$$

$$\underbrace{\left[\left(\boldsymbol{r}_i + \boldsymbol{R}(q_i)\boldsymbol{r}^i_{\text{anc}}\right) - \left(\boldsymbol{r}_j + \boldsymbol{R}(q_j)\boldsymbol{r}^j_{\text{anc}}\right)\right]_z}_{\Phi_3} = 0, \tag{7.73c}$$

where $\boldsymbol{R}(q)$ is the corresponding rotation matrix of the quaternion q. From the equations above it is clear that the geometric constraint characterizing the ball-in-socket joint can be expressed as three holonomic constraints on vector form as

$$\boldsymbol{\Phi}(\boldsymbol{s}) = \begin{bmatrix} \Phi_1(\boldsymbol{s}) \\ \Phi_2(\boldsymbol{s}) \\ \Phi_3(\boldsymbol{s}) \end{bmatrix} = 0. \tag{7.74}$$

Note that the small example is not only illustrative; it actually provides us with a recipe for deriving different joint types. In conclusion, a holonomic constraint is equivalent to removing a degree of freedom from the system, which means that we can find a generalized position vector with one less entry than the spatial position vector.

By differentiation with respect to time, we can derive a *kinematic constraint* from each holonomic constraint

$$\frac{d}{dt}\boldsymbol{\Phi}_l(\boldsymbol{s}) = \frac{\partial \boldsymbol{\Phi}}{\partial \boldsymbol{s}}\frac{d\boldsymbol{s}}{dt} \tag{7.75a}$$

$$= \underbrace{\frac{\partial \boldsymbol{\Phi}}{\partial \boldsymbol{s}}}_{\boldsymbol{J}_\Phi}\boldsymbol{S}\,\boldsymbol{u} \tag{7.75b}$$

$$= 0. \tag{7.75c}$$

The matrices $\frac{\partial \boldsymbol{\Phi}}{\partial \boldsymbol{s}} \in \mathbb{R}^{m\times 14}$ and $\boldsymbol{J}_\Phi \in \mathbb{R}^{m\times 12}$ are called Jacobians; they describe relations between velocities in different coordinate representations. Finally, we have the kinematic constraint

$$\boldsymbol{J}_\Phi \boldsymbol{u}_l = 0. \tag{7.76}$$

Performing another differentiation w.r.t. time leads us to the acceleration constraint

$$\frac{d^2}{dt^2}\boldsymbol{\Phi}(\boldsymbol{s}(t)) = \frac{d}{dt}\left(\boldsymbol{J}_\Phi \boldsymbol{u}\right) \tag{7.77a}$$

$$= \frac{d}{dt}\left(\boldsymbol{J}_\Phi\right)\boldsymbol{u} + \boldsymbol{J}_\Phi \frac{d}{dt}\left(\boldsymbol{u}\right) \tag{7.77b}$$

$$= 0, \tag{7.77c}$$

from which we conclude that

$$\boldsymbol{J}_\Phi \dot{\boldsymbol{u}} = -\dot{\boldsymbol{J}}_\Phi \boldsymbol{u}. \tag{7.78}$$

For our velocity-based formulation we have no use for the acceleration constraint; however, if we set up a force-based formulation, we would need to augment the Newton-Euler equations with these acceleration constraints.

It is well known that the generalized constraint force exerted by a holonomic constraint can be written as

$$\boldsymbol{F}_\Phi = \boldsymbol{J}_\Phi^T \boldsymbol{\lambda}_\Phi. \tag{7.79}$$

This follows from the principle of virtual work described in Section 22.6. The $\boldsymbol{\lambda}_\Phi \in \mathbb{R}^m$ is a vector of Lagrange multipliers. They account for the reaction forces coming from the joint bearings; the Lagrange multipliers can take any real value, both positive and negative. Observe that the dimension of $\boldsymbol{\lambda}_\Phi$ depends on the number of constraints on the joint. Therefore, we conclude that we have as many independent reaction forces as there are constraints.

7.5.2 Non-Holonomic Constraints

A non-holonomic constraint is a differential constraint that cannot be integrated; however in this context, we define a non-holonomic constraint as a constraint that cannot be put into the form of a holonomic constraint (7.71). There are many different kinds of non-holonomic constraints, and we will restrict ourselves to a certain kind, namely those called unilateral constraints.

The non-holonomic constraint between two bodies B_i and B_j can, by definition, be written as a function Ψ of time and generalized position vector $\boldsymbol{s} \in \mathbb{R}^{14}$, such that we always have

$$\Psi(t, \boldsymbol{s}) \geq 0. \tag{7.80}$$

The condition for a contact can be modeled by $(1+\eta)$ time-independent non-holonomic constraints, that is,

$$\boldsymbol{\Psi}(\boldsymbol{s}) \geq 0. \tag{7.81}$$

This looks very different from the contact conditions we have seen previously, but don't be concerned; the connection with our previous derivations will be made clear later on. Taking the time derivative gives us a kinematic contact constraint,

$$\frac{d}{dt}\boldsymbol{\Psi}(\boldsymbol{s}) = \frac{\partial \boldsymbol{\Psi}}{\partial \boldsymbol{s}}\frac{d\boldsymbol{s}}{dt} \tag{7.82a}$$

$$= \underbrace{\frac{\partial \boldsymbol{\Psi}}{\partial \boldsymbol{s}}\boldsymbol{S}}_{\boldsymbol{J}_\Psi}\boldsymbol{u} \tag{7.82b}$$

$$= \boldsymbol{J}_\Psi \boldsymbol{u} \tag{7.82c}$$

$$\geq 0, \tag{7.82d}$$

where $\boldsymbol{J}_\Psi \in \mathbb{R}^{(1+\eta)\times 12}$ is the Jacobian of the contact constraint. Taking the time derivative one more time yields an acceleration constraint

$$\frac{d^2}{dt^2}\boldsymbol{\Psi}(\boldsymbol{s}(t)) = \frac{d}{dt}\left(\boldsymbol{J}_\Psi \boldsymbol{u}\right) \tag{7.83a}$$

$$= \dot{\boldsymbol{J}}_\Psi \boldsymbol{u} + \boldsymbol{J}_\Psi \dot{\boldsymbol{u}} \tag{7.83b}$$

$$\geq 0. \tag{7.83c}$$

The generalized constraint force exerted by the contact constraint can be written as

$$\boldsymbol{F}_\Psi = \boldsymbol{J}_\Psi^T \boldsymbol{\lambda}_\Psi, \tag{7.84}$$

where $\boldsymbol{\lambda}_\Psi \in \mathbb{R}^{1+\eta}$ is the vector of Lagrange multipliers. Unlike the Lagrange multipliers used for the joint reaction forces, the Lagrange multipliers for the contacts can only take nonnegative values, that is,

$$\boldsymbol{\lambda}_\Psi \geq 0. \tag{7.85}$$

As pointed out by Anitscu and Potra [Anitescu et al., 2002], one should be careful about the constraint $\frac{d}{dt}\boldsymbol{\Psi}(\boldsymbol{s}) \geq 0$, because if we have

$$\boldsymbol{\Psi}(\boldsymbol{s}) > 0 \tag{7.86}$$

indicating a potential future contact, this does not imply that

$$\frac{d}{dt}\boldsymbol{\Psi}(\boldsymbol{s}) > 0. \tag{7.87}$$

Only so-called active contacts, where

$$\boldsymbol{\Psi}(\boldsymbol{s}) = 0, \tag{7.88}$$

require this. This boils down to the fact that separated contacts are allowed to move toward each other until they become touching contacts, and a touching contact can either continue with being a touching contact, or it can become a separated contact.

Momentarily reintroducing the subscript for the contact ordering, we can write all the kinematic constraints and force contributions as

$$\boldsymbol{J}_{\Psi_k}\boldsymbol{u}_k \geq 0, \quad \text{where} \quad \boldsymbol{J}_{\Psi_k} \in \mathbb{R}^{(1+\eta)\times 12}, \tag{7.89a}$$

$$\boldsymbol{f}_{\Psi_k} = \boldsymbol{J}_{\Psi_k}^T \boldsymbol{\lambda}_{\Psi_k}, \quad \text{where} \quad \boldsymbol{\lambda}_{\Psi_k} \in \mathbb{R}^{1+\eta}. \tag{7.89b}$$

Concatenating them into matrix equations, we have

$$\boldsymbol{J}_{\text{contact}}\boldsymbol{u} = 0, \tag{7.90a}$$

$$\boldsymbol{f}_{\text{contact}} = \boldsymbol{J}_{\text{contact}}^T \boldsymbol{\lambda}_{\text{contact}}, \tag{7.90b}$$

where $\boldsymbol{u} \in Re^{6n}$ is the generalized velocity vector (Section 7.1), $\boldsymbol{u} = \left[\boldsymbol{v}_1, \boldsymbol{\omega}_1, \boldsymbol{v}_2, \boldsymbol{\omega}_2, \cdots, \boldsymbol{v}_n, \boldsymbol{\omega}_n\right]^T$, and $\boldsymbol{\lambda}_{\text{contact}} \in \mathbb{R}^{K(1+\eta)}$ is the concatenated vector of all the Lagrange multipliers.

$$\boldsymbol{\lambda}_{\text{contact}} = \left[\boldsymbol{\lambda}_{\Psi_1}^1, \ldots, \boldsymbol{\lambda}_{\Psi_1}^{(\eta+1)}, \ldots, \boldsymbol{\lambda}_{\Psi_K}^1, \ldots, \boldsymbol{\lambda}_{\Psi_K}^{(\eta+1)}\right]^T. \tag{7.91}$$

The $\boldsymbol{J}_{\text{contact}} \in \mathbb{R}^{K(1+\eta)\times 6n}$ is the system Jacobian for all the contacts, and it is given by

$$\boldsymbol{J}_{\text{contact}} = \begin{bmatrix} \boldsymbol{J}_{\Psi_1}^1 & \cdots & \cdots & \cdots & \cdots & \cdots & \boldsymbol{J}_{\Psi_1}^n \\ \vdots & & & & & & \vdots \\ \boldsymbol{J}_{\Psi_k}^1 & \cdots & \boldsymbol{J}_{\Psi_k}^i & \cdots & \boldsymbol{J}_{\Psi_k}^j & \cdots & \boldsymbol{J}_{\Psi_k}^n \\ \vdots & & & & & & \vdots \\ \boldsymbol{J}_{\Psi_K}^1 & \cdots & \cdots & \cdots & \cdots & \cdots & \boldsymbol{J}_{\Psi_K}^n \end{bmatrix}. \tag{7.92}$$

This Jacobian is extremely sparse since the k'th contact only involves two bodies i and j, meaning that the only nonzero entries in the k'th row of $\boldsymbol{J}_{\text{contact}}$ are the columns corresponding to the bodies i and j

$$\begin{bmatrix} \boldsymbol{J}_{\Psi_k}^i & \boldsymbol{J}_{\Psi_k}^j \end{bmatrix} = \boldsymbol{J}_{\Psi_k}. \tag{7.93}$$

We will now prove that

$$\boldsymbol{C}\left(\boldsymbol{N}\boldsymbol{f} + \boldsymbol{D}\boldsymbol{\beta}\right) \equiv \boldsymbol{J}_{\text{contact}}^T \boldsymbol{\lambda}_{\text{contact}}. \tag{7.94}$$

The above equation follows from straightforward computations and permutations of the left-hand side of

$$\boldsymbol{C}\left(\boldsymbol{N}\boldsymbol{f} + \boldsymbol{D}\boldsymbol{\beta}\right) = \boldsymbol{C}\boldsymbol{N}\boldsymbol{f} + \boldsymbol{C}\boldsymbol{D}\boldsymbol{\beta} \tag{7.95a}$$

$$= \underbrace{\begin{bmatrix} \boldsymbol{C}\boldsymbol{N} & \boldsymbol{C}\boldsymbol{D} \end{bmatrix}}_{\pi\left(\boldsymbol{J}_{\text{contact}}^T\right)} \underbrace{\begin{bmatrix} \boldsymbol{f} \\ \boldsymbol{\beta} \end{bmatrix}}_{\pi\left(\boldsymbol{\lambda}_{\text{contact}}\right)} \tag{7.95b}$$

$$= \pi\left(\boldsymbol{J}_{\text{contact}}^T \boldsymbol{\lambda}_{\text{contact}}\right), \tag{7.95c}$$

where $\pi(\cdot)$ is a permutation. Now we simply swap rows and columns, such that

$$\boldsymbol{\lambda}^1_{\Psi_k} = f_k, \tag{7.96a}$$

$$\boldsymbol{\lambda}^2_{\Psi_k} = \beta_{1_k}, \tag{7.96b}$$

$$\vdots \quad \vdots$$

$$\boldsymbol{\lambda}^{(\eta+1)}_{\Psi_k} = \beta_{\eta_k}, \tag{7.96c}$$

and the relation between the Jacobian, $\boldsymbol{J}_{\text{contact}}$, and the matrices $\boldsymbol{C}$, $\boldsymbol{N}$, and $\boldsymbol{D}$ is clear.

7.5.3 A Unified Notation for Unilateral and Bilateral Constraints

Now we'll show that both bilateral and unilateral constraints are added to the govern system of equations of motion through the same notion of Jacobian and Lagrange multipliers.

Momentarily reintroducing the subscripting on both the joint and contact ordering, we have K contacts and L joints, and we can write all their kinematic constraints and force contributions as

$$\boldsymbol{J}_{\Phi_l}\boldsymbol{u}_l = 0, \quad \text{where} \quad \boldsymbol{J}_{\Phi_l} \in \mathbb{R}^{m_l \times 12}, \tag{7.97a}$$

$$\boldsymbol{J}_{\Psi_k}\boldsymbol{u}_k \geq 0, \quad \text{where} \quad \boldsymbol{J}_{\Psi_k} \in \mathbb{R}^{(1+\eta)\times 12}, \tag{7.97b}$$

$$\boldsymbol{f}_{\Phi_l} = \boldsymbol{J}^T_{\Phi_l}\boldsymbol{\lambda}_{\Phi_l}, \quad \text{where} \quad \boldsymbol{\lambda}_{\Phi_l} \in \mathbb{R}^{m_l}, \tag{7.97c}$$

$$\boldsymbol{f}_{\Psi_k} = \boldsymbol{J}^T_{\Psi_k}\boldsymbol{\lambda}_{\Psi_k}, \quad \text{where} \quad \boldsymbol{\lambda}_{\Psi_k} \in \mathbb{R}^{1+\eta}. \tag{7.97d}$$

Following the same recipe as in Section 7.5.2 for concatenating these into matrix notations, we get

$$\boldsymbol{J}_{\text{joint}}\boldsymbol{u} = 0, \quad \text{where} \quad \boldsymbol{J}_{\text{joint}} \in \mathbb{R}^{(\sum_l^L m_l)\times 6n}, \tag{7.98a}$$

$$\boldsymbol{J}_{\text{contact}}\boldsymbol{u} \geq 0, \quad \text{where} \quad \boldsymbol{J}_{\text{contact}} \in \mathbb{R}^{K(1+\eta)\times 6n}, \tag{7.98b}$$

$$\boldsymbol{f}_{\text{joint}} = \boldsymbol{J}^T_{\text{joint}}\boldsymbol{\lambda}_{\text{joint}}, \quad \text{where} \quad \boldsymbol{\lambda}_{\text{joint}} \in \mathbb{R}^{\sum_l^L m_l}, \tag{7.98c}$$

$$\boldsymbol{f}_{\text{contact}} = \boldsymbol{J}^T_{\text{contact}}\boldsymbol{\lambda}_{\text{contact}}, \quad \text{where} \quad \boldsymbol{\lambda}_{\text{contact}} \in \mathbb{R}^{K(1+\eta)}. \tag{7.98d}$$

The Jacobian $\boldsymbol{J}_{\text{contact}}$ and the Lagrange multiplier vector $\boldsymbol{\lambda}_{\text{contact}}$ was given in (7.92) and (7.91). The system joint Jacobian $\boldsymbol{J}_{\text{joint}}$ and the joint Lagrange multiplier vector $\boldsymbol{\lambda}_{\text{joint}}$ follows the same pattern and is given as

$$\boldsymbol{J}_{\text{joint}} = \begin{bmatrix} \boldsymbol{J}^1_{\Phi_1} & \cdots\cdots\cdots\cdots\cdots\cdots & & & \boldsymbol{J}^n_{\Phi_1} \\ \vdots & & & & \vdots \\ \boldsymbol{J}^1_{\Phi_l} & \cdots \quad \boldsymbol{J}^i_{\Phi_l} & \cdots & \boldsymbol{J}^j_{\Phi_l} \quad \cdots & \boldsymbol{J}^n_{\Phi_l} \\ \vdots & & & & \vdots \\ \boldsymbol{J}^1_{\Phi_L} & \cdots\cdots\cdots\cdots\cdots\cdots & & & \boldsymbol{J}^n_{\Phi_L} \end{bmatrix}. \tag{7.99}$$

This Jacobian is inherently extremely sparse, since the l'th joint only involves two bodies i and j, meaning that the only nonzero entries in the l'th row of $\boldsymbol{J}_{\text{joint}}$ are the columns corresponding to the bodies i and j

$$\begin{bmatrix} \boldsymbol{J}^i_{\Phi_l} & \boldsymbol{J}^j_{\Phi_l} \end{bmatrix} = \boldsymbol{J}_{\Phi_l}, \tag{7.100}$$

and

$$\boldsymbol{\lambda}_{\text{joint}} = \left[\boldsymbol{\lambda}^1_{\Phi_1}, \ldots, \boldsymbol{\lambda}^{m_1}_{\Phi_1}, \ldots, \boldsymbol{\lambda}^1_{\Phi_K}, \ldots, \boldsymbol{\lambda}^{m_K}_{\Phi_K}\right]^T. \tag{7.101}$$

Using the matrix notation to write constraint forces of both bilateral and unilateral constraint, the generalized acceleration vector can be written as

$$\dot{\boldsymbol{u}} = \boldsymbol{M}^{-1}\left(\boldsymbol{f}_{\text{contact}} + \boldsymbol{f}_{\text{joint}} + \boldsymbol{f}_{\text{ext}}\right) \tag{7.102a}$$

$$= \boldsymbol{M}^{-1}\left(\boldsymbol{J}^T_{\text{contact}}\boldsymbol{\lambda}_{\text{contact}} + \boldsymbol{J}^T_{\text{joint}}\boldsymbol{\lambda}_{\text{joint}} + \boldsymbol{f}_{\text{ext}}\right). \tag{7.102b}$$

This is a completely general way to add constraints; it will be further explored in the remainder of this chapter. In the end it will also lead to a general and efficient implementation framework.

7.6 Joint Modeling

In this section we will derive the machinery for modeling joints and later joint limits as well as joint motors. We will start by introducing a submatrix pattern of the Jacobian matrix. Hereafter, we will describe joint error, connectivity, and error reduction.

For the $l'th$ joint constraint, we can write the kinematic constraint as

$$\boldsymbol{J}_l \boldsymbol{u}_l = 0. \tag{7.103}$$

Since we will focus on joint types, we will omit writing the subscript indicating the joint ordering, that is, for a given joint type we simply write the kinematic constraint as $\boldsymbol{J}\boldsymbol{u} = 0$. There is a remarkable submatrix pattern of the Jacobians, which we will use extensively, because later on it will make the assembly of the system matrix easier, that is, $\boldsymbol{A}$. Writing the generalized velocity vector with its subvectors as

$$\boldsymbol{J}\boldsymbol{u} = 0, \tag{7.104a}$$

$$\begin{bmatrix} \boldsymbol{J}^i_{\text{lin}} & \boldsymbol{J}^i_{\text{ang}} & \boldsymbol{J}^j_{\text{lin}} & \boldsymbol{J}^j_{\text{ang}} \end{bmatrix} \begin{bmatrix} \boldsymbol{v}_i \\ \boldsymbol{\omega}_i \\ \boldsymbol{v}_j \\ \boldsymbol{\omega}_j \end{bmatrix} = 0. \tag{7.104b}$$

Observe that there is a part of the Jacobian matrix that is only multiplied with the linear velocity of body i, which is denoted $\boldsymbol{J}^i_{\text{lin}}$, a part that is only multiplied by the angular part of body i, $\boldsymbol{J}^i_{\text{ang}}$, and so on. In fact we can interpret

$$\boldsymbol{J}^i_{\text{lin}}\boldsymbol{v}_i + \boldsymbol{J}^i_{\text{ang}}\boldsymbol{\omega}_i, \tag{7.105}$$

as the velocity of the joint bearings on body i, and

$$\boldsymbol{J}^j_{\text{lin}}\boldsymbol{v}_j + \boldsymbol{J}^j_{\text{ang}}\boldsymbol{\omega}_j, \tag{7.106}$$

as the velocity of the joint bearing on body j. It is now obvious that in order to keep the joint bearings together, the bearings must move with the same velocity and the sum must therefore be zero. This observation provides us with a strategy for designing the Jacobians: given the body velocities, set up a matrix equation, such that the relative velocity in the direction of the joint bearings is always zero.

7.6.1 Joint Error

By now it should be clear that the kinematic constraints are constraints on the velocities, not the positions; meaning that both numerical errors and errors stemming from internal approximations can sneak into the computations of the positions as the simulation proceeds. Imagine that some positional error has occurred, such that there is a positional *displacement* of the joint bearings and/or a misalignment of the joint bearings. This error could be reduced by adjusting the velocities of the joint bearings, such that the error is smaller in the following simulation step. Therefore we augment our kinematic constraints with a velocity error correction term, $\boldsymbol{b}$

$$\boldsymbol{J}\boldsymbol{u} = \boldsymbol{b}. \tag{7.107}$$

To illustrate, we will present a simple one-dimensional example: imagine two particles that can move along a line, where the particles are jointed together, such that their positions are always equal. Their kinematic constraint will then be

$$\boldsymbol{v}_i - \boldsymbol{v}_j = 0. \tag{7.108}$$

Now imagine that some error is present

$$\boldsymbol{r}_{\text{err}} = \boldsymbol{r}_j - \boldsymbol{r}_i, \tag{7.109}$$

with $\|\boldsymbol{r}_{\text{err}}\| > 0$. To adjust the velocities so that this error is eliminated within some time Δt, we require that

$$\underbrace{\boldsymbol{v}_i - \boldsymbol{v}_j}_{\boldsymbol{J}\boldsymbol{u}} = \underbrace{\frac{\boldsymbol{r}_{\text{err}}}{\Delta t}}_{\boldsymbol{b}}, \tag{7.110a}$$

$$\boldsymbol{J}\boldsymbol{u} = \boldsymbol{b}. \tag{7.110b}$$

If joint or limits is subject to an initial error and incident links are at rest, then error terms will accelerate the links; so not only will the error be corrected, but also bodies will continue to move afterward. This is obviously an unwanted effect!

The error correction should not add kinetic energy to the system. In fact, the error correction has the same effect as using Newton's collision law for solving simultaneous collisions [Baraff, 1989]. An acceptable and practical workaround is to use an error reduction parameter to control the rate of error correction, which will be discussed in Section 7.6.3.

7.6.2 Connectivity

We will describe the connectivity and movements of all joints by using *anchor points* and *joint axes*. An anchor point is a point in space, where two points, one from each incident body are always perfectly aligned. The placement of an anchor point relative to a body, i, is given by a body frame vector, $\boldsymbol{r}_{\text{anc}}^{\;i}$. The position of the anchor point in the world coordinate system (WCS) w.r.t. to body i is given by

$$\boldsymbol{r}_{\text{anc}}^{\;\text{wcs}} = \boldsymbol{r}_i + \boldsymbol{R}(q_i)\boldsymbol{r}_{\text{anc}}^{\;i}. \tag{7.111}$$

A joint axis describes an allowed direction of movement, such as an axis of rotation or a direction of sliding. The joint axis is given by a 3D unit vector, $s_{\text{axis}}^{\text{wcs}}$. In Section 7.7 we will explain the details in describing different joint types using the notation of anchor points and joint axes.

This way of describing the connectivity is very similar to the paired joint coordinate frames described in Featherstone [Featherstone, 1998]. In comparison, anchor points correspond to the placement of the origin of the joint frames and joint axes correspond to the orientation of the joint frames, such as the z-axis of the joint coordinate frame. Alternative notations for describing the connectivity of jointed mechanisms are used in some literature [Featherstone, 1998, Craig, 1986].

7.6.3 Error Reduction Parameter

The kind of approach for simulating joints that we are outlining in this paper belongs to a class of algorithms referred to as *Full-Coordinate methods* because every body in a jointed mechanism is described by the full set of rigid body motion coordinates.

An alternative approach is the *Reduced Coordinate methods*, where a good example is Featherstone's algorithm [Featherstone, 1998]. The central idea is that only the relative motion of bodies between joints needs to be described; only the relative coordinates of the joints are therefore needed.

The main difference between the two approaches is that Reduced Coordinate methods explicitly work with joint parameters. The position and placement of the links are derived from these joint parameters. With a Full-Coordinate method, we work explicitly on the links and we need to derive joint parameters if needed. There are some benefits and disadvantages of these methods, which we will describe shortly.

The Reduced Coordinate methods are often computationally faster, since they have fewer variables to work on, and since they are often implemented by recursive algorithms like Armstrong and Featherstone [Armstrong et al., 1985, Featherstone, 1998]. These recursive algorithms are often limited to tree-like mechanisms and only with great difficulty can these recursive algorithms be extended to handle closed loops and contacts.

The Full-Coordinate methods are not limited by any kind of topology, but they are often more computationally demanding, because they must describe all the constraints on each link's rigid body motion. Reduced Coordinate methods need only to describe the free movement, which is often of lesser dimension.

Many people prefer the Full-Coordinate methods because they think the notation is easier to read and work with. Reduced Coordinate methods appear to have long and difficult terms representing *coriolis* and *centripetal accelerations*.

From a computer animation viewpoint, numerical errors in a Full-Coordinate method seem to be much more noticeable than in a Reduced Coordinate method. This is because errors in the body coordinates will split joints apart and introduce an effect called drifting because links that supposedly should be jointed together are drifting apart. Reduced Coordinate methods do not suffer from the drifting problem, since no matter how big numerical errors one obtains, the simulation will always show bodies connected properly.

In conclusion, with Full-Coordinate methods we can expect drifting problems; there are two ways these can arise in a working simulator:

- The user interacts with a mechanism and forgets to set the correct position or orientation of all the links in a mechanism.

- During the simulation, errors can creep in that result in the links drifting away from their joints.

In Section 7.7, we describe the kinematic constraints of different joint types and we will introduce some error correcting terms. These are all multiplied by a coefficient, k_{corr}, which denotes a measure of the rate of error correction. The idea is as follows: for each joint we will have an error reduction parameter, k_{erp}

$$0 \leq k_{\text{erp}} \leq 1. \tag{7.112}$$

Its value is a measure for how much error reduction should occur in the next simulation step. A value of zero means that there is no error correction at all; a value of one means that the error should be totally eliminated.

If we let the duration of time in the next simulation step be denoted by a characteristic time-step, Δt, then the following constant is a measure of rate of change

$$k_{\text{fps}} = \frac{1}{\Delta t}. \tag{7.113}$$

The coefficient k_{cor} can now be determined as

$$k_{\text{cor}} = k_{\text{erp}} k_{\text{fps}}. \tag{7.114}$$

Setting $k_{\text{erp}} = 1$ is not recommended, since various internal approximations can cause the errors not to be completely fixed. The Open Dynamics Engine [ODE, 2005] uses the same approach for correcting errors. They recommend using a value around 0.8.

7.7 Joint Types

In this section we will derive the Jacobians for several different kinds of joint types needed for the kinematic constraints explained in the previous sections.

7.7.1 Ball-in-Socket Joint

A *ball-in-socket joint* allows arbitrary rotation between two bodies as illustrated in Figure 7.10. We already know that a ball-in-socket joint removes three DOFs, so we conclude that the Jacobian, $\boldsymbol{J}_{\text{ball}}$, for the ball is a 3×12 matrix. From our previous example in Section 7.5.1 it should not come as a surprise that the submatrix of the Jacobian is given by

$$\boldsymbol{J}_{\text{ball}} = \left[\boldsymbol{J}^i_{\text{lin}}, \boldsymbol{J}^j_{\text{lin}}, \boldsymbol{J}^i_{\text{ang}}, \boldsymbol{J}^j_{\text{ang}} \right], \tag{7.115}$$

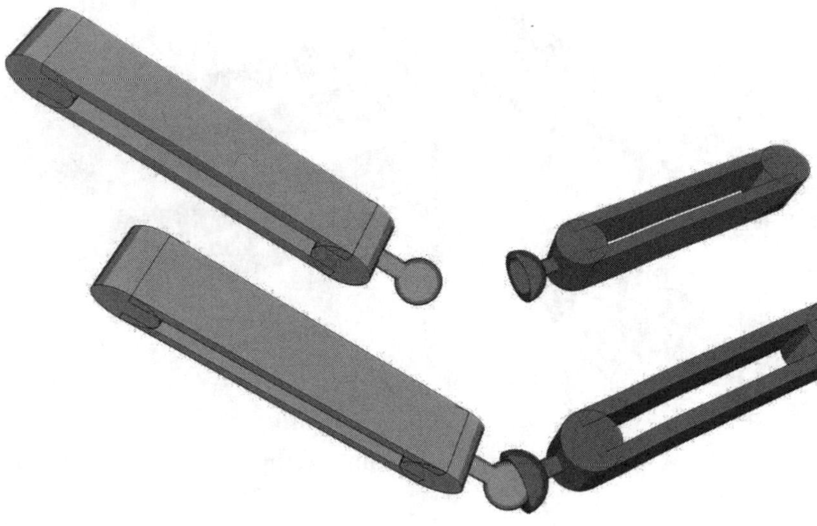

Figure 7.10: A ball-in-socket joint example.

where

$$J^i_{\text{lin}} = \begin{bmatrix} 1 & 0 & 0 \\ 0 & 1 & 0 \\ 0 & 0 & 1 \end{bmatrix}, \tag{7.116a}$$

$$J^j_{\text{lin}} = \begin{bmatrix} -1 & 0 & 0 \\ 0 & -1 & 0 \\ 0 & 0 & -1 \end{bmatrix}, \tag{7.116b}$$

$$J^i_{\text{ang}} = -\left(R(q_i) r^i_{\text{anc}}\right)^{\times}, \tag{7.116c}$$

$$J^j_{\text{ang}} = \left(R(q_j) r^j_{\text{anc}}\right)^{\times}, \tag{7.116d}$$

and where $J^i_{\text{lin}} \in \mathbb{R}^{3\times3}$, $J^i_{\text{ang}} \in \mathbb{R}^{3\times3}$, $J^j_{\text{lin}} \in \mathbb{R}^{3\times3}$, $J^j_{\text{ang}} \in \mathbb{R}^{3\times3}$, and the velocity error correcting term, $b_{\text{ball}} \in \mathbb{R}^3$, is given by

$$b_{\text{ball}} = k_{\text{cor}} \left(r_j + R(q_j) r^j_{\text{anc}} - r_i - R(q_i) r^i_{\text{anc}} \right). \tag{7.117}$$

7.7.2 Hinge Joint

A *hinge joint*, also called a *revolute joint*, only allows relative rotation around a specified joint axis as illustrated in Figure 7.11. We describe the joint by an anchor point placed on the axis of rotation and a joint axis, $s_{\text{axis}}^{\text{wcs}}$, given by a unit vector in the world coordinate system. We only have one DOF, meaning that the hinge joint places five constraints on the relative movement. Hence the Jacobian, J_{hinge} is a 5×12 matrix

$$J_{\text{hinge}} = \begin{bmatrix} J^i_{\text{lin}} & J^i_{\text{ang}} & J^j_{\text{lin}} & J^j_{\text{ang}} \end{bmatrix}, \tag{7.118}$$

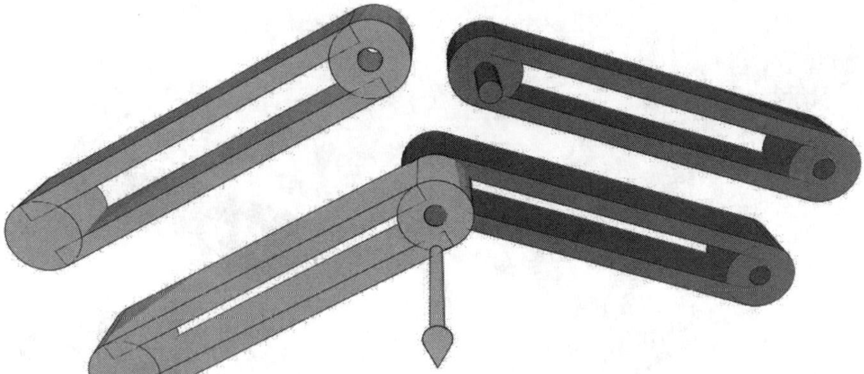

Figure 7.11: A hinge joint example.

where $\boldsymbol{J}^i_{\text{lin}} \in \mathbb{R}^{5\times3}$, $\boldsymbol{J}^i_{\text{ang}} \in \mathbb{R}^{5\times3}$, $\boldsymbol{J}^j_{\text{lin}} \in \mathbb{R}^{5\times3}$, $\boldsymbol{J}^j_{\text{ang}} \in \mathbb{R}^{5\times3}$, and $\boldsymbol{b}_{\text{hinge}} \in \mathbb{R}^5$. A hinge joint has the same kind of positional constraints as the ball-in-socket joint, so we can immediately borrow the first three rows of the ball-in-socket Jacobian and the error measure, and we only have to extend the hinge Jacobian with two more rows, which will constrain the rotational freedom from the ball-in-socket joint to only one axis of rotation.

The strategy for adding the two rotational constraints is as follows: since we only want to allow rotations around the joint axis, only the relative angular velocity of the two bodies with respect to the joint axis is allowed to be nonzero, that is,

$$\boldsymbol{s}_{\text{axis}} \cdot (\boldsymbol{\omega}_i - \boldsymbol{\omega}_j) \neq 0. \tag{7.119}$$

The relative angular velocity with any other axis orthogonal to $\boldsymbol{s}_{\text{axis}}$ must be zero.

In particular, if we let the two vectors $\boldsymbol{t}_1{}^{\text{wcs}}, \boldsymbol{t}_2{}^{\text{wcs}} \in \mathbb{R}^3$ be two orthogonal unit vectors, and require them to be orthogonal to the joint axis $\boldsymbol{s}_{\text{axis}}^{\text{wcs}}$, then

$$\boldsymbol{t}_1{}^{\text{wcs}} \cdot (\boldsymbol{\omega}_i - \boldsymbol{\omega}_j) = 0, \tag{7.120a}$$
$$\boldsymbol{t}_2{}^{\text{wcs}} \cdot (\boldsymbol{\omega}_i - \boldsymbol{\omega}_j) = 0. \tag{7.120b}$$

From these two equations we have the two needed kinematic constraints and we can write the hinge

Jacobian as follows:

$$J^i_{\text{lin}} = \begin{bmatrix} 1 & 0 & 0 \\ 0 & 1 & 0 \\ 0 & 0 & 1 \\ 0 & 0 & 0 \\ 0 & 0 & 0 \end{bmatrix}, \tag{7.121a}$$

$$J^j_{\text{lin}} = \begin{bmatrix} -1 & 0 & 0 \\ 0 & -1 & 0 \\ 0 & 0 & -1 \\ 0 & 0 & 0 \\ 0 & 0 & 0 \end{bmatrix}, \tag{7.121b}$$

$$J^i_{\text{ang}} = \begin{bmatrix} -\left(R(q_i) r^i_{\text{anc}}\right)^{\times} \\ (t_1{}^{\text{wcs}})^T \\ (t_2{}^{\text{wcs}})^T \end{bmatrix}, \tag{7.121c}$$

$$J^j_{\text{ang}} = \begin{bmatrix} \left(R(q_j) r^j_{\text{anc}}\right)^{\times} \\ -(t_1{}^{\text{wcs}})^T \\ -(t_2{}^{\text{wcs}})^T \end{bmatrix}. \tag{7.121d}$$

For the error-measure term, we already have the first three error measures from the ball-in-socket joint taking care of positional errors. Two further error measures are needed for rotational misalignment around any nonjoint axes.

If we store the joint axis with respect to both body frames, s^i_{axis} and s^j_{axis}, then computing the joint axis directions in the world coordinate system with respect to each of the incident bodies gives

$$s_i{}^{\text{wcs}} = R(q_i) s^i_{\text{axis}}, \tag{7.122a}$$

$$s_j{}^{\text{wcs}} = R(q_j) s^j_{\text{axis}}. \tag{7.122b}$$

If $s_i{}^{\text{wcs}} = s_j{}^{\text{wcs}}$, then there is obviously no error in the relative hinge orientation between the bodies. If there is an error, then the bodies must be rotated such that $s_i{}^{\text{wcs}}$ and $s_j{}^{\text{wcs}}$ are equal. This can be done as follows: imagine the angle between the two vectors is θ_{err}, then we can fix the relative error by rotation of θ_{err} radians around the axis

$$u = s_i{}^{\text{wcs}} \times s_j{}^{\text{wcs}}. \tag{7.123}$$

Let's say that we want to correct the error by the angle θ_{cor} within the time Δt, which could be the size of the time-step in some time-stepping algorithm, then we would need a relative angular velocity of magnitude

$$\|\boldsymbol{\omega}_{\text{cor}}\| = \frac{\theta_{\text{cor}}}{\Delta t} \tag{7.124a}$$
$$= \frac{k_{\text{erp}}\theta_{\text{err}}}{\Delta t} \tag{7.124b}$$
$$= k_{\text{erp}}\frac{1}{\Delta t}\theta_{\text{err}} \tag{7.124c}$$
$$= k_{\text{erp}}k_{\text{fps}}\theta_{\text{err}} \tag{7.124d}$$
$$= k_{\text{cor}}\theta_{\text{err}}. \tag{7.124e}$$

The direction of this correcting angular velocity is dictated by the $\boldsymbol{u}$-vector, since

$$\boldsymbol{\omega}_{\text{cor}} = \|\boldsymbol{\omega}_{\text{cor}}\| \frac{\boldsymbol{u}}{\|\boldsymbol{u}\|} \tag{7.125a}$$
$$= k_{\text{cor}}\theta_{\text{err}}\frac{\boldsymbol{u}}{\|\boldsymbol{u}\|} \tag{7.125b}$$
$$= k_{\text{cor}}\theta_{\text{err}}\frac{\boldsymbol{u}}{\sin\theta_{\text{err}}}. \tag{7.125c}$$

In the last step we used that $\boldsymbol{s}_i{}^{\text{wcs}}$ and $\boldsymbol{s}_j{}^{\text{wcs}}$ are unit vectors, such that

$$\|\boldsymbol{u}\| = \left\|\boldsymbol{s}_i{}^{\text{wcs}} \times \boldsymbol{s}_j{}^{\text{wcs}}\right\| = \sin\theta_{\text{err}}. \tag{7.126}$$

We expect the error to be small, so it is reasonable to use the small angle approximation, where $\theta_{\text{err}} \approx \sin\theta_{\text{err}}$, i.e.,

$$\boldsymbol{\omega}_{\text{cor}} = k_{\text{cor}}\boldsymbol{u}. \tag{7.127}$$

We know that $\boldsymbol{u}$ is orthogonal to $\boldsymbol{s}_{\text{axis}}^{\text{wcs}}$, so we project it onto the vectors $\boldsymbol{t}_1{}^{\text{wcs}}$ and $\boldsymbol{t}_2{}^{\text{wcs}}$, and we end up with the error measure

$$\boldsymbol{b}_{\text{hinge}} = k_{\text{cor}} \begin{bmatrix} \left(\boldsymbol{r}_j + \boldsymbol{R}(q_j)\boldsymbol{r}^j_{\text{anc}} - \boldsymbol{r}_i - \boldsymbol{R}(q_i)\boldsymbol{r}^i_{\text{anc}}\right) \\ \boldsymbol{t}_1{}^{\text{wcs}} \cdot \boldsymbol{u} \\ \boldsymbol{t}_2{}^{\text{wcs}} \cdot \boldsymbol{u} \end{bmatrix}. \tag{7.128}$$

7.7.3 Slider Joint

The *slider joint* only allows translation in a single direction, as shown in Figure 7.12. Hence there is only one DOF, so the Jacobian of the slider joint, $\boldsymbol{J}_{\text{slider}}$, must be a 5×12 matrix

$$\boldsymbol{J}_{\text{slider}} = \begin{bmatrix} \boldsymbol{J}^i_{\text{lin}} & \boldsymbol{J}^i_{\text{ang}} & \boldsymbol{J}^j_{\text{lin}} & \boldsymbol{J}^j_{\text{ang}} \end{bmatrix}, \tag{7.129}$$

where $\boldsymbol{J}^i_{\text{lin}} \in \mathbb{R}^{5\times 3}$, $\boldsymbol{J}^i_{\text{ang}} \in \mathbb{R}^{5\times 3}$, $\boldsymbol{J}^j_{\text{lin}} \in \mathbb{R}^{5\times 3}$, and $\boldsymbol{J}^j_{\text{ang}} \in \mathbb{R}^{5\times 3}$. We will use the first three rows of the Jacobian to ensure that the two bodies connected by the slider joint do not rotate relative to each other, hence we require that they have identical angular velocity.

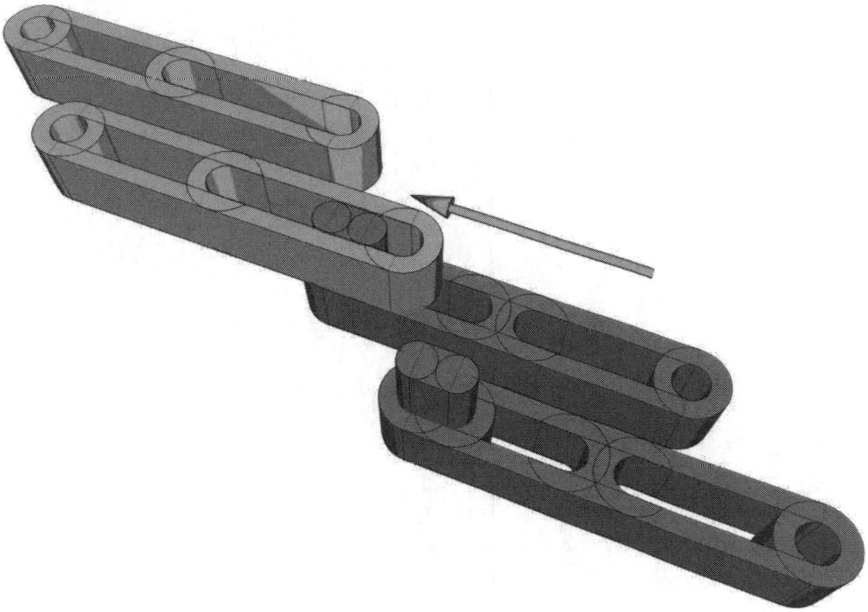

Figure 7.12: A slider joint example.

The last two rows of the Jacobian is used to make sure that the bodies only move relatively in the direction of the joint axis, $\boldsymbol{s}_{\text{axis}}^{\text{wcs}}$. This is done as follows: first we note the following relation between the bodies' linear velocities

$$\boldsymbol{v}_j = \boldsymbol{v}_i + \boldsymbol{\omega}_i \times \boldsymbol{c} + \boldsymbol{v}_{\text{slider}}, \tag{7.130}$$

where $\boldsymbol{c} = \boldsymbol{r}_j - \boldsymbol{r}_i$, and $\boldsymbol{v}_{\text{slider}}$ is the joint velocity along the slider axis. Recalling that $\boldsymbol{\omega}_i = \boldsymbol{\omega}_j$, we can rewrite the velocity relation as follows:

$$\boldsymbol{v}_j = \boldsymbol{v}_i + \boldsymbol{\omega}_i \times \boldsymbol{c} + \boldsymbol{v}_{\text{slider}}, \tag{7.131a}$$

$$-\boldsymbol{v}_{\text{slider}} = \boldsymbol{v}_i - \boldsymbol{v}_j + \boldsymbol{\omega}_i \times \boldsymbol{c}, \tag{7.131b}$$

$$-\boldsymbol{v}_{\text{slider}} = \boldsymbol{v}_i - \boldsymbol{v}_j + \frac{\boldsymbol{\omega}_i + \boldsymbol{\omega}_j}{2} \times \boldsymbol{c}. \tag{7.131c}$$

From the joint axis, $\boldsymbol{s}_{\text{axis}}^{\text{wcs}}$, we can compute two orthogonal vectors $\boldsymbol{t}_1{}^{\text{wcs}}$ and $\boldsymbol{t}_2{}^{\text{wcs}}$. By the workings of a slider joint we know that we may never have any relative velocities in the directions of the two vectors $\boldsymbol{t}_1{}^{\text{wcs}}$ and $\boldsymbol{t}_2{}^{\text{wcs}}$. That is,

$$0 = \boldsymbol{t}_1{}^{\text{wcs}} \cdot \left(-\boldsymbol{v}_{\text{slider}}\right), \tag{7.132a}$$

$$0 = \boldsymbol{t}_2{}^{\text{wcs}} \cdot \left(-\boldsymbol{v}_{\text{slider}}\right). \tag{7.132b}$$

From these two equations we can derive the remaining two rows in the Jacobian slider matrix, and we find

$$\boldsymbol{J}_{\text{lin}}^{i} = \begin{bmatrix} 0 & 0 & 0 \\ 0 & 0 & 0 \\ 0 & 0 & 0 \\ & (\boldsymbol{t}_1{}^{\text{wcs}})^T & \\ & (\boldsymbol{t}_2{}^{\text{wcs}})^T & \end{bmatrix}, \tag{7.133a}$$

$$\boldsymbol{J}_{\text{lin}}^{j} = \begin{bmatrix} 0 & 0 & 0 \\ 0 & 0 & 0 \\ 0 & 0 & 0 \\ & -(\boldsymbol{t}_1{}^{\text{wcs}})^T & \\ & -(\boldsymbol{t}_2{}^{\text{wcs}})^T & \end{bmatrix}, \tag{7.133b}$$

$$\boldsymbol{J}_{\text{ang}}^{i} = \begin{bmatrix} 1 & 0 & 0 \\ 0 & 1 & 0 \\ 0 & 0 & 1 \\ & \frac{1}{2}\boldsymbol{c} \times \boldsymbol{t}_1{}^{\text{wcs}} & \\ & \frac{1}{2}\boldsymbol{c} \times \boldsymbol{t}_2{}^{\text{wcs}} & \end{bmatrix}, \tag{7.133c}$$

$$\boldsymbol{J}_{\text{ang}}^{j} = \begin{bmatrix} -1 & 0 & 0 \\ 0 & -1 & 0 \\ 0 & 0 & -1 \\ & \frac{1}{2}\boldsymbol{c} \times \boldsymbol{t}_1{}^{\text{wcs}} & \\ & \frac{1}{2}\boldsymbol{c} \times \boldsymbol{t}_2{}^{\text{wcs}} & \end{bmatrix}. \tag{7.133d}$$

Now we will look at the error term, $\boldsymbol{b}_{\text{slider}} \in \mathbb{R}^5$. The first tree entries are used for rotational misalignment between the two links, such as sliding along a bend axis. The last two are used for fixing parallel positional displacement of the joint axis.

As for the hinge joint, we derived an angular velocity to correct the misalignment error of θ_{err} radians. The magnitude of this correcting angular velocity is as before

$$\begin{aligned} \|\boldsymbol{\omega}_{\text{cor}}\| &= \frac{\theta_{\text{cor}}}{\Delta t} && (7.134\text{a}) \\ &= \frac{k_{\text{erp}}\theta_{\text{err}}}{\Delta t} && (7.134\text{b}) \\ &= k_{\text{erp}}\frac{1}{\Delta t}\theta_{\text{err}} && (7.134\text{c}) \\ &= k_{\text{erp}}k_{\text{fps}}\theta_{\text{err}} && (7.134\text{d}) \\ &= k_{\text{cor}}\theta_{\text{err}}. && (7.134\text{e}) \end{aligned}$$

As before, the direction of this correcting angular velocity is dictated by an rotation axis given by some unit $\boldsymbol{u}$-vector

$$\begin{aligned} \boldsymbol{\omega}_{\text{cor}} &= \|\boldsymbol{\omega}_{\text{cor}}\|\, \boldsymbol{u} && (7.135\text{a}) \\ &= k_{\text{cor}}\theta_{\text{err}}\boldsymbol{u}. && (7.135\text{b}) \end{aligned}$$

However, unlike previously, the correcting angular velocity will be derived as follows: let the rotational misalignment be given by the quaternion, q_{err}, then we have

$$q_{\text{err}} = [s, \boldsymbol{v}], \tag{7.136a}$$

$$q_{\text{err}} = \left[\cos\left(\frac{\theta_{\text{err}}}{2}\right), \sin\left(\frac{\theta_{\text{err}}}{2}\right)\boldsymbol{u}\right]. \tag{7.136b}$$

The error is suspected to be small, so the small angle approximation is reasonable and we find

$$\frac{\theta_{\text{err}}}{2}\boldsymbol{u} \approx \sin\left(\frac{\theta_{\text{err}}}{2}\right)\boldsymbol{u} = \boldsymbol{v}. \tag{7.137}$$

Using this in our formula for the correcting angular velocity, we get

$$\boldsymbol{\omega}_{\text{cor}} = k_{\text{cor}} 2\boldsymbol{v}. \tag{7.138}$$

This will be the first three entries in the $\boldsymbol{b}_{slider}$-vector.

We can describe the current joint position by an offset vector, $\boldsymbol{r}_{\text{off}}^{\text{wcs}}$, which indicates the initial difference between the body centers, that is,

$$\boldsymbol{r}_{\text{off}}^{\text{j}} = \boldsymbol{R}(q_j)^T(\boldsymbol{r}_j - \boldsymbol{r}_i). \tag{7.139}$$

Observe this offset vector is computed when the joint initially was set up, that is, before simulation, and it is a constant. The corresponding offset in the world coordinate system is then simply found as

$$\boldsymbol{r}_{\text{off}}^{\text{wcs}} = \boldsymbol{R}(q_j)\boldsymbol{r}_{\text{off}}^{\text{j}}. \tag{7.140}$$

If there is no parallel displacement of the joint axis, then the vector, $\boldsymbol{c} - \boldsymbol{r}_{\text{off}}^{\text{wcs}}$ will have no components orthogonal to the joint axis. From this observation we have the last two entries in the vector $\boldsymbol{b}_{\text{slider}}$,

$$\boldsymbol{b}_{\text{slider}} = k_{\text{cor}}\begin{bmatrix} 2\boldsymbol{v} \\ \boldsymbol{t}_1^{\text{wcs}} \cdot \left(\boldsymbol{c} - \boldsymbol{r}_{\text{off}}^{\text{wcs}}\right) \\ \boldsymbol{t}_2^{\text{wcs}} \cdot \left(\boldsymbol{c} - \boldsymbol{r}_{\text{off}}^{\text{wcs}}\right) \end{bmatrix}. \tag{7.141}$$

7.7.4 Hinge-2 Joint

The *hinge-2 joint* is also called a *wheel joint* because its motion resembles that of a turning front wheel on a car. Therefore, we will explain the workings of this joint type by the example of a car wheel as shown in Figure 7.13.

The wheel joint is the same as a series of two hinge joints. Its motion is described by a rotation axis, $\boldsymbol{s}_{\text{axis}_1}^{i}$, given by a unit vector in the body frame of body i, and another rotation axis, $\boldsymbol{s}_{\text{axis}_2}^{j}$, given as a unit vector in the body frame of body j.

In the following, we will implicitly assume that body i is the car and body j is the wheel. Using this convention, the axes are referred to as the steering axis or suspension axis and the motor axis.

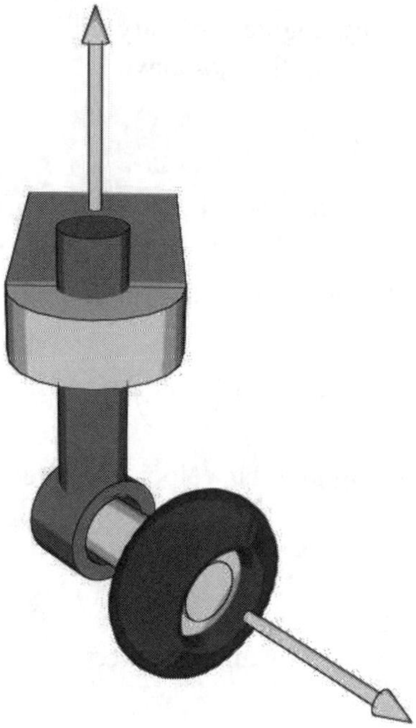

Figure 7.13: A car wheel joint example.

We will also use an anchor point like before, where both axes are going through this anchor point. We will assume that the axes do not lie along the same line, and that they are always separated by the initial angle, θ, between them.

From the description, it is clear that the joint has two DOFs, from which we know that the wheel joint Jacobian must have dimension 4×12

$$\boldsymbol{J}_{\text{wheel}} = \begin{bmatrix} \boldsymbol{J}^i_{\text{lin}} & \boldsymbol{J}^i_{\text{ang}} & \boldsymbol{J}^j_{\text{lin}} & \boldsymbol{J}^j_{\text{ang}} \end{bmatrix}, \tag{7.142}$$

where $\boldsymbol{J}^i_{\text{lin}} \in \mathbb{R}^{4\times 3}$, $\boldsymbol{J}^i_{\text{ang}} \in \mathbb{R}^{4\times 3}$, $\boldsymbol{J}^j_{\text{lin}} \in \mathbb{R}^{4\times 3}$, and $\boldsymbol{J}^j_{\text{ang}} \in \mathbb{R}^{4\times 3}$.

Following the same recipe as previously, we reuse the ball-in-socket joint for the positional constraints and we are now left only with the fourth row in the Jacobian matrix.

Let's compute the joint axis in the world coordinate system

$$\boldsymbol{s}_i{}^{\text{wcs}} = \boldsymbol{R}(q_i)\boldsymbol{s}_{\text{axe}}{}^i, \tag{7.143a}$$

$$\boldsymbol{s}_j{}^{\text{wcs}} = \boldsymbol{R}(q_j)\boldsymbol{s}_{\text{axe}}{}^j, \tag{7.143b}$$

then the constrained rotational DOF is dictated by a rotational axis orthogonal to the two rotation axes, that is,

$$\boldsymbol{u} = \boldsymbol{s}_i{}^{\text{wcs}} \times \boldsymbol{s}_j{}^{\text{wcs}}. \tag{7.144}$$

For the hinge to keep its alignment, we must ensure that there is no relative rotation around this axis

$$\boldsymbol{u} \cdot \boldsymbol{\omega}_i - \boldsymbol{u} \cdot \boldsymbol{\omega}_j = 0. \tag{7.145}$$

This give us the missing fourth row of the Jacobian matrix

$$\boldsymbol{J}^i_{\text{lin}} = \begin{bmatrix} 1 & 0 & 0 \\ 0 & 1 & 0 \\ 0 & 0 & 1 \\ 0 & 0 & 0 \end{bmatrix}, \tag{7.146a}$$

$$\boldsymbol{J}^j_{\text{lin}} = \begin{bmatrix} -1 & 0 & 0 \\ 0 & -1 & 0 \\ 0 & 0 & -1 \\ 0 & 0 & 0 \end{bmatrix}, \tag{7.146b}$$

$$\boldsymbol{J}^i_{\text{ang}} = \begin{bmatrix} \left(\boldsymbol{R}(\boldsymbol{q_i})\boldsymbol{r}^{\boldsymbol{i}}_{\text{anc}}\right)^{\times} \\ \boldsymbol{u}^T \end{bmatrix}, \tag{7.146c}$$

$$\boldsymbol{J}^j_{\text{ang}} = -\begin{bmatrix} \left(\boldsymbol{R}(\boldsymbol{q_j})\boldsymbol{r}^{\boldsymbol{j}}_{\text{anc}}\right)^{\times} \\ \boldsymbol{u}^T \end{bmatrix}. \tag{7.146d}$$

From the ball-in-socket joint we also have the first three entries of the error term, $\boldsymbol{b}_{\text{wheel}} \in \mathbb{R}^4$. Therefore, we only need to come up with the fourth entry to reestablish the angle θ between the two joint axes. Let's say that the current angle is given by ϕ, then we need a correcting angular velocity of magnitude

$$\|\boldsymbol{\omega}_{\text{cor}}\| = \frac{\theta_{\text{cor}}}{\Delta t} \tag{7.147a}$$

$$= \frac{k_{\text{erp}}\left(\theta - \phi\right)}{\Delta t} \tag{7.147b}$$

$$= k_{\text{erp}} \frac{1}{\Delta t}\left(\theta - \phi\right) \tag{7.147c}$$

$$= k_{\text{erp}} k_{\text{fps}}\left(\theta - \phi\right) \tag{7.147d}$$

$$= k_{\text{cor}}\left(\theta - \phi\right). \tag{7.147e}$$

We can now write the error-term vector as

$$\boldsymbol{b}_{\text{wheel}} = k_{\text{cor}} \begin{bmatrix} \boldsymbol{b}_{\text{ball}} \\ (\theta - \phi) \end{bmatrix}. \tag{7.148}$$

Finally, two more tricks are possible: first, one rotates the axes of the ball-in-socket joints, such that the first constraining axis is along the suspension axis, which allows one to model suspension by modulating the translational error in the ball-in-socket joint along its first axis. Second, a small angle approximation for the fourth entry in the error-term vector may be used [ODE, 2005].

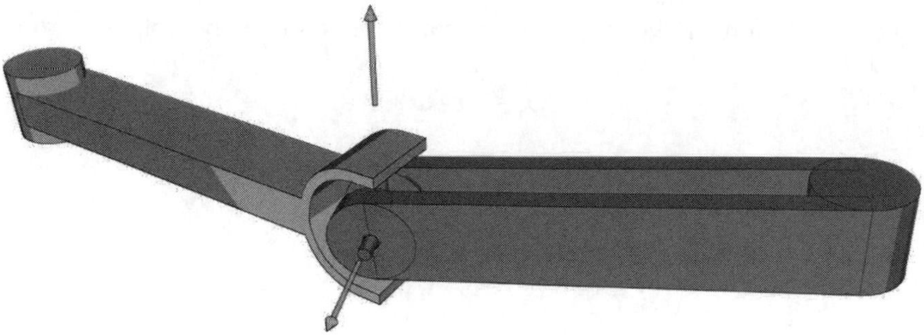

Figure 7.14: A universal joint example.

7.7.5 Universal Joint

The *universal joint* is in some sense similar to the wheel joint, and is described similarly by the two joint axes

$$s^i_{\text{axe}_1}, \tag{7.149a}$$
$$s^j_{\text{axe}_2}, \tag{7.149b}$$

and an anchor point, which the two axes run through. The difference from the wheel joint is that it is further required that axis two makes an angle of $\pi/2$ with axis one. An example of a universal joint is shown in Figure 7.14.

We notice again that we have two DOFs, and the Jacobian matrix of the universal joint, $J_{\text{universal}}$, must be a 4×12 matrix

$$J_{\text{universal}} = \begin{bmatrix} J^i_{\text{lin}} & J^i_{\text{ang}} & J^j_{\text{lin}} & J^j_{\text{ang}} \end{bmatrix}. \tag{7.150}$$

Since this joint type has derivations almost identical to previous types, we will ease on notation and go through the steps faster. We start out by reusing the ball-in-socket joint for the positional constraints, and then we compute the constrained rotation axis

$$u = s_i^{\text{wcs}} \times s_j^{\text{wcs}}, \tag{7.151}$$

along which we know there must be no relative angular velocity. We can now write the Jacobian matrix for the universal joint as

$$J^i_{\text{lin}} = \begin{bmatrix} 1 & 0 & 0 \\ 0 & 1 & 0 \\ 0 & 0 & 1 \\ 0 & 0 & 0 \end{bmatrix}, \tag{7.152a}$$

$$J^j_{\text{lin}} = \begin{bmatrix} -1 & 0 & 0 \\ 0 & -1 & 0 \\ 0 & 0 & -1 \\ 0 & 0 & 0 \end{bmatrix}, \tag{7.152b}$$

$$J^i_{\text{ang}} = \begin{bmatrix} \left(R(q_i)r^i_{\text{anc}}\right)^{\times} \\ u^T \end{bmatrix}, \tag{7.152c}$$

$$J^j_{\text{ang}} = -\begin{bmatrix} \left(R(q_j)r^j_{\text{anc}}\right)^{\times} \\ u^T \end{bmatrix}. \tag{7.152d}$$

We already have the first three entries of the vector, $b_{\text{universal}}$, and we must find the fourth. We do this by first looking at the magnitude of the correcting angular velocity

$$\|\omega_{\text{cor}}\| = \frac{\theta_{\text{cor}}}{\Delta t} \tag{7.153a}$$

$$= \frac{k_{\text{erp}}\left(\phi - \frac{\pi}{2}\right)}{\Delta t} \tag{7.153b}$$

$$= k_{\text{cor}}\left(\phi - \frac{\pi}{2}\right), \tag{7.153c}$$

where ϕ denotes the current angle between the two joint axis. If ϕ is close to $\pi/2$, then

$$\phi - \frac{\pi}{2} \approx \cos(\phi) \tag{7.154a}$$

$$= {s_i}^{\text{wcs}} \cdot {s_j}^{\text{wcs}}. \tag{7.154b}$$

We can now write the error-term vector as

$$b_{\text{universal}} = k_{\text{cor}} \begin{bmatrix} b_{\text{ball}} \\ -{s_i}^{\text{wcs}} \cdot {s_j}^{\text{wcs}} \end{bmatrix}. \tag{7.155}$$

7.7.6 Fixed Joint

For *fixed joints*, we know that it constrains two bodies completely from any relative movement, and it therefore has zero DOFs, from which we know that the Jacobian matrix, $J_{\text{fixed}} \in \mathbb{R}^{6\times12}$

$$J_{\text{universal}} = \begin{bmatrix} J^i_{\text{lin}} & J^i_{\text{ang}} & J^j_{\text{lin}} & J^j_{\text{ang}} \end{bmatrix}. \tag{7.156}$$

The fixed joint is described by an anchor point, and initially we compute an offset vector and store it in the body frame of body i

$$\boldsymbol{r}_{\text{off}}^{\text{i}} = \boldsymbol{r}_i - \boldsymbol{r}_j. \tag{7.157}$$

Observe this offset vector is computed when the joint initially was set up prior to simulation, and it is a constant. The corresponding offset in the world coordinate system is then found by

$$\boldsymbol{r}_{\text{off}}^{\text{wcs}} = R(q_i)\boldsymbol{r}_{\text{off}}^{\text{i}}. \tag{7.158}$$

Since we have a fixed joint, both incident bodies must be rotating with the same angular velocity and the linear velocities must obey the relation

$$\boldsymbol{v}_j = \boldsymbol{v}_i + \boldsymbol{\omega}_i \times \boldsymbol{r}_{\text{off}}^{\text{wcs}}. \tag{7.159}$$

From all this we can now set up the Jacobian matrix as

$$\boldsymbol{J}_{\text{lin}}^{i} = \begin{bmatrix} 1 & 0 & 0 \\ 0 & 1 & 0 \\ 0 & 0 & 1 \\ 0 & 0 & 0 \\ 0 & 0 & 0 \\ 0 & 0 & 0 \end{bmatrix}, \tag{7.160a}$$

$$\boldsymbol{J}_{\text{lin}}^{j} = \begin{bmatrix} -1 & 0 & 0 \\ 0 & -1 & 0 \\ 0 & 0 & -1 \\ 0 & 0 & 0 \\ 0 & 0 & 0 \\ 0 & 0 & 0 \end{bmatrix}, \tag{7.160b}$$

$$\boldsymbol{J}_{\text{ang}}^{i} = \begin{bmatrix} & -\left(\boldsymbol{r}_{\text{off}}^{\text{wcs}}\right)^{\times} & \\ 1 & 0 & 0 \\ 0 & 1 & 0 \\ 0 & 0 & 1 \end{bmatrix}, \tag{7.160c}$$

$$\boldsymbol{J}_{\text{ang}}^{j} = \begin{bmatrix} 0 & 0 & 0 \\ 0 & 0 & 0 \\ 0 & 0 & 0 \\ -1 & 0 & 0 \\ 0 & -1 & 0 \\ 0 & 0 & -1 \end{bmatrix}. \tag{7.160d}$$

Similarly, the error term is straightforward, since most of it was presented for the ball-in-socket joint, $\boldsymbol{b}_{\text{ball}}$, from where we get the first three entries, for positional error, and from the slider joint, $\boldsymbol{b}_{\text{slider}}$. We may reuse the first three entries to take care of any rotational errors. We can now write the $\boldsymbol{b}_{\text{fixed}}$ vector as

$$\boldsymbol{b}_{\text{fixed}} = k_{\text{cor}} \begin{bmatrix} \left(\boldsymbol{r}_i + \boldsymbol{R}(q_i)\boldsymbol{r}_{\text{anc}}^{i} - \boldsymbol{r}_j - \boldsymbol{R}(q_j)\boldsymbol{r}_{\text{anc}}^{j}\right) \\ 2\boldsymbol{v} \end{bmatrix}, \tag{7.161}$$

where $\boldsymbol{v}$ comes from the quaternion representing the rotational error

$$q_{\text{err}} = [s, \boldsymbol{v}]\,. \tag{7.162}$$

7.7.7 Contact Point

As we have explained, contact constraints are completely different from joint constraints, but they too, are described by a Jacobian matrix. As we will show, this Jacobian matrix $\boldsymbol{J}_{\text{contact}}$, can be expressed in the same submatrix pattern as the joint Jacobians; one can even construct an error correcting term.

From previously, we know that the contact Jacobian has $1 + \eta$ constraints, so it is $(1 + \eta)$-by-12 dimensional matrix,

$$\boldsymbol{J}_{\text{contact}} = \begin{bmatrix} \boldsymbol{J}_{\text{lin}}^{i} & \boldsymbol{J}_{\text{ang}}^{i} & \boldsymbol{J}_{\text{lin}}^{j} & \boldsymbol{J}_{\text{ang}}^{j} \end{bmatrix}. \tag{7.163}$$

The first row corresponds to the normal force constraints and the remaining η rows correspond to the *tangential friction constraints*, that is,

$$\boldsymbol{J}_{\text{lin}}^{i} = \begin{bmatrix} -\boldsymbol{n}^{t} \\ -\boldsymbol{D}_{k}^{T} \end{bmatrix}, \tag{7.164a}$$

$$\boldsymbol{J}_{\text{lin}}^{j} = \begin{bmatrix} \boldsymbol{n}^{t} \\ \boldsymbol{D}_{k}^{T} \end{bmatrix}, \tag{7.164b}$$

$$\boldsymbol{J}_{\text{ang}}^{i} = \begin{bmatrix} -\left(\boldsymbol{r_i} \times \boldsymbol{n}\right)^{T} \\ -\left(\boldsymbol{r_i} \times \boldsymbol{D}_k\right)^{T} \end{bmatrix}, \tag{7.164c}$$

$$\boldsymbol{J}_{\text{ang}}^{j} = \begin{bmatrix} \left(\boldsymbol{r_j} \times \boldsymbol{n}\right)^{T} \\ \left(\boldsymbol{r_j} \times \boldsymbol{D}_k\right)^{T} \end{bmatrix}. \tag{7.164d}$$

If the penetration constraints are violated, then an error correcting vector, $\boldsymbol{b}_{\text{contact}} \in \mathbb{R}^{1+\eta}$, can be used as

$$\boldsymbol{b}_{\text{contact}} = k_{\text{cor}} \begin{bmatrix} d_{\text{penetration}} \\ \boldsymbol{0} \end{bmatrix}. \tag{7.165}$$

where $d_{\text{penetration}}$ is the penetration depth. These observations regarding the submatrix patterns of the Jacobians of both the contact and joint constraints allow us to implement these kind of constraints using almost the same kind of data structure.

7.8 Joint Limits

It is not always enough just to set up a joint, even though the relative motion is constrained to move only in a consistent manner w.r.t. the joint, other constraints need our attention. For instance, in the real world we cannot find a jointed mechanism with a sliding joint that has an infinitely long joint axis. In other words, we need some way to model the extent of a sliding joint. We will do this modeling by setting up *joint limits*. To be specific, we will treat joint limits on a sliding joint and a hinge joint.

The general approach we will take here for introducing joint limits is very similar to the way we use unilateral constraints for enforcing normal nonpenetration constraints at the contact points. In a sense, setting joint limits this way is nothing more than a slightly exotic way of computing contact points for normal force constraints disguised as joint limits.

7.8.1 Slider Joint Limits

Recall that in specifying the slider joint we used an offset vector, which was the initial difference between the origin of the body frames; that is, at time $t = 0$, we compute

$$\boldsymbol{r}_{\text{off}}^{\text{j}} = \boldsymbol{R}(q_j)^T (\boldsymbol{r}_j - \boldsymbol{r}_i). \tag{7.166}$$

As before, the initial offset w.r.t. the bodies current location in the world coordinate system is computed as

$$\boldsymbol{r}_{\text{off}}^{\text{wcs}} = R(q_j)\boldsymbol{r}_{\text{off}}^{\text{j}}. \tag{7.167}$$

Now letting $\boldsymbol{c} = \boldsymbol{r}_j - \boldsymbol{r}_i$, we can compute the current displacement, $\boldsymbol{r}_{\text{dis}}$, along the joint axis as

$$\boldsymbol{r}_{\text{dis}} = \boldsymbol{c} - \boldsymbol{r}_{\text{off}}^{\text{wcs}}. \tag{7.168}$$

Taking the dot product with the joint axis, $\boldsymbol{s}_{\text{axe}}^{\text{wcs}}$, gives a signed distance measure of the displacement along the joint axis,

$$d_{\text{dis}} = \boldsymbol{s}_{\text{axe}}^{\text{wcs}} \cdot \boldsymbol{r}_{\text{dis}}. \tag{7.169}$$

When the joint limits are imposed on the slider joint, we want to be able to specify a lower-distance limit, d_{lo}, and an upper-distance limit, d_{hi}. If one of these are violated, for instance,

$$d_{\text{dis}} \leq d_{\text{lo}}, \tag{7.170}$$

then we will add a new unilateral constraint. This constraint specifies that the relative velocity of the joint along the joint axis must be such that the displacement does not move beyond the limit. For a slider joint that means we require

$$\boldsymbol{s}_{\text{axe}}^{\text{wcs}} \cdot (\boldsymbol{v}_j - \boldsymbol{v}_i) \geq 0. \tag{7.171}$$

We immediately see that this is equivalent to a 1×12 dimensional Jacobian matrix, $\boldsymbol{J}_{\text{slider}}^{\text{lo}}$, where

$$\boldsymbol{J}_{\text{lin}}^{i} = -\left(\boldsymbol{s}_{\text{axe}}^{\text{wcs}}\right)^T, \tag{7.172a}$$

$$\boldsymbol{J}_{\text{lin}}^{j} = \left(\boldsymbol{s}_{\text{axe}}^{\text{wcs}}\right)^T, \tag{7.172b}$$

$$\boldsymbol{J}_{\text{ang}}^{i} = \boldsymbol{0}, \tag{7.172c}$$

$$\boldsymbol{J}_{\text{ang}}^{j} = \boldsymbol{0}. \tag{7.172d}$$

However, this would be the wrong Jacobian to use because when we look at the reaction forces from the joint limit, this Jacobian will not model the torques coming from the limiting force, only the linear contribution is included.

We will now remodel the Jacobian to include all the force and torque contributions. Let's say that the position of the joint limit is given by the vectors: $\boldsymbol{r}_{\text{lim}_i}{}^{\text{wcs}}$ and $\boldsymbol{r}_{\text{lim}_j}{}^{\text{wcs}}$. These vectors are specified in the world coordinate system and are running from the respective body centers to the position of the joint limit.

Now say that some force, $\boldsymbol{F}$, is acting on body i at the joint limit, then the force is required to be parallel with the joint axis $\boldsymbol{s}_{\text{axe}}{}^{\text{wcs}}$. The force contribution to body j is $-\boldsymbol{F}$ according to Newton's third law of motion. The limit force also result in a torque on body i

$$\boldsymbol{\tau}_{\text{lim}_i} = \boldsymbol{r}_{\text{lim}_i}{}^{\text{wcs}} \times \boldsymbol{F}, \tag{7.173}$$

and a torque on body j,

$$\boldsymbol{\tau}_{\text{lim}_j} = -\boldsymbol{r}_{\text{lim}_j}{}^{\text{wcs}} \times \boldsymbol{F}. \tag{7.174}$$

For a slider joint we must also require that these torques do not induce a relative angular velocity of the two bodies, meaning that angular momentum should remain unchanged. From Euler's equation, we get

$$\boldsymbol{\tau}_{\text{lim}_i} + \boldsymbol{\tau}_{\text{lim}_j} = 0. \tag{7.175}$$

Recalling that the corresponding reaction force is given by

$$\boldsymbol{F}_{\text{slider}}^{\text{lo}} = \left(\boldsymbol{J}_{\text{slider}}^{\text{lo}}\right)^T \lambda_{\text{lo}}, \tag{7.176}$$

where λ_{lo} is a nonnegative Lagrange multiplier. This suggest that the Jacobian should look like

$$\boldsymbol{J}_{\text{lin}}^{i} = -\left(\boldsymbol{s}_{\text{axe}}{}^{\text{wcs}}\right)^T, \tag{7.177a}$$

$$\boldsymbol{J}_{\text{lin}}^{j} = \left(\boldsymbol{s}_{\text{axe}}{}^{\text{wcs}}\right)^T, \tag{7.177b}$$

$$\boldsymbol{J}_{\text{ang}}^{i} = \left(\boldsymbol{r}_{\text{lim}_i}{}^{\text{wcs}} \times \boldsymbol{s}_{\text{axe}}{}^{\text{wcs}}\right)^T, \tag{7.177c}$$

$$\boldsymbol{J}_{\text{ang}}^{j} = -\left(\boldsymbol{r}_{\text{lim}_j}{}^{\text{wcs}} \times \boldsymbol{s}_{\text{axe}}{}^{\text{wcs}}\right)^T. \tag{7.177d}$$

However, it is not obvious that $\boldsymbol{J}_{\text{ang}}^{i}\boldsymbol{\omega}_i + \boldsymbol{J}_{\text{ang}}^{j}\boldsymbol{\omega}_j = 0$, also to avoid computing the vectors $\boldsymbol{r}_{\text{lim}_i}{}^{\text{wcs}}$ and $\boldsymbol{r}_{\text{lim}_j}{}^{\text{wcs}}$ during simulation it would be nice to remove them from the expressions.

Observe that the vector, $\boldsymbol{c} = \boldsymbol{r}_j - \boldsymbol{r}_i$, can be written as, $\boldsymbol{c} = \boldsymbol{r}_{\text{lim}_i}{}^{\text{wcs}} - \boldsymbol{r}_{\text{lim}_j}{}^{\text{wcs}}$. We will now show that with the $\boldsymbol{c}$-vector we can obtain:

$$\boldsymbol{r}_{\text{lim}_i}{}^{\text{wcs}} \times \boldsymbol{F} = \frac{1}{2}\boldsymbol{c} \times \boldsymbol{F} = \frac{1}{2}\left(\boldsymbol{r}_{\text{lim}_i}{}^{\text{wcs}} - \boldsymbol{r}_{\text{lim}_j}{}^{\text{wcs}}\right) \times \boldsymbol{F}, \tag{7.178a}$$

$$\boldsymbol{r}_{\text{lim}_j}{}^{\text{wcs}} \times \boldsymbol{F} = -\frac{1}{2}\boldsymbol{c} \times \boldsymbol{F} = -\frac{1}{2}\left(\boldsymbol{r}_{\text{lim}_i}{}^{\text{wcs}} - \boldsymbol{r}_{\text{lim}_j}{}^{\text{wcs}}\right) \times \boldsymbol{F}. \tag{7.178b}$$

From the second equation we have

$$\boldsymbol{r}_{\text{lim}_j}{}^{\text{wcs}} \times \boldsymbol{F} = -\frac{1}{2}\boldsymbol{r}_{\text{lim}_i}{}^{\text{wcs}} \times \boldsymbol{F} + \frac{1}{2}\boldsymbol{r}_{\text{lim}_j}{}^{\text{wcs}} \times \boldsymbol{F}, \tag{7.179}$$

which yields

$$\frac{1}{2}\boldsymbol{r}_{\text{lim}_j}^{\text{wcs}} \times \boldsymbol{F} = -\frac{1}{2}\boldsymbol{r}_{\text{lim}_i}^{\text{wcs}} \times \boldsymbol{F}, \tag{7.180}$$

and substituting this into the first equation yields

$$\begin{aligned}
\boldsymbol{r}_{\text{lim}_i}^{\text{wcs}} \times \boldsymbol{F} &= \frac{1}{2}\left(\boldsymbol{r}_{\text{lim}_i}^{\text{wcs}} - \boldsymbol{r}_{\text{lim}_j}^{\text{wcs}}\right) \times \boldsymbol{F} && (7.181a)\\
&= \frac{1}{2}\boldsymbol{r}_{\text{lim}_i}^{\text{wcs}} \times \boldsymbol{F} - \frac{1}{2}\boldsymbol{r}_{\text{lim}_j}^{\text{wcs}} \times \boldsymbol{F} && (7.181b)\\
&= \frac{1}{2}\boldsymbol{r}_{\text{lim}_i}^{\text{wcs}} \times \boldsymbol{F} - \left(-\frac{1}{2}\boldsymbol{r}_{\text{lim}_i}^{\text{wcs}} \times \boldsymbol{F}\right), && (7.181c)\\
\boldsymbol{r}_{\text{lim}_i}^{\text{wcs}} \times \boldsymbol{F} &= \boldsymbol{r}_{\text{lim}_i}^{\text{wcs}} \times \boldsymbol{F}. && (7.181d)
\end{aligned}$$

This proves (7.178a). Repeating the steps but interchanging equations easily derives (7.178b). Observe also that the sum of the two equations is equal to zero as required by Euler's equation. We can now rewrite the angular parts of the Jacobian as

$$\begin{aligned}
\boldsymbol{J}_{\text{lin}}^{i} &= -\left(\boldsymbol{s}_{\text{axe}}^{\text{wcs}}\right)^T, && (7.182a)\\
\boldsymbol{J}_{\text{lin}}^{j} &= \left(\boldsymbol{s}_{\text{axe}}^{\text{wcs}}\right)^T, && (7.182b)\\
\boldsymbol{J}_{\text{ang}}^{i} &= \frac{1}{2}\left(\boldsymbol{c} \times \boldsymbol{s}_{\text{axe}}^{\text{wcs}}\right)^T, && (7.182c)\\
\boldsymbol{J}_{\text{ang}}^{j} &= -\frac{1}{2}\left(\boldsymbol{c} \times \boldsymbol{s}_{\text{axe}}^{\text{wcs}}\right)^T. && (7.182d)
\end{aligned}$$

To verify that $\boldsymbol{J}_{\text{ang}}^{i}\boldsymbol{\omega}_i + \boldsymbol{J}_{\text{ang}}^{j}\boldsymbol{\omega}_j = 0$, we insert (7.182c) and (7.182d) and find

$$\begin{aligned}
&\frac{1}{2}\left(\boldsymbol{c} \times \boldsymbol{s}_{\text{axe}}^{\text{wcs}}\right)^T \boldsymbol{\omega}_i - \frac{1}{2}\left(\boldsymbol{c} \times \boldsymbol{s}_{\text{axe}}^{\text{wcs}}\right)^T \boldsymbol{\omega}_j = 0, && (7.183a)\\
\Rightarrow\quad &\frac{1}{2}\left(\boldsymbol{c} \times \boldsymbol{s}_{\text{axe}}^{\text{wcs}}\right)^T \left(\boldsymbol{\omega}_i - \boldsymbol{\omega}_j\right) = 0, && (7.183b)
\end{aligned}$$

and because we have a slider joint $\boldsymbol{\omega}_i = \boldsymbol{\omega}_j$. In conclusion, we see that with the Jacobian in (7.183), both the kinematic constraints are satisfied, and the reaction forces are prober.

Putting it all together, we have the complementarity constraint

$$\boldsymbol{J}_{\text{slider}}^{\text{lo}}\boldsymbol{u} \geq 0, \quad \text{compl. to} \quad \lambda_{\text{lo}} \geq 0. \tag{7.184}$$

An error correcting term, $\boldsymbol{b}_{\text{slider}}^{\text{lo}}$ is easily added to the right side of the kinematic constraint as

$$\begin{aligned}
\boldsymbol{b}_{\text{slider}}^{\text{lo}} &= k_{\text{erp}}\frac{d_{\text{lo}} - d_{\text{dis}}}{\Delta t} && (7.185a)\\
&= k_{\text{cor}} d_{\text{err}}, && (7.185b)
\end{aligned}$$

where we have set $d_{\text{err}} = d_{\text{lo}} - d_{\text{dis}}$.

In conclusion, we have derived a single linear complementarity constraint for the lower joint limit of a slider joint. The same approach can be used to derive a single linear complementarity constraint for the upper limit. It should be apparent that all that is really needed is to negate the Jacobian, that is,

$$\boldsymbol{J}_{\text{slider}}^{\text{hi}} = -\boldsymbol{J}_{\text{slider}}^{\text{lo}}, \tag{7.186}$$

and the error term

$$\boldsymbol{b}_{\text{slider}}^{\text{hi}} = k_{\text{erp}} \frac{d_{\text{hi}} - d_{\text{dis}}}{\Delta t} \tag{7.187a}$$

$$= k_{\text{cor}} d_{\text{err}}. \tag{7.187b}$$

7.8.2 Hinge Joint Limits

There really is not much difference between setting limits on a slider joint and a hinge joint. The major difference is that the joint axis now describes a rotation axis, and instead of distances, we use angle measures.

If we store the initial relative rotation of two bodies in the quaternion, q_{ini}, then we can compute the current relative rotation of the two bodies as

$$q_{\text{rel}} = q_j^* q_i q_{\text{ini}}^*. \tag{7.188}$$

This quaternion corresponds to a rotation of θ radians around the unit axis, $\boldsymbol{v}$, that is the angle measured from i to j around the joint axis,

$$q_{\text{rel}} = \left[\cos\left(\frac{\theta}{2}\right), \sin\left(\frac{\theta}{2}\right)\boldsymbol{v}\right]. \tag{7.189}$$

Using standard trigonometry and taking care of the double representation of rotations by picking the smallest angle solution, one can extract the angle from the quaternion of relative rotation. Specifically, taking the dot product with the vector part of the quaternion, $\sin\frac{\theta}{2}$, is obtained since $\boldsymbol{v}\cdot\boldsymbol{v} = 1$, now arctan can be used to obtain $\frac{\theta}{2}$.

As we did in the case of the slider joint, we want to impose a low- and high-joint limit, θ_{lo} and θ_{hi}. If, for instance, the lower limit is violated as

$$\theta \le \theta_{\text{lo}}, \tag{7.190}$$

then we will add a new unilateral constraint, which specifies that the relative angular velocity of the joint around the joint axis must be such that the angle does not move beyond the limit. For a hinge joint this means that we must require

$$\boldsymbol{s}_{\text{axe}}^{\text{wcs}} \cdot (\boldsymbol{\omega}_j - \boldsymbol{\omega}_i) \ge 0. \tag{7.191}$$

We immediately see that this is equivalent to a 1×12 dimensional Jacobian matrix, $\boldsymbol{J}_{\text{hinge}}^{\text{lo}}$, where

$$\boldsymbol{J}_{\text{lin}}^{i} = \boldsymbol{0}, \tag{7.192a}$$

$$\boldsymbol{J}_{\text{lin}}^{j} = \boldsymbol{0}, \tag{7.192b}$$

$$\boldsymbol{J}_{\text{ang}}^{i} = -\left(\boldsymbol{s}_{\text{axe}}^{\text{wcs}}\right)^T, \tag{7.192c}$$

$$\boldsymbol{J}_{\text{ang}}^{j} = \left(\boldsymbol{s}_{\text{axe}}^{\text{wcs}}\right)^T. \tag{7.192d}$$

The corresponding reaction force from the joint limit is given by

$$\boldsymbol{F}_{\text{hinge}}^{\text{lo}} = \left(\boldsymbol{J}_{\text{hinge}}^{\text{lo}}\right)^T \lambda_{\text{lo}}, \tag{7.193}$$

where λ_{lo} is a nonnegative Lagrange multiplier. We see that we have the complementarity constraint

$$\boldsymbol{J}_{\text{hinge}}^{\text{lo}} \boldsymbol{u} \geq 0, \quad \text{compl. to} \quad \lambda_{\text{lo}} \geq 0. \tag{7.194}$$

An error correcting term, $\boldsymbol{b}_{\text{hinge}}^{\text{lo}}$, is added to the right side of the kinematic constraint as

$$\boldsymbol{b}_{\text{hinge}}^{\text{lo}} = k_{\text{erp}} \frac{\theta_{\text{lo}} - \theta}{\Delta t} \tag{7.195a}$$

$$= k_{\text{cor}} \theta_{\text{err}}, \tag{7.195b}$$

where $\theta_{\text{err}} = \theta_{\text{lo}} - \theta$.

The constraints for the high limit of the hinge joint is obtained by negating the Jacobian

$$\boldsymbol{J}_{\text{hinge}}^{\text{hi}} = -\boldsymbol{J}_{\text{hinge}}^{\text{lo}}, \tag{7.196}$$

and the error term is given by,

$$\boldsymbol{b}_{\text{hinge}}^{\text{hi}} = k_{\text{erp}} \frac{\theta_{\text{hi}} - \theta}{\Delta t} \tag{7.197a}$$

$$= k_{\text{cor}} \theta_{\text{err}}. \tag{7.197b}$$

7.8.3 Generalization of Joint Limits

In the previous sections we derived constraint equations specific for low- and high-joint limits on slider and hinge joints. Fortunately, it is possible to extend these ideas to a more general framework. For instance, the concept of a reach cone, i.e., multiple angular joint limits, is often used in biomechanics to describe the limited movement of the shoulder or hip joints in the human skeleton [Wilhelms et al., 2001].

In fact, we could formulate the allowable configuration space or the reachable region for a joint, by an implicit function, $C(\ldots) \in \mathbb{R}$, of the joint parameters. For the slider and hinge joints, the joint parameters are the displacement and the angle, which we will specify with the generalized joint parameter vector, $\boldsymbol{q}$, as a function of the generalized position vector, $\boldsymbol{s}$. Furthermore, the implicit function has the following characteristics,

$$C(\boldsymbol{q}(\boldsymbol{s})) < 0 \quad \text{Outside}, \tag{7.198a}$$

$$C(\boldsymbol{q}(\boldsymbol{s})) = 0 \quad \text{On boundary}, \tag{7.198b}$$

$$C(\boldsymbol{q}(\boldsymbol{s})) > 0 \quad \text{Inside}. \tag{7.198c}$$

We can now reformulate positional constraints as

$$C(\boldsymbol{q}(\boldsymbol{s})) \geq 0. \tag{7.199}$$

Differentiation w.r.t. time leads to the kinematic constraint,

$$\frac{d}{dt}C(\boldsymbol{q}(\boldsymbol{s})) = \underbrace{\frac{dC(\boldsymbol{q}(\boldsymbol{s}))}{d\boldsymbol{q}}\frac{d\boldsymbol{q}}{d\boldsymbol{s}}}_{\boldsymbol{J}_C}\underbrace{\frac{d\boldsymbol{s}}{dt}}_{\boldsymbol{u}} \tag{7.200a}$$

$$= \boldsymbol{J}_C\boldsymbol{u} \tag{7.200b}$$

$$\geq 0, \tag{7.200c}$$

which could be augmented with an error reduction term

$$\boldsymbol{J}_C\boldsymbol{u} \geq \boldsymbol{b}_C. \tag{7.201}$$

The reaction forces are determined by

$$\boldsymbol{F}^C_{\text{reaction}} = \boldsymbol{J}_C^T\boldsymbol{\lambda}_C, \tag{7.202}$$

where $\boldsymbol{\lambda}_C$ is a vector of nonnegative Lagrange multipliers. Finally, we have the complementarity constraints,

$$\boldsymbol{J}_C\boldsymbol{u} - \boldsymbol{b}_C \geq 0, \quad \text{compl. to} \quad \boldsymbol{\lambda}_C \geq 0. \tag{7.203}$$

The constraints in terms of the Jacobian and the error term should be added to the system equations, whenever a joint limit has been violated or its boundary has been reached. This is completely analogous to collision detection; enforcing joint limits in this manner is therefore not much different from finding contacts and computing normal forces.

Observe that in a force-based formulation, the kinematic joint limit constraints should be differentiated w.r.t. time to get the acceleration constraints needed for augmenting the system equations.

7.9 Joint Motors

With joints and joint limits, we are capable of modeling the range of relative motion between two bodies. We will now look at one way to control the motion that is taking place.

A *joint motor* applies torque or force to a joint's degrees of freedom to induce movement. The joint motor model uses two parameters for this: a desired speed, v_{desired}, and the maximum torque or force, $\lambda_{\max}$, that can be applied to reach the desired speed.

From past sections we have seen that the error correcting term can be used to adjust velocities. The same principle can be used to drive a joint toward a desired speed by

$$\boldsymbol{J}_{\text{motor}}\boldsymbol{u} \geq \boldsymbol{b}_{\text{motor}}, \tag{7.204a}$$

$$\begin{bmatrix}\boldsymbol{J}^i_{\text{lin}} & \boldsymbol{J}^i_{\text{ang}} & \boldsymbol{J}^j_{\text{lin}} & \boldsymbol{J}^j_{\text{ang}}\end{bmatrix}\begin{bmatrix}\boldsymbol{v}_i\\ \boldsymbol{\omega}_i\\ \boldsymbol{v}_j\\ \boldsymbol{\omega}_j\end{bmatrix} \geq \boldsymbol{b}_{\text{motor}}. \tag{7.204b}$$

For a one DOF joint like a slider and a hinge joint, the motor Jacobian will have dimension 1×12, and the right-hand side will be a scalar. In fact,

$$\boldsymbol{b}_{\text{motor}} = v_{\text{desired}}. \tag{7.205}$$

The Jacobian is also easy to derive for these two cases

$$\boldsymbol{J}_{\text{motor}}^{\text{slider}} = \left[\boldsymbol{s}_{\text{axe}}^{\text{wcs}}, \boldsymbol{0}, -\boldsymbol{s}_{\text{axe}}^{\text{wcs}}, \boldsymbol{0}\right], \tag{7.206a}$$

$$\boldsymbol{J}_{\text{motor}}^{\text{hinge}} = \left[\boldsymbol{0}, -\boldsymbol{s}_{\text{axe}}^{\text{wcs}}, \boldsymbol{0}, \boldsymbol{s}_{\text{axe}}^{\text{wcs}}\right]. \tag{7.206b}$$

The motor force is given by the relation

$$\boldsymbol{F}_{\text{motor}} = \boldsymbol{J}_{\text{motor}}^{T} \lambda_{\text{motor}}, \tag{7.207}$$

where λ_{motor} is a Lagrange multiplier, that can be interpreted as a measure of the magnitude of the joint force along the degrees of freedom in the joint. By setting upper and lower limits on λ_{motor}, we can model the aspect of the maximum available force, that is,

$$-\lambda_{\max} \leq \lambda_{\text{motor}} \leq \lambda_{\max}. \tag{7.208}$$

Finally, we require the force and the desired velocity term to be complementary to each other, that is,

$$\boldsymbol{J}_{\text{motor}} \boldsymbol{u} \geq \boldsymbol{b}_{\text{motor}}, \quad \text{compl. to} \quad |\lambda_{\text{motor}}| \leq \lambda_{\max}. \tag{7.209}$$

The basic idea behind this is that if the velocity exceeds the desired velocity, then the motor force should work at its maximum to bring the velocity back to the desired speed.

On the other hand, if the desired speed has been reached, then the motor force can assume any value between 0 and $|\lambda_{\max}|$ to keep the desired speed.

In conclusion, we have developed linear complementarity constraints with both upper and lower limits for joint motors. The theory we have outlined can be extended to more complex joint types in a straightforward manner, simply by formulating Jacobians for their degree of freedom movement.

Another aspect of joint motors, which comes in handy, is that they can be used to model friction in joints. This is done by setting the desired velocity to zero and the maximum force to some constant value; then all joint motion will be slowed down by the *frictional motor force*.

To drive the joints to a specified position, a positional joint motor would simply be a hybrid of the joint limit model and the joint motor models we have outlined. The trick lies in setting the lower- and upper-joint limits equal to the wanted position, and then limiting the motor force as we did in this section.

In contrast to real-life motors and engines, the presented motor controls capture the essential idea of limited power and the need for controlling the speed. Higher-level controllers could be added to a simulator (motor programs) for manipulating the joint motors, but this is out of the scope of this book.

```
Algorithm fixed-time-step(s^t, u^t, Δt)
  s' = s^t + ΔtSu^t
  λ = LCP(s', u^t)
  u^{t+Δt} = u^t + M^{-1} (J^T λ + Δt f_ext)
  s^{t+Δt} = s^t + ΔtSu^{t+Δt}
  return s^{t+Δt}
End algorithm
```

Figure 7.15: Fixed Time-Stepping.

7.10 Time-Stepping Methods

In order to calculate the movement of rigid bodies, the simulation loop needs to advance the simulation time. This process is called a *time-stepping method* or *time control*. Knowing how to compute contact and constraint forces or impulses at collisions, the time-stepping method sets up a scheme that integrates the forces in order to obtain the motion of the rigid bodies. In the following, we will discuss mainly fixed time-stepping methods.

The matrices $\boldsymbol{M}$, $\boldsymbol{C}$, $\boldsymbol{N}$, and $\boldsymbol{D}$ depend on the generalized position vector $\boldsymbol{s}$, which itself is dependent on time.

In some simulators the time dependency is ignored and the simulator uses a fixed time-stepping routine, such as is the case of the Open Dynamics Engine [ODE, 2005]. The general idea is illustrated in Figure 7.15, and the main advantage is that only a single LCP problem is solved per time-step. Unfortunately, it also leads to penetrations and drifting problems. In the Open Dynamics Engine several heuristics are used to overcome these problems: constraint Force Mixing, Error Reduction Parameter, and a specialized position update. These heuristics will be discussed in this section.

Now we will discuss the detection of contacts. There are several ways to approach this for the pseudocode in Figure 7.15. One way is to invoke the collision detection at time t and hope for the best, but new contacts might develop during the time from t to $t + \Delta t$. The future contacts that are overlooked at time t could potentially end up as violated contacts at time $t + \Delta t$. That is, deeply penetrating contacts. This is illustrated in Figure 7.16.

Stewart and Trinkle [Stewart et al., 1996] propose a *retroactive detection approach* to detecting overlooked future contacts. First, all contacts are detected at time t, then a fixed time-step is taken, and finally all contacts at time $t + \Delta t$ are detected. If any new and violated contacts are found, then these contacts are added to the set of contacts found at time t, the simulation is then rewound to time t, and a new fixed time-step is taken. These steps are repeated until all the necessary contacts have been found. Pseudocode can be found in Figure 7.17. Although it is obvious that only a finite number of contacts exist, and that the algorithm sooner or later will have detected all contacts necessary for preventing penetration, it is, however, not obvious how many iterations the algorithm will take, and it is therefore difficult to say anything useful about the time-complexity. The retroactive detection of contacts is similar to the contact tracking algorithm described in Section 14.3.

Detecting a future contact at an early stage can have an undesirable effect, in essence, a contact that appears at time $t + \Delta t$ is resolved at time t. This would make objects appear to have a force field or

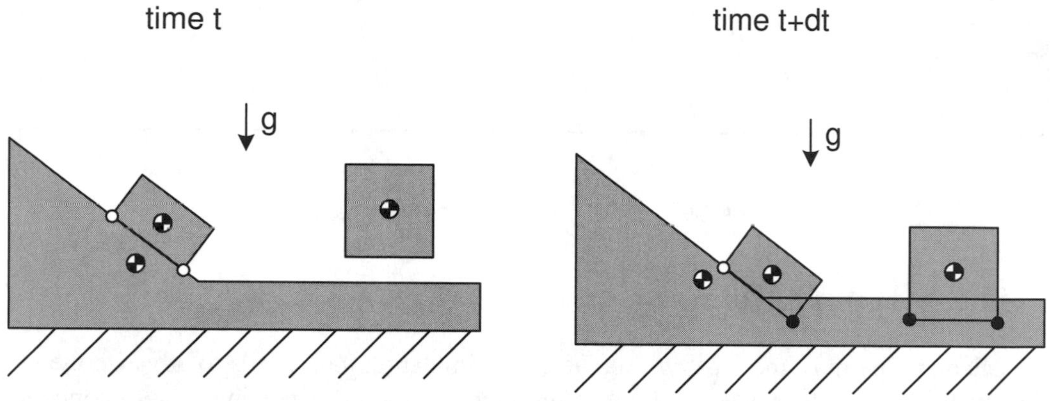

Figure 7.16: 2D illustration of the problem with violated contacts in a fixed time-stepping due to overlooking potential future contact. Small white circles show valid contacts and black small circles show violated contacts. Notice that contacts not detected at time t will be detected as violated contacts at time $t + dt$.

```
Algorithm retroactive-1(s^t, u^t, Δt)
  repeat
    S_contacts = collision detection(s^t)
    s^{t+Δt} = fixed-time-step(s^t, u^t, Δt)
    S'_contacts = collision detection(s^{t+Δt})
    if violated contacts in S'_contacts then
      for all contacts c ∈ S'_contacts do
        if c violated and c ∉ S_contacts then
          add c to S_contacts
      next c
    else
      return s^{t+Δt}
    end if
  until forever
End algorithm
```

Figure 7.17: Retroactive Detection of Contacts in a Fixed Time-Stepping Method.

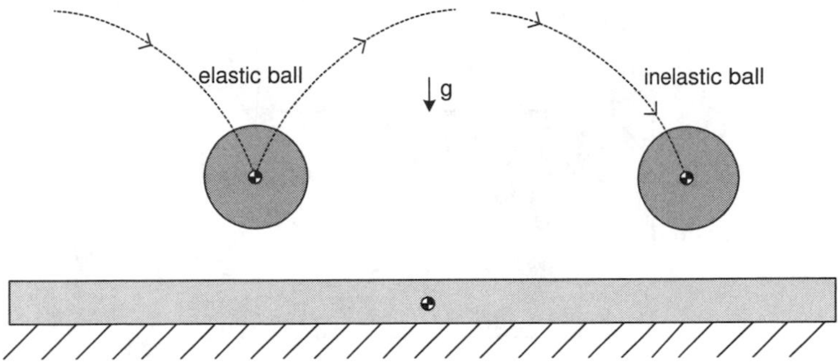

Figure 7.18: 2D example showing visual artifacts of resolving future contacts at time t. The elastic ball never touches the fixed box before it bounces; the inelastic ball is hanging in the air after its impact.

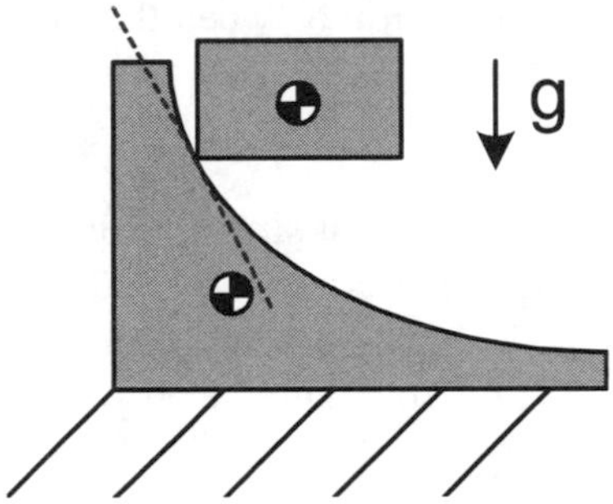

Figure 7.19: System moving along a concave boundary of the admissible region in configuration space.

envelope surrounding them, preventing other objects from actually touching them. Most noticeable, this could cause an object hanging in the air, as shown in Figure 7.18. If we are simulating fast moving and bouncing objects, it is unlikely that an observer would notice the visual artifacts, but if the time-step is big enough, the artifacts illustrated in Figure 7.18 may annoy an observer. To remedy this effect, one could either lower the time-step size, which causes a performance degradation, or one could remodel the error terms to take into account that a contact does not exist at time t. This approach was elaborated on in Section 7.3.

Time-stepping methods may result in penetrations when the system moves along concave boundaries of the admissible region in configuration space [Anitescu et al., 1997, Stewart, 2000]. Configuration space is the vector space consisting of the concatenation of the generalized position and velocity vectors. The admissible region is the subspace of states that make physical sense, like states that do not cause a penetration. A simple example is illustrated in Figure 7.19. As can be seen in the figure, the dotted line indicates the normal constraint; therefore the box is allowed to move along this line. Furthermore, since the lower fixed object is concave at the touching contact point, a penetration will always occur no matter how small a step the box moves along the dotted line. This indicates that situations will arise where all necessary contacts have been detected, but still the algorithm will find violated contacts causing an infinite loop since the *if*-statement in the pseudocode of Figure 7.17 always will be true. This seems to be an unsolved

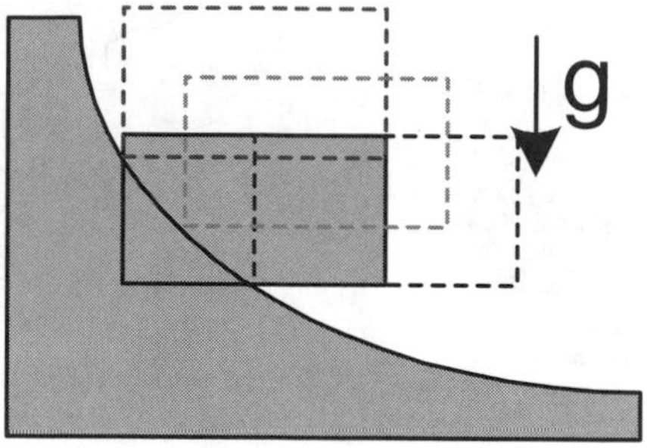

Figure 7.20: Different ways to project a violated contact back into a valid contact. The horizontal projection does not change the potential energy of the box; both the vertical and the inclined projections increase the potential energy. In the following time-step, the added potential energy is transformed into kinetic energy, resulting in a more violent collision between the two objects.

problem in the literature.

Stewart and Trinkle [Stewart, 2000] suggest that simple projection can be used to eliminate the problem of penetrations as a result of moving along concave boundaries in configuration space. They state, however, that care must be taken to avoid losing energy in the process. In [Baraff, 1995] a displacement is computed by using a first-order system $\boldsymbol{A}\boldsymbol{f} = \boldsymbol{b}$, where $\boldsymbol{A}$ only contains normal and bilateral constraints. In our notation, this corresponds to

$$\boldsymbol{A} = \begin{bmatrix} \boldsymbol{N}^T\boldsymbol{C}^T\boldsymbol{M}^{-1}\boldsymbol{C}\boldsymbol{N} & \boldsymbol{N}^T\boldsymbol{C}^T\boldsymbol{M}^{-1}\boldsymbol{J}_\Phi \\ \boldsymbol{J}_\Phi^T\boldsymbol{M}^{-1}\boldsymbol{C}\boldsymbol{N} & \boldsymbol{J}_\Phi^T\boldsymbol{M}^{-1}\boldsymbol{J}_\Phi \end{bmatrix}. \tag{7.210}$$

The $\boldsymbol{b}$-vector contains the signed constraint errors. From the solution, $\boldsymbol{f}$, the derivative, $\dot{\boldsymbol{s}}$, can be computed as described in Section 7.14. Now using $\Delta s = \dot{\boldsymbol{s}}$, a displacement can be obtained as $\boldsymbol{s}^{t+\Delta t} = \boldsymbol{s}^{t+\Delta t} + \Delta s$ (see [Baraff, 1995] for more details).

Solving penetration errors by projection can change the potential energy of the system, thus changing the total energy in the system. Figure 7.20 illustrates the energy problem with the projection method. In the figure, three possible projections of the box are shown as dashed boxes. Due to the gravitational field $\boldsymbol{g}$, both the vertical and the inclined projections will increase the energy of the system, while only the horizontal projection will maintain the same energy level. If the geometries are mirrored in the vertical direction, then the vertical and inclined projections will result in a loss of energy. In other words, projection must be done in such a way that the potential energy remains unchanged. It is not obvious to us how a general method of projection can be designed to fulfill this.

Another approach for handling penetration errors is to use constraint stabilization. This can intuitively be explained as inserting small damped virtual springs between objects at those places where penetration errors are detected. In Section 7.6 and 7.7, the constraint-based method was extended with error correcting terms that stabilized the constraints. An error reduction parameter was used to control the amount of error correction. In case of large errors, or over-eager error reduction, stabilization can cause severe alterations of the simulated motion because the stabilization is accelerating objects apart in order to fix the error.

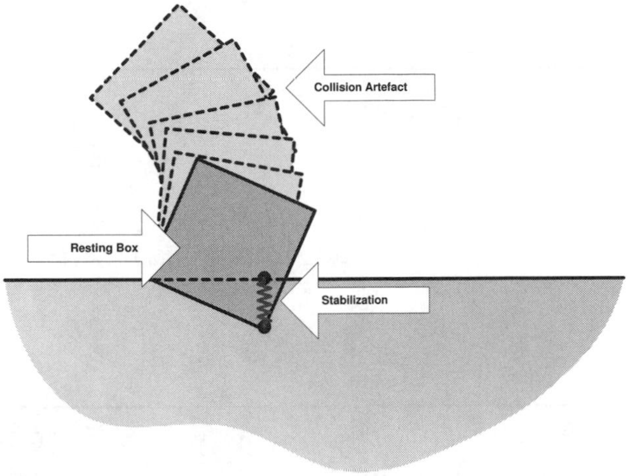

Figure 7.21: Example of constraint stabilization on a violated contact of a resting box causing the box to bounce off the resting surface.

Thus the stabilization adds kinetic energy to the system; in severe cases stabilization can cause a shock-like effect on constraints with large errors. The artifact of stabilization is illustrated in Figure 7.21. Several approaches exist for minimizing the problem, but none of them completely removes it. By lowering the time-step size, the magnitude of constraint errors would also be lowered, thus decreasing the chance of large constraint errors and degrading performance. Lowering the error reduction parameter minimizes the chance of stabilization being too eager; the drawback is that error correction will take longer, thus increasing the chance of an observer noticing deep penetrations of objects. Finally, constraints can be made softer by using Constraint Force Mixing as described in Section 7.13. This has the same drawbacks as lowering the error reduction parameter; furthermore, it removes kinetic energy from the system. Thus if used too aggressively, objects appear lazier than they should.

The matrices $\boldsymbol{M}$, $\boldsymbol{C}$, $\boldsymbol{N}$, and $\boldsymbol{D}$ depend on time; the constraint-based method should rightly be formulated as a nonlinear complementarity problem (NCP). A NCP can be solved iteratively by using a fix-point algorithm as shown in Figure 7.22.

In [Anitescu et al., 1997] an explicit time-stepping method is used together with retroactive detection of collisions. We have outlined the general control flow in Figure 7.23. The main idea is to halt the simulation at the time of an impact and then handle the impact before proceeding with the simulation. In [Anitescu et al., 1997], two LCP problems are set up and used to solve for postvelocities of the impact. This is done using Poisson's hypotheses for handling the compression and decompression phases of an impact. In [Baraff, 1989], a simpler approach is used based on Newton's impact law. This leads to nearly the same kind of LCP problem we have outlined. Later in [Anitescu et al., 2002], an even simpler collision model is used, which only supports completely inelastic collisions. The methods in [Anitescu et al., 1997, Baraff, 1989, Anitescu et al., 2002] are termed simultaneous collision methods; we will not treat these further. Another possibility is to use a so-called sequential collision method, which is treated in more detail in Section 6.2.4.

```
Algorithm fixpoint(s^t, u^t, Δt)
  s' = s^t + ΔtSu^t
  repeat
    λ = LCP(s', u^t)
    u' = u^t + M^{-1} (J^T λ + Δt f_ext)
    s'' = s'
    s' = s^t + ΔtSu'
  until |s' − s''| < ε_fix
  s^{t+Δt} = s'
  return s^{t+Δt}
End algorithm
```

Figure 7.22: Fix-point-Iteration algorithm, Typical values according to [Sauer et al., 1998] are $\Delta t \leq 10^{-3}$ and $\epsilon_{fix} \leq 10^{-4}$.

```
Algorithm retroactive-2(s^t, u^t, Δt)
  s' = s^t
  u' = u^t
  h = Δt/n_steps
  t = 0
  while t < Δt do
    s'' = s' + hSu'
    λ = LCP(s'', u')
    if no collision then
      t = t + h
      s' = s''
      u' = u^t + M^{-1} ((J^T λ + Δt f_ext)
    else
      let t_toi be time of impact
      apply collision model
      ...
      t = t_toi
    end if
  end while
  s^{t+Δt} = s'
  return s^{t+Δt}
End algorithm
```

Figure 7.23: Explicit time-stepping with Retroactive Detection of Colliding Contacts.

```
dt = T_target - T
do
  simulate-forward(dt)
  if intersection
    rewind-simulation()
    dt = dt/2
  else if contact
    collision-resolving()
    T = T + dt
    dt = T_target - T
  end if
while T<T_target
```

Figure 7.24: Example of retroactive advancement based on a bisection root search algorithm.

In [Anitescu et al., 2002] the same control flow is used in an implicit-time-stepping method, the major difference being the way the LCP is formed. We have chosen to omit the implicit version, since it is out of scope for the kind of applications we have in mind.

7.10.1 Numerical Issues with Retroactive Time Control

Due to numerical truncation and roundoff errors, thresholding is a necessary evil in order to determine the type of contact between two objects, A and B. Using a threshold value ε, an often-used rule of thumb for determining the contact state is as follows:

- if A and B are separated by ε, then there is no contact
- if distance between A and B is less than ε, then there is contact
- if penetration between A and B is no more than ε, then there is contact
- if penetration between A and B is more than ε, then A and B are intersecting

Now we'll review a typical retroactive advancement of the simulation. That is, if time control is handled in a root searching manner, the general idea is to watch out for penetrations and then backtrack the simulation to the time of impact when they occur. This is illustrated in Figure 7.24. Of course, more elaborate and intelligent root search schemes can be used, but the bisection scheme in Figure 7.24 suffices for our discussion in this section.

Suppose A and B are in resting contact and penetrate each other with a penetration of ε, and imagine that during the forward simulation a small numerical drift causes A and B to interpenetrate with a depth greater than ε. As can be seen from the pseudocode, the root searching algorithm will be fooled into thinking that a collision has occurred, even though no collision has occurred. Consequently, the root searching algorithm will begin to backtrack in order to search for the time of impact. The result will be a never-ending search for a nonexistent root. Even if a root is determined within a threshold value, the subsequent attempt to advance the simulation is doomed to repeat a new root search for the same nonexistent root. In other words, the simulation will either go into an infinite loop never advancing the simulation, or alternatively, the system will end up in a faulty state with penetrations greater than ε.

One possible strategy to avoid the above-mentioned problems would be to adapt a more advanced thresholding method, using one threshold for the root searching algorithm and another threshold value for determining the type of contact [Baraff, 1995]. However, it is extremely difficult to get such an approach to work efficiently and robustly in practice. Another way out would be to penalize penetrations by a force-feedback term. However, what you get is all the troubles of penalty methods, and there is no guarantee that the error will be within a certain limit, since a penalty force like a spring does not impose a hard constraint.

If your simulator is already based on a penalty method, you have nothing to worry about; however, retroactive advancement is a very bad choice for a penalty-based simulator; instead, fixed time-stepping is often the preferred choice. On the other hand, if your simulator is a constraint-based simulator, it seems daunting to add penalty forces to it, since it essentially will turn your simulator into a hybrid simulator. Not only can you get the advantages from both types of simulator, but also you can inherit all the sicknesses.

In our opinion, a far better approach for resolving the problem is to displace objects when their penetration depth is greater than a certain tolerance correction value. For example, set the tolerance correction to

$$\delta = \frac{3}{4}\varepsilon, \tag{7.211}$$

whenever the penetration depth increases beyond δ, objects are displaced to reduce or remove penetrations. This resolution technique will guarantee that you never will get into problems with your main simulation loop. However, there are some drawbacks; a displacement could change the potential energy of an object. If the energy is increased, the subsequent simulation might transform the potential energy into kinetic energy, causing objects to begin jittering and jumping around. In our opinion, it is more pleasing to look at a simulation where potential energy vanishes. Our main point is that displacements should occur such that the potential energy is nonincreasing.

7.10.2 Unavoidable Penetrations

In some cases, penetrations are simply unavoidable due to the discrete time-stepping. This can be hard to grasp, so we will present a small example, originally presented in [Ilerhøj, 2004], illustrating how penetrations can occur. The example uses the fixed semi-implicit time-stepping method given in Figure 7.15. In the initial state the rod is moving to the right and the box is fixed as seen in Figure 7.25. The time-stepping method first tries to guess the next position by doing a fake position update, $t' = t + \Delta t$. This fake position is first used to determine contact points shown as small solid circles, and then the velocities are updated at the fake position. As shown in the figure, the velocity update predicts a tipping movement of the rod at the fake position. Now the time-stepping method will use the velocities computed at the fake position to update the real position. However, the tipping movement will cause an unwanted penetration of the rod and the box. A rule of thumb is that penetrations can occur in the same order as the order of the time-stepping method used. To be specific, the fixed semi-implicit time-stepping method introduced in Section 7.10 is of first order, i.e., $O(h)$, where h denotes the step-size. The errors accumulate linearly with the number of steps n, such that the error after n steps is proportional to nh. This might appear to be bad, however from a convergence theory point of view, lowering h will guarantee better accuracy, and

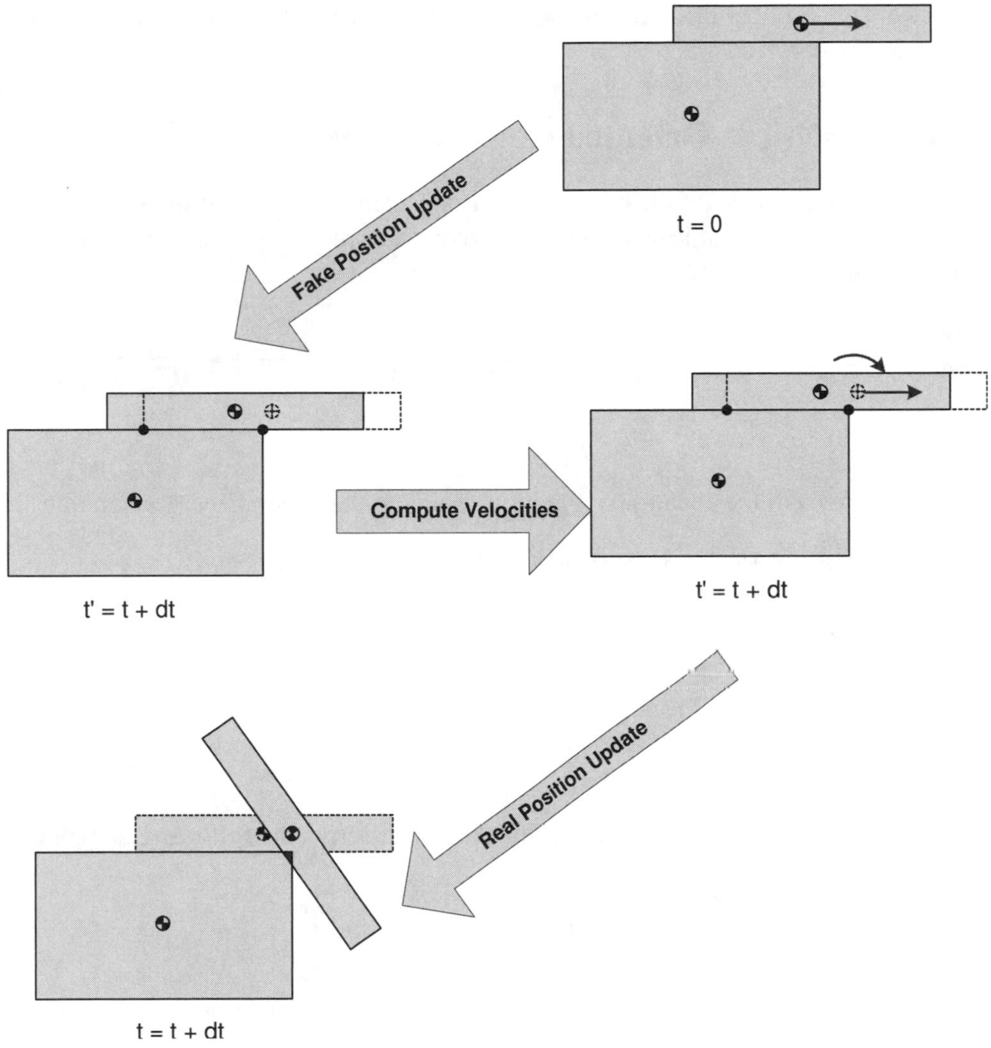

Figure 7.25: Penetrations can occur with fixed semi-implicit time-stepping.

in the limit $h \mapsto 0$ a perfect solution will be found. In practice this is not feasible, since all limiting cases cannot be reached on a computer with finite precision arithmetic; even if the limiting cases were possible it would take far too long to compute. Therefore, a better and practical approach is to pick a step size, such that the errors never grow large enough for an end-user to notice them.

Another example of unavoidable penetrations is the configuration shown in Figure 7.19. Here the problem is that we have a linear discretization, but a higher order surface. The numerics cannot see the higher order and do not care about it.

7.11 A Unified Object-Oriented Constraint Design

From past chapters we learned that four types of constraints can be expressed by using Jacobians. These are joint constraints, contacts, joint limits, and joint motors. For these types of constraints we derived the following kinematic constraints

$$\boldsymbol{J}_{\text{joint}}\boldsymbol{u} = \boldsymbol{b}_{\text{joint}}, \tag{7.212a}$$

$$\boldsymbol{J}_{\text{contact}}\boldsymbol{u} \geq \boldsymbol{b}_{\text{contact}}, \tag{7.212b}$$

$$\boldsymbol{J}_{\text{limit}}\boldsymbol{u} \geq \boldsymbol{b}_{\text{limit}}, \tag{7.212c}$$

$$\boldsymbol{J}_{\text{motor}}\boldsymbol{u} \geq \boldsymbol{b}_{\text{motor}}. \tag{7.212d}$$

Adding the reaction forces to the equations of motion results in the generalized acceleration vector

$$\dot{\boldsymbol{u}} = \boldsymbol{M}^{-1}\left(\boldsymbol{J}_{\text{joint}}^T\boldsymbol{\lambda}_{\text{joint}} + \boldsymbol{J}_{\text{contact}}^T\boldsymbol{\lambda}_{\text{contact}} + \boldsymbol{J}_{\text{limit}}^T\boldsymbol{\lambda}_{\text{limit}} + \boldsymbol{J}_{\text{motor}}^T\boldsymbol{\lambda}_{\text{motor}} + \boldsymbol{f}_{\text{ext}}\right), \tag{7.213}$$

with the following limits on the Lagrange multipliers

$$-\infty \leq \boldsymbol{\lambda}_{\text{joint}} \leq \infty, \tag{7.214a}$$

$$0 \leq \boldsymbol{\lambda}_{\text{contact}} \leq \infty, \tag{7.214b}$$

$$0 \leq \boldsymbol{\lambda}_{\text{limit}} \leq \infty, \tag{7.214c}$$

$$-\boldsymbol{\lambda}_{\text{max}} \leq \boldsymbol{\lambda}_{\text{motor}} \leq \boldsymbol{\lambda}_{\text{max}}. \tag{7.214d}$$

Performing the usual discretization steps and substitutions, we derive the following complementarity formulation

$$\underbrace{\begin{bmatrix} \boldsymbol{A}_{11} & \boldsymbol{A}_{12} \\ \boldsymbol{A}_{21} & \boldsymbol{A}_{22} \end{bmatrix}}_{\boldsymbol{A}} \underbrace{\begin{bmatrix} \boldsymbol{\lambda}_{\text{joint}} \\ \boldsymbol{\lambda}_{\text{contact}} \\ \boldsymbol{\lambda}_{\text{limit}} \\ \boldsymbol{\lambda}_{\text{motor}} \\ \boldsymbol{\lambda}_{\text{aux}} \end{bmatrix}}_{\boldsymbol{\lambda}} + \underbrace{\begin{bmatrix} \boldsymbol{J}_{\text{joint}}\left(\boldsymbol{u} + \Delta t \boldsymbol{M}^{-1}\boldsymbol{f}_{\text{ext}}\right) - \boldsymbol{b}_{\text{joint}} \\ \boldsymbol{J}_{\text{contact}}\left(\boldsymbol{u} + \Delta t \boldsymbol{M}^{-1}\boldsymbol{f}_{\text{ext}}\right) - \boldsymbol{b}_{\text{contact}} \\ \boldsymbol{J}_{\text{limit}}\left(\boldsymbol{u} + \Delta t \boldsymbol{M}^{-1}\boldsymbol{f}_{\text{ext}}\right) - \boldsymbol{b}_{\text{limit}} \\ \boldsymbol{J}_{\text{motor}}\left(\boldsymbol{u} + \Delta t \boldsymbol{M}^{-1}\boldsymbol{f}_{\text{ext}}\right) - \boldsymbol{b}_{\text{motor}} \\ \boldsymbol{b}_{\text{aux}} \end{bmatrix}}_{\boldsymbol{b}} \geq \boldsymbol{0}, \tag{7.215}$$

where

$$\boldsymbol{A}_{11} = \begin{bmatrix} \boldsymbol{J}_{\text{joint}}\boldsymbol{M}^{-1}\boldsymbol{J}_{\text{joint}}^T & \boldsymbol{J}_{\text{joint}}\boldsymbol{M}^{-1}\boldsymbol{J}_{\text{contact}}^T & \boldsymbol{J}_{\text{joint}}\boldsymbol{M}^{-1}\boldsymbol{J}_{\text{limit}}^T & \boldsymbol{J}_{\text{joint}}\boldsymbol{M}^{-1}\boldsymbol{J}_{\text{motor}}^T \\ \boldsymbol{J}_{\text{contact}}\boldsymbol{M}^{-1}\boldsymbol{J}_{\text{joint}}^T & \boldsymbol{J}_{\text{contact}}\boldsymbol{M}^{-1}\boldsymbol{J}_{\text{contact}}^T & \boldsymbol{J}_{\text{contact}}\boldsymbol{M}^{-1}\boldsymbol{J}_{\text{limit}}^T & \boldsymbol{J}_{\text{contact}}\boldsymbol{M}^{-1}\boldsymbol{J}_{\text{motor}}^T \\ \boldsymbol{J}_{\text{limit}}\boldsymbol{M}^{-1}\boldsymbol{J}_{\text{joint}}^T & \boldsymbol{J}_{\text{limit}}\boldsymbol{M}^{-1}\boldsymbol{J}_{\text{contact}}^T & \boldsymbol{J}_{\text{limit}}\boldsymbol{M}^{-1}\boldsymbol{J}_{\text{limit}}^T & \boldsymbol{J}_{\text{limit}}\boldsymbol{M}^{-1}\boldsymbol{J}_{\text{motor}}^T \\ \boldsymbol{J}_{\text{motor}}\boldsymbol{M}^{-1}\boldsymbol{J}_{\text{joint}}^T & \boldsymbol{J}_{\text{motor}}\boldsymbol{M}^{-1}\boldsymbol{J}_{\text{contact}}^T & \boldsymbol{J}_{\text{motor}}\boldsymbol{M}^{-1}\boldsymbol{J}_{\text{limit}}^T & \boldsymbol{J}_{\text{motor}}\boldsymbol{M}^{-1}\boldsymbol{J}_{\text{motor}}^T \end{bmatrix}, \tag{7.216}$$

and $\boldsymbol{A}_{12}, \boldsymbol{A}_{22}, \boldsymbol{A}_{21}$, and $\boldsymbol{b}_{\text{aux}}$ corresponds to a permutation of the third row and column in (7.60), that is the auxiliary constraints needed to model the frictional force. This is complementary to

$$\underbrace{\begin{bmatrix} -\infty \\ 0 \\ 0 \\ -\boldsymbol{\lambda}_{\text{max}} \\ 0 \end{bmatrix}}_{\boldsymbol{\lambda}_{\text{low}}} \leq \boldsymbol{\lambda} \leq \underbrace{\begin{bmatrix} \infty \\ \infty \\ \infty \\ \boldsymbol{\lambda}_{\text{max}} \\ \infty \end{bmatrix}}_{\boldsymbol{\lambda}_{\text{high}}}. \tag{7.217}$$

where complementarity is understood coordinate-wise and is best explained by introducing the vector $\boldsymbol{w}$

$$\boldsymbol{w} = \boldsymbol{A}\boldsymbol{\lambda} + \boldsymbol{b}. \tag{7.218}$$

The i'th coordinate of $\boldsymbol{w}$ is paired with the i'th coordinate of $\boldsymbol{\lambda}$. Complementarity means that for all i, one of the three conditions below holds

$$\boldsymbol{\lambda}_i = \boldsymbol{\lambda}_{\text{low}_i}, \boldsymbol{w}_i \geq 0, \tag{7.219a}$$

$$\boldsymbol{\lambda}_i = \boldsymbol{\lambda}_{\text{high}_i}, \boldsymbol{w}_i \leq 0, \tag{7.219b}$$

$$\boldsymbol{\lambda}_{\text{low}_i} < \boldsymbol{\lambda}_i < \boldsymbol{\lambda}_{\text{high}_i}, \boldsymbol{w}_i = 0. \tag{7.219c}$$

Figure 7.26 helps illustrate the complementarity conditions in equation (7.219). Notice that as long as $\boldsymbol{\lambda}_i$ is within its lower and upper bounds, $\boldsymbol{w}_i$ is forced to zero. The vector $\boldsymbol{w}_i$ is only nonzero at the lower and upper bounds. Usually, the LCP is formulated with $\boldsymbol{\lambda}_{\text{low}} = 0$ and $\boldsymbol{\lambda}_{\text{high}} = \infty$, in which case the above definition reduces to the familiar notation

$$\boldsymbol{\lambda} \geq \boldsymbol{0} \quad \text{compl. to} \quad \boldsymbol{w} \geq \boldsymbol{0}. \tag{7.220}$$

We refer the reader to [Cottle et al., 1992, Murty, 1988] for more details on LCP or Section 19.10.

To ease notation further, we may concatenate all the Jacobians into a single matrix,

$$\boldsymbol{J} = \begin{bmatrix} \boldsymbol{J}_{\text{joint}} \\ \boldsymbol{J}_{\text{contact}} \\ \boldsymbol{J}_{\text{limit}} \\ \boldsymbol{J}_{\text{motor}} \end{bmatrix}. \tag{7.221}$$

Similarly we may concatenate all the error correcting terms,

$$\boldsymbol{b}_{\text{error}} = \begin{bmatrix} \boldsymbol{b}_{\text{joint}} \\ \boldsymbol{b}_{\text{contact}} \\ \boldsymbol{b}_{\text{limit}} \\ \boldsymbol{b}_{\text{motor}} \end{bmatrix}, \tag{7.222}$$

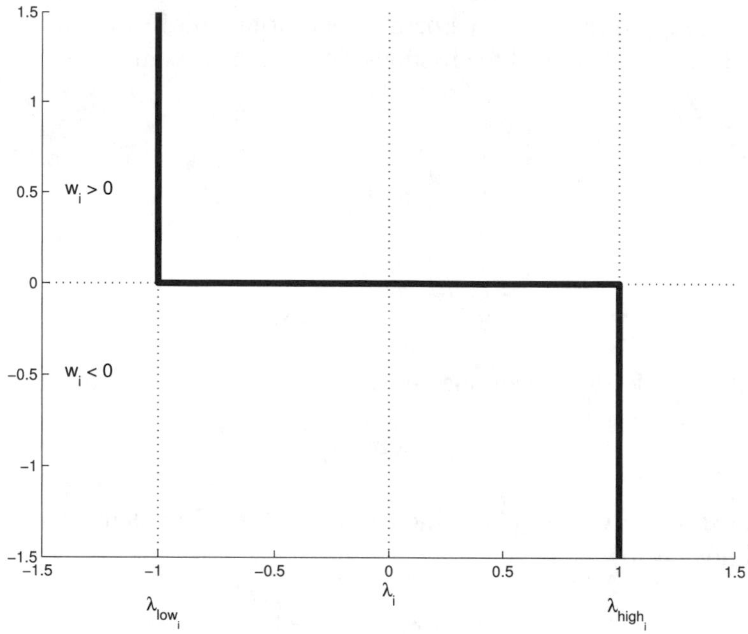

Figure 7.26: The complementarity condition on the i'th variable.

and we may thus write

$$\underbrace{\begin{bmatrix} \boldsymbol{J}\boldsymbol{M}^{-1}\boldsymbol{J}^T & \boldsymbol{A}_{12} \\ \boldsymbol{A}_{21} & \boldsymbol{A}_{22} \end{bmatrix}}_{\boldsymbol{A}} \boldsymbol{\lambda} + \underbrace{\begin{bmatrix} \boldsymbol{J}\left(\boldsymbol{u} + \Delta t \boldsymbol{M}^{-1}\boldsymbol{f}_{\text{ext}}\right) - \boldsymbol{b}_{\text{error}} \\ \boldsymbol{b}_{\text{aux}} \end{bmatrix}}_{\boldsymbol{b}} \geq \boldsymbol{0} \tag{7.223}$$

complementary to

$$\boldsymbol{\lambda}_{\text{low}} \leq \boldsymbol{\lambda} \leq \boldsymbol{\lambda}_{\text{high}}. \tag{7.224}$$

Having rewritten the complementarity formulation into this form allows us to compute the system matrix very efficiently. Notice also how easy we can write the generalized acceleration vector with the new notation,

$$\dot{\boldsymbol{u}} = \boldsymbol{M}^{-1}\left(\boldsymbol{J}^T\boldsymbol{\lambda} + \boldsymbol{f}_{\text{ext}}\right). \tag{7.225}$$

When assembling the system matrix, we must first allocate space for all matrices involved, and then set up the subblock structure for each individual constraint. We evaluate each constraint, i.e., compute joint axes, joint positions, joint errors, and so on. That is, all information needed in the Jacobian matrix and the corresponding error term for each constraint, including any auxiliary constraints are evaluated.

Care must be taken in the evaluation since joint limits and motors depend on the joints they are attached to, and joint motors and limits must therefore not be evaluated before the joints they are attached to.

After having performed the evaluation, we can determine which constraints are currently active and which are nonactive. The nonactive constraints can simply be dropped from further consideration in the current assembly. As an example, the joint limit is nonactive whenever the joint has not reached its outer limit.

Knowing how many active constraints there are, we can compute the dimensions of the matrices involved. For each constraint we will query how many rows its Jacobian matrix contains and we will query how many auxiliary variables there are. Summing these up we are able to determine the total dimensions of the matrices and vectors needed in the assembly.

During these summations it is also possible to assign indices for the subblocks for each and every constraint, where its Jacobian matrix, error term, and the auxiliary variable data should be mapped to. Figure 7.27 shows the pseudocode. Observe that substantial memory savings can be achieved by using a simple sparse matrix representation of the matrices $\boldsymbol{M}^{-1}$ and $\boldsymbol{J}$, as shown in the pseudocode as well. We can now start filling in data in the matrices $\boldsymbol{M}^{-1}$ and $\boldsymbol{J}$, and the vector $\boldsymbol{b}_{\text{error}}$, together with the parts of the system matrix $\boldsymbol{A}$ and the right-hand side $\boldsymbol{b}$ containing the auxiliary data. Also, external forces, limits, and the generalized velocity vector are easily dealt with as shown in Figure 7.28. Using these matrices it is quite easy to compute (7.223) in a straightforward manner. The only real difficulty is that one must be careful about the sparse representation of the matrices $\boldsymbol{M}^{-1}$ and $\boldsymbol{J}^{-1}$.

We have completed what we set out to do in this section. A unified framework for handling both contact point constraints with friction and joint constraints with both motors and limits have been derived.

The framework allows a modularized and object-oriented design of all the constraints in a simulator. This object oriented design is outlined in Figure 7.29. In the figure we have omitted details regarding assembly of the jointed mechanism (linking bodies together with joints, and adding limits and motors).

7.12 Modified Position Update

When the new generalized position vector is computed as

$$\boldsymbol{s}^{t+\Delta t} = \boldsymbol{s}^{t} + \Delta t \boldsymbol{S} \boldsymbol{u}^{t+\Delta t}, \tag{7.226}$$

then we call it a position update. In the position update written above, an infinitesimal orientation update is used. This is fast to compute, but can occasionally cause inaccuracies for bodies that are rotating at high speed; especially when joined to other bodies.

For instance, in a car simulation, four wheels might be attached to a chassis with a wheel joint. When driving the car the wheels may rotate in incorrect directions, as though the joints were somehow becoming ineffective. The problem is observed when the car is moving fast and turning. The wheels appear to rotate out of their proper constraints as though the wheel axes have been bent. If the wheels are rotating slowly, or the turn is made slowly, the problem is less apparent. The problem is that the high rotation speed of the wheels is causing numerical errors. A finite orientation update can be used to reduce such inaccuracies. This is more costly to compute, but will be more accurate for high-speed rotations. High-speed rotations can result in many types of errors in a simulation, and a finite orientation update will only fix one of those sources of error.

We will now outline a modified position update like the one used in the Open Dynamics Engine [ODE, 2005]. For each body B_i we want to be able at configuration design time to set a kind of bit flag indicating if the body should be updated using the infinite or finite update method. In case of the finite

```
Algorithm allocate(...)
  C = set of all constraints
  $n_{\text{jacobian}} = 0$
  for each constraint c ∈ C do
    c.evaluate()
    if not c.active() then
      remove c from C
    end if
    c.setJacobianIndex($n_{\text{jacobian}}$)
    $n_{\text{jacobian}} += $ c.getNumberOfJacobianRows()
  next c

  $n_{\text{auxiliary}} = 0$
  for each constaint c ∈ C do
    c.setAuxiliaryIndex($n_{\text{jacobian}} + n_{\text{auxiliary}}$)
    $n_{\text{auxiliary}} += $ c.getNumberOfAuxiliaryVars()
  next c

  $\boldsymbol{J} = matrix(n_{\text{jacobian}}, 12)$
  $\boldsymbol{b}_{\text{error}} = vector(n_{\text{jacobian}})$
  $n_{\text{total}} = n_{\text{jacobian}} + n_{\text{auxiliary}}$
  $\boldsymbol{A} = matrix(n_{\text{total}}, n_{\text{total}})$
  $\boldsymbol{b} = vector(n_{\text{total}})$
  $\boldsymbol{\lambda} = vector(n_{\text{total}})$
  $\boldsymbol{\lambda}_{\text{low}} = vector(n_{\text{total}})$
  $\boldsymbol{\lambda}_{\text{high}} = vector(n_{\text{total}})$

  B = set of all bodies
  $n_{\text{body}}$ = B.size()
  $\boldsymbol{M}_{\text{inv}} = matrix(3, 6n_{\text{body}})$
  $\boldsymbol{u} = vector(6n_{\text{body}})$
  $\boldsymbol{f}_{\text{ext}} = vector(6n_{\text{body}})$
End algorithm
```

Figure 7.27: Allocate system matrix and setup subblock structure for constraints.

```
Algorithm fillIn(...)
  C = set of all active constraints
  for each constaint c ∈ C do
    i = c.getJacobianIndex()
    j = i + c.getNumberOfJacobianRows()
    J^i_lin = J_(i..j),(0..2)
    J^j_lin = J_(i..j),(3..5)
    J^i_ang = J_(i..j),(6..8)
    J^j_ang = J_(i..j),(9..11)
    c.getLinearJacobian_i(J^i_lin)
    c.getLinearJacobian_j(J^j_lin)
    c.getAngularJacobian_i(J^i_ang)
    c.getAngularJacobian_j(J^j_ang)
    c.getErrorTerm(b_error,(i..j))
    c.getJacobianLowLimit(λ_low,(i..j))
    c.getJacobianHighLimit(λ_high,(i..j))
  next c
  for each constaint c ∈ C do
    i = c.getAuxiliaryIndex()
    j = i + c.getNumberOfAuxiliaryVars()
    A_rows = A_(i..j),(0..n_total-1)
    A_cols = A_(0..n_total-1),(i..j)
    c.getAuxiliaryRowsAndColumns(A_rows, A_cols)
    c.getAuxiliaryLowLimit(λ_low,(i..j))
    c.getAuxiliaryHighLimit(λ_high,(i..j))
    c.getAuxiliaryRightHandSide(b_(i..j))
  next c
  B = set of all bodies
  for each body b ∈ B do
    i = 6 b.getIndex()
    j = i + 6
    b.getMassInvMatrix(M_inv,(i..i+3,0..2))
    b.getInertiaInvMatrix(M_inv,(i+3..i+5,3..5))
    b.getLinearVelocity(u_i..i+2)
    b.getAngularVelocity(u_i+3..i+5)
    b.getExternalForce(f_ext,(i..i+2))
    b.getExternalTorque(f_ext,(i+3..i+5))
    b.getInertiaMatrix(I)
    b.getAngularVelocity(ω)
    f_ext,(i+3..i+5) -= ω × Iω
  next b
End algorithm
```

Figure 7.28: Fill-in data in subblock structure for constraints and bodies.

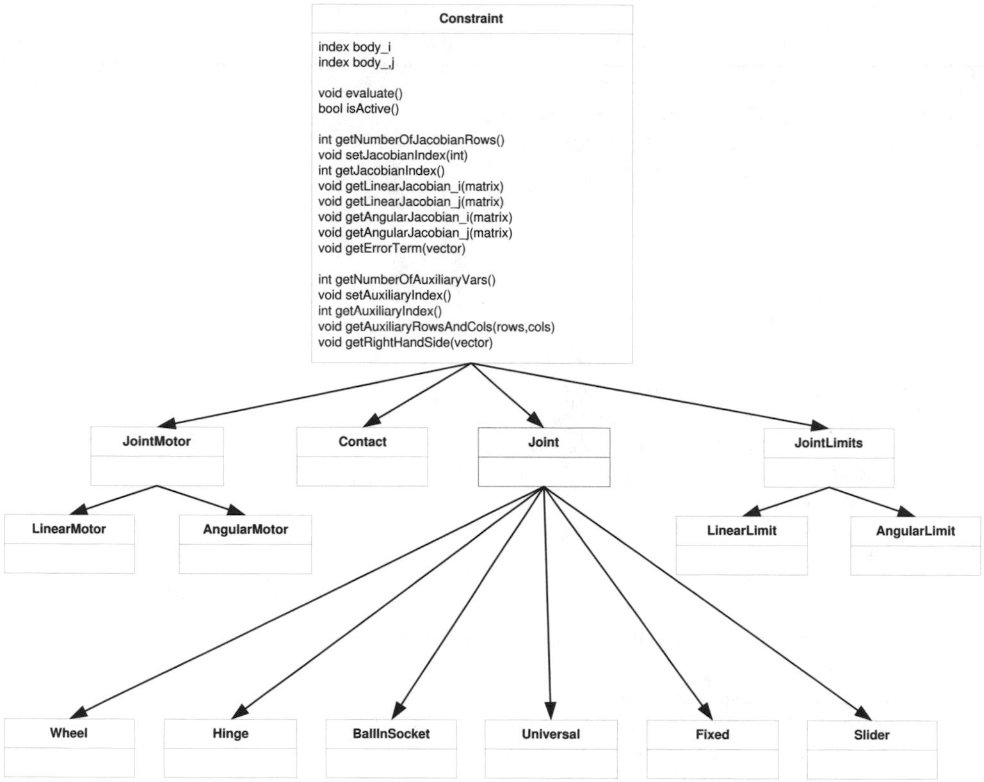

Figure 7.29: The Constraints Design. Observe the unification of contacts and joints.

update we want to compute a rotation, q, corresponding to the radians traveled around the rotation axis in the time interval Δt, that is, the rotation angle θ is given by

$$\theta = \Delta t \left\|\boldsymbol{\omega}_i\right\|_2, \tag{7.227}$$

where the rotation axis is

$$\boldsymbol{u} = \frac{\boldsymbol{\omega}_i}{\left\|\boldsymbol{\omega}_i\right\|_2}. \tag{7.228}$$

The corresponding quaternion q is then given as

$$q = \left[\cos\left(\frac{\theta}{2}\right), \boldsymbol{u}\sin\left(\frac{\theta}{2}\right)\right]. \tag{7.229}$$

This can be rewritten as follows:

$$
\begin{aligned}
q &= \left[\cos\left(\frac{\theta}{2}\right), \boldsymbol{u}\sin\left(\frac{\theta}{2}\right)\right] && (7.230a)\\
&= \left[\cos\left(\frac{\theta}{2}\right), \frac{\boldsymbol{\omega}_i}{\left\|\boldsymbol{\omega}_i\right\|_2}\sin\left(\frac{\Delta t\left\|\boldsymbol{\omega}_i\right\|_2}{2}\right)\right] && (7.230b)\\
&= \left[\cos\left(\frac{\theta}{2}\right), \boldsymbol{\omega}_i\frac{\sin\left(\frac{\Delta t\|\boldsymbol{\omega}_i\|_2}{2}\right)}{\left\|\boldsymbol{\omega}_i\right\|_2}\right] && (7.230c)\\
&= \left[\cos\left(\frac{\theta}{2}\right), \frac{\Delta t}{2}\boldsymbol{\omega}_i\frac{\sin\left(\frac{\Delta t\|\boldsymbol{\omega}_i\|_2}{2}\right)}{\frac{\Delta t\|\boldsymbol{\omega}_i\|_2}{2}}\right] && (7.230d)\\
&= \left[\cos\left(\frac{\Delta t\left\|\boldsymbol{\omega}_i\right\|_2}{2}\right), \frac{\Delta t}{2}\boldsymbol{\omega}_i\mathrm{sinc}\left(\frac{\Delta t\left\|\boldsymbol{\omega}_i\right\|_2}{2}\right)\right]. && (7.230e)
\end{aligned}
$$

Introducing the notation $h = \Delta t/2$, and $\theta = \left\|\boldsymbol{\omega}_i\right\|_2 h$, we end up with

$$q = \left[\cos\left(\theta\right), \boldsymbol{\omega}_i\mathrm{sinc}\left(\theta\right)h\right], \tag{7.231}$$

where

$$\mathrm{sinc}\left(x\right) \sim \begin{cases} 1 - \frac{x^2}{6} & \text{if } |x| < \varepsilon, \\ \frac{\sin(x)}{x} & \text{otherwise.} \end{cases} \tag{7.232}$$

In order to avoid division by zero we have patched the sinc function around zero by using a Taylor expansion for small values $\varepsilon = 10^{-4}$. Furthermore, we want to be able to do both a full finite orientation update and a partial finite orientation update. We have already taken care of the full finite orientation update, and for the partial finite orientation update we split the angular velocity vector into a component $\boldsymbol{\omega}_{\text{finite}}$ along a specified finite rotation axis $\boldsymbol{r}_{\text{axis}}$, and a component $\boldsymbol{\omega}_{\text{infinite}}$ orthogonal to it, that is,

$$
\begin{aligned}
\boldsymbol{\omega}_{\text{finite}} &= \left(\boldsymbol{r}_{\text{axis}}\cdot\boldsymbol{\omega}_i\right)\boldsymbol{r}_{\text{axis}}, && (7.233a)\\
\boldsymbol{\omega}_{\text{infinite}} &= \boldsymbol{\omega}_i - \boldsymbol{\omega}_{\text{finite}}. && (7.233b)
\end{aligned}
$$

First, a finite update is done with $\boldsymbol{\omega}_{\text{finite}}$ followed by an infinite update done with $\boldsymbol{\omega}_{\text{infinite}}$

$$
\begin{aligned}
q_i &= qq_i, && (7.234a)\\
q_i &= q_i + \Delta t Q_i\boldsymbol{\omega}_{\text{infinite}}. && (7.234b)
\end{aligned}
$$

A partial finite orientation update can be useful in a situation like the previously mentioned wheel problem; we simply set the finite rotation axis equal to the hinge axis. Figure 7.30 shows the pseudocode for the position update on body B_i.

```
Algorithm position-update (i, Δt)
  r_i = r_i + Δt v_i
  if finite rotation on i then
    if finite rotation axis on i then
      ω_finite = (r_axis · ω_i) r_axis
      ω_infinite = ω_i − ω_finite
      Δt = Δt/2
      θ = (r_axis · ω_i) Δt
      q_s = cos(θ)
      q_v = (sinc(θ)Δt) ω_finite
    else
      Δt = Δt/2
      θ = ||ω_i||_2 * Δt
      q_s = cos(θ)
      q_v = (sinc(θ)Δt) ω_i
    end if
    q = [q_s, q_v]
    q_i = q q_i
    if finite rotation axis on i then
      q_i = q_i + Δt Q_i ω_infinite
    end if
  else
    q_i = q_i + Δt Q_i ω_i
  end if
  normalize(q_i)
End Algorithm
```

Figure 7.30: Position update on i'th body.

7.13 Constraint Force Mixing

The constraint equation for a joint has the form

$$\boldsymbol{J}\boldsymbol{u} = \boldsymbol{b}, \tag{7.235}$$

where $\boldsymbol{u}$ is a velocity vector for the bodies involved, $\boldsymbol{J}$ is the Jacobian matrix with one row for every degree of freedom the joint removes from the system, and $\boldsymbol{b}$ is the error correcting term.

The constraint forces, that is, the reaction forces from the joint bearings are computed by

$$\boldsymbol{F} = \boldsymbol{J}^T\boldsymbol{\lambda}, \tag{7.236}$$

where $\boldsymbol{\lambda}$ is a vector of Lagrange multipliers and has the same dimension as $\boldsymbol{b}$. The Open Dynamics Engine [ODE, 2005] adds a new twist to these equations by reformulating the constraint equation as

$$\boldsymbol{J}\boldsymbol{u} = \boldsymbol{b} - \boldsymbol{K}_{\text{cmf}}\boldsymbol{\lambda}, \tag{7.237}$$

Where $\boldsymbol{K}_{\text{cmf}}$ is a square diagonal matrix. The matrix $\boldsymbol{K}_{\text{cmf}}$ mixes the resulting constraint force with the constraint. A nonzero (positive) value of a diagonal entry of $\boldsymbol{K}_{\text{cmf}}$ allows the original constraint equation to be violated by an amount proportional to $\boldsymbol{K}_{\text{cmf}}$ times the restoring force $\boldsymbol{\lambda}$. Solving for $\boldsymbol{\lambda}$ gives

$$M\ddot{\boldsymbol{u}} = M\frac{\boldsymbol{u}^{\Delta t+t} - \boldsymbol{u}}{\Delta t} = \boldsymbol{J}^T\boldsymbol{\lambda}, \tag{7.238}$$

from which we isolate $\boldsymbol{u}^{\Delta t+t}$ as

$$\boldsymbol{u}^{\Delta t+t} = \boldsymbol{u} + \Delta t M^{-1}\boldsymbol{J}^T\boldsymbol{\lambda}. \tag{7.239}$$

Assuming that the constraint equation holds at time $t + \Delta t$ and substituting the expression for $\boldsymbol{u}^{\Delta t+t}$ into the constraint equation, we get

$$\boldsymbol{J}\boldsymbol{u}^{\Delta t+t} = \boldsymbol{b} - \boldsymbol{K}_{\text{cmf}}\boldsymbol{\lambda}, \tag{7.240a}$$

$$\boldsymbol{J}\boldsymbol{u} + \Delta t\boldsymbol{J}M^{-1}\boldsymbol{J}^T\boldsymbol{\lambda} = \boldsymbol{b} - \boldsymbol{K}_{\text{cmf}}\boldsymbol{\lambda}. \tag{7.240b}$$

Collecting $\boldsymbol{\lambda}$ terms on the left side we get

$$\left(\boldsymbol{J}\boldsymbol{M}^{-1}\boldsymbol{J}^T + \frac{1}{\Delta t}\boldsymbol{K}_{\text{cmf}}\right)\boldsymbol{\lambda} = \frac{1}{\Delta t}\left(\boldsymbol{b} - \boldsymbol{J}\boldsymbol{u}\right), \tag{7.241}$$

from which it is clear that the $\boldsymbol{K}_{\text{cmf}}$ matrix is added to the diagonal of the original system matrix.

According to [ODE, 2005], using only positive values in the diagonal of $\boldsymbol{K}_{\text{cmf}}$ has the benefit of moving the system away from singularities and improves factorization accuracy.

This twist of the constraint equations is known as constraint force mixing, and the diagonal entries of the matrix $\boldsymbol{K}_{\text{cmf}}$ controls the amount of mixing that is done.

7.14 First-Order World

First-order world simulation is greatly inspired by the way Aristotle saw and described the world at his time. These misconceptions were later rectified by Newton in his three laws of motion. Regardless, a first-order world is useful in animation for error correction and precise positioning of objects. Aristotle's basic views were:

1. Heavier objects fall faster.
2. To keep an object in motion at constant velocity, a constant force is needed.

The problem with the second statement was in not realizing that in addition to the pulling or pushing force, there are other forces involved, typically friction and air or water resistance. Fortunately, these misconceptions are of great practical use in computer animation and also in more serious applications such as virtual prototyping for example, [Redon et al., 2003].

Figure 7.31: A sequence in a first-order world simulation share two identical objects that are aligned. The left box is pulled to the right. Observe that both the left and right boxes are equally affected.

Figure 7.32: A sequence in a first-order world simulation where two objects of different mass are aligned. The left box has less mass than the right box. The left box is pulled to the right. Observe that the heavier box on the right is less affected than light box on the left in comparison with Figure 7.31.

A first-order world is useful due to its controllability. In Newtonian mechanics, objects keep moving or sliding after user interaction, making it hard to accurately position objects interactively in a virtual world. On the other hand, in a first-order world, an object would stop immediately after a user stops pushing it.

Ease of interaction can be obtained by merely translating objects, but such an approach does not take care of the rotational movement induced by collisions, etc. In a first-order world, misalignments between objects are handled through simulation.

For instance, if a light misaligned object is pushed against a heavy perfectly aligned object, then the simulation will automatically align the two objects w.r.t. each other. Furthermore, the light object will be aligned more than the heavier object. Figures 7.31 and 7.32 show a few frames of a first-order world simulation where two objects are automatically aligned. As seen in Figure 7.31 and 7.32 a first-order world simulation is well suited for aligning objects and it respects their mass and inertia. This smooth alignment is very attractive in many virtual environments; this also makes a first-order world simulation an ideal tool for correcting simulation errors [Baraff, 1995]. An example of this is shown in Figure 7.33.

In a second-order system we have a state function, $\boldsymbol{s}(t)$, for a rigid body

$$\boldsymbol{s}(t) = \begin{bmatrix} \boldsymbol{r} \\ q \\ \boldsymbol{P} \\ \boldsymbol{L} \end{bmatrix}, \quad \text{and} \quad \dot{\boldsymbol{s}}(t) = \begin{bmatrix} \boldsymbol{v} \\ \frac{1}{2}\boldsymbol{\omega} q \\ \boldsymbol{F} \\ \boldsymbol{\tau} \end{bmatrix}, \tag{7.242}$$

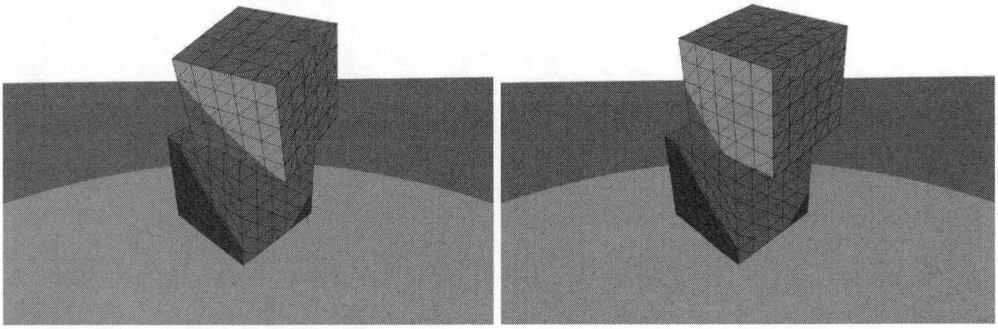

Figure 7.33: First-order world simulation used to correct penetration error. Left shows initial state, right shows the corrected state. Observe that when corrected, the upper box is both translated and rotated.

where

$$\boldsymbol{v} = \frac{\boldsymbol{P}}{m}, \quad \text{and} \quad \boldsymbol{\omega} = \boldsymbol{I}^{-1}\boldsymbol{L}, \tag{7.243}$$

or equivalently, we have

$$\boldsymbol{s}(t) = \begin{bmatrix} \boldsymbol{r} \\ q \\ \boldsymbol{v} \\ \boldsymbol{\omega} \end{bmatrix}, \quad \text{and} \quad \dot{\boldsymbol{s}}(t) = \begin{bmatrix} \boldsymbol{v} \\ \frac{1}{2}\boldsymbol{\omega} q \\ \frac{\boldsymbol{F}}{m} \\ \boldsymbol{I}^{-1}\left(\boldsymbol{\tau} - \boldsymbol{\omega} \times L\right) \end{bmatrix}. \tag{7.244}$$

In a first-order system, the state function for a rigid body simplifies to

$$\boldsymbol{s}(t) = \begin{bmatrix} \boldsymbol{r} \\ q \end{bmatrix}, \quad \text{and} \quad \dot{\boldsymbol{s}}(t) = \begin{bmatrix} \frac{\boldsymbol{F}}{m} \\ \frac{1}{2}\boldsymbol{I}^{-1}\boldsymbol{\tau} q \end{bmatrix}. \tag{7.245}$$

Observe that the difference is that force relates directly to velocity, that is,

$$\boldsymbol{F} = m\boldsymbol{v}, \tag{7.246}$$

$$\boldsymbol{\tau} = \boldsymbol{I}\boldsymbol{\omega}. \tag{7.247}$$

This is the first-order world equivalent to the Newton-Euler equations of motion. Thus, in a first-order world there is velocity but no acceleration, and first-order worlds are therefore very useful for evaluating system kinematics. In a first-order system, the dynamics equation $\boldsymbol{F} = m\boldsymbol{v}$ dictates that objects have no intrinsic velocity of their own; equivalently, the velocity at any given instant depends completely on the forces acting at that instant. This means that velocity-based damping and friction are nonexistent in a first-order world, and that inertial forces due to velocity are absent. As we will see later, these consequences greatly simplify the contact modeling compared to a second-order world obeying the Newton-Euler equations of motion.

7.14.1 Single Point of Contact

Now we'll study a single point of contact, $\boldsymbol{p}_k$, between two bodies i and j. Let $\boldsymbol{r}_i$ and $\boldsymbol{r}_j$ be the center of mass position of the bodies, then the two vectors from the center of mass to the point of contact are found as

$$\boldsymbol{r}_{ki} = \boldsymbol{p}_k - \boldsymbol{r}_i, \tag{7.248}$$

$$\boldsymbol{r}_{kj} = \boldsymbol{p}_k - \boldsymbol{r}_j. \tag{7.249}$$

The change in velocity of the contact point with respect to each body are

$$\Delta \boldsymbol{u}_i = \Delta \boldsymbol{v}_i + \Delta \boldsymbol{\omega}_i \times \boldsymbol{r}_{ki}, \tag{7.250}$$

$$\Delta \boldsymbol{u}_j = \Delta \boldsymbol{v}_j + \Delta \boldsymbol{\omega}_j \times \boldsymbol{r}_{kj}. \tag{7.251}$$

In a first-order world, a change in velocity corresponds to a change in force. For the time being we will ignore all other forces in the system except for the forces acting at the contact point. This means that the change in force is simply the force acting at the contact point, and for body j we have

$$\Delta \boldsymbol{v}_j = \frac{\boldsymbol{F}}{m_j}, \tag{7.252}$$

$$\Delta \boldsymbol{\omega}_j = \boldsymbol{I}_j^{-1} \left(\boldsymbol{r}_{kj} \times \boldsymbol{F} \right), \tag{7.253}$$

where $\boldsymbol{F}$ is the force acting on body j. Assuming the law of reaction equals action, we must have that the force on body i is given by $-\boldsymbol{F}$, yielding the following equations for body i

$$\Delta \boldsymbol{v}_i = -\frac{\boldsymbol{F}}{m_i}, \tag{7.254}$$

$$\Delta \boldsymbol{\omega}_i = -\boldsymbol{I}_i^{-1} \left(\boldsymbol{r}_{ki} \times \boldsymbol{F} \right). \tag{7.255}$$

Now let us compute the relative change in contact velocity as

$$\boldsymbol{u} = \left(\Delta \boldsymbol{u}_j - \Delta \boldsymbol{u}_i \right). \tag{7.256}$$

Substituting previous results yield

$$\boldsymbol{u} = \left(\left(\Delta \boldsymbol{v}_j + \boldsymbol{\Delta} \omega_j \times \boldsymbol{r}_{kj} \right) - \left(\Delta \boldsymbol{v}_i + \boldsymbol{\Delta} \omega_i \times \boldsymbol{r}_{ki} \right) \right), \tag{7.257a}$$

$$\boldsymbol{u} = \left(\left(\frac{\boldsymbol{F}}{m_j} + \left(\boldsymbol{I}_j^{-1} \left(\boldsymbol{r}_{kj} \times \boldsymbol{F} \right) \right) \times \boldsymbol{r}_{kj} \right) - \left(-\frac{\boldsymbol{F}}{m_i} + \left(-\boldsymbol{I}_i^{-1} \left(\boldsymbol{r}_{ki} \times \boldsymbol{F} \right) \right) \times \boldsymbol{r}_{ki} \right) \right) \tag{7.257b}$$

Using the cross matrix notation for the cross products we can isolate $\boldsymbol{F}$ as

$$\boldsymbol{u} = \left(\left(\frac{\boldsymbol{F}}{m_j} + \left(\boldsymbol{I}_j^{-1}\left(\boldsymbol{r_{kj}}^{\times}\boldsymbol{F}\right)\right)\boldsymbol{r_{kj}}^{\times}\right) - \left(-\frac{\boldsymbol{F}}{m_i} + \left(-\boldsymbol{I}_i^{-1}\left(\boldsymbol{r_{ki}}^{\times}\boldsymbol{F}\right)\right)\boldsymbol{r_{ki}}^{\times}\right)\right) \tag{7.258a}$$

$$= \left(\frac{1}{m_j} + \frac{1}{m_i}\right)\boldsymbol{F} - \left(\boldsymbol{r_{kj}}^{\times}\boldsymbol{I}_j^{-1}\boldsymbol{r_{kj}}^{\times}\right)\boldsymbol{F} - \left(\boldsymbol{r_{ki}}^{\times}\boldsymbol{I}_i^{-1}\boldsymbol{r_{ki}}^{\times}\right)\boldsymbol{F} \tag{7.258b}$$

$$= \left(\frac{1}{m_j} + \frac{1}{m_i}\right)\boldsymbol{F} - \left(\boldsymbol{r_{kj}}^{\times}\boldsymbol{I}_j^{-1}\boldsymbol{r_{kj}}^{\times} + \boldsymbol{r_{ki}}^{\times}\boldsymbol{I}_i^{-1}\boldsymbol{r_{ki}}^{\times}\right)\boldsymbol{F} \tag{7.258c}$$

$$= \underbrace{\left(\left(\frac{1}{m_j} + \frac{1}{m_i}\right)\boldsymbol{1} - \left(\boldsymbol{r_{kj}}^{\times}\boldsymbol{I}_j^{-1}\boldsymbol{r_{kj}}^{\times} + \boldsymbol{r_{ki}}^{\times}\boldsymbol{I}_i^{-1}\boldsymbol{r_{ki}}^{\times}\right)\right)\boldsymbol{F}}_{\boldsymbol{K}} \tag{7.258d}$$

$$\boldsymbol{u} = \boldsymbol{K}\boldsymbol{F}. \tag{7.258e}$$

The matrix $\boldsymbol{K}$ is the familiar collision matrix [Mirtich, 1996], and we have derived the same relationship between force and contact point velocity in a first-order world as we have done earlier for collision impulses and contact point velocities in a second-order world. Measuring the relative contact velocity in the normal direction only $\boldsymbol{n}$, yields

$$u_n = \boldsymbol{n}^T\boldsymbol{u} = \boldsymbol{n}^T\left(\boldsymbol{K}\boldsymbol{F}\right), \tag{7.259}$$

and restricting the contact force $\boldsymbol{F}$, to be parallel to the normal direction is simply

$$u_n = \left(\boldsymbol{n}^T\boldsymbol{K}\boldsymbol{n}\right)f, \tag{7.260}$$

where f is a scalar denoting the magnitude of the force $\boldsymbol{F}$, and u_n is likewise a scalar denoting the magnitude of relative contact velocity in the normal direction.

7.14.1.1 Penetration Correction

The previously derived relation (7.260) provides a convenient way for projecting penetrating bodies out of each other. The idea is as follows: set up (7.260), such that you solve for the force $\boldsymbol{F}$, which will yield a change in the relative contact velocity $\boldsymbol{u}$, that will correct the penetration during the next time-step h.

Let the penetration depth be given by the distance d, then the correcting velocity at the contact points must be

$$u_n = \frac{d}{h}, \tag{7.261}$$

and solving for the correcting force yields

$$f = \frac{\frac{\boldsymbol{d}}{h}}{\boldsymbol{n}^T\boldsymbol{K}\boldsymbol{n}}. \tag{7.262}$$

Now use $\boldsymbol{F} = \boldsymbol{n}f$ in the state function (7.245) to perform a single forward Euler step. This yields a position update, which will correct the penetration between the two objects, that is,

$$r_i^{t+1} = r_i^t + h\frac{(-F)}{m_i}, \tag{7.263}$$

$$q_i^{t+1} = q_i^t + h\frac{1}{2}\left(I_i^{-1}\left(r_{ki} \times (-F)\right)\right) q_i^t, \tag{7.264}$$

$$r_j^{t+1} = r_j^t + h\frac{F}{m_j}, \tag{7.265}$$

$$q_j^{t+1} = q_j^t + h\frac{1}{2}\left(I_j^{-1}\left(r_{kj} \times F\right)\right) q_j^t. \tag{7.266}$$

In the above we have applied a forward Euler scheme, meaning that we have linearized the sought displacements. The correction is therefore only correct to within first-order, but in practice this is seldom a problem, since most simulation paradigms try to prevent penetrations, indicating that penetration errors are likely to be small and only require small corrections.

7.14.1.2 Continuous Motion

The constraint forces needed in a first-order world simulation can also be derived from (7.258e). Taking external forces into account, say forces F^i_{ext} and F^j_{ext} and torques τ^i_{ext} and τ^j_{ext} working on bodies i and j respectively, then it is seen by substituting the forces into (7.257a) that (7.258e) changes into the form

$$u = KF + b, \tag{7.267}$$

where b is given by,

$$b = \frac{F^j_{\text{ext}}}{m_j} - \frac{F^i_{\text{ext}}}{m_i} + I_j^{-1}\tau^j_{\text{ext}} \times r_{kj} - I_i^{-1}\tau^i_{\text{ext}} \times r_{ki}. \tag{7.268}$$

Here F denotes the constraint force at the contact point, which must prevent penetration from occurring. This implies that the relative contact velocity in the normal direction must be nonnegative, since a first-order world is frictionless. According to the principle of virtual work it makes sense to require that the constraint force is parallel to the normal direction; also the bodies are allowed to separate, which means that the constraint force can only be repulsive. To summarize we have

$$u_n \geq 0, \quad \text{and} \quad f \geq 0. \tag{7.269}$$

Furthermore, u_n and f must be complementarity, meaning that if u_n initially is greater than zero, then there is no need of a constraint force, that is,

$$u_n > 0 \Rightarrow f = 0. \tag{7.270}$$

On the other hand, if we have constraint force acting at the contact point, then the normal velocity must be zero, that is,

$$f > 0 \Rightarrow u_n = 0. \tag{7.271}$$

In conclusion, we discover a linear complementarity condition similar to (7.21).

7.14.2 Multiple Contact Points

In this section we will extend the machinery for a two body problem to handle an n-body system.

Let $\boldsymbol{u}_k$ denote the change in relative contact velocity and at the k'th contact, then

$$\boldsymbol{u}_k = \Delta \boldsymbol{u}_{j_k} - \Delta \boldsymbol{u}_{i_k}. \tag{7.272}$$

As previously, we also have

$$\Delta \boldsymbol{u}_{i_k} = \Delta \boldsymbol{v}_{i_k} + \Delta \boldsymbol{\omega}_{i_k} \times \boldsymbol{r}_{ki_k}, \tag{7.273}$$

$$\Delta \boldsymbol{u}_{j_k} = \Delta \boldsymbol{v}_{j_k} + \Delta \boldsymbol{\omega}_{j_k} \times \boldsymbol{r}_{kj_k}, \tag{7.274}$$

however this time we do not have a single contact force contributing to the k'th contact. To get the total force and torque contributing to the k'th contact we have to sum over all forces and torques. Using the indexing introduced in Section 7.1 we write

$$\Delta \boldsymbol{v}_{j_k} = \frac{\boldsymbol{F}_{\text{ext}}^{j_k} + \sum_{h, j_h = j_k} \boldsymbol{F}_h - \sum_{h, i_h = i_k} \boldsymbol{F}_h}{m_{j_k}}, \tag{7.275}$$

$$\Delta \boldsymbol{\omega}_{j_k} = \boldsymbol{I}_{j_k}^{-1} \left(\boldsymbol{\tau}_{\text{ext}}^{j_k} + \left(\sum_{h, j_h = j_k} \boldsymbol{r}_{hj_h} \times \boldsymbol{F}_h \right) - \left(\sum_{h, i_h = j_k} \boldsymbol{r}_{hi_h} \times \boldsymbol{F}_h \right) \right), \tag{7.276}$$

where $\boldsymbol{F}_h$ is the contact force at the h'h contact point. If we perform the same substitutions as done in the case of a single point of contact (7.267), then the contributions from the external forces and torques can be collected in a single vector $\boldsymbol{b}_k$. The contribution stemming from the contact forces can then be written as a linear combination,

$$\boldsymbol{u}_k = \left(\sum_h \boldsymbol{K}_{kh} \boldsymbol{F}_h \right) + \boldsymbol{b}_k, \tag{7.277}$$

where

$$\boldsymbol{K}_{kh} = \begin{cases} \left(\frac{1}{m_{j_k}} + \frac{1}{m_{i_k}} \right) \boldsymbol{1} - \left(\boldsymbol{r}_{kj_k}{}^{\times} \boldsymbol{I}_{j_k}^{-1} \boldsymbol{r}_{hj_k}{}^{\times} + \boldsymbol{r}_{ki_k}{}^{\times} \boldsymbol{I}_{i_k}^{-1} \boldsymbol{r}_{hi_k}{}^{\times} \right) & \text{if } i_h = i_k \text{ and } j_h = j_k, \\ \left(\frac{-1}{m_{i_k}} \right) \boldsymbol{1} + \left(\boldsymbol{r}_{ki_k}{}^{\times} \boldsymbol{I}_{i_k}^{-1} \boldsymbol{r}_{hi_h}{}^{\times} \right) & \text{if } i_h = i_k \text{ and } j_h \neq j_k, \\ \left(\frac{-1}{m_{j_k}} \right) \boldsymbol{1} + \left(\boldsymbol{r}_{kj_k}{}^{\times} \boldsymbol{I}_{j_k}^{-1} \boldsymbol{r}_{hi_h}{}^{\times} \right) & \text{if } i_h = j_k \text{ and } j_h \neq i_k, \\ \left(\frac{1}{m_{i_k}} \right) \boldsymbol{1} - \left(\boldsymbol{r}_{ki_k}{}^{\times} \boldsymbol{I}_{i_k}^{-1} \boldsymbol{r}_{hj_h}{}^{\times} \right) & \text{if } j_h = i_k \text{ and } i_h \neq j_k, \\ \left(\frac{1}{m_{j_k}} \right) \boldsymbol{1} - \left(\boldsymbol{r}_{kj_k}{}^{\times} \boldsymbol{I}_{j_k}^{-1} \boldsymbol{r}_{hj_h}{}^{\times} \right) & \text{if } j_h = j_k \text{ and } i_h \neq i_k, \\ \boldsymbol{0} & \text{otherwise.} \end{cases} \tag{7.278}$$

If we only consider relative contact velocity in the normal direction, and only allow contact forces to be parallel with the contact normals, then it is easily seen that the equation transforms into

$$u_{nk} = \boldsymbol{n}_k^T \boldsymbol{u}_k = \left(\sum_h \boldsymbol{n}_k^T \boldsymbol{K}_{kh} \boldsymbol{n}_h f_h \right) + \boldsymbol{b}_k, \tag{7.279}$$

where f_h denotes the magnitude of the h'th contact force. The equations for all the relative normal contact velocities can now be written as in a single matrix equation,

$$\underbrace{\begin{bmatrix} u_{n0} \\ \vdots \\ u_{nK-1} \end{bmatrix}}_{\boldsymbol{a}} = \underbrace{\begin{bmatrix} \boldsymbol{n}_0^T \boldsymbol{K}_{00} \boldsymbol{n}_0 & \dots & \boldsymbol{n}_0^T \boldsymbol{K}_{0K-1} \boldsymbol{n}_{K-1} \\ \vdots & & \vdots \\ \boldsymbol{n}_{K-1}^T \boldsymbol{K}_{K-10} \boldsymbol{n}_0 & \dots & \boldsymbol{n}_{K-1}^T \boldsymbol{K}_{K-1K-1} \boldsymbol{n}_{K-1} \end{bmatrix}}_{\boldsymbol{A}} \underbrace{\begin{bmatrix} f_0 \\ \vdots \\ f_{K-1} \end{bmatrix}}_{\boldsymbol{x}} + \underbrace{\begin{bmatrix} \boldsymbol{n}_0^T \boldsymbol{b}_0 \\ \vdots \\ \boldsymbol{n}_{K-1}^T \boldsymbol{b}_{K-1} \end{bmatrix}}_{\boldsymbol{b}}, \tag{7.280}$$

$$\Rightarrow \boldsymbol{a} = \boldsymbol{A}\boldsymbol{f} + \boldsymbol{b}. \tag{7.281}$$

This equation is a similar equation to (7.25), and recalling the definition of the contact Jacobian in Section 7.7.7 and the assembly process in Section 7.11, we immediately generalize,

$$\boldsymbol{A} = \boldsymbol{J}_{\text{contact}} \boldsymbol{M}^{-1} \boldsymbol{J}_{\text{contact}}^T, \tag{7.282}$$

$$\boldsymbol{b} = \boldsymbol{J}_{\text{contact}} \boldsymbol{M}^{-1} \boldsymbol{f}_{\text{ext}}. \tag{7.283}$$

Note that in a first-order world $\boldsymbol{f}_{\text{ext}}$ does not contain inertial forces. An LCP can now be formulated for the continuous movement of a first-order world as

$$\boldsymbol{a} \geq 0, \boldsymbol{f} \geq 0, \quad \text{and} \quad \boldsymbol{f}^T \boldsymbol{a} = 0. \tag{7.284}$$

A penetration correcting force can be computed by redefining the $\boldsymbol{b}$-vector

$$\boldsymbol{b} = \frac{1}{h} \begin{bmatrix} -d_0 \\ \vdots \\ -d_{K-1} \end{bmatrix}, \tag{7.285}$$

and then solving the same LCP as we formulated above. For the case of a single-point contact, we could solve the linear system. But for multiple contact points, the projection of a penetration of one contact point might fix the penetration of another, and this induces a complementarity condition where there can be no correcting force if there is no penetration. On the other hand, if there is a correcting force, the penetration depth must be zero.

7.15 Previous Work

Impulse-based simulation was introduced by Hahn [Hahn, 1988], where time integrals of contact forces were used to model the interactions. In recent times, Mirtich [Mirtich, 1996] worked with impulse-based simulation using a slightly different approach, where contact forces were modeled as collision impulse trains. Hahn's and Mirtich's work represent two different ways of thinking of impulse-based simulation: as a time integral and as a sum of delta functions approximating the corresponding time integral. Mirtich's work led to a new simulation paradigm as discussed in Chapter 6. Hahn's work could be interpreted as an early predecessor to the velocity-based formulation.

Stewart and Trinkle [Stewart et al., 1996, Stewart et al., 2000, Stewart, 2000] made a new impulse-based method. Their method is now known as Stewart's method. Like Hahn's method, Stewart's method also computes the time integrals of the contact forces, and it has since inspired many: Anitescu and Potra [Anitescu et al., 1997] extended the method to guarantee existence of the solution; Sauer and Schömer [Sauer et al., 1998] extended with a linearized contact condition; Song *et al.* [Song et al., 2003] used a semi-implicit time-stepping model for frictional compliant contact; and most recently, an implicit time-stepping method for stiff multibody dynamics by Anitescu and Potra [Anitescu et al., 2002] and Hart and Anitescu introduced a constraint stabilization [Hart et al., 2003] method.

Even though Stewart's method is an impulse-based method, it looks and feels like a typical constraint-based method, such as the one formulated by Baraff [Baraff, 1994, Baraff, 2001], Trinkle, Pang, Sudarsky, and Lo [Trinkle et al., 1995], Trinkle, Tzitzoutis, and Pang [Trinkle et al., 2001], and Pfeiffer and Glocker [Pfeiffer et al., 1996a]. These are termed force-based formulations and Stewart's is termed an impulse-based or velocity-based formulation.

Stewart and Trinkle originally used position constraints in their formulation; these position constraints ensure nonpenetration, but suffer from existence problems unless all contact normals are linearly independent.

Anitescu and Potra's velocity-based formulation always guarantees a solution, but there is one drawback: penetrations might occur when the system moves along concave boundaries of the admissible region in configuration space. Another side effect from the velocity-based formulation is that special attention must be added to separating contacts moving toward each other. If these are present, they will be treated as if they were in colliding contact; this could leave objects hanging in the air. Anitescu and Potra propose a time-stepping algorithm that correctly handles this side effect, but other authors tend to forget the problem.

Stewart and Trinkle suggest that simple projection can be used to eliminate this problem, but care must be taken to avoid losing energy in the process. However, they do not mention how one should do the projection.

Stewart and Trinkle [Stewart et al., 2000] suggest using contact tracking (it could be coined "retroactive detection" as well) to avoid the problem of explicitly determining all potential active contact constraints. That is, once a solution is found, the constraints at time $t + \Delta t$ are checked. If any one is found to be violated it is added to the set of active contact constraints and the problem is resolved once more. This of course, increases the amount of computations; often this is undesirable. For instance, in the Open Dynamics Engine, a fixed time-stepping advancement is chosen and any errors occurring are reduced by using penalty forces. The strategy is: don't try to prevent errors, but fix or reduce them if they occur. Another issue (which is not obvious, at least to us) is: is it possible to use a retroactive detection of contact constraints when we know there is a problem with concave boundaries of the admissible region of configuration space?

Sauer and Schömer [Sauer et al., 1998] use a linearized contact condition; they say this is for potential contact constraints and they require the assumption that during their fixpoint-iteration contact constraints do not change topologically, i.e., $(E, E) \mapsto (V, E)$. It is not obvious to us why this is required.

In the summary section of Stewart and Trinkle's paper [Stewart et al., 2000], there are some thoughts on how their method can be extended to handle a nonzero coefficient of restitution. They suggest stopping at collision times, which in our opinion is not an attractive choice. Actually their thoughts are based on the work by Anitescu and Potra. In the Open Dynamics Engine a slightly different approach is used similar to [Baraff, 1989].

Part III

The Dynamics of Deformable Objects

Deformable objects cover all object types that are not rigid, and thus span a wide range of different object types with different physical properties, such as jelly, cloth, biological tissue, water, wind, and fire.

Deformable objects are considered more difficult to deal with than rigid body simulation for several reasons. First, is the complexity of variables needed to describe the motion of a single object exploded in magnitude compared to a single rigid object. For a rigid object, only the motion and orientation of its center of mass are needed; for a deformable object every little particle needs to be described. Second, since deformable objects could potentially self-intersect, both the geometric problem of detecting self-intersections and the collision resolving are unpleasant problems to deal with. Third, the physics of deformable objects is described by a constitutive law describing relationships between physical properties inside the object, such as stress and strain. Although a constitute law often can be recognized as Newton's second law of motion, a student often needs to learn a multitude of new mathematical notations, terminology, and physical properties, such as calculus of variation, stress, strain, etc., in order to master its application to deformable objects.

The dynamics of deformable objects have been well known by physicists for the last 200 years or so. The mathematical models are well developed and the engineering community has been simulating computer models of deformable objects almost since the beginning of computers. Compared with this long history, it is not until recently that physically based animation of deformable objects has been introduced to the computer graphics community by the pioneering work of Terzopoulos *et al.* in 1987 [Terzopoulos et al., 1987].

Computer animation differs from traditional engineering applications in several aspects. First, the computational resources are low and the demand for fast performance and high visual details are weighted much higher than accurate computation. Second, computer animation is more concerned with showing interesting motion such as object deformation or fracture, than with the end results. Computational grids in computer animation are extremely coarse compared to the grids used in engineering, and stability and robustness is strongly favored over accuracy and precision. Consequently, computer animation is often based on implicit time-stepping methods with large time-steps, rather than explicit methods with small time-steps as preferred in engineering disciplines. Finally, computer animation is about making tools such as Maya® or 3DMax® for artistic and creative people, which have little respect for the real world. That is, a material may be given unrealistic properties, which produce an entertaining motion on a computer screen, but which do not correspond to any existing materials. Furthermore, objects may be forced into unnatural poses, simply because the poses are funny. The implication is that although physics-based animation uses physics as its foundation, physics-based animation must be able to cope with unphysical situations robustly.

In the beginning, people used rather simple constitute models in computer animation. Simple linear models between stress and strain of isotropic materials were applied. The quest for higher realism has moved the computer graphics community toward more advanced constitute models, since in animation large deformations are sought, and materials found in nature exhibit complex nonlinearities under large deformations. Recently, there has been an increased focus in the computer graphics community on improved handling of large deformations. The constitutive laws are often solved on mesh grids, but simulating large deformations can severely damage the integrity of a mesh grid. For instance, mesh elements can be inverted or entangled. There have been attempts to remodel the underlying physical models by introducing force-terms that counter these effects, or strategies for dynamically remeshing or simply

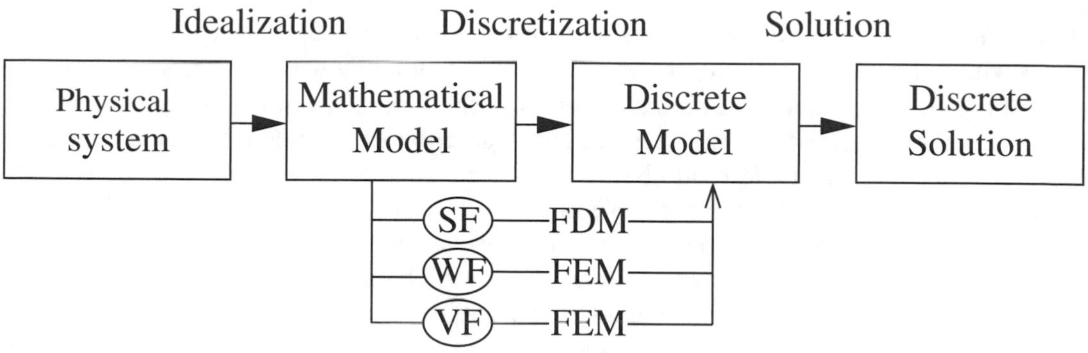

Figure III.1: Analysis process in computational mechanics.

deleting erogenous mesh elements. However, many of these solutions exhibit visual artifacts, such as mesh elements that pop out during simulation.

Deformable objects in computer animation have found their way to the movie theater: movies such as Monsters Inc.® use implicit constraint-based cloth animation [Baraff et al., 1998] with untangling of mesh elements [Baraff et al., 2003b], Phantom Menace® uses a guaranteed non self-intersecting time-stepping method for cloth animation [Bridson et al., 2002], and The Rise of the Machines® used a fold preserving and increasing method [Bridson et al., 2003]. In computer games methods based on *over-relaxation* have become widely popular [Jakobsen, 2001].

The scope on the theory of deformable objects in this book is to establish the basic foundation. Our main intention is to focus on describing the constitutive models and their implementation. We refrain from the problems of mesh inversion and entangling and refer the interested reader to [Irving et al., 2004] and [Baraff et al., 2003b].

The *field of mechanics* can be divided into four different subparts: theoretical, applied, computational, and experimental. In *theoretical mechanics*, the fundamental laws and principles of mechanics are studied. In *applied mechanics*, the theory is applied to science and engineering applications by constructing mathematical models of physical phenomenon. In *computational mechanics*, actual problems are solved by combining the mathematical models with numerical methods, leading to an implementation on a computer that is then simulated. In *experimental mechanics*, observations of the physical laws, the mathematical models, and the numerical simulations are compared. In computer animation, the field of computational mechanics is used together with a plethora of simplifying assumptions that lead to faster simulations.

The field of computational mechanics is highly interdisciplinary. It uses applied mathematics and numerical analysis, computer science, and theoretical and applied mechanics to arrive at a discrete model that can be solved on a computer. The analysis process that leads to a discrete model is illustrated in Figure III.1. Going from a physical system to a mathematical model is a process known as idealization. This stems from the fact that the real world is seldom ideal, especially when trying to express a phenomenon as a mathematical equation. The problem is expressed in an ideal situation that allows it to be formulated mathematically. Discretization is the process of reducing the continuum of the mathematical model to a finite algebraic system. In Figure III.1 three subpaths are shown at the discretization: *Strong form* (*SF*),

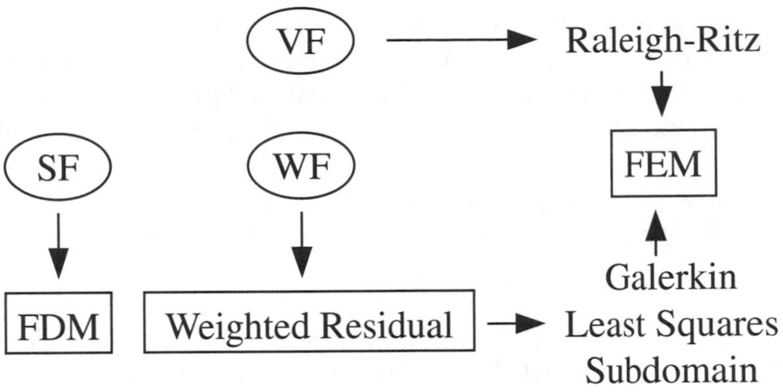

Figure III.2: Discretization of strong form, variational form, and weak form.

Weak form (*WF*), and *Variational form* (*VF*). Strong form is a system of ordinary or partial differential equations in space and/or time together with a set of boundary conditions. It is called strong because the system is satisfied at each point of the problem domain. Weak form is a weighted integral equation that relaxes the strong form in a domain-averaging sense. Variational form is a functional whose stationary conditions generate the weak and the strong forms. Variational calculus is used to pass from one form to another: strong to weak form, or the other way around, variational to weak form, or variational to strong form. Going from variational to strong form is essentially what is taught in variational calculus, whereas the inverse problem of going from strong to variational form is not always possible. However, sometimes it can be done, as will be shown for a simple example below.

Problems stated in strong form are a well-established part of calculus and mathematical physics. As an example, Newton's second law $\boldsymbol{F} = m\boldsymbol{a}$ is a strong form equation. The reason that the variational and weak forms are used instead of the strong form is the following: a variational form functionally expresses all properties of a model: field equations, natural boundary conditions, and conservation laws. The functionals are scalars and therefore invariant to coordinate transformations, so variational form transforms between different coordinate systems. Both variational form and weak form are used in discrete methods of approximation on computers. Variational form and weak form characterize quantities like mass, momentum, and energy. Variational form and weak form lead naturally to conservation laws. Variational form and weak form systematize the treatment of boundary and interface conditions with discrete schemes.

The continuum mathematical models in strong form, variational form, or weak form initially have an infinite degree of freedom. The discretization process reduces this to a finite set of algebraic equations that can be solved in reasonable time. The discretization process for the different forms leads to different approximation methods as characterized in Figure III.2. The strong form is usually discretized using the *Finite Difference Method* (*FDM*) where the derivatives are replaced with differences. This is an easy process for regular domains and boundary conditions, but becomes complicated for arbitrary geometry of boundary conditions. The weak form is discretized using the *Weighted Residual Method*. This consists of a lot of subclasses with names like *Galerkin*, *Petrov-Galerkin*, *Subdomain*, *Finite Volume Method*, and *Method of Least Squares*. All these subclasses are called trial function methods. The weighted residual method gives approximate solutions everywhere in the domain. In earlier times, the weighted residual method was solved by hand but the invention of the *Finite Element Method* (*FEM*) made a computer implementation possible. The variational form is discretized using the *Raleigh-Ritz method*, which is a special subclass of the Galerkin weighted residual method. Originally, the finite element method was developed in this way.

To illustrate the different terminology introduced above, consider the following simple example. Let $y = y(x)$ be a function satisfying the following ordinary differential equation

$$y'' = y + 2, \quad 0 \leq x \leq 2. \tag{III.1}$$

This is a strong form since the *ordinary differential equation* (*ODE*) is to be satisfied at each point in the problem domain $x \in [0, 2]$. Equation (III.1) alone is not sufficient to specify a solution. It needs to be paired with a set of boundary conditions. Two examples are

$$y(0) = 1, \qquad y(2) = 4, \tag{III.2a}$$

$$y(0) = 1, \qquad y'(0) = 0. \tag{III.2b}$$

Equation (III.1) together with the boundary conditions specified in (III.2a) defines a *boundary value problem* (*BVP*), which typically models problems in space. Equation (III.1) together with the boundary conditions specified in (III.2b) defines an *initial value problem* (*IVP*), which typically models problems in time.

Consider the boundary value problem consisting of (III.1)) and (III.2a). This is the top box in Figure III.3. The residual is defined as $r(x) = y'' - y - 2$. The strong form in (III.1) is equivalent to $r(x) = 0, \forall x \in [0, 2]$. The residuals for the boundary conditions can be written as $r_0 = y(0) - 1$ and $r_2 = y(2) - 4$.

Now, multiply the residual $r(x)$ by a weighting function $w(x)$ and integrate over the domain $[0, 2]$, multiply r_0, r_2 by weights w_0, w_2, and add them to get

$$\int_0^2 r(x)w(x)dx + r_0 w_0 + r_2 w_2 = 0. \tag{III.3}$$

The problem is now on weighted integral form, which is a weak form. The reason for calling it weak is that functions other than (III.1) with boundary conditions (III.2a) may satisfy the weak form in (III.3). This is shown in the top part of the middle box of Figure III.3.

If the weight functions w, w_0, w_2 are written as variations of functions v, v_0, v_2, the weak form in (III.3) is converted to the variational statement

$$\int_0^2 r(x)\delta v(x)dx + r_0 \delta v_0 + r_2 \delta v_2 = 0, \tag{III.4}$$

where δ is the variation symbol. The functions v are called test functions. This is shown in the bottom part of the middle box in Figure III.3.

For this example, the inverse problem of variational calculus has a solution. The functional

$$J[y] = \int_0^2 \left[\frac{1}{2} \left(y''\right)^2 - \frac{1}{2} y^2 + 2y \right] dx, \tag{III.5}$$

restricted to y's that satisfies the boundary value problem is stationary in a variational calculus sense. Equation (III.1) is called the *Euler-Lagrange equation* of the functional in (III.5). This is shown in the bottom box of Figure III.3, which is now completely described.

Strong Form (SF)

Boundary Value Problem (BVP)

$$y'' = y + 2, \quad y = y(x), x \in [0, 2]$$
$$y(0) = 1, \quad y(2) = 4$$

Weak Form (WF)

Weighted Residual Form

$$\int_0^2 r(x)w(x)dx + r_0 w_0 + r_2 w_2 = 0$$

Variational Statement

$$\int_0^2 r(x)\delta v(x)dx + r_0 \delta v_0 + r_2 \delta v_2 = 0$$

Variational Form (VF)

Functional

$$J[y] = \int_0^2 \left[\frac{1}{2} (y'')^2 - \frac{1}{2} y^2 + 2y \right] dx$$
$$y(0) = 1, \quad y(2) = 4$$

Figure III.3: All the forms used in the simple example.

8

Particle Systems

Particles are the easiest objects to animate. They are objects that have position, velocity, and mass, but no spatial extend, i.e., neither moment of inertia nor torque. Particles have been used to animate a large variety of behaviors, such as gases, water (see Chapter 11), fire, rubber, clothes, flocking, rigid bodies, etc. Several sections in this chapter are given in the spirit of [Baraff et al., 2003a, Baraff et al., 1998].

8.1 Newtonian Particle Systems

Newtonian particles are the most common and are governed by *Newton's second law*

$$\boldsymbol{f} = m\ddot{\boldsymbol{r}} \Leftrightarrow \ddot{\boldsymbol{r}} = \boldsymbol{f}/m, \tag{8.1}$$

where $\boldsymbol{r}(t) = [x_1, x_2, x_3]^T$ is the position of the particle at time t, and $\ddot{\boldsymbol{r}} = [\ddot{x}_1, \ddot{x}_2, \ddot{x}_3]^T = \frac{d^2\boldsymbol{r}(t)}{dt^2}$ is the instantaneous acceleration of the particle. The equation, $\ddot{\boldsymbol{r}} = \boldsymbol{f}/m$, contains a second-order derivative, hence it is a *second-order differential equation.* First-order equations are the simplest to solve, and any linear higher-order differential equations can be converted to a system of coupled first-order differential equations.

Newton's second law (8.1) is converted into two coupled first-order differential equations by projecting the particles into *phase space* where a point in phase space is denoted by its position *and* velocity:

$$\mathbf{p} = \begin{bmatrix} \boldsymbol{r} \\ \boldsymbol{v} \end{bmatrix} = \begin{bmatrix} \boldsymbol{r} \\ \dot{\boldsymbol{r}} \end{bmatrix}. \tag{8.2}$$

The velocity is naturally found as the instantaneous change of position, $\dot{\boldsymbol{r}} = \boldsymbol{v} = \frac{d\boldsymbol{r}(t)}{dt}$, and when $\boldsymbol{r} \in \mathbb{R}^3$ as typical in 3D computer graphics, then $\boldsymbol{v} \in \mathbb{R}^3$, and hence $\mathbf{p} \in \mathbb{R}^6$.

The second-order differential equation is changed into two first-order differential equations, one for $\boldsymbol{r}$ and one for $\boldsymbol{v}$, which are coupled through $\dot{\boldsymbol{r}} = \boldsymbol{v}$. The instantaneous change is thus

$$\dot{\mathbf{p}} = \begin{bmatrix} \boldsymbol{v} \\ \boldsymbol{a} \end{bmatrix} = \begin{bmatrix} \dot{\boldsymbol{r}} \\ \dot{\boldsymbol{v}} \end{bmatrix} = \begin{bmatrix} \dot{\boldsymbol{r}} \\ \ddot{\boldsymbol{r}} \end{bmatrix}. \tag{8.3}$$

In a simple explicit solution of this system of first-order differential equations, the velocity at time t is used to update the particle position for time $t + h$, while the acceleration at time t is used to update the particle velocity for time $t + h$. Hence, the effect of setting forces at time t will first have an influence on the particle's position at time $t + 2h$. This will be discussed in detail in the following sections.

8.2 Solving Ordinary Differential Equations

For a *system of particles*, we assume that the forces are given for all relevant interactions and positions, therefore we know the accelerations acting on any particle at any time. We will also assume that the initial positions and velocities for all particles are known. The problem is now an initial value problem on the form $\dot{\mathbf{p}}(t) = \mathbf{F}(\mathbf{p}(t))$ under the condition $\mathbf{p}(t_0) = \mathbf{p}_0 = [\boldsymbol{r}_0, \dot{\boldsymbol{r}}_0]^T$, where we wish to solve for some $t > 0$. Most initial value problems in particle animation do not have a closed form solution; instead they must be solved by discrete approximations, such as *Euler's explicit* or *implicit* scheme. These techniques are discussed in detail in Chapter 23. The simplest method for solving first-order differential equations is by *explicit Euler integration*; this is the only method that we will discuss here.

Assume that time is discretized as follows:

$$t_{i+1} = h + t_i. \tag{8.4}$$

A second-order accurate approximation of the position at time t_{i+1} is given by the first-order *Taylor Series*

$$\mathbf{p}(t_{i+1}) = \mathbf{p}(t_i) + h\dot{\mathbf{p}}(t_i) + \mathcal{O}(h^2). \tag{8.5}$$

Since we know the initial value of $\mathbf{p}(t_0)$ and since we know $\mathbf{F}(\mathbf{p}(t)) = [\dot{x}, \boldsymbol{f}(t)/m]^T$, then we may approximate $\mathbf{p}(t_1)$ as

$$\mathbf{p}(t_1) \simeq \mathbf{p}(t_0) + h\mathbf{F}(\mathbf{p}(t_0)), \tag{8.6}$$

which is equivalent to

$$\begin{bmatrix} \boldsymbol{r}_1 \\ \dot{\boldsymbol{r}}_1 \end{bmatrix} \simeq \begin{bmatrix} \boldsymbol{r}_0 \\ \dot{\boldsymbol{r}}_0 \end{bmatrix} + h \begin{bmatrix} \dot{\boldsymbol{r}}_0 \\ \boldsymbol{f}(t_0)/m \end{bmatrix}. \tag{8.7}$$

The following steps are thus calculated as

$$\begin{bmatrix} \boldsymbol{r}_{i+1} \\ \dot{\boldsymbol{r}}_{i+1} \end{bmatrix} \simeq \begin{bmatrix} \boldsymbol{r}_i \\ \dot{\boldsymbol{r}}_i \end{bmatrix} + h \begin{bmatrix} \dot{\boldsymbol{r}}_i \\ \boldsymbol{f}(t_i)/m \end{bmatrix}. \tag{8.8}$$

It should be noted that there is a time difference between the solutions of the position and velocity differential equation, since the velocity calculated at time t_i is used to update the position of the particle at time t_{i+1}. This is the price paid for solving higher-order differential equations as a system of coupled first-order differential equations, and for animation purposes it is usually not a problem. Explicit Euler solutions to ordinary differential equations are very simple to implement, and it is very fast to compute each iteration. However, they are neither *stable* with respect to large steps, h, nor very *accurate*, which is demonstrated in Figure 8.1. Figure 8.1(a) shows the iso-energy values of a rotational symmetric system. Assuming that the speed is initially zero, then the correct solution would be the particular circle that the particle was positioned on initially. However, the second-order *Taylor approximation* extrapolates the solution with a finite step size, which implies that the particle will leave whichever circle it is currently on. Instability is demonstrated in Figure 8.1(b). Again, assuming that the initial speed is zero, then the correct solution is the iso-energy lines shown in the figure and the correct solution is the convergence of the particle on the center horizontal line. However, if the step size is set too high, then the particle will diverge in this particular example, since the Taylor approximation will extrapolate to positions with increasing forces.

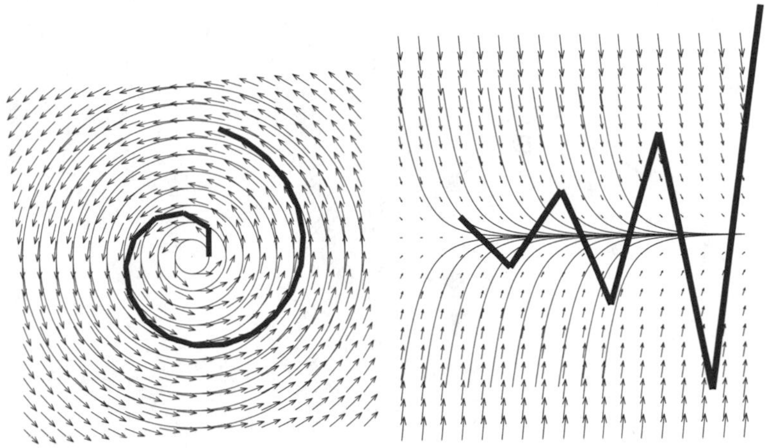

(a) (b)

Figure 8.1: Euler's method is neither accurate (a) nor stable (b).

The phase-space solution to the second-order differential equation simultaneously solves for position and velocity. Using first-order Euler integration,

$$\begin{bmatrix} \boldsymbol{r}(t+h) \\ \boldsymbol{v}(t+h) \end{bmatrix} = \begin{bmatrix} \boldsymbol{r}(t) \\ \boldsymbol{v}(t) \end{bmatrix} + h \begin{bmatrix} \boldsymbol{v}(t) \\ \boldsymbol{a}(t) \end{bmatrix} + \mathcal{O}(h^2),$$

Verlet [Verlet, 1967] suggested simplifying using the approximation,

$$\boldsymbol{r}(t-h) = \boldsymbol{r}(t) - h\boldsymbol{v}(t) + \frac{1}{2}h^2\boldsymbol{a}(t) + \mathcal{O}(h^3) \tag{8.9a}$$

$$\Rightarrow \boldsymbol{v}(t) = \frac{\boldsymbol{r}(t) - \boldsymbol{r}(t-h)}{h} + \frac{1}{2}h\boldsymbol{a}(t) + \mathcal{O}(h^2), \tag{8.9b}$$

which may be inserted into a second-order integration

$$\boldsymbol{r}(t+h) = \boldsymbol{r}(t) + h\boldsymbol{v}(t) + \frac{1}{2}h^2\boldsymbol{a}(t) + \mathcal{O}(h^3) \tag{8.10a}$$

$$= -\boldsymbol{r}(t-h) + 2\boldsymbol{r}(t) + h^2\boldsymbol{a}(t) + \mathcal{O}(h^3). \tag{8.10b}$$

This is called *Verlet integration*. A consequence of the scheme is that velocity is represented implicitly by the previous and current positions.

An important part in physics-based animation is *collision detection* and *response*. A particularly simple solution exists for Verlet integration, since Verlet integration does not store velocities. Hence, when a particle is found to penetrate an obstacle, then a simple collision response projects out of the obstacle along the shortest path. The cancellation of the velocity normal to the obstacle surface is thus automatic

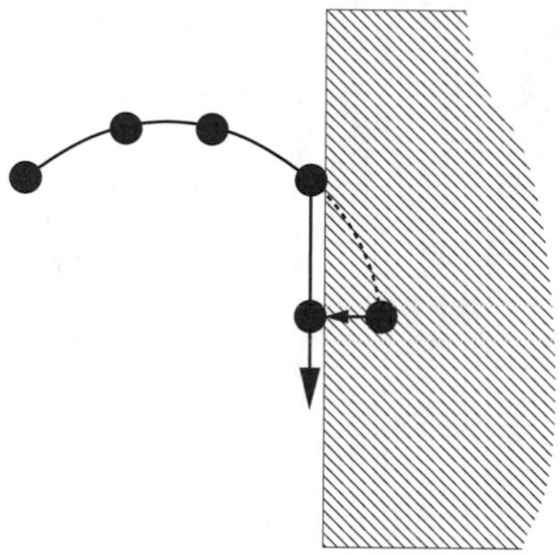

Figure 8.2: A particle trajectory colliding with a wall. When a particle moves into a wall, it is projected the shortest distance out again.

in Verlet integration as illustrated in Figure 8.2! The idea was introduced to the graphics community by [Provot, 1995] and discussed in [Baraff et al., 1998]. Later [Wagenaar, 2001] extended the method, which was put to use in [Jakobsen, 2001]. In the graphics community, the idea was extended into the impulse-based domain of cloth simulation by [Bridson et al., 2002]. With some freedom of interpretation you could even claim that the *shock propagation* from [Guendelman et al., 2003] is related to this way of thinking about constraints.

8.3 Hooke's Spring Law

The motion of two particles connected with a *spring* is governed by *Hooke's Spring Law* (Robert Hooke, 1635–1703), and it is given as

$$m_i \ddot{x}_i = k_s (x_j - x_i) \quad \text{and} \quad m_j \ddot{x}_j = -k_s (x_j - x_i). \tag{8.11}$$

where k_s is the spring coefficient, and where we have aligned the x-axis of the coordinate system along the spring. This may be reformulated as

$$\ddot{x} = -k \left(\frac{1}{m_j} + \frac{1}{m_i} \right) x \quad \Rightarrow \quad \mu \ddot{x} = -k_s x, \tag{8.12}$$

using $x = x_j - x_i$ and $\mu = \frac{m_i m_j}{m_i + m_j}$ and is called the reduced mass. Hence, Hooke's undamped spring law is essentially a one-object *harmonic oscillator harmonic oscillator* as discussed in Section 22.4. A one-object harmonic oscillator, such as a single particle connected to a wall with a spring may be described as

$$f_{\text{spring}} = -k_s x. \tag{8.13}$$

Newton's second law of motion of a particle with mass m is then

$$m\ddot{x} = -k_s x \quad \Rightarrow \quad m\ddot{x} + k_s x = 0, \tag{8.14}$$

and the analytical solution may be found to be

$$\begin{aligned} x &= B \sin(\omega_0 t) + C \cos(\omega_0 t) && (8.15a) \\ &= A \cos(\omega_0 t + \phi). && (8.15b) \end{aligned}$$

The *natural frequency* is given as, $\omega_0 = \sqrt{\frac{k_s}{m}}$, B and C are constants determined by *initial conditions*, and ϕ is the corresponding phase.

The harmonic oscillator will continue its movement indefinitely unless it is interfered with by other objects. This is unrealistic, since in the real world, springs lose energy due to the production of heat through the movement itself and *air friction*. This dissipation of energy is often modeled using a *damping viscosity force*

$$F_{\text{damping}} = -k_d \dot{x}, \tag{8.16}$$

which implies that

$$\begin{aligned} m\ddot{x} &= -k_s x - k_d \dot{x} && (8.17a) \\ &\Rightarrow m\ddot{x} + k_d \dot{x} + k_s x = 0 && (8.17b) \\ &\Rightarrow \ddot{x} + \frac{k_d}{m}\dot{x} + \frac{k_s}{m} x = 0, && (8.17c) \end{aligned}$$

for which the analytical solution is

$$x = A \exp\left(-\frac{\gamma}{2} t\right) \cos(\omega_1 t + \phi), \tag{8.18}$$

using

$$\omega_0^2 = \frac{k}{m}, \quad \gamma = \frac{b}{m}, \quad \omega_1 = \sqrt{\omega_0^2 - \frac{\gamma^2}{4}}, \tag{8.19}$$

and A and ϕ are constants determined from initial conditions. Solutions are only real valued when $\omega_0^2 - \frac{\gamma^2}{4} \geq 0$. Writing the *damped harmonic oscillator* as

$$x = A(t) \cos(\omega_1 t + \phi) = A \exp\left(-\frac{\gamma}{2} t\right) \cos(\omega_1 t + \phi) \tag{8.20}$$

and comparing to the undamped harmonic oscillator (8.15b), we see that

- the amplitude of the damped oscillator is exponential decaying.
- the frequency ω_1 of the damped oscillator is less than the frequency, ω_0, of the undamped oscillator.

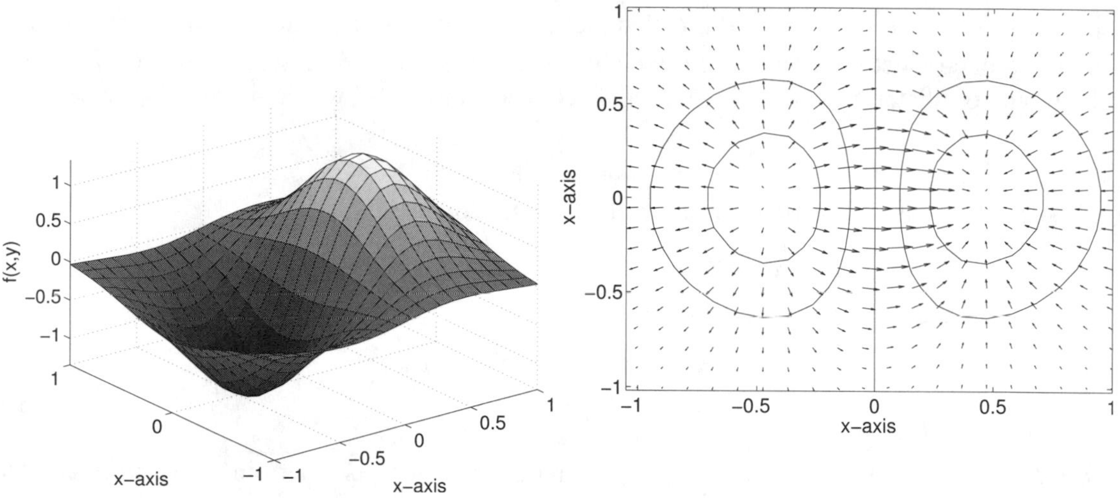

Figure 8.3: An energy function and the corresponding potential field. The positive slope acts as an attractor and the negative slope is a repellent.

8.4 Particle Forces

The behavior of particles is controlled through the forces $\boldsymbol{f}$. Typical forces are *potential forces*, which are gradients of *energy functions*. An example of an energy function and its potential field is shown in Figure 8.4. If no other forces are acting on the particle, then it will follow curves, where the potential field on every point on the curve is tangent to the curve.

Particle systems are conceptually simple; there are many systems, that with clever applications, make use of only a few types of force fields. These are usually grouped into the following categories: *unary forces*, which act independently on each particle, for example,

Gravity

$$\boldsymbol{f} = \begin{bmatrix} 0 \\ -g \\ 0 \end{bmatrix}, \tag{8.21}$$

Viscous Drag

$$\boldsymbol{f} = -k_d \dot{\boldsymbol{r}}, \tag{8.22}$$

Air Drag

$$\boldsymbol{f} = -k_d \left\| \boldsymbol{r} \right\|_2 \dot{\boldsymbol{r}}, \tag{8.23}$$

where the second coordinate is assumed to be the vertical direction, g is the gravitational strength, and k_d is either the *viscosity* or *air friction coefficients*; *N-ary forces* which are the interaction between groups of particles, for example,

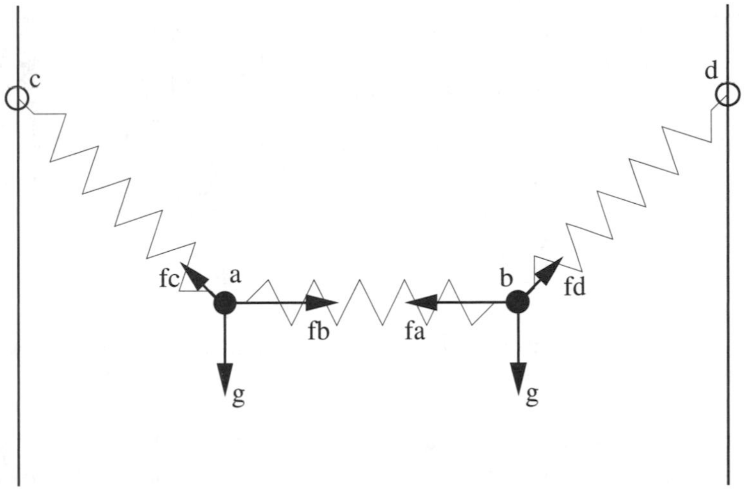

Figure 8.4: An example of a system of particles, where two particles, a and b, are connected to each other and immobile points of a wall at c and d. All forces are spring or gravity forces.

Hooke's Law for Damped Spring

$$\boldsymbol{f}_a = -\boldsymbol{f}_b = -\left[k_s(|\mathbf{l}| - R) + k_d \frac{\dot{\mathbf{l}} \cdot \mathbf{l}}{|\mathbf{l}|}\right] \frac{\mathbf{l}}{|\mathbf{l}|}, \tag{8.24}$$

where a and b are two particles connected with a spring, k_s is the spring constant, $\mathbf{l} = \boldsymbol{r}_a - \boldsymbol{r}_b$ is the vector connecting the two particles, $\dot{\mathbf{l}} = \boldsymbol{v}_a - \boldsymbol{v}_b$ is the vector of instantaneous change, and R is the length of the spring at rest. The final category is spatial interactions, which are interactions on single or groups of particles that depend on their spatial position. Some of these forces are illustrated in Figure 8.4

8.4.1 Deformable Surfaces

Classically, *cloth* was modeled by using *mass-spring systems* [Provot, 1995]. These are essentially particle systems with a set of predefined springs between pairs of particles. The cloth is modeled as a regular 2D grid where the grid nodes correspond to particles. The cloth can be animated by moving the particles, which will deform the regular grid.

Springs are not created at random between the cloth particles, but a certain structure is used to mimic cloth properties. Three types of springs are used: structural springs, shearing springs, and bending springs. These spring types are illustrated in Figure 8.5.

Structural springs are created between each pair of horizontal and vertical particle neighbors in the regular 2D springs. The purpose of structural springs is to resist stretching and compression of the cloth. This kind of spring is usually initialized with very high spring coefficients and with a rest length equal to the interparticle distance.

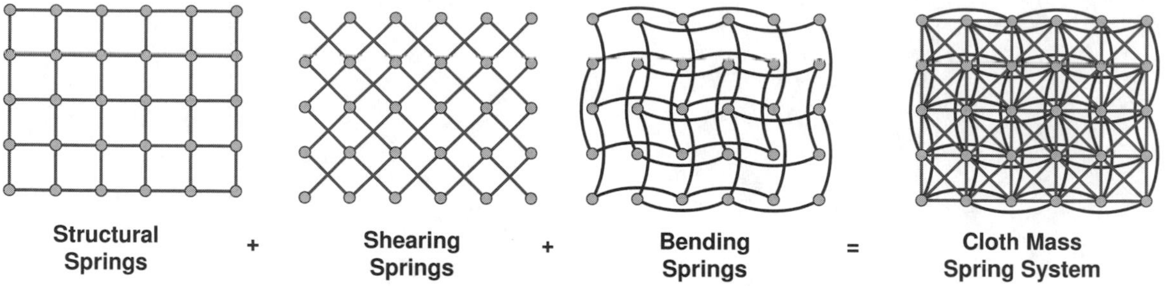

Figure 8.5: Structural, shearing, and bending springs in a cloth mesh.

Shearing springs are used to make sure that the cloth does not shear, i.e., a square piece of cloth should stay squared and not turn into an oblong diamond shape. The spring coefficient of these springs is usually set less than the structural springs. Shearing springs are created between diagonal direction in the regular grid. Thus a particle at grid location (i, j) will have shearing springs to particles at grid locations: $(i+1, j+1)$, $(i+1, j-1)$, $(i-1, j+1)$, and $(i-1, j-1)$.

Bending springs are inserted to make sure the cloth will not have sharp ridges when folded. These springs are usually not very strong, since natural cloth does not strongly resist bending. The springs are created along the horizontal and vertical grid lines, but only between every second particle. That is, particles at grid location i, j are connected with bending springs to particles at grid locations: $(i+2, j)$, $(i-2, j)$, $(i, j+2)$, and $(i, j-2)$.

It is straightforward to create these springs for a rectilinear grid of particles and it offers an easy way to model a rectangular piece of cloth. Spring coefficients can be tuned to model different kinds of cloth types: cotton, polyester, etc., as discussed in [House et al., 2000].

One deficiency with modeling cloth this way is that it is limited to rectangular pieces of cloth. This is very limiting when, for instance, modeling animation cloth on an animated person. Nevertheless, we will focus on a generalization made in [OpenTissue, 2005], which can be applied to *unstructured meshes* such as arbitrary triangle meshes.

The generalization is based on the observation that structural springs correspond to a 1-neighborhood stencil in the rectilinear grid; shearing and bending springs correspond to a 2-neighborhood stencil. Similar neighborhoods can be defined in an unstructured mesh. We let the vertices of the mesh correspond to particles, the cost of every edge in the mesh is set to 1, and for each particle the shortest paths to all other particles is computed. If we want to create 1-neighborhood-type springs, then springs are created to all particles having a cost less than or equal to 1. If we also want to add 2-neighborhood-type springs, then springs are created to all particles with a cost less than or equal to 2. 3-neighborhood springs and so on are created in a similar fashion. Figure 8.6 illustrate the springs created for a single chosen vertex.

Generally speaking, the larger the neighborhood size used, the more rigid the resulting object appears to be. In fact, if the neighborhood size is large enough, springs will be created between every pair of particles in the mesh, and if the spring constants also are large, then the object will appear completely rigid. Thus we refer to the neighborhood size as the *rigidity factor*. The *spring creation method* was named *surface springs* in [OpenTissue, 2005].

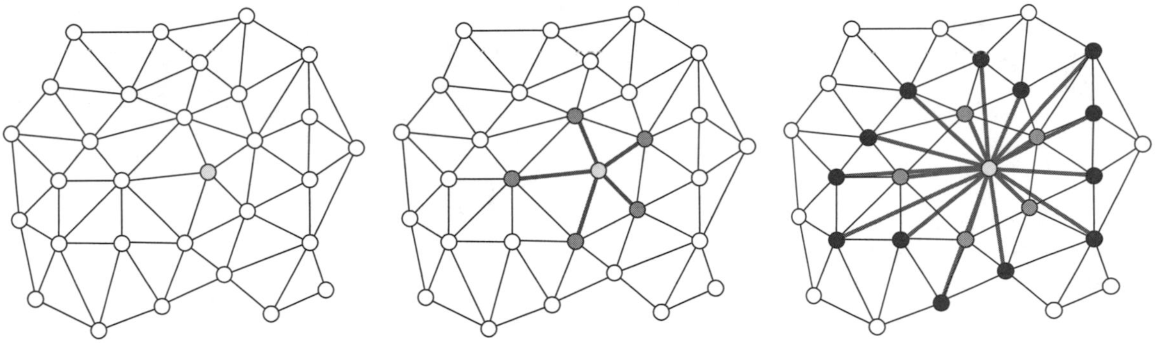

(a) 0 neighborhood (b) 1 neighborhood (c) 2 neighborhood

Figure 8.6: Surface springs (thick lines) created for a chosen mesh vertex.

The path cost computation can be implemented elegantly by performing a *breadth-first traversal* on each particle in the mesh. Once the traversal reaches particles lying further away than the rigidity factor, the traversal is stopped. Figure 8.7 illustrates a pseudocode implementation of the breadth-first traversal algorithm for creating surface springs. Observe that creating a rectangular mesh and applying the surface spring creation method with a rigidity factor of two, will yield the traditional cloth mesh. In Figure 8.8 are examples of a cow with rigidity factors 1–3, and in Figures 8.9–8.11 is the animation when the cow falls under gravity.

8.4.2 Deformable Solids

The spring modeling ideas introduced in the previous section can be extended from surfaces to solids. For instance, given a 3D rectilinear grid, structural, shearing, and bending springs can be extended straightforwardly to the 3D case. However, one needs to consider *spatial diagonals* as well as *shearing diagonals*. Shearing diagonals will prevent area loss; spatial diagonals will counteract volume loss. The generalization to *unstructured solid meshes* is also easily performed with the so-called *volume mesh*, such as a *tetrahedral mesh*. The algorithm shown in Figure 8.7 can be applied unchanged to this type of mesh. In Figure 8.12 is the cow simulation for an unstructured mesh.

Unfortunately, in practice a rectilinear grid or a volume mesh of the solid is not always available, but instead a 2D surface mesh of the object is given. To make a solid mesh, a *voxelization* of the interior of the surface could be performed and the resulting voxels could be used as a basis for creating a rectilinear grid structure resembling the solid object. To keep particle and spring numbers as low as possible, a coarse voxelization is often applied. The surface mesh can then be coupled to the grid-structure by initially mapping each vertex into the grid-cube containing it. During animation, the vertex position can be updated when the rectilinear grid deforms by using *trilinear interpolation* of the deformed positions of the grid nodes of the containing grid cube. The *mesh coupling* idea is a well-known technique for deformable objects [M.M̃üller, 2004b, M.M̃üller, 2004a].

```
algorithm create-surface-springs(rigidity, mesh)
  for each vertex V of mesh
    S = empty set of vertices
    traverse(V, V, 0, S)
    for vertices in S unmark them
  next V
end algorithm

algorithm traverse(V,A,distance,S)
  if distance >= rigidity then
    return
  S = S union A
  mark A
  for each edge E of A do
    let B be other vertex of E
    if B not marked then
      if not exist spring (A,B) then
        create spring(A,B)
      end if
      traverse(V,B,distance+1,S)
    end if
  next E
end algorithm
```

Figure 8.7: Pseudocode for breadth-first traversal creation of springs in a mesh.

In [Jansson et al., 2002b, Jansson et al., 2002a] it is shown how spring models can be modeled based on rectilinear grids. Furthermore, a mesh-coupling technique is adapted, although in their approach only structural springs are initially created. During animation it is tested whether particles come too close, i.e., whether the interdistance between particles drops below a user-specified threshold. In that case, a spring is created dynamically on the fly and kept active until the interparticle distance is increased beyond a spring-breaking threshold distance specified by the end user.

A solid model can be created from the surface mesh by clever insertion of springs. This approach has been explored in [Mosegaard, 2003], where a *cone-based spring creation method* was presented. The idea herein is readily generalized to create *volume preserving springs* for *surface meshes*. Such a generalized approach will be presented in the following.

Given an unstructured surface mesh, we let the vertices denote particles. Initially *angle-weighted vertex normals* [Aanæs et al., 2003] are computed. These normals are favored, since they are independent of the tessellation of the mesh. For each vertex a cone is created, the cone will have apex at the vertex position, and the angle-weighted vertex normal will denote the cone axis. Next, all other vertices are tested for inclusion inside the vertex cone. For each vertex found inside the cone, a spring is created between the apex vertex and the contained vertex. The idea is illustrated in 2D in Figure 8.13.

The cone angle works as a rigidity factor in very much the same way as the neighborhood size used previously. The larger the angle, the more springs will be created, and the surface mesh will have more resistance toward collapsing. The creation method is independent of the specific tessellation. Even meshes

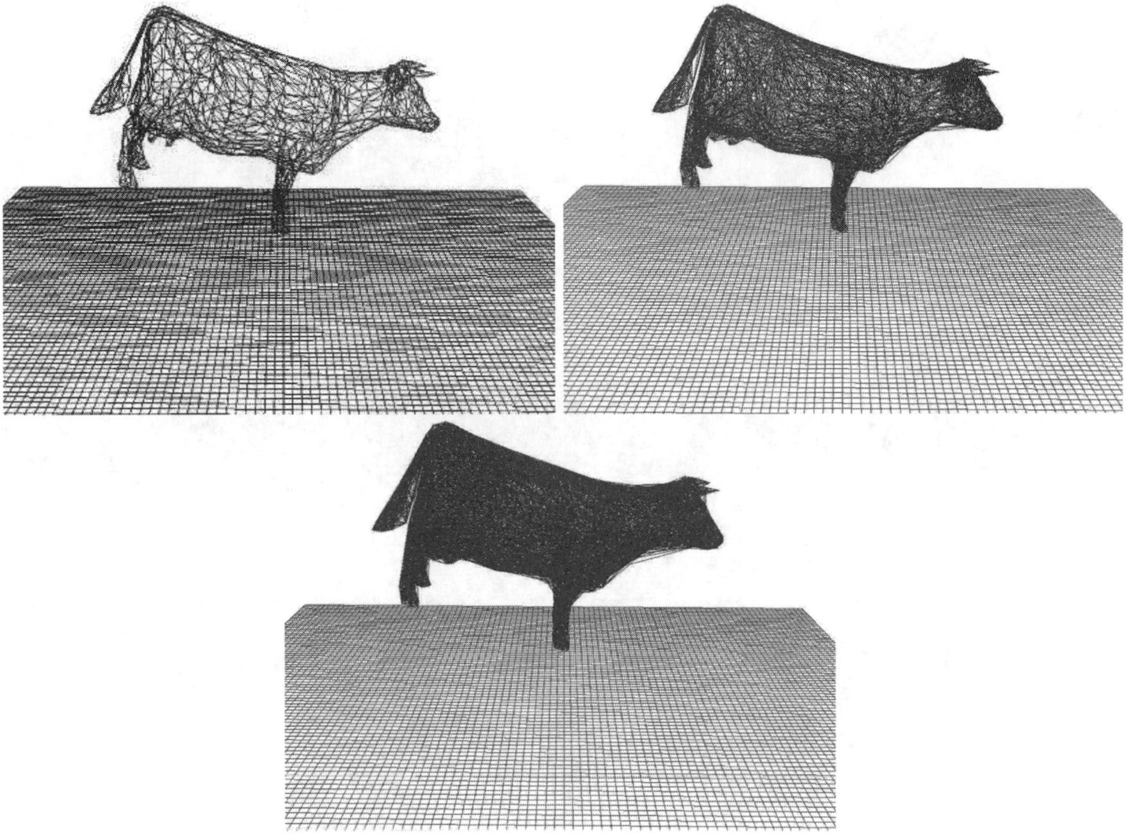

Figure 8.8: A cow setup with rigidity factor equal to 1–3 from top to bottom. Simulations are shown in Figures 8.9–8.11 respectively.

with faulty topology can be handled, since only vertex positions are used.

One drawback with this spring creation method is that if the cone angle is too small, it may occur that no vertices are found to lie inside the cone angles, and an insufficient number of springs will be created. One possible remedy of this problem is to make the cone angle adaptive; for instance, dependent on the local surface curvature, i.e., the angle is inverse reciprocal to the largest principal curvature or the like.

A computational cheap alternative to the spring cone creation method is to use an *inward mesh extrusion* instead. Here an inward mesh extrusion is performed, for instance, by shrinking the original mesh by moving vertices inward along vertex normal directions. It is advantageous to use a vertex normal definition that determines normals independently of mesh tessellation [Aanæs et al., 2003]; the extrusion lengths can be computed to ensure non-self-intersections as done in [Erleben et al., 2004].

Having obtained the extruded mesh surface, it is now a simple matter to create springs based on *mesh connectivity*

and pairing extruded vertices with their originals. This is illustrated in Figure 8.14, where it can be seen how to create structural and shearing springs.

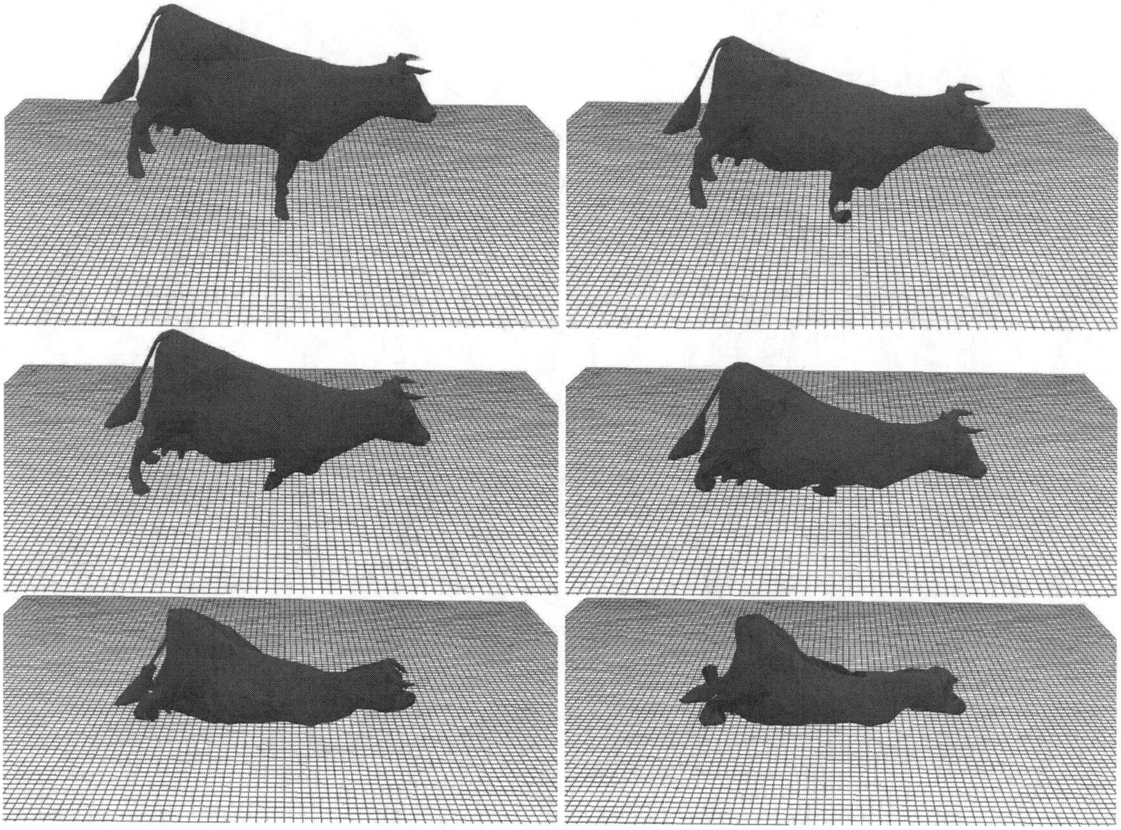

Figure 8.9: A cow being deformed under gravity with rigidity factor equal to 1. Compare with Figures 8.10 and 8.11

Compared with the other methods for solids, this method has the advantage of being simple to implement and very fast. Furthermore, since only a minimum of internal particles are created (vertices of extruded surface), the method has a performance advantage compared to the voxelization approach described previously.

It should be noted that a voxelization approach often requires a watertight surface mesh; otherwise the voxelization may be error prone. Methods do exist [Nooruddin et al., 2003] using *layered depth images* (*LDI*) for creating binary images that can be used for repairing a polygonal mesh or moving least squares approaches [Shen et al., 2004], which creates implicit surface models.

It may be more attractive to be able to work directly on a *degenerate mesh*, i.e., one with *topological errors*, such as edges having more than two incident neighboring faces. Especially, graphics artists or content creators are famous for producing meshes, which are a very poor starting point for creating a model for a physical simulation. Thus, to circumvent these problems, one approach is to accept life as it is, and simply use methods that are robust and stable toward artistic errors in visual content. The cone-

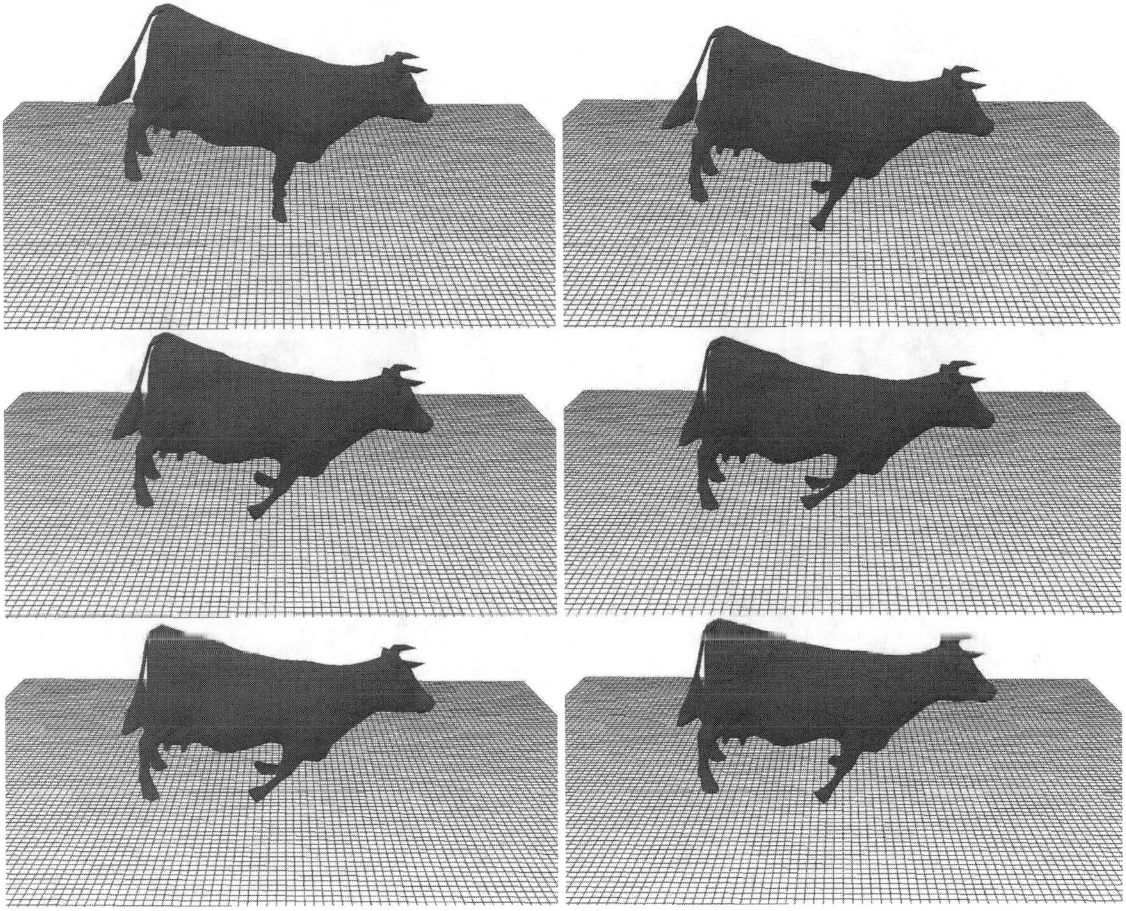

Figure 8.10: A cow being deformed under gravity with rigidity factor equal to 2. Compare with Figures 8.9 and 8.11

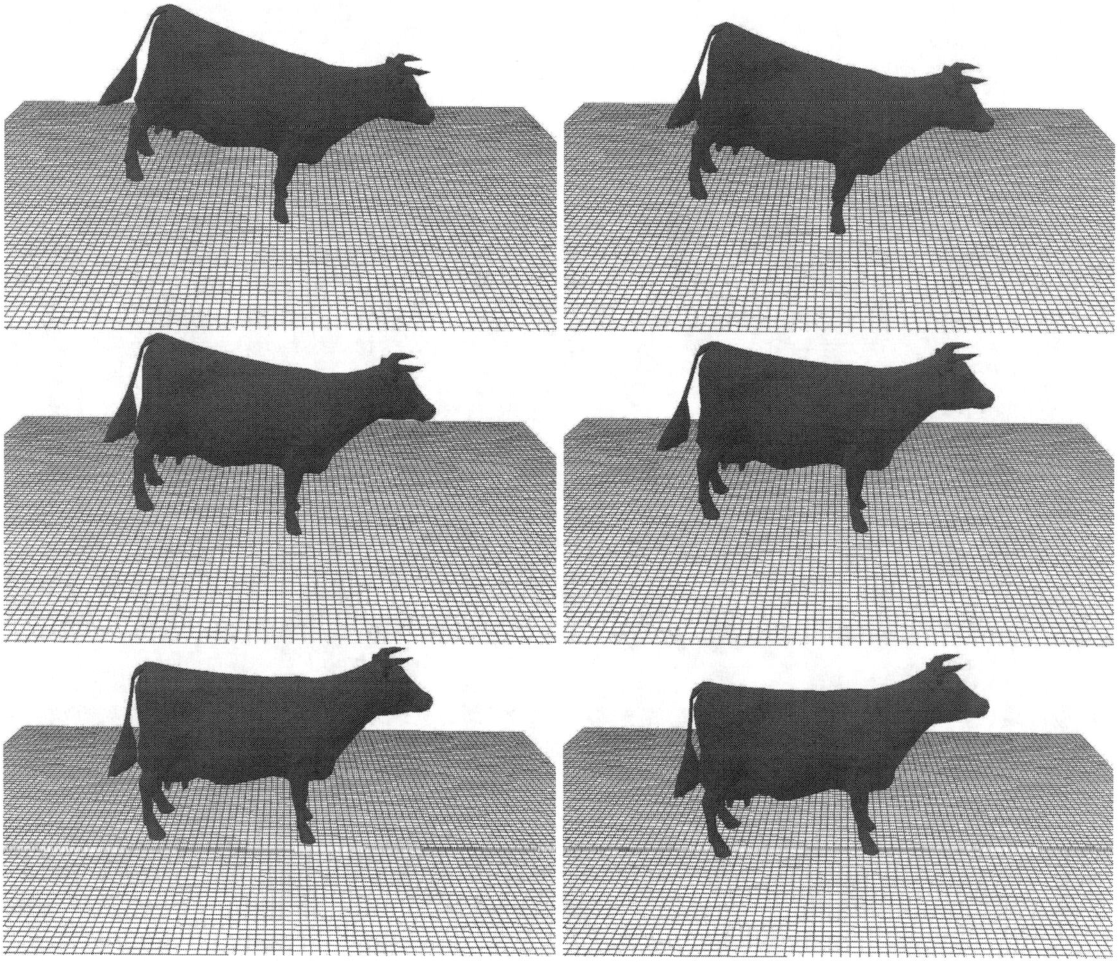

Figure 8.11: A cow being deformed under gravity with rigidity factor equal to 3. Compare with Figures 8.9 and 8.10

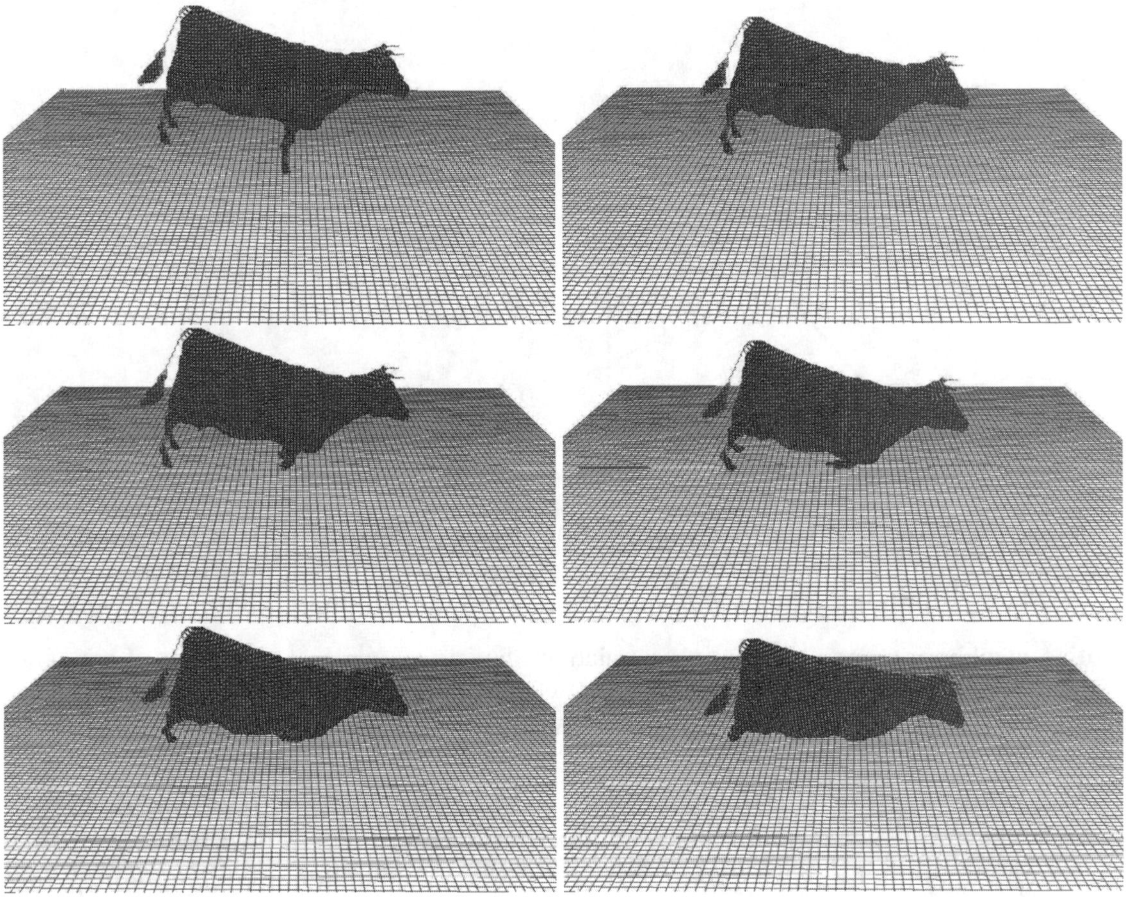

Figure 8.12: Simulation using springs created from cubes in a voxelization of a cow mesh.

based spring creation method and the breadth-first traversal spring creation methods can both be used on such faulty meshes. Whereas the other spring creation methods often rely on a perfect error-free mesh, sometimes even a watertight mesh.

8.4.3 Deformable Plants

More organic-like shapes such as plants and trees are also easily modeled by particle systems with clever spring creations.

A simple straw of grass may be modeled as a string of particles like pearls on a string. Structural springs and bending springs are inserted to provide the string with stiffness as shown in Figure 8.15. The same principle can be applied to model ropes, grass, and hair. If more stiffness is wanted, more springs can be created in a similar fashion to using 3- and 4-neighborhoods etc. Another possibility is to introduce *angular springs*. Here a rest angle, θ_{rest}, is assigned between the two lines running through three

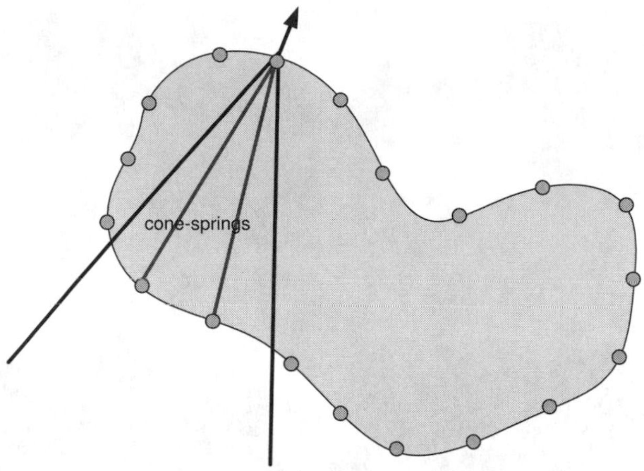

Figure 8.13: Angle-weighted cones used for creating springs, which add internal structure to a surface mesh.

consecutive neighboring particles. During simulation, the current angle, θ, is computed and an energy function can be designed as $E = -\frac{1}{2}k(\theta - \theta_{\text{rest}})^2$, where k is a kind of spring coefficient. The negative gradient of the energy function yields a restoring penalty torque that can be applied to the particles. In Section 8.5, we will show how energy functions can be designed in a general way and used to add forces to the particles.

If more complex structures are needed, branches can be added to the model to give a treelike effect. However, extra springs must be inserted between the branches and the tree trunk. This schematic is shown in Figure 8.16. In order to appear realistic in a real application, the above particle models must be rendered properly. For the treelike model, a mesh coupling similar to traditional skin-deformation can by used to model the geometry of the trunk and branches. Leaves and finer structures are more easily handled by

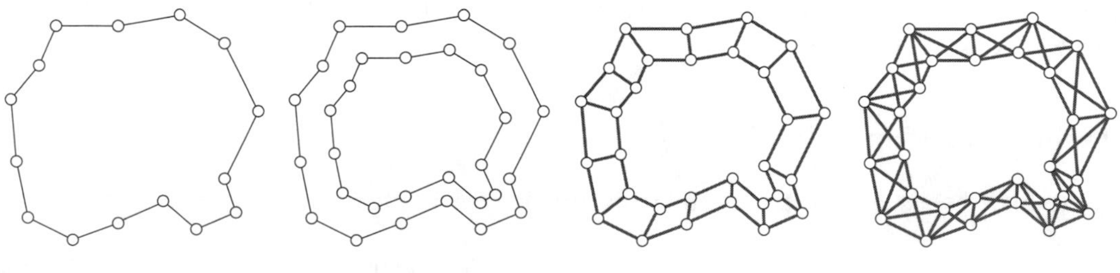

(a) Original Surface Mesh (b) Inward Extrusion (c) Structural Springs (d) Structural and Shearing Springs

Figure 8.14: Spring creation based on inward mesh extrusion. Springs are shown as thickened lines.

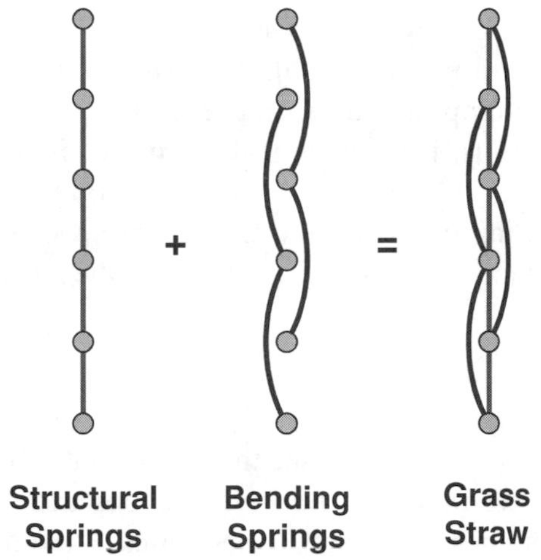

Figure 8.15: A simple grass straw mass-spring model.

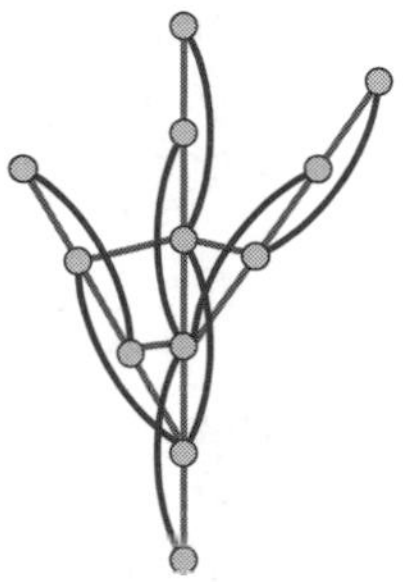

Figure 8.16: A simple tree mass-spring model. Notice springs between branches and trunk.

adding small texture maps (also known as billboards) attached to particles.

8.4.4 Pressure Forces

Pressure forces are based on traditional thermodynamics, and they can by used to model balloonlike objects, which are often called *pressure soft bodies* [Matyka et al., 2003]. Such objects allow for interesting effects such as inflation, or creating fluffy looking deformable objects, as shown in Figure 8.18.

Initially, a particle system based on a watertight two-manifold is set up; for instance, by creating surface springs using the method for unstructured meshes outlined in Section 8.4.1.

From physics, it is given that the norm of a pressure force $\boldsymbol{F}$ acting on a surface is given as the pressure, P, divided by the area, A, of the surface, that is,

$$\|\boldsymbol{F}\|_2 = \frac{P}{A}. \tag{8.25}$$

The direction is given by the normal, $\boldsymbol{n}$, of the surface, that is, $\boldsymbol{F} = (P/A)\boldsymbol{n}$.

We will assume that the pressure inside the object is evenly distributed, which is a good assumption for *systems in equilibrium*. The assumption implies that each face on the surface of the unstructured mesh is subject to the same pressure. Thus, if the area of the i'th face is A_i, then the magnitude of the force acting on that face is given by P/A_i. However, our particles correspond to the vertices of the mesh, so in order to distribute the force acting on the face to the vertices, we assume that the face force is evenly distributed to each vertex of the face. Thus, for C_i vertices on the face, for the j'th vertex of the face the force $\boldsymbol{f}_j$ is added

$$\boldsymbol{f}_j = \boldsymbol{n}_j \frac{P}{A_i C_i}, \tag{8.26}$$

where $\boldsymbol{n}_j$ is the normal of the vertex. Of course, this is not entirely physically accurate, but for fine tessellated objects with good aspect ratio, i.e., no slivers or obscured triangles, this is a fairly good approximation. In practice the error does not affect the aesthetics of the motion, and a plausible balloonlike effect is easily achieved.

The only problem with the approach so far is that the value of P is unknown. Letting P be user specified allows the user to control the pressure forces by altering the value of P directly. But such an approach cannot model the effect of an increasing internal pressure as an object gets squeezed, nor can it model the falling internal pressure of an extended object. This implies that we need to consider the change in volume of the object. Fortunately, the *Ideal Gas Law*

$$PV = nRT, \tag{8.27}$$

may be used for just that. The constant R is known as the *gas constant*, n is the number of molar of gas proportional to the number of molecules of gas, T is the temperature, and V is the volume of the gas. The ideal gas law can be used to compute the internal pressure inside the object: first, the current volume of the object is computed and then the pressure is found as

$$P = \frac{nRT}{V}. \tag{8.28}$$

For animation purposes it is impractical to specify n and R; instead it is easier to specify an initial internal pressure P_{initial}, and then compute

$$c_{\text{nRT}} = P_{\text{initial}} V_{\text{initial}}, \tag{8.29}$$

where V_{initial} is the initial volume. Having computed the constant c_{nRT}, the pressure can now be computed as

$$P = \frac{c_{\text{nRT}}}{V}. \tag{8.30}$$

This approach also allows an easy way to interact with the pressure forces. Letting the user change P_{initial} over the course of animation, and then recomputing the constant c_{nRT} yields an easy and intuitive way of controlling inflation and deflation of the object.

Figure 8.17 illustrates the pressure force computations in pseudocode.

```
algorithm apply-pressure-force(mesh)
  V = volume(mesh)
  P =  nRT / V
  update(normals(mesh))
  for each face F in mesh do
    C = count(vertices(F))
    A = area(F)
    f = P/ A C
    for each vertex v in F do
      let n be normal of v
      force(v) = force(v) + f*n
    next v
  next F
end algorithm
```

Figure 8.17: Pressure force computations.

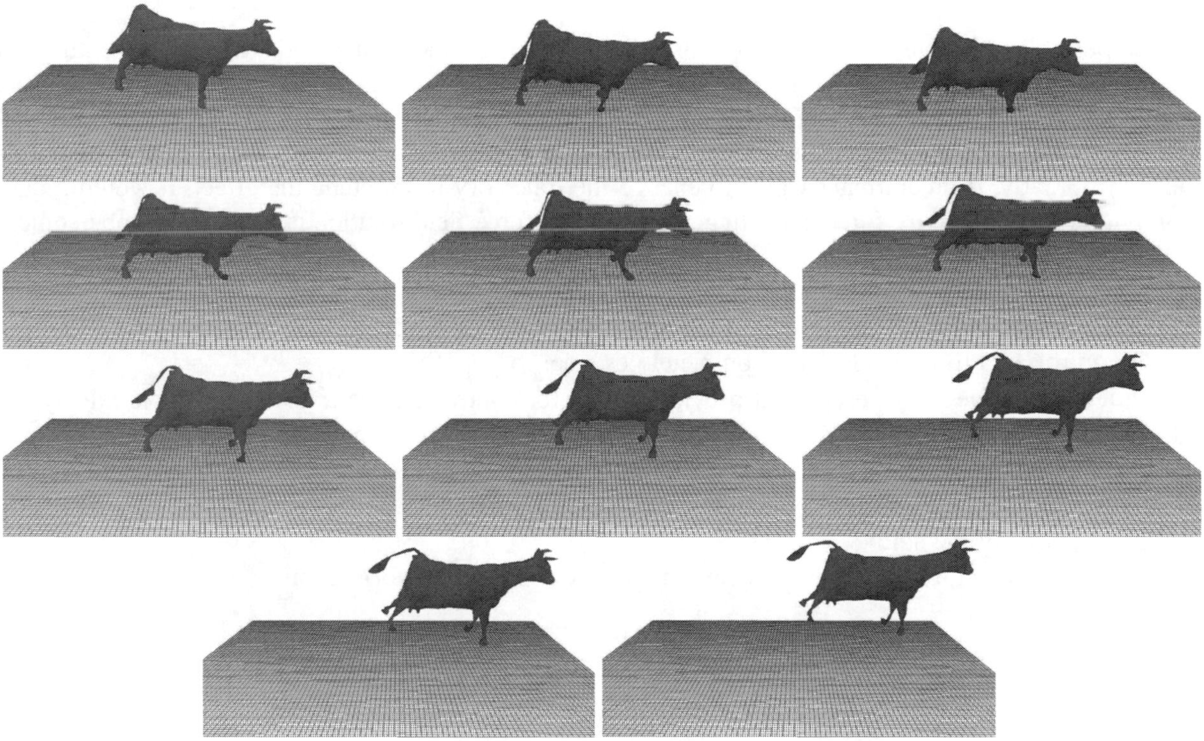

Figure 8.18: Cow falling under gravity while being inflated.

8.4.5 Force Fields

The last type of force example we will present is based on interpolation. A flow field of either forces or velocities can be computed offline, and sampled on some grid structure or other spatial arrangement. Particles are then let loose, and during simulation their spatial positions are used to look up their position in a grid arrangement. Hereafter, the flow-field values are interpolated and applied to the particle. This was used in [Rasmussen et al., 2003] to create large scale effects, such as nuclear explosions in a movie production.

8.4.6 Spline-Trajectory Controlled Particle System

In some cases, one wants to plan how force fields lie in space to give an overall control of the *particle trajectories*. Imagine some kind of animation effect of smoke or fire traveling though a building; that is, going through one door, turning around a corner, moving along the ceiling, and out through another door. We have a general idea of the average particle trajectory, which is a completely planned motion. The fine details and perhaps turbulent behavior of the particulates should be dynamically simulated as the particles move along the trajectory. This is feasible because if the trajectory goes through some obstacle, such as a chair or table, then we want particles to interact in a physically plausible way with the obstacles but still keep on track.

One possible solution is to use a huge force field sampled on a regular grid, wherein the entire configuration, i.e., the whole building, is contained. However, this is not a good choice: first, it is infeasible, since it will require a huge amount of memory to store the samples. Second, it would be computationally disadvantageous to initialize the force field with values, such that particles would follow a predefined trajectory. Finally, if an animator wants to change the trajectory to fine tune the effect, it would require recomputation of the entire force field. In conclusion, the force field solution is slow and cumbersome to work with in this case.

Another solution is to insert attraction and repulsive force field on some algebraic form to control the particle trajectory. However, in practice it requires a lot of tuning to receive the wanted effect, there is no explicit control, and the particles may completely escape.

The technique we will present next provides a tool for controlling the trajectory of a particle system in the way we just described. The method is inspired by the work in [Rasmussen et al., 2003].

Let the trajectory be defined by a *B-spline* as described in Chapter 24 (other spline types could be used, but we favor B-splines). Then the animator can easily control and change the trajectory by manipulating the control points of the spline.

Given a spline parameter u, one can compute the corresponding world point $\boldsymbol{p}(u)$ by

$$\boldsymbol{p}(u) = \sum_{i=0}^{n} N_{i,K}(u)\boldsymbol{P}_i \tag{8.31}$$

where $N_{i,K}$ is the i'th basis function of K'th order and $\boldsymbol{P}_i$ is the i'th control point. There is a total of $n+1$ control points. The evaluation of the spline point shown here is not very efficient but it is sufficient to give intuition behind the described method. Efficient spline implementation is outlined in Chapter 24.

For simplicity, we will assume that the spline is a sufficient *regular spline*. That is, we assume that it has no cusps and that the first- and second-order derivatives, the tangent and normal vectors, are always nonzero. It is thus possible to assign an intrinsic coordinate frame to each point, u, along the spline in a unique and well-defined way. First, we compute the tangent vector, $\boldsymbol{t}(u)$, by straightforward differentiation of (8.31), thus

$$\boldsymbol{t}(u) = \sum_{i=0}^{n} \frac{dN_{i,K}(u)}{du} \boldsymbol{P}_i \tag{8.32}$$

The normal vector $\boldsymbol{n}(u)$ is then given by

$$\boldsymbol{n}(u) = \sum_{i=0}^{n} \frac{d^2 N_{i,K}(u)}{du^2} \boldsymbol{P}_i \tag{8.33}$$

The cross product yields the binormal vector $\boldsymbol{b}(u)$. The vectors $\boldsymbol{t}(u)$, $\boldsymbol{n}(u)$, and $\boldsymbol{b}(u)$, are generally not unit vectors unless the spline-parameter u is identical to the arc length. Therefore, we perform a normalization of the three vectors. We now have three linear-independent vectors, all orthogonal to each other; thus normalization yields an orthonormal basis,

$$\boldsymbol{F}(u) = \begin{bmatrix} \frac{\boldsymbol{t}(u)}{\|\boldsymbol{t}(u)\|_2} & \frac{\boldsymbol{n}(u)}{\|\boldsymbol{n}(u)\|_2} & \frac{\boldsymbol{b}(u)}{\|\boldsymbol{b}(u)\|_2} \end{bmatrix} \tag{8.34}$$

$$= \begin{bmatrix} \boldsymbol{x}(u) & \boldsymbol{y}(u) & \boldsymbol{z}(u) \end{bmatrix} \tag{8.35}$$

where we have introduced the shorthand notation $\boldsymbol{x}(u)$, $\boldsymbol{y}(u)$, and $\boldsymbol{z}(u)$ for the unit axis coordinate vectors. The coordinate frame $\boldsymbol{F}$ is also known as the *Frenet frame*. The spline can thus be seen as a rotational warp of the initial Frenet frame $\boldsymbol{F}(0)$. At time point u, along the spline the frame will have orientation $\boldsymbol{F}(u)$ and origin will have been translated to $\boldsymbol{p}(u)$. The particles will live in this strange coordinate system whenever the forces applied to the particles need to be evaluated.

Say a particle is located at some world coordinate position $\boldsymbol{r}_{\text{wcs}}(t)$, where t denotes the current time. The closest point on the spline is found, $\boldsymbol{p}(u)$, and the world coordinate position is transformed into the warped spline coordinate frame by the coordinate transform

$$\boldsymbol{r}_{\text{spline}}(t) = \boldsymbol{F}(u)^T \left(\boldsymbol{r}_{\text{wcs}}(t) - \boldsymbol{p}(u).\right) \tag{8.36}$$

Notice that if $\boldsymbol{p}(u)$ is truly the closest point on the spline, then $\boldsymbol{r}_{\text{spline}}(t)$ should have a component along the $\boldsymbol{t}$-axis of $\boldsymbol{F}(u)$.

We place 2D grids at each distinct knot-value of the spline. This is equivalent to placing the 2D grid at the data points of the spline. This is illustrated in 2D in Figure 8.19. The grids are placed such that the spline goes through the center of the grid. The x-axis and y-axis of the grid are aligned with the n-axis and b-axis of the Frenet frame at the spline point where the grid is located. The general idea is to find the two 2D grids, where the particle lies in between, as shown in Figure 8.20. It is a rather trivial task to find these grids, once the closest point on the spline has been determined. If the closest point corresponds to spline-parameter value u, then the grid lying before is located at the largest knot-value u_-, such that $u_- < u$. Similarly, the grid lying after the particle is located at the smallest knot-value u_+, where $u_+ > u$.

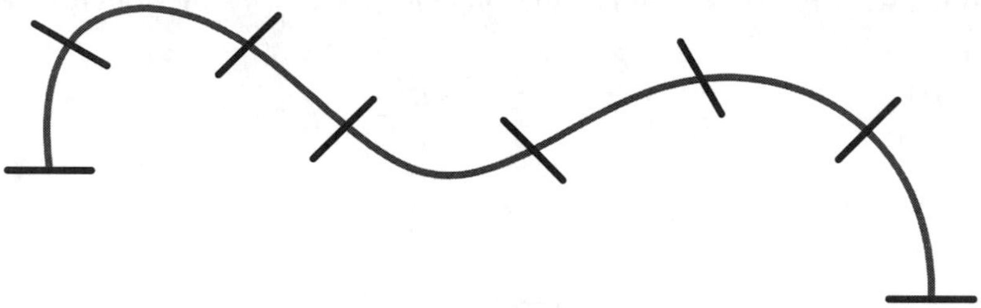

Figure 8.19: 2D grids places at distinct knot values.

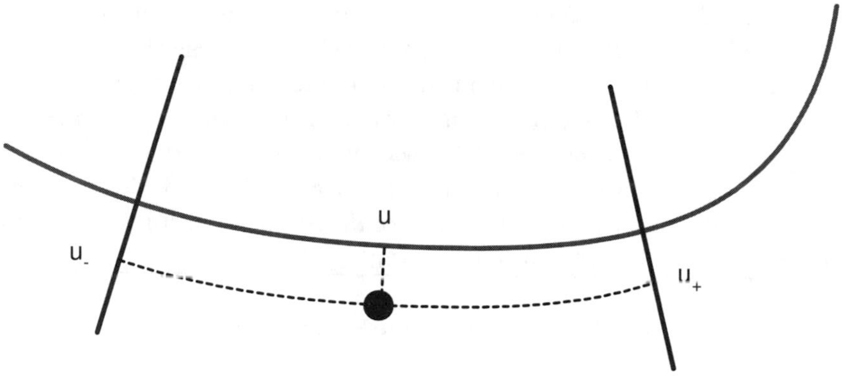

Figure 8.20: A particle with closest point on spline at u is located between two grids at position u_- and u_+.

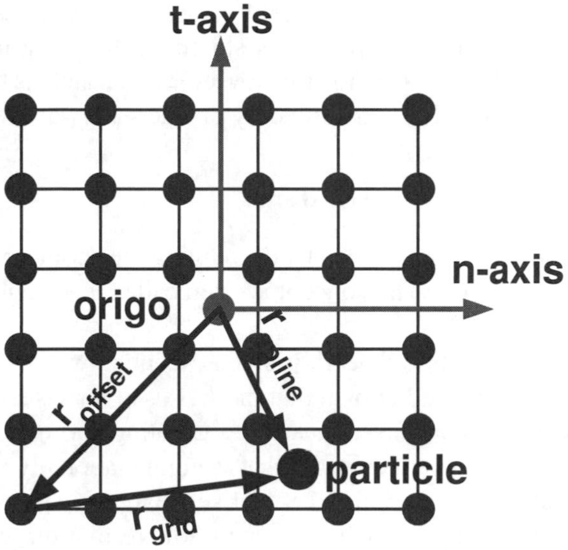

Figure 8.21: Illustration showing how particle positions are mapped onto a 2D grid, using the Frenet frame. Observe that the spline goes through the center of the grid. Grid node with indices (0,0) is therefore offset by $\boldsymbol{r}_{\text{offset}}$.

Next, we map the particle position onto the two grids using the Frenet frame axes. Figure 8.21 illustrates the coordinate mapping process.

First, we must account for the spline going through the midpoint of the 2D grid, a priori this offset, $\boldsymbol{r}_{\text{offset}}$ is known, therefore we get the particle position with respect to the smallest grid node by

$$\boldsymbol{r}_{\text{grid}} = \boldsymbol{r}_{\text{spline}} - \boldsymbol{r}_{\text{offset}} \tag{8.37}$$

Hereafter, we project $\boldsymbol{r}_{\text{grid}}$ onto the normal and binormal axis. If the grid resolution along the axes is given by Δy and Δz, then the particle is located in the grid cell given by indices

$$y = \left\lfloor \frac{\boldsymbol{y} \cdot \boldsymbol{r}_{\text{grid}}}{\Delta y} \right\rfloor \tag{8.38}$$

$$z = \left\lfloor \frac{\boldsymbol{z} \cdot \boldsymbol{r}_{\text{grid}}}{\Delta z} \right\rfloor \tag{8.39}$$

Knowing the cell indices, it is trivial to perform a *bilinear interpolation* of the values stored in the four corner nodes of the cell, which the particle is mapped into. Thus, we now have two grid-interpolated values $f(u_-)$ and $f(u_+)$, the value at the particle position can now be found by a linear interpolation of the found grid values, that is,

$$f(u) = \frac{u_+ - u}{u_+ - u_-} f(u_-) + \frac{u - u_-}{u_+ - u_-} f(u_+). \tag{8.40}$$

The technique can be used to define any kind of field values. In the example we used to derive our equations, we simply assumed that a scalar field was stored in the 2D grids placed along the spline. However, the formulas are identical if we were to store a vector field, such as the force field. The 2D grids could be placed at other positions than those identified by distinct knot values of the spline.

8.4.7 Free-Form Deformation Particle System

Sometimes increased performance can be obtained by decoupling the geometry used for visualization from the dynamics model used for simulation. The concept is often called *mesh coupling* [Müller et al., 2004a] or a *cartoon mesh* [Hauser et al., 2003].

Most of the modeling techniques described in previous sections were based on creating springs directly from a given surface mesh. It is well known that meshes used for visualization have a large number of triangular faces—millions of faces are not unheard of. Creating springs for a particle system resembling such a large mesh will yield a dynamic model that is computationally intractable for real time and even interactive usage. Fortunately, it is possible to render such large meshes very efficiently using graphics hardware. Therefore, it is a viable approach to create a low-resolution dynamics/physical model for computing deformations in a physical plausible way, and then apply the computed deformation to the high-resolution mesh, which should be used for visualization. Another benefit from mesh coupling is that the problem of error-prone meshes mentioned earlier can be circumvented rather elegantly, as we will illustrate in the following.

We will demonstrate a method based on *free-form deformations* (*FFD*). Free-form deformation is one of the early techniques in computer graphics [Sederberg et al., 1986] for animating deformations. Here we will briefly present the general idea.

Initially we will set up a *B-spline tensor*, i.e., a 3D array of control points, where $\boldsymbol{P}_{i,j,k}$ denotes the (i, j, k)'th element of the array, and the B-spline basis functions $N_{i,K}(s)$, $N_{j,K}(t)$, and $N_{k,K}(u)$, where K is the order of the spline, and the indices i, j, and k indicate the beginning of the knot-interval where the spline is evaluated (is dependent on). See Appendix 24 for an introduction to B-splines.

Then the point, $\boldsymbol{p}$, corresponding to the spline parameters s, t, and u in the spline tensor is computed as

$$\boldsymbol{p}(s,t,u) = \sum_{k=0}^{n_k}\sum_{j=0}^{n_j}\sum_{i=0}^{n_i} N_{i,K}(s)N_{j,K}(t)N_{k,K}(u)\boldsymbol{P}_{i,j,k}, \tag{8.41}$$

where $n_i + 1$, $n_j + 1$, and $n_k + 1$ is the number of control points along the i-, j-, and k-axes. Exploiting the fact that the basis function is only evaluated on a finite support of the *knot vector* leads to efficient implementations (see [Hoschek et al., 1993, Piegl et al., 1995] for details). In the case of B-splines, the basis functions are polynomials of order K, (8.41) and are simply a weighted sum of vectors, where the weights are given by polynomials.

The control point array is set up so that all control points lie in a 3D rectangular grid, axes aligned with the world coordinate frame. It is trivial to see that in case of B-splines, keeping two parameters fixed while varying the last yields straight orthogonal lines aligned with the world coordinate system.

Picking a uniform knot vector in this initial position, the world coordinate system and the spline parameter space are in perfect alignment, except for a shifting, given by the value of the control point

```
Algorithm init(Mesh mesh)
  P = new vector3[n_i+1][n_j+1][n_k+1]
  p_ min = vector3(-infty,-infty,-infty)
  p_max = - p_min
  for each vertex v in mesh
    p_min = min(p_min, v.position)
    p_max = max(p_max, v.position)
  next v
  p_min = p_min - vector3(border,border,border)
  di = (p_max_i - p_min_i) / n_i
  dj = (p_max_j - p_min_j) / n_j
  dk = (p_max_k - p_min_k) / n_k
  P[0][0][0] = p_min
  for(int k=0;k<=n_k;++k)
    for(int j=0;j<=n_j;++j)
      for(int i=0;i<=n_i;++i)
        P[i][j][k] = P[0][0][0] + vector3(i*di,j*dj,k*dk);
  for each vertex v in mesh
    v.parameter = v.position - P[0][0][0]
  next v
End algorithm
```

Figure 8.22: Initialization of control point grid and mapping of mesh vertices into spline parameter space.

with lowest coordinates. This means that mesh vertices are easily mapped into the spline parameter space by storing the original value of the vertex positions minus the minimum coordinate control point. During simulation the control point positions are altered, whereby the spline parameter space is warped. The coupled mesh can be reevaluated by using the original vertex position as spline parameters in (8.41). The computed position is then used when rendering the mesh.

Figures 8.22 and 8.23 illustrate the initialization process and rendering process of FFD mesh coupling. The figures are oversimplified to show the main concepts clearly. In practice, any kind of splines and knot vector could be used; it will only complicate the initial mapping of mesh vertices into the spline parameter space. Also the reevaluation of mesh vertex positions could be implemented far more efficiently than the brute-force evaluation we have outlined here.

We will now explain how to create a dynamic model for simulation using the FFD grid. A particle is created at each control point in the array. The array partitions a region of space into cubes, such that the cube labeled by (i, j, k) consists of particles: (i, j, k), $(i+1, j, k)$, $(i, j+1, k)$, $(i+1, j+1, k)$, $(i, j, k+1)$, $(i+1, j, k+1)$, $(i, j+1, k+1)$, and $(i+1, j+1, k+1)$. When assigning mass value to particle (i, j, k), look up the number of vertices from the mesh mapped into the eight neighboring cubes given by the labels $(i-1, j-1, k)$, $(i-1, j, k)$, $(i, j-1, k)$, (i, j, k), $(i-1, j-1, k+1)$, $(i-1, j, k+1)$, $(i, j-1, k+1)$, and $(i, j, k+1)$. The mass of the particle is found by the total number of mesh vertices in the neighboring cubes divided by eight and multiplied by some user-specified density value. Pseudocode for calculating the particle masses is given in Figure 8.24. Next, structural, shearing, and bending springs are created between the control point particles. The details of such a spring creation method were explained in Section 8.4.2.

```
Algorithm show-mesh(Mesh mesh)
  for each vertex v in mesh
    s = v.parameter.s
    t = v.parameter.t
    u = v.parameter.u
    v.position =  sum_k sum_j sum_i N_iK(s) N_jK(t) N_kK(u) P[i,j,k]
  next v
  draw mesh
end algorithm
```

Figure 8.23: Evaluation of vertex positions before drawing coupled mesh.

```
algorithm mass-assignment(density)
  for each particle p in system
    i,j,k = index of p
    C1 = cube[i-1,j-1,k]
    C2 = cube[i-1,j,k]
    C3 = cube[i,j-1,k]
    C4 = cube[i,j,k]
    C5 = cube[i-1,j-1,k+1]
    C6 = cube[i-1,j,k+1]
    C7 = cube[i,j-1,k+1]
    C8 = cube[i,j,k+1]
    mass(p) = density* (vertices(C1)+...+vertex(C8))/8
  next p
end algorithm
```

Figure 8.24: Mass computation of particles

We now essentially have a physical model, consisting of the control point particles interconnected with springs. We can subject the particles to any external forces, whereby the control point particles will move and deform the spline parameter space. After the simulation, the coupled mesh vertices are reevaluated using the deformed control points, and the coupled mesh is redrawn.

Essentially we can choose two ways in which the FFD particle system can interact with the surroundings: either the collision detection or response is applied directly to the control point particles.

This is a simple and straightforward solution. It lends itself to a simple particle system implementation since there is only a one-way communication with the coupled mesh, i.e., there is no feedback from the coupled mesh to the FFD particle system. The coupled mesh is completely dependent on the FFD particles. This solution also poses a performance advantage since the count of control point particles is expected to be extremely low compared with the number of vertices in the coupled mesh.

On the downside, the interactions can appear quite unrealistic, since the grid of FFD particles has nothing in common with the deforming geometry of the coupled mesh, except that we know the convex hull of the control points encloses the underlying geometry.

To create a more plausible interaction with the surroundings, we need two-way communications between the coupled mesh and the FFD particles. This can be accomplished by performing collision detection between the deforming coupled mesh and the environment. This will generate a set of contact points (see Chapter 14 for details on contact determination) between the coupled mesh and some other obstacles in the configuration.

Here we will assume that an arbitrary simulation method is used to compute collision impulses or contact forces that should be applied at the contact point in order to prevent penetration, and thereby cause a deformation.

To keep things simple at this point, we will simply perform penetration tests between the coupled mesh vertices and other obstacles. This means that a generated contact point will have the same position in world space as a deformed mesh vertex.

We can thus remap the contact point into the spline parameter space by looking up the spline parameters of the deformed vertex. The spline parameters will indicate the cube in the FFD grid which the deformed mesh vertex was originally mapped into. Thus, we have the idea of performing a reverse interpolation for finding equivalent contact forces/impulses to apply at the corner control point particles of that cube.

From Newton's second law we know forces obey the superposition principle, which means that given the contact force, $\boldsymbol{F}$ applied at the deformed vertex position $\boldsymbol{r}$, then

$$\boldsymbol{F} = \boldsymbol{f}_1 + \cdots + \boldsymbol{f}_8 \tag{8.42}$$

where $\boldsymbol{f}_i$ is the force applied to the i'th particle. In addition, it seems reasonable to require some balance of torque, thus

$$\boldsymbol{r} \times \boldsymbol{F} = \boldsymbol{r}_1 \times \boldsymbol{f}_1 + \cdots + \boldsymbol{r}_8 \times \boldsymbol{f}_8 \tag{8.43}$$

where $\boldsymbol{r}_i$ is the current position of the i'th control point particle. These two equations thus define two requirements for an inverse interpolation. We need to determine the particle forces.

Using the skew-symmetric *cross product matrix* defined in Theorem 18.4, this yields a system of equations

$$\underbrace{\begin{bmatrix} \boldsymbol{I} & \boldsymbol{I} & \boldsymbol{I} & \boldsymbol{I} & \boldsymbol{I} & \boldsymbol{I} & \boldsymbol{I} & \boldsymbol{I} \\ \boldsymbol{r}_1{}^{\times} & \boldsymbol{r}_2{}^{\times} & \boldsymbol{r}_3{}^{\times} & \boldsymbol{r}_4{}^{\times} & \boldsymbol{r}_5{}^{\times} & \boldsymbol{r}_6{}^{\times} & \boldsymbol{r}_7{}^{\times} & \boldsymbol{r}_8{}^{\times} \end{bmatrix}}_{\boldsymbol{A}} \underbrace{\begin{bmatrix} \boldsymbol{f}_1 \\ \boldsymbol{f}_2 \\ \boldsymbol{f}_3 \\ \boldsymbol{f}_4 \\ \boldsymbol{f}_5 \\ \boldsymbol{f}_6 \\ \boldsymbol{f}_7 \\ \boldsymbol{f}_8 \end{bmatrix}}_{\boldsymbol{f}} = \underbrace{\begin{bmatrix} \boldsymbol{F} \\ \boldsymbol{r} \times \boldsymbol{F} \end{bmatrix}}_{\boldsymbol{b}} \tag{8.44}$$

$$\boldsymbol{A}\boldsymbol{f} = \boldsymbol{b} \tag{8.45}$$

Notice that $\boldsymbol{A} \in \mathbf{R}^{6\times 24}$, $\boldsymbol{f} \in \mathbf{R}^{24\times 1}$, and $\boldsymbol{b} \in \mathbf{R}^{6\times 1}$, thus we have more unknowns than equations, and the system is underdetermined In general, this means that we have more than one solution to our problem and as a practical consequence $\boldsymbol{A}$ cannot be inverted. To circumvent these difficulties, we can simply

```
algorithm reverse-interpolation(di,dj,dk)
  clear forces
  for each contact point cp
    v = corresponding vertex of cp
    s,t,u = v.parameters
    i,j,k = s/di, t/dj u/dk

    p1 = particle[i,j,k]
    p2 = particle[i+1,j,k]
    ...
    p8 = particle[i+1,j+1,k+1]

    solve for f1,..., f8

    add f1 to p1
    ...
    add f8 to p8
  next cp
end algorithm
```

Figure 8.25: Applying contact forces from coupled mesh to FFD particles.

use a *singular value decomposition* (*SVD*) solution or *pseudoinverse* of $\boldsymbol{A}$ to obtain the *minimum norm solution*.

An SVD decomposition of $\boldsymbol{A}$ yields $\boldsymbol{A} = \boldsymbol{U}\boldsymbol{D}\boldsymbol{V}^T$, where $\boldsymbol{D}$ is a diagonal square matrix with singular values in the diagonal. The matrices $\boldsymbol{U}$ and $\boldsymbol{V}$ are orthogonal in the sense that their columns are orthonormal. A minimum norm solution to the problem is then given by

$$\boldsymbol{f} = \boldsymbol{V}\boldsymbol{D}^{-1}\left(\boldsymbol{U}^T\boldsymbol{b}\right) \tag{8.46}$$

The solution minimizes the norm of the residual $\boldsymbol{r} = \boldsymbol{A}\boldsymbol{f} - \boldsymbol{b}$ (see [Press et al., 1999b] for more details on SVD. Figure 8.25 illustrates the force computation).

Control-point particle collision impulses $\boldsymbol{j}_1, \ldots \boldsymbol{j}_8$ can be computed in a similar fashion given some simulation methods, which can compute the impulse $\boldsymbol{J}$ to apply at the contact points. The main difference from the contact force computation is that impulses instantaneously change the velocities at the particles they are applied at, whereas contact forces are accumulated into a force vector, which is used in a numerical integration scheme.

8.5 Energy Systems

Forces are the handles for controlling the behavior of a particle system. Many forces are easily adapted from physics to a specific animation system, such as gravity, viscosity, and spring forces. Nevertheless, animation systems often have other forces that are not based on reality, but are added for convenience. As an example, if a particle is not allowed to penetrate an object, then a force field is often applied around the object. For example, a force field around a sphere could be produced by an *energy* or *potential function*, such as

$$E(\boldsymbol{r}) = \|\boldsymbol{r} - \boldsymbol{r}_0\|_2 - R \tag{8.47a}$$

$$= \sqrt{(\boldsymbol{r} - \boldsymbol{r}_0) \cdot (\boldsymbol{r} - \boldsymbol{r}_0)} - R, \tag{8.47b}$$

where $\boldsymbol{r}_0$ is the center of the sphere, and R is its radius. The *implicit function* E is positive outside and negative inside the sphere. The gradient of E may be used to define the direction of the repulsive force,

$$\frac{\partial E(\boldsymbol{r})}{\partial \boldsymbol{r}} = \frac{2(\boldsymbol{r} - \boldsymbol{r}_0)}{2\sqrt{(\boldsymbol{r} - \boldsymbol{r}_0) \cdot (\boldsymbol{r} - \boldsymbol{r}_0)}} \tag{8.48a}$$

$$= \frac{\boldsymbol{r} - \boldsymbol{r}_0}{\sqrt{(\boldsymbol{r} - \boldsymbol{r}_0) \cdot (\boldsymbol{r} - \boldsymbol{r}_0)}} \tag{8.48b}$$

since it always points away from the center of the sphere and has length 1,

$$\left\| \frac{\partial E(\boldsymbol{r})}{\partial \boldsymbol{r}} \right\|_2^2 = \left\| \frac{\boldsymbol{r} - \boldsymbol{r}_0}{\sqrt{(\boldsymbol{r} - \boldsymbol{r}_0) \cdot (\boldsymbol{r} - \boldsymbol{r}_0)}} \right\|_2^2 \tag{8.49a}$$

$$= \frac{\boldsymbol{r} - \boldsymbol{r}_0}{\sqrt{(\boldsymbol{r} - \boldsymbol{r}_0) \cdot (\boldsymbol{r} - \boldsymbol{r}_0)}} \cdot \frac{\boldsymbol{r} - \boldsymbol{r}_0}{\sqrt{(\boldsymbol{r} - \boldsymbol{r}_0) \cdot (\boldsymbol{r} - \boldsymbol{r}_0)}} \tag{8.49b}$$

$$= 1. \tag{8.49c}$$

Having a repulsive force in all of space is typically not useful and the repulsive force is therefore often made strong only near the object. This may be done as

$$\boldsymbol{f}_{\text{sphere},\boldsymbol{r}_0}(\boldsymbol{r}) = c e^{-\max(0, E(\boldsymbol{r})/\sigma)} \frac{\partial E(\boldsymbol{r})}{\partial \boldsymbol{r}}, \tag{8.50}$$

where c and σ are constants to control the strength and the width of the repulsive field. In this example, we have used a clamped exponential force, such that the force field diminishes quickly away from the surface, and such that the maximum force is limited to avoid stiff ordinary differential equations. An example is shown in Figure 8.26.

As illustrated in the above example, forces may be designed as gradients of energy, potential, or *penalty functions*. Such vector fields are also known as potential fields. The potential function for Hooke's undamped spring law for two particles at position $\boldsymbol{a}$ and $\boldsymbol{b}$, is given by

$$E_{ab} = \frac{1}{2} k_s (|\boldsymbol{l}| - R)^2, \tag{8.51}$$

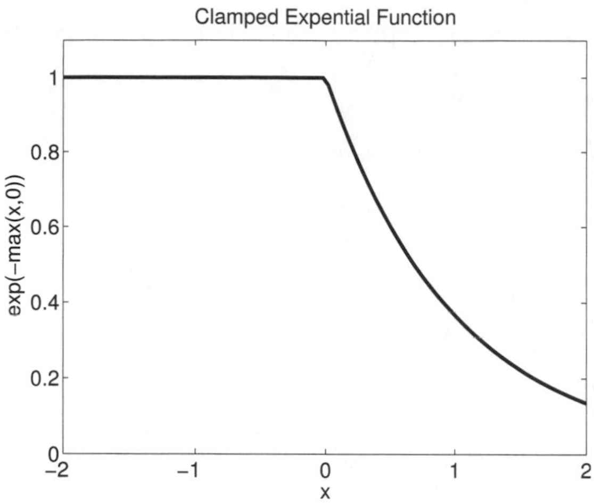

Figure 8.26: An often-used strength for a repulsive force is the clamped exponential function.

Distance preservation	$E_{ab} = \frac{1}{2}k_s \left(\left\|\boldsymbol{r}_b - \boldsymbol{r}_a\right\|_2 - R\right)^2$
Area preservation	$E_{abc} = \frac{1}{2}k_a \left(\left\|(\boldsymbol{r}_b - \boldsymbol{r}_a) \times (\boldsymbol{r}_c - \boldsymbol{r}_a)\right\|_2 - A\right)^2$
Volume preservation	$E_{abcd} = \frac{1}{2}k_a \left(\det([\boldsymbol{r}_b - \boldsymbol{r}_a \vert \boldsymbol{r}_c - \boldsymbol{r}_a \vert \boldsymbol{r}_d - \boldsymbol{r}_a]) - V\right)^2$

Table 8.1: Distance-, area-, and volume-preserving energy systems.

where, $\boldsymbol{l} = \boldsymbol{r}_b - \boldsymbol{r}_a$. This is easily verified by calculating the gradients of E_{ab} with respect to $\boldsymbol{r}_a$:

$$\boldsymbol{f}_a = -\frac{\partial E_{ab}}{\partial \boldsymbol{r}_a} \tag{8.52a}$$

$$= -k_s(|\boldsymbol{l}| - R)\,\frac{\partial(|\boldsymbol{l}| - R)}{\partial \boldsymbol{r}_a} \tag{8.52b}$$

$$= -k_s(|\boldsymbol{l}| - R)\,\frac{-2\boldsymbol{r}_b + 2\boldsymbol{r}_a}{2|\boldsymbol{l}|} \tag{8.52c}$$

$$= k_s(|\boldsymbol{l}| - R)\frac{\boldsymbol{l}}{|\boldsymbol{l}|}, \tag{8.52d}$$

and with a similar calculation for $\boldsymbol{r}_b$. Hooke's Law may be viewed as a distance-preserving energy function. Area and volume-preserving energy functions may be defined in a similar way [Teschner et al., 2004], as summarized in Table 8.1. In the table reference, lengths, areas, and volumes are given as R, A, and V, for the corresponding parallelograms. In case the reference areas and volumes are given as triangular area and tetrahedral volume, then the norms should be divided by the factors $\frac{1}{2}$ and $\frac{1}{6}$ respectively.

8.6 Constraint Dynamics

Stiffness constraints are difficult to integrate in Euler methods with springs, since these lead to stiff ordinary differential equations. However, there is a special case when $k_s \to \infty$, which may be solved directly. Use

$$\boldsymbol{l}(t) = \boldsymbol{r}_b(t) - \boldsymbol{r}_a(t) \tag{8.53a}$$

$$\Delta l(t) = |\boldsymbol{l}(t)| - r. \tag{8.53b}$$

Since the Δl is antisymmetric in $\boldsymbol{r}_a$ and $\boldsymbol{r}_b$, solving for $\Delta l(t+h) = 0$ implies that

$$\boldsymbol{r}_a(t+h) = \frac{\Delta l}{2} \frac{\boldsymbol{l}}{|\boldsymbol{l}|} \tag{8.54a}$$

$$\boldsymbol{r}_b(t+h) = -\frac{\Delta l}{2} \frac{\boldsymbol{l}}{|\boldsymbol{l}|}. \tag{8.54b}$$

Iterating over all the stiff springs and applying (8.54) until only minor changes are performed is termed *relaxation*. Using Verlet integration together with relaxation and projection for nonpenetration is beneficial because velocities are represented implicitly in the Verlet integration method. The implication is that when positions are altered by relaxation or projection, then velocities are implicitly modified to match the enforced constraints [Jakobsen, 2001].

In general, *hard constraints* can be enforced by adding constraint forces. In the following, we will discuss a general energy function, which is given as an implicit function $E(\boldsymbol{r})$, for which the constraints are fulfilled for all positions $\boldsymbol{r}'$ where $E(\boldsymbol{r}') = 0$. Points on a unit sphere centered at the origin, $E(\boldsymbol{r}) = \frac{1}{2}(\boldsymbol{r} \cdot \boldsymbol{r} - 1)$ is an example. For points on the surface $\boldsymbol{r}'$, we have $E(\boldsymbol{r}') = 0$, and the velocities ensuring that $E = 0$ are found by requiring,

$$\frac{\partial}{\partial t} E = \boldsymbol{r} \cdot \frac{d\boldsymbol{r}}{dt} = 0. \tag{8.55}$$

Likewise, accelerations fulfilling the constraint must satisfy

$$\frac{\partial^2}{\partial t^2} E = \frac{d\boldsymbol{r}}{dt} \cdot \frac{d\boldsymbol{r}}{dt} + \boldsymbol{r} \cdot \frac{d^2\boldsymbol{r}}{dt^2} = 0. \tag{8.56}$$

An arbitrary force $\boldsymbol{f}$ will most likely not fulfill the above constraint, and we therefore seek a constraint force $\boldsymbol{\phi}$. We can add to $\boldsymbol{f}$ such that the constraint is fulfilled, that is,

$$\frac{d^2\boldsymbol{r}}{dt^2} = \frac{\boldsymbol{f} + \boldsymbol{\phi}}{m} \tag{8.57a}$$

$$\Rightarrow \frac{d\boldsymbol{r}}{dt} \cdot \frac{d\boldsymbol{r}}{dt} + \boldsymbol{r} \cdot \frac{\boldsymbol{f} + \boldsymbol{\phi}}{m} = 0 \tag{8.57b}$$

$$\Rightarrow \boldsymbol{r} \cdot \boldsymbol{\phi} = -m \frac{d\boldsymbol{r}}{dt} \cdot \frac{d\boldsymbol{r}}{dt} - \boldsymbol{r} \cdot \boldsymbol{f}. \tag{8.57c}$$

The dimensionality of ϕ is typically three, hence the above equation determines one out of three unknowns. To determine the remaining unknowns we require that the force neither add nor subtracts energy to the system. This is the *Principle of Virtual Work*. Given the kinetic energy as

$$T = \frac{1}{2} m \frac{d\boldsymbol{r}}{dt} \cdot \frac{d\boldsymbol{r}}{dt}, \tag{8.58}$$

the principle of virtual work requires that

$$\frac{\partial T}{\partial t} = m \frac{d\boldsymbol{r}}{dt} \cdot \frac{d^2\boldsymbol{r}}{dt^2} \tag{8.59a}$$

$$= \frac{d\boldsymbol{r}}{dt} \cdot (\boldsymbol{f} + \boldsymbol{\phi}) \tag{8.59b}$$

$$= \frac{d\boldsymbol{r}}{dt} \cdot \boldsymbol{f}. \tag{8.59c}$$

Hence,

$$\frac{d\boldsymbol{r}}{dt} \cdot \boldsymbol{\phi} = 0. \tag{8.60}$$

We now have two out of three unknowns for $\boldsymbol{\phi}$. The final equation is obtained by requiring that (8.60) must be satisfied for every $\frac{d\boldsymbol{r}}{dt}$ fulfilling (8.55), which leads us to conclude that $\boldsymbol{\phi}$ must be proportional to $\boldsymbol{r}$, that is,

$$\boldsymbol{\phi} = \lambda \boldsymbol{r}, \tag{8.61}$$

The Lagrange multiplier λ is found by inserting (8.61) into (8.57b), i.e.,

$$\frac{\partial^2}{\partial t^2} E = \frac{d\boldsymbol{r}}{dt} \cdot \frac{d\boldsymbol{r}}{dt} + \boldsymbol{r} \cdot \frac{d^2\boldsymbol{r}}{dt^2} \tag{8.62a}$$

$$= \frac{d\boldsymbol{r}}{dt} \cdot \frac{d\boldsymbol{r}}{dt} + \boldsymbol{r} \cdot \frac{\boldsymbol{f} + \boldsymbol{\phi}}{m} \tag{8.62b}$$

$$= \frac{d\boldsymbol{r}}{dt} \cdot \frac{d\boldsymbol{r}}{dt} + \boldsymbol{r} \cdot \frac{\boldsymbol{f} + \lambda \boldsymbol{r}}{m} \tag{8.62c}$$

$$= 0, \tag{8.62d}$$

and λ is found to be,

$$\lambda = \frac{-m \frac{d\boldsymbol{r}}{dt} \cdot \frac{d\boldsymbol{r}}{dt} - \boldsymbol{r} \cdot \boldsymbol{f}}{\boldsymbol{r} \cdot \boldsymbol{r}}. \tag{8.63}$$

For a system of particles, these equations generalize as follows: we generate a *state vector* as the concatenation of particle positions

$$\boldsymbol{q} = \begin{bmatrix} \boldsymbol{r}_1 \\ \boldsymbol{r}_2 \\ \vdots \\ \boldsymbol{r}_n \end{bmatrix}. \tag{8.64}$$

Newton's second law for the complete system can then be written as

$$F = M\ddot{q}, \tag{8.65}$$

where F is the concatenation of force according to (8.65) and the mass matrix M is diagonal on the form of $M = \mathrm{diag}(m_1, m_1, m_1, m_2, m_2, m_2, m_3, \ldots, m_n)$. Similarly to the single particle system, we form a global constraint vector function $C(q)$, such that the constraints are fulfilled, when

$$C(q) = \dot{C}(q) = 0. \tag{8.66}$$

By differentiation, we find that this is equivalent to

$$\dot{C}(q) = \frac{\partial C(q)}{\partial q}\dot{q} \tag{8.67a}$$

$$= J\dot{q}. \tag{8.67b}$$

The matrix J is called the *Jacobian* of C. Differentiation once more gives us

$$\ddot{C}(q) = \dot{J}\dot{q} + J\ddot{q} \tag{8.68a}$$

$$= \frac{\partial \dot{C}(q)}{\partial q}\dot{q} + \frac{\partial C(q)}{\partial q}\ddot{q}. \tag{8.68b}$$

Note that the calculation of $\dot{J}$ involves 3×3 dimensional matrix,

$$\dot{J} = \frac{\partial J}{\partial q}\dot{q} \tag{8.69}$$

but the evaluation of $\frac{\partial J}{\partial q}$ can be avoided by using an explicit representation for $\dot{C}$ as shown in (8.68b).

Now we will find a global constraint force Φ, which causes no work. Newton's second equation then becomes

$$\ddot{q} = M^{-1}(F + \Phi), \tag{8.70}$$

and as for (8.57b) we write

$$\ddot{C}(q) = \dot{J}\dot{q} + JM^{-1}(F + \Phi) = 0 \tag{8.71}$$

Using the principle of virtual work, we find the solution to the vector Φ by requiring that it must not contribute work. Writing the kinetic energy as

$$T = \frac{1}{2}\dot{q}^T M\dot{q}, \tag{8.72}$$

we find the work as the time derivative of the energy,

$$\dot{T} = \ddot{q}^T M\dot{q}, \tag{8.73a}$$

$$= \left(M^{-1}(F + \Phi)\right)^T M\dot{q}, \tag{8.73b}$$

$$= (F^T + \Phi^T)M^{-1^T} M\dot{q}, \tag{8.73c}$$

$$= (F^T + \Phi^T)M^{-1} M\dot{q}, \tag{8.73d}$$

$$= F^T\dot{q} + \Phi^T\dot{q}. \tag{8.73e}$$

```
Algorithm ParticleSystemStep(m,p,v,N,delta)
  // Calculate new forces
  for i = 0 to N
    f(i) = calculateForces(p,v,N)
  end
  // Calculate constraint forces
  for i = 0 to N
    c(i) = calculateConstraints(m,p,v,N)
  end
  // Calculate the velocity in phase-space
  for i = 0 to N
    dp = [v,(f+c)/m]
  end
  // Update the position in phase-space
  p = p+delta*dp
end algorithm
```

Figure 8.27: Explicit fixed time-stepping of a simple general-purpose particle system.

For $\boldsymbol{\Phi}$ not to contribute work, we thus require that

$$\boldsymbol{\Phi}^T \dot{\boldsymbol{q}} = 0. \tag{8.74}$$

For this to hold for any $\boldsymbol{q}$, and using (8.66) and (8.67b) we conclude that

$$\boldsymbol{\Phi} = \boldsymbol{J}^T \boldsymbol{\lambda}, \tag{8.75}$$

where $\boldsymbol{\lambda}$ is a vector of Langrangians. Inserting (8.75) into (8.71) we find

$$0 = \dot{\boldsymbol{J}}\dot{\boldsymbol{q}} + \boldsymbol{J}\boldsymbol{M}^{-1}(\boldsymbol{F} + \boldsymbol{\Phi}) \tag{8.76a}$$

$$= \dot{\boldsymbol{J}}\dot{\boldsymbol{q}} + \boldsymbol{J}\boldsymbol{M}^{-1}(\boldsymbol{F} + \boldsymbol{J}^T\boldsymbol{\lambda}) \tag{8.76b}$$

and with a simple rewrite we conclude that

$$\boldsymbol{J}\boldsymbol{M}^{-1}\boldsymbol{J}^T\boldsymbol{\lambda} = -\dot{\boldsymbol{J}}\dot{\boldsymbol{q}} - \boldsymbol{J}\boldsymbol{M}^{-1}\boldsymbol{F}. \tag{8.77}$$

Unfortunately, numerical implementations of (8.77) introduce drifts. It is therefore useful to add a damped spring force to the system

$$\boldsymbol{J}\boldsymbol{M}^{-1}\boldsymbol{J}^T\boldsymbol{\lambda} = -\dot{\boldsymbol{J}}\dot{\boldsymbol{q}} - \boldsymbol{J}\boldsymbol{M}^{-1}\boldsymbol{F} - k_s\boldsymbol{C} - k_d\dot{\boldsymbol{C}}, \tag{8.78}$$

for some suitable *spring* and *damping constants* k_s and k_d.

In [Baraff et al., 2003a] Witkin presents a simple algorithm simulating particle systems with constraints, which is sketched in Figure 8.27. The mass is given in `m`, the point phase space is `p`, the number of particles is `N`, and the magnitude of a single step in the ordinary integration is given by `delta`. The function `calculateForces(p,N)` calculates the forces for the specific system. For example, for a piece of cloth it could be the sum of spring forces for the nearest particles on the grid of the cloth, and `calculateConstraints(m,p,N)` calculates the relevant constraint forces, such as collision response with a sphere.

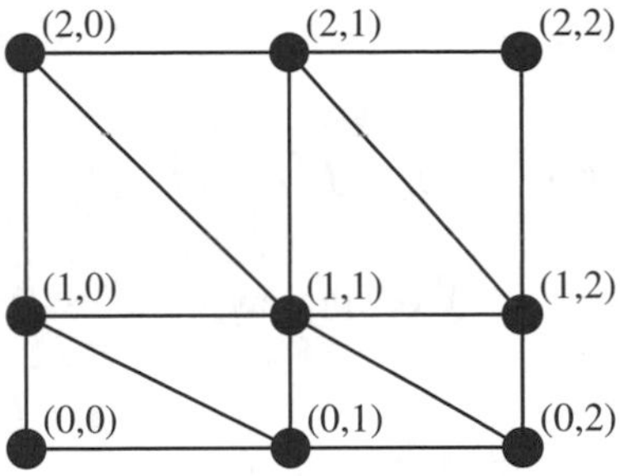

Figure 8.28: A piece of cloth is modeled as a grid of particles connected in triangular mesh. The coordinate pair denotes the particle index.

8.7 Large Steps in Cloth Simulation

In [Baraff et al., 1998] the authors present an implicit method for simulating cloth with a particle system. The basic setup is shown in Figure 8.28, where the particles are defined on a grid and connected in a *triangular mesh*. Defining the general position for the total system $\boldsymbol{r}$ as

$$\boldsymbol{r} = \begin{bmatrix} \boldsymbol{r}_1 \\ \boldsymbol{r}_2 \\ \vdots \\ \boldsymbol{r}_n \end{bmatrix}, \tag{8.79}$$

we write Newton's second law of motion as

$$\boldsymbol{M}\ddot{\boldsymbol{r}} = \boldsymbol{f}(\boldsymbol{r}, \dot{\boldsymbol{r}}) \tag{8.80}$$

where $\boldsymbol{f}$ is the corresponding general force vector, and $\boldsymbol{M}$ is a diagonal matrix with $[m_1, m_2, \ldots, m_n]$ along the diagonal. For cloth, typical internal forces considered are bending, stretching, and shearing, while external forces are typically gravity and collision constraints.

8.7.1 Implicit Integration for Cloth Animation

Cloth strongly opposes stretching, while it easily allows bending, and this implies that the system becomes stiff. Some advocate explicit methods due to the importance of high-frequency response for realistic-looking images [Kačić-Alesić et al., 2003]. However, *explicit integration* of the forces requires an enormous number of small steps in order to avoid instabilities. An *implicit integration* scheme is defined as

$$\begin{bmatrix} \boldsymbol{r}(t+h) \\ \dot{\boldsymbol{r}}(t+h) \end{bmatrix} = \begin{bmatrix} \boldsymbol{r}(t) \\ \dot{\boldsymbol{r}}(t) \end{bmatrix} + h \begin{bmatrix} \dot{\boldsymbol{r}}(t+h) \\ \ddot{\boldsymbol{r}}(t+h) \end{bmatrix} \tag{8.81a}$$

$$= \begin{bmatrix} \boldsymbol{r}(t) \\ \dot{\boldsymbol{r}}(t) \end{bmatrix} + h \begin{bmatrix} \dot{\boldsymbol{r}}(t+h) \\ \boldsymbol{M}^{-1}\boldsymbol{f}\left(\boldsymbol{r}(t+h), \dot{\boldsymbol{r}}(t+h)\right) \end{bmatrix}. \tag{8.81b}$$

To solve the system we assume that $\boldsymbol{f}$ is linear, that is, $\boldsymbol{f}$ may be written on the form

$$\boldsymbol{f}\left(\boldsymbol{r}(t+h), \dot{\boldsymbol{r}}(t+h)\right) = \boldsymbol{f}\left(\boldsymbol{r}(t), \dot{\boldsymbol{r}}(t)\right) + h \nabla \boldsymbol{f} \begin{bmatrix} \dot{\boldsymbol{r}}(t) \\ \ddot{\boldsymbol{r}}(t) \end{bmatrix}, \tag{8.82}$$

where $\nabla \boldsymbol{f}$ is the *Jacobian matrix* taken at t. We can now write (8.81b) as

$$\begin{bmatrix} \boldsymbol{r}(t+h) \\ \dot{\boldsymbol{r}}(t+h) \end{bmatrix} = \begin{bmatrix} \boldsymbol{r}(t) \\ \dot{\boldsymbol{r}}(t) \end{bmatrix} + h \begin{bmatrix} \dot{\boldsymbol{r}}(t+h) \\ \boldsymbol{M}^{-1} \left(\boldsymbol{f}(t) + h \nabla \boldsymbol{f} \begin{bmatrix} \dot{\boldsymbol{r}}(t) \\ \ddot{\boldsymbol{r}}(t) \end{bmatrix} \right) \end{bmatrix}, \tag{8.83}$$

where we have used $\boldsymbol{f}(t) = \boldsymbol{f}\left(\boldsymbol{r}(t), \dot{\boldsymbol{r}}(t)\right)$ for shorthand. Rewriting this equation in terms of the sought updates,

$$\begin{bmatrix} \Delta \boldsymbol{r}(t) \\ \Delta \dot{\boldsymbol{r}}(t) \end{bmatrix} = \begin{bmatrix} \boldsymbol{r}(t+h) - \boldsymbol{r}(t) \\ \dot{\boldsymbol{r}}(t+h) - \dot{\boldsymbol{r}}(t) \end{bmatrix} \tag{8.84}$$

and expanding the Jacobian, we find

$$\begin{bmatrix} \Delta \boldsymbol{r}(t) \\ \Delta \dot{\boldsymbol{r}}(t) \end{bmatrix} = h \begin{bmatrix} \dot{\boldsymbol{r}}(t) + \Delta \dot{\boldsymbol{r}}(t) \\ \boldsymbol{M}^{-1} \left(\boldsymbol{f}(t) + h \frac{\partial \boldsymbol{f}(t)}{\partial \boldsymbol{r}} \dot{\boldsymbol{r}}(t) + h \frac{\partial \boldsymbol{f}(t)}{\partial \dot{\boldsymbol{r}}} \ddot{\boldsymbol{r}}(t) \right) \end{bmatrix}. \tag{8.85}$$

Then we replace $\dot{\boldsymbol{r}}(t)$ $\ddot{\boldsymbol{r}}(t)$ with their forward difference approximations,

$$\dot{\boldsymbol{r}}(t) \simeq \frac{\boldsymbol{r}(t+h) - \boldsymbol{r}(t)}{h} = \frac{\Delta \boldsymbol{r}(t)}{h} \tag{8.86a}$$

$$\ddot{r}(t) \simeq \frac{\dot{\boldsymbol{r}}(t+h) - \dot{\boldsymbol{r}}(t)}{h} = \frac{\Delta \dot{\boldsymbol{r}}(t)}{h} \tag{8.86b}$$

to give

$$\begin{bmatrix} \Delta \boldsymbol{r}(t) \\ \Delta \dot{\boldsymbol{r}}(t) \end{bmatrix} = h \begin{bmatrix} \dot{\boldsymbol{r}}(t) + \Delta \dot{\boldsymbol{r}}(t) \\ \boldsymbol{M}^{-1} \left(\boldsymbol{f}(t) + h \frac{\partial \boldsymbol{f}(t)}{\partial \boldsymbol{r}} \frac{\Delta \boldsymbol{r}(t)}{h} + h \frac{\partial \boldsymbol{f}(t)}{\partial \dot{\boldsymbol{r}}} \frac{\Delta \dot{r}(t)}{h} \right). \end{bmatrix} \tag{8.87}$$

Finally, we insert the top row in the bottom,

$$\Delta \dot{\boldsymbol{r}}(t) = h \boldsymbol{M}^{-1} \left(\boldsymbol{f}(t) + \frac{\partial \boldsymbol{f}(t)}{\partial \boldsymbol{r}} h \left(\dot{\boldsymbol{r}}(t) + \Delta \dot{\boldsymbol{r}}(t) \right) + \frac{\partial \boldsymbol{f}(t)}{\partial \dot{\boldsymbol{r}}} \Delta \dot{\boldsymbol{r}}(t) \right). \tag{8.88}$$

We now have an equation only depending on $\boldsymbol{M}$, $\dot{\boldsymbol{r}}(t)$, the first-order structure of $\boldsymbol{f}\left(\boldsymbol{r}(t), \dot{\boldsymbol{r}}(t)\right)$, and $\Delta \dot{\boldsymbol{r}}(t)$, and for which the latter may be isolated as

$$\left(\mathbf{1} - h^2 \boldsymbol{M}^{-1} \frac{\partial \boldsymbol{f}(t)}{\partial \boldsymbol{r}} - h \boldsymbol{M}^{-1} \frac{\partial \boldsymbol{f}(t)}{\partial \dot{\boldsymbol{r}}} \right) \Delta \dot{\boldsymbol{r}}(t) = h \boldsymbol{M}^{-1} \left(\boldsymbol{f}(t) + h \frac{\partial \boldsymbol{f}(t)}{\partial \boldsymbol{r}} \dot{\boldsymbol{r}}(t) \right), \tag{8.89}$$

where $\mathbf{1}$ is the identity matrix. This equation may be solved for $\Delta \dot{\boldsymbol{r}}(t)$, and $\Delta \boldsymbol{r}(t)$ may be then be calculated using the top row of (8.87).

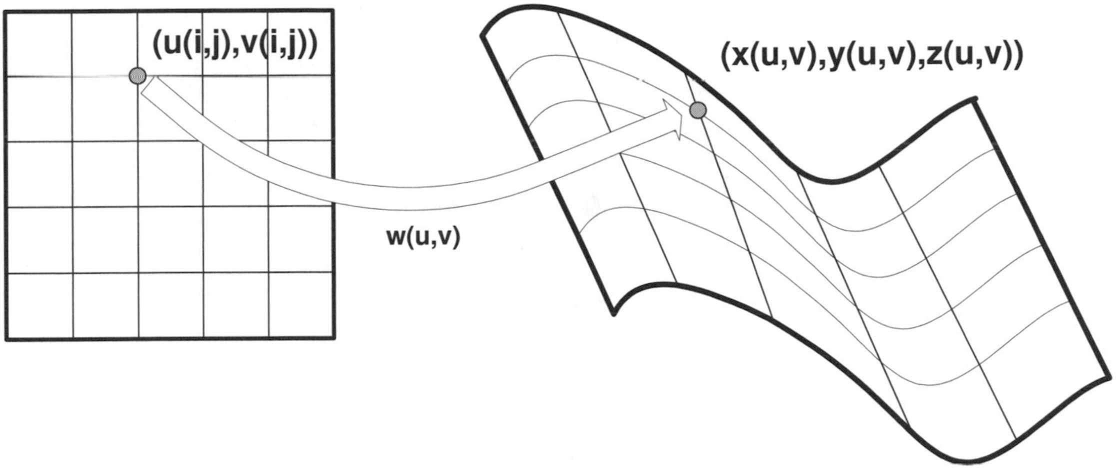

Figure 8.29: Mapping between indices, intrinsic, and world coordinates.

8.7.2 Cloth Forces, Damping, and Constraints

In [Baraff et al., 1998] the constraints are formulated as positive vector functions $\boldsymbol{C}$, that must be minimized. Energy is calculated as squares of constraint functions, $E = \frac{k}{2}\boldsymbol{C}^T\boldsymbol{C}$, and the forces are found as derivatives of the energy functions, $f = \frac{\partial E}{\partial \boldsymbol{r}_i} = -k\frac{\partial \boldsymbol{C}}{\partial \boldsymbol{r}_i}\boldsymbol{C}$.

To define the stretching, bending, and shearing forces, let's consider a piece of cloth that has topology as a plane, implying that the cloth can be spread out in a single layer on a plane without holes. Consider a coordinate system intrinsic to the cloth, $(u(i,j), v(i,j))$, where (i,j) are the indices of a particle. This coordinate system is unaffected by stretching, bending, or shearing, and is used to denote the relative positions of the particles with respect to each other, when the cloth is most at rest. We can then calculate the mapping between the intrinsic and the world coordinates

$$\boldsymbol{x}(i,j) = \begin{bmatrix} x(i,j) \\ y(i,j) \\ z(i,j) \end{bmatrix} = \boldsymbol{w}(u(i,j), v(i,j)). \tag{8.90}$$

This is depicted in Figure 8.29.

Cloth strongly resists stretching, and we may define the amount of stretching by the functions $\frac{\partial \boldsymbol{w}}{\partial u}$ and $\frac{\partial \boldsymbol{w}}{\partial v}$ for the stretch in the u and v directions on the cloth respectively. We will assume that $\left\|\frac{\partial \boldsymbol{w}}{\partial u}\right\|_2 = \left\|\frac{\partial \boldsymbol{w}}{\partial v}\right\|_2 = 1$ when the cloth is at rest. Assuming for a moment that the indices (i,j) are continuous variables, we write the change in world coordinate $\boldsymbol{x}(i,j)$ as a function of index i and j respectively,

$$\frac{\partial \boldsymbol{x}}{\partial i} = \frac{\partial \boldsymbol{w}}{\partial u}\frac{\partial u}{\partial i} + \frac{\partial \boldsymbol{w}}{\partial v}\frac{\partial v}{\partial i}, \tag{8.91a}$$

$$\frac{\partial \boldsymbol{x}}{\partial j} = \frac{\partial \boldsymbol{w}}{\partial u}\frac{\partial u}{\partial j} + \frac{\partial \boldsymbol{w}}{\partial v}\frac{\partial v}{\partial j}. \tag{8.91b}$$

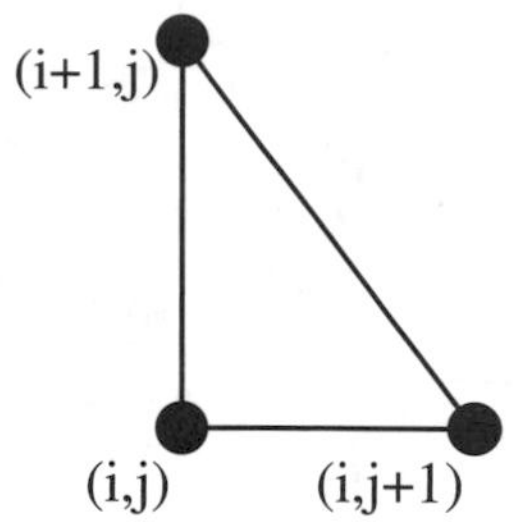

Figure 8.30: Three neighboring particles in the cloth mesh

On matrix form this gives

$$\begin{bmatrix} \frac{\partial \boldsymbol{x}}{\partial i} \\ \frac{\partial \boldsymbol{x}}{\partial j} \end{bmatrix} = \begin{bmatrix} \frac{\partial u}{\partial i} & \frac{\partial v}{\partial i} \\ \frac{\partial u}{\partial j} & \frac{\partial v}{\partial j} \end{bmatrix} \begin{bmatrix} \frac{\partial \boldsymbol{w}}{\partial u} \\ \frac{\partial \boldsymbol{w}}{\partial v} \end{bmatrix}. \tag{8.92}$$

Thus, given three neighboring particles as shown in Figure 8.30, we may estimate $\frac{\partial \boldsymbol{w}}{\partial u}$ and $\frac{\partial \boldsymbol{w}}{\partial v}$ by finite differences and matrix inversion as

$$\begin{bmatrix} \frac{\partial \boldsymbol{w}}{\partial u} \\ \frac{\partial \boldsymbol{w}}{\partial v} \end{bmatrix} = \begin{bmatrix} u(i+1,j) - u(i,j) & v(i+1,j) - v(i,j) \\ u(i,j+1) - u(i,j) & v(i,j+1) - v(i,j) \end{bmatrix}^{-1} \begin{bmatrix} \boldsymbol{x}(i+1,j) - \boldsymbol{x}(i,j) \\ \boldsymbol{x}(i,j+1) - \boldsymbol{x}(i,j) \end{bmatrix}. \tag{8.93}$$

The matrix in u and v is constant, hence $\frac{\partial \boldsymbol{w}}{\partial u}$ and $\frac{\partial \boldsymbol{w}}{\partial v}$ are a function of $\boldsymbol{x}$, and the constraint function is therefore defined to be

$$\boldsymbol{C}_{\text{stretch}}(\boldsymbol{x}) = \alpha \begin{bmatrix} \left\| \frac{\partial \boldsymbol{w}}{\partial u} \right\|_2 - 1 \\ \left\| \frac{\partial \boldsymbol{w}}{\partial v} \right\|_2 - 1 \end{bmatrix}, \tag{8.94}$$

where α is a user-specified constant controlling the relative strength of the stretch constraint. Likewise, we define shearing energy by measuring the angular change performed by the mapping,

$$\boldsymbol{C}_{\text{shear}} = \beta \frac{\partial \boldsymbol{w}}{\partial u} \cdot \frac{\partial \boldsymbol{w}}{\partial v}, \tag{8.95}$$

where β is a user constant controlling the relative strength of the shear constraint. This is an approximation to $\cos\theta$, with θ being the angle between the vectors, and the approximation depends on β, since this controls the relative enforcement of $\boldsymbol{C}_{\text{shear}}$.

For the bending constraint, we define it to be proportional with the curvature of the cloth, which in turn is proportional with the angle between two neighboring triangle normals, that is,

$$C_{\text{bend}} = \gamma \cos^{-1}(\boldsymbol{n}_1 \cdot \boldsymbol{n}_2), \tag{8.96}$$

where $\boldsymbol{n}_1$ are the normals $\boldsymbol{n}_2$, and γ is a user constant controlling the relative strength of the stretch constraint.

Strong forces require strong damping forces to stabilize the numerical integration. It has been suggested to use the constraint function to define damping forces [Baraff et al., 1998] as follows:

$$\boldsymbol{d}_i = -k_d \frac{\partial \boldsymbol{C}}{\partial \boldsymbol{r}_i} \dot{\boldsymbol{C}}. \tag{8.97}$$

Inserting this into (8.89) we need to calculate the derivatives

$$\frac{\partial \boldsymbol{d}_i}{\partial \boldsymbol{r}_j} = -k_d \left(\frac{\partial \boldsymbol{C}}{\partial \boldsymbol{r}_i} \frac{\partial \dot{\boldsymbol{C}}}{\partial \boldsymbol{r}_j} + \frac{\partial^2 \boldsymbol{C}}{\partial \boldsymbol{r}_i \partial \boldsymbol{r}_j} \dot{\boldsymbol{C}} \right) \tag{8.98a}$$

$$\frac{\partial \boldsymbol{d}_i}{\partial \dot{\boldsymbol{r}}_j} = -k_d \left(\frac{\partial \boldsymbol{C}}{\partial \boldsymbol{r}_i} \frac{\partial \boldsymbol{C}}{\partial \boldsymbol{r}_j}^T \right). \tag{8.98b}$$

At points of contact between the cloth and other impenetrable objects, or as specified by the user, constraint forces must be applied. Instead of introducing springs with high spring constants, the mass may be set to infinity. At first glance this seems awkward, however, since (8.89) uses the inverse mass, setting a mass to infinity is equivalent to setting its inverse mass to zero. To complicate matters further, a particle in contact with a planar surface will only be constrained in the direction normal to the surface, and we need only set the inverse mass to zero in the normal direction. As an example, consider a single particle, $\boldsymbol{r}_i$: Newton's second law may be written on matrix form as

$$\ddot{\boldsymbol{r}}_i = \frac{1}{m_i} \boldsymbol{f}_i = \begin{bmatrix} \frac{1}{m_i} & 0 & 0 \\ 0 & \frac{1}{m_i} & 0 \\ 0 & 0 & \frac{1}{m_i} \end{bmatrix} \boldsymbol{f}_i, \tag{8.99}$$

in which case we may impose a constraint along one of the coordinate axes by setting the corresponding element in the diagonal to zero. The extension of the inverse mass to a matrix was done by multiplication with the identity matrix, $\frac{1}{m_i}\mathbf{1}$, and constraining along an axis could be considered as the operation $\frac{1}{m_i}(\mathbf{1} - \boldsymbol{\Xi})$, where $\boldsymbol{\Xi}$ is a zero matrix except at the relevant diagonal element to be constrained, which is one. In general we have

$$(\mathbf{1} - \boldsymbol{\xi}\boldsymbol{\xi}^T)\boldsymbol{\xi} = \mathbf{0}, \tag{8.100}$$

when $\xi = [\xi_1, \xi_2, \xi_3]^T$ is a unit vector. To verify, we simply expand the products in three dimensions,

$$(\mathbf{1} - \boldsymbol{\xi}\boldsymbol{\xi}^T)\boldsymbol{\xi} = \boldsymbol{\xi} - \begin{bmatrix} \xi_1^2 & \xi_1\xi_2 & \xi_1\xi_3 \\ \xi_1\xi_2 & \xi_2^2 & \xi_2\xi_3 \\ \xi_1\xi_3 & \xi_2\xi_3 & \xi_3^2 \end{bmatrix} \boldsymbol{\xi} \tag{8.101a}$$

$$= \boldsymbol{\xi} - \begin{bmatrix} \xi_1^3 + \xi_1\xi_2^2 + \xi_1\xi_3^2 \\ \xi_1^2\xi_2 + \xi_2^3 + \xi_2\xi_3^2 \\ \xi_1^2\xi_3 + \xi_2^2\xi_3 + \xi_3^3 \end{bmatrix} \tag{8.101b}$$

$$= \boldsymbol{\xi} - \begin{bmatrix} \xi_1(\xi_1^2 + \xi_2^2 + \xi_3^2) \\ \xi_2(\xi_1^2 + \xi_2^2 + \xi_3^2) \\ \xi_3(\xi_1^2 + \xi_2^2 + \xi_3^2) \end{bmatrix} \tag{8.101c}$$

$$= 0. \tag{8.101d}$$

Thus we may specify the constraints in 0–3 directions by letting the inverse mass matrix be

$$\boldsymbol{M}_i^{-1} \begin{cases} \frac{1}{m_i} & \text{for 0 constraints,} \\ \frac{1}{m_i}\left(\mathbf{1} - \boldsymbol{\xi}\boldsymbol{\xi}^T\right) & \text{for 1 constraint,} \\ \frac{1}{m_i}\left(\mathbf{1} - \boldsymbol{\xi}\boldsymbol{\xi}^T - \boldsymbol{\eta}\boldsymbol{\eta}^T\right) & \text{for 2 constraints,} \\ 0 & \text{for 3 constraints,} \end{cases} x \tag{8.102}$$

where $\boldsymbol{\xi}$ and $\boldsymbol{\eta}$ are mutually orthogonal vectors.

Finally, [Baraff et al., 1998] has had success with solving the above system with the conjugate gradient method.

9

Continuum Models with Finite Differences

In this chapter we will discuss *continuum models* with *finite differences* for the simulation of *deformable objects*. This was first presented for the animation community in [Terzopoulos et al., 1987] and later widely discussed [Kelager et al., 2005]. The model typically leads to rubbery objects, as illustrated in Figure 9.1.

The original method was designed using finite differencing, but many have later turned finite elements as the computational model. The finite element method will be discussed in Chapter 10.

9.1 A Model for Deformable Objects

A deformable object can be identified as a point cloud. The positions of these points describe the geometry of the object. Any point of a deformable object can at any time be identified by a set of unique parameter values. We call these parameter values the *material coordinates* and denote them with the symbol $\boldsymbol{a}$. For a solid, $\boldsymbol{a} = [a_1, a_2, a_3]^T$, for a surface, $\boldsymbol{a} = [a_1, a_2]^T$, and for a curve, $\boldsymbol{a} = [a_1]$.

As the object deforms, points belonging to the object move. The position of an object point is a time-varying vector depending on the material coordinates. A point belonging to an object in Euclidean space is denoted $\boldsymbol{r}$ and is given by

$$\boldsymbol{r}(\boldsymbol{a}, t) = [r_1(\boldsymbol{a}, t), r_2(\boldsymbol{a}, t), r_3(\boldsymbol{a}, t)]. \tag{9.1}$$

In Figure 9.2, we show the relationship between a surface described by material coordinates and the points in Euclidean space.

The deformation of an object is modeled using *elastic forces*. When an object is in its rest shape, meaning that it is undeformed, there is no *elastic energy* stored in the object, but when the object is

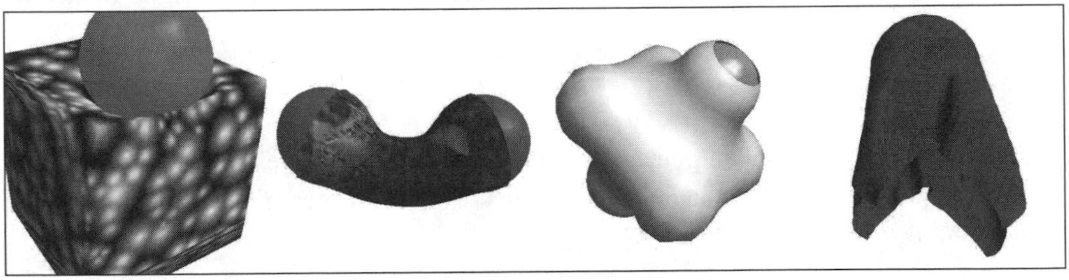

Figure 9.1: Examples of models using the continuum formulation, kindly provided by Micky Kelager and Anders Fleron, at the time of writing students at the Department of Computer Science, University of Copenhagen.

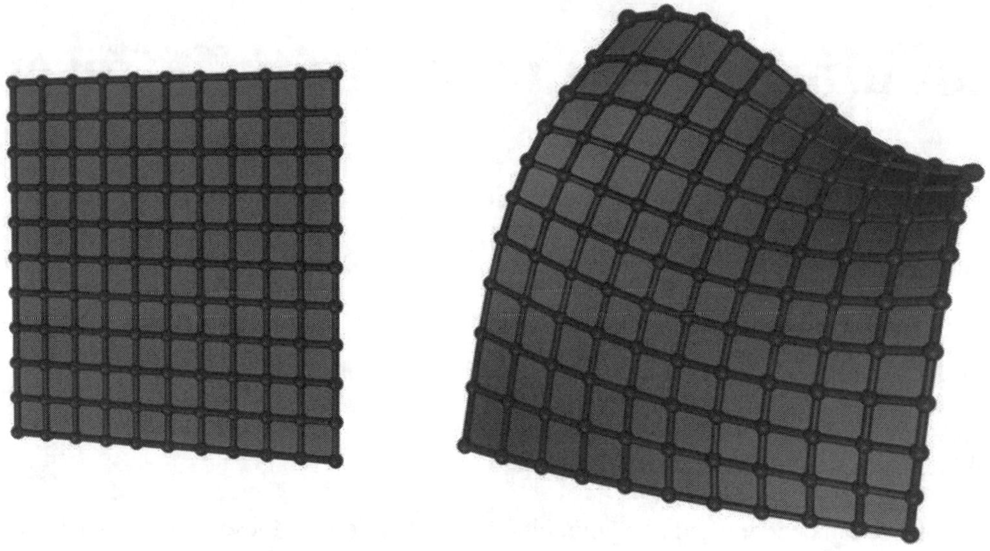

Figure 9.2: Parameterization of a deformable object.

deformed, an elastic energy is built up in the object. The deformed object wants to return to its rest shape, which is equivalent to minimizing the elastic energy stored in the object. Thus, simulating deformable objects is all about energy minimization.

The deformation of an object in a given point is denoted with a *potential elastic energy* function $\mathcal{E} = \mathcal{E}(\boldsymbol{r}(\boldsymbol{a},t))$. This energy should be independent of rigid-body movement.

We work in a continuum model, which means that we consider the object as a whole, and not just a representation of the object, for instance, its center of mass. This means that a *differential volume* of the object is assigned a *density of mass*, a *density of energy*, a *density of damping*, and so on. Thus, in the limiting case, we have a mass density function, an energy density function, etc., describing the distribution of densities at any point in the object.

The *Lagrangian density*, see Section 22.5, is an energy density function, and it can be written as

$$\mathcal{L} = \frac{1}{2}\mu(\boldsymbol{a})\left(\frac{d\boldsymbol{r}(\boldsymbol{a},t)}{dt}\right)^2 - \mathcal{E}(\boldsymbol{r}(\boldsymbol{a},t)). \tag{9.2}$$

Here $\mu(\boldsymbol{a})$ is the mass density in a given point, and the derivative of $\boldsymbol{r}$ with respect to time, describes the velocity of motion. The object deforms due to some applied *external forces*, $\boldsymbol{f}^{(a)}$, and the deformation is damped by a *damping force*, $\boldsymbol{f}^{(d)}$, given by

$$\boldsymbol{f}^{(a)} = \boldsymbol{f}(\boldsymbol{r}(\boldsymbol{a},t),t), \tag{9.3a}$$

$$\boldsymbol{f}^{(d)} = -\gamma(\boldsymbol{a})\frac{d\boldsymbol{r}(\boldsymbol{a},t)}{dt}, \tag{9.3b}$$

where $\gamma(\boldsymbol{a})$ is the *damping density*. The damping force resists deformation, while the applied external force can be a sum of several different kinds of forces. Examples of these external forces are given later in Section 9.4.

9.1.1 The Lagrangian Formulation

The *equations of motion* for a continuous object can be described by the *Lagrangian formulation.* The theory and derivations can be found in Section 22.5. The specific equation we use for our model, Equation (22.186), is repeated here:

$$\frac{d}{dt}\left(\frac{\partial \mathcal{L}}{\partial \frac{\partial \boldsymbol{r}}{\partial t}}\right) - \frac{\delta \mathcal{L}}{\delta \boldsymbol{r}} = \mathcal{Q}. \tag{9.4}$$

Now let us try to substitute the expression for the Lagrangian density of our deformable model, (9.2), into the above Lagrangian formulation:

$$\frac{d}{dt}\left(\frac{\partial\left(\frac{1}{2}\mu(\boldsymbol{a})\left(\frac{d\boldsymbol{r}(\boldsymbol{a},t)}{dt}\right)^2 - \mathcal{E}(\boldsymbol{r}(\boldsymbol{a},t))\right)}{\partial \frac{\partial \boldsymbol{r}(\boldsymbol{a},t)}{\partial t}}\right) - \frac{\delta\left(\frac{1}{2}\mu(\boldsymbol{a})\left(\frac{d\boldsymbol{r}(\boldsymbol{a},t)}{dt}\right)^2 - \mathcal{E}(\boldsymbol{r}(\boldsymbol{a},t))\right)}{\delta \boldsymbol{r}(\boldsymbol{a},t)} = \mathcal{Q}. \tag{9.5}$$

If we carry out the partial derivatives on the left side of the equation, we obtain

$$\frac{d}{dt}\left(\mu(\boldsymbol{a})\left(\frac{d\boldsymbol{r}(\boldsymbol{a},t)}{dt}\right)\right) + \frac{\delta \mathcal{E}(\boldsymbol{r}(\boldsymbol{a},t))}{\delta \boldsymbol{r}(\boldsymbol{a},t)} = \mathcal{Q}. \tag{9.6}$$

The quantity $\mathcal{Q}$ is the total sum of applied forces. In our model, these are the external forces, $\boldsymbol{f}^{(a)}$, and the damping force, $\boldsymbol{f}^{(d)}$. Substituting the expressions from (9.3) for these forces yields

$$\frac{d}{dt}\left(\mu(\boldsymbol{a})\left(\frac{d\boldsymbol{r}(\boldsymbol{a},t)}{dt}\right)\right) + \frac{\delta \mathcal{E}(\boldsymbol{r}(\boldsymbol{a},t))}{\delta \boldsymbol{r}(\boldsymbol{a},t)} = \boldsymbol{f}(\boldsymbol{r},t(\boldsymbol{a},t)) - \gamma(\boldsymbol{a})\frac{d\boldsymbol{r}(\boldsymbol{a},t)}{dt}. \tag{9.7}$$

If we move the damping force to the left side, and exchange absolute derivatives with partial derivatives wherever possible, we get our *Lagrangian model* for a deformable object under motion:

$$\frac{\partial}{\partial t}\left(\mu(\boldsymbol{a})\left(\frac{\partial \boldsymbol{r}(\boldsymbol{a},t)}{\partial t}\right)\right) + \gamma(\boldsymbol{a})\frac{\partial \boldsymbol{r}(\boldsymbol{a},t)}{\partial t} + \frac{\delta \mathcal{E}(\boldsymbol{r}(\boldsymbol{a},t))}{\delta \boldsymbol{r}(\boldsymbol{a},t)} = \boldsymbol{f}(\boldsymbol{r}(\boldsymbol{a},t),t), \tag{9.8}$$

where $\boldsymbol{r}(\boldsymbol{a},t)$ is the position of material point $\boldsymbol{a}$ at time t, $\mu(\boldsymbol{a})$ is the mass density, $\gamma(\boldsymbol{a})$ is the damping density, $\boldsymbol{f}\left(\boldsymbol{r}(\boldsymbol{a},t),t\right)$ is the applied external forces, and $\mathcal{E}\left(\boldsymbol{r}(\boldsymbol{a},t)\right)$ is potential energy due to the elastic deformation of the body. The derived equation is an exact match of the deformable model introduced in [Terzopoulos et al., 1987].

To ease notation, we omit the explicit dependencies on position $\boldsymbol{a}$, and time t. The equation of motion is then reduced to

$$\mu\frac{\partial^2 \boldsymbol{r}}{\partial t^2} + \gamma\frac{\partial \boldsymbol{r}}{\partial t} + \frac{\delta \mathcal{E}\left(\boldsymbol{r}\right)}{\delta \boldsymbol{r}} = \boldsymbol{f}\left(\boldsymbol{r},t\right). \tag{9.9}$$

We find a connection with classical mechanics when we assign labels to the different parts of the equation. For example, μ has dimension of mass, and $\frac{\partial^2 \boldsymbol{r}}{\partial t^2}$ is acceleration; thus $\mu \frac{\partial^2 \boldsymbol{r}}{\partial t^2}$ is mass times acceleration, which we denote with $m \cdot a$. Similarly, we find that γ has dimension of viscosity, $\frac{\partial \boldsymbol{r}}{\partial t}$ has dimension of velocity, and combined they have dimension of force, e.g., $\gamma \frac{\partial \boldsymbol{r}}{\partial t} = F_{\text{viscous}}$. Continuing this, we can put a label on each of the terms in the equation of motion, which yields:

$$\underbrace{\mu \frac{\partial^2 \boldsymbol{r}}{\partial t^2}}_{m \cdot a} + \underbrace{\gamma \frac{\partial \boldsymbol{r}}{\partial t}}_{F_{\text{viscous}}} + \underbrace{\frac{\delta \mathcal{E}(\boldsymbol{r})}{\delta \boldsymbol{r}}}_{F_{\text{elastic}}} = \underbrace{\boldsymbol{f}(\boldsymbol{r}, t)}_{F_{\text{external}}}. \tag{9.10}$$

Doing so, we can gather the viscous, elastic, and external force, as $F_{\text{total}} = F_{\text{external}} - (F_{\text{viscous}} + F_{\text{elastic}})$. With this notation, we find that our equation of motion is equivalent to Newton's second law:

$$m \cdot a = F_{\text{total}}. \tag{9.11}$$

Normally, we think of Newton's second law used directly on one body. In the Lagrangian formulation, the body is parameterized. It is therefore a continuous description.

9.1.2 Designing the Energy Functional

The $\mathcal{E}(\boldsymbol{r}(\boldsymbol{a}, t))$ functional describes the potential elastic energy of our deformable object. This functional is only dependent on the form of the object. We do not want our object to change form, depending on its position in the world, so we need a description of form that is invariant to rigid body motion.

Differential geometry is well suited to describe the local shape of any kind of object. Therefore, we can use this description to set up an energy functional, which penalizes a deforming shape with respect to its natural or initial shape. When the simulation is run a force will be applied, pulling the body toward its natural shape, until equilibrium is reached. Thus, penalizing is equivalent to energy minimization and the *equilibrium shape* is equal to energy minimum.

The *first fundamental form* or the *metric tensor* is a measuring tool for points in an object. It describes how to measure distances between points in the object, independent of the world coordinate frame. For a point $\boldsymbol{r}$ in our parameterized object, the metric tensor

$$G = \begin{bmatrix} G_{11} & G_{12} \\ G_{21} & G_{22} \end{bmatrix}, \tag{9.12}$$

is a symmetric matrix with elements defined by

$$G_{ij}(\boldsymbol{r}(\boldsymbol{a})) = \frac{\partial \boldsymbol{r}}{\partial a_i} \cdot \frac{\partial \boldsymbol{r}}{\partial a_j}. \tag{9.13}$$

The differential distance between two nearby points with material coordinates $\boldsymbol{a}$ and $\boldsymbol{a} + d\boldsymbol{a}$ is then found by

$$dl = \sum_{i,j} G_{ij}(\boldsymbol{r}(\boldsymbol{a}))\, da_i da_j. \tag{9.14}$$

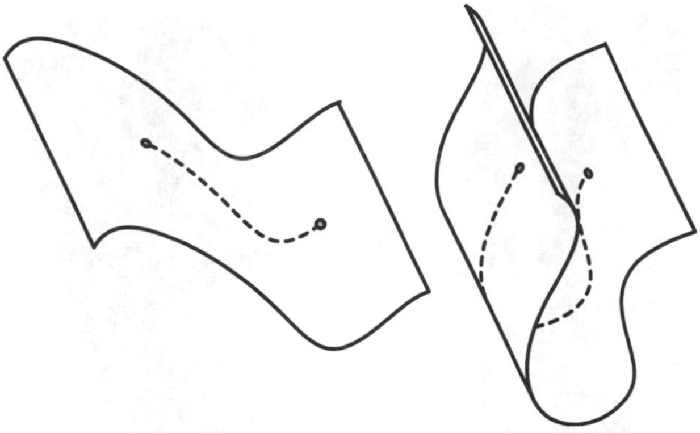

Figure 9.3: Distance between points on surface is independent of the mean curvature.

For 3D solid objects, the metric tensor is a 3×3 matrix. If two solids have the same shape, their metric tensors are identical functions of $\boldsymbol{a}$. However, for 2D surfaces, this description is no longer sufficient. The distance between points on a surface is independent of the *mean curvature* of the surfaces as seen in Figure 9.3, so we need to look at the *second fundamental form* or the *curvature tensor*. For a point in our parameterized surface, the elements of the curvature tensor, B, are defined as

$$B_{ij}\left(\boldsymbol{r}(\boldsymbol{a})\right) = \boldsymbol{n} \cdot \frac{\partial^2 \boldsymbol{r}}{\partial a_i \cdot \partial a_j}, \tag{9.15}$$

where $\boldsymbol{n} = \left[n_1, n_2, n_3\right]^T$ is the unit surface normal. If two surfaces have the same shape, their 2×2 metric tensors, G, as well as their 2×2 curvature tensors, B, are identical functions of $\boldsymbol{a}$.

Finally, if we restrict our deformable objects to 1D curves, we need yet another measurement to account for twisting, in order to decide if two curves have the same shape, as illustrated in Figure 9.4. The metric and curvature tensors are now reduced to scalars, called *arc length* s and *curvature* κ. Since the curve can twist, we need to compare their *torsion* τ, which is defined as

$$\tau = \boldsymbol{n} \cdot \left(\boldsymbol{t} \times \boldsymbol{n}\right)', \tag{9.16}$$

where $\boldsymbol{t}$ is the tangent, $(\boldsymbol{t} \times \boldsymbol{n})$ is the binormal, and $(\boldsymbol{t} \times \boldsymbol{n})'$ is differentiation of the binormal with respect to the arc length parameterization. In the following, we will restrict the description to 2D surfaces. It is easy to incorporate the torsion for curves, or remove the curvature for solids.

In the model for a deformable object, (9.8), the external forces working on the object are countered by internal forces. The internal elastic force

$$F_{\text{elastic}} = \frac{\delta \mathcal{E}\left(\boldsymbol{r}\right)}{\delta \boldsymbol{r}}, \tag{9.17}$$

deals with the elastic energy that is produced when the deformable object has a shape that is different from its rest shape. We want to model the energy in a way that resembles real-life elastic objects. For example, when compressing a rubber ball, it returns to its natural ball shape when the pressure is released. We can

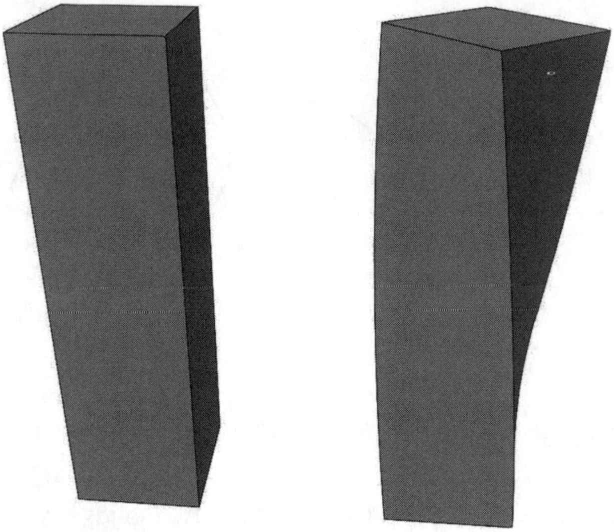

Figure 9.4: The shapes of two curves depend on torsion. Image shows two curves, with same arch length and curvature metrics, but with different torsion.

model this behavior for our deformable object, by requiring that the material points at the deformation should have an increased elastic energy. This ensures that the elastic force makes the material points want to seek their natural *rest shape*, e.g., the undeformed object. We further want the model to have a low elastic energy when deformation is small, and a high elastic energy when deformation is large. A simple, but reasonable, model of the elastic energy $\mathcal{E}(\boldsymbol{r}(\boldsymbol{a},t))$ in an object being deformed is the difference between the fundamental forms of the object in its deformed state and in its rest shape. We denote the fundamental forms of the object in its natural rest shape with a superscript 0; that is, G^0 is the metric tensor, and B^0 is the curvature tensor for the object in its natural rest shape. This elastic energy can be written as

$$\mathcal{E}(\boldsymbol{r}) = \int_{\Omega} \left\|G - G^0\right\|_{\eta}^2 + \left\|B - B^0\right\|_{\xi}^2 \quad da_1 da_2, \tag{9.18}$$

where Ω is the domain of the deformable object and $\|\cdot\|_{\eta}$ and $\|\cdot\|_{\xi}$ are weighted matrix norms. This model for the elastic energy has the nice properties that it is zero for rigid body motion and that it includes the fewest partial derivatives necessary to restore a deformable object to its natural shape.

9.2 Model Relaxation

In the previous sections we derived a mathematical model for a deformable object. The mathematical model is now converted to a discrete model with nice numerical properties and efficiently solvable on a computer. The numerical property we aim for is that small errors, due to imprecision and round-off, are not amplified, but rather dissipated. Choosing this strategy has some tradeoffs. The motion is often damped by the dissipation. The more dissipation, the more damped the motion appears to be. In contrast, the more damping, the more abrupt, violent, and destructive change can be applied to the deformable object, without the animation blowing up. From a computer graphics viewpoint, efficiency often implies taking very large, fixed time-steps, with comparatively low time-complexity.

We start by simplifying the expression for the elastic energy. Thereafter, we work through the mathematics of calculating the variational derivatives of the elastic force, which leads us to another simplification. When this is done, we show how to discretize the simplified equation of motion in space. Finally, the resulting system, which has been converted from a partial differential equation to a system of coupled ordinary differential equations, is discretized through time and ready to be implemented.

9.2.1 Simplification of the Elastic Force

In the previous section, we derived an expression for the elastic energy, when the object was deformed away from its natural shape. Using the *weighted Frobenius norm*, also called the *Hilbert-Schmidt norm* [Weisstein, 2004], which is defined as

$$\|A\|_w = \sqrt{\sum_{i,j} w_{ij}|A_{ij}|^2}, \tag{9.19}$$

we can rewrite (9.18) as follows:

$$\mathcal{E}(\boldsymbol{r}) = \int_\Omega \left\|G - G^0\right\|_\eta^2 + \left\|B - B^0\right\|_\xi^2 \quad da_1 da_2, \tag{9.20a}$$

$$= \int_\Omega \sum_{i,j=1}^{2} \left(\eta_{ij}\left(G_{ij} - G_{ij}^0\right)^2 + \xi_{ij}\left(B_{ij} - B_{ij}^0\right)^2\right) da_1 da_2. \tag{9.20b}$$

The weighting matrices, η and ξ will control the strength of restoration of the first and second fundamental form, respectively.

9.2.2 The Variational Derivative

With the above simplification of the elastic energy functional, we are now ready to find an expression for the elastic force, $F_{\text{elastic}} = \frac{\delta \mathcal{E}(\boldsymbol{r})}{\delta \boldsymbol{r}}$. The *variational derivative*

of a potential energy functional can be interpreted as a force as explained in Section 22.3. Calculating the variational derivative also corresponds to finding the function that minimizes the functional as described in Chapter 21. That means that by calculating the variational derivative, we find an expression of the elastic force that seeks to minimize the elastic energy.

To better follow the derivations, we split (9.20b) into two parts. The first, S, dealing with the first fundamental form, and the other, T, dealing with the second fundamental form:

$$S = \sum_{i,j=1}^{2} \eta_{ij} \left(G_{ij} - G^0_{ij}\right)^2, \tag{9.21a}$$

$$T = \sum_{i,j=1}^{2} \xi_{ij} \left(B_{ij} - B^0_{ij}\right)^2. \tag{9.21b}$$

These terms will be developed individually, using the calculus of Variation (see Chapter 21).

9.2.2.1 Variational Derivative of S

We will now derive the variational derivative of S. The function S on expanded form is

$$S = \eta_{11} \left(G_{11} - G^0_{11}\right)^2 + \eta_{12} \left(G_{12} - G^0_{12}\right)^2 + \eta_{21} \left(G_{21} - G^0_{21}\right)^2 + \eta_{22} \left(G_{22} - G^0_{22}\right)^2. \tag{9.22}$$

Since G is symmetric, we choose $\eta_{12} = \eta_{21}$. Using the fact that $G_{ij} = \frac{\partial \boldsymbol{r}}{\partial a_i} \cdot \frac{\partial \boldsymbol{r}}{\partial a_j}$, the expression becomes

$$S = \eta_{11} \left(\frac{\partial \boldsymbol{r}}{\partial a_1} \cdot \frac{\partial \boldsymbol{r}}{\partial a_1} - G^0_{11}\right)^2 + 2\eta_{12} \left(\frac{\partial \boldsymbol{r}}{\partial a_1} \cdot \frac{\partial \boldsymbol{r}}{\partial a_2} - G^0_{12}\right)^2 + \eta_{22} \left(\frac{\partial \boldsymbol{r}}{\partial a_2} \cdot \frac{\partial \boldsymbol{r}}{\partial a_2} - G^0_{22}\right)^2. \tag{9.23}$$

Introducing the shorthand $\boldsymbol{r}_{a_i} = \frac{\partial \boldsymbol{r}(\boldsymbol{a})}{\partial a_i}$, the equation becomes

$$S = \eta_{11} \left(\boldsymbol{r}_{a_1} \cdot \boldsymbol{r}_{a_1} - G^0_{11}\right)^2 + 2\eta_{12} \left(\boldsymbol{r}_{a_1} \cdot \boldsymbol{r}_{a_2} - G^0_{12}\right)^2 + \eta_{22} \left(\boldsymbol{r}_{a_2} \cdot \boldsymbol{r}_{a_2} - G^0_{22}\right)^2, \tag{9.24}$$

which may also be written as

$$\mathcal{S}(\boldsymbol{r}) = \int_\Omega S\left(a_1, a_2, \boldsymbol{r}, \boldsymbol{r}_{a_1}, \boldsymbol{r}_{a_2}\right) da_1 da_2. \tag{9.25}$$

The first variational derivative of $\mathcal{S}$ is defined by

$$\frac{\delta \mathcal{S}}{\delta \boldsymbol{r}} = S_{\boldsymbol{r}} - \partial_{a_1} S_{\boldsymbol{r}_{a_1}} - \partial_{a_2} S_{\boldsymbol{r}_{a_2}}. \tag{9.26}$$

Observe that nowhere does S depend explicitly on $\boldsymbol{r}$, so $S_{\boldsymbol{r}} = 0$. That means we end up with

$$\begin{aligned} \frac{\delta \mathcal{S}}{\delta \boldsymbol{r}} = &- \partial_{a_1} \left[\underbrace{4\eta_{11} \left(\boldsymbol{r}_{a_1} \cdot \boldsymbol{r}_{a_1} - G^0_{11}\right)}_{\alpha_{11}} \boldsymbol{r}_{a_1} + \underbrace{4\eta_{12} \left(\boldsymbol{r}_{a_1} \cdot \boldsymbol{r}_{a_2} - G^0_{12}\right)}_{\alpha_{12}} \boldsymbol{r}_{a_2} \right] \\ &- \partial_{a_2} \left[\underbrace{4\eta_{12} \left(\boldsymbol{r}_{a_1} \cdot \boldsymbol{r}_{a_2} - G^0_{12}\right)}_{\alpha_{12}} \boldsymbol{r}_{a_1} + \underbrace{4\eta_{22} \left(\boldsymbol{r}_{a_2} \cdot \boldsymbol{r}_{a_2} - G^0_{22}\right)}_{\alpha_{22}} \boldsymbol{r}_{a_2} \right]. \end{aligned} \tag{9.27}$$

Cleaning up we have

$$\frac{\delta \mathcal{S}}{\delta \boldsymbol{r}} = -\partial_{a_1}\left[\alpha_{11}\boldsymbol{r}_{a_1} + \alpha_{12}\boldsymbol{r}_{a_2}\right] - \partial_{a_2}\left[\alpha_{12}\boldsymbol{r}_{a_1} + \alpha_{22}\boldsymbol{r}_{a_2}\right]. \tag{9.28}$$

Using the product rule we can now write

$$\begin{aligned}\frac{\delta \mathcal{S}}{\delta \boldsymbol{r}} =& -\left(\partial_{a_1}\alpha_{11}\right)\boldsymbol{r}_{a_1} - \alpha_{11}\boldsymbol{r}_{a_1a_1} - \left(\partial_{a_1}\alpha_{12}\right)\boldsymbol{r}_{a_2} - \alpha_{12}\boldsymbol{r}_{a_1a_2}\\ &-\left(\partial_{a_2}\alpha_{12}\right)\boldsymbol{r}_{a_1} - \alpha_{12}\boldsymbol{r}_{a_2a_1} - \left(\partial_{a_2}\alpha_{22}\right)\boldsymbol{r}_{a_2} - \alpha_{22}\boldsymbol{r}_{a_2a_2},\end{aligned} \tag{9.29}$$

which can be reduced to

$$\frac{\delta \mathcal{S}}{\delta \boldsymbol{r}} = -\sum_{i,j=1}^{2} \partial_{a_i}\alpha_{ij}\boldsymbol{r}_{a_j}, \tag{9.30a}$$

$$\alpha_{ij} = \tilde{\eta}_{ij}\left(G_{ij} - G_{ij}^0\right), \tag{9.30b}$$

$$\tilde{\eta}_{ij} = 4\eta_{ij}. \tag{9.30c}$$

This is the expression of the variation of the first fundamental form. The constant η_{ij} is user specified, hence we might as well consider $\tilde{\eta}_{ij}$ as the user-specified parameter. This will be our practice in the remainder of this chapter.

9.2.2.2 Variational Derivative of T

Following the same procedure for T, using the fact that $B_{ij} = \boldsymbol{n} \cdot \boldsymbol{r}_{a_ja_i}$, and choosing $\xi_{12} = \xi_{21}$, yields

$$T = \xi_{11}\left(\boldsymbol{n}\cdot\boldsymbol{r}_{a_1a_1} - B_{11}^0\right)^2 + 2\xi_{12}\left(\boldsymbol{n}\cdot\boldsymbol{r}_{a_1a_2} - B_{12}^0\right)^2 + \xi_{22}\left(\boldsymbol{n}\cdot\boldsymbol{r}_{a_2a_2} - B_{22}^0\right)^2. \tag{9.31}$$

We can then write the T-part of the energy functional as

$$\mathcal{T}(\boldsymbol{r}) = \int_\Omega T\left(a_1, a_2, \boldsymbol{r}, \boldsymbol{r}_{a_1}, \boldsymbol{r}_{a_2}, \boldsymbol{r}_{a_1a_1}, \boldsymbol{r}_{a_1a_2}, \boldsymbol{r}_{a_2a_2}\right) da_1 da_2. \tag{9.32}$$

The first variational derivative of T is defined by

$$\frac{\delta \mathcal{T}}{\delta \boldsymbol{r}} = T_{\boldsymbol{r}} - \partial_{a_1}T_{\boldsymbol{r}_{a_1}} - \partial_{a_2}T_{\boldsymbol{r}_{a_2}} + \partial_{a_1a_1}T_{\boldsymbol{r}_{a_1a_1}} + 2\partial_{a_1a_2}T_{\boldsymbol{r}_{a_1a_2}} + \partial_{a_2a_2}T_{\boldsymbol{r}_{a_2a_2}}. \tag{9.33}$$

Again, we see that $T_{\boldsymbol{r}} = 0$, so

$$\begin{aligned}\frac{\delta \mathcal{T}}{\delta \boldsymbol{r}} = & -\partial_{a_1}\partial_{\boldsymbol{r}_{a_1}}\left[\xi_{11}\left(\boldsymbol{n}\cdot\boldsymbol{r}_{a_1a_1} - B^0_{11}\right)^2 + 2\xi_{12}\left(\boldsymbol{n}\cdot\boldsymbol{r}_{a_1a_2} - B^0_{12}\right)^2 + \xi_{22}\left(\boldsymbol{n}\cdot\boldsymbol{r}_{a_2a_2} - B^0_{22}\right)^2\right] \\ & -\partial_{a_2}\partial_{\boldsymbol{r}_{a_2}}\left[\xi_{11}\left(\boldsymbol{n}\cdot\boldsymbol{r}_{a_1a_1} - B^0_{11}\right)^2 + 2\xi_{12}\left(\boldsymbol{n}\cdot\boldsymbol{r}_{a_1a_2} - B^0_{12}\right)^2 + \xi_{22}\left(\boldsymbol{n}\cdot\boldsymbol{r}_{a_2a_2} - B^0_{22}\right)^2\right] \\ & +\partial_{a_1a_1}\partial_{\boldsymbol{r}_{a_1a_1}}\left[\xi_{11}\left(\boldsymbol{n}\cdot\boldsymbol{r}_{a_1a_1} - B^0_{11}\right)^2 + 2\xi_{12}\left(\boldsymbol{n}\cdot\boldsymbol{r}_{a_1a_2} - B^0_{12}\right)^2 + \xi_{22}\left(\boldsymbol{n}\cdot\boldsymbol{r}_{a_2a_2} - B^0_{22}\right)^2\right] \\ & +2\partial_{a_1a_2}\partial_{\boldsymbol{r}_{a_1a_2}}\left[\xi_{11}\left(\boldsymbol{n}\cdot\boldsymbol{r}_{a_1a_1} - B^0_{11}\right)^2 + 2\xi_{12}\left(\boldsymbol{n}\cdot\boldsymbol{r}_{a_1a_2} - B^0_{12}\right)^2 + \xi_{22}\left(\boldsymbol{n}\cdot\boldsymbol{r}_{a_2a_2} - B^0_{22}\right)^2\right] \\ & +\partial_{a_2a_2}\partial_{\boldsymbol{r}_{a_2a_2}}\left[\xi_{11}\left(\boldsymbol{n}\cdot\boldsymbol{r}_{a_1a_1} - B^0_{11}\right)^2 + 2\xi_{12}\left(\boldsymbol{n}\cdot\boldsymbol{r}_{a_1a_2} - B^0_{12}\right)^2 + \xi_{22}\left(\boldsymbol{n}\cdot\boldsymbol{r}_{a_2a_2} - B^0_{22}\right)^2\right].\end{aligned} \tag{9.34}$$

Taking care of the first partial differentiation using the differentiation rule in (18.173), gives

$$\begin{aligned}\frac{\delta \mathcal{T}}{\delta \boldsymbol{r}} = & -\partial_{a_1}\left[2\xi_{11}\left(\boldsymbol{n}\cdot\boldsymbol{r}_{a_1a_1} - B^0_{11}\right)\boldsymbol{n}^T_{\boldsymbol{r}_{a_1}}\boldsymbol{r}_{a_1a_1} + 4\xi_{12}\left(\boldsymbol{n}\cdot\boldsymbol{r}_{a_1a_2} - B^0_{12}\right)\boldsymbol{n}^T_{\boldsymbol{r}_{a_1}}\boldsymbol{r}_{a_1a_2}\right. \\ & \qquad \left. +2\xi_{22}\left(\boldsymbol{n}\cdot\boldsymbol{r}_{a_2a_2} - B^0_{22}\right)\boldsymbol{n}^T_{\boldsymbol{r}_{a_1}}\boldsymbol{r}_{a_2a_2}\right] \\ & -\partial_{a_2}\left[2\xi_{11}\left(\boldsymbol{n}\cdot\boldsymbol{r}_{a_1a_1} - B^0_{11}\right)\boldsymbol{n}^T_{\boldsymbol{r}_{a_2}}\boldsymbol{r}_{a_1a_1} + 4\xi_{12}\left(\boldsymbol{n}\cdot\boldsymbol{r}_{a_1a_2} - B^0_{12}\right)\boldsymbol{n}^T_{\boldsymbol{r}_{a_2}}\boldsymbol{r}_{a_1a_2}\right. \\ & \qquad \left. +2\xi_{22}\left(\boldsymbol{n}\cdot\boldsymbol{r}_{a_2a_2} - B^0_{22}\right)\boldsymbol{n}^T_{\boldsymbol{r}_{a_2}}\boldsymbol{r}_{a_2a_2}\right] \\ & +\partial_{a_1a_1}\left[2\xi_{11}\left(\boldsymbol{n}\cdot\boldsymbol{r}_{a_1a_1} - B^0_{11}\right)\boldsymbol{n}\right] \\ & +2\partial_{a_1a_2}\left[4\xi_{12}\left(\boldsymbol{n}\cdot\boldsymbol{r}_{a_1a_2} - B^0_{12}\right)\boldsymbol{n}\right] \\ & +\partial_{a_2a_2}\left[2\xi_{22}\left(\boldsymbol{n}\cdot\boldsymbol{r}_{a_2a_2} - B^0_{22}\right)\boldsymbol{n}\right].\end{aligned} \tag{9.35}$$

As for the S-case, we introduce a symbol representing the part of the equation that concerns the fundamental form. Specifically, we set

$$\beta_{11} = 2\xi_{11}\left(\boldsymbol{n}\cdot\boldsymbol{r}_{a_1a_1} - B^0_{11}\right) = \tilde{\xi}_{11}\left(\boldsymbol{n}\cdot\boldsymbol{r}_{a_1a_1} - B^0_{11}\right), \tag{9.36a}$$

$$\beta_{12} = 4\xi_{12}\left(\boldsymbol{n}\cdot\boldsymbol{r}_{a_1a_2} - B^0_{12}\right) = \tilde{\xi}_{12}\left(\boldsymbol{n}\cdot\boldsymbol{r}_{a_1a_2} - B^0_{12}\right), \tag{9.36b}$$

$$\beta_{22} = 2\xi_{22}\left(\boldsymbol{n}\cdot\boldsymbol{r}_{a_2a_2} - B^0_{22}\right) = \tilde{\xi}_{22}\left(\boldsymbol{n}\cdot\boldsymbol{r}_{a_2a_2} - B^0_{22}\right). \tag{9.36c}$$

The parameters ξ_{ij} are user specified. For η_{ij}, for convenience we introduce $\tilde{\xi}_{ij}$ as the new user-specified parameters, and finally we may write the variational derivative of $\mathcal{T}$ as

$$\begin{aligned}\frac{\delta \mathcal{T}}{\delta \boldsymbol{r}} = & -\partial_{a_1}\left[\beta_{11}\boldsymbol{n}^T_{\boldsymbol{r}_{a_1}}\boldsymbol{r}_{a_1a_1} + \beta_{12}\boldsymbol{n}^T_{\boldsymbol{r}_{a_1}}\boldsymbol{r}_{a_1a_2} + \beta_{22}\boldsymbol{n}^T_{\boldsymbol{r}_{a_1}}\boldsymbol{r}_{a_2a_2}\right] \\ & -\partial_{a_2}\left[\beta_{11}\boldsymbol{n}^T_{\boldsymbol{r}_{a_2}}\boldsymbol{r}_{a_1a_1} + \beta_{12}\boldsymbol{n}^T_{\boldsymbol{r}_{a_2}}\boldsymbol{r}_{a_1a_2} + \beta_{22}\boldsymbol{n}^T_{\boldsymbol{r}_{a_2}}\boldsymbol{r}_{a_2a_2}\right] \\ & +\partial_{a_1a_1}\beta_{11}\boldsymbol{n} + 2\partial_{a_1a_2}\beta_{12}\boldsymbol{n} + \partial_{a_2a_2}\beta_{22}\boldsymbol{n}.\end{aligned} \tag{9.37}$$

This equation is the variational derivative of the part of the energy-functional that concerns the second fundamental form. As can be seen, it is rather complex, so we would like to approximate it with something simpler, which can be done in many ways.

In [Terzopoulos et al., 1987], an approximation of the T-part is chosen by an analogy to the S-part without any theoretical justification. Our derivation shows how this approximation can be justified. First we ignore all first-order terms, which seems reasonable since curvature describes a second-order property. Then we replace the normal $\boldsymbol{n}$ with $\boldsymbol{r}_{a_i a_j}$, which can be justified as follows: the first derivative of a point on a curve is the tangent, the second derivative corresponds to a normal. We then arrive at the following approximation:

$$\frac{\delta \mathcal{T}}{\delta \boldsymbol{r}} \approx \partial_{a_1 a_1} \beta_{11} \boldsymbol{r}_{a_1 a_1} + 2 \partial_{a_1 a_2} \beta_{12} \boldsymbol{r}_{a_1 a_2} + \partial_{a_2 a_2} \beta_{11} \boldsymbol{r}_{a_2 a_2}. \tag{9.38}$$

As can be seen, the above approximation is very similar to (9.30). The only difference is the different multiplicative constant hidden in the β_{12} term. Rescaling this term can be done without changing the fundamental properties of this term. To see this, we can study the analogy with gradient descent. Here, the negative gradient always points in the minimum direction. Thus, the direction remains the same, regardless of any chosen multiplicative constant. This implies that during minimization, we always walk in the direction of the minimum. The multiplicative term only determines how long the steps are. With this justification, we arrive at the final approximation for the T-term:

$$\frac{\delta \mathcal{T}}{\delta \boldsymbol{r}} \approx \sum_{i,j=1}^{2} \partial_{a_i a_j} \left(\beta_{ij} \boldsymbol{r}_{a_i a_j} \right), \tag{9.39a}$$

$$\beta_{ij} = \tilde{\xi}_{ij} \left(\boldsymbol{n} \cdot \boldsymbol{r}_{a_i a_j} - B^0_{ij} \right). \tag{9.39b}$$

9.2.2.3 The Complete Variational Derivative

This concludes the derivation of the approximating vector expression for the variational derivative of the energy potential, yielding the following relation:

$$\boldsymbol{e} = \frac{\delta \mathcal{E}}{\delta \boldsymbol{r}} \approx \boldsymbol{e}(\boldsymbol{r}) = \sum_{i,j=1}^{2} -\partial_{a_i} \left(\alpha_{ij} \boldsymbol{r}_{a_j} \right) + \partial_{a_i a_j} \left(\beta_{ij} \boldsymbol{r}_{a_i a_j} \right), \tag{9.40a}$$

$$\alpha_{ij} = \tilde{\eta}_{ij} \left(G_{ij} - G^0_{ij} \right), \tag{9.40b}$$

$$\beta_{ij} = \tilde{\xi}_{ij} \left(B_{ij} - B^0_{ij} \right). \tag{9.40c}$$

The size of the elastic force vector, $\boldsymbol{e}$, describes the elasticity inherent at a point in a deformable object. This is an internal property of the object, and it increases as the object deforms at the intrinsic position. So, the elasticity, $\boldsymbol{e}$, is the elastic force that should work on a point to minimize the deformation.

9.2.3 Understanding the Model

The two constitutive equations (9.40b) and (9.40c) model the governing behavior of the elastic motion. Comparing them with *Hooke's Spring Law*, described in Section 22.4, which states that

$$\boldsymbol{F} = -k\boldsymbol{x}, \tag{9.41}$$

where x is a *displacement vector*, and k is the spring constant, we can see a resemblance. The $\tilde{\eta}$ and $\tilde{\xi}$ tensors both work as spring constants, albeit without the $-$ sign, and the difference of the fundamental form of the deformed object, from the fundamental form of the undeformed object, can be seen as displacement. This means, that the behavior of the elasticity is actually a spring model, with the fundamental forms as the units of measurements.

The first part of (9.40a), can be seen as the tension constraint on the elasticity. Inspecting the metric tensor,

$$G = \begin{bmatrix} G_{11} & G_{12} \\ G_{21} & G_{22} \end{bmatrix} \tag{9.42a}$$

$$= \begin{bmatrix} \frac{\partial \boldsymbol{r}}{\partial a_1} \cdot \frac{\partial \boldsymbol{r}}{\partial a_1} & \frac{\partial \boldsymbol{r}}{\partial a_1} \cdot \frac{\partial \boldsymbol{r}}{\partial a_2} \\ \frac{\partial \boldsymbol{r}}{\partial a_2} \cdot \frac{\partial \boldsymbol{r}}{\partial a_1} & \frac{\partial \boldsymbol{r}}{\partial a_2} \cdot \frac{\partial \boldsymbol{r}}{\partial a_2} \end{bmatrix}, \tag{9.42b}$$

we can see the significance of the different entries. The two elements, G_{11} and G_{22}, are the squared vector norm of the derivative in each of the coordinate directions. These entries measure the length in each direction, and compared with the rest state, G^0, determine stretching or compression of the material. The entries $G_{12} = G_{21}$ measure the angle between the two coordinate directions, since the dot product is defined as

$$\boldsymbol{x} \cdot \boldsymbol{y} = \frac{\cos\theta}{|\boldsymbol{x}||\boldsymbol{y}|}. \tag{9.43}$$

Together with G^0, they represent an angle constraint.

The constants $\tilde{\eta}_{ij}$ contains the weights of the *metric tensor*, and can be written as

$$\tilde{\eta} = \begin{bmatrix} \tilde{\eta}_{11} & \tilde{\eta}_{12} \\ \tilde{\eta}_{21} & \tilde{\eta}_{22} \end{bmatrix}, \tag{9.44}$$

with $\tilde{\eta}_{ij} \geq 0$. The $\tilde{\eta}_{11}$ and $\tilde{\eta}_{22}$ terms describe the resistance to length deformations in the two directions, while $\tilde{\eta}_{12} = \tilde{\eta}_{21}$ describe resistance to shearing. To simulate a material that behaves like soft rubber, one can use a small $\tilde{\eta}$, while a larger $\tilde{\eta}$ will model a less stretchable material, such as paper. In practice, it is seen that, if some $\tilde{\eta}_{ij} > 1$ and for large time steps, then the system tends to become *unstable* [Kelager et al., 2005].

The second part of (9.40a), can be seen as the curvature constraint on the elasticity. Inspecting the curvature tensor,

$$B = \begin{bmatrix} B_{11} & B_{12} \\ B_{21} & B_{22} \end{bmatrix} \tag{9.45a}$$

$$= \begin{bmatrix} \boldsymbol{n} \cdot \frac{\partial^2 \boldsymbol{r}}{\partial a_1^2} & \boldsymbol{n} \cdot \frac{\partial^2 \boldsymbol{r}}{\partial a_1 \cdot \partial a_2} \\ \boldsymbol{n} \cdot \frac{\partial^2 \boldsymbol{r}}{\partial a_2 \cdot \partial a_1} & \boldsymbol{n} \cdot \frac{\partial^2 \boldsymbol{r}}{\partial a_2^2} \end{bmatrix}, \tag{9.45b}$$

we find that B_{11} and B_{22} measure bending in each of the two coordinate directions, with $B_{12} = B_{21}$ measures twisting of the coordinate frame projected onto the normal. Comparing the values with the rest state, B^0, we have a measure of how the surface deforms with regard to bending and rotation.

The constants $\tilde{\xi}_{ij}$ contains the weights of the curvature tensor. These can be collected in a *rigidity tensor*

$$\tilde{\xi} = \begin{bmatrix} \tilde{\xi}_{11} & \tilde{\xi}_{12} \\ \tilde{\xi}_{21} & \tilde{\xi}_{22}, \end{bmatrix} \tag{9.46}$$

where $\tilde{\xi}_{11}$ and $\tilde{\xi}_{22}$ describe the resistance to bending, and $\tilde{\xi}_{12} = \tilde{\xi}_{21}$ describes resistance to twisting. To model surfaces with flexible bending properties, like cloth, $\tilde{\xi}$ should be close to zero. A thin metal plate, which has a high resistance to bending, should have a larger $\tilde{\xi}$. In practice, it is often seen that the system stays stable, by keeping the values $\tilde{\xi}_{ij} < 1$ [Christensen et al., 2004].

9.3 Discretizing the Model Relaxation

In the previous section, we derived a simplified approximation of the original partial equation given in (9.18). This approximation resulted in a vector expression, repeated here for convenience:

$$\boldsymbol{e} = \sum_{i,j=1}^{2} -\partial_{a_i}\left(\alpha_{ij}\boldsymbol{r}_{a_j}\right) + \partial_{a_i a_j}\left(\beta_{ij}\boldsymbol{r}_{a_i a_j}\right), \tag{9.47a}$$

$$\alpha_{ij} = \tilde{\eta}_{ij}\left(G_{ij} - G_{ij}^0\right), \tag{9.47b}$$

$$\beta_{ij} = \tilde{\xi}_{ij}\left(B_{ij} - B_{ij}^0\right). \tag{9.47c}$$

This expression for the elastic force is continuous in the material coordinates $\boldsymbol{a}$ of the deformable object. To be able to implement this, we need to discretize it, thereby transforming the original partial differential equation (9.8) into a system of ordinary differential equations. This system can then be converted to a matrix-vector form, which is easily implemented and solved on a computer. In this section, we will use the standard technique of finite difference approximations as described in Section 20.2, to calculate the different derivatives involved in the expressions. The deformable surface is described by a continuous mapping from material coordinates $\boldsymbol{a} = [a_1, a_2]^T$ to world coordinates $\boldsymbol{r}(\boldsymbol{a}) = [r_x, r_y, r_z]^T$. The domain of the material coordinates is a unit square, $0 \leq a_1, a_2 \leq 1$. We discretize the material domain into a regular $M \times N$-sized grid of nodes, with an internode spacing of h_1 and h_2, given by

$$h_1 = \frac{1}{M-1}, \tag{9.48a}$$

$$h_2 = \frac{1}{N-1}. \tag{9.48b}$$

This is illustrated in Figure 9.5. We will use square brackets to indicate that we approximate a continuous function $\boldsymbol{r}(a_1, a_2)$, on the discrete grid, where $0 \leq m \leq M-1$ and $0 \leq n \leq N-1$. For example, $\boldsymbol{r}[m,n] = \boldsymbol{r}(mh_1, nh_2)$.

By analogy to particle systems presented in Chapter 8, a grid node can be thought of as a particle. The metric tensor G can then be thought of as structural springs, and the curvature tensor B as bending springs.

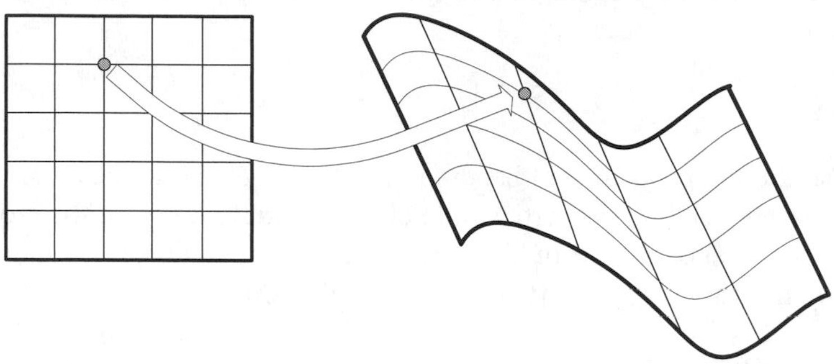

Figure 9.5: Discretization of the material coordinate domain.

9.3.1 Finite Difference Operators

To ease notation in the following, we will introduce symbolic names for the *finite difference operators* needed. The symbol D indicates a finite difference operator. The subscripts denote the material coordinate axis along which the difference is performed. The superscript $+$ indicates a forward difference, while a $-$ indicate a backward difference.

The forward first difference operators are defined by:

$$D_1^+(\boldsymbol{u})\,[m,n] = (\boldsymbol{u}\,[m+1,n] - u\,[m,n])\,/h_1, \tag{9.49a}$$
$$D_2^+(\boldsymbol{u})\,[m,n] = (\boldsymbol{u}\,[m,n+1] - u\,[m,n])\,/h_2. \tag{9.49b}$$

Similarly, the backward first difference operators are defined by

$$D_1^-(\boldsymbol{u})\,[m,n] = (\boldsymbol{u}\,[m,n] - u\,[m-1,n])\,/h_1, \tag{9.50a}$$
$$D_2^-(\boldsymbol{u})\,[m,n] = (\boldsymbol{u}\,[m,n] - u\,[m,n-1])\,/h_2. \tag{9.50b}$$

The forward and backward cross difference operators, can then be defined as

$$D_{12}^+(\boldsymbol{u})\,[m,n] = D_{21}^+(\boldsymbol{u})\,[m,n] = D_1^+\left(D_2^+(\boldsymbol{u})\right)[m,n]\,, \tag{9.51a}$$
$$D_{12}^-(\boldsymbol{u})\,[m,n] = D_{21}^-(\boldsymbol{u})\,[m,n] = D_1^-\left(D_2^-(\boldsymbol{u})\right)[m,n]\,. \tag{9.51b}$$

The central second difference operators can then be defined as

$$D_{11}(\boldsymbol{u})\,[m,n] = D_1^-\left(D_1^+(\boldsymbol{u})\right)[m,n]\,, \tag{9.52a}$$
$$D_{22}(\boldsymbol{u})\,[m,n] = D_2^-\left(D_2^+(\boldsymbol{u})\right)[m,n]\,. \tag{9.52b}$$

Finally, we define combined second difference operators, $D_{ij}^{(+)}$ and $D_{ij}^{(-)}$, that means: use the forward or backward cross differential operator, when $i \neq j$, and the second central difference operator D_{ii}, otherwise.

9.3.2 Discretizing the Elastic Force

With the above operators, it is very easy to write up the discrete versions of the elastic force F_{elastic}. First, the two continuous versions of the constitutive functions, α and β, given by

$$\alpha_{ij}(\boldsymbol{a}, \boldsymbol{r}) = \tilde{\eta}_{ij}(\boldsymbol{a}) \left(G_{ij} - G^0_{ij}\right) = \tilde{\eta}_{ij}(\boldsymbol{a}) \left(\frac{\partial \boldsymbol{r}}{\partial a_i} \cdot \frac{\partial \boldsymbol{r}}{\partial a_j} - G^0_{ij}\right), \tag{9.53a}$$

$$\beta_{ij}(\boldsymbol{a}, \boldsymbol{r}) = \tilde{\xi}_{ij}(\boldsymbol{a}) \left(B_{ij} - B^0_{ij}\right) = \tilde{\xi}_{ij}(\boldsymbol{a}) \left(\boldsymbol{n} \cdot \frac{\partial^2 \boldsymbol{r}}{\partial a_i \cdot \partial a_j} - B^0_{ij}\right), \tag{9.53b}$$

are discretized to yield

$$\alpha_{ij}\left[m,n\right] = \tilde{\eta}_{ij}\left[m,n\right] \left(D^+_i(\boldsymbol{r})\left[m,n\right] \cdot D^+_i(\boldsymbol{r})\left[m,n\right] - G^0_{ij}\left[m,n\right]\right), \tag{9.54a}$$

$$\beta_{ij}\left[m,n\right] = \tilde{\xi}_{ij}\left[m,n\right] \left(\boldsymbol{n}\left[m,n\right] \cdot D^{(+)}_{ij}(\boldsymbol{r})\left[m,n\right] - B^0_{ij}\left[m,n\right]\right), \tag{9.54b}$$

where the initial tensors, G^0 and B^0, can be calculated analytically, or by using the same finite difference operators on a discretization of the rest shape. The finite difference operators appears to give higher stability. Hence, the continuous elastic force, given by

$$\boldsymbol{e}(\boldsymbol{r}) = \sum_{i,j=1}^{2} -\frac{\partial}{\partial a_i}\left(\alpha_{ij}\frac{\partial \boldsymbol{r}}{\partial a_j}\right) + \frac{\partial^2}{\partial a_i \partial a_j}\left(\beta_{ij}\frac{\partial^2 \boldsymbol{r}}{\partial a_i \partial a_j}\right), \tag{9.55}$$

can be discretized to yield

$$\boldsymbol{e}\left[m,n\right] = \sum_{i,j=1}^{2} -D^-_i(\boldsymbol{p})\left[m,n\right] + D^{(-)}_{ij}(\boldsymbol{q})\left[m,n\right], \tag{9.56a}$$

$$\boldsymbol{p} = \alpha_{ij}\left[m,n\right] D^+_j(\boldsymbol{r})\left[m,n\right], \tag{9.56b}$$

$$\boldsymbol{q} = \beta_{ij}\left[m,n\right] D^{(+)}_{ij}(\boldsymbol{r})\left[m,n\right]. \tag{9.56c}$$

Notice that the final discretization uses a combination of forward and backward difference operators. This combination results in a central difference approximation for $\boldsymbol{r}$.

The elastic force has been separated in two parts, $\boldsymbol{p}\left[m,n\right]$ and $\boldsymbol{q}\left[m,n\right]$, to emphasize the fact that they are fields of the same size as the discretized surface $\boldsymbol{r}\left[m,n\right]$. It therefore makes sense to apply the finite difference operators on these fields as well. That means, to calculate the elastic force $\boldsymbol{e}$ for a given material point $\boldsymbol{r}\left[m,n\right]$, we only need to look in the neighborhood of the material point. This is the key in understanding how to perform the actual implementation, which is described next.

9.3.3 The Stiffness Matrix

With the discretization in place, we now want to derive a matrix-vector equation for the elastic force. In the following description, we look at a deformable surface consisting of $M \times N$ material points. Let us collect all the particle positions, $\boldsymbol{r}[m,n]$, in one large MN dimensional vector, $\underline{\mathrm{r}}$. We then want to reformulate the discretization, in such a way, that we can calculate the elastic force of all the particles simultaneously, by the expression

$$\underline{\mathrm{e}} = \mathbf{K}(\underline{\mathrm{r}})\underline{\mathrm{r}}, \tag{9.57}$$

where $\underline{\mathrm{e}}$ is an MN dimensional vector containing the elastic force for all material points. The matrix $\mathbf{K}(\underline{\mathrm{r}})$, with dimensions $MN \times MN$, is called the *stiffness matrix*.

To assemble the stiffness matrix, we need to have a closer look at the discretizations of the elastic force. We will evaluate the finite differences to see which material point positions are involved in calculating the elastic force for a single material point. We will discover that the material points involved all lie in a close neighborhood, which gives an analogy to *discrete filtering kernels*, also called *stencils*.

9.3.3.1 The α Stencil

Expanding the first part of (9.56a), we get

$$\begin{aligned}\sum_{i,j=1}^{2} -D_i^-(\boldsymbol{p})[m,n] = &- D_1^-\left(\alpha_{11}[m,n]\,D_1^+(\boldsymbol{r})[m,n]\right)\\ &- D_1^-\left(\alpha_{12}[m,n]\,D_2^+(\boldsymbol{r})[m,n]\right)\\ &- D_2^-\left(\alpha_{21}[m,n]\,D_1^+(\boldsymbol{r})[m,n]\right)\\ &- D_2^-\left(\alpha_{22}[m,n]\,D_2^+(\boldsymbol{r})[m,n]\right).\end{aligned} \tag{9.58}$$

Taking only the first part of this, and evaluating, first the backward difference operator, then the forward difference operator, we find

$$-D_1^-\left(\alpha_{11}[m,n]\,D_1^+(\boldsymbol{r})[m,n]\right)$$

$$= \frac{-\alpha_{11}[m,n]\,D_1^+(\boldsymbol{r})[m,n] + \alpha_{11}[m-1,n]\,D_1^+(\boldsymbol{r})[m-1,n]}{h_1} \tag{9.59a}$$

$$= \frac{-\alpha_{11}[m,n]\left(\boldsymbol{r}[m+1,n] - \boldsymbol{r}[m,n]\right) + \alpha_{11}[m-1,n]\left(\boldsymbol{r}[m,n] - \boldsymbol{r}[m-1,n]\right)}{h_1^2} \tag{9.59b}$$

$$= -\frac{\alpha_{11}[m,n]}{h_1^2}\boldsymbol{r}[m+1,n] + \frac{\alpha_{11}[m,n] + \alpha_{11}[m-1,n]}{h_1^2}\boldsymbol{r}[m,n] - \frac{\alpha_{11}[m-1,n]}{h_1^2}\boldsymbol{r}[m-1,n]. \tag{9.59c}$$

Doing the same for the other parts of the summation, and gathering terms, we can write the results as a 3×3 stencil,

$$S_\alpha[m,n] : \quad \begin{array}{|c|c|c|}\hline 0 & -\frac{\alpha_{21}[m,n-1]}{h_1h_2} - \frac{\alpha_{22}[m,n-1]}{h_2^2} & \frac{\alpha_{21}[m,n-1]}{h_1h_2} \\ \hline -\frac{\alpha_{11}[m-1,n]}{h_1^2} - \frac{\alpha_{12}[m-1,n]}{h_1h_2} & \begin{array}{c}\frac{\alpha_{11}[m,n]+\alpha_{11}[m-1,n]}{h_1^2}\\ +\frac{\alpha_{12}[m,n]+\alpha_{21}[m,n]}{h_1h_2}\\ +\frac{\alpha_{22}[m,n]+\alpha_{22}[m,n-1]}{h_2^2}\end{array} & -\frac{\alpha_{11}[m,n]}{h_1^2} - \frac{\alpha_{21}[m,n]}{h_1h_2} \\ \hline \frac{\alpha_{12}[m-1,n]}{h_1h_2} & -\frac{\alpha_{12}[m,n]}{h_1h_2} - \frac{\alpha_{22}[m,n]}{h_2^2} & 0 \\ \hline\end{array} \tag{9.60}$$

```
Algorithm compute-alpha()
    for m=0 to M-1
      for n=0 to N-1
        alpha_11[m][n] = alpha_12[m][n] = alpha_22[m][n] = 0
        vector3 D11_r =  (r_cur[m+1][n] - r_cur[m-1][n])/ 2 h_1
        vector3 D22_r =  (r_cur[m][n+1] - r_cur[m][n-1])/ 2 h_2
        alpha_11[m][n] = eta_11[m][n]*( D1_r * D1_r  - G0_11[m][n])
        alpha_12[m][n] = eta_12[m][n]*( D1_r * D2_r - G0_12[m][n])
        alpha_22[m][n] = eta_22[m][n]*( D2_r * D2_r - G0_22[m][n])
      next m
    next n
End algorithm
```

Figure 9.6: Pseudocode showing how to compute the alpha grid. Von Neumann boundary conditions as described in Section 9.3.7 should be applied to the grid of current particle positions.

corresponding to the grid positions,

$$\begin{array}{|c|c|c|}\hline [m-1,n-1] & [m,n-1] & [m+1,n-1] \\ \hline [m-1,n] & [m,n] & [m+1,n] \\ \hline [m-1,n+1] & [m,n+1] & [m+1,n+1] \\ \hline \end{array} \tag{9.61}$$

Now the α-stencil, S_α, can be seen as a filter that can be applied on the positional grid, $\boldsymbol{r}$. When applying this filter at position $\boldsymbol{r}\,[m,n]$, we effectively calculate (9.58).

Figure 9.6 illustrates in pseudocode how to compute α.

9.3.3.2 The β Stencil

Expanding the second part of (9.56a), we get

$$\begin{aligned}\sum_{i,j=1}^{2} D_{ij}^{(-)}(\boldsymbol{q})\,[m,n] =& D_{11}\beta_{11}\,[m,n]\, D_{11}(\boldsymbol{r})\,[m,n] \\ &+ D_{12}^{-}\beta_{12}\,[m,n]\, D_{12}^{+}(\boldsymbol{r})\,[m,n] \\ &+ D_{21}^{-}\beta_{21}\,[m,n]\, D_{21}^{+}(\boldsymbol{r})\,[m,n] \\ &+ D_{22}\beta_{22}\,[m,n]\, D_{22}(\boldsymbol{r})\,[m,n]\,.\end{aligned} \tag{9.62}$$

As for the α-stencil, we can expand this expression fully by substituting the expressions for the finite difference operators, and collect terms. This time, due to the use of the central and cross difference operators, the result is a 5×5 stencil,

$$
S_\beta : \quad
\begin{array}{|c|c|c|c|c|}
\hline
0 & 0 & S_\beta\,[m, n-2] & 0 & 0 \\
\hline
0 & S_\beta\,[m-1, n-1] & S_\beta\,[m, n-1] & S_\beta\,[m+1, n-1] & 0 \\
\hline
S_\beta\,[m-2, n] & S_\beta\,[m-1, n] & S_\beta\,[m, n] & S_\beta\,[m+1, n] & S_\beta\,[m+2, n] \\
\hline
0 & S_\beta\,[m-1, n+1] & S_\beta\,[m, n+1] & S_\beta\,[m+1, n+1] & 0 \\
\hline
0 & 0 & S_\beta\,[m, n+2] & 0 & 0 \\
\hline
\end{array}
\quad , \qquad (9.63)
$$

where the nonzero entries in each row are given by:

$$S_\beta[m, n-2] = (\beta_{22}\,[m, n-1])\,/h_2^4, \tag{9.64a}$$

$$S_\beta[m-1, n-1] = (\beta_{12}\,[m-1, n-1] + \beta_{21}\,[m-1, n-1])\,/(h_1^2 h_2^2), \tag{9.64b}$$

$$S_\beta[m, n-1] = (-\beta_{12}\,[m, n-1] - \beta_{12}\,[m-1, n-1] - \beta_{21}\,[m, n-1] - \beta_{21}\,[m-1, n-1])\,/(h_1^2 h_2^2)$$
$$\qquad + (-2\beta_{22}\,[m, n] - 2\beta_{22}\,[m, n-1])\,/h_2^4, \tag{9.64c}$$

$$S_\beta[m+1, n-1] = (\beta_{12}\,[m, n-1] + \beta_{21}\,[m, n-1])\,/(h_1^2 h_2^2), \tag{9.64d}$$

$$S_\beta[m-2, n] = (\beta_{11}\,[m-1, n])\,/h_1^4, \tag{9.64e}$$

$$S_\beta[m-1, n] = (-2\beta_{11}\,[m, n] - 2\beta_{11}\,[m-1, n])\,/h_1^4$$
$$\qquad + (-\beta_{12}\,[m-1, n] - \beta_{12}\,[m-1, n-1] - \beta_{21}\,[m-1, n] - \beta_{21}\,[m-1, n-1])\,/(h_1^2 h_2^2), \tag{9.64f}$$

$$S_\beta[m, n] = (\beta_{11}\,[m+1, n] + 4\beta_{11}\,[m, n] + \beta_{11}\,[m-1, n])\,/h_1^4$$
$$\qquad + (\beta_{12}\,[m, n] + \beta_{12}\,[m, n-1] + \beta_{21}\,[m-1, n] + \beta_{21}\,[m-1, n-1])\,/(h_1^2 h_2^2)$$
$$\qquad + (\beta_{21}\,[m, n] + \beta_{12}\,[m, n-1] + \beta_{21}\,[m-1, n] + \beta_{21}\,[m-1, n-1])\,/(h_1^2 h_2^2)$$
$$\qquad + (\beta_{22}\,[m, n+1] + 4\beta_{22}\,[m, n] + \beta_{22}\,[m, n-1])\,/h_2^4, \tag{9.64g}$$

$$S_\beta[m+1, n] = (-2\beta_{11}\,[m+1, n] - 2\beta_{11}\,[m, n])\,/h_1^4$$
$$\qquad + (-\beta_{12}\,[m, n] \quad \beta_{12}\,[m, n-1] - \beta_{21}\,[m, n] - \beta_{21}\,[m, n-1])\,/(h_1^2 h_2^2), \tag{9.64h}$$

$$S_\beta[m+2, n] = (\beta_{11}\,[m+1, n])\,/h_1^4, \tag{9.64i}$$

$$S_\beta[m-1, n+1] = (\beta_{12}\,[m-1, n] + \beta_{21}\,[m-1, n])\,/(h_1^2 h_2^2), \tag{9.64j}$$

$$S_\beta[m, n+1] = (-\beta_{12}\,[m, n] - \beta_{12}\,[m-1, n] - \beta_{21}\,[m, n] - \beta_{21}\,[m-1, n])\,/(h_1^2 h_2^2)$$
$$\qquad + (-2\beta_{22}\,[m, n+1] - 2\beta_{22}\,[m, n])\,/h_2^4, \tag{9.64k}$$

$$S_\beta[m+1, n+1] = (\beta_{12}\,[m, n] + \beta_{21}\,[m, n])\,/(h_1^2 h_2^2), \tag{9.64l}$$

$$S_\beta[m, n+2] = (\beta_{22}\,[m, n+1])\,/h_2^4. \tag{9.64m}$$

Again, when applying the S_β stencil to a node, given by $r\,[m, n]$ in the positional grid, the result is an evaluation of (9.62).

Figure 9.7 illustrates how to compute β in pseudocode.

```
Algorithm compute-beta()
    for m=0 to M
      for n=0 to N
        beta_11[m][n] =  beta_12[m][n] = beta_22[m][n] = 0
        vector3 D11_r = (r_cur[m+1][n] - r_cur[m-1][n])/2*h_1
        vector3 D22_r = (r_cur[m][n+1] - r_cur[m][n-1])/2*h_1
        vector3 D12_r = (r_cur[m+1][n+1] - r_cur[m+1][n]
                        - r_cur[m][n+1] + r_cur[m][n])/h_1*h_2
        beta_11[m][n] = xhi_11[m][n]*(n[m][n]*D11_r - B0_11[m][n])
        beta_12[m][n] = xhi_12[m][n]*(n[m][n]*D12_r - B0_12[m][n])
        beta_22[m][n] = xhi_22[m][n]*(n[m][n]*D22_r - B0_22[m][n])
      next m
    next n
End algorithm
```

Figure 9.7: Pseudocode showing how to compute the beta grid. Before invocation the normals for each grid node must have been computed. Von Neumann boundary conditions as described in Section 9.3.7 should be applied to the grid of current particle positions.

9.3.3.3 The Combined Stencil

To evaluate the complete (9.56a), we combine the S_α and S_β stencils, arriving at:

$S_c =$

0	0	$S_\beta[m, n-2]$	0	0
0	$S_\alpha[m-1, n-1]$ $+S_\beta[m-1, n-1]$	$S_\alpha[m, n-1]$ $+S_\beta[m, n-1]$	$S_\alpha[m+1, n-1]$ $+S_\beta[m+1, n-1]$	0
$S_\beta[m-2, n]$	$S_\alpha[m-1, n]$ $+S_\beta[m-1, n]$	$S_\alpha[m, n]$ $+S_\beta[m, n]$	$S_\alpha[m+1, n]$ $+S_\beta[m+1, n]$	$S_\beta[m+2, n]$
0	$S_\alpha[m-1, n+1]$ $+S_\beta[m-1, n+1]$	$S_\alpha[m, n+1]$ $+S_\beta[m, n+1]$	$S_\alpha[m+1, n+1]$ $+S_\beta[m+1, n+1]$	0
0	0	$S_\beta[m, n+2]$	0	0

. (9.65)

This stencil includes all of (9.56a) and contains all the information needed to understand how to assemble the stiffness matrix $\mathbf{K}$.

9.3.3.4 Assembling the Stiffness Matrix

The analogy to filter operations in the above derivations of the stencils can now help us to understand how to construct the stiffness matrix $\mathbf{K}$. The result of the matrix-vector multiplication, $\underline{e} = \mathbf{K}(\underline{r})\underline{r}$, is that $\underline{e}$ contains the elastic force for all the material points described by $\underline{r}$. Unfolding the positional grid to the vector $\underline{r}$ can be done as shown by the pseudocode shown in Figure 9.8. A single row in $\mathbf{K}$ should mask out the needed material points in $\underline{r}$, and apply the combined stencil S_c on these particles. For the sake

```
for i = 0 to MN-1 do
  m = div(i,M)
  n = mod(i,N)
  r(i) = r[m,n]
next i
```

Figure 9.8: Pseudocode for unfolding positional grid.

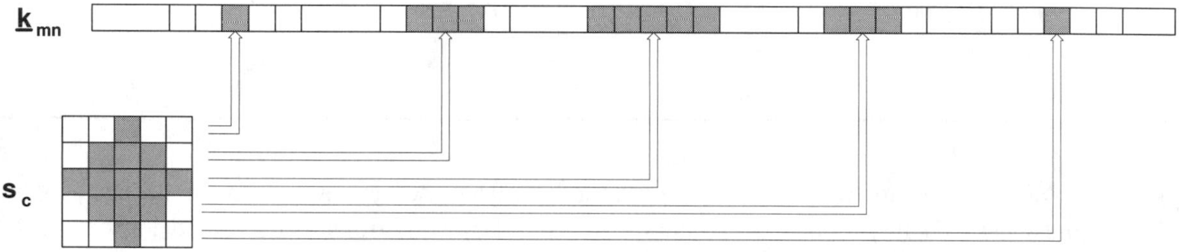

Figure 9.9: Row $\underline{k}_i$ of the stiffness matrix K comes from unfolding the combined stencil S_c.

of clarity, let us look at how to calculate the elastic force $\underline{e}_i$ for the particle $\underline{r}_i$, where position i in the MN-vectors corresponds to index $[m, n]$ in the grid. Unfolding the elasticity grid and the positional grid, the matrix-vector equation (9.57), will look like this:

$$\begin{bmatrix} \underline{e}_0 \\ \vdots \\ \underline{e}_i \\ \vdots \\ \underline{e}_{MN-1} \end{bmatrix} = \begin{bmatrix} \underline{k}_0^T \\ \vdots \\ \underline{k}_i^T \\ \vdots \\ \underline{k}_{MN-1}^T \end{bmatrix} \begin{bmatrix} \underline{r}_0 \\ \vdots \\ \underline{r}_i \\ \vdots \\ \underline{r}_{MN-1} \end{bmatrix}, \tag{9.66}$$

where $\underline{k}_{ij}^T$ is the rows of the stiffness matrix $\mathbf{K}$. The row, $\underline{k}_i^T$, corresponding to the elastic force calculation for particle $\underline{r}_i$, looks like Figure 9.9.

That is, the combined 5×5 stencil, S_c, has been unwrapped and the individual rows has been placed in the proper positions in the corresponding row of the stiffness matrix. Note that all the other entries are zero, which, in effect, ensures that only the needed particles are used in the calculation.

The other rows of $\mathbf{K}$ are just shifted version of row $\underline{k}_i$. This results in a stiffness matrix with a very nice structure, as seen in Figure 9.10. It only contains five subbands, each with five bands, with all the other entries being zero. So it is a square, banded, sparse matrix. This again means that we can use all sorts of nice matrix vector solvers to quickly calculate the elastic force of all the particles.

In Figure 9.11 the assembly of the stiffness matrix is outlined in pseudocode.

Figure 9.10: Structure of the stiffness matrix K.

```
Algorithm assembly-K()
 K = 0
 for i = 0 to MN-1
   m = mod(i,M)
   n = div(i,N)
   for s = m-2 to m+2
     for t = n-2 to n+2
       K(i, sM+t) = Sc(s,t)
     next t
   next s
 next i
End algorithm
```

Figure 9.11: Pseudocode for assembly of the stiffness matrix K.

9.3.4 A System of Ordinary Differential Equations

Having dealt with the elastic force, we are ready to look at the rest of the equation of motion (9.8), that is,

$$\frac{\partial}{\partial t}\left(\mu(\boldsymbol{a})\left(\frac{\partial \boldsymbol{r}(\boldsymbol{a},t)}{\partial t}\right)\right)+\gamma(\boldsymbol{a})\frac{\partial \boldsymbol{r}(\boldsymbol{a},t)}{\partial t}+\frac{\delta \mathcal{E}(\boldsymbol{r}(\boldsymbol{a},t))}{\delta \boldsymbol{r}(\boldsymbol{a},t)}=\boldsymbol{f}(\boldsymbol{r}(\boldsymbol{a},t),t). \tag{9.67}$$

In the general case, the density distribution function could be dependent on time, both directly, and indirectly, through the material coordinates, as in $\mu(\boldsymbol{a}(t),t)$. However, for our specific purpose, we will consider the density distribution function to be directly dependent upon the material coordinates only. This is justified by creating a fixed rectangular grid embedded in the object, where nodes correspond to a fixed material coordinate point. This simplifies the equation of motion to

$$\mu(\boldsymbol{a})\frac{\partial^2 \boldsymbol{r}(\boldsymbol{a},t)}{\partial t^2}+\gamma(\boldsymbol{a})\frac{\partial \boldsymbol{r}(\boldsymbol{a},t)}{\partial t}+\frac{\delta \mathcal{E}(\boldsymbol{r}(\boldsymbol{a},t))}{\delta \boldsymbol{r}(\boldsymbol{a},t)}=\boldsymbol{f}(\boldsymbol{r}(\boldsymbol{a},t),t). \tag{9.68}$$

For the elastic force, we have chosen to approximate with $\mathbf{K}(\underline{\mathrm{r}})\underline{\mathrm{r}}$, where $\underline{\mathrm{r}}$ is the MN element-sized concatenated vector of particle positions. To be able to use $\underline{\mathrm{r}}$ everywhere in (9.68), we need to represent the discrete versions of the mass densities, $\mu[m,n]$, and the damping densities, $\gamma[m,n]$, as well as the external forces, in a proper form.

For the discrete mass densities, $\mu[m,n]$, we construct a diagonal $MN \times MN$-dimensional mass matrix M with the $\mu[m,n]$ values in the diagonal. Similarly, we construct a *damping matrix* C with the discrete damping values $\gamma[m,n]$, in the diagonal. Finally, we create a MN-sized vector $\underline{\mathrm{f}}$, that gathers all the discrete external forces.

With these constructs, we are able to construct the fully spatial discretization of (9.68) as:

$$\mathbf{M}\frac{\partial^2 \underline{\mathrm{r}}}{\partial t^2}+\mathbf{C}\frac{\partial \underline{\mathrm{r}}}{\partial t}+\mathbf{K}(\underline{\mathrm{r}})\underline{\mathrm{r}}=\underline{\mathrm{f}}. \tag{9.69}$$

The original formulation, which is a system of nonlinear partial differential equations, has now been converted to a system of nonlinear ordinary differential equations.

9.3.5 Temporal Discretization

To simulate the deformation, the system of ordinary differential equations, (9.69), needs to be integrated through time. In order to favor stability and robustness over accuracy, an *implicit integration* scheme can be applied. For ease and speed, we also want the system to be linear, which is not the case for the system in (9.69). However, linearizing the system through a series of numerical steps will result in the semi-implicit method known as the Terzopoulos method [Terzopoulos et al., 1987].

The time-dependent factors in (9.69) can be approximated by the discrete first- and second-order accurate central differences given by

$$\frac{\partial \underline{\mathrm{r}}}{\partial t}=\frac{\underline{\mathrm{r}}_{t+\Delta t}-\underline{\mathrm{r}}_{t-\Delta t}}{2\Delta t}, \tag{9.70a}$$

$$\frac{\partial^2 \underline{\mathrm{r}}}{\partial t^2}=\frac{\underline{\mathrm{r}}_{t+\Delta t}-2\underline{\mathrm{r}}_{t}+\underline{\mathrm{r}}_{t-\Delta t}}{\Delta t^2}, \tag{9.70b}$$

where the subscripts on $\underline{r}$ means evaluate $\underline{r}$ at the time indicated by the subscript. This results in a linear approximation to the nonlinear system. Now, we evaluate $\underline{f}$ at time t, and $\underline{e}$ at time $t + \Delta t$. That is:

$$\underline{e}_{t+\Delta t} = \mathbf{K}(\underline{r}_t)\underline{r}_{t+\Delta t}. \tag{9.71}$$

These evaluations, together with the discrete time approximations from (9.70a) and (9.70b), are plugged into (9.69) to yield:

$$\mathbf{M}\frac{\underline{r}_{t+\Delta t} - 2\underline{r}_t + \underline{r}_{t-\Delta t}}{\Delta t^2} + \mathbf{C}\frac{\underline{r}_{t+\Delta t} - \underline{r}_{t-\Delta t}}{2\Delta t} + \mathbf{K}(\underline{r}_t)\underline{r}_{t+\Delta t} = \underline{f}_t, \tag{9.72}$$

which can be expanded to:

$$\frac{1}{\Delta t^2}\mathbf{M}\underline{r}_{t+\Delta t} - \frac{2}{\Delta t^2}\mathbf{M}\underline{r}_t + \frac{1}{\Delta t^2}\mathbf{M}\underline{r}_{t-\Delta t} + \frac{1}{2\Delta t}\mathbf{C}\underline{r}_{t+\Delta t} - \frac{1}{2\Delta t}\mathbf{C}\underline{r}_{t-\Delta t} + \mathbf{K}(\underline{r}_t)\underline{r}_{t+\Delta t} = \underline{f}_t. \tag{9.73}$$

We then collect $\underline{r}_{t+\Delta t}$ terms on the left-hand side, and get:

$$\left[\mathbf{K}(\underline{r}_t) + \left(\frac{1}{\Delta t^2}\mathbf{M} + \frac{1}{2\Delta t}\mathbf{C}\right)\right]\underline{r}_{t+\Delta t} = \underline{f}_t + \frac{2}{\Delta t^2}\mathbf{M}\underline{r}_t - \left(\frac{1}{\Delta t^2}\mathbf{M} - \frac{1}{2\Delta t}\mathbf{C}\right)\underline{r}_{t-\Delta t}. \tag{9.74}$$

The left-hand side can be written as

$$\mathbf{A}_t\underline{r}_{t+\Delta t} \quad \text{with} \quad \mathbf{A}_t = \mathbf{K}(\underline{r}_t) + \left(\frac{1}{\Delta t^2}\mathbf{M} + \frac{1}{2\Delta t}\mathbf{C}\right). \tag{9.75}$$

To arrive at an *implicit scheme*, we want the right-hand side to have a $\left(\frac{1}{\Delta t^2}\mathbf{M} + \frac{1}{2\Delta t}\mathbf{C}\right)\underline{r}_t$-term. We expand and rearrange, and get:

$$\mathbf{A}_t\underline{r}_{t+\Delta t} = \underline{f}_t + \frac{2}{\Delta t^2}\mathbf{M}\underline{r}_t - \left(\frac{1}{\Delta t^2}\mathbf{M} - \frac{1}{2\Delta t}\mathbf{C}\right)\underline{r}_{t-\Delta t} \tag{9.76a}$$

$$= \underline{f}_t + \frac{1}{\Delta t^2}\mathbf{M}\underline{r}_t + \frac{1}{\Delta t^2}\mathbf{M}\underline{r}_t - \frac{1}{\Delta t^2}\mathbf{M}\underline{r}_{t-\Delta t} + \frac{1}{2\Delta t}\mathbf{C}\underline{r}_{t-\Delta t}. \tag{9.76b}$$

By adding and subtracting the term $\frac{1}{2\Delta t}\mathbf{C}\underline{r}_t$, we contribute nothing to the equation. Doing this and rearranging again, we get

$$\mathbf{A}_t\underline{r}_{t+\Delta t} = \underline{f}_t + \frac{1}{\Delta t^2}\mathbf{M}\underline{r}_t + \frac{1}{\Delta t^2}\mathbf{M}\underline{r}_t - \frac{1}{\Delta t^2}\mathbf{M}\underline{r}_{t-\Delta t} + \frac{1}{2\Delta t}\mathbf{C}\underline{r}_{t-\Delta t} + \frac{1}{2\Delta t}\mathbf{C}\underline{r}_t - \frac{1}{2\Delta t}\mathbf{C}\underline{r}_t \tag{9.77a}$$

$$= \underline{f}_t + \frac{1}{\Delta t^2}\mathbf{M}\underline{r}_t + \frac{1}{2\Delta t}\mathbf{C}\underline{r}_t + \frac{1}{\Delta t^2}\mathbf{M}\underline{r}_t - \frac{1}{2\Delta t}\mathbf{C}\underline{r}_t - \frac{1}{\Delta t^2}\mathbf{M}\underline{r}_{t-\Delta t} + \frac{1}{2\Delta t}\mathbf{C}\underline{r}_{t-\Delta t} \tag{9.77b}$$

$$= \underline{f}_t + \left(\frac{1}{\Delta t^2}\mathbf{M} + \frac{1}{2\Delta t}\mathbf{C}\right)\underline{r}_t + \left(\frac{1}{\Delta t^2}\mathbf{M} - \frac{1}{2\Delta t}\mathbf{C}\right)\underline{r}_t - \left(\frac{1}{\Delta t^2}\mathbf{M} + \frac{1}{2\Delta t}\mathbf{C}\right)\underline{r}_{t-\Delta t} \tag{9.77c}$$

$$= \underline{f}_t + \left(\frac{1}{\Delta t^2}\mathbf{M} + \frac{1}{2\Delta t}\mathbf{C}\right)\underline{r}_t + \left(\frac{1}{\Delta t^2}\mathbf{M} - \frac{1}{2\Delta t}\mathbf{C}\right)\left(\underline{r}_t - \underline{r}_{t-\Delta t}\right) \tag{9.77d}$$

$$= \underline{f}_t + \left(\frac{1}{\Delta t^2}\mathbf{M} + \frac{1}{2\Delta t}\mathbf{C}\right)\underline{r}_t + \left(\frac{1}{\Delta t}\mathbf{M} - \frac{1}{2}\mathbf{C}\right)\frac{1}{\Delta t}\left(\underline{r}_t - \underline{r}_{t-\Delta t}\right) \tag{9.77e}$$

$$= \underline{f}_t + \left(\frac{1}{\Delta t^2}\mathbf{M} + \frac{1}{2\Delta t}\mathbf{C}\right)\underline{r}_t + \left(\frac{1}{\Delta t}\mathbf{M} - \frac{1}{2}\mathbf{C}\right)\underline{v}_t. \tag{9.77f}$$

```
Algorithm time-step(dt)
  M = mass matrix...
  C = damping matrix...
  r_cur = current position...
  r_old = old positions...
  f = external_forces...
  assemble_stiffness_matrix(K)
  MpC = ( M/(dt*dt) + C/(2*dt))
  A = K + MpC
  MmC = (M /dt - C/2)
  v = (r_cur - r_old)/dt
  g = f + MpC*r_cur + MmC*v
  solve(A,r_new,g)
  r_old = r_cur
  r_cur = r_new
End algorithm
```

Figure 9.12: Complete pseudocode for a single time-step.

In the last line, we recognized and substituted the implicit given velocity at time t, $\underline{v}_t = \frac{1}{\Delta t}\left(\underline{r}_t - \underline{r}_{t-\Delta t}\right)$. Looking at the SI-units of the right-hand side, we find that all terms have dimension of force. Therefore, we can call the right-hand side for the effective force vector, $\underline{g}_t$.

To summarize, we have derived a *semi-implicit integration* scheme described by the sparse, banded, linear system

$$\mathbf{A}_t \underline{r}_{t+\Delta t} = \underline{g}_t, \tag{9.78}$$

with the system matrix

$$\mathbf{A}_t = \mathbf{K}(\underline{r}_t) + \left(\frac{1}{\Delta t^2}\mathbf{M} + \frac{1}{2\Delta t}\mathbf{C}\right), \tag{9.79}$$

and the effective force vector

$$\underline{g}_t = \underline{f}_t + \left(\frac{1}{\Delta t^2}\mathbf{M} + \frac{1}{2\Delta t}\mathbf{C}\right)\underline{r}_t + \left(\frac{1}{\Delta t}\mathbf{M} + \frac{1}{2}\mathbf{C}\right)\underline{v}_t, \tag{9.80}$$

with

$$\underline{v}_t = \frac{1}{\Delta t}\left(\underline{r}_t - \underline{r}_{t-\Delta t}\right). \tag{9.81}$$

Figure 9.12 shows a pseudocode version of the complete algorithm, using the pseudocode from Figure 9.11.

9.3.6 Numerical Issues

Given initial conditions, $\underline{r}_0$ and $\underline{v}_0$, the above sparse linear system can be solved by inverting the system matrix

$$\underline{r}_{t+\Delta t} = \mathbf{A}_t^{-1}\underline{g}_t, \tag{9.82}$$

using an appropriate numerical solver, for example *Choleski decomposition* or *LU factorization*. However, the real win comes from exploiting the properties of the system matrix **A** from (9.79). This consists of the stiffness matrix plus a positive diagonal matrix, so all the properties of the stiffness matrix still hold. This means that we can use an iterative solver, like the *conjugate gradient* method as described in Section 18.2, to solve the system matrix. This allow us to simulate deformations, represented by a large amount of material coordinates, and still be able to visualize the results in real time.

If the entries in the stiffness matrix are very small, these values will become very large, when inverted. This is a problem for any method of solving the system of equations, but a simple and effective solution is to clamp all contributions to the stiffness matrix that are below a certain threshold, to zero.

Another issue concerns the boundaries of the discretized grid. Some sort of boundary conditions need to be implemented, to ensure that the finite difference operators do not break down. The easiest way to implement a boundary condition is to extend the grid with a border all around it. This border can then be initialized with whatever value is proper for a specific boundary condition. The filter operations are then defined on all values of the original grid. This is similar to the way filtering is implemented in, for example, Matlab®. For example, a natural boundary condition, also known as a von Neumann condition, requires the gradient to be constant across the boundary. This can be simulated by ensuring that the forward and cross difference operators in (9.56b) and (9.56c) return zero. To implement this, the border values need to be set to the same values that are right inside the boundary.

9.3.7 Von Neumann Boundary Conditions

We will now show how to implement simple *von Neumann boundary conditions* on a rectangular grid.

Let $r[i][j]$ denote the grid node at position (i, j). Let the $M \times N$ computational grid be represented on a grid of dimension $(M + 2) \times (N + 2)$. The computational grid, that is, where we solve the Dynamics, is given by the ranges $i \in 1..M$ and $j \in 1..N$. Indices outside these ranges are used to set up boundary conditions.

The central difference of r at grid locations $(1, \cdot)$ in horizontal direction is given by the formula:

$$D_{11}(r[i][j]) = \frac{r[i+1][j] - r[i-1][j]}{2h_1}. \tag{9.83}$$

Obviously, when $i = 1$, $r[i-1][j]$ lies outside the computational grid. To handle this boundary case, imagine that the surface is smooth and continuous and that the surface has infinite extension. It is then fair to assume that we can estimate the direction of $r[i-1][j]$ by the tangent of the surface at $r[i][j]$, as shown in Figure 9.13. That is

$$r[0][j] = r[1][j] - (r[2][j] - r[1][j]) \tag{9.84}$$

$$= 2r[1][j] - r[2][j]. \tag{9.85}$$

Inserting this into the *central difference scheme* yields

$$D_{11}(r[1][j]) = \frac{r[2][j] - (2r[1][j] - r[2][j])}{2h_1} \tag{9.86}$$

$$= \frac{r[2][j] - r[1][j]}{h_1}. \tag{9.87}$$

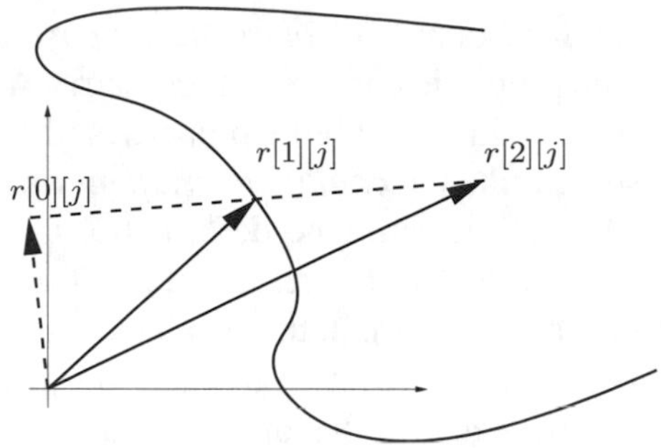

Figure 9.13: An imaginary point to the left of the left boundary.

This is recognized as a forward difference. Hereby we have shown that it makes sense to use Equation 9.84.

A similar case exists when $i = M$. This time $r[i+1][j]$ is undefined, and applying the same machinery suggests that

$$r[M+1][j] = r[M][j] - (r[M-1][j] - r[M][j]) \tag{9.88}$$

$$= 2r[M][j] - r[M-1][j]. \tag{9.89}$$

In order to verify that the value is meaningful, (9.88) is inserted into the central difference formula

$$D_{11}(r[M][j]) = \frac{(2r[M][j] - r[M-1][j]) - r[M-1][j]}{2h_1} \tag{9.90}$$

$$= \frac{r[M][j] - r[M-1][j]}{h_1}. \tag{9.91}$$

It is seen that this is in fact a backward difference.

The same approach applied to the horizontal direction yields the boundary values

$$r[i][0] = 2r[i][1] - r[i][2], \tag{9.92}$$

$$r[i][N+1] = 2r[i][N] - r[i][N-1]. \tag{9.93}$$

Notice that the four corner values are unused, that is, $r[0][0]$, $r[0][N+1]$, $r[M+1][0]$, and $r[M+1][N+1]$. Also, no left and right values are set for the top and bottom row. Similar, no top and bottom values are set for the left and right borders.

A central finite difference scheme for mixed partials can lead to trouble at the corner points because the values $r[0][0]$, $r[0][N+1]$, $r[M+1][0]$, and $r[M+1][N+1]$ are undefined. Using the same assumption about a continuous smooth surface yields the computational low-cost estimations of the corner values

$$r[0][0] = 2r[1][1] - r[2][2], \tag{9.94}$$

$$r[0][N+1] = 2r[1][N] - r[2][N-1], \tag{9.95}$$

$$r[M+1][0] = 2r[M][1] - r[M-1][2], \tag{9.96}$$

$$r[M+1][N+1] = 2r[M][N] - r[M-1][N-1]. \tag{9.97}$$

```
Algorithm apply-neumann(r,M,N)
  for i=0, j=1 to N
    r[i-1][j] =  2*r[i][j] - r[i+1][j]
  for i=M, j=1 to N
    r[i+1][j] =  2*r[i][j] - r[i-1][j]
  for j=0, i=1 to M
    r[i][j-1] =  2*r[i][j] - r[i][j+1]
  for j=N, i=1 to M
    r[i][j+1] =  2*r[i][j] - r[i][j-1]
  r[0][0] = 2 r[1][1] - r[2][2]
  r[0][N+1] = 2 r[1][N] - r[2][N-1]
  r[M+1][0] = 2 r[M][1] - r[M-1][2]
  r[M+1][N+1] = 2 r[M][N] - r[M-1][N-1]
End algorithm
```

Figure 9.14: Pseudocode showing how to apply von Neumann boundary conditions to a computational grid r, where a central difference scheme is applied.

A more elaborate scheme can of course be used, but we favor the above due to its simplicity and the fact that corner points are based on known values and not other boundary values, set along the horizontal and vertical lines outside the computational grid. In Figure 9.14 the pseudocode for applying von Neumann boundary conditions is given.

The boundary conditions we have applied are accurate enough to first order. Thus, if large discretizations are used (large h_0 and h_1), then boundary values will have large errors. Furthermore, if higher-order difference schemes are applied, that is, $O(n^p)$ with $p > 1$, then the scheme is more accurate than the boundary values. In the latter case one might want to devise a higher-order method for determining the off-surface points. This is, however, not needed for the Terzopoulos method, and we leave this as an exercise for the reader.

9.3.8 Dirichlet Boundary Conditions

Although not used in the Terzopoulos method, we will outline a simple implementation for *Dirichlet boundary conditions*. For this, a scalar computational grid s is used, with the same dimension as in Section 9.3.7. A Dirichlet boundary condition can now be set as $s[i][j] = 0$, or any other constant value.

These kind of boundary conditions are easily applied simply by setting values in the computational grid, before using it to perform any computations.

9.4 The External Forces

The external force, $\boldsymbol{f}(\boldsymbol{r}, t)$, in our model is the sum of several different kinds of forces. These external forces can be used to add realistic behavior to the model. A list of some examples of such external forces are

Gravity

Gravity force is acting on everything that has a mass. It is given by

$$\boldsymbol{f}_{\text{gravity}} = \mu(\boldsymbol{a})\boldsymbol{g}, \tag{9.98}$$

where $\boldsymbol{g}$ is the gravitational field. This is usually defined as a constant downward pointing value, $\boldsymbol{g} = \left[0, -9.82\text{m}/\text{s}^2, 0\right]^T$, but could be set to any other constant value.

Spring Forces

Spring forces are produced form springs between fixed material points, $\boldsymbol{a}_0$, and fixed points in the world, $\boldsymbol{r}_0$,

$$\boldsymbol{f}_{\text{spring}}(t) = k\left(\boldsymbol{r}_0 - \boldsymbol{r}(\boldsymbol{a}_0, t)\right). \tag{9.99}$$

Viscous Forces

Viscous forces measure the resistance to motion in a fluid-like substance. For example, a viscous force is given as

$$\boldsymbol{f}_{viscous}(\boldsymbol{a}, t) = c\left(\boldsymbol{n}(\boldsymbol{a}, t) \cdot \boldsymbol{v}_r(\boldsymbol{a}, t)\right)\boldsymbol{n}(\boldsymbol{a}, t) \quad \forall \boldsymbol{a} \in \Gamma, \tag{9.100}$$

where c is the viscosity coefficient, the strength of the viscous force, $\boldsymbol{n}$, is the unit surface normal, and $\boldsymbol{v}_r(\boldsymbol{a}, t)$ is the relative surface velocity to the constant stream velocity $\boldsymbol{u}$. That is,

$$\boldsymbol{v}_r(\boldsymbol{a}, t) = \boldsymbol{u} - \frac{\partial \boldsymbol{r}(\boldsymbol{a}, t)}{\partial t}. \tag{9.101}$$

As an example of a viscous force, consider a ball rolling toward a puddle of water. When the ball rolls through the water, it will slow down, due to the viscosity of the water.

9.4.1 Contact Forces

Contact forces are the key to interacting with the deformable model. Consider an impenetrable rigid object, for example, a stick, being pressed against the deformable object. Wherever the rigid object comes in contact with the deformable object, the material points of the deformable object need to be forced away, such that no penetrations occur. We will describe two methods to implement contact forces. One is by using penalty forces, as in [Terzopoulos et al., 1987]. The other is a projection method, as used in [Jakobsen, 2001], which utilizes the implicitly given velocity.

Contact forces can be modeled by *penalty forces*, as follows. We define a *potential energy function*, $V(\boldsymbol{r})$:

$$V(\boldsymbol{r}) = c\exp\left(\frac{-\phi(\boldsymbol{r})}{\epsilon}\right). \tag{9.102}$$

Here, c and ϵ are user-defined constants, used to fine-tune the shape of the potential. The function $\phi(\boldsymbol{r})$ is the inside/outside function of the object. It provides a measure of the *penetration depth* at those places where an object is in contact with something else. In Figure 9.15, the potential energy function is plotted.

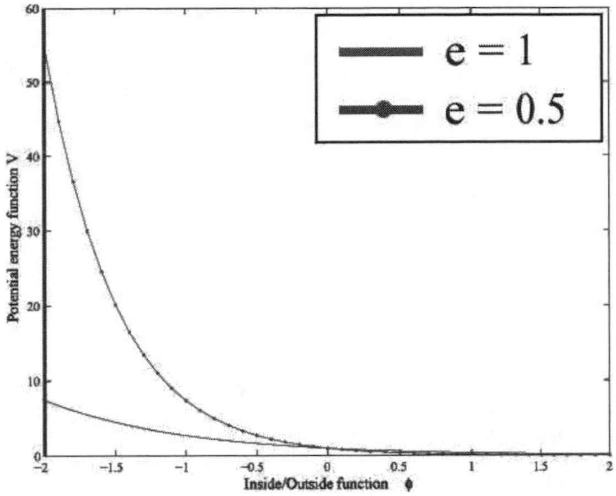

Figure 9.15: Potential energy function for $c = 1$ and different values of ϵ.

Conservative forces can be written as the negative gradient of a scalar field. Following this idea, we compute the negative gradient of the potential energy function:

$$-\nabla V(\boldsymbol{r}) = c\frac{\nabla \phi(\boldsymbol{r})}{\epsilon} \exp\left(\frac{-\phi(\boldsymbol{r})}{\epsilon}\right). \tag{9.103}$$

Finally, the contact force is determined as the projection of the negative gradient of the potential energy function onto the surface normal.

$$\boldsymbol{f}_{\text{contact}} = -\left(\nabla V \cdot \boldsymbol{n}\right)\boldsymbol{n}. \tag{9.104}$$

By substitution, we derive the final formula for the penalty force

$$\boldsymbol{f}_{\text{contact}}(\boldsymbol{r}) = c\left(\frac{\nabla \phi(\boldsymbol{r})}{\epsilon} \exp\left(\frac{-\phi(\boldsymbol{r})}{\epsilon}\right) \cdot \boldsymbol{n}(\boldsymbol{r})\right)\boldsymbol{n}(\boldsymbol{r}). \tag{9.105}$$

9.4.1.1 Collision Response

The *projection method* is a relatively simple method for *collision response*: it projects material points that have penetrated an impenetrable object, back to the surface of the object. Since the numerical scheme described in Section 9.3.5 calculates the velocities of the material points implicitly, the position update does not result in the position and velocities becoming out of sync. If another numerical scheme is used, where the velocities are explicitly calculated, the synchronization of positions and velocities would be harder to ensure. The projection method corresponds to iterative over-relaxation. In the limiting case, it can be seen as infinitely stiff springs that immediately return material points to the wanted position.

The projection method can be implemented as an extra step that is performed after all material positions have been updated. Simply run through all material points and project the penetrating points back to the surface in the normal direction. A multiplicative constant, $c > 0$, can be used to control the strength of the projection. In this way, c can be thought of as a *restitution coefficient*.

10

The Finite Element Method

In physics-based animation the *Finite Element Method* (*FEM*) is becoming the dominant method for animating deformable objects. The theory from mechanics is well established, but can be rather daunting. However, when applying a set of simplifying assumptions, the mathematics involved becomes much simpler. The following will concentrate on the special case of simulating deformable objects constructed from materials that are isotropic and further assume that the deformations involved are small.

Continuum mechanics deal with the prediction and calculation of the effect of applying an external load to some object with physical properties. The theory of elasticity is the part of continuum mechanics that deals with elastic materials, materials that return to their initial configurations, when the external load is removed.

When studying the relationship between forces and deformation, some of the concepts needed are *stress*, *strain*, *equilibrium*, and *displacement*. Stress is the strength of the force from interactions such as stretching, squeezing, or twisting, and stress is often characterized as force per unit area. Strain is the resulting deformation. The stress-strain relationship defines how a deformable object deforms under a given force. When forces are applied to the object, it deforms to a configuration of points, in which the energy of the object is in equilibrium. The information needed for animation is the displacement of the vertices of the underlying mesh in equilibrium.

This chapter is devoted to the basics of FEM in computer animation, and we will give the theoretical background for the static, isotropic stress/strain, finite element method, and we will show how FEM is used in animation. We will not treat fracturing [O'Brien et al., 1999, O'Brien et al., 2002a, Müller et al., 2004a], cutting [Molino et al., 2004], nor diagonalization [Irving et al., 2004] the recent finite volume method [Teran et al., 2003]. We also only consider tetrahedral elements, unlike, for instance, cubical elements as in [Müller et al., 2004b].

10.1 Tetrahedral Geometry

An often-used tessellation for surfaces is a triangular mesh. The corresponding tessellation for volumes is a tetrahedral mesh. These are the building blocks of the finite element method, and therefore in the following we will shortly review tetrahedral geometry.

A *tetrahedron* is defined by four nodes locally labeled 0, 1, 2, and 3, and we will use the convention that the labels are assigned such that the coordinates of nodes, $\boldsymbol{x}_0$, $\boldsymbol{x}_1$, $\boldsymbol{x}_2$, and $\boldsymbol{x}_3$ span a positive volume,

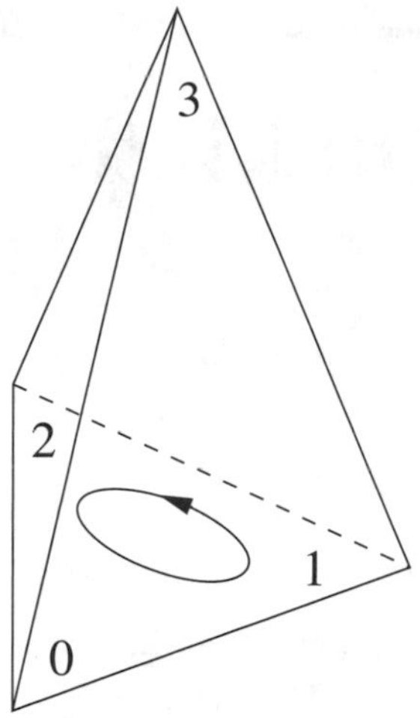

Figure 10.1: Geometry of a tetrahedron.

that is

$$V = \frac{1}{6} \det\left(\left[\boldsymbol{x}_1 - \boldsymbol{x}_0 \mid \boldsymbol{x}_2 - \boldsymbol{x}_0 \mid \boldsymbol{x}_3 - \boldsymbol{x}_0\right]\right) \tag{10.1a}$$

$$= \frac{1}{6} \begin{vmatrix} x_1 - x_0 & x_2 - x_0 & x_3 - x_0 \\ y_1 - y_0 & y_2 - y_0 & y_3 - y_0 \\ z_1 - z_0 & z_2 - z_0 & z_3 - z_0 \end{vmatrix} \tag{10.1b}$$

$$\geq 0, \tag{10.1c}$$

with $|\cdot|$ as the determinant operator. This is the case, when $\boldsymbol{x}_0$, $\boldsymbol{x}_1$, and $\boldsymbol{x}_2$ form a positive cycle as seen from $\boldsymbol{x}_3$. An example is shown in Figure 10.1. Such a tetrahedron is the element we use in the finite element method for 3D problems.

To every tetrahedron we attribute a unique, global index with values $e, f, \dots \in \{0, 1, 2, \dots, K\}$. Likewise, all nodes of a tetrahedra mesh have a unique global index with values $i, j, \dots \in \{0, 1, 2, \dots, N\}$, where $N \leq 4K$. For each tetrahedron e, the nodes also have a local index with values $m, n, \ldots \in \{0, 1, 2, 3\}$. The implication is that while the global index i is unique for a given node, then for each node indexed by i there will be a number of local indices $m, n, \ldots$, corresponding to each tetrahedron e that share the i'th node To make matters worse, we will often need to switch between the global and local indices for a given node. Ironically, the finite element method appears to be complex, but the core is just work and force balance, however the indexing is often the greatest challenge.

All nodes have a coordinate vector, and the coordinate vector of the nth node is $\boldsymbol{x}_n = [x_n, y_n, z_n]^T$. These indices are illustrated in Figure 10.2.

The finite element method considers not only the nodes of the tetrahedra, but the full continuum of positions inside each tetrahedron. A point inside a tetrahedron is parametrized by a set of local coordinates,

$$w_0, w_1, w_2, w_3, \tag{10.2}$$

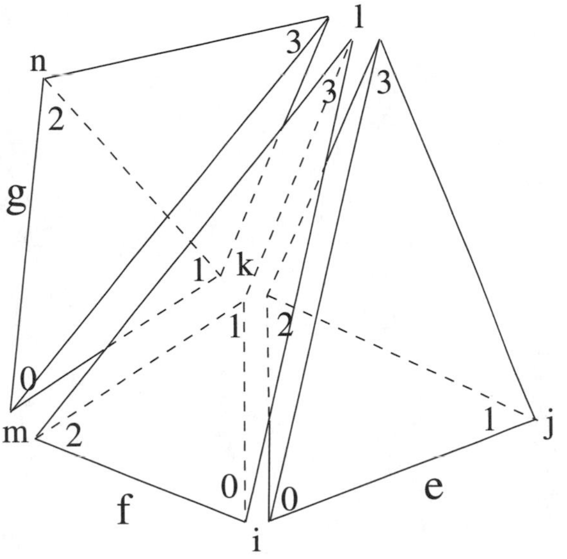

Figure 10.2: Tetrahedra mesh notation convention. Three tetrahedral elements are shown, with global indices e, f, and g. The nodes of element e have global indices i, j, k, l.

where the value of w_n is 1 at node n, zero at the remaining nodes, and a linear function in between. Furthermore,

$$w_0 + w_1 + w_2 + w_3 = 1, \tag{10.3}$$

and these coordinates are often called *natural coordinates* or *Barycentric coordinates*. An illustration of the tetrahedra natural coordinates is shown in Figure 10.3, where Figure 10.3(a) shows the point inside the tetrahedron, and Figure 10.3(b) shows planes of equal values of w_0. Any function f linear in x, y, and z that takes the values f_n at the nodes may be interpolated in terms of the natural coordinates using,

$$f(w_0, w_1, w_2, w_3) = f_0 w_0 + f_1 w_1 + f_2 w_2 + f_3 w_3 = \sum_{n=0}^{3} f_n w_n. \tag{10.4}$$

With this linear relationship on the four nodes of the tetrahedron, we can, for example, compute the coordinate of any point inside the tetrahedron in terms of the natural coordinates as,

$$\boldsymbol{x}(w_0, w_1, w_2, w_3) = \boldsymbol{x}_0 w_0 + \boldsymbol{x}_1 w_1 + \boldsymbol{x}_2 w_2 + \boldsymbol{x}_3 w_3. \tag{10.5}$$

Linear polynomial for interpolating a scalar field $f(x, y, z)$ at a given position $\boldsymbol{p} = [1, x, y, z]^T$ inside the tetrahedron is given as,

$$f(x, y, z) = a_0 + a_1 x + a_2 y + a_3 z = \boldsymbol{p}^T \boldsymbol{a}, \tag{10.6}$$

where the a's are the polynomial coefficients (to be determined) and $\boldsymbol{a} = [a_0, a_1, a_2, a_3]^T$. Given the values of $f_0 = f(x_0, y_0, z_0), \ldots, f_3 = f(x_3, y_2, z_3)$, at the four tetrahedron corner points, $\boldsymbol{x}_0 =$

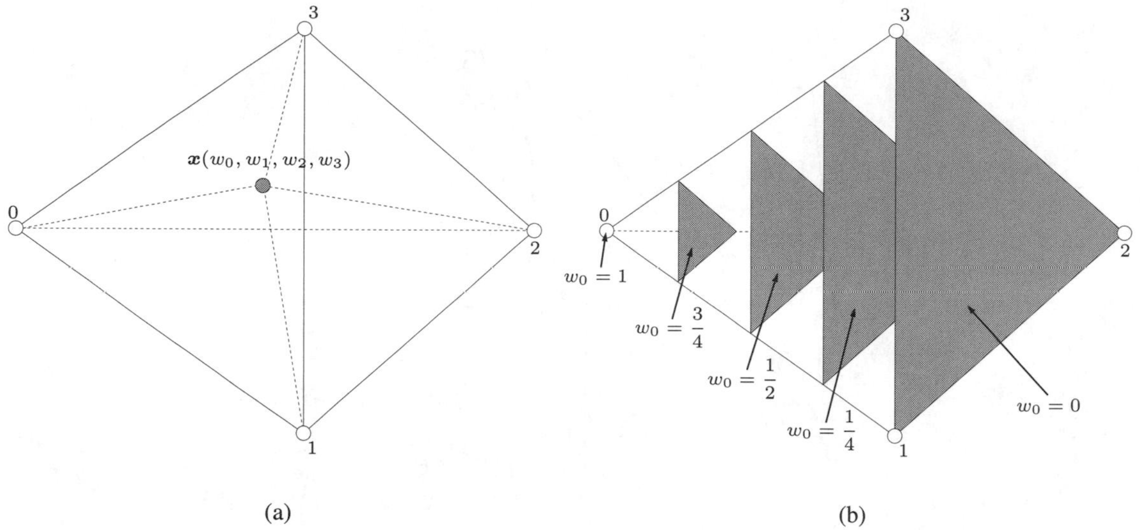

Figure 10.3: Tetrahedra natural coordinates. In (a) is shown a general point inside a tetrahedron, and in (b) are shown planes of equal values of w_0.

$[x_0, y_0, z_0]^T, \ldots, \boldsymbol{x}_3 = [x_3, y_3, z_3]^T$, we can set up the linear system

$$\begin{bmatrix} f_0 \\ f_1 \\ f_2 \\ f_3 \end{bmatrix} = \begin{bmatrix} 1 & x_0 & y_0 & z_0 \\ 1 & x_1 & y_1 & z_1 \\ 1 & x_2 & y_2 & z_2 \\ 1 & x_3 & y_3 & z_3 \end{bmatrix} \begin{bmatrix} a_0 \\ a_1 \\ a_2 \\ a_3 \end{bmatrix} = \boldsymbol{P}\boldsymbol{a}. \tag{10.7}$$

The matrix $\boldsymbol{P}$ is invertible as long as the four points are in *general position*, meaning that no point can be written as a linear combination of any of the three other points. This is the case whenever a tetrahedron is not collapsed into a triangle, line, or point. For four points in general position we can solve the polynomial coefficients as,

$$\boldsymbol{a} = \boldsymbol{P}^{-1} \begin{bmatrix} f_0 \\ f_1 \\ f_2 \\ f_3 \end{bmatrix}. \tag{10.8}$$

For any point $\boldsymbol{p} = [1, x, y, z]^T$ we thus have,

$$f(x, y, z) = \boldsymbol{p}^T \boldsymbol{P}^{-1} \begin{bmatrix} f_0 \\ f_1 \\ f_2 \\ f_3 \end{bmatrix}. \tag{10.9}$$

Denoting the n'th column of $\boldsymbol{p}^T \boldsymbol{P}^{-1}$ by N_n we have

$$f(x, y, z) = \begin{bmatrix} N_0 & N_1 & N_2 & N_3 \end{bmatrix} \begin{bmatrix} f_0 \\ f_1 \\ f_2 \\ f_3 \end{bmatrix} = \sum_{n=0}^{3} \boldsymbol{N}_n f_n, \tag{10.10}$$

In case f is a vector field, then each coordinate can be interpolated independently.

$$\boldsymbol{f}(x, y, z) = \begin{bmatrix} \boldsymbol{N}_0 & \boldsymbol{N}_1 & \boldsymbol{N}_2 & \boldsymbol{N}_3 \end{bmatrix} \begin{bmatrix} \boldsymbol{f}_0 \\ \boldsymbol{f}_1 \\ \boldsymbol{f}_2 \\ \boldsymbol{f}_3 \end{bmatrix} = \sum_{n=0}^{3} \boldsymbol{N}_n \boldsymbol{f}_n, \tag{10.11}$$

where

$$\boldsymbol{N}_n = \begin{bmatrix} N_n & 0 & 0 \\ 0 & N_n & 0 \\ 0 & 0 & N_n \end{bmatrix} \tag{10.12}$$

Let us now try to look at the barycentric coordinates, $w_0, \ldots, w_1$ of the point $[x, y, z]^T$. These can also be used for interpolation

$$f(x, y, z) = w_0 f_0 + w_1 f_1 + w_2 f_2 + w_3 f_3 = \boldsymbol{w}^T \begin{bmatrix} f_0 \\ f_1 \\ f_2 \\ f_3 \end{bmatrix} \tag{10.13}$$

From the coordinates of the four points and the condition $1 = w_0 + w_1 + w_2 + w_3$ we can set up the linear system

$$\begin{bmatrix} 1 \\ x \\ y \\ z \end{bmatrix} = \begin{bmatrix} 1 & 1 & 1 & 1 \\ x_0 & x_1 & x_2 & x_3 \\ y_0 & y_1 & y_2 & y_3 \\ z_0 & z_1 & z_2 & z_3 \end{bmatrix} \begin{bmatrix} w_0 \\ w_1 \\ w_2 \\ w_3 \end{bmatrix}, \tag{10.14a}$$

$$\Updownarrow$$

$$\boldsymbol{p} = \boldsymbol{Q}\boldsymbol{w}. \tag{10.14b}$$

Since the four points are in general position $\boldsymbol{Q}$ is invertible, and we can solve for $\boldsymbol{w}$ as,

$$\boldsymbol{w} = \boldsymbol{Q}^{-1}\boldsymbol{p}. \tag{10.15}$$

Insertion into the barycentric interpolation formula yields

$$f(x,y,z) = \left(\boldsymbol{Q}^{-1}\boldsymbol{p}\right)^T \begin{bmatrix} f_0 \\ f_1 \\ f_2 \\ f_3 \end{bmatrix} \tag{10.16a}$$

$$= \boldsymbol{p}^T \boldsymbol{Q}^{-T} \begin{bmatrix} f_0 \\ f_1 \\ f_2 \\ f_3 \end{bmatrix}. \tag{10.16b}$$

Comparison with the polynomial interpolation derivation we see that $\boldsymbol{P} = \boldsymbol{Q}^T$, furthermore we notice that $w_n = N_n$ in the case f is a scalar, and $\boldsymbol{N}_n = \text{diag}(w_n, w_n, w_n)$, when $\boldsymbol{f}$ is a 3D vector. Hence, not surprisingly, it is seen that barycentric interpolation is just linear polynomial interpolation.

10.2 Elastic Solids with Finite Element Models

The finite element method is a procedure for obtaining numerical approximations to the solution of boundary value problems. The general idea is to formulate a deformation of a solid as the matrix equation,

$$\boldsymbol{K}\boldsymbol{u} = \boldsymbol{f}, \tag{10.17}$$

where $\boldsymbol{K}$ is a symmetric, positive definite, *stiffness matrix*, $\boldsymbol{u}$ is a vector of *nodal displacements*, and $\boldsymbol{f}$ is a vector of external *node forces*. The goal is to solve for the value of $\boldsymbol{u}$. To simplify the problem, the entire computational domain is replaced by the union of disjoint subdomains called finite elements. These subdomains are tetrahedra in a volume mesh. Other volume types may be used, but the tetrahedral geometry is often the computationally most feasible for computer animation.

In computer animations, the *Three-Dimensional Linear Elastostatics Model* is typically used and will be described in the rest of this chapter. It uses the following assumptions:

1. The deformations involved are small, in which case the relationship between *stress* and *strain* are well approximated by a linear model.
2. Only elastic materials are considered, thereby ignoring the *viscous stress*.
3. Only *isotropic materials* are considered, which implies that elasticity matrix can be described by two parameters only.
4. The object is in *static equilibrium*, which allows us to ignore *inertia forces*.

In the following, we will derive the three-dimensional linear elastostatics model for computer animation.

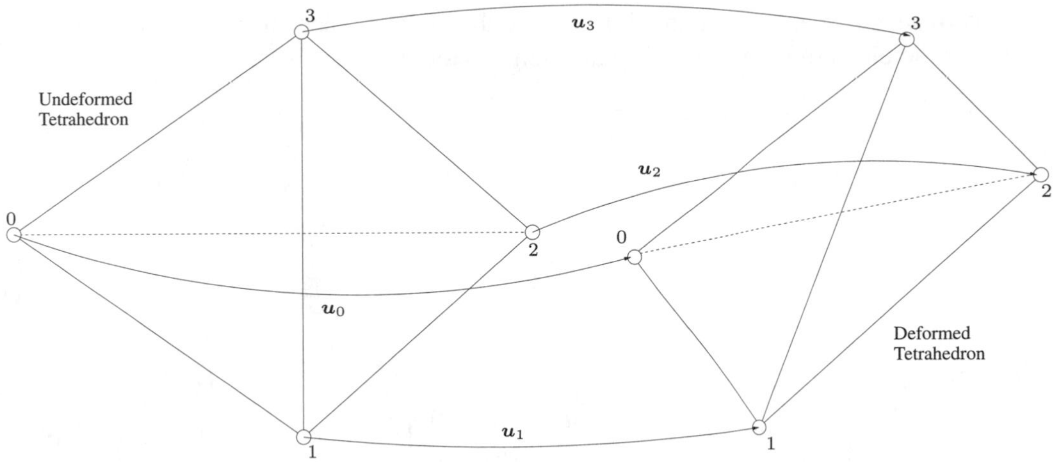

Figure 10.4: Deformation of a tetrahedron is given as a set of displacement vectors.

10.2.1 Displacement and Shape Functions

The *displacement function* at a given point $\boldsymbol{x} = [x, y, z]^T$ in the object, is given as

$$\boldsymbol{u} = \begin{bmatrix} u^x \\ u^y \\ u^z \end{bmatrix} = \boldsymbol{x} - \boldsymbol{x}_u, \tag{10.18}$$

where u^x is the displacement along the x-axis, u^y is the displacement along the y-axis, and u^z is the displacement along the z-axis. Thus, every point $\boldsymbol{x}_u$ in the undeformed object corresponds to point $\boldsymbol{x} = \boldsymbol{x}_u + \boldsymbol{u}$ in the deformed object. This is illustrated in Figure 10.4. Here the traditional finite element literature adds a further level of complexity by considering material properties, which both $\boldsymbol{x}$ and $\boldsymbol{x}_u$ depend on. However, we will not need these for the deformations we will discuss in this chapter.

The deformable object is discretized into tetrahedral elements, where each node has a deformation $\boldsymbol{u}_n = \boldsymbol{x}_n - \boldsymbol{x}_{un}$. A linear approximation to the displacement function inside an element e from its nodal values is given as,

$$\boldsymbol{u}(w_0, w_1, w_2, w_3) = \begin{bmatrix} \boldsymbol{u}_0 \mid \boldsymbol{u}_1 \mid \boldsymbol{u}_2 \mid \boldsymbol{u}_3 \end{bmatrix} \begin{bmatrix} w_0 \\ w_1 \\ w_2 \\ w_3 \end{bmatrix} \tag{10.19a}$$

$$= \begin{bmatrix} u_0^x & u_1^x & u_2^x & u_3^x \\ u_0^y & u_1^y & u_2^y & u_3^y \\ u_0^z & u_1^z & u_2^z & u_3^z \end{bmatrix} \begin{bmatrix} w_0 \\ w_1 \\ w_2 \\ w_3 \end{bmatrix}, \tag{10.19b}$$

Thus, the natural coordinates w_n form a finite dimensional basis for the space spanned by the tetrahedron.

It is often convenient in an implementation to have the nodal displacements arranged node-wise as a single vector. For the element e, the node displacement vector $\boldsymbol{u}^e$ is given as:

$$\boldsymbol{u}^e = \begin{bmatrix} \boldsymbol{u}_0 \\ \boldsymbol{u}_1 \\ \boldsymbol{u}_2 \\ \boldsymbol{u}_3 \end{bmatrix} \tag{10.20a}$$

$$= \begin{bmatrix} u_0^x & u_0^y & u_0^z & u_1^x & u_1^y & u_1^z & \cdots & u_3^z \end{bmatrix}^T. \tag{10.20b}$$

Hence, using

$$\boldsymbol{N}_n = \begin{bmatrix} w_n & 0 & 0 \\ 0 & w_n & 0 \\ 0 & 0 & w_n \end{bmatrix}, \tag{10.21}$$

we may now rewrite the linear interpolation in (10.19a) as,

$$\boldsymbol{u} = \begin{bmatrix} \boldsymbol{N}_0 & \boldsymbol{N}_1 & \boldsymbol{N}_2 & \boldsymbol{N}_3 \end{bmatrix} \begin{bmatrix} \boldsymbol{u}_0 \\ \boldsymbol{u}_1 \\ \boldsymbol{u}_2 \\ \boldsymbol{u}_3 \end{bmatrix} \tag{10.22a}$$

$$= \sum_{n=0}^{3} \boldsymbol{N}_n \boldsymbol{u}_n \tag{10.22b}$$

$$= \boldsymbol{N}\boldsymbol{u}^e, \tag{10.22c}$$

where $\boldsymbol{N} = \begin{bmatrix} \boldsymbol{N}_0 & \boldsymbol{N}_1 & \boldsymbol{N}_2 & \boldsymbol{N}_3 \end{bmatrix}$, and where the submatrices $\boldsymbol{N}_n$ are called the *shape functions*.

10.2.2 Strain

To describe the deformation of an object, a measurement is needed. We use the *linear Cauchy strain matrix*, defined in Section 22.7, which relates the displacement $\boldsymbol{u}$ to the strain, $\boldsymbol{\varepsilon}$. In 3D the strain matrix is given as

$$\boldsymbol{\varepsilon} = \begin{bmatrix} \varepsilon_{11} & \varepsilon_{12} & \varepsilon_{13} \\ \varepsilon_{21} & \varepsilon_{22} & \varepsilon_{23} \\ \varepsilon_{31} & \varepsilon_{32} & \varepsilon_{33} \end{bmatrix}, \tag{10.23}$$

where

$$\varepsilon_{ij} = \frac{1}{2}\left(\frac{\partial u_i}{\partial x_j} + \frac{\partial u_j}{\partial x_i}\right), \tag{10.24}$$

and where $x_1 = x$, $x_2 = y$, and $x_3 = z$ has been introduced for notational convenience. The matrix ε is symmetric, and its six independent components may conveniently be rewritten on vector form as,

$$
\begin{aligned}
\boldsymbol{\varepsilon} &= \begin{bmatrix}\varepsilon_{11} & \varepsilon_{22} & \varepsilon_{33} & \gamma_{12} & \gamma_{13} & \gamma_{23}\end{bmatrix}^T && (10.25a)\\
&= \begin{bmatrix} \frac{\partial u_1}{\partial x_1} \\ \frac{\partial u_2}{\partial x_2} \\ \frac{\partial u_3}{\partial x_3} \\ \frac{\partial u_1}{\partial x_2} + \frac{\partial u_2}{\partial x_1} \\ \frac{\partial u_1}{\partial x_3} + \frac{\partial u_3}{\partial x_1} \\ \frac{\partial u_2}{\partial x_3} + \frac{\partial u_3}{\partial x_2} \end{bmatrix} && (10.25b)\\
&= \begin{bmatrix} \frac{\partial}{\partial x_1} & 0 & 0 \\ 0 & \frac{\partial}{\partial x_2} & 0 \\ 0 & 0 & \frac{\partial}{\partial x_3} \\ \frac{\partial}{\partial x_2} & \frac{\partial}{\partial x_1} & 0 \\ \frac{\partial}{\partial x_3} & 0 & \frac{\partial}{\partial x_1} \\ 0 & \frac{\partial}{\partial x_3} & \frac{\partial}{\partial x_2} \end{bmatrix} \begin{bmatrix} u_1 \\ u_2 \\ u_3 \end{bmatrix} && (10.25c)\\
&= \boldsymbol{S}\boldsymbol{u}. && (10.25d)
\end{aligned}
$$

where $\gamma_{ij} = 2\varepsilon_{ij}$. The matrix $\boldsymbol{S}$ is an operator similar to the gradient. The first three components of the strain measures stretching in the coordinate directions, while the last three components measure shearing.

A linear interpolation of the relation between strains and nodal displacements inside a finite element may be obtained by combining (10.25) with the linear approximation from (10.22):

$$
\boldsymbol{\varepsilon} = \boldsymbol{S}\boldsymbol{N}\boldsymbol{u}^e = \boldsymbol{B}\boldsymbol{u}^e, \tag{10.26}
$$

where the matrix $\boldsymbol{B} = \boldsymbol{S}\boldsymbol{N}$. Naturally $\boldsymbol{B}$ has a block structure similar to $\boldsymbol{N}$, i.e.,

$$
\boldsymbol{B} = \boldsymbol{S}\begin{bmatrix}\boldsymbol{N}_0 & \boldsymbol{N}_1 & \boldsymbol{N}_2 & \boldsymbol{N}_3\end{bmatrix} = \begin{bmatrix}\boldsymbol{B}_0 & \boldsymbol{B}_1 & \boldsymbol{B}_2 & \boldsymbol{B}_3\end{bmatrix}, \tag{10.27}
$$

where $\boldsymbol{B}_n = \boldsymbol{S}\boldsymbol{N}_n$ for $n = 0, 1, 2, 3$. Straightforward evaluation gives,

$$\boldsymbol{B}_n = \begin{bmatrix} \frac{\partial}{\partial x_1} & 0 & 0 \\ 0 & \frac{\partial}{\partial x_2} & 0 \\ 0 & 0 & \frac{\partial}{\partial x_3} \\ \frac{\partial}{\partial x_2} & \frac{\partial}{\partial x_1} & 0 \\ \frac{\partial}{\partial x_3} & 0 & \frac{\partial}{\partial x_1} \\ 0 & \frac{\partial}{\partial x_3} & \frac{\partial}{\partial x_2} \end{bmatrix} \begin{bmatrix} w_n & 0 & 0 \\ 0 & w_n & 0 \\ 0 & 0 & w_n \end{bmatrix} \tag{10.28a}$$

$$= \begin{bmatrix} b_n & 0 & 0 \\ 0 & c_n & 0 \\ 0 & 0 & d_n \\ c_n & b_n & 0 \\ d_n & 0 & b_n \\ 0 & d_n & c_n \end{bmatrix}, \tag{10.28b}$$

where $b_n = \frac{\partial w_n}{\partial x_1}$, $c_n = \frac{\partial w_n}{\partial x_2}$, and $d_n = \frac{\partial w_n}{\partial x_3}$.

When computing the stiffness matrix we are interested in derivatives of the N_n's with respect to the x-, y-, and z- coordinates. From (10.9) we see

$$\frac{d\boldsymbol{N}_n}{dx} = \boldsymbol{P}^{-1}_{1,n}, \tag{10.29a}$$

$$\frac{d\boldsymbol{N}_n}{dy} = \boldsymbol{P}^{-1}_{2,n}, \tag{10.29b}$$

$$\frac{d\boldsymbol{N}_n}{dz} = \boldsymbol{P}^{-1}_{3,n}, \tag{10.29c}$$

where we have used zero-indexing. Instead of actually computing the inverse of the 4×4 $\boldsymbol{P}$ matrix, a computationally more efficient solution exists, which only requires us to solve for a 3×3 system. This is achieved using the following theorem,

Theorem 10.1

Let $\boldsymbol{x}_n = [x_n, y_n, z_n]^T$ for $n = 0, 1, 2, 3$, and define

$$\mathbf{e}_{10} = \boldsymbol{x}_1 - \boldsymbol{x}_0, \tag{10.30a}$$

$$\mathbf{e}_{20} = \boldsymbol{x}_2 - \boldsymbol{x}_0, \tag{10.30b}$$

$$\mathbf{e}_{30} = \boldsymbol{x}_3 - \boldsymbol{x}_0. \tag{10.30c}$$

Furthermore, define the matrix $\boldsymbol{P}$ as,

$$\begin{bmatrix} 1 & \boldsymbol{x}_0^T \\ 1 & \boldsymbol{x}_1^T \\ 1 & \boldsymbol{x}_2^T \\ 1 & \boldsymbol{x}_3^T \end{bmatrix} \tag{10.31}$$

and the matrix $\mathbf{E}$ as,

$$\boldsymbol{E} = \begin{bmatrix} \mathbf{e}_{10} \\ \mathbf{e}_{20} \\ \mathbf{e}_{30} \end{bmatrix} = \begin{bmatrix} (x_1 - x_0) & (y_1 - y_0) & (z_1 - z_0) \\ (x_2 - x_0) & (y_2 - y_0) & (z_2 - z_0) \\ (x_3 - x_0) & (y_3 - y_0) & (z_3 - z_0) \end{bmatrix}. \tag{10.32}$$

Then the matrices $\boldsymbol{P}$ and $\mathbf{E}$ are related according to,

$$\det \boldsymbol{P} = \det \boldsymbol{E}, \tag{10.33a}$$

$$\boldsymbol{P}^{-1}_{n+1,m+1} = \boldsymbol{E}^{-1}_{n,m}. \tag{10.33b}$$

Proof of Theorem 10.1:

It is simple to show that $\det \boldsymbol{P} = \det \boldsymbol{E}$, and this is left as an exercise for the reader. To prove (10.33b) we use Cramer's rule,

$$\boldsymbol{P}^{-1}_{n,m} = \frac{(-1)^{n+m} \det \boldsymbol{P}_{mn}}{\det \boldsymbol{P}}, \tag{10.34}$$

where $\det \boldsymbol{P}_{mn}$ is the determinant of $\boldsymbol{P}$ with the m'th row and n'th column removed. By straightforward computation we verify that

$$-1^{(n+1)+(m+1)} = -1^{n+m}, \tag{10.35}$$

and what remains to be proven is that

$$\det \boldsymbol{P}_{n+1,m+1} = \det \boldsymbol{E}_{nm}, \tag{10.36}$$

A total of 9 cases exist for this, but here we will only show a single case and leave the remaining cases for the reader. Setting $n = 1$ and $m = 0$ implies that

$$\det \boldsymbol{P}_{12} = \det \boldsymbol{E}_{01}. \tag{10.37}$$

or equivalently that

$$\det \begin{bmatrix} 1 & x_0 & z_0 \\ 1 & x_2 & z_2 \\ 1 & x_3 & z_3 \end{bmatrix} = \det \begin{bmatrix} x_2 - x_0 & z_2 - z_0 \\ x_3 - x_0 & z_3 - z_0 \end{bmatrix}, \tag{10.38}$$

which is trivially true. □

Thus we have

$$\boldsymbol{P}^{-1} = \begin{bmatrix} \cdot & \cdots \\ \vdots & \boldsymbol{E}^{-1} \end{bmatrix}. \tag{10.39}$$

As can be seen from (10.29), for $n > 0$ we have,

$$\frac{dN_n}{dx} = \boldsymbol{E}^{-1}_{0,n-1}, \tag{10.40a}$$

$$\frac{dN_n}{dy} = \boldsymbol{E}^{-1}_{1,n-1}, \tag{10.40b}$$

$$\frac{dN_n}{dz} = \boldsymbol{E}^{-1}_{2,n-1}. \tag{10.40c}$$

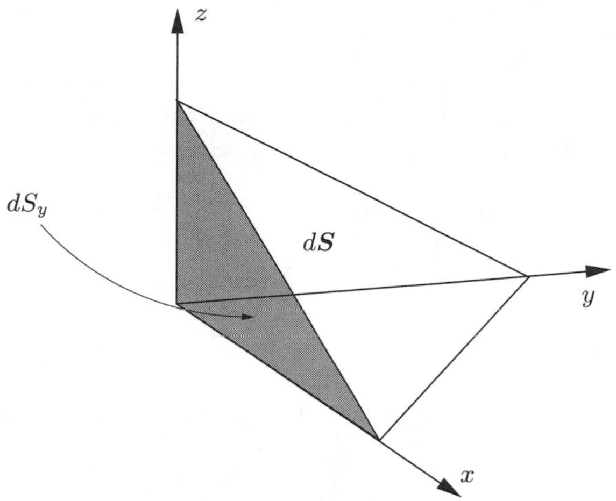

Figure 10.5: The projection of surface element $d\boldsymbol{S}$ onto the $x - z$ plane.

For $n = 0$ we cannot use the above equations, since the first column of $\boldsymbol{P}^{-1}$ is missing. Instead we use the normalization of barycentric coordinates,

$$w_0 = 1 - w_1 - w_2 - w_3. \tag{10.41}$$

Taking the derivate of w_n w.r.t. x, y, and z yields

$$\frac{dN_0}{dx} = 1 - \boldsymbol{E}_{00}^{-1} - \boldsymbol{E}_{01}^{-1} - \boldsymbol{E}_{02}^{-1}, \tag{10.42a}$$
$$\frac{dN_0}{dy} = 1 - \boldsymbol{E}_{10}^{-1} - \boldsymbol{E}_{11}^{-1} - \boldsymbol{E}_{12}^{-1}, \tag{10.42b}$$
$$\frac{dN_0}{dz} = 1 - \boldsymbol{E}_{20}^{-1} - \boldsymbol{E}_{21}^{-1} - \boldsymbol{E}_{22}^{-1}. \tag{10.42c}$$

The notation $b_n = \frac{dN_n}{dx}$, $c_n = \frac{dN_n}{dy}$, and $d_n = \frac{dN_n}{dz}$ is used. Furthermore all the derivatives are returned as four $\boldsymbol{B}$-vectors, where

$$\boldsymbol{B}_n \sim \begin{bmatrix} b_n & c_n & d_n \end{bmatrix}^T. \tag{10.43}$$

10.2.3 Stress

Stress is defined as force per unit area, the standard unit for stress is the same as the unit for pressure, that is pascal (Pa). Start by considering a surface element $d\boldsymbol{S}$, which may be represented in terms of the unit surface elements as $[dS_x, dS_y, dS_z]^T$, where dS_y is the area projection onto the $x - z$ plane as illustrated in Figure 10.5. If the force df_x is applied along the x-axis of the material surface dS_y orthogonal to the x and z axes, then the shear stress, σ_{xy}, is

$$\sigma_{xy} = \frac{df_x}{dS_y}. \tag{10.44}$$

Similar the normal stress, σ_{yy}, is

$$\sigma_{yy} = \frac{df_y}{dS_y}. \tag{10.45}$$

Consider all forces along all coordinate axes df_x, df_y, and df_z applied to all surface directions dS_x, dS_y, and dS_z. These forces yield what is known as Cauchy's stress hypothesis [Lautrup, 2005]:

$$\begin{bmatrix} df_x \\ df_y \\ df_z \end{bmatrix} = \begin{bmatrix} \sigma_{xx}dS_x + \sigma_{xy}dS_y + \sigma_{xz}dS_z \\ \sigma_{yx}dS_x + \sigma_{yy}dS_y + \sigma_{yz}dS_z \\ \sigma_{zx}dS_x + \sigma_{zy}dS_y + \sigma_{zz}dS_z \end{bmatrix}, \tag{10.46}$$

where each coefficient σ_{ij} depends on position and time. We can collect the coefficients into a stress matrix $\boldsymbol{\sigma}$:

$$\boldsymbol{\sigma} = \begin{bmatrix} \sigma_{xx} & \sigma_{xy} & \sigma_{xz} \\ \sigma_{yx} & \sigma_{yy} & \sigma_{yz} \\ \sigma_{zx} & \sigma_{zy} & \sigma_{zz} \end{bmatrix}. \tag{10.47}$$

A very general condition that is imposed on the stress matrix is symmetry, which means

$$\sigma_{ij} = \sigma_{ji}. \tag{10.48}$$

This reduces the stress matrix from 9 components to only 6. We thus write it in vector form as

$$\boldsymbol{\sigma} = \begin{bmatrix} \sigma_{xx} & \sigma_{yy} & \sigma_{zz} & \sigma_{xy} & \sigma_{zx} & \sigma_{zy} \end{bmatrix}^T. \tag{10.49}$$

The proofs of Cauchy's stress hypothesis and symmetry of the stress matrix can be found in [Lautrup, 2005, Chapter 9]. The six independent stress components may then be related to the six corresponding strains ε by the linear matrix equation

$$\boldsymbol{\sigma} = \boldsymbol{D}\boldsymbol{\varepsilon}. \tag{10.50}$$

This equation is *Hooke's Spring Law* generalized to elastic solids, which can help in the interpretation. Think of stress as a sort of spring force, and strain as a sort of spring elongation.

The *isotropic elasticity matrix* $\boldsymbol{D}$, described in Section 22.7, is defined as

$$\boldsymbol{D} = \frac{Y}{(1+\nu)(1-2\nu)} \begin{bmatrix} 1-\nu & \nu & \nu & 0 & 0 & 0 \\ \nu & 1-\nu & \nu & 0 & 0 & 0 \\ \nu & \nu & 1-\nu & 0 & 0 & 0 \\ 0 & 0 & 0 & \frac{1-2\nu}{2} & 0 & 0 \\ 0 & 0 & 0 & 0 & \frac{1-2\nu}{2} & 0 \\ 0 & 0 & 0 & 0 & 0 & \frac{1-2\nu}{2} \end{bmatrix}, \tag{10.51}$$

where Y is *Young's modulus*. Young's modulus is a measure of instretchability, such that a large Young's modulus implies that the material is hard to stretch. Some typical values are 200GPa for steel, 0.05GPa for rubber, and 0.032GPa for cork. The coefficient $-1 < \nu \leq 1/2$ is the *Poisson's ratio*, and it is only in rare instances negative. The Poisson's ratio describes how much a material contracts in the direction transverse to stretching. Negative values imply that the material gets thicker when stretched. Typical values are $1/2$ for incompressible materials such as rubber, 0.33 for steel, and almost 0 for cork.

10.2.4 Balancing Work

In the following will we derive the stiffness matrix equation for a single tetrahedron.

Stress, discussed in Section 10.2.3, is the governing force internally in a solid material. External forces are applied either to the nodes or to the tetrahedral surfaces. The forces acting at the nodes of the e'th tetrahedral element is written as

$$\boldsymbol{q}^e = \begin{bmatrix} \boldsymbol{q}_0 \\ \boldsymbol{q}_1 \\ \boldsymbol{q}_2 \\ \boldsymbol{q}_3 \end{bmatrix}, \tag{10.52}$$

and nodal forces come from the neighboring tetrahedra inside a mesh. External distributed load on the boundary of the tetrahedra, such as an instrument pressing against an organ, is called traction, $\boldsymbol{t}$, and has unit force per area. In short, the following forces are present for the isolated system consisting of a single tetrahedron:

- Stress forces are internal forces
- Nodal forces are external forces
- Load forces are external forces

Assume that we are given a *virtual displacement* of the nodes of tetrahedron e termed $\delta \boldsymbol{u}^e$, such that every node is moved to a new displacement, $(\boldsymbol{u}^e)' = \boldsymbol{u}^e + \delta \boldsymbol{u}^e$. During the virtual displacement work is performed in the system. The corresponding displacement for every point inside the tetrahedron may be obtained using our interpolation equation, and the result may be used to calculate the strain and stress for every point inside the tetrahedron, using (10.22) and (10.53b). Hence, we find,

$$\delta \boldsymbol{u} = \boldsymbol{N} \delta \boldsymbol{u}^e, \tag{10.53a}$$

$$\delta \boldsymbol{\varepsilon} = \boldsymbol{B} \delta \boldsymbol{u}^e, \tag{10.53b}$$

However, our goal is the opposite: given a set of forces, what is the resulting displacement. Our strategy will be to use the work balance equation, since the amount of work performed by the surface of a tetrahedron must equal the accumulation of work done by its interior. This is also known as *static equilibrium*, and for our system of nodal, surface, and volume forces it is given as,

$$\int_{\Omega^e} W_\sigma \, dV = W_q + \int_{\delta\Omega^e} W_t \, dA, \tag{10.54}$$

where Ω^e and $\delta\Omega^e$ are points inside and on the surface of the tetrahedron respectively. This equation is known as the *Work Balance Equation*. The internal work per unit volume performed by the stress forces is given as,

$$W_\sigma = (\delta \boldsymbol{\varepsilon})^T \boldsymbol{\sigma}, \tag{10.55}$$

the external work performed by the nodal forces, $\boldsymbol{q}^e$ is given as,

$$W_q = (\delta \boldsymbol{u}^e)^T \boldsymbol{q}^e, \tag{10.56}$$

and the external work per unit area performed by the external distributed load is given as,

$$W_t = (\delta \boldsymbol{u})^T \boldsymbol{t}. \tag{10.57}$$

Substituting (10.55), (10.56), and (10.57) into the work balance equation (10.54), we find

$$\int_{\Omega^e} (\delta \boldsymbol{\varepsilon})^T \boldsymbol{\sigma} \, dV = (\delta \boldsymbol{u}^e)^T \boldsymbol{q}^e + \int_{\delta\Omega^e} (\delta \boldsymbol{u})^T \boldsymbol{t} \, dA. \tag{10.58}$$

Substituting by (10.53a) and (10.53b) gives

$$\int_{\Omega^e} (\boldsymbol{B} \delta \boldsymbol{u}^e)^T \boldsymbol{\sigma} \, dV = (\delta \boldsymbol{u}^e)^T \boldsymbol{q}^e + \int_{\delta\Omega^e} (\boldsymbol{N} \delta \boldsymbol{u}^e)^T \boldsymbol{t} \, dA. \tag{10.59}$$

Expanding the transpose operator, and moving the constant virtual displacement outside the integrals gives,

$$(\delta \boldsymbol{u}^e)^T \int_{\Omega^e} \boldsymbol{B}^T \boldsymbol{\sigma} \, dV = (\delta \boldsymbol{u}^e)^T \left(\boldsymbol{q}^e + \int_{\delta\Omega^e} \boldsymbol{N}^T \boldsymbol{t} \, dA \right). \tag{10.60}$$

Since this equation must hold for any virtual displacement $\delta \boldsymbol{u}^e$, we conclude that the multipliers must be equal, i.e.,

$$\int_{\Omega^e} \boldsymbol{B}^T \boldsymbol{\sigma} \, dV = \boldsymbol{q}^e + \int_{\delta\Omega^e} \boldsymbol{N}^T \boldsymbol{t} \, dA. \tag{10.61}$$

Although appearing complex, the terms under the integral are simple to evaluate. To achieve this, we first substitute (10.50) followed by (10.26) to get,

$$\int_{\Omega^e} \boldsymbol{B}^T \boldsymbol{D} \boldsymbol{\varepsilon} \, dV = \boldsymbol{q}^e + \int_{\delta\Omega^e} \boldsymbol{N}^T \boldsymbol{t} \, dA \tag{10.62a}$$

$$\Downarrow$$

$$\int_{\Omega^e} \boldsymbol{B}^T \boldsymbol{D} \boldsymbol{B} \boldsymbol{u}^e \, dV = \boldsymbol{q}^e + \int_{\delta\Omega^e} \boldsymbol{N}^T \boldsymbol{t} \, dA. \tag{10.62b}$$

The matrices $\boldsymbol{B}$ and $\boldsymbol{D}$ are constant w.r.t. the integration as are the nodal displacements $\boldsymbol{u}^e$, hence we find that

$$\boldsymbol{B}^T \boldsymbol{D} \boldsymbol{B} \boldsymbol{u}^e \int_{\Omega^e} dV = \boldsymbol{q}^e + \int_{\delta\Omega^e} \boldsymbol{N}^T \boldsymbol{t} \, dA \tag{10.63a}$$

$$\Downarrow$$

$$\boldsymbol{B}^T \boldsymbol{D} \boldsymbol{B} \boldsymbol{u}^e V^e = \boldsymbol{q}^e + \int_{\delta\Omega^e} \boldsymbol{N}^T \boldsymbol{t} \, dA, \tag{10.63b}$$

where V^e is the volume of the tetrahedron respectively. Introducing the *element stiffness matrix*

$$\boldsymbol{K}^e = \boldsymbol{B}^T \boldsymbol{D} \boldsymbol{B} V^e, \tag{10.64}$$

and the *element surface force*,

$$\boldsymbol{f}^e = \int_{\delta\Omega^e} \boldsymbol{N}^t \boldsymbol{t} \, dA, \tag{10.65}$$

we finally have the matrix equation,

$$\boldsymbol{K}^e \boldsymbol{u}^e = \boldsymbol{q}^e + \boldsymbol{f}^e, \tag{10.66}$$

where $\boldsymbol{K}^e \in \mathbb{R}^{12\times 12}$ is the element stiffness matrix, $\boldsymbol{u}^e \in \mathbb{R}^{12}$ is the nodal displacements, $\boldsymbol{q}^e \in \mathbb{R}^{12}$ is the nodal forces, and $\boldsymbol{f}^e \in \mathbb{R}^{12}$ is the element force.

10.2.5 Assembling the Work Balance Equation for all Tetrahedra

In the previous section we saw that the work balance for a single tetrahedron resulted in a simple matrix equation in terms of the nodal forces and displacements. We have such an equation for each tetrahedron in a mesh, and these equations will be tied together in this section.

Newton's third law dictates that in static equilibrium all forces at a point must sum to zero. Thus, for a given node i, all the nodal forces coming from neighboring tetrahedra must sum to zero. Assume that $n, m, \ldots$ are the local indices in elements $e, f, \ldots$ that correspond to the global index i, then the *force balance equation* may be written as,

$$\boldsymbol{q}_n^e + \boldsymbol{q}_m^f + \cdots = 0. \tag{10.67}$$

To obtain a computationally more efficient form, we first investigate the structure of $\boldsymbol{K}^e$. It is defined as $\boldsymbol{K}^e = \boldsymbol{B}^T \boldsymbol{D} \boldsymbol{B} V^e$, and since

$$\boldsymbol{B} = \begin{bmatrix} \boldsymbol{B}_0 & \boldsymbol{B}_1 & \boldsymbol{B}_2 & \boldsymbol{B}_3, \end{bmatrix} \tag{10.68}$$

we can decompose $\boldsymbol{K}^e$ into submatrices

$$\boldsymbol{K}^e = \begin{bmatrix} \boldsymbol{B}_0^T \\ \boldsymbol{B}_1^T \\ \boldsymbol{B}_2^T \\ \boldsymbol{B}_3^T \end{bmatrix} \boldsymbol{D} \begin{bmatrix} \boldsymbol{B}_0 & \boldsymbol{B}_1 & \boldsymbol{B}_2 & \boldsymbol{B}_3 \end{bmatrix} V^e \tag{10.69a}$$

$$= \begin{bmatrix} \boldsymbol{B}_0^T \boldsymbol{D} \boldsymbol{B}_0 V^e & \boldsymbol{B}_0^T \boldsymbol{D} \boldsymbol{B}_1 V^e & \boldsymbol{B}_0^T \boldsymbol{D} \boldsymbol{B}_2 V^e & \boldsymbol{B}_0^T \boldsymbol{D} \boldsymbol{B}_3 V^e \\ \boldsymbol{B}_1^T \boldsymbol{D} \boldsymbol{B}_0 V^e & \boldsymbol{B}_1^T \boldsymbol{D} \boldsymbol{B}_1 V^e & \boldsymbol{B}_1^T \boldsymbol{D} \boldsymbol{B}_2 V^e & \boldsymbol{B}_1^T \boldsymbol{D} \boldsymbol{B}_3 V^e \\ \boldsymbol{B}_2^T \boldsymbol{D} \boldsymbol{B}_0 V^e & \boldsymbol{B}_2^T \boldsymbol{D} \boldsymbol{B}_1 V^e & \boldsymbol{B}_2^T \boldsymbol{D} \boldsymbol{B}_2 V^e & \boldsymbol{B}_2^T \boldsymbol{D} \boldsymbol{B}_3 V^e \\ \boldsymbol{B}_3^T \boldsymbol{D} \boldsymbol{B}_0 V^e & \boldsymbol{B}_3^T \boldsymbol{D} \boldsymbol{B}_1 V^e & \boldsymbol{B}_3^T \boldsymbol{D} \boldsymbol{B}_2 V^e & \boldsymbol{B}_3^T \boldsymbol{D} \boldsymbol{B}_3 V^e \end{bmatrix}. \tag{10.69b}$$

Using the notation $\boldsymbol{K}_{nm}^e = \boldsymbol{B}_n^T \boldsymbol{D} \boldsymbol{B}_m V^e$ we simplify the above to

$$\boldsymbol{K}^e = \begin{bmatrix} \boldsymbol{K}_{00}^e & \boldsymbol{K}_{01}^e & \boldsymbol{K}_{02}^e & \boldsymbol{K}_{03}^e \\ \boldsymbol{K}_{10}^e & \boldsymbol{K}_{11}^e & \boldsymbol{K}_{12}^e & \boldsymbol{K}_{13}^e \\ \boldsymbol{K}_{20}^e & \boldsymbol{K}_{21}^e & \boldsymbol{K}_{22}^e & \boldsymbol{K}_{23}^e \\ \boldsymbol{K}_{30}^e & \boldsymbol{K}_{31}^e & \boldsymbol{K}_{32}^e & \boldsymbol{K}_{33}^e \end{bmatrix}. \tag{10.70}$$

The matrix $\boldsymbol{K}^e$ has a special symmetry for isotropic materials:

$$\left(\boldsymbol{B}_n^T \boldsymbol{D} \boldsymbol{B}_m V^e\right)^T = \boldsymbol{B}_m^T \boldsymbol{D} \boldsymbol{B}_n V^e \tag{10.71}$$

since $\boldsymbol{D}$ is symmetric for isotropic materials. Hence the submatrices are related as,

$$\left(\boldsymbol{K}_{ij}^{e}\right)^{T} = \boldsymbol{K}_{ji}^{e}, \tag{10.72}$$

which is conveniently used in calculating $\boldsymbol{K}^e$. Furthermore, writing the elasticity matrix $\boldsymbol{D}$ as,

$$\boldsymbol{D} = \begin{bmatrix} D_0 & D_1 & D_1 & 0 & 0 & 0 \\ D_1 & D_0 & D_1 & 0 & 0 & 0 \\ D_1 & D_1 & D_0 & 0 & 0 & 0 \\ 0 & 0 & 0 & D_2 & 0 & 0 \\ 0 & 0 & 0 & 0 & D_2 & 0 \\ 0 & 0 & 0 & 0 & 0 & D_2 \end{bmatrix}, \tag{10.73}$$

where $D_0 = \frac{Y(1-\nu)}{(1+\nu)(1-2\nu)}$, $D_1 = \frac{Y\nu}{(1+\nu)(1-2\nu)}$, and $D_2 = \frac{Y(1-2\nu)}{2(1+\nu)(1-2\nu)}$, and we evaluate $\boldsymbol{K}_{nm}^{e}$ to be,

$$\boldsymbol{K}_{nm}^{e} = \begin{bmatrix} b_n & 0 & 0 \\ 0 & c_n & 0 \\ 0 & 0 & d_n \\ c_n & b_n & 0 \\ d_n & 0 & b_n \\ 0 & d_n & c_n \end{bmatrix}^{T} \begin{bmatrix} D_0 & D_1 & D_1 & 0 & 0 & 0 \\ D_1 & D_0 & D_1 & 0 & 0 & 0 \\ D_1 & D_1 & D_0 & 0 & 0 & 0 \\ 0 & 0 & 0 & D_2 & 0 & 0 \\ 0 & 0 & 0 & 0 & D_2 & 0 \\ 0 & 0 & 0 & 0 & 0 & D_2 \end{bmatrix} \begin{bmatrix} b_m & 0 & 0 \\ 0 & c_m & 0 \\ 0 & 0 & d_m \\ c_m & b_m & 0 \\ d_m & 0 & b_m \\ 0 & d_m & c_m \end{bmatrix} V^e \tag{10.74a}$$

$$= \begin{bmatrix} D_0 b_n b_m + D_2(c_n c_m + d_n d_m) & D_1 b_n c_m + D_2 c_n b_m & D_1 b_n d_m + D_2 d_n b_m \\ D_1 c_n b_m + D_2 b_n c_m & D_0 c_n c_m + D_2(b_n b_m + d_n d_m) & D_1 c_n d_m + D_2 d_n c_m \\ D_1 d_n b_m + D_2 b_n d_m & D_1 d_n c_m + D_2 c_n d_m & D_0 d_n d_m + D_2(b_n b_m + c_n c_m) \end{bmatrix} V^e, \tag{10.74b}$$

The nodal force coming from the e'th element onto the i'th node in global index and n'th node in local e index, we have that

$$\boldsymbol{q}_n^e = \boldsymbol{K}_{n0}^e \boldsymbol{u}_0^e + \boldsymbol{K}_{n1}^e \boldsymbol{u}_1^e + \boldsymbol{K}_{n2}^e \boldsymbol{u}_2^e + \boldsymbol{K}_{n3}^e \boldsymbol{u}_3^e - \boldsymbol{f}_n^e, \tag{10.75}$$

where $\boldsymbol{u}_n^e$ is the displacement of the n'th node in element e. The force balance on the i'th node in global indices corresponding to $n, \ldots$ in local $e, \ldots$ element indices. Thus,

$$0 = \sum_{\mathcal{T}_i} \boldsymbol{K}_{n0}^e \boldsymbol{u}_0^e + \boldsymbol{K}_{n1}^e \boldsymbol{u}_1^e + \boldsymbol{K}_{n2}^e \boldsymbol{u}_2^e + \boldsymbol{K}_{n3}^e \boldsymbol{u}_3^e - \boldsymbol{f}_n^e \tag{10.76}$$

where $\mathcal{T}_i$ is the set of tetrahedra including node with global index i and corresponding local index n.

We will now show how to assemble all the force equations into a single and easily invertible system of equations. The assembly is best explained through examples. Consider the 2-tetrahedra mesh shown in Figure 10.6. The two tetrahedra e and f share a node, l, and therefore only have one coupling. The node l has local index 3 and 0 in tetrahedra e and f respectively. Hence we have one force balance equation, which sums over e and f,

$$\begin{aligned} 0 = {} & \boldsymbol{K}_{30}^e \boldsymbol{u}_0^e + \boldsymbol{K}_{31}^e \boldsymbol{u}_1^e + \boldsymbol{K}_{32}^e \boldsymbol{u}_2^e + \boldsymbol{K}_{33}^e \boldsymbol{u}_3^e - \boldsymbol{f}_3^e \\ & + \boldsymbol{K}_{00}^f \boldsymbol{u}_0^f + \boldsymbol{K}_{01}^f \boldsymbol{u}_1^f + \boldsymbol{K}_{02}^f \boldsymbol{u}_2^f + \boldsymbol{K}_{03}^f \boldsymbol{u}_3^f - \boldsymbol{f}_0^f. \end{aligned} \tag{10.77}$$

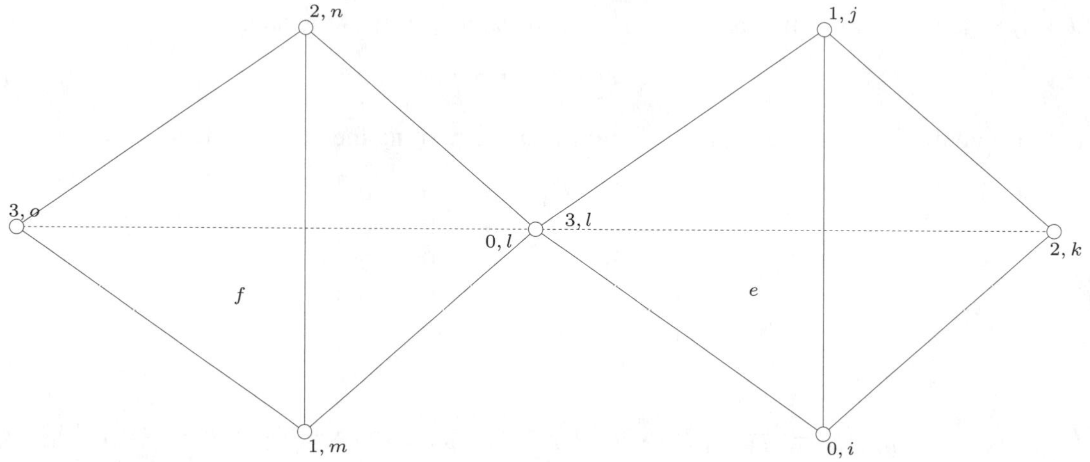

Figure 10.6: A mesh consisting of two tetrahedra coupled at node l.

To simplify the above equation we wish to write it on the form,

$$\boldsymbol{K}\boldsymbol{u} = \boldsymbol{f}, \tag{10.78}$$

where $\boldsymbol{K}$ is the assembly of all the tetrahedral stiffness matrices, $\boldsymbol{u}$ is a vector of all the concatenated displacements, and $\boldsymbol{f}$ is likewise an assembly of external forces. The first step to achieve this is to identify the local nodal indices with their global counterparts as $\boldsymbol{u}_i = \boldsymbol{u}_0^e$, $\boldsymbol{u}_j = \boldsymbol{u}_1^e$, ..., and thus we write,

$$\begin{aligned} 0 = \boldsymbol{K}_{30}^e\boldsymbol{u}_i + \boldsymbol{K}_{31}^e\boldsymbol{u}_j + \boldsymbol{K}_{32}^e\boldsymbol{u}_k + \boldsymbol{K}_{33}^e\boldsymbol{u}_l - \boldsymbol{f}_3^e \\ + \boldsymbol{K}_{00}^f\boldsymbol{u}_l + \boldsymbol{K}_{01}^f\boldsymbol{u}_m + \boldsymbol{K}_{02}^f\boldsymbol{u}_n + \boldsymbol{K}_{03}^f\boldsymbol{u}_o - \boldsymbol{f}_0^f. \end{aligned} \tag{10.79}$$

Then we collect terms in front of the nodal displacements to get,

$$\begin{bmatrix} \boldsymbol{K}_{30}^e & \boldsymbol{K}_{31}^e & \boldsymbol{K}_{32}^e & (\boldsymbol{K}_{33}^e + \boldsymbol{K}_{00}^f) & \boldsymbol{K}_{01}^f & \boldsymbol{K}_{02}^f & \boldsymbol{K}_{03}^f \end{bmatrix} \begin{bmatrix} \boldsymbol{u}_i \\ \boldsymbol{u}_j \\ \boldsymbol{u}_k \\ \boldsymbol{u}_l \\ \boldsymbol{u}_m \\ \boldsymbol{u}_n \\ \boldsymbol{u}_o \end{bmatrix} - (\boldsymbol{f}_3^e + \boldsymbol{f}_0^f) = 0 \tag{10.80}$$

This has the form of (10.78) with

$$\boldsymbol{K} = \begin{bmatrix} \boldsymbol{K}_{30}^e & \boldsymbol{K}_{31}^e & \boldsymbol{K}_{32}^e & (\boldsymbol{K}_{33}^e + \boldsymbol{K}_{00}^f) & \boldsymbol{K}_{01}^f & \boldsymbol{K}_{02}^f & \boldsymbol{K}_{03}^f \end{bmatrix}, \tag{10.81a}$$

$$\boldsymbol{u} = \begin{bmatrix} \boldsymbol{u}_i & \boldsymbol{u}_j & \boldsymbol{u}_k & \boldsymbol{u}_l & \boldsymbol{u}_m & \boldsymbol{u}_n & \boldsymbol{u}_o \end{bmatrix}^T, \tag{10.81b}$$

$$\boldsymbol{f} = \boldsymbol{f}_3^e + \boldsymbol{f}_0^f. \tag{10.81c}$$

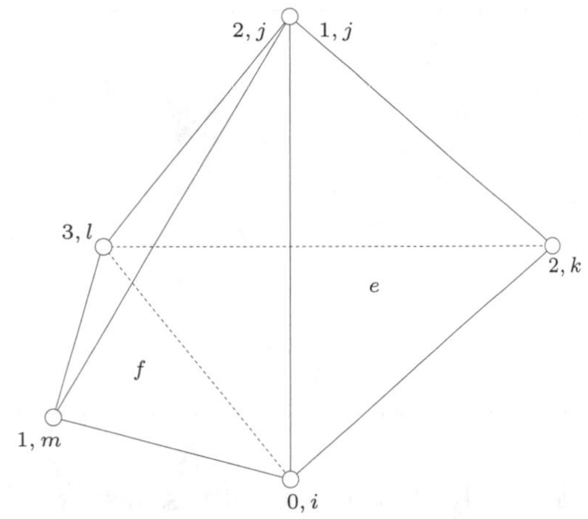

Figure 10.7: A mesh consisting of two tetrahedra coupled at nodes l.

A more complicated configuration is shown in Figure 10.7, where a mesh is shown consisting of two tetrahedra sharing a face, which is therefore coupled at the nodes i, j, and l, which have local coordinates $0, 1, 3$ and $0, 2, 3$ in elements e and f respectively. Hence we have three force balance equations, which sums over e and f,

$$0 = \boldsymbol{K}^e_{00}\boldsymbol{u}^e_0 + \boldsymbol{K}^e_{01}\boldsymbol{u}^e_1 + \boldsymbol{K}^e_{02}\boldsymbol{u}^e_2 + \boldsymbol{K}^e_{03}\boldsymbol{u}^e_3 - \boldsymbol{f}^e_0 + \boldsymbol{K}^f_{00}\boldsymbol{u}^f_0 + \boldsymbol{K}^f_{01}\boldsymbol{u}^f_1 + \boldsymbol{K}^f_{02}\boldsymbol{u}^f_2 + \boldsymbol{K}^f_{03}\boldsymbol{u}^f_3 - \boldsymbol{f}^f_0, \tag{10.82a}$$

$$0 = \boldsymbol{K}^e_{10}\boldsymbol{u}^e_0 + \boldsymbol{K}^e_{11}\boldsymbol{u}^e_1 + \boldsymbol{K}^e_{12}\boldsymbol{u}^e_2 + \boldsymbol{K}^e_{13}\boldsymbol{u}^e_3 - \boldsymbol{f}^e_1 + \boldsymbol{K}^f_{20}\boldsymbol{u}^f_0 + \boldsymbol{K}^f_{21}\boldsymbol{u}^f_1 + \boldsymbol{K}^f_{22}\boldsymbol{u}^f_2 + \boldsymbol{K}^f_{23}\boldsymbol{u}^f_3 - \boldsymbol{f}^f_2, \tag{10.82b}$$

$$0 = \boldsymbol{K}^e_{30}\boldsymbol{u}^e_0 + \boldsymbol{K}^e_{31}\boldsymbol{u}^e_1 + \boldsymbol{K}^e_{32}\boldsymbol{u}^e_2 + \boldsymbol{K}^e_{33}\boldsymbol{u}^e_3 - \boldsymbol{f}^e_3 + \boldsymbol{K}^f_{30}\boldsymbol{u}^f_0 + \boldsymbol{K}^f_{31}\boldsymbol{u}^f_1 + \boldsymbol{K}^f_{32}\boldsymbol{u}^f_2 + \boldsymbol{K}^f_{33}\boldsymbol{u}^f_3 - \boldsymbol{f}^f_3, \tag{10.82c}$$

Again we identify the global displacement with the local and write,

$$0 = \boldsymbol{K}^e_{00}\boldsymbol{u}_i + \boldsymbol{K}^e_{01}\boldsymbol{u}_j + \boldsymbol{K}^e_{02}\boldsymbol{u}_k + \boldsymbol{K}^e_{03}\boldsymbol{u}_l - \boldsymbol{f}^e_0 + \boldsymbol{K}^f_{00}\boldsymbol{u}_i + \boldsymbol{K}^f_{01}\boldsymbol{u}_m + \boldsymbol{K}^f_{02}\boldsymbol{u}_j + \boldsymbol{K}^f_{03}\boldsymbol{u}_l - \boldsymbol{f}^f_0, \tag{10.83a}$$

$$0 = \boldsymbol{K}^e_{10}\boldsymbol{u}_i + \boldsymbol{K}^e_{11}\boldsymbol{u}_j + \boldsymbol{K}^e_{12}\boldsymbol{u}_k + \boldsymbol{K}^e_{13}\boldsymbol{u}_l - \boldsymbol{f}^e_1 + \boldsymbol{K}^f_{20}\boldsymbol{u}_i + \boldsymbol{K}^f_{21}\boldsymbol{u}_m + \boldsymbol{K}^f_{22}\boldsymbol{u}_j + \boldsymbol{K}^f_{23}\boldsymbol{u}_l - \boldsymbol{f}^f_2, \tag{10.83b}$$

$$0 = \boldsymbol{K}^e_{30}\boldsymbol{u}_i + \boldsymbol{K}^e_{31}\boldsymbol{u}_j + \boldsymbol{K}^e_{32}\boldsymbol{u}_k + \boldsymbol{K}^e_{33}\boldsymbol{u}_l - \boldsymbol{f}^e_3 + \boldsymbol{K}^f_{30}\boldsymbol{u}_i + \boldsymbol{K}^f_{31}\boldsymbol{u}_m + \boldsymbol{K}^f_{32}\boldsymbol{u}_j + \boldsymbol{K}^f_{33}\boldsymbol{u}_l - \boldsymbol{f}^f_3, \tag{10.83c}$$

```
K = 0
f = 0
for all tetrahedra e do
  for each node m of e do
    find global index i of m
    for each node n of e do
      find global index j of n
      K_{j,i} += K^e_{n,m}
    next n
    f_i += f^e_m
  next m
next e
```

Figure 10.8: Pseudocode for the assembly of the global stiffness matrix $\boldsymbol{K}$ and the global force vector $\boldsymbol{f}$.

Finally we gather the equations on the form of (10.78) and find,

$$\boldsymbol{0} = \begin{bmatrix} \boldsymbol{K}^e_{00} + \boldsymbol{K}^f_{00} & \boldsymbol{K}^e_{01} + \boldsymbol{K}^f_{02} & \boldsymbol{K}^e_{02} & \boldsymbol{K}^e_{03} + \boldsymbol{K}^f_{03} & \boldsymbol{K}^f_{01} \\ \boldsymbol{K}^e_{10} + \boldsymbol{K}^f_{20} & \boldsymbol{K}^e_{11} + \boldsymbol{K}^f_{22} & \boldsymbol{K}^e_{12} & \boldsymbol{K}^e_{13} + \boldsymbol{K}^f_{23} & \boldsymbol{K}^f_{21} \\ \boldsymbol{K}^e_{30} + \boldsymbol{K}^f_{30} & \boldsymbol{K}^e_{31} + \boldsymbol{K}^f_{32} & \boldsymbol{K}^e_{32} & \boldsymbol{K}^e_{33} + \boldsymbol{K}^f_{33} & \boldsymbol{K}^f_{31} \end{bmatrix} \begin{bmatrix} \boldsymbol{u}_i \\ \boldsymbol{u}_j \\ \boldsymbol{u}_k \\ \boldsymbol{u}_l \\ \boldsymbol{u}_m \end{bmatrix} - \begin{bmatrix} \boldsymbol{f}^e_0 + \boldsymbol{f}^f_0 \\ \boldsymbol{f}^e_1 + \boldsymbol{f}^f_2 \\ \boldsymbol{f}^e_3 + \boldsymbol{f}^f_3 \end{bmatrix} \tag{10.84}$$

Thus we identify,

$$\boldsymbol{K} = \begin{bmatrix} \boldsymbol{K}^e_{00} + \boldsymbol{K}^f_{00} & \boldsymbol{K}^e_{01} + \boldsymbol{K}^f_{02} & \boldsymbol{K}^e_{02} & \boldsymbol{K}^e_{03} + \boldsymbol{K}^f_{03} & \boldsymbol{K}^f_{01} \\ \boldsymbol{K}^e_{10} + \boldsymbol{K}^f_{20} & \boldsymbol{K}^e_{11} + \boldsymbol{K}^f_{22} & \boldsymbol{K}^e_{12} & \boldsymbol{K}^e_{13} + \boldsymbol{K}^f_{23} & \boldsymbol{K}^f_{21} \\ \boldsymbol{K}^e_{30} + \boldsymbol{K}^f_{30} & \boldsymbol{K}^e_{31} + \boldsymbol{K}^f_{32} & \boldsymbol{K}^e_{32} & \boldsymbol{K}^e_{33} + \boldsymbol{K}^f_{33} & \boldsymbol{K}^f_{31} \end{bmatrix} \tag{10.85a}$$

$$\boldsymbol{u} = \begin{bmatrix} \boldsymbol{u}_i \\ \boldsymbol{u}_j \\ \boldsymbol{u}_k \\ \boldsymbol{u}_l \\ \boldsymbol{u}_m \end{bmatrix} \tag{10.85b}$$

$$\boldsymbol{f} = \begin{bmatrix} \boldsymbol{f}^e_0 + \boldsymbol{f}^f_0 \\ \boldsymbol{f}^e_1 + \boldsymbol{f}^f_2 \\ \boldsymbol{f}^e_3 + \boldsymbol{f}^f_3 \end{bmatrix} \tag{10.85c}$$

The *general assembly* is shown as pseudocode in Figure 10.8. The assembly will assemble all the local stiffness matrices into one global stiffness matrix, such that

$$\boldsymbol{K}\boldsymbol{u} = \boldsymbol{f} \tag{10.86}$$

where

$$\boldsymbol{u} = [\boldsymbol{u}_0, \boldsymbol{u}_1, \boldsymbol{u}_2, \dots]^T \tag{10.87}$$

and

$$\boldsymbol{f} = [\boldsymbol{f}_0, \boldsymbol{f}_1, \boldsymbol{f}_2, \ldots]^T. \tag{10.88}$$

In computer animation forces are often set directly on nodes through the global $\boldsymbol{f}$-vector instead of indirectly through local surface traction, $\boldsymbol{t}$, in which case the computation of $\boldsymbol{f}_m^e$ is omitted in the pseudocode.

Deformation of tetrahedral meshes can now be calculated by applying the external forces, calculating the global stiffness matrix, and solving the linear system,

$$\boldsymbol{u} = \boldsymbol{K}^{-1}\boldsymbol{f}. \tag{10.89}$$

This system may be solved efficiently, for example, using the conjugate gradient method, but the result is only static deformations. In the following we will extend the method to dynamic animation.

Using a global stiffness matrix is not the most efficient approach, and a computationally more efficient approach will be shown later.

10.2.6 Inertia and Damping Forces

In this section we will show how to extend the equations of motion to include *inertia* and *damping forces*. This is done straightforwardly by adding the corresponding work-energy terms to the derivation in Section 10.2.4.

Inertia forces originate from the movement of inertia, i.e., inertia forces are mass times acceleration. For a virtual displacement, $\delta\boldsymbol{u}$, the work performed by the inertia force per unit volume is,

$$W_{\text{inertia}} = \delta\boldsymbol{u}^T \rho \ddot{\boldsymbol{u}}, \tag{10.90}$$

where ρ is the mass density and $\ddot{\boldsymbol{u}}$ is the double time derivative of $\boldsymbol{u}$. Likewise, for a linear damping force per unit volume, the work performed is

$$W_{\text{damping}} = \delta\boldsymbol{u}^T c \dot{\boldsymbol{u}} \tag{10.91}$$

where c is the *damping coefficient* and $\dot{\boldsymbol{u}}$ is the time derivative of $\boldsymbol{u}$. To include inertia and damping forces we extend the work balance equation (10.54) as,

$$\int_{\Omega^e} W_{\text{inertia}}\, dV + \int_{\Omega^e} W_{\text{damping}}\, dV + \int_{\Omega^e} W_\sigma\, dV = W_q + \int_{\delta\Omega^e} W_t\, dA, \tag{10.92}$$

The values of $\delta\boldsymbol{u}$ may be interpolated from the nodal values, $\delta\boldsymbol{u} = \boldsymbol{N}\delta\boldsymbol{u}^e$, and assuming that we also have access to time derivatives at the nodal values, we may equally have $\dot{\boldsymbol{u}} = \boldsymbol{N}\dot{\boldsymbol{u}}^e$ and $\ddot{\boldsymbol{u}} = \boldsymbol{N}\ddot{\boldsymbol{u}}^e$. Thus, as we expand the two new terms in (10.92) we find that

$$\int_{\Omega^e} \delta\boldsymbol{u}^T \rho \ddot{\boldsymbol{u}}\, dV + \int_{\Omega^e} \delta\boldsymbol{u}^T c \dot{\boldsymbol{u}}\, dV + \int_{\Omega^e} W_\sigma\, dV = W_q + \int_{\delta\Omega^e} W_t\, dA, \tag{10.93a}$$

$$\Downarrow$$

$$\int_{\Omega^e} (\boldsymbol{N}\delta\boldsymbol{u}^e)^T \rho \boldsymbol{N}\ddot{\boldsymbol{u}}^e\, dV + \int_{\Omega^e} (\boldsymbol{N}\delta\boldsymbol{u}^e)^T c \boldsymbol{N}\dot{\boldsymbol{u}}^e\, dV + \int_{\Omega^e} W_\sigma\, dV = W_q + \int_{\delta\Omega^e} W_t\, dA. \tag{10.93b}$$

The displacements $\delta \boldsymbol{u}^e$ and $\boldsymbol{u}^e$ are constant w.r.t. the integration, and they may be moved outside the integration. Further introducing the *element mass matrix*,

$$\boldsymbol{M}^e = \int_{\Omega^e} \boldsymbol{N}^T \boldsymbol{N} \rho \, dV, \tag{10.94}$$

and the *element damping matrix*,

$$\boldsymbol{C}^e = \int_{\Omega^e} \boldsymbol{N}^T \boldsymbol{N} c \, dV, \tag{10.95}$$

and expanding the remaining terms as described in Section 10.2.4, we find

$$(\delta \boldsymbol{u}^e)^T \boldsymbol{M}^e \ddot{\boldsymbol{u}}^e + (\delta \boldsymbol{u}^e)^T \boldsymbol{C}^e \dot{\boldsymbol{u}}^e + (\delta \boldsymbol{u}^e)^T \boldsymbol{K}^e \boldsymbol{u}^e = (\delta \boldsymbol{u}^e)^T \boldsymbol{q}^e + (\delta \boldsymbol{u}^e)^T \boldsymbol{f}^e, \tag{10.96a}$$

$$\Downarrow$$

$$(\delta \boldsymbol{u}^e)^T \left(\boldsymbol{M}^e \ddot{\boldsymbol{u}}^e + \boldsymbol{C}^e \dot{\boldsymbol{u}}^e + \boldsymbol{K}^e \boldsymbol{u}^e \right) = (\delta \boldsymbol{u}^e)^T \left(\boldsymbol{q}^e + \boldsymbol{f}^e \right). \tag{10.96b}$$

Again, since this is valid for any virtual displacement $\delta \boldsymbol{u}^e$, we conclude that

$$\boldsymbol{M}^e \ddot{\boldsymbol{u}}^e + \boldsymbol{C}^e \dot{\boldsymbol{u}}^e + \boldsymbol{K}^e \boldsymbol{u}^e = \boldsymbol{q}^e + \boldsymbol{f}^e, \tag{10.97}$$

Since $\boldsymbol{u}^e = \boldsymbol{x}^e - \boldsymbol{x}_u^e$, then $\dot{\boldsymbol{u}}^e = \dot{\boldsymbol{x}}^e$ and $\ddot{\boldsymbol{u}}^e = \ddot{\boldsymbol{x}}^e$. Thus,

$$\boldsymbol{M}^e \ddot{\boldsymbol{x}}^e + \boldsymbol{C}^e \dot{\boldsymbol{x}}^e + \boldsymbol{K}^e (\boldsymbol{x}^e - \boldsymbol{x}_u^e) = \boldsymbol{f}_{\text{ext}}^e \tag{10.98}$$

where we have used the shorthand, $\boldsymbol{f}_{\text{ext}}^e = \boldsymbol{q}^e + \boldsymbol{f}^e$. Assembling the total system into a single matrix equation we have,

$$\boldsymbol{M}\ddot{\boldsymbol{x}} + \boldsymbol{C}\dot{\boldsymbol{x}} + \boldsymbol{K}(\boldsymbol{x} - \boldsymbol{x}_u) = \boldsymbol{f}_{\text{ext}} \tag{10.99}$$

10.2.7 Computing the Mass Matrix

A mass matrix is a discrete representation of a continuous mass distribution. The element mass matrix is defined as

$$\boldsymbol{M}^e = \int_{\Omega^e} \boldsymbol{N}^T \boldsymbol{N} \rho \, dV, \tag{10.100}$$

and is called consistent. Considering the scalar case where $N_n \in \mathbb{R}$, and assuming that ρ is constant over each tetrahedral element and using the linear shape functions, the above definition (10.100) results in

$$\boldsymbol{M}^e = \rho \int_{\Omega^e} \begin{bmatrix} (N_0 N_0) & (N_0 N_1) & (N_0 N_2) & (N_0 N_3) \\ (N_1 N_0) & (N_1 N_1) & (N_1 N_2) & (N_1 N_3) \\ (N_2 N_0) & (N_2 N_1) & (N_2 N_2) & (N_2 N_3) \\ (N_3 N_0) & (N_3 N_1) & (N_3 N_2) & (N_3 N_3) \end{bmatrix} dV. \tag{10.101}$$

Using [Cook et al., 2002, pp. 266],

$$\int_{\Omega^e} \boldsymbol{N}_0^a \boldsymbol{N}_1^b \boldsymbol{N}_2^c \boldsymbol{N}_3^d \, dV = \frac{6V^e a! b! c! d!}{(3 + a + b + c + d)!}, \tag{10.102}$$

we find that

$$\boldsymbol{M}^e = \rho \frac{V^e}{20} \begin{bmatrix} 2 & 1 & 1 & 1 \\ 1 & 2 & 1 & 1 \\ 1 & 1 & 2 & 1 \\ 1 & 1 & 1 & 2 \end{bmatrix}, \tag{10.103}$$

or equivalently

$$M_{ij}^e = \rho \frac{V^e}{20} (1 + \delta_{ij}), \tag{10.104}$$

where δ_{ij} is the Kronecker delta. In the vector case where $\boldsymbol{N}_n \in \mathbb{R}^{3\times3}$, this means that for the tetrahedral element

$$\boldsymbol{M}^e = \rho \frac{V^e}{20} \begin{bmatrix} 2 & 2 & 2 & 1 & 1 & 1 & 1 & 1 & 1 & 1 & 1 & 1 \\ 2 & 2 & 2 & 1 & 1 & 1 & 1 & 1 & 1 & 1 & 1 & 1 \\ 2 & 2 & 2 & 1 & 1 & 1 & 1 & 1 & 1 & 1 & 1 & 1 \\ & & & & & & & & & & & \\ 1 & 1 & 1 & 2 & 2 & 2 & 1 & 1 & 1 & 1 & 1 & 1 \\ 1 & 1 & 1 & 2 & 2 & 2 & 1 & 1 & 1 & 1 & 1 & 1 \\ 1 & 1 & 1 & 2 & 2 & 2 & 1 & 1 & 1 & 1 & 1 & 1 \\ & & & & & & & & & & & \\ 1 & 1 & 1 & 1 & 1 & 1 & 2 & 2 & 2 & 1 & 1 & 1 \\ 1 & 1 & 1 & 1 & 1 & 1 & 2 & 2 & 2 & 1 & 1 & 1 \\ 1 & 1 & 1 & 1 & 1 & 1 & 2 & 2 & 2 & 1 & 1 & 1 \\ & & & & & & & & & & & \\ 1 & 1 & 1 & 1 & 1 & 1 & 1 & 1 & 1 & 2 & 2 & 2 \\ 1 & 1 & 1 & 1 & 1 & 1 & 1 & 1 & 1 & 2 & 2 & 2 \\ 1 & 1 & 1 & 1 & 1 & 1 & 1 & 1 & 1 & 2 & 2 & 2 \end{bmatrix}. \tag{10.105}$$

Notice that in order to obtain the global/system mass matrix an assembly similar to the stiffness matrix assembly must be carried out. Further, the global $\boldsymbol{M}$ matrix will have the same subblock pattern as the global $\boldsymbol{K}$ matrix.

A consistent mass matrix is often not used in computer graphics. Instead an ad hoc matrix called the *lumped mass matrix* is used, which is obtained by placing particle masses at the nodes. This corresponds to shifting all the masses in the rows of (10.103) onto the diagonal. In 3D this yields the element mass

```
for each node n
  mass(n) = 0
next n
for each tetrahedron e
  for each node n of e
    mass(n) += ρ V^e/4
  next n
next e
```

Figure 10.9: Pseudocode for calculating the lumped mass matrix.

matrix

$$
\boldsymbol{M}^e = \rho\frac{V^e}{4}\begin{bmatrix}
1 & 0 & 0 & 0 & 0 & 0 & 0 & 0 & 0 & 0 & 0 & 0 \\
0 & 1 & 0 & 0 & 0 & 0 & 0 & 0 & 0 & 0 & 0 & 0 \\
0 & 0 & 1 & 0 & 0 & 0 & 0 & 0 & 0 & 0 & 0 & 0 \\
0 & 0 & 0 & 1 & 0 & 0 & 0 & 0 & 0 & 0 & 0 & 0 \\
0 & 0 & 0 & 0 & 1 & 0 & 0 & 0 & 0 & 0 & 0 & 0 \\
0 & 0 & 0 & 0 & 0 & 1 & 0 & 0 & 0 & 0 & 0 & 0 \\
0 & 0 & 0 & 0 & 0 & 0 & 1 & 0 & 0 & 0 & 0 & 0 \\
0 & 0 & 0 & 0 & 0 & 0 & 0 & 1 & 0 & 0 & 0 & 0 \\
0 & 0 & 0 & 0 & 0 & 0 & 0 & 0 & 1 & 0 & 0 & 0 \\
0 & 0 & 0 & 0 & 0 & 0 & 0 & 0 & 0 & 1 & 0 & 0 \\
0 & 0 & 0 & 0 & 0 & 0 & 0 & 0 & 0 & 0 & 1 & 0 \\
0 & 0 & 0 & 0 & 0 & 0 & 0 & 0 & 0 & 0 & 0 & 1
\end{bmatrix}. \tag{10.106}
$$

Thus, a lumped mass matrix is diagonal whereas a consistent mass matrix is not. Observe that the consequence is that the global mass matrix also becomes diagonal, and thus the assembly simply becomes an iteration over all tetrahedra, while incrementing the nodal mass by one fourth of the tetrahedral mass. This is demonstrated in Figure 10.9. Since V and ρ are positive for all elements, both the element mass matrices and the global mass matrices are symmetric positive definite matrices.

The advantage of lumping is less storage and higher performance. The disadvantage is that discontinuity is introduced in the displacement field. [O'Brien et al., 2002b] state that the errors in lumping is negligible for small-size, course meshes such as those used in computer graphics. There does exist alternative approaches for computing mass matrices; we refer the interested reader to [Cook et al., 2002] for more details.

10.3 Stiffness Warping

The linear elastic method introduced in the previous sections is only valid for small deformations. This is due to the fact that the *linear Cauchy strain tensor* ε used in the calculation of the *stiffness matrix* $\boldsymbol{K}$ is

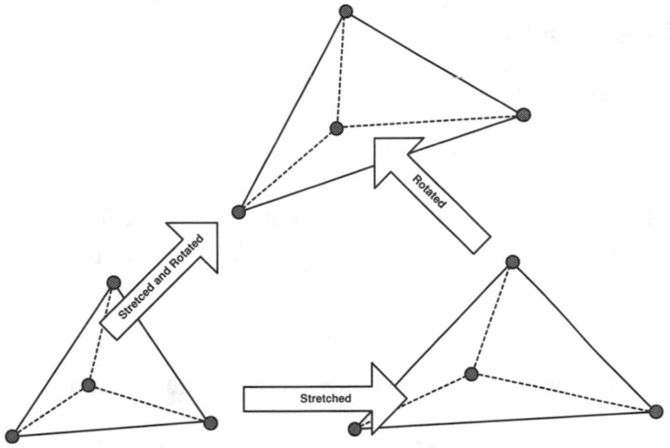

Figure 10.10: Illustration of the stiffness warping concept

a first-order approximation to the *nonlinear Green-Lagrange strain tensor*, as explained in Section 22.7. When the deformable object is subject to large rotational deformations, then the result is an unrealistic growth in volume. However, it is not a viable solution to use a higher-order approximation to the strain tensor for animation purposes, since this leads to systems of nonlinear equations, which are hard to solve.

In [Müller et al., 2004a], a method was shown that removes the artifacts that linear elastic forces introduces, while keeping the governing equations linear. Consider the elastic force acting on a single tetrahedral element e, as described in (10.89) and repeated here for convenience

$$\boldsymbol{f}^e = \boldsymbol{K}^e \left(\boldsymbol{x}^e - \boldsymbol{x}^e_u\right) = \boldsymbol{K}^e \boldsymbol{x}^e + \boldsymbol{f}^e_u, \tag{10.107}$$

where $\boldsymbol{u}^e = \boldsymbol{x}^e - \boldsymbol{x}^e_u$, and where $\boldsymbol{x}^e$ and $\boldsymbol{x}^e_u$ are the positions of the four vertices of a tetrahedron at its deformed and undeformed state, $\boldsymbol{K}^e$ is the element stiffness matrix, and $\boldsymbol{f}^e_u = \boldsymbol{K}^e \boldsymbol{x}^e_u$ is the force offsets.

Assume that the rotational part of the deformation $\boldsymbol{R}^e$ for the tetrahedron e is known. The *stiffness warping* concept consists of rotating the deformed positions back into the undeformed frame, calculating the elastic force in this frame, and rotating the result back to the deformed frame. This is illustrated in Figure 10.10, and can be written as

$$\boldsymbol{f}^e = \boldsymbol{R}^e \boldsymbol{K}^e \left(\boldsymbol{R}^{e-1} \boldsymbol{x}^e - \boldsymbol{x}^e_u\right) \tag{10.108a}$$

$$= \boldsymbol{R}^e \boldsymbol{K}^e \boldsymbol{R}^{e-1} \boldsymbol{x}^e - \boldsymbol{R}^e \boldsymbol{K}^e \boldsymbol{x}^e_u \tag{10.108b}$$

$$= \boldsymbol{K}^{e\prime} \boldsymbol{x}^e + \boldsymbol{f}^{e\prime}_u, \tag{10.108c}$$

where $\boldsymbol{R}^e$ is a 12×12 matrix that contains the 3×3 rotation matrix along its diagonal. By doing so, the elastic forces are the same as if the regular linear forces were calculated in a rotated coordinate frame.

Stiffness warping is not without peril, since it does suffer from element inversion, when a model is compressed violently. Recently a diagonalization method has been introduced to deal with the inversion problem [Irving et al., 2004], but this method is outside the scope of this book.

10.3.1 Stiffness Warping Assembly

For an assembled system, the linear elastostatic model is,

$$\boldsymbol{K}\boldsymbol{u} = \boldsymbol{K}(\boldsymbol{x} - \boldsymbol{x}_u) = \boldsymbol{f}, \tag{10.109}$$

where $\boldsymbol{u} = \boldsymbol{x} - \boldsymbol{x}_u$ is the nodal displacement, $\boldsymbol{x}$ is the current position and $\boldsymbol{x}_u$ is the original position, $\boldsymbol{f}$ is the nodal forces, and $\boldsymbol{K}$ is the stiffness matrix. Using $\boldsymbol{f}_u = -\boldsymbol{K}\boldsymbol{x}_u$ as the force offset vectors, we have

$$\boldsymbol{f} = \boldsymbol{K}\boldsymbol{x} + \boldsymbol{f}_u. \tag{10.110}$$

Let $\boldsymbol{R}$ denote the current orientation, then $\boldsymbol{R}^{-1}$ rotates back to the original frame, which means we have,

$$\boldsymbol{f} = \boldsymbol{R}\boldsymbol{K}(\boldsymbol{R}^{-1}\boldsymbol{x} - \boldsymbol{x}_u), \tag{10.111a}$$

$$\boldsymbol{f} = \boldsymbol{R}\boldsymbol{K}\boldsymbol{R}^{-1}\boldsymbol{x} - \boldsymbol{R}\boldsymbol{K}\boldsymbol{x}_u. \tag{10.111b}$$

So with stiffness warping we have to compute

$$\boldsymbol{K}' = \boldsymbol{R}\boldsymbol{K}\boldsymbol{R}^{-1}, \tag{10.112a}$$

$$\boldsymbol{f}'_u = -\boldsymbol{R}\boldsymbol{K}\boldsymbol{x}_u. \tag{10.112b}$$

For N nodes the system stiffness matrix $\boldsymbol{K}'$ is a $3N \times 3N$ symmetric and sparse matrix. It would be insane to actually allocate such a matrix; instead the matrix is stored inside the nodes of the volume mesh.

Each node stores a row of $\boldsymbol{K}'$ and the corresponding entries of the $\boldsymbol{f}'_u$ vector. That is, the i'th node stores all nonzero 3×3 subblocks of the i'th row of the stiffness matrix, and it also stores the i'th 3D subvector of $\boldsymbol{f}_u$. Let $\mathcal{T}_i$ denote the set of all tetrahedral elements sharing global node i, then the assembly of the warped stiffness matrix can be written as,

$$\boldsymbol{K}'_{ij} = \sum_{i \sim n \text{ and } j \sim m} \boldsymbol{R}^e \boldsymbol{K^e}_{nm} \boldsymbol{R}^{eT}. \tag{10.113}$$

Furthermore, the assembly of the force offset vector

$$\boldsymbol{f'_{ui}} = \sum_{i \sim n} -\boldsymbol{R}^e \boldsymbol{K}^e_{nm} \boldsymbol{x}_{um}. \tag{10.114}$$

Notice that this can be optimized: letting the indices i, j, k, and m denote global indices of e such that the global index i corresponds to local index n. Then the contribution from element e can be written as,

$$\begin{aligned} &- \boldsymbol{R}^e \boldsymbol{K}^e_{nn} \boldsymbol{x}_{un} - \boldsymbol{R}^e \boldsymbol{K}^e_{nm} \boldsymbol{x}_{um} - \boldsymbol{R}^e \boldsymbol{K}^e_{no} \boldsymbol{x}_{uo} - \boldsymbol{R}^e \boldsymbol{K}^e_{np} \boldsymbol{x}_{up} \\ &\quad = -\boldsymbol{R}^e (\boldsymbol{K}^e_{nn} \boldsymbol{x}_{un} + \boldsymbol{K}^e_{nm} \boldsymbol{x}_{um} + \boldsymbol{K}^e_{no} \boldsymbol{x}_{uo} + \boldsymbol{K}^e_{np} \boldsymbol{x}_{up}), \end{aligned} \tag{10.115}$$

which saves us a few matrix multiplications, and we then finally have

$$\boldsymbol{f}'_{ui} = \sum_{n \sim i} -\boldsymbol{R}^e (\boldsymbol{K}^e_{nn} \boldsymbol{x}_{un} + \boldsymbol{K}^e_{nm} \boldsymbol{x}_{um} + \boldsymbol{K}^e_{no} \boldsymbol{x}_{uo} + \boldsymbol{K}^e_{np} \boldsymbol{x}_{up}). \tag{10.116}$$

```
for each element e do
  for each node i of e do
    tmp = 0
    for each node j of e do
      tmp += Ke_ij * xo_j
    next j
    f0'_i -= Re*tmp
  next i
next e
```

Figure 10.11: Pseudocode for calculating f_u.

```
for each element e do
  for each node i of e do
    for each node j of e do
      if i >= j then
        tmp = Re Ke_ij Re^{T}
        K'_ij +=  tmp
        if j > i then
          K'_ji +=  trans(tmp)
        end if
      end if
    next j
  next i
next e
```

Figure 10.12: Pseudocode for assembly process for the warped stiffness matrix.

Assuming that f'_{un} is initially cleared to zero for all n. This results in the implementation strategy shown in Figure 10.11. Also the stiffness matrix can be optimized slightly by exploiting the symmetry property. The symmetry indicates that it is sufficient to only compute the upper triangular and diagonal parts. The lower triangular parts can be found simply be taking the transpose of the upper triangular parts. Thus, the e'th tetrahedral element contributes with

$$\boldsymbol{K}'_{ij} += \boldsymbol{R}^e \boldsymbol{K}^e_{nm} \boldsymbol{R}^{eT}, \tag{10.117a}$$

$$\boldsymbol{K}'_{ji} += \boldsymbol{R}^e \boldsymbol{K}^e_{mn} \boldsymbol{R}^{eT} = (\boldsymbol{R}^e \boldsymbol{K}^e_{mn} \boldsymbol{R}^{eT})^T, \tag{10.117b}$$

where $i \sim n$ and $j \sim m$, and since $\boldsymbol{K}^e_{mn} = (\boldsymbol{K}^e_{nm})^T$. Assuming that all $\boldsymbol{K}'_{ij}$ is initially cleared to zero this results in the implementation strategy shown in Figure 10.12.

Note that if $\boldsymbol{R}^e$ is initially set to the identity matrix, then the stiffness warping reduces to the traditional assembly of stiffness matrix (as it is used in linear elastostatics). Also notice that whenever $\boldsymbol{R}^e$ changes, then the stiffness matrix assembly must be recalculated. This is done after each position update. Furthermore, if the i'th node is set to be fixed, this corresponds to letting $\boldsymbol{K}'_{ii} = \mathbf{1}$, and $\boldsymbol{K}'_{ij}$ and $\boldsymbol{K}'_{ji}$ be zero for all j not equal to i. This is known as a Dirichlet boundary condition. However, we do not use this during the assembly. Instead we assemble the $\boldsymbol{K}'$ matrix as though there were no fixed nodes. Later, when we use the $\boldsymbol{K}'$ matrix in computations such as $\boldsymbol{K}'\boldsymbol{x}$, we simply test whether $\boldsymbol{x}_j$ is fixed. If this is the case, then it is multiplied by the j'th column of $\boldsymbol{K}'$, i.e., $\boldsymbol{K}'_{*j}$. If so, we simply do nothing! This is computationally more tractable, and it also allow us to more easily turn nodes fixed and unfixed dynamically during animation.

10.3.2 Orientation Computation

In order to perform the stiffness warping assembly described in the previous section, we need to be able to estimate the rotational warp of each individual tetrahedron. The most elegant method is to find the transform using barycentric coordinates [Müller et al., 2004a], and this method will be described below.

Let the deformed corners be $\boldsymbol{x}_0$, $\boldsymbol{x}_1$, $\boldsymbol{x}_2$, and $\boldsymbol{x}_3$ and the undeformed corners $\boldsymbol{x}_{u0}$, $\boldsymbol{x}_{u1}$, $\boldsymbol{x}_{u2}$, and $\boldsymbol{x}_{u3}$. Examining point $\boldsymbol{x}_u = [x, y, z, 1]^T$ inside the undeformed tetrahedron is written as,

$$\boldsymbol{x}_u = \begin{bmatrix} \boldsymbol{x}_{u0} & \boldsymbol{x}_{u1} & \boldsymbol{x}_{u2} & \boldsymbol{x}_{u3} \\ 1 & 1 & 1 & 1 \end{bmatrix} \begin{bmatrix} w_0 \\ w_1 \\ w_2 \\ w_3 \end{bmatrix} = \boldsymbol{P}\boldsymbol{w}. \tag{10.118}$$

The corresponding point in the deformed tetrahedron has the same barycentric coordinates, which mean,

$$\boldsymbol{x} = \begin{bmatrix} \boldsymbol{x}_0 & \boldsymbol{x}_1 & \boldsymbol{x}_2 & \boldsymbol{x}_3 \\ 1 & 1 & 1 & 1 \end{bmatrix} \begin{bmatrix} w_0 \\ w_1 \\ w_2 \\ w_3 \end{bmatrix} = \boldsymbol{X}\boldsymbol{w}. \tag{10.119}$$

We can now use (10.118) to solve for $\boldsymbol{w}$ and insert the solution into (10.119) to get,

$$\boldsymbol{x} = \boldsymbol{X}\boldsymbol{P}^{-1}\boldsymbol{x}_u. \tag{10.120}$$

The matrix $\boldsymbol{X}\boldsymbol{P}^{-1}$ transforms $\boldsymbol{x}_u$ into $\boldsymbol{x}$. Since both $\boldsymbol{P}$ and $\boldsymbol{X}$ have their fourth rows equal to $\boldsymbol{1}$, it can be shown that their product has the block structure

$$\boldsymbol{X}\boldsymbol{P}^{-1} = \begin{bmatrix} \boldsymbol{G} & \boldsymbol{a} \\ \boldsymbol{0}^T & 1 \end{bmatrix}, \tag{10.121}$$

and this is recognized as a transformation matrix of homogeneous coordinates. The $\boldsymbol{a}$ vector gives the translation, the $\boldsymbol{G}$ matrix includes, scaling, shearing, and rotation.

We thus need to extract the rotational matrix $\boldsymbol{R}$ from $\boldsymbol{G}$. In [Müller et al., 2004a] the authors suggest using Polar Decompositions [Shoemake et al., 1992, Etzmuss et al., 2003]. However, a simpler although more imprecise approach would simply be to apply a Gram-Schmidt orthonormalization to transform $\boldsymbol{G}$ into an orthonormal matrix. This seems to work quite well in practice. We have not observed any noteworthy visual difference in using polar decomposition or orthonormalization.

Since we are only interested in the G part of (10.121), we can compute this more efficiently exploiting the fact that barycentric coordinates sum up to one. If we substitute $w_0 = 1 - w_1 - w_2 - w_3$ in (10.118) and (10.119), then we can ignore the fourth rows, since they simply state $1 = 1$, i.e.,

$$\boldsymbol{x}_u = \begin{bmatrix} \boldsymbol{x}_{u0} & \boldsymbol{x}_{u1} & \boldsymbol{x}_{u2} & \boldsymbol{x}_{u3} \end{bmatrix} \begin{bmatrix} 1 - w_1 - w_2 - w_3 \\ w_1 \\ w_2 \\ w_3 \end{bmatrix}, \tag{10.122}$$

which is

$$\boldsymbol{x}_u = \begin{bmatrix} \boldsymbol{x}_{u0} & (\boldsymbol{x}_{u1} - \boldsymbol{x}_{u0}) & (\boldsymbol{x}_{u2} - \boldsymbol{x}_{u0}) & (\boldsymbol{x}_{u3} - \boldsymbol{x}_{u0}) \end{bmatrix} \begin{bmatrix} 1 \\ w_1 \\ w_2 \\ w_3 \end{bmatrix}. \tag{10.123}$$

Moving the first column to the left-hand side we get,

$$\boldsymbol{x}_u - \boldsymbol{x}_{u0} = \begin{bmatrix} (\boldsymbol{x}_{u1} - \boldsymbol{x}_{u0}) & (\boldsymbol{x}_{u2} - \boldsymbol{x}_{u0}) & (\boldsymbol{x}_{u3} - \boldsymbol{x}_{u0}) \end{bmatrix} \begin{bmatrix} w_1 \\ w_2 \\ w_3 \end{bmatrix}. \tag{10.124}$$

Introducing $\mathbf{e}_{10} = \boldsymbol{x}_{u1} - \boldsymbol{x}_{u0}$, $\mathbf{e}_{20} = \boldsymbol{x}_{u2} - \boldsymbol{x}_{u0}$, $\mathbf{e}_{30} = \boldsymbol{x}_{u3} - \boldsymbol{x}_{u0}$, and $\boldsymbol{E} = [\mathbf{e}_{10}, \mathbf{e}_{20}, \mathbf{e}_{30}]$, we have,

$$\boldsymbol{x}_u - \boldsymbol{x}_{u0} = \boldsymbol{E} \begin{bmatrix} w_1 \\ w_2 \\ w_3 \end{bmatrix}, \tag{10.125}$$

and similar for (10.119) we have,

$$\boldsymbol{x} - \boldsymbol{x}_0 = \boldsymbol{E}' \begin{bmatrix} w_1 \\ w_2 \\ w_3 \end{bmatrix}, \tag{10.126}$$

where $\boldsymbol{E}' = [\mathbf{e}'_{10}\mathbf{e}'_{20}\mathbf{e}'_{30}]$ and $\mathbf{e}'_{10} = \boldsymbol{x}_1 - \boldsymbol{x}_0$, $\mathbf{e}'_{20} = \boldsymbol{x}_2 - \boldsymbol{x}_0$, $\mathbf{e}'_{30} = \boldsymbol{x}_3 - \boldsymbol{x}_0$. Now inverting (10.125) and inserting the result into (10.126) yields,

$$\boldsymbol{x} - \boldsymbol{x}_0 = \boldsymbol{E}'\boldsymbol{E}^{-1}(\boldsymbol{x}_u - \boldsymbol{x}_{u0}). \tag{10.127}$$

By comparison with (10.121) we see that

$$\boldsymbol{G} = \boldsymbol{E}'\boldsymbol{E}^{-1}. \tag{10.128}$$

Using Cramer's rule the inverse of $\boldsymbol{E}$ can be written as

$$\boldsymbol{E}^{-1} = \frac{1}{6V} \begin{bmatrix} (\mathbf{e}_{20} \times \mathbf{e}_{30})^T \\ (\mathbf{e}_{30} \times \mathbf{e}_{10})^T \\ (\mathbf{e}_{10} \times \mathbf{e}_{20})^T \end{bmatrix}. \tag{10.129}$$

This can easily be confirmed by straightforward computation

$$\boldsymbol{E}^{-1}\boldsymbol{E} = \boldsymbol{1}. \tag{10.130a}$$

Using the notation

$$\boldsymbol{n}_1 = \frac{1}{6V}\boldsymbol{e}_{20} \times \boldsymbol{e}_{30}, \tag{10.131a}$$

$$\boldsymbol{n}_2 = \frac{1}{6V}\boldsymbol{e}_{30} \times \boldsymbol{e}_{10}, \tag{10.131b}$$

$$\boldsymbol{n}_3 = \frac{1}{6V}\boldsymbol{e}_{10} \times \boldsymbol{e}_{20}, \tag{10.131c}$$

we write,

$$\boldsymbol{E}^{-1} = \begin{bmatrix} \boldsymbol{n}_1^T \\ \boldsymbol{n}_2^T \\ \boldsymbol{n}_3^T \end{bmatrix}, \tag{10.132}$$

and we finally have,

$$\boldsymbol{G} = \begin{bmatrix} \boldsymbol{e}'_{10} & \boldsymbol{e}'_{20} & \boldsymbol{e}'_{30} \end{bmatrix} \begin{bmatrix} \boldsymbol{n}_1^T \\ \boldsymbol{n}_2^T \\ \boldsymbol{n}_3^T \end{bmatrix}. \tag{10.133}$$

Observe that $\boldsymbol{E}'$ is very inexpensive to compute and all nonprimed quantities $\{\boldsymbol{n}_1, \boldsymbol{n}_2, \boldsymbol{n}_3\}$ can be precomputed and stored on a per tetrahedron basis given sufficiently available memory. Even in case where memory is not available $\boldsymbol{n}_1$, $\boldsymbol{n}_2$, and $\boldsymbol{n}_3$ are quite cheap to compute.

10.3.3 Plasticity

The total strain of the e'th element is given by

$$\boldsymbol{e}_{\text{total}} = \boldsymbol{B}\boldsymbol{u}^e \tag{10.134}$$

Where $\boldsymbol{u}^e$ is the nodal displacement, i.e., $\boldsymbol{u}^e = \boldsymbol{x} - \boldsymbol{x}_u$. Applying the idea of stiffness warping we have

$$\boldsymbol{e}_{\text{total}} = \boldsymbol{B}((\boldsymbol{R}^e)^{-1}\boldsymbol{x} - \boldsymbol{x}_u) \tag{10.135}$$

where $\boldsymbol{R}^e$ is the rotational deformation of the e'th tetrahedral element.

The elastic strain is given as the total strain minus the plastic strain

$$\boldsymbol{e} = \boldsymbol{e}_{\text{total}} - \boldsymbol{e}_{\text{plastic}} \tag{10.136}$$

$\boldsymbol{e}_{\text{plastic}}$ is initial initialized to zero. During simulation the plastic strain is constantly updates as follows. If elastic strain exceeds c_{yield}, then it is added to plastic strain by c_{creep}

```
if ||\vec e||_2 > c_yield then
   e_plastic += dt*std::min(T->m_creep,(1.0/dt)) e
```

If plastic strain exceeds $c_{\max}$, then it is clamped to maximum magnitude

```
if ||e_plastic|| > c_max then
  e_plastic = (e_plastic/|e_plastic|) c_max
```

The plastic strain causes plastic forces in the material

$$\boldsymbol{f}_{\text{plastic}} = \boldsymbol{R}^e \boldsymbol{K}^e \boldsymbol{u}^e_{\text{plastic}}. \tag{10.137}$$

Using $\boldsymbol{e}_{\text{plastic}} = \boldsymbol{B}\boldsymbol{u}^e_{\text{plastic}}$ we find,

$$\boldsymbol{f}_{\text{plastic}} = \boldsymbol{R}^e \boldsymbol{K}^e \boldsymbol{B}^{-1} \boldsymbol{e}_{\text{plastic}} \tag{10.138a}$$

$$\boldsymbol{f}_{\text{plastic}} = \boldsymbol{R}^e (V^e \boldsymbol{B}^T \boldsymbol{D}\boldsymbol{B}) \boldsymbol{B}^{-1} \boldsymbol{e}_{\text{plastic}} \tag{10.138b}$$

$$\boldsymbol{f}_{\text{plastic}} = \boldsymbol{R}^e (V^e \boldsymbol{B}^T \boldsymbol{D}) \boldsymbol{e}_{\text{plastic}} \tag{10.138c}$$

Introducing the plasticity matrix $\boldsymbol{P}^e = (V^e \boldsymbol{B}^T \boldsymbol{E})$ we have,

$$\boldsymbol{f}_{\text{plastic}} = \boldsymbol{R}^e \boldsymbol{P}^e \boldsymbol{e}_{\text{plastic}}. \tag{10.139}$$

The plastic forces can be computed efficiently by exploiting the structure of the $\boldsymbol{B}_n$ and $\boldsymbol{D}$ matrices as,

$$\boldsymbol{B}_n = \begin{bmatrix} b_n & 0 & 0 \\ 0 & c_n & 0 \\ 0 & 0 & d_n \\ c_n & b_n & 0 \\ d_n & 0 & b_n \\ 0 & d_n & c_n, \end{bmatrix}, \tag{10.140a}$$

$$\boldsymbol{D} = \begin{bmatrix} D_0 & D_1 & D_1 & 0 & 0 & 0 & \\ D_1 & D_0 & D_0 & 0 & 0 & 0 & \\ D_1 & D_1 & D_0 & 0 & 0 & 0 & \\ 0 & 0 & 0 & D_2 & 0 & 0 & 0 \\ 0 & 0 & 0 & 0 & D_2 & 0 & \\ 0 & 0 & 0 & 0 & 0 & D_2 & \end{bmatrix}. \tag{10.140b}$$

This implies that the product $\boldsymbol{B}_n^T \boldsymbol{D}$ is

$$\boldsymbol{B}_n^T \boldsymbol{D} = \begin{bmatrix} b_n D_0 & b_n D_1 & b_n D_1 & c_n D_2 & d_n D_2 & 0 \\ c_n D_1 & c_n D_0 & c_n D_1 & b_n D_2 & 0 & d_n D_2 \\ d_n D_1 & d_n D_1 & d_n D_0 & 0 & b_n D_2 & c_n D_2 \end{bmatrix}. \tag{10.141}$$

Notice that even though this is a 3×6 matrix with $18 - 3 = 15$ nonzero elements it actually only contains 9 different values. In fact, these values could be precomputed and stored in each tetrahedron. Furthermore they could be premultiplied by the volume of the tetrahedron to yield the matrix,

$$\boldsymbol{P}_n^e = V^e \boldsymbol{B}_n^T \boldsymbol{D}. \tag{10.142}$$

The plastic force that should be subtracted from node n is then computed in each iteration as

$$\boldsymbol{f}_n = \boldsymbol{R}^e \boldsymbol{P}^e_n \boldsymbol{e}_{\text{plastic}}. \tag{10.143}$$

Instead of allocating another set of temporary variables to hold the plastic forces, it is much easier to simply add the plastic forces to the external force vector. Thus saving memory.

10.4 Time Integration

The equation of motion has the following form (where $\boldsymbol{u} = \boldsymbol{x} - \boldsymbol{x}_u$, and $\dot{\boldsymbol{x}}$ is derivative w.r.t. time)

$$\boldsymbol{M}\ddot{\boldsymbol{x}} + \boldsymbol{C}\dot{\boldsymbol{x}} + \boldsymbol{K}(\boldsymbol{x} - \boldsymbol{x}_u) = \boldsymbol{f}_{\text{ext}}. \tag{10.144}$$

Implicit discretization, means we evaluated $\boldsymbol{x}$ and $\boldsymbol{v} = \dot{\boldsymbol{x}}$ at time $i+1$. Furthermore, using $\ddot{\boldsymbol{x}} = \frac{\boldsymbol{v}^{i+1} - \boldsymbol{v}^i}{\Delta t}$ and $\dot{\boldsymbol{x}} = \boldsymbol{v}^{i+1}$, we have

$$\boldsymbol{M}\frac{\boldsymbol{v}^{i+1} - \boldsymbol{v}^i}{\Delta t} + \boldsymbol{C}\boldsymbol{v}^{i+1} + \boldsymbol{K}(\boldsymbol{x}^{i+1} - \boldsymbol{x}_u) = \boldsymbol{f}_{\text{ext}}, \tag{10.145}$$

and since $\boldsymbol{x}^{i+1} = \boldsymbol{x}^i + \boldsymbol{v}^{i+1}\Delta t$,

$$\boldsymbol{M}\frac{\boldsymbol{v}^{i+1} - \boldsymbol{v}^i}{\Delta t} + \boldsymbol{C}\boldsymbol{v}^{i+1} + \boldsymbol{K}((\boldsymbol{x}^i + \boldsymbol{v}^{i+1}\Delta t) - \boldsymbol{x}_u) = \boldsymbol{f}_{\text{ext}}, \tag{10.146a}$$

$$\Downarrow$$

$$\boldsymbol{M}\frac{\boldsymbol{v}^{i+1} - \boldsymbol{v}^i}{\Delta t} + \boldsymbol{C}\boldsymbol{v}^{i+1} + \boldsymbol{K}\boldsymbol{x}^i + \Delta t\boldsymbol{K}\boldsymbol{v}^{i+1} - \boldsymbol{K}\boldsymbol{x}_u = \boldsymbol{f}_{\text{ext}}, \tag{10.146b}$$

$$\Downarrow$$

$$\boldsymbol{M}\boldsymbol{v}^{i+1} - \boldsymbol{M}\boldsymbol{v}^i + \Delta t\boldsymbol{C}\boldsymbol{v}^{i+1} + \Delta t^2\boldsymbol{K}\boldsymbol{v}^{i+1} = \Delta t(\boldsymbol{f}_{\text{ext}} - \boldsymbol{K}\boldsymbol{x}^i + \boldsymbol{K}\boldsymbol{x}_u), \tag{10.146c}$$

$$\Downarrow$$

$$(\boldsymbol{M} + \Delta t\boldsymbol{C} + \Delta t^2\boldsymbol{K})\boldsymbol{v}^{i+1} = \boldsymbol{M}\boldsymbol{v}^i + \Delta t(\boldsymbol{f}_{\text{ext}} - \boldsymbol{K}\boldsymbol{x}^i + \boldsymbol{K}\boldsymbol{x}_u). \tag{10.146d}$$

Let $\boldsymbol{f}_u = -\boldsymbol{K}\boldsymbol{x}_u$, then

$$(\boldsymbol{M} + \Delta t\boldsymbol{C} + \Delta t^2\boldsymbol{K})\boldsymbol{v}^{i+1} = \boldsymbol{M}\boldsymbol{v}^i - \Delta t(\boldsymbol{K}\boldsymbol{x}^i + \boldsymbol{f}_u - \boldsymbol{f}_{\text{ext}}), \tag{10.147}$$

so we need to solve $\boldsymbol{A}\boldsymbol{v}^{i+1} = \boldsymbol{b}$ for $\boldsymbol{v}^{i+1}$, where

$$\boldsymbol{A} = (\boldsymbol{M} + \Delta t\boldsymbol{C} + \Delta t^2\boldsymbol{K}), \tag{10.148a}$$

$$\boldsymbol{b} = \boldsymbol{M}\boldsymbol{v}^i - \Delta t(\boldsymbol{K}\boldsymbol{x}^i + \boldsymbol{f}_u - \boldsymbol{f}_{\text{ext}}). \tag{10.148b}$$

This is termed a velocity update. The matrix $\boldsymbol{A}$ and the vector $\boldsymbol{b}$ are most efficiently assembled in a manner similar to the stiffness matrix assembly discussed in Section 10.2.5. That means that each node stores the corresponding row and right-hand side of $\boldsymbol{A}\boldsymbol{v} = \boldsymbol{b}$.

```
Algorithm time-step
  if(stiffness_warp)
    update-orientation
  else
    reset-orientation
  stiffness-assembly
  add-plasticity-force
  dynamics assembly (A,b)
  conjugate_gradient(A,v,b);
  position_update
End algorithm
```

Figure 10.13: A time-stepping algorithm for the finite element method.

The matrix $\boldsymbol{A}$ is a symmetric matrix, which implies that we can solve $\boldsymbol{A}\boldsymbol{v}^{i+1} = \boldsymbol{b}$ efficiently by using a conjugate gradient solver. In [Müller et al., 2004a] 20 iterations were used.

After the velocity update we perform a position update

$$\boldsymbol{x}^{i+1} = \boldsymbol{x}^i + \boldsymbol{v}^{i+1}\Delta t. \tag{10.149}$$

Notice that a fully implicit scheme requires $\boldsymbol{K}^{i+1}$, however for linear elastic materials $\boldsymbol{K}$ is constant. The time-stepping algorithm is summarized in Figure 10.13. In practice a time-step the order of $\Delta t = 0.01$ seconds can be used without any problems.

The damping matrix $\boldsymbol{C}$ can be computed in various ways. Often a linear combination of the mass and stiffness matrix, known as *Rayleigh damping*, is used

$$\boldsymbol{C} = \alpha \boldsymbol{M} + \beta \boldsymbol{K} \tag{10.150}$$

where α and β is known as the *mass damping* and *stiffness damping coefficients* respectively. In practice we often only apply mass damping with $\alpha = 0.2$ and no stiffness damping $\beta = 0$. This has the computational benefit that if $\boldsymbol{M}$ is a lumped mass matrix, then $\boldsymbol{C}$ becomes a diagonal matrix. Furthermore one does not even need storage for $\boldsymbol{C}$, since it is given implicitly by $\boldsymbol{M}$.

10.5 Mesh Coupling

Due to the complexity of the dynamics of finite element methods, it is often convenient to separate the visual geometry from the geometry used to compute the dynamics. This makes it possible to use highly detailed visual representation of objects, while using a computationally low-cost coarse volume mesh for computing the dynamics.

A technique for doing this is called *mesh coupling* or cartoon meshing. Below we describe how it is used together with tetrahedral meshes. It is, however, a general approach and can be used with other types of geometries. Free-form deformation lattices as discussed in Section 8.4.7 are another very common example of mesh coupling.

The first step in mesh coupling is to bind the vertices of the surface mesh to the tetrahedral elements of the volume mesh. A *spatial hashing* algorithm is easily used to find vertex-tetrahedron pairs, where the vertex is embedded inside the tetrahedron. The actual test is done by first computing the barycentric coordinates of the vertex with respect to a tetrahedron in question. The vertex is embedded in the tetrahedron, when $0 \leq w_i \leq 1$. In practice, we need to apply threshold testing to counter numerical precision problems, and as a consequence it may happen that vertices lying close to a face of a tetrahedron gets reported twice: once for the tetrahedron embedding it and once for the neighboring tetrahedron. Therefore, a quick rejection test can be performed: if the vertex is already embedded in a tetrahedron, then it is simply ignored.

Before rendering each frame, we must update the vertex positions to reflect the underlying deformation of the tetrahedral mesh. This is done using the barycentric coordinates, such that the new vertex position is given by,

$$\boldsymbol{c} = w_0\boldsymbol{x}_0 + w_1\boldsymbol{x}_1 + w_2\boldsymbol{x}_2 + w_3\boldsymbol{x}_3, \tag{10.151}$$

where $\boldsymbol{x}_0$, $\boldsymbol{x}_1$, $\boldsymbol{x}_2$, and $\boldsymbol{x}_3$ are the nodal coordinates of the tetrahedron, which the vertex was bounded to.

If stiffness warping is used, the element rotation, $\boldsymbol{R}^e$, can be used to update the undeformed vertex normal, $\boldsymbol{n}_0$, into the deformed vertex normal, $\boldsymbol{n}$, by,

$$\boldsymbol{n} = \boldsymbol{R}^e\boldsymbol{n}_0 \tag{10.152}$$

Often a tetrahedra mesh is used with a conservative coverage of the surface mesh. That means that one is guaranteed that all vertices of the surface mesh are embedded inside one unique tetrahedron. However, mesh coupling can be used in cases where only one have partial coverage. The solution is to bind a vertex to the closest tetrahedron. Even though the vertex lies outside the tetrahedral mesh, the barycentric coordinates extend the deformation of the tetrahedra mesh beyond its surface.

10.6 Finite Element Method in the Literature

Finite element method has been used to model hand grasping a ball [Gourret et al., 1989] and muscle simulation [Chen et al., 1992]. An implicit finite element method was used in [Hirota et al., 2001] to simulate elastic solids in contact. They used their method for simulating the muscles in a bending knee. In [O'Brien et al., 1999] the authors used static isotropic elastic finite element method with additive plasticity to simulate crack initiation and propagation in three dimensional volumes, i.e., brittle fracture. Later in [O'Brien et al., 2002a] both brittle and ductile fracture were simulated. [O'Brien et al., 2002b] used dynamic isotropic elastic finite element method to extract modal vibration modes of rigid bodies. The vibration modes where then used to synthesizing sound in rigid body simulations.

In [Teran et al., 2003] the finite volume method was introduced to the graphics community, and it was shown to be identical to the classical FEM when using linear basis functions and constant strain tetrahedra. The finite volume method has the great advantage that it easily supports different constitutive models. Furthermore, it does not require the assembly process to compute elastic and damping forces.

In [Irving et al., 2004] they extended the finite volume method with a diagonalization method capable of handling inverted tetrahedral elements. They also introduced multiplicative plastic flow and a method for plastic control to achieve prescribed deformations to aid animation control by animators. A rigid-body collision law and improved Newmark time-stepping method were also described.

In [Irving et al., 2005] the finite volume method was generalized for other types of elements than tetrahedra, but it was indicated that tetrahedra were the most cost-efficient element for computer animation purposes. In [Teran et al., 2005] a framework is presented for simulating skeletal muscles with the finite volume method using a transversely isotropic, quasi-incompressible constitutive model that incorporated muscle fiber fields. Inverted elements were handled using diagonalization.

To overcome the computational disadvantage of linear, isotropic, elastic finite element method, many have applied modal analysis, see [Pentland et al., 1989]. Later [James et al., 2002] moved the ideas onto GPUs by a method called Dynamic Response Textures. [Hauser et al., 2003] introduced the idea of using model modes from dynamic linear elastic finite element model to achieve interactive deformations. Later [Choi et al., 2005] extended the ideas to include rotational warps in order to overcome the volume growth in large deformations.

[Müller et al., 2004b] used the finite element method based on cubical elements of uniform size to simulate objects represented by surface meshes. They used a mesh coupling idea and added a fracture technique. [Müller et al., 2004a] improved on the original ideas in [Müller et al., 2002], where a rotational warp was applied to the elastic forces in the stiffness matrix assembly. In the later work they included mesh-coupling, plasticity, and fracturing. Furthermore, they rectified the problem of ghost-forces by computing the rotational warp on elements instead of on a per node basis.

11

Computational Fluid Dynamics

The animation of fluid phenomena is widely used in the film industry and of growing importance in the gaming industry. The physics of fluid dynamics has been successfully described by the Navier-Stokes equation since about 1821, although later investigation into turbulent phenomena has added considerable knowledge about the behavior of fluids at high velocities, etc. The Navier-Stokes model is usually used to predict the motion of fluid particles or volumes inside a fluid, but the model is also a good description of the behavior of gaseous phenomena such as smoke at speeds less than the speed of sound. For animation, the interface between water and air is equally important, since water waves visually dominate water scenes. For animating water waves, there are two competing models, one developed by Gerstner in 1809 and an adaptation of Navier-Stokes to shallow water situations. A detailed review of the origins of water wave theory is given in [Craik, 2004]. This chapter starts by describing the model of water waves leading to Gerstner's model, followed by a description of the Navier-Stokes equations and their applications and implementations.

11.1 Waves

The most prominent visual feature of water is its surface. In the following, we will discuss equations for waves with emphasis on Gerstner's theory.

11.1.1 Cosine Waves

The simplest model of water waves is sinusoidal, meaning that the profile of a wave at a fixed time is well described by a sum of sine and cosine functions. Therefore, waves are typically described by the parameters *amplitude* and *frequency* using a sum of cosine basic functions,

$$f_{A,L}(x) = A(x) \cos\left(\frac{2\pi(x + \phi(x))}{L}\right), \tag{11.1}$$

where x is the spatial coordinate, A is the amplitude of the wave, ϕ is its phase, and L is its wavelength. An example of a circular wave is shown in Figure 11.1. Furthermore, simple waves interact by addition. Waves propagate through space

$$f_{A,L,C}(x,t) = A(x,t) \cos\left(\frac{2\pi(x + \phi(x) - Ct)}{L}\right), \tag{11.2}$$

where t is the time parameter and C is the wave propagation speed.

From an artistic point of view, the pure sinusoidal wave functions in (11.2) tend to be too smooth at the top; it has been suggested by [Finch et al., 2004] simply to raise the cosine to some sufficiently pleasing

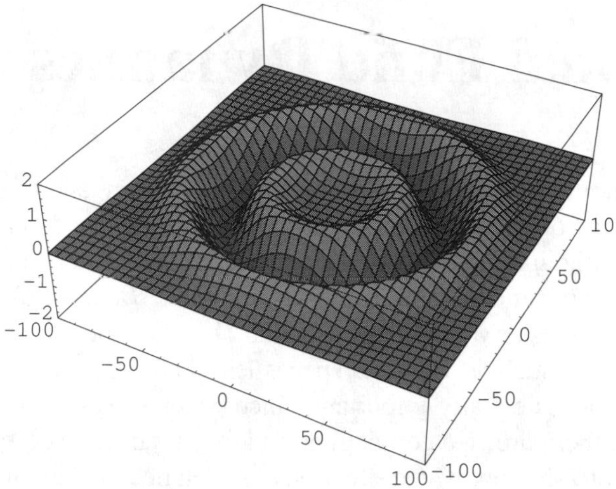

Figure 11.1: The snapshot of a circular water wave modeled as a radially symmetric cosine function.

power as follows:

$$f(x,t) = A(x,t)\left(2\left(\frac{\cos\left(\frac{2\pi(x-Ct)}{L}\right)+1}{2}\right)^k - 1\right), \tag{11.3}$$

and normalize the cosine function to span the range from -1 to 1. An example of the result for $k = 2.5$ is shown in Figure 11.2, and as shown, a consequence of the power function is that the waves also become flatter at the bottom.

11.1.2 Gravity Waves

Gravity waves are the most dominating waves in typical ocean scenes. They arise from the differential effect across the water-air interface. A simple model that may be used for small amplitude waves is *Airy's Model* [Airy, 1845] (George Biddell Airy 1801–1892), where the velocity of the wave propagation is proportional to the water height as

$$C(x) = \sqrt{\frac{gL}{2\pi}\tanh\left(\frac{2\pi h(x)}{L}\right)}, \tag{11.4}$$

with h being water height and $g = 9.82\frac{\text{m}}{\text{sec}^2}$ being the gravitational acceleration. As illustrated in Figure 11.3, $\tanh(x) \to 1$ for $x \to \infty$ and $\tanh(x) \to x$ as $x \to 0$. This implies that

$$C(x) = \begin{cases} \sqrt{\frac{gL}{2\pi}} & h \to \infty, \\ \sqrt{gh(x)} & h \to 0, \end{cases} \tag{11.5}$$

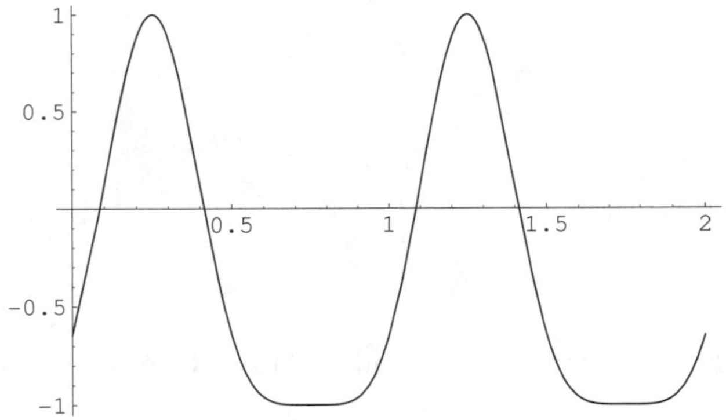

Figure 11.2: Cosine waves may be made sharper at their peak by raising the cosine function to some power k, here $k = 2.5$.

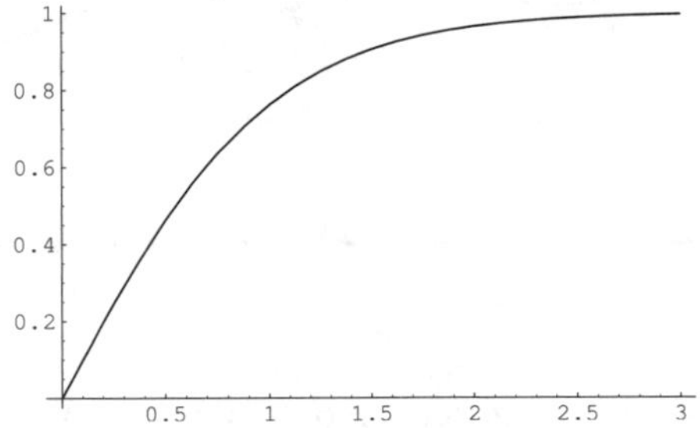

Figure 11.3: The function tanh is asymptotically 1 at infinity and linear at 0.

and as a consequence, waves will tend to move perpendicular to shorelines as illustrated in Figure 11.4. This is because for a single wave front the parts of the front that are close to the beach will move slower than parts of the back, which are further away.

As a wave moves forward, the water particles for an *ideal wave* typically move in circular paths as illustrated in Figure 11.5. An accurate model for a particle in a single wave is the Gerstner Model [Gerstner, 1802] (Franz Joseph von Gerstner 1756–1832). Since individual waves move locally in a particular direction, we may accurately describe the motion of a single water molecule as

$$\begin{bmatrix} x(t) \\ z(t) \end{bmatrix} = \begin{bmatrix} x_0 - A \exp\left(\frac{2\pi z_0}{L}\right) \sin\left(\frac{2\pi(x_0 - Ct)}{L}\right) \\ z_0 + A \exp\left(\frac{2\pi z_0}{L}\right) \cos\left(\frac{2\pi(x_0 - Ct)}{L}\right) \end{bmatrix}, \tag{11.6}$$

where $[x_0, z_0]^T$ is the position of the particle relative to the surface at some initial reference time, A is the radius of the circular path, L is the wavelength, and C is the particle's speed. At the surface, $z_0 = 0$, hence

$$\begin{bmatrix} x(t) \\ z(t) \end{bmatrix} = \begin{bmatrix} x_0 - A \sin\left(\frac{2\pi(x_0 - Ct)}{L}\right) \\ A \cos\left(\frac{2\pi(x_0 - Ct)}{L}\right) \end{bmatrix}, \tag{11.7}$$

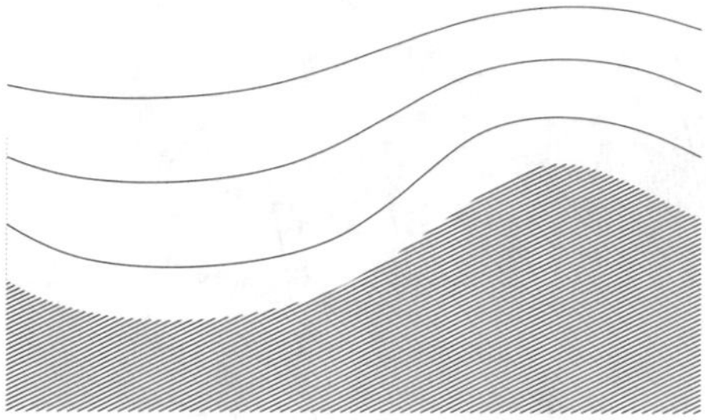

Figure 11.4: Waves approaching a shore will tend to become parallel with the shoreline

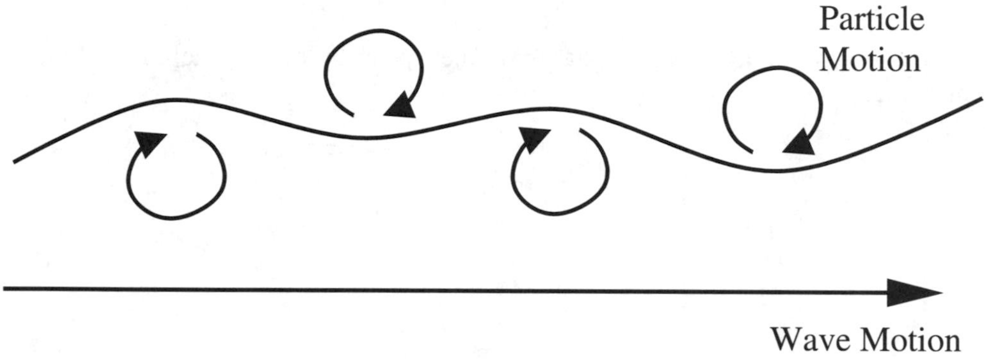

Figure 11.5: For ideal waves, the water particles move in circles, when a wave propagates forward.

and the particle velocity is in a global coordinate system

$$\begin{bmatrix} v_x(t) \\ v_z(t) \end{bmatrix} = \begin{bmatrix} \frac{2\pi CA}{L} \cos\left(\frac{2\pi(x_0 - Ct)}{L}\right) \\ \frac{2\pi CA}{L} \sin\left(\frac{2\pi(x_0 - C_i t)}{L}\right) \end{bmatrix} = v_0 \begin{bmatrix} \cos\left(\frac{2\pi(x_0 - Ct)}{L}\right) \\ \sin\left(\frac{2\pi(x_0 - C_i t)}{L}\right) \end{bmatrix}. \tag{11.8}$$

Moving to a local coordinate system

$$\alpha = \frac{2\pi(x_0 - Ct)}{L}, \tag{11.9}$$

implies that

$$\begin{bmatrix} x(\alpha) \\ z(\alpha) \end{bmatrix} = \begin{bmatrix} x_0 - A\sin\left(\frac{2\pi(x_0 - Ct)}{L}\right) \\ A\cos\left(\frac{2\pi(x_0 - Ct)}{L}\right) \end{bmatrix} \tag{11.10a}$$

$$= \begin{bmatrix} \frac{\alpha L}{2\pi} + Ct - A\sin\alpha \\ A\cos\alpha \end{bmatrix}. \tag{11.10b}$$

Investigating a snapshot by setting $t = 0$, and analyzing the profile for varying α, which is proportional to x_0 gives

$$\begin{bmatrix} x(\alpha) \\ z(\alpha) \end{bmatrix} = \begin{bmatrix} \frac{\alpha L}{2\pi} - A\sin\alpha \\ A\cos\alpha \end{bmatrix}. \tag{11.11}$$

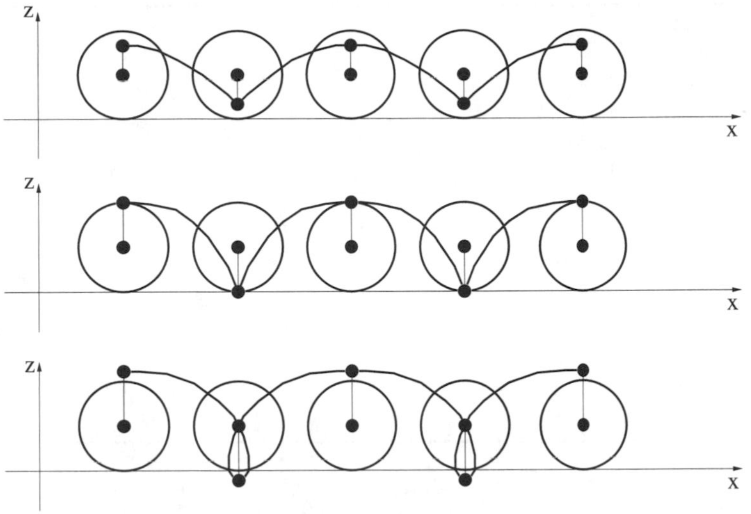

Figure 11.6: A trochoid curve is generated by rolling a circle along a line and noting the points swept by a line along the radius. If the line is not longer than the radius of the circle, then the curve is a function.

This is a trochoid with A as the radius of a rolling circle, and $\frac{L}{2\pi}$ is the distance from center to a fixpoint being traced on the rolling circle. Examples of trochoids are shown in Figure 11.6, where the top has $\frac{L}{2\pi} < A$, middle has $\frac{L}{2\pi} = A$, and the bottom has $\frac{L}{2\pi} > A$, which is no longer a model for water waves. To generate a wave profile, several water particles are tracked simultaneously, and the profile is generated by joining neighboring particles with a line. A procedure for generating Gerstner waves in one dimension is given in Figure 11.7. In Figure 11.8 is the output of this algorithm. The figure shows the wave profile at a fixed time, together with the trace of a water particle. As can be seen, the water particle is moving in an elliptical fashion. The ellipse is a consequence of the nonunit aspect ratio of the graph, since the movement is truly circular according to (11.11). Further on a horizontal line in the figure we see the project of the x-coordinate. As we can see, the density along the x-axis is highest at the wave top, which is convenient, since this is where the curvature of the wave is highest and where there is therefore a need for finer sampling in order to preserve the wave profile.

The 1D Gerstner wave is extended to two dimensions in two steps: first, by extending (11.7) with the y-coordinate, and then rotating the result around $[x_0, y_0]^T$,

$$\begin{bmatrix} x(t) \\ y(t) \\ z(t) \end{bmatrix} = \begin{bmatrix} x_0 \\ y_0 \\ 0 \end{bmatrix} + \boldsymbol{R_z} \begin{bmatrix} -A \sin\left(\frac{2\pi(x_0 - Ct)}{L}\right) \\ 0 \\ A\cos\left(\frac{2\pi(x_0 - Ct)}{L}\right) \end{bmatrix}, \tag{11.12}$$

where $\boldsymbol{R_z}$ is the specialized rotation matrix,

$$\boldsymbol{R_z} = \begin{bmatrix} \cos\theta & \sin\theta & 0 \\ -\sin\theta & \cos\theta & 0 \\ 0 & 0 & 1 \end{bmatrix}, \tag{11.13}$$

```
algorithm gerstner()
  N = 10
  x0 = 1:N
  x = zeros(1,N)   z = zeros(1,N)
  A = 0.5
  C = 1
  L = 10

  for t = 1 to N step 0.1
    for i = 1 to N
      x(i) = x0(i) -A*sin(2*pi*(x0(i)-C*t)/L)
      z(i) = A*cos(2*pi*(x0(i)-C*t)/L)
    end
    plot(x,z)
  end
```

Figure 11.7: Pseudocode for generating propagating Gerstner waves in 1D.

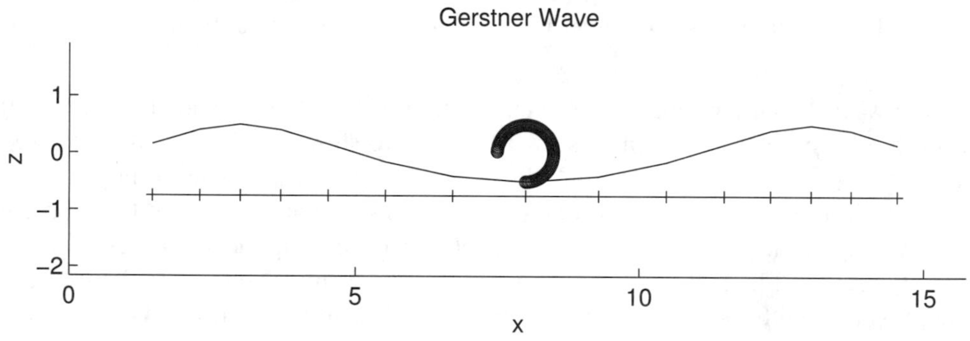

Figure 11.8: The Gerstner wave and a circulating particle.

which rotates a three dimensional point θ degrees around the z-axis.

Finally, it may be desired to limit the spatial extend of the wave along the y-axis by multiplying with a window,

$$\begin{bmatrix} x(t) \\ y(t) \\ z(t) \end{bmatrix} = \begin{bmatrix} x_0 \\ y_0 \\ 0 \end{bmatrix} + \boldsymbol{R_z} \begin{bmatrix} -w(y(t),\sigma) A \sin\left(\frac{2\pi(x_0 - Ct)}{L}\right) \\ 0 \\ w(y(t),\sigma) A \cos\left(\frac{2\pi(x_0 - Ct)}{L}\right) \end{bmatrix}, \tag{11.14}$$

where σ specifies the width of the window. An example of a window function is the unnormalized Gaussian function

$$G(x,\sigma) = \exp\left(-\frac{x^2}{2\sigma^2}\right), \tag{11.15}$$

which contains 76% of its mass in the interval $[-\sigma, \sigma]$.

A consequence of the circular paths of the particles in an ideal wave (11.11) is that there is no net transport of water except near the shoreline. In deep water, the particle speed is found as the length of the particle velocity (11.8),

$$Q = \left\| \begin{bmatrix} v_x(t) \\ v_z(t) \end{bmatrix} \right\|_2 = v_0 = \frac{2\pi CA}{L} \tag{11.16}$$

Hence, if the particle speed exceeds the wave propagation speed, then the particles escape the wave and the waves break, which typically results in white foam on the top of the waves. That is, wave breaking occurs when

$$Q > C, \tag{11.17}$$

which implies that

$$\frac{2\pi CA}{L} > C, \tag{11.18a}$$

$$\Downarrow$$

$$2\pi > \frac{L}{A}. \tag{11.18b}$$

Hence, the breaking of a wave is independent of the wave speed, but only depends on the ration of the wavelength L and the wave's amplitude A. Wave breaking is typically visualized by emitting white particles from the top of the wave or by using texture maps to visualize foam [Jensen, 2001].

Waves interact by addition. Consider the example of a particle originally at $[x_0, y_0, 0]$ being moved according to a number of unclamped Gerstner waves. Adding the waves gives

$$\begin{bmatrix} x(t) \\ y(t) \\ z(t) \end{bmatrix} = \begin{bmatrix} x_0 \\ y_0 \\ 0 \end{bmatrix} + \boldsymbol{R_z} \begin{bmatrix} -A\sin\left(\frac{2\pi(x_0 - Ct)}{L}\right) \\ 0 \\ A\cos\left(\frac{2\pi(x_0 - Ct)}{L}\right) \end{bmatrix} + \boldsymbol{R'_z} \begin{bmatrix} -A'\sin\left(\frac{2\pi(x_0 - C't)}{L'}\right) \\ 0 \\ A'\cos\left(\frac{2\pi(x_0 - C't)}{L'}\right) \end{bmatrix} + \dots \tag{11.19}$$

$$= \begin{bmatrix} x_0 \\ y_0 \\ 0 \end{bmatrix} + \begin{bmatrix} -\cos(\theta)A\sin\left(\frac{2\pi(x_0 - Ct)}{L}\right) - \cos(\theta')A'\sin\left(\frac{2\pi(x_0 - C't)}{L'}\right) - \dots \\ \sin(\theta)A\sin\left(\frac{2\pi(x_0 - Ct)}{L}\right) + \sin(\theta')A'\sin\left(\frac{2\pi(x_0 - C't)}{L'}\right) + \dots \\ A\cos\left(\frac{2\pi(x_0 - Ct)}{L}\right) + A'\cos\left(\frac{2\pi(x_0 - C't)}{L'}\right) + \dots \end{bmatrix} \tag{11.20}$$

$$= \begin{bmatrix} x_0 \\ y_0 \\ 0 \end{bmatrix} + \begin{bmatrix} -\sum_i \cos(\theta_i)A_i\sin\left(\frac{2\pi(x_0 - C_it)}{L_i}\right) \\ \sum_i \sin(\theta_i)A_i\sin\left(\frac{2\pi(x_0 - C_it)}{L_i}\right) \\ \sum_i A_i\cos\left(\frac{2\pi(x_0 - C_it)}{L_i}\right) \end{bmatrix}. \tag{11.21}$$

However, it is not simple to determine the breaking point of the resulting waves, since it requires that the resulting velocities of the wave and the particle are calculated. Wave breaking is therefore often left for an animating artist.

In the literature on partial differential equations, Burger's equation is often introduced for its simple but nonlinear characteristics [Collatz, 1986, Morton et al., 1994]. Burger's equation models the breaking of waves, but it has not yet found practical value in computer animation.

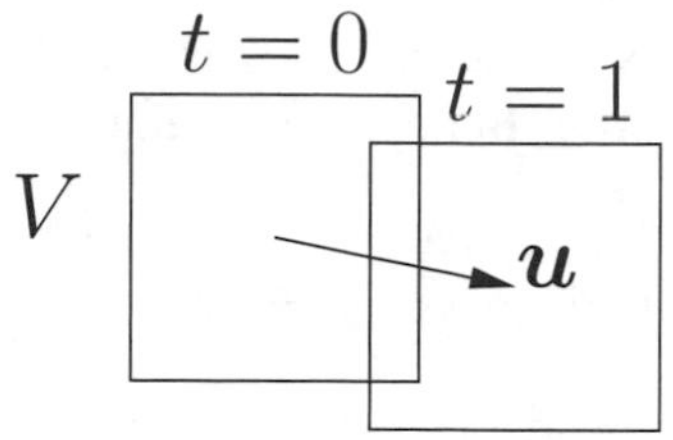

Figure 11.9: The substantive or total derivative estimate the time derivative as a volume is moved in a velocity field.

11.2 Fluid Motion

In this section we will introduce the general subject of fluid mechanics [Tritton, 1988]. A recent survey on the origins of fluid mechanics is given in [Craik, 2004].

The most important physical properties of fluids are *velocity* $\boldsymbol{u}$, *density* ρ, *pressure* p, *temperature* T, and *shear viscosity* η and the *kinematic viscosity* μ, which are macroscopic averages. It is often useful to check physical equations according to their units, and the *International System* (*SI*)standard units for the above properties are $[\boldsymbol{u}] = \mathrm{m\,s^{-1}}$, $[\rho] = \mathrm{kg\,m^{-3}}$, $[p] = \mathrm{N\,m^{-2}}$, $[T] = \mathrm{K}$, $[\eta] = \mathrm{Pa\,s}$, and $[\mu] = \frac{\mathrm{N\,s}}{\mathrm{m^2}}$. For our purpose, they only make sense within some interval of scale much larger than mean free path of the molecule and much smaller than the scale of the total system. The selected scale will be considered the unit scale in the rest of this chapter.

A major problem in fluid dynamics is deciding between a coordinate system fixed in space or on the particle, also known as the Eulerian and Lagrangian coordinate systems respectively. Although apparently trivial, some of the properties of a fluid such as velocity and acceleration are best described in the Lagrangian system, while density, pressure, and temperature are better described in the Eulerian system. In this chapter, we will first discuss the Navier-Stokes equations in the Eulerian coordinate systems along the lines of [Tritton, 1988], followed by a discussion of smooth particle hydrodynamics, which is a particle approach using the Lagrangian coordinate system.

11.2.1 Derivative Operators for Vector Fields

Fluid mechanics heavily relies on the differential notation derived in Chapter 18.3 and summarized in Table 26.2. Furthermore, our choice of the Eulerian coordinate system makes the identification of a single particle impossible, and applying Newton's second law on a fixed position would not be correct, since different particles occupy a fixed volume at different times. However, the fluid flow gives an indication of the average motion of particles per unit volume. As an example, consider the temperature change by time as a volume is tracked in a velocity field, where the general situation is depicted in Figure 11.9. Assume that we are tracking a particle with coordinates $[x(t), y(t), z(t)]$ in three dimensions, that the time varying temperature field is given as $T : \mathbb{R}^4 \to \mathbb{R}$, and that the temperature of the particle is determined as $T(x(t), y(t), z(t), t)$. Then the *total derivative* with respect to t is found to be

$$\frac{dT}{dt} = \frac{\partial T}{\partial t} + \frac{\partial T}{\partial x}\frac{dx}{dt} + \frac{\partial T}{\partial y}\frac{dy}{dt} + \frac{\partial T}{\partial z}\frac{dz}{dt} \tag{11.22a}$$

$$= \frac{\partial T}{\partial t} + \frac{\partial T}{\partial x}u + \frac{\partial T}{\partial y}v + \frac{\partial T}{\partial z}w, \tag{11.22b}$$

using $\boldsymbol{u} = [u, v, w]^T$ as the velocity vector of the particle. This is the change of temperature in the fluid, following the fluid, also called the substantial derivative. The substantial operator for a flow $\boldsymbol{u}$ and in a dimensionless formulation is given as

$$\frac{d}{dt} = \frac{\partial}{\partial t} + \boldsymbol{u} \cdot \nabla, \tag{11.23}$$

where $\nabla = \nabla_{[x,y,t]^T}$ is the spatial gradient operator, which will be assumed in the rest of this chapter. Newton's second law of motion in terms of the substantial derivative per unit volume is found to be

$$\rho \frac{d}{dt}\boldsymbol{u} = \boldsymbol{F} \tag{11.24a}$$

$$\Downarrow$$

$$\rho\left(\frac{\partial}{\partial t} + \boldsymbol{u} \cdot \nabla\right)\boldsymbol{u} = \boldsymbol{F}, \tag{11.24b}$$

where $\boldsymbol{F}$ is the sum forces acting on the volume.

11.2.2 Euler's Equations

Euler (Leonhard Euler 1707–1783) was the first to formulate an equation of the motion of fluids using Newton's second equation, and the pressure gradient as an internal force [Euler, 1755], augmented with an equation for mass conservation under the assumption of incompressible fluids

$$\rho\left(\frac{\partial}{\partial t} + \boldsymbol{u} \cdot \nabla\right)\boldsymbol{u} = -\nabla P, \tag{11.25a}$$

$$\nabla \cdot \boldsymbol{u} = 0 \tag{11.25b}$$

and these equations are commonly known as *Euler's equations*.

The mass conservation equation (11.25b) is a consequence of Gauss' divergence theorem (18.142): consider a closed region of a fluid V as shown in Figure 11.10. The total mass in this volume is given as

$$\text{mass of } V = \int_V \rho \, dV, \tag{11.26}$$

where dV is a unit volume element also known as a three form. The scalar ρ is the fluid density, calculated as the average molecular mass per unit of volume. As the fluid flows, mass will enter and exit this region

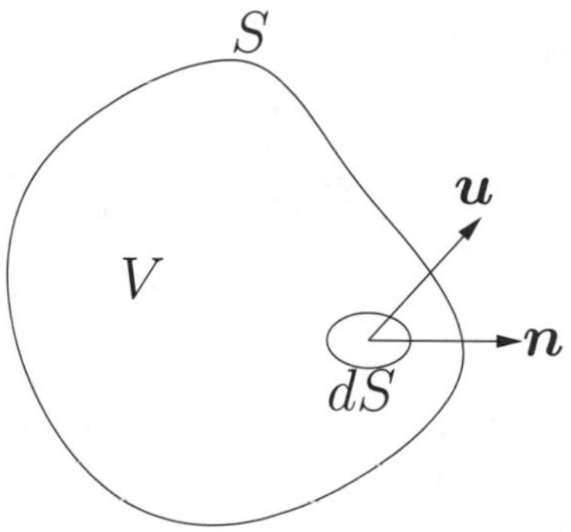

Figure 11.10: A volume V completely inside the fluid.

across its surface S. Use dS to denote an area element of the border also known as a two-form, and use $\boldsymbol{n}$ as the outward normal to the border. The amount of mass loss may now be calculated as,

$$\text{Loss of mass from } V = \int_S \rho \boldsymbol{u} \cdot \boldsymbol{n} \, dS. \tag{11.27}$$

Setting the time derivative of (11.26) equal to minus (11.27) we get

$$\frac{d}{dt} \int_V \rho \, dV = \int_V \frac{\partial}{\partial t} \rho \, dV = - \int_S \rho \boldsymbol{u} \cdot \boldsymbol{n} \, dS. \tag{11.28}$$

Letting V shrink until the change in density is constant inside V, the integration in the middle equation is redundant,

$$\lim_{V \to 0} \int_V \frac{\partial}{\partial t} \rho \, dV = - \frac{\partial}{\partial t} \rho V \tag{11.29}$$

implying that the same limit for the r.h.s. of (11.28) is given as

$$\frac{\partial}{\partial t} \rho = - \lim_{V \to 0} \frac{1}{V} \int_S \rho \boldsymbol{u} \cdot \boldsymbol{n} \, dS = -\text{div} \rho \boldsymbol{u} = -\nabla \cdot (\rho \boldsymbol{u}), \tag{11.30}$$

by the definition of the divergence operator, div, and where $\nabla = \nabla_{[x,y,z]^T}$ is the spatial gradient operator. This is the *conservation of mass* equation also known as the *continuity equation*. Often the terms are rearranged as

$$\frac{\partial}{\partial t} \rho + \nabla \cdot (\rho \boldsymbol{u}) = 0. \tag{11.31}$$

When the density is constant, this implies that

$$\rho \nabla \cdot \boldsymbol{u} = 0, \tag{11.32a}$$

$$\Downarrow$$

$$\nabla \cdot \boldsymbol{u} = 0. \tag{11.32b}$$

and the fluid is called an *incompressible fluid*.

11.2.3 The Naiver-Stokes Equations

Euler's equation ignores the *friction* between water molecules, and Navier (Claude Louis Marie Henri Navier 1785–1836) was the first to derive the equations including friction from a pure theoretical consideration [Navier, 1822],

$$\rho \left(\frac{\partial}{\partial t} + \boldsymbol{u} \cdot \nabla \right) \boldsymbol{u} = -\nabla p + \mu \nabla^2 \boldsymbol{u} + \boldsymbol{F}^{\text{external}}, \tag{11.33a}$$

$$\nabla \cdot \boldsymbol{u} = 0 \tag{11.33b}$$

where $\boldsymbol{F}^{\text{external}}$ are the external forces such as gravity and the motion of solid objects in the fluid. Navier determined the *kinematic viscosity*, μ, as a function of molecular spacing, but did not attach any physical significance to it. Stokes (George Gabriel Stokes 1819–1903) later derived the same equations [Stokes, 1845], where he made the physical meaning of μ clear as the magnitude of the fluid's viscosity. The kinematic viscosity is related to the *shear viscosity* as $\mu = \frac{\eta}{\rho}$. These equations are therefore now known as *Navier-Stokes equations.* If $\|\nabla p\|_2 \gg \|\mu \nabla^2 \boldsymbol{u}\|_2$, then the fluid is called a *viscous fluid*, and in the opposite case, where $\|\nabla p\|_2 \ll \|\mu \nabla^2 \boldsymbol{u}\|_2$, then the fluid is an *inviscid fluid.*

A finite difference solution to the Navier-Stokes equations are found using the *Helmholtz-Hodge decomposition* [Harris, 2004].

Theorem 11.1 (Helmholtz-Hodge decomposition)
Given a Domain $\mathcal{D}$, its border $\delta\mathcal{D}$, normals to the border $\boldsymbol{n}$, and a scalar field p, then a vector field $\boldsymbol{w}$ can be decomposed into

$$\boldsymbol{w} = \boldsymbol{u} + \nabla p, \tag{11.34}$$

where $\nabla \cdot \boldsymbol{u} = 0$, and $\boldsymbol{u} \cdot \boldsymbol{n} = 0$

The proof is rather complicated, and is therefore omitted in this text; instead, see [Denaro, 2003]. The implications of Helmholtz-Hodge decomposition are that

1. Given a general vector field $\boldsymbol{w}$, we may then find a scalar field p by taking the divergence on both sides of (11.34),

$$\nabla \cdot \boldsymbol{w} = \nabla \cdot (\boldsymbol{u} + \nabla p) \tag{11.35a}$$

$$= \nabla \cdot \boldsymbol{u} + \nabla^2 p \tag{11.35b}$$

$$= \nabla^2 p. \tag{11.35c}$$

   The equation $\nabla \cdot \boldsymbol{w} = \nabla^2 p$ is a *Poisson equation*, and is solved straight forwardly with a central finite difference approximation.

2. Given the vector field $\boldsymbol{w}$ and the corresponding scalar field p, we may now calculate a divergence-free vector field as

$$\boldsymbol{u} = \boldsymbol{w} - \nabla p. \tag{11.36}$$

Object Type	u_1	u_2	T	Description
Concrete	0	0	T_0	Small amount of turbulence
Rough Wall	$-u_0$	0	T_0	Much turbulence
Smooth Plastic	u_0	0	T_0	Laminar flow
Radiator	0	0	T_k	Heat convection
Open Window	0	v_0	T_k	Heat is blowing into scene

Table 11.1: Some useful border conditions [Foster et al., 1997].

Hence, given a solution to the Navier-Stokes equations at time t for $\boldsymbol{u}$, p, and $\boldsymbol{F}^{\text{external}}$ a numerical solution for $t + \Delta t$ is obtained by first performing an explicit finite differencing step of (11.33a) to produce a divergence-full vector field $\boldsymbol{w}$, then (11.33b) is solved in two steps: first by solving the Poisson equation (11.35c) for p, and then by calculating the divergence-free field $\boldsymbol{u}$ using (11.36). Examples of such implementations are given in [Foster et al., 1997, Harris, 2004].

Boundary conditions are typically handled in a pragmatic manner as follows: a fluid cannot pass through a impermeable rigid body, and the relative velocity of the fluid at that point must be zero, or

$$\boldsymbol{u} \cdot \boldsymbol{n} = \boldsymbol{U} \cdot \boldsymbol{n}, \tag{11.37}$$

where $\boldsymbol{n}$ is the normal of the boundary and $\boldsymbol{U}$ is its velocity vector. Furthermore, there should be no slip between the wall and fluid right next to it, amounting to no relative tangential velocity

$$\boldsymbol{u} \times \boldsymbol{n} = \boldsymbol{U} \times \boldsymbol{n}. \tag{11.38}$$

Combining (11.37) and (11.38) we must have

$$\boldsymbol{u} = \boldsymbol{U}. \tag{11.39}$$

In [Foster et al., 1997], the border conditions in Table 11.1 have been found to be useful.

A two-dimensional example of pseudocode implementing incompressible, viscous Navier-Stokes equations is given in Figure 11.11. The gradient of the pressure term in the first Navier-Stokes step may actually be ignored, since it is effectively added by the solution to the Poisson equations. This is the so-called *projection method* [Harris, 2004]. Nevertheless, we have chosen to keep it in the above code for pedagogical reasons. On a personal note, we find it appealing, that although the equations appear difficult, the actual implementation is rather short.

11.2.4 Navier-Stokes for Dry Air

For a gas, Boyle and Charles noted that the three thermodynamic variables pressure, p, molar volume, α, and temperature T depends on each other. The molar volume is related to the density, ρ, the number of molecules, n, and the volume, V, as $\alpha = \frac{1}{\rho} = \frac{V}{n}$. For an ideal gas, the dependency is simply called the *Ideal Gas Law*,

$$pV = nRT, \tag{11.40}$$

```
algorithm navierStokes()
  dt = 1/15
  nu = 10
  h = 0.1

  while(i < T)
    // Perform a step in the Navier-Stokes direction
    du = -u*dx(u) - v*dy(u) + nu*(dxx(u) + dyy(u))
    dv = -u*dx(v) - v*dy(v) + nu*(dxx(u) + dyy(u))
    u = u + dt*du
    v = v + dt*dv
    [u,v,p] = setBoundaries(u,v,p)

    // Solve Poisson Equations
    gradDotU = (dx(u)+dy(v))/dTau
    while(max(abs(p-pOld)) > 10^(-3)
      pOld = p
      p = p + h*(dxx(p) + dyy(p) - gradDotU)
    end

    // Adjust velocity field to become divergence free
    u = u - dx(p)
    v - v - dy(p)

    // Set boundary conditions appropriately
    [u,v,p] = setBoundaries(u,v,p)

    plotVectorField(u,v,p)
    i = i+di
  end while
end algorithm
```

Figure 11.11: Pseudocode for implementing incompressible viscous Navier-Stokes equations. The unspecified functions `dx`, `dy`, `dxx`, and `dyy` perform central finite differencing of first and second order, `setBoundaries` clamps values according to chosen boundary conditions, and `plotVectorField` presents the resulting vector field in some suitable graphical manner.

where $R = 8.314\frac{\mathrm{N}}{\mathrm{m}^2\ \mathrm{mol\ K}}$ is the ideal gas constant. Ideal gases do not exist, but are nevertheless a good approximation of gas behavior under normal conditions, which is attractive in computer graphics that usually are concerned with animating everyday phenomena. Disregarding chemical, magnetic, and electrical effects, the first law of thermodynamics states that the rate of heat addition, $\frac{dq}{dt}$, is

$$\frac{dq}{dt} = \frac{dE_{\text{int}}}{dt} + \frac{dW}{dt}, \tag{11.41}$$

where E_{int} is the internal energy and W is the work done by the gas on its surroundings due to expansion. For an ideal, *inviscid gas*,

$$\frac{dE_{\text{int}}}{dt} = c_v \frac{dT}{dt}, \tag{11.42}$$

$$\frac{dW}{dt} = p\frac{d\alpha}{dt}, \tag{11.43}$$

where c_v is the specific heat coefficient for constant volume. There is also a specific heat coefficient for constant pressure, c_p, and these are related for a mono-atomic ideal gas as

$$c_p - c_v = R, \tag{11.44}$$

implying that [Haltiner et al., 1980],

$$\frac{dq}{dt} = \alpha\frac{dp}{dt} + \left(1 + \frac{R}{c_v}\right)p\frac{d\alpha}{dt} = \alpha\frac{dp}{dt} + \frac{c_p}{c_v}p\frac{d\alpha}{dt} \tag{11.45}$$

The equations (11.30), (11.33a), (11.40), and (11.43) constitute a complete system of equations describing the motion of dry air.

11.2.5 Navier-Stokes with Heat Convection

For a incompressible, viscous fluid, the *Boussinesq approximation* is often used [Tritton, 1988]. In the Boussinesq approximation, the only fluid property considered is the density, and it is only considered when the density variation gives rise to a gravitational force. Assuming that the density varies slightly from some reference density ρ_0, for example, in a neighboring point, then the density in a particular point as

$$\rho = \rho_0 + \Delta\rho \tag{11.46}$$

Since we are ignoring nongravity effects, the continuity equation (11.30) is simply $\nabla \cdot \boldsymbol{u} = 0$, and we calculate the change in moment as $\rho_0 \frac{d}{dt}\boldsymbol{u}$. However, gravity effects causes the third term in (11.33a) to become,

$$\boldsymbol{F} = \rho\boldsymbol{g} = \rho_0\boldsymbol{g} + \Delta\rho\boldsymbol{g} \tag{11.47}$$

The gravitational acceleration can be rewritten as the gradient of a scalar field, $\boldsymbol{g} = -\nabla G$, using $G = gz$ with z being the direction up. Newton's second law for fluids (11.33a) is then written as

$$\rho_0\frac{d}{dt}\boldsymbol{u} = -\nabla(p + \rho_0 G) + \mu\nabla^2\boldsymbol{u} + \Delta\rho\boldsymbol{g} = -\nabla P + \mu\nabla^2\boldsymbol{u} + \Delta\rho\boldsymbol{g}. \tag{11.48}$$

with $P = p + \rho_0 G$. Hence, if the density is constant, then (11.48) simplifies to (11.33a) except for the correction of the pressure term for the height. If the pressure does not appear directly in the boundary conditions, this correction of the hydrostatic pressure has no physical significance. When there is a density variation, then the last term will cause an effect when $\frac{d}{dt}\boldsymbol{u} \ll \boldsymbol{g}$, and in this case, we may use a linearizing of the density variation

$$\Delta\rho = -\gamma\rho_0\Delta T \tag{11.49}$$

with γ as the coefficient of expansion of the fluid. Inserting (11.49) into (11.48) gives

$$\rho_0\frac{d}{dt}\boldsymbol{u} = -\nabla P + \mu\nabla^2\boldsymbol{u} - \gamma\rho_0\Delta T\boldsymbol{g}. \tag{11.50}$$

The term $\gamma\rho_0\Delta T\boldsymbol{g}$ is known as the buoyancy force. An additional equation for the temperature is needed, and in the Boussinesq approximation it is assumed that

$$\frac{dq}{dt} = \rho c_p\frac{d}{dt}T - k_T\nabla^2 T, \tag{11.51}$$

where k_T is the thermal conductivity coefficient. See [Tritton, 1988] for arguments for using c_p instead of c_v. In a fixed coordinate system, the temperature field is thus governed by

$$\frac{\partial T}{\partial t} = \frac{k_T}{\rho c_v}\nabla^2 T - \nabla\cdot(T\boldsymbol{u}) + \frac{1}{\rho c_v}\frac{dq}{dt}. \tag{11.52}$$

Equations (11.30), (11.50), and (11.51) are the basic computational fluid dynamical equations with convection.

11.2.6 Navier-Stokes with Concentration Variations

Analogous to (11.49), the Boussinesq approximation may be used to model concentration variations as

$$\Delta\rho = -\gamma\rho_0\Delta c \tag{11.53}$$

where c is the concentration. Newton's second law then becomes

$$\rho_0\frac{d}{dt}\boldsymbol{u} = -\nabla P + \mu\nabla^2\boldsymbol{u} - \gamma\rho_0\Delta c\boldsymbol{g}. \tag{11.54}$$

Again, analogous to heat convection, the concentration is governed by diffusion,

$$\rho c_p\frac{d}{dt}c = k_c\nabla^2 c, \tag{11.55}$$

where k_c is the thermal conductivity coefficient.

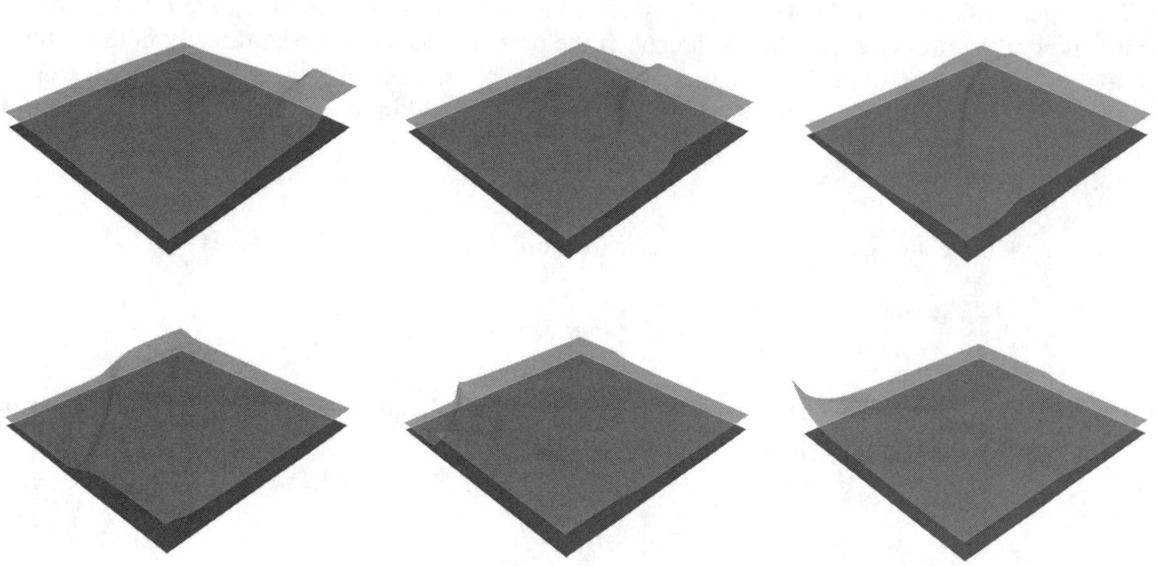

Figure 11.12: Snapshots from a shallow-water animation.

11.2.7 Shallow Water

So far, the discussion on Navier-Stokes equation have been for fluids fully enclosed in some solid volume. In contrast, the Gerstner equation discussed in Section 11.1.2 is mainly concentrating on the water surface. A connection is given through the shallow water equation [Saint-Venant, 1871, Haltiner et al., 1980, Layton et al., 2002], and an example of a shallow-water computation is shown in Figure 11.12. The shallow water equation is much more powerful than the Gerstner equation, since it is dynamic and allows for easy interaction between the fluid and boundaries. The shallow-water equation assumes an incompressible and inviscid fluid, and they will be derived in the following.

Assume a column of fluid of height, h, and base area B. Then the total mass of fluid at the base over the area B is

$$m = hB\rho, \tag{11.56}$$

which corresponds to a force on the base and in the direction of gravity as

$$f = mg. \tag{11.57}$$

The pressure at the base is therefore

$$p = \frac{f}{B} = hg\rho. \tag{11.58}$$

Hence, the pressure term in (11.33a) simplifies as

$$\nabla p = g\rho\nabla h. \tag{11.59}$$

For large-scale motions of the fluid, the vertical acceleration may be ignored, and the fluid is said to be in *hydrostatic equilibrium*. This implies that Newton's second law of motion simplifies to

$$\rho\left(\frac{\partial}{\partial t}+\boldsymbol{u}\cdot\nabla\right)\boldsymbol{u}=-g\rho\nabla h+\mu\nabla^2\boldsymbol{u}+\boldsymbol{F}^{\text{external}}, \tag{11.60}$$

where only changes in the horizontal plane are nonzero, that is, the above equation reduces to the two,

$$\rho\left(\frac{\partial u}{\partial t}+u\frac{\partial u}{\partial x}+v\frac{\partial u}{\partial y}\right)=-g\rho\frac{\partial h}{\partial x}+\mu\left(\frac{\partial^2 u}{\partial x^2}+\frac{\partial^2 u}{\partial y^2}\right)+\boldsymbol{F}_1^{\text{external}}, \tag{11.61a}$$

$$\rho\left(\frac{\partial v}{\partial t}+u\frac{\partial v}{\partial x}+v\frac{\partial v}{\partial y}\right)=-g\rho\frac{\partial h}{\partial y}+\mu\left(\frac{\partial^2 v}{\partial x^2}+\frac{\partial^2 v}{\partial y^2}\right)+\boldsymbol{F}_2^{\text{external}}, \tag{11.61b}$$

for $\boldsymbol{u}=[u,v,w]^T$. The mass preservation in terms of the height is found by first integrating (11.30) by z,

$$\frac{\partial u}{\partial x}+\frac{\partial v}{\partial y}+\frac{\partial w}{\partial z}=0, \tag{11.62a}$$

$$\Downarrow$$

$$\int_0^h\frac{\partial u}{\partial x}+\frac{\partial v}{\partial y}+\frac{\partial w}{\partial z}\,dz=\left(\frac{\partial u}{\partial x}+\frac{\partial v}{\partial y}\right)h+w_h-w_0=0. \tag{11.62b}$$

Since w_0 is the vertical speed at the bottom, this term must vanish. On the other hand, w_h is the rate of rise at the fluid surface, hence

$$w_0=0, \tag{11.63a}$$

$$w_h=\frac{dh}{dt}. \tag{11.63b}$$

Inserting into (11.62b) it is found that

$$\left(\frac{\partial u}{\partial x}+\frac{\partial v}{\partial y}\right)h=-\frac{dh}{dt}=-\frac{\partial h}{\partial t}-u\frac{\partial h}{\partial x}-v\frac{\partial h}{\partial y} \tag{11.64a}$$

$$\Downarrow$$

$$\left(\frac{\partial u}{\partial x}+\frac{\partial v}{\partial y}\right)h+\frac{\partial h}{\partial t}+u\frac{\partial h}{\partial x}-v\frac{\partial h}{\partial y}=0. \tag{11.64b}$$

The *shallow water equations* are now obtained by using $\boldsymbol{F}^{\text{external}}=[0,0,g]^T$ and assuming inviscid fluid, that is, that $\left\|\mu\nabla^2\boldsymbol{u}\right\|_2\ll\|\nabla p\|_2$, hence

$$\frac{\partial u}{\partial t}+u\frac{\partial u}{\partial x}+v\frac{\partial u}{\partial y}=-g\frac{\partial h}{\partial x}, \tag{11.65a}$$

$$\frac{\partial v}{\partial t}+u\frac{\partial v}{\partial x}+v\frac{\partial v}{\partial y}=-g\frac{\partial h}{\partial y}, \tag{11.65b}$$

$$\frac{\partial h}{\partial t}+u\frac{\partial h}{\partial x}+v\frac{\partial h}{\partial y}=-\left(\frac{\partial u}{\partial x}+\frac{\partial v}{\partial y}\right)h. \tag{11.65c}$$

A simple finite difference using central approximations and zero flow at the borders may be used, however the implicit *semi-Lagrangian time integration* scheme as implemented in [Layton et al., 2002] is superior in performance and stability and has been used to produce the animation shown in snapshots in Figure 11.12.

The implicit semi-Lagrangian time implementation of the shallow water equations is based on the Eulerian formulation given above, where the physical parameters are computed on the grid. However, the velocity field is approximated, as if it had been calculated by following individual particles, which yields a semi-Lagrangian formulation. That is, the substantial derivatives in (11.65) are replaced with ordinary derivatives

$$\frac{du}{dt} = -g\frac{\partial h}{\partial x}, \tag{11.66a}$$

$$\frac{dv}{dt} = -g\frac{\partial h}{\partial y}, \tag{11.66b}$$

$$\frac{dh}{dt} = -\left(\frac{\partial u}{\partial x} + \frac{\partial v}{\partial y}\right) h, \tag{11.66c}$$

and the ordinary derivatives are estimated by tracking a hypothetical particle located at grid point (i, j) using forward differences,

$$\frac{du}{dt} = \frac{u(t + \Delta t) - \tilde{u}(t)}{\Delta t} + \mathcal{O}(\Delta t), \tag{11.67a}$$

$$\frac{dv}{dt} = \frac{v(t + \Delta t) - \tilde{v}(t)}{\Delta t} + \mathcal{O}(\Delta t), \tag{11.67b}$$

$$\frac{dh}{dt} = \frac{h(t + \Delta t) - \tilde{h}(t)}{\Delta t} + \mathcal{O}(\Delta t). \tag{11.67c}$$

The functions $\tilde{u}$, $\tilde{v}$, and $\tilde{h}$ are only given implicitly in the Eulerian formalism and have to be estimated. Using the current values of u, v, and h at grid point (i, j), we assume that these are a good approximation of their values in the previous step, and the departure point of the hypothetical particle at (i, j) is thus assumed to be

$$\begin{bmatrix} \tilde{x}(t - \Delta t) \\ \tilde{y}(t - \Delta t) \end{bmatrix} = \begin{bmatrix} x(t) \\ y(t) \end{bmatrix} - \Delta t \begin{bmatrix} u(t) \\ v(t) \end{bmatrix} + \mathcal{O}(\Delta t). \tag{11.68}$$

We may thus estimate the values of $\tilde{u}$, $\tilde{v}$, and $\tilde{h}$ by bilinear interpolation, that is,

$$\begin{aligned}\tilde{u} = {} & (1 - a)(1 - b)\, u(\lfloor \tilde{x} \rfloor, \lfloor \tilde{y} \rfloor) + (1 - a)b\, u(\lfloor \tilde{x} \rfloor, \lceil \tilde{y} \rceil) \\ & + ab\, u(\lceil \tilde{x} \rceil, \lceil \tilde{y} \rceil) + a(1 - b)\, u(\lceil \tilde{x} \rceil, \lfloor \tilde{y} \rfloor),\end{aligned} \tag{11.69a}$$

$$\begin{aligned}\tilde{v} = {} & (1 - a)(1 - b)\, v(\lfloor \tilde{x} \rfloor, \lfloor \tilde{y} \rfloor) + (1 - a)b\, v(\lfloor \tilde{x} \rfloor, \lceil \tilde{y} \rceil) \\ & + ab\, v(\lceil \tilde{x} \rceil, \lceil \tilde{y} \rceil) + a(1 - b)\, v(\lceil \tilde{x} \rceil, \lfloor \tilde{y} \rfloor),\end{aligned} \tag{11.69b}$$

$$\begin{aligned}\tilde{h} = {} & (1 - a)(1 - b)\, h(\lfloor \tilde{x} \rfloor, \lfloor \tilde{y} \rfloor) + (1 - a)b\, h(\lfloor \tilde{x} \rfloor, \lceil \tilde{y} \rceil) \\ & + ab\, h(\lceil \tilde{x} \rceil, \lceil \tilde{y} \rceil) + a(1 - b)\, h(\lceil \tilde{x} \rceil, \lfloor \tilde{y} \rfloor).\end{aligned} \tag{11.69c}$$

where $a = \tilde{x} - \lfloor\tilde{x}\rfloor$ and $b = \tilde{y} - \lfloor\tilde{y}\rfloor$, and $\lfloor\cdot\rfloor$ and $\lceil\cdot\rceil$ are the floor and ceiling operators respectively. Discretizing (11.66) in time implicitly and using (11.67) gives,

$$\frac{u(t+\Delta t) - \tilde{u}(t)}{\Delta t} = -g\frac{\partial h(t+\Delta t)}{\partial x}, \tag{11.70a}$$

$$\frac{v(t+\Delta t) - \tilde{v}(t)}{\Delta t} = -g\frac{\partial h(t+\Delta t)}{\partial y}, \tag{11.70b}$$

$$\frac{h(t+\Delta t) - \tilde{h}(t)}{\Delta t} = -\left(\frac{\partial u(t+\Delta t)}{\partial x} + \frac{\partial v(t+\Delta t)}{\partial y}\right) h(t). \tag{11.70c}$$

To produce a single equation, we first calculate the derivative (11.70a) with respect to x,

$$\frac{\partial}{\partial x}\frac{u(t+\Delta t) - \tilde{u}(t)}{\Delta t} = -\frac{\partial}{\partial x}g\frac{\partial h(t+\Delta t)}{\partial x}, \tag{11.71a}$$

$$\Downarrow$$

$$\frac{\frac{\partial u(t+\Delta t)}{\partial x} - \frac{\partial \tilde{u}(t)}{\partial x}}{\Delta t} = -g\frac{\partial^2 h(t+\Delta t)}{\partial x^2}, \tag{11.71b}$$

assuming that g is independent on x. This implies that

$$\frac{\partial u(t+\Delta t)}{\partial x} = \frac{\partial \tilde{u}(t)}{\partial x} - \Delta t g\frac{\partial^2 h(t+\Delta t)}{\partial x^2}. \tag{11.72}$$

Likewise, we calculate the derivative of (11.70b) with respect to y to give,

$$\frac{\partial}{\partial y}\frac{v(t+\Delta t) - \tilde{v}(t)}{\Delta t} = -\frac{\partial}{\partial y}g\frac{\partial h(t+\Delta t)}{\partial y}, \tag{11.73a}$$

$$\Downarrow$$

$$\frac{\frac{\partial v(t+\Delta t)}{\partial y} - \frac{\partial \tilde{v}(t)}{\partial y}}{\Delta t} = -g\frac{\partial^2 h(t+\Delta t)}{\partial y^2}, \tag{11.73b}$$

which implies that

$$\frac{\partial v(t+\Delta t)}{\partial y} = \frac{\partial \tilde{v}(t)}{\partial y} - \Delta t g\frac{\partial^2 h(t+\Delta t)}{\partial y^2}. \tag{11.74}$$

We can now eliminate $u(t+\Delta t)$ and $v(t+\Delta t)$ in (11.70c) using (11.72) and (11.74) as,

$$\frac{h(t+\Delta t) - \tilde{h}(t)}{\Delta t} = -\left(\frac{\partial \tilde{u}(t)}{\partial x} - \Delta t g\frac{\partial^2 h(t+\Delta t)}{\partial x^2} + \frac{\partial \tilde{v}(t)}{\partial y} - \Delta t g\frac{\partial^2 h(t+\Delta t)}{\partial y^2}\right) h(t), \tag{11.75}$$

and when we rearrange the terms we find,

$$h(t+\Delta t) = \tilde{h}(t) - \Delta t h(t)\left(\frac{\partial \tilde{u}(t)}{\partial x} - \Delta t g\frac{\partial^2 h(t+\Delta t)}{\partial x^2} + \frac{\partial \tilde{v}(t)}{\partial y} - \Delta t g\frac{\partial^2 h(t+\Delta t)}{\partial y^2}\right). \tag{11.76}$$

Finally, a numerical scheme is obtained by using first- and second-order central differences for the spatial derivatives to give

$$\begin{aligned}
h(x,y,t+\Delta t) &= \tilde{h}(x,y,t) \\
&\quad - \Delta t h(x,y,t)\frac{\partial \tilde{u}(x,y,t)}{\partial x} + (\Delta t)^2 h(x,y,t) g \frac{\partial^2 h(x,y,t+\Delta t)}{\partial x^2} \\
&\quad - \Delta t h(x,y,t)\frac{\partial \tilde{v}(x,y,t)}{\partial y} + (\Delta t)^2 h(x,y,t) g \frac{\partial^2 h(x,y,t+\Delta t)}{\partial y^2}, \qquad (11.77)\\
&= \tilde{h}(x,y,t) \\
&\quad - \Delta t h(x,y,t)\frac{\tilde{u}(x+1,y,t) - \tilde{u}(x+1,y,t)}{2\Delta x} \\
&\quad + (\Delta t)^2 h(x,y,t) g \frac{h(x+1,y,t+\Delta t) - 2h(x,y,t+\Delta t) + h(x-1,y,t+\Delta t)}{\Delta x^2} \\
&\quad - \Delta t h(x,y,t)\frac{\tilde{v}(x,y+1,t) - \tilde{v}(x,y-1,t)}{2\Delta y} \\
&\quad + (\Delta t)^2 h(x,y,t) g \frac{h(x,y+1,t+\Delta t) - 2h(x,y,t+\Delta t) + h(x,y-1,t+\Delta t)}{\Delta y^2}.
\end{aligned} \tag{11.78}$$

This equation is nonlinear since it contains products of h's. Nevertheless, terms involving $h(t+\Delta t)$ may be isolated,

$$\begin{aligned}
h(x,y,t+\Delta t) &- (\Delta t)^2 h(x,y,t) g \frac{h(x+1,y,t+\Delta t) - 2h(x,y,t+\Delta t) + h(x-1,y,t+\Delta t)}{\Delta x^2} \\
&+ (\Delta t)^2 h(x,y,t) g \frac{h(x,y+1,t+\Delta t) - 2h(x,y,t+\Delta t) + h(x,y-1,t+\Delta t)}{\Delta y^2} \\
&= \tilde{h}(x,y,t) - \Delta t h(x,y,t)\frac{\tilde{u}(x+1,y,t) - \tilde{u}(x+1,y,t)}{2\Delta x} \\
&\quad - \Delta t h(x,y,t)\frac{\tilde{v}(x,y+1,t) - \tilde{v}(x,y-1,t)}{2\Delta y},
\end{aligned} \tag{11.79}$$

and when assuming that $h(x,y,t)$ is constant on the left-hand side the system may be solved as a linear tridiagonal system for $h(t+\Delta t)$ based on $h(t)$. The entire algorithm is shown in Figure 11.13. Although the shallow water equations do not contain any diffusion terms, the waves will slowly diminish, since the velocities are smoothed implicitly by the bilinear interpolation and the time integration performed in the numerical scheme.

The boundary conditions are important for this method. It is our experience that setting the derivative of h across the boundary to be zero, and setting u and v to be zero at the boundary, gives useful results. This implies that the height-field is relatively unaffected by the boundary, while the velocity outside the fluid is zero. More technically, the boundary condition on h is of the type von Neumann described in Section 9.3.7, while the boundary condition on u and v is of the type Dirichlet described in Section 9.3.8.

```
algorithm shallowWater(float h[][], int N, float T)
  u = zeros(N,N)
  v = zeros(N,N)
  dt = 0.1
  g=9.82
  t=0

  while(t < T)
    t=t+dt     // Perform a step in the Shallow-Water equation

    // Estimate departure points using (11.68)
    [xfrom,yfrom] = computeDeparturePoint(x,y)

    // Estimate values of u,v,h at departure points using (11.69)
    [hTilde, uTilde, vTilde] = EstimateDepartureState(h,u,v,xfrom,yfrom)

    // Solve for h(t+dt) using (11.79)
    h = ShallowWaterStep(h,u,v,g,hTilde,uTilde,vTilde)

    // Update u(t+dt) and v(t+dt) using (11.67)
    [u,v] = UpdateVelocities(h,u,v,g,uTilde,vTilde)
  end
end algorithm
```

Figure 11.13: Pseudocode for the shallow water equation.

11.3 Smoothed Particle Hydrodynamics

In the Eulerian view of fluid dynamics, the fluid is considered a density and it is therefore complicated to attribute notions of velocity and acceleration to it. In contrast, in the Lagrangian view, the fluid is considered a collection of particles, for which velocity and acceleration are natural descriptors, but in contrast, parameters such as density, pressure, and temperature are more difficult to define. In the following, we will describe smoothed particle hydrodynamics, which is a Lagrangian implementation of the Navier-Stokes equations, where kernels are the central issues for estimating the parameters of density, pressure, and temperature. This text is based on [Shao et al., 2003, Müller et al., 2003, Roy, 1995, Monaghan, 1992, Monaghan, 1988].

Consider a fluid represented as a collection of particles. Each particle represents a certain volume V_i, and carries position, mass, and velocity. We will attribute each particle with other quantities such as fluid density $\rho_i = m_i/V_i$, pressure p_i, and temperature T_i, however it does not make sense to talk of the density of a particle, since this is a macroscopic quantity. These macroscopic quantities should therefore only be obtained as weighted averages of the neighboring particles. Assuming the general case, we are given a scalar quantity A_j for each particle j. Then in any position $\boldsymbol{r}$ we may interpolate this scalar quantity using

$$\text{Gaussian} \quad K(\boldsymbol{r}) = \tfrac{1}{k}\exp\left(-\tfrac{\|\boldsymbol{r}\|_2^2}{2}\right).$$

$$\text{B-Spline} \quad K(\boldsymbol{r}) = \tfrac{1}{k}\begin{cases} \tfrac{2}{3} - \|\boldsymbol{r}\|_2^2 + 1.5\,\|\boldsymbol{r}\|_2^5, & 0 \le \|\boldsymbol{r}\|_2\ 1, \\ \tfrac{(2-\|\boldsymbol{r}\|_2)^3}{6}, & 1 \le \|\boldsymbol{r}\|_2 < 2 \\ 0, & \text{otherwise.} \end{cases}$$

$$\text{Q-spline} \quad K(\boldsymbol{r}) = \tfrac{1}{k}\begin{cases} (3-\|\boldsymbol{r}\|_2)^5 - 6(2-\|\boldsymbol{r}\|_2)^5 + 15(1-\|\boldsymbol{r}\|_2)^5, & 0 \le \|\boldsymbol{r}\|_2 < 1, \\ (3-\|\boldsymbol{r}\|_2)^5 - 6(2-\|\boldsymbol{r}\|_2)^5, & 1 \le \|\boldsymbol{r}\|_2 < 2, \\ (3-\|\boldsymbol{r}\|_2)^5, & 2 \le \|\boldsymbol{r}\|_2 < 3, \\ 0 & \text{otherwise.} \end{cases}$$

Table 11.2: Some smoothing kernels often used in smoothed particle hydrodynamics. For simplicity, we have used $W(\boldsymbol{r}, \sigma) = K(\boldsymbol{r}/\sigma)$, and k is the normalization constant enforcing (11.81c).

a spatial *averaging function* W as follows:

$$A(\boldsymbol{r}) = \sum_{j=1}^{N} A_j \frac{m_j}{\rho_j} W(\boldsymbol{r} - \boldsymbol{r}_j, \sigma). \tag{11.80}$$

The particular choice of $\frac{m_j}{\rho_j}$ will be discussed below. Let us for the moment concentrate on the function W. This function is known as an averaging function or *smoothing kernel*, and σ is some parameter relating to its width. For the interpolation to be useful, we will have to require a number of constraints on W:

$$W(\boldsymbol{r}, \sigma) \ge 0, \tag{11.81a}$$

$$W(\boldsymbol{r}, \sigma) = W(-\boldsymbol{r}, \sigma), \tag{11.81b}$$

$$\int W(\boldsymbol{r})\, d\boldsymbol{r} = 1, \tag{11.81c}$$

which in words are positivity, rotational symmetry, and unit integral. Positivity is necessary in order to ensure that it is an averaging function. Rotational symmetry is often useful to ensure invariance w.r.t. rotations of the coordinate system, and unit integral ensures that maxima and minima are not enhanced.

Many kernels have been proposed in the literature, some of the more popular are shown in Table 11.2. In [Hongbin et al., 2005] these have been compared for stable fields. A stable field is a flow field that does not vary with space and the comparison has been performed w.r.t. the kernel's estimation error of the function and first-order derivatives. It is concluded that the Gaussian and the Q-spline are the best kernels, and since the Gaussian is the kernel introducing the least structure [Weickert et al., 1997], in the remainder of this chapter, we will only consider the Gaussian kernel. The isotropic *Gaussian kernel* in n dimensions is given by

$$G(\boldsymbol{r}, \sigma) = \frac{1}{(2\pi\sigma^2)^{\frac{3}{2}}} \exp\left(\frac{-\boldsymbol{r}^T\boldsymbol{r}}{2\sigma^2}\right), \tag{11.82}$$

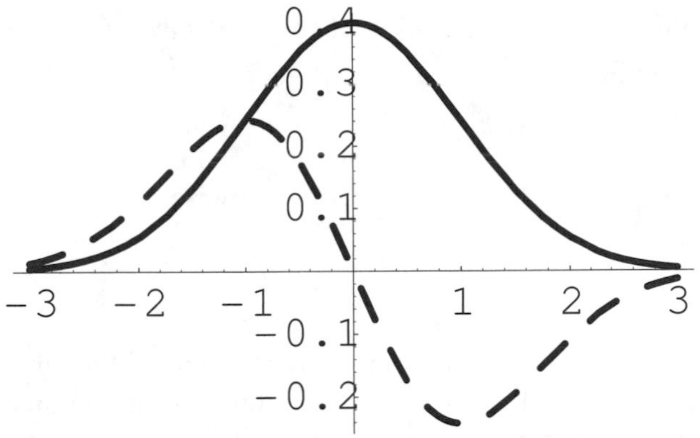

Figure 11.14: The Gaussian weighting function and its derivative.

using $\sigma > 0$. It may be verified, that the Gaussian fulfills the constraints in (11.81). The Gaussian kernel is infinitely differentiable, and since it is the only term in (11.80) that depends directly on space, we conclude that (11.80) is also infinitely differentiable. That is, the partial derivative of A w.r.t. space is given as

$$\frac{\partial^n}{\partial x^\alpha \partial y^\beta \partial z^\gamma} A(\boldsymbol{r}) = \sum_{j=1}^{N} \rho_j \frac{m_j}{\rho_j} \frac{\partial^n}{\partial x^\alpha \partial y^\beta \partial z^\gamma} G(\boldsymbol{r} - \boldsymbol{r}_j, \sigma) \tag{11.83}$$

where $n = \alpha + \beta + \gamma$. In Figure 11.14 is a graph of a one-dimensional Gaussian together with its first-order derivative. The Gaussian is special in many respects: the Gaussian maximizes uncertainty when only mean value and standard deviation are known [Shannon et al., 1949], and it is the kernel that introduces the least structure when varying its scale, σ, [Weickert et al., 1997]. Since σ may be seen as proportional to downsampling of the domain with a factor σ, we will refer to σ as the scale of the kernel and hence of (11.80).

It should be noted that the Gaussian only fulfills (11.81c) on a continuous, infinite domain such as $\mathbb{R}^3$ or a 3D torus. However, approximations may be used for discrete, finite size domains by sampling the Gaussian and renormalizing the Gaussian to enforce (11.81c). This will be assumed in the following.

Now let's return to the factor $\frac{m_j}{\rho_j}$ appearing in (11.80). By using $\rho_j = \frac{m_j}{V_j}$, where V_j is the volume implicitly attributed to the particle j, we find that $\frac{m_j}{\rho_j} = V_j$. Furthermore, consider the interpolated density function. Using (11.80) with ρ instead of A we find

$$\rho(\boldsymbol{r}) = \sum_{j=1}^{N} \rho_j \frac{m_j}{\rho_j} W(\boldsymbol{r} - \boldsymbol{r}_j, \sigma) \tag{11.84a}$$

$$= \sum_{j=1}^{N} m_j W(\boldsymbol{r} - \boldsymbol{r}_j, \sigma). \tag{11.84b}$$

For a finite domain of volume V and properly renormalized Gaussian, then $W \to \frac{1}{V}$ as $\sigma \to \infty$, hence $\rho = \frac{1}{V} \sum_{j=1}^{N} m_j$, which is the correct density at infinite scale. This is certainly the correct density, when viewing the system from infinitely afar. Likewise, when $\sigma \to 0$ then $G \to \delta(\|\boldsymbol{r} - \boldsymbol{r}_j\|)$, where δ is the *Dirac delta function* and defined as

$$\delta(x) = \begin{cases} \infty, & \text{if } x = 0, \\ 0, & \text{otherwise}, \end{cases} \tag{11.85a}$$

$$\int \delta(x) = 1 \tag{11.85b}$$

This implies that that the density is infinite at each particle, which although physically unrealistic, corresponds to assigning the mathematical mass m_j to an infinitely small volume of space, which naturally would result in infinite density. We thus conclude that for the density function, the coefficients $\frac{m_j}{\rho_j}$ are correct.

Now consider the more complicated example of an incompressible, homogeneous Navier-Stokes equation for an ideal gas and including a temperature gradient. In the Eulerian view, these equations are as follows:

$$\frac{\partial \boldsymbol{u}}{\partial t} = -(\boldsymbol{u} \cdot \nabla)\boldsymbol{u} - \frac{1}{\rho}\nabla p + \nu \nabla^2 \boldsymbol{u} + \boldsymbol{F}, \tag{11.86a}$$

$$\nabla \cdot \boldsymbol{u} = 0, \tag{11.86b}$$

$$\frac{\partial T}{\partial t} = \lambda \nabla^2 T - \nabla \cdot (T\boldsymbol{u}) \tag{11.86c}$$

$$pV = nRT \tag{11.86d}$$

However, smoothed particle hydrodynamics is based on the Lagrangian view, where particles are treated rather than densities. Therefore, we should not use the normal derivative instead of the substantiate derivative, which simplifies (11.86a) to

$$\boldsymbol{a}_j = -\frac{1}{\rho}\nabla p + \nu \nabla^2 \boldsymbol{u} + \boldsymbol{F}, \tag{11.87}$$

Further, and in contrast to (11.86b), conservation of mass is simply obtained by neither removing nor introducing particles.

According to (11.80) and (11.83) the gradient of pressure is calculated as,

$$-\nabla p(\boldsymbol{r}) = -\sum_{j=1}^{N} p_j \frac{m_j}{\rho_j} \nabla W(\boldsymbol{r} - \boldsymbol{r}_j, \sigma). \tag{11.88}$$

First, note that due to (11.81b) W is an even function, which implies that the derivatives along each axis is an even function, hence antisymmetric, and $\nabla W(0, \sigma) = 0$. Nevertheless, (11.88) is not without problems. Consider a two particle system distance $d\boldsymbol{r} = \boldsymbol{r}_1 - \boldsymbol{r}_2$ apart with identical densities and mass, $\rho = \rho_1 = \rho_2$ and $m = m_1 = m_2$. Using (11.88) we find the force from the pressure gradient at each particle to be

$$-\nabla p(\boldsymbol{r}_1) = -p_2 \frac{m}{\rho} \nabla W(d\boldsymbol{r}, \sigma), \tag{11.89a}$$

$$-\nabla p(\boldsymbol{r}_2) = -p_1 \frac{m}{\rho} \nabla W(-d\boldsymbol{r}, \sigma) \tag{11.89b}$$

$$= p_1 \frac{m}{\rho} \nabla W(d\boldsymbol{r}, \sigma), \tag{11.89c}$$

where we have used the antisymmetry of the gradient of W in (11.89c). Thus, when $p_1 \neq p_2$, the magnitude of the forces differ on each particle, and the system therefore does not fulfill Newton's first law.

To enforce Newton's first law for the pressure gradient, a simple symmetrization has been suggested [Müller et al., 2003], where the smoothed pressure gradient is calculated as

$$-\nabla p(\boldsymbol{r}_i) = -\sum_{j=1}^{N} \frac{p_i + p_j}{2} \frac{m_j}{\rho_j} \nabla W(\boldsymbol{r}_i - \boldsymbol{r}_j, \sigma). \tag{11.90}$$

For the two-particle system above, this results in a symmetric force on each particle

$$-\nabla p(\boldsymbol{r}_1) = -\frac{p_1 + p_2}{2} \frac{m}{\rho} \nabla W(d\boldsymbol{r}, \sigma) \tag{11.91a}$$

$$= \nabla p(\boldsymbol{r}_2). \tag{11.91b}$$

Similarly, the smoothed viscosity is also antisymmetric for two-particle systems

$$\nu \nabla^2 \boldsymbol{v}(\boldsymbol{r}) = \nu \sum_{j=1}^{N} \boldsymbol{v}_j \frac{m_j}{\rho_j} \nabla^2 W(\boldsymbol{r} - \boldsymbol{r}_j, \sigma). \tag{11.92}$$

In this case, it has suggested to symmetrize by considering velocity differences [Müller et al., 2003]

$$\nu \nabla^2 \boldsymbol{v}(\boldsymbol{r}_i) = \nu \sum_{j=1}^{N} (\boldsymbol{v}_j - \boldsymbol{v}_i) \frac{m_j}{\rho_j} \nabla^2 W(\boldsymbol{r} - \boldsymbol{r}_j, \sigma). \tag{11.93}$$

Finally, the surface of a smoothed particle hydrodynamical system may be expressed as the surface where the density (11.84) is given as some user-specified constant c as

$$S = \{\boldsymbol{r} \mid \rho(\boldsymbol{r}) = c\}, \tag{11.94}$$

and the surface may be tessellated, for example, using marching cubes [Lorensen et al., 1987] or splatting [Rusinkiewicz et al., 2000]. The gradient of the surface is useful for visualization, and it may be found as the gradient of the density take where $\rho = c$, that is,

$$\boldsymbol{n} = \{\nabla \rho \mid \rho(\boldsymbol{r}) = c\}. \tag{11.95}$$

Finally, the smoothed particle hydrodynamics may be augmented with a surface tension term

$$\boldsymbol{F}^{\text{surface}} = \tau h \boldsymbol{n}, \tag{11.96}$$

where τ is the surface tension coefficient, and h is the mean curvature, which is readily obtained as [Florack, 1997, p. 167],

$$h = \frac{1}{2}\frac{(\rho_y^2 + \rho_z^2)\rho_{xx} + (\rho_x^2 + \rho_z^2)\rho_{yy} + (\rho_x^2 + \rho_y^2)\rho_{zz} - 2\rho_x\rho_y\rho_{xy} - 2\rho_x\rho_z\rho_{xz} - 2\rho_y\rho_z\rho_{yz}}{(\rho_x^2 + \rho_y^2 + \rho_z^2)^{3/2}}, \tag{11.97}$$

taken at $\rho = c$.

Part IV

Collision Detection

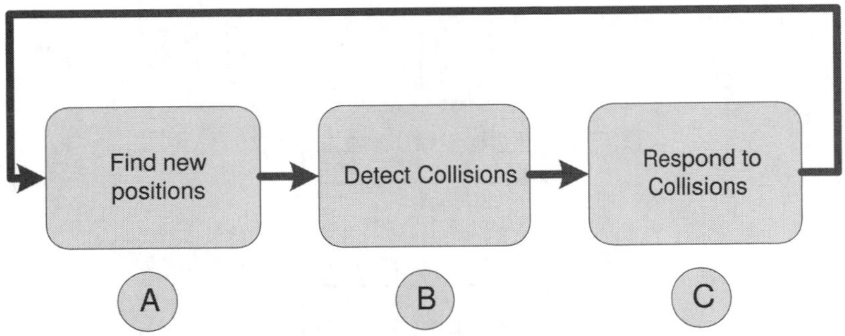

Figure IV.1: The simulation loop.

During the course of physics-based animation, objects come in contact with each other. The contact region must be resolved so that objects bounce or slide off each other or come to rest upon each other. In order to simulate these effects it is necessary to infer details about the shape of the contact regions. This is the aim of *collision detection* in physics-based animation. Collision detection is therefore a purely geometrical problem.

The *simulation loop* is the simplest way of describing the interaction between a *simulation method* and the collision detection. The simulation loop [Mirtich et al., 1995] illustrates the basic interaction between collision detection and the simulation method as shown in Figure IV.1.

First, the simulation method updates the position of the objects and/or their shape, then the collision detection finds the regions of contact or penetration between the objects, and finally the regions of contact are reacted to in a proper physical manner by the simulator.

In physics-based animation, collision detection often becomes the bottleneck, since a collision query needs to be performed in every simulation step in order to determine contacting and colliding objects. Animations can have many objects, all of which may have a complex geometry, such as polygonal soups of several thousands facets, and it is therefore a computationally heavy burden to perform collision detection, and it can be difficult to obtain real-time interaction.

Hubbard [Hubbard, 1993] was among the first to address these specific kinds of problems encountered in physics-based animation. Initially, collision detection appears to be an $O(n^2)$ algorithm, since any two triangles may be intersecting. Instead of running an expensive pairwise collision test between every pair of objects, Hubbard introduced the concepts of *broad-phase* and *narrow-phase collision detection* still widely in use today. The main idea is to reduce the computational load by performing a coarse test in order to prune an unnecessary pair test. This is broad-phase collision detection.

The actual reduced pairwise testing is the narrow-phase collision detection. After the narrow-phase collision detection, a postprocessing phase, called contact determination [Bouma et al., 1993], is usually carried out. Its purpose is to take the output from the narrow-phase collision detection and turn it into meaningful data for the simulation method. It is possible to further extend the collision detection with a fourth phase, termed the spatial-temporal coherence phase. The spatial-temporal coherence phase is essentially responsible for exploiting cached information and breaking down the computation in smaller independent pieces [Erleben, 2005].

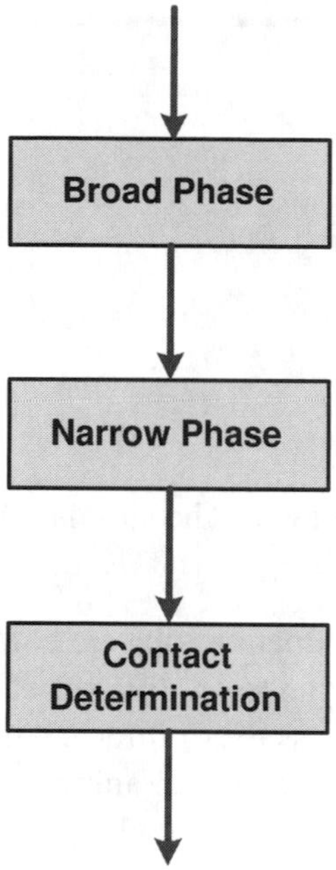

Figure IV.2: The three phases of collision detection.

Part IV is dedicated to the three phases: broad-phase collision detection, narrow-phase collision detection, and contact determination. These are depicted in Figure IV.2. Due to space considerations we will limit ourselves to treat only polygonal objects. Part IV is organized as follows: in Chapter 12 we will introduce the reader to basic principles, and treat broad-phase collision detection in detail. In Chapter 13 we will introduce the reader to narrow-phase collision detection algorithms, and in Chapter 14 we discuss contact determination. The remaining chapters, Chapter 15, Chapter 16, and Chapter 17 are dedicated to specific treatment of various narrow-phase collision detection algorithms.

12

Broad-Phase Collision Detection

It is computationally very expensive to test two arbitrary objects for collision and to determine their contact regions. As a simple example, imagine a scene consisting of two complex tentacle objects, like the ones shown in Figure 12.1(a). In this case, each object has roughly 10,000 faces. A naïve approach would be to clip every face from an object against the faces of the other object. Such an algorithm would, in the worst-case, have a quadratic running time, $\mathcal{O}(m^2)$, where m is number of faces; this brute approach is therefore seldom used in practice. A better approach is to store an object in a spatial data structure as described in Chapter 15, which often brings the worst-case time complexity down to that of doing a complete traversal of a treelike structure, $\mathcal{O}(m \log m)$. Even better would be to use a signed distance map approach as described in Section 17.1, which would consist of looking up every vertex of one object in a distance field of the other object. This requires $\mathcal{O}(m)$, assuming there is an upper bound on the number of vertices in a single face, as often is the case for triangular meshes. In special cases for rigid and convex objects an expected $\mathcal{O}(1)$ time complexity can be achieved. To summarize, for two arbitrary deforming and moving tentacle objects with a total of m faces, the worst-case time complexity ranges from $\mathcal{O}(m)$ to $\mathcal{O}(m^2)$. Since m can become quite large, it is easily seen that in the general case, the pairwise testing will be computationally intensive. Doing physics-based animation with only two objects is often not enough, and even simple scenes often have a handful of objects, as shown in Figure 12.1(b). This is called the *n-body problem*, n being the number of objects.

We can deal with the n-body problem by considering every possible pairwise test of the n objects in the scene. In the worst-case this would require

$$\frac{n\,(n-1)}{2} \approx O(n^2) \tag{12.1}$$

pairwise tests. However, in practice it is rare that all objects are momentarily in contact with each other. For instance, a single sphere would expect, on average, to be in contact with at most six other spheres in a box full of rigid spheres, and in such a case we would expect only $\mathcal{O}(6n)$ pairwise test to result in actual contact being detected.

Since objects in physics-based animation is prohibited from deeply interpenetrating each other, we can, on average, expect to do better than $\mathcal{O}(n^2)$ pairwise testing, and one of the goals of *broad-phase collision detection* is to quickly prune expensive and unnecessary pairwise tests. It is important to observe that broad-phase collision detection does not change the worst-case time complexity; nevertheless it does ease the workload.

Figure 12.2 shows how a broad-phase collision detection algorithm can be used in a simple collision detection engine. In order for a broad-phase collision detection algorithm to be efficient, we stride toward an algorithm capable of pruning an unnecessary pair test in constant time and with a very low time constant. From computational geometry [Berg et al., 1997, O'Rourke, 1998], we know traditional algorithms, such as: *point location* and *range searching*, as illustrated in Figure 12.3. These algorithms efficiently solve problems, such as

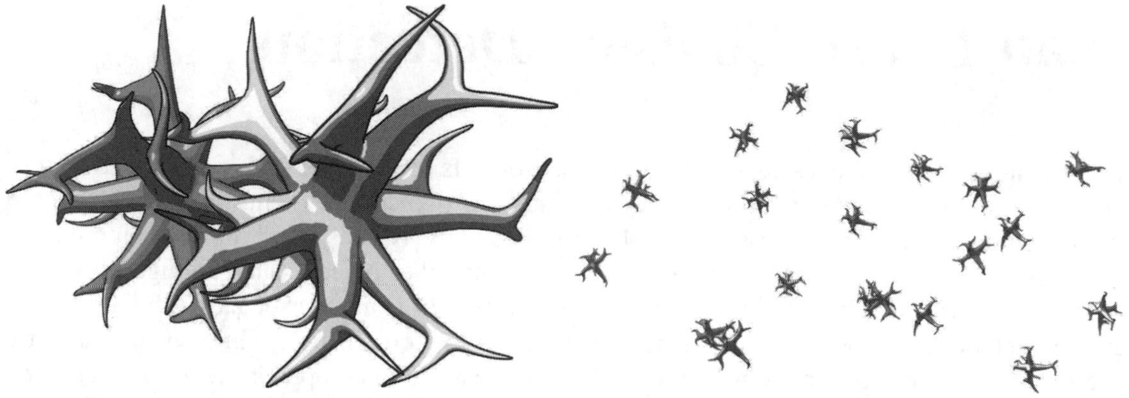

(a) 2 objects, 11066 faces each

(b) 20 objects = 190 pairs

Figure 12.1: Illustration showing why collision detection is computationally heavy.

```
algorithm collision detection(C:Contacts)
  pairs = broad-phase()
  clear C   for each pair p in pairs do
    proximity = narrow-phase(p)
    contact = contact-determination(proximity)
    add contact to C
  next p
end algorithm
```

Figure 12.2: A simple collision detection engine.

- Which box contains a given point?
- Which boxes overlap a given box?

This seems to be useful for broad-phase collision detection algorithm. Therefore, an initial idea would be to approximate each object by a box, and then apply the traditional computational geometry algorithm. Unfortunately, such an approach is doomed to be inefficient in the context of physics-based animation, since two important things have escaped our attention: we need to consider all possible pairs of overlap, and these need to be considered as time progresses forward in a simulation. In conclusion, in broad-phase collision detection we want to solve problems, such as

- Which boxes overlap each other?
- Which boxes overlap in the next iteration?

These are also known as *multiple queries* and *all-pair problems*.

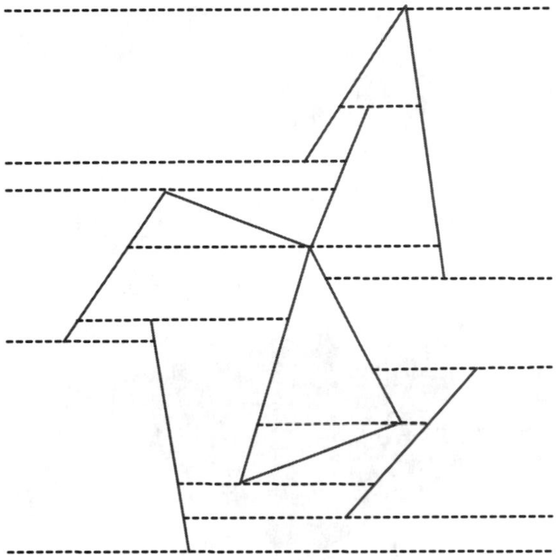

(a) Point Location Data Structure: line end-points are used to create horizontal lines, creating an arrangement of trapezoids.

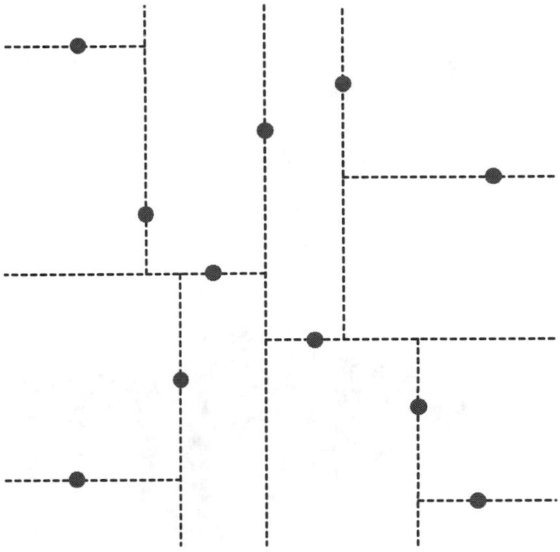

(b) Range Searching: a recursive subdivision of space is done by splitting space into two halves at every point.

Figure 12.3: Traditional algorithms from computational geometry.

In physics-based animation, objects move and deform over time, e.g., in Figure 12.4 frames from a simple rigid body simulation are shown, and the broad-phase collision detection algorithm should be run at each of these frames. To perform fast simulation, we need an algorithm with low complexity and low constants, such as dynamic algorithms, which we'll discuss later. In the following, we will introduce the four principles used for constructing a dynamic algorithm, followed by an outline of three popular algorithms for doing broad-phase collision detection: Exhaustive Search, also known as the All-Pair Test, Coordinate Sorting, also known as Sweep and Prune, and Hierarchical Hash tables, also known as Multilevel Grids.

12.1 The Four Principles for Dynamic Algorithms

To obtain fast broad-phase collision detection algorithms the following *four principles* are helpful:

- The Approximation Principle
- The Locality Principle

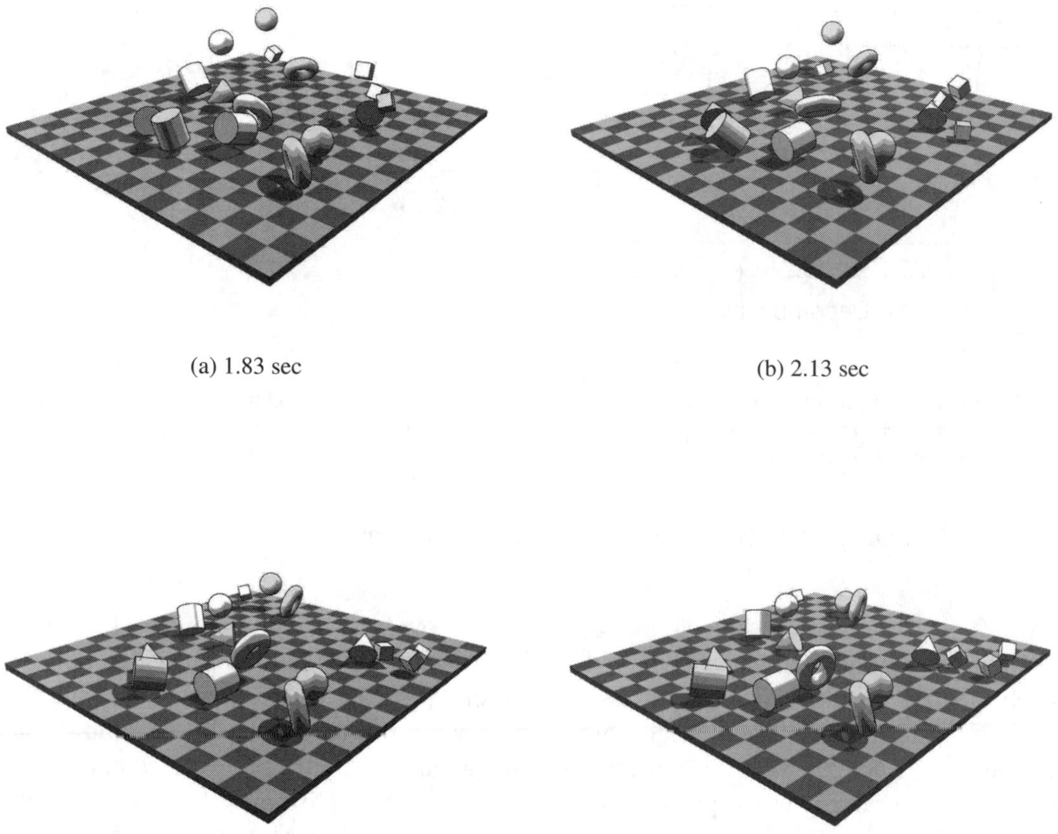

(a) 1.83 sec

(b) 2.13 sec

(c) 2.43 sec

(d) 2.71 sec

Figure 12.4: Frames of a rigid body simulation.

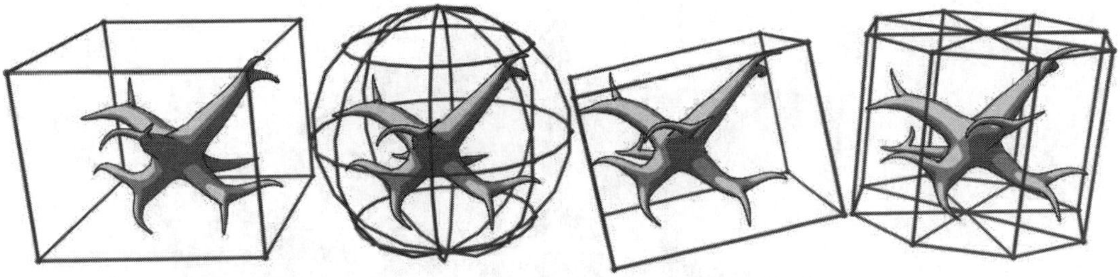

Figure 12.5: The Approximation Principle. A complex tentacle geometry is approximated by an AABB, a sphere, an OBB, and a cylinder.

- The Coherence Principle
- The Kinematic Principle

The Approximation Principle Complex geometry of an object can be approximated with a simpler geometry, which is known as the *Approximation Principle principle!approximation*. Some frequently used approximation geometries are:

- *Spheres*
- *Axes Aligned Bounding Boxes* (*AABB*)
- *Oriented Bounding Boxes* (*OBB*)
- *Cylinders*

These are illustrated in Figure 12.5. The choice of approximation geometry has an impact on the time constants of a broad-phase algorithm, and the general rule of thumb is that more complex geometry means higher time constants.

Here, *complexity* is used vaguely; the number of parameters needed to describe the size and location of a volume is one definition: a sphere needs four parameters, an AABB needs six parameters, a cylinder needs eight parameters, and an OBB needs nine parameters. However, there are other definitions, for example, describing the shape by the order of curved surfaces or the number of faces. The theory of shape complexity is huge, and the interested reader may wish to investigate Stochastic Complexity [Rissanen, 1989] and Fractal Dimensions [Mandelbrot, 2004, Halsey et al., 1986]

Typically, a scene consists of many objects in the order of 100–1000 and for a dynamic, real-time animation, we will have to approximate many objects frequently. This indicates that it should be easy and fast to find the approximating geometry. In contrast, more complex geometry means better pruning of unnecessary pair tests. The choice of tradeoff is thus similar to the choice of volume type in bounding volume hierarchies, as discussed in Chapter 15. However, we know of no work examining this trade-off for broad-phase collision detection. We believe that simpler geometries will be preferable, since a more complex test is done later by the narrow-phase collision detection. In the broad-phase collision detection algorithms we have chosen to present in this book, we have decided to use AABBs because:

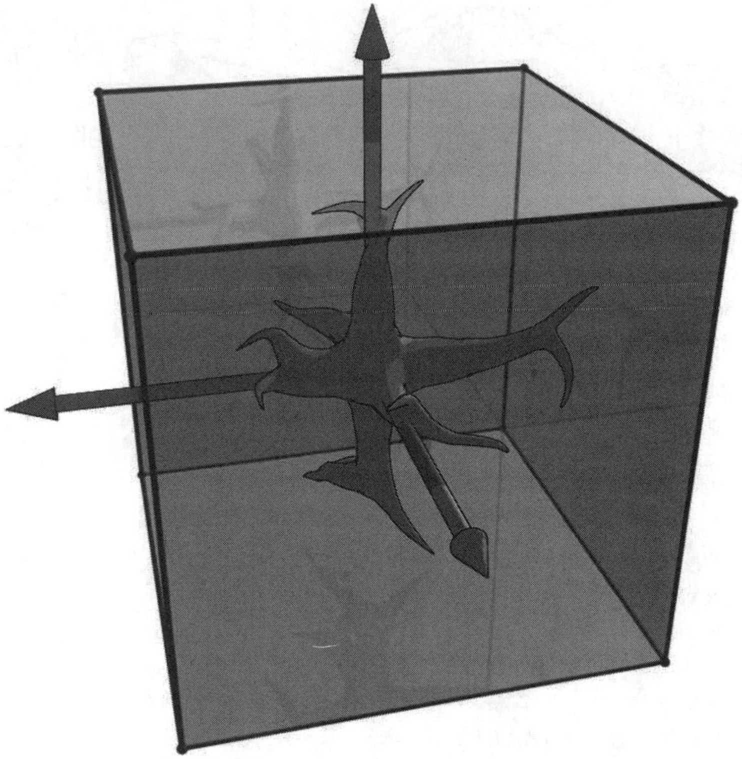

Figure 12.6: Sides of AABB are orthogonal to the coordinate frame, whose axes are shown with arrows.

- They are easy and fast to compute given a maximum distance from the center of mass of a body to any point on the body surface
- They are fast to do an overlap test with
- They generalize to any dimension

This is also true for spheres. However, later we will present two algorithms: sweep and prune and hierarchical hash tables, that only work with AABBs. The exhaustive search algorithm, which we will present can use any kind of volume. In practice, as a rule of thumb, one should choose the simplest volume that can be used with the chosen algorithm and which best describes the shape of the objects. As an example, if one chooses the exhaustive search algorithm and has sphere-like objects, then a sphere volume is going to be the best choice. We will now go into the details of an AABB.

An AABB is a box whose sides are orthogonal to the *world coordinate system* (*WCS*) axes as illustrated in Figure 12.6. Sometimes other coordinate frames are chosen, e.g., the model frame in which the object was modeled, however, for the purpose of broad-phase collision detection, we will only consider the WCS.

We can represent an AABB by two points: the minimum point $\boldsymbol{r}_{min}$ and the maximum point $\boldsymbol{r}_{max}$. These are defined as the corners of the AABB with minimum and maximum coordinates, as illustrated in

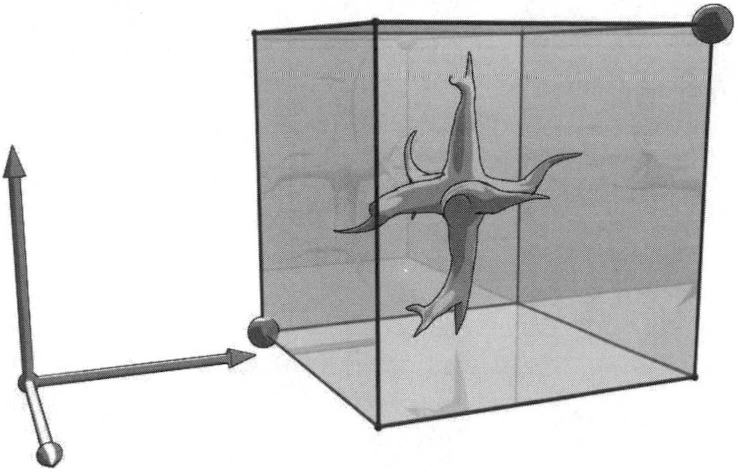

Figure 12.7: Minimum and maximum points of an AABB.

Figure 12.7.

A brute-force approach for computing the minimum and maximum point is to iterate over every face vertex and determine the minimum and maximum coordinates as illustrated in Figure 12.8. This will result in the tightest-fitting AABB with the best pruning capabilities. Unfortunately, this approach is infeasible for objects with many vertices as the ones shown in Figure 12.1(a). The brute method is sometimes the only alternative; for instance, if an object is deforming and there is no way to predict the bounds of deformation. However, sometimes, faster algorithms that compute a looser fitting AABB can be used, e.g., if the objects are rigid bodies, then a looser fitting AABB method can be constructed by first determining an enclosing sphere, and then finding the AABB enclosing the sphere.

In order to find an enclosing sphere, we will introduce a preprocessing step where we determine the maximum distance, d_{max}, from the center of mass to the surface of an object, A

$$d_{max} = \max\left(\|\boldsymbol{p}\|_2, \quad \boldsymbol{p} \in A\right). \tag{12.2}$$

This is illustrated in Figure 12.9. For a polyhedron object, d_{max} can be computed by iterating over all the vertices of the object. For each vertex, the difference between its position and the center of mass is computed, and then it is tested if the length of the difference vector exceeds the previously known distance to the surface. The observant reader might object that this iteration is more expensive than the iteration used to compute a tight AABB, but recall that the computation is done only once as a preprocessing step, whereas the tight AABB computation is performed in each and every query. The pseudocode for this algorithm is shown in Figure 12.10. For an object represented by splines or NURBS, a similar strategy could be used, by exploiting the convex hull property of their control points. Implicit surface representations are more difficult, but their surface could be sampled [Witkin et al., 1994].

```
algorithm bruteAABB(M: Mesh)
 min = (infty, infty, infty)
  max = min
  for each vertex v in M do
    if v.x < min.x then
      min.x = v.x
    end if
    ...
    if v.x > max.x then
      max.x = v.x
    end if
    ...
  next v
  return min and max
end algorithm
```

Figure 12.8: Brute-force computation of an AABB.

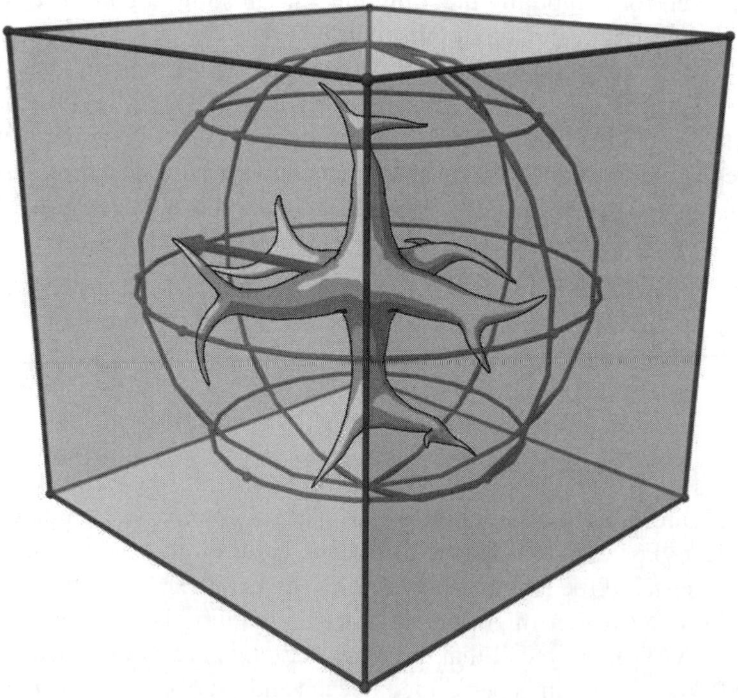

Figure 12.9: Maximum radius to surface of an object.

```
algorithm compute-d_max(O : Object)
  V = vertices(O)
  d_max = 0
  for each v ∈ V do
    if d_max < ||v − r_cm||_2 then
      d_max = ||v − r_cm||_2
  next v
end algorithm
```

Figure 12.10: Maximum radius computation for a rigid polyhedron object.

Knowing d_{max}, the minimum point is computed as

$$r_{min} = r_{cm} - \begin{bmatrix} d_{max} \\ d_{max} \\ d_{max} \end{bmatrix}, \tag{12.3}$$

and the maximum point is given as

$$r_{max} = r_{cm} + \begin{bmatrix} d_{max} \\ d_{max} \\ d_{max} \end{bmatrix}. \tag{12.4}$$

Observe that since d_{max} is precomputed once, finding the AABB is a constant time operation with extremely low constants, since it only requires a total of six simple floating-point operations. An example AABB is shown in Figure 12.11; notice that although the AABB is not the best fit, it is very fast to compute.

If we look at two boxes i and j along a coordinate axis of the WCS, then we can describe the boxes on the axis by two intervals

$$[b_i \dots e_i] \quad \text{and} \quad [b_j \dots e_j], \tag{12.5}$$

where

$$b_i < e_i \quad \text{and} \quad b_j < e_j. \tag{12.6}$$

These AABB intervals are illustrated in Figure 12.12. Observe that the intervals can be found by projecting the minimum point and the maximum point, i.e., the b and e-values onto the axis in question. The bs and es are also sometimes called the endpoints. Clearly if box i and box j overlap along a given axis, then we must have

$$b_j < b_i \leq e_j \quad \text{or} \quad b_i \leq b_j < e_i. \tag{12.7}$$

If they are separated, then we must have

$$e_i < b_j \quad \text{or} \quad e_j < b_i. \tag{12.8}$$

Exactly one of these four conditions is always true, and the other three are always false, as shown in Figure 12.13. Furthermore, if, and only if, their intervals along all coordinates axes overlap, only then

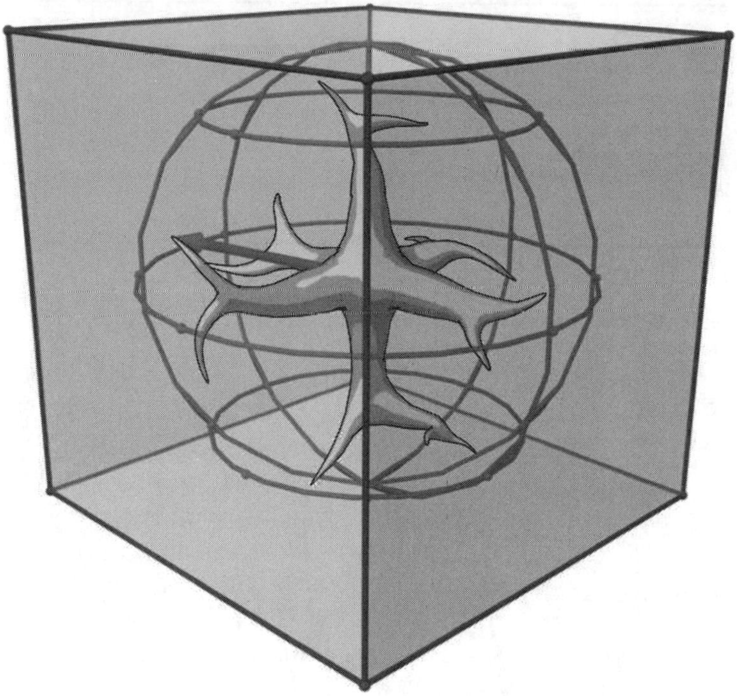

Figure 12.11: An example of an AABB computed by the fast computation method.

will the two AABBs overlap. As a consequence, in 3 dimensions the problem has been reduced to three one-dimensional problems: we simply count the number of overlaps along each of the WCS axes. If the number of overlapping axes is equal to three, then we conclude that the two AABBs overlap. Figure 12.14 shows the pseudocode for this overlap test. In contrast, for objects approximated with spheres, a distance computation in $3D$ space would be needed. Thus, in the case of spheres, one cannot exploit the property of dimension reduction of the AABBs. Comparing the actual costs of sphere testing and AABB testing, using squared distances spheres required 4 multiplications, 6 additions, and 1 comparison, where AABBs are handled with only 12 comparisons and 3 logical tests. Thus, spheres are marginally more expensive when considering just a single pairwise test.

The Locality Principle Another key observation for broad-phase collision detection algorithms is that only close neighbors need to be considered when determining overlaps between the approximating geometries. This is termed the *Locality Principle*. This principle essentially states that objects lying sufficiently far away from each other do not need to be considered as overlapping and can easily be ignored.

The idea is perhaps best illustrated by the example as shown in Figure 12.15. Here 28 objects are placed in a world, posing $(28 \cdot 27)/2 = 378$ possible pair test. Many of these are trivially superfluous, for instance, the leftmost object is so far away from the rightmost object that it would be unnecessary to do a pairwise test between the two objects. If we draw arrows between the center of masses of the objects, which are close neighbors, then the potential set of pairwise tests drop to only 42 in the present case,

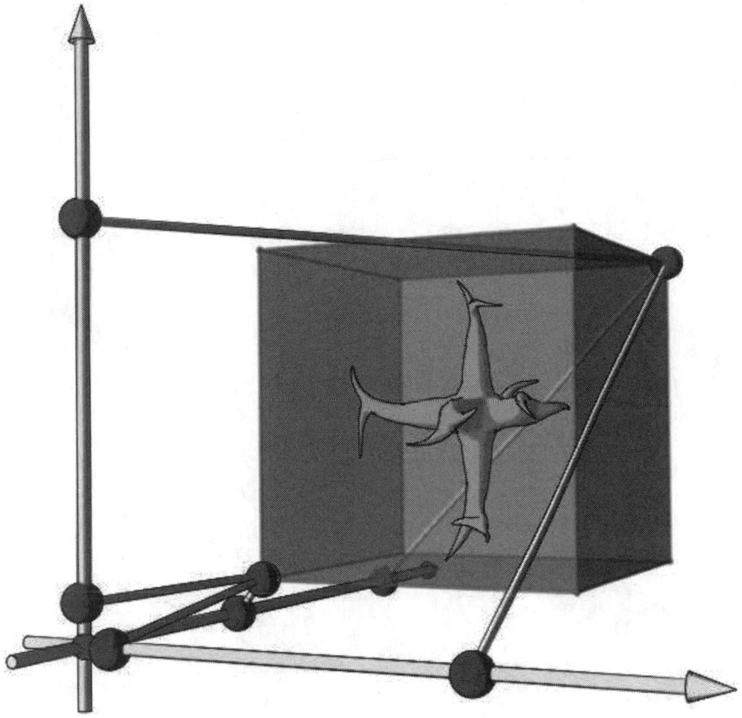

Figure 12.12: AABB intervals along a coordinate axis.

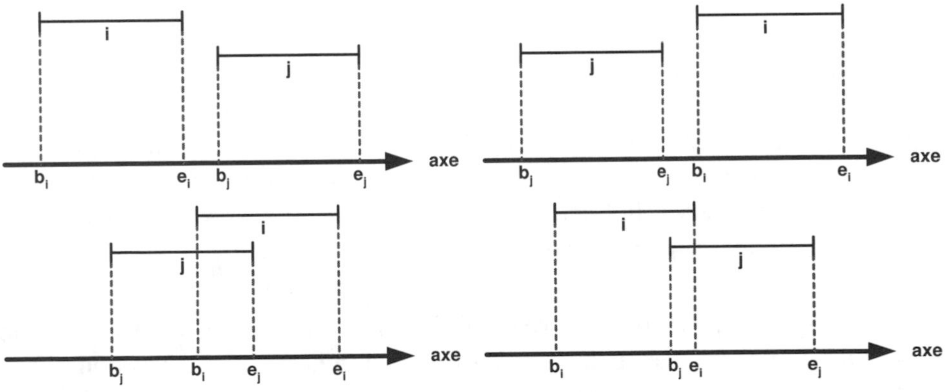

Figure 12.13: Possible conditions for detecting interval overlap of two AABBs.

```
algorithm AABB-overlap(i,j : AABB)
  if ( b_jx < b_ix ≤ e_jx or b_ix ≤ b_jx < e_ix ) and
     ( b_jy < b_iy ≤ e_jy or b_iy ≤ b_jy < e_iy ) and
     ( b_jz < b_iz ≤ e_jz or b_iz ≤ b_jz < e_iz ) then
    return true
  return false
end algorithm
```

Figure 12.14: Pseudocode for overlap test between two AABBs.

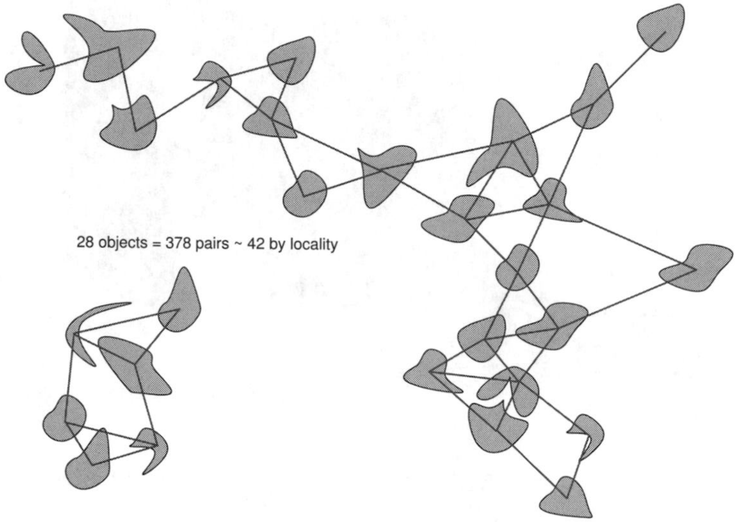

Figure 12.15: The Locality Principle. Total number of object pairs is far greater than the number of edges between nearby objects. These indicate possible object pairs where it make sense to test for collision.

yielding a speedup factor of $378/42 = 9$.

In order to exploit the locality principle to its fullest, one needs to come up with a way to determine when things are sufficiently far away. Computing a generalized Voronoi diagram [O'Rourke, 1998, Berg et al., 1997] from scratch in order to determine the close neighbors would be much too expensive; therefore, other methods are needed. In Section 12.3 and Section 12.4 we will show two examples where coordinate sorting and gridding is used to exploit the locality principle.

The Coherence Principle The third principle is the *Coherence Principle*, and by coherence we mean a measure of how much things change. Low coherence would indicate a configuration, where objects are nearly teleporting around in the world, and high coherence would be the exact opposite, where objects move smoothly around.

The rigid bodies in a rigid body simulator have high coherence, if the time-step is not too big. In Figure 12.16, an example is shown where a number of rigid bodies is falling under gravity with a time-step of 0.3 seconds. Observe how object positions and orientations only change a little bit from frame to frame. This is an example of coherence.

Coherence comes in many flavors, four different kinds of coherence are usually considered in the context of physics-based animation. They are:

- Spatial Coherence
- Geometric Coherence
- Frame Coherence
- Temporal Coherence

The first two address the shape and position of objects in the world, where high coherence would indicate that objects are placed nicely. In the following, we will think of this as a measure of how nicely objects are aligned, and how much overlap they pose. The last two kinds of coherence are indications of how objects evolve, that is, how they move and deform as the simulation proceeds.

High coherence indicates that we would have to compute almost the exact same result in the next iteration of our simulation method, which suggests that we can reuse previously computed results from the last iteration to obtain the correct results for the current iteration. This is what we mean by the phrase *dynamic algorithm*, not to be confused with dynamic programming.

The Kinematics Principle When we can benefit from knowing something about the objects trajectory in the near future, we say that we exploit the *Kinematics Principle*, which is the fourth principle. This comes in handy when proximity information about near future colliding objects is needed. Figure 12.17 shows an example of where knowledge of the trajectory could be used to predict a collision between the red sphere and the green box and between the red and blue spheres. The knowledge could be used to minimize the number of times we actually have to stop the simulation and do collision detection. In the case of the example, collision detection only needs to be performed twice: once at each time of impact. This is, for instance, useful in order to obtain accurate information for computing *Time of Impact* (*TOI*) estimates. Another example of usage is when four-dimensional collision detection is used, such as space-time bounds (S-bounds).

12.2 Exhaustive Search

An *exhaustive search* is the brute-force approach for doing broad-phase collision detection. Brute-force is testing the AABBs of every possible object pair against each other. For this reason, it is also commonly called the *all-pair test*. The time complexity is therefore

$$\binom{n}{2} = \frac{n(n-1)}{2} \approx O(n^2). \tag{12.9}$$

A pseudocode version of the algorithm is presented in Figure 12.18 and as can be seen from the pseudocode, exhaustive search only exploits the principle of approximation. At first this algorithm might seem to be a poor choice due to its quadratic running time. However, it does pose some nice features:

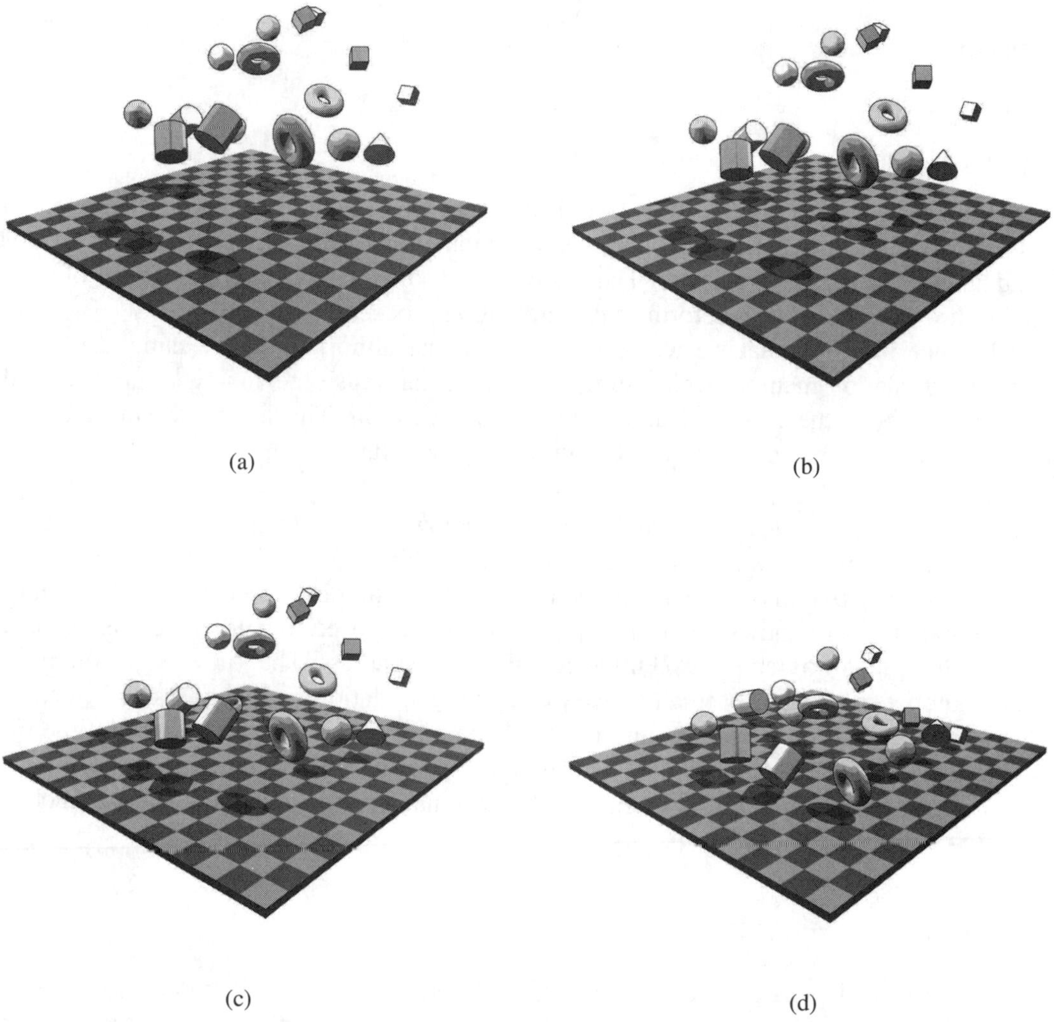

Figure 12.16: High coherence in a rigid body simulation. Even though objects have moved a lot as seen globally, they are more or less still placed similarly as seen relative with respect to each other.

Figure 12.17: The Kinematics Principle. Considering future trajectories of the spheres, it is possible to predict possible future collisions.

```
algorithm exhaustive-search(B : bodies)
  for each b ∈ B do
    compute AABB of b
  next b

  for each (b, b')_{b≠b'} ∈ B do
    if AABB(b) overlap AABB(b') then
      report overlap of (b, b')
  next (b, b')
end algorithm
```

Figure 12.18: Pseudocode for the exhaustive search algorithm.

- It is simple and fast to implement
- It has extremely low time constants (when using AABBs)
- It is applicable to any kind of bounding volume geometry

This means that it is practical for small-sized configurations and its simplicity further ensures that it is unlikely to be the point of failure. Other more advanced algorithms require a bit of hard work to implement and debug. For configurations up to sizes of order $10 - 100$ objects it is our experience that Exhaustive Search outperforms both Sweep and Prune and Hierarchical Hash tables, as discussed in the following.

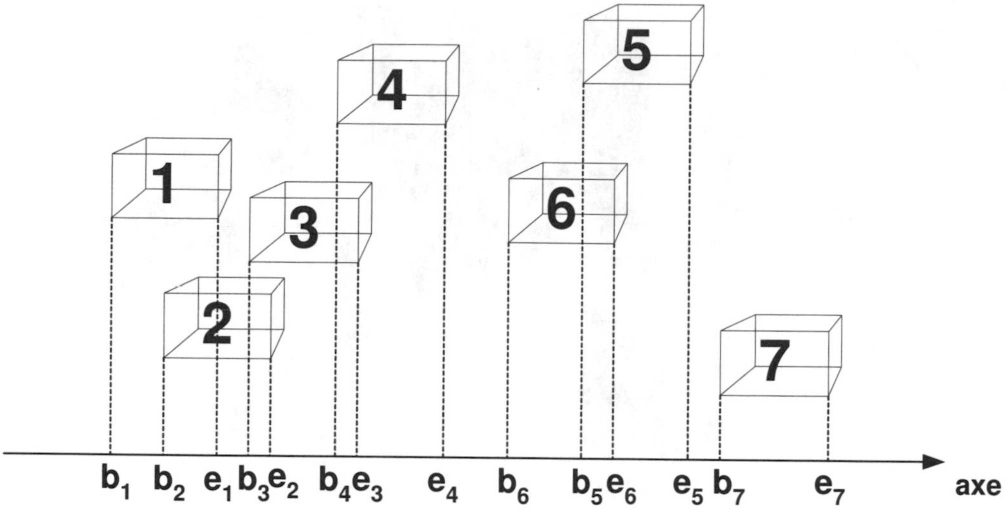

Figure 12.19: AABBs on a single coordinate axis.

12.3 Sweep and Prune

It is possible to obtain a far better time complexity than the Exhaustive Search algorithm. In this section we will outline an algorithm based on a *sweep line* approach: it has a linear expected running time and is called *Sweep and Prune* or *coordinate sorting* [Baraff et al., 2003a, Lin et al., 1994].

We will begin with introducing the algorithm in the 1D case, where the AABBs simply are bounded intervals on the coordinate axis. The situation is depicted in Figure 12.19. First, all the interval endpoints are sorted in increasing order along the coordinate axis, assuming for now that no two endpoints have the same coordinate value. The idea is to let a sweep line go from minus infinity to infinity along the coordinate axis, and update a status set, S, with every endpoint encountered. It is the purpose of this status set to keep indices of those objects whose interval is currently crossing the sweep line as illustrated in Figure 12.20. The update rule of the status set when the sweep line hits an interval endpoint is:

- If the sweep-line hits a starting endpoint, i.e., b_i, then object i is added to the status set S.

- If the sweep-line hits an ending endpoint, i.e., e_i, then object i is removed from the status set S.

It is immediately observed that the status set indicates which AABBs overlap along the coordinate axis, and we can report all overlapping AABBs on the coordinate axis by extending the two update rules with an extra auxiliary rule:

- When object i is about to be added to S, we report overlaps between i and all other objects currently in S.

The extension to higher dimensions is straightforward. We simply perform a sweep along each coordinate axis; afterward we count the number of times the same overlap has been seen. If we count the

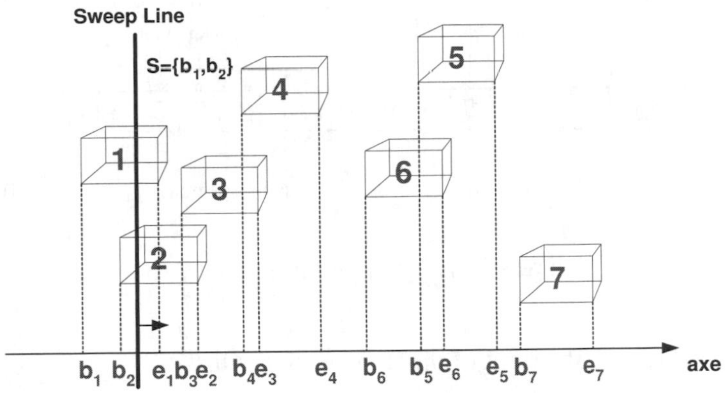

Figure 12.20: The sweep line and the status set.

same number of overlaps as the number of dimensions, we immediately know that the two corresponding AABBs overlap. This implies that all overlaps found on one coordinate axis should be matched against all overlaps found on the other axis, which is a quadratic algorithm in the number of overlaps. However, by introducing a counter table and modifying the update rules of the sweep-line slightly, we can get rid of the unpleasant quadratic time matching. The modification is as follows (for three dimensions):

- Use a table of counters, where each counter keeps track of the number of coordinate axes two AABBs i and j overlap on.
- When body i is about to be added to S we increment the counters between i and every other body currently in S.
- If a counter between two bodies reaches the value 3, then we report an overlap between the two bodies.

We now have Sweep and Prune in its most basic and pure form. If the endpoints are sorted along the coordinate axis, it runs in linear time in the number of AABBs, which is very attractive. However, there is nothing that guarantees that the endpoints will be sorted upon invocation of the Sweep and Prune algorithm, and the algorithm therefore requires a presorting along all coordinate axes indicating that the computational complexity is $\mathcal{O}(n \log n)$ [Cormen et al., 1994], where n is the number of AABBs. This is still better than the quadratic $\mathcal{O}(n^2)$ running time of Exhaustive Search, but we can do even better by taking a close look at the sorting of the endpoints.

Sweep and Prune requires that a list is sorted in increasing order. There are several sorting algorithms [Cormen et al., 1994] available for doing this: quicksort, bubblesort, insertion sort, etc. We will use *insertion sort*; later it will become clear why. For now, we will summarize how insertion sort works. For more details, we refer to [Cormen et al., 1994]:

- Insertion sort scans the unsorted list from left to right
- When a number is encountered, which is smaller than its leftmost neighbor, then insertion sort:

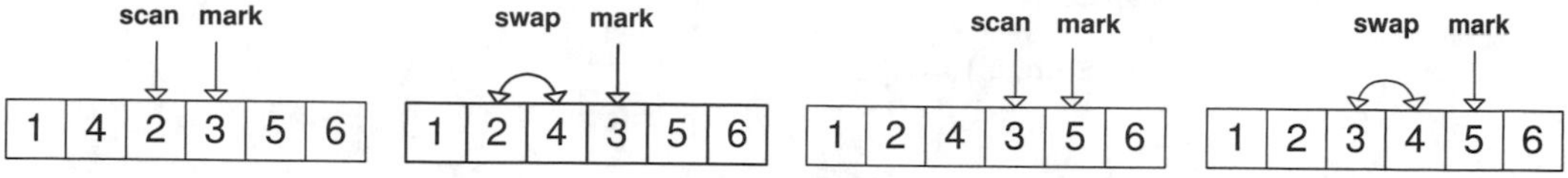

(a) First mark (b) Swap (c) Next mark (d) Second swap

Figure 12.21: Example of insertion sort.

1. Marks the position to the right of the number in the list.
2. The number is then repeatedly swapped with its leftmost neighbor until the number is greater than or equal to the leftmost neighbor.
3. The original scan is continued from the marked position.

An example of how insertion works is shown in Figure 12.21. The worst-case time complexity of insertion sort is $\mathcal{O}(n^2)$. This occurs if numbers in the initial unsorted list are sorted in decreasing order from left to right, in which case every number encountered in the scan is swapped to the front of the list, that is,

$$\underbrace{0+1+2+3+\cdots+(n-1)}_{n\text{- terms}} = \frac{n(n-1)}{2} \approx \mathcal{O}(n^2). \tag{12.10}$$

If the list is nearly sorted in increasing order then insertion sort behaves much better. Only a few numbers need to be swapped and they need not be swapped a very long way. Therefore, in this case, insertion sort runs in expected $\mathcal{O}(n)$ time. This indicates that depending on how badly sorted the endpoints are, we can expect Sweep and Prune to have a linear time complexity and a quadratic time complexity as lower and upper limits.

Fortunately in the context of physics-based animation, we can expect a high coherence, which means that the intervals of the AABBs along the coordinate axis only change slightly from invocation to invocation of the Sweep and Prune algorithm. If we save the sorted intervals from the previous invocation, and use these for the input to the current invocation of Sweep and Prune algorithm, then high coherence implies that insertion sort can sort them in linear time, $\mathcal{O}(n)$. We have now found a broad-phase collision detection algorithm which runs in expected $\mathcal{O}(n)$ time.

Nevertheless, there are still situations where Sweep and Prune has a quadratic running time as shown in Figure 12.22. Here a 2D rigid body simulation is shown, where five rigid balls are falling under gravity along the y-axis and colliding with a fixed object. The balls are only slightly displaced, such that at the frame after the impact, their order along the y-axis is reversed. In this case, insertion sort is passed a list of interval endpoints along the y-axis, which is sorted in reverse order. Luckily, in our experience this is more a theoretical issue than a practical issue.

It is possible to optimize the Sweep and Prune algorithm even more. Inspired by how the interval endpoint list was reused from the previous invocation of the algorithm, we will now try to reuse the list of reported overlaps from the previous invocation as well. For this purpose we will extend our counter table

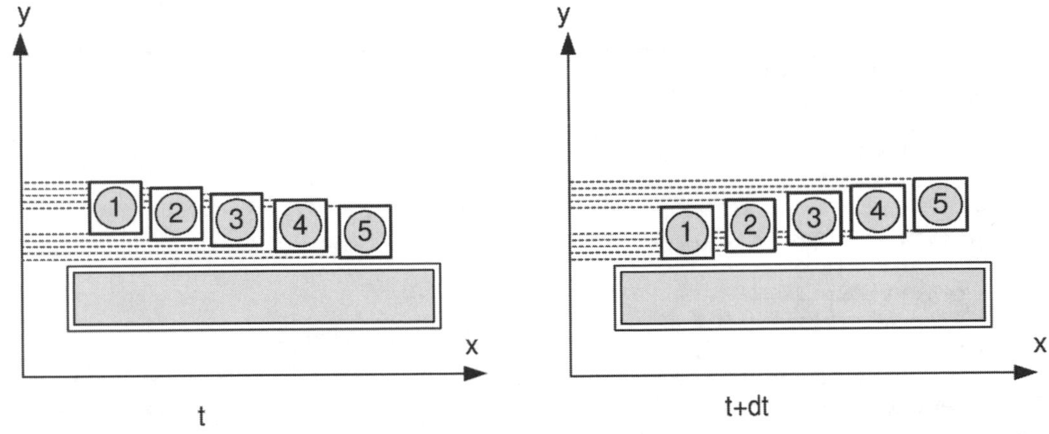

Figure 12.22: Bad case for the Sweep and Prune algorithm resulting in quadratic running time.

to also include a pointer for a counter into the list of reported overlaps, if an overlap is reported for that counter. Now let us examine what happens during the swapping operation of insertion sort.

- Imagine insertion sort is swapping b_i to the left of e_j, that is previously $e_j < b_i$ but now $e_j > b_i$. This indicates that i and j are now overlapping, so their counter is incremented and if its value is three, an overlap is reported.
- The opposite might also occur if e_j is swapped to the left of b_i, meaning that i and j no longer overlap. This time the counter between i and j is decremented and if a reported overlap exists, then it is removed in constant time by using the overlap pointer between i and j.
- If insertion sort tries to swap b_i and b_j, then we do nothing. Similarly, we do nothing if it tries to swap e_i and e_j.

With these modifications, we no longer need to have the sweep line and the status set represented explicitly. The update actions of the sweep line is performed implicitly, when insertion sort performs a swap between two endpoints. The pseudocode for sorting one coordinate axis in the Sweep and Prune algorithm can be seen in Figure 12.23.

So far we have assumed that no two endpoints have the same coordinate value along a given coordinate axis. If this happens, the algorithm will not report an overlap. In practice this can have fatal consequences. A missing overlap means that no contacts are detected further down the collision detection pipeline, thus the simulator might fail to react on a touching contact. An example of such a simulation is shown in Figure 12.24. We will now deal with this degenerate case: if we apply the rule that b's are to come before e's, then the inner while loop in Figure 12.23 becomes

```
While scan < left  or ( scan = left and  left=e and scan=b) Do
```

The implication of this is that touching AABBs will also be reported. This is useful, since the surface of the enclosing object could be touching the surface of the enclosing AABB.

```
algorithm coordinate-sort-axis(L : List(endpoints))
  scan = head(L)
  while L unsorted do
    mark = right(scan),left = left(scan)
    while scan < left do
      if scan = b_i and left = e_j then
        increment counter(i,j)
        if counter(i,j)=3 then
          report overlap(i,j)
      else if scan = e_j and left = b_i then
        decrement counter(i,j)
        if counter(i,j)=2 then
          remove overlap(i,j)
      end if
      scan = left,left = left(scan)
    end while
    scan = mark
  end while
end algorithm
```

Figure 12.23: Sweep and Prune pseudocode.

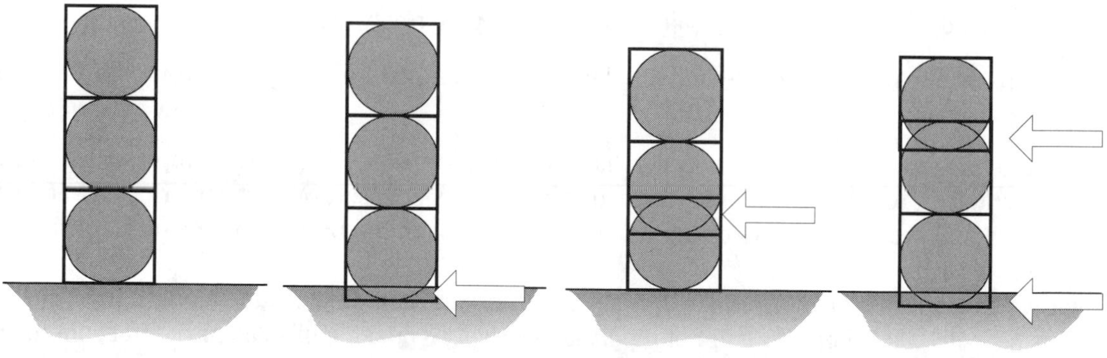

Figure 12.24: Illustration that missing detection of overlaps in the broad-phase collision detection algorithm can result in bad simulation behavior. A resting stack of rigid spheres in a gravitational field with their AABBs superimposed. Simulation frames are shown from left to right, reported overlaps and detection of contacts only occur at places marked with an arrow. Observe that penetrations occur due to the lack of collision resolving.

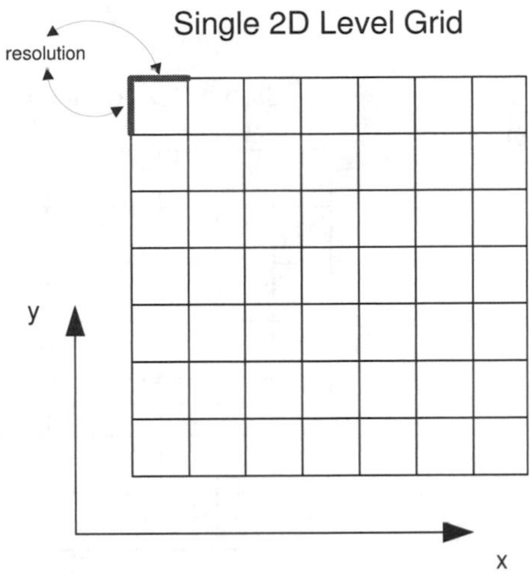

Figure 12.25: A single-level grid.

12.4 Hierarchical Hash Tables

Another approach to broad-phase collision detection is to use a spatial data structure, such as a rectilinear grid. Mirtich [Mirtich, 1996] introduced a *multilevel gridding* algorithm, known as *hierarchical hash tables*, which will be explained in this section.

Consider the simulated world divided into a rectilinear grid using the same size grid spacing along all coordinate axis. Such a spatial subdivision is called a tiling. The bounded region, where the simulation is expected to take place, can be represented by a minimum and maximum point in a manner similar to an AABB. A resolution of the cells can then be given as the edge size of the grid cells as illustrated in Figure 12.25 for a 2D example. If we have a tiling and a given *cell resolution*, ρ, every cell can be uniquely identified by a triplet (α, β, γ) in 3D. The triplet consist of set of order indices indicating the order of a cell along the respective coordinate axis. The idea of triplets is illustrated for the 2D case in Figure 12.26. These triplets uniquely identify a given cell in the tiling and can be used as hash keys. Given an arbitrary point, $\boldsymbol{p}$, we can find the triplet of the enclosing cell in the tiling as

$$\tau(\boldsymbol{p}, \rho) = \left(\left\lfloor \frac{\boldsymbol{p}_x - \boldsymbol{t}_x}{\rho} \right\rfloor, \left\lfloor \frac{\boldsymbol{p}_y - \boldsymbol{t}_y}{\rho} \right\rfloor, \left\lfloor \frac{\boldsymbol{p}_z - \boldsymbol{t}_z}{\rho} \right\rfloor \right) = (\alpha, \beta, \gamma) . \tag{12.11}$$

Here $\boldsymbol{t}$ is the minimum point of the minimum cell.

Using (12.11), all cells in the tiling that overlap with a given AABB are easily found by identifying the triplets spanned by the mapping of the minimum, $\boldsymbol{p}_{\text{min}}$, and maximum point, $\boldsymbol{p}_{\text{max}}$, of the given AABB, that is, all triplets satisfying the relation

$$\tau(\boldsymbol{p}_{min}, \rho) \leq (\alpha, \beta, \gamma) \leq \tau(\boldsymbol{p}_{max}, \rho). \tag{12.12}$$

The idea is illustrated in the 2D case on Figure 12.27. If every cell can store the AABBs that it overlaps

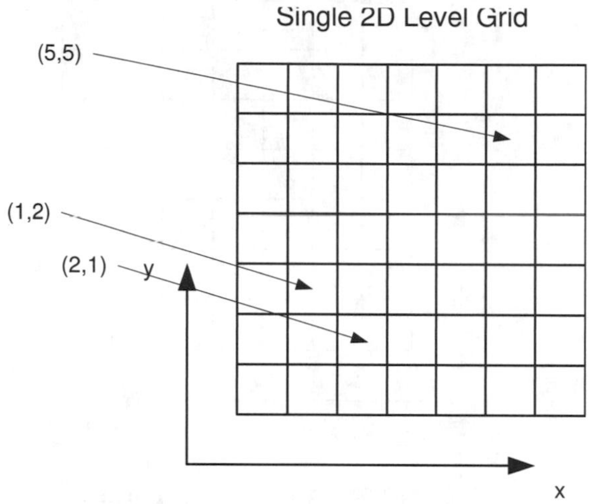

Figure 12.26: Example of triplets in 2D.

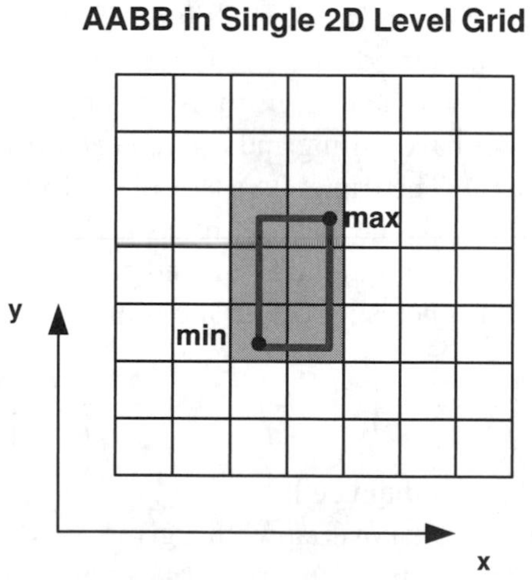

Figure 12.27: Triplets spanned by AABB.

```
algorithm store(b: AABB)
  for each c where τ(p_min, ρ) ≤ c ≤ τ(p_max, ρ) do
    for each b' ∈ c do
      counter(b,b') = counter(b,b') +1
      if counter(b,b')=1 then
        report overlap(b,b')
    next b'
    add b to c
  next c
end algorithm
```

Figure 12.28: Pseudocode for storing AABB in single-level grid.

with, then we have a data structure we can use for broad-phase collision detection. All we need is a table of counters, where each counter remembers the number of cells where two AABBs, i and j, both were mapped to.

If the counter has value zero, then no cell exists where both i and j were mapped to. If a counter has value one, then there exists exactly one cell, where both i and j have been mapped to. If the counter has value two, then there exists two different cells, and so on.

In the Exhaustive Search and Sweep and Prune algorithms we required the actual AABBs to overlap; this is not necessary for gridding algorithms. Sometimes a gridding algorithm reports AABBs as being overlapping, if there exists at least one cell in the tiling where they both are mapped to. In this case, overlapping means that the approximate geometry (i.e., the AABBs) of the objects lie sufficiently close. Of course one could extend such a gridding algorithm with an extra test, which examines for overlap with approximate geometry. Therefore, in the remainder of this section we say overlapping whenever we mean that there exists a cell where two AABBs are both mapped to.

This indicates a way to report AABBs lying sufficiently close to each other: when an AABB is mapped into the tiling, the counters between the newly added AABB and those already stored in a cell is incremented by one. If during this operation we encounter a counter that is incremented to the value one, then it is the first time this overlap between the two AABBs is seen. The pseudocode for storing an AABB in the grid is shown in Figure 12.28.

The next time the single-level gridding algorithm is invoked we must start by clearing the tiling, which may be done by removing AABB in a similar way to how they were added. The difference is that this time the counters are decremented, and when they reach a value of zero any reported overlap is removed. The pseudocode for the removal operation is shown in Figure 12.29.

With the remove and store operations, we are now capable of using the tiling for doing broad-phase collision detection, simply by iterating over all AABBs. For each AABB, we first remove it from the tiling using its position from the last invocation. Then we update the position of the AABB for the current invocation before finally storing the AABB in the tiling. The pseudocode for the algorithm is shown in Figure 12.30. Notice that we need to know both the old and new position of the AABBs.

It is possible to apply some optimization to the gridding algorithm just described. Clearly a lot of remapping is performed by the repeated removal and addition of an AABB. If we have high coherence, it

```
algorithm remove(b : AABB)
  for each c where τ(p_min, ρ) ≤ c ≤ τ(p_max, ρ) do
    remove b from c
    for each b' ∈ c do
      counter(b,b') = counter(b,b') - 1
      if counter(b,b')=0 then
        remove reported overlapb,b')
    next b'
  next c
end algorithm
```

Figure 12.29: Pseudocode for removing AABB from a single-level grid.

```
algorithm single-level(B : Bodies)
  for each b ∈ B do
    remove(AABB(b))
    compute new position of b
    store(AABB(b))
  next b
end algorithm
```

Figure 12.30: Single-level gridding algorithm for broad-phase collision detection.

is very likely that an AABB is remapped to the same cells in the tiling, and unnecessary computations are thus taking place. We can remedy this by exploiting cached information from the previous invocation of the gridding algorithm. If we cache the location of the minimum and maximum points of the AABB from the previous invocation, then we can perform a test in the current invocation to see whether the current positions of the minimum and maximum points of the AABB maps to the same triplets as in the previous invocation. We only need to remap an AABB if the minimum and maximum points map to different triples than they did in the previous invocation.

The simple gridding algorithm we have outlined so far, is not without problems. If ρ is too big, then the algorithm is no better than Exhaustive Search, since every AABB will be mapped to the same triplet. If ρ is too small, then we will spend a lot of time on mapping AABBs into the tiling. To avoid this we would like the cells to be of the same size as the AABBs of the objects. However, the size of the objects can vary greatly, so it is impossible to decide a good value of ρ that would work for all objects. In conclusion, the single-level gridding algorithm is a good choice when all objects are of similar size.

For objects varying greatly in size we can use multiple levels in the gridding algorithm. Assume that we have multiple tilings, for instance, m different tilings, each with its own resolution, and assume that the i'th tiling has the resolution denoted by ρ_i. Furthermore, assume that all the tilings can be sorted according to their resolutions, such that

$$0 < \rho_m < \rho_{m-1} < \rho_{m-1} < \cdots < \rho_2 < \rho_1. \tag{12.13}$$

We define the size of an AABB, B to mean

$$\text{size}(B) = \max\left(\boldsymbol{r}_{max_x} - \boldsymbol{r}_{min_x}, \boldsymbol{r}_{max_y} - \boldsymbol{r}_{min_y}, \boldsymbol{r}_{max_z} - \boldsymbol{r}_{min_z}\right). \tag{12.14}$$

We would like to have some means to describe how well B fits into a given tiling, say the j'th tiling. In order to do so we will introduce two constants α and β as lower and upper bound of the fitness. We require that there exist a resolution ρ_j, such that

$$\alpha \leq \frac{\text{size}(B)}{\rho_j} \leq \beta \quad \text{and} \quad 0 < \alpha < 1 \leq \beta, \tag{12.15}$$

is fulfilled. By picking specific values for α and β, we can control our sense of fitness. If $\alpha = 0.5$ and $\beta = 1.0$ in (12.15), then it means that B must have a length that is from 0.5 to 1.0 times the width of the cells at resolution ρ_j.

Naturally, not all our resolutions will fulfill this constraint for a given AABB, and there might even be more than one resolution fulfilling the constraint. In order to define a unique best-fitting resolution for a given AABB, we pick the largest resolution fulfilling the constraint. That is, for B we have

$$\text{res}(B) = \max\left(\rho_k \quad \middle| \quad \alpha \leq \frac{\text{size}(B)}{\rho_k} \leq \beta\right), \tag{12.16}$$

which is the maximum value of ρ fulfilling the constraint. The largest resolution is picked such that if B was mapped into the corresponding tiling, then we will map B to fewer cells than if we had picked a smaller resolution fulfilling the constraint. The semantics can be quite confusing, however, we adopt the convention that

- Higher resolution (larger value of j in ρ_j) means smaller cell size (i.e. smaller ρ value)
- Lower resolution (smaller value of j in ρ_j) means larger cell size (i.e. larger ρ value)

Figure 12.31 shows a 1D example of the definitions introduced so far. In the example, tilings of different resolutions are drawn on top of each other. The thick lines indicate the ρ-values of the tilings. When we work with multiple levels, we will store (and remove) an AABB in all levels with a resolution that is lower (having larger ρ-value) than or equal to the resolution of the AABB itself. Figure 12.32 illustrates how an AABB, A, is mapped into the 1D multilevel tiling shown in Figure 12.31. The filled box indicates the resolution of A, and as can be seen, A has the resolution of the tiling with a cell size similar to the size of A.

The reporting of overlaps is handled a little differently from the case of the single-level algorithm introduced previously: the counter between two AABBs, i and j, is only updated at resolution k if

$$\rho_k = \max \text{res}(b_i), \text{res}(b_j). \tag{12.17}$$

This condition essentially masks out the tiling having the best resolution for detecting an overlap between i and j. The condition should be obvious, since we cannot use a minimum resolution value because only one of the AABBs is mapped at this level. The maximum resolution value is the first level, where both

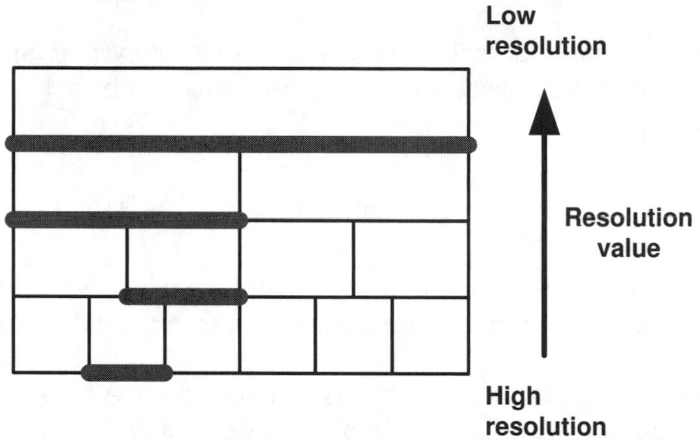

Figure 12.31: 1D multilevel gridding, showing correspondence between resolution definitions.

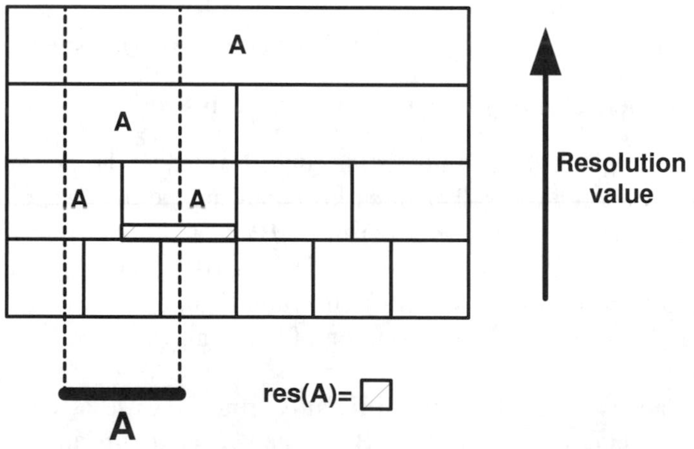

Figure 12.32: 1D multilevel gridding, showing the mapping of an AABB

AABBs are mapped into, and therefore the level with the best resolution for detecting overlap between the two AABBs.

Figure 12.33(a) shows an example where two AABBs, A and B, are mapped into the multilevel grid. In Figure 12.33(b) is another AABB, C, about to be mapped into the tilings. We leave it to the reader as an exercise to determine the proper counter values. The pseudocode for the multilevel gridding algorithm is shown in Figure 12.34, the multilevel store operation is shown in Figure 12.35, and the multilevel remove operation is shown in Figure 12.36. The time complexity for updating the multilevel gridding algorithm is linear, $\mathcal{O}(n)$, since the number of levels are limited and the α-β constraint equation gives an upper limit on the number of cells that overlap an AABB, such that it takes constant time to store or remove an AABB from the multilevel grid. Since we have n AABBs, it must take linear time to update the multilevel grid. However, the total time complexity depends on the maximum number of AABBs mapped into a single cell. If we denote this number by m, then the time complexity of the entire algorithm is $\mathcal{O}(n + m^2)$. In practice, the number of tilings and their resolutions, together with the α and β constants are chosen such that $m^2 \lll n$, and such that the quadratic term can be ignored.

There are some additional benefits of using multilevel gridding. The time complexity is independent on the configuration. We saw in the case of Sweep and Prune, that for some configurations, one could expect the worst-case quadratic time complexity. The multilevel gridding algorithm does not suffer from this weakness. Another advantage is that coherence does not change the time complexity, it only reduces the workload, while Sweep and Prune was highly dependent on high coherence in order to perform well.

There are drawbacks, however, of this algorithm as well: in order for multilevel gridding to be efficient in practice, one needs a good hash table implementation, which is not as common as list and tree data structures. The worst drawback is that the algorithm may require a huge memory usage, in particular if parameters are chosen poorly. In comparison, Exhaustive Search does not use any memory at all, and the Sweep and Prune algorithm only needs the counter table, which in worst-case is $\mathcal{O}(n^2)$, but in practice, often is $\mathcal{O}(n)$, and the interval endpoint lists, which is $\mathcal{O}(n)$. The multilevel gridding algorithm also needs a counter table as Sweep and Prune, however the multiple tilings can consume quite a lot of memory: letting d be the dimension, m the number of levels, and ρ the maximum resolution value, then the memory consumption of this spatial subdivision scale in the worst-case is $\mathcal{O}(\frac{md}{\rho})$. In our experience, multilevel gridding is competitive with Sweep and Prune for medium-sized configurations, as the memory usage grows large for the multilevel gridding algorithm page swapping degrades performance and Sweep and Prune becomes superior.

12.5 Using the Kinematics Principle

In the three broad-phase collision detection algorithms we have presented, we have used the approximation principle and the coherence and locality principles, but none of the algorithms have exploited the kinematics principle. In this section we will present some ideas for how this last principle can be put to use.

Sweeping volumes [Mirtich, 1996] is one way of incorporating knowledge about the future. These come in many different variations, but they all share the same properties:

- They are volumes in 3D space.

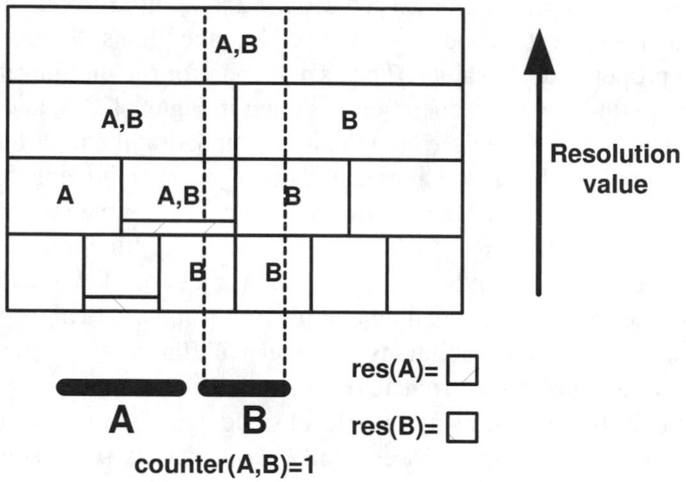

(a) box A and B are mapped

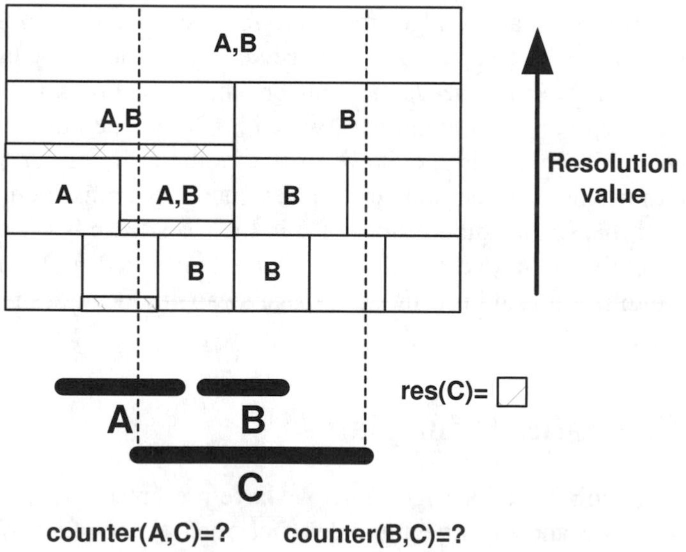

(b) Box C is mapped

Figure 12.33: Updating of counter value in a multilevel grid algorithm.

```
algorithm multilevel(B : Bodies)
  for each b ∈ B do
    ρ = res(AABB(b))
    for each tiling t where res(t) ≤ ρ do
      remove(AABB(b), t)
    next t
    compute new position of b
    for each tiling t where res(t) ≤ ρ do
      store(AABB(b))
    next t
  next b
end algorithm
```

Figure 12.34: The multilevel gridding algorithm.

```
algorithm store(b : AABB, T : Tiling)
  for each c ∈ C where τ(p_min, ρ_T) ≤ c ≤ τ(p_max, ρ_T) do
    for each b' ∈ c do
      if ρ_T = max(res(b), res(b')) then
        counter(b, b') = counter(b, b') +1
        if counter(b, b')=1 then
          report overlapb, b')
      end if
    next b'
    add b to c
  next c
end algorithm
```

Figure 12.35: The multilevel gridding store operation.

```
algorithm remove(b : AABB, T : Tiling)
  for each c ∈ C where τ(p_min, ρ_T) ≤ c ≤ τ(p_max, ρ_T) do
    remove b from c
    for each B' ∈ c do
      if ρ_T = max(res(b), res(b')) then
        counter(b, b') = counter(b, b') - 1
        if counter(b, b')=0 then
          remove reported overlapb, b')
      end if
    next b'
  next c
end algorithm
```

Figure 12.36: The multilevel gridding remove operation.

- They represent the space an object travels through in a given time duration $t - t_{cur}$.
- They are often not tight, meaning they cover more space than the objects travel through; however, they are always an upper bound.

Here we will derive a sweeping volume, which is an AABB, but our idea is not specific for AABBs and could be applied to other volume types as well. From kinematics, we know something about the trajectory of an object:

$$\boldsymbol{a}_{cm} = \frac{d\boldsymbol{v}_{cm}}{dt} = \frac{d^2\boldsymbol{r}_{cm}}{dt^2}. \tag{12.18}$$

In order to find a formula for the trajectory of an object, we will try to integrate the acceleration to find $\boldsymbol{r}_{cm}$ as a function of time. If we assume that the acceleration is constant in the near future, then

$$\frac{d^2\boldsymbol{r}_{cm}}{dt^2} = \boldsymbol{a}_{cm}, \tag{12.19a}$$

$$\int_{t_{cur}}^{t} \frac{d^2\boldsymbol{r}_{cm}}{dt^2} dt = \int_{t_{cur}}^{t} \boldsymbol{a}_{cm} dt, \tag{12.19b}$$

$$\frac{d\boldsymbol{r}_{cm}}{dt} = \boldsymbol{v}_{cm} + \boldsymbol{a}_{cm} t. \tag{12.19c}$$

Integrating once more, w.r.t. time yields

$$\int_{t_{cur}}^{t} \frac{d\boldsymbol{r}_{cm}}{dt} dt = \int_{t_{cur}}^{t} (\boldsymbol{v}_{cm} + \boldsymbol{a}_{cm} t)\, dt, \tag{12.20a}$$

$$\boldsymbol{r}_{cm}(t) = \boldsymbol{r}_{cm} + \boldsymbol{v}_{cm} t + \frac{1}{2}\boldsymbol{a}_{cm} t^2. \tag{12.20b}$$

We thus have a function describing how the center of mass moves in the near future assuming that it moves with constant acceleration. In the limit of very small time steps ($t \to t_{\text{cur}}$), this is a fair assumption, and the trajectory computed will be a close approximation to the true trajectory of the object. Convergence theory indicates that the approximation will be better and better the smaller time-steps we use. In the theoretical limit the approximation will be exact. Therefore, the basic idea is to find the extreme points of the trajectory along the coordinate axes of WCS and then place an AABB enclosing the object at these extreme points. This is done by first placing smaller AABBs around each of the extreme positions enclosing the object at these positions. Afterward, one large AABB is found enclosing all the smaller ones. This final large AABB is computed as the sweeping volume of the object. This seems straightforward; we only need to figure out:

- How do we find the extreme points?
- How do we find an enclosing AABB of a set of smaller AABBs?

We observe that the trajectory is described by a second-order polynomial, so its curve is a parabola. If we assume that gravity is the only force acting on the object, then $\boldsymbol{a}_{cm}$ is pointing downward (i.e., $[0, -1, 0]^T$).

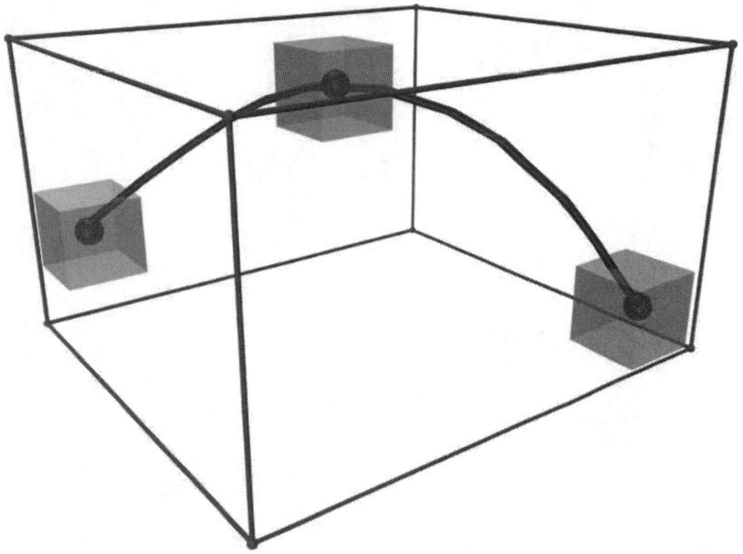

Figure 12.37: An AABB sweeping volume example. Sweeping volume is computed as the AABB covering the AABBs of object in initial, top, and final position.

The extreme points will then be the starting and ending point of the parabola and the top point. The large enclosing AABB is found by taking the minimum and maximum coordinates of all the smaller AABBs. The construction algorithm is shown in Figure 12.37.

Space-time bounds [Cameron, 1990] also describe how an object moves in the near future, but they are very different from sweeping volumes. They represent the time dimension, hence for a 2D object the space-time bound will be a 3D volume, and for a 3D object the space-time bound will be a 4D volume. We usually work in 3D and thinking of 4D volumes might be a little difficult, but the benefits are

- Even though sweeping volumes intersect, the space-time bounds might not.
- With space-time bounds we can find the exact time of the intersection.

In conclusion, the extra dimension give us more detail of the movement.

13

Introduction to Narrow-Phase Collision Detection

There is a large number of *narrow-phase collision detection* algorithms, far too many to fit into a single chapter in this book. Therefore, this short chapter serves as a brief introduction to concepts and goals in narrow-phase collision detection, which we need to know before talking about contact determination in Chapter 14. Later, in Chapter 15, Chapter 16, and Chapter 17 we will treat different groups of narrow-phase collision detection algorithms in depth.

Broad-phase collision detection lists pairs of potential colliding objects, and the narrow-phase collision detection examines each of these pairs in detail. For each pair of objects, the narrow-phase collision detection determines whether the objects are separated, touching, or penetrating. Most existing algorithms for narrow-phase collision detection are capable of returning much more detailed information, such as:

- separation distance
- penetration depth
- separation axis
- closest points
- closest features

The choice of the right narrow-phase collision detection algorithm depends on the later stages in the *animation pipeline*; some examples are:

- closest points can be used in contact determination
- separation distance/axis may be needed for the computation of *Time of Impact* (*TOI*)
- penetration depth is required for calculating *contact forces* and *backtracking*

There is a wealth of literature on narrow-phase collision detection algorithms, and many different approaches have been investigated. Spatial subdivision algorithms, like Binary Space-Partitioning (BSP) tree [Melax, 2001], octree [Tzafestas et al., 1996, Ganovelli et al., 2000, Erleben et al., 2003b], k-d trees, and grids [Ganovelli et al., 2000, Erleben et al., 2003b]; feature-based algorithms, like polygonal intersection [Moore et al., 1988], Lin-Canny [Ponamgi et al., 1997], V-Clip [Mirtich, 1998b], and SWIFT [Ehmann et al., 2001]; recursive search methods, like [Sundaraj et al., 2000] and simplex-based, like GJK [Gilbert et al., 1988, Bergen, 2001]. Lately, volume-based methods, such as generalized Voronoi diagrams [Hoff, III et al., 1999] and signed distance maps [Guendelman et al., 2003, Bridson et al., 2003,

Hirota, 2002] have become popular. Finally, there are algorithms based on bounding volume hierarchies. It is beyond the scope of this chapter to explain all of these algorithms; we refer the reader to Chapter 15, Chapter 16, and Chapter 17 for more details.

Narrow-phase collision detection algorithms are naturally divided into four main groups:

- *Spatial Data Structures* such as spatial subdivisions and bounding volume hierarchies
- feature-based
- simplex-based
- volume-based

In the *spatial subdivisions*, we approach the problem of collision detection by building a data structure containing the geometry. The data structure is built by subdividing the object into pieces, for instance, by clipping the object recursively by planes. Bounding volume hierarchies are very similar to this, but while spatial subdivisions do not respect the underlying features of the geometry, bounding volume hierarchies do. As an example, a subdivision algorithm might clip a face in a polygonal mesh into two pieces, each stored in different locations of the data structure, while a bounding volume hierarchy never does this. It will treat each face as an unsplitable atomic entity. More detail is found in Chapter 15.

A *feature-based algorithm* works directly on the features of an object. For polygonal meshes, the features are the vertices, edges, and faces. A simple feature-based approach would clip every face of one mesh against all the faces of the other mesh and vice versa. If the clipped result ends up being empty, then no penetration of the objects has occurred, but if the result is not empty, then there will be a penetrating volume of the objects. Feature-based algorithms are discussed in detail in Chapter 16.

A *simplex-based algorithm* is based on a simplex, which is the convex hull of an affinely independent set of points. We will not go into further details here, but instead, we refer the reader to [Gilbert et al., 1988, Cameron, 1997, Bergen, 1999, Bergen, 2001, Bergen, 2003b]. Simplex-based algorithms often work by incrementally improving upon a simplex, which approximates the configuration space of the objects. The subject has a mathematical nature, which tends to discourage some people.

Volume-based algorithms have a volumetric view of the objects. An example could be the sampling of the signed distance function of an object onto a 3D rectilinear grid. In such a case, the closest points and separation distances from a given location from the object can be found by looking up values and gradients in the signed distance grid. These kind of algorithms are rather new compared to the spatial data structures, feature-based, and simplex-based algorithms. Volume-based algorithms will be discussed in Chapter 17.

The major challenges for narrow-phase collision detection are deforming geometry, self-intersections, and penetration depths. For deforming geometry, the spatial data structures need to be updated in every invocation of the narrow-phase collision detection algorithm, which is time consuming. Simplex- and feature-based algorithms usually assume objects are convex, which might not hold after a deformation. Volume-based methods pose some of the same problems for deforming geometry as the spatial data structures, e.g., a deformation would require an update of the signed distance map. *Self-intersections* are unpleasant by nature, which is seen by an example: for a polygonal mesh, every face is touching its neighboring faces, indicating a collision, but not a self-intersection. Search and traversal methods pose difficulties in effectively pruning away unnecessary tests. Existing algorithms for calculating penetration depths are extremely slow.

In summary, narrow-phase collision detection algorithms solve the problem of determining whether two objects intersect (*intersection query*) or how far apart they are (*proximity query*). Narrow-phase collision detection algorithms often need to be superseded by a *contact determination* algorithm, which is the subject of the next chapter.

14

Contact Determination

The task of computing regions of contact from the output of the narrow-phase collision detection algorithm is called *contact determination*, and it is a pure geometrical problem. Before we can present algorithms for contact determination, it is important to define what we mean by a region of contact and how it should be represented.

The reader should be familiar with concepts and goals of narrow-phase collision detection as described in Chapter 13. Detailed knowledge of specific narrow-phase collision detection algorithms is not required for reading this chapter.

14.1 Contact Regions, Normals, and Planes

A touching point between the surfaces of two objects is called a *contact point*. In practice however, this is not always a suitable representation. Quite often a simulation method needs information about the neighborhood of a touching point, i.e., the shape. At the point of contact of two smooth surfaces, the surfaces will have coinciding tangent planes, and these tangent planes serve as a good linear approximation to the two surfaces at the point of contact. We call such a tangent plane the *plane of contact*, and its normal the *contact normal*.

In a computer world, we work with polygonal objects and we cannot always take the *myopic view* of the real world. Polygonal objects are inherently discontinuous over the edges and vertices. Therefore, a slightly different approach is often used to represent the neighborhood information for contact points between polygonal objects. The contact point is represented by two features, one from each polyhedra, and the point of contact is usually computed as the closest point between the two features. Such a representation is called a *Principal Contact* (*PC*). For polyhedron objects we have three different kinds of features: a vertex, V, an edge, E, and a face, F. Due to symmetry, we only have six different types of principal contacts: (V, V), (V, E), (V, F), (E, E), (E, F), and (F, F). Figure 14.1 illustrates the six different principal contacts. Observe that the closest point is not uniquely defined in all cases, and that some types of principal contacts represent entire continuous regions of infinitely many contact points. These problems will be deferred for later treatment in this section.

Since objects are represented by features; it seems natural to use them for representing contact points. It is quite easy to deduce information about the shape of the surface in a neighborhood of a single touching point. For instance, in the case of an (F, V) contact, the contact plane is obviously picked unambiguously as the plane of the face. Finally, it is easier to recognize the same contact point evolving over time (i.e., a temporal touching point) based on a pair of features rather than a 3D world location, because the features will temporarily be the same pair by coherence, whereas the 3D world location could change substantially.

The finite precision of floating point representation introduces some problems in connection to touching contacts: intuitively we define a touching contact as the point between two objects where the distance is exactly zero. However, numerical imprecision will make such a distance slightly nonzero, typically in

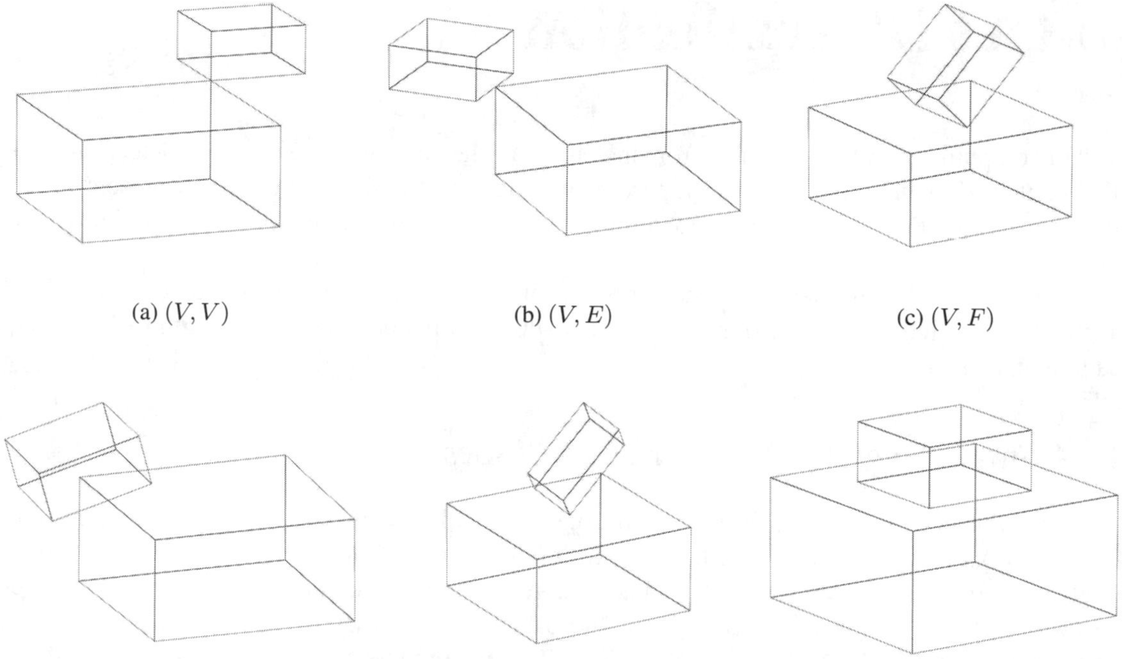

(a) (V,V) (b) (V,E) (c) (V,F)

(d) (E,E) (e) (E,F) (f) (F,F)

Figure 14.1: The six different principal contact types.

the range of 10^{-7}–10^{-15}, depending on the precision of computation. To help reduce such problems, we introduce a *collision envelope*

around each object, as illustrated in Figure 14.2. The collision envelope works as a slightly soft enlargement of the objects, defining a field around the object where it can consider touching contact with other objects. That is, whenever the distance between the closest points of a feature pair is less than the collision envelope, then the corresponding contact point is said to be a touching contact. The closest points between a feature pair using a collision envelope might no longer be exactly the same for a touching contact. To remedy, the point of contact, $\boldsymbol{p}$, is usually computed as the mean of the closest points of the two features, $\boldsymbol{p}_A$ and $\boldsymbol{p}_B$

$$\boldsymbol{p} = \frac{\boldsymbol{p}_A + \boldsymbol{p}_B}{2}. \tag{14.1}$$

Thus, given two features, one from object A and one from object B, we need to be able to compute the closest points between the features. In case of a (V,V) contact type, the closest points are simply given by the vertex positions. In the case of an (E,V) contact type, we can project the position $\boldsymbol{v}$ of the vertex V onto the edge E running from position $\boldsymbol{o}$ to position $\boldsymbol{d}$ and having direction $\boldsymbol{u}$

$$\boldsymbol{p}_E = \boldsymbol{o} + ((\boldsymbol{v} - \boldsymbol{o}) \cdot \boldsymbol{u})\, \boldsymbol{u}, \tag{14.2}$$

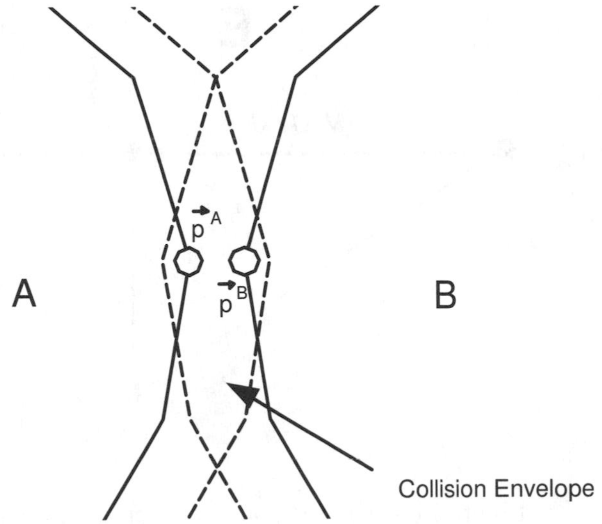

Figure 14.2: The collision envelope.

where $\boldsymbol{u} = \boldsymbol{d} - \boldsymbol{o}$. If the projection lies between the two positions $\boldsymbol{o}$ and $\boldsymbol{d}$, then the projection indicates the closest point on the edge. If the projection lies outside the endpoints of the edge, then the closest endpoint to the projection is taken to be the closest point. Figure 14.3 illustrates the (E, V) contact type. In case of a (V, F) contact type, we project the position, $\boldsymbol{v}$, of the vertex V onto the face plane of the face F, represented by a face normal, $\boldsymbol{n}$, and an arbitrary point, $\boldsymbol{f}$, on the face,

$$\boldsymbol{p}_F = \boldsymbol{v} - ((\boldsymbol{v} - \boldsymbol{f}) \cdot \boldsymbol{n})\, \boldsymbol{n}. \tag{14.3}$$

This is illustrated in Figure 14.4. If the projected vertex lies inside the face boundary, then its position gives the closest point on the face. If it lies outside, we can repeat the (V, E) case for each boundary edge of the face in order to find the closest edge and the closest point on this edge.

The case of an (E_1, E_2) contact type is a little more difficult. Assume that the closest points, $\boldsymbol{p}_{E_1}$ and $\boldsymbol{p}_{E_2}$, between the two edges are given. Then

$$\boldsymbol{p}_{E_1} = \boldsymbol{o}_1 + \left((\boldsymbol{p}_{E_2} - \boldsymbol{o}_1) \cdot \boldsymbol{u}_1\right) \boldsymbol{u}_1, \tag{14.4}$$

and

$$\boldsymbol{p}_{E_2} = \boldsymbol{o}_2 + \left((\boldsymbol{p}_{E_1} - \boldsymbol{o}_2) \cdot \boldsymbol{u}_2\right) \boldsymbol{u}_2. \tag{14.5}$$

Inserting equation (14.5) into equation (14.4) yields

$$\boldsymbol{p}_{E_1} = \boldsymbol{o}_1 + \left(\left(\boldsymbol{o}_2 + \left((\boldsymbol{p}_{E_1} - \boldsymbol{o}_2) \cdot \boldsymbol{u}_2\right) \boldsymbol{u}_2 - \boldsymbol{o}_1\right) \cdot \boldsymbol{u}_1\right) \boldsymbol{u}_1. \tag{14.6}$$

Isolating $\boldsymbol{P}_{E_1}$ results in

$$\boldsymbol{p}_{E_1} = \boldsymbol{o}_1 + \left(\frac{(\boldsymbol{o}_2 - \boldsymbol{o}_1) \cdot (\boldsymbol{u}_1 - k\boldsymbol{u}_2)}{1 - k^2}\right) \boldsymbol{u}_1, \tag{14.7}$$

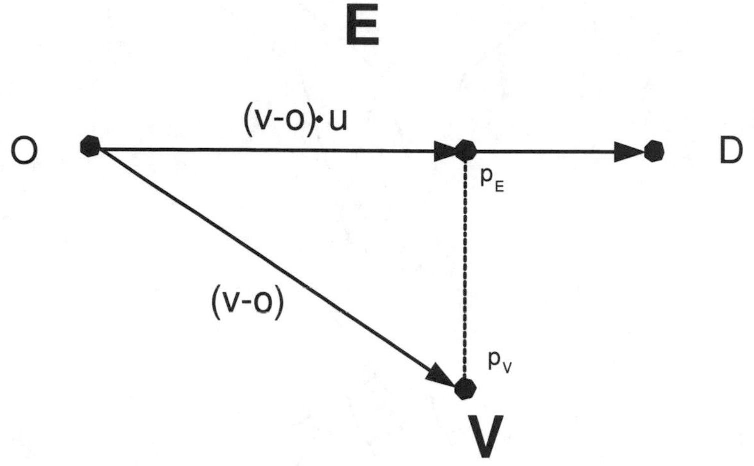

Figure 14.3: Closest point between vertex and edge.

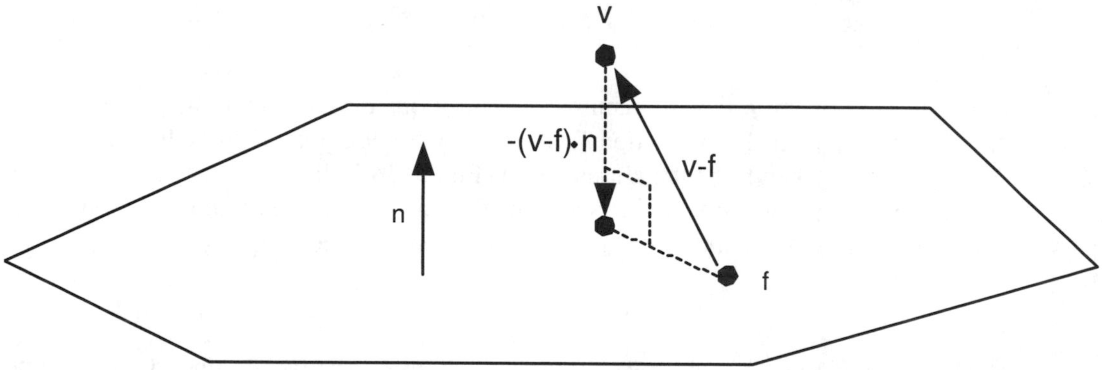

Figure 14.4: Projection of a vertex onto a face.

where $k = \boldsymbol{u}_1 \cdot \boldsymbol{u}_2$. Finally, we can find $\boldsymbol{p}_{E_2}$ by applying the (E, V) case. The two remaining cases of the (E, F) contact type and the (F, F) contact type can be handled by decomposing them into a set of the cases we already know how to handle. If the edge E runs between vertices O and D and the boundary edges of F is given by $\{(E, E_1), (E, E_2), \ldots\}$, then we can decompose the case (E, F) as follows:

$$(E, F) \rightarrow \{(O, F), (D, F), (E, E_1), (E, E_2), \ldots\} \tag{14.8}$$

If the boundary of the face F_1 is defined by the edges $\{E_0^1, E_1^1, E_2^1, \ldots\}$ and the boundary of face F_2 by $\{E_0^2, E_1^2, E_2^2, \ldots\}$, then we can decompose (F_1, F_2) into

$$(F_1, F_2) \rightarrow \{(E_0^1, F_2), (E_1^1, F_2), \ldots, (F_1, E_0^2), (F_1, E_1^2), \ldots\}. \tag{14.9}$$

Actually, from this we can deduce that all contact points can be represented by three cases: (V, E), (E, E), and (V, F), which is the smallest set of principal contact types we can use to represent contact points. The

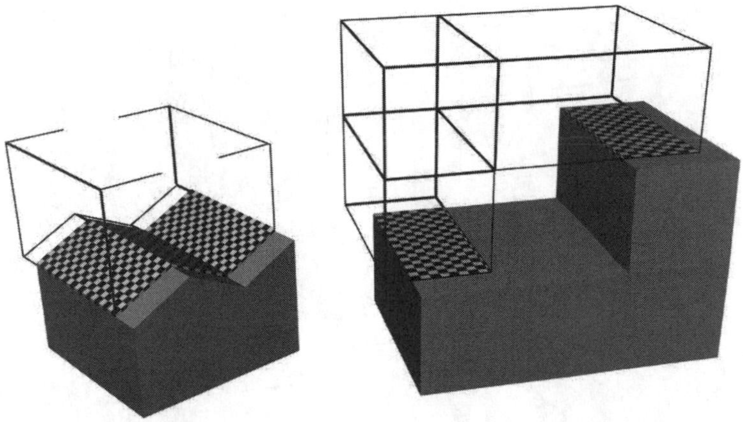

Figure 14.5: Contact regions of polyhedra objects.

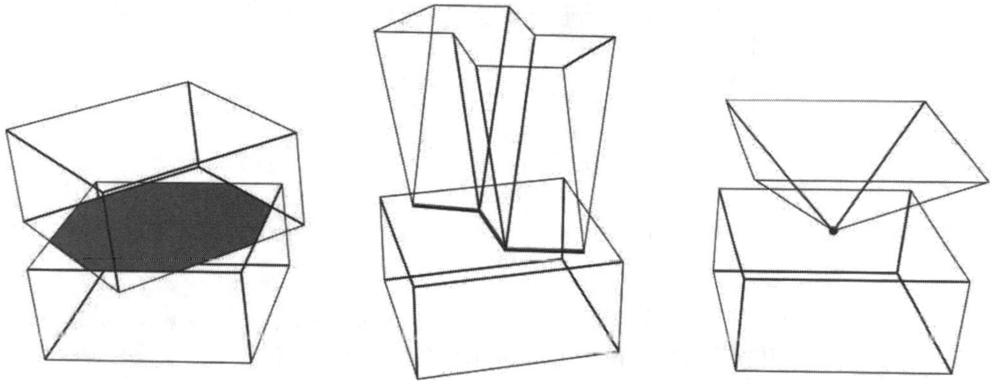

Figure 14.6: Examples of contact geometry between polyhedral objects.

observant reader will have noticed that the (V, V) case is not included. This is because the contact point could equally be represented by an (V, E) case. We will later elaborate on this redundancy in contact point representation.

We define the *contact region* as the intersection of the two objects. Figure 14.5 shows two polyhedra examples. Notice we can have multiple regions between two objects and regions are not necessarily planar. For polyhedra objects, the contact region is a polygonal area, which consist of:

- single points
- line segments
- or closed polygons (perhaps with holes)

Figure 14.6 shows three examples of contact geometry between polyhedral objects. For convex polyhedra, the contact regions is particularly simple. It is either a single point, a single line segment, or a closed planar

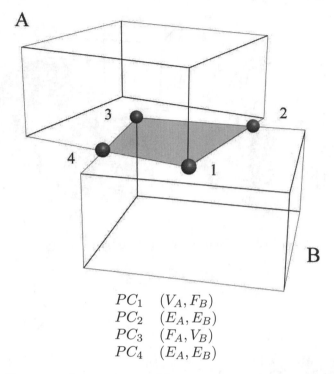

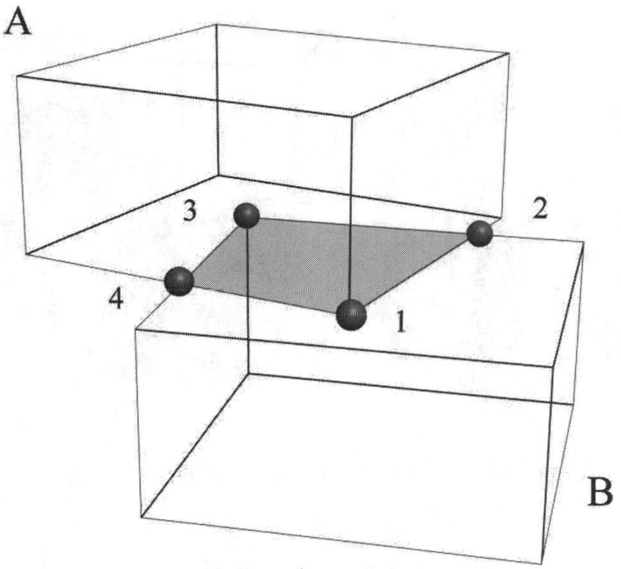

$$\begin{array}{ll} PC_1 & (V_A, F_B) \\ PC_2 & (E_A, E_B) \\ PC_3 & (F_A, V_B) \\ PC_4 & (E_A, E_B) \end{array}$$

Figure 14.7: Contact region represented by polygonal vertices of the intersection.

convex polygon without holes. This indicates that we can represent contact regions by the vertices of the polygonal regions. It is easy to determine principal contacts for representing these polygonal vertices. The set of principal contacts used for representing the polygonal vertices is called a *contact formation* (*CF*). Figure 14.7 illustrates the idea. In the figure, the CF consists of the principal contacts PC_1, PC_2, PC_3, and PC_4.

The usage of contact formations is much more general and can be used even in the case of penetration, as Figure 14.8 illustrates. In the figure, the CF could consist of the principal contacts,

$$\begin{array}{ll} PC_1 & (E_A, F_B), \\ PC_2 & (E_A, F_B), \\ PC_3 & (E_A, F_B), \\ PC_4 & (E_A, F_B). \end{array}$$

It is apparent that the definition of a contact formation gives a valuable tool for representing contact regions, but unfortunately the representation of a CF is not unique. Figure 14.9 shows an example where a single (V, F) or four (E, F) contact points representing the same contact region.

When objects touch in real life, the contact normals are parallel to surface normals at the point of contact, but this is not true for polyhedra objects as Figure 14.10 shows. Two methods for computing contact normals can be used. We may pick the normal of the feature with the highest dimension, and in case both features have the same dimension, we make a random pick. Alternatively, we can compute

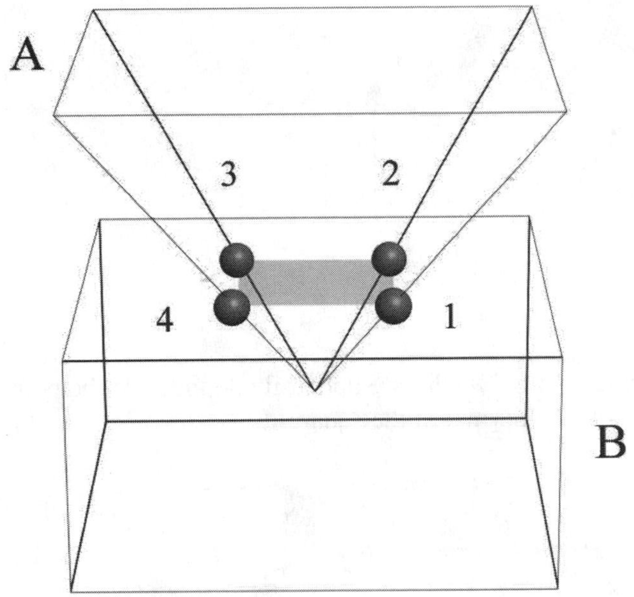

Figure 14.8: A penetrating contact formation.

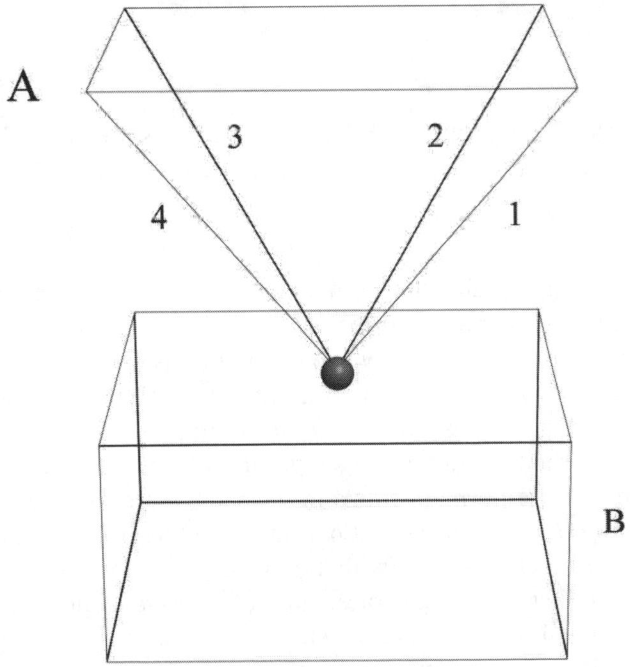

Figure 14.9: Nonunique contact formation.

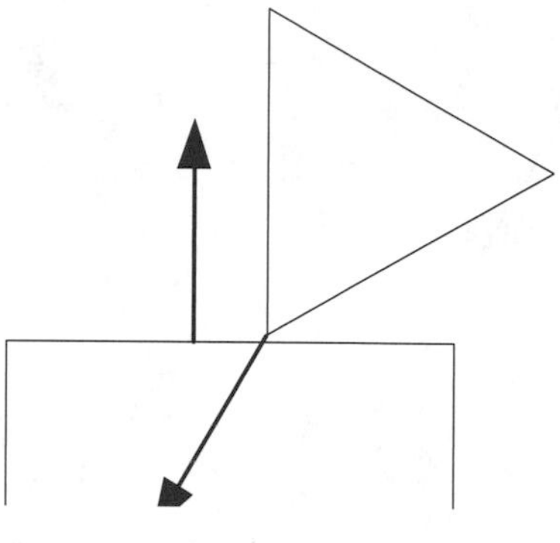

Figure 14.10: Contact normals for polyhedra are not easily defined. At the point of contact, the normal of the triangle is nonparallel with the normal of the square.

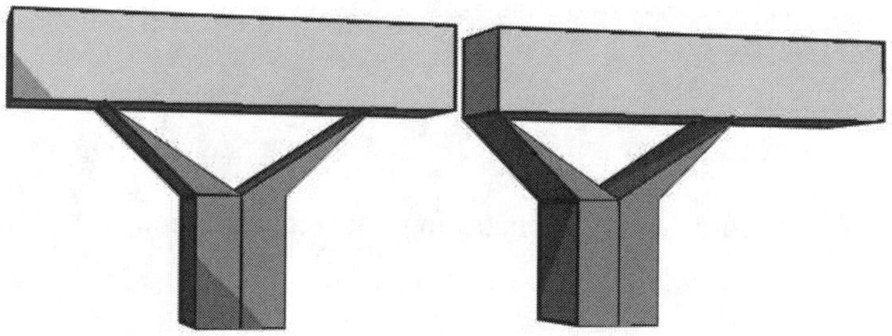

Figure 14.11: A discontinuous change of contact normal. A box slides from left to right, when the left lower corners of the box reach the tip of the Y-shape, normals are picked randomly from the (V, V) contacts.

the normal as a unit vector along the direction of the closest points between a pair of features. The first method suffers from discontinuity of contact normals, meaning that as a simulation proceeds, the direction of the contact normal can change abruptly even when the motion is smooth, as illustrated in Figure 14.11. In the figure, a box slides smoothly across a supporting object. In the first frame all normals are pointing downward (we have (F, V) contact types), but at the instant the box reaches the state shown in the last frame, the contact normals on the left side of the supporting object would be picked randomly from the (V, V) contact type. None of these normals points in the same direction as the face normals previously used. One remedy is to exploit caching of contact normals from previous frames to avoid abrupt changes of the normals. However, this solution comes with a bookkeeping cost. In practice, the problem is often ignored. The argument being that these types of contact often have a short lifespan so an end user will never notice the problem in a real-time simulation. The second method for computing the contact normal obviously breaks down in cases where the closest distance of the features is zero. In such cases, one often resorts to using the first method for computing contact normals.

Knowing the contact point, $\boldsymbol{p}$, and the contact normal, $\boldsymbol{n}$, of a touching contact, we can define a contact

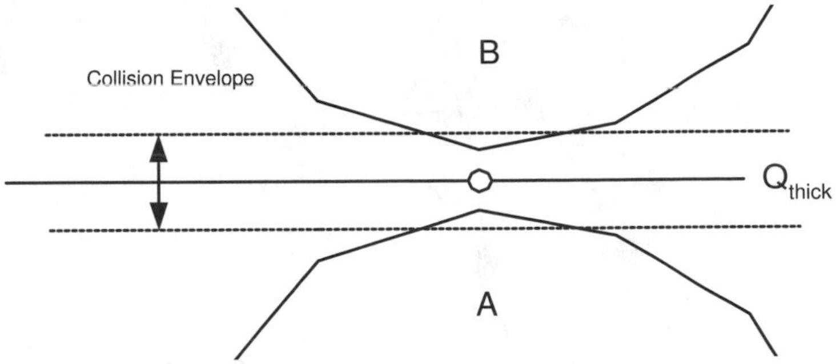

Figure 14.12: A thick contact plane.

plane as the set of all points, $\boldsymbol{x}$, that fulfills the equation of a plane

$$\{\boldsymbol{x} \quad | \quad (\boldsymbol{x} - \boldsymbol{p}) \cdot \boldsymbol{n} = 0\}\,. \tag{14.10}$$

Observe that for convex polyhedra, all touching contacts lie in the same plane, when no penetration occurs.

In this section we have given definitions of principal contacts and contact formations. We have discussed difficulties in computing contact points and contact normals; we have also treated the uniqueness problem of contact formations. In Section 14.2 and Section 14.3 we will present two different algorithms for computing the contact formation between two objects. The algorithms make use of the definitions and concept introduced so far.

14.2 A Geometrical Algorithm

Assume that we are given the two closest features and two convex polyhedra, for instance, by *V-Clip* (see Section 16.3) or *GJK*

[Gilbert et al., 1988, Cameron, 1997, Bergen, 1999, Bergen, 2001, Bergen, 2003b]. If they are within the collision envelope, then we have a touching contact between the convex polyhedra. We will now develop a simple algorithm to determine the CF. In the first step of the algorithm

- the two features will be the first principal contact in our CF
- the touching principal contact will be used to determine a contact plane Q

Since we are using a collision envelope, we will make Q a thick plane as shown in Figure 14.12. Because the objects are convex, we know that all other features, which might cause a touching contact, must lie within Q. So we start at the initial feature of object A and examine features in a breadth first traversal over the mesh of object A. When a feature is found lying inside the thick plane Q, it is added to the *impact zone*, $\boldsymbol{Z}_A$, of object A. The impact zone is thus the set of touching features. If a feature is encountered lying outside Q, then the neighbors are not considered for further traversal. That is, we start at the first feature and examine neighboring features recursively. If all points of a feature, X_A, are inside Q, then we

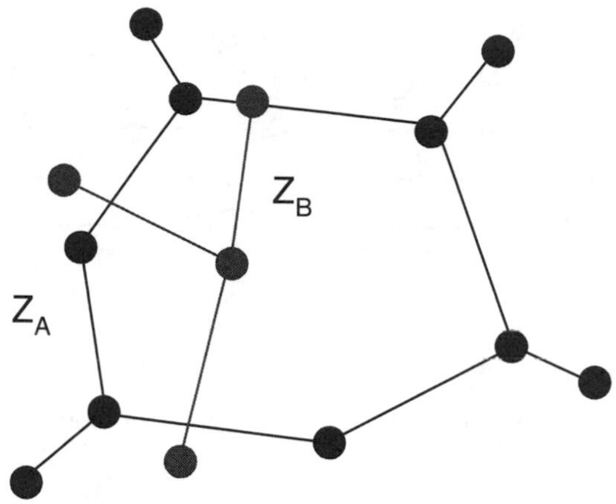

Figure 14.13: Projected impact zones for both objects.

add feature to impact zone, Z_A. Afterward, the same procedure is repeated for object B and we will have two sets of features, Z_A and Z_B.

If we project the impact zones Z_A and Z_B onto (the thin) Q, then we have reduced our problem of finding principal contacts to a two-dimensional problem. An example of how the projected impact zones could look like is shown in Figure 14.13. One way to think of these impact zones is as the print pattern of a wet soccer ball on the ground. The projected pattern corresponds to features; principal contacts can therefore be determined by examining how the two patterns intersect each other.

To examine the intersection of the patterns, we first test projected edges from Z_A for intersection against projected edges of Z_B, features that we considered to be open point sets. If an intersection is found, we add the corresponding pair of edge features as a contact point to the CF. Figure 14.14 illustrates the edge-edge case. Afterward, we test projected vertices from Z_A against projected faces of Z_B. If a vertex is found to lie inside the boundary of a face, then a corresponding (V, F) contact is added to the contact formation. Hereafter, the roles of A and B are interchanged as illustrated in Figure 14.16. Similarly, we test projected vertices against projected edges. Figure 14.17 illustrates this step for our example. In the final step, we test projected vertices against projected vertices. In the example, there is none of these kind of intersections. Looking at all the intersecting projected features we can build the contact formation for the touching convex objects.

The algorithm we have presented is fairly simple, and it is quite easy to implement. The concept of using the thickening plane is a great way to combat numerical imprecision, and it is our experience that it works well in practice. If objects become highly tessellated, then the algorithm will return many principal contacts in the CF lying inside the polygonal intersection. It is possible to add a further postprocessing step eliminating these principal contacts by computing the convex hull. The observant reader might argue that the algorithm is ineffective due to the pairwise testing of projected features, which would lead to an quadratic time complexity. However, the number of projected features is usually low, and the quadratic time complexity will therefore be insignificant compared to the time consumed by the narrow-phase collision detection algorithm. In case the number of projected features grows exceedingly large, a sweep line

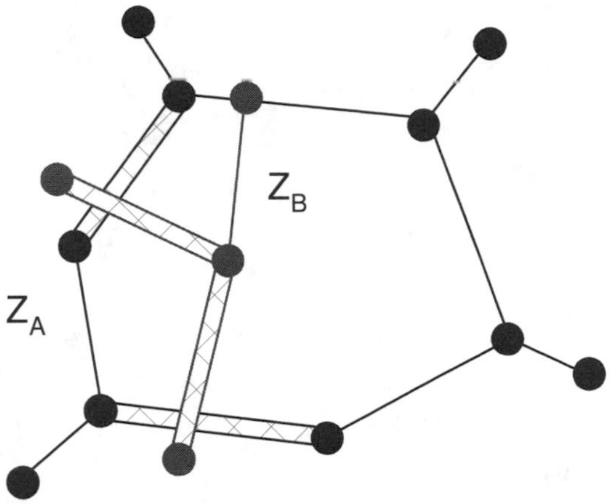

Figure 14.14: Edge intersections of the projected impact zones.

or spatial data structure approach could be used to reduce the quadratic time complexity.

14.3 A Contact Tracking Algorithm

Now we will look at an entirely different kind of contact determination algorithm, called *contact tracking* [Mirtich, 1998a]. The algorithm is applicable to arbitrary shaped polyhedra, but only usable if a retroactive detection is used, that is, a *backtracking time-control algorithm*. We will assume that the narrow-phase collision detection is capable of returning pairs of intersecting features as is the case for bounding volume hierarchies (BVHs) discussed in Chapter 15.

A backtracking algorithm means that the time control allows for penetrations to occur; when this happens, the simulator is rewound to a state where penetrations disappear. If a contact point is missing, then the simulation method will not be able to apply contact forces and/or contact impulses where they are needed. As a consequence, penetrations will occur at these points, when the simulation is run forward. This means that when we detect penetrating features, they actually represent a missing contact point. Therefore, we can add a penetrating pair of features to the set of potential principal contacts in the CF.

After we have added potential principal contacts, we let the time control backtrack the simulation, and next time the contact determination algorithm is invoked, we validate the set of potential principal contacts to form the actual CF used to compute the contact forces and/or impulses.

When we validate the potential principal contacts, we require that their closest points are within the collision envelope and that the closest points must be within the corresponding external *Voronoi regions* of the features. Voronoi regions are discussed in Chapter 16. All principal contacts not fulfilling these requirements are removed from the CF. A 2D example of the algorithm is shown in Figure 14.18.

One problem with the contact-tracking algorithm is that we can get redundant principal contacts. For instance, if an edge penetrates a face, then both the edge and the endpoint lying below the face could be used to represent the principal contact. We could compute the actual contact points of all principal contacts and remove those with identical coordinates, but it would be better to use the concept of the smallest set

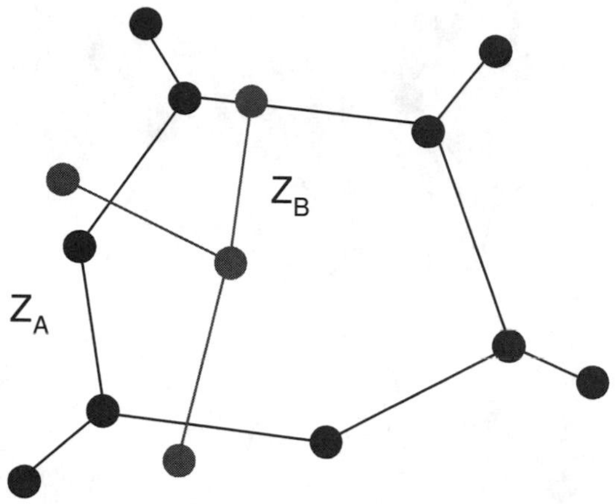

Figure 14.15: Intersection test of projected vertices of A against projected faces of B.

of principal contact types.

The contact tracking algorithm appears to be much more ad hoc than the geometrical approach, and it is impossible to assert anything about its time complexity because it is highly intervened with the backtracking of the simulator. However, the method is easily implemented and works well in practice.

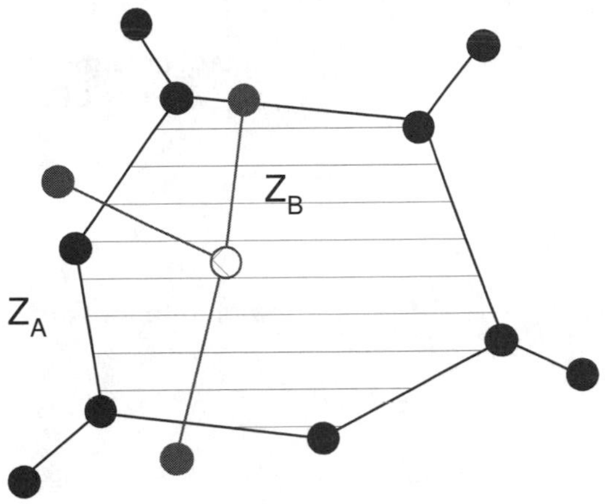

Figure 14.16: Intersection test of projected vertices of B against projected faces of A.

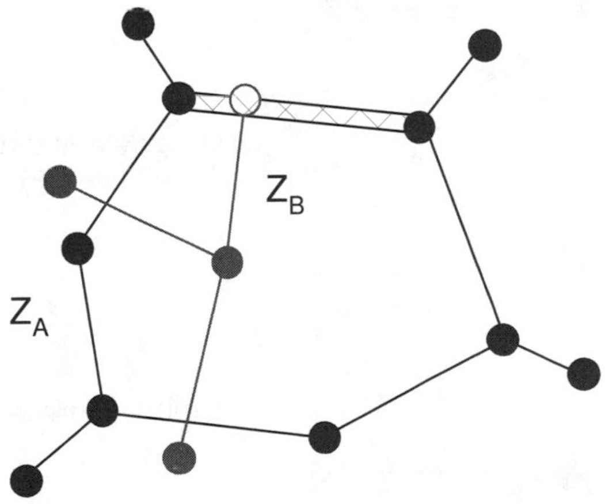

Figure 14.17: Intersection test of projected vertices against projected edges.

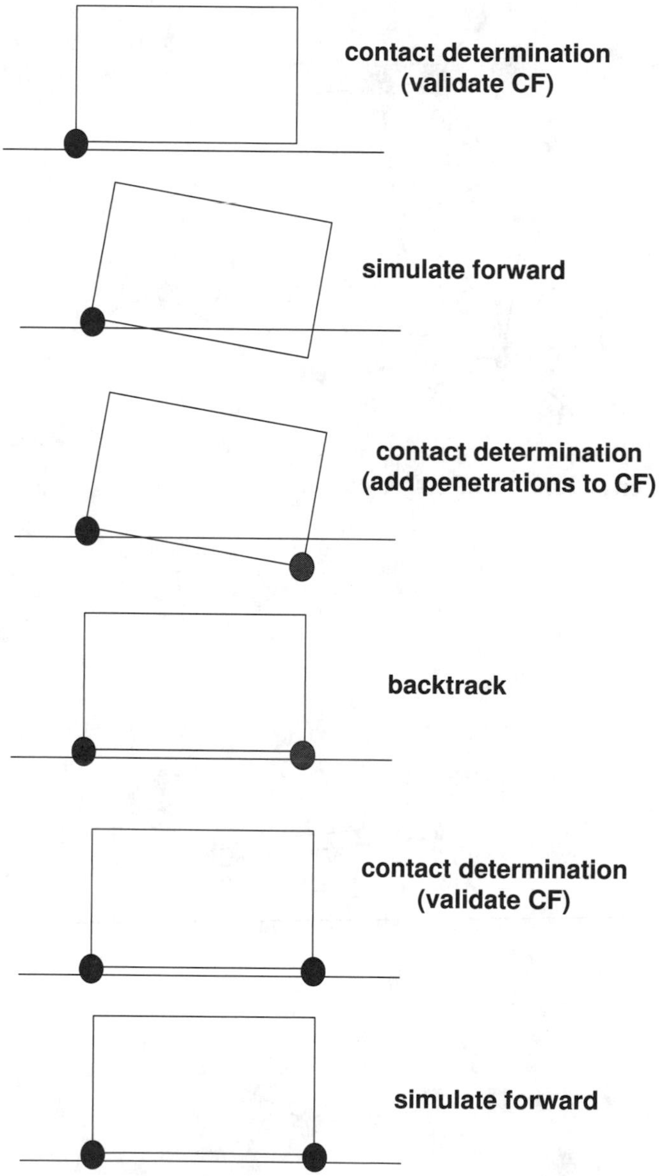

Figure 14.18: 2D example of contact tracking algorithm.

15

Bounding Volume Hierarchies

There are two types of spatial data structures: *spatial subdivision* and *bounding volume hierarchies* (*BVH*). Spatial subdivision recursively partitions the embedded space of an object, whereas bounding volume hierarchies are based on a recursive partitioning of the primitives of an object as stated in [Gottschalk, 2000].

Using spatial partitioning has the disadvantage that splitting of polygons is usually unavoidable. This may increase the depth of the tree data structure, which is undesirable for performance reasons. Besides, the cells produced by the partitioning tend not to cover the objects tightly, thus making the cells less suitable for determining contact status when models are close together. This is a disadvantage in physics-based animation where contact status needs to be determined very efficiently. Due to these problems with spatial partitioning and space considerations in this book, we will not treat spatial partitioning here. Instead we will focus on an in-depth treatment of bounding volume hierarchies.

Bounding volume hierarchies are popular and widely used in computer graphics for ray tracing [Goldsmith et al., 1987], and in animation for cloth animation [Bridson et al., 2003], since they are applicable to a more general shape than most feature-based and simplex-based algorithms. They tend to generate smaller hierarchies than spatial subdivision algorithms and they offer a graceful degradation of objects, which is highly useful when accuracy is to be traded for performance.

A bounding volume hierarchy (BVH) is a discrete representation of all levels of details. At the first level, we have a coarse representation with less-to-no detail, usually a single *bounding volume* (*BV*) of the object. At the next level, more detail of the object is represented, and we say we have a finer scale. This level is often constructed by splitting the original object into disjunct partitions and placing bounding volumes around each partitioning. The following levels reveal more details of the object in a recursive fashion, by splitting the geometry of each disjunct partition at the previous level into several disjunct subpartitions and placing a bounding volume around each of these subpartitions. The finest level of the representation—the finest scale—is the object primitives, such as lines, triangles, or tetrahedra.

The successive scale refinement naturally introduces a parent-child relationship between bounding volumes at succeeding levels, with the topology of a tree; therefore, the data structure is called a bounding volume hierarchy.

15.1 Tandem Traversal

Tandem traversal is an algorithm for testing overlap between two BVHs. We will introduce tandem traversal with an example. Consider a 2D stick object, as shown in Figure 15.1. The sticks are referred to as the geometrical primitives or simply the primitives. In this example, we will use bounding circles, implying that at the first level we place a single bounding circle enclosing the entire stick object as shown in Figure 15.2. In order to obtain a more detailed version, the stick object is further divided into three disjunct partitions: the first partition is given by the two topmost sticks, the next partition is given by the two connected bottom-right sticks, and the last partition is given by the two leftover sticks. Enclosing

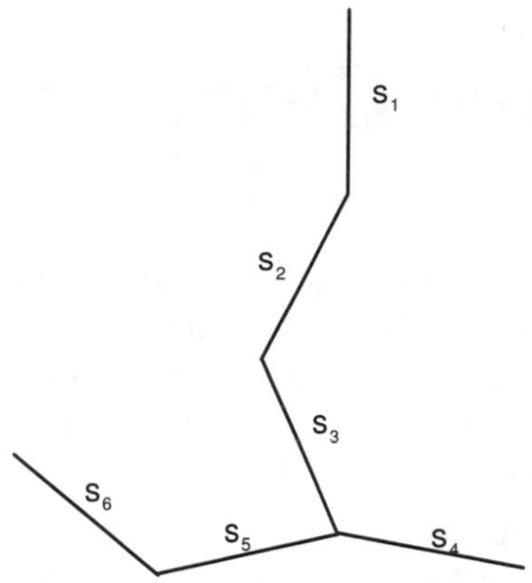

Figure 15.1: A 2D stick object; sticks are label $S_1, \ldots, S_6$.

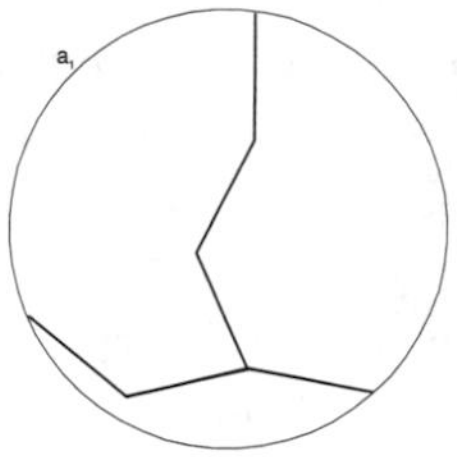

Figure 15.2: A single circle, a_1, enclosing the 2D stick object shown in Figure 15.1.

circles are placed around each of these partitions, as shown in Figure 15.3. Each of these three new circles is linked to the initial circle representing the entire object. Finally, each of the three disjunct partitions are split into two disjunct partitions, and for our example this is the finest level, since each partition now contains a single stick. Enclosing circles are placed around each of these partitions, as shown in Figure 15.4. The new circles are linked to the parent circles from the previous level shown in Figure 15.3. The bounding volumes at the finest level are called the leaves. Quite often the leaves are annotated by the geometry they enclose, in which case the BVH is annotated. We can now draw the tree of the BVH we just constructed, as can be seen from Figure 15.5, using the labels introduced in Figure 15.1, Figure 15.2, Figure 15.3, and Figure 15.4. This is an example of an annotated BVH. Drawing all the levels superimposed on top of each other, as shown in Figure 15.6, we will gain more insight into how BVs at different levels relate to each other. Notice that a BV does not necessarily enclose its children BVs; only the geometry enclosed by its children needs to be strictly enclosed. Hence:

Property 15.1 (BV Property)
A Bounding Volume (BV) is defined such that: a BV at level i encloses the geometry of all its children at level $i-1$.

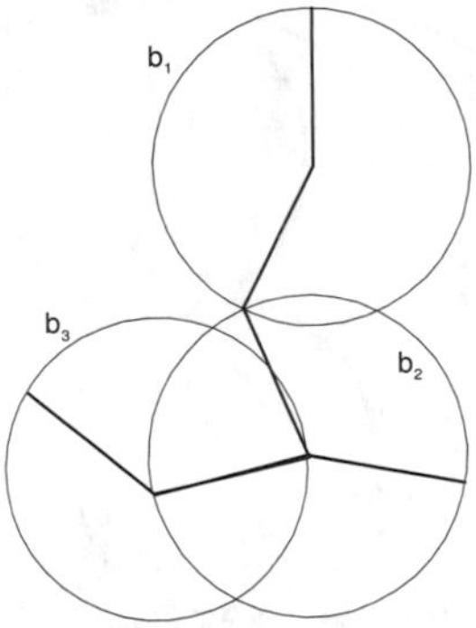

Figure 15.3: Three circles: b_1, b_2, and b_3 enclosing three disjunct partitions of the 2D stick object as shown in Figure 15.1. Notice that circles might overlap; it is the underlying geometry that is partitioned into disjoint sets.

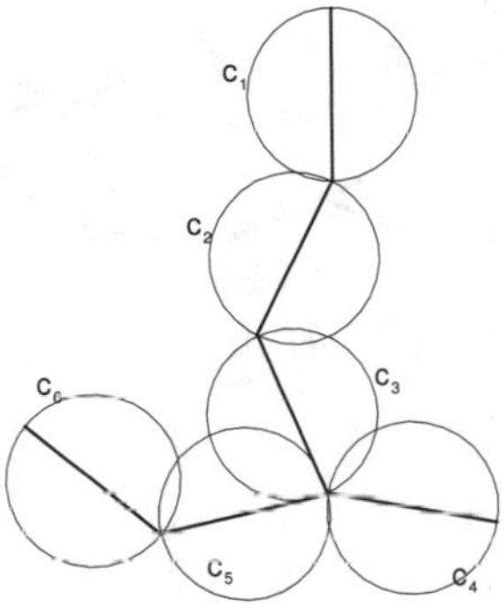

Figure 15.4: Circles: C_1, C_2, C_3, C_4, C_5, and C_6 at the finest level. Each enclosing a single stick of the object, as shown in Figure 15.1.

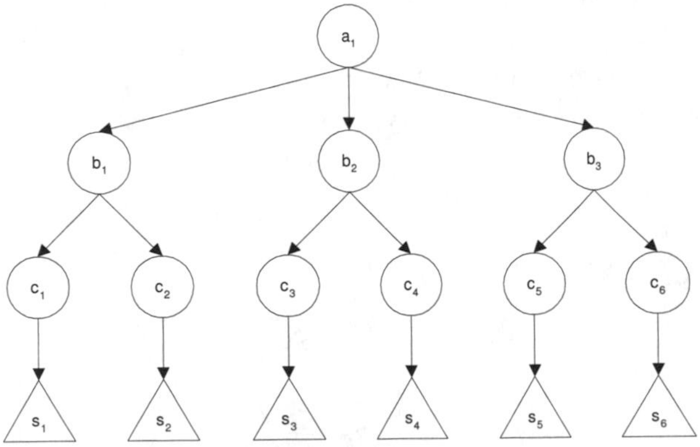

Figure 15.5: Tree topology of BVH built in.

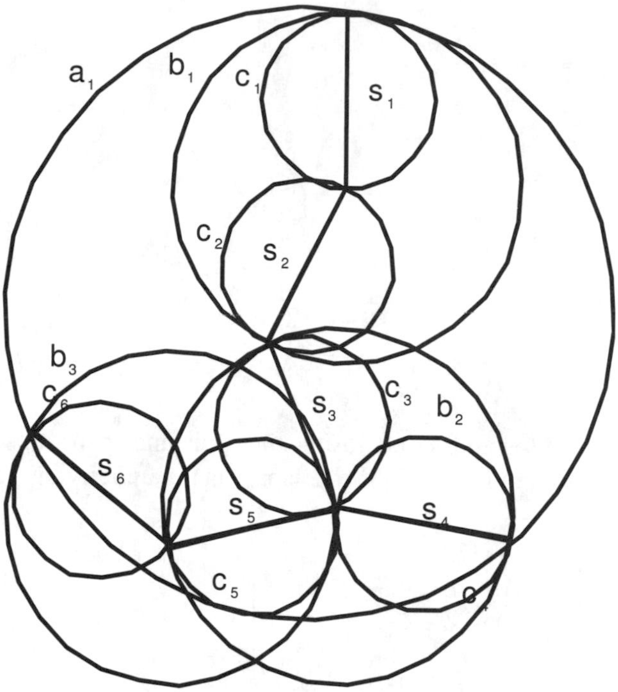

Figure 15.6: All bounding circles of the BVH shown in Figure 15.5 drawn on top of each other.

It is important to notice that Property 15.1 only says something about how tight, but not how loose, a BV can be fitted to its children. For instance, it might be useful to build a BVH such that parent BVs enclose all the geometry of the children BVs.

Now let us try to see how we can use the BVH data structure. Imagine two identical and overlapping stick objects, as shown in Figure 15.7. In the following, they will be referred to as the left and right object. In order to determine whether the stick objects overlap, we will recursively examine their BVHs. Starting at the two root bounding volumes, we see these overlaps, as shown in Figure 15.8. If the root bounding volumes had not been overlapping, we could immediately conclude that it would be impossible for the two objects to be colliding, using Property 15.1. Unfortunately, we cannot infer the opposite, and

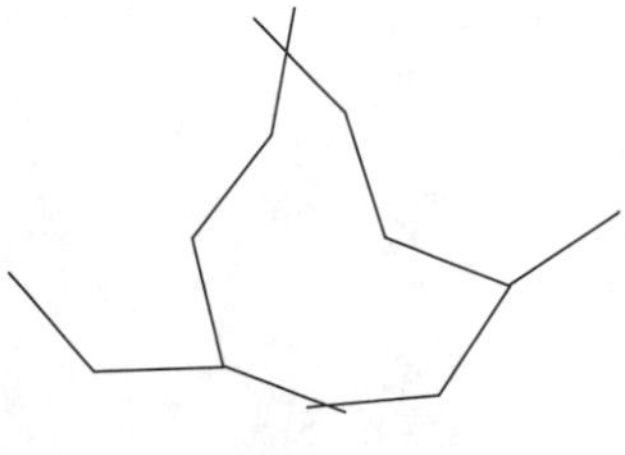

Figure 15.7: Two identical and overlapping stick objects, each is identical to the stick object in Figure 15.1.

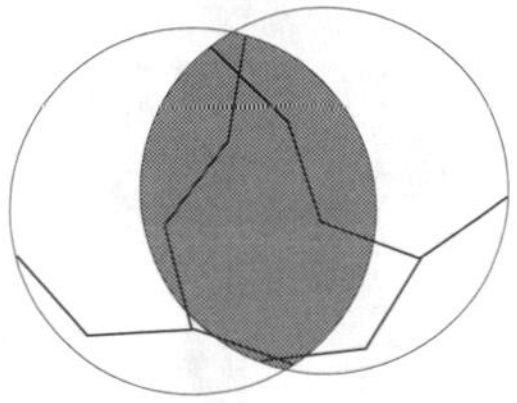

Figure 15.8: Root BVs overlap, indicating possible collision at a finer level.

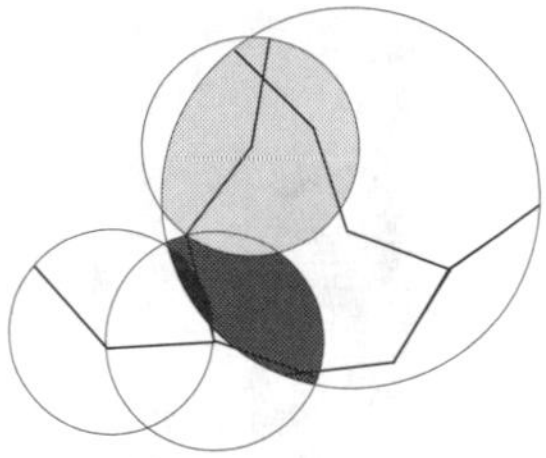

Figure 15.9: Left root BV from Figure 15.8 has been replaced by its children.

we must look for an answer at a lower scale. We do this by replacing one of the root volumes by its children, say the left one, and we will have the situation depicted in Figure 15.9. This is called descending because we are picking a path to move down the hierarchy toward the leaves. The rule for picking which volume to descend along is called the traversal rule. As can be seen from the figure, we now have three circles from the left hierarchy, which we test for overlap against the root circle from the right hierarchy. Again, an overlap means that a collision might occur at the finest scale, and a separation means that no collision is possible. In our case, all three circles of the left hierarchy overlap with the root circle of the right hierarchy. To lower the chance of finding overlapping BVs, we replace the largest volume with its children, as shown in Figure 15.10. We now test each of the three right circles against the three left circles yielding a total of nine *pairwise tests*. Luckily only two of the nine pairwise tests are overlapping,

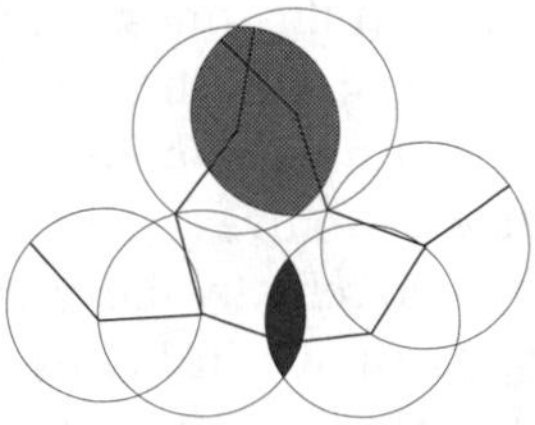

Figure 15.10: Right root BV from Figure 15.9 has been replaced by its children.

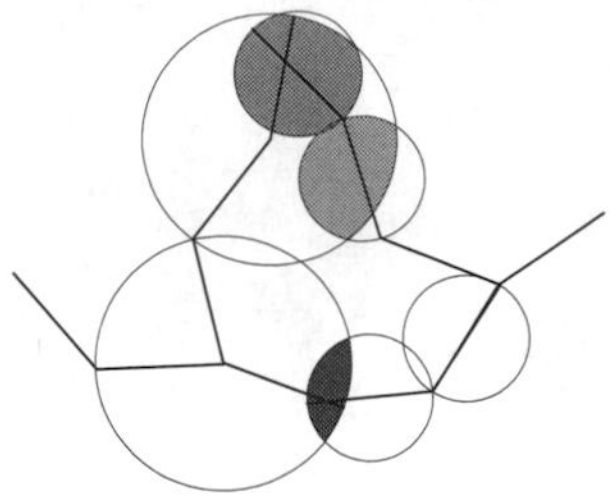

Figure 15.11: Overlapping circles from the right object in Figure 15.10 have been replaced by their children.

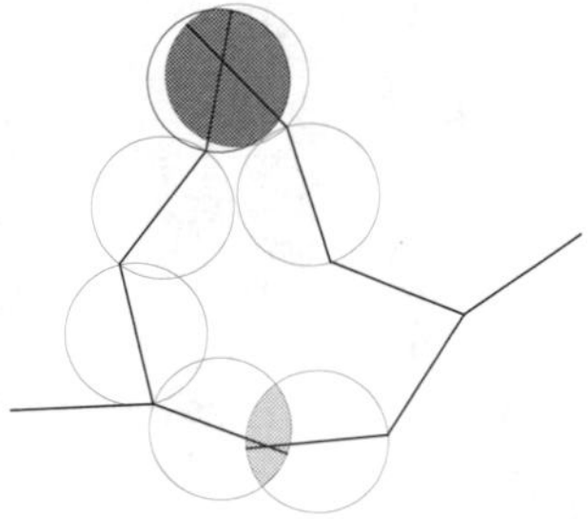

Figure 15.12: Overlapping circles with largest volume in Figure 15.11 have been replaced by their children.

indicating a collision at a finer scale. The remaining seven pairwise tests are nonoverlapping and can thus be discarded from further consideration. This is called pruning. The two pairwise overlapping cases are between circles of the same size, so we randomly choose to descend down the right hierarchy illustrated in Figure 15.11. Here the top circle from the left hierarchy is tested against the two topmost circles from the right hierarchy, and the bottom circle from the left hierarchy is tested against the two bottom most circles from the right hierarchy. The bottom circle from the left hierarchy and the bottom rightmost circle from the right hierarchy are nonoverlapping and are therefore pruned. We pick the largest volume to descend along giving us the situation in Figure 15.12. At this finest level, only two BVs are overlapping, the two topmost circles and the two bottommost circles, all other pairs of circles are pruned. Having reached the leaves of the BVHs, the only way we can obtain more details about the collision between the two stick objects is by considering the annotated primitives. This can be done in two different ways. In the first method, we replace the BVs from one hierarchy by the enclosed primitives, and test these primitives against the BVs from the other hierarchy, as shown in Figure 15.13. If the pairwise primitive-BV test indicates overlap the remaining overlapping BVs are replaced by their enclosed primitives, and we are now left with pairwise primitive tests, as shown in Figure 15.14. From these pairwise primitive tests we can now return a precise description of the overlapping of the two stick objects.

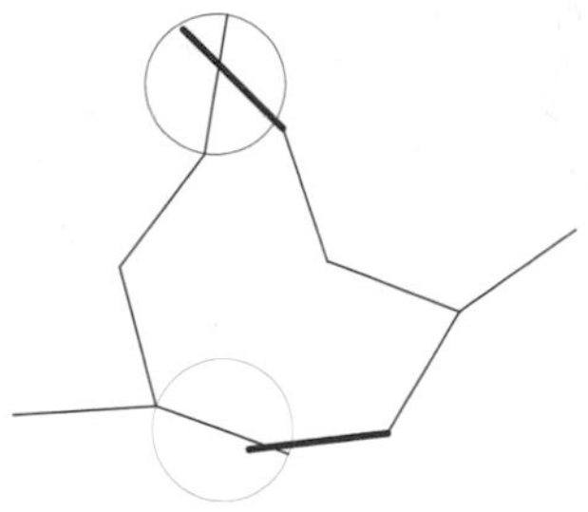

Figure 15.13: Replacing overlapping leaf circles from right object in Figure 15.12 with annotated primitives.

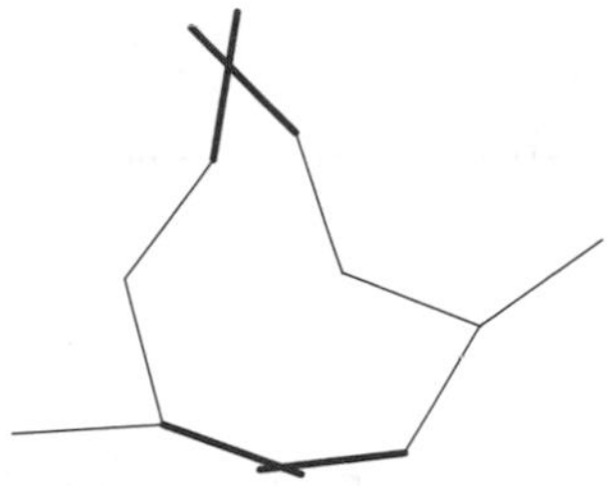

Figure 15.14: Replacing overlapping leaf circles from left object in Figure 15.13 with annotated primitives.

The other method simply skips the step of testing primitives against BVs. This has the benefit of simplifying the implementation efforts, since one can skip the code for overlapping tests between BVs and primitives and only consider the two cases of pairwise BVs and pairwise primitives. Although the pairwise BV and primitive testing is often less expensive than the pairwise primitive testing and could lead to further going directly for the pairwise primitive testing, it means a reduction in the number of iterations are needed. Therefore, there is a tradeoff between the number of iterations and the complexity in the overlap testing.

The *recursive collision query* we performed in the example above is called a recursive tandem traversal because two hierarchies are traversed simultaneously in a recursive manner. Figure 15.15 illustrates a pseudocode version of the collision query algorithm. In practice, it is often a bad choice to implement the *recursive tandem traversal* by using recursive calls [Gottschalk, 2000] because the number of primitives in an object can be quite large and the hierarchies for such large objects will be even larger. Hence, the number of recursive calls could potentially be very large, leading to a memory stack overflow on the memory heap.

Fortunately the recursive traversal is easily rewritten into an *iterative traversal* by using a *first-in-first-out queue* (*FIFO*): initially, the root bounding volumes are pushed onto the queue, then a loop is set up, popping the two first pairs of volumes from the queue, and the overlapping test is performed as usual.

```
algorithm recursive(A : BV, B : BV )
  if not colliding(A,B) then
    return

  if leaf(A) and leaf(B) then
    contact-determination(A,B)
    continue
  end if

  if descend(A) then
    for all children C of A do
      recursive(C,B)
    next C
  if descend(B) then
    for all children C of B do
      recursive(A,C)
    next C
end algorithm
```

Figure 15.15: Recursive tandem traversal collision query.

However, when the actual descend is about to be performed, instead of invoking a method recursively, the descended volumes are pushed onto the queue and thus processed later in the loop. Figure 15.16 shows an iterative version of the pseudocode from Figure 15.15. Algorithmic variations can be applied to the traversal scheme. For instance, alternative traversal orders could be used: preorder, in-order, or post-order. The first corresponds to a breadth-first traversal, the last two are similar to depth-first traversals. Observe that if a stack is used instead of a queue in the iterative traversal, then we will have a depth-first traversal instead of a breadth-first traversal.

The idea of using a queue can be taken one step further by introducing a priority on the pairwise BV tests. This is useful, if one wants to perform a *time-critical tandem traversal*. In most cases there will be more than two objects in a world; a time-critical query would be to consider all pairs of colliding objects. The broad-phase collision detection, of course, returns all such pairs that need to be considered (see Chapter 12); therefore, all pairs of root BVs are initially pushed onto the queue and given a priority. Afterward, a loop is set up similar to the pseudocode shown in Figure 15.16. The only difference is that an extra condition is added to the loop, testing whether more time is available for performing the collision query. Figure 15.17 outlines the pseudocode for a time-critical collision query. It is important to notice that all object pairs are handled simultaneously: since each BV pair pushed onto Q gets a priority, we will descend simultaneously through all BVHs according to whatever priority rule is applied. For more details, see [O'Sullivan et al., 1999, Dingliana et al., 2000].

15.2 Coordinate Space Updates

We'll examine some of the details in performing the collision queries in Figure 15.15, Figure 15.16, and Figure 15.17. We need to consider at least two kinds of coordinate spaces when we perform a query.

```
algorithm iterative(A : BV, B : BV )
  Queue Q
  push(Q, A, B)
  while not Q empty do
    pop(Q, A, B)
    if not colliding(A, B) then
      continue
    if leaf(A) and leaf(B) then
      contact-determination(A, B)
      continue
    end if
    if descend(A) then
      for all children C of A do
        push(Q, C, B)
      next C
    if descend(B) then
      for all children C of B do
        push(Q, A, C)
      next C
  end while
end algorithm
```

Figure 15.16: Iterative Collision Query.

```
algorithm time-critical(...)
  Queue Q

  O = results from broad-phase
  for all pairs of overlap (A, B) ∈ O do
    push(Q, A, B)
  next (A, B)

  while not Q empty and time left do
    pop(Q, A, B)
    ...
  end while
end algorithm
```

Figure 15.17: Time-Critical Collision Query. BV pairs are kept in a queue; during traversal, pairs are popped off the queue and tested until time is up or the queue is empty.

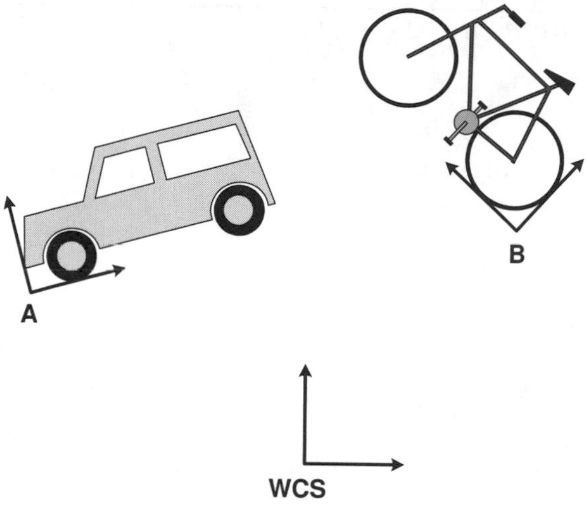

Figure 15.18: Geometries A and B are defined in their model spaces, which are placed in a common world coordinate system.

Usually the object geometry is created off-line in another application, and the coordinate space in which the object was initially created is called the *model space*, or *model frame*. When the object is used in an animation or simulation, it is moving around in a coordinate space called the *world coordinate system* (*WCS*). WCS is a fixed global coordinate frame, and any motion can be described absolutely in it. The model frame is fixed w.r.t. to the object, meaning that if the object moves and translates in the world coordinate system, then so does the model frame.

BVHs are built from the geometry of an object, therefore it is most natural to represent them in the model frame. When we perform an overlap test between two BVs from different objects, we need to bring these into a common coordinate frame in order to perform the test. This action is called BV updating or simply updating. Different updates need to be considered for rigid and deformable objects. Deformable objects are usually represented in WCS, and during a simulation, the world coordinate position and shape of the individual geometric primitives of the deformable object are altered, causing the initial BVH to become misaligned. Deformable objects thus require a different kind of update involving possible rebuilding, rebalancing, and refitting of BVHs. This will be treated in Section 15.7. For rigid objects, three possibilities are available for BV updating. Consider two objects A and B, as shown in Figure 15.18. We can transform the BV from the model frame of A into the model frame of B or vice versa, and these two kinds of transformations are referred to as a *model space update*. The third and last possibility is to transform both BVs from their model frames into the common world coordinate system, which is called a *world space update*.

A third local coordinate system often used for rigid objects is the body frame. This is an object-fixed coordinate frame with the origin placed at the center of mass and the axes aligned with the principal axes of inertia. During simulation, it is the body frame of a rigid object which is moved, and before starting a

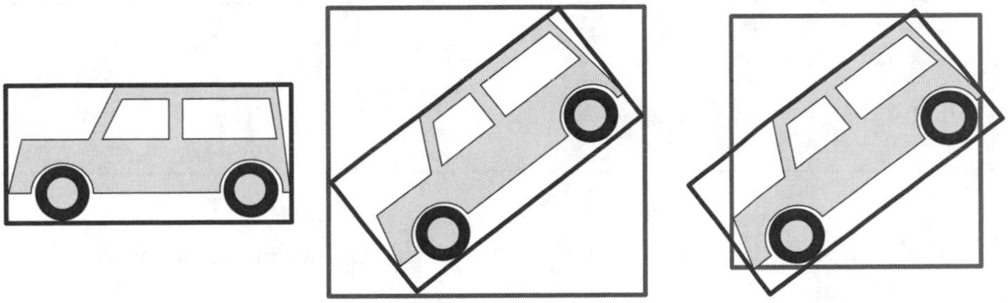

Figure 15.19: An original AABB is rotated into an OBB, two strategies are shown to make the OBB an AABB again: an expensive refitting of the BV yields optimal tight fit (RIGHT), or a cheap wrapping yields a loose fitting (MIDDLE).

collision query we must first determine where the model frame is placed in the world coordinate system before we can apply either a model space update or a world space update to the BVs. Fortunately, the transformation between the body frame and model frame is always the same and needs to be found only once at initialization time.

For BVs aligned to a specific frame such as an *axes aligned bounding box* (*AABB*), a rotational motion will make the AABB nonaligned, that is, turn it into an *oriented bounding box* (*OBB*). Thus the BV updating for AABBs not only involves coordinate transformations but also requires a realignment. Figure 15.19 illustrates the problem together with two solutions. Refitting the BV is computationally expensive, since it requires us to examine all the geometric primitives covered by the BV and find the smallest AABB. The benefit is that the new AABB will have a tight fit, and thus provide the best pruning capability. Another less expensive approach is to place an AABB around the OBB, thus avoiding having to examine all the geometry covered by the BV. This is a fast and cheap solution, but the new BV will be loose, implying a worsened pruning capability. The loose method is commonly referred to as approximate, dynamic updating or simply, wrapping. The difference between the two methods is illustrated in Figure 15.19.

Some geometries are nonaligned, such as OBBs, and nonaligned BV types do not require refitting. Some BV types are even more favorable. For instance, *spheres* are completely independent of their orientation, implying that only their positions need to be considered for the update.

There is both a performance and a fitting aspect to the model space update, since only one BV needs to be updated, implying half the work compared to a world space update. Only the updated BV might suffer from a looser fit, in contrast to a world space update where both BVs might suffer from a looser fit. Due to the performance and fitting benefits, model space updating is often preferred over world space updating.

Figure 15.20 contains pseudocode for a model space update, and Figure 15.21 contains pseudocode for a world space update.

In every single BV comparison, at least one BV update is taking place; as we saw in the simple stick object example in Section 15.1, a single BV can be part of many BV comparisons. In the example, we first tested two root BVs, but in the second iteration only one of these was descended, resulting in several BV comparisons between children and a root. Thus the root BV might be wastefully updated at each

```
algorithm colliding(A_A, B_B)
  Let T_AB be transform from B to A
  B_A = T_AB(B_B)
  return overlap(A_A, B_A)
end algorithm
```

Figure 15.20: Model space update from model frame of B, to model frame of A. Subscript-denoted coordinate space representation.

```
algorithm colliding(A_A, B_B)
  Let T_WCS,A be transform from A to WCS
  Let T_WCS,B be transform from B to WCS
  A_WCS = T_WCS,A(A_A)
  B_WCS = T_WCS,B(B_B)
  return overlap(A_WCS, B_WCS)
end algorithm
```

Figure 15.21: World space update. Subscript-denoted coordinate space representation.

comparison. This should be avoided by using a caching strategy, for example.

A simple approach to update caching is to let the node in the hierarchy have two BVs associated with it: one native BV, which is the BV originally created in the model space, and a second BV, which is the updated BV together with a time stamp of the current collision query. During a comparison, one first examines the time stamp of the nodes. If a node does not have an up-to-date time stamp, then the second BV is updated by using the current transformation on the native BV. Finally, the time stamp is set to reflect that the BV has been updated. After having taken care of time stamp testing and possible BV updating, an overlap test can be performed between the two updated BVs. This strategy is simple, but there are some drawbacks. First, the amount of storage needed for a BVH is almost doubled, since two BVs are needed for each node in the hierarchy instead of just one. Second, it places some restrictions on world space updates, since two identical objects cannot share the same BVH data structure. Nevertheless, there is no problem for the model space update, since there is no problem in testing the native BV against the updated BV in a shared BVH. That is, for a world update, the second BV update will overwrite the first.

15.3 Approximating and Hybrid BVHs

Figure 15.22 shows a space fighter. The space fighter is a polygonal model consisting of little more than 80,000 faces. If we were to build a traditional balanced binary BVH, where each leaf covers exactly one face, then we will need a binary tree with $80,000 + (80,000 - 1) = 159.999 \approx 160K$ nodes. The kind of object shown is suitable for a gaming context, but in this context, a BVH of $160K$ nodes would be considered gigantic and of little practical usage.

To obtain a workable representation for a time-critical application such as a game, we will start by

Figure 15.22: A space fighter polygon mesh.

approximating the object. As can be seen in the first row of Figure 15.23, we have done a volume sampling of the object. We have manually placed a set of primitive BV types: cylinders, spheres, and OBBs. The BVs are placed such that they closely resemble the object. Observe that at some places the original object sticks outside the volume sampling; other places the volume sampling floats a little bit over the object. This is perfectly legal for an approximation.

The BVs in the volume sampling will be used as leaf nodes in the resulting BVH. The topology of the resulting BVH is drawn to the left of the space fighter as it is being built.

Next we will try to find the parents of the leaf nodes. This is done by merging close leaf volumes, and then approximating them by a suitable BV type. In the next row, we see how the cylinders and OBBs of the three wings have been merged into three OBBs. In the next step, the cockpit part and the three wings are merged into a single root sphere.

Counting the number of nodes in the final BVH, we see that the BVH contains a total of 16 nodes, yielding an improvement of a factor of $160,000/16 \approx 10000$ in size. The decrease in size is not only reflected in storage requirements, but also the performance of a collision detection query is drastically improved.

In this example, we have chosen not to annotate the leaves of the BVH with the primitives they cover. This means that a collision detection query will determine penetration based solely on the leaf BV geometries. The kind of hierarchy shown in Figure 15.23 is termed an approximating *heterogeneous BVH* or an approximating *hybrid BVH*. It is called approximating because the leaves only approximate the true shape (surface) of the underlying object. The phrase heterogeneous or hybrid reflects the fact that different kinds of BV types are used. The opposite, where only a single BV type is used, is sometime referred to as a *homogeneous BVH*.

Approximating hybrids are particularly effective, but it is difficult to automate the construction of

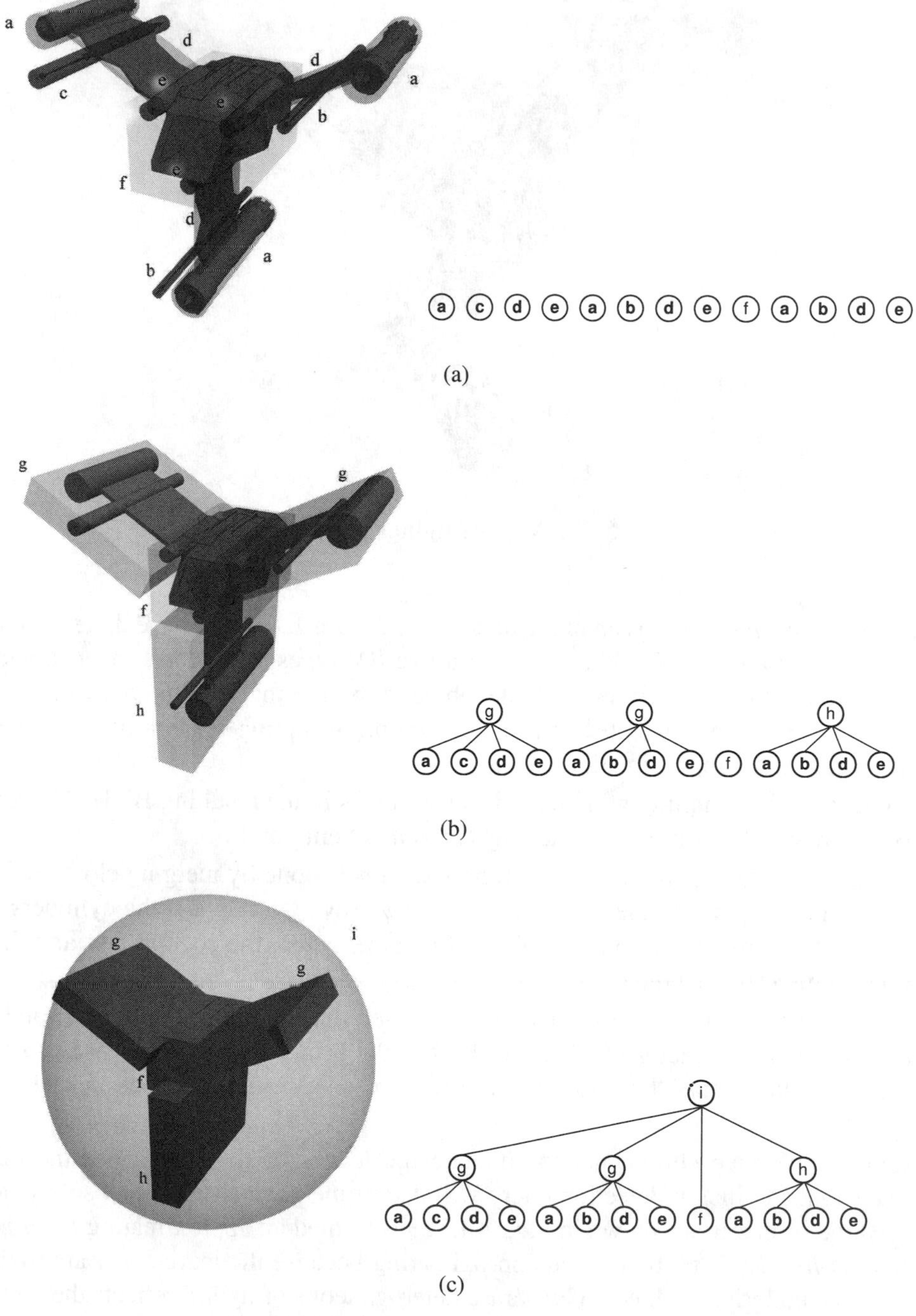

Figure 15.23: Example of an approximating heterogeneous BVH. BVH is built bottom up using a volume sampling for the leaves.

approximating hybrid BVHs. Such hierarchies are quite common in computer games and often they are hand-modeled as illustrated, which is a tedious, time-consuming, and error-prone approach. In our opinion, the most difficult part of an automatic construction method is to obtain the initial volume sampling, also called an object segmentation. Two different policies can be applied for a volume sampling: *fully conservative coverage* or *sample-based coverage*.

Figure 15.24 illustrates how the approximating hybrid BVH is used in a collision query. The figure should be read in a top-down manner. The left column shows the result of the recursive BV overlap test, and the right column shows how the corresponding traversal rule replaces an overlapping BV with its children. Observe that the traversal rules will pick the largest volume to descend. If two overlapping volumes are the same size, a random volume is picked. The recursive collision query ends when two leaf BVs are tested for overlap. In this illustrative example the collision query ends with having found a touching contact between two cylinders, one from each space fighter.

As can be seen from Figures 15.23 and 15.24, an *approximating BVH* provides a progressive refinement of an object. In a collision query, this property can be used to interrupt the collision query if available time is exhausted, and use the overlapping BVs at the level where the query was interrupted to form a contact point for the collision resolving. Usually sphere trees are used for this [Hubbard, 1996, O'Sullivan et al., 1999, Dingliana et al., 2000, Bradshaw et al., 2004].

15.4 Performance and Complexity

To achieve a good performance of a collision query, one seeks good pruning capabilities of the BVs in the BVH. This implies that a BV comparison is capable of rejecting a pair of BVs for further processing at the earliest possible level. Obtaining good pruning capabilities has an impact on both the topology of hierarchy and the fitness of BVs. There is not a single overall goal for constructing a BVH with good pruning capabilities, but rather it's a tradeoff between different properties of the BVs. As a consequence it becomes very application dependent to pick the best way to build a BVH.

We saw some properties of the BVs in a BVH from the simple stick object example in Section 15.1. At each level of the hierarchy, the primitives covered by a single BV at that level are also covered by the union of that BV's children at the next level, and the leaf nodes in the hierarchy each cover a single primitive. Furthermore, child BVs can extend beyond the space of their parent, and sibling BVs can overlap each other.

It is important the BVs are as tight fitting as possible to be able to reject a BV comparison at an early stage, simply because tighter fitting BVs cover a smaller space and thus it is less likely that other BVs will cover the same space.

A similar argument holds for reducing the amount of overlap between siblings in the hierarchy. A large overlap between siblings indicates that they cover the same space, thus a traversal might descend simultaneously down two paths in the hierarchy. If there were no overlap between siblings, the traversal is more likely to pick only one of the paths. In practice, trying to reduce the overlap between siblings implies looser fitting BVs and vice versa, thus the two desired properties for obtaining good pruning capabilities are conflicting.

To reduce overlap while having a tight fit of BVs, one could adopt more complex BV shapes, such as those with increasing complexity: spheres are simple, axes aligned bounding volumes (AABBs), oriented

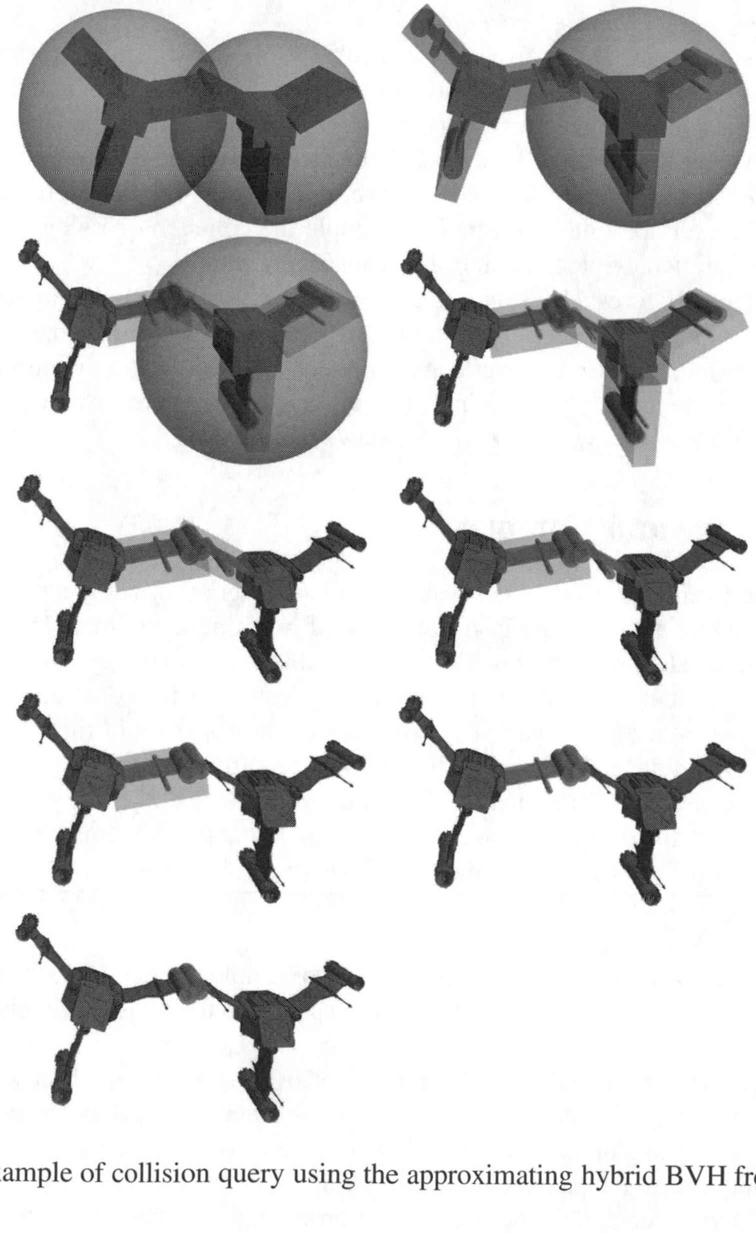

Figure 15.24: Example of collision query using the approximating hybrid BVH from Figure 15.23.

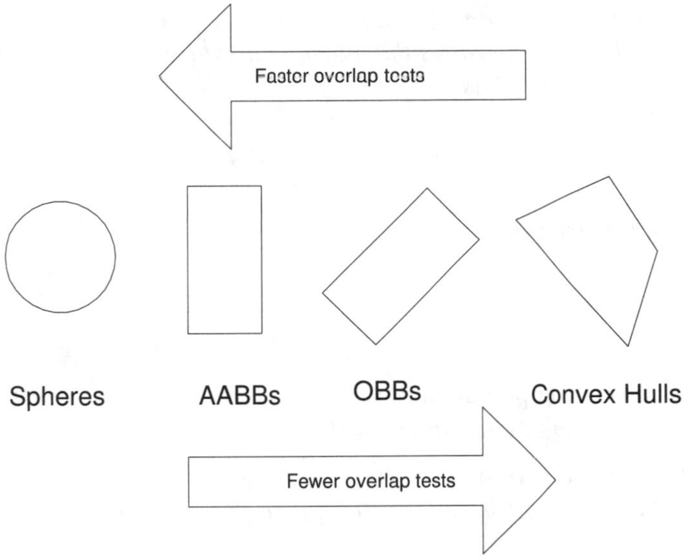

Figure 15.25: Tradeoff between BV geometry complexity, number of overlap tests performed in a traversal, and the cost of performing a single overlap test.

bounding boxes (OBBs), and convex hulls. In general, one could choose any kind of BVs, convex or non-convex. We only need to know how to fit it to a subset of primitives, and how to detect overlaps between two BV.

Theoretically, we could pick a very complex BV fulfilling our two requirements for good pruning capabilities; however, this will not resolve our problem of obtaining good performance due to tradeoffs between BV geometry complexity, cost of BV overlap tests, and number of overlap tests.

Imagine having picked a complex geometry with perfect pruning capabilities, implying tightest possible fit and no overlap between sibling BVs. The traversal algorithm would pick the optimal path down the hierarchies during a traversal such that no wrong path is examined. In such a case, the number of overlap tests is reduced to a bare minimum. Unfortunately, the cost of performing an overlap test between two complex geometries is expected to increase with complexity, and therefore it might be better to have picked a simpler geometry, with a cheaper overlap test, even though we will perform a number of unnecessary overlap tests due to the loss in pruning capability. This is illustrated in Figure 15.25.

Two definitions for measuring the *tightness of a BV* are presented in [Zachmann et al., 2003b]:

Definition 15.1 (Tightness by *Hausdorff Distance*)
Let B be a BV, G some geometry covered by B. The Hausdorff distance, $h(B,G)$, is defined to be

$$h(B,G) = \max_{\boldsymbol{b}\in B} \min_{\boldsymbol{g}\in G} d\left(\boldsymbol{b},\boldsymbol{g}\right), \tag{15.1}$$

where $\mathbf{b}$ *is a point on the surface of* B *and* $\mathbf{g}$ *is a point on the geometry.* G, $d(\cdot,\cdot)$ *is the distance between two points. The Hausdorff distance measures the maximal distance of* B *to the nearest point in* G. *Let the diameter of the geometry* G *be defined as*

$$diam(G) = \max_{\boldsymbol{g},\boldsymbol{f}\in G} d\left(\boldsymbol{g},\boldsymbol{f}\right), \tag{15.2}$$

then we can define a tightness measure, τ, *as*

$$\tau = \frac{h(B,G)}{diam(G)}. \tag{15.3}$$

The Hausdorff distance can be computationally extensive and numerically sensitive to compute. A tightness measure based on volume can therefore be used:

Definition 15.2 (Tightness by Volume)
Let $C(B)$ *be the set of children of a BV* B, *let* $vol(B)$ *be the volume of a BV* B, *then tightness,* τ, *can be defined as*

$$\tau = \frac{vol(B)}{\sum_{c\in C(B)} vol(c)}. \tag{15.4}$$

If $L(B)$ *is the set of leaf BVs beneath* B, *then an alternative tightness definition can be used:*

$$\tau = \frac{vol(B)}{\sum_{l\in L(B)} vol(l)}. \tag{15.5}$$

The topology of the tree structure can be described by the number of children a nonleaf node has. If all nonleaf nodes have n children, then we have an n-ary tree. A frequently used case is $n = 2$, which is also called a binary tree. The number of children is often referred to as the cardinality or the degree. Given the maximum degree, d, and the number of primitives, n, the height, h, of the complete tree is at least

$$h \geq \lceil \log_d (n) \rceil, \tag{15.6}$$

where equality only holds when the tree is balanced. The height of a tree is defined as the number of nodes encountered on the longest path from any leaf node to the root node. Furthermore, the BVH will have at most, $2n - 1$ nodes and n of these are leaves. This follows quite easily, since a binary tree will have the smallest (sensible) degree, and any higher degree will lower the number of internal nodes. These bounds on BVH height and node count only hold when leaf nodes cover exactly one distinct primitive.

The topology of the BVH can also play an important role for the performance of a collision query. Often, balanced binary trees are wanted since these are known to have good search properties. However, as our previous examples show, a hierarchy does not need to be binary. In fact, quad-trees and octrees have been reported to be significantly faster than binary trees [Mezger et al., 2003, Larsson et al., 2001]. Furthermore, as far as we know, there have been no experiments showing that binary balanced BVHs are always the best choice. For instance, one could argue that for approximating BVHs queries, it would be feasible to have the BVH balanced w.r.t. volume [Somchaipeng et al., 2004].

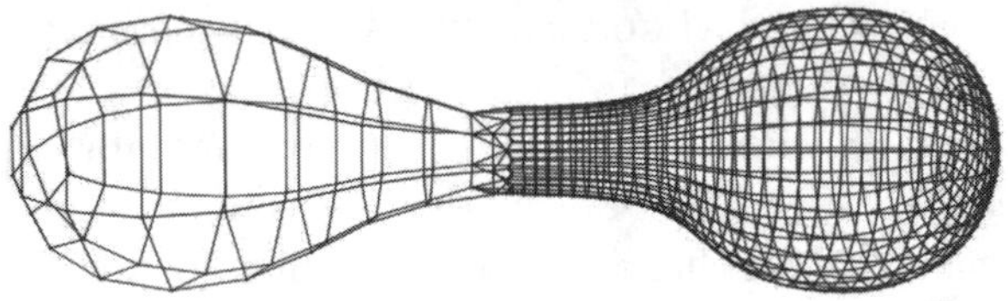

Figure 15.26: Dumbbell, showing two ends with nearly equal volume, but with a large difference in number of primitives.

As an example, imagine a dumbbell figure where one end is finally tessellated, and the other end has a coarse tessellation as shown in Figure 15.26. From a volume-approximating viewpoint, both ends are equal, since they have nearly the same amount of volume inside them. From a surface point of view, one end is much heavier than the other and requires a finer subdivision. Thus, creating a balanced hierarchy w.r.t. volume and number of primitives will be focused quite differently.

For surface-based BVHs, OBBs are superior over spheres and AABBs [Gottschalk, 2000]. AABBs [Bergen, 1997, Larsson et al., 2001] are the preferred choice for deformable objects. The reason is that during simulation, the BVs in the BVH constantly need to be updated, and the cost of refitting an OBB is very expensive compared with the cost of refitting an AABB. Hence, AABBs can outperform OBBs, even though OBBs have better pruning capabilities. For volume-based methods, spheres are often the preferred choice [Hubbard, 1996, O'Sullivan et al., 1999, Bradshaw et al., 2004].

In general, one tries to keep the overall size of the BVH as small as possible; with a small height these two properties are known to improve the speed of a search through the tree structure. Obviously for a surface-based BVH, the number of primitives have a direct impact on these two desired properties, since increasing the number of primitives will make the BVH large and increase the height as well.

Let's summarize the characteristic of a good BVH:

- small size
- small height
- good pruning capabilities; no overlap between BVs at the same level and smallest fitting BVs
- balanced hierarchy—in terms of data structure and in terms of volume

Frequently, the time required to perform a collision query is approximated by the linear combination

$$T = N_v T_v + N_p T_p \tag{15.7}$$

Here, N_v and N_p denote the number of overlap tests for bounding volumes and primitives respectively, and T_v and T_p denote the corresponding average times to perform these tests.

Generally speaking, one seeks to make N_v and N_p as small as possible by picking the bounding volume with the best pruning capability for the problem at hand. Also T_v and T_p should be as small as possible by choosing simpler geometries. Unfortunately, these two minimization goals are conflicting as explained earlier.

The particular query in question also has an impact on the running time. If a close proximity query is performed, for example, a cloth falling over an object, then N_p is likely to increase rapidly. The primitive testing is in many cases more expensive than the simpler bounding volume overlap testing.

A third term should be included in the time cost, such that the BV updating is taken into account. This was suggested in [Klosowski et al., 1998] yielding

$$T = N_v T_v + N_p T_p + N_u T_u \tag{15.8}$$

This update term covers transforming BVs into the same coordinate frame before performing an overlap test. This transform might include a dynamic update of the BV geometry itself. For instance, if an AABB BVH is built and kept in the model space of a rigid object, then the model frame will have a different orientation than the world frame during rotational motion, indicating that the AABBs are no longer AABBs, but have become OBBs.

One resolution to the problem would be to update the OBB into an AABB, such that an AABB overlap test can be performed. The drawback is that the updated AABB could have a much looser fit than the OBB. This was discussed in detail earlier; we refer the reader to Figure 15.19. Another approach would be to perform a more expensive overlap test, capable of dealing with the OBB instead of the AABB.

For *deformable objects*, the updating cost is a little different. It is actually more of a refitting cost, implying that the average time T_u might not be a constant. As an example, imagine a simple update strategy as follows: before a query, the two BVHs are updated in a bottom-up fashion, leafs are refitted to cover their annotated primitive, internal nodes are refitted to tightly cover the primitives given by the union of the primitives covered by their children, and the root is refitted to cover all primitives. Obviously, the leaf refitting is very cheap, and the closer an internal node is to the root, the more expensive the update will be. Deformable objects will be treated more thoroughly in Section 15.7.

Lower and upper bounds on a balanced binary BVH consisting of ideal BVs have been proven [Gottschalk, 2000]. An ideal BV is defined as one with perfect pruning capability, that is, it is so tight fitting that it only overlaps with other BVs if the covered geometry overlaps. Suppose we have two models each consisting of n primitives. Assume that the BVHs are perfectly balanced using ideal BVs. If the models are touching and there are $k > 0$ contacts, then the number of BV tests required to identify all k contacts is at least

$$\nu_l(n,k) = 2\log_2(n^2/k) + 2k - 1, \tag{15.9}$$

and at most

$$\nu_u(n,k) = 2k\log_2(n^2/k) + 2k - 1. \tag{15.10}$$

Obviously the lower bound on the number of ideal BV tests is also a lower bound of real BV tests. The upper bound represents the worst-case performance for ideal BVs, and therefore it represents a lower bound on the worst-case performance for ordinary BVs.

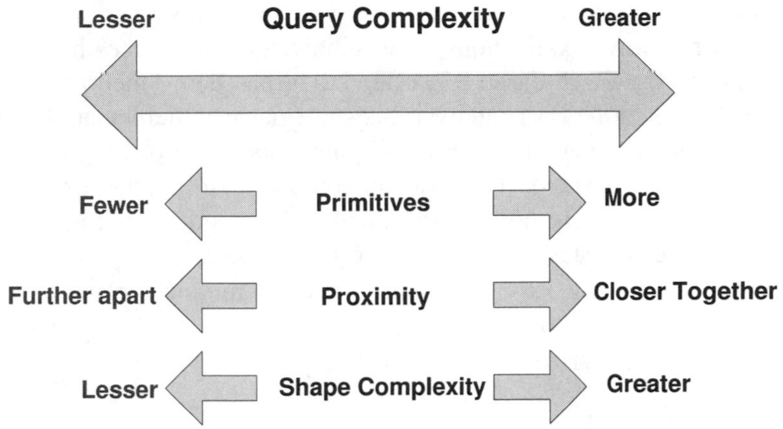

Figure 15.27: The performance impact of primitive count, proximity type, and shape complexity on a collision query.

Of course, in the real world there is no such thing as an ideal BV, and we are left with real BVs. A worst-case time complexity for real BVs is difficult to derive, if possible at all, due to the many factors involved—the complexity of the object shape, the number of primitives in the object, the BV geometry, the topology of the BVH, etc.

Of course, it is possible to construct situations where the worst imaginable time complexity will be $O(n^2)$; for instance, if one were to create and place two objects, such that all their primitives were intersecting each other. However, in physics-based animation we often work with objects that resemble real world objects, implying that the geometry for solids is a connected nonintersecting twofold, and at least in their rest shape they are nonintersecting with themselves. A $O(n^2)$ time complexity is therefore not likely to occur. Figure 15.27 illustrates our discussions on the time complexity of a collision query.

15.5 Hierarchy Construction Methods

There are many approaches for building BVHs. They can be classified into three main classes: top-down, bottom-up, and incremental methods. Their names reflect how the BVH is traversed during creation of the nodes in the hierarchy. In Section 15.1 and in Section 15.3 we described two different ways for obtaining the example BVHs: the stick object applied a top-down method, whereas the star fighter model used a bottom-up approach. We have not shown any examples of an incremental method, but here, the general idea is to extend a BVH incrementally. Incremental methods are, to our knowledge, not widely used in collision detection. Each of the three main groups can be further subdivided into subgroups.

Top-down methods can be grouped as being based on a subdivision scheme or a statistical approach. Both of these subgroups are treated in detail in Section 15.5.1.

Bottom-up methods come in two flavors, depending on whether a volume-based BVH or a surface BVH is wanted. Volume-based BVHs usually start out by performing some sort of volume sampling of an object. Medial surfaces are very popular for volume sampling. Alternatively, diffusion-based methods, such as using scale space and deep structure may be used [Somchaipeng et al., 2004]. Alternatives are convex decompositions or simply voxelizations; even subdivisions by octrees have been used to obtain a volume sampling of an object. Surface-based BVHs tend to be based on a merging strategy. Here, BVs are initially formed for the leaves of the BVH and various strategies can then be applied to pick BVs, which undergo a merging operation. Theoretically, it is an all-pair problem for picking two BVs, and even worse if a higher degree of the BVH is wanted. The problem could be cast into a optimization problem. Graph theory is also a popular choice, where nodes correspond to BVs and edges to possible merges. Greedy algorithms for picking edge-candidates for merges are often adopted.

Incremental methods are governed by two main problems: finding a place to insert a BV and then updating the BVH [Zachmann et al., 2003b].

The various methods are summarized here:

Top-down methods

- Statistical approach
- Subdivision

Bottom-up methods

- Volume sampling
  - Structural information (medial surfaces)
  - Diffusion
  - Convex decomposition, voxelization
- Merging
  - Optimization problems
  - Graph theory
  - Greedy (deterministic) algorithms

Incremental methods

- Inserting a BV, updating hierarchy

In the following subsections we will treat both top-down and bottom-up methods in more detail; incremental methods are only briefly touched.

15.5.1 Top-Down Methods

A *top-down method* usually adopts a *fit-and-split strategy*, where for a given collection of primitives, a BV is fitted to cover all the primitives, and then the collection is partitioned into two or more groups. For each group a new BV is fitted and the collection is partitioned again. This is repeated until each group only contains a single primitive. Figure 15.28 illustrates the basic idea in pseudocode. Two operations need to be considered in order to apply a top-down method:

```
algorithm fit-and-split(parent,primitives)
  bv = BV(primitives)
  add bv as child to parent
  groups  = split(primitives)
  for each g in groups do
    fit-and-split(bv,g)
  next g
end algorithm
```

Figure 15.28: Fit-and-split strategy of a top-down method.

Fitting Given a collection of primitives and a BV type, how do we find the smallest and tightest fitting BV?

Splitting Given a collection of primitives and the degree, d, how do we split the collection into d groups?

The task of fitting a BV to a collection of primitives is deferred to Section 15.6. In this section we will only consider the task of splitting a collection of primitives into two or more groups.

Top-down methods are easily implemented. They are probably also the most common used in practice. Most *splitting methods* seek a binary partitioning of the primitives resulting in binary BVHs. It is easier to split a set of primitives into two disjunct groups than into three or four groups simply because given a single primitive, one only needs to consider a single yes-no decision. It is also desirable to make the BVH balanced, to give it a good overall worst-case seeking complexity. Having balanced binary BVHs yields an $O(\log_2 n)$ depth (height) for n primitives.

Most splitting methods are based on the idea of first choosing a splitting axis to indicate a direction of splitting. Hereafter, a splitting point on the axis is often determined and a splitting or dividing plane can be set up, having the axis as normal and containing the splitting point. Having obtained a *splitting plane*, one is left with the task of deciding which side of the plane a primitive is mapped to. Most often the decision is based on the position of the centroid of the primitive w.r.t. the splitting plane. Figure 15.29 contains 2D illustrations of the concepts and terms we have introduced.

Without clever search structures the partitioning of k primitives takes $O(k)$ time. If the fitting process is also $O(k)$ for k primitives, then the BVH building process has the same recurrence relation as quicksort, that is, expected $O(n \log n)$. If the BVH is reasonably balanced however, the worst-case running time is $O(n^2)$. If the fitting is not linear in the number of primitives, but for instance $O(n \log n)$, which is the case when a convex hull computation is involved, then the BVH building takes $O(n \log^2 n)$.

15.5.1.1 A Subdivision Method

Using a *subdivision* method for finding the *splitting plane* is often fast and simple. For instance, in [Klosowski, 1998] a splitting plane orthogonal to the x-, y-, or z-axis is picked based upon the following criteria:

Min Sum: Choose the axis that minimizes the sum of the volumes of the two resulting children.

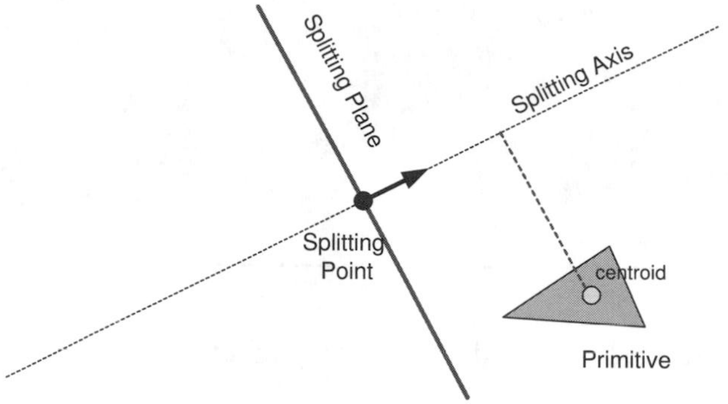

Figure 15.29: Often-used terms and concepts in top-down methods.

Min Max: Choose the axis that minimizes the larger of the volumes of the two resulting children.

Longest Side: Choose the axis along which the BV is longest.

The last method does not make much sense if spheres are used, but works great for AABBs, k-DOPs, OBBs, or similar BV types. The idea in min sum and min max is to try out all axes, and pick an axis according to some greedy optimization strategy. They both require that six BVs must be computed, one pair for each axis, involving six fitting operations.

An alternative algorithm not restricted to using a splitting plane orthogonal to the coordinates axis works by taking as input a set F of BVs each enclosing one primitive and a set C of points, which are the barycenters of the primitives. The algorithm starts by finding $\mathbf{c}_i, \mathbf{c}_j \in C$ with almost maximal distance. In [Zachmann, 1998], a nearoptimal pair is found by a simple $O(n)$ heuristic. Then a splitting axis parallel to $\overline{c_i c_j}$ is determined and C is sorted along that axis, which induces a sorting on F. After these initial steps, which are done for every recursion, F can be split in two parts F_1 and F_2. To start with $F_1 = f_i$, $F_2 = f_j$, where f_i, f_j are associated to c_i, c_j, respectively, then, all other $f \in F$ are treated in an iterative manner one by one and assigned to either F_1 or F_2, according to whichever BV increases the least. If both BVs of F_1 and F_2 increase equally and in particular, if they do not increase at all, then f is added to the set, which has the least polygons.

According to [Zachmann, 1998], the algorithm produces good trees that are fairly well balanced. Furthermore, the algorithm is geometrically robust and can be applied to all unstructured models, that is, no adjacency information is needed or connectivity restrictions required. A very strong point of the algorithm is that it is capable of dealing with degenerate primitives, such as polygons collapsing to lines, points, or worse.

15.5.1.2 A Statistical Method

In order to increase the pruning capabilities of the BVH, we seek to make BVs fat, that is, we would like to avoid having long thin BVs. These span a large area of space, thus increasing the chance of overlapping a lot of other BVs. If the BV is more like a cubic or spherical shape, it will in a sense, be more local,

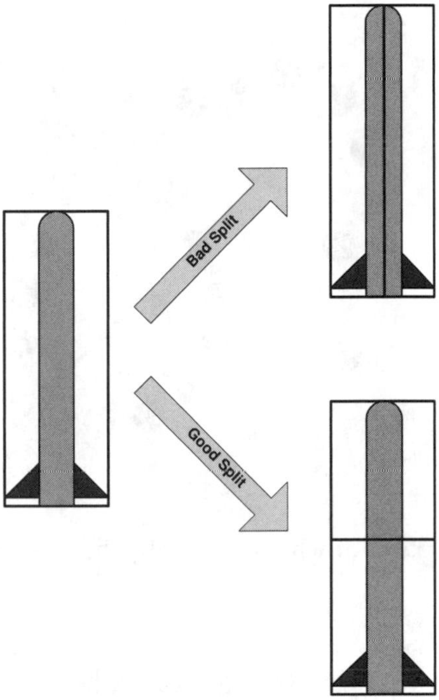

Figure 15.30: 2D example of a bad split and a good split.

implying a better chance for pruning. Therefore, splitting along the axis of maximum spread increases the chance of creating more fat BVs than long thin BVs. Figure 15.30 illustrates the idea in a 2D Example where a rocket object is shown, together with a bad and good split. In the following, we will consider the theory for spatial point distributions and derive the *covariance matrix*. Afterward, we will give some hints on how to generalize the results.

Consider Figure 15.31. We have drawn a set of points in 2D and assume that we want to split along an axis with *maximum variance*. In general, we have a point set with N Points:

$$P = \{\boldsymbol{p}_1, \boldsymbol{p}_2, \ldots \boldsymbol{p}_N\} . \tag{15.11}$$

Usually the points belong to 3D space, that is,

$$\boldsymbol{p}_i \in \mathbf{R^3}, \quad \text{for } i = 1, \ldots, N. \tag{15.12}$$

The mean is given by

$$\boldsymbol{m} = \frac{1}{N} \sum_i \boldsymbol{p}_i. \tag{15.13}$$

The direction of the maximum variance is denoted by the vector $\boldsymbol{n}$. As can be seen from Figure 15.31, it is quite easy for a human being to intuitively pick $\boldsymbol{n}$. If we subtract the mean from each $\boldsymbol{p}_i$ we get a new

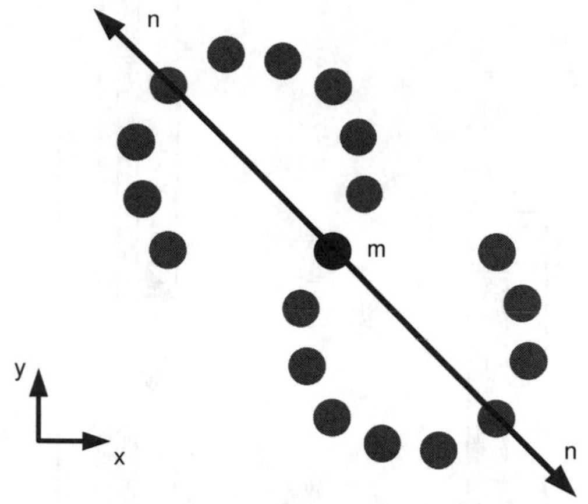

Figure 15.31: Illustration of what is meant by the axis of maximum spread.

point set:

$$Q = \{\boldsymbol{q}_1, \boldsymbol{q}_2, \ldots, \boldsymbol{q}_N\}, \tag{15.14}$$

where

$$\boldsymbol{q}_i = \boldsymbol{p}_i - \boldsymbol{m}, \quad \text{for } i = 1, \ldots, N. \tag{15.15}$$

The direction, $\boldsymbol{n}$, of maximal variance is also the direction that maximizes the square sum of the projection of Q onto $\boldsymbol{n}$,

$$v = \frac{1}{N} \sum_i (\boldsymbol{n} \cdot \boldsymbol{q}_i)^2. \tag{15.16}$$

We want to maximize v w.r.t. $\boldsymbol{n}$ under the condition that $enorm\boldsymbol{n} = 1$. This is equivalent to maximizing the expression

$$v + \lambda (\boldsymbol{n} \cdot \boldsymbol{n} - 1), \tag{15.17}$$

where λ is a Lagrange multiplier. The maximum must occur at zero derivative, so we differentiate with respect to n_x, n_y and n_z

$$\frac{d}{dn_x} \left(\frac{1}{N} \sum_i (\boldsymbol{n} \cdot \boldsymbol{q}_i)^2 + \lambda (\boldsymbol{n} \cdot \boldsymbol{n} - 1) \right) = 0, \tag{15.18a}$$

$$\frac{d}{dn_y} \left(\frac{1}{N} \sum_i (\boldsymbol{n} \cdot \boldsymbol{q}_i)^2 + \lambda (\boldsymbol{n} \cdot \boldsymbol{n} - 1) \right) = 0, \tag{15.18b}$$

$$\frac{d}{dn_z} \left(\frac{1}{N} \sum_i (\boldsymbol{n} \cdot \boldsymbol{q}_i)^2 + \lambda (\boldsymbol{n} \cdot \boldsymbol{n} - 1) \right) = 0. \tag{15.18c}$$

For the derivative w.r.t. n_x we get

$$\frac{d}{dn_x}\left(\frac{1}{N}\sum_i (\boldsymbol{n}\cdot\boldsymbol{q}_i)^2 + \lambda(\boldsymbol{n}\cdot\boldsymbol{n}-1)\right) = 0, \tag{15.19a}$$

$$\Downarrow$$

$$\frac{1}{N}\sum_i \frac{d}{dn_x}\left(n_x q_{ix} + n_y q_{iy} + n_z q_{iz}\right)^2 + \lambda\frac{d}{dn_x}\left(n_x^2 + n_y^2 + n_z^2 - 1\right) = 0, \tag{15.19b}$$

$$\Downarrow$$

$$\frac{1}{N}\sum_i 2\left(n_x q_{ix} + n_y q_{iy} + n_z q_{iz}\right) q_{ix} + \lambda 2 n_x = 0, \tag{15.19c}$$

$$\Downarrow$$

$$\frac{1}{N}\sum_i \left(n_x q_{ix} + n_y q_{iy} + n_z q_{iz}\right) q_{ix} + \lambda n_x = 0. \tag{15.19d}$$

Obviously we get similar equations for the derivative w.r.t. n_y and n_z, so we end up with

$$\frac{1}{N}\sum_i \left(n_x q_{ix} + n_y q_{iy} + n_z q_{iz}\right) q_{ix} + \lambda n_x = 0, \tag{15.20a}$$

$$\frac{1}{N}\sum_i \left(n_x q_{ix} + n_y q_{iy} + n_z q_{iz}\right) q_{iy} + \lambda n_y = 0, \tag{15.20b}$$

$$\frac{1}{N}\sum_i \left(n_x q_{ix} + n_y q_{iy} + n_z q_{iz}\right) q_{iz} + \lambda n_z = 0. \tag{15.20c}$$

We can rewrite this into a matrix equation

$$\underbrace{\begin{bmatrix} \frac{1}{N}\sum_i q_{ix}^2 & \frac{1}{N}\sum_i q_{iy}q_{ix} & \frac{1}{N}\sum_i q_{iz}q_{ix} \\ \frac{1}{N}\sum_i q_{ix}q_{iy} & \frac{1}{N}\sum_i q_{iy}^2 & \frac{1}{N}\sum_i q_{iz}q_{iy} \\ \frac{1}{N}\sum_i q_{ix}q_{iz} & \frac{1}{N}\sum_i q_{iy}q_{iz} & \frac{1}{N}\sum_i q_{iz}^2 \end{bmatrix}}_{C} \begin{bmatrix} n_x \\ n_y \\ n_z \end{bmatrix} = -\lambda \begin{bmatrix} n_x \\ n_y \\ n_z \end{bmatrix} \tag{15.21}$$

That is,

$$C\boldsymbol{n} = -\lambda\boldsymbol{n} \tag{15.22}$$

The matrix C is symmetric and is called the covariance matrix. Furthermore, this is an *eigenvalue problem* with $\boldsymbol{n}$ and λ as eigenvector and eigenvalue of C. Hence the *eigenvector* with maximum *eigenvalue* is the splitting axis. Splitting can now occur in two ways:

- Divide the primitives into two disjunct sets, by using a splitting plane at the mean.
- Project the centroids of the primitives onto the splitting axis and find the median. Then use a splitting plane running through the median.

```
algorithm bottom-up(L)
  C = L
  while |C| > 1 do
    set P empty
    while C not empty do
      choose subset S from C
      B = BV(S)
      add S as children to B
      add B to P
    end
    C = P
  end
  root = C
end algorithm
```

Figure 15.32: Pseudocode illustration of a general bottom-up method. Taking a set, L, of leaf BVs as argument, the set C denotes the children BVs and P the new parent BV.

Picking the median over the mean ensures a balanced BVH, however, using the median over the mean yields no improvement on the running times of a collision query [Klosowski et al., 1998]. Numerical experiments indicate the mean outperformed the median.

Although covariance clearly shows how to obtain a sensible splitting axis, it is by no mean trivial to do so. There are many pitfalls involved in computing a good covariance matrix for a set of primitives. We deal with this in full detail in Section 15.6.1.

The *splatter method* [Klosowski, 1998] is slightly different. It consists of first projecting the centroids of the primitives onto each of the three coordinate axes and then calculating the variance of each of the resulting distributions. Hereafter, one chooses the axis yielding the largest variance.

15.5.2 Bottom-Up Methods

In *bottom-up methods* the idea is to start by fitting BVs for the leaves of the BVH and then merging the leaves of subsequential nodes until the root is reached. A new BV must be created after each merge covering the entire subtree.

Given n primitives, then $n-1$ merges are required in order to build the BVH. Determining an enclosing BV after a merge can be done in $O(1)$ time, if one simply lets the BV enclose the geometry of the immediate children. For k primitives in the subtree, a fitting, which examines all the covered primitives one by one will take $O(k)$. If extremal points or a similar measure is sought, then the complexity is $O(k \log k)$. The total BVH construction time would be $O(n)$, $O(n \log n)$, and $O(n \log^2 n)$ using these fitting strategies respectively. Of course, here we have implicitly assumed that it takes $O(1)$ time to decide which nodes should be merged into a new parent node.

A pseudocode illustration of the basic idea of a bottom-up method is shown in Figure 15.32. There are two main difficulties in a bottom-up method:

- picking a subset of BVs at level l, which should form a parenting BV at level $l-1$

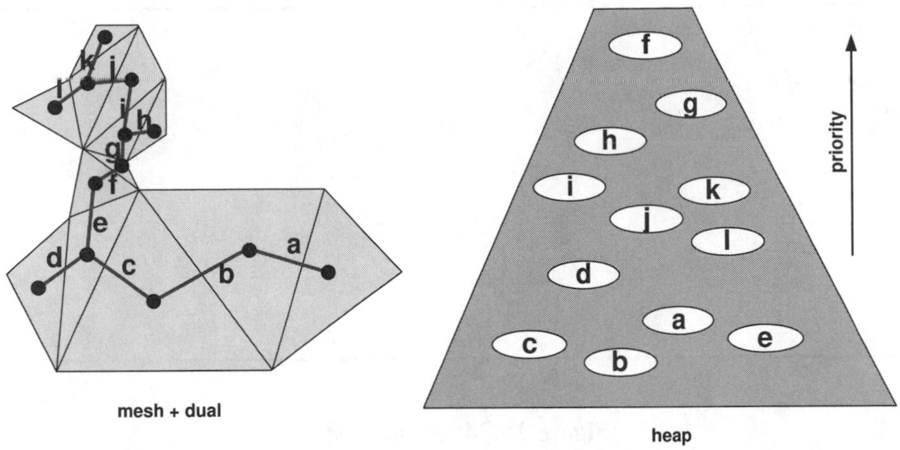

Figure 15.33: Basic data structures used by the bottom-up mesh connectivity method.

- computing the BV at level $l - 1$

In the following, we will treat the first problem and defer the second to Section 15.6.

15.5.2.1 Mesh Connectivity

Mesh connectivity is the dominant strategy for applying BVHs to deformable objects [Volino et al., 1998, Volino et al., 2000, Larsson et al., 2001, Bridson et al., 2002, Bergen, 1997]. [Larsson et al., 2001] reports a performance increase of up to 10% for the collision query when using mesh connectivity. Deformable objects will be treated further in Section 15.7. Here, we will describe a bottom-up construction method from [OpenTissue, 2005], inspired by [Hubbard, 1996, Larsson et al., 2001, Bridson et al., 2002].

Given a mesh, the topology can be used to guide the bottom-up construction. Initially, leaf BVs are created, such that they cover exactly one face in the mesh. At the same time, a graph data structure is being built to represent the dual graph of the mesh. The dual graph is constructed as follows: a node is created in the graph for every face, and edges are inserted between nodes in the graph if their corresponding faces are neighbors in the mesh as illustrated in Figure 15.33. The graph edges describe potential merges of leaf nodes into parent nodes. During initialization, all edges are assigned a priority penalizing a potential merge between the BVs stored in the end nodes. All the edges are then inserted into a priority heap, allowing the algorithm to incrementally pick the edge with minimum priority. Thus the edge, which represents the two BVs that are most beneficial, are merged into a parent BV. Whenever a merge operation is performed, the corresponding graph edge is collapsed, thereby melting the two end nodes of the edge into a single node. The main loop of this algorithm is shown in pseudocode in Figure 15.34. When an edge collapse occurs, one has to guard against inconsistencies in the graph data structure. For instance, if multiple edges exist between the two merging end nodes, self-loops will exist in the resulting graph, and these must be removed during the edge collapse since it makes no sense to merge a node with the node itself. There is a direct correspondence between a node in the graph and a BV node. Therefore, we keep

```
algorithm construct(G)
  Heap Q
  for all edges e ∈ G do
    e.priority = cost(e)
    add e to Q
  next e
  while Q not empty do
    e = pop(Q)
    collapse(e, G, Q)
    sort Q
  end
end algorithm
```

Figure 15.34: Main loop.

a pointer to the current BV, which the node represents. Furthermore, we keep track of the height this BV has in the BVH that is being built.

Due to BV fitting, it is beneficial to keep track of the mesh geometry that is covered by a graph node, thus every time we collapse an edge in the graph, the resulting node will contain the union of the geometry covered by the two end nodes before the edge collapses.

After a merging operation, some edges in the graph will have updated one of their end nodes to the merged node, thus they need to get their priority updated. The heap must also be updated to reflect changes in priorities.

Figure 15.35 contains the details of an edge collapse operation in pseudocode. The cost function, used to assign priorities to the graph edges, can be used to control the overall topology of the BVH. A useful practical cost function consists of the sum of the heights of the BVs stored in the end nodes. This cost will try to favor a balanced BVH.

Other criteria could be the volume that a resulting BV would have if a merge was carried out, thereby favoring smallest possible BVs. However, there is no telling if a greedy pick of smallest BV would yield a final BVH where all nodes are as small as possible.

A real-life example of a BVH built with the mesh connectivity method is shown in Figure 15.36. The bottom-up method we have outlined is not specific for mesh connectivity, but rather a general graph-based algorithm driven by a greedy deterministic optimization algorithm. This implies that the graph does not need to be built from the dual graph of a mesh; instead, it could be the dual graph of the generalized Voronoi diagram of a volume sampling, which could be used to build approximating hybrid BVHs as shown in Figure 15.23.

15.5.3 Incremental Methods

Incremental methods are based on an insertion principle. Initially the BVH is empty, and BVs from an elementary set are inserted one by one into the hierarchy [Zachmann et al., 2003b]. Most incremental methods have complexity $O(n \log n)$ [Zachmann et al., 2003b]. The elementary set of BVs can be thought of as the set of leaf BVs in the resulting BVH. The elementary set of BVs could consist of a set of BVs,

```
algorithm collapse(e,G,Q)
  [S,D] =getEndNodes(e)
  add D.geo to S.geo
  B = BV(S.geo)
  add S.bv and D.bv as children to B
  S.bv = B
  S.height = min(S.height, H.height) + 1
  for all edges h between S and D do
    remove h from G
    remove h from Q
  next h
  for all edges h incidient to D do
    move h from D to S
  next h
  delete D from G
  for all edges h incident to S do
    h.priority = cost(h)
  next h
end algorithm
```

Figure 15.35: Edge collapse operation.

Figure 15.36: Illustration of AABB BVH built using mesh connectivity, left image shows original polygonal mesh, middle image shows mesh with leaf AABBs superimposed, right image shows all AABBS at height four in the BVH.

```
algorithm incremental(B)
  while B not empty do
    choose b ∈ B
    if BVH empty then
      root = b
      continue
    else
      ν = root
      while ν ≠ leaf do
        choose child ν' of ν
        ν = ν'
      end while
    end if
    insert b into ν
  end while
end algorithm
```

Figure 15.37: A typical incremental construction method taking an elementary set, B, of BVs as argument.

where each BV in the set encloses a uniquely determined primitive. In other words, for a polygonal soup, each polygon is enclosed by a single BV, and all these BVs form the elementary set. The elementary set could also be built from an object segmentation, i.e., a volume sampling of an object can be a set of known BV geometry types.

The general idea is to traverse the BVH built so far in order to find a node, which dictates an insertion point for the next elementary BV. We'll label the insertion point node ν and the elementary node that should be inserted, b. A pseudocode illustration is presented in Figure 15.37. When a suitable ν is found, an insertion will take place. In a typical insertion, ν will be the parent of b. If ν was a leaf prior to insertion, an extra sibling node must be created, which will contain the elementary BV originally stored in ν.

Having inserted a new BV in the BVH, the BV properties of all the ancestors might have been destroyed. In order to correct this one could traverse the insertion path backward from the newly inserted BV to the root, and while doing so update every BV node on the path to cover its children.

Many variations over this scheme exist, however they all must deal with three basic problems:

- picking the next b from B, such that a good BVH will be built
- choosing the best child ν' during the traversal of the insertion path
- applying a good strategy to update the BVs on the insertion path after the insertion has taken place

An optimization strategy can be applied to make these decisions by attributing bs with a cost function and nodes ν in the BVH with another cost function, and then making choices which minimize the cost.

15.6 Smallest Enclosing Volume

Many types of BVs have been presented in the literature. The three most simple and widespread are spheres, AABBs, and OBBs. In the following, we will describe fitting methods for these. We refer the interested reader to references in Section 15.9 for more details on other types of BVs.

15.6.1 Fitting an OBB

A frequently used representation for an OBB is a center position, $\boldsymbol{c}$, and an orientation, $\boldsymbol{R}$, given as a rotation matrix. Each column in $\boldsymbol{R}$ is a unit vector along a major axis of the OBB, and three half length extents along the three axes of the OBB. Thus, in a precomputation step the half length extents are computed. Let's for a moment assume that the orientation of the OBB is given as

$$\boldsymbol{R} = \begin{bmatrix} \boldsymbol{v}_1 & \boldsymbol{v}_2 & \boldsymbol{v}_3 \end{bmatrix}. \tag{15.23}$$

For the vertices, $\boldsymbol{p}_i$ with $i \in [1..k]$, of the set of primitives, we could compute the upper and lower extremes along each axis of the sought OBB by

$$u^1 = \max\left(\boldsymbol{v}_1 \cdot \boldsymbol{p}_1, \ldots, \boldsymbol{v}_1 \cdot \boldsymbol{p}_k\right), \tag{15.24a}$$
$$u^2 = \max\left(\boldsymbol{v}_2 \cdot \boldsymbol{p}_1, \ldots, \boldsymbol{v}_2 \cdot \boldsymbol{p}_k\right), \tag{15.24b}$$
$$u^3 = \max\left(\boldsymbol{v}_3 \cdot \boldsymbol{p}_1, \ldots, \boldsymbol{v}_3 \cdot \boldsymbol{p}_k\right), \tag{15.24c}$$
$$l^1 = \min\left(\boldsymbol{v}_1 \cdot \boldsymbol{p}_1, \ldots, \boldsymbol{v}_1 \cdot \boldsymbol{p}_k\right), \tag{15.24d}$$
$$l^2 = \min\left(\boldsymbol{v}_2 \cdot \boldsymbol{p}_1, \ldots, \boldsymbol{v}_2 \cdot \boldsymbol{p}_k\right), \tag{15.24e}$$
$$l^3 = \min\left(\boldsymbol{v}_3 \cdot \boldsymbol{p}_1, \ldots, \boldsymbol{v}_3 \cdot \boldsymbol{p}_k\right). \tag{15.24f}$$

The width w, height h, and depth d of the OBB would be given by

$$w = u^1 - l^1, \tag{15.25a}$$
$$h = u^2 - l^2, \tag{15.25b}$$
$$d = u^3 - l^3. \tag{15.25c}$$

The half length extents are therefore given by $(w/2, h/2, d/2)$, and finally the center of the OBB by

$$\boldsymbol{c} = \frac{1}{2}\left(l^1 + u^1\right)\boldsymbol{v}^1 + \frac{1}{2}\left(l^2 + u^2\right)\boldsymbol{v}^2 + \frac{1}{2}\left(l^3 + u^3\right)\boldsymbol{v}^3. \tag{15.26}$$

In conclusion, knowing the orientation of the OBB, it is quite easy to compute its center and extents. Unfortunately, that was under the assumption of known orientation of the OBB.

Generally speaking, if the set of primitives has a long and thin shape, so should the tightest enclosing OBB fitting the set of primitives. Covariance as discussed in Section 15.5.1.2 provides us with a powerful tool for finding an enclosing volume. For instance, we could use the axis of maximum variance to set up an orientation for an OBB. Figure 15.38 shows a 2D example where extremal points along the axes

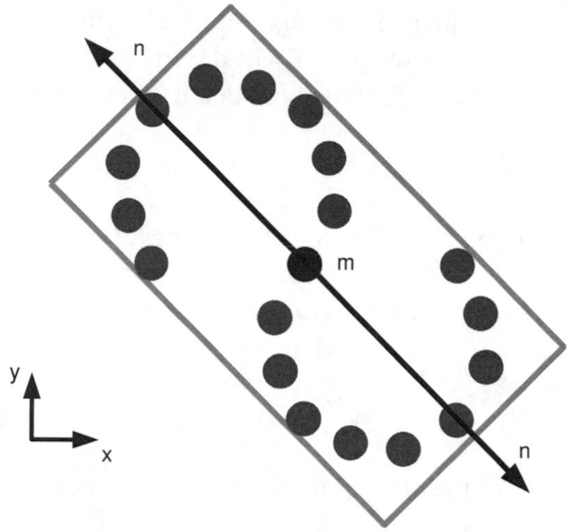

Figure 15.38: Using maximum variance to find the orientation of OBB.

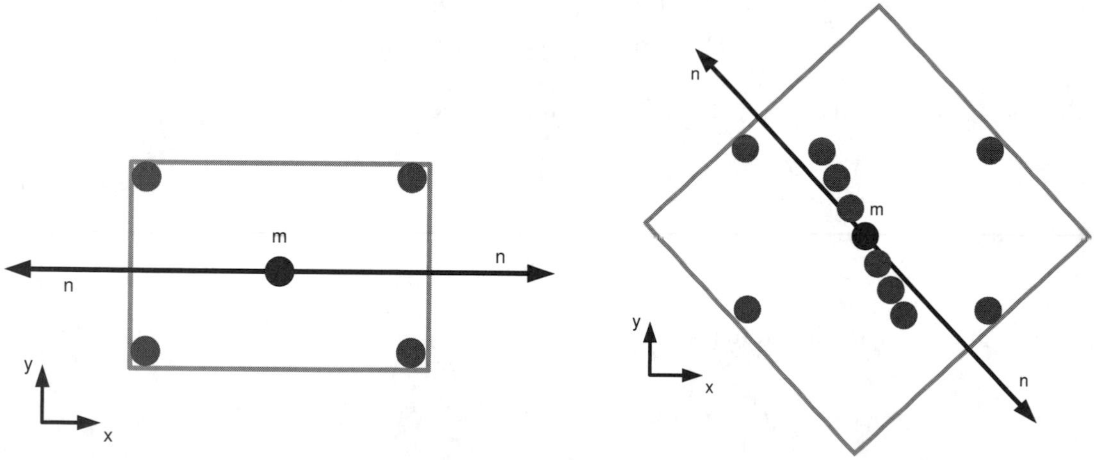

(a) No misalignment

(b) Misalignment caused by internal nodes

Figure 15.39: Influence of interior vertices causing a significant misalignment of the enclosing OBB.

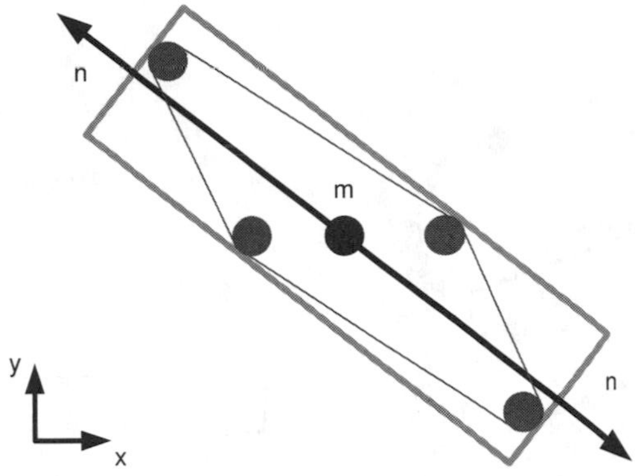

Figure 15.40: Using points lying on the convex hull only to avoid misalignment caused by interior points.

of maximum variance are used to compute an OBB. However, this headless approach suffers from some difficulties arising form the distribution of the points. For instance, the influence of interior vertices can cause an arbitrary misalignment of the enclosing OBB, as illustrated in Figure 15.39(b). To get around this, we could try to eliminate the contribution of interior points to the covariance. For instance, we could compute the convex hull of the set of points and then only use the points lying on the surface of the convex hull, thus ignoring all points lying inside the convex hull, as illustrated in Figure 15.40. It appears from Figure 15.40 that we have solved all our troubles, but misalignment could still in fact occur. If there is a nonuniform distribution of points on the convex hull, it could cause an arbitrary bad misalignment, as can be seen from Figure 15.41. The problem could be seen as a sampling artifact, and one way to remedy it would be to resample the surface of the convex hull with points to obtain a uniform distribution. However, this is a costly operation to perform and by no means as trivial as it may sound. A far better solution is to take the limiting case where we resampled the surface of the convex hull with infinitely many points, such that they would cover the entire surface in a uniform manner. This actually corresponds to integrating over the surface of the convex hull as shown in Figure 15.41(b).

Although this method is general, some point sets can still cause misalignment due to special symmetry, such as is illustrated in Figure 15.42. There are currently no known methods to get around this. The covariance-based method we have outlined does not yield optimal OBBs, and they can easily be shown to be suboptimal. In Figure 15.43 the nonoptimality of the covariance-based alignment method is illustrated. In Figure 15.43(a), an initial object with its covariance-aligned OBB is shown. In Figure 15.43(b) a slightly altered object is shown superimposed on the original object. The object has been altered so that its convex hull still lies inside the original OBB, shown with dotted lines. The alteration is shown grayed. The change in shape causes the covariance alignment to pick another orientation of the OBB, shown with solid lines. The change in orientation causes a slight change in the extents of the OBB. Because the altered OBB covers the altered object, and the altered object covers the initial object, then the altered OBB also covers the initial object. By construction, the initial OBB covers the altered object. In essence we have two distinct OBBs both covering two different objects.

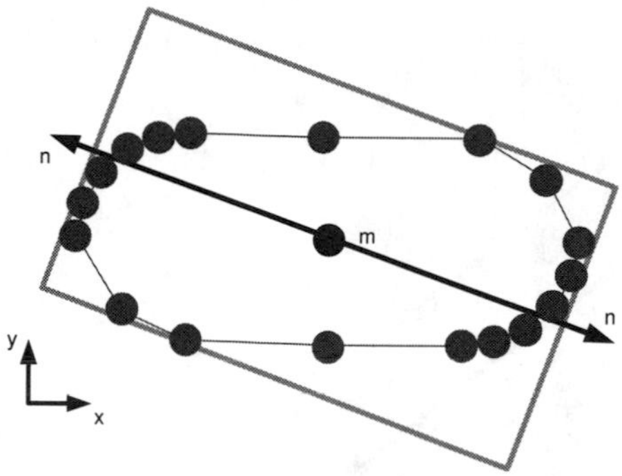

(a) Misalignment caused by nonuniform point distribution.

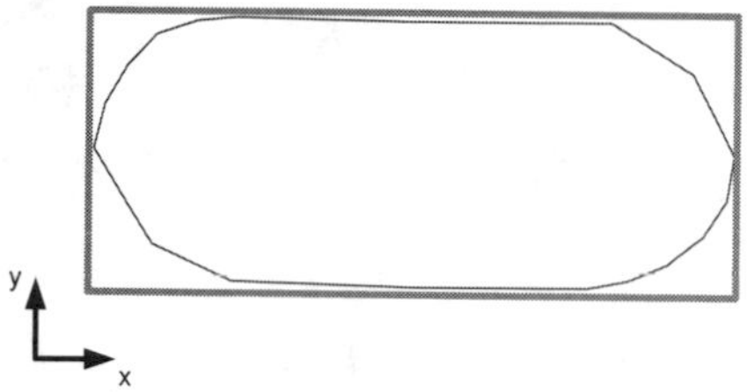

(b) Integrate covariance over surface of convex hull to avoid misalignment.

Figure 15.41: Nonuniform distribution of points on the convex hull causing misalignment of OBB.

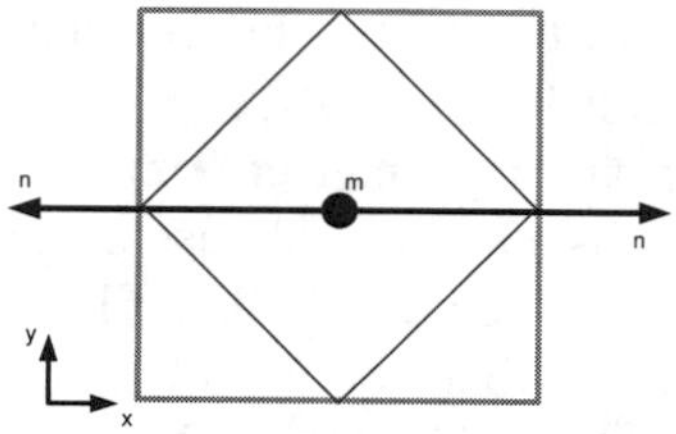

Figure 15.42: Special geometry causing bad misalignment; square has same statistical spread in all directions, any may be a chosen orientation. The figure illustrates the worst-case fit.

Now let us try to derive formulas for integrating the covariance matrix over the surface of the convex hull. Let $\boldsymbol{x}$ denote a random point on the surface of the convex hull, then the entries of the covariance matrix

$$\boldsymbol{C} = \begin{bmatrix} C_{00} & C_{01} & C_{02} \\ C_{10} & C_{11} & C_{12} \\ C_{20} & C_{21} & C_{22} \end{bmatrix}, \tag{15.27}$$

is by definition given as

$$C_{ij} = E\left[\boldsymbol{x}_i \boldsymbol{x}_j\right] - E\left[\boldsymbol{x}_i\right] E\left[\boldsymbol{x}_j\right] \quad \forall i, j \in [0..2], \tag{15.28}$$

where $E[\cdot]$ is the statistical expectation operator, and $\boldsymbol{x}_i$ and $\boldsymbol{x}_j$ is the i'th and j'th coordinate of the random point. This is the statistical definition of covariance in comparison to the geometrical definition in (15.21). If we let S denote the surface of the convex hull and dA a differential area element, then the

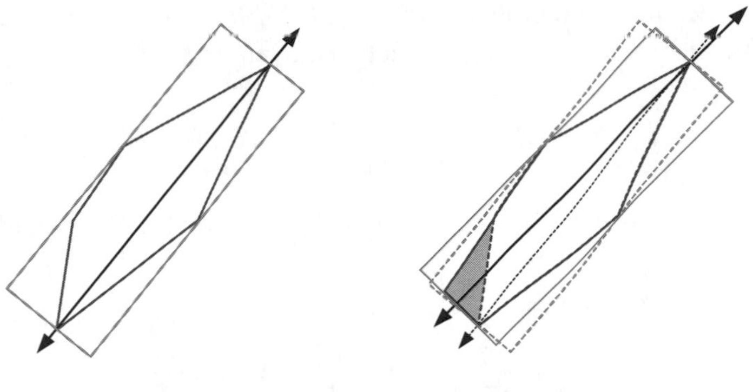

(a) Initial object with its covariance-aligned OBB.

(b) Slightly altered object inside initial OBB, however, covariance-aligned OBB is different.

Figure 15.43: Covariance-aligned OBBs are suboptimal.

expectations above is by definition given as

$$E[\boldsymbol{x}_i] = \frac{\int_S \boldsymbol{x}_i dA}{\int_S dA}, \tag{15.29a}$$

$$E[\boldsymbol{x}_j] = \frac{\int_S \boldsymbol{x}_j dA}{\int_S dA}, \tag{15.29b}$$

$$E[\boldsymbol{x}_i \boldsymbol{x}_j] = \frac{\int_S \boldsymbol{x}_i \boldsymbol{x}_j dA}{\int_S dA}. \tag{15.29c}$$

Without loss of generality we will assume that the surface of the convex hull consists of a set of triangles, T^k for $k = 1, \ldots, K$. If this is not the case, these triangles can easily be obtained by standard triangularization methods [Berg et al., 1997, O'Rourke, 1998]. The three vertices of the k'th triangle are given by $\boldsymbol{p}^k$, $\boldsymbol{q}^k$, and $\boldsymbol{r}^k$. A parameterization of the k'th triangle is written as

$$\boldsymbol{x}(s,t) = \boldsymbol{p}^k + \boldsymbol{u}^k s + \boldsymbol{v}^k t, \quad \text{where} \quad s \in [0,1], t \in [0, 1-s], \tag{15.30}$$

and the area of the k'th triangle, A^k, is written as

$$A^k = \frac{1}{2} \left\| \boldsymbol{u}^k \times \boldsymbol{v}^k \right\|_2, \tag{15.31}$$

where $\boldsymbol{u}^k = q^k - p^k$ and $\boldsymbol{v}^k = r^k - p^k$. The total integrals over the surface S can be viewed as the sum of integrals over each of the triangles. In particular, the denominator in the above equations is

$$\int_S dA = \sum_k \int_{T^k} dA. \tag{15.32}$$

Now the main idea is to change the integration variable to s and t, such that we can use our parameterization to evaluate the expectation integrals in (15.29a), (15.29b), and (15.29c). The change of variable, when integrating any function $f(s,t)$ over the triangle, is given by

$$\int_{T^k} f dA = \left\| \boldsymbol{u}^k \times \boldsymbol{v}^k \right\|_2 \int_0^1 \int_0^{1-s} f(s,t) dt ds. \tag{15.33}$$

Applying this strategy to the denominator in (15.29a), (15.29b), and (15.29c) yields

$$\int_S dA = \sum_k \int_{T^k} dA \tag{15.34a}$$

$$= \sum_k \left\| \boldsymbol{u}^k \times \boldsymbol{v}^k \right\|_2 \int_0^1 \int_0^{1-s} dt ds \tag{15.34b}$$

$$= \sum_k \left\| \boldsymbol{u}^k \times \boldsymbol{v}^k \right\|_2 \int_0^1 (1-s)\, ds \tag{15.34c}$$

$$= \sum_k \left\| \boldsymbol{u}^k \times \boldsymbol{v}^k \right\|_2 \frac{1}{2} \tag{15.34d}$$

$$= \sum_k A^k = A. \tag{15.34e}$$

The area of the convex hull is thus the sum of all triangle areas. Applying the same recipe to the enumerator in (15.29a) yields

$$E\left[\boldsymbol{x}_i\right] = \frac{1}{A} \int_S \boldsymbol{x}_i dA \tag{15.35a}$$

$$= \frac{1}{A} \sum_k \int_{T^k} \boldsymbol{x}_i^k dA, \tag{15.35b}$$

and changing the integration variable and substituting parameterization give

$$\int_{T^k} \boldsymbol{x}_i^k dA = \left\| \boldsymbol{u}^k \times \boldsymbol{v}^k \right\|_2 \int_0^1 \int_0^{1-s} \boldsymbol{x}_i^k dt ds \tag{15.36a}$$

$$= \left\| \boldsymbol{u}^k \times \boldsymbol{v}^k \right\|_2 \int_0^1 \int_0^{1-s} \left(\boldsymbol{p}^k + \boldsymbol{u}^k s + \boldsymbol{v}^k t \right)_i dt ds \tag{15.36b}$$

$$= \left(\left\| \boldsymbol{u}^k \times \boldsymbol{v}^k \right\|_2 \int_0^1 \int_0^{1-s} \boldsymbol{p}^k + \boldsymbol{u}^k s + \boldsymbol{v}^k t dt ds \right)_i . \tag{15.36c}$$

Notice that subscript refers to the i'th coordinate. Trivially solving the integrals yields

$$\int_{T^k} \boldsymbol{x}_i^k dA = \left(\left\| \boldsymbol{u}^k \times \boldsymbol{v}^k \right\|_2 \frac{1}{6} \left(\boldsymbol{p}^k + \boldsymbol{q}^k + \boldsymbol{r}^k \right) \right)_i . \tag{15.37}$$

Rewriting, we get

$$\int_{T^k} \boldsymbol{x}_i^k dA = \left(\left(\frac{1}{2} \left\| \boldsymbol{u}^k \times \boldsymbol{v}^k \right\|_2 \right) \left(\frac{1}{3} \left(\boldsymbol{p}^k + \boldsymbol{q}^k + \boldsymbol{r}^k \right) \right) \right)_i \tag{15.38a}$$

$$= A^k \boldsymbol{m}_i, \tag{15.38b}$$

where $m^k = \frac{1}{3}\left(\boldsymbol{p}^k + \boldsymbol{r}^k + \boldsymbol{q}^k\right)$ is mean of the k'th triangle. Back substitution leads to the following solution for the first expectation

$$E\left[\boldsymbol{x}_i\right] = \sum_k A^k \boldsymbol{m}_i. \tag{15.39}$$

It is trivial to see that by the same derivation, the solution to the second expectation is given as

$$E\left[\boldsymbol{x}_j\right] = \sum_k A^k \boldsymbol{m}_j. \tag{15.40}$$

The exact same approach can now be applied to the third and last expectation integral, that is,

$$E\left[\boldsymbol{x}_i \boldsymbol{x}_j\right] = \frac{1}{A} \int_S \boldsymbol{x}_i \boldsymbol{x}_j dA \tag{15.41a}$$

$$= \frac{1}{A} \sum_k \int_{T^k} \boldsymbol{x}_i^k \boldsymbol{x}_j^k dA. \tag{15.41b}$$

Changing integration variables and substituting the triangle parameterization leads to the following results with a bit of mathematical handiwork:

$$E\left[\boldsymbol{x}_i \boldsymbol{x}_j\right] = \frac{1}{A} \sum_k \frac{2A^k}{24} \left(9\boldsymbol{m}_i^k \boldsymbol{m}_j^k + \boldsymbol{p}_i^k \boldsymbol{p}_j^k + \boldsymbol{q}_i^k \boldsymbol{q}_j^k + \boldsymbol{r}_i^k \boldsymbol{r}_j^k \right). \tag{15.42}$$

The derivation is long and quite trivial so we refer the interested reader to [Gottschalk, 2000] for a detailed proof. By back substituting into the definition of covariance we obtain the desired result

$$C_{ij} = E\left[\boldsymbol{x}_i \boldsymbol{x}_j\right] - E\left[\boldsymbol{x}_i\right] E\left[\boldsymbol{x}_j\right] \tag{15.43a}$$

$$= \frac{1}{A} \sum_k \frac{1}{24} \left(9\boldsymbol{m}_i^k \boldsymbol{m}_j^k + \boldsymbol{p}_i^k \boldsymbol{p}_j^k + \boldsymbol{q}_i^k \boldsymbol{q}_j^k + \boldsymbol{r}_i^k \boldsymbol{r}_j^k \right) - \boldsymbol{m}_i^S \boldsymbol{m}_j^S, \tag{15.43b}$$

where $\boldsymbol{m}^S$ is the mean point of the entire surface. Observe that the covariance matrix is symmetrical, meaning that only six entries need to be evaluated.

15.6.2 Fitting an AABB

The axes aligned bounding box (AABB) was treated in detail in Chapter 12, and may be considered a special case of an OBB, where the orientation is given as

$$\boldsymbol{R} = \begin{bmatrix} \boldsymbol{v}_1 & \boldsymbol{v}_2 & \boldsymbol{v}_3 \end{bmatrix}, \text{and } \boldsymbol{v}_1 = [1,0,0]^T, \boldsymbol{v}_2 = [0,1,0]^T, \boldsymbol{v}_3 = [0,0,1]^T. \tag{15.44}$$

Therefore, we can compute the minimum and maximum points of an AABB by

$$u^1 = \max\left(\boldsymbol{v}_1 \cdot \boldsymbol{p}_1, \ldots, \boldsymbol{v}_1 \cdot \boldsymbol{p}_k\right), \tag{15.45a}$$
$$u^2 = \max\left(\boldsymbol{v}_2 \cdot \boldsymbol{p}_1, \ldots, \boldsymbol{v}_2 \cdot \boldsymbol{p}_k\right), \tag{15.45b}$$
$$u^3 = \max\left(\boldsymbol{v}_3 \cdot \boldsymbol{p}_1, \ldots, \boldsymbol{v}_3 \cdot \boldsymbol{p}_k\right), \tag{15.45c}$$
$$l^1 = \min\left(\boldsymbol{v}_1 \cdot \boldsymbol{p}_1, \ldots, \boldsymbol{v}_1 \cdot \boldsymbol{p}_k\right), \tag{15.45d}$$
$$l^2 = \min\left(\boldsymbol{v}_2 \cdot \boldsymbol{p}_1, \ldots, \boldsymbol{v}_2 \cdot \boldsymbol{p}_k\right), \tag{15.45e}$$
$$l^3 = \min\left(\boldsymbol{v}_3 \cdot \boldsymbol{p}_1, \ldots, \boldsymbol{v}_3 \cdot \boldsymbol{p}_k\right), \tag{15.45f}$$

and then we have

$$\boldsymbol{r}_{min} = \left[l^1, l^2, l^3\right]^T, \quad \text{and} \quad \boldsymbol{r}_{max} = \left[u^1, u^2, u^3\right]^T. \tag{15.46}$$

Notice that there is no need to save the orientation, since it is given implicitly.

15.6.3 Fitting a Sphere

We'll first consider some simple cases where the set of primitives we want to enclose consists of a set of one point, two points, three points, and four points. We label these points as $\boldsymbol{v}_0$, $\boldsymbol{v}_1$, $\boldsymbol{v}_2$, and $\boldsymbol{v}_3$. Also, we assume that all points are in general position, that is, no four points lie in the same plane, no three points lie on the same line, and no two points have equal coordinates.

In case we only have a single point, we can trivially find an enclosing sphere by setting the center, $\boldsymbol{c}$, equal to the point and the radius, r, to zero:

$$\boldsymbol{c} = \boldsymbol{v}_0, \tag{15.47a}$$
$$r = 0. \tag{15.47b}$$

In case we have two points, they must both lie on the surface of the smallest enclosing sphere, meaning that they are equidistant from the center of the enclosing sphere

$$\boldsymbol{c} = \tfrac{1}{2}\left(\boldsymbol{v}_1 - \boldsymbol{v}_0\right) + \boldsymbol{v}_0, \tag{15.48a}$$
$$r = \tfrac{1}{2}\left\|\boldsymbol{v}_1 - \boldsymbol{v}_0\right\|_2. \tag{15.48b}$$

In the case where we have more than two points, and if all points do not lie on the surface of the enclosing sphere, then we can reduce the problem to the trivial case above.

So without further fuss, we assume that all points lie on the surface of the smallest enclosing sphere, implying that they are all equidistant from the center of the sphere. Let n denote the number of points, either three or four, then we have

$$\left\|\boldsymbol{c} - \boldsymbol{v}_i\right\|_2 = r \quad 0 \leq i \leq n. \tag{15.49}$$

If we take the square and rewrite the above constraints, we have

$$\left(\boldsymbol{c} - \boldsymbol{v}_i\right) \cdot \left(\boldsymbol{c} - \boldsymbol{v}_i\right) = r^2, \tag{15.50a}$$
$$\Downarrow$$
$$\boldsymbol{c} \cdot \boldsymbol{c} - \boldsymbol{c} \cdot \boldsymbol{v}_i - \boldsymbol{v}_i \cdot \boldsymbol{c} + \boldsymbol{v}_i \cdot \boldsymbol{v}_i = r^2, \tag{15.50b}$$

for all $0 \leq i < n$. If we subtract the equation $i = 0$ from all the equations with $i > 0$, then we find

$$\boldsymbol{c} \cdot \boldsymbol{c} - \boldsymbol{c} \cdot \boldsymbol{v}_i - \boldsymbol{v}_i \cdot \boldsymbol{c} + \boldsymbol{v}_i \cdot \boldsymbol{v}_i - (\boldsymbol{c} \cdot \boldsymbol{c} - \boldsymbol{c} \cdot \boldsymbol{v}_0 - \boldsymbol{v}_0 \cdot \boldsymbol{c} + \boldsymbol{v}_0 \cdot \boldsymbol{v}_0)\, d = r^2 - r^2, \tag{15.51a}$$

$$\Downarrow$$

$$-\boldsymbol{c} \cdot \boldsymbol{v}_i - \boldsymbol{v}_i \cdot \boldsymbol{c} + \boldsymbol{v}_i \cdot \boldsymbol{v}_i + \boldsymbol{c} \cdot \boldsymbol{v}_0 + \boldsymbol{v}_0 \cdot \boldsymbol{c} - \boldsymbol{v}_0 \cdot \boldsymbol{v}_0 = 0, \tag{15.51b}$$

$$\Downarrow$$

$$-2\boldsymbol{v}_i \cdot \boldsymbol{c} + 2\boldsymbol{v}_0 \cdot \boldsymbol{c} - 2\boldsymbol{v}_0 \cdot \boldsymbol{v}_0 = -\boldsymbol{v}_i \cdot \boldsymbol{v}_i - \boldsymbol{v}_0 \cdot \boldsymbol{v}_0. \tag{15.51c}$$

We now add $+2\boldsymbol{v}_i \cdot \boldsymbol{v}_0$ to both sides of the equation to give

$$-2\boldsymbol{v}_i \cdot \boldsymbol{c} + 2\boldsymbol{v}_0 \cdot \boldsymbol{c} - 2\boldsymbol{v}_0 \cdot \boldsymbol{v}_0 + 2\boldsymbol{v}_i \cdot \boldsymbol{v}_0 = -\boldsymbol{v}_i \cdot \boldsymbol{v}_i - \boldsymbol{v}_0 \cdot \boldsymbol{v}_0 + 2\boldsymbol{v}_i \cdot \boldsymbol{v}_0, \tag{15.52a}$$

$$\Downarrow$$

$$(\boldsymbol{v}_i - \boldsymbol{v}_0) \cdot (\boldsymbol{c} - \boldsymbol{v}_0) = \tfrac{1}{2} (\boldsymbol{v}_i - \boldsymbol{v}_0) \cdot (\boldsymbol{v}_i - \boldsymbol{v}_0), \tag{15.52b}$$

$$\Downarrow$$

$$(\boldsymbol{v}_i - \boldsymbol{v}_0) \cdot (\boldsymbol{c} - \boldsymbol{v}_0) = \tfrac{1}{2} \|\boldsymbol{v}_i - \boldsymbol{v}_0\|_2^2. \tag{15.52c}$$

Using the matrix and vector notation

$$\boldsymbol{M} = \begin{bmatrix} \boldsymbol{v}_1 - \boldsymbol{v}_0 \\ \boldsymbol{v}_2 - \boldsymbol{v}_0 \\ \vdots \\ \boldsymbol{v}_i - \boldsymbol{v}_0 \end{bmatrix}, \quad \boldsymbol{b} = \begin{bmatrix} \frac{1}{2} \|\boldsymbol{v}_1 - \boldsymbol{v}_0\|_2^2 \\ \frac{1}{2} \|\boldsymbol{v}_2 - \boldsymbol{v}_0\|_2^2 \\ \vdots \\ \frac{1}{2} \|\boldsymbol{v}_i - \boldsymbol{v}_0\|_2^2 \end{bmatrix}, \tag{15.53}$$

we can write the derivations for all the equations $0 < i < n$ as

$$\boldsymbol{M} (\boldsymbol{c} - \boldsymbol{v}_0) = \boldsymbol{b}, \tag{15.54}$$

which allows us to write the solution for the center of the enclosing sphere as

$$\boldsymbol{c} = \boldsymbol{v}_0 + \boldsymbol{M}^{-1}\boldsymbol{b}, \tag{15.55}$$

and the radius as

$$r = \|\boldsymbol{c} - \boldsymbol{v}_0\|_2 = \left\|\boldsymbol{M}^{-1}\boldsymbol{b}\right\|_2. \tag{15.56}$$

In the case where we have three points, which lie in the same plane, then the sphere center will also lie in that plane and $\boldsymbol{M} \in \mathbb{R}^{2\times2}$. For four points, $\boldsymbol{M} \in \mathbb{R}^{3\times3}$. $\boldsymbol{M}$ will always be invertible [Eberly, 2005a] regardless of the number of points.

A randomized algorithm can now be used to compute the minimum enclosing sphere of a point set with $n \geq 1$ points using the above results. The idea is a simple trial and error strategy, where a minimum sphere is first constructed from a subset of the point set, and then it is verified whether all points lie inside the sphere. If so, the algorithm terminates, and if not, a new point has been found lying outside the sphere. The new point is then used as a surface point in the computation of a new minimum enclosing sphere. The algorithm continues in this manner until all points lie inside the sphere. The algorithm is called the Welzl algorithm [Welzl, 1991, Berg et al., 1997], and Figure 15.6.3 shows a pseudocode version of the algorithm. For more details, we refer the reader to [Welzl, 1991, Berg et al., 1997].

```
function mini-ball(P)
  return compute-mini-ball(π(P),∅)

function compute-mini-Ball(P,R)
  if P = ∅ or |R| = 4
    D =circumscribed-sphere(R)
  else
    p = tail(P)
    D = compute-mini-Ball(P − {p}, R)
    if p ∉ D
      D = compute-mini-Ball(P − {p}, R ∪ {p})
      move p to head of P
  return D
```

Figure 15.44: Welzl algorithm for computing minimum enclosing sphere.

15.7 Handling Deformable Objects

Deformable objects are challenging for BVHs. Typically, a BVH will be calculated for an object's initial rest shape, but during a simulation the deformation of the object will cause the BVH to come out of sync with the object shape. Even worse, the deformations can be so extreme that self-intersections can also occur.

15.7.1 Updating the BVH

The simplest solution to getting the BVH to cover the geometry after a deformation is to rebuild it from scratch; however, this is not computationally very attractive, and prohibits real-time or even interactive use of the BVH.

A faster approach is to refit the current misaligned BVH. Reports have shown that it is about 10 times faster to refit an AABB tree of a triangle mesh than to rebuild the AABB tree [Bergen, 1997]. In general, if we have a fast method like $O(1)$ to refit a parent BV to cover its children BVs, then we could simply traverse the BVH in a bottom-up fashion. For example, for a deformable object, a leaf usually covers a single polygon, indicating that it is fast to refit the leaf BVs, and if refitting of parents based on their children BVs is fast, such as time $O(1)$, then the algorithm runs in $O(n)$ complexity. This is a so-called bottom-up update used by many [Bergen, 1997, Volino et al., 1998, Volino et al., 2000, Bridson et al., 2002, Mezger et al., 2003]. It is a fast and simple scheme, but has several drawbacks.

First of all, the bottom-up update requires one to traverse the entire BVH, which may not be a serious drawback for self-intersections, since in this case it is likely that all BVs will be visited in the collision query anyway.

A second problem with the bottom-up update is that not all BV types can be updated in $O(1)$ time. Some BV types, like AABBs and k-DOPs, share the nice property that if they tightly cover their children BV, then they also tightly cover the geometry of their children [Larsson et al., 2003]. Therefore, it is sufficient only to consider the children BV geometries when refitting a BV of these types, yielding a

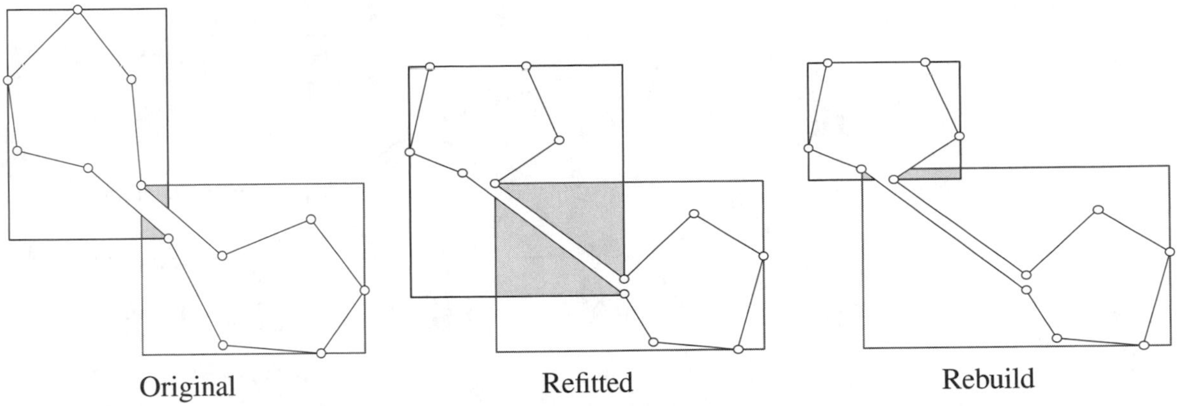

Figure 15.45: Illustration of refitting versus rebuilding. The two children AABBs of the root AABB are shown in the figure. Observe the large sibling overlap that occurs with refitting.

complexity of $O(d)$, where d is the branching factor, usually a small constant such that $O(d) \approx O(1)$. Other BV types, such as OBBs or spheres, require us to examine all the geometry covered by the subtree of a BV in order to refit with a tight BV. If the subtree covers k primitives, then a good OBB fit can be obtained in $O(k \log k)$, implying a worse-case $O(n^2 \log n)$ complexity for the entire update. A good sphere fit can usually be obtained in expected $O(k)$ complexity yielding a total of $O(n^2)$.

A third problem with the bottom-up update is that even in case of tight refitted BVs, pruning capabilities can deteriorate, due to an increasing overlap between sibling BVs. Deformations that keep the adjacency relation intact have been reported to have no significant performance deterioration for intersection [Bergen, 1997].

Figure 15.45 illustrates the problem of large overlap between sibling BVs, and shows how this problem could have been avoided by rebuilding the BVH. The first drawback of having to traverse the entire BVH can be avoided by a top-down approach, such that only those BVs used in a collision query are refitted.

If two objects are distant, then only their root BVs will need to be updated, and if two deformable objects overlap only in a few places, then the tandem traversal will only require refitting of a few BVs. However, the top-down approach will not yield good performance when we consider self-intersections or close parallel proximities, such as cloth or skin on a human being, where every primitive is in contact with at least one primitive from the other object. In these cases, a collision query will traverse almost the entire BVHs of both objects and require most of the tree to be refitted.

One advantage of the top-down method is that it is easily added to the collision query. During a world space or model space update, one simply also refits the two BVs. The top-down method also suffers from the two other problems that the bottom-up method had: for certain BV types, tight refitting is slow, and pruning capabilities can deteriorate, even with tight refitting sibling.

Finally, comparing top-down with bottom-up methods, we can see that bottom-up methods rely on the fact that the children have been refitted prior to refitting a BV, which is not required for the top-down method. Thus, unless we want to evaluate the children, their children, and so on before refitting a BV, we need to come up with a clever way of avoiding the traversal of the entire BVH. In [Larsson et al., 2001]

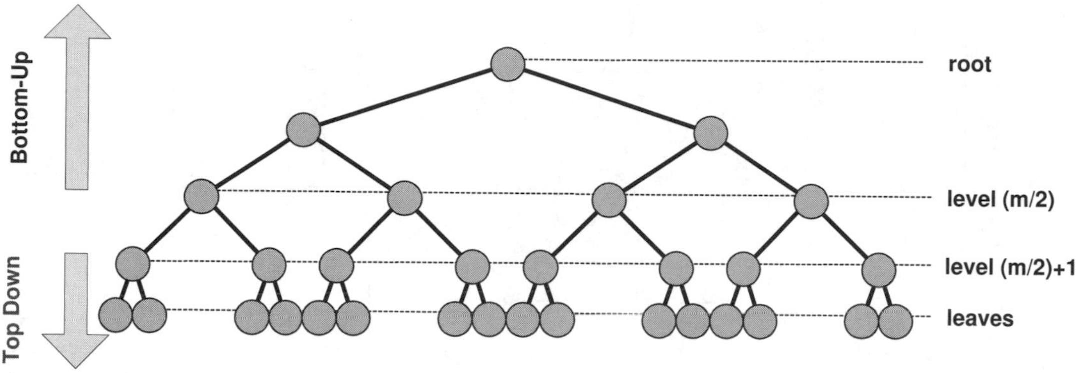

Figure 15.46: Illustration of hybrid update, first levels of BVH are refitted bottom-up, the levels below $m/2$ are refitted in a top-down fashion.

the problem is solved by letting each BV in the hierarchy store the primitives covered by its subtree. Thus, in a top-down update method, one can simply refit a BV to cover the primitives stored in the BV. However, as pointed out by the authors, this results in a memory drawback.

A hybrid update is suggested in [Larsson et al., 2001] where a bottom-up update is mixed with a top-down update, in the hope that a combination will give the advantages of both methods. The main idea is to try to minimize the number of BV updates. For a tree with depth m, the hybrid update method initially updates the $m/2$ first levels bottom up. During a collision query, when nonupdated BVs are reached, they can either be updated top-down as needed, or a specified number of levels in their subtrees can be updated using a bottom-up method. Figure 15.46 illustrates the basic idea of the hybrid update method. According to [Larsson et al., 2001] their method is roughly five times faster than [Bergen, 1997]. One will also observe that their numerical experiments hint that the complexity of the hybrid update method is similar to the bottom-up method, although the constants seem to be half as big for the hybrid update as for the bottom-up update (see Figure 3 in [Larsson et al., 2001]).

15.7.2 Handling Self-Intersections

By the nature of physical objects, their surfaces are fully connected and closed, implying that all primitives are in touching contact with their immediate neighbors. Thus, even without *self-intersections*, we will have $O(n)$ contacts in a deformable object consisting of n primitives. Equation (15.10) therefore implies that without self-intersections, we should not expect to perform a collision query better than

$$2n\log_2(n) + 2n - 1 \approx O(n\log_2 n). \tag{15.57}$$

For a deformable object, this is a lower bound, because we cannot exploit the idea of pruning as we did for static objects. Since every part of an object obviously collides with itself, taking a BVH and testing it against itself will cause us to traverse all the way down all the paths to the leaves.

Using the tandem traversal blindly will produce a lot of redundant work as we will show later. The literature has proposed two solutions to improve upon the complexity and redundancies of the traversal

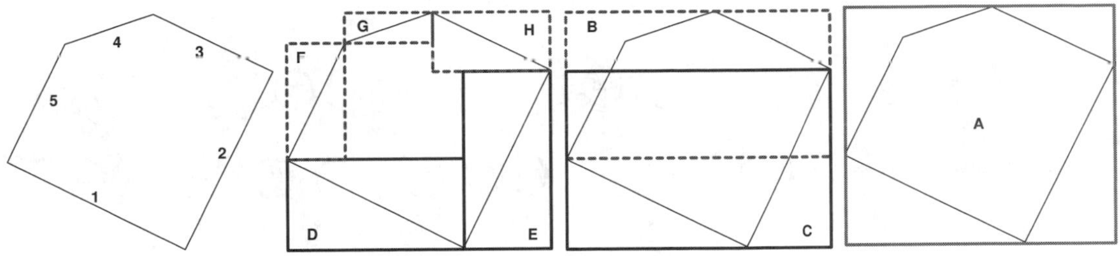

Figure 15.47: Simple 2D example BVH for self-intersection query. The figure shows the original, finest, mid, and coarsest levels.

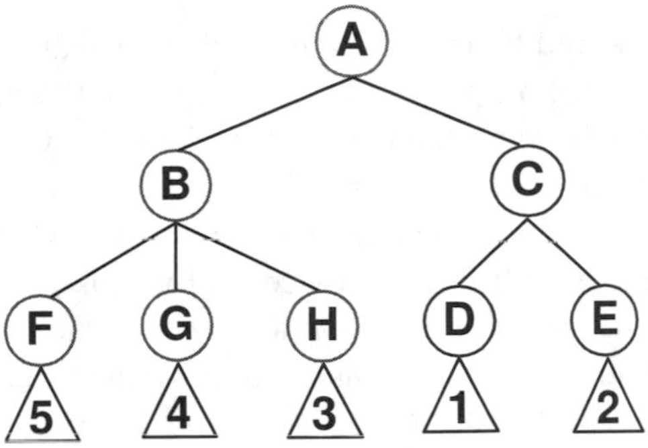

Figure 15.48: Topology of BVH from Figure 15.47.

problem: extending the overlap test in the tandem traversal with several other kinds of tests and using a single traversal instead of a tandem traversal.

The traditional tandem traversal can be extended to include self-intersection by making sure that primitive pair testing is only performed if the primitives do not share a common point such as a vertex of a face. This will disregard immediate neighbors and the primitive itself from primitive pair testing.

We'll study the problems of using BVHs blindly for self-intersection testing by a simple example. In Figure 15.47 we show a small stick figure consisting of five sticks forming a diamond together with the BVs that form a BVH. The topology of the BVH is shown in Figure 15.48. Observe that we have chosen AABBs and that the BVH was built using mesh connectivity. A *bounding volume test tree* (*BVTT*) is shown in Figure 15.49, which is the result of performing a tandem traversal of the BVH shown in Figure 15.48 against itself. From the figure it is evident that the pruning capabilities have degraded completely for a self-intersection test. Only in the C-G overlap were the traversals able to prune, as shown grayed in the figure. From the BVTT we see that a total of 40 BV overlap tests are performed, from which 8 primitive pair tests are performed.

In comparison with a brute all-sticks against all-sticks, which yields 10 tests, disregarding redundant tests will result in only 5 primitive pair tests. Obviously, the brute-force approach out performs the BVH

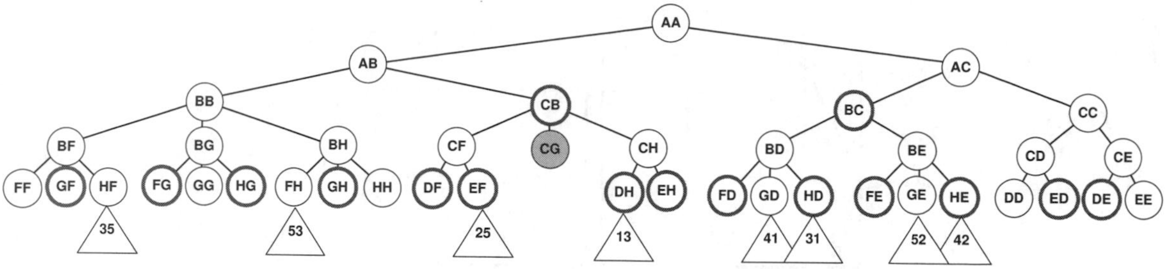

Figure 15.49: Bounding Volume Test Tree (BVTT), each node represents a BV test, children represent a descend in the tandem traversal, and primitive pair testing is shown as annotated triangles.

in this case.

In a real application, objects would be much bigger, and the extent of a single primitive would be far less than the extent of the entire model, implying that for a bigger BVH the traversal will be able to better prune those primitives lying distant from each other, such as the C-G overlap test in the example above. In conclusion, for large n, the BVH will beat the all-pair $O(n^2)$ complexity with its $O(n \log_2 n)$ complexity.

Some properties should be noted from the example: out of the 40 BV overlap test, 16 of them had redundancies, implying that 8 of these where done twice. In four cases, these redundant BV overlap tests led to primitive pair tests, implying that two primitive tests were done twice. We also see that if one can catch redundant tests lying close to the root, substantial improvements can be made. For instance, in the case of the redundant C-B and B-C test, only one of their subtrees needs to be explored, thus pruning the B-C tree would reduce the work with 9 BV overlap tests and 4 primitive tests.

Since we already know that every leaf of the BVH will collide with the BVH, there is really no need to perform a tandem traversal. Instead, we can perform a single traversal. The idea is to iterate over all leaf BVs, testing each of them recursively against the entire BVH. The pseudocode for the *single traversal* is presented in Figure 15.50. For completeness, we have shown the BVTT in Figure 15.51 using a single traversal for self-intersection testing of the BVH shown in Figure 15.48. In comparison with Figure 15.49, notice that we perform just slightly better. This time there is a total of 38 BV overlap tests. We still perform the same amount of primitive pair tests, and there are still 16 redundant BV overlap tests; however, there is one difference. The redundancies are all leaf BV overlap tests—no internal redundant BV overlap tests exists. However, we can still not beat the brute-force method for the example. Another important observation is that the BVTTs for the single traversal have less height than the BVTT for the tandem traversal.

A *modified tandem traversal* is presented in [Volino et al., 2000] for self-intersection testing. Figure 15.52 shows the modified self-intersection traversal in pseudocode. The modified traversal exploits the fact that there is no need to test a BV against itself. It completely removes all redundant overlap tests, since the recursive sibling testing is invoked such that a tandem traversal is run only once between two children. To see the advantage of this traversal, a BVTT is shown in Figure 15.53. As seen in the figure, the number of overlap tests has dropped to 12, and the number of primitive tests is 3. The self-test algorithm is invoked 8 times. There is no redundant overlap tests or primitive tests. This modified traversal beats the brute-force approach, and it avoids the redundant leaf BV testing, which the single traversal

```
algorithm self-intersect(A : BVH )
  for all leaf BVs B in A do
    single(root,B)
  next B
end algorithm

algorithm single(A : BV, B : BV )
  Queue Q
  push(Q, A)
  while not Q empty do
    pop(Q, A)
    if not colliding(A, B) then
      continue
    if leaf(A) then
      contact-determination(A, B)
    else
      for all children C of A do
        push(Q, C)
      next C
    end if
  end while
end algorithm
```

Figure 15.50: Single traversal for self-intersection testing.

suffers from.

Mezger *et al.* [Mezger et al., 2003] have extended the work in [Volino et al., 1998] by using a top-down splitting approach for building k-DOP trees, and a BV inflation technique, where applied, to accommodate proximity queries of a moving and deforming object. Furthermore, they have extended the *curvature testing* used by [Volino et al., 1998, Volino et al., 2000], with several other heuristics. We refer the reader to [Mezger et al., 2003] for more details. Here we will limit ourselves to present the basic idea behind the curvature testing extension.

As we have seen, the adjacent structural nature of primitives causes a performance degradation on the BVH traversals, leading to deep BVTTs traversing all the way down to leaf BV tests. Both the tandem, single, and modified traversals we have presented seem to suffer from these artifacts. However, these problems will be remedied by extending the traversals with a curvature test.

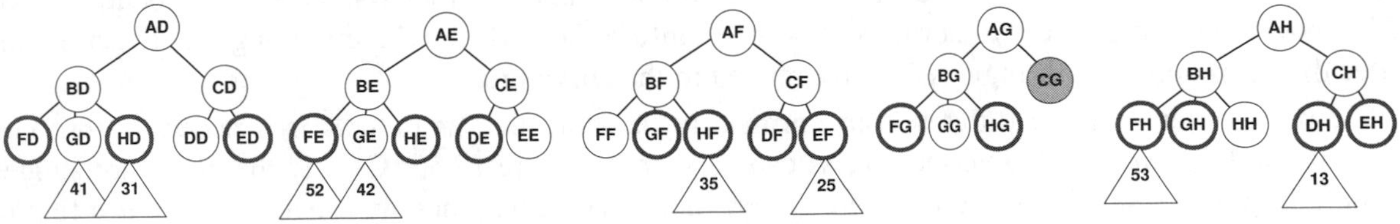

Figure 15.51: Bounding Volume Test Tree (BVTT) for single traversal. Compare with Figure 15.49.

```
algorithm self-test(A:BV)
  if leaf A then
    return
  end if
  for all children C of A do
    self-test(C)
    for all children D right of C do
      recursive(C,D)
    next D
  next C
end algorithm
```

Figure 15.52: Modified traversal for self-intersection testing. Siblings are tested against each other using the traditional recursive tandem traversal (see Figure 15.15); a child is tested against itself by a recursive call on all of its children.

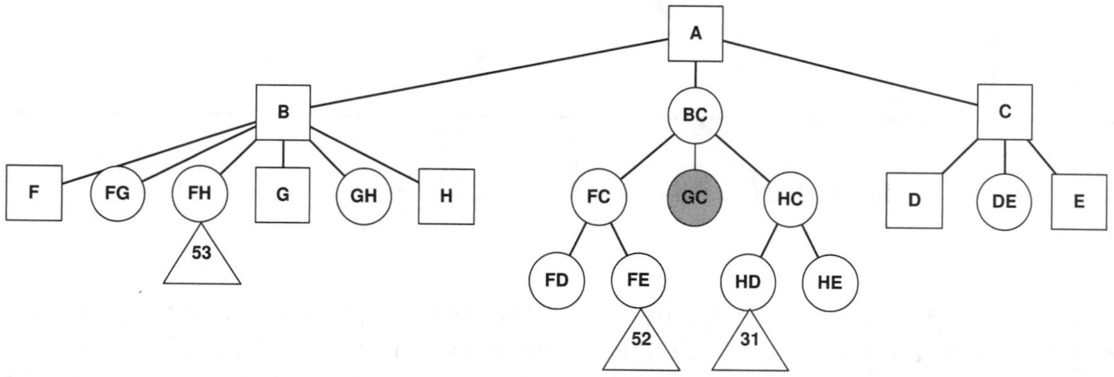

Figure 15.53: BVTT of modified traversal from Figure 15.52 on BVH from Figure 15.48. Square nodes denote calls to self-test, circles are calls to recursive tandem traversal.

In Figure 15.54, we show a simple example: A stick is bent from being completely flat to self-intersecting. We would like to formalize this measure of bending, such that we could use it in a BVH traversal. If we, for instance, knew a surface was flat, then there would be no need to perform any self-intersection testing on the surface. Looking at the normals of the stick, these tell us something about how much the stick is being bent. In the 2D case, it is obvious that in order for the stick to bend over and self-intersect, there must be two normals at some point on the surface where the angle between them is greater than π radians. This angle is directly related to the curvature.

The requirement for the difference in normals to be more than π radians is a necessity, but not a sufficient condition for a self-intersection, as can be seen in Figure 15.55. Clearly the curvature suggests that there might be a self-intersection where there is none. Thus, we can only use a curvature test to prune away flat cases, not curled up cases. Moving into 3D from 2D complicates matters a little bit, since we now have a 2D surface bending in 3D space.

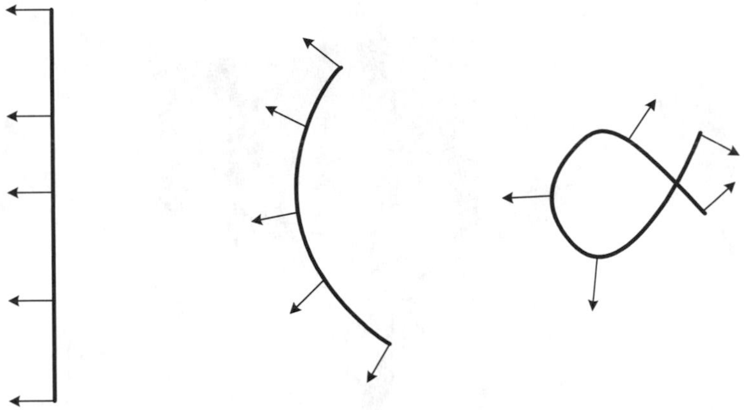

Figure 15.54: A stick bending in 2D with self-intersection.

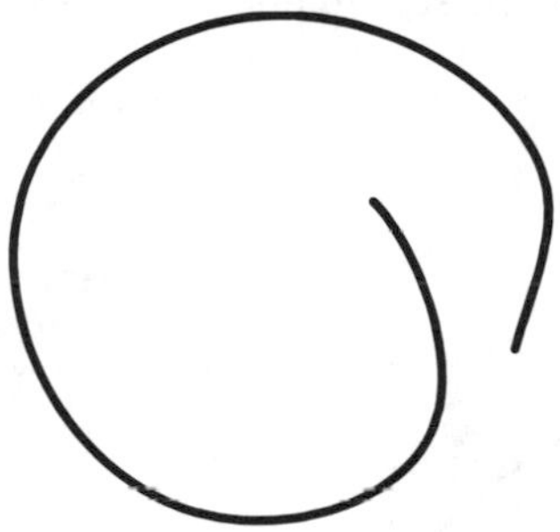

Figure 15.55: A stick where curvature indicates a self-intersection, but there is none.

The problem is that even though the curvature indicates a flat surface, the surface might still be self-intersecting, such as the example of an elastic rubber sheet lying on a table, where two corners meet without bending the sheet too much out of the plane. Figure 15.56 illustrates the problem. A sufficient criteria is to require that the projected surface boundary onto a plane nearly coplanar with the flat surface does not self-intersect. These observations lead to the following definition:

Definition 15.3 (Curvature Criteria)
A continuous surface, S, with boundary, C, does not have any self-intersections when the following criteria are met:

- *there exists a vector $\boldsymbol{v}$ for which the normal $\boldsymbol{n}(\mathbf{p})$ at every point $\mathbf{p} \in S$ fulfill*

$$\boldsymbol{v} \cdot \boldsymbol{n} > 0 \tag{15.58}$$

- *the projection of C onto the plane orthogonal to $\boldsymbol{v}$ has no self-intersections*

The definition is illustrated in Figure 15.57. When we apply the curvature test, we will need to update

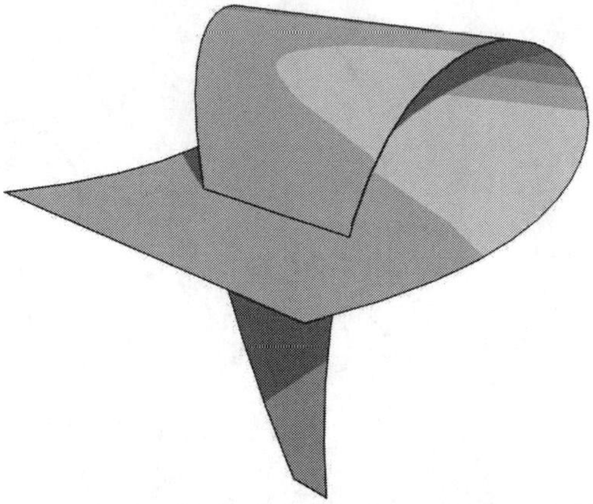

Figure 15.56: A 2D self-intersecting surface in 3D space.

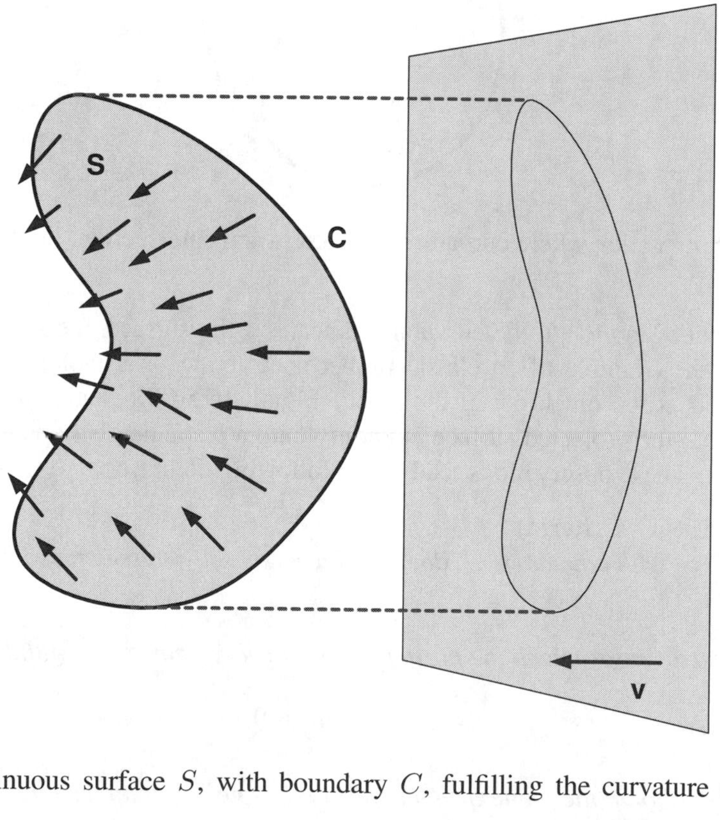

Figure 15.57: A continuous surface S, with boundary C, fulfilling the curvature criteria (see Definition 15.3).

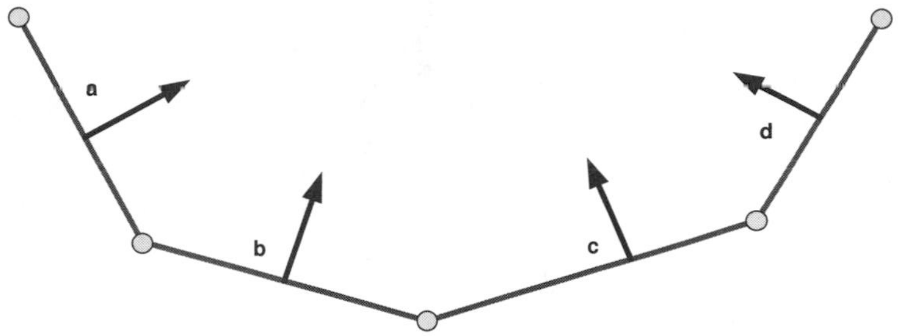

Figure 15.58: An example surface region, consisting of four faces, a, b, c, and d with their respective normals.

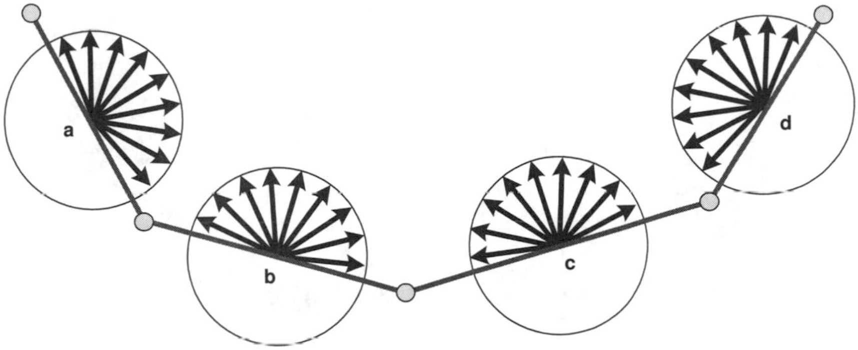

Figure 15.59: Curvature information stored for leaf BVs.

the BVH with curvature information. Here we implicitly assume that a mesh-connectivity was used to build the BVH, implying that a BV node in the BVH covers a surface region. Its parent BV will cover a larger surface region, being the union of the BV node and its siblings. Furthermore, the parent surface region is a connected region implying that for two arbitrary points a continuous and unbroken curve can be drawn on the surface connecting the two points.

Instead of trying to compute how big the normal angles are for each surface region, it is more efficient to store the half space, from which a vector $\boldsymbol{v}$ can be found. Figure 15.58 shows a simple model we will use to illustrate the idea. Here a simple surface region is shown, consisting of four faces: a, b, c, and d. The corresponding BVH consists of $4 + 3 = 7$ BVs: four leafs, two intermediate BVs each covering half of the surface, and one root BV covering the entire surface.

For each leaf BV we will store the half space, from which a valid $\boldsymbol{v}$-vector can be found for the corresponding surface as illustrated in Figure 15.59. Here circle cones are used to represent the valid directions for $\boldsymbol{v}$-vectors. When the BVH is updated in a bottom-up fashion, the curvature information can easily be propagated from the leaf BVs to the root BV. The half-space cone for a valid $\boldsymbol{v}$-vector for a parent BV is found as the intersection of the half-space cones for its children. This is illustrated in Figure 15.60. In the figure, the big arrows point in the direction of a parent BV. Observe that one can

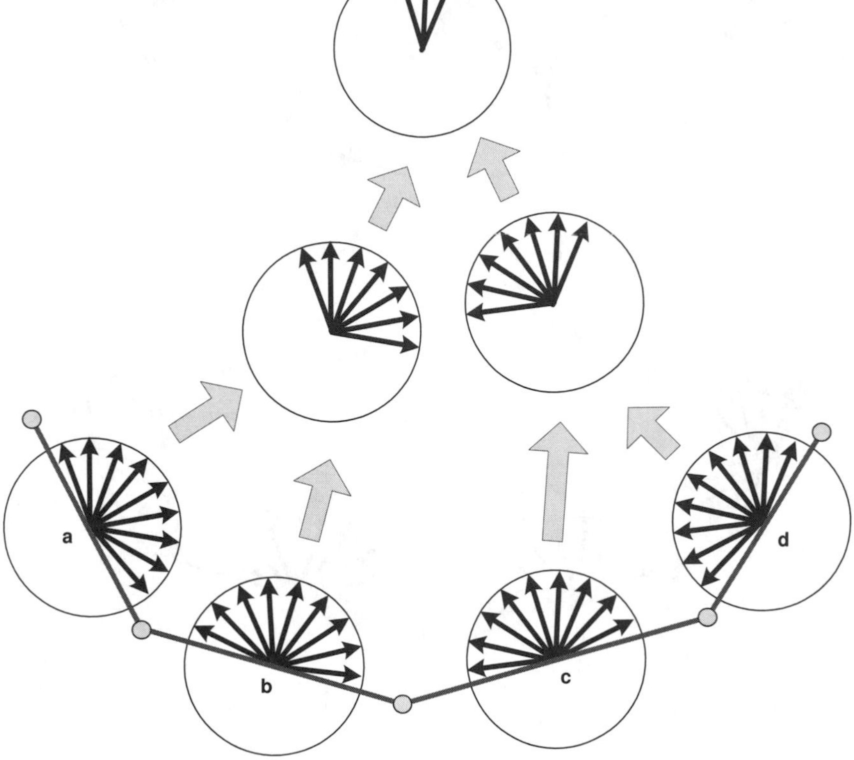

Figure 15.60: Curvature information propagated from leaf BVs to root BV.

easily find a suitable $\boldsymbol{v}$-vector from the half-space cone of the root, which will work as a $\boldsymbol{v}$-vector for the entire surface.

In practice, one does not store an actual half-space cone. Instead, the space of possible $\boldsymbol{v}$-vectors is discretized onto a fixed set of directions. These directions could, for instance, be picked from an axis-aligned unit cube as follows: each vertex, edge middle, and face middle yields a vector direction, providing us with a total of 26 directions. Other geometries are discussed in [Volino et al., 2000].

The benefit of the discretization is that half spaces can be efficiently implemented as bit-patterns. For instance, the 26 direction cubes can be encoded by attributing each BV in the BVH with a 32-bit unsigned integer, where each of the 26 first bits indicates whether the normal direction would be a valid $\boldsymbol{v}$-vector for the surface region covered by the BV. During propagation of curvature information from leaf BVs to root BV, the curvature information of a parent is easily found by taking the bit-wise AND of all the bit-patterns of the children BVs.

The self-intersection testing from Figure 15.52 is easily extended with the curvature testing. If the curvature criteria passes for a surface covered by a BV, then the recursion stops. This is shown in Fig-

```
algorithm self-test(A : BV )
  v = get v-vector of A
  if valid v then
    if not projectedBoundaryIntersect(A,v) then
      return
    end if
  end if
  if leaf A then
    return
  end if
  for all children C of A do
    self-test(C)
    for all children D right of C do
      recursive(C, D, true)
    next D
  next C
end algorithm
```

Figure 15.61: Modified traversal with curvature testing.

ure 15.61. Observe that the recursive tandem traversal has been extended with an extra argument, which we will explain in detail shortly. When testing siblings against each other, we would also like to exploit the benefits of the curvature test. Obviously, the BVs of the siblings will overlap if the surfaces covered by the sibling BVs are adjacent, that is, they share a common border. So we cannot hope to rely on the BV overlap test to prune the nearly flat adjacent surface regions covered by two sibling BVs. The BV overlap testing, however, will still work fine for pruning nonadjacent surfaces. Figure 15.62 illustrates the usefulness of the BV overlap test compared to the curvature test. As seen from Figure 15.62, we would like to extend the recursive tandem traversal with a curvature test when we are dealing with two BVs that represent adjacent surface regions. The extended recursive tandem traversal is shown in Figure 15.63. The pseudocode in Figure 15.63 seems straightforward, but we have omitted one detail for clarity: how does one determine whether two surface regions are adjacent? As suggested by [Volino et al., 2000], each BV in the BVH is annotated with a list of surface vertices lying on the boundary of the surface region covered by the BV. The list only contains vertices indicating adjacency with another surface. In other words, no two vertices are added to the vertex list of the BV representing the same adjacency information. The vertex list can be created initially, when the BVH is being built. Thus, there is no need to update any adjacency information during simulation. An adjacency test can now be performed by comparing the vertex lists of two regions: if they share a vertex, then the regions are deemed to be adjacent. Theoretically speaking, cases could be conceived where the vertex list could be rather long, implying an expensive adjacency test. However, [Volino et al., 2000] report that for the usual cases, the lists hardly exceed six vertices, meaning that the adjacency can be considered to have constant complexity. Figure 15.64 shows an example of two vertex lists for two surface regions. According to [Volino et al., 2000], the boundary intersection testing is never decisive in the final collision detection process, and is therefore not performed. We would like to note that the boundary testing only makes sense for a surface with an open boundary, implying that it is superfluous for closed surfaces. [Volino et al., 2000] reports that the curvature testing yields an algorithm

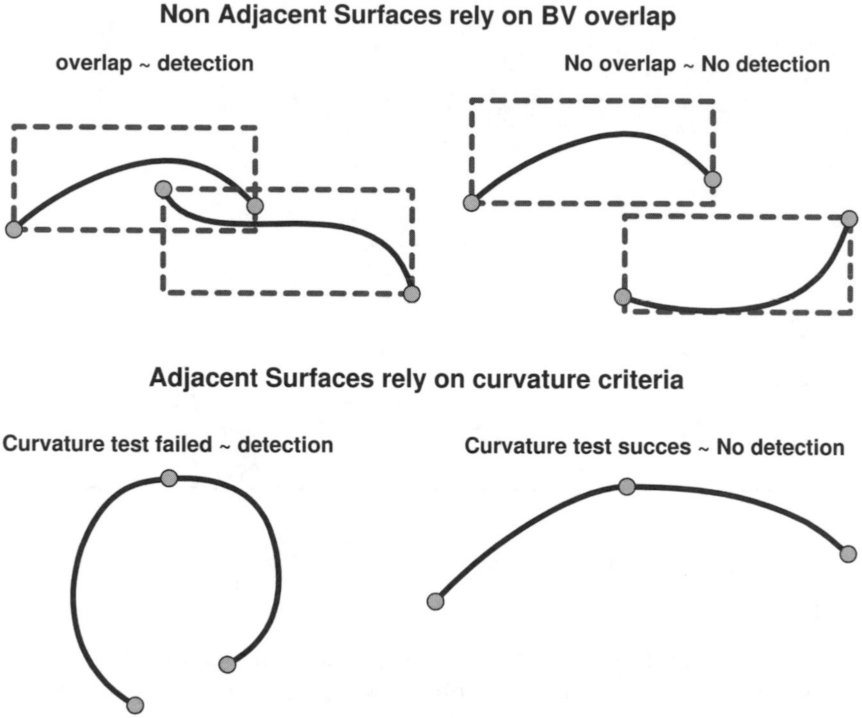

Figure 15.62: Illustration showing that the BV overlap test is well suited for nonadjacent surfaces, but for adjacent surfaces the curvature test is better.

that is linear in the number of colliding faces, which is far better than the $O(n \log n)$ lower bound we have for the simple-minded use of the traversals.

15.8 Contact Determination with BVHs

When using BVHs for physics-based simulation, we are interested in obtaining a set of contact points as explained in Chapter 14. Typically a *contact determination* algorithm is used for processing the results from a narrow-phase collision detection algorithm. This approach can also be taken when using BVHs by enqueuing primitive pairs as the collision query algorithm encounters them, for example, in line eight of Figure 15.16. However, a separate contact determination phase is usually not needed when using BVHs, but can instead be intervened with the collision query. That is, during the collision query a contact determination routine is invoked, which processes two primitive pairs, such as two triangles, and produces a set of contact points, which is enqueued as the collision result of the BVH collision query. This section discusses this approach to contact determination, while doing the collision detection queries of BVHs. As will be explained, the main problem with this approach is that certain degenerate cases result in multiple reports of identical contact points. A few examples of degenerate cases is shown in Figure 15.65

```
algorithm recursive(A : BV, B : BV, adjacent )
  if not colliding(A, B) then
    return
  end if
  if adjacent then
    adjacent = AdjacentState(A,B)
    if adjacent then
      v = get v-vector of (A, B)
      if valid v then
        if not projectedBoundaryIntersect(A,B,v) then
          return
        end if
      end if
    end if
  end if
  if leaf(A) and leaf(B) then
    contact-determination(A, B)
    return
  end if
  if descend(A) then
    for all children C of A do
      recursive(C, B, adjacent)
    next C
  end if
  if descend(B) then
    for all children C of B do
      recursive(A, C, adjacent)
    next C
  end if
end algorithm
```

Figure 15.63: Recursive tandem traversal extended with curvature testing.

and Figure 15.70. Self-intersection adds yet another complication to these multiplicities, as illustrated in Figure 15.74.

Multiple reported identical contact points are undesired in physical simulation due to several reasons: first, they provide a performance decrease in iterative methods for collision resolving. However, they seldom cause different physical behavior or problems with the computations involved in the iterative collision resolving. Second, imagine that collision resolving is done by back-projecting penetrating contacts, that is, the first time a contact is encountered it will be projected to resolve penetration. If the new projected state is not reflected in the remaining multiple reported contacts, then further excessive projections will be carried out, yielding a final unwanted position. Finally, in the case of simultaneous collision resolving, such as the constraint method in Chapter 7, multiple reported identical contact points lead to numerical instability in the system matrix, meaning that not only do they cause a performance decrease, but they could also result in unsolvability of the numerical methods.

Generally we could take two avenues to handle the problem. First, we could introduce a postprocessing

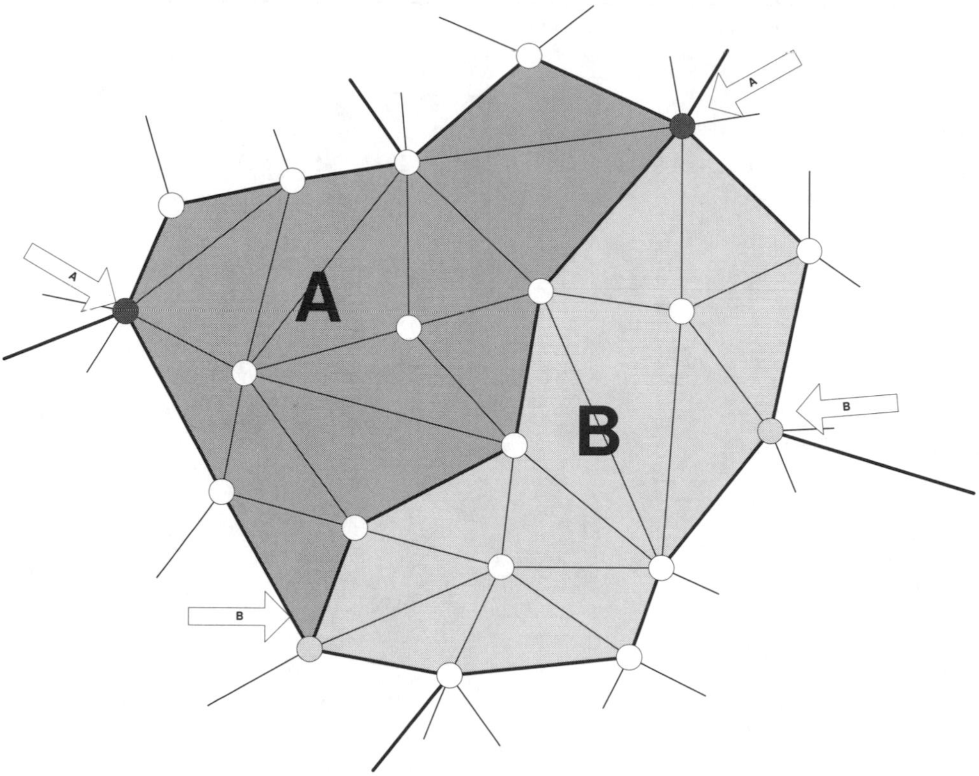

Figure 15.64: Illustration showing vertex lists for two surface regions, A and B. Notice that only a very few number of vertices is needed to capture all adjacency information about the two surfaces.

step of the BVH collision query, which filters out multiple reported contact points, and second, we could devise some sort of clever bookkeeping during the traversal query, which is able to prune away multiple contact points before they are even considered. The first solution is really just a reintroduction of a contact determination phase to the collision detection engine, and therefore really not interesting. Besides, the filtering needed indicates, at worst, an $O(n^2)$ time-complexity, which is undesirable. Therefore, we will focus on the second solution here.

When doing physics-based animation, there are two kinds of collision detection queries that interest us: interference and proximity queries. An *interference query* will search for the actual intersection between two objects, while a *proximity query* will search for the nearest parts of two objects. The important thing to notice is that an interference query only works when penetrations have occurred, whereas a proximity query will return results even when objects are separated by a small threshold. Interference queries could prove to be a problem in simulation since the simulation method tries to avoid penetrations. Contact tracking is a possible way to resolve this, however, proximity testing is far better but requires knowledge of the movement of the objects as will be discussed in Section 15.8.2.

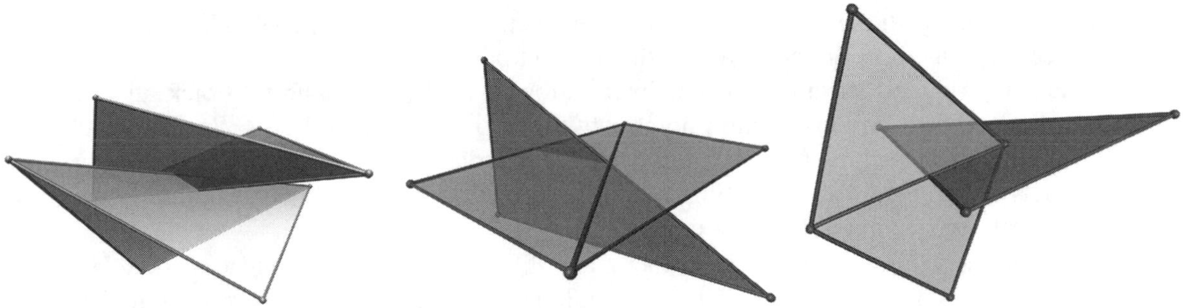

(A) (B) (C)

Figure 15.65: Interference queries can lead to multiple reported (E, F) contacts.

15.8.1 Interference Query

Contact points between polygonal objects are often represented by a pair of features, such as (V, V), (V, E), (V, F), (E, E), (E, F), and (F, F), where V is a vertex, E is an edge, and F is face. This was introduced in Chapter 14.1. For polygonal objects, (E, F) contact points are sufficient for representing the vertices of intersection between two objects, which will be the focus for *interference query* in the following. Case A in Figure 15.65 illustrates this. Here, two objects, each consisting of two triangles, are intersecting each other. Observe that the (E, F) intersections result in four intersection points, which describe the vertices in the polyline representing the intersection between the two objects.

Case B shows a more difficult case, where one of the intersection points is given by an edge-edge intersection. However, one could just as easily pick one of the faces of the square object together with the intersecting edge from the triangular object, yielding an (E, F) contact point representing the same intersection point as the (E, E) contact point. There is some ambiguity in picking a face from the square object, since both faces yield the same intersection point, but two different contact points. Recall that contact points are uniquely identified by the features that constitute them, not by the position of the point in 3D space.

The case could become even more complicated. Imagine moving the square object such that the intersecting edge intersects one of the end points of the edge from the triangular object. Now the ambiguity in contact point representation is even higher; a single (V, E) type, or one of two (E, E) types or one of five (E, F) types could be picked. However, the important thing to notice is we can pick an (E, F) contact type.

Case C shows another challenging case. Here, one intersection point is given by an (E, E) contact point type and can be resolved in the same manner as we just discussed for case B. The main difficulty illustrated by this example is that the other intersection point, which is given by a (V, F) contact point type, consists of the vertex of the square object and the face of the triangular object. Again, we see that we could pick one of the incident edges of the vertex from the square object, which is not coplanar with the face of the triangular object. Again we end up with an (E, F) type of contact, and again we have the same ambiguity in picking an edge, since both the edges lying above and below the triangular face will result in a contact point representing the same intersection point. We did ignore the edge from the square object that is coplanar with the face of the triangular object. Picking this edge would result in a very bad situation, since this edge is collinear with the other contact point.

In conclusion, we see that in the case of intersection, it is always possible to pick an (E, F) type contact point to represent any intersection point between two polygonal objects. We also conclude that there is an ambiguity in picking the (E, F) contact. This indicates a nonuniqueness, when we want to identify contacts by the features constituting them. The nonuniqueness would be devastating for any kind of bookkeeping algorithm and is therefore unwanted.

If we allowed reporting types of contact other than (E, F), then the nonuniqueness could be removed by always picking the contact representing the lowest dimension of features: a vertex has zero dimensions, an edge has one dimension, and a face has two dimensions.

Theorem 15.1 (Uniqueness of Contact Point Representation)
Let F_A and F_B be the features from objects A and B, and let $dim(\cdot)$ be a function returning the dimension of a feature, then F_A and F_B constitute a unique contact point, if, and only if,

$$dim(F_A) + dim(F_B) = \min(dim(F'_A) + dim(F'_B)), \tag{15.59}$$

where F'_A and F'_B could be any neighboring features of the features F_A and F_B, including the features themselves in direct contact with the intersection point.

It should now be easily seen that in case A the four (E, F) contacts have the lowest dimension, in case B it is the (E, F) contact and the (E, E) contact that have the lowest sum, and in case C it is the (E, E) contact and the (V, F) contact. Observe that by this rule we can never have an (F, F) type contact, since it will always be possible to decompose such a contact into a set of contacts with lower dimension.

Proof of Theorem 15.1:

(V, V) **case:** The neighbors of a vertex are the incident edges and the incident faces. Therefore, picking the neighbors of either the vertex of object A or B will increase the dimension sum.

(V, E) **case:** The only possible way of reducing the dimension sum is if the edge could be replaced by one of its neighboring endpoints. However, this would indicate that the end vertex is touching the intersection point, and a (V, V) type would be the correct answer. If the intersection point is not touching the endpoints, then the edge can only be updated to one of its neighboring faces, which will indicate an increase in the dimension sum. The vertex itself cannot be replaced by any of its neighbors since this would imply an increase in the dimension sum as well.

(V, F) **case:** The same arguments as previously apply to the vertex; the face has only lower dimensional neighbors, the edges and vertices on its perimeter. If the intersection point is not touching the perimeter, then we cannot reduce the dimension sum.

(E, E) **case:** Obviously, none of the edges can be replaced by their neighboring faces, since this will result in a dimension increase. The only possibility for a reduction, is to replace one or both edges with one of their neighboring end vertices. This would mean that the intersection point is touching the end vertices and that the replacement would be valid and correct and result in either a (V, E) or (V, V) type case, which we already have proved.

(E, F) **case:** The only possibility for decreasing dimension of E is by picking one of its end-points, which is impossible, unless the intersection point touches one of them, in which case we are in (V, F) case, which we have already proved. The only possibility left is replacement of F by one of its neighbors, but this is impossible, if they are not touching the intersection point. □

Usually a good rule of thumb is to treat the case analysis by testing the most restrictive cases first. In our case that would mean:

theorem 15.1 (Rule of most restrictive case first)
Given two triangles, it is first verified whether there are any (V, V) contacts, then (V, E) types, followed by (V, F), (E, E), and ending with (E, F) types.

In this way, testing the most restrictive cases first will allow us to disregard the special cases of higher dimensional cases. As an example, imagine we have a (V, V) type of contact. Having reported this contact, we need not consider the cases where the edge on a (V, E) contact reduces to one of its end-point vertices.

The Proof 5 and Theorem 15.1 can straightforwardly be combined into an algorithm for contact determination based on a case analysis. A pseudocode version of this algorithm is shown in Figure 15.66.

As seen from the pseudocode, there are roughly 102 lookups, which is quite a lot of tests for previously reported contacts. This is computationally infeasible unless a very cheap lookup method is available. If BVH data structures are not shared among objects, meaning for instance, that two identical box objects would each have their own instance of a BVH, then a cheap lookup function can be constructed by observing the fact that a single nonface feature can only be part of exactly one reported contact point. All features could therefore be attributed by a pointer to the reported contact they are part of, and thus provide a cheap constant time test for previously reported contacts. Of course, all contact pointers of the features must be reset to null prior to a query.

If one only cares about knowing whether a feature could be part of a new contact point, then a more efficient time-stamping scheme could be adopted: instead of a contact point pointer, each feature is attributed with a time-stamp. Whenever a feature pair is used to report a contact point, then their time-stamps are updated with the current time. Whenever one encounters a feature pair and wants to know if these could constitute a new contact point that should be reported, one simply tests that both their time-stamps are less than the current time. If this is true, then a new contact point can be reported.

The proposed idea of using a pointer or time-stamp requires a huge memory usage, since objects cannot share the same BVH instance. Observe however, that when working with deformable objects, separate instances are needed, since two geometries can deform in many different ways. The consequence is that the updated BVHs do not look the same even though the initial geometry of two deformable objects were identical. This implies that the outlined strategy for a fast lookup method is feasible for interference detection of deformable objects.

If BVHs are shared among objects, which is often the case for rigid objects, another lookup method must be devised. A simple solution would be to give every feature a unique index, and then use the indices to look up contact point information in a map or similar data structure.

Consider case A once again. Assume we are using the contact determination outlined above. Then, as can be seen in Figure 15.65, the upper object has two faces; we'll label them F_A and F_B. Similarly,

```
void interference-detection-by-case-analysis(T_A,T_B)
  for all vertex pairs (V_A,V_B) where V_A in T_A and V_B in T_B
    if (V_A,V_B) not reported before then
      if dist(V_A,V_B)<ε then
        report (V_A,V_B)
      end if
    end if
  next (V_A,V_B)

  for all vertices V_A in T_A and all edges E_B inT_B
    if (V_A,E_B) not reported before (V_A,V_E) where V_E in  E_B then
      if dist(V_A,E_B)<ε then
        report (V_A,E_B)
      end if
    end if
  next (V_A,E_B)
  repeat above loop with A and B reversed

  for all vertices V_A in T_A
   if dist(V_A,T_B)<ε and V_A inside perimeter of T_B then
     report (V_A,T_B)
   end if
  next V_A
  repeat above loop with A and B reversed

  for all vertex pairs (E_A,E_B) where E_A in T_A and E_B in T_B
    if (E_A,E_B) not reported before then
      if no mixed endpoints vertex pairs of E_A or E_B reported then
        if dist(E_A,E_B)<ε then
          report (E_A,E_B)
        end if
      end if
    end if
  next (E_A,E_B)

  for all edges E_A in T_A
   if no endpoints of E_A have been reported then
     if E_A intersect T_B inside perimeter then
       report (E_A,T_B)
     end if
   end if
  next E_A
  repeat above loop with A and B reversed
end algorithm
```

Figure 15.66: Contact determination by case analysis for interference queries.

the lower object has two faces; we'll label these F_C and F_D. F_A and F_B share a common edge, labeled E_{upper}. Similarly, the faces from the lower object share an edge, which we'll label E_{lower}. As seen from the figure, both faces of the upper object intersect with both faces of the lower object. This means that during a BVH traversal the following pairs of primitive test will be generated.

Leaf tests		Contact Points
(f_A, F_C)	$\rightarrow$	$(E_{\text{upper}} - F_C), (E_{\text{lower}} - F_A)$
(f_A, F_D)	$\rightarrow$	$(E_{\text{upper}} - F_D), (E_{\text{lower}} - F_A)$
(f_B, F_C)	$\rightarrow$	$(E_{\text{upper}} - F_C), (E_{\text{lower}} - F_B)$
(f_B, F_D)	$\rightarrow$	$(E_{\text{upper}} - F_D), (E_{\text{lower}} - F_B)$

The rightmost column shows the possible contact points that can be generated from each pairwise primitive test. The table shows that four unique contact points will exist, as we expected. However, the table also shows that each contact point will be reported twice if we do not guard against multiple reported contact points. This artifact is unavoidable and comes from the fact that neighboring triangles share features. Therefore, it is a problem one always has to consider when using BVHs. The contact determination algorithm we have outlined, will prevent this artifact. In our discussion so far we have implicitly assumed that we have complete topology information about the underlying geometry. If this is not the case, such as for a triangle soup, we are in real trouble, because the same edge and vertices might be redundantly stored in a triangle soup. Therefore, it is nontrivial to uniquely identify features.

We will now outline another more practical approach to the problem of interference intersection. The main idea is to consider only (E, F) contact point types, since these are sufficient for representing any intersection. As previously explained, there is sometimes an ambiguity in picking (E, F) contacts, for example, case B and C in Figure 15.65. The ambiguity implies that two different (E, F) contacts might be reported, which represent the same intersection point. In the following, we will ignore this ambiguity problem. This is not as bad as it might seem, since in practice these degenerate cases rarely exist, and even if they do, they are short-termed. The reason for this is that cases like B and C in Figure 15.65 require perfectly aligned and positioned objects. In a general simulation, numerical inaccuracies and round off errors will cause small perturbations, even in the case of perfectly aligned objects. However, theoretically speaking, there is a danger for some of the problems we discussed earlier regarding badly conditioned numerics for simultaneous collision resolving. If an iterative method is chosen instead, the proposed intersection strategy that we will outline will not prove to be a problem.

Let's label the vertices of a triangle in counterclockwise order by v_0, v_1, and v_2. Then the edges of a triangle are given by the pairs of vertices $(v_0 - v_1)$, $(v_1 - v_2)$, and $(v_2 - v_0)$. Given two triangles T_A and T_B, there is a potential of six (E, F) contact points. The interference algorithm starts out by an exhaustive test of all six potential contact points, as shown in Figure 15.67. Now let's consider the steps involved in taking care of a single edge-face test. First we need to ensure that we do not have multiple reported identical edge-face contacts. This can be done by the strategies we elaborated on previously.

If we pass the test for multiple reported contact points, then we need to determine whether there really is a possibility of an edge-face contact. This can be done by testing the signed distance of the edge vertices w.r.t. the face plane. However, we need to consider the C case shown in Figure 15.65. What should we do if the signed distance is zero? In the case of the horizontal edge characterized by both vertices having zero distance, we simply ignore it. Since we are looking for interference, it seems appropriate to favor edges

```
algorithm practical-interference(T_a, T_b)
  do-Edge-Face(T_A.v_0, T_A.v_1, T_B)
  do-Edge-Face(T_A.v_1, T_A.v_2, T_B)
  do-Edge-Face(T_A.v_2, T_A.v_0, T_B)
  do-Edge-Face(T_B.v_0, T_B.v_1, T_A)
  do-Edge-Face(T_B.v_1, T_B.v_2, T_A)
  do-Edge-Face(T_B.v_2, T_B.v_0, T_A)
end algorithm
```

Figure 15.67: Edge-face interference tests of two triangles.

lying mostly on the backside of the triangle. Therefore, we will ignore edges where all vertices have a nonnegative signed distance w.r.t. to the face plane. Looking at case C in Figure 15.65, this means that we prune the coplanar edge and the edge on the front side of the face of the triangular object.

Having determined that the edge actually crosses the plane of the triangle, we can now compute the intersection point between the edge and the plane of the triangle. This is done by parameterization of the edge, and if the edge is given by the vertices $\boldsymbol{v}_0$ and $\boldsymbol{v}_1$, then any point on the edge can be given by the parameterization

$$\boldsymbol{u}(t) = (\boldsymbol{v}_1 - \boldsymbol{v}_0)\, t + \boldsymbol{v}_0, \quad \text{where} \quad t \in [0..1]\,. \tag{15.60}$$

Due to the linearity of the edge, the signed distance of any point is given by

$$\text{dist}(\text{plane}(T), \boldsymbol{u}(t)) = (\text{dist}(\text{plane}(T), \boldsymbol{v}_1) - \text{dist}(\text{plane}(T), \boldsymbol{v}_0))\, t + \text{dist}(\text{plane}(T), \boldsymbol{v}_0). \tag{15.61}$$

The intersection is given by the fact that the signed distance w.r.t. the face plane is zero. Exploiting this fact in the above equation allows us to solve for the parameterization parameter. This yields

$$t = \frac{\text{dist}(\text{plane}(T), \boldsymbol{v}_0)}{\text{dist}(\text{plane}(T), \boldsymbol{v}_0) - \text{dist}(\text{plane}(T), \boldsymbol{v}_1)}. \tag{15.62}$$

Knowing the value of the t-parameter, the intersection point can be computed by using the parameterization. Having found the intersection point, we can now detect if the edge-face case we are testing constitutes a new contact point by testing whether the intersection point lies inside the triangle boundary. *Barycentric coordinates*, to be explained below, are very efficient for determining whether a point lies inside a triangle, and we will therefore use these in the last part of our test. The barycentric coordinates w_0, w_1, and w_2 are defined such that

$$\boldsymbol{u}'(t) = w_0 \boldsymbol{v}_0 + w_1 \boldsymbol{v}_1 + w_2 \boldsymbol{v}_2 \tag{15.63}$$

is the point in the plane of the triangle closest to $\boldsymbol{u}(t)$. If $0 \leq w_0, w_1, w_2 \leq 1$, then the point lies inside or on the perimeter of the triangle. Computing the barycentric coordinates, w_0, w_1, and w_2 of $\boldsymbol{u}(t)$ implies solving the linear system

$$\begin{bmatrix} (\boldsymbol{v}_0 - \boldsymbol{v}_2) \cdot (\boldsymbol{v}_0 - \boldsymbol{v}_2) & (\boldsymbol{v}_0 - \boldsymbol{v}_2) \cdot (\boldsymbol{v}_1 - \boldsymbol{v}_2) \\ (\boldsymbol{v}_0 - \boldsymbol{v}_2) \cdot (\boldsymbol{v}_1 - \boldsymbol{v}_2) & (\boldsymbol{v}_1 - \boldsymbol{v}_2) \cdot (\boldsymbol{v}_1 - \boldsymbol{v}_2) \end{bmatrix} \begin{bmatrix} w_0 \\ w_1 \end{bmatrix} = \begin{bmatrix} (\boldsymbol{v}_0 - \boldsymbol{v}_2) \cdot (\boldsymbol{u} - \boldsymbol{v}_2) \\ (\boldsymbol{v}_1 - \boldsymbol{v}_2) \cdot (\boldsymbol{u} - \boldsymbol{v}_2) \end{bmatrix}, \tag{15.64a}$$

$$w_0 + w_1 + w_2 = 1. \tag{15.64b}$$

We introduce the shorthand notation

$$\begin{bmatrix} a_{11} & a_{12} \\ a_{12} & a_{22} \end{bmatrix} \begin{bmatrix} w_0 \\ w_1 \end{bmatrix} = \begin{bmatrix} b_1 \\ b_2 \end{bmatrix}. \tag{15.65}$$

Isolating w_1 from the second equation yields

$$w_1 = \frac{b_2 - a_{12}w_0}{a_{22}} \tag{15.66a}$$

$$= \frac{b_2}{a_{22}} - \frac{a_{12}}{a_{22}}w_0, \tag{15.66b}$$

and substituting this into the first gives

$$a_{11}w_0 + a_{12}((b_2 - a_{12}w_0)/a_{22}) = b_1, \tag{15.67a}$$

$$\Downarrow$$

$$a_{11}w_0 + (a_{12}/a_{22})b_2 - a_{12}(a_{12}/a_{22})w_0 = b_1, \tag{15.67b}$$

$$\Downarrow$$

$$(a_{11} - a_{12}(a_{12}/a_{22}))w_0 = b_1 - (a_{12}/a_{22})b_2. \tag{15.67c}$$

Letting $f = a_{12}/a_{22}$ gives

$$m = \frac{a_{11} - a_{12}}{f}, \tag{15.68a}$$

$$n = b_1 - fb_2, \tag{15.68b}$$

we have

$$w_0 = \frac{n}{m}, \tag{15.69a}$$

$$w_1 = \frac{b_2}{a_{22}} - fw_0, \tag{15.69b}$$

$$w_2 = 1 - w_0 - w_1. \tag{15.69c}$$

Since we always have $a_{11} > 0$ and $a_{22} > 0$, a solution will always exist regardless of the value of a_{12}, b_1, and b_2. A pseudocode implementation of the computation of the barycentric coordinates is shown in Figure 15.68. We have now walked through all the details of the edge-face testing. A complete pseudocode version of the test is given in Figure 15.69.

15.8.2 Proximity Query

A *proximity query* is the process of finding nearest and possible touching parts of two objects. The concept of contact points is easily expanded to cover separated objects as the closest points between features of two polygonal objects. Thus, the term contact point is used even for objects in close proximity without contact.

```
algorithm barycentric-coords(v_0, v_1, v_2, u)
    a_11 = (v_0 - v_2) · (v_0 - v_2)
    a_12 = (v_0 - v_2) · (v_1 - v_2)
    a_22 = (v_1 - v_2) · (v_1 - v_2)
    b_1 = (v_0 - v_2) · (u - v_3)
    b_2 = (v_1 - v_2) · (u - v_3)
    f = a_12/a_22
    m = (a_11 - a_12 f)
    n = b_1 - (b_2 f)
    w_0 = n/m
    w_1 = b_2/a_22 - f w_0
    w_2 = 1 - w_0 - w_1
    return (w_0, w_1, w_2)
end algorithm
```

Figure 15.68: Computation of barycentric coordinates.

```
algorithm do-Edge-Face(v_0, v_1, T)
    if existEdgeFace(v_0, v_1, T) then
      return
    end if
    d_0 = dist(plane(T), v_0)
    d_1 = dist(plane(T), v_1)
    if d_0 >= 0 and d_1 >= 0 then
      return
    end if
    if d_0 < 0 and d_1 < 0 then
      return
    end if
    u = intersection(v_0, v_1, T)
    (w_0, w_1, w_2) =barycentric-coords(v_0, v_1, v_2, u)
    if inside(w_0, w_1, w_2) then
      report (v_0, v_1, T)
    end if
end algorithm
```

Figure 15.69: Edge-face interference test

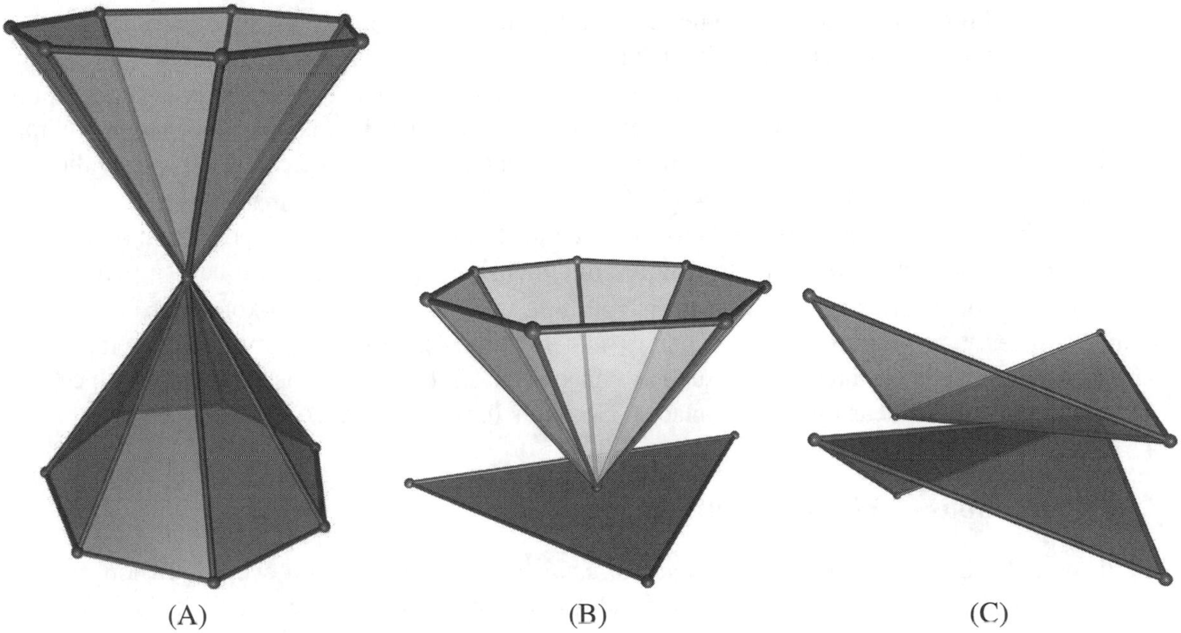

Figure 15.70: Proximity queries can lead to multiple reported (V, F) contacts (A and B) or (E, E) contacts (C).

When doing proximity queries, we could apply the same strategy for reporting unique contact points as presented in the previous section. However, a simpler strategy is available based on the following: in the case of a proximity query, (V, F) and (E, E) contact points are sufficient for representing any contact region between two polygonal objects. Since there are no penetrations, there is no need for (E, F) contact points.

As in the case of interference, we encounter the problems of ambiguity and multiple reported identical contact points. The latter being a consequence of neighboring triangles sharing common boundaries, as explained in the previous section. Here, we'll briefly study the problem of ambiguity and convince ourselves that (V, F) and (E, E) contact types are sufficient.

Looking at case A in Figure 15.70, we see that the minimum dimension contact is a (V, V) type, which is a unique contact for this sort of touching contact. However, we could just as well have picked any pair of edges, one from the upper object and one from the lower object, or we could have picked the vertex from one of the objects and an arbitrary face from the other object. It is obvious that we can suffice with (V, F) and (E, E) contact types for this kind of touching contact, and it is apparent that the ambiguity for this case is really bad. The number of possible contact points for representing the same touching point is quadratic in the number of features containing the touching point. However, in any simulation system, this kind of contact will occur rarely, and even if something similar is set up, numerical accuracies and round-offs will add perturbations.

In case B in Figure 15.70, we have a trivial example of a (V, F) type of contact. In this case there is no ambiguity, however, imagine moving the cone such that the vertex lies on top of the border of the triangle. The touching point could still be represented by the (V, F) contact, but again we have ambiguity in choosing a representation for the touching contact.

The C case in Figure 15.70 illustrates the ideal (E, E) type of contact, where there is no ambiguity in the representation. However, displacing one of the objects, such that the touching point on the common edge is moved to the boundary of the other object, results in ambiguity of the contact representation.

Actually, case B and C show why it is (V, F) and (E, E) contact types that are the smallest set of contact types that suffice for representing a touching contact region between two polygonal objects, since in these two cases the contact types are the minimum dimension representing the touching point.

Usually collision queries are invoked at discrete times. This leads to well-known artifacts, such as tunneling—objects that pass through each other (see Chapter 6.4). For proximity queries with BVHs, it can also lead to unexpected interference, such as penetration of objects. This is undesirable, since we are seeking only touching or near-touching contacts. This calls for continuous collision detection.

15.8.3 Continuous Collision Detection

Unlike discrete collision detection, *continuous collision detection* deals with every collision event in a given time span. There are two flavors of continuous collision detection. We can either look forward in time, from the current instance of invocation to the next expected instance, or we can look backward in time, from the current instance of invocation to the previous instance.

Assuming that the time-step is small, it is justified to look upon the motion between the two instances of time as being linear. The error in this assumption is linear in the size of the time-step, h, that is, $O(h)$. From a convergence theory point of view, we can simply let the time-step go to zero and the approximation would be exact. In practice, this is of course, impossible, but the error can be made so small that it is negligible compared to errors coming from numerical inaccuracies and round off.

Having assumed linear motion, we can compute the space swept by a single triangle over the time-step. Say that the three vertices of a triangle move with velocities $\boldsymbol{u}_0$, $\boldsymbol{u}_1$, and $\boldsymbol{u}_2$, then we expect the triangle to be at the candidate positions given by

$$\boldsymbol{v}_0' = \boldsymbol{v}_0 + h\boldsymbol{u}_0, \tag{15.70a}$$
$$\boldsymbol{v}_1' = \boldsymbol{v}_1 + h\boldsymbol{u}_1, \tag{15.70b}$$
$$\boldsymbol{v}_2' = \boldsymbol{v}_2 + h\boldsymbol{u}_2. \tag{15.70c}$$

If we look backward, the candidate positions would be

$$\boldsymbol{v}_0' = \boldsymbol{v}_0 - h\boldsymbol{u}_0, \tag{15.71a}$$
$$\boldsymbol{v}_1' = \boldsymbol{v}_1 - h\boldsymbol{u}_1, \tag{15.71b}$$
$$\boldsymbol{v}_2' = \boldsymbol{v}_2 - h\boldsymbol{u}_2. \tag{15.71c}$$

Or even better, if we cached vertex positions, then we would know the exact candidate position, without having to compute them as above. Instead, we could estimate the linear velocity they must have moved with as

$$u_0 = \frac{v_0 - v_0'}{h}, \tag{15.72a}$$

$$u_1 = \frac{v_1 - v_1'}{h}, \tag{15.72b}$$

$$u_2 = \frac{v_2 - v_2'}{h}. \tag{15.72c}$$

A simple approach to continuous collision detection is to update the BVH prior to a collision query, in the same way we would do for a deformable object. The only difference is in how the leaf-bounding volumes are updated. Traditionally, these would enclose the geometry at the current instant of time. However, for continuous collision detection, we would make it enclose the geometry both at the current position and at the candidate position. So in the case of AABBs this would imply

$$p_{\text{min}} = \min\left(v_0, v_1, v_2, v_0', v_1', v_2'\right), \tag{15.73a}$$

$$p_{\text{max}} = \max\left(v_0, v_1, v_2, v_0', v_1', v_2'\right). \tag{15.73b}$$

Observe that the update of the BVH is the same regardless of the flavor of the continuous collision detection. The only difference lies in how the candidate positions are picked.

The approach we have described here is most convenient for deformable objects, where the BVHs are not shared among objects, and BVHs are updated anyway to adapt to the deformation of objects. For rigid objects, continuous collision detection can be made more efficient simply by updating the pairwise BVs during the traversal, but before they are tested against each other for collision (see [Eberly, 2005b, Eberly, 2005c] for an example or [Redon et al., 2002, Redon, 2004b, Redon, 2004b, Redon et al., 2004b, Redon et al., 2004a] for more details on continuous collision detection).

During a query traversal when two overlapping leaf bounding volumes are encountered, this indicates a possible contact over the time-step we are looking at. Therefore, the contact determination needs to find the point in time where a touching contact first appears.

The contact determination works by examining all possible contact types, exactly as we did in the case of interference. However, this time we look for (V, F) and (E, E) contacts. The pseudocode is shown in Figure 15.71. In each of the contact cases, first we will try to find the time of collision and then perform the contact determination of the geometries at their positions at that time.

Due to our assumption of linear motion over the time interval, h, the time of contact must be characterized by the vertex lying in the face plane in the case of a (V, F) contact or by the two edges being coplanar in the case of an (E, E) contact. Regardless of the case, we seek a point in time where four points all lie in the same plane.

The idea is to use three points to compute a plane normal, and then use one of the three points to find a distance between the plane and the origin. Finally, the fourth point is used for a point in the plane test. For convenience, in the case of the (V, F), let us label the points of the triangle in counterclockwise order: x_1, x_2, and x_3 and the point of the vertex x_4. In the case of an (E, E) type, we label the end-points of the first edge x_1 and x_2, and the end-points of the second edge x_3 and x_4. The corresponding velocities are in both cases labeled u_1, u_2, u_3, and u_4. Now we'll set up two vectors $x_2 - x_1$ and $x_3 - x_1$, and

```
algorithm practical-proximity(T_a, T_b)
  do-Vertex-Face(T_A.v_0, T_B)
  do-Vertex-Face(T_A.v_1, T_B)
  do-Vertex-Face(T_A.v_2, T_B)

  do-Vertex-Face(T_B.v_0, T_A)
  do-Vertex-Face(T_B.v_1, T_A)
  do-Vertex-Face(T_B.v_2, T_A)

  do-Edge-Edge(T_A.v_0, T_A.v_1, T_B.v_0, T_B.v_1)
  do-Edge-Edge(T_A.v_1, T_A.v_2, T_B.v_0, T_B.v_1)
  do-Edge-Edge(T_A.v_2, T_A.v_0, T_B.v_0, T_B.v_1)

  do-Edge-Edge(T_A.v_0, T_A.v_1, T_B.v_1, T_B.v_2)
  do-Edge-Edge(T_A.v_1, T_A.v_2, T_B.v_1, T_B.v_2)
  do-Edge-Edge(T_A.v_2, T_A.v_0, T_B.v_1, T_B.v_2)

  do-Edge-Edge(T_A.v_0, T_A.v_1, T_B.v_2, T_B.v_0)
  do-Edge-Edge(T_A.v_1, T_A.v_2, T_B.v_2, T_B.v_0)
  do-Edge-Edge(T_A.v_2, T_A.v_0, T_B.v_2, T_B.v_0)
end algorithm
```

Figure 15.71: Practical proximity contact determination between two triangles.

take the cross product of these two to obtain a plane normal

$$\boldsymbol{n} = ((\boldsymbol{x}_2 - \boldsymbol{x}_1) \times (\boldsymbol{x}_3 - \boldsymbol{x}_1)\,. \tag{15.74}$$

The point $\boldsymbol{x}_1$ must lie in the plane, so the distance, d, to the origin is given by

$$d = \boldsymbol{n} \cdot \boldsymbol{x}_1. \tag{15.75}$$

In order for the last point to lie in the plane, then its distance to the plane must be zero, that is,

$$\boldsymbol{n} \cdot \boldsymbol{x}_4 - d = 0. \tag{15.76}$$

Substitution leads to

$$((\boldsymbol{x}_2 - \boldsymbol{x}_1) \times (\boldsymbol{x}_3 - \boldsymbol{x}_1)) \cdot (\boldsymbol{x}_4 - \boldsymbol{x}_1) = 0. \tag{15.77}$$

Whenever this equation is fulfilled, the four points will lie in the same plane. The last thing we need to consider is the motion of the points. That is, we have

$$((\boldsymbol{x}_2(t) - \boldsymbol{x}_1(t)) \times (\boldsymbol{x}_3(t) - \boldsymbol{x}_1(t))) \cdot (\boldsymbol{x}_4(t) - \boldsymbol{x}_1(t)) = 0, \tag{15.78}$$

and we want to determine the smallest nonnegative value $t < h$, which makes the above equation true.

Now we find

$$x_1(t) = x_1 + u_1 t, \tag{15.79a}$$
$$x_2(t) = x_2 + u_2 t, \tag{15.79b}$$
$$x_3(t) = x_3 + u_3 t, \tag{15.79c}$$
$$x_4(t) = x_4 + u_4 t. \tag{15.79d}$$

By substitution we have

$$(((x_2 - x_1) + (u_2 - u_1)\,t) \times ((x_3 - x_1) + (u_3 - u_1)\,t)) \cdot ((x_4 - x_1) + (u_4 - u_1)\,t) = 0. \tag{15.80}$$

This is a cubic polynomial, and an analytical solution exists. Its three roots can be found, and the vertice's positions can thus be found at the specific times. A rounding error may hide a collision at the boundary between two time-steps; a test at the end of the time-step $t = h$ should therefore by performed [Bridson et al., 2002].

Having found the point in time where the four points are coplanar, the (V, F) case is similar to the (E, F) case in the interference testing after having found the intersection point. The difference is that the vertex position at the time of contact replaces the intersection point. The pseudocode in Figure 15.72 illustrates the basic idea. We will now focus on the (E, E) case. As in the (V, F) case, we first find the roots, and then we examine the geometries in ascending order.

For simplicity we let x_1, x_2, x_3, and x_4 denote the edge geometry positions at the instance in time corresponding to a root. First we test whether the edges are parallel. This is the case, when

$$(x_2 - x_1) \times (x_4 - x_3) = 0. \tag{15.81}$$

In practice, an equality test will not work, so we use a threshold test instead. If the test succeeds, then a dimension reduction technique can be used by projecting the vertices of one edge onto the line running through the edge. However, one could also simply drop the case, since if a touching contact exists, it could just as well be represented by two (V, F) type contacts. Therefore, we will only consider the general case where the two edges are in general position, that is, there is exactly one touching point between them.

Parameterization of the two edges with the a and b parameters, yields

$$x_1 + a\,(x_2 - x_1)\,, \tag{15.82a}$$
$$x_3 + b\,(x_4 - x_3)\,. \tag{15.82b}$$

The touching point between the two lines must also be the closest point, and the closest point is characterized by the minimum distance, so we seek the values of a and b, which minimizes

$$\sqrt{((x_1 + a\,(x_2 - x_1)) - (x_3 + b\,(x_4 - x_3)))^2}. \tag{15.83}$$

Taking the derivative w.r.t. a and b yields the so-called normal equations,

$$\begin{bmatrix} (x_2 - x_1)\cdot(x_2 - x_1) & -(x_2 - x_1)\cdot(x_4 - x_3) \\ -(x_2 - x_1)\cdot(x_4 - x_3) & (x_4 - x_3)\cdot(x_4 - x_3) \end{bmatrix} \begin{bmatrix} a \\ b \end{bmatrix} = \begin{bmatrix} (x_2 - x_1)\cdot(x_3 - x_1) \\ -(x_4 - x_3)\cdot(x_3 - x_1) \end{bmatrix}. \tag{15.84}$$

```
algorithm do-Vertex-Face(v,T)
  if existVertexFace(v,T) then
    return
  end if
  for each root t in ascending order do
    x1 = T.v1 + tT.u1
    x2 = T.v2 + tT.u2
    x3 = T.v3 + tT.u3
    x4 = v + tv.u
    H = triangle(x1, x2, x3)          d0 = dist(plane(H), x4)
    d1 = dist(plane(H), x4)
    if d0 >= 0 and d1 >= 0 then
      return
    end if
    if d0 < 0 and d1 < 0 then
      return
    end if
    u = intersection(x4, H)
    (w0, w1, w2) =barycentric-coords(x1, x2, x3, x4)
      if inside(w0, w1, w2) then
        report (v,T)
        return
      end if
  next t
end algorithm
```

Figure 15.72: Vertex-face proximity test.

Solving for a and b, we can compute the closest points between the two lines running through the two edges. If a and b both are not below zero or above one, then a contact point can be reported. The pseudocode is outlined in Figure 15.73. When looking backward in time we are actually seeking the first point of contact. This point in space is attractive for simulation methods, since it implies the point in time a simulation should be rewound in order to avoid penetration.

15.8.4 Self-Intersection

Self-intersection queries add one more complication to the contact determination discussed in the previous sections. Observing that neighboring faces touch each other along common boundaries, trivially leads to a self-intersection along these common boundaries. In Figure 15.74, two triangle faces are shown, and during a query of self-collision, the bounding volumes of these two faces trivially intersect each other leading to a primitive test between the two faces. However, we already know that the two faces would result in contact points being reported corresponding to the shared boundary between the faces. A simple prescreening can be applied to the contact determination avoiding the unpleasanties of this problem. The prescreening consists of a quick rejection, and we only run contact determination on triangular faces, which do not share any nodes. Thus, no immediate neighboring triangles will yield any contact points.

```
algorithm do-Egde-Edge(x'_1, x'_2, x'_3, x'_4)
  if existEdgeEdge(x'_1, x'_2, x'_3, x'_4) then
    return
  end if
  for each root t in ascending order do
    x_1 = x'_1 + t u_1
    x_2 = x'_2 + t u_2
    x_3 = x'_3 + t u_3
    x_4 = x'_4 + t u_4
    if (x_2 - x_1) × (x_4 - x_3) > ε then
      return
    end if
    (a, b) =closest-point(x_1, x_2, x_3, x_4)
    if 0 < a < 1 and 0 < b < 1 then
        report (x'_1, x'_2, x'_3, x'_4)
        return
      end if
  next t
end algorithm
```

Figure 15.73: Edge-edge proximity test.

15.9 Previous Work

Bounding volume hierarchies have been around for a long time. Consequently, there is a huge wealth of literature on bounding volume hierarchies. Most addresses homogeneous bounding volume hierarchies and top-down construction methods. A great variety of different types of bounding volumes has been reported: spheres [Hubbard, 1996, Palmer, 1995, Dingliana et al., 2000], axes aligned bounding boxes (AABBs) [Bergen, 1997, Larsson et al., 2001], oriented bounding boxes (OBBs) [Gottschalk et al., 1996, Gottschalk, 2000], discrete orientation polytypes (k-DOPs) [Klosowski et al., 1998, Zachmann, 1998], quantized orientation slabs with primary orientations (QuOSPOs) [He, 1999], spherical shell and swept sphere volumes (SSVs) [Krishnan et al., 1998, Larsen et al., 1999]. In general, it has been discovered that

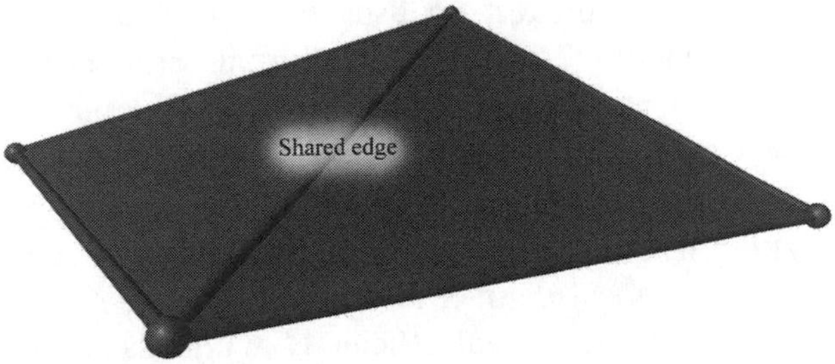

Figure 15.74: Self-intersection needs special treatment of neighboring faces, since neighborship implies self-intersection along common edges.

there is a tradeoff between the complexity of the geometry of a bounding volume and the speed of its overlap test and the number of overlap tests in a query.

In contrast to bounding volumes types, only a little has been written on approximating bounding volume hierarchies. To our knowledge, [Hubbard, 1993] pioneered the field, where octrees combined with simulated annealing were used to construct a sphere tree. In [Palmer et al., 1995, Palmer, 1995], a superior bottom-up construction method was added, which is based on medial surface (M-reps) [Hubbard, 1996]. More recently, [O'Sullivan et al., 1999, Dingliana et al., 2000] used approximating sphere-trees built in a top-down fashion based on an octree for time critical collision detection, and [Bradshaw et al., 2004] used an adaptive m-rep approximation based on a top-down construction algorithm.

Even less has been written about heterogeneous bounding volume hierarchies, although object hierarchies of different primitive volume types are a widely used concept in most of today's simulators [ODE, 2005, Vortex, 2005, Karma, 2005]. The SSVs [Larsen et al., 1999] is one of the most recent publications. The general belief is, however, that heterogeneous bounding volumes do not change the fundamental algorithms, but merely introduce a raft of other problems. It is also believed that heterogeneous bounding volumes could provide better and more tightly fitting bounding volumes resulting in higher convergence toward the true shape volume of the objects. This could mean an increase in the pruning capabilities and a corresponding increase in performance.

Most of the work with bounding volume hierarchies has addressed objects that are represented by polygonal models. Many experiments also indicate that OBBs (and other rectangular volumes) provide the best convergence for polygonal models [Gottschalk et al., 1996, Gottschalk, 2000, Zachmann, 1998, Larsen et al., 1999], while spherical volumes are believed to converge best toward the volume. The underlying query algorithms for penetration detection, separation distance, and contact determination of bounding volume hierarchies have not changed much. In their basic form, these algorithms are nothing more than simple traversals [Gottschalk, 2000]. The stack-list traversal [Zachmann et al., 2003a] is thread-safe and overcomes the problem of inefficient updating of BVs, meaning that queries can be done in parallel even though they share the same BVH data structure.

M-rep-based methods are the state of art for bottom-up construction methods [Hubbard, 1996] and top-down construction [Bradshaw et al., 2004]. For deformable objects such as cloth, bottom-up construction based on mesh topology [Volino et al., 1995, Volino et al., 2000, Bridson et al., 2002] is the preferred choice. In [Bergen, 1997], a median-based top-down method was proposed for building an AABB tree. [Larsson et al., 2001] suggested using a mesh connectivity tree in a top-down construction method. Extensions to deformable surfaces by curvature test are discussed in [Volino et al., 1995, Volino et al., 2000], In [Larsson et al., 2003] an update method for morphing deformation based on blending is proposed. The method out performs their hybrid update method [Larsson et al., 2001], but is not as generally applicable.

In [Bergen, 1997], initial AABB trees are built in local object coordinate systems. The trees are built using classical top-down splitting methods, and the entire AABB tree is updated in a bottom-up fashion ensuring that making parent AABBs enclose their children AABBs. During runtime, the AABB trees are moved causing the local defined AABBs to become OBBs. A variation of the separation axis overlap test method is used to deal efficiently with this problem. Self-intersections are treated in [Volino et al., 1995, Volino et al., 2000] by organizing the boundary of an object into a hierarchical representation of subsurfaces, each of which has no self-intersections. The BucketTree algorithm [Hirota, 2002, Ganovelli et al., 2000] is, in our opinion, interesting because it takes a different approach to updating a spatial data structure, which is easily extended to more complex scenarios. Instead of updating the spatial data structure at every iteration, a fast method is used to remap primitives into the spatial data structure. In [Larsson et al., 2001], a top-down method is used for building AABBs in order to handle deformation of arbitrary vertex positioning of meshes, and mesh connectivity is analyzed when splitting parents to children. Furthermore, in order to minimize the number of AABB updates, the method uses a top-down update approach while doing a tandem traversal. A bottom-up update method is used on the remaining subtree when at predefined depth.

Even though there are several ways for constructing bounding volume hierarchies, there has been a tendency to use top-down methods. Some believe that bottom-up methods would be superior to top-down methods in the sense that smaller and tighter bounding volume hierarchies can be constructed. Most recent work with bounding volume hierarchies has focused on trying out new kinds of bounding volumes, figuring out better methods for fitting a bounding volume to a subset of an object's underlying geometry, finding faster and better overlap test methods, and comparing homogeneous bounding volume hierarchies of different bounding volume types with each other. In order to improve performance of traversal algorithms, depth control, layered bounding volumes, caching bounding volumes, and shared bounding volumes have been studied.

Depth control: In time-critical applications it can sometimes be beneficial to set a limit on the depth a traversal is allowed to proceed in a bounding volume hierarchy, thereby trading accuracy for performance [Hubbard, 1993].

Layered bounding volumes: Having recognized the tradeoffs between the complexity of the geometry of the bounding volumes and their overlap test speed, simpler geometries are tried out first in order to get a quick rejection test. Spheres are most commonly used [Gottschalk, 2000, Eberly, 2005b].

Caching bounding volumes: Caching bounding volumes from previous invocations create witnesses that can exploit spatial and temporal coherence [Gottschalk, 2000, Eberly, 2005b].

Shared bounding volumes: This changes a hierarchy from a tree into a DAG [Hubbard, 1996].

16

Feature-Based Algorithms

A *feature-based algorithm* works directly on the features of an object. For polygonal meshes, the features are the vertices, edges, and faces of the meshes. In other words, a feature is a geometric primitive, and we therefore classify a narrow-phase collision detection algorithm as being feature based whenever the algorithm works directly on the geometric primitives of the objects. This is a broad classification and there is a wealth of literature on feature-based narrow-phase collision detection algorithms, and many different approaches have been investigated: polygonal intersection [Moore et al., 1988], Lin-Canny [Ponamgi et al., 1997], V-Clip [Mirtich, 1998b], SWIFT [Ehmann et al., 2001], and recursive search methods [Sundaraj et al., 2000], just to mention a few.

16.1 CULLIDE

The naive approach to the collision detection problem would be to take every geometric primitive and test it against every other primitive, which leads to a brute-force, all-triangle pair clipping algorithm, with complexity $O(n^2)$.

Quadratic complexity algorithms are unattractive in physics-based animation; nevertheless, exhaustive pair testing is not dependent on spatial structures and is generally applicable to arbitrary complex shapes with all kinds of degeneracies, such as holes, open boundaries, flipped faces, etc.

Exhaustive search algorithms make no real distinction between handling self-intersections and object-object intersections, leading to improvements investigated in the literature.

To avoid the all pair testing, the ideas of broad-phase collision detection can be exploited; for instance, each primitive could be bounded by a single *AABB* followed by a sweep and prune algorithm (see Section 12.3) in order to quickly find potential overlapping triangle pairs. This approach appears to be superior, since the method should run an expected $O(n)$ time, and since it's generally applicable to both deformable objects, open surfaces, and even triangle soups. However, it useless for the following reasons [Hirota, 2002]: We need to keep close-pair counters for counting the number of axes that two AABBs overlap, and the storage requirement is likely to be $O(n^2)$ due to the neighborhood relation of primitives. For volumetric meshes such as tetrahedra meshes, every tetrahedra inside an object shares triangular faces with at least four other neighboring tetrahedra. AABB boxes for volumetric meshes will thus overlap by this structural relationship, and a lot of false AABB overlaps will be reported.

Graphics hardware may be used to speed up collision detection, and in [Govindaraju et al., 2003] *CULLIDE* is proposed to prune primitives from a *potentially colliding set* (*PCS*) as an efficient preprocessing step prior to an exhaustive search.

Initially, the PCS contains all objects. All elements of the PCS are then rendered in a two-pass algorithm, first in a forward order and then in reverse order.

While rendering objects, *visibility queries* are done to remove elements from the PCS, which is known not to be colliding with any other elements in the PCS. After the second pass, fully visible objects are removed from the PCS. This strategy is applied iteratively until no more changes are made to the PCS. Hereafter, one can perform exact collision detection on the primitives that are left in the PCS.

Other algorithms based on stencil and/or depth testing also use graphics hardware to accelerate collision detection [Hoff III et al., 2001, III et al., 2002, Heidelberger et al., 2003, Heidelberger et al., 2004]. These algorithms require read back of either the stencil and/or depth buffers, which can be expensive on commodity graphics hardware.

The CULLIDE algorithm is based on visibility queries, computed by image-space occlusion queries, which are supported on most graphics hardware. Occlusion queries have low bandwidth, unlike buffer read-backs, and are therefore cheap to perform on commodity graphics hardware (for more specific details see [SGI, 2005]). An occlusion query returns the number of rasterized fragments, which passed the depth test. Setting up the prober depth test, it is thus possible to count how many pixels are occluded by other objects already rendered onto the screen.

Given an environment of n objects, $O_1, O_2, \ldots, O_n$, each represented as a collection of triangles, we want to find out which objects overlap and compute the overlapping triangles. If an object O_i is not in the PCS, then O_i does not collide with any object in the PCS. This property is used to prune object pairs, which need to be considered for exact collision detection. Given a set S of objects, we test the relative visibility of an object O with respect to S, by testing if any parts of O are occluded by S. If we rasterize all objects in S, then O is considered fully visible when all fragments generated by rasterization of O have a depth value less than the corresponding pixels in the frame buffer, where we assume that depth values increase as we go into the screen. If O were colliding with something in S, then some fragments must be behind those rasterized from S, when rasterizing O. This is not the same as saying that we always have a collision when fragments of O are found to be behind those from S. On the other hand, if we know that all fragments of O are in front of all those from S, then O can not be colliding with anything in S. This observation leads to the following lemma:

Lemma 16.1 (Noncolliding Object)
An object O does not collide with a set of objects S, when O is fully visible with respect to S.

We will use this lemma to prune objects from the PCS. The naive approach for this would be to test each object in the PCS against all remaining objects, however this leads to an $O(n^2)$ complexity. An efficient approach can be derived from the following lemma:

Lemma 16.2
For n objects, $O_1, \ldots, O_n$, in the potentially colliding set (PCS) and two sets $S_{i-1} = \{O_1, \ldots, O_{i-1}\}$ and $S_{i+1} = \{O_{i+1}, \ldots, O_n\}$. If object O_i is fully visible both w.r.t. S_{i-1} and S_{i+1} then O_i is fully visible w.r.t. the set $S = S_{i-1} \cup S_{i+1}$. Hence O_i is fully visible w.r.t. to all other objects in PCS

We can use the Lemma 16.2 to prune objects from the PCS in linear time, by iterating over the objects in two passes. When object O_i is treated in the first pass, it is tested if O_i is fully visible w.r.t. S_{i-1}. After having performed the test, we can add O_i to S_{i-1} simply by rasterizing O_i to obtain $S_i = S_{i-1} \cup O_i$. Now we are ready to test O_{i+1} against S_i. In the second pass, the object order is reversed, implying that O_i is tested against S_{i+1}. Adding O_i to S_{i+1} we get the set $S_i = S_{i+1} \cup O_i$, and we are ready to test object O_{i-1} for full visibility against S_i. This two-pass algorithm is shown in pseudocode in Figure 16.1. If an object O_i were determined to be fully visible in both render passes, then we know that it is fully visible w.r.t.

```
algorithm reduce( PCS )
  clearDepthBuffer()
  for each o in PCS do
    DepthTest( GREATER_EQUAL )
    DepthMask( FALSE )
    BeginOcclusionQuery()
    render o
    EndOcclusionQuery()
    fullyVisible(o) = (GetQueryObject(o)==NONE)
    DepthTest( LESS )
    DepthMask( TRUE )
    render o
  next o
  reverse PCS
  clearDepthBuffer()
  for each o in PCS do
    DepthTest( GREATER_EQUAL )
    DepthMask( FALSE )
    BeginOcclusionQuery()
    render o
    EndOcclusionQuery()
    fullyVisible(o) &= (GetQueryObject(o)==NONE)
    DepthTest( LESS )
    DepthMask( TRUE )
    render o
  next o
  remove all fully visible o from PCS
end algorithm
```

Figure 16.1: Reduction of the PCS in CULLIDE.

both S_{i-1} and S_{i+1}. Thus, according to Lemma 16.1 O_i can be safely removed from PCS. The pruning algorithm has linear complexity in the number of objects in the PCS.

It can be somewhat difficult to see through the logic of the depth test and depth mask operations in the algorithm listed in Figure 16.1, so we will present here a small example, where the PCS consists of five objects labeled a, b, c, d, and e (in that order) as seen in Figure 16.2. Notice that the depth values at the far and near clipping plane are $z = 1$ and $z = 0$ During the first render pass:

- When object a is rendered, all z-values are one. Thus, the greater-than-equal depth test fails on all fragments being rendered, and the fully visible flag for a is set. Finally, a is written to the depth buffer, and the next object is b.
- Object b lies in front of a, implying that its z-values are all less than those currently in the z-buffer. Thus b is also set to be fully visible.
- Finally, object c is rendered and set to be fully visible, since all z-values are less than those stored in the z-buffer.

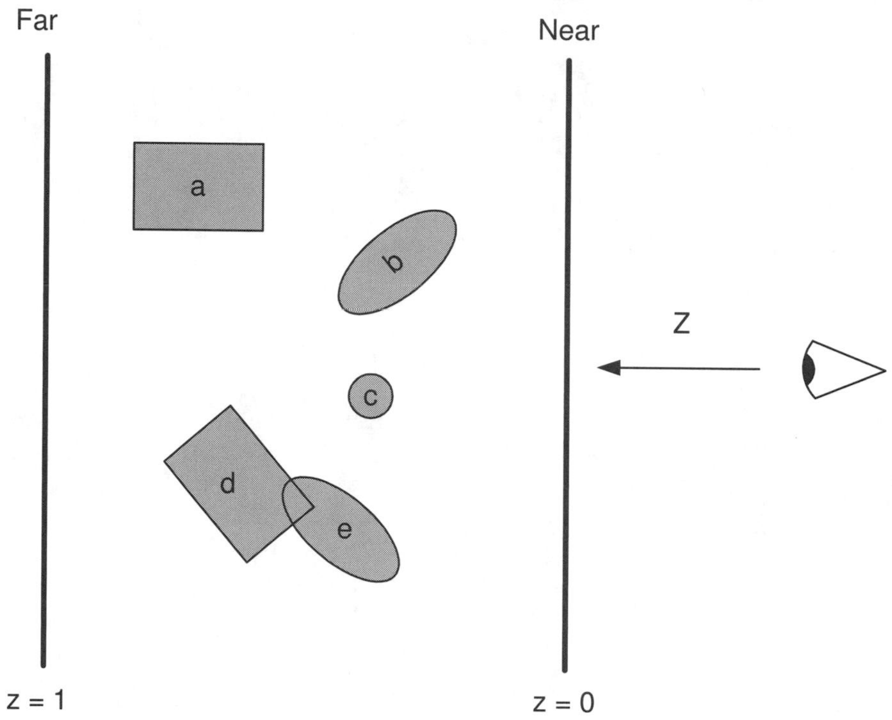

Figure 16.2: Small CULLIDE example.

- When object d is rendered something different occurs: a small part lies behind object c, so object d will not be set to be fully visible since some fragments will fail the greater-than-equal test.

- Similarly, when rendering object e, some parts are lying behind objects d, causing fragments to pass the greater-than-equal test.

In the second pass, the objects are rendered in reverse order:

- Object e will be found to not occlude anything, being the first object that is rendered. However, object e was determined as not being fully visible in the first pass, so no changes are made to the state of object e.

- When rendering, object d fragments will pass the greater-than-equal test, no changes are made to object d as it was already determined to be not fully visible in the first pass.

- Object c lies in front of anything else being rendered so far; since it was determined to be fully visible in both the first and second pass, it is declared to be a fully visible object.

- A similar thing happens for object b.

```
algorithm CULLIDE( Objects )
  PCS = Objects
  do
    reduce(PCS)
    for each o in PCS do
      if o not primitive then
        remove o from PCS
        add subobjects of o to PCS
      end if
    next o
  while non primitive objects exist in PCS
end algorithm
```

Figure 16.3: Main loop of CULLIDE.

- Object a lies in front of object b, thus fragments will pass the greater-than-equal test and the state of object a is set to be non fully visible.

When removing objects from the PCS only b and c were determined to be fully visible, thus a, d, and e are left in the PCS. Performing an iteration more will prune object a, and we are left with only object d and e, which will never be pruned from the PCS and in the end will be passed along for exact collision detection.

To minimize the number of triangles that are up for rasterization, a *hierarchical decomposition* of objects can be devised. Initially each object is enclosed by an AABB. Then the reduce algorithm is performed three times, using the three world axis as projection axes. Hereafter the AABB representation of the objects can be replaced by a set of subobjects, which are used in the next reduction step of the PCS. Each time a reduction has been performed, objects in the PCS are replaced by subobjects. Eventually objects in the PCS will be decomposed into their respective triangles. The finally output from CULLIDE will therefore be a set of potentially colliding triangles.

CULLIDE could be initialized with each triangle initially being an object in the PCS, however this approach will have poor performance. It is beneficial to use a subobject to quickly home in on regions of objects with colliding triangles. Since a fully visible subobject may mean that several hundred or even thousands of triangles are pruned in one reduction step. The subobjects can be computed dynamically on the fly. For instance, by collecting a subset of k triangles making up the object into a single subobject, another k triangles into another subobject, and so forth.

To recap the idea is to iteratively continue decomposing objects in the PCS into subobjects, until all objects in the PCS consist of a single primitive, i.e., a single triangle. Figure 16.3 illustrates the idea in pseudocode.

CULLIDE has many benefits, no precomputed data structures are required, no topology information is needed, no temporal coherence is exploited. Thus, CULLIDE is applicable to both static and deformable objects—even flying triangle soups can be dealt with. Furthermore, the triangle count is also allowed to change from iteration to iteration. Many factors have an impact on the overall algorithm, object count, subobject strategy, number of triangles, projection direction used during the reduce algorithm, etc. We refer the interested reader to [Govindaraju et al., 2003] for details on a performance analysis of CULLIDE. In [Boldt et al., 2004], the CULLIDE algorithm has been extended to handle self-intersections. There are however, serious performance issues that must be addressed.

16.2 Optimal Spatial Hashing

In the previous section, we saw how the brute-force of graphics hardware was exploited to speed up naive exhaustive searching to prune unneeded primitive pair tests. In this section, we will present *optimal spatial hashing* [Teschner et al., 2003]. This algorithm does not use graphics hardware; instead, spatial locality is exploited. The algorithm is designed for deformable objects represented by a tetrahedra mesh, but it can be equally well applied to a triangular mesh or soup. The conversion is straightforward and we leave this as an exercise for the reader. optimal spatial hashing uses a two-pass algorithm. First, vertices are mapped into a hash map, and in the next pass, tetrahedras are tested against the hash map to find potential colliding vertices. The novelty is that it is not the tetrahedra that are stored into the hash map as is done in other gridding algorithms as suggested in *BucketTree*

[Ganovelli et al., 2000].

Given an infinite uniform rectilinear grid in 3D space, characterized by a user-specified grid cell size, l, we can discretize any given point, $\boldsymbol{r} = [x, y, z]^T$, in space

$$\boldsymbol{p} = \left[\left\lfloor \frac{x}{l} \right\rfloor, \left\lfloor \frac{y}{l} \right\rfloor, \left\lfloor \frac{z}{l} \right\rfloor\right]^T \tag{16.1}$$

The integer coordinate, $\boldsymbol{p}$, can be thought of as a 3D index, mapping the point $\boldsymbol{r}$ into a uniquely determined index. A full 3D grid of cells would require a prohibitive amount of storage, so instead, we will use a 1D *hash map* and a *hash function*, $\text{hash}(\cdot)$, which maps a discretized point into a 1D index. The hash function suggested in [Teschner et al., 2003] is

$$\text{hash}(\boldsymbol{p}) = (xp_1 \text{ xor } yp_2 \text{ xor } zp_3) \mod n, \tag{16.2}$$

where p_1, p_2, and p_3 are large prime numbers, e.g., 73856093, 19349663, and 83492791, as used in [Teschner et al., 2003]. The value n is the hash table size, ideally also a prime number. Although in [Teschner et al., 2003], the hash table size varies according to 99, 199, 299, etc. There is no guarantee that discretized points mapped to two different grid cells will not map to the same hash cell. Traditionally, this is called a collision.

The algorithm makes two passes; a first pass discretizes the position of each vertex of the tetrahedra using (16.1). The vertices are then stored into the hash cells using (16.2). In the second pass, the minimum enclosing AABB is found for each tetrahedron. This AABB is defined by two points in space, a minimum and maximum coordinate point. Using (16.1), a span of discretized points covered by the enclosing AABB is calculated. For each discretized point in this span the hash function is used to find the hash cell, containing vertices mapped into the same grid cell as the discretized point currently being treated.

All nodes in the found hash cell are then tested for inclusion in the tetrahedron currently being treated. If a node is part of the tetrahedron, it is trivially rejected. However, if the node is not part of the tetrahedron currently being treated, and the position of the node is inside the tetrahedron, a contact point is reported.

```
class HashCell
  Timestamp  T
  list<Node> nodes

class HashMap
  Timestamp T
  vector<HashCell> cell
```

Figure 16.4: Hash map data structure.

To avoid clearing the entire hash table before each collision query, a clever time-stamping strategy can be applied instead. Each query is given a unique time-stamp; similarly, each hash cell has a time-stamp. When a vertex is mapped to a hash cell, it is first tested if the time-stamp is different from the current time-stamp of the query. If so, the hash cell is cleared before adding the vertex to the hash cell and the time-stamp of the hash cell is updated to that of the current query. In the second pass, one must make sure to only test against hash cells spanned by the AABB, which have a time-stamp equal to the current query.

The point in the tetrahedron inclusion test is done by computing the *barycentric coordinates* of the point also used in Section 15.8. The barycentric coordinates, w_1, w_2, w_3, and w_4 of the point $\boldsymbol{r}$ w.r.t. to the tetrahedron defined by the vertex positions $\boldsymbol{p}_1$, $\boldsymbol{p}_2$, $\boldsymbol{p}_3$,and $\boldsymbol{p}_4$ is given by

$$\boldsymbol{r} = w_1\boldsymbol{p}_1 + w_2\boldsymbol{p}_2 + w_3\boldsymbol{p}_3 + w_4\boldsymbol{p}_4, \tag{16.3}$$

where

$$w_1 + w_2 + w_3 + w_4 = 1, \tag{16.4}$$

which is trivially solved. Observe that one only needs to store three of the barycentric coordinates. The other is implicitly given by the last constraint. Having found the barycentric coordinates, the given point lies inside the tetrahedron if

$$w_1 \geq 0, w_2 \geq 0, w_3 \geq 0 \quad \text{and} \quad w_1 + w_2 + w_3 \leq 1. \tag{16.5}$$

Here we assumed that w_4 was given implicitly by the other coordinates. Figure 16.4 illustrates the data structures in pseudocode. The first pass is shown in pseudocode in Figure 16.5. The second pass is given in pseudocode in Figure 16.6. The overlap algorithm is shown in Figure 16.7.

The edge tetrahedron intersection case is ignored in the Optimized Spatial Hashing algorithm. At first hand, this might seem flawed. However, according to [Teschner et al., 2003], there are two reasons for not considering edge intersections. First, the performance of the algorithm would decrease substantially, while the relevance of the edge test is unclear in the case of densely sampled objects. Second, the algorithm was developed to be integrated into physically based environments, where penetrating vertices are easily dealt with, whereas edge intersections are uncommon and costly.

Obviously, the first pass of the algorithm is linear in the number of vertices, n, since both the discretization and the hash function takes $O(1)$ time, The second pass is more difficult to analyze. Clearly the number of tetrahedra is not going to be larger than the number of vertices, since four vertices are used

```
algorithm first-pass(H:HashMap,V:Vertices)
  for each v in V do
    p = discretized(v.pos)
    h = hash-func(p)
    if H.cell[h].T not equal H.T then
       H.cell[h].nodes.clear()
       H.cell[h].T = H.T
     end if
     H.cell[h].nodes.add(v)
  next v
end algorithm
```

Figure 16.5: Pseudocode for the first pass.

```
algorithm second-pass(H:Hashmap,T:Tetrahedra)
  for each t in T do
    A = AABB(t)
    m = discretized(A.min)
    M = discretized(A.max)
    for each p, m <= p <= M do
       h = hash-func(p)
       if H.cell[h].T equal H.T then
         for each n H.cell[h].nodes do
            if n not part of t and n inside t then
               create contact(n,t)
            end if
         next n
       end if
    next p
  next t
end algorithm
```

Figure 16.6: Pseudocode for the second pass.

```
algorithm spatial-hashing(H:Hashmap,T:Tetrahedra,V:Vertices)
  inc H.T
  first-pass(H,V)
  second-pass(H,T)
end algorithm
```

Figure 16.7: Pseudocode for the spatial hashing algorithm.

to define each tetrahedra. If p is the average number of cells intersected by a tetrahedron, and q is the average number of vertices per cell, then the complexity is of order $O(npq)$. If the cell size is chosen to be proportional to the average tetrahedron size, then p is constant under that assumption that the aspect ratio of the tetrahedra does not vary too much. If there are no hash collisions, then the average number of tetrahedra per cell is constant and so is q, since there are at most four times as many vertices as tetrahedra in a cell. Since p and q can be regarded as constants, the complexity of the algorithm is linear in the number of primitives, that is, $O(n)$.

In [Teschner et al., 2003] numerical results are given supporting the following statements:

- The method is linear in the number of primitives and not objects.
- Hash table size influences performance; it should be large enough to avoid too many colliding entries in the hash map.
- Grid cell size should be set to the average tetrahedra edge length to achieve the best performance.

The problem of varying aspect ratio is not mentioned in [Teschner et al., 2003]. Most likely because it is not encountered in the test cases, where all tetrahedra appears to be of uniform size implying that the enclosing AABBs are cubes of the same size, ideally suited for hashing in a uniform grid as pointed out by [Mirtich, 1996]. In [Mirtich, 1996], hierarchical hashing is used to circumvent the problem of large variance in aspect ratio.

16.3 The Voronoi-Clip Algorithm

To avoid the all triangle-pair exhaustive search comparison feature, tracking algorithms have been proposed, such as *Lin-Canny* [Lin et al., 1994, Lin et al., 1998], *Voronoi-Clip* [Mirtich, 1998b], and *SWIFT* [Ehmann et al., 2000a, Ehmann et al., 2000b]. In the following we will present the Voronoi-Clip (*V-Clip*) algorithm as an example of a feature tracking algorithm.

The main idea of V-Clip is to iteratively optimize either the minimum distance between two convex polyhedra or improve upon the localization of the closest point between the two polyhedra.

The minimum distance and closest points between the two convex polyhedra are given implicitly by two features: a vertex, an edge, or a face, one from each polyhedra. V-Clip estimates the minimum distance and closest points by a feature pair. In each iteration of the algorithm, V-Clip updates the features of the feature pair with their neighbors to minimize the minimum known distance or localization of the closest points. The algorithm iteratively continues to update these features until the closest point or an interpenetration is found.

Before we can go into details of the V-Clip algorithm, we will need to work out some geometric definitions that allow us to more clearly describe features and regions of space around a convex object. We will do this in Section 16.3.1. If the reader is familiar with *Voronoi regions* and the *closest feature pair theorem*, it should be safe to skip directly to Section 16.3.2, where the V-Clip algorithm is explained in detail.

16.3.1 Definitions and Notation

The V-Clip algorithm is concerned with features of a polygonal object that are either a vertex (V), an edge (E), or a face (F). We consider each feature type to be a closed set, i.e., an edge will include its end-points and a face will include its boundary edges. Mathematically, we describe each of the feature types as follows:

- A vertex V is a point $\boldsymbol{v} \in \mathbb{R}^3$.
- An edge, E, is a line running from vertex O to vertex D, and we can parameterize it as follows:

$$\boldsymbol{e}(t) = (\boldsymbol{d} - \boldsymbol{o})\,t + \boldsymbol{o} \quad \text{for} \quad 0 \leq t \leq 1 \tag{16.6}$$

- A face, F, is represented by its boundary edges and a face plane, $P(F)$, which we can describe by

$$\boldsymbol{p} \cdot \boldsymbol{n} - w = 0. \tag{16.7}$$

  Here $\boldsymbol{p}$ is any point in the face plane, $\boldsymbol{n}$ is the outward pointing face normal, and w is the orthogonal distance from the origin to the face plane.

Note that we will be working with *convex polyhedra* and the boundary edges of a face will therefore form a planar convex polygon without any holes. Furthermore, no coplanar faces are present in the polyhedra. If a mesh contains coplanar faces, then these must be merged into a single convex face.

Definition 16.1 (Signed Distance Map for a Plane)
We define the signed distance function from a point $\boldsymbol{p}$ to a plane Q to be

$$D_Q(\boldsymbol{p}) = \boldsymbol{p} \cdot \boldsymbol{n} - w, \tag{16.8}$$

where the plane unit normal is $\boldsymbol{n}$ and distance to the origin is w.

Any given point $\boldsymbol{p}$ may be classified with respect to a plane Q using D_Q as:

$D_Q(\boldsymbol{p}) < 0$	$\boldsymbol{p}$ is in back of Q
$D_Q(\boldsymbol{p}) = 0$	$\boldsymbol{p}$ is on Q
$D_Q(\boldsymbol{p}) > 0$	$\boldsymbol{p}$ is in front of Q

The signed distance map can also be used to find the intersection between an edge, E, and a plane, Q. By substituting the edge parameterization into the definition of the signed distance map, an analytical expression for the signed distance map of any point along the edge may be derived using (16.6) as follows:

$$D_Q(\boldsymbol{e}(t)) = D_Q((\boldsymbol{d} - \boldsymbol{o})t + \boldsymbol{o}) \tag{16.9a}$$
$$= \boldsymbol{n} \cdot \boldsymbol{d}t - \boldsymbol{n} \cdot \boldsymbol{o}t + \boldsymbol{n} \cdot \boldsymbol{o} - w \tag{16.9b}$$
$$= \boldsymbol{n} \cdot \boldsymbol{d}t - wt - \boldsymbol{n} \cdot \boldsymbol{o}t + wt + \boldsymbol{n} \cdot \boldsymbol{o} - w \tag{16.9c}$$
$$= (\boldsymbol{n} \cdot \boldsymbol{d} - w)t - (\boldsymbol{n} \cdot \boldsymbol{o} - w)t + (\boldsymbol{n} \cdot \boldsymbol{o} - w) \tag{16.9d}$$
$$= (D_Q(\boldsymbol{d}) - D_Q(\boldsymbol{o}))\,t + D_Q(\boldsymbol{o}). \tag{16.9e}$$

At the intersection point between the edge and the plane, $D_Q(\mathbf{e}(t)) = 0$, which means that

$$0 = (D_Q(\mathbf{d}) - D_Q(\mathbf{o}))\,t + D_Q(\mathbf{o}), \tag{16.10a}$$

$$t = \frac{D_Q(\mathbf{o})}{D_Q(\mathbf{o}) - D_Q(\mathbf{d})}. \tag{16.10b}$$

Hence, we only need to compute the t-value corresponding to the intersection point with the plane as long as the edge is not parallel to the plane. For a given t-value, we know:

$t \leq 0$	The staring point $\boldsymbol{o}$ is the closest point on the edge to the plane Q.
$0 \leq t \leq 1$	Point of intersection is $\mathbf{e}(t)$.
$t \geq 1$	The end-point $\boldsymbol{d}$ is closest point to the plane Q.

Definition 16.2 (Edge-Plane Intersection)
Given a plane Q and a noncoplanar parameterized edge

$$e(t) = (\mathbf{d} - \mathbf{o})\,t + \mathbf{o}, \tag{16.11}$$

where $0 \leq t \leq 1$*, then the intersection point between the edge and plane is given by the parameter* t*,*

$$t = \frac{D_Q(\mathbf{o})}{D_Q(\mathbf{o}) - D_Q(\mathbf{d})}, \tag{16.12}$$

as long as $0 \leq t \leq 1$*.*

It is common practice to define a topological neighborhood relation between features such that only features in touching contact are neighbors. We will, however, require a more strict definition of neighborhood.

Definition 16.3 (Feature Neighborhood)
The neighbors of a feature are defined to be

Vertex *all incident edges*

Edge *the two incident faces and the two end-points*

Face *all boundary edges*

In our definition of neighborhood relationship we have implicitly assumed that all polyhedra are closed twofolds; that is, we have a watertight object surface, where each edge is shared by exactly two faces. Notice that the neighborhood relation definition is a symmetric definition, meaning that if feature A by definition is a neighbor of feature B, then feature B is also by definition a neighbor of feature A. As implied, our neighborhood relation definition is a strong definition. A weaker definition could be made where faces and vertices are also allowed to be neighbors.

Our neighborhood relation definition is not more prohibitive than the weaker definition, in the sense that given two arbitrary features on the polyhedra surface, it is possible to walk from one feature to the other, by going from neighbor to neighbor. The difference is that the path using the weak definition will be shorter in some cases.

The concept of a *Voronoi diagram* can be extended to a polyhedral object: in a Voronoi diagram a cell (or region) of a site point delimits a subspace, where all points are known to lie closer to the site than any other site. This kind of information is useful for locating sites closest to a given point. Polyhedral objects do not pose point sites, but features; the definition below therefore extends the Voronoi concept to include polygonal features.

Definition 16.4 (External Voronoi Region)
An external Voronoi region $VR(X)$ of a feature, X, from a polyhedron, O, is defined as:

The set of points outside O lying closer or just as close to X than to any other feature.

It is important to notice that we only consider the space lying outside an object. Although it is possible to define internal Voronoi regions as well [Lin et al., 1998], we will not need those for our treatment of V-Clip.

Introducing a distance function $D(\boldsymbol{p}, X)$, which gives the minimum distance between a point $\boldsymbol{p}$ and a feature X, allows us to express the definition of an external Voronoi region in more mathematical terms as

$$\text{VR}(X) = \left\{ \boldsymbol{p} \quad \text{where} \quad D(\boldsymbol{p}, X) = \min_i \left\{ D(\boldsymbol{p}, X_i) \right\} \quad \text{and} \quad \boldsymbol{p} \notin O. \right\} \tag{16.13}$$

We will now define the concept of Voronoi planes, which will turn out to be very useful for describing the boundary of the external Voronoi regions.

Definition 16.5 (Voronoi Plane)
A Voronoi plane separates the Voronoi regions between two neighboring features, X and Y. We define it to be

$$VP(X, Y) = VR(X) \cap VR(Y) \tag{16.14}$$

.

Noticc that any point $\boldsymbol{p}$, which belongs to $\text{VP}(X, Y)$, has the same minimum distance to both X and Y.

It is easily seen from our definition of neighborhood relation and the fact that features are closed sets, that a convex polyhedron has two types of *Voronoi planes*: edge-vertex Voronoi planes and edge-face Voronoi planes.

Definition 16.6 (Edge-Vertex Voronoi Plane)
The edge-vertex Voronoi plane, $VP(E, V)$ is the plane with normal parallel to $\boldsymbol{u} = \boldsymbol{o} - \boldsymbol{d}$ and with point $\boldsymbol{v}$ on it.

Definition 16.6 is demonstrated in Figure 16.8.

Definition 16.7 (Edge-Face Voronoi Plane)
The edge-face Voronoi plane, $VP(E, F)$, is the plane with normal orthogonal to the normal of F and with all points of E on it.

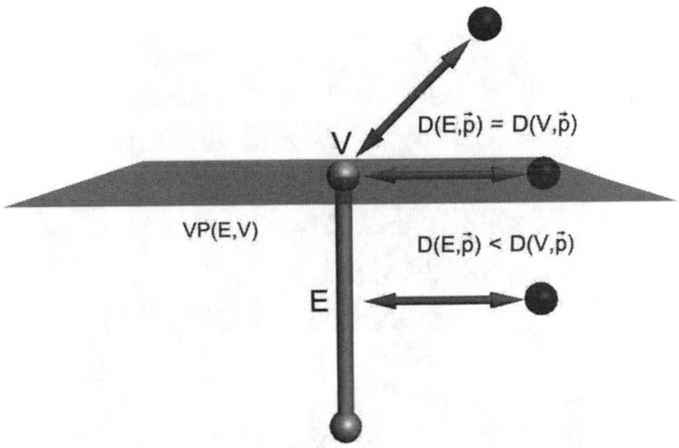

Figure 16.8: Edge-vertex Voronoi plane.

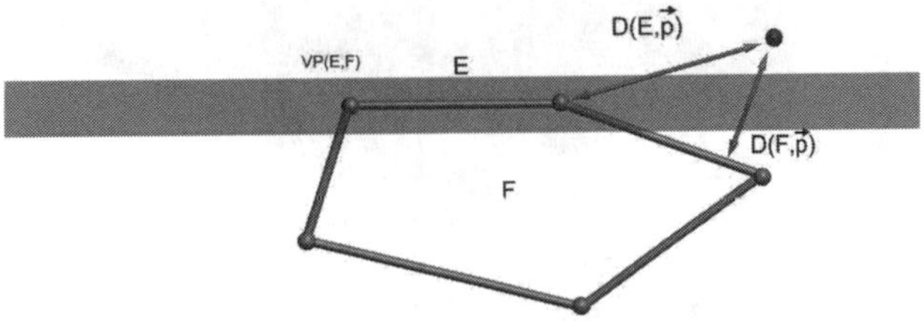

Figure 16.9: Edge-face Voronoi plane.

Definition 16.7 is demonstrated in Figure 16.9. There are some properties of the two kinds of Voronoi-planes that are worth more investigation, since they will have an impact on the details of the V-Clip algorithm.

An edge-vertex Voronoi plane, VP(E, V), divides space into two point sets: a set where all points definitely lie closer to E than to V, and another set where the points lie just as close to E as to V. This is shown in Figure 16.8. An edge-face Voronoi plane, VP(E, F), also divides space into two point sets: a set where we will certainty know that all points lie closer to F than to E, and another set where we just do not know whether F or E is the closest feature. This is illustrated in Figure 16.9. By our definition of features, we have three different kinds of Voronoi regions: a vertex Voronoi region (VR(V)), an edge Voronoi region (VR(E)), and a face Voronoi region (VR(F)). We will now give precise definitions of how these three kinds of Voronoi regions are represented by Voronoi planes.

Definition 16.8 (Vertex Voronoi Region)
The boundary of the vertex Voronoi region, VR(V), is given by the edge-vertex Voronoi planes, VP(E_i, V), between the vertex, V, and all incident edges, E_i, to V. We choose the convention that normals are pointing into the vertex Voronoi region.

Definition 16.8 is demonstrated in Figure 16.10.

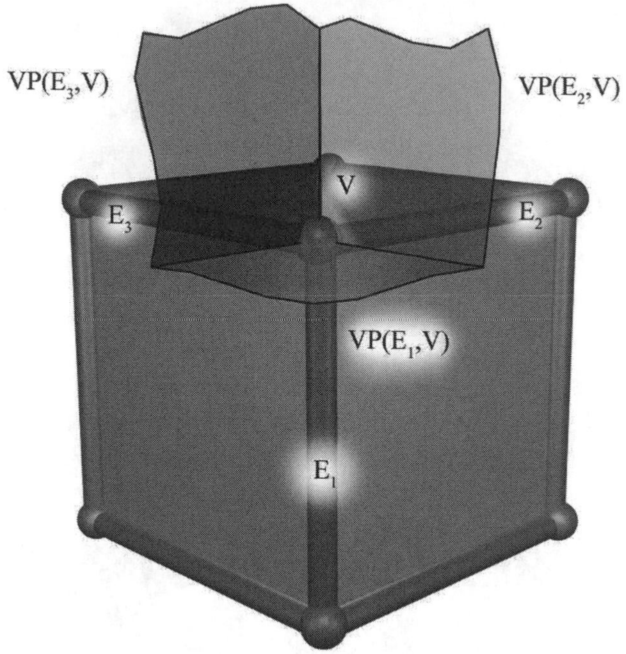

Figure 16.10: A vertex Voronoi region and the edge-vertex Voronoi planes defining its boundary.

Definition 16.9 (Edge Voronoi Region)
The boundary of the edge Voronoi region, VR(E), is represented by two edge-vertex Voronoi planes, VP(E,O) and VP(E,D), and two edge-face Voronoi planes, VP(E,F_i)s. We choose the convention that normals are pointing out of the Voronoi region. See Figure 16.11.

Definition 16.10 (Face Voronoi Region)
The boundary of the face Voronoi region, VR(F), is given by the edge-face Voronoi planes, VP(E_i,F), where the E_is are the boundary edges of F, and the face plane of F. We choose the convention that normals are pointing into the Voronoi region. See Figure 16.12.

In our precise representation of the three Voronoi regions, we have carefully stated the orientation of the Voronoi planes making up the boundaries between the Voronoi regions. This was done in such a manner that the normal direction of one region is not conflicting with the normal direction of neighboring Voronoi regions.

We now have all the necessary geometric background to state the main theorem, which the V-Clip algorithm relies on.

Theorem 16.3 (Closest Feature Pair)
Let A and B be two convex polyhedra and let P be a feature from A and Q a feature from B. Now let the points $\mathbf{p} \in P$ and $\mathbf{q} \in Q$ be the closest points between P and Q. If

$$\mathbf{p} \in VR(Q) \quad and \quad \mathbf{q} \in VR(P), \tag{16.15}$$

Figure 16.11: An edge Voronoi region and the Voronoi planes defining its boundary.

then no other points from A and B lie closer to each other than $\mathbf{p}$ and $\mathbf{q}$. In which case we say that P and Q are the closest features between A and B.

The proof of this theorem follows trivially from contradiction and the properties of the Voronoi regions (see [Mirtich, 1998b] for details). Figure 16.13 shows some examples illustrating the theorem.

16.3.2 Overview of V-Clip

V-Clip performs a greedy search for two features (X, Y) that fulfill the closest feature pair theorem, Theorem 16.3. Throughout the algorithm, V-Clip keeps track of a current feature pair (X, Y). The current feature pair is an estimate for the closest proximity between the two polyhedra, especially the closest distance between the two features $D(X, Y)$ is an estimate for the closest distance between the two polyhedra. In each iteration, V-Clip incrementally replaces either X or Y with one of their respective neighbors. The replacement is only done if the neighboring feature either decreases the currently estimated minimum distance or improves upon the localization of the closest points.

If we have a feature pair (X, Y), and we are about to update X with Z, then

$$(X, Y) \mapsto (Z, Y) \Rightarrow \begin{cases} D(Z, Y) < D(X, Y) & \text{If } \dim(Z) > \dim(X), \\ D(Z, Y) = D(X, Y) & \text{If } \dim(Z) < \dim(X), \end{cases} \tag{16.16}$$

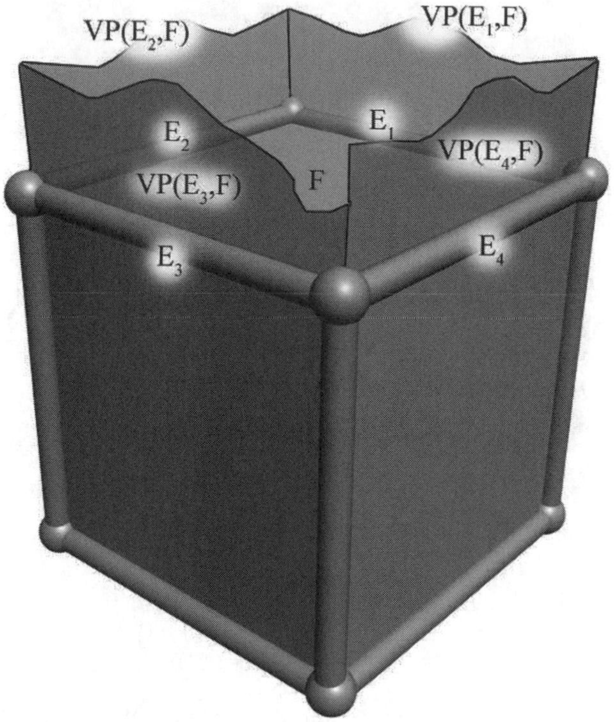

Figure 16.12: A face Voronoi region and the Voronoi planes defining its boundary.

where dim$(\cdot)$ denotes the dimension of a feature. In other words, if dim(Z) is greater than dim(X), the minimum distance will decrease, if dim(Z) is less than dim(x) the minimum distance is unchanged, but the localization of the closest points between the polyhedra is improved. Figure 16.14 shows examples clarifying these statements. In Figure (a), a face F is updated with one of its boundary edges, E', i.e., a lower dimensional feature; the minimum distance between the feature pairs remains unchanged, but we now have a better idea of where we should look for the closest point. In Figure (b) we have a vertex, V, making up the initial feature pair with E. By our neighborhood relation definition, the only possible updates would be to replace the vertex with one of its incident edges, E' or E''. Hence, regardless of which edge is used to update the vertex, the minimum distance between the feature pair becomes smaller.

Our definition of neighborhood relation guarantees that we never have a face-face feature pair, (F, F). Thus, we have only five possible states that the algorithm can be in as depicted in Figure 16.15. In the figure, the possible feature updates that can occur are shown. A dotted arrow indicates a lower dimensional update, and a solid arrow indicates a higher dimensional update. From the figure, it is intuitively clear that V-Clip will terminate, since each update aggressively improves the answer, and since there are only a finite number of features, so there can only be a finite number of updates.

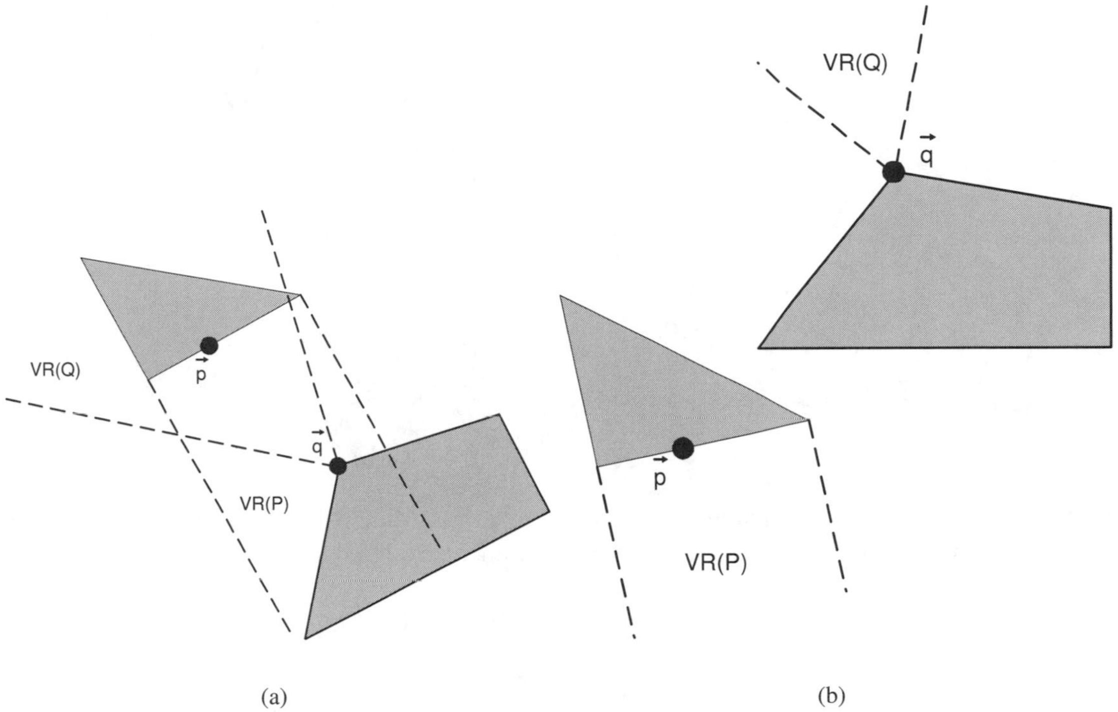

Figure 16.13: Examples of the closest feature pair theorem. In Figure (a) the closest points from edge P and vertex Q lie inside each of the other Voronoi regions, implying that P and Q are closest features. In Figure (b) this is no longer true.

16.3.3 Edge Clipping

The core of the algorithm is based on the use of *edge clipping* to determine a neighboring feature with which to perform an update. An edge E is clipped against the Voronoi planes of a Voronoi region $\text{VR}(X)$. Since E runs from origin O to destination D, it is possible to determine whether an intersection point with a Voronoi plane of $\text{VR}(X)$ indicates that the edge is entering or leaving the Voronoi region. We will also remember the neighboring features causing the Voronoi planes that the edge intersect, when it enters and leaves the Voronoi region, $\text{VR}(X)$.

If any intersection points are found, these indicate possible updates. In Figure 16.16 a simplified conceptual drawing is shown clarifying the idea behind the edge clipping. As can be seen in the figure, the Voronoi plane intersection indicates that feature X should be updated with its neighboring feature Z and not W. Of course the update should only be performed if the intersecting feature either decreases the minimum distance or improves upon the localization. Later we will present methods for testing these requirements. The edge clipping can thus be seen as a heuristic that guides the greedy search of possible neighboring features with which to update the current feature pair.

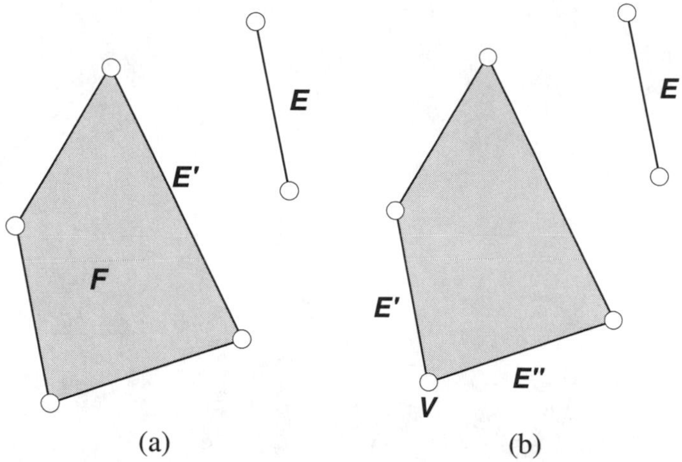

Figure 16.14: Examples showing feature updates. In (a) a lower dimensional update, $(F, E) \rightarrow (E', E)$, improving localization of closest points. In (b) a higher dimensional update $(V, E) \rightarrow (E', E)$ or (E'', E), improving minimum distance.

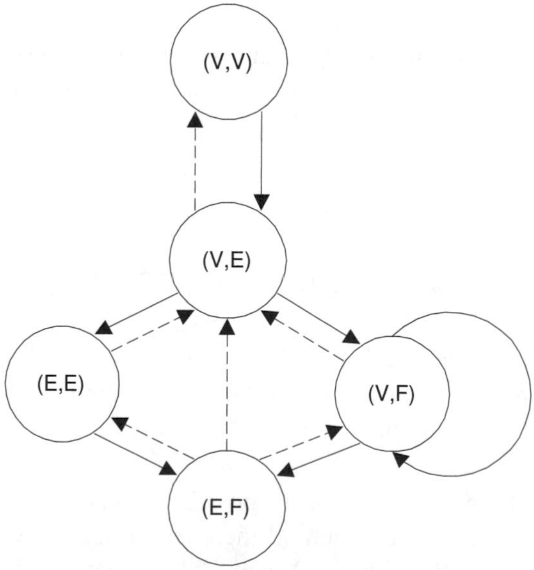

Figure 16.15: State diagram of the V-Clip algorithm. Dotted arrows are lower dimensional updates and solid arrows are higher dimensional updates.

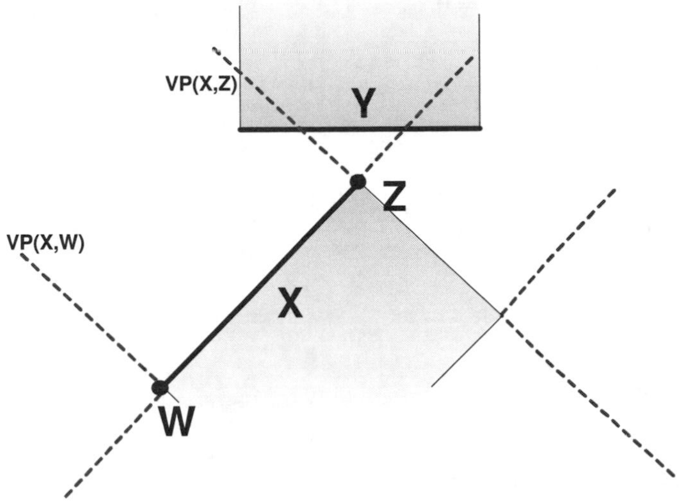

Figure 16.16: Edge Y is clipped against Voronoi planes of X: VP(X, W) and VP(X, Z), edge Y is intersecting Voronoi plane defined by feature Z, thus Z is a possible feature with which to update X.

The actual edge clipping is nothing more than a simple *Cyrus-Beck clipping* [Foley et al., 1996]. Figure 16.17 shows the edge-clipping algorithm in pseudocode. Notice that the sign of the distance on the end-points are used to determine whether the intersection point is an entering point or a leaving point. Observe further that the algorithm iteratively updates the best known entering and/or leaving point by keeping track of the parameter t-value for the intersection point.

When an edge is tested against a Voronoi region, there can be four different cases:

- Either the edge is fully enclosed inside all the Voronoi planes of the Voronoi region or the edge is partially enclosed, meaning that it is sticking out through at least one of the Voronoi planes.
- It might also be the case that the edge is excluded due to lying entirely on the outside of a Voronoi plane. We call this simple exclusion.
- The last possibility is that the edge lies outside the Voronoi region, but in such a way that it is not simply excluded. We call this compound exclusion.

The four cases are shown in Figure 16.18. The results from the edge-clip algorithm shown in Figure 16.17 can be used to determine which of the four cases we are dealing with.

$$\text{clip-edge} \Rightarrow \begin{cases} t_{in} = 0, t_{out} = 1, N_{in} = N_{out} = null & \text{If enclosed} \\ 0 < t_{in} < t_{out} < 1, N_{in} \neq N_{out} \neq null & \text{If partial enclosed} \\ t_{in} = 0, t_{out} = 1, N_{in} = N_{out} \neq null & \text{If simple exclusion} \\ t_{in} > t_{out} & \text{If compound exclusion} \end{cases} \tag{16.17}$$

```
algorithm clip-edge(E, X, S, t_in = 0, t_out = 1, N_in = N_out = ε )
  for all P ∈ S do
    N = neighbor feature of X that causes P
    d_O = sign_{X≠E'} * D(P, E.O), d_D = sign_{X≠E'} * D(P, E.D)
    if d_O < 0 and d_D < 0 then
      N_in = N_out = N
      return false
    else if d_O < 0 then
      t = d_O/(d_O − d_D)
      if t > t_in then
        t_in = t, N_in = N
        if t_in > t_out then return false
      end if
    else if d_D < 0 then
      t = d_O/(d_O − d_D)
      if t < t_out then
        t_out = t, N_out = N
        if t_in > t_out then return false
      end if
    next P
  return true
end algorithm
```

Figure 16.17: Edge-clipping pseudocode.

Depending on the case, it is possible to devise a feature update strategy. In the case of a partial enclosed edge, we have two t-values, t_{in} and t_{out}, indicating points on the edge, where a feature other than X might be closer to E. The possibilities are as follows: either there is no intersection with a Voronoi plane, in which case the t-value corresponds to an end vertex of the edge itself, and which suggests that the edge itself should be updated with the vertex, or a t-value might correspond to an intersection between E and some VP(N, X), which may indicate that X should be updated with its neighbor, N, constituting the intersecting Voronoi plane.

16.3.4 The Derivative Test

Given a pair of t-values from the edge-clipping algorithm described previously, we will now present a simple test to determine whether the corresponding features will decrease the minimum distance or improve upon localization.

Looking at the sign of the derivative of the distance function between E and X, $D'(X, \mathbf{e}(t))$, the best feature to update X with can be determined as summarized in Table 16.1. The idea is that if the derivative of the distance function is negative, then the distance is decreasing, if the sign is positive, then the signed distance is increasing. Hence, to minimize the minimum distance we want to pick features where the sign of the derivative of the distance function is negative. In the case of full enclosement, there is no need to update X, but perhaps we need to update E. This is done by picking the end vertex of E with the smallest distance to X. The entire strategy of determining what feature to update based on the derivative of the

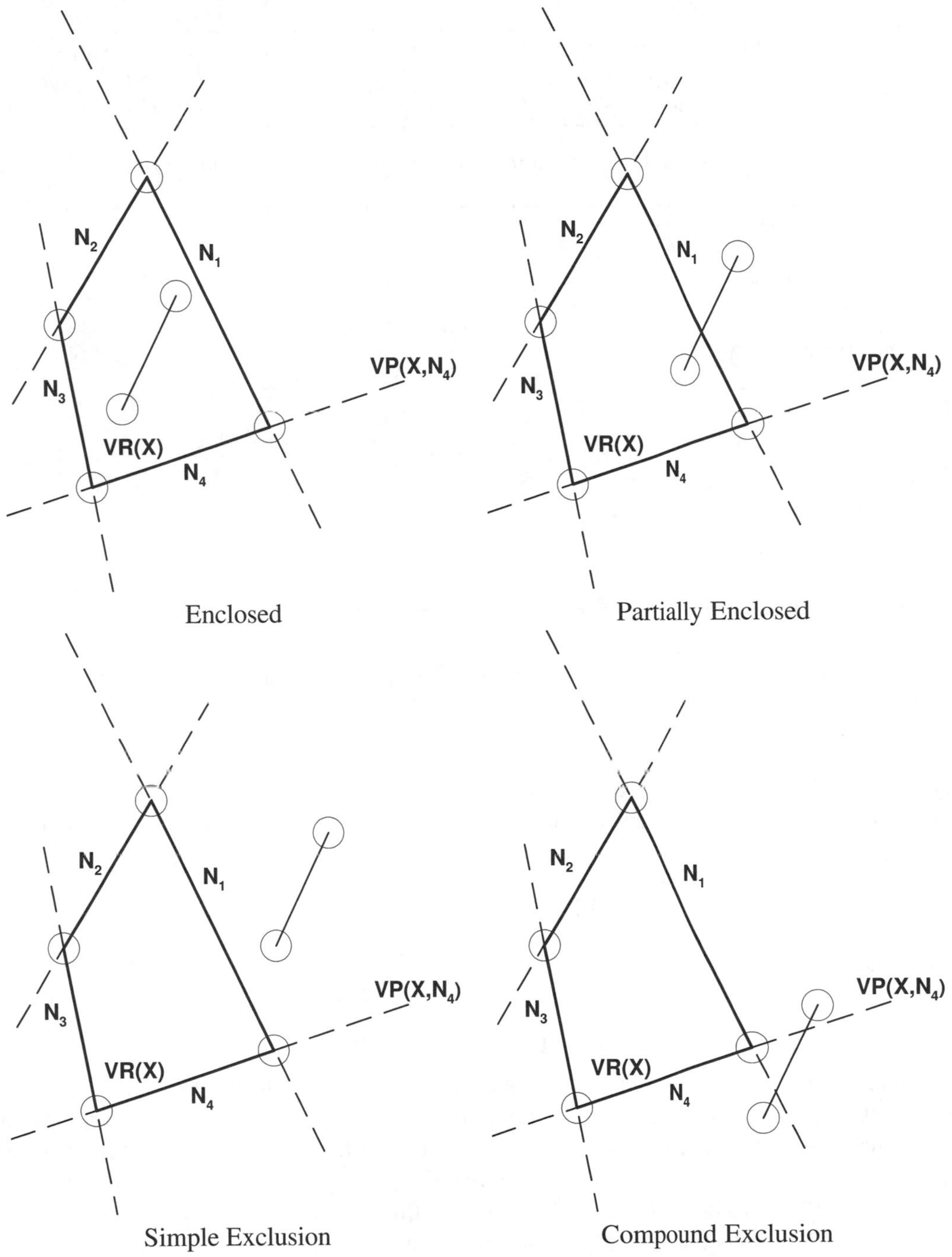

Figure 16.18: Four different cases for edge intersection with a Voronoi region $\mathrm{VR}(X)$ bounded by Voronoi planes: $\mathrm{VP}(X, N_1), \ldots, \mathrm{VP}(X, N_4)$.

Sign	Best Interval	Update
$D'(X, \boldsymbol{e}(t_{in})) > 0$	$[0, t_{in}[$	$(X, E) \mapsto (N_{in}, E)$
$D'(X, \boldsymbol{e}(t_{out})) < 0$	$]t_{out}, 1]$	$(X, E) \mapsto (N_{out}, E)$
$D'(X, \boldsymbol{e}(t_{in})) < 0$ and $D'(X, \boldsymbol{e}(t_{out})) > 0$	$[t_{in}, t_{out}]$	$(X, E) \mapsto (X, E)$

Table 16.1: Signed derivative tests and corresponding feature updates.

```
algorithm derivative-test(E, X, t_in, t_out, N_in, N_out)
  if X not an edge
    δ_in = sign[D'(X, e(t_in]))]
    δ_out = sign[D'(X, e(t_out]))]
  else
    δ_in = sign[D'(N_in, e(t_in))]
    δ_out = sign[D'(N_out, e(t_out))]
  end if
  if N_in ≠ null and δ_in > 0
    return N_in
  else if N_out ≠ null and δ_out < 0
    return N_out
  end if
  return X
end algorithm
```

Figure 16.19: Pseudocode showing how to determine what feature X should be updated with. Before this test, E has been clipped against VR(X) or a subset hereof.

signed distance map is called the *derivative test*.

If X is a vertex, then an analytical expression of the sign of the derivative of the distance function $D'(X, \boldsymbol{e}(t))$ can be derived

$$\text{sign}[D'(V, \boldsymbol{e}(t))] = \text{sign}[\boldsymbol{u} \cdot (\boldsymbol{e}(t) - \boldsymbol{v})] \tag{16.18}$$

If X is a face then

$$\text{sign}[D'(F, \boldsymbol{e}(t))] = \begin{cases} +\text{sign}[\boldsymbol{u} \cdot \boldsymbol{n}] & \text{If } D(F, \boldsymbol{e}(t)) > 0 \\ -\text{sign}[\boldsymbol{u} \cdot \boldsymbol{n}] & \text{If } D(F, \boldsymbol{e}(t)) < 0 \end{cases} \tag{16.19}$$

Fortunately, it turns out that the case where X is an edge is not needed. The derivative test is used to handle full enclosement and partial enclosement; the remaining two cases are simple exclusion and compound exclusion. In the case of simple exclusion, we can update with the feature causing the exclusion, except in the case of an (E, F) state, due to the edge-face Voronoi plane property, as shown in Figure 16.9. This property makes it difficult to determine whether the violating feature is in fact also the closest feature to the edge. Figure 16.20 shows the case of simple exclusion. The solution to the problem is to search the perimeter of the face in order to find the closest feature to the edge. In most cases of compound exclusion, we can reuse the derivative test for doing the update. The pseudocode in Figure 16.19 shows the details of the derivative test.

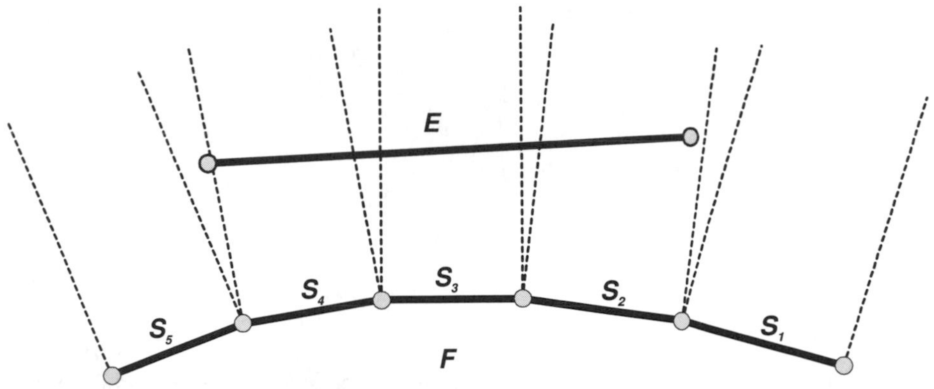

Figure 16.20: Face exclusion. Edge E is simply excluded by S_1, S_2, S_3, S_4, and S_5. A search must be done to find the closest feature S_3.

16.3.5 Dealing with Penetrations

Penetration can only be detected in the (V, F) and (E, F) states of the V-Clip algorithm. In the (E, F) case a penetration is detected if the edge intersects the face plane and the intersection point lies inside the edge-face Voronoi planes of the face Voronoi Region. The (V, F) state is not obviously dealt with, since a local minimum can cause confusion, as shown in Figure 16.21. From the figure it is clear that it is not enough to test whether the vertex lies beneath the face plane. If this was the case, then all face planes of the object must be searched. If a single face plane is found where the vertex lies in front as depicted in the right picture of Figure 16.21, then the current face is replaced with another face of the object where the signed distance to the vertex is positive and greater than the signed distance to any other face plane.

16.3.6 The Internal States of V-Clip

In the previous sections we have presented the reader with all the technicalities of the V-Clip algorithm. We have finally reached the point where the internal workings of the five states in Figure 16.15 can be described.

16.3.6.1 The Vertex-Vertex State

The vertex-vertex case is dealt with simply by applying a brute-force test using the closest feature pair theorem, Theorem 16.3. That is, one vertex is tested for inclusion by the edge-Voronoi planes of the other vertex and vice versa. If a Voronoi plane is found violating the closest feature pair theorem, the vertex is updated to the corresponding edge defining the violating Voronoi plane. The pseudocode is shown in Figure 16.22.

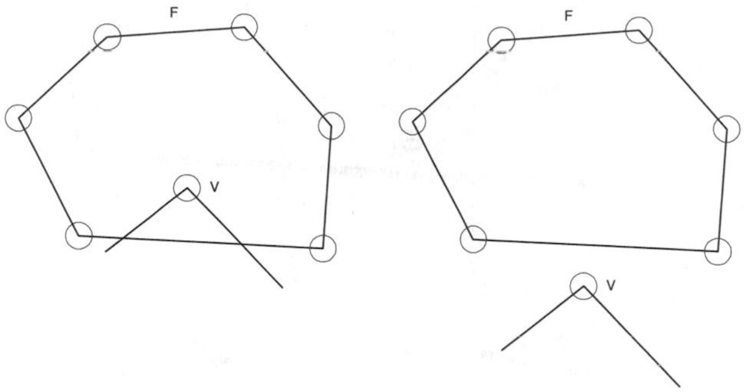

Figure 16.21: Local minimum problem of the (V, F) case; in the left and in the right picture V lies inside the Voronoi planes of F; in the left image V is also clearly beneath the face plane, and it is sensible to conclude that a penetration has occurred. However, the same arguments apply to the right picture, but no penetration occurs here.

```
algorithm vertex-vertex-state(V1, V2 )
  for all P = VP(V1, E) ∈ VR(V1) do
    if D(P, V2) < 0 then
      V1 ↦ E
      return continue
  repeat all of the above with V1 and V2 interchanged
  return done
end algorithm
```

Figure 16.22: Pseudocode for the vertex-vertex state of V-Clip.

16.3.6.2 The Vertex-Edge State

In the vertex-edge state, the vertex is tested for inclusion of the Voronoi planes making up the edge-Voronoi region. If a violating plane is found, then the edge is updated to the neighboring feature defining the violating Voronoi plane. If the vertex is determined to lie inside the edge Voronoi region, then the edge is clipped against the Voronoi region of the vertex. Afterward, it is determined which one of the four edge intersection cases is being dealt with, and an appropriate action is taken as explained previously in Section 16.3.3 and Section 16.3.4. Figure 16.23 illustrates a pseudocode version of the vertex-edge state.

16.3.6.3 The Vertex-Face State

In the vertex-face state, it is first tested if the vertex lies inside the Voronoi places of the face Voronoi region. If the vertex is found to lie outside a Voronoi plane, a simple exclusion must have been found, and the face can be updated to the edge defining the violated Voronoi plane. If the vertex is found to lie inside all the Voronoi planes of the face Voronoi region, it is tested whether any of the incident edges of the vertex is pointing toward the face. If such an edge exists, going along it will decrease the minimum

```
algorithm vertex-edge-state(V,E )
  for all P = VP(E,N) ∈ VR(E) do
    if D(P,V) > 0 then
      E ↦ N
      return continue
    end if
  clip-edge(E,V,VR(V),t_in,t_out,N_in,N_out)
  if E simply excluded then
    V ↦ N_in
  else
    derivative-test(E,V,t_in,t_out,N_in,N_out)
  if V is updated then
    return continue
  else
    return done
  end if
end algorithm
```

Figure 16.23: Pseudocode for the vertex edge state of V-Clip.

distance to the face. Thus the vertex is updated to the edge pointing toward the face.

If all of the above tests pass, we know that neither the vertex nor the face can be updated, and a last test is performed where the signed distance of the vertex w.r.t. the face plane is computed in order to figure out if a separation has occurred, in which case a final state of the algorithm has been found. If the vertex is found to lie beneath the face plane, we can either have a penetration or a local minimum (see Figure 16.21). If we have penetration, we have reached a final state and the algorithm terminates. If a local minimum is detected, the face is updated with another face and V-Clip iterates once again. A pseudocode version of the vertex-face state is given in Figure 16.24.

16.3.6.4 The Edge-Edge State

The edge-edge state is specially compared with the other states. Here each edge is clipped against the other Voronoi region of the other edge, but the clipping is done in a two-pass manner.

First an edge is clipped against the edge-vertex Voronoi planes of the other edge. These are known to be parallel, thus only a simple exclusion is done or a derivative test must be performed. This is illustrated in Figure 16.25. Notice that if E_3 were fully enclosed, the derivative test would not perform any update. If no update occurs in the first pass, then the edge is clipped against the edge-face Voronoi planes of the other edge in the second pass. Again, either a simple exclusion is found or a derivative test must be performed. Figure 16.26 illustrates the idea in pseudocode.

16.3.6.5 The Edge-Face State

The last remaining state in the V-Clip algorithm is the edge-face state. Here the edge is first clipped against the Voronoi planes of the face. If either a simple or compound exclusion is found, a search along the face

```
algorithm vertex-face-state(V,F)
  for all P = VP(F,E) ∈ VR(F) do
    if D(P,V) < 0 then
      F ↦ E
      return continue
    end if
  P = plane(F)
  for all neighbors E to V do
    V' = endpoint of E not equal to V
    if D(P,V)sign[D(P,V) − D(P,V')] > 0 then
      return continue
  if D(P,V) > 0 then
    return done
  return localmin(V,F)
end algorithm
```

Figure 16.24: Pseudocode for the vertex face state of V-Clip.

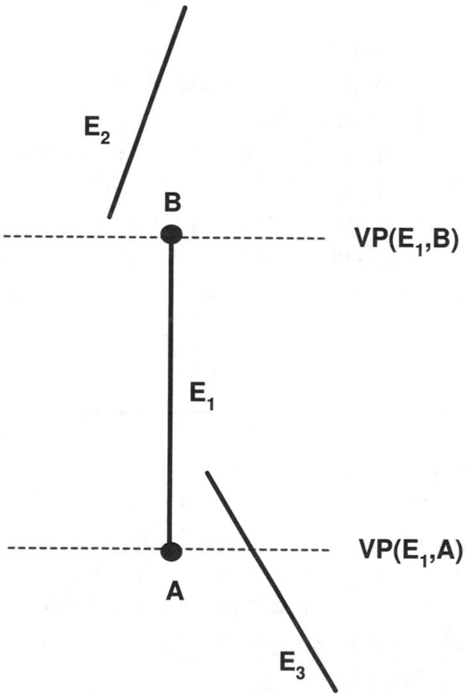

Figure 16.25: Figure showing that edge-vertex Voronoi planes of edge E_1 are parallel.Two things might happen when clipping another edge against these planes: either it is simply excluded as E_2 or it is not as E_3, in which case a derivative test is needed.

```
algorithm edge-edge-state(E1, E2 )
  S = edge-vertex Voronoi planes of E1
  clip-edge(E2, E1, S, t_in, t_out, N_in, N_out)
  if E2 simply excluded by VP(E1, V) then
    E1 ↦ V
  else
    derivative-test(E2, E1, t_in, t_out, N_in, N_out)
  if E1 was updated then
    return continue
  S = edge-face Voronoi planes of E1
  //Very important do not reset t-values and N-values
  clip-edge(E2, E1, S, t_in, t_out, N_in, N_out)
  if E2 simply excluded by VP(E1, F) then
    E1 ↦ F
  else
    derivative-test(E2, E1, t_in, t_out, N_in, N_out)
  if E1 was updated then
    return continue
  repeat all of the above with E1 and E2 interchanged
  return done
end algorithm
```

Figure 16.26: Pseudocode for the edge-edge state of V-Clip.

perimeter is initiated to determine the closest feature to the edge, and the face is updated to that feature. In the case that the edge is fully or partially enclosed, it is tested if the edge intersects the face plane, in which case the algorithm terminates in a penetrating state.

If the edge does not intersect the face plane, then the sign of the derivative of the signed distance map is used to determine the course of action. This is done by testing whether the sign of the derivative of the signed distance indicates that the minimum distance decreases when one moves along the edge toward the face. If so, the edge is updated with the end-point that one is moving toward. Notice that if the minimum distance does not decrease, it means that the edge is partially enclosed and it intersects a Voronoi plane defined by a boundary edge of the face. The face is thus updated to the boundary edge. The pseudocode version of the edge-face state is shown in Figure 16.27.

16.3.7 V-Clip in Perspective

V-Clip is an improvement of the Lin-Canny algorithm [Lin et al., 1994]. Given the current feature pair, the Lin-Canny algorithm works by computing the actual closest points between one of the features and the neighboring features of the other feature. The other feature is then updated to the neighboring feature having a smaller distance to the closest point. V-Clip has three advantages over the Lin-Canny algorithm. V-Clip never computes the actual closest points between feature pairs or the distance between them. This makes V-Clip more robust and stable toward numerical precision and round-off errors. Furthermore, numerical experiments indicate that V-Clip is faster than Lin-Canny. The final benefit comes from V-Clip being able to handle intersecting objects. The original Lin-Cannny would enter an infinite loop if objects

```
function edge-face-state(E,F )
  clip-edge(E,F,VR(F) − plane(F),t_in,t_out,N_in,N_out)
  if E excluded then
    F ↦ closest edge or vertex on F to E
    return continue
  d_in = D(F,e(t_in))
  d_out = D(F,e(t_out))
  if d_in d_out ≤ 0 then
    return penetration
  if D'(F,e(t_in)) ≥ 0 then
    if N_in ≠ null then
      F ↦ N_in
    else
      E ↦ E.O
  else
    if N_out ≠ null then
      F ↦ N_out
    else
      E ↦ E.D
  return done
end algorithm
```

Figure 16.27: Pseudocode for the edge-face state of V-Clip.

were intersecting, however, Lin-Canny were later extended with so-called *internal pseudo Voronoi regions* [Lin et al., 1998], allowing it to handle intersecting objects. A drawback of both algorithms is that they only work on convex polygonal objects.

16.4 Recursive Search Algorithms

The last feature-based algorithms, we will present are *recursive search algorithms* [Joukhadar et al., 1996, Joukhadar et al., 1998, Joukhadar et al., 1999, Sundaraj et al., 2000]. Recursive search algorithms search over the surface mesh to localize contacts between two objects. These algorithms typically exploit the topology of the faces in a mesh in order to perform a fast search for contacting faces given an initial colliding pair of faces.

We will describe the algorithm presented in [Sundaraj et al., 2000]. The algorithm needs a pre-processing step, where another algorithm such as V-Clip, BVH, etc. determines an initial pair of colliding faces, these are passed along as input arguments to the algorithm. The algorithm then proceeds in three stages. First a contour of collision is found, then inner and outer boundaries are determined, and finally the contact elements are determined.

The initial pair of colliding faces are used to seed the first stage of the algorithm. A recursive search is initiated where all neighboring triangle pairs that are colliding are traversed in an iterative manner. When a colliding triangle pair is encountered during the search, it is added to a set called the contour of collision. The pseudocode in Figure 16.28 illustrates an iterative version of the recursive search. Observe that the

```
algorithm contour-of-collision(F_A,F_B:faces)
  list contour
  Queue Q
  Q.push (F_A,F_B)
  while Q not empty
    (F_A,F_B) = Q.pop
    contour.add (F_A,F_B)
    mark F_A and F_B as contour faces
    for all non-contour neighbors N_A of F_A
      for all non-contour neighbors N_B of F_B
        if N_A collides with N_B then
          Q.push(N_A,N_B)
        end if
      next N_B
    next N_A
  end while
  return contour
end algorithm
```

Figure 16.28: Recursive search method to find contour of collision.

topology of the surface mesh is used to recursively trace a contour of colliding faces. Thus, only the exact intersecting boundaries of the two objects are traversed.

Hereafter, the second stage is initiated. In this state, neighboring faces of the contour of collision are recursively visited and added to a set containing the inner boundary or another set containing the outer boundary. To test whether a neighboring face N, of a face A is part of the inner or outer boundary, the face plane of the colliding face B of A is used. If N lies in front of the face plane of B, then N belongs to the outer boundary, if N lies behind the face plane of B, then it belongs to the inner boundary. The idea is illustrated in Figure 16.29. Here two faces A and B lying on the contour of collision are shown. The two neighboring faces N_1 and N_2 of face A are tested against the face plane of face B. N_1 is lying above the face plane of B and is thus added to the outer boundary, N_2 lies below the plane and is therefore added to the inner boundary. Care must be taken that neighboring faces are not visited more than once, since two faces lying on the contour of collision could share the same neighboring face. This is, however, easily avoided by flagging faces; also, faces already added to the contour of collision should be ignored. A pseudocode version of the second stage is given in Figure 16.30.

In the last stage of the algorithm, contact elements are recursively searched. Initially we visit all the neighboring faces of the inner boundary. If these are not part of the contour or the outer boundary, then they are added as contact elements. Afterward, their neighbors are recursively searched and so on, until all contact elements are found. Thus, the contact elements are those faces entirely embedded inside the surface of the other object. Figure 16.31 illustrates the idea in pseudocode.

Looking at the complexity of the algorithm, we see that the first and second stages are linear in the number of intersecting faces, whereas the last stage is linear in the number of contact elements. Thus, the overall complexity is output sensitive.

As explained, the algorithm is not addressing the problem of self-intersecting nor is the problem

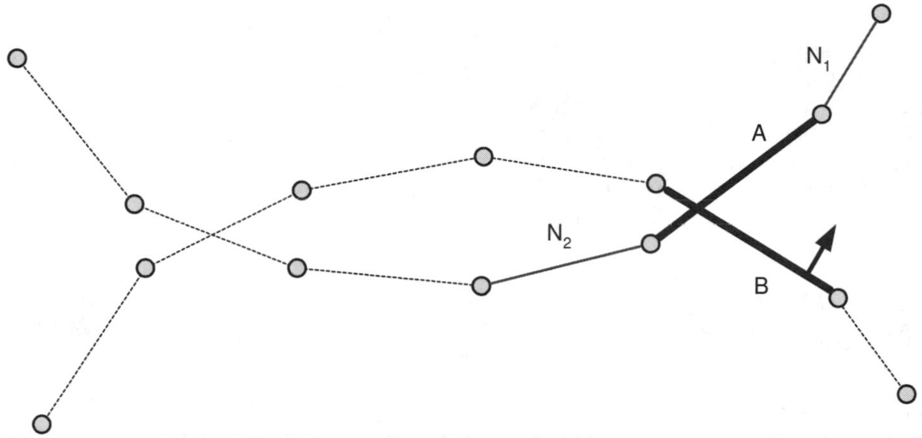

Figure 16.29: Inner and outer boundary test. Neighboring faces of face A are tested against face plane of face B.

```
algorithm inner-outer-boundary(contour)
  list inner
  list outer
  for each pair of faces F_A,F_B in contour
    for all non-marked neighbors N_A of F_A
      if N_A in front of F_B then
        outer.add(N_A)
        mark N_A as outer boundary
      else
        inner.add(N_A)
        mark N_A as inner boundary
      end if
    next N_A
    for all non-contour neighbors N_B of F_B
      ... same as above with A and B interchanged
    next N_B
  next F_A,F_B
  return inner and outer
end algorithm
```

Figure 16.30: Search method to find inner and outer boundary of the contour of collision.

```
algorithm contact-elements(inner)
  list contact
  Queue Q
  Q.push(inner)
  while Q not empty do
    F = Q.pop()
    for all neighbors N of F
      if N is not contact, outer, inner or contour then
        mark N as contact
        contact.add(N)
        Q.push(N)
      end if
    next N
  end while
  return contact
end algorithm
```

Figure 16.31: Recursive search method to traverse contact elements.

addressed in [Sundaraj et al., 2000], however the extension seems trivial. As noted earlier, the algorithm needs a preprocessing step feeding an initial pair of colliding faces. In [Sundaraj et al., 2000] this was done by using *GJK* on a *convex decomposition* of the objects. The result of the algorithm is a set of intersecting faces (the contour of collision) and a set containing faces fully embedded inside the surface of the other object. Thus the algorithm returns an explicit representation of the entire intersection volume between the two objects. It is not obvious how the algorithm can be extended in a general context to work with multiple contact areas. In [Sundaraj et al., 2000] every convex component of the decomposition was tested against each other to overcome this problem.

Aside from the problem of seeding the algorithm with pairs of colliding faces from all contact areas, the algorithm has the advantage of being applicable to both static and deformable objects.

17

Volume-Based Algorithms

Volumetric representations of objects may be used for doing collision detection. Many algorithms, which we have chosen to classify as volume-based, combine the classical *geometric algorithms* treated in previous chapters with the so-called *image-based techniques* or *object space algorithms*. As indicated, the image-based algorithms see objects as 3D images. Often *signed distance maps* are used as these 3D images. However, there are also volume-based methods, which work on tessellated manifolds. The phrase "image-space techniques" refers to objects being rendered into an image (see [Govindaraju et al., 2003]). We have therefore classified volume-based methods as methods which are not limited to the boundary representation of objects.

There is a large number of algorithms for volume-based methods, and we will therefore limit ourselves to present two different algorithms, which illustrates the idea of using a volume-based representation well. Most of the volume-based algorithms are conceptually based on the same idea, but use different techniques for computing distance fields, layered depth images, etc. We do not see much point in delving into whether stencil buffers, GPUs, or OpenGL extensions are used for producing the volume-based representations due to the rapid development in graphics hardware.

17.1 Distance Maps

Implicit functions are useful for describing the shape of an object; consider the *implicit function* describing the surface of the unit sphere

$$f_{\text{unit sphere}}(\boldsymbol{p}) = x^2 + y^2 + z^2 - 1$$

This function has the property that given a point $\boldsymbol{p} = [x, y, z]^T$:

$f_{\text{unit sphere}}(\boldsymbol{p}) < 0$	$\boldsymbol{p}$ is inside the unit sphere
$f_{\text{unit sphere}}(\boldsymbol{p}) > 0$	$\boldsymbol{p}$ is outside the unit sphere
$f_{\text{unit sphere}}(\boldsymbol{p}) = 0$	$\boldsymbol{p}$ is on the surface of the unit sphere

This is beneficial since we have a way to determine in constant time whether an arbitrary point collides with the unit sphere.

A *signed distance map* is a special case of an implicit function. The signed distance map, $\phi(\cdot)$, is defined such that given an arbitrary point in space, $\boldsymbol{p}$, the value $\phi(\boldsymbol{p})$ gives the signed Euclidean distance to the closest point on the surface of the object. If the point $\boldsymbol{p}$ is outside the object the sign is positive. If the point is inside the object the sign is negative. In particular, if the signed distance is zero the point lies on the surface of the object. A signed distance map has the property that the magnitude of the gradient is one, and the gradient is normal to the object surface. Therefore, a contact normal can be found by using the gradient at the given point.

It is rare that one can find an analytical expression for the signed distance map for arbitrary convex objects. Even in those few cases where this might be possible, such an analytical expression will be far too expensive to evaluate. Instead, the signed distance map is represented by sampling it. A popular and widespread data structure for doing this is a rectilinear grid. The object is embedded in this grid, and each node in the grid keeps the signed distance to the closest point on the object surface. The sampled signed distance function is called a signed distance field or signed distance map.

Signed distance fields can be computed in many ways, e.g., the fast marching method [Sethian, 1999, Osher et al., 2003], characteristic scan conversion [Mauch, 2000], prism scan [Sigg et al., 2003], and distance meshes [III et al., 2002, Sud et al., 2004] can compute signed distance maps on regular grids. However, adaptive representations also exist [Frisken et al., 2000], where the signed distance map is stored in an octree representation in order to save memory at the price of the lookup cost in octree. In our description of the algorithm, for simplicity, we will assume that uniform grids are used.

Given two objects A and B, the method in [Guendelman et al., 2003] works by taking the vertices of A and looking them up in the signed distance function of B. If a negative distance is found, then a contact point is generated. Afterward, the vertices of B are looked up in the signed distance map of A. In [Guendelman et al., 2003] a double representation of each object is stored and used to handle *collision detection* and *contact generation*. Each object is represented by a triangular mesh and a signed distance map. The method in [Guendelman et al., 2003] is tailored for rigid bodies, and thus a convenient object-space frame is set up where the center of mass is at the origin, and the axes aligned with the principal axes of inertia. Both the triangular mesh and the signed distance grid ϕ are stored in this object-space. This means that when vertices of A are looked up in B, then they must be transformed from object space of A into object space of B, and vice versa.

When a given point is looked up in the signed distance grid, it is very unlikely that the point will be perfectly aligned with a grid node, and in order to obtain a signed distance value at non-grid node positions an interpolation is therefore needed. We use a trilinear interpolation of the eight neighboring grid nodes.

The algorithm as described is fairly easy to understand and straightforward to implement. One major drawback is that it ignores edge-edge intersections: if a coarse tessellation is given, such as 12 triangular faces for a cube, only the eight corners will be used to find contact points. This implies that no contact points will be found for the case of two cubes, one resting slightly rotated on top of the other. In [Guendelman et al., 2003] it is suggested to handle the problem by intersecting the edges with the zero-level set contour and flag the deepest penetrating point on the edge as a sample point. Furthermore, an edge-length threshold test can be used to determine which edges should be subjected to this more thorough test.

Several acceleration methods can be applied to speed up a collision query. If more storage is allowed, one can store min-max-values and in-outside markers for the signed distance map grid. Thus, one will have a quick rejection test to avoid having to do the more expensive trilinear interpolation. This sort of extra information has an even more dramatic impact on octree-based grids, allowing a lookup to terminate at an early level in the hierarchy.

The simplicity of the method implies that it is very cheap to test a single vertex for penetration, however, since a fine tessellation is needed a large number of vertices is expected, and looking up each vertex can degrade performance. To remedy this, vertices can be stored in a bounding volume hierarchy (see Chapter 15), where the BVH is tested for overlap with the box enclosing the distance grid. Only those points found to be inside the distance grid box are actually tested against the distance map.

Another possible avenue for improving performance is through parallelism, where a single vertex test is completely independent of all other vertex tests, and they can thus be performed in parallel.

A problem encountered in practice with highly tessellated objects is that they generate large contact point sets. Often we only want to use contact points at the corners of the convex polygon of a contact area between two rigid bodies. The method just described will in most cases generate contact points sampled uniformly over the entire contact area. A postprocessing or filtering step must thus be performed to prune unneeded contacts. Otherwise the performance of a typical constraint-based rigid body simulation will degrade horribly.

One approach to contact filtering would be to divide contacts into disjoint sets based on their penetration distance and contact normals. That is, only contacts with the same penetration and contact normal direction within numerical threshold can be found in the same contact set. After having divided the contacts into disjoint sets, the convex polygon of the contacts in each set is found in a plane orthogonal to the common contact normal. All contacts not lying on the vertices of the convex polygon can now be pruned. It is possible to prune the contact sets further if a minimum size is wanted, see [Bouma et al., 1993] for more details.

The method we have just described has another benefit from a contact generation viewpoint. Each contact is uniquely determined by the triangle mesh vertex that generated it. It is thus easy to uniquely identify the same contact point in two subsequent iterations of a simulation, which can be exploited to cache temporal information about contacts. For instance, to obtain smooth transitions when objects move over discontinuities, see Section 14.1.

17.2 Layered Depth Image

A graphics hardware accelerated approach is presented in [Heidelberger et al., 2003] based on computing a *layered depth image* (*LDI*) for the *volume of intersection* s(*VoI*) between two objects.

An LDI of an object is very similar to a scan conversion of a polygon, see [Foley et al., 1996]. A scan conversion algorithm scans lines through a polygon, keeping track of when a line enters and when it leaves the polygon. These entry and exit points are used to determine spans across the scan line, where pixels should be rasterized. An LDI is very similar, and parallel scan lines are shot orthogonally along an image plane, and the depth of exit and entry points are recorded in the LDI data structure. A volume representation of the VoI is thus created consisting of spans lying inside and outside the object. Figure 17.1 illustrates the basic idea of an LDI. The algorithm proceeds in three stages: first, the intersection volume of the enclosing object AABBs is found. This intersection is itself an AABB if it exists; if it does not exist, there is no chance that the two objects collide. The intersecting AABB is called the volume of interest (VoI). The first stage is illustrated in Figure 17.2. Second, two LDIs are computed, one for each object in the VoI. The LDIs can be computed efficiently using graphics hardware, to be elaborated on below. The LDI computation to a specific representation such as triangular meshes, patches, quads, etc., requires watertight object surfaces. Figure 17.3 shows the second stage. Third, the two computed LDIs are used to determine whether a collision has taken place. This can be done in one of two ways. The two LDIs can be combined into one LDI representing the intersecting volume of the two objects. If no volume is found, it is known that the two objects are not colliding. On the other hand, if a intersecting volume

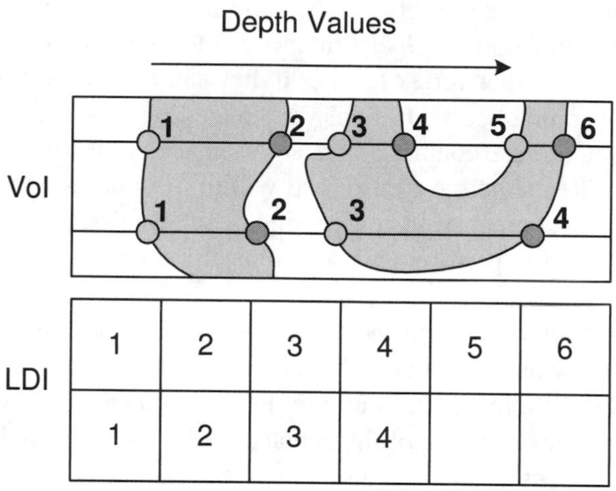

Figure 17.1: Two-pixel LDI of Volume of Intersection (VoI).

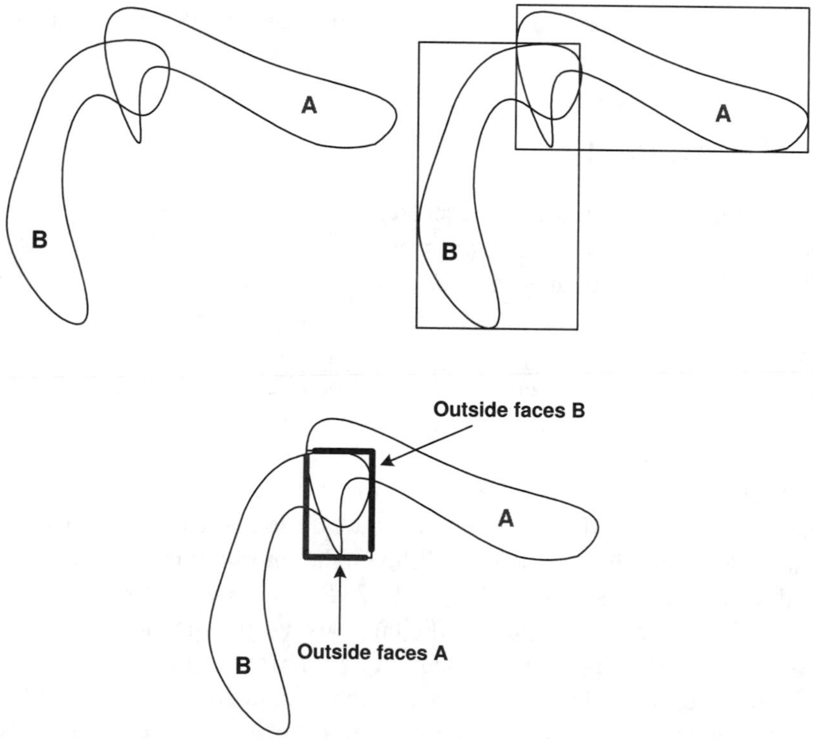

Figure 17.2: First stage of the LDI algorithm, AABBs are used to find VoI.

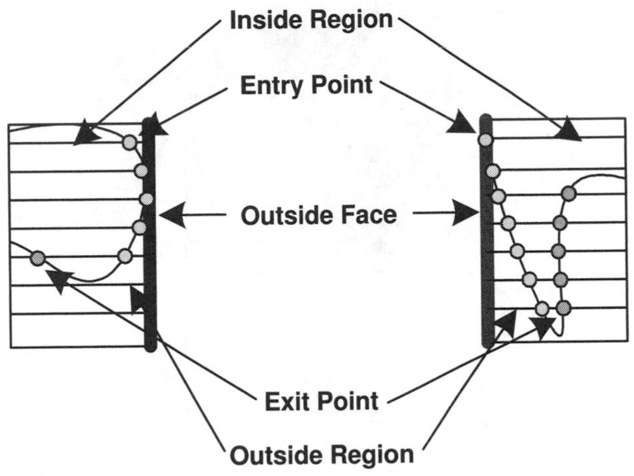

Figure 17.3: Second stage of the LDI algorithm, LDIs of objects are computed in VoI.

is found, the objects are colliding and an exact representation of the overlapping parts of the objects is found. The overlap is found in a similar manner as the approach used in the previous section: first, the vertices of one object lying inside the VoI is looked up in the LDI of the other object. If the vertex lies in an inside span, then a collision has taken place. Second, the vertices of the other object is processed in a similar fashion. If a colliding vertex is found, it can be used to generate a contact point at the position of the vertex. In Figure 17.4 it is shown, how the LDIs in Figure 17.3 are combined into an LDI representing the intersection volume. To guarantee proper boundary conditions, the LDI is rendered for each object from the outside. As shown in Figure 17.2, outside faces of object A are opposite to outside faces of B, and we choose to render the LDI for each object from opposite outside faces, as shown in Figure 17.3. This guarantees that the LDI will start from an outside region. In particular, the first layer of points in the LDI will be entry points, the next exit points, and so on.

If one of the objects is fully contained within the other object, the VoI will be equal to the AABB of the contained object, and it is thus impossible to find an outside face for the object with the enclosing AABB. The solution to the problem is to extend the VoI by picking one of the faces and extruding it until it touches the side of the enclosing AABB. This is illustrated in Figure 17.5. In [Heidelberger et al., 2003] it is suggested to pick the opposite faces with minimum distance in between, which works as a fast heuristic since the depth complexity, total maximum number of entry, and exit points along any scan line of the LDIs is minimized.

17.2.1 Computing LDI Using OpenGL

To generate the LDIs, we set up an orthographic projection. We use the selected outside face as the near plane and the opposite face as the far plane. The remaining faces define the top, bottom, left, and right planes of the view volume. The LDI is rendered using a multipass approach, where each object is rendered

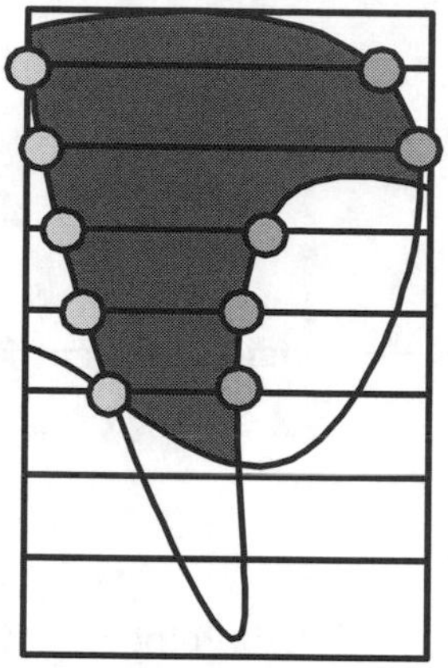

Figure 17.4: Third stage of the LDI algorithm; the two object LDIs are combined.

$n_{\max}$ times, and where $n_{\max}$ denotes the maximum depth complexity of the objects inside the VoI. This gives an $O(n_{\max})$ complexity. Depth testing, face culling, and color buffer are disabled; only the stencil test are used.

In the first render pass, only the first fragment is allowed to pass the stencil test, and thus write its depth value to the z-buffer. The subsequent stencil tests is set to fail, but still the stencil buffer is incremented. After the first render pass, the depth buffer contains an object layer in the LDI and the stencil buffer contains a map of the depth complexity. We can therefore find $n_{\max}$ by reading back the stencil buffer and searching for the maximum value. The values stored in the depth buffer are copied to the first layer in the LDI.

Additional rendering passes are then performed from 2 to $n_{\max}$. This time the stencil test is changed. The idea is that in the n'th pass, the first $n-1$ fragments fail the stencil test, while the stencil buffer is incremented, and only the n'th rasterized fragment is allowed to pass the stencil test, writing to the depth buffer. Thus after the n'th render pass the n'th LDI object layer can thus be read back from the depth buffer.

A pseudocode version of the LDI generation for a single object is shown in Figure 17.6. As can be seen from the pseudocode, the fragments generated in the LDI are in arbitrary order, which means that the LDI must be sorted before it can be used. For each pixel, only the n_p layers are sorted, where n_p is the depth complexity of that particular pixel. If $n_p < n_{\max}$ then the remaining layers $n_p + 1$ to $n_{\max}$ are ignored.

Two simple optimizations are possible: the depth buffer can be tiled, such that each layer has its own tile, and such that only a single read-back is necessary for the additional passes. In the first pass the stencil and depth buffers are packed into a single buffer using the `GL_NV_packed_depth_stencil` extension such that only a single read-back is necessary in the first render pass.

Compared to algorithms that compute a signed distance map of the intersecting volume such as [III et al., 2002], the LDI based method has a lower bandwidth, since the LDI representation requires much less storage than a signed distance map. This is an advantage, since high bandwidth is an Achilles'

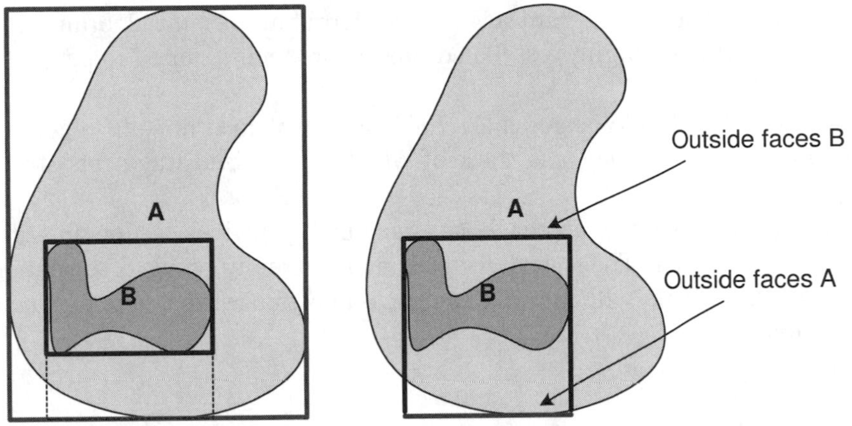

Figure 17.5: Extending VoI to get outside faces of object A.

```
Algorithm LDI(...)
  //First render pass
  glClear(GL DEPTH_BUFFER_BIT or GL_STENCIL_BUFFER_BIT)
  glStencilFunc(GL_GREATER,1,0xFF)
  glStencilOp(GL_INCR,GL_INCR,GL_INCR)
  render object
  depth complexity = glReadBack(stencil buffer)
  n_max = max(depthcomplexity)
  layer[1] = glReadBack(depth buffer)
  // Passes from 2 to n_max
  n = 2
  while n <= n_max do
    glClear(GL_DEPTH_BUFFER_BIT or GL_STENCIL_BUFFER_BIT)
    glStencilFunc(GL_GREATER,n,0xFF)
    glStencilOp(GL_KEEP,GL_INCR,GL_INCR)
    render object
    layer[n] = glReadBack(depth buffer)
    n = n+1
  end while
End algorithm
```

Figure 17.6: Pseudocode of LDI generation of an object.

heel in today's commodity graphics hardware due to high read-back latencies.

As described, the algorithm is capable of computing the intersection volume. However, if the vertex in LDI approach is used instead during the third stage of the algorithm, then the algorithm will suffer from missing edge-edge intersection, and highly tessellated objects are then required to get realistic collision handling in simulation.

In [Heidelberger et al., 2003, Heidelberger et al., 2004] it is explained how the algorithm can be extended to handle self-intersections by keeping track of whether rasterized fragments stem from front-facing or back-facing faces.

Compared to the signed distance map approach explained in the previous section, this algorithm is not as well suited for contact generation. The signed distance map inherently provides separation/penetration distances and contact normals, while with the LDI approach a postprocessing step must be performed to determine this information.

17.3 Previous Work

In [Hoff III et al., 2001] a hybrid geometric method and image-based method is presented for doing 2D geometric proximity queries using graphics hardware. Here a geometric approach based on bounding volume hierarchies is used to quickly reject intersecting objects or to home in on overlapping regions. Signed distance maps are then computed for the overlapping regions and intersecting pixels of two objects are found by a multipass rendering scheme. Separation and penetration distances are found simply by looking up distance measures in the signed distance maps. Gradients provide contact normals, penetration directions, and separation distances. The technique for computing the generalized Voronoi diagrams in [Hoff, III et al., 1999] is used for computing the signed distance maps. However, the method is only for 2D objects and the problem of self-intersecting deforming objects is not addressed.

The work in [Hoff III et al., 2001] was extended into 3D in [III et al., 2002]. The method was also extended to handle self-intersections by applying the classical parity test used in the shadow volume algorithm.

In [Hirota et al., 2000] elastic bodies are simulated using distance fields, a FEM is used where an initial precomputed signed distance field on an undeformed tetrahedral mesh is deformed as the simulation progresses. The idea is to find the tetrahedron enclosing a point p, given the barycentric coordinates, u_1, u_2, u_3, and u_4; of the point $\boldsymbol{p}$ the deformed distance is found by a linear interpolation of the undeformed distance values, d_1, d_2, d_3, and d_4 at the nodes of the enclosing tetrahedron, that is,

$$d = u_1 d_1 + u_2 d_2 + u_3 d_3 + u_4 d_4$$

The barycentric coordinates are found easily by solving

$$\boldsymbol{p} = u_1 \boldsymbol{p}_1 + u_2 \boldsymbol{p}_2 + u_3 \boldsymbol{p}_3 + u_4 \boldsymbol{p}_4$$

subject to $u_1 + u_2 + u_3 + u_4 = 1$. The method is applicable to both static and deformable objects. Furthermore, it handles self-intersection and interpenetration in a unified manner. However, several details are not explained, such as how one determines which points should be looked up in which tetrahedra.

In addition, it is not discussed what to do about handling edge-face intersections (where there are no penetrating points).

The work is extended in [Fisher et al., 2001] where a lazy evaluation of AABB BVHs is used to quickly locate regions of interest (overlapping tetrahedra) before doing linear interpolation of the penetration depth at the tetrahedra nodes as we described above. The deformed distance field is partially updated in the region indicated by the overlapping AABBs.

In [Bridson et al., 2003] the work from [Bridson et al., 2002] is extended. Cloth environment collisions are detected by looking up cloth mesh vertices in a signed distance map and the signed distance maps are used for generating contacts between cloth and environment interactions. Signed distance maps of the static objects are precomputed on regular grids. During simulation of the cloth, vertices in the cloth mesh are looked up in the regular grids by trilinear interpolation. Gradients of the signed distance field provide contact normals. The cloth meshes are highly tessellated and edge intersections (i.e., where end vertices do not intersect the static object) are ignored. Furthermore, a fold-and-wrinkle preserving technique is presented, which exploits the signed distance map to project interpenetrating cloth out of objects in the scene.

In [Guendelman et al., 2003], a double representation of rigid objects is proposed for each object a mesh and a signed distance field is stored in the objects local coordinate system; during simulation, contacts are generated by looking up mesh vertices from one object in the signed distance field of another object and vice versa. BVHs are suggested for storing vertices and speeding up the collision queries. As with many other methods edge-intersections are ignored and the method relies on having a fine tessellation of the rigid objects.

In [Baciu et al., 2002] a hardware-assisted method for self-collision of deformable surfaces is described based on image-based intersections; triangle surfaces are divided into so-called (π, β) surfaces, where π is a unit vector, such that for any surface normal n, we have $\pi \cdot n > \cos\beta$, where $0 \leq \beta \leq \pi/2$. The idea is now simply to render the surfaces along their π direction and test for intersection (compare this with Definition 15.3).

In [Fuhrmann et al., 2003], a method is suggested for computing signed distance fields of deformable objects. A new sign function definition is introduced and used for open surfaces (such as cloth which does not have an inside-outside), collisions detection is performed by looking vertices up in the signed distance fields, edge intersections are handled by introducing an offset (making vertices hover over the surface), and the edge midpoints are used for proximity tests to avoid particles getting trapped in surface gaps. In our opinion, these methods are ad hoc methods, which reduce the chance for getting in trouble, but they do not solve the problem of not handling the edge intersection case.

In [Heidelberger et al., 2004] an image space technique is presented; it is based on layered depth images combined with face orientation information. The method handles both collision and self-collision. However, the paper never goes into detail about how to generate contacts (separation/penetration distance and normals) based on layered depth images.

In [Hirota et al., 2001, Hirota, 2002], the undeformed distance field of a deforming object is used to define a continuous gap function. The distance field is referred to as material depth and is stored in the nodes of a tetrahedral mesh, which is used for FEM simulation of soft tissue.

Part V

Mathematics and Physics for Animation

Physics-based animation in computer graphics relies heavily on standard methods from mathematics, physics, and engineering. In Part V we give thorough introductions to the main topics used from these fields in relation to physics-based animation in computer graphics. These chapters were actually our starting point for writing this book, and even though many of the topics are expected to be standard knowledge for the intended reader, we have chosen to include this part for the sake of completeness. For further reading, we recommend:

Algebra, Calculus, Analysis, and Geometry:

- [Adams, 1995]
- [Bronshtein et al., 1997]
- [Hansen, 1988]
- [Koenderink, 1990]
- [Kreyszig, 1993]
- [Magnus et al., 1988]
- [Messer, 1994]

Numerical Analysis:

- [Ames, 1969]
- [Boor, 1978]
- [Burden et al., 1997]
- [Eriksson et al., 1996]
- [Golub et al., 1996]
- [Morton et al., 1994]
- [Press et al., 1999a]

Linear Complementarity Problems:

- [Cottle et al., 1992]
- [Murty, 1988]

Classical Mechanics:

- [Arnold, 1989]
- [Boas, 1983]
- [Goldsmith et al., 1987]
- [Kleppner et al., 1978]

Continuum Mechanics and Fluid Dynamics:

- [Lautrup, 2005]
- [Tritton, 1988]

18

Vectors, Matrices, and Quaternions

This chapter will give a brief introduction to the notation we use for vectors, matrices, and quaternions. The notation is greatly inspired by [Weisstein, 2005b, Elbek, 1994]. We will assume that a Cartesian coordinate system is used unless otherwise and explicitly stated.

18.1 Vectors

A *vector* is a geometric tool with a head and a tail for the representation of length and direction, but not position. All parallel vectors with identical length are thus geometrically identical. Vectors may be used to represent position by placing the tail at the origin of our coordinate system, but care should be taken since position and vectors translate differently: a position changes during a translation, while a vector remains unchanged.

A vector representation is an ordered list of *scalars*, and an example of a vector is

$$\boldsymbol{v} = \begin{bmatrix} v_1 \\ v_2 \\ \vdots \\ v_n \end{bmatrix}, \tag{18.1}$$

where the scalars v_i are called the elements or components of the vector. We write that $\boldsymbol{v}$ is an n-dimensional vector as $\boldsymbol{v} \in \mathbb{R}^n$. A basic property of a vector is its length.

Definition 18.1 (Vector Length)
The (Euclidean) length of the vector $\boldsymbol{v} \in \mathbb{R}^n$ is

$$\|\boldsymbol{v}\|_2 = \sqrt{v_1^2 + v_2^2 + \cdots + v_n^2}. \tag{18.2}$$

A unit vector is a vector with length 1, and the zero vector, **0**, *has length zero.*

Vectors are additive and have three different products: scalar-vector, dot, and cross products.

Definition 18.2 (Vector Addition)
The addition of two vectors $\boldsymbol{a}, \boldsymbol{b} \in \mathbb{R}^n$ is

$$\boldsymbol{a} + \boldsymbol{b} = \begin{bmatrix} a_1 + b_1 \\ a_2 + b_2 \\ \vdots \\ a_n + a_n \end{bmatrix}. \tag{18.3}$$

Definition 18.3 (Scalar-Vector Product)
The product between a scalar $k \in \mathbb{R}$ and a vector $\boldsymbol{v} \in R^n$ is

$$k\boldsymbol{v} = \begin{bmatrix} kv_1 \\ kv_2 \\ \vdots \\ kv_n \end{bmatrix}. \tag{18.4}$$

Definition 18.4 (Dot Product)
The dot product between two vectors $\boldsymbol{a}, \boldsymbol{b} \in \mathbb{R}^n$,

$$\boldsymbol{a} \cdot \boldsymbol{b} = \sum_{i=1}^{n} a_i b_i. \tag{18.5}$$

Definition 18.5 (Cross Product)
The cross product of two vectors $\boldsymbol{a}, \boldsymbol{b} \in \mathbb{R}^3$ is

$$\boldsymbol{a} \times \boldsymbol{b} = \begin{bmatrix} a_2b_3 - a_3b_2 \\ a_3b_1 - a_1b_3 \\ a_1b_2 - a_2b_1 \end{bmatrix}. \tag{18.6}$$

Two vectors are perpendicular, denoted $\boldsymbol{a} \perp \boldsymbol{b}$, when $\boldsymbol{a} \cdot \boldsymbol{b} = 0$, and they are parallel, $\boldsymbol{a} \parallel \boldsymbol{b}$, when $\boldsymbol{a} \times \boldsymbol{b} = \boldsymbol{0}$. The dot product is proportional to the lengths of the vectors and the angle between them as

$$\boldsymbol{a} \cdot \boldsymbol{b} = \|\boldsymbol{a}\|_2 \; \|\boldsymbol{b}\|_2 \cos\theta, \tag{18.7}$$

where θ is the angle between them and the dot product of a vector with itself is naturally the squared length of the vector, $\boldsymbol{v} \cdot \boldsymbol{v} = \|v\|_2^2$. The length of a cross product is

$$\|\boldsymbol{a} \times \boldsymbol{b}\|_2 = \|\boldsymbol{a}\|_2 \; \|\boldsymbol{b}\|_2 \sin\theta. \tag{18.8}$$

The dot product is commutative,

$$\boldsymbol{a} \cdot \boldsymbol{b} = \boldsymbol{b} \cdot \boldsymbol{a}, \tag{18.9}$$

associative with scalars

$$(k\boldsymbol{a}) \cdot \boldsymbol{b} = k\left(\boldsymbol{a} \cdot \boldsymbol{b}\right), \tag{18.10}$$

and distributive with addition

$$\boldsymbol{a} \cdot (\boldsymbol{b} + \boldsymbol{c}) = \boldsymbol{a} \cdot \boldsymbol{b} + \boldsymbol{a} \cdot \boldsymbol{c}. \tag{18.11}$$

The cross product is neither commutative,

$$\boldsymbol{a} \times \boldsymbol{b} = -\boldsymbol{b} \times \boldsymbol{a}, \tag{18.12}$$

nor associative with cross product,

$$\boldsymbol{a} \times (\boldsymbol{b} \times \boldsymbol{c}) = \boldsymbol{b}(\boldsymbol{a} \cdot \boldsymbol{c}) - \boldsymbol{c}(\boldsymbol{a} \cdot \boldsymbol{b}). \tag{18.13}$$

However, it is distributive with addition as

$$\boldsymbol{a} \times (\boldsymbol{b} + \boldsymbol{c}) = \boldsymbol{a} \times \boldsymbol{b} + \boldsymbol{a} \times \boldsymbol{c}, \tag{18.14}$$

and associative with scalar products as

$$(k\boldsymbol{a}) \times \boldsymbol{b} = k\,(\boldsymbol{a} \times \boldsymbol{b})\,. \tag{18.15}$$

The cross product of $\boldsymbol{a}$ and $\boldsymbol{b}$ is perpendicular to both $\boldsymbol{a}$ and $\boldsymbol{b}$.

Definition 18.6 (Coordinate Systems)
An n-dimensional coordinate system *is a set of n vectors, $\boldsymbol{e}_i \in \mathbb{R}^n$, $\quad i = 1 \ldots n$, called the* basis, *and a zero point, called the* origin. *For a 3D space, the coordinates are commonly called $i = x, y, z$. The vectors must span the n-dimensional space, that is, all positions of the space must be reachable as a linear combination of the basis,*

$$\boldsymbol{x} = a_1\boldsymbol{e}_1 + a_2\boldsymbol{e}_2 + \cdots + a_n\boldsymbol{e}_n. \tag{18.16}$$

The coefficients a_i are the representation of the vector $\boldsymbol{a}$ in the basis $\boldsymbol{e}_i$. When

$$\boldsymbol{e}_i \cdot \boldsymbol{e}_j = \begin{cases} 1, & \text{if } i = j, \\ 0, & \text{otherwise}, \end{cases} \tag{18.17}$$

then the vectors constitute an orthonormal basis, *and the coordinate system is called* orthogonal.

Two nonparallel vectors and their cross product $(\boldsymbol{a}, \boldsymbol{b}, \boldsymbol{a} \times \boldsymbol{b})$ make up a right-handed coordinate system. Right-handed coordinate systems are related to determinants discussed in Definition 18.23. An often-used coordinate systems is the *body frame* coordinate system, which is placed and aligned conveniently with respect to an object. We denote a vector in coordinates in a body frame as $\boldsymbol{a}^{\text{BF}}$. In parallel, a single global coordinate system is almost always needed, and this is sometimes called the *world coordinate system (WCS)*, $\boldsymbol{a}^{\text{WCS}}$.

A construction often appearing in vector equations is the space product.

Definition 18.7 (Space Product)
For $\boldsymbol{a}, \boldsymbol{b}, \boldsymbol{c} \in \mathbb{R}^3$ the space product is given as

$$\boldsymbol{a} \times \boldsymbol{b} \cdot \boldsymbol{c} = \begin{bmatrix} a_1(b_2c_3 - b_3c_2) \\ a_2(b_3c_1 - b_1c_3) \\ a_3(b_1c_2 - b_2c_1) \end{bmatrix} \tag{18.18a}$$

$$= \det([\boldsymbol{a}|\boldsymbol{b}|\boldsymbol{c}]) \tag{18.18b}$$

where $\det()$ *is the determinant discussed in Definition 18.23*

The space product measures the volume of the parallelepiped spanned by the vectors $\boldsymbol{a}$, $\boldsymbol{b}$, and $\boldsymbol{c}$, as shown in Figure 18.1. It is invariant under interchanging of the cross product and the dot product, and cyclic permutations of the vectors.

In animation we often use vectors to express dynamic quantities, where we consider vectors as functions of time, $\boldsymbol{a}(t) : \mathbb{R} \to \mathbb{R}^n$ and analyze their change with time.

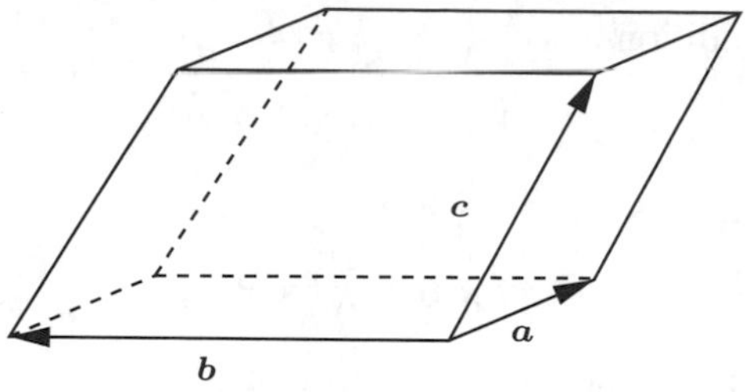

Figure 18.1: Three vectors defining a parallelepiped.

Definition 18.8 (Time Derivative of a Vector)
For a time varying vector, $\boldsymbol{v}(t) : \mathbb{R} \rightarrow \mathbb{R}^n$, the derivative w.r.t. time is given as

$$\frac{d\boldsymbol{v}}{dt} = \begin{bmatrix} \frac{dv_1}{dt} \\ \frac{dv_2}{dt} \\ \vdots \\ \frac{dv_n}{dt} \end{bmatrix}. \tag{18.19}$$

Definition 18.9 (Derivative of a Dot Product)
The time derivative a dot product between two vectors $\boldsymbol{a}, \boldsymbol{b} : \mathbb{R} \rightarrow \mathbb{R}^n$ is

$$\frac{d}{dt}(\boldsymbol{a} \cdot \boldsymbol{b}) = \frac{d\boldsymbol{a}}{dt} \cdot \boldsymbol{b} + \boldsymbol{a} \cdot \frac{d\boldsymbol{b}}{dt}, \tag{18.20}$$

.

Definition 18.10 (Derivative of a Cross Product)
Assuming that two vectors $\boldsymbol{a}$ and $\boldsymbol{b}$ vary with a variable t, then the derivative of their cross product is

$$\frac{d}{dt}(\boldsymbol{a} \times \boldsymbol{b}) = \frac{d\boldsymbol{a}}{dt} \times \boldsymbol{b} + \boldsymbol{a} \times \frac{d\boldsymbol{b}}{dt}. \tag{18.21}$$

Derivatives of vector fields are treated in Section 18.3.

Definition 18.11 (Vector Norm)
A vector norm on $\mathbb{R}^n$ is a function $\|\cdot\|$, from $\mathbb{R}^n$ into $\mathbb{R}$ with the following properties:

(i) $\|\boldsymbol{r}\| > 0$ *for* $\boldsymbol{r} \neq \boldsymbol{0}$, *and* $\|\boldsymbol{r}\| = 0$ *if, and only if,* $\boldsymbol{r} = \boldsymbol{0}$,

(ii) $\|\alpha \boldsymbol{r}\| = |\alpha| \, \|\boldsymbol{r}\|$ *for all* $\boldsymbol{r} \in \mathbb{R}^n$ *and* $\alpha \in \mathbb{R}$,

(iii) $\|\boldsymbol{r} + \boldsymbol{y}\| \leq \|\boldsymbol{r}\| + \|\boldsymbol{y}\|$ *for all* $\boldsymbol{r}, \boldsymbol{y} \in \mathbb{R}^n$.

Many norms are possible, two such are the l_2 and the l_∞ norms.

Definition 18.12 (The l_2 and l_∞ norms)
The l_2 and l_∞ norms for the vector $\boldsymbol{r} = [r_0, r_1, \dots, r_{n-1}]^T$ are defined by

$$\|\boldsymbol{r}\|_2 = \sqrt{\left(\sum_{i=0}^{n-1} r_i^2\right)} \quad \text{and} \quad \|\boldsymbol{r}\|_\infty = \max_{0 \le i \le n-1} |r_i| \tag{18.22}$$

The l_2 norm is called the Euclidean norm of the vector $\boldsymbol{r}$. For a vector $\boldsymbol{r} \in \mathbb{R}^n$ the norms are related by

$$\|\boldsymbol{r}\|_\infty \le \|\boldsymbol{r}\|_2 \le \sqrt{n}\,\|\boldsymbol{r}\|_\infty . \tag{18.23}$$

18.2 Matrices

A set of m linear equations in n variables may be written on the following form

$$u_1 = a_{11}v_1 + a_{12}v_2 + \cdots + a_{1n}v_n \tag{18.24a}$$

$$u_2 = a_{21}v_1 + a_{22}v_2 + \cdots + a_{2n}v_n \tag{18.24b}$$

$$\vdots$$

$$u_m = a_{m1}v_1 + a_{m2}v_2 + \cdots + a_{mn}v_n, \tag{18.24c}$$

where a_{ij} are the coefficients. This is written on *matrix* form as

$$\boldsymbol{u} = \boldsymbol{A}\boldsymbol{v}, \tag{18.25}$$

where $\boldsymbol{A}$ is the table of scalars a_{ij},

$$\boldsymbol{A} = \begin{bmatrix} a_{11} & a_{12} & \dots & a_{1n} \\ a_{21} & a_{22} & \ddots & \vdots \\ a_{m1} & a_{m2} & \dots & a_{mn} \end{bmatrix}. \tag{18.26}$$

The scalars a_{ij} are also called the *matrix elements*, and the matrix is said to have m rows and n columns, and we write $\boldsymbol{A} \in \mathbb{R}^{m \times n}$. A square matrix has $m = n$. A matrix with either $m = 1$ or $n = 1$ is called a row or column vector respectively.

Definition 18.13 (Diagonal Matrix)
A square matrix, $\mathbf{D}$, is called diagonal if, and only if,:

$$d_{ij} = 0 \text{ when } i \neq j. \tag{18.27}$$

That is, only the entries d_{ii}, may be different from zero in a diagonal matrix.

Definition 18.14 (Lower Triangular Matrix)
A matrix, $\mathbf{L}$, is lower triangular if, and only if,:

$$l_{ij} = 0 \text{ when } i < j. \tag{18.28}$$

That is, there are only values below the diagonal.

Definition 18.15 (Upper Triangular Matrix)
A matrix, U, is upper triangular if, and only if,:

$$u_{ij} = 0 \text{ when } i > j. \tag{18.29}$$

That is, there are only values above the diagonal.

A strictly lower or upper triangular matrix is a lower or upper triangular matrix, which has zero diagonal as well.

Definition 18.16 (Identity Matrix)
The diagonal matrix:

$$\mathbf{1} = \begin{pmatrix} 1 & 0 & \dots & 0 \\ 0 & 1 & & \vdots \\ \vdots & & \ddots & 0 \\ 0 & \dots & 0 & 1 \end{pmatrix}, \tag{18.30}$$

is called the identity matrix. Often in the literature, the identity matrix is denoted I. Unfortunately, in classical mechanics the I-notation is often used to mean an inertia tensor, which is why we use $\mathbf{1}$ for the identity matrix.

Matrices are additive and have two matrix products defined.

Definition 18.17 (Matrix-Matrix Addition)
The addition of two equal sized matrices, $A, B \in \mathbb{R}^{m \times n}$, is

$$C = A + B, \tag{18.31}$$

where $c_{ij} = a_{ij} + b_{ij}$.

Definition 18.18 (Matrix-Scalar Multiplication)
Given a scalar $k \in \mathbb{R}$ and a matrix $A \in \mathbb{R}^{m \times n}$, the product,

$$B = kA, \tag{18.32}$$

is given as

$$b_{ij} = ka_{ij}. \tag{18.33}$$

Definition 18.19 (Matrix-Matrix Multiplication)
Given two matrices $A \in \mathbb{R}^{m \times n}$ and $B \in \mathbb{R}^{o \times m}$, then the product

$$C = BA, \tag{18.34}$$

is defined as,

$$c_{ij} = \sum_{p=1}^{n} b_{ip} a_{pj}. \tag{18.35}$$

The result is the matrix C, where $C \in \mathbb{R}^{o \times n}$. Its product is undefined, when the number of columns in B differs from the number of rows in A. The identity matrix $\mathbf{1}$ is the neutral element for matrix multiplication.

Definition 18.20 (Transpose Matrix)
The transpose of $\boldsymbol{A}$ is written as $\boldsymbol{A}^T$, and is found as

$$\boldsymbol{B} = \boldsymbol{A}^T \tag{18.36a}$$
$$\Downarrow$$
$$b_{ij} = a_{ji}. \tag{18.36b}$$

Naturally, transpose is its own inverse,

$$\left(\boldsymbol{A}^T\right)^T = \boldsymbol{A}, \tag{18.37}$$

But further,

$$(\boldsymbol{A}+\boldsymbol{B})^T = \boldsymbol{A}^T + \boldsymbol{B}^T, \tag{18.38}$$

and

$$(\boldsymbol{A}\boldsymbol{B})^T = \boldsymbol{B}^T\boldsymbol{A}^T. \tag{18.39}$$

for matrices $\boldsymbol{A}$ and $\boldsymbol{B}$.

Definition 18.21 (Inverse Matrix)
The inverse matrix of $\boldsymbol{A} \in \mathbb{R}^{n\times n}$ is written as $\boldsymbol{A}^{-1}$, and the following property must hold for the inverse matrix

$$\boldsymbol{A}^{-1}\boldsymbol{A} = \boldsymbol{A}\boldsymbol{A}^{-1} = \boldsymbol{1}. \tag{18.40}$$

The inverse of a matrix product is,

$$(\boldsymbol{A}\boldsymbol{B})^{-1} = \boldsymbol{B}^{-1}\boldsymbol{A}^{-1}, \tag{18.41}$$

and further

$$\left(\boldsymbol{A}^{-1}\right)^{-1} = \boldsymbol{A}. \tag{18.42}$$

Finally,

$$\left(\boldsymbol{A}^T\right)^{-1} = \left(\boldsymbol{A}^{-1}\right)^T \tag{18.43}$$

A square matrix, $\boldsymbol{A}$, has an inverse if, and only if, $\det(\boldsymbol{A}) \neq 0$. Common methods for calculating the inverse of a square matrix are: Gauss-Jordan elimination, Gaussian elimination, and LU decomposition, which can be found described in [Press et al., 1999a]. The reader may also consult Chapter 19, where iterative methods for solving systems of linear equations are described.

Definition 18.22 (Trace of a Matrix)
The trace of a square matrix $\boldsymbol{A} \in \mathbb{R}^{n\times n}$ is given as

$$\operatorname{Tr}(\boldsymbol{A}) = \sum_{i=1}^{n} a_{ii}. \tag{18.44}$$

The trace is invariant under the transpose operator,

$$\operatorname{Tr}(\boldsymbol{A}) = \operatorname{Tr}\left(\boldsymbol{A}^T\right), \tag{18.45}$$

it is associative with scalars,

$$\mathrm{Tr}(k\boldsymbol{A}) = k\,\mathrm{Tr}(\boldsymbol{A}), \tag{18.46}$$

for any scalar $k \in \mathbb{R}$*. The trace is further distributive w.r.t. addition,*

$$\mathrm{Tr}(\boldsymbol{A}+\boldsymbol{B}) = \mathrm{Tr}(\boldsymbol{A}) + \mathrm{Tr}(\boldsymbol{B}), \tag{18.47}$$

and invariant under multiplication,

$$\mathrm{Tr}(\boldsymbol{A}\boldsymbol{B}) = \mathrm{Tr}(\boldsymbol{B}\boldsymbol{A}). \tag{18.48}$$

Definition 18.23 (Determinant of a Matrix)
The determinant is only defined for square matrices. The determinant of $\boldsymbol{A} \in \mathbb{R}^{2\times 2}$ *is,*

$$\begin{aligned}
|\boldsymbol{A}| &= \det(\boldsymbol{A}) && (18.49a)\\
&= \det\left(\begin{bmatrix} a_{11} & a_{12}\\ a_{21} & a_{22}\end{bmatrix}\right) && (18.49b)\\
&= \begin{vmatrix} a_{11} & a_{12}\\ a_{21} & a_{22}\end{vmatrix} && (18.49c)\\
&= a_{11}a_{22} - a_{21}a_{12}. && (18.49d)
\end{aligned}$$

The determinant for $\boldsymbol{A} \in \mathbb{R}^{n\times n}$ *is defined recursively as*

$$\begin{aligned}
\begin{vmatrix} a_{11} & a_{12} & \cdots & a_{1n}\\ a_{21} & a_{22} & \cdots & a_{2n}\\ \vdots & \vdots & \ddots & \vdots\\ a_{n1} & a_{n2} & \cdots & a_{nn}\end{vmatrix} &= a_{11}\begin{vmatrix} a_{22} & a_{23} & \cdots & a_{2n}\\ a_{32} & a_{33} & \cdots & a_{3n}\\ \vdots & \vdots & \ddots & \vdots\\ a_{n2} & a_{n3} & \cdots & a_{nn}\end{vmatrix} - a_{12}\begin{vmatrix} a_{21} & a_{23} & \cdots & a_{2n}\\ a_{31} & a_{32} & \cdots & a_{3n}\\ \vdots & \vdots & \ddots & \vdots\\ a_{n1} & a_{n3} & \cdots & a_{nn}\end{vmatrix} +\\
&\quad \cdots \pm \begin{vmatrix} a_{21} & a_{22} & \cdots & a_{2(n-1)}\\ a_{31} & a_{32} & \cdots & a_{3(n-1)}\\ \vdots & \vdots & \ddots & \vdots\\ a_{n1} & a_{n2} & \cdots & a_{n(n-1)}\end{vmatrix} && (18.50a)\\
&= \sum_{i=1}^{n} (-1)^{i+j} a_{ij} \boldsymbol{M}_{ij}, && (18.50b)
\end{aligned}$$

where $\boldsymbol{M}_{ij}$ *is the minor of matrix* $\boldsymbol{A}$ *produced by removing row* i *and column* j *in* $\boldsymbol{A}$*.*

The determinant is commutative with inversion,

$$\det \boldsymbol{A}^{-1} = \left(\det(\boldsymbol{A})\right)^{-1}, \tag{18.51}$$

and it is distributive w.r.t. matrix multiplication,

$$\det(\boldsymbol{A}\boldsymbol{B}) = \det(\boldsymbol{A})\det(\boldsymbol{B}), \tag{18.52}$$

when matrices $\boldsymbol{A}$ *and* $\boldsymbol{B}$ *are invertible.*

The determinant is a tool often used when solving linear systems of equations, and it has geometrical importance, since it is related to the area of parallelepipeds formed by two vectors $\boldsymbol{u}, \boldsymbol{v} \in \mathbb{R}^2$ is given as $\det([\boldsymbol{u}|\boldsymbol{v}])$. In n dimensions, the volume of the parallelepiped spanned by the vectors $\boldsymbol{v}_1, \ldots, \boldsymbol{v}_n$ is given as $\det([\boldsymbol{v}_1|\ldots|\boldsymbol{v}_n])$, and the sign is the orientation of the parallelepiped. That is, in the usual three-space, the unit vectors $\boldsymbol{e}_x$, $\boldsymbol{e}_y$, and $\boldsymbol{e}_z$ have a positive determinant in a *right-handed coordinate system*, that is, $\det([\boldsymbol{e}_x|\boldsymbol{e}_y|\boldsymbol{e}_z]) = 1$, while a *left-handed coordinate system* has a negative determinant. These coordinate systems are in mirror relation like the right and left hand as indicated by the difference in sign of the determinant.

Definition 18.24 (Orthogonal Matrix)
A matrix, $\boldsymbol{R}$, is said to be orthogonal, if, and only if,

$$\boldsymbol{R}^T = \boldsymbol{R}^{-1}. \tag{18.53}$$

As a consequence,

$$\boldsymbol{R}^T\boldsymbol{R} = \boldsymbol{1} \tag{18.54}$$

As a consequence of Definition 18.24, the row or its column vectors form an orthonormal basis.

theorem 18.1 (Rotation Matrix)
An orthogonal matrix is a rotation (and possibly a mirroring) transformation.

theorem 18.2 (Coordinate Transformation)
Assume that we have two orthogonal coordinate systems labeled BF and WCS, and three unit vectors: $\boldsymbol{r}_1, \boldsymbol{r}_2, \boldsymbol{r}_3 \in \mathbb{R}^n$, given with respect to WCS, and such that they are parallel with the axes of BF. That is, $\boldsymbol{r}_1 \perp \boldsymbol{r}_2 \perp \boldsymbol{r}_3$. We now construct a matrix $\boldsymbol{R} \in \mathbb{R}^{n\times 3}$, such that its columns are equal to $\boldsymbol{r}_1$, $\boldsymbol{r}_2$, and $\boldsymbol{r}_3$. The $\boldsymbol{R}$ will transform a vector $\boldsymbol{x}$ given with respect to BF into the corresponding vector given with respect to WCS, that is,

$$\boldsymbol{R} = \left[\boldsymbol{r}_1 \mid \boldsymbol{r}_2 \mid \boldsymbol{r}_3\right] \tag{18.55}$$

$$\Downarrow$$

$$\boldsymbol{R}\boldsymbol{x}^{BF} = \boldsymbol{x}^{WCS}, \tag{18.56}$$

where $\left[\boldsymbol{r}_1 \mid \boldsymbol{r}_2 \mid \boldsymbol{r}_3\right]$ is the matrix produced by concatenating the three column vectors. The inverse, $\boldsymbol{R}^{-1} = \boldsymbol{R}^T$, will have $\boldsymbol{r}_1^T$, $\boldsymbol{r}_2^T$, and $\boldsymbol{r}_3^T$ as rows, and $\boldsymbol{R}^T$ will transform $\boldsymbol{x}$ given in WCS into the corresponding vector in BF, that is,

$$\boldsymbol{R}^T = \begin{bmatrix} \boldsymbol{r}_1^T \\ \boldsymbol{r}_2^T \\ \boldsymbol{r}_3^T \end{bmatrix} \tag{18.57}$$

$$\Downarrow$$

$$\boldsymbol{R}^T\boldsymbol{x}^{WCS} = \boldsymbol{x}^{BF}, \tag{18.58}$$

where $\boldsymbol{R}^T$ is produced by concatenating the three row vectors.

Proof of Theorem 18.2:
Let's start by examining $\boldsymbol{R}$, where the columns are given by $\boldsymbol{r}_1$, $\boldsymbol{r}_2$, and $\boldsymbol{r}_3$. Since $\boldsymbol{R}$ is a linear transformation, it is enough to show that the axes of BF transforms into the axes of WCS. Let's begin with the first axis of BF.

$$\boldsymbol{R}\boldsymbol{r}_1^{\text{BF}} = \boldsymbol{R}\begin{bmatrix}1\\0\\0\end{bmatrix} \tag{18.59a}$$

$$= \begin{bmatrix}\boldsymbol{r}_1 \mid \boldsymbol{r}_2 \mid \boldsymbol{r}_3\end{bmatrix}\begin{bmatrix}1\\0\\0\end{bmatrix} \tag{18.59b}$$

$$= \boldsymbol{r}_1 \tag{18.59c}$$

$$= \boldsymbol{r}_1^{\text{WCS}} \tag{18.59d}$$

Similarly, we find for the second and third axes, $\boldsymbol{R}\boldsymbol{r}_2^{\text{BF}} = \boldsymbol{r}_2^{\text{WCS}}$ and $\boldsymbol{R}\boldsymbol{r}_3^{\text{BF}} = \boldsymbol{r}_3^{\text{WCS}}$. We have now proven the first half of our theorem. The column version of $\boldsymbol{R}$ is a rotation matrix, and the row version is its transpose, implying that it is the inverse rotation. This completes our proof. □

Definition 18.25 (Symmetric Matrix)
A matrix $\boldsymbol{A}$ is a symmetric matrix, if it is equal to its transpose matrix, that is,

$$\boldsymbol{A} = \boldsymbol{A}^T. \tag{18.60}$$

For every matrix $\boldsymbol{B}$, both $\boldsymbol{B}^T\boldsymbol{B}$ and $\boldsymbol{B}\boldsymbol{B}^T$ are symmetric.

theorem 18.3 (Properties of a Symmetric Matrix)
A symmetric matrix $\boldsymbol{A}$ has the property that it can be written as

$$\boldsymbol{A} = \boldsymbol{R}\boldsymbol{D}\boldsymbol{R}^T, \tag{18.61}$$

where $\boldsymbol{R}$ is an orthogonal matrix and $\boldsymbol{D}$ is a diagonal matrix.

Proof of Theorem 18.3:
We evaluate the transpose of (18.61)

$$\boldsymbol{A}^T = (\boldsymbol{R}\boldsymbol{D}\boldsymbol{R}^T)^T \tag{18.62a}$$

$$= (\boldsymbol{D}\boldsymbol{R}^T)^T\boldsymbol{R}^T \tag{18.62b}$$

$$= (\boldsymbol{R}^T)^T\boldsymbol{D}^T\boldsymbol{R}^T \tag{18.62c}$$

$$= \boldsymbol{R}\boldsymbol{D}\boldsymbol{R}^T, \tag{18.62d}$$

where we repeatedly used (18.39), and the fact that both the double transpose and the transpose of a diagonal matrix are the identity operation. Since (18.61) and (18.62d) are identical, we have proven the theorem.
□

Definition 18.26 (Skew Symmetric Matrix)
A matrix $\boldsymbol{A}$ is said to be skew symmetric if its transpose is equal to its negation,

$$\boldsymbol{A}^T = -\boldsymbol{A}, \tag{18.63}$$

implying that the diagonal is zero. Every square matrix $\boldsymbol{B}$ can be decomposed into a sum of a symmetric and skew-symmetric matrix,

$$\boldsymbol{B} = \frac{1}{2}\left(\boldsymbol{B} + \boldsymbol{B}^T\right) + \left(\boldsymbol{B} - \boldsymbol{B}^T\right). \tag{18.64}$$

theorem 18.4 (Cross Product Matrix)
The cross product between two three-dimensional vectors $\boldsymbol{a}$ and $\boldsymbol{b}$ can be written as a matrix product using the cross product matrix. The cross product matrix is defined as follows:

$$\boldsymbol{a}^{\times} = \begin{pmatrix} 0 & -a_z & a_y \\ a_z & 0 & -a_x \\ -a_y & a_x & 0 \end{pmatrix}, \tag{18.65}$$

where we have

$$\boldsymbol{a} \times \boldsymbol{b} = \boldsymbol{a}^{\times}\boldsymbol{b}. \tag{18.66}$$

Proof of Theorem 18.4:
By straightforward computation of the cross product between the two vectors $\boldsymbol{a}$ and $\boldsymbol{b}$ we get

$$\boldsymbol{a} \times \boldsymbol{b} = \begin{pmatrix} a_y b_z - b_y a_z \\ b_x a_z - a_x b_z \\ a_x b_y - b_x a_y \end{pmatrix} = \boldsymbol{a}^{\times}\boldsymbol{b}. \tag{18.67}$$

□

theorem 18.5 (Properties of the Cross Product Matrix)
The cross product matrix is skew symmetrical.

Proof of Theorem 18.5:
If we transpose the cross product matrix from Theorem 18.4, then we get

$$\boldsymbol{a}^{\times T} = \begin{pmatrix} 0 & a_z & -a_y \\ -a_z & 0 & a_x \\ a_y & -a_x & 0 \end{pmatrix} = -\boldsymbol{a}^{\times}, \tag{18.68}$$

and we have shown what we wanted. □

There are several useful rules for the cross product matrix. We have listed some of them below:

$$\begin{aligned} \boldsymbol{a}^{\times}\boldsymbol{b} &= \boldsymbol{a}^T\boldsymbol{b}^{\times} & (18.69) \\ \boldsymbol{a}^{\times}\boldsymbol{b} &= -\boldsymbol{b}^T\boldsymbol{a}^{\times} & (18.70) \\ \boldsymbol{a}^{\times}\boldsymbol{b} &= \boldsymbol{b}^{\times}\boldsymbol{a} & (18.71) \end{aligned}$$

It is not difficult to prove these rules by using Theorem 18.4 and Theorem 18.5. We will leave this as an exercise for the reader.

Definition 18.27 (Eigenvalues and Eigenvectors)
Given a matrix $\boldsymbol{A}$, a scalar λ, and a vector $\boldsymbol{v}$, such that

$$\boldsymbol{A}\boldsymbol{v} = \lambda\boldsymbol{v}. \tag{18.72}$$

The scalar λ is called the eigenvalue of $\boldsymbol{A}$ and $\boldsymbol{v}$ is called the corresponding right eigenvector of $\boldsymbol{A}$. The similar equation

$$\boldsymbol{u}^T\boldsymbol{A} = \lambda\boldsymbol{u}^T, \tag{18.73}$$

define the left eigenvector. Left and right eigenvalues are equivalent, but this does not hold in general for left and right eigenvectors. Nevertheless, it is often sufficient to consider the right eigenvector, and it is thus referred to as the *eigenvector.*

Letting $\boldsymbol{V} = [\boldsymbol{v}_1|\boldsymbol{v}_2|\dots|\boldsymbol{v}_n]$ be the matrix formed by all the right eigenvectors of a matrix $\boldsymbol{A} \in \mathbb{R}^{n\times n}$ and $\boldsymbol{D} = diag(\lambda_1, \lambda_2, \dots, \lambda_n)$ be a diagonal matrix of corresponding eigenvalues, then we can write the full system of eigenvalues and vectors as

$$\boldsymbol{A}\boldsymbol{V} = \boldsymbol{V}\boldsymbol{D}, \tag{18.74}$$

and equivalently for the left eigenvectors.

$$\boldsymbol{U}^T\boldsymbol{A} = \boldsymbol{D}\boldsymbol{U}^T. \tag{18.75}$$

The left eigenvector is the right eigenvector of the transpose matrix A^T, since

$$\boldsymbol{u}^T\boldsymbol{A} = \lambda\boldsymbol{u}^T, \tag{18.76a}$$

$$\Downarrow$$

$$\left(\boldsymbol{u}^T\boldsymbol{A}\right)^T = \left(\lambda\boldsymbol{u}^T\right)^T, \tag{18.76b}$$

$$\Downarrow$$

$$\boldsymbol{A}^T\boldsymbol{u} = \lambda\boldsymbol{u}. \tag{18.76c}$$

theorem 18.6 (Left and Right Eigenvectors of a Symmetrical Matrix)
The left and right eigenvectors of a symmetric matrix are identical.

Proof of Theorem 18.6:
For a symmetric matrix, $\boldsymbol{A} = \boldsymbol{A}^T$, hence by (18.76c) we realize that a left eigenvector is also a right eigenvector. Since the eigen system only has n eigenvalues and vectors, where $\boldsymbol{A} \in \mathbb{R}^{n\times n}$, then we conclude that the left and right eigenvectors are identical. □

theorem 18.7 (Orthogonality of Eigenvectors)
Right and left eigenvectors are orthogonal on each other, that is if $\boldsymbol{v}_i$ and $\boldsymbol{u}_j$ are right and left eigenvectors for a matrix $\boldsymbol{A}$ corresponding to eigenvalue λ_i and λ_j, then

$$\boldsymbol{v}_i \cdot \boldsymbol{u}_j = 0, \quad when \quad i \neq j. \tag{18.77}$$

Proof of Theorem 18.7:
Starting with (18.74) and (18.75) and applying the matrices of left and right eigenvectors we find that

$$U^T A V = U^T V D, \tag{18.78a}$$
$$U^T A V = D U^T V, \tag{18.78b}$$

and we conclude that $(U^T V)D = D(U^T V)$. Since D is a diagonal vector, then so must $U^T V$ be. This completes our proof. □

Eigenvalues and eigenvectors are related up to a scaling constant, i.e., if λ and u are corresponding eigenvalues and eigenvectors solving (18.72), then $c\lambda$ and $\frac{1}{c}u$ is also a solution to (18.72) for any constant $c \neq 0$.

theorem 18.8 (Eigenvalues and Eigenvectors of a Symmetrical Matrix)
For a symmetrical matrix A we have:

$$A = R D R^T, \tag{18.79}$$

where R is an orthogonal matrix. Choosing eigenvectors of A to be unit vectors, then the columns of R will be the eigenvalues of A and the diagonal of D will hold the corresponding eigenvalues.

Proof of Theorem 18.8:
Assuming that U and V are the system of unit right and left eigenvectors of matrix A. Multiplying (18.74) with the left eigenvectors we find that

$$A V U^T = V D U^T. \tag{18.80}$$

Since A is symmetric we know that the left and right eigenvectors are identical. Writing $R = U = V$ we find,

$$A R R^T = R D R^T, \tag{18.81a}$$
$$\Downarrow$$
$$A = R D R^T, \tag{18.81b}$$

since $R R^T = 1$. □

Definition 18.28 (Positive Definite)
A symmetrical matrix A is positive definite, if and only if

$$v^T A v > 0 \textit{ for all } v \neq 0 \tag{18.82}$$

theorem 18.9 (Properties of a Positive Definite Matrix)
A positive definite matrix, A, can be written as

$$A = R D R^T, \tag{18.83}$$

where R is an orthogonal matrix, and D is a diagonal matrix. Furthermore, all the diagonal elements of D are strictly positive, $d_{ii} > 0, \forall i \in [0 \ldots n]$.

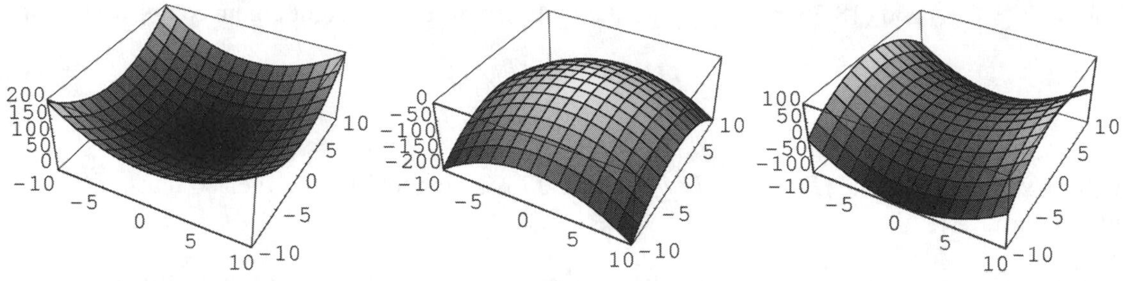

(a) (b) (c)

Figure 18.2: Visualizing positive-definite, negative-definite, and indefinite matrices.

When discussing the definiteness of matrices, it is useful to have the pictures in Figure 18.2 in mind. In the figure is shown the visualization of the function,

$$f(\boldsymbol{r}) = \boldsymbol{r}^T \boldsymbol{A} \boldsymbol{r}, \tag{18.84}$$

for the following three matrices,

$$\text{Positive-definite } \boldsymbol{A} = \begin{bmatrix} 1 & 0 \\ 0 & 1 \end{bmatrix}, \tag{18.85a}$$

$$\text{Negative-definite } \boldsymbol{A} = \begin{bmatrix} -1 & 0 \\ 0 & -1 \end{bmatrix}, \tag{18.85b}$$

$$\text{indefinite } \boldsymbol{A} = \begin{bmatrix} 1 & 0 \\ 0 & -1 \end{bmatrix}. \tag{18.85c}$$

For the positive-definite, negative-definite, and indefinite matrices, there is a single minimum, maximum, and saddle point respectively at $[0, 0]^T$.

Proof of Theorem 18.9:
The form of $\boldsymbol{A}$ follows directly from Theorem 18.3. In order to show the positivity of $\boldsymbol{D}$, we will use Definition 18.28 and write

$$\boldsymbol{v}^T \boldsymbol{A} \boldsymbol{v} > 0. \tag{18.86}$$

Using Theorem 18.3, we get

$$\boldsymbol{v}^T \boldsymbol{R} \boldsymbol{D} \boldsymbol{R}^T \boldsymbol{v} > 0. \tag{18.87}$$

Finally, with a little rewriting we have

$$\left(\boldsymbol{R}^T \boldsymbol{v}\right)^T \boldsymbol{D} \left(\boldsymbol{R}^T \boldsymbol{v}\right) > 0. \tag{18.88}$$

The expression $\boldsymbol{R}^T\boldsymbol{v}$ corresponds to a rotation of the vector $\boldsymbol{v}$, so using $\boldsymbol{w} = \boldsymbol{R}^T\boldsymbol{v}$, we can rewrite our equation into

$$\boldsymbol{w}^T\boldsymbol{D}\boldsymbol{w} > 0. \tag{18.89}$$

We know that $\boldsymbol{D}$ is a diagonal matrix, and the equation can therefore be rewritten into

$$d_{11}w_1^2 + \cdots + d_{nn}w_n^2 > 0. \tag{18.90}$$

Since $\boldsymbol{w}$ is a rotation of the vector $\boldsymbol{v}$ with the property,

$$\boldsymbol{v} \neq \boldsymbol{0}, \tag{18.91}$$

then it must also hold that

$$\boldsymbol{w} \neq \boldsymbol{0}. \tag{18.92}$$

That is, there always exist one or more nonzero elements of $\boldsymbol{w}$, $w_i \neq 0$. Therefore, we must have

$$w_i^2 \geq 0 \text{ for all } i \in [1 \ldots n]. \tag{18.93}$$

The equation in (18.90) holds for an arbitrary vector $\boldsymbol{w} \neq \boldsymbol{0}$. Hence, choose $\boldsymbol{w}$ such that $w_j = 0$ for all $j \in [1 \ldots (k-1), (k+1) \ldots n]$, then by (18.90) we conclude that $d_{kk} > 0$, and this must hold for all $d_{kk}, k \in [1 \ldots n]$. This completes our proof. □

Definition 18.29 (Positive Semidefinite)
A symmetrical matrix $\boldsymbol{A}$ is called positive semidefinite if, and only if,

$$\boldsymbol{v}^T\boldsymbol{A}\boldsymbol{v} \geq 0 \textit{ for all } \boldsymbol{v} \neq \boldsymbol{0}. \tag{18.94}$$

theorem 18.10 (Properties of a Positive Semidefinite Matrix)
A positive semidefinite matrix $\boldsymbol{A}$ can be written as

$$\boldsymbol{A} = \boldsymbol{R}\boldsymbol{D}\boldsymbol{R}^T, \tag{18.95}$$

where $\boldsymbol{R}$ is an orthogonal matrix, $\boldsymbol{D}$ is a diagonal matrix, and all the diagonal elements of $\boldsymbol{D}$ are non-negative, $d_{ii} \geq 0, i \in [1 \ldots n]$.

Proof of Theorem 18.8:
The proof of this is almost identical to the proof of Theorem 18.9, and will be left to the reader as an exercise. □

theorem 18.11 (Elliptical Level Sets of a Positive Definite Matrix)
Given a positive definite matrix $\boldsymbol{M}$ and a constant scalar c, then all vectors $\boldsymbol{v}$ that satisfy

$$c = \boldsymbol{v}^T\boldsymbol{M}\boldsymbol{v}, \tag{18.96}$$

will lie on an ellipse.

Proof of Theorem 18.11:
Since $\boldsymbol{M}$ is symmetrical, there exists an orthogonal matrix $\boldsymbol{R}$ and a diagonal matrix $\boldsymbol{D}$, such that

$$c = \boldsymbol{v}^T \boldsymbol{M} \boldsymbol{v} \tag{18.97a}$$
$$= \boldsymbol{v}^T \boldsymbol{R} \boldsymbol{D} \boldsymbol{R}^T \boldsymbol{v} \tag{18.97b}$$
$$= \left(\boldsymbol{R}^T \boldsymbol{v}\right)^T \boldsymbol{D} \left(\boldsymbol{R}^T \boldsymbol{v}\right). \tag{18.97c}$$

The term $\boldsymbol{R}^T \boldsymbol{v}$ corresponds to a rotation of the vector $\boldsymbol{v}$. Writing $\boldsymbol{w} = \boldsymbol{R}^T \boldsymbol{v}$, we get

$$c = \boldsymbol{w}^T \boldsymbol{D} \boldsymbol{w}. \tag{18.98}$$

Since $\boldsymbol{D}$ is a diagonal matrix, we may rewrite the equation as

$$c = d_{11} w_1^2 + \cdots + d_{nn} w_n^2. \tag{18.99}$$

Finally, since all $d_{ii} > 0$, we realize that the equation represents an ellipse. ☐

theorem 18.12 (Ellipses as a Representation of Eigen Structure)
Referring to the proof of Theorem 18.11, the elliptical structure,

$$c = d_1 w_1^2 + \cdots + d_n w_n^2, \tag{18.100}$$

corresponds to the ellipse given by

$$c = d_1 v_1^2 + \cdots + d_n v_n^2, \tag{18.101}$$

rotated by $\boldsymbol{R}^T$, and the axes are related as

$$\boldsymbol{R}^T = \left[\boldsymbol{w}_1 | \boldsymbol{w}_2 | \ldots | \boldsymbol{w}_n\right] \tag{18.102}$$

From this we note that the first axis corresponds to the first column of $\boldsymbol{R}$, and it follows that the i'th non-rotated axis corresponds to the i'th column of the matrix $\boldsymbol{R}$. Recalling that $\boldsymbol{R}$ consists of the eigenvectors of $\boldsymbol{M}$, then we can conclude that the i'th axis of the ellipse,

$$c = \boldsymbol{v}^T \boldsymbol{M} \boldsymbol{v}, \tag{18.103}$$

is the i'th eigenvector of $\boldsymbol{M}$, and the eigenvalues are the scaling of the axes.

Definition 18.30 (Matrix Norm)
A matrix norm is defined for square matrices, $\boldsymbol{A} \in \mathbb{R}^{n \times n}$ and is a function $\|\cdot\|$, from $\mathbb{R}^{n \times n}$ into $\mathbb{R}$ with the following properties,

(i) $\|\boldsymbol{A}\| > 0$ *for* $\boldsymbol{A} \in \mathbb{R}^{n \times n}$, $\boldsymbol{A} \neq \boldsymbol{0}$, *and* $\|\boldsymbol{A}\| = 0$ *if, and only if,* $\boldsymbol{A} = \boldsymbol{0}$.

(ii) $\|\alpha \boldsymbol{A}\| = |\alpha| \, \|\boldsymbol{A}\|$ *for all* $\boldsymbol{A} \in \mathbb{R}^{n \times n}$ *and* $\alpha \in \mathbb{R}$,

(iii) $\|\boldsymbol{A} + \boldsymbol{B}\| \leq \|\boldsymbol{A}\| + \|\boldsymbol{B}\|$ *for all* $\boldsymbol{A}, \boldsymbol{B} \in \mathbb{R}^{n \times n}$.

(iv) $\|\boldsymbol{AB}\| \leq \|\boldsymbol{A}\| \, \|\boldsymbol{B}\|$ *for all* $\boldsymbol{A}, \boldsymbol{B} \in \mathbb{R}^{n \times n}$.

Several useful norms exists such as the matrix p-norm, Frobenius norm, and the spectral norm,

Definition 18.31 (Matrix p-norm)
The matrix p-norm is defined as,

$$\|\boldsymbol{A}\|_p = \max_{\|\boldsymbol{r}\|_p = 1} \|\boldsymbol{A}\boldsymbol{r}\|_p \tag{18.104}$$

for any scalar $1 \leq p \leq \infty$.

Definition 18.32 (Frobenius Norm)
The Frobenius norm of a matrix $\boldsymbol{A} \in \mathbb{R}^{m \times n}$ *is defined as,*

$$\|\boldsymbol{A}\|_F = \sqrt{\operatorname{Tr}\left(\boldsymbol{A}\boldsymbol{A}^T\right)} = \sqrt{\sum_{i=1}^{m} \sum_{j=1}^{m} a_{ij}^2}. \tag{18.105}$$

Definition 18.33 (Spectral Norm)
The spectral norm of a matrix $\boldsymbol{A}$ *is given as the square root of the maximum eigenvalue of* $\boldsymbol{A}^T\boldsymbol{A}$, *or equivalently,*

$$\|\boldsymbol{A}\|_2 = \max_{\|\boldsymbol{r}\|_2 \neq 0} \frac{\|\boldsymbol{A}\boldsymbol{r}\|_2}{\|\boldsymbol{r}\|_2}. \tag{18.106}$$

18.3 Scalar and Vector Fields

A *scalar field* is a function defined in every point of space, $f : \mathbb{R}^n \rightarrow \mathbb{R}$, e.g. $f(x, y, z)$ in 3D space. It is useful to think of a scalar field as a gray-valued image, where each position has a scalar value, the image intensity. A *vector field* and a *matrix field* is equivalently a vector and a matrix function defined in every point of space, e.g., the gradient vector of a scalar field, $\phi : \mathbb{R}^n \rightarrow \mathbb{R}^m$, e.g. $[\frac{\partial f(x,y,z)}{\partial x}, \frac{\partial f(x,y,z)}{\partial y}, \frac{\partial f(x,y,z)}{\partial z}]^T$. Fields often vary with time.

18.3.1 Differential Forms

Following [Magnus et al., 1988] we will calculate the derivatives of matrix equations using differentials also know as *differential forms*. The *differential* or *total derivative* of a function $f(x, y, z)$ is given as,

$$df = \frac{\partial f}{\partial x} dx + \frac{\partial f}{\partial y} dy + \frac{\partial f}{\partial z} dz \tag{18.107}$$

where $\frac{\partial f}{\partial x}$ etc., are the partial derivatives and dx etc., are the unit differentials. The differential may be thought of as a mapping from vectors into numbers. Pictorially, the differential is tangent where the partial derivatives $\frac{\partial f}{\partial x}$ etc. are the tangent vectors, and the differentials dx etc., are the coordinates. This is illustrated in Figure 18.3.

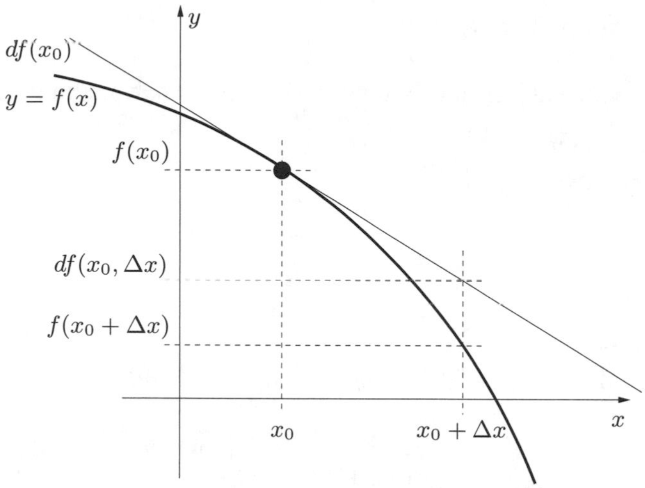

Figure 18.3: A function f, its tangent at x_0, and the corresponding differential.

Consider the simplest *matrix function*,

$$\boldsymbol{F}(\boldsymbol{x}) = \boldsymbol{A}\boldsymbol{x}, \tag{18.108}$$

where the vector $\boldsymbol{x} \in \mathbb{R}^n$ is the vector field of Cartesian coordinates, and assume that $\boldsymbol{A} \in \mathbb{R}^{m \times n}$ is a constant matrix independent of position. Then for every point $\boldsymbol{x}$ we conclude that the matrix function $\boldsymbol{F} : \mathbb{R}^n \rightarrow \mathbb{R}^m$. Expanding the terms we find,

$$f_1(\boldsymbol{x}) = a_{11}x_1 + a_{12}x_2 + \cdots + a_{1n}x_n \tag{18.109a}$$

$$f_2(\boldsymbol{x}) = a_{21}x_1 + a_{22}x_2 + \cdots + a_{2n}x_n \tag{18.109b}$$

$$\vdots$$

$$f_m(\boldsymbol{x}) = a_{m1}x_1 + a_{m2}x_2 + \cdots + a_{mn}x_n, \tag{18.109c}$$

where x_i is the i'th coordinate for the position $\boldsymbol{x}$ in space. For each equation we now calculate the differential, and since x_i is the coordinate function, then it only depends on the i coordinate, that is

$$\frac{\partial x_i}{\partial x_j} = \begin{cases} 1 & \text{if } i = j, \\ 0 & \text{otherwise.} \end{cases} \tag{18.110}$$

Therefore, the differentials of each equation are simply,

$$df_1 = a_{11}dx_1 + a_{12}dx_2 + \cdots + a_{1n}dx_n \tag{18.111a}$$

$$df_2 = a_{21}dx_1 + a_{22}dx_2 + \cdots + a_{2n}dx_n \tag{18.111b}$$

$$\vdots$$

$$df_m = a_{m1}dx_1 + a_{m2}dx_2 + \cdots + a_{mn}dx_n, \tag{18.111c}$$

which we may summarize as,

$$dF = A dx, \tag{18.112}$$

and in analogue to scalar derivatives we say that A is the derivative of F w.r.t. x.

To find the partial derivatives of a matrix expression, we may thus calculate the differential of the expression and identify the leading term of the corresponding unit differentials. However, since the partial derivatives of matrix equations are closely linked to the *Taylor series*, it is often simpler to calculate the derivatives as the linear part of $F(X + dX) - F(X)$, (see Chapter 20 for a discussion of Taylor series). The Taylor series to first order is given as,

$$F(X + \Delta X) = F(X) + \frac{\partial F}{\partial X}\Delta X + \mathcal{O}(\|\Delta X\|^2), \tag{18.113}$$

and taking $\Delta X \to 0$ we identify the matrix $\frac{\partial F}{\partial X}$ as the derivative of F w.r.t. X. Again, for every position or matrix X this is simply the process of approximating the matrix function F with a linear function dF. The matrix coefficient $\frac{\partial F}{\partial X}$ is often called the Jacobian and is intimately related to the gradient operator to be discussed in the next section. The Taylor series gives us an interpretation of the total derivative as the change of F when we move in some specific direction ΔX.

theorem 18.13 (Differential of a Constant Matrix)
The differential of a constant matrix A is zero,

$$dA = 0. \tag{18.114}$$

The proof follows immediately, since the Jacobian is zero.

theorem 18.14 (Differential of a Scalar-Matrix Product)
Given $k \in \mathbb{R}$ and a matrix X, then

$$d(kX) = k\,dX, \tag{18.115}$$

and hence $\frac{d(kX)}{dX} = k$.

Proof of Theorem 18.14
We evaluate $F(X + dX) - F(X)$ for $F(X) = kX$:

$$k(X + dX) - kX = k\,dX, \tag{18.116}$$

and the linear term is trivially identified to be k. □

theorem 18.15 (Differential of a Matrix Sum)
Given two matrices X and Y then

$$d(X + Y) = dX + dY, \tag{18.117}$$

and hence $\frac{d(X+Y)}{dX} = \frac{d(X+Y)}{dY} = 1$.

Proof of Theorem 18.15:
We evaluate $\boldsymbol{F}(\boldsymbol{X}+d\boldsymbol{X},\boldsymbol{Y}+d\boldsymbol{Y})-\boldsymbol{F}(\boldsymbol{X},\boldsymbol{Y})$ for $\boldsymbol{F}(\boldsymbol{X},\boldsymbol{Y})=\boldsymbol{X}+\boldsymbol{Y}$:

$$(\boldsymbol{X}+d\boldsymbol{X})+(\boldsymbol{Y}+d\boldsymbol{Y})-(\boldsymbol{X}+\boldsymbol{Y})=d\boldsymbol{X}+d\boldsymbol{Y}, \tag{18.118}$$

and the linear terms are both trivially identified to be 1. □

theorem 18.16 (Differential of a Matrix-Matrix Product)
Given two matrices $\boldsymbol{X}\in\mathbb{R}^{m\times o}$ *and* $\boldsymbol{Y}\in\mathbb{R}^{o\times n}$*, then*

$$d(\boldsymbol{Y}\boldsymbol{X})=(d\boldsymbol{Y})\boldsymbol{X}+\boldsymbol{Y}\,d\boldsymbol{X}, \tag{18.119}$$

and hence $\frac{d(\boldsymbol{Y}\boldsymbol{X})}{d\boldsymbol{X}}=\boldsymbol{Y}$.

Proof of Theorem 18.16:
We evaluate $\boldsymbol{F}(\boldsymbol{X}+d\boldsymbol{X},\boldsymbol{Y}+d\boldsymbol{Y})-\boldsymbol{F}(\boldsymbol{X},\boldsymbol{Y})$ for $\boldsymbol{F}(\boldsymbol{X},\boldsymbol{Y})=\boldsymbol{Y}\boldsymbol{X}$:

$$(\boldsymbol{Y}+d\boldsymbol{Y})(\boldsymbol{X}+d\boldsymbol{X})-(\boldsymbol{Y}\boldsymbol{X})=(d\boldsymbol{Y})\boldsymbol{X}+\boldsymbol{Y}\,d\boldsymbol{X}+d\boldsymbol{Y}\,d\boldsymbol{X}, \tag{18.120}$$

and the linear term for $d\boldsymbol{X}$ is identified to be $\boldsymbol{Y}$, while the linear term for $d\boldsymbol{Y}$ is more complicated, since matrix multiplication does not commute. There exists an extended set of operations to write such equations on a simpler form called the vec operator and the Kronecker product, but their definition and usage is outside the scope of this book. The interested reader is urged to consult [Magnus et al., 1988]. □

Lemma 18.1 (Differential of a Linear Transformation of Vectors)
A simpler result than Theorem 18.16 is obtained for the product between a constant matrix $\boldsymbol{A}\in\mathbb{R}^{m\times n}$ *and a vector* $\boldsymbol{x}\in\mathbb{R}^{n\times 1}$*:*

$$d(\boldsymbol{A}\boldsymbol{x})=\boldsymbol{A}\,d\boldsymbol{x}, \tag{18.121}$$

since $d\boldsymbol{A}=0$*, and the linear term is thus* $\boldsymbol{A}$.

Lemma 18.2 (Differential of a Quadratic Form)
From Theorem 18.16 we also easily derive the partial derivatives of a common quadratic involving matrices $\boldsymbol{Y}\in\mathbb{R}^{n\times n}$ *and* $\boldsymbol{x},\boldsymbol{Z}\in\mathbb{R}^{n\times 1}$*:*

$$d(\boldsymbol{x}^T\boldsymbol{Y}\boldsymbol{z})=(d\boldsymbol{x}^T)\boldsymbol{Y}\boldsymbol{z}+\boldsymbol{x}^T(d\boldsymbol{Y})\boldsymbol{z}+\boldsymbol{x}^T\boldsymbol{Y}\,d\boldsymbol{z}. \tag{18.122}$$

The linear term w.r.t. $d\boldsymbol{z}$ *is* $\boldsymbol{x}^T\boldsymbol{Y}$*. Furthermore,* $(d\boldsymbol{x}^T)\boldsymbol{Y}\boldsymbol{x}$ *is a scalar, and it is therefore invariant under the transpose operator. Hence, we may rearrange the first term to be* $\boldsymbol{x}^T\boldsymbol{Y}^T\,d\boldsymbol{x}$*, and we identify the linear term w.r.t.* $d\boldsymbol{x}$ *to be* $\boldsymbol{x}^T\boldsymbol{Y}^T$*. Again we find that the linear term w.r.t.* $d\boldsymbol{Y}$ *is difficult to write on a simple form, since matrix multiplication does not commute. Finally, in the specific case of* $\boldsymbol{x}=\boldsymbol{z}$*, then the above simplifies to*

$$d(\boldsymbol{x}^T\boldsymbol{Y}\boldsymbol{x})=\boldsymbol{x}^T(\boldsymbol{Y}^T+\boldsymbol{Y})\,d\boldsymbol{x}+\boldsymbol{x}^T(d\boldsymbol{Y})\boldsymbol{x}. \tag{18.123}$$

theorem 18.17 (Differential of an Inverse)
Given an invertible matrix $\boldsymbol{X}\in\mathbb{R}^{n\times n}$*, then*

$$d\boldsymbol{X}^{-1}=-\boldsymbol{X}^{-1}(d\boldsymbol{X})\boldsymbol{X}^{-1}. \tag{18.124}$$

Proof of Theorem 18.17:
Since $\mathbf{1} = \boldsymbol{X}\boldsymbol{X}^{-1} = \boldsymbol{X}^{-1}\boldsymbol{X}$ we have,

$$0 = d\mathbf{1} = d(\boldsymbol{X}\boldsymbol{X}^{-1}) = (d\boldsymbol{X})\boldsymbol{X}^{-1} + \boldsymbol{X}\,d\boldsymbol{X}^{-1}, \tag{18.125}$$

Isolating $d\boldsymbol{X}^{-1}$ we find

$$d\boldsymbol{X}^{-1} = -\boldsymbol{X}^{-1}(d\boldsymbol{X})\boldsymbol{X}^{-1}. \tag{18.126}$$

□

theorem 18.18 (Differential of a Trace)
Given a matrix $\boldsymbol{X} \in \mathbb{R}^{n\times n}$, then

$$d\,\mathrm{Tr}(\boldsymbol{X}) = \mathrm{Tr}(d\boldsymbol{X}). \tag{18.127}$$

Proof of Theorem 18.18:
We evaluate $\boldsymbol{F}(\boldsymbol{X} + d\boldsymbol{X}) - \boldsymbol{F}(\boldsymbol{X})$ for $\boldsymbol{F}(\boldsymbol{X}) = \mathrm{Tr}(\boldsymbol{X})$:

$$\mathrm{Tr}(\boldsymbol{X} + d\boldsymbol{X}) - \mathrm{Tr}(\boldsymbol{X}) = \mathrm{Tr}(d\boldsymbol{X}). \tag{18.128}$$

□

18.3.2 The Gradient Operator

The gradient operator is an essential operator for fields, and it is used in computational fluid dynamics just as commonly as the derivative operator. We have therefore reserved a full section for it and its relatives. The symbol for the gradient is most often the Greek letter Nabla.

Definition 18.34 (Nabla Operator)
The nabla or "del" differential operator in three dimensional space is defined as

$$\nabla = \boldsymbol{e}_x\frac{\partial}{\partial x} + \boldsymbol{e}_y\frac{\partial}{\partial y} + \boldsymbol{e}_z\frac{\partial}{\partial z}, \tag{18.129}$$

where $\boldsymbol{e}_x$, $\boldsymbol{e}_y$, and $\boldsymbol{e}_z$ are the coordinate axes using Einstein's summation convention, *we can write the nabla operator as*

$$\nabla = \boldsymbol{e}_i\frac{\partial}{\partial i} \tag{18.130}$$

where it is understood that the right-hand side is a sum over i, where i iterates over the names of the coordinate axes in the space the operator is used, $i =' x',' y',' z'$. A final notation in 3D is

$$\partial_{\boldsymbol{x}} = \frac{\partial}{\partial \boldsymbol{x}} = \nabla, \tag{18.131}$$

where $\boldsymbol{x}$ represents the complete domain, e.g., for a 3D function $\boldsymbol{x} = [\boldsymbol{e}_x, \boldsymbol{e}_y, \boldsymbol{e}_z]^T$ or more commonly simplified to $\boldsymbol{x} = [x, y, z]^T$. If only parts of the domain are specified, e.g., $\nabla_{[x,z]^T}$, then the nabla operator is restricted to the corresponding subspace, that is,

$$\nabla_{[x,z]^T} = \begin{bmatrix} \frac{\partial}{\partial x} \\ \frac{\partial}{\partial z} \end{bmatrix}. \tag{18.132}$$

This is not to be confused with a directional derivative discussed in Theorem 18.19 and 18.39.

Definition 18.35 (Gradient of a Scalar Field)
Applying the Nabla operator on a gradient field f gives the gradient vector field:

$$\nabla f = \nabla f, \tag{18.133}$$

which for $f : \mathbb{R}^3 \to \mathbb{R}$ gives,

$$\nabla f = \begin{bmatrix} \frac{\partial f(x,y,z)}{\partial x} \\ \frac{\partial f(x,y,z)}{\partial y} \\ \frac{\partial f(x,y,z)}{\partial z} \end{bmatrix}. \tag{18.134}$$

The gradient denotes the direction in which the scalar field increases, and its length is equal to the derivative of the scalar field in the gradient direction. Furthermore,

$$\oint_C \nabla f \cdot d\boldsymbol{r} = \oint_C \nabla f \cdot \boldsymbol{t}\, dr = 0, \tag{18.135}$$

which states that the circular integral of the gradient operator on a closed curve, $r \in C$, is zero, where $\mathbf{t}$ is the tangent to the curve.

Definition 18.36 (Gradient of a Vector Field)
The gradient of a vector field, $\phi : \mathbb{R}^n \to \mathbb{R}^m$ is

$$\nabla \phi = \begin{bmatrix} \nabla \phi_1^T \\ \nabla \phi_2^T \\ \vdots \\ \nabla \phi_m^T \end{bmatrix} = \begin{bmatrix} \frac{\partial \phi_1}{\partial x_1} & \frac{\partial \phi_1}{\partial x_2} & \cdots & \frac{\partial \phi_1}{\partial x_n} \\ \frac{\partial \phi_2}{\partial x_1} & \frac{\partial \phi_2}{\partial x_2} & \cdots & \frac{\partial \phi_2}{\partial x_n} \\ \vdots & \vdots & \ddots & \vdots \\ \frac{\partial \phi_m}{\partial x_1} & \frac{\partial \phi_m}{\partial x_2} & \cdots & \frac{\partial \phi_m}{\partial x_n} \end{bmatrix}, \tag{18.136}$$

which is also known as the Jacobian matrix. *Notice that there is an inconsistency in the use of the gradient operator between the scalar and vector fields, where the former writes the gradient as a column vector and the latter as row vectors. This convention, used in most literature to reduce the number of transpose operations in equations involving the Jacobian [Cottle et al., 1992, Section 2.1.19]. When $m = n = 3$, we get*

$$\nabla \phi = \begin{bmatrix} \frac{\partial \phi_1}{\partial x} & \frac{\partial \phi_1}{\partial y} & \frac{\partial \phi_1}{\partial z} \\ \frac{\partial \phi_2}{\partial x} & \frac{\partial \phi_2}{\partial y} & \frac{\partial \phi_2}{\partial z} \\ \frac{\partial \phi_3}{\partial x} & \frac{\partial \phi_3}{\partial y} & \frac{\partial \phi_3}{\partial z} \end{bmatrix}. \tag{18.137}$$

Sometimes only parts of the Jacobian are used, and a common notation is $\nabla_{\boldsymbol{r}}$, where $\boldsymbol{r}$ is a vector of parameters to ϕ, e.g. $\boldsymbol{r} = [x_i, x_j, x_k]$ meaning

$$\nabla_{\boldsymbol{r}} \phi = \begin{bmatrix} \frac{\partial \phi_1}{\partial x_i} & \frac{\partial \phi_1}{\partial x_j} & \frac{\partial \phi_1}{\partial x_k} \\ \frac{\partial \phi_2}{\partial x_i} & \frac{\partial \phi_2}{\partial x_j} & \frac{\partial \phi_2}{\partial x_k} \\ \vdots & \vdots & \vdots \\ \frac{\partial \phi_m}{\partial x_i} & \frac{\partial \phi_m}{\partial x_j} & \frac{\partial \phi_m}{\partial x_k} \end{bmatrix}. \tag{18.138}$$

Definition 18.37 (Divergence of a Vector Field)
Applying the Nabla operator on a vector field $\boldsymbol{\phi}$ using the dot product gives the divergence scalar field:

$$\nabla \cdot \boldsymbol{\phi} = div\, \boldsymbol{\phi}, \tag{18.139}$$

which for $\boldsymbol{\phi} : \mathbb{R}^3 \rightarrow \mathbb{R}^3$ is given as,

$$\nabla \cdot \boldsymbol{\phi} = \frac{\partial \phi_1}{\partial x} + \frac{\partial \phi_2}{\partial y} + \frac{\partial \phi_3}{\partial z}. \tag{18.140}$$

where ϕ_1, ϕ_2, and ϕ_3 are the x, y, and z components of the vector fields, hence a scalar field.

The divergence theorem *or* Gauss' theorem *is expressed using the divergence operator,*

$$\int_V \nabla \cdot \boldsymbol{\phi}\, d\boldsymbol{v} = \oint_S \boldsymbol{\phi} \cdot d\boldsymbol{a} = \oint_S \boldsymbol{\phi} \cdot \boldsymbol{n}\, da, \tag{18.141}$$

which states that the integral of the divergence of a vector field $\boldsymbol{\phi}$ over a closed volume $\boldsymbol{v} \in V$ is equivalent to the integral of flow through the surface $\boldsymbol{a} \in S$, where $\boldsymbol{n}$ is the normal to the surface. In the limit of an infinitesimal volume,

$$\nabla \cdot \boldsymbol{\phi} = \lim_{V \rightarrow 0} \frac{1}{V} \oint_{\boldsymbol{S}} \boldsymbol{\phi} \cdot \boldsymbol{n}\, d\boldsymbol{a}, \tag{18.142}$$

and thus it is seen, that the divergence is the point-wise flow through the surface of the point.

Definition 18.38 (Rotation of a Vector Field)
Applying the Nabla operator on a vector field $\boldsymbol{\phi}$ using the cross product gives the rotation vector field:

$$\nabla \times \boldsymbol{\phi} = curl\, \boldsymbol{\phi}, \tag{18.143}$$

which is also sometimes called rot. For $\boldsymbol{\phi} : \mathbb{R}^3 \rightarrow \mathbb{R}^3$ is given as

$$\nabla \times \boldsymbol{\phi} = \begin{bmatrix} \frac{\partial \phi_3}{\partial y} - \frac{\partial \phi_2}{\partial z} \\ \frac{\partial \phi_1}{\partial z} - \frac{\partial \phi_3}{\partial x} \\ \frac{\partial \phi_2}{\partial x} - \frac{\partial \phi_1}{\partial y} \end{bmatrix}. \tag{18.144}$$

If the rotation of a vector field is zero, $\nabla \times \boldsymbol{\phi}$, then $\boldsymbol{\phi}$ is a gradient field, i.e., there exists a scalar field g such that $\boldsymbol{\phi} = \nabla g$.

The rotation theorem *or* Stokes' theorem *is expressed using the rotation operator:*

$$\int_S \nabla \times \boldsymbol{\phi} \cdot d\boldsymbol{a} = \int_S \nabla \times \boldsymbol{\phi} \cdot \boldsymbol{n}\, da = \oint_C \boldsymbol{\phi} \cdot d\boldsymbol{l} = \oint_C \boldsymbol{\phi} \cdot \boldsymbol{t}\, dl, \tag{18.145}$$

which states that rotation of a vector field along a closed curve $\boldsymbol{l} \in C$ is equal to the integral of the field over any surface $\boldsymbol{a} \in S$, which has C as its border. The vectors $\boldsymbol{n}$ and $\boldsymbol{t}$ are the normal to the surface S and tangent to the curve C respectively. In the limit,

$$\boldsymbol{n} \cdot (\nabla \times \boldsymbol{\phi}) = \lim_{S \rightarrow 0} \frac{1}{S} \oint_C \boldsymbol{\phi} \cdot \boldsymbol{t}\, dl, \tag{18.146}$$

and we may interpret the normal part of the rotation of a vector field as rotation of the point.

theorem 18.19 (Directional Derivative of a Scalar Field)
The change of a scalar field in the direction ϕ may be written as

$$\frac{df}{d\phi} = (\phi \cdot \nabla) f. \tag{18.147}$$

When $|\phi| = 1$, then $\frac{d}{d\phi}$ is called the directional derivative or 'ϕ gradient f'. Assuming $f(x, y, z) : \mathbb{R}^3 \to \mathbb{R}$ and $\phi = [\phi_1, \phi_2, \phi_3]^T \in \mathbb{R}^3$ then

$$\frac{df}{d\phi} = \phi_1 \frac{\partial f}{\partial x} + \phi_2 \frac{\partial f}{\partial y} + \phi_3 \frac{\partial f}{\partial z}. \tag{18.148}$$

Definition 18.39 (Directional Derivative of a Vector Field)
The change in a vector field ψ, when moving along the vector field ϕ, is another vector field $(\phi \cdot \nabla)\psi$, which is called 'ϕ gradient ψ'.

$$\frac{d\psi}{d\phi} = (\phi \cdot \nabla)\psi = (\nabla \psi)\, \phi \tag{18.149}$$

When $|\phi| = 1$, then $\frac{d}{d\phi}$ is called the directional derivative. For $\phi, \psi : \mathbb{R}^3 \to \mathbb{R}^3$ it is found that

$$\frac{d\psi}{d\phi} = \begin{bmatrix} \phi_1 \frac{\partial \psi_1}{\partial x} + \phi_2 \frac{\partial \psi_1}{\partial y} + \phi_3 \frac{\partial \psi_1}{\partial z} \\ \phi_1 \frac{\partial \psi_2}{\partial x} + \phi_2 \frac{\partial \psi_2}{\partial y} + \phi_3 \frac{\partial \psi_2}{\partial z} \\ \phi_1 \frac{\partial \psi_3}{\partial x} + \phi_2 \frac{\partial \psi_3}{\partial y} + \phi_3 \frac{\partial \psi_3}{\partial z} \end{bmatrix}. \tag{18.150}$$

In this case, the $\phi \cdot \nabla$ is applied component-wise on the elements of ψ.

theorem 18.20 (Gradient of a Scalar-Scalar Product)
The gradient of a (point-wise) product of two scalar fields, f and g, is a vector field given as

$$\nabla(fg) = g\nabla f + f\nabla g. \tag{18.151}$$

theorem 18.21 (Gradient of a Scalar-Vector Product)
The gradient of a the (point-wise) product of a scalar field, f, and a vector field ϕ is

$$\nabla (f\phi) = f\nabla\phi + \phi\,(\nabla f)^T \tag{18.152}$$

theorem 18.22 (Divergence of a Scalar-Vector Product)
The divergence of the (point-wise) product of a scalar field f and a vector field ϕ is a scalar given as

$$\nabla \cdot (f\phi) = \phi \cdot (\nabla f) + f(\nabla \cdot \phi). \tag{18.153}$$

theorem 18.23 (Rotation of a Scalar-Vector Product)
The rotation of the (point-wise) product of a scalar field f and a vector field ϕ is a vector given as

$$\nabla \times (f\phi) = f\,(\nabla \times \phi) + (\nabla f) \times \phi. \tag{18.154}$$

theorem 18.24 (Gradient of a Dot Product)
The gradient of a (point-wise) dot product between two vector fields $\boldsymbol{\phi}$ and $\boldsymbol{\psi}$ is

$$\nabla(\boldsymbol{\phi}\cdot\boldsymbol{\psi}) = (\nabla\boldsymbol{\phi})^T\boldsymbol{\psi} + (\nabla\boldsymbol{\psi})^T\boldsymbol{\phi} = (\boldsymbol{\phi}\cdot\nabla)\boldsymbol{\psi} + \boldsymbol{\phi}\times(\nabla\times\boldsymbol{\psi}) + (\boldsymbol{\psi}\cdot\nabla)\boldsymbol{\phi} + \boldsymbol{\psi}\times(\nabla\times\boldsymbol{a}). \quad (18.155)$$

theorem 18.25 (The Divergence of a Cross Product)
The divergence of a (point-wise) cross product between two vector fields $\boldsymbol{\phi}$ and $\boldsymbol{\psi}$ is,

$$\nabla\cdot(\boldsymbol{\phi}\times\boldsymbol{\psi}) = (\nabla\times\boldsymbol{\phi})\cdot\boldsymbol{\psi} - \boldsymbol{\phi}\cdot(\nabla\times\boldsymbol{\psi})\,. \quad (18.156)$$

theorem 18.26 (The Rotation of a Cross Product)
The rotation of a (point-wise) cross product between two vector fields $\boldsymbol{\phi}$ and $\boldsymbol{\psi}$ is,

$$\nabla\times(\boldsymbol{\phi}\times\boldsymbol{\psi}) = (\nabla\cdot\boldsymbol{\psi})\,\boldsymbol{\phi} - (\nabla\cdot\boldsymbol{\phi})\,\boldsymbol{\psi} + (\boldsymbol{\psi}\cdot\nabla)\,\boldsymbol{\phi} - (\boldsymbol{\phi}\cdot\nabla)\,\boldsymbol{\psi}. \quad (18.157)$$

theorem 18.27 (The Divergence of a Gradient Field: The Laplace Operator)
The Laplace operator,

$$\nabla\cdot\nabla = \nabla^2, \quad (18.158)$$

on a scalar field yields a scalar field, which for $f : \mathbb{R}^3 \to \mathbb{R}$ gives

$$\nabla^2 f = \frac{\partial^2 f}{\partial x^2} + \frac{\partial^2 f}{\partial y^2} + \frac{\partial^2 f}{\partial z^2}. \quad (18.159)$$

theorem 18.28 (The Rotation of a Gradient Field Vanishes)
The rotation of a gradient of a scalar field is zero,

$$\nabla\times(\nabla f) = 0. \quad (18.160)$$

theorem 18.29 (The Divergence of a Rotation Vanishes)
The divergence of a rotation of a vector field is zero,

$$\nabla\cdot(\nabla\times\boldsymbol{\phi}) = 0. \quad (18.161)$$

theorem 18.30 (The Rotation of a Rotation)
The Rotation of a Rotation is given as

$$\nabla\times\nabla\times\boldsymbol{\phi} = \nabla\,(\nabla\cdot\boldsymbol{\phi}) - \nabla^2\boldsymbol{\phi}, \quad (18.162)$$

where $\nabla^2\boldsymbol{\phi} = [\nabla^2\phi_1, \nabla^2\phi_2, \nabla^2\phi_3]^T$ is used for shorthand.

theorem 18.31 (Gradient of a Constant Linear Transformation of a Vector Field)
The gradient of a vector field $\boldsymbol{\phi} : \mathbb{R}^3 \to \mathbb{R}^3$ under constant transformation $\boldsymbol{A} \in \mathbb{R}^{3\times3}$ is,

$$\nabla(\boldsymbol{A}\boldsymbol{\phi}) = \boldsymbol{A}\nabla\boldsymbol{\phi} \quad (18.163)$$

Proof of Theorem 18.31:
To prove we first expand the equation as

$$\nabla(\boldsymbol{A}\boldsymbol{\phi}) = \nabla \begin{bmatrix} a_{11}\phi_1 + a_{12}\phi_2 + a_{13}\phi_3 \\ a_{21}\phi_1 + a_{22}\phi_2 + a_{23}\phi_3 \\ a_{31}\phi_1 + a_{32}\phi_2 + a_{33}\phi_3 \end{bmatrix} \tag{18.164a}$$

$$= \begin{bmatrix} \frac{\partial(a_{11}\phi_1+a_{12}\phi_2+a_{13}\phi_3)}{\partial x} & \frac{\partial(a_{11}\phi_1+a_{12}\phi_2+a_{13}\phi_3)}{\partial y} & \frac{\partial(a_{11}\phi_1+a_{12}\phi_2+a_{13}\phi_3)}{\partial z} \\ \frac{\partial(a_{21}\phi_1+a_{22}\phi_2+a_{23}\phi_3)}{\partial x} & \frac{\partial(a_{21}\phi_1+a_{22}\phi_2+a_{23}\phi_3)}{\partial y} & \frac{\partial(a_{21}\phi_1+a_{22}\phi_2+a_{23}\phi_3)}{\partial z} \\ \frac{\partial(a_{31}\phi_1+a_{32}\phi_2+a_{33}\phi_3)}{\partial x} & \frac{\partial(a_{31}\phi_1+a_{32}\phi_2+a_{33}\phi_3)}{\partial y} & \frac{\partial(a_{31}\phi_1+a_{32}\phi_2+a_{33}\phi_3)}{\partial z} \end{bmatrix}. \tag{18.164b}$$

Considering the first element we find,

$$\frac{\partial(a_{11}\phi_1 + a_{12}\phi_2 + a_{13}\phi_3)}{\partial x} = a_{11}\frac{\partial\phi_1}{\partial x} + a_{12}\frac{\partial\phi_2}{\partial x} + a_{13}\frac{\partial\phi_3}{\partial x}, \tag{18.165}$$

since the elements of $\boldsymbol{A}$ are constant. Extending the calculation on the first element to the full matrix and separating the terms gives,

$$\nabla(\boldsymbol{A}\boldsymbol{\phi}) = \begin{bmatrix} a_{11} & a_{12} & a_{13} \\ a_{21} & a_{22} & a_{23} \\ a_{31} & a_{32} & a_{33} \end{bmatrix} \begin{bmatrix} \frac{\partial\phi_1}{\partial x} & \frac{\partial\phi_1}{\partial y} & \frac{\partial\phi_1}{\partial z} \\ \frac{\partial\phi_2}{\partial x} & \frac{\partial\phi_2}{\partial y} & \frac{\partial\phi_2}{\partial z} \\ \frac{\partial\phi_3}{\partial x} & \frac{\partial\phi_3}{\partial y} & \frac{\partial\phi_3}{\partial z} \end{bmatrix} \tag{18.166a}$$

$$= \boldsymbol{A}\nabla\boldsymbol{\phi}. \tag{18.166b}$$

This completes our proof. □

theorem 18.32 (Directional Derivative of a Constant Linear Transformation of a Vector Field)
The change in direction $\boldsymbol{\phi} : \mathbb{R}^3 \rightarrow \mathbb{R}^3$ of a vector $\boldsymbol{\psi} : \mathbb{R}^3 \rightarrow \mathbb{R}^3$ under constant transformation $\boldsymbol{A} \in \mathbb{R}^{3\times 3}$ is,

$$\frac{d\boldsymbol{A}\boldsymbol{\psi}}{d\boldsymbol{\phi}} = (\boldsymbol{\phi}\cdot\nabla)\boldsymbol{A}\boldsymbol{\psi} = \boldsymbol{A}\left((\boldsymbol{\phi}\cdot\nabla)\boldsymbol{\psi}\right) = \boldsymbol{A}\frac{d\boldsymbol{\psi}}{d\boldsymbol{\phi}}. \tag{18.167}$$

Proof of Theorem 18.32:
To prove, we write

$$(\boldsymbol{\phi}\cdot\nabla)\boldsymbol{A}\boldsymbol{\psi} = \left(\nabla\left(\boldsymbol{A}\boldsymbol{\psi}\right)\right)\boldsymbol{\phi} \tag{18.168a}$$

$$= \left(\boldsymbol{A}\nabla\boldsymbol{\psi}\right)\boldsymbol{\phi} \tag{18.168b}$$

$$= \boldsymbol{A}\left(\left(\nabla\boldsymbol{\psi}\right)\boldsymbol{\phi}\right) \tag{18.168c}$$

$$= \boldsymbol{A}\left(\boldsymbol{\phi}\cdot\nabla\right)\boldsymbol{\psi} \tag{18.168d}$$

which completes our proof. □

theorem 18.33 (Gradient of a Constant Quadratic Form of Vector Fields)
For $\boldsymbol{\phi}, \boldsymbol{\psi} : \mathbb{R}^3 \rightarrow \mathbb{R}^3$ and a constant transformation $\boldsymbol{A} \in \mathbb{R}^{3\times 3}$ the gradient of the quadratic form $\boldsymbol{\phi}^T\boldsymbol{A}\boldsymbol{\psi}$ is given by,

$$\nabla(\boldsymbol{\phi}^T\boldsymbol{A}\boldsymbol{\psi}) = (\nabla\boldsymbol{\phi})^T(\boldsymbol{A}\boldsymbol{\psi}) + (\nabla\boldsymbol{\psi})^T\boldsymbol{A}^T\boldsymbol{\phi}. \tag{18.169}$$

Proof of Theorem 18.33:
Expanding the equation we find,

$$\nabla(\boldsymbol{\phi}^T \boldsymbol{A}\boldsymbol{\psi}) = \nabla(\boldsymbol{\phi} \cdot \boldsymbol{A}\boldsymbol{\psi}) \tag{18.170a}$$
$$= (\nabla\boldsymbol{\phi})^T(\boldsymbol{A}\boldsymbol{\psi}) + (\nabla(\boldsymbol{A}\boldsymbol{\psi}))^T\boldsymbol{\phi} \tag{18.170b}$$
$$= (\nabla\boldsymbol{\phi})^T\boldsymbol{A}\boldsymbol{\psi} + (\boldsymbol{A}\nabla\boldsymbol{\psi})^T\boldsymbol{\phi} \tag{18.170c}$$
$$= (\nabla\boldsymbol{\phi})^T\boldsymbol{A}\boldsymbol{\psi} + (\nabla\boldsymbol{\psi})^T\boldsymbol{A}^T\boldsymbol{\phi}. \tag{18.170d}$$

□

In the special case where $\boldsymbol{\phi} = \boldsymbol{\psi}$, we find that $\nabla(\boldsymbol{\phi}^T\boldsymbol{A}\boldsymbol{\phi}) = (\nabla\boldsymbol{\phi})^T(\boldsymbol{A} + \boldsymbol{A}^T)\boldsymbol{\phi}$.

18.4 Functional Derivatives

Functional derivatives are a generalization of the derivative operator that occurs in calculus of variation. Instead of differentiation, a function w.r.t. a variable, a functional is differentiated w.r.t. a function. See Chapter 21 for details on the sense of functional derivatives. The essence is that in functional derivatives, it is allowed take derivatives w.r.t. function names.

theorem 18.34 (Functional Derivative of a Scalar Field)
Given a scalar field, $f(\boldsymbol{x}, \boldsymbol{u})$, where $\boldsymbol{x}$ is the independent variable and $\boldsymbol{u}$ is the dependent variable, i.e., $\boldsymbol{u}(\boldsymbol{x})$. The functional derivative w.r.t. $\boldsymbol{u}$ is $\frac{\partial f}{\partial \boldsymbol{u}}$. The functional derivative treats dependent variables as independent w.r.t. to differentiation.

The above theorem is best understood with an example.

theorem 18.35 (Functional Derivative of a Scalar-Scalar Product)
Given two scalar fields, f, g, the functional derivative of their product w.r.t. a dependent vector field $\boldsymbol{u}$ is

$$\partial_{\boldsymbol{u}}(fg) = g\partial_{\boldsymbol{u}}f + f\partial_{\boldsymbol{u}}g \tag{18.171}$$

Proof of Theorem 18.35:
Write the functional derivative using the specialized gradient operator as

$$\partial_{\boldsymbol{u}}(fg) = \nabla_{\boldsymbol{u}}(fg) \tag{18.172a}$$
$$= \begin{bmatrix} \frac{\partial(fg)}{\partial u_1} \\ \frac{\partial(fg)}{\partial u_2} \\ \frac{\partial(fg)}{\partial u_3} \end{bmatrix} \tag{18.172b}$$
$$= \begin{bmatrix} g\frac{\partial(f)}{\partial u_1} + f\frac{\partial(g)}{\partial u_1} \\ g\frac{\partial(f)}{\partial u_2} + f\frac{\partial(g)}{\partial u_2} \\ g\frac{\partial(f)}{\partial u_3} + f\frac{\partial(g)}{\partial u_3} \end{bmatrix} \tag{18.172c}$$
$$= g\partial_{\boldsymbol{u}}f + f\partial_{\boldsymbol{u}}g \tag{18.172d}$$

□

theorem 18.36 (Functional Derivative of a Dot Product)
Given two vector fields $\boldsymbol{\phi}, \boldsymbol{\psi}$, the functional derivative of their dot product w.r.t. a dependent vector field $\boldsymbol{u}$ is

$$\partial_{\boldsymbol{u}} (\boldsymbol{\phi} \cdot \boldsymbol{\psi}) = (\partial_{\boldsymbol{u}} \boldsymbol{\phi})^T \boldsymbol{\psi} + (\partial_{\boldsymbol{u}} \boldsymbol{\psi})^T \boldsymbol{\phi} \tag{18.173}$$

Proof of Theorem 18.36:
Assume that $\boldsymbol{\phi}, \boldsymbol{\psi} \in \mathbb{R}^3$, and that they are depending on $\boldsymbol{u}$, then we expand the dot product as

$$\begin{aligned}
\partial_{\boldsymbol{u}} (\boldsymbol{\phi} \cdot \boldsymbol{\psi}) &= \partial_{\boldsymbol{u}}(\phi_1\psi_1 + \phi_2\psi_2 + \phi_3\psi_3) && (18.174a)\\
&= \partial_{\boldsymbol{u}}(\phi_1\psi_1) + \partial_{\boldsymbol{u}}(\phi_2\psi_2) + \partial_{\boldsymbol{u}}(\phi_3\psi_3) && (18.174b)\\
&= \psi_1\partial_{\boldsymbol{u}}(\phi_1) + \phi_1\partial_{\boldsymbol{u}}(\psi_1) + \psi_2\partial_{\boldsymbol{u}}(\phi_2) + \phi_2\partial_{\boldsymbol{u}}(\psi_2) + \psi_3\partial_{\boldsymbol{u}}(\phi_3) + \phi_3\partial_{\boldsymbol{u}}(\psi_3) && (18.174c)\\
&= (\partial_{\boldsymbol{u}}\boldsymbol{\phi})^T \boldsymbol{\psi} + (\partial_{\boldsymbol{u}}\boldsymbol{\psi})^T \boldsymbol{\phi}. && (18.174d)
\end{aligned}$$

This completes our proof. □

A special case is the functional derivative of a squared length,

$$\partial_{\boldsymbol{u}} (\boldsymbol{\phi}^T \boldsymbol{\phi}) = 2(\partial_{\boldsymbol{u}}\boldsymbol{\phi})^T \boldsymbol{\phi}. \tag{18.175}$$

theorem 18.37 (Functional Derivative of an Independent Linear Transformation)
The functional derivative of an independent transformation of a vector field $\boldsymbol{\phi}$ w.r.t. the vector field $\boldsymbol{u}$ is,

$$\partial_{\boldsymbol{u}} (\boldsymbol{A}\boldsymbol{\phi}) = \boldsymbol{A}\partial_{\boldsymbol{u}}\boldsymbol{\phi} \tag{18.176}$$

Proof of Theorem 18.37:
Assume that $\boldsymbol{\phi} : \mathbb{R}^3 \rightarrow \mathbb{R}^3$ and $\boldsymbol{A} \in \mathbb{R}^{3\times 3}$, then

$$\begin{aligned}
\partial_{\boldsymbol{u}} (\boldsymbol{A}\boldsymbol{\phi}) &= \partial_{\boldsymbol{u}} \begin{bmatrix} a_{11}\phi_1 + a_{12}\phi_2 + a_{13}\phi_3 \\ a_{21}\phi_1 + a_{22}\phi_2 + a_{23}\phi_3 \\ a_{31}\phi_1 + a_{32}\phi_2 + a_{33}\phi_3 \end{bmatrix} && (18.177a)\\
&= \begin{bmatrix} \partial_{\boldsymbol{u}}(a_{11}\phi_1 + a_{12}\phi_2 + a_{13}\phi_3) \\ \partial_{\boldsymbol{u}}(a_{21}\phi_1 + a_{22}\phi_2 + a_{23}\phi_3) \\ \partial_{\boldsymbol{u}}(a_{31}\phi_1 + a_{32}\phi_2 + a_{33}\phi_3) \end{bmatrix} && (18.177b)\\
&= \begin{bmatrix} a_{11}\partial_{\boldsymbol{u}}\phi_1 + a_{12}\partial_{\boldsymbol{u}}\phi_2 + a_{13}\partial_{\boldsymbol{u}}\phi_3 \\ a_{21}\partial_{\boldsymbol{u}}\phi_1 + a_{22}\partial_{\boldsymbol{u}}\phi_2 + a_{23}\partial_{\boldsymbol{u}}\phi_3 \\ a_{31}\partial_{\boldsymbol{u}}\phi_1 + a_{32}\partial_{\boldsymbol{u}}\phi_2 + a_{33}\partial_{\boldsymbol{u}}\phi_3 \end{bmatrix} && (18.177c)\\
&= \boldsymbol{A}\partial_{\boldsymbol{u}}\boldsymbol{\phi}. && (18.177d)
\end{aligned}$$

This completes our proof. □

theorem 18.38 (Functional Derivatives of a constant Quadratic Form)
Given two vector fields $\boldsymbol{\phi}$ and $\boldsymbol{\psi}$ and an independent linear transformation $\boldsymbol{A}$, the functional derivative w.r.t. the vector field $\boldsymbol{u}$ is

$$\partial_{\boldsymbol{u}}(\boldsymbol{\phi}^T \boldsymbol{A}\boldsymbol{\psi}) = (\partial_{\boldsymbol{u}}\boldsymbol{\phi})^T \boldsymbol{A}\boldsymbol{\psi} + (\partial_{\boldsymbol{u}}\boldsymbol{\psi})^T \boldsymbol{A}^T \boldsymbol{\phi} \tag{18.178}$$

Proof of Theorem 18.38:

$$\partial_{\boldsymbol{u}}(\boldsymbol{\phi}^T \boldsymbol{A}\boldsymbol{\psi}) = \partial_{\boldsymbol{u}}(\boldsymbol{\phi} \cdot (\boldsymbol{A}\boldsymbol{\psi})) \tag{18.179a}$$
$$= (\partial_{\boldsymbol{u}}\boldsymbol{\phi})^T (\boldsymbol{A}\boldsymbol{\psi}) + (\partial_{\boldsymbol{u}}(\boldsymbol{A}\boldsymbol{\psi}))^T \boldsymbol{\phi} \tag{18.179b}$$
$$= (\partial_{\boldsymbol{u}}\boldsymbol{\phi})^T \boldsymbol{A}\boldsymbol{\psi} + (\boldsymbol{A}\partial_{\boldsymbol{u}}\boldsymbol{\psi})^T \boldsymbol{\phi} \tag{18.179c}$$
$$= (\partial_{\boldsymbol{u}}\boldsymbol{\phi})^T \boldsymbol{A}\boldsymbol{\psi} + (\partial_{\boldsymbol{u}}\boldsymbol{\psi})^T \boldsymbol{A}^T \boldsymbol{\phi} \tag{18.179d}$$

□

In the special case, where $\boldsymbol{\phi} = \boldsymbol{\psi}$, then $\partial_{\boldsymbol{u}}(\boldsymbol{\phi}^T \boldsymbol{A}\boldsymbol{\phi}) = (\partial_{\boldsymbol{u}}\boldsymbol{\phi})^T \left(\boldsymbol{A} + \boldsymbol{A}^T\right) \boldsymbol{\phi}$.

theorem 18.39 (Functional Derivative of a Normal Vector)
Consider two vector fields $\boldsymbol{\phi}$ and $\boldsymbol{\psi}$. If $\boldsymbol{\phi}$ is independent of $\boldsymbol{\psi}$ then the functional derivative of their cross product w.r.t. $\boldsymbol{\psi}$ is

$$\partial_{\boldsymbol{\psi}} (\boldsymbol{\psi} \times \boldsymbol{\phi}) = -\partial_{\boldsymbol{\psi}} (\boldsymbol{\phi} \times \boldsymbol{\psi}) \tag{18.180a}$$
$$= -\partial_{\boldsymbol{\psi}} (\boldsymbol{f}^{\times} \boldsymbol{\psi}) \tag{18.180b}$$
$$= -\boldsymbol{f}^{\times} \partial_{\boldsymbol{\psi}} \boldsymbol{\psi} \tag{18.180c}$$
$$= -\boldsymbol{f}^{\times}. \tag{18.180d}$$

Likewise, if $\boldsymbol{\psi}$ is independent of $\boldsymbol{\phi}$ then the functional derivative of their cross product w.r.t. $\boldsymbol{\phi}$ is

$$\partial_{\boldsymbol{\phi}} (\boldsymbol{\psi} \times \boldsymbol{\phi}) = \boldsymbol{g}^{\times}. \tag{18.181}$$

Now consider a normal vector field given by

$$\boldsymbol{n} = \frac{\boldsymbol{\psi} \times \boldsymbol{\phi}}{|\boldsymbol{\psi} \times \boldsymbol{\phi}|}. \tag{18.182}$$

Its derivative w.r.t. $\boldsymbol{\psi}$ is

$$\partial_{\boldsymbol{\psi}} \boldsymbol{n} = \partial_{\boldsymbol{\psi}} \left(\frac{\boldsymbol{\psi} \times \boldsymbol{\phi}}{\|\boldsymbol{\psi} \times \boldsymbol{\phi}\|_2} \right) \tag{18.183a}$$
$$= \partial_{\boldsymbol{\psi}} \left(\frac{\boldsymbol{\psi} \times \boldsymbol{\phi}}{(\boldsymbol{\psi} \times \boldsymbol{\phi} \cdot \boldsymbol{\psi} \times \boldsymbol{\phi})^{1/2}} \right) \tag{18.183b}$$
$$= \partial_{\boldsymbol{\psi}} \left((\boldsymbol{\psi} \times \boldsymbol{\phi}) \left((\boldsymbol{\psi} \times \boldsymbol{\phi})^T (\boldsymbol{\psi} \times \boldsymbol{\phi}) \right)^{-\frac{1}{2}} \right). \tag{18.183c}$$

Using (18.152) we find

$$\partial_{\boldsymbol{\psi}} \boldsymbol{n} = (\partial_{\boldsymbol{\psi}} (\boldsymbol{\psi} \times \boldsymbol{\phi})) \left((\boldsymbol{\psi} \times \boldsymbol{\phi})^T (\boldsymbol{\psi} \times \boldsymbol{\phi}) \right)^{-\frac{1}{2}} + (\boldsymbol{\psi} \times \boldsymbol{\phi}) \left[\partial_{\boldsymbol{\psi}} \left(\left((\boldsymbol{\psi} \times \boldsymbol{\phi})^T (\boldsymbol{\psi} \times \boldsymbol{\phi}) \right)^{-\frac{1}{2}} \right) \right]^T, \tag{18.184}$$

and using (18.180d) *and* (18.173) *on the square brackets term, we get*

$$n_{\psi} = -\boldsymbol{f}^{\times}\left((\boldsymbol{\psi}\times\boldsymbol{\phi})^T(\boldsymbol{\psi}\times\boldsymbol{\phi})\right)^{-\frac{1}{2}} - \frac{1}{2}(\boldsymbol{\psi}\times\boldsymbol{\phi})\left((\boldsymbol{\psi}\times\boldsymbol{\phi})^T(\boldsymbol{\psi}\times\boldsymbol{\phi})\right)^{-\frac{3}{2}}\left[2\left(\boldsymbol{f}^{\times}\boldsymbol{f}^{\times}\right)^T(\boldsymbol{\psi}\times\boldsymbol{\phi})\right]^T \tag{18.185}$$

Simplifying by using Theorem 18.5 get

$$\partial_{\boldsymbol{\psi}}\boldsymbol{n} = -\boldsymbol{f}^{\times}\left(\left(\boldsymbol{f}^{\times T}\boldsymbol{\psi}\right)^T\boldsymbol{f}^{\times T}\boldsymbol{\psi}\right)^{-\frac{1}{2}} - \left(\left(\boldsymbol{f}^{\times T}\boldsymbol{\psi}\right)^T\boldsymbol{f}^{\times T}\boldsymbol{\psi}\right)^{-\frac{3}{2}}\left(-\boldsymbol{f}^{\times}\boldsymbol{\psi}\right)\left[\boldsymbol{f}^{\times T}\boldsymbol{f}^{\times T}\left(-\boldsymbol{f}^{\times}\boldsymbol{\psi}\right)\right]^T \tag{18.186a}$$

$$= -\boldsymbol{f}^{\times}\left(\boldsymbol{\psi}^T\boldsymbol{f}^{\times}\boldsymbol{f}^{\times T}\boldsymbol{\psi}\right)^{-\frac{1}{2}} - \left(\boldsymbol{\psi}^T\boldsymbol{f}^{\times}\boldsymbol{f}^{\times T}\boldsymbol{\psi}\right)^{-\frac{3}{2}}\boldsymbol{f}^{\times}\boldsymbol{\psi}\boldsymbol{\psi}^T\boldsymbol{f}^{\times T}\boldsymbol{f}^{\times}\boldsymbol{f}^{\times} \tag{18.186b}$$

18.5 Quaternions

A quaternion is a 4D complex number, which may be used to represent rotations in 3D space. A thorough treatment of quaternions is given in [Dam et al., 1998].

Definition 18.40 (Quaternion)
A quaternion is defined to be a real number and three imaginary numbers. Typically a quaternion q is written as:

$$q = s + x\tilde{i} + y\tilde{j} + z\tilde{k}, \tag{18.187}$$

where $\tilde{i}$, $\tilde{j}$, and $\tilde{k}$ are the imaginary axes. Alternatively, the quaternion q may be written as

$$q = [s, \boldsymbol{v}] = [s, (x, y, z)] = [s, x, y, z]\,. \tag{18.188}$$

Definition 18.41 (Quaternion Product)
Two quaternions $q = [s, \boldsymbol{v}]$ and $q' = [s', \boldsymbol{v}']$ are multiplied with each other as follows:

$$qq' = \left[ss' - \boldsymbol{v}\cdot\boldsymbol{v}', s\boldsymbol{v}' + s'\boldsymbol{v} + \boldsymbol{v}\times\boldsymbol{v}'\right]. \tag{18.189}$$

Definition 18.42 (Conjugated Quaternion)
The conjugated quaternion of $q = [s, \boldsymbol{v}]$ is defined to be

$$q^* = [s, -\boldsymbol{v}]. \tag{18.190}$$

theorem 18.40 (Conjugate of a Product of Quaternions)
For the conjugated of the product of two quaternions: $q = [s, (x, y, z)]$ and $q' = [s', (x', y', z')]$ we have

$$(qq')^* = q'^*q^*. \tag{18.191}$$

Proof of Theorem 18.40:
We will prove the equality by straightforward computation of the left-hand side and the right-hand side. From the left-hand side we have

$$(qq')^* = \left[ss' - \boldsymbol{v} \cdot \boldsymbol{v}', s\boldsymbol{v}' + s'\boldsymbol{v} + \boldsymbol{v} \times \boldsymbol{v}'\right]^* \tag{18.192a}$$

$$= \left[ss' - \boldsymbol{v} \cdot \boldsymbol{v}', -s\boldsymbol{v}' - s'\boldsymbol{v} - \boldsymbol{v} \times \boldsymbol{v}'\right], \tag{18.192b}$$

and from the right-hand side we get

$$q'^* q^* = [s', -\boldsymbol{v}'][s, -\boldsymbol{v}] \tag{18.193a}$$

$$= [ss' - \boldsymbol{v} \cdot \boldsymbol{v}', -s'\boldsymbol{v} - s\boldsymbol{v}' + \boldsymbol{v}' \times \boldsymbol{v}] \tag{18.193b}$$

$$= [ss' - \boldsymbol{v} \cdot \boldsymbol{v}', -s'\boldsymbol{v} - s\boldsymbol{v}' - \boldsymbol{v} \times \boldsymbol{v}']. \tag{18.193c}$$

By comparison, we discover that the left-hand side is equal to the right-hand side. This completes our proof. □

Definition 18.43 (Inner Product of Quaternions)
The inner product between two quaternions $q = [s, (x, y, z)]$ *and* $q' = [s', (x', y', z')]$ *is defined as follows*

$$q \cdot q' = ss' + \boldsymbol{v} \cdot \boldsymbol{v}'. \tag{18.194}$$

Definition 18.44 (The Norm of a Quaternion)
The norm (or length) of a quaternion is defined by

$$\|q\| = \sqrt{q \cdot q} = \sqrt{qq^*}. \tag{18.195}$$

theorem 18.41 (An Unit Quaternion is a Rotation)
A quaternion, with norm equal to 1*, is called a unit quaternion. If we have the unit quaternion,*

$$q = [\cos\theta, \boldsymbol{n}\sin\theta], \tag{18.196}$$

then it represents a rotation of 2θ *radians around the normalized axis* $\boldsymbol{n}$*.*

theorem 18.42 (Quaternion Rotation)
Given $p = [0, \boldsymbol{r}]$ *and a unit quaternion* $q = [\cos\theta, \boldsymbol{n}\sin\theta]$*, then the rotation of* p *is given by,*

$$p' = qpq^* \tag{18.197}$$

where p' *is* p *rotated by* 2θ *radians around the axis* $\boldsymbol{n}$*.*

theorem 18.43 (Compound Rotations)
Given $p = [0, \boldsymbol{r}]$ *and two unit quaternions* q *and* q'*, then the rotation of* p *first by* q *and then with* q' *is given by the quaternion*

$$r = q'q \tag{18.198}$$

The theorem states that composition of rotations is equivalent to product of quaternions.

Proof of Theorem 18.43:
From Theorem 18.42 we have:

$$p' = qpq^* \tag{18.199}$$

now p' must be rotated by q', using the same theorem yields:

$$\begin{aligned} p'' &= q'p'q'^* && (18.200a)\\ &= q'(qpq^*)q'^* && (18.200b)\\ &= (q'q)p(q'q)^* && (18.200c)\\ &= rpr^* && (18.200d) \end{aligned}$$

which is what we wanted to prove. □

theorem 18.44 (Conversion from Rotation Matrix to Quaternion)
Given a rotation matrix, $\boldsymbol{M}$, then the corresponding quaternion $q = [s, (x, y, z)]$ is given by:

$$\begin{aligned} s &= \frac{1}{2}\sqrt{\boldsymbol{M}_{11} + \boldsymbol{M}_{22} + \boldsymbol{M}_{33} + 1} && (18.201a)\\ x &= \frac{\boldsymbol{M}_{32} + \boldsymbol{M}_{23}}{4s} && (18.201b)\\ y &= \frac{\boldsymbol{M}_{13} + \boldsymbol{M}_{31}}{4s} && (18.201c)\\ z &= \frac{\boldsymbol{M}_{21} + \boldsymbol{M}_{12}}{4s} && (18.201d) \end{aligned}$$

If the rotation angle is π radians (180 degrees) then the value of the trace of the rotation matrix is -1. This means that the value of s will be zero, and it will become impossible to compute the x, y, and z values.

If the conversion is done on a computer then one would also have to consider the numerical inaccuracies as the trace of the rotation matrix gets close to -1.

theorem 18.45 (Conversion from Quaternion to Rotation Matrix)
Given a unit quaternion $q = [s, (x, y, z)]$, the corresponding rotation matrix is:

$$\boldsymbol{M} = \begin{pmatrix} 1 - 2(y^2 + z^2) & 2xy - 2sz & 2sy + 2xz \\ 2xy + 2sz & 1 - 2(x^2 + z^2) & -2sx + 2yz \\ -2sy + 2xz & 2sx + 2yz & 1 - 2(x^2 + y^2) \end{pmatrix} \tag{18.202}$$

theorem 18.46 (The Time Derivative of the Quaternion)
Given a body with an orientation represented by the rotation $q(t_0)$, and an angular velocity of $\boldsymbol{\omega}(t)$, then the time derivative of the orientation is given by:

$$\dot{q}(t_0) = \frac{1}{2}[0, \boldsymbol{\omega}(t_0)]q(t_0) \tag{18.203}$$

Using $\omega = [0, \boldsymbol{\omega}(t_0)]$, this can be written as:

$$\dot{q} = \frac{1}{2}\omega q \tag{18.204}$$

Proof of Theorem 18.46:
The angular velocity $\omega(t)$ means that the body rotates $\|\omega(t)\|_2$ radians per second around the axis given by $\frac{\omega(t)}{\|\omega(t)\|_2}$. After Δt seconds the body must be rotated by:

$$r(t) = [\cos \frac{\|\omega(t)\|_2 \Delta t}{2}, \frac{\omega(t)}{\|\omega(t)\|_2} \sin \frac{\|\omega(t)\|_2 \Delta t}{2}] \tag{18.205}$$

Where Δt is some infinitely small value, such that we can assume that the angular acceleration is effectively constant. The orientation of the body after Δt seconds must then be:

$$q(t_0 + \Delta t) = r(t_0)q(t_0) \tag{18.206}$$

If we substitute $t = t_0 + \Delta t$ and the expression for $r(t_0)$, then we have the following equation for the orientation of the body:

$$q(t) = [\cos \frac{\|\omega(t_0)\|_2 (t - t_0)}{2}, \frac{\omega(t_0)}{\|\omega(t_0)\|_2} \sin \frac{\|\omega(t_0)\|_2 (t - t_0)}{2}]q(t_0) \tag{18.207}$$

Now all we need to do is to differentiate this equation with respect to time and remember to evaluate the final expression at time $t = t_0$ (this is essentially the same as taking the limit of $q(t_0 + \Delta t) - q(t_0)$ as Δt goes to zero). Doing so yields:

$$\dot{q}(t) = \frac{d}{dt}\left([\cos \frac{\|\omega(t_0)\|_2 (t - t_0)}{2}, \sin \frac{\|\omega(t_0)\|_2 (t - t_0)}{2} \frac{\omega(t_0)}{\|\omega(t_0)\|_2}]q(t_0)\right) \tag{18.208a}$$

$$= \frac{d}{dt}\left([\cos \frac{\|\omega(t_0)\|_2 (t - t_0)}{2}, \sin \frac{\|\omega(t_0)\|_2 (t - t_0)}{2} \frac{\omega(t_0)}{\|\omega(t_0)\|_2}]\right) q(t_0) \tag{18.208b}$$

$$= \left[\frac{d}{dt}\left(\cos \frac{\|\omega(t_0)\|_2 (t - t_0)}{2}\right), \frac{d}{dt}\left(\sin \frac{\|\omega(t_0)\|_2 (t - t_0)}{2} \frac{\omega(t_0)}{\|\omega(t_0)\|_2}\right)\right] q(t_0) \tag{18.208c}$$

$$= \left[-\frac{\|\omega(t_0)\|_2}{2} \sin \frac{\|\omega(t_0)\|_2 (t - t_0)}{2}, \frac{\|\omega(t_0)\|_2}{2} \cos \frac{\|\omega(t_0)\|_2 (t - t_0)}{2} \frac{\omega(t_0)}{\|\omega(t_0)\|_2}\right] q(t_0) \tag{18.208d}$$

$$= \left[-\frac{\|\omega(t_0)\|_2}{2} \sin 0, \frac{\|\omega(t_0)\|_2}{2} \cos 0 \frac{\omega(t_0)}{\|\omega(t_0)\|_2}\right] q(t_0) \tag{18.208e}$$

$$= \left[0, \frac{\|\omega(t_0)\|_2}{2} \frac{\omega(t_0)}{\|\omega(t_0)\|_2}\right] q(t_0) \tag{18.208f}$$

$$= \frac{1}{2} [0, \omega(t_0)]\, q(t_0) \tag{18.208g}$$

This completes the proof. □

theorem 18.47 (Quaternion Matrix)

$$\frac{1}{2}\boldsymbol{\omega}_i q_i = \boldsymbol{Q}_i \boldsymbol{\omega}_i, \tag{18.209}$$

where

$$\boldsymbol{Q}_i = \frac{1}{2}\begin{bmatrix} -x_i & -y_i & -z_i \\ s_i & z_i & -y_i \\ -z_i & s_i & x_i \\ y_i & -x_i & s_i \end{bmatrix}. \tag{18.210}$$

Proof of Theorem 18.47:
Let us start by writing the quaternion product rule, for two quaternions $q = [s, \boldsymbol{v}]$ and $q' = [s', \boldsymbol{v}']$,

$$qq' = \left[ss' - \boldsymbol{v} \cdot \boldsymbol{v}', s\boldsymbol{v}' + s'\boldsymbol{v} + \boldsymbol{v} \times \boldsymbol{v}'\right]. \tag{18.211}$$

We will now use this product rule on the left side of (18.209), and we get

$$\frac{1}{2}\boldsymbol{\omega}_i q_i = \frac{1}{2}[0, \boldsymbol{\omega}_i][s_i, \boldsymbol{v}_i] \tag{18.212a}$$

$$= \frac{1}{2}[0s_i - \boldsymbol{\omega}_i \cdot \boldsymbol{v}_i, 0\boldsymbol{v}_i + s_i\boldsymbol{\omega}_i + \boldsymbol{\omega}_i \times \boldsymbol{v}_i] \tag{18.212b}$$

$$= \frac{1}{2}[-\boldsymbol{v}_i \cdot \boldsymbol{\omega}_i, s_i\boldsymbol{\omega}_i - \boldsymbol{v}_i \times \boldsymbol{\omega}_i] \tag{18.212c}$$

$$= \frac{1}{2}\left[-\boldsymbol{v}_i^T\boldsymbol{\omega}_i, \begin{bmatrix} s_i & 0 & 0 \\ 0 & s_i & 0 \\ 0 & 0 & s_i \end{bmatrix}\boldsymbol{\omega}_i - \boldsymbol{v}_i{}^{\times}\boldsymbol{\omega}_i\right] \tag{18.212d}$$

We are now almost finished. We only have to remember that $\boldsymbol{v}_i = [x_i, y_i, z_i]^T$ and use the definition of the cross product matrix (18.65), this yields

$$\frac{1}{2}\boldsymbol{\omega}_i q_i = \frac{1}{2}\left[\begin{bmatrix} -x_i & -y_i & -z_i \end{bmatrix}, \left(\begin{bmatrix} s_i & 0 & 0 \\ 0 & s_i & 0 \\ 0 & 0 & s_i \end{bmatrix} - \begin{bmatrix} 0 & -z_i & y_i \\ z_i & 0 & -x_i \\ -y_i & x_i & 0 \end{bmatrix}\right)\right]\boldsymbol{\omega}_i \tag{18.213a}$$

$$= \frac{1}{2}\begin{bmatrix} -x_i & -y_i & -z_i \\ s_i & z_i & -y_i \\ -z_i & s_i & x_i \\ y_i & -x_i & s_i \end{bmatrix}\boldsymbol{\omega}_i \tag{18.213b}$$

Comparing this with the (18.210) for $\boldsymbol{Q}_i$ we conclude that

$$\frac{1}{2}\boldsymbol{\omega}_i q_i = \boldsymbol{Q}_i \boldsymbol{\omega}_i. \tag{18.214}$$

We have proved what we wanted. □

19

Solving Linear Systems of Equations

Often in physics-based animation, we have to solve sets of linear equations. Popular sources for algorithms are [Press et al., 1999a, Golub et al., 1996], which we follow in this chapter.

A *linear set of equations* may be written as

$$a_{11}r_1 + a_{12}r_2 + \cdots + a_{1N}r_N = b_1, \tag{19.1a}$$

$$a_{21}r_1 + a_{22}r_2 + \cdots + a_{2N}r_N = b_2, \tag{19.1b}$$

$$\vdots$$

$$a_{M1}r_1 + a_{M2}r_2 + \cdots + a_{MN}r_N = b_M, \tag{19.1c}$$

or in matrix form as

$$\boldsymbol{A}\boldsymbol{r} = \boldsymbol{b}, \tag{19.2}$$

where $\boldsymbol{A} = \{a_{ij}\} \in \mathbb{R}^{N\times M}$, $\boldsymbol{r} = [r_1, r_2, \ldots, r_N]^T$, and $\boldsymbol{b} = [b_1, b_2, \ldots, b_N]^T$. The typical situation is that $\boldsymbol{A}$ and $\boldsymbol{b}$ are given, and that we wish to solve for $\boldsymbol{r}$. As an example, consider the equations

$$2r_1 + 4r_2 = 4, \tag{19.3a}$$

$$-3r_1 + r_2 = 2, \tag{19.3b}$$

which are shown in Figure 19.1. The solution is the point where the lines cross at $[-2/7, 8/7]^T$.

When $M < N$ there are fewer equations than unknowns, and the system cannot be solved without extra constraints. In the case that $M = N$, there exists a solution as long as $\det \boldsymbol{A} \neq 0$ (see Definition 18.23 for a definition of the determinant). If $\det \boldsymbol{A} = 0$, then the system is degenerated and can be reduced to yield a system of equations with fewer than M equations. Numerically speaking, the determinant may be near the round-off error, and is thus considered as a degenerated system of equations. In the case that $M > N$, then the system is over constrained and there is typically not an exact solution, in which case only an approximation may be found, which minimizes $E(\boldsymbol{r}) = \|\boldsymbol{A}\boldsymbol{r} - \boldsymbol{b}\|$.

In the following, we will assume that $M = N$ and that $\det \boldsymbol{A} \neq 0$. The conceptually simplest method for solving for $\boldsymbol{r}$ in (19.2) is to invert $\boldsymbol{A}$ and apply it on both sides of the equation

$$\boldsymbol{r} = \boldsymbol{A}^{-1}\boldsymbol{b}. \tag{19.4}$$

19.1 Gauss Elimination

Gauss elimination is a method for inverting the matrix, in which case it is also referred to as *Gauss-Jordan elimination*, and when followed by *back substitution* may be used to solve a system of linear equations

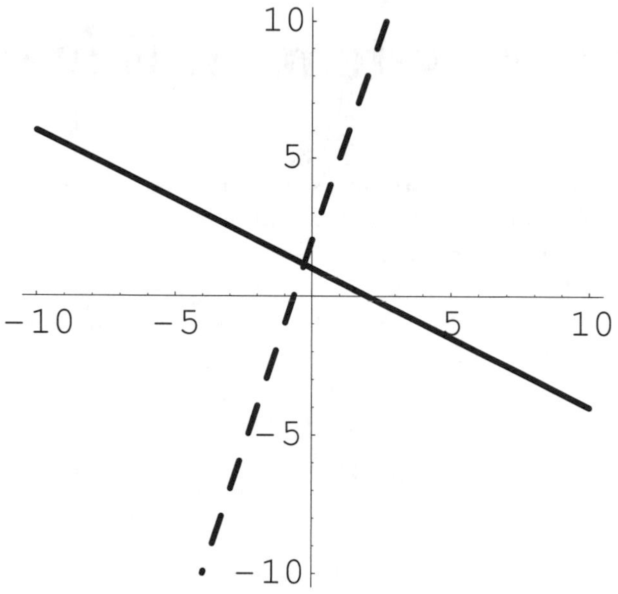

Figure 19.1: Two lines given by the implicit equations in (19.3a)—solid and (19.3b)—dashed.

directly. It is often used as an introductory method, although it neither is the most memory conserving nor the fastest method.

For Gauss elimination we just consider a system of equations, $\boldsymbol{A}\boldsymbol{r} = \boldsymbol{b}$, while for Gauss-Jordan elimination, the system (19.2) is augmented with the inverse matrix $\boldsymbol{C} = \boldsymbol{A}^{-1}$, such that $\boldsymbol{A}\boldsymbol{C} = \boldsymbol{A}\boldsymbol{A}^{-1} = \mathbf{1}$, where $\mathbf{1}$ is the identity matrix. We write as follows:

$$\boldsymbol{A}\left[\boldsymbol{r} \mid \boldsymbol{C}\right] = \left[\boldsymbol{b} \mid \mathbf{1}\right] \tag{19.5a}$$

$$\begin{bmatrix} a_{11} & a_{12} & \dots & a_{1N} \\ a_{21} & a_{22} & \dots & a_{2N} \\ \vdots & & \ddots & \\ a_{N1} & a_{N2} & \dots & a_{NN} \end{bmatrix} \begin{bmatrix} r_1 & c_{11} & c_{12} & \dots & c_{1N} \\ r_2 & c_{21} & c_{22} & \dots & c_{2N} \\ \vdots & & & \ddots & \\ r_N & c_{N1} & c_{N2} & \dots & c_{NN} \end{bmatrix} = \begin{bmatrix} b_1 & 1 & 0 & \dots & 0 \\ b_2 & 0 & 1 & \dots & 0 \\ \vdots & & & \ddots & \\ b_N & 0 & 0 & \dots & 1 \end{bmatrix} \tag{19.5b}$$

Gauss elimination and Gauss-Jordan elimination rely on the same process of reordering information in the above equation without destroying its solution, such that the coefficients in $\boldsymbol{A}$ are replaced with an identity matrix, in which case $\boldsymbol{C}$ will be replaced with $\boldsymbol{A}^{-1}$ and $\boldsymbol{r}$ will contain the solution to the system. The system on form (19.5) may be rearranged in three different ways without destroying the solution to (19.2):

Interchange two rows in $\boldsymbol{A}$:

Since $\boldsymbol{A}\boldsymbol{r} = \boldsymbol{b}$ and $\boldsymbol{A}\boldsymbol{C} = \mathbf{1}$ are decoupled in (19.5), we realize that interchanging two rows in $\boldsymbol{A}$ requires that the corresponding rows in both $\boldsymbol{b}$ and $\mathbf{1}$ are interchanged, and amounts to writing the original equations in a different order. As an example, interchanging rows one and two is equivalent to writing the system of equations as

$$a_{21}r_1 + a_{22}r_2 + \cdots + a_{2N}r_N = b_2, \tag{19.6a}$$

$$a_{11}r_1 + a_{12}r_2 + \cdots + a_{1N}r_N = b_1, \tag{19.6b}$$

$$\vdots$$

$$a_{N1}r_1 + a_{N2}r_2 + \cdots + a_{NN}r_N = b_N, \tag{19.6c}$$

which clearly does not change its solution. The same argument holds for $\boldsymbol{AC} = \boldsymbol{1}$.

Interchange two columns in A:
Interchanging two columns in $\boldsymbol{A}$ implies that the corresponding rows in $\boldsymbol{r}$ and $\boldsymbol{C}$ must be interchanged. As an example, interchanging columns one and two is equivalent to writing the system of equations as

$$a_{12}r_2 + a_{11}r_1 + \cdots + a_{1N}r_N = b_1, \tag{19.7a}$$

$$a_{22}r_2 + a_{21}r_1 + \cdots + a_{2N}r_N = b_2, \tag{19.7b}$$

$$\vdots$$

$$a_{N2}r_2 + a_{N1}r_1 + \cdots + a_{NN}r_N = b_N, \tag{19.7c}$$

which clearly does not change its solution. The same argument holds for $\boldsymbol{AC} = \boldsymbol{1}$. However, in contrast to the interchanging of rows, the first element of the solution in $\boldsymbol{r}$ is now to be found on position two, hence, we need to track the interchanging of columns in order to unscramble the final solution to the original ordering.

Replace a row in A with the linear combination of itself with any other row in A:
Replacing a row in $\boldsymbol{A}$ with the linear combination of itself with any other row in $\boldsymbol{A}$ will not destroy the solution as long as the same linear combination is performed on the same rows in $\boldsymbol{b}$ and $\boldsymbol{1}$. When using $\boldsymbol{A}_{i*}$ to denote the i'th row in $\boldsymbol{A}$, we may, as an example, replace row two with $\boldsymbol{A}_{2*} - \frac{a_{21}}{a_{11}}\boldsymbol{A}_{1*}$, which is equivalent to replacing the second equation in (19.1) with

$$(a_{21}r_1 + a_{22}r_2 + \cdots + (a_{2N})r_N) - \frac{a_{21}}{a_{11}}(a_{11}r_1 + a_{12}r_2 + \cdots + a_{1N}r_N) = b_1 - \frac{a_{21}}{a_{11}}b_2, \tag{19.8a}$$

$$\Downarrow$$

$$\left(a_{21} - \frac{a_{21}}{a_{11}}a_{11}\right)r_1 + \left(a_{22} - \frac{a_{21}}{a_{11}}a_{12}\right)r_2 + \cdots + \left(a_{2N} - \frac{a_{21}}{a_{11}}a_{1N}\right)r_N = b_1 - \frac{a_{21}}{a_{11}}b_2, \tag{19.8b}$$

$$\Downarrow$$

$$\left(a_{22} - \frac{a_{21}}{a_{11}}a_{12}\right)r_2 + \cdots + \left(a_{2N} - \frac{a_{21}}{a_{11}}a_{1N}\right)r_N = b_1 - \frac{a_{21}}{a_{11}}b_2. \tag{19.8c}$$

The same argument holds for $\boldsymbol{AC} = \mathbf{1}$.

In (19.8), we see that the dependency on the first equation in the second equation may be factored out. This is the essence of elimination; that is, if we first eliminate the dependency on the first equation in equations $2 \ldots N$, then we may eliminate the dependency on the resulting second equation in resulting $3 \ldots N$ equations and recurse until we have obtained an equation of the form

$$\boldsymbol{Ur} = \boldsymbol{b}', \tag{19.9}$$

where $\boldsymbol{U} = \{u_{ij}\}$ is an upper triangular matrix, that is,

$$u_{11}r_1 + u_{12}r_2 + \cdots + u_{1N}r_N = b'_1, \tag{19.10a}$$

$$u_{22}r_2 + \cdots + u_{2N}r_N = b'_2, \tag{19.10b}$$

$$\vdots$$

$$u_{NN}r_N = b'_N, \tag{19.10c}$$

for Gauss elimination or with the added and reordered matrices $\boldsymbol{C}'$ and $\mathbf{1}'$ for Gauss-Jordan.

For Gauss-Jordan elimination, the reordered matrix $\boldsymbol{C}$ is now equal to the inverse of $\boldsymbol{A}$, and we may thus use this to compute the solution for $\boldsymbol{r}$. In the case of Gauss elimination, we may perform *back substitution*, as follows: the last equation in (19.10) is to solve for $r_N = \frac{b'_N}{u_{NN}}$, which in turn may be use to solve for $r_{N-1} = \frac{b'_{N-1} - u_{NN}r_N}{u_{(N-1)N}}$, and recursively for the rest of $\boldsymbol{r}$.

Both the Gauss-elimination and the Gauss-Jordan elimination are numerically unstable, since if the leading coefficient of the term to be eliminated is zero, then elimination is impossible; that is, elimination will fail in (19.8) if $a_{11} = 0$ or close to the round-off error. The solution is to perform a *pivot*; that is, interchange rows and/or columns to avoid such a situation. Although not completely safe, it is usually enough to interchange rows such that the equation with the largest leading coefficient is to be eliminated in the remaining equations.

19.2 LU Decomposition

Any matrix $\boldsymbol{A}$ may be factorized into two triangular matrices,

$$\boldsymbol{LU} = \boldsymbol{A} \tag{19.11}$$

such that $\boldsymbol{L}$ and $\boldsymbol{U}$ are lower and upper triangular matrices,

$$\boldsymbol{L} = \begin{bmatrix} l_{11} & 0 & 0 & \dots & 0 \\ l_{21} & l_{22} & 0 & \dots & 0 \\ \vdots & & & \ddots & \\ l_{N1} & l_{N2} & l_{N3} & \dots & l_{NN} \end{bmatrix}, \tag{19.12a}$$

$$\boldsymbol{U} = \begin{bmatrix} u_{11} & u_{12} & u_{13} & \dots & u_{NN} \\ 0 & u_{22} & u_{23} & \dots & u_{2N} \\ \vdots & & & \ddots & \\ 0 & 0 & 0 & \dots & u_{NN} \end{bmatrix}. \tag{19.12b}$$

This is known as *LU decomposition*. Using LU decomposition, we may solve (19.2) by *back substitution* in two steps. That is, write (19.2) as

$$\boldsymbol{L}\boldsymbol{U}\boldsymbol{r} = \boldsymbol{b}, \tag{19.13a}$$

$$\Downarrow$$

$$\boldsymbol{L}\boldsymbol{p} = \boldsymbol{b} \tag{19.13b}$$

where

$$\boldsymbol{p} = \boldsymbol{U}\boldsymbol{r}. \tag{19.14}$$

That is, using forward substitution, which is equivalent to back substitution, may be used first to solve for p in (19.13b) and then back substitution may be used to solve for $\boldsymbol{r}$ in (19.14).

The triangular matrices $\boldsymbol{L}$ and $\boldsymbol{U}$ contain $N^2 + N$ unknowns, while $\boldsymbol{A}$ only has N^2 coefficients, since the diagonal is nonzero in both $\boldsymbol{L}$ and $\boldsymbol{U}$. As a consequence, we must find further N equations to solve for $\boldsymbol{L}$ and $\boldsymbol{U}$ in (19.11). In *Crout's algorithm*

[Press et al., 1999a, p. 44] $l_{ii} = 1$ is used, in which case the coefficient a_{ij} may be written as

$$a_{ij} = l_{i*}u_{*j}. \tag{19.15}$$

```
algorithm Crout(A)
  N = size(A)
  L = zeros(N,N)
  U = zeros(N,N)
  for i=1:N
    L(i,i) = 1;
  for j=1:N
    for i=1:j
      U(i,j) = A(i,j) - L(i,1:i-1)*U(1:i-1,j)
    for i=j+1:N
      L(i,j) = (A(i,j) - L(i,1:j-1)*U(1:j-1,j))
  end
end
```

Figure 19.2: Pseudocode for Crout's algorithm for LU decomposition without pivot.

Examining the first few coefficients, we find that

$$a_{11} = l_{11}u_{11} = u_{11}, \tag{19.16a}$$
$$a_{12} = l_{11}u_{12} = u_{12}, \tag{19.16b}$$
$$\vdots$$
$$a_{21} = l_{21}u_{11}, \tag{19.16c}$$
$$a_{22} = l_{21}u_{12} + l_{22}u_{22} = l_{21}u_{12} + u_{22}, \tag{19.16d}$$
$$a_{23} = l_{21}u_{13} + l_{22}u_{23} = l_{21}u_{13} + u_{23}, \tag{19.16e}$$
$$\vdots$$
$$a_{31} = l_{31}u_{11}, \tag{19.16f}$$
$$a_{32} = l_{31}u_{12} + l_{32}u_{22}, \tag{19.16g}$$
$$a_{33} = l_{31}u_{13} + l_{32}u_{23} + l_{33}u_{33} = l_{31}u_{13} + l_{32}u_{23} + u_{33}, \tag{19.16h}$$
$$a_{34} = l_{31}u_{14} + l_{32}u_{24} + l_{33}u_{34} = l_{31}u_{14} + l_{32}u_{24} + u_{34}, \tag{19.16i}$$
$$\vdots$$

Thus, we may use a_{1*} to solve for u_{1*} in (19.16a), (19.16b), etc., and using this knowledge we may solve for l_{*1} in (19.16c), (19.16f), etc. We now only need to determine the coefficients of $\boldsymbol{L}$ and $\boldsymbol{U}$ in the $(2 \ldots N) \times (2 \ldots N)$ submatrices. In (19.16d) we realize that the coefficients l_{21} and u_{12} are now known. Hence, we may solve for u_{22}, and likewise we may solve for u_{23} in (19.16e) and the remaining coefficients in u_{2*}. Having u_{1*}, l_{*1}, and u_{2*} we may solve for l_{*2} in (19.16g) etc., and we thus only need to determine the coefficients of $\boldsymbol{L}$ and $\boldsymbol{U}$ in the $(3 \ldots N) \times (3 \ldots N)$ submatrices, and the remaining coefficients follow by induction. This is the basis of Crout's algorithm, which is shown in Figure 19.2. Pivoting is also part of Crout's algorithm and is discussed, for example, in [Press et al., 1999a, p. 46]; however, we will omit this for clarity.

In the special case when $\boldsymbol{A}$ is symmetric and positive-definite, (see Section 18.2 for a definition), then we may write

$$\boldsymbol{L}\boldsymbol{L}^T = A \tag{19.17}$$

and the LU-decomposition becomes particularly simple, since the last loop in Figure 19.2 is not needed because of the symmetry. This is known as *Choleski decomposition*, and it can be shown that Cholesky decomposition is very stable and needs no pivoting.

19.3 Singular Value Decomposition

Singular value decomposition (*SVD*) is a method for solving for $\boldsymbol{r}$ in

$$\boldsymbol{A}\boldsymbol{r} = \boldsymbol{b}, \tag{19.18}$$

when $\boldsymbol{r} \in \mathbb{R}^n$, $\boldsymbol{b} \in \mathbb{R}^m$, and $\boldsymbol{A} \in \mathbb{R}^{m \times n}, m \geq n$ is singular or close to singular. The fact that $m \geq n$ implies that there are more equations than unknown, in which case the system is called and *over-constrained system*.

Any matrix $\boldsymbol{A} \in \mathbb{R}^{m \times n}, m \geq n$ can be written on the following form:

$$\boldsymbol{A} = \boldsymbol{U}\boldsymbol{D}\boldsymbol{V}^T, \tag{19.19}$$

where $\boldsymbol{D} \in \mathbb{R}^{n \times n}$ is a diagonal matrix, and where $\boldsymbol{U} \in \mathbb{R}^{m \times n}$ and $\boldsymbol{V} \in \mathbb{R}^{n \times n}$ are both orthogonal, i.e., their column vectors form an orthonormal basis. For these reasons, the inverse of $\boldsymbol{A}$ is immediately found to be

$$\boldsymbol{A}^{-1} = \boldsymbol{V}\boldsymbol{D}^{-1}\boldsymbol{U}^T, \tag{19.20}$$

where $\left(\boldsymbol{D}^{-1}\right)_{ii} = \frac{1}{d_{ii}}$. However, when $\boldsymbol{A}$ is singular or close to singular, then there will be diagonal elements d_{ii}, which are close to zero, and $\boldsymbol{D}^{-1}$ will have diagonal values that are near infinity. Singularity of $\boldsymbol{A}$ means that there are areas in $\Omega \subseteq \mathbb{R}^n$, where $\boldsymbol{A}\tilde{\boldsymbol{r}} = 0, \tilde{\boldsymbol{r}} \in \Omega$. The set Ω is called the *nullspace*. A consequence is that $\tilde{\boldsymbol{r}}$ may be added to any given solution $\boldsymbol{r} \notin \Omega$, while still fulfilling the equation,

$$\boldsymbol{A}\left(\boldsymbol{r} + \tilde{\boldsymbol{r}}\right) = \boldsymbol{A}\boldsymbol{r} = \boldsymbol{b}, \tag{19.21}$$

The implication is that the solution is undetermined, and we must choose a value. There are two cases to consider: either $\boldsymbol{b}$ is reachable for some $\boldsymbol{r}$, in which case $\boldsymbol{b}$ is said to be in the range of $\boldsymbol{A}$, or otherwise there is no $\boldsymbol{r}$ which solves the system. In both cases, the choice by singular value decomposition is to set $\frac{1}{d_{ii}} = 0$ in (19.20), when $d_{ii} \simeq 0$. When $\boldsymbol{b}$ is in the range of $\boldsymbol{A}$, this is equivalent to picking the value of $\boldsymbol{r}$, which minimizes $\|\boldsymbol{r}\|_2$. When $\boldsymbol{b}$ is not in the range of $\boldsymbol{A}$, this is equivalent to picking $\boldsymbol{r}$ which minimizes $\|\boldsymbol{A}\boldsymbol{r} - \boldsymbol{b}\|_2$. See [Press et al., 1999a, p. 62] for a simple proof. An algorithm for computing the singular value decomposition is given in [Golub et al., 1996, Section 8.6].

19.4 Linear Least Squares

A method related to singular value decomposition is the method of *linear least squares*, which as singular value decomposition seeks the minimum of

$$\boldsymbol{r}^* = \arg\min_{\boldsymbol{r}} \|\boldsymbol{A}\boldsymbol{r} - \boldsymbol{b}\|_2^2 . \tag{19.22}$$

The origin of the linear least square problem is fitting: given a set of data-values $\{x_j, y_j\}, j = 1 \ldots m$, we wish to find the parameters $\boldsymbol{a} \in \mathbb{R}^m$ of a function f such as the coefficients of the polynomial

$$f(\boldsymbol{a}, x) = \sum_{i=1}^{m} a_i x^{i-1}, \tag{19.23}$$

which minimizes the quadratic distance

$$\boldsymbol{a}^* = \arg\min_{\boldsymbol{a}} \sum_{j=1}^{n} \left(\frac{f(\boldsymbol{a}, x_j) - y_j}{\sigma_j} \right)^2 . \tag{19.24}$$

The coefficients σ_j are a measure of error on the j'th data-value, and if nothing is known or presupposed, then $\sigma_j = 1$. We will assume in the following that $\sigma_j = 1$. In general, $\boldsymbol{y}_j, \boldsymbol{f}, \boldsymbol{x} \in \mathbb{R}^n$ are vector functions, in which case we write

$$\boldsymbol{f}(x) = \sum_{i=1}^{m} a_i \boldsymbol{x}_i(x) = \boldsymbol{X}_x \boldsymbol{a}, \tag{19.25}$$

where $\boldsymbol{x}_i(x)$ are any functions but often form an orthonormal basis. Since we give m data values, we can at most determine m parameters, hence, $\boldsymbol{a} \in \mathbb{R}^m$ and we may fix $\boldsymbol{X} = \boldsymbol{x}_i(x_j), \boldsymbol{X} \in \mathbb{R}^{n \times m}$, which is called *design matrix*. Thus, our minimization problem is reduced to

$$\boldsymbol{a}^* = \arg\min_{\boldsymbol{a}} \|\boldsymbol{X}\boldsymbol{a} - \boldsymbol{y}\|_2^2 , \tag{19.26}$$

and we find complete resemblance with the singular value decomposition method. Minimum is obtained when

$$\frac{\partial \|\boldsymbol{X}\boldsymbol{a} - \boldsymbol{y}\|_2^2}{\partial \boldsymbol{a}} = 0. \tag{19.27}$$

To obtain the partial derivative we first rewrite the squared Euclidean norm

$$\|\boldsymbol{X}\boldsymbol{a} - \boldsymbol{y}\|_2^2 = (\boldsymbol{X}\boldsymbol{a} - \boldsymbol{y})^T (\boldsymbol{X}\boldsymbol{a} - \boldsymbol{y}) \tag{19.28a}$$

$$= \boldsymbol{a}^T \boldsymbol{X}^T \boldsymbol{X}\boldsymbol{a} - \boldsymbol{a}^T \boldsymbol{X}^T \boldsymbol{y} - \boldsymbol{y}^T \boldsymbol{X}\boldsymbol{a} - \boldsymbol{y}^T \boldsymbol{y} \tag{19.28b}$$

$$= \boldsymbol{a}^T \boldsymbol{X}^T \boldsymbol{X}\boldsymbol{a} - 2\boldsymbol{y}^T \boldsymbol{X}\boldsymbol{a} - \boldsymbol{y}^T \boldsymbol{y}, \tag{19.28c}$$

using $a^T X^T y = y^T X a$, since scalars are invariant to the transpose operator. Following Chapter 18.3.1, we perform the mechanical exercise of calculating the *differential* in order to evaluate (19.27):

$$\begin{aligned} d\,\|Xa - y\|_2^2 &= d\left(a^T X^T X a - 2y^T X a - y^T y\right) && (19.29a)\\ &= \left(da^T\right) X^T X a + a^T \left(dX^T\right) X a + a^T X^T \left(dX\right) a + a^T X^T X\, da \\ &\quad - 2\left(\left(dy^T\right) X a + y^T \left(dX\right) a + y^T X\, da\right) \\ &\quad - \left(\left(dy^T\right) y + y^T\, dy\right). && (19.29b) \end{aligned}$$

We are only interested in the linear terms involving da, and using sloppy notation, we write

$$\begin{aligned} \frac{\partial\,\|Xa - y\|_2^2}{\partial a} &= \frac{\left(da^T\right) X^T X a + a^T X^T X\, da - 2y^T X\, da}{da} && (19.30a)\\ &= 2a^T X^T X - 2y^T X, && (19.30b) \end{aligned}$$

where we again made use of the invariance of scalars to the transpose operator. The coefficients a that optimize (19.26) are found by solving $a^T X^T X - y^T X = 0$, or equivalently by rearrangement and application of the transpose operator

$$X^T X a = X^T y. \tag{19.31}$$

This may be solved using Gauss-elimination. The matrix $X^T X$ is positive-definite hence invertible, and this is often written as $a = \left(X^T X\right)^{-1} X^T y$, where the matrix $\left(X^T X\right)^{-1} X^T$ is known as the *pseudoinverse*, and the system may be solved using Cholesky decomposition.

19.5 The Jacobi and Gauss-Seidel Methods

Iterative methods for solving linear systems of equations are often rejected in the classical literature because they converge very slowly toward an accurate solution. In animation, high precision is most often not a major concern, and the iterative solutions are favored, since they very quickly produce solutions that are sufficiently accurate for typical animation problems.

An iterative method can be stated as

$$r^{\,k+1} = f(r^{\,k}), \tag{19.32}$$

where the superscript k denotes the iteration. The iteration is continued until a fixed point is reached,

$$r^{\,*} = f(r^{\,*}). \tag{19.33}$$

Here, $r^{\,*}$ is a solution, and the limit of the sequence $\left\{r^{\,0}, r^{\,1}, \ldots, r^{\,*}\right\}$. Converges will be discussed later in Section 19.7. Iterative methods are very effective for solving large sparse matrix systems of the form (19.2). The first step to bring such a system onto the form of (19.32) is to decompose A into a sum of three matrices: a strictly lower matrix L, a diagonal matrix D, and a strictly upper matrix U, such that

$$A = L + D + U. \tag{19.34}$$

This implies that

$$(\boldsymbol{L} + \boldsymbol{D} + \boldsymbol{U})\,\boldsymbol{r} = \boldsymbol{b}, \tag{19.35a}$$
$$\Downarrow$$
$$\boldsymbol{D}\boldsymbol{r} = \boldsymbol{b} - (\boldsymbol{L} + \boldsymbol{U})\,\boldsymbol{r}. \tag{19.35b}$$

As long as $\boldsymbol{A}$ and hence $\boldsymbol{D}$ have nonzero diagonal elements, we can invert $\boldsymbol{D}$ and write

$$\boldsymbol{r} = \boldsymbol{D}^{-1}\boldsymbol{b} - \boldsymbol{D}^{-1}(\boldsymbol{L} + \boldsymbol{U})\,\boldsymbol{r}, \tag{19.36a}$$
$$\Downarrow$$
$$\boldsymbol{r} = \boldsymbol{c} + \boldsymbol{T}\boldsymbol{r}, \tag{19.36b}$$

where $\boldsymbol{c} = \boldsymbol{D}^{-1}\boldsymbol{b}$, and $\boldsymbol{T} = -\boldsymbol{D}^{-1}(\boldsymbol{L} + \boldsymbol{U})$. Thus we have found a linear equation of (19.2) on the form (19.33). If the vector $\boldsymbol{r}$ is a solution to the system, then (19.36) is on a fixed point. If $\boldsymbol{r}$ is not a solution, we may use (19.36) as an update rule by imposing an iteration number as

$$\boldsymbol{r}^{k+1} = \boldsymbol{c} + \boldsymbol{T}\boldsymbol{r}^{k}, \tag{19.37}$$

All iterative methods on this form are called stationary iterative methods, if neither the matrix $\boldsymbol{T}$ nor the vector $\boldsymbol{c}$ depend upon the iteration count k. In the following, we will treat stationary methods and defer nonstationary methods until Section 19.9.

Since $\boldsymbol{D}$ is a diagonal matrix, then $\boldsymbol{D}^{-1}$ is also diagonal, and it is very easy to show that $\left(\boldsymbol{D}^{-1}\right)_{ij} = \frac{1}{a_{ij}}$. Hence, the iterative scheme may be calculated as

$$\boldsymbol{r}_i^{k+1} = \frac{\left(\boldsymbol{b}_i - \sum_{j=0}^{i-1} l_{i,j}\boldsymbol{r}_j^{k} - \sum_{j=i+1}^{n-1} u_{i,j}\boldsymbol{r}_j^{k}\right)}{a_{i,i}} \tag{19.38}$$

This scheme is the *Jacobi method* and a pseudocode version is shown in Figure 19.3 From the figure it can be seen that the algorithm iterates until a convergence test succeeds. Stopping criteria will be discussed in detail in Section 19.7.

Looking closely at (19.38), we see that when updating $\boldsymbol{r}_i^{k+1}$, then we have already computed $\boldsymbol{r}_j^{k+1}$ for all $j < i$, and we may use the most recent values in the computation of $\boldsymbol{r}_i^{k+1}$ to get a faster solution. Our update rule now becomes

$$\boldsymbol{r}_i^{k+1} = \frac{\left(\boldsymbol{b}_i - \sum_{j=0}^{i-1} l_{i,j}\boldsymbol{r}_j^{k+1} - \sum_{j=i+1}^{n-1} u_{i,j}\boldsymbol{r}_j^{k}\right)}{a_{i,i}}, \tag{19.39}$$

which is known as *Gauss-Seidel method*. Pseudocode for the Gauss-Seidel method is listed in Figure 19.4. For a closer examination of the Gauss-Seidel method, we rewrite (19.39) by multiplying both sides by $a_{i,i}$ and collecting all $k+1$'th terms on the left-hand side,

$$a_{i,i}\boldsymbol{r}_i^{k+1} + \sum_{j=0}^{i-1} l_{i,j}\boldsymbol{r}_j^{k+1} = \boldsymbol{b}_i - \sum_{j=i+1}^{n-1} u_{i,j}\boldsymbol{r}_j^{k}. \tag{19.40}$$

```
algorithm Jacobi(A,x,b)
  r = initial guess
  for k=0,1,2,3,... do
    for i=0 to n-1 do
      delta = 0
      for j=0 to i-1 do
        delta += A(i,j)*r(j)
      next j
      for j=i+1 to n-1 do
        delta += A(i,j)*r(j)
      next j
      rNext(i) = (b(i) - delta)/A(i,i)
    next i
    r = rNext
    check convergence, continue if necessary
  next k
end algorithm
```

Figure 19.3: Pseudocode for the Jacobi method.

```
algorithm Gauss-Seidel(A,x,b)
  r = initial guess
  for k=0,1,2,3,... do
    for i=0 to n-1 do
      delta = 0
      for j=0 to i-1 do
        delta += A(i,j)*r(j)
      next j
      for j=i+1 to n-1 do
        delta += A(i,j)*r(j)
      next j
      r(i) = (b(i) - delta)/A(i,i)
    next i
    check convergence, continue if necessary
  next k
end algorithm
```

Figure 19.4: The Gauss-Seidel method.

It now follows that

$$(\boldsymbol{D}+\boldsymbol{L})\,\boldsymbol{r}^{\,k+1}=\boldsymbol{b}-\boldsymbol{U}\boldsymbol{r}^{\,k}, \tag{19.41}$$

and by inverting $\boldsymbol{D}+\boldsymbol{L}$ we find that

$$\boldsymbol{r}^{\,k+1}=(\boldsymbol{D}+\boldsymbol{L})^{-1}\left(\boldsymbol{b}-\boldsymbol{U}\boldsymbol{r}^{\,k}\right), \tag{19.42a}$$

$$\Downarrow$$

$$\boldsymbol{r}^{\,k+1}=\boldsymbol{T}\boldsymbol{r}^{\,k}+\boldsymbol{c}, \tag{19.42b}$$

where we have used $\boldsymbol{T}=-\left(\boldsymbol{D}+\boldsymbol{L}\right)^{-1}\boldsymbol{U}$, and $\boldsymbol{c}=\left(\boldsymbol{D}+\boldsymbol{L}\right)^{-1}\boldsymbol{b}$. The Jacobi and Gauss-Seidel update equations (19.36) and (19.42) are on the same form, which implies that the same study of convergence will apply for both. We refer the interested reader to [Burden et al., 1997] for details.

In general, the Gauss-Seidel method is considered superior to the Jacobi method; however, there are systems where one converges and the other does not and vice versa. From a computational viewpoint, the major difference between the Jacobi method and the Gauss-Seidel method is that in the Jacobi method all variables depend only on the solution from the previous iteration and can thus be updated in parallel. In contrast, the Gauss-Seidel method partly depends on both the previous and the current solution and is thus sequential in nature. Furthermore, the Gauss-Seidel method depends on the order in which the variables are updated. This implies that if we compute the solution, $\boldsymbol{r}^{\,k}$, and then repeat the computation with a reordering, $\pi(\cdot)$, of the variables to obtain the solution, $\pi(\boldsymbol{r})^{\,k}$, then it is very likely that we find

$$\boldsymbol{r}^{\,k}\neq\pi(\boldsymbol{r})^{\,k}. \tag{19.43}$$

Thus, reordering can affect the rate of convergence of the Gauss-Seidel method, which may be exploited to increase convergence rate.

19.6 Successive Over Relaxation

Suppose that $\boldsymbol{r}^{\,k}$ is an approximation to the linear system $\boldsymbol{A}\boldsymbol{r}=\boldsymbol{b}$, then we may calculate the approximation residual as

$$\boldsymbol{\rho}^{\,k}=\boldsymbol{A}\boldsymbol{r}^{\,k}-\boldsymbol{b}. \tag{19.44}$$

Let $\left\{\boldsymbol{\rho}_i^{\,k}\right\}$ denote the sequence of residual vectors for the Gauss-Seidel method, corresponding to the sequence of solutions $\left\{\boldsymbol{r}_i^{\,k}\right\}$. The subscript might appear confusing; it refers to the currently known solution in the k'th iteration just before updating the i'th variable. Inserting the Gauss-Seidel update rule (19.39) into (19.44) we find the m'th coordinate of $\boldsymbol{\rho}_i^{\,k+1}$ to be

$$\boldsymbol{\rho}_{mi}^{\,k+1}=\boldsymbol{b}_m-\sum_{j=0}^{i-1}a_{m,j}\boldsymbol{r}_j^{\,k+1}-\sum_{j=i+1}^{n-1}a_{m,j}\boldsymbol{r}_j^{\,k}-a_{m,i}\boldsymbol{r}_m^{\,k} \tag{19.45}$$

$$=\boldsymbol{b}_m-\sum_{j=0}^{i-1}a_{m,j}\boldsymbol{r}_j^{\,k+1}-\sum_{j=i}^{n-1}a_{m,j}\boldsymbol{r}_j^{\,k} \tag{19.46}$$

If we look at the i'th coordinate, we have

$$\boldsymbol{\rho}_{ii}^{k+1} = \boldsymbol{b}_i - \sum_{j=0}^{i-1} a_{i,j}\boldsymbol{r}_j^{k+1} - \sum_{j=i+1}^{n-1} a_{i,j}\boldsymbol{r}_j^{k} - a_{i,i}\boldsymbol{r}_i^{k} \tag{19.47}$$

$$a_{i,i}\boldsymbol{r}_i^{k} + \boldsymbol{\rho}_{ii}^{k+1} = \boldsymbol{b}_i - \sum_{j=0}^{i-1} a_{i,j}\boldsymbol{r}_j^{k+1} - \sum_{j=i+1}^{n-1} a_{i,j}\boldsymbol{r}_j^{k}$$

Looking at the left-hand side and comparing with (19.39), we see that it is equal to $a_{i,i}\boldsymbol{r}_i^{k+1}$, so we have

$$a_{i,i}\boldsymbol{r}_i^{k} + \boldsymbol{\rho}_{ii}^{k+1} = a_{i,i}\boldsymbol{r}_i^{k+1} \tag{19.48}$$

Or if we rearrange terms we get

$$\boldsymbol{r}_i^{k+1} = \boldsymbol{r}_i^{k} + \frac{\boldsymbol{\rho}_{ii}^{k+1}}{a_{i,i}}. \tag{19.49}$$

Until now we only rewrite the update step in terms of the residual vector. We can gain more insight into the Gauss-Seidel method by repeating the above steps for the $i+1$'th variable update, which is

$$\begin{aligned}\boldsymbol{\rho}_{i,i+1}^{k+1} &= \boldsymbol{b}_i - \sum_{j=0}^{i} a_{i,j}\boldsymbol{r}_j^{k+1} - \sum_{j=i+1}^{n-1} a_{i,j}\boldsymbol{r}_j^{k} \\ &= \underbrace{\boldsymbol{b}_i - \sum_{j=0}^{i-1} a_{i,j}\boldsymbol{r}_j^{k+1} - \sum_{j=i+1}^{n-1} a_{i,j}\boldsymbol{r}_j^{k}}_{a_{i,i}\boldsymbol{r}_i^{k+1}} - a_{i,i}\boldsymbol{r}_i^{k+1} \\ &= 0\end{aligned}$$

The last step follows from (19.39). Thus, the Gauss-Seidel method is characterized by choosing $\boldsymbol{r}_i^{k+1}$ in such a way that the i'th component of $\boldsymbol{\rho}_{i+1}^{k+1}$ is zero. Reducing one coordinate of the residual vector to zero is not generally the most efficient way to reduce the overall size of the vector $\boldsymbol{\rho}_{i+1}^{k+1}$. We need to choose $\boldsymbol{r}_i^{k+1}$ to make $\left\|\boldsymbol{\rho}_{i+1}^{k+1}\right\|$ small. Modifying (19.49) to

$$\boldsymbol{r}_i^{k+1} = \boldsymbol{r}_i^{k} + \omega\frac{\boldsymbol{\rho}_{ii}^{k+1}}{a_{i,i}} \tag{19.50}$$

where $\omega > 0$. For certain values of ω, the norm of the residual vector is reduced and this leads to faster convergence. The ω parameter is a relaxation of the Gauss-Seidel method, and the new iterative scheme is called *successive over relaxation* (*SOR*). When $0 < \omega < 1$ the method is termed under-relaxation, and when $1 < \omega$ the method is call over relaxation. Notice that when $\omega = 1$ the method is simply the Gauss-Seidel method.

```
algorithm SOR(A,x,b)
  r = initial guess
  for k=0,1,2,3,... do
    for i=0 to n-1 do
      delta = 0
      for j=0 to i-1 do
        delta += A(i,j)*r(j)
      next j
      for j=i+1 to n-1 do
        delta += A(i,j)*r(j)
      next j
      delta = (b(i) - delta)/A(i,i)
      r(i) = r(i) + w(delta - r(i))
    next i
    check convergence, continue if necessary
  next k
end algorithm
```

Figure 19.5: The SOR method.

Insert (19.47) into (19.50) to reformulate the SOR method into a more implementation friendly equation,

$$\boldsymbol{r}_i^{\,k+1} = \boldsymbol{r}_i^{\,k} + \omega \frac{\boldsymbol{b}_i - \sum_{j=0}^{i-1} a_{i,j} \boldsymbol{r}_j^{\,k+1} - \sum_{j=i+1}^{n-1} a_{i,j} \boldsymbol{r}_j^{\,k} - a_{i,i} \boldsymbol{r}_i^{\,k}}{a_{i,i}} \tag{19.51}$$

$$= (1-\omega)\,\boldsymbol{r}_i^{\,k} + \frac{\omega}{a_{i,i}} \left(\boldsymbol{b}_i - \sum_{j=0}^{i-1} a_{i,j} \boldsymbol{r}_j^{\,k+1} - \sum_{j=i+1}^{n-1} a_{i,j} \boldsymbol{r}_j^{\,k} \right), \tag{19.52}$$

whose pseudocode is shown in Figure 19.5. To determine the matrix form of the SOR method we rewrite (19.52) as

$$a_{i,i} \boldsymbol{r}_i^{\,k+1} + \omega \sum_{j=0}^{i-1} a_{i,j} \boldsymbol{r}_j^{\,k+1} = (1-\omega)\, a_{i,i} \boldsymbol{r}_i^{\,k} + \omega \boldsymbol{b}_i - \omega \sum_{j=i+1}^{n-1} a_{i,j} \boldsymbol{r}_j^{\,k}, \tag{19.53}$$

from which we see that

$$(\boldsymbol{D} + \omega \boldsymbol{L})\, \boldsymbol{r}^{\,k+1} = ((1-\omega)\,\boldsymbol{D} - \omega \boldsymbol{U})\, \boldsymbol{r}^{\,k} + \omega \boldsymbol{b} \tag{19.54}$$

or

$$\boldsymbol{r}^{\,k+1} = (\boldsymbol{D} + \omega \boldsymbol{L})^{-1} ((1-\omega)\,\boldsymbol{D} - \omega \boldsymbol{U})\, \boldsymbol{r}^{\,k} + \omega\, (\boldsymbol{D} + \omega \boldsymbol{L})^{-1} \boldsymbol{b} \tag{19.55}$$

If we let $\boldsymbol{T} = (\boldsymbol{D} + \omega \boldsymbol{L})^{-1} ((1-\omega)\,\boldsymbol{D} - \omega \boldsymbol{U})$, and $\boldsymbol{c} = \omega\,(\boldsymbol{D} + \omega \boldsymbol{L})^{-1} \boldsymbol{b}$, then we see that the SOR method can be written on the form

$$\boldsymbol{r}^{\,k+1} = \boldsymbol{T} \boldsymbol{r}^{\,k} + \boldsymbol{c}. \tag{19.56}$$

Jacobi Method	$r^{k+1} = D^{-1}\left(b - (L+U)\,r^{k}\right)$
Gauss-Seidel	$r^{k+1} = D^{-1}\left(b - Lr^{k+1} - Ur^{k}\right)$
Successive over relaxation	$r^{k+1} = r^{k} + \omega\left(D^{-1}\left(b - Lr^{k+1} - Ur^{k}\right) - r^{k}\right)$

Table 19.1: Matrix forms of the three iterative Matrix solvers for the system $(L + D + U)r = b$.

In short, the SOR method has the same form as the Jacobi and the Gauss-Seidel methods.

We end this section by listing the matrix forms of the three iterative matrix solver methods in Table 19.1.

19.7 Stopping Criteria for Iterative Solvers

A major point of any practical implementation of any iterative solver is to determine when to stop the iterations. A combination of stopping criteria is often used, such as a maximum on the number of iterations, and convergence tests.

It is often a good idea to specify a maximum limit on the number of iterations that one is willing to use in an iterative method. There are mainly two good reasons for this. In a time-critical computation one wants to control how much time is spent on a computation, a maximum limit can help enforce this. In case the problem is unsolvable (i.e., diverges), an iterative method would loop forever, and the loop must therefore be stopped by a maximum iteration limit.

This is typically done by some form of stopping test based on the convergence of the method. A convergence test is a test for how close the vector r^{r+1} is to a fixed point (see (19.33)).

Definition 19.1 (Convergence)
An infinite sequence $\left\{r^{k}\right\}_{k=0}^{\infty} = \left\{r^{0}, x^{1}, r^{2}, \ldots\right\}$ *of vectors in* $\mathbb{R}^n$ *is said to converge to* r^{*} *w.r.t. the vector norm* $\|\cdot\|$ *if, given any* $\varepsilon > 0$, *there exist an integer* $N(\varepsilon)$ *such that*

$$\left\| r^{k} - r^{*} \right\| < \varepsilon \qquad \textit{for all} \quad k \geq N(\varepsilon). \tag{19.57}$$

As is seen from Definition 19.1, the concept of a vector norm is vital to defining convergence. In theory, any vector norm can be used, but we will only consider the l_2 and the l_∞ norms, see Definition 18.11 and Definition 18.12. Often the convergence test will consist of several stopping criteria used in combination.

An absolute estimate for the error can be taken by measuring the difference between the solutions of two succeeding iterations, r^{k+1} and r^{k}. The simplest stopping criteria is to allow for a user-specified threshold, ε, and to consider the sequence to have converged, when

$$\left\| r^{k+1} - r^{k} \right\| < \varepsilon. \tag{19.58}$$

By comparison with Definition 19.1 it is evident that the test will succeed in case the iterative method converges. Nevertheless, if convergence is very slow, then this method will fail. Even worse, there exists divergent sequences where $r^{k+1} - r^{k}$ converges to zero, as the following example illustrates:

Example 19.1

Let the sequence $\left\{x^{k}\right\}_{k=1}^{\infty}$ *of real numbers be defined by*

$$x^{k} = \sum_{r=1}^{k} \frac{1}{r} \tag{19.59}$$

Now the limit of the difference is

$$\lim_{k\to\infty}\left(x^{k} - x^{k-1}\right) = \lim_{k\to\infty}\left(\sum_{r=1}^{k}\frac{1}{r} - \sum_{r=1}^{k-1}\frac{1}{r}\right) = \lim_{k\to\infty}\left(\frac{1}{k}\right) = 0 \tag{19.60}$$

However,

$$\lim_{k\to\infty} x^{k} = \lim_{k\to\infty}\left(\sum_{r=1}^{k}\frac{1}{r}\right) = \infty \tag{19.61}$$

meaning that the sequence is divergent.

As an alternative to the absolute error measure, a measure of relative error is sometimes applied,

$$\frac{\left\|\boldsymbol{r}^{k+1} - \boldsymbol{r}^{k}\right\|}{\left\|\boldsymbol{r}^{k+1}\right\|} < \varepsilon. \tag{19.62}$$

Observe that the $k+1$'th solution must be nonzero in order for the relative test to work. Often the l_∞ norm is used, since it is cheap to compute and is much more robust toward numerical deficiencies, such as overflow and underflow, in contrast to the l_2 norm.

Using Landau symbols, see (20.11), we may define the rate of convergence as when

$$x^{k} = \alpha + O(\beta^{k}) \tag{19.63}$$

then we say that x^{k} converges to α with rate of convergence $O(\beta^{k})$. In many cases, the sequence $\left\{\beta^{k}\right\}$ has the form

$$\beta^{k} = \frac{1}{k^p} \tag{19.64}$$

for some number $p > 0$. We consider the largest value of p so that $x^{k} = \alpha + O(1/k^p)$ to describe the rate at which x^{k} converges to α.

We have given this formal presentation of rate of convergence because iterative methods might reorder the variables such that variables with the slowest rate of convergence are updated before variables with faster rate of convergence. In practice, the relative convergence test is not used. Instead, the magnitudes of absolute error of the individual variables are used as an ad hoc measure of rate of convergence, that is, if

$$|\boldsymbol{r}_i^{k+1} - \boldsymbol{r}_i^{k}| < |\boldsymbol{r}_j^{k+1} - \boldsymbol{r}_j^{k}| \tag{19.65}$$

The i'th variable is considered to converge faster than the j'th variable. This ad hoc way of measuring rate of convergence allows a simple approach in practice, where variables are reordered in decreasing order w.r.t. the absolute error.

19.8 The Gradient Descent Method

The *gradient descent* method [Press et al., 1999a, Golub et al., 1996, Shewchuk, 1994] is a nonstationary iterative process, meaning that its parameters, $\boldsymbol{T}$ and $\boldsymbol{c}$, change with time, hence, our model problem has the following form:

$$\boldsymbol{r}^{k+1} = \boldsymbol{c}_k + \boldsymbol{T}_k \boldsymbol{r}^{k}. \tag{19.66}$$

The gradient descent method has its root in minimization. Assuming that we wish to minimize the quadratic equation,

$$E(\boldsymbol{r}) = \frac{1}{2}\boldsymbol{r}^T \boldsymbol{A}\boldsymbol{r} - \boldsymbol{r}^T\boldsymbol{b} + c, \tag{19.67}$$

then a common approach is to follow the gradient of E,

$$\nabla E(\boldsymbol{r}) = \frac{1}{2}\boldsymbol{A}\boldsymbol{r} + \frac{1}{2}\boldsymbol{A}^T\boldsymbol{r} - \boldsymbol{b} \tag{19.68a}$$

$$= \frac{1}{2}\left(\boldsymbol{A} + \boldsymbol{A}^T\right)\boldsymbol{r} - \boldsymbol{b}, \tag{19.68b}$$

in the negative direction. That is, using a forward Euler scheme we write

$$\boldsymbol{r}^{k+1} = \boldsymbol{r}^{k} - \alpha \nabla E(\boldsymbol{r}^{k}), \tag{19.69}$$

where α some positive constant. This is known as the *gradient descent* method, and with sufficiently small α's will minimize (19.67). When the gradient is zero, then the Euler scheme will be at a stationary point, and (19.67) will be at an extremal point. It is readily seen that $\frac{1}{2}\left(\boldsymbol{A} + \boldsymbol{A}^T\right)\boldsymbol{r} = \boldsymbol{b}$ is a stationary point, and in case $\boldsymbol{A}$ is symmetric then (19.68) will reduce to

$$\nabla E(\boldsymbol{r}) = \boldsymbol{A}\boldsymbol{r} - \boldsymbol{b}, \tag{19.70}$$

which will be stationary, when $\boldsymbol{A}\boldsymbol{r} = \boldsymbol{b}$. Hence, for positive-definite symmetric matrices, minimizing (19.67) is equivalent to solving (19.2). Geometrically positive-definite matrices have a structure similar to $x^2 + y^2$, and the gradient field is thus radiating from the global minimum as illustrated in Figure 19.6(a) and 19.6(d). In Figure 19.6 is the graph and gradient field plotted for

$$f(\boldsymbol{r}) = \boldsymbol{r}^T \boldsymbol{A}\boldsymbol{r}, \tag{19.71}$$

using the following three matrices,

$$\text{Positive-definite}\,\boldsymbol{A} = \begin{bmatrix} 1 & 0 \\ 0 & 1 \end{bmatrix}, \tag{19.72a}$$

$$\text{Negative-definite}\,\boldsymbol{A} = \begin{bmatrix} -1 & 0 \\ 0 & -1 \end{bmatrix}, \tag{19.72b}$$

$$\text{Indefinite}\,\boldsymbol{A} = \begin{bmatrix} 1 & 0 \\ 0 & -1 \end{bmatrix}. \tag{19.72c}$$

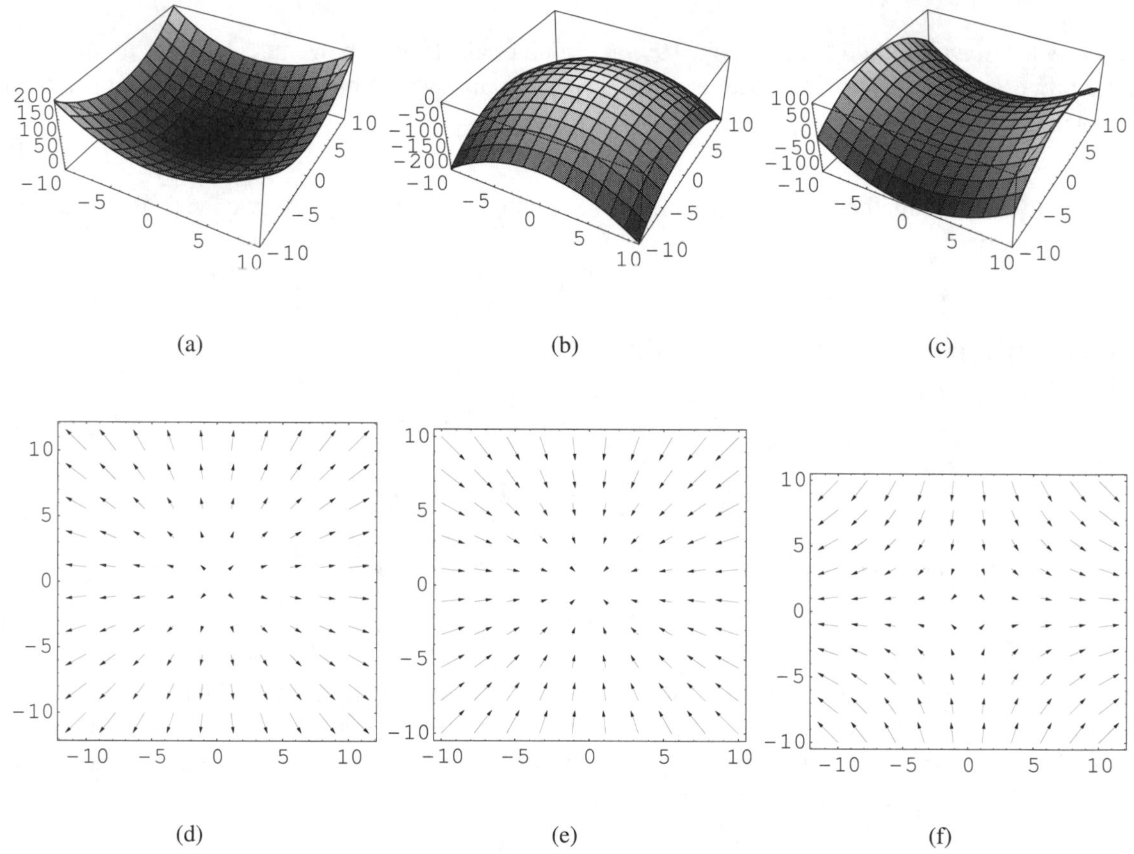

Figure 19.6: Visualizing positive-definite, negative-definite, and indefinite matrices and their corresponding gradient fields.

It is visually clear that for the negative-definite matrix then the gradient descent algorithm will converge toward a point at infinity. Of course, the maximum could be found by simply modifying the algorithm to perform a gradient ascent instead. Worse are the indefinite matrices, which should not be expected to converge to the saddle point.

In the remainder of this chapter we will assume that $\boldsymbol{A}$ is symmetric and positive-definite. Rather than choosing small values for α, we could instead search for the value of α minimizing (19.67), which is equivalent to searching for the minimum along the line starting at $\boldsymbol{r}^{\,k}$ and with direction $\nabla E(\boldsymbol{r}^{\,k})$. This is known as a *line search*. To discuss the line searching procedure, we'll first introduce the notion of error and residual. Assuming that the optimum is located at $\boldsymbol{r}^{\,*}$, and that the current position is $\boldsymbol{r}^{\,k}$, then the error in position is given as

$$\boldsymbol{\epsilon}^{\,k} = \boldsymbol{r}^{\,k} - \boldsymbol{r}^{\,*}, \tag{19.73}$$

while the residual or error in $\boldsymbol{b}$ is

$$\boldsymbol{\rho}^{k} = \boldsymbol{b} - \boldsymbol{A}\boldsymbol{r}^{k}. \tag{19.74}$$

Using (19.73) and (19.70) we find that

$$\begin{aligned}
\boldsymbol{\rho}^{k} &= -\boldsymbol{A}\boldsymbol{\epsilon}^{k} && (19.75a)\\
&= -\nabla E(\boldsymbol{r}^{k}.) && (19.75b)
\end{aligned}$$

In the line search algorithm, we search for the value of α in (19.69) that minimizes (19.67); hence, we write the quadratic energy parameterized by α, differentiate and find the zero point

$$\begin{aligned}
0 &= \frac{d}{d\alpha} E(\boldsymbol{r}^{k+1}(\alpha)) && (19.76a)\\
&= \nabla E(\boldsymbol{r}^{k+1}(\alpha))^T \frac{d}{d\alpha}\boldsymbol{r}^{k+1}(\alpha) && (19.76b)\\
&= \nabla E(\boldsymbol{r}^{k+1}(\alpha))^T \nabla E(\boldsymbol{r}^{k}). && (19.76c)
\end{aligned}$$

Thus, we should choose α such that the new search direction is orthogonal to the previous. Using (19.75), (19.74), and (19.69) we may determine α as follows:

$$\begin{aligned}
0 &= \nabla E(\boldsymbol{r}^{k+1}(\alpha))^T \nabla E(\boldsymbol{r}^{k}) && (19.77a)\\
&= \boldsymbol{\rho}^{k+1^T} \nabla E(\boldsymbol{r}^{k}) && (19.77b)\\
&= \left(\boldsymbol{b} - \boldsymbol{A}\boldsymbol{r}^{k+1}\right)^T \nabla E(\boldsymbol{r}^{k}) && (19.77c)\\
&= \left(\boldsymbol{b} - \boldsymbol{A}\left(\boldsymbol{r}^{k} - \alpha\nabla E(\boldsymbol{r}^{k})\right)\right)^T \nabla E(\boldsymbol{r}^{k}) && (19.77d)\\
&= \left(\boldsymbol{\rho}^{k} + \alpha\boldsymbol{A}\nabla E(\boldsymbol{r}^{k})\right)^T \nabla E(\boldsymbol{r}^{k}) && (19.77e)\\
&= \left(-\nabla E(\boldsymbol{r}^{k}) + \alpha\boldsymbol{A}\nabla E(\boldsymbol{r}^{k})\right)^T \nabla E(\boldsymbol{r}^{k}), && (19.77f)
\end{aligned}$$

which implies that

$$\begin{aligned}
\alpha &= \frac{\nabla E(\boldsymbol{r}^{k})^T \nabla E(\boldsymbol{r}^{k})}{\nabla E(\boldsymbol{r}^{k})^T \boldsymbol{A}^T \nabla E(\boldsymbol{r}^{k})} && (19.78a)\\
&= \frac{(\boldsymbol{\rho}^{k})^T \nabla \boldsymbol{\rho}^{k}}{(\boldsymbol{\rho}^{k})^T \boldsymbol{A}^T \boldsymbol{\rho}^{k})}, && (19.78b)
\end{aligned}$$

and where the transpose of $\boldsymbol{A}$ can be ignored since it is a symmetric matrix. The complete algorithm is shown in pseudocode in Figure 19.10.

```
Algorithm GradientDescent(A,b,r)
  do
    residual = b-A*r
    alpha = (r'*r)/(r'*A*r)
    r = r+alpha*residual
  until residual sufficiently small
end algorithm
```

Figure 19.7: Pseudocode for the gradient descent algorithm on (19.67) for a symmetric, positive-definite matrix $\boldsymbol{A}$.

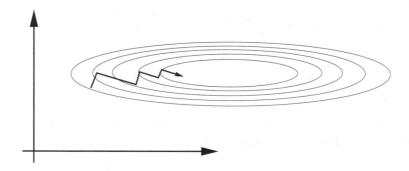

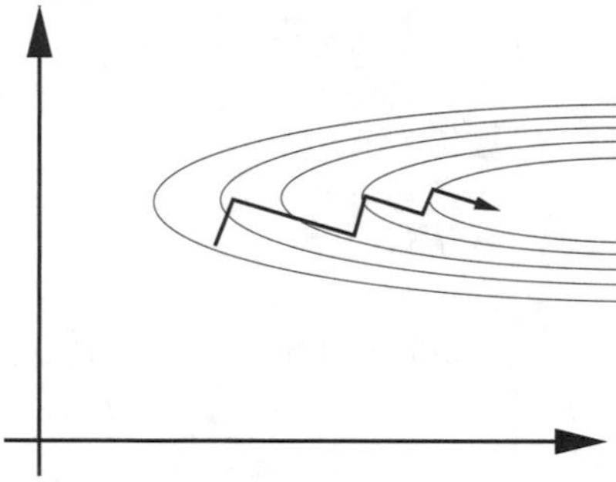

Figure 19.8: Isophotes of an elongated energy function. At each step, the search direction is parallel to the gradient of the energy function.

19.9 The Conjugate Gradient Method

Gradient descent often is the method of choice where more complicated methods must give up. Nevertheless, it is rather slow, since it will tend to take repeated steps in similar directions. This is especially the case when the energy function is deep and elongated, as shown in Figure 19.8. It would seem better to avoid searching in directions previously investigated, and hence make a sequence of orthogonal directions, $\{\boldsymbol{d}^0, \boldsymbol{d}^1, \ldots, \boldsymbol{d}^N\}$, such that

$$\boldsymbol{r}^{k+1} = \boldsymbol{r}^k + \alpha_k \boldsymbol{d}^k. \tag{19.79}$$

This is the *conjugate gradient descent* method. The consequence would be that once a direction had been investigated, then it would not be used again. Then the stationary point would be found in N iterations, where N is the dimensionality of $\boldsymbol{r}$. As a consequence, the error at $k+1$ must be perpendicular to the direction at k, and thus

$$(\boldsymbol{d}^k)^T \boldsymbol{\epsilon}^{k+1} = 0, \tag{19.80}$$

as illustrated in Figure 19.9. Thus, inserting (19.73) and (19.79) we find that

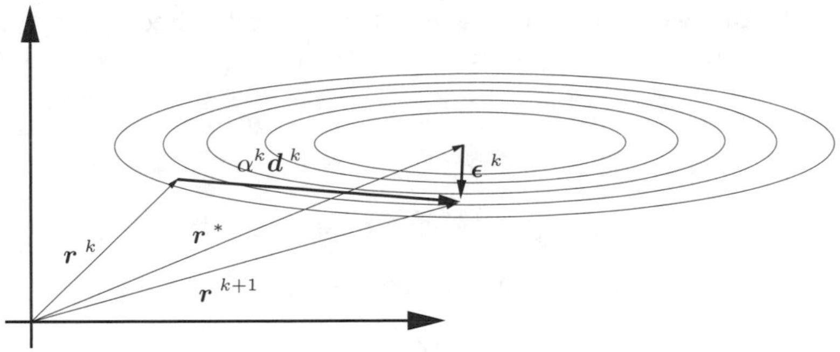

Figure 19.9: Optimal distance along $d^{\,k}$ is such that $\alpha^k d^{\,k}$ is perpendicular to ϵ^{k+1}.

$$
\begin{aligned}
(\boldsymbol{d}^{\,k})^T \boldsymbol{\epsilon}^{\,k+1} &= (\boldsymbol{d}^{\,k})^T \left(\boldsymbol{r}^{\,k+1} - \boldsymbol{r}^{\,*}\right) && (19.81a)\\
&= (\boldsymbol{d}^{\,k})^T \left(\boldsymbol{r}^{\,k} + \alpha^k \boldsymbol{d}^{\,k} - \boldsymbol{r}^{\,*}\right) && (19.81b)\\
&= (\boldsymbol{d}^{\,k})^T \left(\boldsymbol{\epsilon}^{\,k} + \alpha^k \boldsymbol{d}^{\,k}\right), && (19.81c)
\end{aligned}
$$

and conclude that

$$
\alpha^k = \frac{-(\boldsymbol{d}^{\,k})^T \boldsymbol{\epsilon}^{\,k}}{(\boldsymbol{d}^{\,k})^T \boldsymbol{d}^{\,k}} \tag{19.82}
$$

Unfortunately, this is not possible without the knowledge of $\boldsymbol{\epsilon}^k$, and if we knew $\boldsymbol{\epsilon}^k$, then we would also know the solution, $\boldsymbol{r}^{\,*}$.

Fortunately, performing the line search method along $\boldsymbol{d}^{\,k}$ in order to find the optimal α^k for a fixed k is solvable. Hence, we start by taking the derivative of (19.67) parameterized by α^k using (19.79):

$$
\begin{aligned}
0 &= \frac{\partial}{\partial \alpha_k} E(\boldsymbol{r}^{\,k+1}(\alpha_k)) && (19.83a)\\
&= \nabla E(\boldsymbol{r}^{\,k+1}(\alpha_k))^T \frac{\partial}{\partial \alpha_k} \boldsymbol{r}^{\,k+1}(\alpha_k) && (19.83b)\\
&= \nabla E(\boldsymbol{r}^{\,k+1}(\alpha_k))^T \boldsymbol{d}^{\,k}. && (19.83c)
\end{aligned}
$$

Using (19.75) and setting the gradient equal to zero we find

$$
\begin{aligned}
0 &= \nabla E(\boldsymbol{r}^{\,k+1}(\alpha_k))^T \boldsymbol{d}^{\,k} && (19.84a)\\
&= \left(\boldsymbol{A}\boldsymbol{\epsilon}^{\,k+1}\right)^T \boldsymbol{d}^{\,k} && (19.84b)\\
&= (\boldsymbol{d}^{\,k})^T \boldsymbol{A}\boldsymbol{\epsilon}^{\,k+1}. && (19.84c)
\end{aligned}
$$

This is essentially the same equation as (19.80) except it is now with the metric $\boldsymbol{A}$ instead of the usual standard Euclidean metric. This is a generalization of orthogonality, and when two vectors fulfill $\boldsymbol{a}^T \boldsymbol{A} \boldsymbol{b} = 0$, then they are said to be *conjugate directions* or $\boldsymbol{A}$*-orthogonal.*

Continuing from (19.84), we rewrite the equation for conjugate directions by inserting (19.73) and (19.79), and we find that

$$(\boldsymbol{d}^{k})^T \boldsymbol{A}\boldsymbol{\epsilon}^{k+1} = (\boldsymbol{d}^{k})^T \boldsymbol{A}(\boldsymbol{r}^{k+1} - \boldsymbol{r}^{*}) \tag{19.85a}$$

$$= (\boldsymbol{d}^{k})^T \boldsymbol{A}(\boldsymbol{r}^{k} + \alpha^k \boldsymbol{d}^{k} - \boldsymbol{r}^{*}) \tag{19.85b}$$

$$= (\boldsymbol{d}^{k})^T \boldsymbol{A}(\boldsymbol{\epsilon}^{k} + \alpha^k \boldsymbol{d}^{k}). \tag{19.85c}$$

Finally, setting the above equal to zero, isolating α^k, and using (19.75) gives

$$\alpha_k = \frac{-(\boldsymbol{d}^{k})^T \boldsymbol{A}\boldsymbol{\epsilon}^{k}}{(\boldsymbol{d}^{k})^T \boldsymbol{A}\boldsymbol{d}^{k}} \tag{19.86a}$$

$$= \frac{-(\boldsymbol{d}^{k})^T \boldsymbol{\rho}^{k}}{(\boldsymbol{d}^{k})^T \boldsymbol{A}\boldsymbol{d}^{k}}. \tag{19.86b}$$

Notice that if we choose $\boldsymbol{d}^{k} = \boldsymbol{\rho}^{k}$, then the method simplifies to gradient descent (19.78).

To find N conjugate directions, $\boldsymbol{d}^{k}$, we will use the *conjugate Gram-Schmidt process*: assume that we have a set of linear independent vectors $\{\boldsymbol{\delta}^{0}, \boldsymbol{\delta}^{1}, \ldots, \boldsymbol{\delta}^{N-1}\}$, for example, the coordinate axes, then we will iteratively produce vectors $\boldsymbol{d}^{k}$ that are $\boldsymbol{A}$-orthogonal to the previous $\{\boldsymbol{d}^{0}, \boldsymbol{d}^{1}, \ldots, \boldsymbol{d}^{k-1}\}$ vectors as follows. Start by setting,

$$\boldsymbol{d}^{0} = \boldsymbol{\delta}^{0}, \tag{19.87}$$

and then for $i = 1..N-1$ iteratively remove dependence on $\boldsymbol{\delta}^{k}$ from the previous selected directions $\boldsymbol{d}^{i}$ by

$$\boldsymbol{d}^{k} = \boldsymbol{\delta}^{k} - \sum_{i=0}^{k-1} \beta_{ki}\boldsymbol{d}^{i}. \tag{19.88}$$

The constants β_{ki} are calculated using $\boldsymbol{A}$-orthogonality, since for any $j < k$ we enforce

$$(\boldsymbol{d}^{k})^T \boldsymbol{A}\boldsymbol{d}^{j} = 0, \tag{19.89}$$

and when expanding with (19.88) it is found that

$$0 = (\boldsymbol{d}^{k})^T \boldsymbol{A}\boldsymbol{d}^{j} \tag{19.90a}$$

$$= \left(\boldsymbol{\delta}^{k} - \sum_{i=0}^{k-1} \beta_{ki}\boldsymbol{d}^{i}\right)^T \boldsymbol{A}\boldsymbol{d}^{j} \tag{19.90b}$$

$$= (\boldsymbol{\delta}^{k})^T \boldsymbol{A}\boldsymbol{d}^{j} - \sum_{i=0}^{k-1} \beta_{ki}(\boldsymbol{d}^{i})^T \boldsymbol{A}\boldsymbol{d}^{j} \tag{19.90c}$$

$$= (\boldsymbol{\delta}^{k})^T \boldsymbol{A}\boldsymbol{d}^{j} - \beta_{kj}(\boldsymbol{d}^{j})^T \boldsymbol{A}\boldsymbol{d}^{j}. \tag{19.90d}$$

Hence, isolating β_{ji} gives,

$$\beta_{kj} = \frac{(\boldsymbol{\delta}^{k})^T \boldsymbol{A}\boldsymbol{d}^{j}}{(\boldsymbol{d}^{j})^T \boldsymbol{A}\boldsymbol{d}^{j}}. \tag{19.91}$$

Using the coordinate axes as the initial set of linear independent vectors $\{\boldsymbol{\delta}^{0}, \boldsymbol{\delta}^{1}, \ldots, \boldsymbol{\delta}^{N-1}\}$ is not optimal. Algorithmically, it's much faster to use the residual at iteration k as $\boldsymbol{\delta}^{k}$. To see this, let's first examine the error. The set $\{\boldsymbol{d}^{k}\}$ gives an orthogonal basis that leads from the initial point $\boldsymbol{r}^{0}$ to the extremum point $\boldsymbol{r}^{*}$; hence, we may write the initial error $\boldsymbol{\epsilon}^{0}$ as a linear combination of $\{\boldsymbol{d}^{k}\}$, i.e.

$$\boldsymbol{\epsilon}^{0} = \boldsymbol{r}^{0} - \boldsymbol{r}^{*} = \sum_{i=0}^{N-1} \gamma^{i} \boldsymbol{d}^{i} \tag{19.92}$$

Using $\boldsymbol{A}$-orthogonality, we may determine the k'th constant γ^{k} as

$$(\boldsymbol{d}^{k})^{T} \boldsymbol{A} \boldsymbol{\epsilon}^{0} = \sum_{i=0}^{N-1} \gamma^{i} (\boldsymbol{d}^{k})^{T} \boldsymbol{A} \boldsymbol{d}^{i} \tag{19.93a}$$

$$= \gamma^{k} (\boldsymbol{d}^{k})^{T} \boldsymbol{A} \boldsymbol{d}^{k} \tag{19.93b}$$

$$\Downarrow$$

$$\gamma_{k} = \frac{(\boldsymbol{d}^{k})^{T} \boldsymbol{A} \boldsymbol{\epsilon}^{0}}{(\boldsymbol{d}^{k})^{T} \boldsymbol{A} \boldsymbol{d}^{k}} \tag{19.93c}$$

Furthermore, using (19.79) we can write

$$\boldsymbol{r}^{k} = \boldsymbol{r}^{0} + \sum_{j=0}^{k-1} \alpha_{j} \boldsymbol{d}^{j}, \tag{19.94}$$

and subtracting $\boldsymbol{r}^{*}$ from both sides we get

$$\boldsymbol{r}^{k} - \boldsymbol{r}^{*} = \boldsymbol{r}^{0} - \boldsymbol{r}^{*} + \sum_{j=0}^{k-1} \alpha_{j} \boldsymbol{d}^{j}, \tag{19.95a}$$

$$\Downarrow$$

$$\boldsymbol{\epsilon}^{k} = \boldsymbol{\epsilon}^{0} + \sum_{j=0}^{k-1} \alpha_{j} \boldsymbol{d}^{j}. \tag{19.95b}$$

This allows us to isolate $\boldsymbol{\epsilon}^{0}$ and insert it into (19.93) to get,

$$\gamma_{k} = \frac{(\boldsymbol{d}^{k})^{T} \boldsymbol{A} \left(\boldsymbol{\epsilon}^{k} - \sum_{j=0}^{k-1} \alpha_{j} \boldsymbol{d}^{j} \right)}{(\boldsymbol{d}^{k})^{T} \boldsymbol{A} \boldsymbol{d}^{k}} \tag{19.96a}$$

$$= \frac{(\boldsymbol{d}^{k})^{T} \boldsymbol{A} \boldsymbol{\epsilon}^{k}}{(\boldsymbol{d}^{k})^{T} \boldsymbol{A} \boldsymbol{d}^{k}} \tag{19.96b}$$

$$= \frac{(\boldsymbol{d}^{k})^{T} \boldsymbol{\rho}^{k}}{(\boldsymbol{d}^{k})^{T} \boldsymbol{A} \boldsymbol{d}^{k}} \tag{19.96c}$$

$$= -\alpha^{k}. \tag{19.96d}$$

The consequence is that for every iteration, we remove a term in the error; that is, inserting (19.92) into (19.95b) and using (19.96) we get

$$\boldsymbol{\epsilon}^{k} = \sum_{i=0}^{N-1} \gamma^i \boldsymbol{d}^{i} + \sum_{j=0}^{k-1} \alpha_j \boldsymbol{d}^{j} \tag{19.97a}$$

$$= \sum_{i=0}^{N-1} \gamma^i \boldsymbol{d}^{i} - \sum_{j=0}^{k-1} \delta_j \boldsymbol{d}^{j} \tag{19.97b}$$

$$= \sum_{i=k}^{N-1} \gamma^i \boldsymbol{d}^{i}. \tag{19.97c}$$

For the final iteration, the method converges, since we have $k = N - 1$ for which case the error is zero.

It is smart to use the residuals first because the residual is orthogonal to the previous search directions. Using (19.83) and (19.75) we see that the residual is orthogonal to the previous search direction,

$$0 = -\nabla E(\boldsymbol{r}^{k}(\alpha_k))^T \boldsymbol{d}^{k-1} = (\boldsymbol{\rho}^{k})^T \boldsymbol{d}^{k-1}. \tag{19.98}$$

Furthermore, the residual is orthogonal to all the previous search directions, that is,

$$(\boldsymbol{\rho}^{k})^T \boldsymbol{d}^{j} = 0 \text{ for } j < k. \tag{19.99}$$

To prove this, consider the sequential buildup of the error using (19.75), (19.79), (19.73), and (19.86),

$$(\boldsymbol{\rho}^{k})^T \boldsymbol{d}^{j} = -(\boldsymbol{\epsilon}^{k})^T \boldsymbol{A}^T \boldsymbol{d}^{j} \tag{19.100a}$$

$$= -(\boldsymbol{\epsilon}^{0} - \sum_{i=0}^{k-1} \alpha^i \boldsymbol{d}^{i})^T \boldsymbol{A}^T \boldsymbol{d}^{j} \tag{19.100b}$$

$$= -(\boldsymbol{\epsilon}^{0})^T \boldsymbol{A}^T \boldsymbol{d}^{j} + \sum_{i=0}^{k-1} \alpha^i (\boldsymbol{d}^{i})^T \boldsymbol{A}^T \boldsymbol{d}^{j} \tag{19.100c}$$

$$= -(\boldsymbol{\epsilon}^{0})^T \boldsymbol{A}^T \boldsymbol{d}^{j} + \alpha^j (\boldsymbol{d}^{j})^T \boldsymbol{A}^T \boldsymbol{d}^{j} \tag{19.100d}$$

$$= -(\boldsymbol{\epsilon}^{0})^T \boldsymbol{A}^T \boldsymbol{d}^{j} - (\boldsymbol{d}^{j})^T \boldsymbol{\rho}^{j} \tag{19.100e}$$

$$= -(\boldsymbol{\epsilon}^{0})^T \boldsymbol{A}^T \boldsymbol{d}^{j} + (\boldsymbol{d}^{j})^T \boldsymbol{A} \boldsymbol{\epsilon}^{j} \tag{19.100f}$$

$$= -(\boldsymbol{\epsilon}^{0})^T \boldsymbol{A}^T \boldsymbol{d}^{j} + (\boldsymbol{d}^{j})^T \boldsymbol{A} (\boldsymbol{\epsilon}^{0} - \sum_{i=0}^{j-1} \alpha^i \boldsymbol{d}^{i}) \tag{19.100g}$$

$$= -(\boldsymbol{\epsilon}^{0})^T \boldsymbol{A}^T \boldsymbol{d}^{j} + (\boldsymbol{d}^{j})^T \boldsymbol{A} \boldsymbol{\epsilon}^{0} \tag{19.100h}$$

$$= 0 \tag{19.100i}$$

The final step to reach the algorithm is to consider a simplification for calculating β_{kj} in (19.91). Since

$$\begin{aligned}
\boldsymbol{\rho}^{\,k+1} &= -\boldsymbol{A}\boldsymbol{\epsilon}^{\,k+1} && (19.101a)\\
&= -\boldsymbol{A}\left(\boldsymbol{r}^{\,k+1} - \boldsymbol{r}^{\,*}\right) && (19.101b)\\
&= -\boldsymbol{A}\left(\boldsymbol{r}^{\,k} + \alpha^k \boldsymbol{d}^{\,k} - \boldsymbol{r}^{\,*}\right) && (19.101c)\\
&= -\boldsymbol{A}\left(\boldsymbol{\epsilon}^{\,k} + \alpha^k \boldsymbol{d}^{\,k}\right) && (19.101d)\\
&= \boldsymbol{\rho}^{\,k} - \alpha^k \boldsymbol{A}\boldsymbol{d}^{\,k}. && (19.101e)
\end{aligned}$$

Multiplying both sides with $(\boldsymbol{\rho}^{\,j})^T$ with get the numerator from (19.91)

$$(\boldsymbol{\rho}^{\,j})^T \boldsymbol{\rho}^{\,k+1} = (\boldsymbol{\rho}^{\,j})^T \boldsymbol{\rho}^{\,k} - \alpha^k (\boldsymbol{\rho}^{\,j})^T \boldsymbol{A}\boldsymbol{d}^{\,k} \tag{19.102a}$$

$$\Downarrow$$

$$(\boldsymbol{\rho}^{\,j})^T \boldsymbol{A}\boldsymbol{d}^{\,k} = \frac{1}{\alpha^k}\left((\boldsymbol{\rho}^{\,j})^T \boldsymbol{\rho}^{\,k} - (\boldsymbol{\rho}^{\,j})^T \boldsymbol{\rho}^{\,k+1}\right). \tag{19.102b}$$

However, since all residuals are orthogonal we get

$$(\boldsymbol{\rho}^{\,j})^T \boldsymbol{A}\boldsymbol{d}^{\,k} = \begin{cases} \frac{(\boldsymbol{\rho}^{\,j})^T \boldsymbol{\rho}^{\,j}}{\alpha^j} & j = k, \\ -\frac{(\boldsymbol{\rho}^{\,j})^T \boldsymbol{\rho}^{\,j}}{\alpha^{j-1}} & j = k+1, \\ 0 & \text{otherwise}, \end{cases} \tag{19.103a}$$

and since β_{kj} is only calculated for $j < k$ we get

$$\beta_{kj} = \begin{cases} -\frac{(\boldsymbol{\rho}^{\,j})^T \boldsymbol{\rho}^{\,j}}{\alpha^{j-1} (\boldsymbol{d}^{\,j-1})^T \boldsymbol{A}\boldsymbol{d}^{\,j-1}} & j = k+1, \\ 0 & \text{otherwise}, \end{cases} \tag{19.104}$$

Finally, the complete algorithm is shown in Figure 19.10. The conjugate gradient method converges in theory to the exact solution in N steps, where N is the dimensionality of $\boldsymbol{r}$. However, round-off errors will cause the solution to deviate from $\boldsymbol{A}$ orthogonality, and hence the convergence will not be perfect after N steps. Furthermore, for large problems it may be desirable to terminate the conjugate gradient iteration before convergence to reduce the computation time for inexact problems.

19.10 The Linear Complementarity Problem

The *Linear Complementarity Problem* (*LCP*) is a well studied mathematical problem (see [Murty, 1988, Cottle et al., 1992]). The linear complementarity problem is used to solve for a discontinuous relationship between two variables such as contact conditions between rigid bodies (see Chapter 7). Linear and quadratic programming is often mentioned in connection with the linear complementarity problem. The

```
Algorithm ConjugateGradient(A,b,r)
  direction = b - A*r
  residual = direction
  for i = 1:length(b)
    alpha = (r'*r)/(direction'*A*direction)
    New_r = r + alpha*direction
    New_residual = residual - alpha*A*direction
    beta = (New_residual'*New_residual)/(residual'*residual)
    direction = New_residual + beta*direction
    r = New_r
    residual = New_residual
  end
end algorithm
```

Figure 19.10: Pseudocode for the conjugate gradient algorithm on (19.67) for a symmetric, positive-definite matrix $\boldsymbol{A}$.

main reason is that a *linear programming* (*LP*) problem can be rephrased as a linear complementarity problem, and a *quadratic programming* (*QP*) problem can be reformulated as a linear complementarity problem. The linear complementarity problem is a general problem, which unifies linear and quadratic programs. Finally, linear programming and quadratic programming are special cases of *mathematical programming*.

Several methods exist for solving linear complementarity problems, there are four main categories of methods: Newton methods, interior point methods, direct methods (also known as pivoting methods), and iterative methods. We refer the interested reader to [Murty, 1988, Cottle et al., 1992] for details.

Implementing a LCP solver can be cumbersome and tricky, fortunately there already exist some solvers. The following is a brief overview of a few existing solvers. For robust simulations PATH from CPNET by Michael Ferris et al. [Path, 2005] is highly recommendable. It is, as far as we know, based on a Newton method. The Lemke algorithm (a pivoting algorithm) is often considered to be a good choice, due to its wide applicability and robustness. The source code accompanying the game physics book by Eberly [Eberly, 2003a] contains an implementation of Lemke's algorithm. Open Dynamics Engine by Russel Smith [ODE, 2005] contains a Dantzig Pivoting algorithm, an iterative Successive-Over-Relaxation (SOR) LCP Solver, and a Conjugate Gradient solver. Also OpenTissue [OpenTissue, 2005] contains implementations of the Dantzig Pivoting algorithm and an iterative SOR/Gauss-Seidel LCP solvers.

The current trend in the Game industry [NovodeX, 2005, ODE, 2005, IO Interactive A/S, 2005] is to use iterative methods for solving LCPs, since these provide a tradeoff between accuracy and speed. Furthermore, iterative methods are well-suited for sparse and extremely large problems. The trade-off property can be exploited in time-critical environments to obtain a solution as accurate as the time permits. Notice that unlike for instance the pivoting algorithms, the iterative methods provides an approximate solution within a given threshold.

In the following we will make use of the inequality relation, $\geq$, for vectors. This is a shorthand to denote that the inequality holds for each pair of components, that is $\boldsymbol{u} = (u_1, u_2, \ldots, u_N)^T \geq$

$(v_1, v_2, \ldots, v_N)^T = \boldsymbol{v}$, if and only if $u_i \geq v_i$ for $1 \leq i \leq N$. Now, let us briefly restate the linear complementarity problem we want to solve,

Definition 19.2 (The Linear Complementarity Problem)
Given a symmetric matrix $\boldsymbol{A} \in \mathbb{R}^{n \times n}$, a vector $\boldsymbol{b} \in \mathbb{R}^n$, a vector of lower limits, $\boldsymbol{x}_{lo} \leq 0$, and upper limits $\boldsymbol{x}_{hi} \geq 0$, where $\boldsymbol{x}_{lo}, \boldsymbol{x}_{hi} \in \mathbb{R}^n$. Find $\boldsymbol{x} \in \mathbb{R}^n$ and $\boldsymbol{w} \in \mathbb{R}^n$ such that

$$\boldsymbol{w} = \boldsymbol{A}\boldsymbol{x} - \boldsymbol{b}, \tag{19.105a}$$

$$\boldsymbol{x}_{lo} \leq \boldsymbol{x} \leq \boldsymbol{x}_{hi}, \tag{19.105b}$$

and for all $i = 0, \ldots, n-1$, one of the three conditions below holds

$$\boldsymbol{x}_i = \boldsymbol{x}_{lo_i}, \quad \boldsymbol{w}_i \geq 0, \tag{19.106a}$$

$$\boldsymbol{x}_i = \boldsymbol{x}_{hi_i}, \quad \boldsymbol{w}_i \leq 0, \tag{19.106b}$$

$$\boldsymbol{x}_{lo_i} < \boldsymbol{x}_i < \boldsymbol{x}_{hi_i}, \quad \boldsymbol{w}_i = 0. \tag{19.106c}$$

Notice that as long as $\boldsymbol{x}_i$ is within its lower and upper limits, $\boldsymbol{w}_i$ is forced to zero. Only at the lower and upper limits is $\boldsymbol{w}_i$ non-zero. Usually, the general LCP is formulated with $\boldsymbol{x}_{\text{lo}} = \boldsymbol{0}$ and $\boldsymbol{x}_{\text{hi}} = \infty$, in which case the above definition reduces to the single set of conditions

$$\boldsymbol{w} = \boldsymbol{A}\boldsymbol{x} - \boldsymbol{b} \geq 0, \tag{19.107a}$$

$$\boldsymbol{x} \geq \boldsymbol{0}, \tag{19.107b}$$

$$\boldsymbol{x}^T\boldsymbol{w} = 0. \tag{19.107c}$$

In multibody dynamics problems the $\boldsymbol{A}$-matrix is often symmetric, unless a linearized friction cone is used, in which case auxiliary variables are used to couple the normal force to the tangential force at a contact point. The $\boldsymbol{A}$-matrix is often positive semi-definite (PSD) or sometimes positive definite (PD). Even if it is PSD, tricks such as damping (adding positive values to the diagonal) can be applied to make it PD. To make a long story short, the $\boldsymbol{A}$-matrix can be made numerically more pleasant, however, the solution will be damped and therefore yield weaker constraint forces.

In this section we will limit ourselves to present iterative methods based on matrix splitting methods. These iterative methods are called projection methods. The main idea is to combine a matrix splitting method (described in Section 19.5 and Section 19.6) with a projection/clamping operation.

Splitting methods can be summarized as follows: we want to solve $Ax = b$, and to do so we introduce a splitting of A as $A = M - N$, hence

$$(\boldsymbol{M} - \boldsymbol{N})\,\boldsymbol{x} = \boldsymbol{b}, \tag{19.108}$$

which gives the iterative scheme,

$$\boldsymbol{M}\boldsymbol{x}^{\,k+1} = b + N\boldsymbol{x}^{\,k}, \tag{19.109}$$

$$\boldsymbol{x}^{\,k+1} = \boldsymbol{M}^{-1}(\boldsymbol{b} + \boldsymbol{N}\boldsymbol{x}^{\,k}). \tag{19.110}$$

The Jacobi method uses $\boldsymbol{M} = \boldsymbol{D}$ and $\boldsymbol{N} = -(\boldsymbol{L} + \boldsymbol{U})$, whereas Gauss-Seidel take $\boldsymbol{M} = (\boldsymbol{D} + \boldsymbol{L})$ and $\boldsymbol{N} = -\boldsymbol{U}$. Here $\boldsymbol{M}^{-1}$ can be understood as a preconditioner to the iterative scheme in (19.110).

The projection operation can be summarized as:

Definition 19.3 (Projection)
Given a vector $\boldsymbol{x} \in \mathbb{R}^n$, a vector of lower limits, $\boldsymbol{x}_{lo} \leq 0$, and upper limits $\boldsymbol{x}_{hi} \geq 0$, where $\boldsymbol{x}_{lo}, \boldsymbol{x}_{hi} \in \mathbb{R}^n$, the projection operation on $\boldsymbol{x}$ is written $(\boldsymbol{x})^+$, and means that for each $j = 0$ to $n-1$

$$\boldsymbol{x}_j^+ = \max\left(\min\left(\boldsymbol{x}_j, \boldsymbol{x}_{hi_j}\right), \boldsymbol{x}_{lo_j}\right). \tag{19.111}$$

As it can be seen from Definition 19.3 the projection operation works element-wise. If a coordinate exceeds a lower or upper limit then it is projected back onto the violated limit. We can now present the iterative LCP solver.

Corollary 19.1 (The iterative LCP solver)
Given a splitting method, an iterative solver to the LCP problem in Definition 19.2, is given by

$$\boldsymbol{x}^{\,k+1} = \left(\boldsymbol{M}^{-1}(\boldsymbol{b} + \boldsymbol{N}\boldsymbol{x}^{\,k})\right)^+. \tag{19.112}$$

According to [Murty, 1988] the only requirement is that $\boldsymbol{A}$ is symmetric. In which case it can be proven that if the sequence of solutions converges to a limit point, then that point will be a solution of the LCP (see Theorem 9.9 pp. 369 in [Murty, 1988]). Furthermore, it can be shown that if $\boldsymbol{A}$ is also PD then the sequence will converge to a solution of the LCP (see Corollary 9.3, pp. 372 in [Murty, 1988]). This is often enough for our purpose. We refer the interested reader to [Murty, 1988] for detailed proofs regarding the general iterative scheme.

Convergence rate, p, can be defined as:

$$lim_{k\to\infty} \frac{\|\mathbf{e}^k\|}{\|\mathbf{e}^{k-1}\|^p} = \lambda, \tag{19.113}$$

where $\mathbf{e}^k$ is the error in the k'th iteration and λ is called the convergence constant. Linear Convergence means $p = 1$, so

$$\left\|\mathbf{e}^k\right\| = \lambda \left\|\mathbf{e}^{k-1}\right\|, \tag{19.114}$$

Whereas quadratic means $P = 2$, and

$$\left\|\mathbf{e}^k\right\| = \lambda \left\|\mathbf{e}^{k-1}\right\|^2 \tag{19.115}$$

The main problem with the iterative method we have presented is that it only has linear convergence. In practice this means that after a certain number of iterations, the improvement per iteration is decreasing. In fact one will always get closer to the solution, but never really hit it. This is unlike direct methods, which is capable of providing the exact solution to the problem. Besides, the speed of convergence of the iterative methods is dependent on the order of the variables.

The theoretical convergence rate of Newton methods is quadratic, even though [Lacoursiere, 2003] only reported linear convergence for multibody dynamics. Interior point methods also have quadratic convergence. The amount of work per iteration in Newton methods is no worse than $O(n^3)$. For direct methods the amount of work per iteration is no worse than $O(n^2)$. Lemke's method needs n iterations to converge which yields a total complexity of $O(n^3)$.

In contrast, the amount of work needed in the iterative method per iteration is only $O(n)$, if an upper bound on the number of iterations can be set. This effectively mean, that the solver is linear in time. Of course the solutions may be horrible, and one need other techniques to remedy these artifacts [Erleben, 2005].

In comparison, Newton methods, direct methods, and interior point methods are more costly per iteration than the iterative methods. On the other hand they often have better convergence properties, implying they only need very few iterations to reach an acceptable solution. Nevertheless, iterative methods are very simple to implement, and in combination with shock-propagation they can deliver acceptable solutions within 5-10 iterations [Erleben, 2005].

20

Taylor Expansion and Derivative Approximations

Many measurements and representations consist of a discrete set of values sampled on a manifold. For example, we may consider an image to be a discrete set of values sampled on a regular grid on a plane, and the surface of a shape may be represented as a discrete set of triangles. To perform differential geometry, we need to assume that the discrete set of values is sampled from an underlying analytical function.

20.1 Taylor Series

In this section we will briefly review Taylor series, since they yield great insight into the approximation of smooth functions. This chapter is inspired by the presentation in [Bronshtein et al., 1997].

Assume that we are given a 1D "well-behaved" function, $f : \mathbb{R} \to \mathbb{R}$, for which all derivatives exist everywhere. That is, the n'th order derivative $f^{(n)}$ is defined in all points. The value of the function f in two points x and $x + h$ are related through the *Taylor series*:

$$f(x+h) = f(x) + hf'(x) + \frac{1}{2}h^2 f''(x) + \frac{1}{6}h^3 f'''(x) + \dots$$
$$= \sum_{i=0}^{\infty} \frac{h^i}{i!} f^{(i)}(x). \tag{20.1}$$

This is also known as the power series; the special case where $x = 0$ is also called the *Maclaurin series*.

As an example, consider the exponential function $f(x) = \exp(x)$. It is arbitrarily differentiable as $f^{(n)} = f$, and $\exp(0) = 1$. Hence,

$$\exp(h) = f(0+h) = \sum_{i=0}^{\infty} \frac{h^i}{i!}, \tag{20.2}$$

and

$$\exp(1) = \sum_{i=0}^{\infty} \frac{1}{i!}. \tag{20.3}$$

Before we give Taylor's theorem, we will first examine the mean value theorem.

Theorem 20.1 (Mean Value Theorem)
For a function $f : \mathbb{R} \to \mathbb{R}$, which is continuous in $[a, b]$ and differentiable in (a, b), there exists an $x_0 \in (a, b)$, such that

$$f'(x_0) = \frac{f(b) - f(a)}{b - a}. \tag{20.4}$$

We can rewrite (20.4) as

$$f(b) = f(a) + (b - a)f'(x_0), \tag{20.5}$$

and using $h = b - a$, and $\theta = \frac{x_0 - a}{k}$, we find

$$f(a + h) = f(a) + hf'(a + \theta h). \tag{20.6}$$

This form of the equation has the spirit of the Taylor theorem.

Theorem 20.2 (Taylor's Theorem)
For a function $f : \mathbb{R} \to \mathbb{R}$, which is $(n + 1)$ times differential on some open interval $x \in (a, b)$, then

$$f(x + h) = \sum_{i=0}^{n} \frac{h^i}{i!} f^{(i)}(x) + R_n(x, h), \tag{20.7}$$

where the remainder on Lagrange's form is given by

$$R_n(x, h) = \frac{h^{n+1}}{(n + 1)!} f^{(n+1)}(x + \theta h), \tag{20.8}$$

and where $\theta \in (0, 1)$ is an unknown constant given by Theorem 20.1.

A function f is said to be an *analytical function* at the point x, if for all $|h| < r > 0$

$$f(x + h) = \sum_{i=0}^{\infty} \frac{h^i}{i!} f^{(i)}(x). \tag{20.9}$$

The largest h, for which the sum converges, is called the *radius of convergence*.
An often-used notation in Taylor expansion is the *Landau symbol* or "Big-O," which disregards the exact form of the remainder by

$$R_n(x, h) = \mathcal{O}(h^{n+1}), \tag{20.10}$$

meaning that given a function $g(x) = \mathcal{O}(f(x))$, then there exists a constant $M \in R$ independent of x, such that

$$|g(x)| < M\,|f(x)| \tag{20.11}$$

for all x possibly limited to some finite interval. Note that the Landau expression $g(x) = \mathcal{O}(f(x))$ is a statement about a set of functions, and we can be tricked into erroneous conclusions. As an example, assume that $g(x) = \mathcal{O}(f(x))$. Since the Landau symbol only defines relations up to some unknown constant M, we can conclude that $3g(x) = \mathcal{O}(f(x))$. This is valid since the two uses of the Landau symbol imply two different constants; but beware it does not imply that $g(x) = 3g(x)$. Nevertheless, it is correct to infer that

$$\mathcal{O}(x^m) + \mathcal{O}(x^n) = \mathcal{O}(x^n), \tag{20.12}$$

when $n \geq m$, and it may also be inferred that

$$x\mathcal{O}(x^n) = \mathcal{O}(x^{n+1}). \tag{20.13}$$

Using Landau symbols, the Taylor series may be written as

$$f(x+h) = \sum_{i=0}^{n} \frac{h^i}{i!} f^{(i)}(x) + \mathcal{O}(h^{n+1}). \tag{20.14}$$

The extension to higher dimensional functions is straightforward, since differentiation is separable. For example, assume we have a 2D function $f : \mathbb{R}^2 \rightarrow \mathbb{R}$, then the Taylor expansion is given as

$$f(x+h, y+k) = \sum_{i=0}^{n} \frac{h^i}{i!} \frac{\partial^i}{\partial x^i} \sum_{j=0}^{m} \frac{k^j}{j!} \frac{\partial^j}{\partial y^j} f(x,y) + \mathcal{O}(h^{n+1}k^{m+1}) \tag{20.15a}$$

$$= \sum_{i=0}^{n} \sum_{j=0}^{m} \frac{h^i k^j}{i! j!} \frac{\partial^{i+j}}{\partial x^i \partial y^j} f(x,y) + \mathcal{O}(h^{n+1}k^{m+1}). \tag{20.15b}$$

Reordering terms we get

$$\begin{aligned} f(x+h, y+k) = f(x,y) &+ h\frac{\partial f(x,y)}{\partial x} + k\frac{\partial f(x,y)}{\partial y} \\ &+ \frac{h^2}{2}\frac{\partial^2 f(x,y)}{\partial x^2} + \frac{k^2}{2}\frac{\partial^2 f(x,y)}{\partial y^2} + hk\frac{\partial^2 f(x,y)}{\partial x \partial y} \dots \end{aligned} \tag{20.16}$$

20.2 Finite Differences by Forward, Backward, and Central Approximations

In the following, we will discuss approximations of derivatives of a function using its neighboring values. The theory to be presented in the following has been inspired by [Eberly, 2003a]. Consider the Taylor expansion of a 1D analytical function around x.

$$f(x+h) = f(x) + hf'(x) + \mathcal{O}(h^2). \tag{20.17}$$

Using this, we may estimate the derivative in x as

$$f'(x) = \frac{f(x+h) - f(x)}{h} + \mathcal{O}(h), \tag{20.18}$$

which is known as the forward difference approximation. Likewise, if we consider

$$f(x-h) = f(x) - hf'(x) + \mathcal{O}(h^2), \tag{20.19}$$

then we get the backward difference approximation,

$$f'(x) = \frac{f(x) - f(x-h)}{h} + \mathcal{O}(h). \tag{20.20}$$

Finally, subtracting (20.19) from (20.17) and solving for f' yields the central difference approximation

$$f'(x) = \frac{f(x+h) - f(x-h)}{2h} + \mathcal{O}(h^2). \tag{20.21}$$

In contrast to the forward and backward difference approximations, the error term in the central difference approximation is one order higher, since the second-order terms in the Taylor expansions cancel.

A finite difference is a linear combination of neighboring function values, hence we may view an approximation as a filter kernel. For example, the kernel for (20.21) would be $\frac{1}{h}[1, 0, -1]$. This principle may be generalized to all linear combinations of neighboring function values.

An approximation of any derivative of an analytical function by a linear combination of neighboring function values will now be derived. The problem is stated as follows: find the linear set of coefficients, c_i, which approximates a d order derivative to p order accuracy as

$$f^{(d)}(x) = \frac{d!}{h^d} \sum_{i=i_{\min}}^{i_{\max}} c_i f(x+ih) + \mathcal{O}(h^p), \tag{20.22}$$

using neighboring values of f with $i_{\max} > i_{\min}$.

To begin, we rearrange terms for mathematical convenience

$$\frac{h^d}{d!} f^{(d)}(x) + \mathcal{O}(h^{d+p}) = \sum_{i=i_{\min}}^{i_{\max}} c_i f(x+ih), \tag{20.23}$$

and insert the infinite Taylor series for f, i.e. $f(x+ih) = \sum_{n=0}^{\infty} \frac{i^n h^n}{n!} f^{(n)}(x)$, on the right-hand side of (20.23). This gives

$$\frac{h^d}{d!} f^{(d)}(x) + \mathcal{O}(h^{d+p}) = \sum_{i=i_{\min}}^{i_{\max}} c_i \sum_{n=0}^{\infty} \frac{i^n h^n}{n!} f^{(n)}(x). \tag{20.24}$$

Truncating the infinite series to $d+p$ order accuracy gives

$$\frac{h^d}{d!} f^{(d)}(x) + \mathcal{O}(h^{d+p}) = \sum_{i=i_{\min}}^{i_{\max}} c_i \sum_{n=0}^{d+p-1} \frac{i^n h^n}{n!} f^{(n)}(x) + \mathcal{O}(h^{d+p}), \tag{20.25}$$

and with a rearrangement of the terms we find that

$$f^{(d)}(x) + \mathcal{O}(h^p) = \sum_{n=0}^{d+p-1} \left(\sum_{i=i_{\min}}^{i_{\max}} i^n c_i \right) \frac{d! h^n}{n! h^d} f^{(n)}(x) + \mathcal{O}(h^p). \tag{20.26}$$

The solution to this system is to choose $\boldsymbol{c} = \{c_i\}$, such that

$$\sum_{i=i_{\min}}^{i_{\max}} i^n c_i = \begin{cases} 1, & \text{if } n = d, \\ 0, & \text{otherwise}, \end{cases} \tag{20.27}$$

or expressed as a matrix equation,

$$\boldsymbol{Ic} = \begin{bmatrix} 1 & 1 & \cdots & 1 \\ i_{\min} & i_{\min+1} & \cdots & i_{\max} \\ i^2_{\min} & i^2_{\min+1} & \cdots & i^2_{\max} \\ \vdots & \vdots & \ddots & \vdots \\ i^{d+p-1}_{\min} & i^{d+p-1}_{\min+1} & \cdots & i^{d+p-1}_{\max} \end{bmatrix} \begin{bmatrix} c_{i\min} \\ c_{i\min+1} \\ c_{i\min+2} \\ \vdots \\ c_{i\max} \end{bmatrix} = \begin{bmatrix} 0 \\ \vdots \\ 0 \\ 1 \\ 0 \\ \vdots \\ 0 \end{bmatrix}, \tag{20.28}$$

where $\boldsymbol{I} = \{i^n\}$. If the extend of the linear approximation is chosen such that $i_{\max} - i_{\min} + 1 = d + p$, then I in (20.27) is a quadratic $(d+p) \times (d+p)$ *Vandermonde matrix*, and the $p+d$ unknown coefficients, c_i, may be shown to have a unique solution. In that case, choosing $i_{\min} = 0$ yields forward difference approximations, $i_{\max} = 0$ yields backward difference approximations, and choosing $i_{\min} = -i_{\max}$ results in the central difference approximations.

To conclude, the d'th order derivative of an analytical function may be approximated to p'th order accuracy as a linear function of the neighboring values using

$$f^{(d)}(x) = \frac{d!}{h^d} \sum_{i=i_{\min}}^{i_{\max}} c_i f(x + ih) + \mathcal{O}(h^p), \tag{20.29}$$

where the coefficients c_i are solved according to (20.27).

21

Calculus of Variation

For a one-dimensional function, $f(x)$, we may seek the extremal points, i.e., the points, x, where the function is either maximal or minimal. If the function is continuous and has a well-defined first-order derivative, the extremal points may be found as $\frac{df(x)}{dx} = 0$. Similarly, *calculus of variation* is concerned with finding extremal functions of functionals, i.e., problems on the form

$$L(f) = \int_a^b \mathcal{L}\, dx, \tag{21.1a}$$

$$\overline{f} = \arg\max_f L(f), \tag{21.1b}$$

where $\mathcal{L}$ is integrable over the domain $x \in [a, b]$ and is a function of x, f, and derivatives of f w.r.t. x. Minimizing problems are also covered by the above formulation since $\max_f \int -\mathcal{L}\, dx$ is the minimum of (21.1). In calculus of variation, the extremal points are also called stationary points. On a historic note, a fundamental result of calculus of variation are the Euler differential equations first described by Euler (Leonhard Euler 1707–1783) in 1744 [Euler, 1744] and later improved by Lagrange (Joseph-Louis Lagrange 1736–1813) in 1755–1762 [Lagrange, 1762]. The Euler-Lagrange equations for various functionals will be derived in this chapter. Below we give a short review of [Hansen, 1988].

21.1 Deriving the Euler-Lagrange Equation

In the following we will derive the simplest of the *Euler-Lagrange equations* for integrals on the form (21.1), where

$$\mathcal{L} = \mathcal{L}\left(x, f(x), \frac{df(x)}{dx}\right) = \mathcal{L}\left(x, f(x), f_x(x)\right), \tag{21.2}$$

and where $f(x)$ and $f_x(x) = \frac{df}{dx}(x)$ are functions depending on the independent variable x. The function f is often referred to as the dependent variable.

To find extremal values of (21.1), we will introduce a Taylor series of functionals as

$$L(f + \Delta f) = L(f) + \Delta f \delta L(f) + \dots, \tag{21.3}$$

where $\delta L(f)$ is the first variation of the functional. Unfortunately, in contrast to the Taylor series developed in Chapter 20, the series in (21.3) depends on f and Δf, which are functions rather than variables. An analytical function may be represented as a vector of samples $[f_1, f_2, \dots, f_n]^T$, which in the limit of infinitely densely sampling is equivalent to the continuous function f. Each sample would in such a case, be a variable, which would imply that f had infinitely many variables. Luckily, the problem can be solved essentially as a one-dimensional problem.

Assume that we are given a function $\overline{f}(x)$, which makes the integral extremal; then the first variation is zero, that is,

$$\delta L(\overline{f}(x)) = 0. \tag{21.4}$$

Introducing a small arbitrary constant, ε, and an arbitrary function, $\eta(x)$, for which

$$\eta(a) = \eta(b) = 0, \tag{21.5}$$

allows us to write the variation of f in the η direction as

$$f(x) = \overline{f}(x) + \varepsilon\eta(x), \tag{21.6}$$

and as a consequence

$$f_x(x) = \overline{f}_x(x) + \varepsilon\eta_x(x). \tag{21.7}$$

For an arbitrary but fixed η, we have converted the infinite-dimensional problem into a one-dimensional problem, i.e., we can write (21.4) as [Hansen, 1988, Equation 1.3 in Section 1.7],

$$\delta L(\overline{f}(x)) = \left[\frac{d}{d\varepsilon} L(\overline{f}(x) + \varepsilon\eta(x))\right]_{\varepsilon=0} = 0. \tag{21.8}$$

Assuming that a and b are independent of ε, and using Leibnitz's rule for differentiation of integrals [Spiegel, 1968, p. 95 Equation 15.14], the differentiation may be moved inside the integral as

$$\delta L(\overline{f}(x)) = \frac{d}{d\varepsilon}\int_a^b \mathcal{L}\left(x, f(x), f_x(x)\right) dx \tag{21.9a}$$

$$= \int_a^b \frac{d}{d\varepsilon}\mathcal{L}\left(x, f(x), f_x(x)\right) dx \tag{21.9b}$$

$$= \int_a^b \frac{\partial \mathcal{L}}{\partial x}\frac{\partial x}{\partial \varepsilon} + \frac{\partial \mathcal{L}}{\partial f}\frac{\partial f}{\partial \varepsilon} + \frac{\partial \mathcal{L}}{\partial f_x}\frac{\partial f_x}{\partial \varepsilon}\, dx \tag{21.9c}$$

$$= \int_a^b \frac{\partial \mathcal{L}}{\partial f}\frac{\partial f}{\partial \varepsilon} + \frac{\partial \mathcal{L}}{\partial f_x}\frac{\partial f_x}{\partial \varepsilon}\, dx, \tag{21.9d}$$

where the last simplification uses $\frac{\partial x}{\partial \varepsilon} = 0$. Recalling the rule for *integration by parts*

$$\int_a^b \phi \frac{d\chi}{dx} dx = [\phi\chi]_a^b - \int_a^b \frac{d\phi}{dx}\chi dx, \tag{21.10}$$

we can rewrite the last terms in (21.9d) as

$$\int_a^b \frac{\partial \mathcal{L}}{\partial f_x}\frac{\partial f_x}{\partial \varepsilon} dx = \int_a^b \frac{\partial \mathcal{L}}{\partial f_x}\left(\frac{d}{dx}\frac{\partial f}{\partial \varepsilon}\right) dx \tag{21.11a}$$

$$= \left[\frac{\partial \mathcal{L}}{\partial f_x}\frac{\partial f}{\partial \varepsilon}\right]_a^b - \int_a^b \left(\frac{d}{dx}\frac{\partial \mathcal{L}}{\partial f_x}\right)\frac{\partial f}{\partial \varepsilon} dx. \tag{21.11b}$$

Inserting first (21.6) and then (21.5) into (21.11b) we find that

$$\int_a^b \frac{\partial \mathcal{L}}{\partial f_x} \frac{\partial f_x}{\partial \varepsilon} dx = \left[\frac{\partial \mathcal{L}}{\partial f_x} \eta(x) \right]_a^b - \int_a^b \left(\frac{d}{dx} \frac{\partial \mathcal{L}}{\partial f_x} \right) \eta(x) dx \tag{21.12a}$$

$$= - \int_a^b \left(\frac{d}{dx} \frac{\partial \mathcal{L}}{\partial f_x} \right) \eta(x) dx. \tag{21.12b}$$

Inserting (21.12b) and (21.6) in (21.9d) and collecting terms for $\eta(x) = \frac{\partial f(x)}{\partial \varepsilon}$, we find that

$$\int_a^b \left[\frac{\partial \mathcal{L}}{\partial f} - \frac{d}{dx} \left(\frac{\partial \mathcal{L}}{\partial f_x} \right) \right] \eta(x) dx = 0. \tag{21.13}$$

Since $\eta(x)$ was chosen as an arbitrary function for which $\eta(a) = \eta(b) = 0$, we must conclude that this is only possible when

$$\frac{\partial \mathcal{L}}{\partial f} - \frac{d}{dx} \left(\frac{\partial \mathcal{L}}{\partial f_x} \right) = 0. \tag{21.14}$$

To conclude, the function $\overline{f}$ is a solution to (21.4), if it is a solution to (21.14).

The *variational derivative* [Goldstein, 1980, Equation 13.63] is the direction in the function space for where L in (21.1) increases the most, and it is found as the difference between the right-hand and left-hand side of (21.14),

$$\frac{\delta}{\delta f} \mathcal{L} = \frac{\partial \mathcal{L}}{\partial f} - \frac{d}{dx} \left(\frac{\partial \mathcal{L}}{\partial f_x} \right). \tag{21.15}$$

21.2 Equation for Many Independent and High-Order Derivatives of 1 Dependent Variable

For more independent variables such as x, y, z, and t, where

$$\mathcal{L} = \mathcal{L} \left(x, y, z, t, f(x,y,z,t), \frac{df(x,y,z,t)}{dx}, \frac{df(x,y,z,t)}{dy}, \frac{df(x,y,z,t)}{dz}, \frac{df(x,y,z,t)}{dt} \right) \tag{21.16a}$$

$$= \mathcal{L} \left(x, y, z, t, f(x,y,z,t), f_x(x,y,z,t), f_y(x,y,z,t), f_z(x,y,z,t), f_t(x,y,z,t) \right), \tag{21.16b}$$

the derivation of (21.14) yields the following simple extension [Hansen, 1988, Equation 5 in Section 2.5],

$$\frac{\partial \mathcal{L}}{\partial f} - \frac{d}{dx} \left(\frac{\partial \mathcal{L}}{\partial f_x} \right) - \frac{d}{dy} \left(\frac{\partial \mathcal{L}}{\partial f_y} \right) - \frac{d}{dz} \left(\frac{\partial \mathcal{L}}{\partial f_z} \right) - \frac{d}{dt} \left(\frac{\partial \mathcal{L}}{\partial f_t} \right) = 0 \tag{21.17}$$

In this case, the variational derivative is given as

$$\frac{\delta}{\delta f} \mathcal{L} = \left(\frac{\partial}{\partial f} - \sum_i \frac{d}{dx_i} \frac{\partial}{\partial f_{x_i}} \right) \mathcal{L}, \tag{21.18}$$

where x_i are the independent variables $x, y, z, \ldots$.

We will now derive the Euler-Lagrange equations for the case where $\mathcal{L}$ in (21.4) depends on higher order derivatives, for example,

$$\mathcal{L} = \mathcal{L}\left(x, y, f(x,y), f_x(x,y), f_y(x,y), f_{xx}(x,y), f_{xy}(x,y), f_{yy}(x,y)\right), \tag{21.19}$$

where $f_{xy} = \frac{d^2 f(x,y)}{dxdy}$ etc.

To simplify, we introduce the following shorthand notation: assume that there are n independent variables, then let $f_{x_i} = \frac{df(x)}{dx_i}$ denote all possible first-order derivatives, and let $f_{x_i x_j} = \frac{d^2 f(x)}{dx_i dx_j}$ denote all possible different second-order derivatives. We may now write

$$\mathcal{L} = \mathcal{L}\left(x_i, f, f_{x_i}, f_{x_i x_j}\right). \tag{21.20}$$

Again we assume that f is a solution and pick an arbitrary constant ε and some unknown function η, which is zero at the border of our domain, and examine (21.8). By straightforward differentiation we get

$$\frac{d}{d\varepsilon}L(f(x)) = \int_{a_1}^{b_1} \cdots \int_{a_n}^{b_n} \left[\frac{\partial \mathcal{L}}{\partial f}\frac{\partial f}{\partial \varepsilon} + \sum_{i=1}^{n} \frac{\partial \mathcal{L}}{\partial f_{x_i}}\frac{\partial f_{x_i}}{\partial \varepsilon} + \sum_{i=1}^{n}\sum_{j=i}^{n} \frac{\partial \mathcal{L}}{\partial f_{x_i x_j}}\frac{\partial f_{x_i x_j}}{\partial \varepsilon}\right] dx_1 \cdots dx_n. \tag{21.21}$$

The first-order terms may be independently integrated by parts and the k'th term is rewritten as

$$\int_{a_1}^{b_1} \cdots \int_{a_n}^{b_n} \frac{\partial \mathcal{L}}{\partial f_{x_k}}\frac{\partial f_{x_k}}{\partial \varepsilon} dx_1 \cdots dx_n = -\int_{a_1}^{b_1} \cdots \int_{a_n}^{b_n} \left(\frac{d}{dx_k}\frac{\partial \mathcal{L}}{\partial f_{x_k}}\right)\frac{\partial f}{\partial \varepsilon} dx_1 \cdots dx_n. \tag{21.22}$$

since $\eta(x_1, \cdots, a_k, \cdots, x_n) = \eta(x_1, \cdots, b_k, \cdots, x_n)) = 0 \quad \forall x_1, \cdots, x_{k-1}, x_{k+1}, \cdots, x_n$. Likewise, the integration by parts for the $h \leq k$'th second derivative term is rewritten as

$$\int_{a_1}^{b_1} \cdots \int_{a_n}^{b_n} \frac{\partial \mathcal{L}}{\partial f_{x_h x_k}}\frac{\partial f_{x_h x_k}}{\partial \varepsilon} dx_1 \cdots dx_n = -\int_{a_1}^{b_1} \cdots \int_{a_n}^{b_n} \left(\frac{d}{dx_h}\frac{\partial \mathcal{L}}{\partial f_{x_h x_k}}\right)\frac{\partial f_{x_k}}{\partial \varepsilon} dx_1 \cdots dx_n \tag{21.23a}$$

$$= \int_{a_1}^{b_1} \cdots \int_{a_n}^{b_n} \left(\frac{d^2}{dx_h dx_k}\frac{\partial \mathcal{L}}{\partial f_{x_h x_k}}\right)\frac{\partial f}{\partial \varepsilon} dx_1 \cdots dx_n, \tag{21.23b}$$

where we repeatedly have used the zero border conditions of η. Gathering all terms yields the Euler-Lagrange equation:

$$\frac{\partial \mathcal{L}}{\partial f} - \sum_i \frac{d}{dx_i}\frac{\partial \mathcal{L}}{\partial f_{x_i}} + \sum_{i=1}^{n}\sum_{j=i}^{n} \frac{d^2}{dx_j dx_i}\frac{\partial \mathcal{L}}{\partial f_{x_i x_j}} = 0 \tag{21.24}$$

and the variational derivative becomes

$$\frac{\delta}{\delta f}\mathcal{L} = \left(\frac{\partial}{\partial f} - \sum_i \frac{d}{dx_i}\frac{\partial}{\partial f_{x_i}} + \sum_{i=1}^{n}\sum_{j=i}^{n} \frac{d^2}{dx_j dx_i}\frac{\partial}{\partial f_{x_i x_j}}\right)\mathcal{L}. \tag{21.25}$$

21.3 Equation for Many Dependent Variables

In the situation where there are several dependent variables, such as $f, g, \ldots$, the integration is over functions on the following form.

$$\mathcal{L} = \mathcal{L}\left(x, f(x), f_x(x), f_{xx}(x), \ldots, g(x), g_x(x), g_{xx}(x), \ldots\right). \tag{21.26}$$

To evaluate the variation we introduce as many extra variables as dependent variables

$$f(x) = \bar{f}(x) + \varepsilon\eta(x), \tag{21.27a}$$
$$g(x) = \bar{g}(x) + \gamma\xi(x), \tag{21.27b}$$
$$\vdots$$

for arbitrary functions η, ξ, ... being zero on the boundaries. The integral is extremal, when the variation w.r.t. $f, g, \ldots$ is zero. That is, we seek to solve the following system of equations:

$$\delta_f L(\overline{f}(x), \overline{g}(x), \ldots) = \left[\frac{d}{d\varepsilon} L(\overline{f}(x) + \varepsilon\eta(x), \overline{g}(x), \ldots)\right]_{\varepsilon=0} = 0, \tag{21.28a}$$
$$\delta_g L(\overline{f}(x), \overline{g}(x), \ldots) = \left[\frac{d}{d\gamma} L(\overline{f}(x), \overline{g}(x) + \gamma\xi(x), \ldots)\right]_{\gamma=0} = 0, \tag{21.28b}$$
$$\vdots$$

where δ_f is the variation with respect to f, etc.

Each equation leads to independent differential equations as derived above, that is, the general solution to the variational problem up to second order may be reformulated as solving the following system of differential equations:

$$\frac{\partial \mathcal{L}}{\partial f^{(m)}} - \sum_i \frac{d}{dx_i} \frac{\partial \mathcal{L}}{\partial f^{(m)}_{x_i}} + \sum_{i=1}^{n} \sum_{j=i}^{n} \frac{d^2}{dx_j dx_i} \frac{\partial \mathcal{L}}{\partial f^{(m)}_{x_i x_j}} = 0, \tag{21.29}$$

where $f^{(m)}$ is the dependent variable and x_k is the independent variable.

The variational derivative is naturally given as

$$\frac{\delta}{\delta \boldsymbol{f}}\mathcal{L} = \begin{bmatrix} \frac{\delta}{\delta f^{(1)}} \\ \frac{\delta}{\delta f^{(2)}} \\ \vdots \\ \frac{\delta}{\delta f^{(M)}} \end{bmatrix} \mathcal{L} = \begin{bmatrix} \frac{\partial \mathcal{L}}{\partial f^{(1)}} - \sum_i \frac{d}{dx_i} \frac{\partial \mathcal{L}}{\partial f^{(1)}_{x_i}} + \sum_{i=1}^{n} \sum_{j=i}^{n} \frac{d^2}{dx_j dx_i} \frac{\partial \mathcal{L}}{\partial f^{(1)}_{x_i x_j}} \\ \frac{\partial \mathcal{L}}{\partial f^{(2)}} - \sum_i \frac{d}{dx_i} \frac{\partial \mathcal{L}}{\partial f^{(2)}_{x_i}} + \sum_{i=1}^{n} \sum_{j=i}^{n} \frac{d^2}{dx_j dx_i} \frac{\partial \mathcal{L}}{\partial f^{(2)}_{x_i x_j}} \\ \vdots \\ \frac{\partial \mathcal{L}}{\partial f^{(M)}} - \sum_i \frac{d}{dx_i} \frac{\partial \mathcal{L}}{\partial f^{(M)}_{x_i}} + \sum_{i=1}^{n} \sum_{j=i}^{n} \frac{d^2}{dx_j dx_i} \frac{\partial \mathcal{L}}{\partial f^{(M)}_{x_i x_j}} \end{bmatrix} \tag{21.30}$$

where $\boldsymbol{f} = [f^{(1)}, f^{(2)}, \ldots, f^{(M)}]^T$ is a vector of M dependent variables.

22

Basic Classical Mechanics

An understanding of basic physics is required to fully understand the physically based modeling that is applied in physics-based animation. In this chapter we briefly present the basic physics required for reading this book.

The first four sections of the chapter are mostly concerned with the basic theory of classical rigid body mechanics. In Section 22.1 we present the equations of motion of rigid bodies. Thereafter, in Section 22.2 we discuss friction, and in Section 22.3 we consider work and energy. Having presented the reader with the theory of rigid bodies in Section 22.4, we will present the basic theory of the harmonic oscillator, which is important for understanding mass-spring systems. Following this, we will introduce the Lagrange formulation in Section 22.5, which may be used when modeling deformable object in physics-based animation. In Section 22.6 we treat the principle of virtual work, which is often used when considering constraint forces. Finally, we close the chapter with an introduction to stress and strain in Section 22.7, which are used to describe the physical properties of elastic objects.

22.1 The Newton-Euler Equations of Motion

In the following, we will introduce the reader to the *equations of motion*, also known as the *Newton-Euler equations*. The theory found here is based on [Kleppner et al., 1978, Goldstein et al., 2002].

22.1.1 The Trajectory of a Particle

A *particle* is defined as a point with mass, but no volume. Hence, a particle is described by its mass, m, and its *trajectory*, $\boldsymbol{r}(t)$, giving the particle position as a function of time, as illustrated in Figure 22.1. The velocity of the particle is defined as the limit of the difference between two succeeding positions as the time-step goes to zero,

$$\boldsymbol{v}(t) = \lim_{\Delta t \to 0} \frac{\boldsymbol{r}(t + \Delta t) - \boldsymbol{r}(t)}{\Delta t} = \lim_{\Delta t \to 0} \frac{\Delta \boldsymbol{r}(t)}{\Delta t} = \frac{d\boldsymbol{r}(t)}{dt} = \dot{\boldsymbol{r}}(t), \tag{22.1}$$

which is depicted in Figure 22.2. That is, the *velocity* is the time-derivative of the position. Similarly, the acceleration is defined as the limit of the change in velocity,

$$\boldsymbol{a}(t) = \lim_{\Delta t \to 0} \frac{\boldsymbol{v}(t + \Delta t) - \boldsymbol{v}(t)}{\Delta t} = \frac{d\boldsymbol{v}(t)}{dt} = \dot{\boldsymbol{v}}(t) = \ddot{\boldsymbol{r}}(t), \tag{22.2}$$

as illustrated in Figure 22.3. That is, the *acceleration* is the double time-derivative of the position.

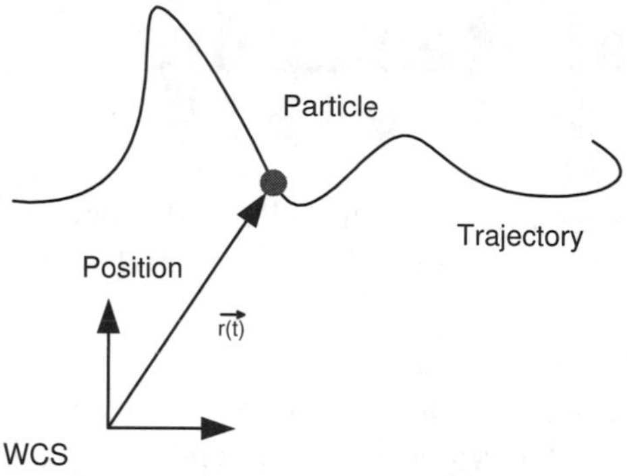

Figure 22.1: A particle trajectory.

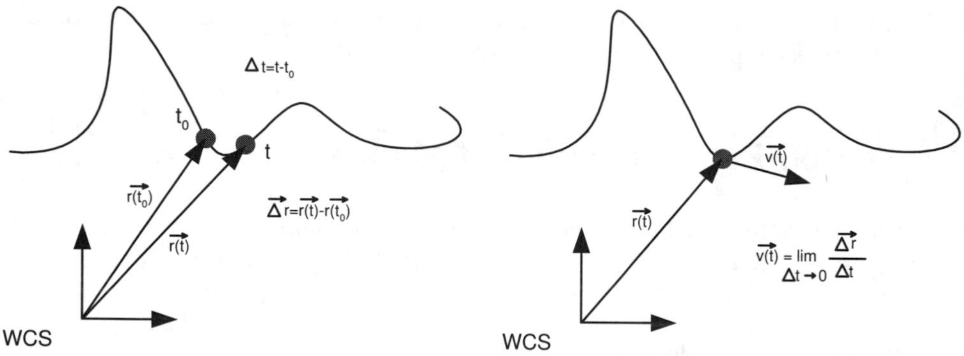

Figure 22.2: The velocity of a particle.

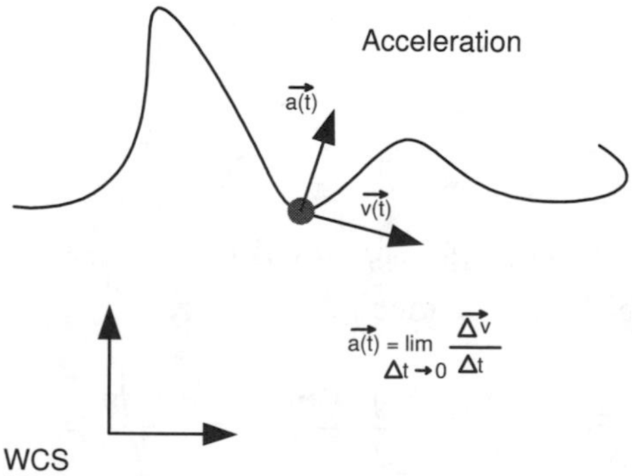

Figure 22.3: The acceleration of a particle.

22.1.2 Newton's Laws of Motion

For pedagogical reasons, we will begin by formulating Newton's law of motion for particle motion. *Newton's first law* of motion states in words that

- Inertial systems exist and an inertial system moves uniformly.
- An isolated particle moves uniformly in an inertial system.

In computer animation, Newton's first law of motion is used to define a global working frame called the *world coordinate system* (*WCS*). The world coordinate system should be thought of as an ideal inertial system, implying that it moves with zero velocity. Of course, in the real world such a coordinate system cannot be uniquely determined, since only relative motion can be measured. Nevertheless, this ideal world coordinate system is useful in computer animation because it provides a global frame of reference in which the motion of all objects in the world may be described uniquely.

Newton's second law of motion defines the linear momentum, $\boldsymbol{p}$, of a particle as

$$\boldsymbol{p} = m\boldsymbol{v}, \tag{22.3}$$

where m is the mass of the particle and $\boldsymbol{v}$ the velocity. Furthermore, Newton's second law states that a force, $\boldsymbol{F}$, has both magnitude and direction. The effect of the force is a change in linear momentum,

$$\boldsymbol{F}(t) = \frac{d\boldsymbol{p}(t)}{dt} = \frac{dm\boldsymbol{v}(t)}{dt} = m\frac{d\boldsymbol{v}(t)}{dt} = m\boldsymbol{a}(t), \tag{22.4}$$

from which we have the relationship force equals mass times acceleration. Note that this is not a definition of force, but rather it describes the effect of a force as an acceleration.

The *point of action* denotes the actual physical point where a force is applied. For a particle, the point of action is simply the position of the particle. The point of action becomes very important when we consider rotational motion later on.

Newton's second law of motion also states that forces obey the superposition principle. That is, if all forces, $\boldsymbol{F}_i$, acting on a particle are known, then the total effect they have on the particle is simply their sum,

$$\boldsymbol{F}_{\text{tot}}(t) = \sum_i \boldsymbol{F}_i(t) = m \sum_i \boldsymbol{a}_i(t) = m\boldsymbol{a}_{\text{tot}}(t). \tag{22.5}$$

Newton's third law states that reaction equals action, and that all forces are due to real-world interactions. The first part of this law comes in two flavors, a weak form and a strong form. The weak law states that

$$\boldsymbol{F}_{AB} = -\boldsymbol{F}_{BA}, \tag{22.6}$$

where a particle A is affected by the force $\boldsymbol{F}_{AB}$ coming from another particle B, and the force $\boldsymbol{F}_{BA}$ is the force that particle A affects particle B with. The strong law requires that F_{AB} and F_{BA} must be central forces, meaning that they must lie on the same line of action, that is, on the line between the two points of action. The two flavors are illustrated in Figure 22.4.

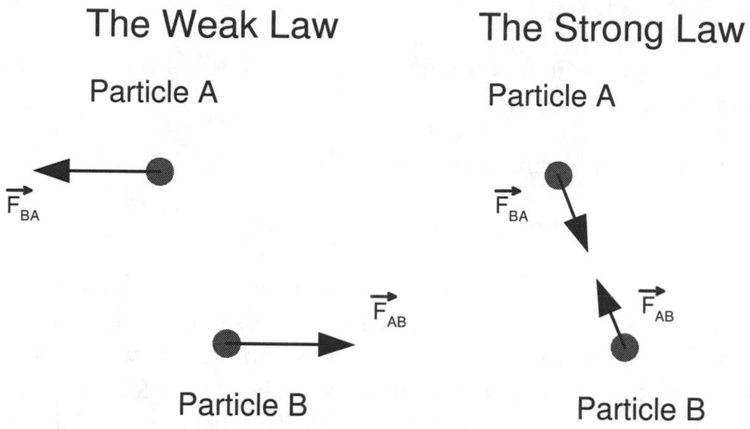

Figure 22.4: The weak and strong form of Newton's third law.

22.1.3 A Particle System

Animating a single particle is trivial, so in the following, Newton's law of motion will be extended to include a *system of particles*. Given N-particles, Newton's second law for the entire system is given as

$$\boldsymbol{F}_1^{\text{tot}} = m_1 \boldsymbol{a}_1^{\text{tot}} \tag{22.7a}$$
$$\boldsymbol{F}_2^{\text{tot}} = m_2 \boldsymbol{a}_2^{\text{tot}} \tag{22.7b}$$
$$\vdots$$
$$\boldsymbol{F}_N^{\text{tot}} = m_N \boldsymbol{a}_N^{\text{tot}}. \tag{22.7c}$$

The forces can now be split into external, $\boldsymbol{F}_i^{\text{ext}}$, and internal forces, $\boldsymbol{F}_i^{\text{int}}$. External forces come from interactions from outside the particle system and internal forces are due to interactions inside the particle system, that is, interactions in between the particles themselves. Splitting the forces gives

$$\boldsymbol{F}_1^{\text{tot}} = \boldsymbol{F}_1^{\text{ext}} + \boldsymbol{F}_1^{\text{int}} = m_1 \boldsymbol{a}_1^{\text{tot}} \tag{22.8a}$$
$$\boldsymbol{F}_2^{\text{tot}} = \boldsymbol{F}_2^{\text{ext}} + \boldsymbol{F}_2^{\text{int}} = m_2 \boldsymbol{a}_2^{\text{tot}} \tag{22.8b}$$
$$\vdots$$
$$\boldsymbol{F}_N^{\text{tot}} = \boldsymbol{F}_N^{\text{ext}} + \boldsymbol{F}_N^{\text{int}} = m_N \boldsymbol{a}_N^{\text{tot}}. \tag{22.8c}$$

Since internal forces are due to other particles, it is found that the total internal force acting on particle i is given by the summation

$$\boldsymbol{F}_i^{\text{int}} = \sum_{j, i \neq j} \boldsymbol{F}_{ji}, \tag{22.9}$$

where $\boldsymbol{F}_{ji}$ is the force with which the j'th particle affects the i'th particle. The sum over all particles may thus be written as

$$\boldsymbol{F}_{\text{tot}} = \sum_i \boldsymbol{F}_i^{\text{ext}} + F_i^{\text{int}} = \sum_i \boldsymbol{F}_i^{\text{ext}} + \sum_i \sum_{j,i \neq j} \boldsymbol{F}_{ji}. \tag{22.10}$$

However, the weak form of Newton's third law states that

$$\boldsymbol{F}_{ji} = -\boldsymbol{F}_{ji}, \tag{22.11}$$

implying that all internal forces cancel each other, that is,

$$\sum_i \sum_{j,i \neq j} \boldsymbol{F}_{ji} = 0. \tag{22.12}$$

This means that the total effect on the entire particle system is given entirely by the sum of the external forces. Hence, we have

$$\boldsymbol{F}_{\text{tot}} = \sum_i \boldsymbol{F}_i^{\text{ext}} \tag{22.13a}$$

$$= \sum_i \left(m_i \boldsymbol{a}_i^{\text{tot}} \right). \tag{22.13b}$$

The total mass, M, of the particle system is given by

$$M = \sum_i m_i. \tag{22.14}$$

We define $\boldsymbol{a}_{\text{cm}}$ as the mass weighted mean of particle accelerations

$$\boldsymbol{a}_{\text{cm}} = \frac{1}{M} \sum_i \left(m_i \ddot{\boldsymbol{r}}_i \right). \tag{22.15}$$

This is called the acceleration of the center of mass (CM) position. Exactly what this center of mass position is, will become clearer later. However, we can now write Newton's second law for a system of particles as

$$\boldsymbol{F}_{\text{tot}} = M \boldsymbol{a}_{\text{cm}}. \tag{22.16}$$

The implication is that the motion of an entire particle system, regardless of the number of particles, may be described as a single particle with mass M. But what is the position of this special particle? Since the acceleration is the double time derivative of a position, $\boldsymbol{a}_{\text{cm}} = \ddot{\boldsymbol{r}}_{\text{cm}}$, we can find the center of mass position, $\boldsymbol{r}_{\text{cm}}$, by integrating the acceleration twice with respect to time.

By the superposition principle (Newton's second law) and the definition of total mass we have

$$\ddot{\boldsymbol{r}}_{\text{cm}} = \frac{1}{M} \sum_i \left(m_i \ddot{\boldsymbol{r}}_i \right). \tag{22.17}$$

Integrating twice with respect to time (and setting integration constants equal to zero), we find that the *position of the center of mass* (*CM*) is

$$\boldsymbol{r}_{\text{cm}} = \frac{1}{M} \sum_i (m_i \boldsymbol{r}_i) . \tag{22.18}$$

That is, the particle system moves like a single particle with position $\boldsymbol{r}_{\text{cm}}$ and mass M.

The Newtonian physics for a real-world object may be derived from a particle system by thinking of a real-world object as a collection of infinitely many particles. Letting the number of particles, N, go to infinity

$$\boldsymbol{r}_{\text{cm}} = \lim_{N \to \infty} \frac{1}{M} \sum_i^N (m_i \boldsymbol{r}_i) = \frac{1}{M} \int \boldsymbol{r}(t)\, dm. \tag{22.19}$$

and introducing the notion of the mass density $\rho = dm/dV$ allows us to rewrite into a volume integral,

$$\boldsymbol{r}_{\text{cm}} = \frac{1}{M} \int_V \rho \boldsymbol{r}\, dV. \tag{22.20}$$

For rigid bodies, the mass density, ρ, is usually assumed to be constant throughout the entire rigid body, implying that the total mass of the rigid body is given by $M = \rho V$.

It is thus concluded that the center of mass of an object behaves as a single particle with position $\boldsymbol{r}_{\text{cm}}$ and mass M. In the above, it has implicitly been assumed that all particles have a fixed relative position w.r.t. each other, and that the particles constitute a rigid body. For simulation purposes, this means that the motion of a rigid body may be found by

$$\frac{d^2 \boldsymbol{r}_{\text{cm}}}{dt^2} = \frac{\boldsymbol{F}}{M}, \tag{22.21}$$

where $\boldsymbol{F}$ is the sum of all external forces. This is a *second-order ordinary differential equation* (*ODE*), which is easily solved as a system of coupled first-order differential equations,

$$\frac{d\boldsymbol{v}_{\text{cm}}}{dt} = \frac{\boldsymbol{F}}{M} \tag{22.22a}$$

$$\frac{d\boldsymbol{r}_{\text{cm}}}{dt} = \boldsymbol{v}_{\text{cm}}. \tag{22.22b}$$

A thorough discussion on ordinary differential equations is found in Section 23.1.

22.1.4 The Body Frame

A brief summary of the previous sections is as follows:

- The world coordinate system (WCS) may be derived from Newton's first law.
- The center of mass (CM) is found using Newton's second law on a particle system.

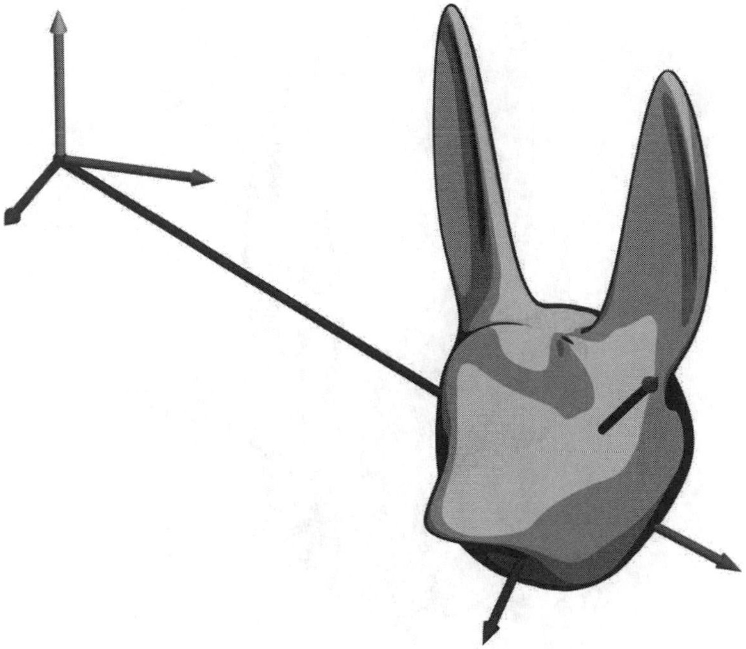

Figure 22.5: The body frame.

From these two results, we know how to describe the motion of the center of mass. However, rigid bodies moving in 3D space not only change position, they also change orientation. In order to describe the rotational movement, a coordinate frame is placed with its origin at center of mass and its axes fixed w.r.t. the orientation of the rigid body. This is known as the *body frame* (*BF*) and is illustrated in Figure 22.5.

One possible way to describe the orientation of the body frame is by *Euler angles*, which can be written in vector form as

$$\boldsymbol{\theta} = \theta_x \boldsymbol{i} + \theta_y \boldsymbol{j} + \theta_z \boldsymbol{k}, \tag{22.23}$$

where $\boldsymbol{i}$, $\boldsymbol{j}$, and $\boldsymbol{k}$ are the *world coordinate axes*, and θ_x, θ_y, and θ_z are scalars. The Euler angles determine the rotation of BF relative to WCS, as depicted in Figure 22.6. Unfortunately, the rotation of objects using Euler angles is not commutative. That is, permuting the order of rotations results in different rotations, as illustrated in Figure 22.7. The $X - Y - Z$ order is commonly called *fixed axis angles* or *roll*, *pitch*, and *yaw* angles.

Although the Euler angles do not commute, their time derivatives are simple to formulate and do commute. These are known as the angular velocity,

$$\boldsymbol{\omega} = \frac{d\theta_x}{dt}\boldsymbol{i} + \frac{d\theta_y}{dt}\boldsymbol{j} + \frac{d\theta_z}{dt}\boldsymbol{k}. \tag{22.24}$$

The direction of the angular velocity gives the rotation axis and the length is the rotation speed.

The absolute value of each component describes how fast the object spins around the corresponding axis, and the sign indicates the direction of rotation around the axis. Positive means counterclockwise and

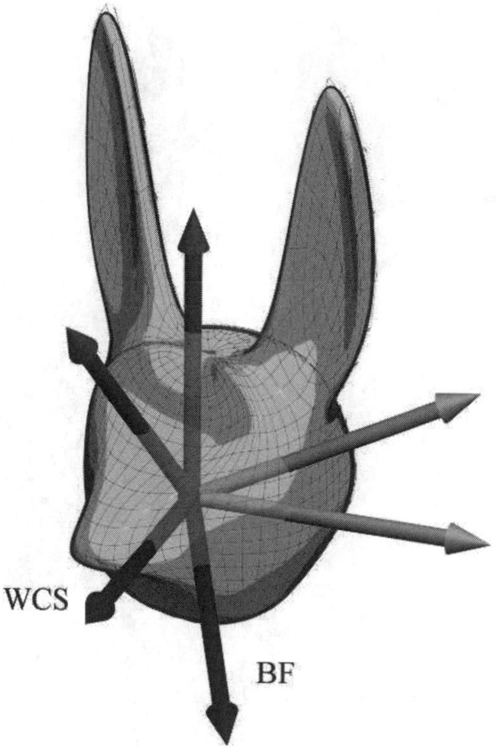

Figure 22.6: The Euler angles describe the orientation of a rigid body.

minus means clockwise. Furthermore, the angular velocity obeys the superposition principle.

To familiarize ourselves with the angular velocity it helps to look at the simple case where $\theta_y = 0$ and $\theta_z = 0$ and $\theta_x = ct$, for some positive constant c. In this case, we derive

$$\boldsymbol{\omega} = \frac{dct}{dt}\boldsymbol{i} + \frac{d0}{dt}\boldsymbol{j} + \frac{d0}{dt}\boldsymbol{k} = \begin{bmatrix} c \\ 0 \\ 0 \end{bmatrix}. \tag{22.25}$$

We see that the angular velocity is a vector along the x-axis, which is also the axis of rotation, the length of the angular velocity is c, which is the rotational speed (traveling distance divided by traveling time). By setting $\theta_z = ct$, we see that we also get a rotation around the z-axis, and the angular velocity now lies in the x-z plane indicating both a rotation around the x and z axes, as expected.

22.1.5 Velocity in a Particle System

Knowing the center of mass position, $\boldsymbol{r}_{\text{cm}}$, of a particle system, then the position, $\boldsymbol{r}_i$, of the i'th particle can be written as

$$\boldsymbol{r}_i = \Delta\boldsymbol{r}_i + \boldsymbol{r}_{\text{cm}}, \tag{22.26}$$

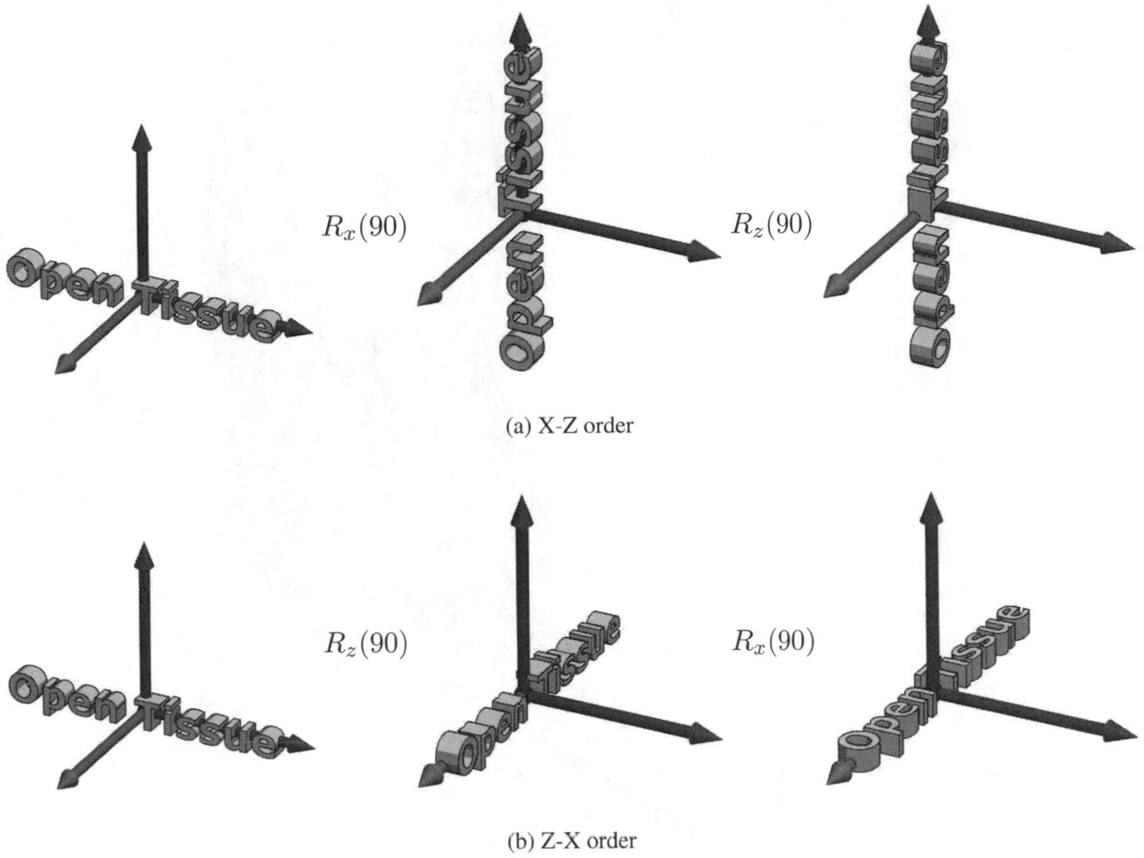

Figure 22.7: Rotation using Euler angles does not commute.

where $\Delta \boldsymbol{r}_i$ is a body-fixed vector, denoting the i'th particle position relative to the center of mass position, as illustrated in Figure 22.8. By differentiation (22.26) w.r.t. time, the velocity of the i'th particle is

$$\boldsymbol{v}_i = \Delta\dot{\boldsymbol{r}}_i + \boldsymbol{v}_{\text{cm}} = \underbrace{\boldsymbol{\omega} \times \Delta\boldsymbol{r}_i}_{\Delta\dot{\boldsymbol{r}}_i} + \boldsymbol{v}_{\text{cm}}. \tag{22.27}$$

Observe that the time derivative of the body-fixed vector $\Delta\boldsymbol{r}_i$ is obtained by the cross product with the angular velocity.

This relation between the time-derivative of a body-fixed vector and the angular velocity will be proven in the following: to ease notation, the particle position in the body frame will be denoted $\boldsymbol{s}$ instead of $\Delta\boldsymbol{r}_i$. The vector, $\boldsymbol{s}$, is rotating around a rotation axis, and the tip of the $\boldsymbol{s}$-vector traces out a circular path. Let the unit vector $\boldsymbol{n}$ denote the rotation axis, and $\Delta\theta$ the rotation angle around $\boldsymbol{n}$. Since the rotation axis passes through the origin of the body frame, the angle, ϕ, between $\boldsymbol{s}$ and $\boldsymbol{n}$ is constant. The circular path of the tip of $\boldsymbol{s}$ has radius $\|\boldsymbol{s}\|_2 \sin(\phi)$, and after some small time-step Δt, the displacement $\Delta\boldsymbol{s}$ of $\boldsymbol{s}$ will

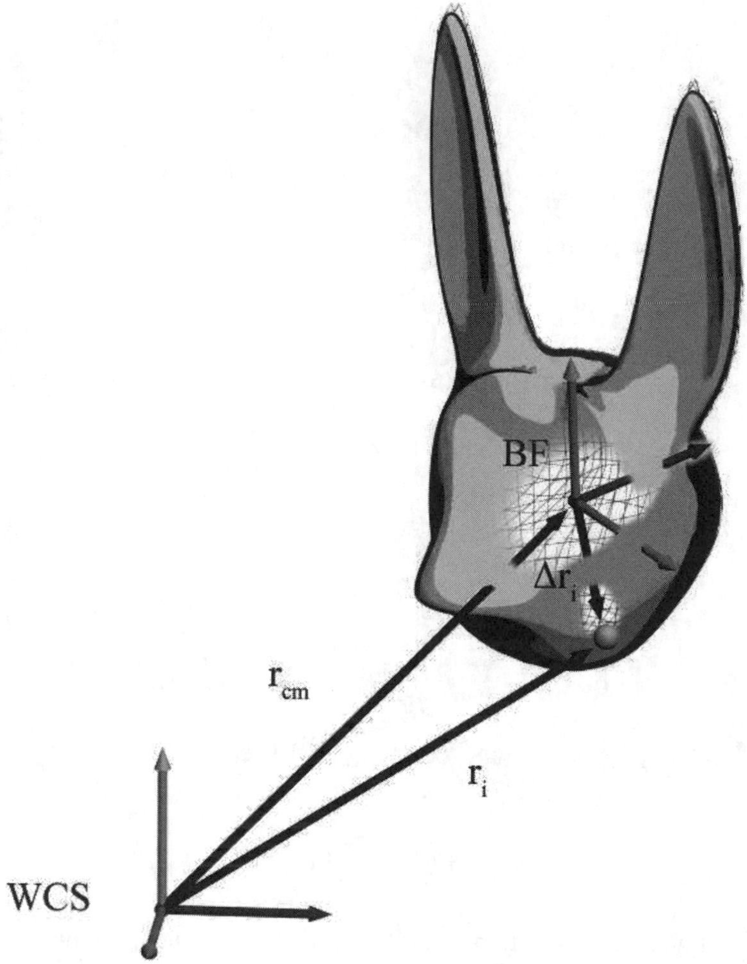

Figure 22.8: The position of the i'th particle in a particle system.

be

$$\Delta \boldsymbol{s} = \boldsymbol{s}(t + \Delta t) - \boldsymbol{s}(t). \tag{22.28}$$

The magnitude of the displacement must then be

$$\|\Delta \boldsymbol{s}\|_2 = 2\,\|\boldsymbol{s}\|_2 \sin(\phi) \sin\left(\frac{\Delta\theta}{2}\right), \tag{22.29}$$

which follows from trigonometry as can be seen in Figure 22.9. The small angle approximation,

$$\sin\left(\frac{\Delta\theta}{2}\right) \approx \frac{\Delta\theta}{2}, \tag{22.30}$$

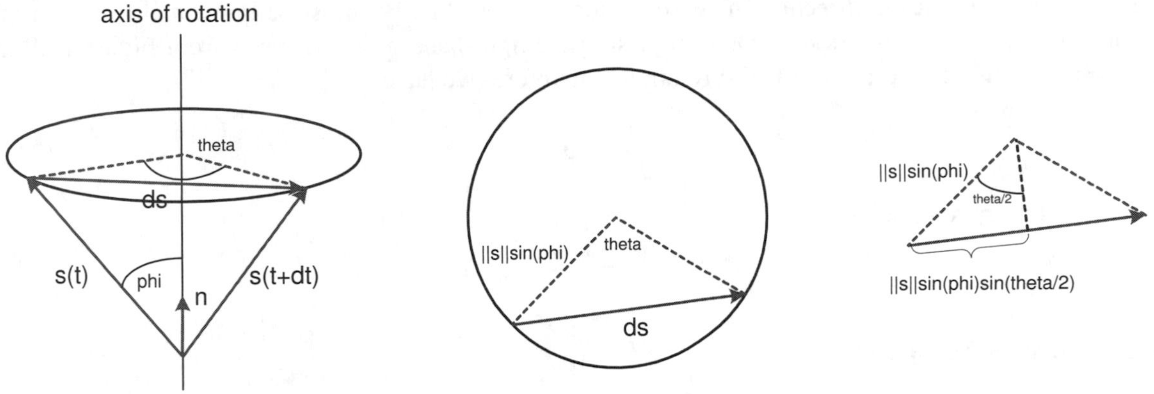

Figure 22.9: The angular velocity.

is good, when $\Delta\theta$ is very small, and hence

$$\|\Delta \boldsymbol{s}\|_2 \approx \|\boldsymbol{s}\|_2 \sin(\phi)\Delta\theta. \tag{22.31}$$

If $\Delta\theta$ occurs in time Δt, then

$$\frac{\|\Delta \boldsymbol{s}\|_2}{\Delta t} \approx \|\boldsymbol{s}\|_2 \sin(\phi)\frac{\Delta\theta}{\Delta t}. \tag{22.32}$$

Taking the limit as $\Delta t \rightarrow 0$, gives

$$\left\|\frac{d\boldsymbol{s}}{dt}\right\|_2 = \lim_{\Delta t \rightarrow 0} \|\boldsymbol{s}\|_2 \sin(\phi)\frac{\Delta\theta}{\Delta t} = \|\boldsymbol{s}\|_2 \sin(\phi)\frac{d\theta}{dt}. \tag{22.33}$$

By definition $\boldsymbol{\omega} = \boldsymbol{n}\frac{d\theta}{dt}$, and thus

$$\|\boldsymbol{\omega}\|_2 = \underbrace{\|\boldsymbol{n}\|_2}_{1} \frac{d\theta}{dt}. \tag{22.34}$$

By substitution, it is found that

$$\left\|\frac{d\boldsymbol{s}}{dt}\right\|_2 = \|\boldsymbol{s}\|_2 \sin(\phi) \|\boldsymbol{n}\|_2 \frac{d\theta}{dt}. \tag{22.35}$$

From the right-hand side it is seen that this is the magnitude of $\boldsymbol{\omega} \times \boldsymbol{s}$,

$$\left\|\frac{d\boldsymbol{s}}{dt}\right\|_2 = \|\boldsymbol{\omega} \times \boldsymbol{s}\|_2 . \tag{22.36}$$

This indicates that either

$$\frac{d\boldsymbol{s}}{dt} = \boldsymbol{\omega} \times \boldsymbol{s} \quad \text{or} \quad \frac{d\boldsymbol{s}}{dt} = \boldsymbol{s} \times \boldsymbol{\omega}. \tag{22.37}$$

However, to ensure that the direction of these vectors are sensible, $\frac{d\boldsymbol{s}}{dt}$ must be tangential to the circular path and pointing in the direction of rotation. Using the right-hand rule, it is seen from Figure 22.9 that $\boldsymbol{\omega} \times \boldsymbol{s}$ points in the same direction as the rotation. Therefore, we have

$$\frac{d\boldsymbol{s}}{dt} = \boldsymbol{\omega} \times \boldsymbol{s}. \tag{22.38}$$

It has thus been proven that

$$\Delta\dot{\boldsymbol{r}}_i = \frac{d\Delta\boldsymbol{r}_i}{dt} = \boldsymbol{\omega} \times \Delta\boldsymbol{r}_i. \tag{22.39}$$

22.1.6 Euler's Equation

The *angular momentum* of a particle, $\boldsymbol{L}$, is defined as

$$\boldsymbol{L} = \boldsymbol{r} \times \boldsymbol{p}, \tag{22.40}$$

where $\boldsymbol{r}$ is the position of the particle, and $\boldsymbol{p} = m\boldsymbol{v}$ is the linear momentum of the particle. The *torque*, $\boldsymbol{\tau}$, of a particle is given by

$$\boldsymbol{\tau} = \boldsymbol{r} \times \boldsymbol{F}, \tag{22.41}$$

where $\boldsymbol{F}$ is the force acting on the particle. It is important to remember which coordinate frame $\boldsymbol{L}$ and $\boldsymbol{\tau}$ are given with respect to, since they have different values in different coordinate frames. The change of the angular momentum is given by its derivative,

$$\frac{d\boldsymbol{L}}{dt} = \frac{d(\boldsymbol{r} \times \boldsymbol{p})}{dt} \tag{22.42a}$$

$$= \frac{d\boldsymbol{r}}{dt} \times \boldsymbol{p} + \boldsymbol{r} \times \frac{d\boldsymbol{p}}{dt} \tag{22.42b}$$

$$= \underbrace{\boldsymbol{v} \times \boldsymbol{p}}_{\boldsymbol{0}} + \boldsymbol{r} \times \boldsymbol{F} \tag{22.42c}$$

$$= \boldsymbol{\tau}. \tag{22.42d}$$

The above relation between angular momentum and torque is known as *Euler's equation*. In words, Euler's equation is a rotational version of Newton's second law.

Euler's equation is the starting point for deriving the formulas for the rotational motion. By the definition of angular momentum and Newton's second law, the total angular momentum, $\boldsymbol{L}_{\text{tot}}$, for a particle system is given as

$$\boldsymbol{L}_{\text{tot}} = \sum_i \boldsymbol{L}_i \tag{22.43a}$$

$$= \sum_i (\boldsymbol{r}_i \times \boldsymbol{p}_i) \tag{22.43b}$$

$$= \sum_i (\boldsymbol{r}_i \times m_i\dot{\boldsymbol{r}}_i). \tag{22.43c}$$

Using $\boldsymbol{r}_i = \Delta\boldsymbol{r}_i + \boldsymbol{r}_{\text{cm}}$, and $\dot{\boldsymbol{r}}_i = \Delta\dot{\boldsymbol{r}}_i + \dot{\boldsymbol{r}}_{\text{cm}}$, the above may be rewritten as

$$\boldsymbol{L}_{\text{tot}} = \sum_i \left((\Delta\boldsymbol{r}_i + \boldsymbol{r}_{\text{cm}}) \times m_i \left(\Delta\dot{\boldsymbol{r}}_i + \dot{\boldsymbol{r}}_{\text{cm}}\right) \right). \tag{22.44}$$

Expanding the cross product and rewriting the summation we find four terms:

$$\begin{aligned} \boldsymbol{L}_{\text{tot}} = &\sum_i \left(\Delta\boldsymbol{r}_i \times m_i \Delta\dot{\boldsymbol{r}}_i\right) + \left(\sum_i m_i \Delta\boldsymbol{r}_i\right) \times \dot{\boldsymbol{r}}_{\text{cm}} \\ &+ \boldsymbol{r}_{\text{cm}} \times \left(\sum_i m_i \dot{\boldsymbol{r}}_{\text{cm}}\right) + \boldsymbol{r}_{\text{cm}} \times \left(\sum_i m_i \Delta\dot{\boldsymbol{r}}_i\right). \end{aligned} \tag{22.45}$$

Although seemingly complicated, this is a useful form for further analysis. To simplify, first use $\Delta\boldsymbol{r}_i = \boldsymbol{r} - \boldsymbol{r}_{\text{cm}}$, which implies that

$$\sum_i m_i \Delta\boldsymbol{r}_i = \sum_i m_i \left(\boldsymbol{r}_i - \boldsymbol{r}_{\text{cm}}\right) \tag{22.46a}$$

$$= \sum_i m_i \boldsymbol{r}_i - \sum_i m_i \boldsymbol{r}_{\text{cm}} \tag{22.46b}$$

$$= \sum_i m_i \boldsymbol{r}_i - \boldsymbol{r}_{\text{cm}} \sum_i m_i \tag{22.46c}$$

Since $M = \sum m_i$, and $\boldsymbol{r}_{\text{cm}} = \frac{1}{M} \sum m_i \boldsymbol{r}_i$, we find that

$$\sum_i m_i \Delta\boldsymbol{r}_i = \sum_i m_i \boldsymbol{r}_i - M\boldsymbol{r}_{\text{cm}} \tag{22.47a}$$

$$= M\boldsymbol{r}_{\text{cm}} - M\boldsymbol{r}_{\text{cm}} \tag{22.47b}$$

$$= \boldsymbol{0}. \tag{22.47c}$$

Furthermore, since the derivative of a constant is zero, it is found that

$$\sum_i m_i \Delta\dot{\boldsymbol{r}}_i = \boldsymbol{0}. \tag{22.48}$$

Using these facts about $\sum m_i \Delta\boldsymbol{r}_i$ and $\sum m_i \Delta\dot{\boldsymbol{r}}_i$ in the equation for the angular momentum, it is found that

$$\boldsymbol{L}_{\text{tot}} = \sum_i (\Delta\boldsymbol{r}_i \times m_i \Delta\dot{\boldsymbol{r}}_i) + \underbrace{\left(\sum_i m_i \Delta\boldsymbol{r}_i\right)}_{\mathbf{0}} \times \dot{\boldsymbol{r}}_{\text{cm}}$$

$$+ \boldsymbol{r}_{\text{cm}} \times \left(\sum_i m_i \dot{\boldsymbol{r}}_{\text{cm}}\right) + \boldsymbol{r}_{\text{cm}} \times \underbrace{\left(\sum_i m_i \Delta\dot{\boldsymbol{r}}_i\right)}_{\mathbf{0}} \tag{22.49a}$$

$$= \sum_i (\Delta\boldsymbol{r}_i \times m_i \Delta\dot{\boldsymbol{r}}_i) + \boldsymbol{r}_{\text{cm}} \times M\boldsymbol{v}_{\text{cm}}. \tag{22.49b}$$

In a similar way, the total torque, $\boldsymbol{\tau}_{\text{tot}}$, of a particle system is found to be

$$\boldsymbol{\tau}_{\text{tot}} = \sum_i \boldsymbol{\tau}_i = \sum_i (\boldsymbol{r}_i \times \boldsymbol{F}_i) = \ldots \tag{22.50a}$$

$$= \sum_i (\Delta\boldsymbol{r}_i \times \boldsymbol{F}_i) + \boldsymbol{r}_{\text{cm}} \times \boldsymbol{F}. \tag{22.50b}$$

By definition, Euler's equation for a particle system is

$$\boldsymbol{\tau}_{\text{tot}} = \frac{d\boldsymbol{L}_{\text{tot}}}{dt} \tag{22.51a}$$

$$\Downarrow$$

$$\sum_i (\Delta\boldsymbol{r}_i \times \boldsymbol{F}_i) + \boldsymbol{r}_{\text{cm}} \times \boldsymbol{F} = \frac{d}{dt}\left(\sum_i (\Delta\boldsymbol{r}_i \times m_i \Delta\dot{\boldsymbol{r}}_i) + \boldsymbol{r}_{\text{cm}} \times M\boldsymbol{v}_{\text{cm}}\right). \tag{22.51b}$$

Differentiating the right-hand side with respect to time gives

$$\sum_i (\Delta\boldsymbol{r}_i \times \boldsymbol{F}_i) + \boldsymbol{r}_{\text{cm}} \times \boldsymbol{F} = \frac{d}{dt}\sum_i (\Delta\boldsymbol{r}_i \times m_i \Delta\dot{\boldsymbol{r}}_i)$$

$$+ \underbrace{\frac{d}{dt}\boldsymbol{r}_{\text{cm}}}_{\boldsymbol{v}_{\text{cm}}} \times M\boldsymbol{v}_{\text{cm}} + \boldsymbol{r}_{\text{cm}} \times \underbrace{\frac{d}{dt}(M\boldsymbol{v}_{\text{cm}})}_{\boldsymbol{F}} \tag{22.52a}$$

$$= \frac{d}{dt}\sum_i (\Delta\boldsymbol{r}_i \times m_i \Delta\dot{\boldsymbol{r}}_i) + \boldsymbol{r}_{\text{cm}} \times \boldsymbol{F}. \tag{22.52b}$$

Observe that we have a $\boldsymbol{r}_{\text{cm}} \times \boldsymbol{F}$ term on both the left- and right-hand sides, which cancels each other. Implying that Euler's equation for a particle system reduces to

$$\underbrace{\sum_i (\Delta\boldsymbol{r}_i \times \boldsymbol{F}_i)}_{\boldsymbol{\tau}_{\text{cm}}} = \frac{d}{dt}\underbrace{\sum_i (\Delta\boldsymbol{r}_i \times m_i \Delta\dot{\boldsymbol{r}}_i)}_{\boldsymbol{L}_{\text{cm}}.}. \tag{22.53}$$

Surprisingly enough, all terms referring to the motion of the center of mass have disappeared, and the remaining terms describe the motion of the particle system around the center of mass. It is concluded that that linear and rotational motion may be treated independently. The equations for $\boldsymbol{L}_{\text{cm}}$ and $\boldsymbol{\tau}_{\text{cm}}$ may be conceptually simplified by introducing the concept of the *inertia tensor*. Briefly explained, the inertia tensor is the rotational equivalent of the total mass. It tells how mass is distributed in an object and thus gives information about how hard it is to rotate an object around any given axis. In the following, we will derive the inertia tensor. Consider the angular momentum of particle system w.r.t. to the center of mass,

$$\boldsymbol{L}_{\text{cm}} = \sum_i \left(\Delta \boldsymbol{r}_i \times m_i \Delta \dot{\boldsymbol{r}}_i\right) \tag{22.54a}$$

$$= \sum_i \left(\Delta \boldsymbol{r}_i \times m_i \left(\boldsymbol{\omega} \times \Delta \boldsymbol{r}_i\right)\right) \tag{22.54b}$$

$$= \sum_i m_i \left(\Delta \boldsymbol{r}_i \times \left(\boldsymbol{\omega} \times \Delta \boldsymbol{r}_i\right)\right). \tag{22.54c}$$

Using $\Delta \boldsymbol{r}_i = [x_i, y_i, z_i]^T$, this can be written as

$$\sum_i m_i \Delta \boldsymbol{r}_i \times \left(\boldsymbol{\omega} \times \Delta \boldsymbol{r}_i\right) = \sum_i m_i \begin{bmatrix} \left(y_i^2 + z_i^2\right) \omega_x - x_i y_i \omega_y - x_i z_i \omega_z \\ -x_i y_i \omega_x + \left(x_i^2 + z_i^2\right) \omega_y - y_i z_i \omega_z \\ -x_i z_i \omega_x - y_i z_i \omega_y + \left(x_i^2 + y_i^2\right) \omega_z \end{bmatrix} \tag{22.55a}$$

$$= \underbrace{\begin{bmatrix} \sum_i m_i \left(y_i^2 + z_i^2\right) & -\sum_i m_i \left(x_i y_i\right) & -\sum_i m_i \left(x_i z_i\right) \\ -\sum_i m_i \left(x_i y_i\right) & \sum_i m_i \left(x_i^2 + z_i^2\right) & -\sum_i m_i \left(y_i z_i\right) \\ \sum_i m_i \left(x_i z_i\right) & -\sum_i m_i \left(y_i z_i\right) & \sum_i m_i \left(x_i^2 + y_i^2\right) \end{bmatrix}}_{\boldsymbol{I}} \begin{bmatrix} \omega_x \\ \omega_y \\ \omega_z \end{bmatrix}. \tag{22.55b}$$

The matrix $\boldsymbol{I}$ is called the inertia tensor

$$\boldsymbol{I} = \begin{bmatrix} \sum_i m_i \left(y_i^2 + z_i^2\right) & -\sum_i m_i \left(x_i y_i\right) & -\sum_i m_i \left(x_i z_i\right) \\ -\sum_i m_i \left(x_i y_i\right) & \sum_i m_i \left(x_i^2 + z_i^2\right) & -\sum_i m_i \left(y_i z_i\right) \\ -\sum_i m_i \left(x_i z_i\right) & -\sum_i m_i \left(y_i z_i\right) & \sum_i m_i \left(x_i^2 + y_i^2\right) \end{bmatrix} = \begin{bmatrix} I_{xx} & I_{xy} & I_{xz} \\ I_{yx} & I_{yy} & I_{yz} \\ I_{zx} & I_{zy} & I_{zz} \end{bmatrix}. \tag{22.56}$$

Using the inertia tensor, the equation for $\boldsymbol{L}_{\text{cm}}$ simplifies to

$$\boldsymbol{L}_{\text{cm}} = \boldsymbol{I}\boldsymbol{\omega}. \tag{22.57}$$

It is observed from (22.56) that the inertia tensor is symmetrical, $\boldsymbol{I} = \boldsymbol{I}^T$. The terms on the diagonal are called products of inertia, and the off-diagonal terms are called moments of inertia. The inertia tensor for a solid object is found by letting the number of particles in the system tend to infinity and rewriting the sum as volume integrals,

$$I_{xx} = \int_V \rho\left(y^2 + z^2\right)\, dV, \tag{22.58a}$$

$$I_{yy} = \int_V \rho\left(x^2 + z^2\right)\, dV, \tag{22.58b}$$

$$I_{zz} = \int_V \rho\left(x^2 + y^2\right)\, dV, \tag{22.58c}$$

$$I_{xy} = -\int_V \rho\,(xy)\, dV, \tag{22.58d}$$

$$I_{xz} = -\int_V \rho\,(xz)\, dV, \tag{22.58e}$$

$$I_{zy} = -\int_V \rho\,(yz)\, dV. \tag{22.58f}$$

Although the inertia tensor, $\boldsymbol{I}$, conceptually simplifies the equation, the underlying mathematics is still complicated, since $\boldsymbol{I}$ is a function of orientation of the object. Fortunately, it can be split it into a sum, and for a particle system it may be written as

$$\boldsymbol{I} = \sum_i m_i \begin{bmatrix} \left(y_i^2 + z_i^2\right) & -\left(x_i y_i\right) & -\left(x_i z_i\right) \\ -\left(x_i y_i\right) & \left(x_i^2 + z_i^2\right) & -\left(y_i z_i\right) \\ -\left(x_i z_i\right) & -\left(y_i z_i\right) & \left(x_i^2 + y_i^2\right) \end{bmatrix} \tag{22.59a}$$

$$= \sum_i m_i \left(\begin{bmatrix} x_i^2 + y_i^2 + z_i^2 & 0 & 0 \\ 0 & x_i^2 + y_i^2 + z_i^2 & 0 \\ 0 & 0 & x_i^2 + y_i^2 + z_i^2 \end{bmatrix} - \begin{bmatrix} x_i^2 & x_i y_i & x_i z_i \\ x_i y_i & y_i^2 & y_i z_i \\ x_i z_i & y_i z_i & z_i^2 \end{bmatrix} \right). \tag{22.59b}$$

This may be recognized as the inner and outer product of the vector $\Delta\boldsymbol{r}_i = \left[x_i y_i z_i\right]^T$, and the equation can be rewritten as

$$\boldsymbol{I} = \sum_i m_i \left(\Delta\boldsymbol{r}_i^T \Delta\boldsymbol{r}_i \mathbf{1} - \Delta\boldsymbol{r}_i \Delta\boldsymbol{r}_i^T\right), \tag{22.60}$$

where $\mathbf{1}$ is the identity matrix. The term $\Delta\boldsymbol{r}_i$ is the rotation, $\boldsymbol{R}$, of some fixed vector, $\boldsymbol{p}_i$, in the body frame, that is,

$$\Delta\boldsymbol{r}_i = \boldsymbol{R}\boldsymbol{p}_i. \tag{22.61}$$

Substituting this gives

$$\boldsymbol{I} = \sum_i m_i \left(\left(\boldsymbol{R}\boldsymbol{p}_i\right)^T \boldsymbol{R}\boldsymbol{p}_i \mathbf{1} - \boldsymbol{R}\boldsymbol{p}_i \left(\boldsymbol{R}\boldsymbol{p}_i\right)^T \right) \tag{22.62a}$$

$$= \sum_i m_i \left(\boldsymbol{p}_i^T \boldsymbol{R}^T \boldsymbol{R}\boldsymbol{p}_i \mathbf{1} - \boldsymbol{R}\boldsymbol{p}_i \boldsymbol{p}_i^T \boldsymbol{R}^T\right) \tag{22.62b}$$

$$= \sum_i m_i \left(\boldsymbol{p}_i^T \boldsymbol{p}_i \mathbf{1} - \boldsymbol{R}\boldsymbol{p}_i \boldsymbol{p}_i^T \boldsymbol{R}^T\right). \tag{22.62c}$$

Since $\boldsymbol{p}_i^T \boldsymbol{p}_i$ is a scalar, the equation can be simplified further with a little mathematical trick:

$$I = \sum_i m_i \left(\boldsymbol{R}\boldsymbol{p}_i^T \boldsymbol{p}_i \boldsymbol{R}^T \boldsymbol{1} - \boldsymbol{R}\boldsymbol{p}_i \boldsymbol{p}_i^T \boldsymbol{R}^T \right) \tag{22.63a}$$

$$= \boldsymbol{R} \left(\underbrace{\sum_i m_i \left(\boldsymbol{p}_i^T \boldsymbol{p}_i \boldsymbol{1} - \boldsymbol{p}_i \boldsymbol{p}_i^T \right)}_{\boldsymbol{I}_{\text{body}}} \right) \boldsymbol{R}^T. \tag{22.63b}$$

Comparing with (22.60), it is found that the inertia tensor may be expressed as the product of a fixed inertia tensor of the body frame and a rotation matrix. The inertia tensor of the body frame is thus given as

$$\boldsymbol{I}_{\text{body}} = \sum_i m_i \left(\boldsymbol{p}_i^T \boldsymbol{p}_i \boldsymbol{1} - \boldsymbol{p}_i \boldsymbol{p}_i^T \right). \tag{22.64}$$

From a computer simulation viewpoint, this is tremendously practical, since $\boldsymbol{I}_{\text{body}}$ can be precomputed, and $\boldsymbol{I}$ can always be found during simulation using the rotation $\boldsymbol{R}$ of the body frame. Given some thought, it should be clear that the inertia tensor on the form $\boldsymbol{I} = \boldsymbol{R}\boldsymbol{I}_{\text{body}}\boldsymbol{R}^T$ is a consequence of the symmetry of $\boldsymbol{I}$, since any symmetric matrix, $\boldsymbol{A}$, may be written as (Theorem 18.3),

$$\boldsymbol{A} = \boldsymbol{R}\boldsymbol{D}\boldsymbol{R}^T, \tag{22.65}$$

where $\boldsymbol{D}$ is a diagonal matrix, with the eigenvalues of $\boldsymbol{A}$ along its diagonal, and $\boldsymbol{R}$ is an orthonormal matrix, where the columns are the eigenvectors of $\boldsymbol{A}$. This indicates a clever initial orientation of the body, where the body frame inertia tensor is a diagonal matrix, and $\boldsymbol{R}$ is then the rotation of this initial body frame. Furthermore, if the columns of the rotation matrix are

$$\boldsymbol{R} = \begin{bmatrix} \boldsymbol{i} & \boldsymbol{j} & \boldsymbol{k} \end{bmatrix}, \tag{22.66}$$

then the columns are the instantaneous placement of the initial body frame's x-, y-, and z-axis. Since these axes are fixed body vectors, their time derivatives can be found simply by taking the cross product with the angular velocity; the time derivative of the rotation matrix is thus,

$$\dot{\boldsymbol{R}} = \begin{bmatrix} \boldsymbol{\omega} \times \boldsymbol{i} & \boldsymbol{\omega} \times \boldsymbol{j} & \boldsymbol{\omega} \times \boldsymbol{k} \end{bmatrix}. \tag{22.67}$$

Using the cross product matrix notation from Theorem 18.4, we have

$$\dot{\boldsymbol{R}} = \boldsymbol{\omega}^\times \boldsymbol{R}. \tag{22.68}$$

22.1.7 Integrating over a Solid Object

There are three commonly used approaches for computing the mass, the center of mass, and the inertia tensor for a solid object.

Analytical Integration: In the first method *volume integration* is computed analytically. Consider an axis-aligned cube with side length $2L$ and constant density, ρ. By definition, the I_{xx} element of the inertia tensor is found as

$$I_{xx} = \rho \int_V \left(y^2 + z^2\right) \, dV \tag{22.69a}$$

$$= \rho \int_{-L}^{L} \int_{-L}^{L} \int_{-L}^{L} \left(y^2 + z^2\right) \, dx \, dy \, dz \tag{22.69b}$$

$$= \rho \frac{16}{3} L^5. \tag{22.69c}$$

The volume of the cube is

$$V = (2L)^3 = 8L^3, \tag{22.70}$$

and therefore it is found that $\rho = \frac{M}{V} = \frac{M}{8L^3}$. Finally, it is found that

$$I_{xx} = \frac{2}{3} M L^2. \tag{22.71}$$

A similar approach may be used for the remaining volume integrals. Unfortunately, the analytical solution is only simple for objects with very simple shape.

Decomposition: The second approach decomposes an object into simpler objects, for instance, small cubes, voxels, as shown in Figure 22.10. The implication is that the analytical approach is tractable for cubes, and if all mass properties are represented w.r.t. the same frame, then the mass properties of the simpler volumes may be added in order to find an approximation to the original object.

$$V = \sum V_i \tag{22.72a}$$

$$M = \sum M_i \tag{22.72b}$$

$$\boldsymbol{r}_{\text{cm}} = \frac{1}{M} \sum M_i \boldsymbol{r}_{\text{cm}_i} \tag{22.72c}$$

$$\boldsymbol{I} = \sum \boldsymbol{I}_i \tag{22.72d}$$

In order to sum the inertia tensor of each cube, we need to rotate and translate each inertia tensor into the same coordinate frame.

Imagine we have an analytical formula for computing the inertia tensor in frame G, and we need to transform the inertia tensor into coordinate frame F. Rotation is simply,

$$\boldsymbol{I}^{\text{F}} = \boldsymbol{R}^{\text{G}\to\text{F}} \boldsymbol{I}^{\text{G}} \boldsymbol{R}^{\text{G}\to\text{F}^T}. \tag{22.73}$$

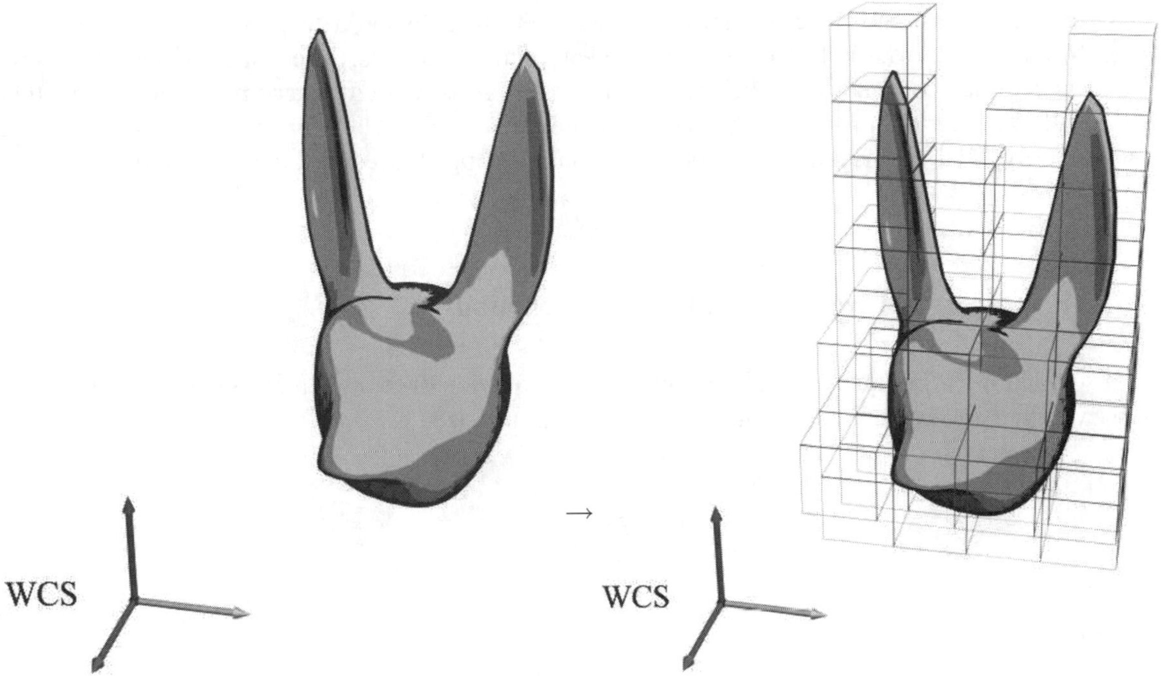

Figure 22.10: A solid object may be decomposed into a set of smaller cubes, voxels.

If frame F is translated by $[x, y, z]^T$ w.r.t. frame G, but both F and G have the same orientation, then inertia tensor can be computed by the *transfer-of-axe theorem* [Kleppner et al., 1978], which states that

$$I_{xx}^F = I_{xx}^G + M\left(y^2 + z^2\right) \tag{22.74a}$$
$$I_{yy}^F = I_{yy}^G + M\left(x^2 + z^2\right) \tag{22.74b}$$
$$I_{zz}^F = I_{zz}^G + M\left(x^2 + y^2\right) \tag{22.74c}$$
$$I_{xy}^F = I_{xy}^G - M\left(xy\right) \tag{22.74d}$$
$$I_{xz}^F = I_{xz}^G - M\left(xz\right) \tag{22.74e}$$
$$I_{zy}^F = I_{zy}^G - M\left(yz\right). \tag{22.74f}$$

Dimension Reduction and Value Propagation: Finally, the integration may be performed using *dimension reduction and value propagation* [Mirtich, 1996]. The basic idea is to use *Stokes'* and *Gauss's theorems* to reduce volume integrals to line integrals. This will not be discussed further.

Comparing the three approaches, the analytical integration is accurate within numerical precision, but also tedious to work with, since complex shapes yield integrals that are difficult to solve analytically by hand. The decomposition approach is quite simple, but requires that one can make a decomposition of simpler volumes, which approximates the real object. The accuracy depends on how close the approximation is to the real object. Decompositions into spheres, boxes, and cylinders are often hand modeled in interactive applications, such as computer games and used for collision detection. These decompositions can therefore easily be reused to compute the needed volume integrals. The last approach of dimension reduction and value propagation can be applied to any polygonal closed surface mesh, and the method is accurate within numerical precision. However, it is not always possible to obtain a closed surface mesh. In practice, polygonal meshes often have open boundaries, flipped faces, and many more degeneracies.

22.1.8 A Summary of Newton's Equations of Motion

Newton's equations of motion for the linear and Euler's equation of rotational motion of a rigid body have been derived in the previous section, and they may be summarized as:

$$\frac{d\boldsymbol{r}_{\text{cm}}}{dt} = \boldsymbol{v}_{\text{cm}} \tag{22.75a}$$

$$\frac{d\boldsymbol{p}_{\text{cm}}}{dt} = \boldsymbol{F} \tag{22.75b}$$

$$\frac{d\boldsymbol{R}}{dt} = \boldsymbol{\omega}^{\times}\boldsymbol{R} \tag{22.75c}$$

$$\frac{d\boldsymbol{L}_{\text{cm}}}{dt} = \boldsymbol{\tau}_{\text{cm}}. \tag{22.75d}$$

The first two described the linear motion, and the following two describe the rotational motion. These four equations are commonly referred to as the Newton-Euler equations of motion.

The three auxiliary equations are

$$\boldsymbol{I}^{-1} = \boldsymbol{R}\boldsymbol{I}_{\text{cm}}^{-1}\boldsymbol{R}^T \tag{22.76a}$$

$$\boldsymbol{\omega} = \boldsymbol{I}^{-1}\boldsymbol{L}_{\text{cm}} \tag{22.76b}$$

$$\boldsymbol{v}_{\text{cm}} = \frac{\boldsymbol{p}_{\text{cm}}}{M}, \tag{22.76c}$$

with the mass and center of mass given by

$$M = \int_V \rho \, dV, \tag{22.77a}$$

$$\boldsymbol{r}_{\text{cm}} = \frac{1}{M}\int_V \rho\boldsymbol{r} \, dV, \tag{22.77b}$$

and the inertia tensor by

$$I_{xx} = \int_V \rho \left(y^2 + z^2\right) \, dV, \tag{22.78a}$$

$$I_{yy} = \int_V \rho \left(x^2 + z^2\right) \, dV, \tag{22.78b}$$

$$I_{zz} = \int_V \rho \left(x^2 + y^2\right) \, dV, \tag{22.78c}$$

$$I_{xy} = -\int_V \rho \left(xy\right) \, dV, \tag{22.78d}$$

$$I_{xz} = -\int_V \rho \left(xz\right) \, dV, \tag{22.78e}$$

$$I_{zy} = -\int_V \rho \left(yz\right) \, dV. \tag{22.78f}$$

The equations of motion are usually rewritten in terms of the *state function*, $\boldsymbol{Y}(t)$ as follows:

$$\boldsymbol{Y}(t) = \begin{bmatrix} \boldsymbol{r}_{\text{cm}} \\ \boldsymbol{R} \\ \boldsymbol{p}_{\text{cm}} \\ \boldsymbol{L}_{\text{cm}} \end{bmatrix} \quad \text{and} \quad \frac{d\boldsymbol{Y}(t)}{dt} = \begin{bmatrix} \boldsymbol{v}_{\text{cm}} \\ \boldsymbol{\omega}^{\times}\boldsymbol{R} \\ \boldsymbol{F} \\ \boldsymbol{\tau}_{\text{cm}} \end{bmatrix}, \tag{22.79}$$

and using *quaternions*, which are described in detail in Section 18.5). Then Theorem 18.46 gives

$$\dot{\boldsymbol{R}} = \boldsymbol{\omega}^{\times}\boldsymbol{R} \quad \Rightarrow \quad \dot{q} = \frac{1}{2}\left[0, \boldsymbol{\omega}\right] q, \tag{22.80}$$

the state function may be written as

$$\boldsymbol{Y}(t) = \begin{bmatrix} \boldsymbol{r}_{\text{cm}} \\ q \\ \boldsymbol{p}_{\text{cm}} \\ \boldsymbol{L}_{\text{cm}} \end{bmatrix} \quad \text{and} \quad \frac{d\boldsymbol{Y}(t)}{dt} = \begin{bmatrix} \boldsymbol{v}_{\text{cm}} \\ \frac{1}{2}\left[0, \boldsymbol{\omega}\right] q \\ \boldsymbol{F} \\ \boldsymbol{\tau}_{\text{cm}} \end{bmatrix}. \tag{22.81}$$

This completes the Newtonian description of the *unconstrained motion* of a rigid body. Knowing the initial position and orientation, the motion of the rigid bodies is found through integrations; see Chapter 23.

22.2 Coulomb's Friction Law

A frequently used friction law is *Coulomb's friction law*, and it will be discussed here for a single-point contact (we refer the reader to [Trinkle et al., 2001] for an example of other friction laws).

Consider two rigid bodies touching at a *single point of contact*, as illustrated in Figure 22.11. At the point of contact the surfaces of the two rigid bodies have parallel surface normals. The direction of the surface normals identifies a unit *contact normal* vector, $\boldsymbol{n}$. The point of contact and the contact normal describes a *contact plane* orthogonal to the contact normal. A unit vector lying in this contact plane is denoted by $\boldsymbol{t}$ and referred to as the tangential direction. A force acting at the contact point is known as a *contact force*, $\boldsymbol{F}_{\text{contact}}$, and is decomposed into two components: a *normal force*, $\boldsymbol{F}_{\boldsymbol{n}}$, parallel to the contact normal direction, and a *friction force*, $\boldsymbol{F}_{\boldsymbol{t}}$, lying in the contact plane.

$$\boldsymbol{F}_{\text{contact}} = \boldsymbol{F}_{\boldsymbol{n}} + \boldsymbol{F}_{\boldsymbol{t}}. \tag{22.82}$$

The normal force is equal in magnitude and opposite to the weight of the objects in the normal direction.

If the relative velocity at the point of contact by the vector, $\boldsymbol{u}$, then the tangential component,

$$\boldsymbol{u}_{\boldsymbol{t}} = \boldsymbol{u} - (\boldsymbol{u} \cdot \boldsymbol{n})\,\boldsymbol{n}, \tag{22.83}$$

describes the amount and direction of sliding between the two rigid bodies.

Coulomb's friction law relates the magnitude of the normal force to the magnitude of the friction force through a coefficient of friction, μ. The actual relationship depends on the state of contact, and there is a total of three different states to distinguish between:

- Dynamic (sliding) friction
- Stable static (dry) friction
- Unstable static (dry) friction

Dynamic (sliding) friction occurs when the two bodies move relative to each other, indicating that the tangential relative velocity is nonzero. In this case, the friction force should attain its maximum possible magnitude, and directly oppose the relative movement. That is,

$$\boldsymbol{u}_{\boldsymbol{t}} \neq 0 \Rightarrow \boldsymbol{F}_{\boldsymbol{t}} = -\mu \frac{\boldsymbol{u}_{\boldsymbol{t}}}{\left\|\boldsymbol{u}_{\boldsymbol{t}}\right\|_2} \left\|\boldsymbol{F}_{\boldsymbol{n}}\right\|_2. \tag{22.84}$$

Stable static (dry) friction occurs when the two bodies do not move relatively to each other, meaning that the relative tangential velocity is zero. In the stable case this relation is maintained, indicating that the relative tangential acceleration is also zero. When these conditions occur Coulomb's friction law states that the magnitude of the friction force is less than or equal to the magnitude of the normal force multiplied by the *friction coefficient*. However, no constraints are placed on the direction of the friction force,

$$\boldsymbol{u}_{\boldsymbol{t}} = 0 \text{ and } \dot{\boldsymbol{u}}_{\boldsymbol{t}} = 0 \quad \Rightarrow \quad \left\|\boldsymbol{F}_{\boldsymbol{t}}\right\|_2 \leq \mu \left\|\boldsymbol{F}_{\boldsymbol{n}}\right\|_2. \tag{22.85}$$

In *unstable static friction*, the conditions for this case are nearly identical to stable static friction; the difference is that the relative tangential acceleration is nonzero, indicating that the tangential velocity is just at the point of becoming nonzero. The magnitude of friction force is required to be as large as is possible in the case of dynamic friction; however, for unstable static friction the direction of the friction force is opposing the direction of the relative tangential acceleration,

$$\boldsymbol{u}_t = 0 \text{ and } \dot{\boldsymbol{u}}_t \neq 0 \quad \Rightarrow \quad \left\|\boldsymbol{F}_{\boldsymbol{t}}\right\|_2 = \mu \left\|\boldsymbol{F}_{\boldsymbol{n}}\right\|_2 \text{ and } \boldsymbol{F}_{\boldsymbol{t}} \cdot \dot{\boldsymbol{u}}_{\boldsymbol{t}} \leq 0. \tag{22.86}$$

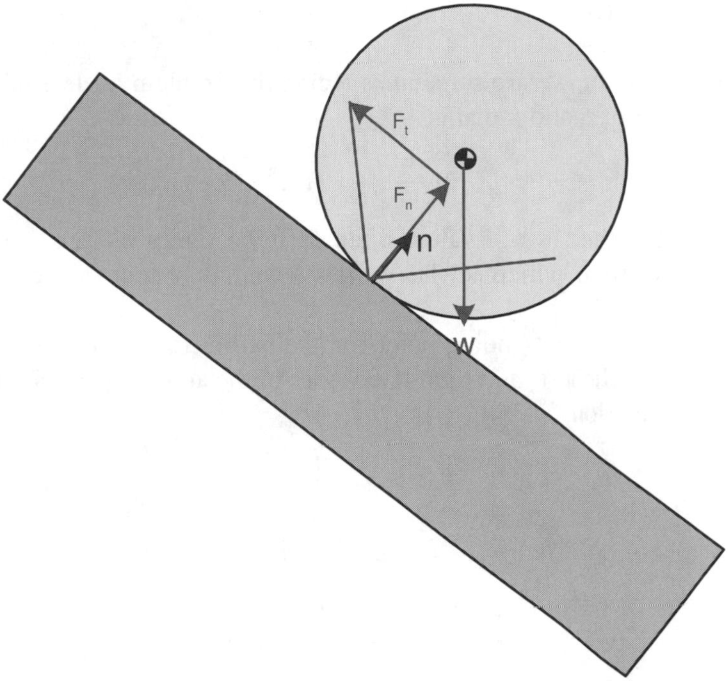

Figure 22.11: 2D illustration of a friction cone of a ball sliding down an inclined plane. $\boldsymbol{W}$ is the weight of the ball.

Observe however, that it is not required that the friction force directly opposes the direction of relative tangential friction. The name unstable indicates that a transition can occur either to dynamic or stable static friction.

An often-used geometric approach for describing the region of legal contact forces that can be applied at a contact point is the *friction cone*. The friction cone is simply the region of space traced out by all possible values of

$$\boldsymbol{F}_{\text{contact}} = \boldsymbol{F}_{\boldsymbol{n}} + \boldsymbol{F}_{\boldsymbol{t}} \tag{22.87}$$

Figure 22.11 shows a 2D example of a friction cone. The slope of the friction cone is dictated by the reciprocal value of the friction coefficient μ. For dynamic friction, the contact force is restricted to lie on a straight line on the surface of the friction cone, and the straight line lies on the side of the friction cone where the relative tangential velocity is pointing away from. For stable static friction, the contact force can be anywhere interior or on the surface of the friction cone. For unstable static friction, the contact force is restrained from being inside the friction cone, and instead it must be on the half-surface lying in the opposite direction of the relative tangential acceleration.

22.3 Work and Energy

Looking at a single particle again, we are sometimes facing the problem of determining the trajectory of the particle given its equation of motion, that is,

$$m\frac{d\boldsymbol{v}}{dt} = \boldsymbol{F}(\boldsymbol{r}). \tag{22.88}$$

The problem with this is that the laws of nature often describe forces as functions of position, that is, $\boldsymbol{F}(\boldsymbol{r})$, and not as functions of time, which is what we really want in order to solve the above equation in a mathematically convenient way.

Imagine we knew the starting and ending points on the particle trajectory. We label these A and B, and then we can integrate both the left- and right-hand sides of the above equation with respect to position and obtain the following derivation

$$\boldsymbol{F}(\boldsymbol{r}) = m\frac{d\boldsymbol{v}}{dt}, \tag{22.89a}$$

$$\int_A^B \boldsymbol{F}(\boldsymbol{r}) \cdot d\boldsymbol{r} = \int_A^B m\frac{d\boldsymbol{v}}{dt} \cdot d\boldsymbol{r}, \tag{22.89b}$$

$$= \int_A^B m\frac{d\boldsymbol{v}}{dt} \cdot \boldsymbol{v}dt. \tag{22.89c}$$

Now we use the following identity rule

$$\frac{1}{2}\frac{d}{dt}\left\|\boldsymbol{A}\right\|_2^2 = \frac{1}{2}\frac{d}{dt}\left(\boldsymbol{A}\cdot\boldsymbol{A}\right), \tag{22.90a}$$

$$= \frac{1}{2}\left(\frac{d\boldsymbol{A}}{dt}\cdot\boldsymbol{A} + \boldsymbol{A}\cdot\frac{d\boldsymbol{A}}{dt}\right), \tag{22.90b}$$

$$= \boldsymbol{A}\cdot\frac{d\boldsymbol{A}}{dt}, \tag{22.90c}$$

which is really just a clever rewriting of the product differentiation rule. Applying the identity to our derivation, we have

$$\int_A^B \boldsymbol{F}(\boldsymbol{r}) \cdot d\boldsymbol{r} = \int_A^B \frac{1}{2}m\frac{d}{dt}\left\|\boldsymbol{v}\right\|_2^2 dt, \tag{22.91a}$$

$$= \frac{1}{2}m\left\|\boldsymbol{v}_B\right\|_2^2 - \frac{1}{2}m\left\|\boldsymbol{v}_A\right\|_2^2. \tag{22.91b}$$

Traditionally, physicists write $v = \left\|\boldsymbol{v}\right\|_2^2$; using this notation we can write:

$$\underbrace{\int_A^B \boldsymbol{F}(\boldsymbol{r}) \cdot d\boldsymbol{r}}_{W_{BA}} = \underbrace{\frac{1}{2}mv_B^2}_{K_B} - \underbrace{\frac{1}{2}mv_A^2}_{K_A}, \tag{22.92a}$$

$$\Downarrow$$

$$W_{BA} = K_B - K_A. \tag{22.92b}$$

Here, $\int_A^B \boldsymbol{F}(\boldsymbol{r}) \cdot d\boldsymbol{r}$ is termed the *work*, W_{BA}, done by force $\boldsymbol{F}$ from A to B; the terms $\frac{1}{2}mv^2$ are called the *kinetic energy* K. Sometimes the notations $K = T = E_{\text{kin}}$ are also used. The simple looking equation

$$W_{BA} = K_B - K_A, \tag{22.93}$$

is known as the *work-energy theorem*. From the above derivations it is seen that the work ΔW done by the force, $\boldsymbol{F}$, in a small displacement $\Delta \boldsymbol{r}$ is

$$\Delta W = \boldsymbol{F} \cdot \Delta \boldsymbol{r}. \tag{22.94}$$

Splitting the force into an orthogonal and parallel component along $\Delta \boldsymbol{r}$, we immediately see that only the component of the force parallel with the path contributes to the work done by the force. Thus, forces orthogonal to the path do not contribute to the work.

If the work integral is not dependent on the actual path between A and B, but only on the positions A and B, then the force $\boldsymbol{F}$ is called a *conservative force*.

Example 22.1

As an example of a conservative force, consider the gravitational field, where $\boldsymbol{F} = m\boldsymbol{g}$. In this case,

$$W_{BA} = \int_A^B \boldsymbol{F}(\boldsymbol{r}) \cdot d\boldsymbol{r}, \tag{22.95a}$$

$$= \int_A^B m\boldsymbol{g} \cdot d\boldsymbol{r}, \tag{22.95b}$$

$$= m\boldsymbol{g} \int_A^B \cdot d\boldsymbol{r}, \tag{22.95c}$$

$$= m\boldsymbol{g} \cdot (\boldsymbol{r}_B - \boldsymbol{r}_A). \tag{22.95d}$$

Usually, $\boldsymbol{g} = [0, 0, -g]^T$, where $g = 9.8\ m/s^2$, so

$$W_{BA} = mg\,(z_A - z_B). \tag{22.96}$$

In conclusion, the work done by gravity depends only on the starting and ending positions.

Whenever we have conservative forces we can write the work integral in the form

$$\int_A^B \boldsymbol{F}(\boldsymbol{r}) \cdot d\boldsymbol{r} = \text{function of}(\boldsymbol{r}_B) - \text{function of}(\boldsymbol{r}_A), \tag{22.97}$$

or

$$\int_A^B \boldsymbol{F}(\boldsymbol{r}) \cdot d\boldsymbol{r} = -U(\boldsymbol{r}_B) + U(\boldsymbol{r}_A), \tag{22.98}$$

where $U(\boldsymbol{r})$ is a function defined by the above expression and U is called the *potential energy*. The sign convention might appear a little awkward at the moment; however, if we look at the work-energy theorem for a conservative force we have:

$$W_{BA} = K_B - K_A \tag{22.99a}$$
$$\Downarrow$$
$$-U_B + U_A = K_B - K_A \tag{22.99b}$$
$$\Downarrow$$
$$K_A + U_A = K_B + U_B, \tag{22.99c}$$

from which the chosen sign convention should be obvious. Sometimes the notation V is used instead of U. However, we will stick with U in this section. Looking at the left-hand side of the equation we see that we only have kinetic and potential energy at A, and the right-hand side only has energies at B, thus the sum $K + U$ is conserved. $K + U$ is called the *mechanical energy*, (sometimes just the energy), and it is often denoted by E or E_{mek}. The conservation of mechanical energy is derived directly from Newton's second law. We say it is a derived law and it is a special case of the more general energy conservation law, which states that if we look at all energies involved (heat, light, mass, etc.) then their sum is conserved.

In our derivation of the *conservation of the mechanical energy*, we assumed that the work was only done by a conservative force. If we have a nonconservative force, we divide the applied force into two terms: one equal to the sum of conservative forces, $\boldsymbol{F}_{\text{C}}$, and another equal to the sum of *nonconservative forces*, $\boldsymbol{F}_{\text{NC}}$,

$$\boldsymbol{F} = \boldsymbol{F}_{\text{C}} + \boldsymbol{F}_{\text{NC}}. \tag{22.100}$$

The total work done by $\boldsymbol{F}$ from A to B is

$$W_{\text{BA}}^{\text{total}} = \int_A^B \boldsymbol{F}(\boldsymbol{r}) \cdot d\boldsymbol{r}, \tag{22.101a}$$
$$= \int_A^B (\boldsymbol{F}_{\text{C}} + \boldsymbol{F}_{\text{NC}}) \cdot d\boldsymbol{r}, \tag{22.101b}$$
$$= \int_A^B \boldsymbol{F}_{\text{C}} + \int_A^B \boldsymbol{F}_{\text{NC}} \cdot d\boldsymbol{r}, \tag{22.101c}$$
$$= -U_B + U_A + \underbrace{\int_A^B \boldsymbol{F}_{\text{NC}} \cdot d\boldsymbol{r}}_{W_{\text{BA}}^{\text{NC}}}, \tag{22.101d}$$
$$= -U_B + U_A + W_{\text{BA}}^{\text{NC}}. \tag{22.101e}$$

The work-energy theorem, $W_{\text{BA}}^{\text{total}} = K_B - K_A$, now has the form

$$-U_B + U_A + W_{\text{BA}}^{\text{NC}} = K_B - K_A, \tag{22.102a}$$

$$\Downarrow$$

$$W_{\text{BA}}^{\text{NC}} = K_B + U_B - K_A - U_A, \tag{22.102b}$$

$$\Downarrow$$

$$W_{\text{BA}}^{\text{NC}} = \underbrace{K_B + U_B}_{E_B} - \underbrace{(K_A + U_A)}_{E_A}, \tag{22.102c}$$

$$\Downarrow$$

$$W_{\text{BA}}^{\text{NC}} = E_B - E_A. \tag{22.102d}$$

We see that the mechanical energy E is no longer constant but depends on the state of the system. A typical and often-used example of a nonconservative force is the friction force. The friction force is parallel to the path, but points in the opposite direction, so $W_{\text{BA}}^{\text{friction}} < 0$. Thus, energy is dissipated from the system implying that $E_B < E_A$. How much E_B decreases depends on how long the particle is moved along the path.

Let's turn our attention back to the definition of potential energy,

$$U_B - U_A = -\int_A^B \boldsymbol{F} \cdot d\boldsymbol{r}. \tag{22.103}$$

Consider the change in potential energy when a particle undergoes the displacement $\Delta \boldsymbol{r}$,

$$U(\boldsymbol{r} + \Delta \boldsymbol{r}) - U(\boldsymbol{r}) = -\int_{\boldsymbol{r}}^{\boldsymbol{r}+\Delta \boldsymbol{r}} \boldsymbol{F}(\boldsymbol{r}') \cdot d\boldsymbol{r}'. \tag{22.104}$$

The left-hand side is the difference in U at the two ends of the path, ΔU. If $\Delta \boldsymbol{r}$ is so small that $\boldsymbol{F}$ does not change significantly over the path, $\boldsymbol{F}$ can be regarded as constant. Thus, we have

$$\Delta U = -\boldsymbol{F} \cdot \Delta \boldsymbol{r}, \tag{22.105a}$$

$$= -\left(F_x \Delta x + F_y \Delta y + F_z \Delta z\right). \tag{22.105b}$$

In the last step, we have written the right-hand side in terms of Coordinates. Another way to write ΔU is as a first-order differential,

$$\Delta U \approx \frac{\partial U}{\partial x}\Delta x + \frac{\partial U}{\partial y}\Delta y + \frac{\partial U}{\partial z}\Delta z, \tag{22.106}$$

combining the equations we have

$$\frac{\partial U}{\partial x}\Delta x + \frac{\partial U}{\partial y}\Delta y + \frac{\partial U}{\partial z}\Delta z \approx -F_x \Delta x - F_y \Delta y - F_z \Delta z. \tag{22.107}$$

In the limit $(\Delta x, \Delta y, \Delta z) \to 0$, the approximation becomes exact. Since Δx, Δy, and Δz are independent, the coefficient on either side of the equation must be equal, meaning

$$F_x = -\frac{\partial U}{\partial x}, \tag{22.108a}$$

$$F_y = -\frac{\partial U}{\partial y}, \tag{22.108b}$$

$$F_z = -\frac{\partial U}{\partial z}. \tag{22.108c}$$

Using the gradient operator, ∇, these three equations are written as

$$\boldsymbol{F} = -\nabla U. \tag{22.109}$$

Not only does this equation allow us to find the force given the potential energy function, but it is also a valuable tool when physicists analyze the stability of a system in terms of energy diagrams. The observation is that $\boldsymbol{F}$ is pointing toward minima of U.

Living in the real world, as humans, we are often quite used to measuring things in terms of absolute measures; energy is a little tricky in this manner. In fact, the value of E is to a certain extent arbitrary, only changes in E have physical significance. Let's look at the potential energy definition once again.

$$U_B - U_A = -\int_A^B \boldsymbol{F} \cdot d\boldsymbol{r} \tag{22.110}$$

defines only the difference in potential energy between A and B and not potential energy itself. For instance, we could add any constant to U_A and the same constant to U_B without violating the above definition, but we would change the value of E, since $E = K + U$.

In the above, we have introduced the concepts of work, mechanical energy, kinetic energy, potential energy, etc. for a single particle. We will now extend the concept of kinetic energy to a particle system, which in the limiting case, yields the kinetic energy for a rigid body (the same recipe was used in section 22.1). For a particle system, the total kinetic energy is simply given by the sum of the kinetic energy of each particle. We have

$$K = \sum_j \frac{1}{2} m_j v_j^2. \tag{22.111}$$

From Section 22.1.5 we know that for a particle in a rigid body,

$$\boldsymbol{v}_j = \boldsymbol{v}_{\text{cm}} + \underbrace{\boldsymbol{\omega} \times \Delta \boldsymbol{r}_j}_{\Delta \boldsymbol{v}_j}, \tag{22.112}$$

where the particle position is given by $\boldsymbol{r}_j = \boldsymbol{r}_{\text{cm}} + \Delta \boldsymbol{r}_j$, so $\Delta \boldsymbol{r}_j$ is a vector from the center of mass to the particle position. Inserting into the kinetic energy, we have

$$K = \sum_j \frac{1}{2} m_j \left(\boldsymbol{v}_{\text{cm}} + \boldsymbol{\omega} \times \Delta \boldsymbol{r}_j\right) \cdot \left(\boldsymbol{v}_{\text{cm}} + \boldsymbol{\omega} \times \Delta \boldsymbol{r}_j\right), \tag{22.113}$$

with some mathematical manipulation this yields

$$K = \sum_j \frac{1}{2} m_j \left(\boldsymbol{v}_{\text{cm}} \cdot \boldsymbol{v}_{\text{cm}} + 2 \left(\boldsymbol{\omega} \times \Delta \boldsymbol{r}_j \right) \cdot \boldsymbol{v}_{\text{cm}} + \left(\boldsymbol{\omega} \times \Delta \boldsymbol{r}_j \right) \cdot \left(\boldsymbol{\omega} \times \Delta \boldsymbol{r}_j \right) \right), \tag{22.114a}$$

$$= \frac{1}{2} M v_{\text{cm}}^2 + \boldsymbol{v}_{\text{cm}} \cdot \sum_j m_j \left(\boldsymbol{\omega} \times \Delta \boldsymbol{r}_j \right) + \sum_j \frac{1}{2} m_j \left(\boldsymbol{\omega} \times \Delta \boldsymbol{r}_j \right) \cdot \left(\boldsymbol{\omega} \times \Delta \boldsymbol{r}_j \right), \tag{22.114b}$$

$$= \frac{1}{2} M v_{\text{cm}}^2 + \underbrace{\boldsymbol{v}_{\text{cm}} \cdot \sum_j m_j \Delta \boldsymbol{v}_j}_{=0} + \sum_j \frac{1}{2} m_j \left(\boldsymbol{\omega} \times \Delta \boldsymbol{r}_j \right) \cdot \left(\boldsymbol{\omega} \times \Delta \boldsymbol{r}_j \right), \tag{22.114c}$$

$$= \frac{1}{2} M v_{\text{cm}}^2 + \frac{1}{2} \sum_j m_j \left(\boldsymbol{\omega} \times \Delta \boldsymbol{r}_j \right) \cdot \left(\boldsymbol{\omega} \times \Delta \boldsymbol{r}_j \right). \tag{22.114d}$$

Using the vector identity $(\boldsymbol{A} \times \boldsymbol{B}) \cdot \boldsymbol{C} = \boldsymbol{A} \cdot (\boldsymbol{B} \times \boldsymbol{C})$, with $\boldsymbol{A} = \boldsymbol{\omega}$, $\boldsymbol{B} = \Delta \boldsymbol{r}_j$, and $\boldsymbol{C} = \boldsymbol{\omega} \times \Delta \boldsymbol{r}_j$, yields

$$K = \frac{1}{2} M v_{\text{cm}}^2 + \frac{1}{2} \sum_j m_j \boldsymbol{\omega} \cdot \left(\Delta \boldsymbol{r}_j \times \left(\boldsymbol{\omega} \times \Delta \boldsymbol{r}_j \right) \right), \tag{22.115a}$$

$$= \frac{1}{2} M v_{\text{cm}}^2 + \frac{1}{2} \boldsymbol{\omega} \cdot \sum_j m_j \left(\Delta \boldsymbol{r}_j \times \left(\boldsymbol{\omega} \times \Delta \boldsymbol{r}_j \right) \right), \tag{22.115b}$$

$$= \frac{1}{2} M v_{\text{cm}}^2 + \frac{1}{2} \boldsymbol{\omega} \cdot \underbrace{\sum_j \left(\Delta \boldsymbol{r}_j \times \left(m_j \Delta \boldsymbol{v}_j \right) \right)}_{\boldsymbol{L}_{\text{cm}}}, \tag{22.115c}$$

$$= \frac{1}{2} M v_{\text{cm}}^2 + \frac{1}{2} \boldsymbol{\omega} \cdot \boldsymbol{L}_{\text{cm}}. \tag{22.115d}$$

Taking the limit and recalling that $\boldsymbol{L} = \boldsymbol{I} \boldsymbol{\omega}$, we end up with the following formula for the kinetic energy of a rigid body:

$$K = \frac{1}{2} M v_{\text{cm}}^2 + \frac{1}{2} \boldsymbol{\omega}^T \boldsymbol{I} \boldsymbol{\omega}. \tag{22.116}$$

The first term is due to translational motion only and the second term is due to rotational motion only; thus, they are respectively called the *translational kinetic energy* and the *rotational kinetic energy*. This concludes out treatment of classical rigid body mechanics.

22.4 The Harmonic Oscillator

In the preceding sections, we treated the basic theory of classical rigid body mechanics. In this section, we will present the basic theory of the harmonic oscillator. A *harmonic oscillator* is a system occurring repeatedly in animation systems and is referred to as springs. First, a single-object system will be discussed followed by a two-object system.

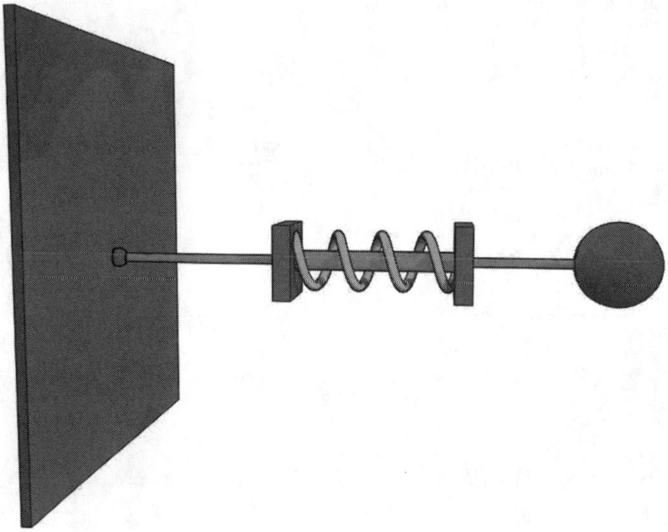

Figure 22.12: The one-mass harmonic oscillator.

22.4.1 The One-Object Harmonic Oscillator

Consider a particle attached to a wall of infinite mass with a *spring*, as shown in Figure 22.12. The spring force given by

$$F_{\text{spring}} = -kx, \tag{22.117}$$

is called *Hooke's spring law*, and $k > 0$ is called the *spring coefficient*. Newton's second law of motion dictates the motion of the particle as

$$m\ddot{x} = -kx, \tag{22.118}$$

which yields the *second-order ordinary differential equation*

$$m\ddot{x} + kx = 0. \tag{22.119}$$

An analytical solution to this equation exists and can be shown to be

$$x = B\sin(\omega_0 t) + C\cos(\omega_0 t), \tag{22.120}$$

where

$$\omega_0 = \sqrt{\frac{k}{m}} \tag{22.121}$$

is known as the *natural frequency*. The constants B and C can be evaluated from the initial position and velocity of the particle. Using the trigonometric identity

$$\cos(a+b) = \cos(a)\cos(b) - \sin(a)\sin(b). \tag{22.122}$$

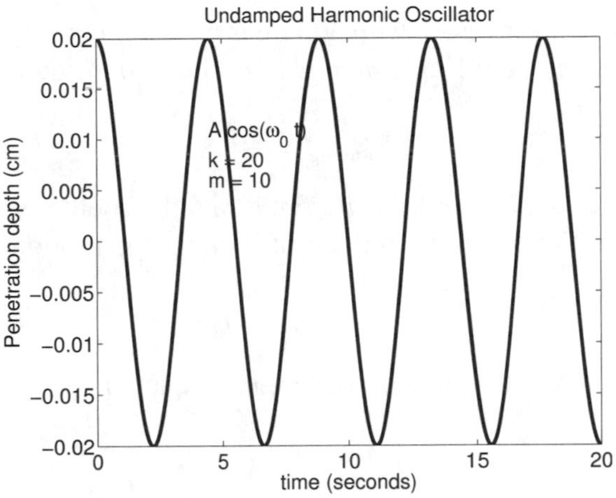

Figure 22.13: The amplitude of an undamped harmonic oscillator plotted as a function of time.

The analytical solution (22.120) can be rewritten as a single cosine function,

$$x = A\cos\left(\omega_0 t + \phi\right). \tag{22.123}$$

Setting (22.123) equal to (22.120) gives

$$A\cos\left(\omega_0 t\right)\cos\left(\phi\right) - A\sin\left(\omega_0 t\right)\sin\left(\phi\right) = B\sin\left(\omega_0 t\right) + C\cos\left(\omega_0 t\right). \tag{22.124}$$

The implication is that

$$A\cos\left(\phi\right) = C, \tag{22.125a}$$
$$A\sin\left(\phi\right) = -B, \tag{22.125b}$$

and that

$$A = \sqrt{B^2 + C^2}, \tag{22.126}$$

and

$$\tan(\phi) = -\frac{B}{C}. \tag{22.127}$$

The particle will follow a cosine motion with *amplitude* A, *frequency* ω_0, and *phase* ϕ. The motion is consequently repetitive with a *period* T,

$$T = \frac{2\pi}{\omega_0} = \frac{2\pi}{\sqrt{\frac{k}{m}}}. \tag{22.128}$$

Figure 22.13 shows an example of a harmonic oscillator.

The idealized harmonic oscillator assumes that there is no loss in energy over time. This is physically unrealistic, and practically not as useful as a *damped harmonic oscillator*. A typical *damping force* is given by

$$F_{\text{damping}} = -b\dot{x}, \tag{22.129}$$

which is commonly referred to as a *linear viscosity force*, and the coefficient $b > 0$ is called the *damping* or *viscosity coefficient*. From Newton's second law of motion, the motion of the damped particle must obey,

$$m\ddot{x} = -kx - b\dot{x}, \tag{22.130}$$

which is equivalent to the second-order ordinary differential equation

$$m\ddot{x} + b\dot{x} + kx = 0, \tag{22.131}$$

or

$$\ddot{x} + \frac{b}{m}\dot{x} + \frac{k}{m}x = 0. \tag{22.132}$$

Using the natural frequency $\omega_0^2 = \frac{k}{m}$ and introducing $\gamma = \frac{b}{m}$, this may be written as

$$\ddot{x} + \gamma\dot{x} + \omega_0^2 x = 0. \tag{22.133}$$

An analytical solution exists and is stated here without proof as

$$x = A\exp\left(-\frac{\gamma}{2}t\right)\cos\left(\omega_1 t + \phi\right), \tag{22.134}$$

where A and ϕ are constants determined from initial conditions, and

$$\omega_1 = \sqrt{\omega_0^2 - \frac{\gamma^2}{4}} \tag{22.135}$$

is the frequency. The frequency ω_1 has real solutions when

$$\omega_0^2 - \frac{\gamma^2}{4} \geq 0 \tag{22.136a}$$

$$\Downarrow$$

$$\frac{k}{m} - \frac{b^2}{4m^2} \geq 0 \tag{22.136b}$$

$$\Downarrow$$

$$4km - b^2 \geq 0. \tag{22.136c}$$

Introducing the notation

$$A(t) = A\exp\left(-\frac{\gamma}{2}t\right), \tag{22.137}$$

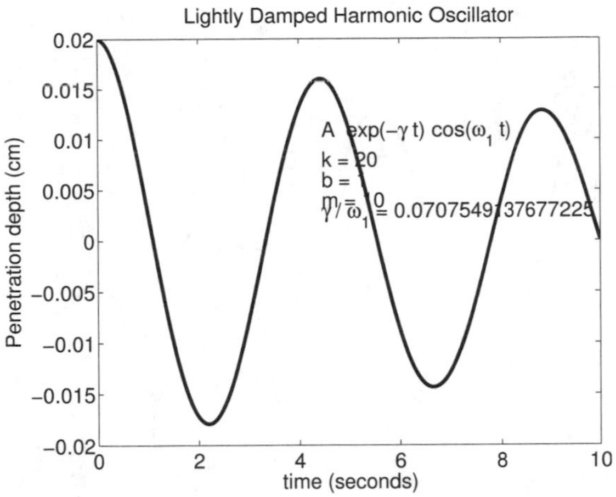

Figure 22.14: The amplitude of a lightly damped harmonic oscillator plotted as a function of time.

the damped harmonic oscillator is written as

$$x = A(t) \cos \left(\omega_1 t + \phi \right), \tag{22.138}$$

which is a cosine wave with a time-varying amplitude.

Comparing the damped harmonic oscillator (22.134) with the undamped harmonic oscillator (22.123), we see that the amplitude of the damped oscillator is exponentially decaying and the frequency ω_1 of the damped oscillator is less than the frequency, ω_0, of the undamped oscillator. In Figure 22.14 the amplitude of a damped harmonic oscillator is shown.

The zero-crossings of the damped harmonic oscillator occurs at equal time intervals by the period

$$T = \frac{2\pi}{\omega_1}. \tag{22.139}$$

Surprisingly though, the peaks of the motion do not lie halfway between the zero-crossings.

The damped motion may be described qualitatively by examining the value of $b^2 - 4mk$ and the ratio of

$$\frac{\gamma}{\omega_1}. \tag{22.140}$$

The motion is:

Over damped, when $b^2 - 4mk > 0$. Two cases of *over-damping* can be distinguished:

Lightly damped, if $\frac{\gamma}{\omega_1} \ll 1$ then $A(t)$ decays very little during the time the cosine makes many zero crossings.

Heavily damped, if $\frac{\gamma}{\omega_1}$ is large then $A(t)$ rapidly goes to zero while the cosine makes only a few oscillations.

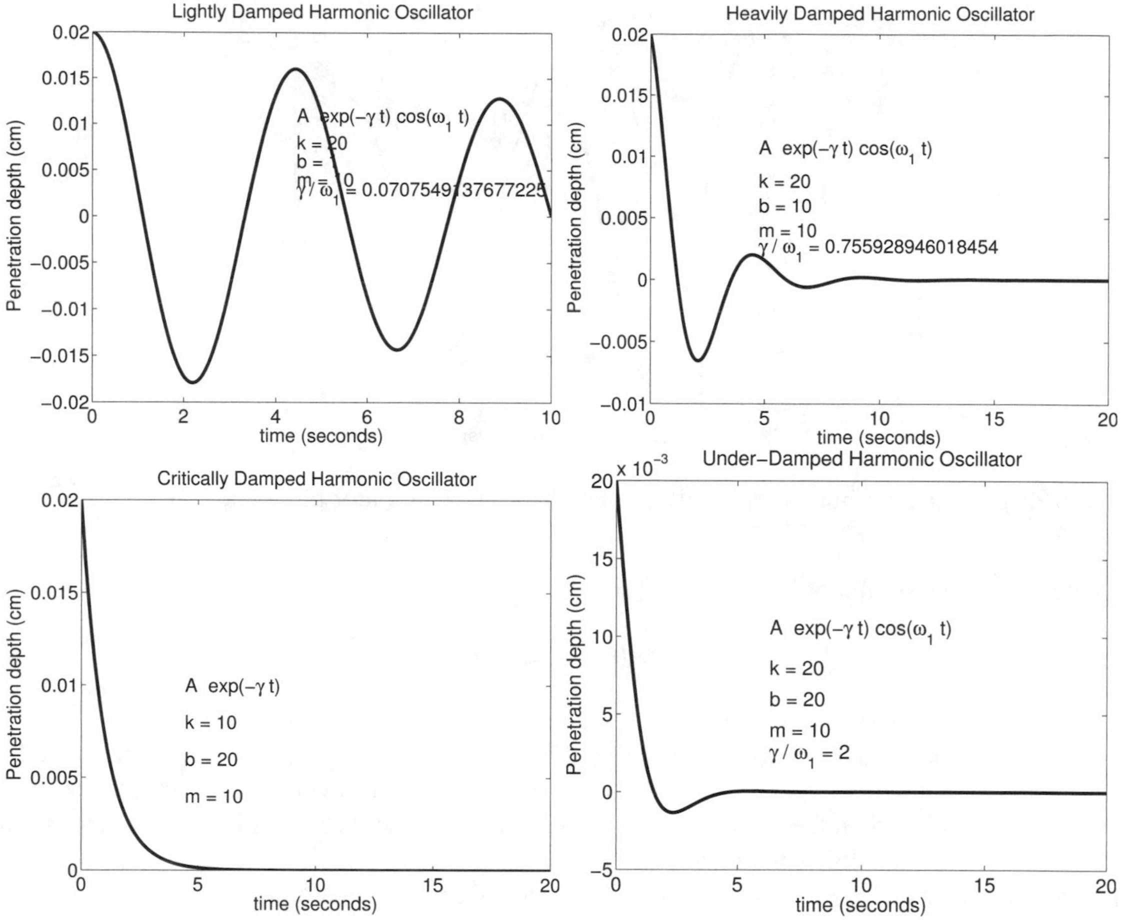

Figure 22.15: A qualitative analysis of a damped harmonic oscillator. Amplitudes are plotted as functions of time.

Critically damped, when $b^2 - 4mk = 0$. In this case, the amplitude tends rapidly to zero (without crossing zero) and flattens out.

Under damped, when $b^2 - 4mk < 0$. In this case, the amplitude decays even faster than in the case of *critical damping*, but the amplitude crosses zero and increases again before flattening out.

Examples of the four categories are illustrated in Figure 22.15.

Using a harmonic oscillator for a mass-spring system (see Section 8.4.1) to model penalty forces (see Chapter 5), reasonable motion is obtained for heavily damped, or at best, critically damped, since oscillating forces such as oscillating contact forces are often undesirable. Furthermore, it is often desirable to require that the amplitude should decay to zero within a time-step, since this will make objects appear rigid.

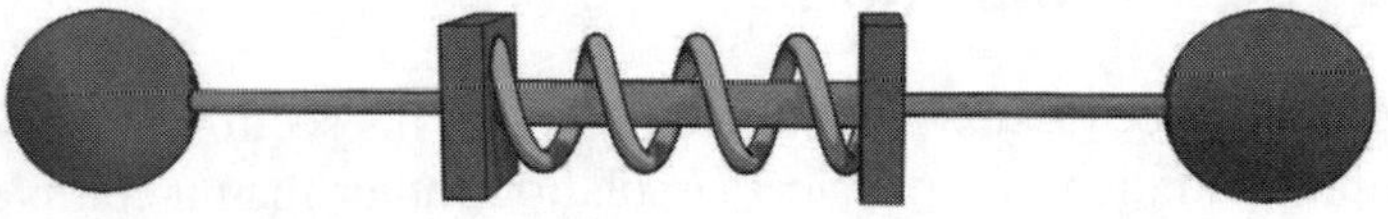

Figure 22.16: The two-body harmonic oscillator.

22.4.2 The Two-Object Harmonic Oscillator

Consider a two-body system, as shown in Figure 22.16, where two particles are connected with a spring and label uniquely by the labels i and j. Hooke's law for this system is given as the following two equations:

$$m_i\ddot{x}_i = k\left(x_j - x_i\right), \qquad (22.141a)$$
$$m_j\ddot{x}_j = -k\left(x_j - x_i\right), \qquad (22.141b)$$

where x_i is the position of the i'th particle and m_i the mass. Similarly, $\boldsymbol{x}_j$ and m_j are the position and mass of the j'th particle. Dividing the first equation by m_i and the second by m_j, yields

$$\ddot{x}_i = k\frac{1}{m_i}\left(x_j - x_i\right), \qquad (22.142a)$$
$$\ddot{x}_j = -k\frac{1}{m_j}\left(x_j - x_i\right), \qquad (22.142b)$$

and subtracting the first from the second yields

$$\ddot{x}_j - \ddot{x}_i = -k\frac{1}{m_j}\left(x_j - x_i\right) - k\frac{1}{m_i}\left(x_j - x_i\right) \qquad (22.143a)$$
$$= -k\left(\frac{1}{m_j} + \frac{1}{m_i}\right)\left(x_j - x_i\right). \qquad (22.143b)$$

The two-object harmonic oscillator has the same motion as the one-object harmonic oscillator. This may be seen by setting, $x = x_j - x_i$, in (22.143b), such that

$$\ddot{x} = -k\left(\frac{1}{m_j} + \frac{1}{m_i}\right)x \qquad (22.144)$$

Introducing the reduced mass as

$$\mu = \frac{m_i m_j}{m_i + m_j}, \qquad (22.145)$$

it is discovered that

$$\mu\ddot{x} = -kx. \qquad (22.146)$$

It is thus concluded that the two-object harmonic oscillator behaves as a one-object system of mass μ.

22.5 The Lagrange Formulation

The *Lagrange formulation* will be discussed in the following. This section is written with an emphasis on obtaining a realistic implementation of a physical simulation rather than a complete physical and mathematical understanding. The scope of this section is the derivation of [Terzopoulos et al., 1987, Equation 1], shown here:

$$\frac{\partial}{\partial t}\left(\mu(\boldsymbol{a})\left(\frac{\partial \boldsymbol{r}}{\partial t}\right)\right) + \gamma(\boldsymbol{a})\frac{\partial \boldsymbol{r}}{\partial t} + \frac{\delta \varepsilon}{\delta \boldsymbol{r}} = \boldsymbol{f}(\boldsymbol{r}, t). \tag{22.147}$$

We will use a notation similar to [Goldstein, 1980]. The physical theory is based on [Goldstein, 1980, Chapters 1, 2 and 13], and the calculus of variation used is discussed in detail in Chapter 21.

22.5.1 Lagrange's Equation

If the total force on each particle in a particle system is zero, then the system is in *equilibrium*, and

$$\boldsymbol{F}_i = 0, \quad \forall i. \tag{22.148}$$

The *virtual work* of all the forces in a virtual displacement, $\delta \boldsymbol{r}_i$, is by definition

$$\sum_i \boldsymbol{F}_i \cdot \delta \boldsymbol{r}_i = 0, \tag{22.149}$$

because all $\boldsymbol{F}_i$s are zero. A *virtual displacement* is an infinitesimal instantaneous fictive displacement, meaning it is infinitely small, there is no time duration, and the displacement never occurs in the real world. Virtual displacements are a useful mathematical trick, which we will use in the following. The only requirement for using virtual displacements is that their use must be consistent with the forces and constraints in the system.

Newton's second law (22.5) for the i'th particle is given by

$$\boldsymbol{F}_i = \dot{\boldsymbol{p}}_i, \tag{22.150a}$$

$$\Downarrow$$

$$\boldsymbol{F}_i - \dot{\boldsymbol{p}}_i = 0. \tag{22.150b}$$

The total force can be split into two: the applied forces, $\boldsymbol{F}_i^{(a)}$, and the constraint forces, $\boldsymbol{F}_i^{(c)}$:

$$\left(\boldsymbol{F}_i^{(a)} + \boldsymbol{F}_i^{(c)}\right) - \dot{\boldsymbol{p}}_i = 0. \tag{22.151}$$

Using a virtual displacement, the work performed is

$$\sum_i \left(\left(\boldsymbol{F}_i^{(a)} + \boldsymbol{F}_i^{(c)}\right) - \dot{\boldsymbol{p}}_i\right) \cdot \delta \boldsymbol{r}_i = 0, \tag{22.152}$$

and expanding the terms gives

$$\sum_i \boldsymbol{F}_i^{(a)} \cdot \delta \boldsymbol{r}_i + \sum_i \boldsymbol{F}_i^{(c)} \cdot \delta \boldsymbol{r}_i - \sum_i \dot{\boldsymbol{p}}_i \cdot \delta \boldsymbol{r}_i = 0. \tag{22.153}$$

Consider a particle constrained to move in a plane. Any constraint force on this particle must be perpendicular to the plane. Since any virtual displacement must be consistent with the constraints in the system, they must lie in the plane and thus be orthogonal to the constraint forces. In this case, the virtual work of the constraint forces is therefore zero. The discussion in the following will be restricted to systems where the net virtual work of the constraint forces is zero. This is *D'Alembert's principle* and reduces (22.153) to:

$$\sum_i \left(\boldsymbol{F}_i^{(a)} - \dot{\boldsymbol{p}}_i \right) \cdot \delta \boldsymbol{r}_i = 0. \tag{22.154}$$

The vectors $\boldsymbol{r}_i$ are not necessarily independent of each other. It is useful to transform them into independent coordinates, q_j. To see why this is useful, recall from linear algebra that a linear combination of a set of independent vectors, $\boldsymbol{v}_i$, can only be zero if all the coefficients, a_i, are zero.

$$a_1 \boldsymbol{v}_1 + \cdots + a_n \boldsymbol{v}_n = 0 \quad \Rightarrow \quad a_1 = \cdots = a_n = 0. \tag{22.155}$$

Hence, given a set of transformed coordinates that are mutually independent and D'Alembert's principle (22.154), we can conclude that $\boldsymbol{F}_i^{(a)} - \dot{\boldsymbol{p}}_i$ are zero for all i. It will be assumed that such a set of independent coordinates exists together with a sct of transformation equations. The transformed coordinates q_i will be called the *generalized coordinates*.

$$\boldsymbol{r}_1 = \boldsymbol{r}_1(q_1, q_2, \ldots, q_n, t), \tag{22.156a}$$
$$\boldsymbol{r}_2 = \boldsymbol{r}_2(q_1, q_2, \ldots, q_n, t), \tag{22.156b}$$
$$\vdots$$
$$\boldsymbol{r}_N = \boldsymbol{r}_N(q_1, q_2, \ldots, q_n, t), \tag{22.156c}$$

where $N > n$, and $k = N - n$ is the redundant degrees of freedoms removed from the representation. Taking the derivative of the i'th particle

$$\boldsymbol{v}_i \equiv \frac{d}{dt}\boldsymbol{r}_i = \sum_k \frac{\partial \boldsymbol{r}_i}{\partial q_k}\dot{q}_k + \frac{\partial \boldsymbol{r}_i}{\partial t}, \tag{22.157}$$

reveals a method for converting between the two set of coordinates, which is the i'th row of the Jacobian of the transformation multiplied by the generalized velocity vector of the system. The virtual displacement in the generalized coordinates $\delta \boldsymbol{r}_i$ is naturally a linear combination of the virtual displacements of the system δq_k through the Jacobian of the transformation:

$$\delta \boldsymbol{r}_i = \sum_k \frac{\partial \boldsymbol{r}_i}{\partial q_k}\delta q_k. \tag{22.158}$$

The virtual displacements are instantaneous; therefore, there is no variation in time to take into account,

$\frac{\partial \boldsymbol{r}_i}{\partial t} = 0$. The first term in (22.154) expressed in generalized coordinates is thus,

$$\sum_i \boldsymbol{F}_i^{(a)} \cdot \delta \boldsymbol{r}_i = \left(\sum_i \boldsymbol{F}_i^{(a)} \cdot \left(\sum_j \frac{\partial \boldsymbol{r}_i}{\partial q_j} \delta q_j \right) \right) \tag{22.159a}$$

$$= \sum_{i,j} \left(\boldsymbol{F}_i^{(a)} \cdot \frac{\partial \boldsymbol{r}_i}{\partial q_j} \delta q_j \right) \tag{22.159b}$$

$$= \sum_j \underbrace{\left(\sum_i \boldsymbol{F}_i^{(a)} \cdot \frac{\partial \boldsymbol{r}_i}{\partial q_j} \right)}_{Q_j} \delta q_j, \tag{22.159c}$$

implying that

$$\sum_i \boldsymbol{F}_i^{(a)} \cdot \delta \boldsymbol{r}_i = \sum_j Q_j \delta q_j, \tag{22.160}$$

where Q_j is called the *generalized force*. The second term in (22.154) expressed in generalized coordinates is

$$\sum_i \dot{\boldsymbol{p}}_i \cdot \delta \boldsymbol{r}_i = \sum_i m_i \ddot{\boldsymbol{r}}_i \cdot \delta \boldsymbol{r}_i \tag{22.161a}$$

$$= \sum_i m_i \ddot{\boldsymbol{r}}_i \cdot \left(\sum_j \frac{\partial \boldsymbol{r}_i}{\partial q_j} \delta q_j \right) \tag{22.161b}$$

$$= \sum_{i,j} m_i \ddot{\boldsymbol{r}}_i \cdot \frac{\partial \boldsymbol{r}_i}{\partial q_j} \delta q_j \tag{22.161c}$$

$$= \sum_j \left(\sum_i m_i \ddot{\boldsymbol{r}}_i \cdot \frac{\partial \boldsymbol{r}_i}{\partial q_j} \right) \delta q_j. \tag{22.161d}$$

The summation in the inner parentheses can be rewritten by using the product rule of differentiation

$$\sum_i m_i \ddot{\boldsymbol{r}}_i \cdot \frac{\partial \boldsymbol{r}_i}{\partial q_j} = \sum_i \left(\frac{d}{dt} \left(m_i \dot{\boldsymbol{r}}_i \cdot \frac{\partial \boldsymbol{r}_i}{\partial q_j} \right) - m_i \dot{\boldsymbol{r}}_i \cdot \frac{d}{dt} \left(\frac{\partial \boldsymbol{r}_i}{\partial q_j} \right) \right) \tag{22.162a}$$

$$= \sum_i \left(\frac{d}{dt} \left(m_i \dot{\boldsymbol{r}}_i \cdot \frac{\partial \boldsymbol{r}_i}{\partial q_j} \right) - m_i \dot{\boldsymbol{r}}_i \cdot \frac{\partial \dot{\boldsymbol{r}}_i}{\partial q_j} \right). \tag{22.162b}$$

Differentiating (22.157) by $\dot{q}_j$ gives

$$\frac{\partial \boldsymbol{v}_i}{\partial \dot{q}_j} = \frac{\partial \boldsymbol{r}_i}{\partial q_j}. \tag{22.163}$$

and inserting into (22.162b) results in

$$\sum_i m_i \ddot{\boldsymbol{r}}_i \cdot \frac{\partial \boldsymbol{r}_i}{\partial q_j} = \sum_i \left(\frac{d}{dt} \left(m_i \boldsymbol{v}_i \cdot \frac{\partial \boldsymbol{v}_i}{\partial \dot{q}_j} \right) - m_i \boldsymbol{v}_i \cdot \frac{\partial \boldsymbol{v}_i}{\partial q_j} \right). \tag{22.164}$$

Rearranging terms and substituting back into (22.161d), it is found that

$$\sum_i \dot{\boldsymbol{p}}_i \cdot \delta \boldsymbol{r}_i = \sum_j \left\{ \frac{d}{dt} \left[\frac{\partial}{\partial \dot{q}_j} \left(\sum_i \frac{1}{2} m_i v_i^2 \right) \right] - \frac{\partial}{\partial q_j} \left(\sum_i \frac{1}{2} m_i v_i^2 \right) \right\} \delta q_j. \tag{22.165}$$

We can now substitute (22.160) and (22.165) into (22.154)

$$\sum_j \left\{ \left[\frac{d}{dt} \left(\frac{\partial T}{\partial \dot{q}_j} \right) - \frac{\partial T}{\partial q_j} \right] - Q_j \right\} \delta q_j = 0, \tag{22.166}$$

where

$$T = \sum_i \tfrac{1}{2} m v_i^2, \tag{22.167}$$

is the total kinetic energy of the system. Since all δq_j are independent, the equation can only hold if the coefficients are zero:

$$\left[\frac{d}{dt} \left(\frac{\partial T}{\partial \dot{q}_j} \right) - \frac{\partial T}{\partial q_j} \right] - Q_j = 0 \tag{22.168a}$$

$$\Downarrow$$

$$\frac{d}{dt} \left(\frac{\partial T}{\partial \dot{q}_j} \right) - \frac{\partial T}{\partial q_j} = Q_j. \tag{22.168b}$$

It will be assumed that the forces constitute a gradient field (Definition 18.38), that is, that they may be found as a gradient operator on a scalar field, V, as

$$\boldsymbol{F}_i^{(a)} = -\nabla_i V, \tag{22.169}$$

where $V(\boldsymbol{r}_1, \boldsymbol{r}_2, \ldots, \boldsymbol{r}_N, t)$ usually denotes the potential energy, and ∇_i is the gradient of V with respect to its coordinates corresponding to $\boldsymbol{r}_i$. The generalized forces then become,

$$Q_j = \sum_i \boldsymbol{F}_i^{(a)} \cdot \frac{\partial \boldsymbol{r}_i}{\partial q_j} \tag{22.170a}$$

$$= -\sum_i \nabla_i V \cdot \frac{\partial \boldsymbol{r}_i}{\partial q_j} \tag{22.170b}$$

$$= -\sum_i \frac{\partial V}{\partial \boldsymbol{r}_i} \cdot \frac{\partial \boldsymbol{r}_i}{\partial q_j} \tag{22.170c}$$

$$= -\frac{\partial V}{\partial q_j}. \tag{22.170d}$$

Inserting this into (22.168b), it is found that

$$\frac{d}{dt}\left(\frac{\partial T}{\partial \dot{q}_j}\right) - \frac{\partial (T-V)}{\partial q_j} = 0. \tag{22.171}$$

Assuming that V is independent of $\partial \dot{q}_j$, which is regularly the case, this is reduced to

$$\frac{d}{dt}\left(\frac{\partial (T-V)}{\partial \dot{q}_j}\right) - \frac{\partial (T-V)}{\partial q_j} = 0. \tag{22.172}$$

The *Lagrange's equation* is found by defining the *Lagrangian* L as

$$L = T - V, \tag{22.173}$$

which results in

$$\frac{d}{dt}\left(\frac{\partial L}{\partial \dot{q}_j}\right) - \frac{\partial L}{\partial q_j} = 0 \tag{22.174}$$

for all j. Observe that if some of the applied forces, $\boldsymbol{f}_i$, could not be derived from a scalar potential, then Lagrange's equation becomes

$$\frac{d}{dt}\left(\frac{\partial L}{\partial \dot{q}_j}\right) - \frac{\partial L}{\partial q_j} = Q_j \tag{22.175}$$

for all j, where

$$Q_j = \sum_i \boldsymbol{f}_i \cdot \frac{\partial \boldsymbol{r}_i}{\partial q_j}. \tag{22.176}$$

22.5.2 Lagrange's Equations from Hamilton's Principle

An alternative derivation of Lagrange's Equations uses *Hamilton's principle.* Hamilton's principle states that the motion of the system from time t_1 to time t_2 is such that the line integral of the Lagrangian,

$$I = \int_{t_1}^{t_2} L \, dt, \tag{22.177}$$

has a stationary value for the actual path of the motion. In other words, Lagrange's equation can be derived by setting the variation of the integral,

$$\delta I = \delta \int_{t_1}^{t_2} L(q_1, \ldots, q_n, \dot{q}_1, \ldots, \dot{q}_n, t) \, dt, \tag{22.178}$$

equal to zero, see Chapter 21 for an introduction to calculus of variation. Forces that cannot be written in terms of potentials are ignored in $\mathcal{L}$ similarly to (22.175).

Calculus of variation assumes a continuous system, however, until now the system has been described by a discrete set of particles given in generalized coordinates, q_is. Fortunately, an object may be considered as the continuous limit of infinitely many small particles. This is similar to thinking of a real-world object as a continuous entity consisting of many, but a finite number of atoms.

In the continuous limit, the index i should be taken to be a *continuous index*, a, of the generalized coordinates,

$$i \simeq a \in \Omega, \tag{22.179}$$

where Ω is the domain (that is, the volume of the object). For simplicity, a single continuous index will be used; nevertheless, the mathematical treatment in the following may easily be generalized to three or more indices.

$$i \simeq \{a_1, a_2, a_3\}. \tag{22.180}$$

One way to think of these continuous indices is as a parameterization of the volume of a deformable object.

Example 22.2

For instance, imagine that the volume is given by the B-spline volume, $B(u, v, w)$, defined as

$$B(u, v, w) = \sum_i \sum_j \sum_k N_i(u) N_j(v) N_k(w) \boldsymbol{P}_{ijk}, \tag{22.181}$$

where N is the B-spline basis function and $\boldsymbol{P}_{ijk}$ are the control points. Here, u, v, and w are the B-spline volume parameters, and they could be used as continuous indices. Given specific values of u, v, and w would uniquely pinpoint a single particle in the material.

Given continuous indices, the Lagrangian is written as an integral,

$$L = \int \mathcal{L}\, da, \tag{22.182}$$

where $\mathcal{L}$ is known as the *Lagrangian density*. The Lagrangian density is a function of time, indices, displacements, and derivatives of displacements,

$$\mathcal{L} = \mathcal{L}\left(a, t, r(a,t), \frac{dr(a,t)}{da}, \frac{dr(a,t)}{dt}\right), \tag{22.183}$$

where $r(a, t)$ is the displacement function, also sometimes called the field quantity. For a deformable object, the displacement $r(a, t)$ would be the displacement of the point, a, from its original placement (that is, $r(a, 0) = 0$) in the deformable object.

Hamilton's Principle can be stated as

$$\delta I = \delta \int_{t_1}^{t_2} \int_\Omega \mathcal{L}\, da\, dt = 0. \tag{22.184}$$

Using calculus of variation, the integral equation is converted to the differential equation,

$$\frac{d}{dt}\left(\frac{\partial \mathcal{L}}{\partial \frac{\partial r}{\partial t}}\right) + \frac{d}{da}\left(\frac{\partial \mathcal{L}}{\partial \frac{\partial r}{\partial a}}\right) - \frac{\partial \mathcal{L}}{\partial r} = 0. \tag{22.185}$$

In general, the displacement vector $\boldsymbol{r}(\boldsymbol{a}, t)$ for a system of independent variables $\boldsymbol{a} = \{a_i\}$ is written in condensed form as

$$\frac{d}{dt}\left(\frac{\partial \mathcal{L}}{\partial \frac{\partial \boldsymbol{r}}{\partial t}}\right) - \frac{\delta \mathcal{L}}{\delta \boldsymbol{r}} = \mathcal{Q}, \tag{22.186}$$

where $\frac{\delta}{\delta \boldsymbol{r}}$ is called the *variational derivative* for a system of independent variables a_i, and it is given as

$$\frac{\delta}{\delta \boldsymbol{r}} = \frac{\partial}{\partial \boldsymbol{r}} - \sum_i \frac{d}{da_i} \frac{\partial}{\partial \frac{\partial \boldsymbol{r}}{\partial a_i}}. \tag{22.187}$$

For integral equations involving second-order derivatives, the variational derivative is given as

$$\frac{\delta}{\delta \boldsymbol{r}} = \frac{\partial}{\partial \boldsymbol{r}} - \sum_i \frac{d}{da_i} \frac{\partial}{\partial \frac{\partial \boldsymbol{r}}{\partial a_i}} + \sum_{i,j} \frac{d^2}{da_j da_i} \frac{\partial}{\partial \frac{\partial^2 \boldsymbol{r}}{\partial a_j \partial a_i}}. \tag{22.188}$$

22.6 Principle of Virtual Work

Virtual work is a method of introducing fictive constraints on an under-constrained system without adding or subtracting energy. It will be shown in this section that the constraint forces can be written as

$$\hat{f} = \boldsymbol{J}^T \boldsymbol{\lambda}, \tag{22.189}$$

where $\hat{f}$ is the constraint force, $\boldsymbol{J}$ is the Jacobian matrix, and $\boldsymbol{\lambda}$ is a vector of *Lagrange multipliers*. From the Newton-Euler equations (see Section 7.1 for details) the generalized acceleration vector can be derived as

$$\ddot{\boldsymbol{s}} = \boldsymbol{M}^{-1}\left(\boldsymbol{f} + \hat{f}\right). \tag{22.190}$$

Here, $\boldsymbol{M}$ is the generalized mass matrix, $\boldsymbol{s}$ is the generalized position vector, and $\boldsymbol{f}$ is the generalized applied force vector.

From a time-independent holonomic constraint, $\boldsymbol{\Phi}(\boldsymbol{s}) = \boldsymbol{0}$, the following kinematic constraint can be derived:

$$\dot{\boldsymbol{\Phi}} = \underbrace{\frac{\partial \boldsymbol{\Phi}}{\partial \boldsymbol{s}}}_{\boldsymbol{J}} \dot{\boldsymbol{s}} \tag{22.191a}$$

$$= \boldsymbol{J}\dot{\boldsymbol{s}} = 0 \tag{22.191b}$$

$$\tag{22.191c}$$

Differentiation w.r.t. time leads to the acceleration constraint

$$\ddot{\boldsymbol{\Phi}} = \dot{\boldsymbol{J}}\dot{\boldsymbol{s}} + \boldsymbol{J}\ddot{\boldsymbol{s}} = 0. \tag{22.192}$$

Here, there are some subtleties concerning the term $\dot{\boldsymbol{J}}$: from the chain rule it can be seen that it involves taking a matrix differentiated w.r.t. a vector

$$\dot{\boldsymbol{J}} = \frac{\partial \boldsymbol{J}}{\partial \boldsymbol{s}} \dot{\boldsymbol{s}}, \tag{22.193}$$

which would imply a 3D tensor. In practice, this can be avoided by using

$$\dot{\boldsymbol{J}} = \frac{\partial \dot{\Phi}}{\partial \boldsymbol{s}}. \tag{22.194}$$

Insertion of $\ddot{\boldsymbol{s}}$ in the acceleration constraint yields

$$\ddot{\boldsymbol{\Phi}} = \dot{\boldsymbol{J}}\dot{\boldsymbol{s}} + \boldsymbol{J}\boldsymbol{M}^{-1}\left(\boldsymbol{f} + \hat{\boldsymbol{f}}\right) = 0, \tag{22.195}$$

and rearranging gives

$$\boldsymbol{J}\boldsymbol{M}^{-1}\hat{\boldsymbol{f}} = -\boldsymbol{J}\boldsymbol{M}^{-1}\boldsymbol{f} - \dot{\boldsymbol{J}}\dot{\boldsymbol{s}}. \tag{22.196}$$

The *principle of virtual work* states that constraint forces do no work, that is,

$$\hat{\boldsymbol{f}} \cdot \dot{\boldsymbol{s}} = 0. \tag{22.197}$$

However, from the constraint problem it is known that $\boldsymbol{J}\dot{\boldsymbol{s}} = 0$, and in combination with the principle of virtual work this leads to

$$\hat{\boldsymbol{f}} = \boldsymbol{J}^T\boldsymbol{\lambda}. \tag{22.198}$$

To get an intuitive grasp of this equation, it may help to think in terms of simple geometry. The rows of the Jacobian $\boldsymbol{J}$ are a collection of vectors, each of which is the gradient of a scalar constraint function. In particular, the i'th row is the gradient of the i'th entry in Φ. In fact, the gradients are the normals to the isosurfaces given by $\boldsymbol{\Phi} = 0$; their directions represent the domains where the solution is not permitted to move into. To ensure this, it is required that the change of state $\dot{\boldsymbol{s}}$ is orthogonal to all those normals. In other words, $\boldsymbol{s}$ is only allowed to change in the tangential direction, and this is exactly what the condition $\boldsymbol{J}\dot{\boldsymbol{s}} = 0$ means. The set of vectors, $\hat{\boldsymbol{f}}$, spanned by $\boldsymbol{J}^T\boldsymbol{\lambda}$ are therefore all orthogonal to the state of change vector $\dot{\boldsymbol{s}} = 0$, and it will therefore always be the case that $\hat{\boldsymbol{f}} \cdot \dot{\boldsymbol{s}} = 0$, which is exactly what the principle of virtual work states.

The Lagrange multipliers may be solved by using $\hat{\boldsymbol{f}} = \boldsymbol{J}^T\boldsymbol{\lambda}$, implying that

$$\boldsymbol{J}\boldsymbol{M}^{-1}\hat{\boldsymbol{f}} = -\boldsymbol{J}\boldsymbol{M}^{-1}\boldsymbol{f} - \dot{\boldsymbol{J}}\dot{\boldsymbol{s}}, \tag{22.199a}$$

$$\Downarrow$$

$$\boldsymbol{J}\boldsymbol{M}^{-1}\boldsymbol{J}^T\boldsymbol{\lambda} = -\boldsymbol{J}\boldsymbol{M}^{-1}\boldsymbol{f} - \dot{\boldsymbol{J}}\dot{\boldsymbol{s}}, \tag{22.199b}$$

from which the vector of Lagrange multipliers, and in turn the constraint forces, may be computed.

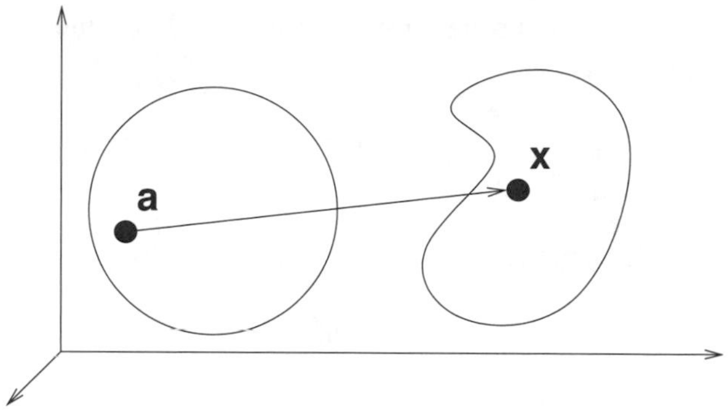

Figure 22.17: A graphical representation of the deformation of an object.

22.7 Stress and Strain

In order to model deformable objects, a way to measure deformation is needed. In this section, we will define measures for deformation and relate them to stress in a deformable object. The field of continuum mechanics has derived a general theory in this respect, which will be described in a condensed form.

Consider an object in an undeformed state, as seen on the left in Figure 22.17. A point within the undeformed object is denoted by the vector $\boldsymbol{a}$, given in material coordinates. When the object is translated, rotated, or deformed, the material at point $\boldsymbol{a}$ changes location. This new location is described by the vector $\boldsymbol{x}$, given in world coordinates. This is illustrated on the right in Figure 22.17. The *displacement* of the material is given as

$$\boldsymbol{u} = \boldsymbol{x} - \boldsymbol{a}. \tag{22.200}$$

For any point $\boldsymbol{a}$ in the material, there exists a mapping toward its actual position in the deformed object, given by $\boldsymbol{x}(\boldsymbol{a})$. This function is undefined if the vector $\boldsymbol{a}$ is outside the material. Knowing the function, one can calculate the change of $\boldsymbol{x}$ with respect to change of $\boldsymbol{a}$ by

$$d\boldsymbol{x} = F d\boldsymbol{a}, \tag{22.201}$$

where F_{ij} is the *deformation gradient* (also known as the Jacobian), given by

$$F_{ij} = \frac{\partial x_i}{\partial a_j}, \tag{22.202}$$

which describes the change in world coordinates with respect to change in material coordinates. The indexes i and j define a particular value of the vectors $\boldsymbol{x}$ and $\boldsymbol{a}$, respectively.

A displacement does not necessarily mean that the object deforms. Rotating and translating the object gives rise to a displacement, but not a deformation. The deformation gradient in (22.202) is invariant to translation, but not to rotation, since the derivative of vector $\boldsymbol{x}$ changes with respect to $\boldsymbol{a}$, as seen in Figure 22.18; but the magnitude does not change. Therefore, it is possible to describe deformation as the change in squared length of $d\boldsymbol{x}$ and $d\boldsymbol{a}$:

$$d\boldsymbol{x}^2 - d\boldsymbol{a}^2 = d\boldsymbol{x}^T d\boldsymbol{x} - d\boldsymbol{a}^T d\boldsymbol{a}. \tag{22.203}$$

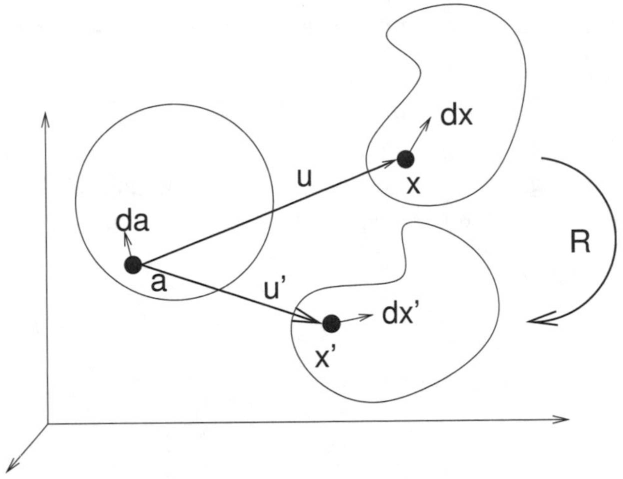

Figure 22.18: A rotation changes the derivative of vector $\boldsymbol{x}$ with respect to $\boldsymbol{a}$; but the magnitude does not change.

Using (22.201), this can be rewritten in terms of material coordinates only, to obtain

$$d\boldsymbol{a}^T F^T F d\boldsymbol{a} - d\boldsymbol{a}^T d\boldsymbol{a} = d\boldsymbol{a}^T \left(F^T F - I\right) d\boldsymbol{a} = d\boldsymbol{a}^T 2\mathcal{E} d\boldsymbol{a}. \tag{22.204}$$

The symbol $\mathcal{E}$ is *Green's strain tensor* also known as the *Lagrangian strain tensor*, defined as

$$\mathcal{E} = \frac{1}{2}\left(F^T F - I\right). \tag{22.205}$$

The Green strain tensor is invariant to rigid body motion. Rewriting it in terms of partials, one obtains

$$\mathcal{E} = \frac{1}{2}\left(\frac{\partial x}{\partial a_i} \cdot \frac{\partial x}{\partial a_j} - \delta_{ij}\right), \tag{22.206}$$

where δ_{ij} is the delta function. Using (22.200), this can further be rewritten in terms of the displacements, by

$$\mathcal{E} = \frac{1}{2}\left(\frac{\partial (u+a)}{\partial a_i} \cdot \frac{\partial (u+a)}{\partial a_j} - \delta_{ij}\right) \tag{22.207a}$$

$$= \frac{1}{2}\left(\frac{\partial u}{\partial a_i} \cdot \frac{\partial u}{\partial a_j} + \frac{\partial u}{\partial a_i} \cdot \frac{\partial a}{\partial a_j} + \frac{\partial a}{\partial a_i} \cdot \frac{\partial u}{\partial a_j} + \frac{\partial a}{\partial a_i} \cdot \frac{\partial a}{\partial a_j} - \delta_{ij}\right) \tag{22.207b}$$

$$= \frac{1}{2}\left(\frac{\partial u}{\partial a_i} \cdot \frac{\partial u}{\partial a_j} + \frac{\partial u_i}{\partial a_j} + \frac{\partial u_j}{\partial a_i}\right). \tag{22.207c}$$

The Green strain tensor contains a quadratic term, which means that analysis of large deformations becomes nonlinear. However, if the displacements are very small, the quadratic term becomes negligible.

This is the assumption for the *Cauchy strain tensor*, which is a first-order approximation to the Green strain tensor, given by

$$\epsilon_{ij} = \frac{1}{2}\left(\frac{\partial u_i}{\partial a_j} + \frac{\partial u_j}{\partial a_i}\right). \tag{22.208}$$

In addition to the strain at a given point, one can calculate the rate of change by taking the derivative with respect to time. For the Green strain tensor, given in (22.206), this becomes

$$\frac{d}{dt}\mathcal{E}_{ij} = \frac{d}{dt}\frac{1}{2}\left(\frac{\partial x}{\partial a_i}\cdot\frac{\partial x}{\partial a_j} - \delta_{ij}\right) = \frac{1}{2}\left(\frac{\partial x}{\partial a_i}\cdot\frac{\partial \dot{x}}{\partial a_j} + \frac{\partial \dot{x}}{\partial a_i}\cdot\frac{\partial x}{\partial a_j}\right). \tag{22.209}$$

From the above, the *strain rate* V is defined as

$$V_{ij} = \frac{\partial x}{\partial a_i}\cdot\frac{\partial \dot{x}}{\partial a_j} + \frac{\partial \dot{x}}{\partial a_i}\cdot\frac{\partial x}{\partial a_j}. \tag{22.210}$$

The stress in a deformable body is related to the strain and the strain-rate. This relationship is determined by the elastic and viscous properties of the material. A way to express this relationship is by the *2nd Piola-Kirchoff stress* tensor S, given by

$$S = S^{(\mathcal{E})} + S^{(V)}. \tag{22.211}$$

The elastic stress, $S^{(\mathcal{E})}$, depends on the Green strain tensor, defined in (22.206), and the viscous stress, $S^{(V)}$, depends on the strain-rate, defined in (22.210). These are given by

$$S_{ij}^{(\mathcal{E})} = \sum_{k=1}^{3}\sum_{l=1}^{3} C_{ijkl}\mathcal{E}_{kl}, \tag{22.212a}$$

$$S_{ij}^{(V)} = \sum_{k=1}^{3}\sum_{l=1}^{3} D_{ijkl}V_{kl}, \tag{22.212b}$$

where the relation between the elastic stress and the strain is given by the *stiffness matrix* C, and the relation between the viscous stress and the strain-rate is given by the *damping matrix* D. In three dimensions, the strain and stress tensors consist of nine values. To fully describe how each of the strain values affects the stress, it requires $9 \times 9 = 81$ coefficients for both the stiffness matrix and the damping matrix. But since $\mathcal{E}$ is symmetric, most of the coefficients of C are redundant, and can be reduced to 6×6 different values. If the material being considered is isotropic, the material properties are independent of direction. Such materials have only two independent variables (that is, elastic constants) in their stiffness and damping matrices, as opposed to the 36 elastic constants in the general anisotropic case.

For isotropic materials, the elastic stress tensor is given by

$$S_{ij}^{(\mathcal{E})} = \sum_{k=1}^{3} \lambda\mathcal{E}_{kk}\delta_{ij} + 2\mu\mathcal{E}_{ij}, \tag{22.213}$$

where μ determines the rigidity of the object, and λ determines the resistance to a change in volume. A similar argument can be done for the viscous stress. Since the strain tensor is symmetric, the strain-rate tensor will also be symmetric. The damping matrix D is therefore reduced to the two values ϕ and ψ, and the viscous stress for isotropic materials is calculated by

$$S_{ij}^{(V)} = \sum_{k=1}^{3} \phi V_{kk} \delta_{ij} + 2\psi v_{ij}. \tag{22.214}$$

The isotropic elastic stress tensor from (22.213) can be conveniently written on matrix-vector form:

$$\begin{bmatrix} S_{11} \\ S_{22} \\ S_{33} \\ S_{23} \\ S_{31} \\ S_{12} \end{bmatrix} = \begin{bmatrix} \lambda + 2\mu & \lambda & \lambda & 0 & 0 & 0 \\ \lambda & \lambda + 2\mu & \lambda & 0 & 0 & 0 \\ \lambda & \lambda & \lambda + 2\mu & 0 & 0 & 0 \\ 0 & 0 & 0 & 2\mu & 0 & 0 \\ 0 & 0 & 0 & 0 & 2\mu & 0 \\ 0 & 0 & 0 & 0 & 0 & 2\mu \end{bmatrix} \begin{bmatrix} \mathcal{E}_{11} \\ \mathcal{E}_{22} \\ \mathcal{E}_{33} \\ \mathcal{E}_{23} \\ \mathcal{E}_{31} \\ \mathcal{E}_{12} \end{bmatrix}, \tag{22.215}$$

using the fact that $\mathcal{E}$ is symmetric.

The *isotropic elastic stress tensor* given above uses the *Lamé coefficients* μ and λ. Often materials are specified using *Young's modulus* E and *Poisson's ratio* ν. To convert from one to the other, one can use the formulas:

$$\lambda = \frac{\nu E}{(1+\nu)(1-2\nu)} \tag{22.216a}$$

$$\mu = \frac{E}{2(1+\nu)}. \tag{22.216b}$$

Inserting these conversions in (22.215), gives the commonly seen stress-strain relationship:

$$\begin{bmatrix} S_{11} \\ S_{22} \\ S_{33} \\ S_{23} \\ S_{31} \\ S_{12} \end{bmatrix} = \frac{E}{(1+\nu)(1-2\nu)} \begin{bmatrix} 1-\nu & \nu & \nu & 0 & 0 & 0 \\ \nu & 1-\nu & \nu & 0 & 0 & 0 \\ \nu & \nu & 1-\nu & 0 & 0 & 0 \\ 0 & 0 & 0 & 1-2\nu & 0 & 0 \\ 0 & 0 & 0 & 0 & 1-2\nu & 0 \\ 0 & 0 & 0 & 0 & 0 & 1-2\nu \end{bmatrix} \begin{bmatrix} \mathcal{E}_{11} \\ \mathcal{E}_{22} \\ \mathcal{E}_{33} \\ \mathcal{E}_{23} \\ \mathcal{E}_{31} \\ \mathcal{E}_{12} \end{bmatrix}. \tag{22.217}$$

Comparing (22.217) with for example, the one given in [Zienkiewicz et al., 2000, Chapter 6], there is a factor of $\frac{1}{2}$ in the difference on the last three diagonal elements. To explain this, write out the entry ϵ_{23} in the Cauchy strain tensor from (22.208):

$$\epsilon_{23} = \frac{1}{2}\left(\frac{\partial u_2}{\partial a_3} + \frac{\partial u_3}{\partial a_2}\right). \tag{22.218}$$

This is the average of the two shear strains. The total of the two shear strains is sometimes used instead:

$$\gamma_{23} = \left(\frac{\partial u_2}{\partial a_3} + \frac{\partial u_3}{\partial a_2}\right), \tag{22.219}$$

which gives rise to the difference. This is sometimes called *engineering shear strain*.

23

Differential Equations and Numerical Integration

Differential equations of interest in animation are often so complicated that it is impossible to find analytical solutions. Therefore, this chapter concentrates on numerical solutions using finite differences for explicit and implicit solution methods. Euler [Euler, 1768] was probably the first to use finite differences for solving differential equations, while many consider Courant, Friedrichs, and Levy's paper [Courant et al., 1928] as the starting point of the modern numerical methods for solving partial differential equations. In this chapter, we will review [Press et al., 1999a, Chapter 16] on ordinary differential equations, [Ames, 1969, Collatz, 1986, Morton et al., 1994, Butcher, 2003] on partial differential equations, [Baraff, 1997a, Baraff, 1997b] on explicit and implicit integration of differential equations, and [Sethian, 1999, Osher et al., 2003] on level-set methods.

A *differential equation* is an equation where the differential of one or more functions appear. They are typically classified as either being ordinary or partial. An *ordinary differential equation* (*ODE*) is an equation of one independent variable x and one dependent variable $y(x)$ and its derivatives. For example, $F[x, y(x), y'(x), y''(x), \ldots] = 0$, where $y^{(n)}(x) = \frac{d^n y}{dx^n}$. A *partial differential equation* (*PDE*) is an equation where partial derivatives occur, such as $F[x, y, z(x,y), z_x(x,y), z_y(x,y), z_{xx}(x,y), \ldots] = 0$, where $z(x,y)$ is the variable depending on the independent variables x and y, and $z_x(x,y) = \frac{\partial z(x,y)}{\partial x}$, etc. The highest order of the derivative occurring in a differential equation is the *order* of the differential equation, and if the differential equation can be written as a polynomial in the dependent variables and their derivatives, then the degree of the equation is also called the degree of the differential equation. A differential equation of degree one is said to be linear.

23.1 Ordinary Differential Equations

Ordinary differential equations may always be reduced to a problem involving only *coupled differential equations* of the form

$$\frac{dx_1(t)}{dt} = \dot{x}_1 = f_1(t, x_1, \ldots x_N), \tag{23.1a}$$

$$\frac{dx_2(t)}{dt} = \dot{x}_2 = f_2(t, x_1, \ldots x_N), \tag{23.1b}$$

$$\vdots$$

$$\frac{dx_N(t)}{dt} = \dot{x}_N = f_N(t, x_1, \ldots x_N), \tag{23.1c}$$

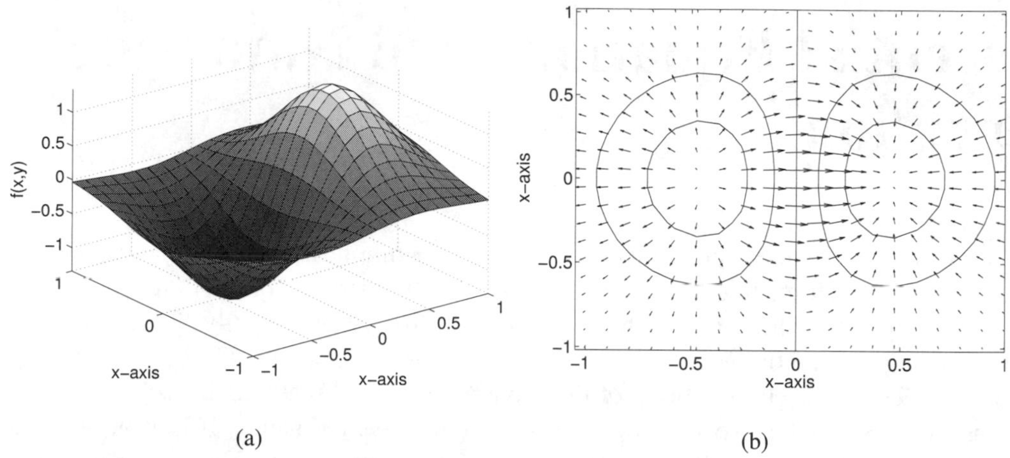

Figure 23.1: A function (a) and its corresponding gradient field (b).

where the expressions f_i are given, together with some *boundary conditions* on x_i. As an example, consider a 2D function $f : \mathbb{R}^2 \to \mathbb{R}$, and its gradient $\nabla f : \mathbb{R}^2 \to \mathbb{R}^2$, as shown in Figure 23.1. The gradient of f is given by

$$\nabla f = \begin{bmatrix} \frac{\partial f}{\partial x_1} \\ \frac{\partial f}{\partial x_2} \end{bmatrix}, \tag{23.2}$$

and solutions to $\dot{\boldsymbol{x}}(t) = \boldsymbol{\phi}(\boldsymbol{x}, t) = -\nabla f$ will be curves $[x_1(t), x_2(t)]^T$, which have $-\nabla f(x, y)$ as tangent. It may be helpful to think of these curves as the paths a ball will follow when it rolls down the hill of f.

For some ordinary differential equations, the analytical solution is simple to find. As an example, consider the ordinary differential equation

$$\dot{x}(t) = \phi(x, t) = -kx(t). \tag{23.3}$$

By writing the differentiation explicitly,

$$\dot{x}(t) = \frac{dx}{dt} = -kx, \tag{23.4}$$

and by rearranging the dx and dt, we find

$$\frac{1}{x} dx = -k\ dt. \tag{23.5}$$

Each side of the equation now denotes a small infinitesimal element in x and t respectively, thus by integrating both sides

$$\int \frac{1}{x}\ dx = -\int k\ dt, \tag{23.6}$$

we may find a solution as

$$\ln x = -kt + c \tag{23.7}$$

with some unknown integration constant c. Isolating x, we conclude that the particular differential equation has the analytical solution,

$$x = e^{-kt+c} = e^c e^{-kt} = Ce^{-kt}, \tag{23.8}$$

and the unknown constant C may be determined if boundary conditions are specified. In spite of the apparent magical rearrangement of differential terms and integration w.r.t. different variables on each side of the equation, it can readily be demonstrated that the above equation is a solution to (23.3)

$$\frac{dx}{dt} = \frac{dCe^{-kt}}{dt} = -kCe^{-kt} = -kx. \tag{23.9}$$

Unfortunately, most differential equations do not have analytical solutions. Instead, their solutions must be approximated by finite differencing schemes, for example.

23.1.1 Explicit Euler Integration

Assume we are given a single first-order ordinary differential equation, $\dot{\boldsymbol{r}}(t) = \boldsymbol{\phi}(t, \boldsymbol{r})$. We think of $\boldsymbol{r} = [x_1, x_2, \ldots, x_N]^T$ as a particle moving on a height field, as shown in Figure 23.1(a), or more precisely, as traveling in a corresponding gradient field $\boldsymbol{\phi}$, as shown in Figure 23.1(b). We thus wish to find the *trajectory*, $\boldsymbol{r}$, of the particle under initial conditions, $\boldsymbol{r}(0) = \boldsymbol{r}_0$; $\dot{\boldsymbol{r}}(0) = \dot{\boldsymbol{r}}_0$.

Examining the Taylor expansion (20.7) for $\boldsymbol{r}$ around t to first order:

$$\boldsymbol{r}(t+h) = \boldsymbol{r}(t) + h\dot{\boldsymbol{r}}(t) + \mathcal{O}(h^2) \tag{23.10a}$$

$$= \boldsymbol{r}(t) + h\boldsymbol{\phi}(t) + \mathcal{O}(h^2). \tag{23.10b}$$

We realize that the function $\boldsymbol{r}$ may be approximated from $\boldsymbol{\phi}$ by iteratively calculating $\boldsymbol{r}(t + ih)$ for $i = 1 \ldots n$ up to the order of precision of h^2 in each step. This procedure is an approximation of

$$\boldsymbol{r}(hT) = \boldsymbol{r}(0) + \sum_{i=0}^{n} h\boldsymbol{\phi}(ih) \simeq \boldsymbol{r}(0) + \int_0^T \boldsymbol{\phi}(t)\, dt, \tag{23.11}$$

where $T = nh$. This is illustrated in Figure 23.2. This is known as *explicit Euler integration*. Unfortunately, the iterative nature of the approximation implies that the error term accumulates. The solution is *simple* to implement and *fast* to compute, but neither *stable* nor very *accurate*! This is demonstrated in Figure 23.3. A vector field is shown in Figure 23.3(a), whose continuous solutions are circles, some of which are indicated. Any explicit solution will give spirals, since any finite step will follow a locally linear approximation of the circular arc, thus leaving the correct solution. This is most prominent near the center, where the curvature of the correct solution is highest. In 23.3(b) we show a vector field whose continuous solutions are translated exponentials. Taking steps that are too large will make the solution diverge, since the locally linear approximation brings the numerical approximation to vectors of gradually increasing size, thus making the numerical approximation explode.

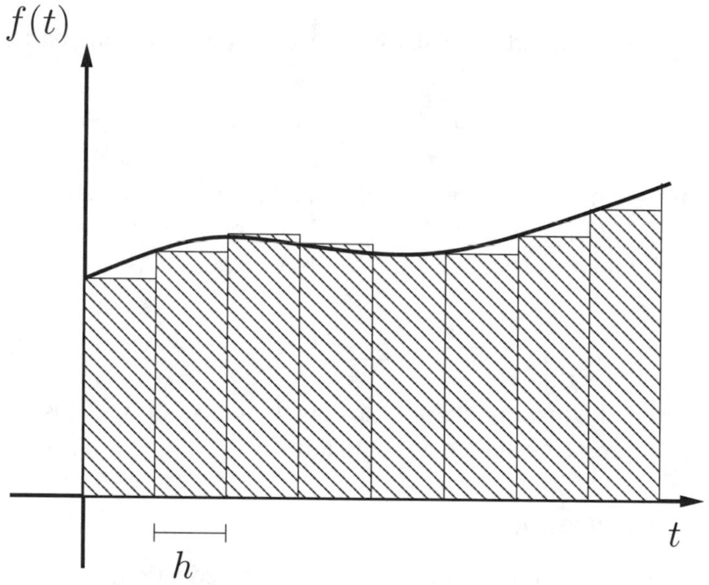

Figure 23.2: The explicit Euler method is an implementation of integration by box counting.

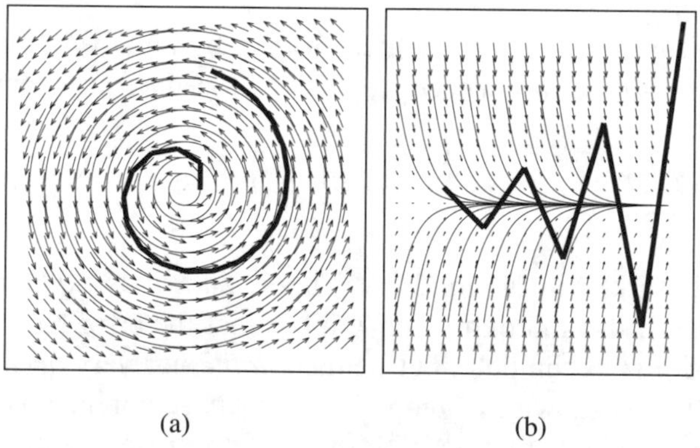

Figure 23.3: Explicit Euler is inaccurate and can be unstable. Arrows denote the velocity field, thin lines are the continuous solutions, and thick lines are a numerical approximation.

23.1.2 Improving Accuracy with the Runge-Kutta Method

The accuracy of Euler's method may be improved by taking into account higher-order terms in the Taylor series. The *midpoint method* (second-order *Runge-Kutta method*) uses the Taylor-series to second order,

$$\boldsymbol{r}(t_{i+1}) = \boldsymbol{r}(t_i) + h\dot{\boldsymbol{r}}(t_i) + \frac{h^2}{2}\ddot{\boldsymbol{r}}(t_i) + \mathcal{O}(h^3). \tag{23.12}$$

Although we are not given $\ddot{\boldsymbol{r}}$, we may find a clever approximation as follows: recall that $\dot{\boldsymbol{r}} = \phi(\boldsymbol{r})$, and therefore

$$\ddot{\boldsymbol{r}} = \frac{\partial\phi(\boldsymbol{r}(t))}{\partial t} = \frac{\partial\phi}{\partial\boldsymbol{r}} \cdot \frac{\partial\boldsymbol{r}}{\partial t} = \nabla\phi(\boldsymbol{r}(t))\,\dot{\boldsymbol{r}} = \nabla\phi(\boldsymbol{r}(t))\,\phi(\boldsymbol{r}(t)). \tag{23.13}$$

Further approximating $\phi(\boldsymbol{r}(t))$ by first-order Taylor series,

$$\phi(\boldsymbol{r}_i + \Delta\boldsymbol{r}) = \phi(\boldsymbol{r}_i) + \nabla\phi(\boldsymbol{r}_i)\,\Delta\boldsymbol{r} + \mathcal{O}(\Delta\boldsymbol{r}^2), \tag{23.14}$$

and cleverly choosing $\Delta\boldsymbol{r} = \frac{h}{2}\phi(\boldsymbol{r}_i)$, we may write

$$\phi(\boldsymbol{r}_i + \frac{h}{2}\phi(\boldsymbol{r}_i)) = \phi(\boldsymbol{r}_i) + \nabla\phi(\boldsymbol{r}_i)\,\frac{h}{2}\phi(\boldsymbol{r}_i) + \mathcal{O}(h^2) \tag{23.15a}$$

$$= \phi(\boldsymbol{r}_i) + \frac{h}{2}\ddot{\boldsymbol{r}}_i + \mathcal{O}(h^2). \tag{23.15b}$$

Thus, by isolating $\frac{h^2}{2}\ddot{\boldsymbol{r}}$ we find

$$\frac{h^2}{2}\ddot{\boldsymbol{r}}_i = h\phi(\boldsymbol{r}_i + \frac{h}{2}\phi(\boldsymbol{r}_i)) - h\phi(\boldsymbol{r}_i) + \mathcal{O}(h^3), \tag{23.16}$$

which may substituted directly into (23.12) as follows:

$$\boldsymbol{r}_{i+1} = \boldsymbol{r}_i + h\dot{\boldsymbol{r}}_i + \frac{h^2}{2}\ddot{\boldsymbol{r}}_i + \mathcal{O}(h^3) \tag{23.17a}$$

$$= \boldsymbol{r}_i + h\phi(\boldsymbol{r}_i + \frac{h}{2}\phi(\boldsymbol{r}_i)) + \mathcal{O}(h^3). \tag{23.17b}$$

Thus, we conclude that by probing ϕ in $\boldsymbol{r}_i + \frac{h}{2}\phi(\boldsymbol{r}_i)$, we have made a more accurate numerical approximation.

Further improvement in accuracy along the approach of the midpoint method is very tedious. However, a general result exists [Butcher, 1963, Hairer et al., 2002, Butcher, 2003].

Definition 23.1 (s-stage Runge-Kutta method)
Given coefficients $b_i, a_{ij}, \in \mathbb{R}, i, j = 1 \ldots s$, and letting $c_i = \sum_{j=1}^{s} a_{ij}$, then an s-stage Runge-Kutta method is given as

$$\boldsymbol{k}_i = \phi\left(t_0 + c_i h, \boldsymbol{r}_0 + h\sum_{j=1}^{s} a_{ij}\boldsymbol{k}_j\right), \tag{23.18a}$$

$$\boldsymbol{r}_1 = \boldsymbol{r}_0 + h\sum_{i=1}^{s} b_i\boldsymbol{k}_i. \tag{23.18b}$$

The method is of

$$\text{order 1 if} \qquad \sum_{i=1}^{s} b_i = 1 \tag{23.19a}$$

$$\text{order 2 if the above and} \sum_{i=1}^{s} b_i c_i = \frac{1}{2} \tag{23.19b}$$

$$\text{order 3 if the above and} \sum_{i=1}^{s} b_i c_i^2 = \frac{1}{3}, \text{ and } \sum_{j=1}^{s}\sum_{i=1}^{s} b_i a_{ij} c_i^2 = \frac{1}{6}. \tag{23.19c}$$

For conditions on higher order are more complicated (see [Hairer et al., 2002, Section III.1] for a derivation).

The coefficients are often depicted as

$$\begin{array}{c|ccc} c_1 & a_{11} & \dots & a_{1s} \\ \vdots & \vdots & & \vdots \\ c_s & a_{s1} & \dots & a_{ss} \\ \hline & b_1 & \dots & b_s \end{array} \tag{23.20}$$

in which case we have

$$\text{explicit Euler}: \qquad \begin{array}{c|c} 0 & 0 \\ \hline & 1 \end{array} \tag{23.21a}$$

$$\text{implicit Euler}: \qquad \begin{array}{c|c} 1 & 1 \\ \hline & 1 \end{array} \tag{23.21b}$$

$$\text{trapezoidal integration}: \qquad \begin{array}{c|cc} 0 & 0 & 0 \\ 1 & 1 & 0 \\ \hline & \frac{1}{2} & \frac{1}{2} \end{array} \tag{23.21c}$$

$$\text{explicit midpoint}: \qquad \begin{array}{c|cc} 0 & 0 & 0 \\ \frac{1}{2} & \frac{1}{2} & 0 \\ \hline & 0 & 1 \end{array} \tag{23.21d}$$

$$\text{4th-order Runge-Kutta integration}: \qquad \begin{array}{c|cccc} 0 & 0 & 0 & 0 & 0 \\ \frac{1}{2} & \frac{1}{2} & 0 & 0 & 0 \\ \frac{1}{2} & 0 & \frac{1}{2} & 0 & 0 \\ 1 & 0 & 0 & 1 & 0 \\ \hline & \frac{1}{6} & \frac{1}{3} & \frac{1}{3} & \frac{1}{6}. \end{array} \tag{23.21e}$$

23.1.3 Adaptive Step Size Control

For many systems, a major reduction in computation time can be obtained by allowing for *adaptive step size*. A simple method for adaptive control of accuracy is *step doubling* (and the analogous step halving), where a big step is compared with the equivalent using two smaller steps. For an explicit Euler, two small steps of size h are found to be

$$\boldsymbol{r}(t+h) = \boldsymbol{r}(t) + h\dot{\boldsymbol{r}}(t) + \mathcal{O}(h^2), \tag{23.22a}$$

$$\boldsymbol{r}(t+2h) = \boldsymbol{r}(t+h) + h\dot{\boldsymbol{r}}(t+h) + \mathcal{O}(h^2) \tag{23.22b}$$

$$= \boldsymbol{r}(t) + h\dot{\boldsymbol{r}}(t) + h\dot{\boldsymbol{r}}(t+h) + \mathcal{O}(h^2). \tag{23.22c}$$

Conversely, a single step of size $2h$ is found to be

$$\boldsymbol{r}_2(t+2h) = \boldsymbol{r}(t) + 2h\dot{\boldsymbol{r}}(t) + \mathcal{O}(h^2), \tag{23.23}$$

and it is seen that the difference between $\boldsymbol{r}(t+2h)$ and $\boldsymbol{r}_2(t+2h)$ depends only on h, and the difference between $\dot{\boldsymbol{r}}(t)$ and $h\dot{\boldsymbol{r}}(t+h)$, that is,

$$\Delta\boldsymbol{r} = \boldsymbol{r}(t+2h) - \boldsymbol{r}_2(t+2h) \tag{23.24a}$$

$$= h\left(\dot{\boldsymbol{r}}(t+h) - \dot{\boldsymbol{r}}(t)\right) + \mathcal{O}(h^2). \tag{23.24b}$$

Thus, when $\Delta\boldsymbol{r}$ is large, doubling will imply a large error of approximation, while h may be safely doubled for small $\Delta\boldsymbol{r}$.

To conclude, step doubling requires three steps, two of size h and one of size $2h$. The extra computation time is often outweighed by the possible doubling of h. Step halving is analogous to the step doubling discussed above.

23.1.4 Implicit Integration

Explicit integration is accurate for small step sizes, h. By step doubling the step size may be adapted to reduce the number of steps dynamically. Nevertheless, there exists a class of differential equations, which requires extremely small steps to converge, and these are called *stiff ordinary differential equations*. As an example, consider a particle unsymmetrically attracted toward $(0,0)$.

$$\dot{\boldsymbol{r}}(t) = \frac{\partial}{\partial t}\begin{bmatrix} x(t) \\ y(t) \end{bmatrix} = \begin{bmatrix} -x(t) \\ -cy(t) \end{bmatrix}, \quad y(t) \neq 0. \tag{23.25}$$

Large c results in unstable or stiff solutions by Euler's method, which is seen by the first step,

$$\boldsymbol{r}(t+h) = \boldsymbol{r}(t) + h\dot{\boldsymbol{r}}(t) = \begin{bmatrix} x(t) \\ y(t) \end{bmatrix} + h\begin{bmatrix} -x(t) \\ -cy(t) \end{bmatrix} = \begin{bmatrix} (1-h)x(t) \\ (1-hc)y(t) \end{bmatrix}. \tag{23.26}$$

In the limit for large h this solution does not converge.

$$\lim_{h\to\infty}\begin{bmatrix} (1-h)x(t) \\ (1-hc)y(t) \end{bmatrix} = \begin{bmatrix} -\infty \\ -\infty \end{bmatrix} \tag{23.27}$$

That is, when $|1-hc| > 1$, then the solution will *diverge* and thus become *unstable*. Conversely, the solution will converge to 0 when $|1-hc| < 1$, which implies that $0 < hc < 2$ or equivalently $h < 2/c$, as $h, c > 0$.

Implicit integration stabilizes Euler's method by solving the equation backward, that is, by solving

$$\boldsymbol{r}(t+h) = \boldsymbol{r}(t) + h\dot{\boldsymbol{r}}(t+h). \tag{23.28}$$

At first glance, this may appear impossible, since it would require a solution to exist in order for us to be able to evaluate $\dot{\boldsymbol{r}}(t+h)$. However, assuming that we are given a vector field $\boldsymbol{\phi}(\boldsymbol{r}(t))$ such that

$$\dot{\boldsymbol{r}}(t+h) = \boldsymbol{\phi}(\boldsymbol{r}(t+h)), \tag{23.29}$$

then it is possible to solve (23.28) when $\boldsymbol{\phi}$ is linear in $\boldsymbol{r}$, that is, when $\boldsymbol{\phi}$ may be written as

$$\boldsymbol{\phi}(\boldsymbol{r}+\delta\boldsymbol{r}) = \boldsymbol{\phi}(\boldsymbol{r}) + \nabla\boldsymbol{\phi}\,\delta\boldsymbol{r}, \tag{23.30}$$

for some fixed $\boldsymbol{r}$ and variable $\delta\boldsymbol{r}$, and where $\nabla\boldsymbol{\phi}$ is the Jacobian of $\boldsymbol{\phi}$ taken in $\boldsymbol{r}$. Cleverly choosing $\delta\boldsymbol{r} = \boldsymbol{r}(t+h) - \boldsymbol{r}(t)$ such that $\boldsymbol{\phi}(\boldsymbol{r}(t+h)) = \boldsymbol{\phi}(\boldsymbol{r}(t)+\delta\boldsymbol{r}) = \boldsymbol{\phi}(\boldsymbol{r}+\delta\boldsymbol{r})$ and inserting (23.30) into (23.28) we find

$$\boldsymbol{r}(t+h) = \boldsymbol{r}(t) + h\left(\boldsymbol{\phi}(\boldsymbol{r}) + \nabla\boldsymbol{\phi}\,\delta\boldsymbol{r}\right), \tag{23.31a}$$

$$\Downarrow$$

$$\boldsymbol{r}(t+h) - \boldsymbol{r}(t) = h\left(\boldsymbol{\phi}(\boldsymbol{r}) + \nabla\boldsymbol{\phi}\,\delta\boldsymbol{r}\right), \tag{23.31b}$$

$$\Downarrow$$

$$\delta\boldsymbol{r} = h\left(\boldsymbol{\phi}(\boldsymbol{r}) + \nabla\boldsymbol{\phi}\,\delta\boldsymbol{r}\right). \tag{23.31c}$$

We can now isolate $\delta\boldsymbol{r}$ as

$$\delta\boldsymbol{r} - h\nabla\boldsymbol{\phi}\,\delta\boldsymbol{r} = h\boldsymbol{\phi}(\boldsymbol{r}), \tag{23.32a}$$

$$\Downarrow$$

$$(\mathbf{1} - h\nabla\boldsymbol{\phi})\,\delta\boldsymbol{r} = h\boldsymbol{\phi}(\boldsymbol{r}), \tag{23.32b}$$

$$\Downarrow$$

$$\left(\frac{1}{h}\mathbf{1} - \nabla\boldsymbol{\phi}\right)\delta\boldsymbol{r} = \boldsymbol{\phi}(\boldsymbol{r}), \tag{23.32c}$$

where $\mathbf{1}$ is the identity matrix. The matrix $\frac{1}{h}\mathbf{1} - \nabla\boldsymbol{\phi}$ is often invertible, since its structure often will be dominated by $\mathbf{1}$, in which case the system may be solved for $\delta\boldsymbol{r}$ as

$$\delta\boldsymbol{r} = \left(\frac{1}{h}\mathbf{1} - \nabla\boldsymbol{\phi}\right)^{-1}\boldsymbol{\phi}(\boldsymbol{r}), \tag{23.33}$$

and in which case

$$\boldsymbol{r}(t+h) = \boldsymbol{r}(t) + \delta\boldsymbol{r}. \tag{23.34}$$

In the example of our particle attracted to $[0,0]^T$, we have $\boldsymbol{\phi}(\boldsymbol{r}) = \dot{\boldsymbol{r}} = [-x, -cy]^T$, hence,

$$\nabla\boldsymbol{\phi} = \begin{bmatrix} -1 & 0 \\ 0 & -c \end{bmatrix}, \tag{23.35}$$

and

$$\frac{1}{h}\mathbf{1} - \nabla\phi = \begin{bmatrix} \frac{1}{h}+1 & 0 \\ 0 & \frac{1}{h}+c \end{bmatrix}, \tag{23.36}$$

whose inverse may be seen to be

$$\left(\frac{1}{h}\mathbf{1} - \nabla\phi\right)^{-1} = \begin{bmatrix} \frac{h}{1+h} & 0 \\ 0 & \frac{h}{1+hc} \end{bmatrix}. \tag{23.37}$$

Thus, the solution for $\delta\boldsymbol{r}$ is therefore

$$\delta\boldsymbol{r} = \left(\frac{1}{h}\mathbf{1} - \nabla\phi\right)^{-1}\phi(\boldsymbol{r}) = \begin{bmatrix} \frac{1}{h}+1 & 0 \\ 0 & \frac{1}{h}+c \end{bmatrix}^{-1} \begin{bmatrix} -x(t) \\ -cy(t) \end{bmatrix} \tag{23.38a}$$

$$= \begin{bmatrix} -\frac{h}{1+h}x(t) \\ -\frac{h}{1+ch}cy(t) \end{bmatrix}. \tag{23.38b}$$

In contrast to (23.27), the implicit solution is unconditionally stable and will converge regardless of the size of h, since

$$\lim_{h\to\infty} \delta\boldsymbol{r} = \begin{bmatrix} -x(t) \\ -\frac{1}{c}cy(t) \end{bmatrix} = \begin{bmatrix} -x(t) \\ -y(t) \end{bmatrix} = -\boldsymbol{r}(t), \tag{23.39}$$

and thus

$$\boldsymbol{r}(t+h) = \boldsymbol{r}(t) + \delta\boldsymbol{r} = \mathbf{0}. \tag{23.40}$$

We conclude that the implicit solution will converge for arbitrarily large h for this example, in contrast to the explicit solution, which requires $h < 2/c$ for convergence.

23.1.5 Semi-Implicit Integration

If ϕ is nonlinear, then a closed-form solution cannot be found. Nevertheless, a linear approximation may be used

$$\phi(\boldsymbol{r}(t+h)) = \phi(\boldsymbol{r}(t)) + \nabla\phi\,\delta\boldsymbol{r} + \mathcal{O}(\|\delta\boldsymbol{r}\|_2^2) \simeq \phi(\boldsymbol{r}(t)) + \nabla\phi\,\delta\boldsymbol{r}, \tag{23.41}$$

ignoring the higher-order terms. The derivations are identical to those presented in the previous section, except they are now approximations. This is known as *semi-implicit integration*. Hence, it is not guaranteed that the solution is stable, but it usually is because the approximation is locally precise.

23.2 Partial Differential Equations

Many differential equations in animation contain partial derivatives and are therefore *partial differential equations* (*PDE* s). We will only treat linear partial differential equations; for nonlinear partial differential equations, see [Ames, 1969, Morton et al., 1994].

23.2.1 Linear First-Order Partial Differential Equation

An example of a linear first-order partial differential equation of a function $u(x, y)$ is

$$Au_x + Bu_y = 0, \tag{23.42}$$

where $u_x = \frac{\partial u(x,y)}{\partial x}$ and $u_y = \frac{\partial u(x,y)}{\partial y}$. This equation can be simplified into a 1D problem by a change of base. Consider the base given by some arbitrary parameters a, b, c, and d:

$$\alpha = ax + by \text{ and } \beta = cx + dy. \tag{23.43}$$

The terms in (23.42) may be rewritten in the new base as

$$u_x = \frac{\partial u}{\partial x} = \frac{\partial u}{\partial \alpha}\frac{\partial \alpha}{\partial x} + \frac{\partial u}{\partial \beta}\frac{\partial \beta}{\partial x} = u_\alpha a + u_\beta c \tag{23.44a}$$

$$u_y = \frac{\partial u}{\partial y} = \frac{\partial u}{\partial \alpha}\frac{\partial \alpha}{\partial y} + \frac{\partial u}{\partial \beta}\frac{\partial \beta}{\partial y} = u_\alpha b + u_\beta d. \tag{23.44b}$$

Inserting (23.44) into (23.42) we find

$$0 = A(u_\alpha a + u_\beta c) + B(u_\alpha b + u_\beta d) = u_\alpha(Aa + Bb) + u_\beta(Ac + Bd). \tag{23.45}$$

Remember that the coordinate shift was arbitrary and does not influence the solution. Hence, we may choose the coordinate system, for which the solution is most easy to find. Consider a system where $Ac + Bd = 0$, for example $c = B$ and $d = -A$. Assuming that $Aa + Bb \neq 0$, we may divide both sides of the equation by $Aa + Bb$ resulting in

$$u_\alpha = 0. \tag{23.46}$$

Hence, the solution does not change in the α direction and is therefore independent on α. On the other hand, there are no bindings in the equation on the solution in the β direction; it can therefore be any differential function in β. Hence, the general solution is

$$u(x, y) = f(\beta) = f(cx + dy) = f(Bx - Ay) \tag{23.47}$$

where f is an arbitrary differentiable function. A single first-order partial differential equation behaves similarly to a hyperbolic second-order differential equation. Numerical solutions will be discussed in Section 23.2.5.

Systems of two first-order partial differential equations may be classified according to the flow of information. Consider two 2D functions $u(x, y)$ and $v(x, y)$ and the following system of equations:

$$a_1 u_x + b_1 u_y + c_1 v_x + d_1 v_y = f_1 \tag{23.48a}$$

$$a_2 u_x + b_2 u_y + c_2 v_x + d_2 v_y = f_2. \tag{23.48b}$$

We will now investigate conditions for unique solutions to the partial derivatives. Assume that the functions u and v have been solved for up to some curve Γ, as illustrated in Figure 23.4. We now wish to

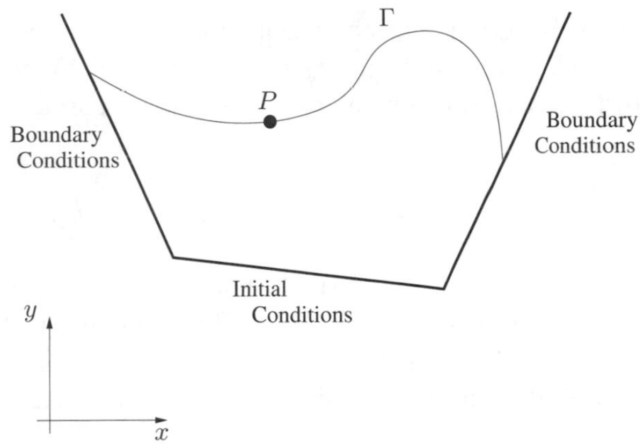

Figure 23.4: An assumed state in the process of solving a differential equation. The solution is assumed found up to the curve Γ.

investigate under what conditions the partial derivatives are uniquely determined at point P on Γ using values of u and v on Γ.

The tangent vector to Γ at P defines a local linear fit to the curve, and assuming that it is nonvertical we may write it as

$$\mu(x) = \alpha x + \beta, \tag{23.49}$$

and on the curve we may write our 2D functions as $u(x, \mu(x))$ and $v(x, \mu(x))$. Hence, the partial derivatives of u and v along the curve are

$$\frac{du}{dx} = u_x + u_y \frac{d\mu}{dx}, \tag{23.50a}$$

$$\frac{dv}{dx} = v_x + v_y \frac{d\mu}{dx}. \tag{23.50b}$$

Since u and v are known on the curve, their derivatives in the tangent direction are also known. Combining (23.48) and (23.50a) results in a system of equations:

$$\begin{bmatrix} a_1 & b_1 & c_1 & d_1 \\ a_2 & b_2 & c_2 & d_2 \\ 1 & \frac{d\mu}{dx} & 0 & 0 \\ 0 & 0 & 1 & \frac{d\mu}{dx} \end{bmatrix} \begin{bmatrix} u_x \\ u_y \\ v_x \\ v_y \end{bmatrix} = \begin{bmatrix} f_1 \\ f_2 \\ \frac{du}{dx} \\ \frac{dv}{dx} \end{bmatrix} \tag{23.51}$$

where all coefficients are known except the partial derivatives of u and v. The system has a unique solution to u_x, u_y, v_x, and v_y, when the determinant of the system matrix is nonzero. When the determinant is zero, that is,

$$(b_2 d_1 - b_1 d_2) + (-b_2 c_1 + b_1 c_2 - a_2 d_1 + a_1 d_2) \frac{d\mu}{dx} + (a_2 c_1 - a_1 c_2) \left(\frac{d\mu}{dx} \right)^2 = 0, \tag{23.52}$$

the system does not have a unique solution. The above equation is called the *characteristic equation.*

Slopes $\frac{d\mu}{dx}$ of the curve Γ at P, which are solutions to the characteristic equation, are called the *characteristic directions*. The differential equation may be classified according to the discriminant of the characteristic equation,

$$(-b_2c_1 + b_1c_2 - a_2d_1 + a_1d_2)^2 - 4(a_2c_1 - a_1c_2)(b_2d_1 - b_1d_2), \tag{23.53}$$

and the characteristic directions may be real and distinct, real and identical, or imaginary, when the discriminant is positive, zero, or negative, respectively. This induces a classification of the system of linear first-order differential equations (23.48), which are called *parabolic* for zero discriminant, *elliptic* for negative discriminant, and *hyperbolic* for positive discriminant. These classes are in a physical setting typically characterized as

Parabolic
A time-dependent, dissipative process that evolves toward a steady state.

Elliptic
A time-independent process, and thus is in its steady state.

Hyperbolic
A time-dependent process that does not evolve toward a steady state.

The characteristic directions are important for the numerical schemes used to produce stable implementations of the partial differential equations to be discussed next.

23.2.2 Linear Second-Order Differential Equations

For a 2D function $u : \mathbb{R}^2 \to \mathbb{R}$, the simplest second-order differential equations are

$$u_{xy} = 0, \tag{23.54}$$

since it is readily verified that

$$u(x, y) = f(x) + g(y), \tag{23.55}$$

is a solution whenever f and g are some arbitrary 1D differential functions. The functions u, which fulfill (23.54), are conceptually produced by translation. Consider a fixed function $g(y) = u(0, y)$. The remainder of u is produced by translating g along x using $f(x)$ as its offset.

The wave equation,

$$\kappa^2 u_{xx} - u_{yy} = 0 \tag{23.56}$$

for some constant $\kappa \neq 0$, is similar to (23.54) in that the solution may be written as two independent differential functions along two directions. Consider the same change in base as (23.43):

$$\alpha = ax + by \text{ and } \beta = cx + dy. \tag{23.57}$$

Continuing from (23.44) it is found that

$$u_{xx} = \frac{\partial u_x}{\partial x} = \frac{\partial u_x}{\partial \alpha}\frac{\partial \alpha}{\partial x} + \frac{\partial u_x}{\partial \beta}\frac{\partial \beta}{\partial x} = (u_{\alpha\alpha}a + u_{\alpha\beta}c)a + (u_{\alpha\beta}a + u_{\beta\beta}c)c, \tag{23.58a}$$

$$u_{yy} = \frac{\partial u_y}{\partial y} = \frac{\partial u_y}{\partial \alpha}\frac{\partial \alpha}{\partial y} + \frac{\partial u_y}{\partial \beta}\frac{\partial \beta}{\partial y} = (u_{\alpha\alpha}b + u_{\alpha\beta}d)b + (u_{\alpha\beta}b + u_{\beta\beta}d)d. \tag{23.58b}$$

Inserting the above equations into (23.56) and rearranging terms results in:

$$\begin{aligned} 0 &= \kappa^2(u_{\alpha\alpha}a^2 + 2u_{\alpha\beta}ac + u_{\beta\beta}c^2) - (u_{\alpha\alpha}b^2 + 2u_{\alpha\beta}bd + u_{\beta\beta}d^2), \\ &= u_{\alpha\alpha}(\kappa^2a^2 - b^2) + 2u_{\alpha\beta}(\kappa^2ac - bd) + u_{\beta\beta}(\kappa^2c^2 - d^2). \end{aligned} \tag{23.59}$$

We now choose a coordinate systems such that

$$\kappa^2a^2 - b^2 = 0, \tag{23.60a}$$

$$\kappa^2c^2 - d^2 = 0, \tag{23.60b}$$

$$\kappa^2ac - bd \neq 0. \tag{23.60c}$$

For example, $b = \kappa a$ and $d = -\kappa c$, which implies that

$$u_{\alpha\beta} = 0, \tag{23.61}$$

and that the solution is:

$$u = f(\alpha) + g(\beta) = f(ax + by) + g(cx + dy) = f(ax + \kappa ay) + g(cx - \kappa cy). \tag{23.62}$$

The constants a and c may, without loss of generality, be chosen to be $a = c = 1$. The solution is the sum of two translated functions. The first term, $f(x + \kappa y)$, is produced as a linear translation with slope κ of a mother function at $y = 0$. Likewise, $g(x - \kappa y)$ is a translation with slope $-\kappa$ of another mother function at $y = 0$. Hence, assuming that κ is positive, then as y is increased, the f function is translated toward smaller x values and g is translated toward larger x values, both with velocity κ.

Any *quasi-linear second-order partial differential equations* may be written on the form

$$Au_{xx} + Bu_{xy} + Cu_{yy} + F(u_x, u_y, f) = 0, \tag{23.63}$$

where $F(u_x, u_y, b)$ is any function of the first-order partial derivatives and a function f not depending on u. The equation is quasi-linear since F may be nonlinear. Analogous to the first-order system, we may classify (23.63) according to its *characteristic equation*. To derive the characteristic equation, consider an equation solved on half of its domain up to the curve Γ, as illustrated in Figure 23.4. The curve Γ may be approximated locally at P along the tangent as the line

$$\mu(x) = \alpha x + \beta. \tag{23.64}$$

Classification	Condition	Characteristic Directions
Parabolic	$B^2 - 4AC = 0$	1
Elliptic	$B^2 - 4AC < 0$	0
Hyperbolic	$B^2 - 4AC > 0$	2

Table 23.1: The classification of a general linear second-order partial differential equation (23.63) according to its characteristic equation.

The derivatives u_{xx}, u_{xy}, and u_{yy} are known along Γ, and we wish to find slopes of Γ for which the derivatives cannot be determined across Γ. On Γ we can write $u_x(x, \mu(x))$ and $u_y(x, \mu(x))$, and since we know u on Γ, then we can calculate the derivatives as

$$\frac{du_x}{dx} = u_{xx} + u_{xy}\frac{d\mu}{dx} \tag{23.65a}$$

$$\frac{du_y}{dx} = u_{xy} + u_{yy}\frac{d\mu}{dx}. \tag{23.65b}$$

Writing the system of equations as

$$\begin{bmatrix} A & B & C \\ 1 & \frac{d\mu}{dx} & 0 \\ 0 & 1 & \frac{d\mu}{dx} \end{bmatrix} \begin{bmatrix} u_{xx} \\ u_{xy} \\ u_{yy} \end{bmatrix} = \begin{bmatrix} 0 \\ \frac{du_x}{dx} \\ \frac{du_y}{dx} \end{bmatrix}. \tag{23.66}$$

The derivatives u_{xx}, u_{xy}, and u_{yy} are undetermined if the system matrix is singular, that is,

$$A\left(\frac{d\mu}{dx}\right)^2 - B\frac{d\mu}{dx} + C = 0, \tag{23.67}$$

which is a second-order equation in $\frac{d\mu}{dx}$. That is, the number of characteristic directions $\frac{d\mu}{dx}$ are determined by the discriminant

$$B^2 - 4AC, \tag{23.68}$$

and the second-order linear partial differential equations (23.63) are classified according to Table 23.1.

The second-order partial differential equation (23.63) may alternatively be transformed into a system of first-order linear equations, for example, by using $v = u_x$ and $w = u_y$, resulting in the system of equations:

$$0 = Av_x + Bv_y + 0w_x + Cw_y,$$

$$0 = 0v_x + 1v_y - 1w_x + 0w_y. \tag{23.69}$$

The two equations are needed since we introduce an extra variable and hence need to fix the added degree of freedom. The first of the equations above can be seen to be (23.63) in disguise, while the second couples v and w by requiring that $v_y = w_x \Leftrightarrow u_{xy} = u_{yx}$. This system of equations can easily be shown to have the same characteristic equation, and this system of first-order equations will therefore have the same characteristic directions as the original second-order equation.

23.2.3 Parabolic Equations

In the following, we will discuss convergence and stability for the parabolic equations. For a parabolic second-order differential equation,

$$Au_{xx} + Bu_{xy} + Cu_{yy} = 0, \tag{23.70}$$

with $B^2 - 4AC = 0$, there is one characteristic direction given by $\frac{d\mu}{dx} = 0$, which implies that μ is constant. The prototypical example of a parabolic differential equation is the *heat diffusion equation*,

$$\frac{\partial u}{\partial t} = \frac{\partial^2 u}{\partial x^2}, \tag{23.71}$$

where t is time and x is the spatial dimension for a 1D signal $u(x, t)$. For the heat diffusion equation $A = 1$ and $B = C = 0$, and the discriminant (23.68) is therefore zero.

Although several methods exist for solving the heat diffusion equation, we solve it with finite differences on a grid $u(i\Delta x, j\Delta t) \simeq U_{i,j}$, where U is an approximation of u. We further impose boundary conditions $U_{x,0} = u(x, 0) = b_1(x)$, $U_{0,t} = u(0, t) = b_2(t)$, and $U_{1,t} = u(1, t) = b_3(t)$.

23.2.3.1 Stability and Convergence for Explicit Solutions.

An *explicit solution* of the heat diffusion equation is found using a forward finite difference operator for the time derivative and a central difference operator for the spatial derivative:

$$\frac{U_{i,j+1} - U_{i,j}}{\Delta t} = \frac{U_{i+1,j} - 2U_{i,j} + U_{i-1,j}}{\Delta x^2} \tag{23.72}$$

Rewriting suggests the following update rule:

$$U_{i,j+1} = mU_{i+1,j} + (1 - 2m)U_{i,j} + mU_{i-1,j}, \tag{23.73}$$

where $m = \frac{\Delta t}{\Delta x^2}$. This is an explicit solution in j, since the solution at time $j + 1$ is explicitly given as a function of prior values of the solution at times j and earlier. The elements on the grid taking part in the computation is often illustrated as a *computational molecule*, as shown in Figure 23.5.

The *truncation error*, T, of the approximation is found by replacing the approximation $U_{i,j}$ with the true solution, $u(x, t) = u(i\Delta x, j\Delta t)$, that is,

$$\frac{u(x, t + \Delta t) - u(x, t)}{\Delta t} = \frac{u(x + \Delta x, t) - 2u(x, t) + u(x - \Delta x, t)}{\Delta x^2} + T(x, t) \tag{23.74}$$

and then inserting the Taylor series for u,

$$\sum_{n=1}^{\infty} \frac{(\Delta t)^{n-1}}{n!} \frac{\partial^n}{\partial t^n} u(x, t) = \sum_{n=1}^{\infty} \frac{(\Delta x)^{n-2}}{n!} \frac{\partial^n}{\partial x^n} u(x, t) + \sum_{n=1}^{\infty} \frac{(-\Delta x)^{n-2}}{n!} \frac{\partial^n}{\partial x^n} u(x, t) + T(x, t). \tag{23.75}$$

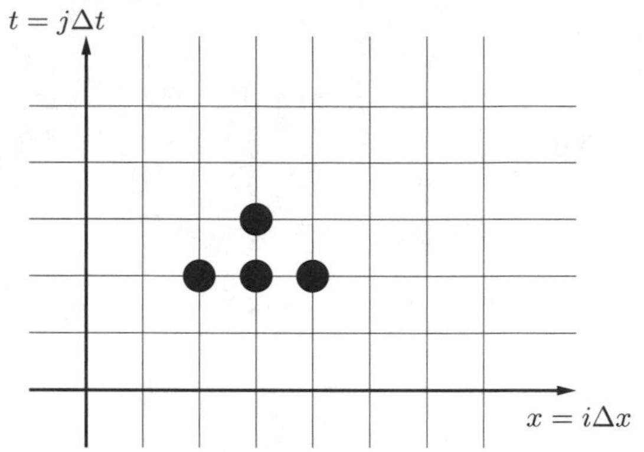

Figure 23.5: The computational molecule for an explicit finite differencing scheme for the heat diffusion equation.

Isolating T gives

$$T(x,t) = \sum_{n=1}^{\infty} \frac{(\Delta t)^{n-1}}{n!} \frac{\partial^n}{\partial t^n} u(x,t) - \sum_{n=1}^{\infty} \frac{(\Delta x)^{n-2} + (-\Delta x)^{n-2}}{n!} \frac{\partial^n}{\partial x^n} u(x,t), \tag{23.76}$$

whose leading terms are

$$T(x,t) = \frac{\partial u(x,t)}{\partial t} + \frac{\Delta t}{2} \frac{\partial^2 u(x,t)}{\partial t^2} - \frac{\partial^2 u(x,t)}{\partial x^2} - \frac{(\Delta x)^2}{12} \frac{\partial^4 u(x,t)}{\partial x^4} + \mathcal{O}(\Delta t^2 + \Delta x^4) \tag{23.77a}$$

$$= \frac{\Delta t}{2} \frac{\partial^2 u(x,t)}{\partial t^2} - \frac{\Delta x^2}{12} \frac{\partial^4 u(x,t)}{\partial x^4} + \mathcal{O}(\Delta t^2 + \Delta x^4). \tag{23.77b}$$

The simplification above was obtained by applying the heat diffusion equation, $u_t = u_{xx}$. From this we observe that the solution has first-order accuracy in Δt, but if $\Delta x^2 = 6\Delta t$, then the method has second-order accuracy in Δt. Furthermore, using the mean value theorem, Theorem 20.1, we realize that there are two constants x_0 and t_0 in the open intervals $x_0 \in (x - \Delta x, x + \Delta x)$ and $t_0 \in (t, t + \Delta t)$, where

$$T(x,t) = \frac{\Delta t}{2} \frac{\partial^2 u(x,t_0)}{\partial t^2} - \frac{\Delta x^2}{12} \frac{\partial^4 u(x_0,t)}{\partial x^4} \tag{23.78a}$$

$$= \frac{\Delta t}{2} \left(\frac{\partial^2 u(x,t_0)}{\partial t^2} - \frac{1}{6m} \frac{\partial^4 u(x_0,t)}{\partial x^4} \right), \tag{23.78b}$$

where $m = \frac{\Delta t}{\Delta x^2}$. Hence, if we assume that u_{tt} and u_{xxxx} are bounded, then the truncation error is $T \to 0$ as $\Delta t, \Delta x \to 0$, and we say that the method is *unconditionally consistent*.

The convergence of a finite difference method is typically studied in two manners—either using Taylor series or Fourier series. These will be described below. For *Taylor convergence*, we write the error as

$$E_{i,j} = U_{i,j} - u(i\Delta x, j\Delta j). \tag{23.79}$$

The approximation U satisfies (23.73) exactly, while u differs by the truncation error, that is,

$$U_{i,j+1} - u(x, t + \Delta j) = m(U_{i+1,j} - u(x + \Delta x, t)) + (1 - 2m)(U_{i,j} - u(x,t)) + m(U_{i-1,j} - u(x - \Delta x, t)) + \Delta t T(x,t) \tag{23.80a}$$

$$\Downarrow$$

$$E_{i,j+1} = mE_{i+1,j} + (1 - 2m)E_{i,j} + mE_{i-1,j} + \Delta t T(x,t). \tag{23.80b}$$

The coefficients in front of E are positive as long as

$$m \geq 0 \text{ and } 1 - 2m \geq 0, \tag{23.81a}$$

$$\Downarrow$$

$$0 \leq m \leq \frac{1}{2}, \tag{23.81b}$$

and in which case

$$|E_{i,j+1}| \leq m|E_{i+1,j}| + (1 - 2m)|E_{i,j}| + m|E_{i-1,j}| + \Delta t|T(x,t)|. \tag{23.82}$$

Since the sum of the coefficients on the right-hand side is always 1, That is, $m + (1 - 2m) + m = 1$, then the sum of the error terms on the right-hand side will never exceed the maximum value, that is,

$$|E_{i,j+1}| \leq \max(|E_{i+1,j}|, |E_{i,j}|, |E_{i-1,j}|) + \Delta t|T(x,t)|. \tag{23.83}$$

Finally, since the approximation agrees with the analytical solution on the boundary, $U_{i,0} = u(i\Delta x, 0)$, then the error must be zero on the boundary,

$$E_{i,0} = 0, \tag{23.84}$$

and by induction we find that

$$|E_{i,j+1}| \leq j\Delta t|T(x,t)|. \tag{23.85}$$

We conclude that the error $E \to 0$ as $\Delta t \to 0$, when $0 \leq m \leq \frac{1}{2}$, and hence the numerical solution approximation converges to the analytical solution.

In *Fourier convergence*, the error is expressed as a Fourier series and the stability is studied as limits on the Fourier coefficients. Let's start by using the *method of splitting*, where it is assumed that u is separable, that is,

$$u(x,t) = f(x)g(t). \tag{23.86}$$

The heat diffusion equation (23.71) then becomes

$$f(x)g'(t) = f''(x)g(t) \tag{23.87a}$$

$$\Downarrow$$

$$\frac{g'(t)}{g(t)} = \frac{f''(x)}{f(x)}. \tag{23.87b}$$

Since both sides of the equation are independent, they must equal a constant,

$$\frac{g'(t)}{g(t)} = \frac{f''(x)}{f(x)} = c, \tag{23.88}$$

and we find that

$$g(t) = \exp(ct), \tag{23.89a}$$
$$f(x) = \sin(x\sqrt{-c}), \tag{23.89b}$$

where we further have to require that $c \leq 0$ for g to be bounded and for f to be real. Thus writing $c = -k^2$, we find

$$u(x,t) = \exp(-k^2 t)\sin(kx), \tag{23.90}$$

and since the solution is independent on k, then any linear combination in k will also be a solution, that is,

$$u(x,t) = \sum_{k=-\infty}^{\infty} a_k \exp(-k^2 t)\sin(kx). \tag{23.91}$$

At the boundary, we have

$$u(x,0) = \sum_{k=-\infty}^{\infty} a_k \sin(kx), \tag{23.92}$$

and we realize that this is a Fourier series with a_k as the Fourier coefficients.

In the finite difference scheme (23.73) we'll assume that the complex exponential is a solution, that is,

$$U_{i,j} = \lambda^j \exp(-ki\Delta x\sqrt{-1}) \tag{23.93a}$$
$$= \lambda U_{i,j-1}, \tag{23.93b}$$

for some constant λ, and where we write $\sqrt{-1}$ explicitly to avoid confusion with the index i, and where $\lambda\exp(\theta\sqrt{-1})$ is the complex exponential,

$$\lambda\exp(\theta\sqrt{-1}) = \lambda\cos(\theta) + \lambda\sqrt{-1}\sin(\theta). \tag{23.94}$$

Using the recursive form of our guess (23.93) in (23.73) and dividing with a factor, U_{ij} we find

$$\frac{\lambda U_{i,j}}{U_{i,j}} = m\frac{U_{i+1,j}}{U_{i,j}} + (1-2m)\frac{U_{i,j}}{U_{i,j}} + m\frac{U_{i-1,j}}{U_{i,j}} \tag{23.95a}$$

$$\Downarrow$$

$$\lambda = m\frac{U_{i+1,j}}{U_{i,j}} + 1 - 2m + m\frac{U_{i-1,j}}{U_{i,j}}, \tag{23.95b}$$

and when we insert (23.94), we find that

$$\lambda = m \exp\left(-k(i+1)\Delta x\sqrt{-1} + ki\Delta x\sqrt{-1}\right) + 1 - 2m$$
$$+ m \exp\left(-k(i-1)\Delta x\sqrt{-1} + ki\Delta x\sqrt{-1}\right) \tag{23.96a}$$
$$= 1 - 2m + m\exp\left(-k\Delta x\sqrt{-1}\right) + m\exp\left(k\Delta x\sqrt{-1}\right) \tag{23.96b}$$
$$= 1 - 2m + 2m\cos(k\Delta x) \tag{23.96c}$$
$$= 1 - 2m\left(1 - \cos(k\Delta x)\right). \tag{23.96d}$$

Thus, we conclude that (23.93) is a solution, when $\lambda = 1 - 2m(1 - \cos(k\Delta x))$ for some k. Since the solution does not depend on k, we further conclude that any linear combination of (23.93) is also a solution, that is,

$$U_{i,j} = \sum_{k=-\infty}^{\infty} a_k \lambda_k^j \exp(-ki\Delta x\sqrt{-1}). \tag{23.97}$$

Again, we find a Fourier series and find that the coefficients a_k are determined by the boundary function $U_{i,0}$. In the continuous solution (23.91), the high frequencies were exponentially damped. In the numerical scheme (23.97), the solution is damped by λ_k^j, and thus requires that $|\lambda_k| \leq 1$ for all k will ensure that the solution does not diverge as $j \to \infty$. The function $|\lambda_k|$ takes its maximum value when $k = \frac{n\pi}{\Delta x}$ for any integer n, in which case

$$1 \geq \lambda_k \geq 1 - 4m. \tag{23.98}$$

Since $|\lambda_k| \leq 1$, we must require that

$$|1 - 4m| \leq 1, \tag{23.99}$$

and for $m \geq 0$ this implies that $m \leq \frac{1}{2}$. Hence, again we find that when $0 \leq m \leq \frac{1}{2}$, then the high frequencies in the solutions will not be amplified and the solution will converge.

Stability conditions for explicit equations typically implies very small iteration steps in the solution. A qualitative argument for this is that the characteristic direction of the heat diffusion equation is $t =$ constant, implying that the flow of information from the boundary conditions is along $t =$ constant. This contradicts the numerical implementation in (23.73), in which the value at $(i, j+1)$ is determined by values at $(i-1, j)$, (i, j), and $(i+1, j)$, implying characteristic directions $\frac{dy}{dx} = \pm\frac{\Delta t}{\Delta x}$, and the characteristic directions only approaches the continuous directions when $\Delta t \to 0$ for some fixed Δx.

23.2.3.2 Stability and Convergence for Implicit Solutions.

The heat diffusion equation may be approximated by an implicit method,

$$\frac{U_{i,j+1} - U_{i,j}}{\Delta t} + \mathcal{O}(\Delta t) = \frac{U_{i+1,j+1} - 2U_{i,j+1} + U_{i-1,j+1}}{\Delta x^2} + \mathcal{O}(\Delta x^2), \tag{23.100}$$

and comparing with the explicit solution (23.72), the spatial derivative u_{xx} has been approximated as a central second-order finite difference approximation at time $j+1$ rather than at time j. The computational molecule for this implicit approximation is shown in Figure 23.6. This suggests an update rule as

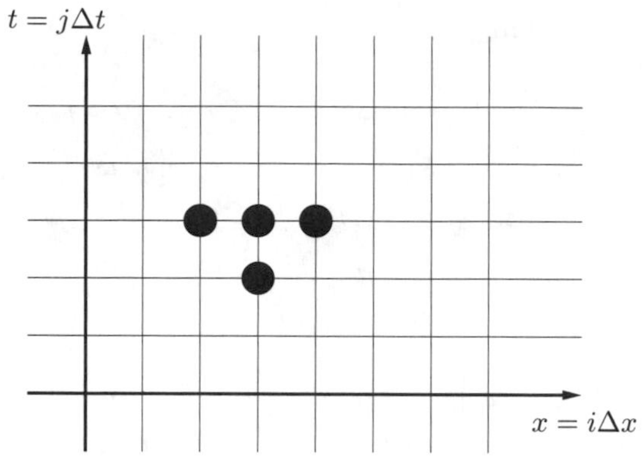

Figure 23.6: The computational molecule for an implicit finite differencing scheme for the heat diffusion equation.

$$-mU_{i+1,j+1} + (1+2m)U_{i,j+1} - mU_{i-1,j+1} = U_{i,j}, \tag{23.101}$$

where $m = \frac{\Delta t}{\Delta x^2}$. This is a linear system of equations in $U_{i,j}$, and the solution for $j+1$ is undetermined without the boundary conditions at $j+1$ in agreement with the continuous solution. As an example, set $u(x,0) = 1$, when $0 < x < 1$, $u(0,t) = 0$, $u(1,t) = 0$, $\Delta x = \Delta t = \frac{1}{4}$, and $i, j = 0, 1, \ldots$. The system of equations is then

$$\begin{bmatrix} 1 & 0 & 0 & 0 & 0 & 0 \\ -m & 1+2m & -m & 0 & 0 & 0 \\ 0 & -m & 1+2m & -m & 0 & 0 \\ 0 & 0 & -m & 1+2m & -m & 0 \\ 0 & 0 & 0 & -m & 1+2m & -m \\ 0 & 0 & 0 & 0 & 0 & 1 \end{bmatrix} \begin{bmatrix} 1 \\ U_{1,j+1} \\ U_{2,j+1} \\ U_{3,j+1} \\ U_{4,j+1} \\ 1 \end{bmatrix} = \begin{bmatrix} 1 \\ U_{1,j} \\ U_{2,j} \\ U_{3,j} \\ U_{4,j} \\ 1 \end{bmatrix}, \tag{23.102}$$

using $m = \frac{\Delta t}{\Delta x^2}$ and starting with $U_{i,0} = 1$. The determinant of the system matrix is $1 + 8m + 21m^2 + 20m^3 + 5m^4$. In general, it can be proven by induction that the determinant is

$$\det A_n = (1+2m)\det A_{n-1} - m^2 \det A_{n-2}, \tag{23.103}$$

for $n > 4$ for systems on the form

$$A_3 = \begin{bmatrix} 1 & 0 & 0 \\ -m & 1+2m & -m \\ 0 & 0 & 1 \end{bmatrix}, \tag{23.104a}$$

$$A_4 = \begin{bmatrix} 1 & 0 & 0 & 0 \\ -m & 1+2m & -m & 0 \\ 0 & -m & 1+2m & -m \\ 0 & 0 & 0 & 1 \end{bmatrix}. \tag{23.104b}$$

$$\vdots$$

Since $m > 0$, it can be seen that $\det A_n > 1$, and that the system matrix always has an inverse. The most common solution is to decompose the system matrix into an LU decomposition (see Section 19.2).

The convergence of this system is most easily studied using Fourier convergence. Similarly, to the explicit method we guess that the complex exponential

$$U_{i,j} = \lambda^j \exp(-ki\Delta x\sqrt{-1}) \tag{23.105a}$$

$$= \lambda U_{i,j-1}, \tag{23.105b}$$

is a solution to the finite difference scheme. Inserting the recursive formulation and dividing by $U_{i,j}$, we find

$$-m\frac{\lambda U_{i+1,j}}{U_{i,j}} + (1+2m)\frac{\lambda U_{i,j}}{U_{i,j}} - m\frac{\lambda U_{i-1,j}}{U_{i,j}} = \frac{U_{i,j}}{U_{i,j}} \tag{23.106a}$$

$$\Downarrow$$

$$\lambda\left(1+2m-m\left(\frac{U_{i+1,j}}{U_{i,j}}+\frac{U_{i-1,j}}{U_{i,j}}\right)\right), = 1 \tag{23.106b}$$

and when we expand the complex exponential, we find that

$$\lambda\left(1+2m-m\left(\exp(-k\Delta x\sqrt{-1})+\exp(+k\Delta x\sqrt{-1})\right)\right) = 1 \tag{23.107a}$$

$$\Downarrow$$

$$\lambda = \frac{1}{1+2m\left(1-\cos(k\Delta x)\right).} \tag{23.107b}$$

Thus, we conclude that (23.105) is a solution, when $\lambda = \left(1+2m\left(1-\cos(k\Delta x)\right)\right)^{-1}$, and since this is independent of k, we further conclude that any linear combination of (23.93) is also a solution, that is,

$$U_{i,j} = \sum_{k=-\infty}^{\infty} a_k \lambda_k^j \exp(-ki\Delta x\sqrt{-1}). \tag{23.108}$$

Again, we find a Fourier series and find that the coefficients, a_k, are determined by the boundary function $U_{i,0}$. In contrast to the explicit approximation, the implicit approximation is unconditionally stable, since

$$\lambda \leq 1. \tag{23.109}$$

23.2.4 Elliptic Equations

In the following, we will discuss convergence and stability for the elliptic equations. For an elliptic differential equation,

$$Au_{xx} + Bu_{xy} + Cu_{yy} = 0, \tag{23.110}$$

with $B^2 - 4AC < 0$, there are no real characteristic directions.

The prototypical example of an elliptic differential equations is the *Laplace equation*:

$$\frac{\partial^2 u}{\partial x^2} + \frac{\partial^2 u}{\partial y^2} + f(x,y) = 0. \tag{23.111}$$

This equation is quite similar to the 2D version of the heat diffusion equation (23.71),

$$\frac{\partial u}{\partial t} = \frac{\partial^2 u}{\partial x^2} + \frac{\partial^2 u}{\partial y^2}, \tag{23.112}$$

and the elliptical equation may be solved as the steady state of this. We will assume that the solution has been obtained somehow, and go on to analyze the truncation and convergence of the following finite differencing scheme: assuming a grid $U_{i,j} \simeq u(i\Delta x, j\Delta y)$ and using central differencing, we find that

$$\frac{U_{i+1,j} - 2U_{i,j} + U_{i-1,j}}{\Delta x^2} + \frac{U_{i,j+1} - 2U_{i,j} + U_{i,j-1}}{\Delta y^2} + f_{i,j} = 0. \tag{23.113}$$

For short, we will write this on operator form

$$L[U] + f = 0. \tag{23.114}$$

The truncation error is found by inserting the true solution u in place of U,

$$\begin{aligned} &\frac{u(x+\Delta x,y) - 2u(x,y) + u(x-\Delta x,y)}{\Delta x^2} \\ &\quad + \frac{u(x,y+\Delta y) - 2u(x,y) + u(x,y-\Delta y)}{\Delta y^2} + f(x,y) = T(x,y), \end{aligned} \tag{23.115}$$

and represent u by its Taylor series,

$$\begin{aligned} &\sum_{n=1}^{\infty} \frac{(\Delta x)^{n-2} + (-\Delta x)^{n-2}}{n!} \frac{\partial^n}{\partial x^n} u(x,y) \\ &\quad + \sum_{n=1}^{\infty} \frac{(\Delta y)^{n-2} + (-\Delta y)^{n-2}}{n!} \frac{\partial^n}{\partial y^n} u(x,y) + f(x,y) = T(x,y). \end{aligned} \tag{23.116}$$

Identifying leading terms,

$$\begin{aligned} T(x,y) &= f(x,y) + \frac{\partial^2}{\partial x^2} u(x,y) + \frac{\partial^2}{\partial y^2} u(x,y) \\ &\quad + \frac{\Delta x^2}{12} \frac{\partial^4}{\partial x^4} u(x,y) + \frac{\Delta y^2}{12} \frac{\partial^4}{\partial y^4} u(x,y) + \mathcal{O}(\Delta x^4 + \Delta y^4) \qquad (23.117a) \\ &= \frac{\Delta x^2}{12} \frac{\partial^4}{\partial x^4} u(x,y) + \frac{\Delta y^2}{12} \frac{\partial^4}{\partial y^4} u(x,y) + \mathcal{O}(\Delta x^4 + \Delta y^4), \qquad (23.117b) \end{aligned}$$

where we have used (23.111) in the last simplification above. As discussed in Chapter 20, this will be limited by some constants M_{x^4} and M_{y^4} as

$$T(x,y) \leq \frac{\Delta x^2}{12} M_{x^4} + \frac{\Delta y^2}{12} M_{y^4} \tag{23.118a}$$
$$= M \tag{23.118b}$$

The convergence of (23.113) is found by studying the error of the approximation as a function of Δx and Δy. The error is defined as

$$e_{i,j} = U_{i,j} - u(i\Delta x, j\Delta y). \tag{23.119}$$

A bound on e may be obtained with the help of a *comparison function*,

$$\Psi_{i,j} = \left(x - i\Delta x - \frac{1}{2}\right)^2 + \left(y - j\Delta y - \frac{1}{2}\right)^2, \tag{23.120}$$

for which the second-order structure is simple. Now we produce a linear combination of (23.119), (23.120), and (23.118b), as

$$\psi_{i,j} = e_{i,j} + \frac{1}{4} T \Psi_{i,j}. \tag{23.121}$$

Applying the finite difference scheme (23.113) to both sides of this equation gives

$$L[\psi]_{i,j} = L[e]_{i,j} + \frac{1}{4} M L[\Psi]_{i,j} \tag{23.122}$$

The first term is evaluated as

$$L[e]_{i,j} = L[U]_{i,j} - L[u](i\Delta x, j\Delta y) \tag{23.123a}$$
$$= -T(i\Delta x, j\Delta y), \tag{23.123b}$$

since $L[U] = -f$ according to (23.113) and $L[u](x,y) = T(x,y) - f(x,y)$ according to (23.115). The second term is evaluated to

$$\frac{1}{4} M L[\Psi]_{i,j} = M, \tag{23.124}$$

since Ψ is a quadratic function that does not contain higher-order terms. Hence, we conclude that

$$L[\psi]_{i,j} = -T(i\Delta x, j\Delta y) + M \geq 0, \tag{23.125}$$

since M is the maximum bound on T. To get a bound on Ψ, we will use the *maximum principle*.

The maximum principle is derived as follows: assume that an operator L is given on the form

$$L[U]_{i,j} = \sum_{k \in \mathcal{N}} a_k U_k - a U_{i,j}, \tag{23.126}$$

where k is some set of neighboring positions $\mathcal{N}$, and where all the coefficients are positive, i.e., $a_k > 0$ and $a > 0$. Furthermore, assume that the coefficients are given such that

$$a \geq \sum_{k \in \mathcal{N}} a_k, \tag{23.127}$$

and that

$$L[U]_{i,j} \geq 0 \tag{23.128}$$

for all coordinates (i, j) in the interior of the domain, then $\Psi_{i,j}$ cannot be greater than the maximum value at the boundary of the domain. This will be proven by contradiction: assume that there was a maximum $U_M \geq 0$ in the interior of the domain, then $L[U] \geq 0 \Rightarrow U_{i,j} \leq \sum_k a_k U_k / a \leq \sum_k a_k U_m / a \leq U_m$. Hence, all values U_k must also be equal to U_M. Applying this argument to the neighboring values iteratively until we reach the maximum at the boundary, we must conclude that the maximum at the boundary is equal to the maximum in the interior, but this is a contradiction.

Hence, for (23.113), we have that the coefficients are positive in the sense of (23.126) and that (23.127) is fulfilled, since $a = \sum_k a_k = \frac{2}{\Delta x^2} + \frac{2}{\Delta y^2}$. Hence, we can conclude that $\Psi_{i,j}$ cannot be greater than its neighbors due to (23.125). Thus, the maximal value must be located on the boundary of the domain, but here $e_{i,j} = 0$, hence,

$$\max_{i,j} \psi_{i,j} = \max \frac{1}{4} M \Psi_{i,j} = \frac{M}{8}. \tag{23.129}$$

Furthermore, since Ψ is nonnegative, we conclude that

$$e_{i,j} = \psi_{i,j} - \frac{1}{4} M \Psi_{i,j} \leq \psi_{i,j} \leq \frac{M}{8} = \frac{\Delta x^2}{96} M_{x^4} + \frac{\Delta y^2}{96} M_{y^4}. \tag{23.130}$$

Similar analysis for $-e_{i,j}$ will show that

$$|e_{i,j}| = |U_{i,j} - u(i\Delta x, j\Delta y)| \leq \frac{\Delta x^2}{96} M_{x^4} + \frac{\Delta y^2}{96} M_{y^4}. \tag{23.131}$$

To conclude, the finite difference scheme (23.113) will converge to the continuous solution as $(\Delta x, \Delta y) \rightarrow 0$.

23.2.5 Hyperbolic Equations

In the following, we will discuss convergence and stability for the hyperbolic equations. First, we will discuss characteristic directions for hyperbolic second-order equations, and then we will study the numerics of the more common hyperbolic first-order equation.

For a hyperbolic second-order differential equation,

$$A u_{xx} + B u_{xy} + C u_{yy} = 0, \tag{23.132}$$

with $B^2 - 4AC > 0$, there are two characteristic directions given by $\frac{d\mu}{dx} = \frac{-B \pm \sqrt{B^2-4AC}}{2A}$. These directions are perpendicular when

$$\begin{bmatrix} 1 \\ \frac{-B+\sqrt{B^2-4AC}}{2A} \end{bmatrix} \cdot \begin{bmatrix} 1 \\ \frac{-B-\sqrt{B^2-4AC}}{2A} \end{bmatrix} = 0, \tag{23.133}$$

that is, when $A = -C$. As an example, consider the *Wave equation*,

$$u_{tt} - u_{xx} = 0,. \tag{23.134}$$

Seeing that $A = -C = 1$ and $B = 0$, we realize that the characteristic directions are perpendicular. The slope of the characteristic direction may be found to be ± 1 by evaluating $\frac{d\mu}{dx}$. The characteristic directions are special, since they simplify the partial differential equation. That is, when transforming the equation to a coordinate system aligned with the characteristic directions,

$$\alpha = x + t, \tag{23.135a}$$
$$\beta = x - t. \tag{23.135b}$$

we may write $u(x,t) = v(\alpha, \beta)$, and we may substitute v for u in (23.134). Evaluating the second-order derivatives of v w.r.t. x and t we find

$$v_{tt} = v_{\alpha\alpha} - 2v_{\alpha\beta} + v_{\beta\beta}, \tag{23.136a}$$
$$v_{xx} = v_{\alpha\alpha} + 2v_{\alpha\beta} + v_{\beta\beta}, \tag{23.136b}$$

and we therefore conclude that (23.134) is equivalent to

$$v_{\alpha\beta} = 0. \tag{23.137}$$

It is readily checked that solutions to this equation are specified by

$$v(\alpha, \beta) = f(\alpha) + g(\beta), \tag{23.138}$$

or equivalently

$$u(x,t) = f(x+t) + g(x-t), \tag{23.139}$$

for any twice differentiable functions f and g. In this example, we see that the hyperbolic equation has a limited *interval of dependence*, as shown in Figure 23.7. More rigorously, if we fix the boundary conditions $u(x,0) = F(x)$ and $u_t(x,0) = F_t(x)$, then we find

$$u(x,0) = f(x) + g(x) = F(x), \tag{23.140a}$$
$$u_t(x,0) = f'(x) - g'(x) = F_t(x). \tag{23.140b}$$

Differentiating (23.140a), we find two equations in f' and g' as

$$f'(x) + g'(x) = F'(x), \tag{23.141a}$$
$$f'(x) - g'(x) = F_t(x), \tag{23.141b}$$

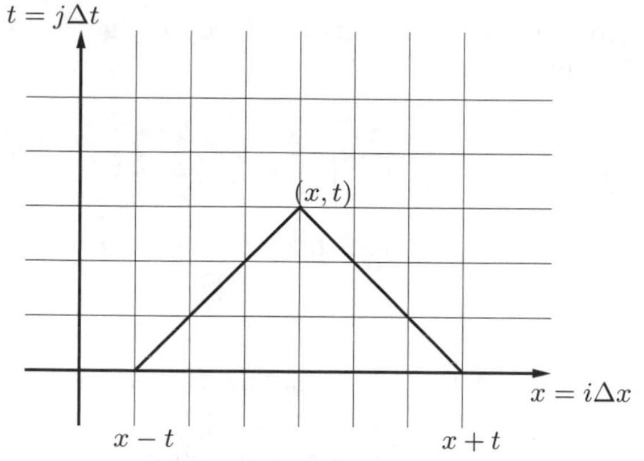

Figure 23.7: The interval of dependence for the wave equation at the point (x, t) in the solution is $[x - t, x + t]$.

and solving for f' and g', we have

$$f'(x) = \frac{1}{2}\left(F'(x) + F_t(x)\right), \tag{23.142a}$$

$$g'(x) = \frac{1}{2}\left(F'(x) - F_t(x)\right). \tag{23.142b}$$

Integrating both equations gives

$$f(x) = \int_0^x f'(x)\,dx = \frac{1}{2}\left(F(x) + \int_0^x F_t(\xi)\,d\xi\right), \tag{23.143a}$$

$$g(x) = \int_0^x g'(x)\,dx = \frac{1}{2}\left(F(x) - \int_0^x F_t(\xi)\,d\xi\right), \tag{23.143b}$$

and thus,

$$u(x,t) = f(x+t) + g(x-t) \tag{23.144a}$$

$$= \frac{1}{2}\left(F(x+t) + \int_0^{x+t} F_t(\xi)\,d\xi\right) + \frac{1}{2}\left(F(x-t) - \int_0^{x-t} F_t(\xi)\,d\xi\right) \tag{23.144b}$$

$$= \frac{1}{2}\left(F(x+t) + F(x-t) + \int_0^{x+t} F_t(\xi)\,d\xi + \int_{x-t}^{0} F_t(\xi)\,d\xi\right) \tag{23.144c}$$

$$= \frac{1}{2}\left(F(x+t) + F(x-t) + \int_{x-t}^{x+t} F_t(\xi)\,d\xi\right). \tag{23.144d}$$

Thus, the values of u at x, t only depend on the values of F at $x + t$, and $x - t$ and on F_t in the interval $[x - t, x + t]$.

The prototypical example of a hyperbolic differential equation is the *linear advection equation*,

$$\frac{\partial u}{\partial t} = -a\frac{\partial u}{\partial x}. \tag{23.145}$$

The solution to the linear advection equation is given by (23.47), as

$$u(x,t) = f(x+at), \tag{23.146}$$

for any differential function f. Comparing with the second-order equation (23.144d), we find that they are similar in the sense that the flow of information is along lines, but in contrast to the second-order equation, the solution to the advection equation depends only on a single point on the boundary $u(x,0) = f(x)$.

Hyperbolic differential equations in several dimensions are rather complex to solve numerically, and we will limit ourselves to the discussion of the simplest case of the linear advection equation (23.145), which is important for the much used Navier-Stokes equation discussed in Section 11.2. In the following, we will approximate the advection equation on a grid $u(i\Delta x, j\Delta t) \simeq U_{i,j}$, where U is an approximation of u. We further impose boundary conditions $U_{x,0} = u(x,0) = b_1(x)$.

23.2.5.1 Stability and Convergence of the Upwind Schemes

The linear advection equation (23.145) is straightforwardly approximated by a forward finite difference in time and either a forward or backward finite difference in space, depending on the characteristic direction. We will assume that $U_{i,j} > 0$, hence,

$$\frac{U_{i,j+1} - U_{i,j}}{\Delta t} = -a\frac{U_{i,j} - U_{i-1,j}}{\Delta x}. \tag{23.147}$$

The truncation error is found in the standard way by replacing U with u represented by its Taylor series,

$$T(x,t) = \frac{u(i\Delta x,(j+1)\Delta t) - u(i\Delta x, j\Delta t)}{\Delta t} + a\frac{u(i\Delta x, j\Delta t) - u((i-1)\Delta x, j\Delta t)}{\Delta x} \tag{23.148a}$$

$$= \sum_{n=1}^{\infty} \frac{\Delta t^{n-1}}{n!}\frac{\partial^n}{\partial t^n}u(x,t) + a\sum_{n=1}^{\infty}\frac{(-\Delta x)^{n-1}}{n!}\frac{\partial^n}{\partial x^n}u(x,t) \tag{23.148b}$$

$$= \frac{\Delta t}{2}\frac{\partial^2}{\partial t^2}u(x,t) + a\frac{-\Delta x}{2}\frac{\partial^2}{\partial x^2}u(x,t) + \mathcal{O}(\Delta t^2 + \Delta x^2) \tag{23.148c}$$

where we have used (23.145) in the last simplification. Thus, $T \to 0$ linearly as $(\Delta t, \Delta x) \to 0$.

The forward finite difference in time and backward difference in space suggest the following update rule:

$$U_{i,j+1} = (1-m)U_{i,j} + mU_{i-1,j}, \tag{23.149}$$

using $m = \frac{a\Delta t}{\Delta x}$. For this update rule, the value at time $(j+1)\Delta t$ depends on the small interval $i\Delta x$, $(i-1)\Delta x$ at time $j\Delta t$, which recursively generalizes to a triangle of dependence as illustrated in Figure 23.8. Comparing with the analytical solution, $u(x,t) = u(x-at,0)$, we realize that the analytical solution can only be properly approximated by this update rule if $a > 0$, and further only if $m \leq 1$. This is the so-called

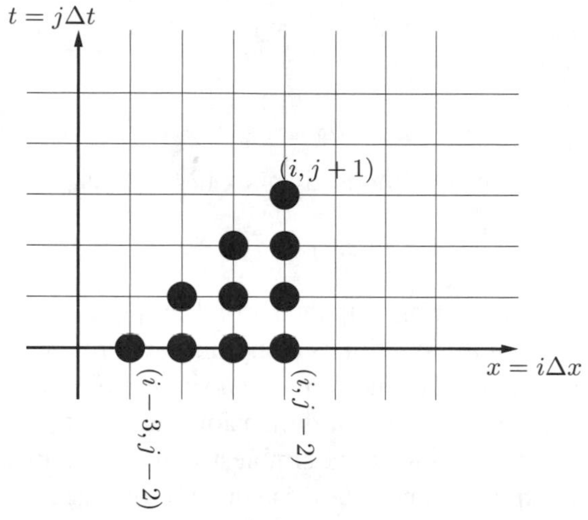

Figure 23.8: The forward time and backward space approximation of the linear advection equation gives a triangular domain of dependence.

CFL condition [Courant et al., 1928], that is, that the flow of information should lie within the numerical triangle of dependency. The CFL condition is a necessary, but not sufficient, condition for convergence.

The Fourier analysis of (23.149) is again based on the guess that

$$U_{i,j} = \lambda^j \exp(ki\Delta x\sqrt{-1}) \tag{23.150}$$

is a solution, and we insert this guess into (23.149), use the recursive formulation, $U_{i,j+1} = \lambda U_{i,j}$, divide by $U_{i,j}$, which gives

$$\frac{\lambda U_{i,j}}{U_{i,j}} = (1-m)\frac{U_{i,j}}{U_{i,j}} + m\frac{U_{i-1,j}}{U_{i,j}} \tag{23.151a}$$
$$\Downarrow$$
$$\lambda = 1 - m + m\exp\left(k(i-1)\Delta x\sqrt{-1} - ki\Delta x\sqrt{-1}\right) \tag{23.151b}$$
$$= 1 - m + m\exp\left(-k\Delta x\sqrt{-1}\right). \tag{23.151c}$$

To find the Fourier convergence, we use the length of a complex number

$$|\alpha + \sqrt{-1}\beta| = \sqrt{\alpha^2 + \beta^2} \tag{23.152}$$

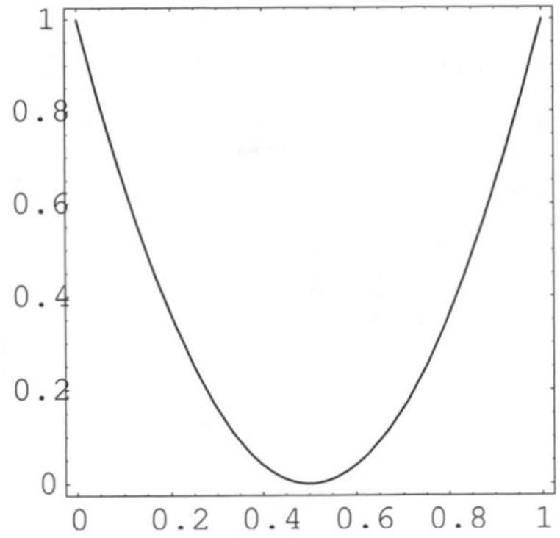

Figure 23.9: The function $1 - 4(1 - m)m$ in the interval $[-1, 1]$.

and evaluate the squared length of λ as

$$
\begin{aligned}
|\lambda|^2 &= |1 - m + m\cos(k\Delta x) - m\sqrt{-1}\sin(k\Delta x)|^2 && (23.153a)\\
&= (1 - m + m\cos(k\Delta x))^2 + (-m\sqrt{-1}\sin(k\Delta x))^2 && (23.153b)\\
&= (1 - m)^2 + 2(1 - m)m\cos(k\Delta x) + m^2\cos^2(k\Delta x) + m^2\sin^2(k\Delta x) && (23.153c)\\
&= (1 - m)^2 + 2(1 - m)m\cos(k\Delta x) + m^2 && (23.153d)\\
&= 1 - 2m + 2m^2 + 2(1 - m)m\cos(k\Delta x) && (23.153e)\\
&= 1 - 2(1 - m)m + 2(1 - m)m\cos(k\Delta x) && (23.153f)\\
&= 1 - 2(1 - m)m(1 \quad \cos(k\Delta x)). && (23.153g)
\end{aligned}
$$

Since the range of cos is [-1,1], we conclude that for $|\lambda| \leq 1$ is equivalent to requiring that $1-4(1-m)m \leq 1$. This is a quadratic function illustrated in Figure 23.9, and we conclude that it is sufficient to require that $m \leq 1$ as also indicated by the CFL condition. This could suggest that the full interval of $a \neq 0$ would be covered by a central differencing scheme in space, that is,

$$
\frac{U_{i,j+1} - U_{i,j}}{\Delta t} + \mathcal{O}(\Delta t) = -a\frac{U_{i+1,j} - U_{i-1,j}}{2\Delta x} + \mathcal{O}(\Delta x^2), \qquad (23.154)
$$

but using (23.150) it may be shown that this scheme has $|\lambda| > 1$ and does therefore not converge. The best choice is therefore to use the *upwind scheme*, where a backward differencing scheme in space is used, when $a > 0$, and a forward difference scheme in space is used, when $a < 0$, that is,

$$
U_{i,j+1} = \begin{cases} (1 - m)U_{i,j} + mU_{i-1,j}, & \text{when } a > 0,\\ (1 + m)U_{i,j} - mU_{i-1,j}, & \text{when } a < 0. \end{cases} \qquad (23.155)
$$

Just as for the case of backward difference in space, when $a > 0$, it may equally be proven that $m \leq 1$ is sufficient for convergence of the forward difference in space. Further investigation into the truncation error will show that the upwind scheme always has an amplitude in the order of $k\Delta x$ and a relative phase error, which vanishes at $k\Delta x = \frac{1}{2}$ (see [Morton et al., 1994, Chapter 4.4] for the derivation).

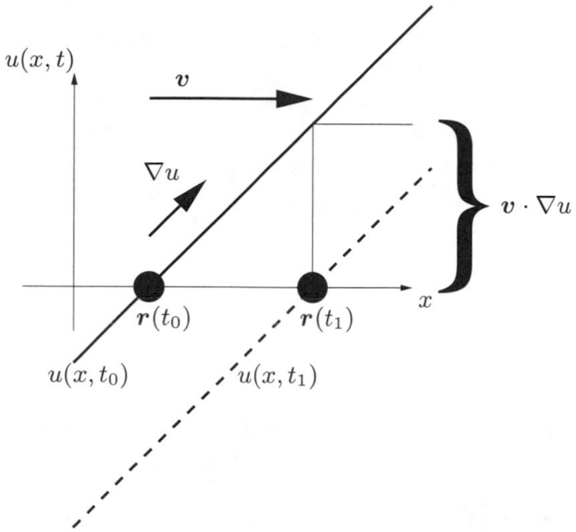

Figure 23.10: Comparing the Lagrangian and the Eulerian method for moving an interface: an interface is moved along an external vector $\boldsymbol{V}$.

23.3 Level-Set Methods

The motion of particles moving in an externally generated velocity field is given as

$$\frac{d\boldsymbol{r}_i(t)}{dt} = \boldsymbol{v}_i(t), \tag{23.156}$$

where $\boldsymbol{r}_i$ and $\boldsymbol{v}_i$ are the position and velocity of particle i at time t. This is a Lagrangian view of the dynamical system discussed in detail in Chapter 8, and it is very useful for animating systems where the configuration of the particles is fixed or nonexisting. For objects that can change topology, such as water that may separate into droplets, the splitting and merging process becomes complicated [McInerney et al., 2000]. When topology may change, it is more natural to define the object boundary as an implicit function, u, and apply the *level set equation* [Osher et al., 1988, Sethian, 1999, Osher et al., 2003]

$$u_t + \boldsymbol{v} \cdot \nabla_x u = 0, \tag{23.157}$$

where u is an implicit function such that

$$u(x, y, z, t) = 0, \tag{23.158}$$

defines the interface between, for example, water and air, and $\boldsymbol{v}$ is now a velocity field sufficiently smooth near the interface. The equivalence of (23.157) with (23.156) is shown in Figure 23.10. The figure shows a particle at its initial position in $\boldsymbol{r}(t_0)$, and later after the application of the velocity vector $\boldsymbol{v}$, resulting in position $\boldsymbol{r}(t_1)$. It is assumed that the time-step is one unit of time. Equivalently, the implicit function $u(x, t)$ intersects the horizontal axis at $u(\boldsymbol{r}, t_0) = 0$ initially, and since the function is locally linear, the addition of $-\boldsymbol{v}\nabla_x u$ will cause the interface to move to $u(\boldsymbol{r}, t_1) = 0$. We thus conclude that the level-set equation (23.157) implements (23.156), when the implicit function is linear in a band $\boldsymbol{v}\nabla_x u$ around its interface.

The most used implicit function is the signed distance map, which for an object with boundary δO is given as

$$d(\boldsymbol{r}) = (-1)^{I(\boldsymbol{r})} \min_{\boldsymbol{r}_O} \|\boldsymbol{r}_O - \boldsymbol{r}\|, \tag{23.159}$$

where $\boldsymbol{r}_O \in \delta O$ is a point on the interface and $I(\boldsymbol{r})$ is the indicator function,

$$I(\boldsymbol{r}) = \begin{cases} 1, & \text{if } \boldsymbol{r} \text{ is inside the object,} \\ 0, & \text{otherwise.} \end{cases} \tag{23.160}$$

The signed distance map is numerically advantageous since $|\nabla_x d| = 1$ in almost all points. It is very convenient for collision detection, since $\operatorname{sgn} d$ can be used to detect intersections between objects. If $d(\boldsymbol{r}) < 0$, then $d(\boldsymbol{r})\nabla_x d(\boldsymbol{r})$ is the shortest route out to the boundary of the object, where $d(\boldsymbol{r}) = 0$.

In contrast to the Lagrangian formulation, where an interface is represented directly as a set of control points or particles, the level-set approach depends on the spatial sampling of the implicit function and speed vector field. This is however, analogous, since finer sampling in space achieves finer representation of the interface, just as adding more particles does in the Lagrangian formulation. Methods also exist for sparse representation of the implicit function, such that the memory requirement can be reduced to be near that of the Lagrangian system. For some systems, $\boldsymbol{v}$ is only determined on the interface, that is, at $d = 0$, and for the level-set method we need to extend the velocities at least to a band around $d = 0$. Since the interface is moving in the normal direction, the most natural solution is to impose constancy in the velocity field along the normal. However, setting $\boldsymbol{v}(\boldsymbol{r})$ to be equal to the velocity of the nearest point on the interface seems to preserve signed distance maps.

We will analyze the simplest case of one space and time dimension,

$$u_t(x, t) = -v \cdot u_x(x, t), \tag{23.161}$$

This equation is the linear advection equation (23.145), which holds for (23.157) in general, hence we must consider the directions of the characteristics. Assuming a grid $U_{i,j} \simeq u(i\Delta x, j\Delta t)$, a forward finite difference in time and an upwind scheme in space gives

$$\frac{U_{i,j+1} - U_{i,j}}{\Delta t} = -\begin{cases} v\frac{U_{i+1,j} - U_{i,j}}{\Delta x}, & \text{if } U_{i,j} \leq 0, \\ v\frac{U_{i,j} - U_{i-1,j}}{\Delta x}, & \text{otherwise.} \end{cases} \tag{23.162}$$

The truncation error is found similarly to (23.148c) to be

$$T(x, t) = \frac{\Delta t}{2}\frac{\partial^2}{\partial t^2}u(x, t) + \begin{cases} v\frac{\Delta x}{2}\frac{\partial^2}{\partial x^2}u(x, t) & \text{if } U_{i,j} \leq 0, \\ v\frac{-\Delta x}{2}\frac{\partial^2}{\partial x^2}u(x, t) & \text{otherwise.} \end{cases} + \mathcal{O}(\Delta t^2 + \Delta x^2) \tag{23.163}$$

Likewise, we find the CFL conditions using (23.153g) to be

$$\Delta t \leq \frac{\Delta x}{v} \tag{23.164}$$

for constant positive velocities, and

$$\Delta t \leq \frac{\Delta x}{\max_x \|v\|_2} \tag{23.165}$$

in general.

24

Open Nonuniform B-Spline Theory

In this section we will present the classical theory of nonuniform B-splines and simultaneously we will derive a c-style pseudocode for efficient implementation of the theory.

The theory of B-splines is a much wider area than the treatment we give in this paper. Therefore, we encourage the reader to look at our references [Piegl et al., 1995, Watt et al., 1992, Hoschek et al., 1993, Boor, 1978, Boehm, 1980, Farin, 1993, Erleben et al., 2003a] if a wider coverage is wanted.

24.1 The B-Spline Basis Functions

A *B-spline* is a parameterized curve in the parameter u. It can be evaluated as the interpolation of a set of basis functions. Therefore, before we look at the B-splines we will describe the B-spline basis functions.

We'll start by defining the *normalized basis function* for the B-spline.

Definition 24.1

The normalized basis functions, $N_{i,k}$, are defined recursively by the Cox de Boor definition. *For $k > 1$:*

$$N_{i,k} = \frac{u - t_i}{t_{i+k-1} - t_i} N_{i,k-1} + \frac{t_{i+k} - u}{t_{i+k} - t_{i+1}} N_{i+1,k-1}, \tag{24.1}$$

and for $k = 1$:

$$N_{i,1} = \begin{cases} 1 & \textit{if } t_i \leq u < t_{i+1}, \\ 0 & \textit{otherwise.} \end{cases} \tag{24.2}$$

The index k is called the order *of the basis function. For a given value of k this definition results in a polynomium of degree $k - 1$. All the t_is are called* knot values, *and are usually arranged in a so-called* knot vector, *T:*

$$T = \left[\ldots, t_{i-1}, t_i, t_{i+1}, t_{i+2}, \ldots\right]^T. \tag{24.3}$$

To better understand the definition (24.1), we will consider a value u that lies between two knot-values

$$t_i \leq u < t_{i+1}. \tag{24.4}$$

Looking at the definition of the B-spline basis functions (24.1), we can easily derive the dependency table shown in Table 24.1. The table should be read bottom-up. Starting at the bottom with the knot vector, one can track all nonzero basis functions up to any wanted k-value. Observe that $N_{i+1,1}$ is zero due to (24.2). The pattern is obvious and we could easily have extended the table to any value of k.

There are three properties, which can be seen immediately from the table and which we are going to put to practical use later on.

$k=3$	0		$N_{i-2,3}$		$N_{i-1,3}$		$N_{i,3}$		0
$k=2$		0		$N_{i-1,2}$		$N_{i,2}$		0	
$k=1$	$\dots$		0		$N_{i,1}$		0		$\dots$
		t_{i-1}		t_i	u	t_{i+1}		t_{i+2}	

Table 24.1: Dependency table showing only nonzero basis functions at the value of u.

1. At the k'th order there are exactly k basis functions, which are different from zero.
2. From the table we can derive that if

$$t_i \le u < t_{i+1}, \tag{24.5}$$

then only

$$N_{i-k+1,k}, \dots, N_{i,k}, \tag{24.6}$$

will be nonzero.

3. Computing the basis functions bottom-up, instead of top-down, will make it possible to reuse previously computed results.

We will use properties one and two to make a sort of fast rejection on which basis functions we need to compute. The third property is obvious from the table, but it requires some work before it can be applied efficiently in a practical implementation.

24.1.1 Implementing the Basis Functions

Let's look at an example. Assume we have

$$t_i \le u < t_{i+1}, \tag{24.7}$$

Then, by the definition of the basis functions, and the properties one and two, we can write up all the nonzero basis functions:

$k = 1$:

$$N_{i,1} = 1. \tag{24.8}$$

$k = 2$:

$$N_{i-1,2} = \frac{u - t_{i-1}}{t_{i+0} - t_{i-1}} N_{i-1,1} + \frac{t_{i+1} - u}{t_{i+1} - t_i} N_{i,1} = \frac{t_{i+1} - u}{t_{i+1} - t_i} N_{i,1}, \tag{24.9a}$$

$$N_{i,2} = \frac{u - t_i}{t_{i+1} - t_i} N_{i,1} + \frac{t_{i+2} - u}{t_{i+2} - t_{i+1}} N_{i+1,1} = \frac{u - t_i}{t_{i+1} - t_i} N_{i,1}. \tag{24.9b}$$

$k = 3$:

$$N_{i-2,3} = \frac{u - t_{i-2}}{t_{i+0} - t_{i-2}} N_{i-2,2} + \frac{t_{i+1} - u}{t_{i+1} - t_{i-1}} N_{i-1,2} = \frac{t_{i+1} - u}{t_{i+1} - t_{i-1}} N_{i-1,2}, \tag{24.10a}$$

$$N_{i-1,3} = \frac{u - t_{i-1}}{t_{i+1} - t_{i-1}} N_{i-1,2} + \frac{t_{i+2} - u}{t_{i+2} - t_i} N_{i,2}, \tag{24.10b}$$

$$N_{i,3} = \frac{u - t_i}{t_{i+2} - t_i} N_{i,2} + \frac{t_{i+3} - u}{t_{i+3} - t_{i+1}} N_{i+1,2} = \frac{u - t_i}{t_{i+2} - t_i} N_{i,2}. \tag{24.10c}$$

We can immediately make a few observations. For instance, if we look at $N_{i-1,3}$, then we observe that the part $\frac{\cdots}{t_{i+2}-t_i} N_{i,2}$ of the second term reappears in the first term of $N_{i,3}$. Another observation we can make is that the first part of $N_{i-2,3}$ is always zero and the same goes for the last part of $N_{i,3}$. This is seen directly from the properties observed from Table 24.1. These two observations can be used to speed up computations.

Looking at the fractions of the knot differences, we see that they appear to be similar for increasing values of k. This similarity can be systematized by introducing two new auxiliary functions called left and right. These are defined as follows:

$$\text{left}(j) = u - t_{i+1-j}, \tag{24.11a}$$

$$\text{right}(j) = t_{i+j} - u. \tag{24.11b}$$

Rewriting the example for $k = 3$, using the auxiliary functions yields:

$$N_{i-2,3} = \frac{\text{left}(3)}{\text{right}(0) + \text{left}(3)} N_{i-2,2} + \frac{\text{right}(1)}{\text{right}(1) + \text{left}(2)} N_{i-1,2}, \tag{24.12a}$$

$$N_{i-1,3} = \frac{\text{left}(2)}{\text{right}(1) - \text{left}(2)} N_{i-1,2} + \frac{\text{right}(2)}{\text{right}(2) + \text{left}(1)} N_{i,2}, \tag{24.12b}$$

$$N_{i,3} = \frac{\text{left}(1)}{\text{right}(2) + \text{left}(1)} N_{i,2} + \frac{\text{right}(3)}{\text{right}(3) + \text{left}(0)} N_{i+1,2}. \tag{24.12c}$$

From this, we can derive the following general relation:

$$M(r,k) = N_{i-(k-r-1),k} \tag{24.13a}$$

$$= \frac{\text{left}(k-r)}{\text{right}(r) - \text{left}(k-r)} N_{i-1,k-1} + \frac{\text{right}(r+1)}{\text{right}(r+1) + \text{left}(k-r-1)} N_{i,k-1}, \tag{24.13b}$$

where

$$0 \le r < k. \tag{24.14}$$

By close examination of (24.9a), (24.9b), (24.10a), (24.10b), and (24.10c) from earlier, we notice that when computing a new k'th level, the only left and right values not already computed are left(k) and right(k). We are now ready to write up pseudocode for computing the values of all nonzero B-spline basis functions $N_{i,k}$ (see Figure 24.1).

```
algorithm BasisFunc(i,u,K,T)
  left = array(K+1)
  right = array(K+1)
  M = array(K)
  left[0]  = u - T[i+1]
  right[0] = T[i] - u

  left[1]  = u - T[i]
  right[1] = T[i+1] - u
  M[0] = 1

  For k = 2 to K do
    left[k] = u - T[i+1-k]
    right[k] = T[i+k] - u

    saved = 0

    For r=0 to k-2
      tmp = M[r]/(right[r+1]+left[k-r-1])
      M[r] = saved + right[r+1]*tmp
      saved = left[k-r-1]*tmp;
    Next r

    M[k-1] = saved

  Next k
  return M
end algorithm
```

Figure 24.1: Pseudocode for computing nonzero B-spline basis functions.

24.1.2 The Derivatives of the Basis Functions

It will prove useful to us later to continue studying the basis functions, as it turns out the derivative of a B-spline can be written as the interpolation of the derivatives of the basis functions. Therefore, we seek a convenient and tractable method for computing the derivative of the basis functions.

We will start by showing the result of computing the first-order derivative of a basis function.

Theorem 24.1 (Derivative of B-Spline Bases)
The first-order derivative of a B-spline basis function is given by

$$\frac{dN_{i,k}}{du} = \frac{k-1}{t_{i+k-1} - t_i} N_{i,k-1} - \frac{k-1}{t_{i+k} - t_{i+1}} N_{i+1,k-1}. \tag{24.15}$$

Proof of Theorem 24.1:
We will prove the equation by induction on k. Setting $k = 2$ we see by direct differentiation of (24.1) that

the derivative would be either

$$\frac{1}{t_{i+k-1} - t_i}, \quad \frac{-1}{t_{i+k} - t_{i+1}}, \quad \text{or } 0 \tag{24.16}$$

depending on what interval u lies within. By direct substitution into (24.15) we can easily verify that (24.15) is true in the case of $k = 2$. Assume now that (24.15) is true for $k - 1$ and that $k > 2$. To prove that (24.15) is true for the k'th case, we start by applying the product rule to (24.1) and get the following,

$$\begin{aligned}\frac{dN_{i,k}}{du} &= \frac{1}{t_{i+k-1} - t_i} N_{i,k-1} - \frac{1}{t_{i+k} - t_{i+1}} N_{i+1,k-1} \\ &+ \frac{u - t_i}{t_{i+k-1} - t_i} \frac{dN_{i,k-1}}{du} + \frac{t_{i+k} - u}{t_{i+k} - t_{i+1}} \frac{dN_{i+1,k-1}}{du}.\end{aligned} \tag{24.17}$$

We substitute (24.15) for the terms $\frac{dN_{i,k-1}}{du}$ and $\frac{dN_{i+1,k-1}}{du}$ and get the following,

$$\begin{aligned}\frac{dN_{i,k}}{du} &= \frac{1}{t_{i+k-1} - t_i} N_{i,k-1} - \frac{1}{t_{i+k} - t_{i+1}} N_{i+1,k-1} \\ &+ \frac{u - t_i}{t_{i+k-1} - t_i} \left(\frac{k-2}{t_{i+k-2} - t_i} N_{i,k-2} - \frac{k-2}{t_{i+k-1} - t_{i+1}} N_{i+1,k-2} \right) \\ &+ \frac{t_{i+k} - u}{t_{i+k} - t_{i+1}} \left(\frac{k-2}{t_{i+k-1} - t_{i+1}} N_{i+1,k-2} - \frac{k-2}{t_{i+k} - t_{i+2}} N_{i+2,k-2} \right).\end{aligned} \tag{24.18}$$

By rearranging terms we get

$$\begin{aligned}\frac{dN_{i,k}}{du} &= \frac{1}{t_{i+k-1} - t_i} N_{i,k-1} - \frac{1}{t_{i+k} - t_{i+1}} N_{i+1,k-1} \\ &+ \frac{k-2}{t_{i+k-1} - t_i} \frac{u - t_i}{t_{i+k-2} - t_i} N_{i,k-2} \\ &+ \frac{k-2}{t_{i+k-1} - t_{i+1}} \left(\frac{t_{i+k} - u}{t_{i+k} - t_{i+1}} - \frac{u - t_i}{t_{i+k-1} - t_i} \right) N_{i+1,k-2} \\ &- \frac{k-2}{t_{i+k} - t_{i+1}} \frac{t_{i+k} - u}{t_{i+k} - t_{i+2}} N_{i+2,k-2}.\end{aligned} \tag{24.19}$$

We perform a mathemagical trick. We add zero to the equation by adding 1 and subtracting 1:

$$\begin{aligned}\frac{dN_{i,k}}{du} &= \frac{1}{t_{i+k-1} - t_i} N_{i,k-1} - \frac{1}{t_{i+k} - t_{i+1}} N_{i+1,k-1} \\ &+ \frac{k-2}{t_{i+k-1} - t_i} \frac{u - t_i}{t_{i+k-2} - t_i} N_{i,k-2} \\ &+ \frac{k-2}{t_{i+k-1} - t_{i+1}} \left(\frac{t_{i+k} - u}{t_{i+k} - t_{i+1}} - 1 + 1 - \frac{u - t_i}{t_{i+k-1} - t_i} \right) N_{i+1,k-2} \\ &- \frac{k-2}{t_{i+k} - t_{i+1}} \frac{t_{i+k} - u}{t_{i+k} - t_{i+2}} N_{i+2,k-2}.\end{aligned} \tag{24.20}$$

Expressed as fractions, we get:

$$\begin{aligned}\frac{dN_{i,k}}{du} &= \frac{1}{t_{i+k-1}-t_i}N_{i,k-1} - \frac{1}{t_{i+k}-t_{i+1}}N_{i+1,k-1}\\ &+ \frac{k-2}{t_{i+k-1}-t_i}\frac{u-t_i}{t_{i+k-2}-t_i}N_{i,k-2}\\ &+ \frac{k-2}{t_{i+k-1}-t_{i+1}}\left(\frac{t_{i+k}-u}{t_{i+k}-t_{i+1}} - \frac{t_{i+k}-t_{i+1}}{t_{i+k}-t_{i+1}}\right.\\ &\left.+\frac{t_{i+k-1}-t_i}{t_{i+k-1}-t_i} - \frac{u-t_i}{t_{i+k-1}-t_i}\right)N_{i+1,k-2}\\ &- \frac{k-2}{t_{i+k}-t_{i+1}}\frac{t_{i+k}-u}{t_{i+k}-t_{i+2}}N_{i+2,k-2}. \end{aligned} \tag{24.21}$$

Setting on common denominators, we get:

$$\begin{aligned}\frac{dN_{i,k}}{du} &= \frac{1}{t_{i+k-1}-t_i}N_{i,k-1} - \frac{1}{t_{i+k}-t_{i+1}}N_{i+1,k-1}\\ &+ \frac{k-2}{t_{i+k-1}-t_i}\frac{u-t_i}{t_{i+k-2}-t_i}N_{i,k-2}\\ &+ \frac{k-2}{t_{i+k-1}-t_{i+1}}\left(\frac{t_{i+k}-u-t_{i+k}+t_{i+1}}{t_{i+k}-t_{i+1}}\right.\\ &\left.+\frac{t_{i+k-1}-t_i-u+t_i}{t_{i+k-1}-t_i}\right)N_{i+1,k-2}\\ &- \frac{k-2}{t_{i+k}-t_{i+1}}\frac{t_{i+k}-u}{t_{i+k}-t_{i+2}}N_{i+2,k-2}. \end{aligned} \tag{24.22}$$

Reduction yields:

$$\begin{aligned}\frac{dN_{i,k}}{du} &= \frac{1}{t_{i+k-1}-t_i}N_{i,k-1} - \frac{1}{t_{i+k}-t_{i+1}}N_{i+1,k-1}\\ &+ \frac{k-2}{t_{i+k-1}-t_i}\frac{u-t_i}{t_{i+k-2}-t_i}N_{i,k-2}\\ &+ \frac{k-2}{t_{i+k-1}-t_{i+1}}\left(\frac{t_{i+1}-u}{t_{i+k}-t_{i+1}} + \frac{t_{i+k-1}-u}{t_{i+k-1}-t_i}\right)N_{i+1,k-2}\\ &- \frac{k-2}{t_{i+k}-t_{i+1}}\frac{t_{i+k}-u}{t_{i+k}-t_{i+2}}N_{i+2,k-2}. \end{aligned} \tag{24.23}$$

Now we are almost at our goal. By rearranging the equation once more, we get:

$$\begin{aligned}\frac{dN_{i,k}}{du} &= \frac{1}{t_{i+k-1}-t_i}N_{i,k-1} - \frac{1}{t_{i+k}-t_{i+1}}N_{i+1,k-1}\\ &+ \frac{k-2}{t_{i+k-1}-t_i}\left(\frac{u-t_i}{t_{i+k-2}-t_i}N_{i,k-2} + \frac{t_{i+k-1}-u}{t_{i+k-1}-t_{i+1}}N_{i+1,k-2}\right)\\ &- \frac{k-2}{t_{i+k}-t_{i+1}}\left(\frac{u-t_{i+1}}{t_{i+k-1}-t_{i+1}}N_{i+1,k-2} + \frac{t_{i+k}-u}{t_{i+k}-t_{i+2}}N_{i+2,k-2}\right).\end{aligned} \tag{24.24}$$

Looking at the terms in the parentheses, we immediately recognize (24.1), which we apply to get the following:

$$\begin{aligned}\frac{dN_{i,k}}{du} &= \frac{1}{t_{i+k-1}-t_i}N_{i,k-1} - \frac{1}{t_{i+k}-t_{i+1}}N_{i+1,k-1}\\ &+ \frac{k-2}{t_{i+k-1}-t_i}N_{i,k-1} - \frac{k-2}{t_{i+k}-t_{i+1}}N_{i+1,k-1}.\end{aligned} \tag{24.25}$$

Cleaning up a bit more we get:

$$\begin{aligned}\frac{dN_{i,k}}{du} &= \frac{(k-2)+1}{t_{i+k-1}-t_i}N_{i,k-1} - \frac{(k-2)+1}{t_{i+k}-t_{i+1}}N_{i+1,k-1}\\ &= \frac{k-1}{t_{i+k-1}-t_i}N_{i,k-1} - \frac{k-1}{t_{i+k}-t_{i+1}}N_{i+1,k-1}.\end{aligned} \tag{24.26}$$

Finally, we can conclude that (24.15) is true. □

Now let us try to look at higher-order derivatives. If we differentiate (24.15), we get:

$$\frac{d^2N_{i,k}}{du^2} = \frac{k-1}{t_{i+k-1}-t_i}\frac{dN_{i,k-1}}{du} - \frac{k-1}{t_{i+k}-t_{i+1}}\frac{dN_{i+1,k-1}}{du}. \tag{24.27}$$

From this, it is not hard to see that a general formula can be written for the j'th derivative:

$$\frac{d^jN_{i,k}}{du^j} = \frac{k-1}{t_{i+k-1}-t_i}\frac{d^{j-1}N_{i,k-1}}{du^{j-1}} - \frac{k-1}{t_{i+k}-t_{i+1}}\frac{d^{j-1}N_{i+1,k-1}}{du^{j-1}}. \tag{24.28}$$

Our results can be generalized into the following theorem.

Theorem 24.2 (Higher-Order Derivatives of B-Spline Bases)
For $j < k$ the higher-order derivatives of a B-spline basis function is given by

$$\frac{d^jN_{i,k}}{du^j} = \frac{(k-1)!}{(k-j-1)!}\sum_{p=0}^{j} a_{j,p}N_{i+p,k-j}, \tag{24.29}$$

with

$$a_{0,0} = 1, \tag{24.30a}$$

$$a_{j,0} = \frac{a_{j-1,0}}{t_{i+k-j} - t_i}, \tag{24.30b}$$

$$a_{j,p} = \frac{a_{j-1,p} - a_{j-1,p-1}}{t_{i+k+p-j} - t_{i+p}}, \tag{24.30c}$$

$$a_{j,j} = -\frac{a_{j-1,j-1}}{t_{i+k} - t_{i+j}}. \tag{24.30d}$$

Proof of Theorem 24.2:

We will now try to prove (24.29) by induction on j. We'll start by examining if the equation holds for $j = 1$. From direct substitution into (24.29) we get the following result:

$$\frac{dN_{i,k}}{du} = \frac{(k-1)!}{(k-2)!}\left(a_{1,0}N_{i,k-1} + a_{1,1}N_{i+1,k-1}\right) \tag{24.31a}$$

$$= (k-1)\left(\frac{a_{0,0}}{t_{i+k-1} - t_i}N_{i,k-1} + \frac{-a_{0,0}}{t_{i+k} - t_{i+1}}N_{i+1,k-1}\right) \tag{24.31b}$$

$$= (k-1)\left(\frac{1}{t_{i+k-1} - t_i}N_{i,k-1} - \frac{1}{t_{i+k} - t_{i+1}}N_{i+1,k-1}\right) \tag{24.31c}$$

$$= \frac{k-1}{t_{i+k-1} - t_i}N_{i,k-1} - \frac{k-1}{t_{i+k} - t_{i+1}}N_{i+1,k-1}. \tag{24.31d}$$

We immediately recognize (24.15) and conclude that (24.29) is true for $j = 1$. Now, we'll assume that (24.29) is true for the case of $j = j - 1$ and we'll try to prove that it also is true in the j'th case. We have

$$\frac{d^{j-1}N_{i,k}}{dt^{j-1}} = \frac{(k-1)!}{(k-(j-1)-1)!}\sum_{p=0}^{j-1} a_{j-1,p}N_{i+p,k-j+1}. \tag{24.32}$$

If we differentiate this once more we get the j'th derivative, that is,

$$\frac{d^jN_{i,k}}{dt^j} = \frac{(k-1)!}{(k-(j-1)-1)!}\sum_{p=0}^{j-1} a_{j-1,p}\frac{dN_{i+p,k-j+1}}{du}. \tag{24.33}$$

Now let us apply (24.15) to the derivative inside the summation:

$$\frac{d^jN_{i,k}}{dt^j} = \frac{(k-1)!}{(k-j)!}\sum_{p=0}^{j-1} a_{j-1,p}\left(\frac{k-j}{t_{i+p+k-j} - t_{i+p}}N_{i+p,k-j} - \frac{k-j}{t_{i+p+k-j+1} - t_{i+p+1}}N_{i+p+1,k-j}\right). \tag{24.34}$$

Rearranging yields:

$$\frac{d^j N_{i,k}}{dt^j} = \frac{(k-1)!}{(k-j-1)!} \sum_{p=0}^{j-1} \left(\frac{a_{j-1,p}}{t_{i+p+k-j} - t_{i+p}} N_{i+p,k-j} - \frac{a_{j-1,p}}{t_{i+p+k-j+1} - t_{i+p+1}} N_{i+p+1,k-j} \right). \tag{24.35}$$

Let's write out the summation into explicit terms. This results in the following:

$$\begin{aligned}\frac{d^j N_{i,k}}{dt^j} = \frac{(k-1)!}{(k-j-1)!} \Bigg(&\frac{a_{j-1,0}}{t_{i+k-j} - t_i} N_{i,k-j} - \frac{a_{j-1,0}}{t_{i+k-j+1} - t_{i+1}} N_{i+1,k-j} \\ &+ \frac{a_{j-1,1}}{t_{i+1+k-j} - t_{i+1}} N_{i+1,k-j} - \frac{a_{j-1,1}}{t_{i+k-j+2} - t_{i+2}} N_{i+2,k-j} \\ &+ \frac{a_{j-1,2}}{t_{i+2+k-j} - t_{i+2}} N_{i+2,k-j} - \frac{a_{j-1,2}}{t_{i+k-j+3} - t_{i+3}} N_{i+3,k-j} \\ &\cdots \\ &+ \frac{a_{j-1,j-1}}{t_{i+k-1} - t_{i+j-1}} N_{i+j-1,k-j} - \frac{a_{j-1,j-1}}{t_{i+k} - t_{i+j}} N_{i+j,k-j} \Bigg). \end{aligned} \tag{24.36}$$

This equation can be rewritten by collecting terms of equal N-factors:

$$\begin{aligned}\frac{d^j N_{i,k}}{dt^j} = \frac{(k-1)!}{(k-j-1)!} \Bigg(&\frac{a_{j-1,0}}{t_{i+k-j} - t_i} N_{i,k-j} \\ &+ \frac{a_{j-1,1} - a_{j-1,0}}{t_{i+1+k-j} - t_{i+1}} N_{i+1,k-j} \\ &+ \frac{a_{j-1,2} - a_{j-1,1}}{t_{i+2+k-j} - t_{i+2}} N_{i+2,k-j} \\ &\cdots \\ &+ \frac{a_{j-1,j-1} - a_{j-1,j-2}}{t_{i+k-1} - t_{i+j-1}} N_{i+j-1,k-j} \\ &- \frac{a_{j-1,j-1}}{t_{i+k} - t_{i+j}} N_{i+j,k-j} \Bigg). \end{aligned} \tag{24.37}$$

Looking at how the a-coefficients in (24.30a)–(24.30d) are defined, we can easily rewrite the equation into the following form:

$$\begin{aligned}\frac{d^j N_{i,k}}{dt^j} = \frac{(k-1)!}{(k-j-1)!} &\left(a_{j,0} N_{i,k-j} + a_{j,1} N_{i+1,k-j} + a_{j,2} N_{i+2,k-j} + \cdots \right. \\ &\left. \cdots + a_{j,j} N_{i+j,k-j} \right), \end{aligned} \tag{24.38}$$

$N_{i,1}$	$N_{i-1,2}$	$N_{i-2,3}$	$N_{i-3,4}$
$t_{i+1} - t_i$	$N_{i,2}$	$N_{i-1,3}$	$N_{i-2,4}$
$t_{i+1} - t_{i-1}$	$t_{i+2} - t_i$	$N_{i,3}$	$N_{i-1,4}$
$t_{i+1} - t_{i-2}$	$t_{i+2} - t_{i-1}$	$t_{i+3} - t_i$	$N_{i,4}$

Table 24.2: M-table example for $k = 4$.

which conveniently can be written as:

$$\frac{d^j N_{i,k}}{dt^j} = \frac{(k-1)!}{(k-j-1)!} \sum_{p=0}^{j} a_{j,p} N_{i+p,k-j}. \tag{24.39}$$

By comparison with (24.29), we can now conclude that it also holds in j'th case. □

24.1.3 Implementing the Derivatives of the Basis Functions

Now we'll turn our attention toward making an efficient implementation. By (24.29) we have

$$\frac{d^j N_{i,k}}{du^j} = \frac{(k-1)!}{(k-j-1)!} \sum_{p=0}^{j} a_{j,p} N_{i+p,k-j}, \qquad j < k. \tag{24.40}$$

and we see that the numerators in (24.30b)–(24.30d) are

$$\Delta T = t_{i+k+p-j} - t_{i+p} \qquad \text{for} \qquad 0 \leq p \leq j. \tag{24.41}$$

By (24.1) we have

$$N_{i+p-1,k-j+1} = \frac{u - t_{i+p-1}}{t_{i+k+p-j-1} - t_{i+p-1}} N_{i+p-1,k-j} + \frac{t_{i+k+p-j} - u}{t_{i+k+p-j} - t_{i+p}} N_{i+p,k-j}. \tag{24.42}$$

Now, if we compare the numerator of the second term to (24.41), we immediately see that they are identical. In other words, we have seen that the knot differences used to compute the N-values can be reused in the computation of the derivatives. We'll create a table, which we call M, and for $0 \leq r < k$ we store values into M as follows:

$$N_{i-k+1+r,k} \rightarrow M_{r,k-1}, \tag{24.43}$$

$$\Delta T \rightarrow M_{k-1,r}. \tag{24.44}$$

The diagonal is special since we will store $N_{i,k}$ in it. In Table 24.2 we have given an example of an M-table to help familiarize you with it. Observe that M contains all the nonzero values of N from the dependency table and it also stores the corresponding knot differences (from the right terms only) in the transpose position of the corresponding N value.

The knot difference we need in the a-coefficient of $N_{i+p,k-j}$ is computed by $N_{i+p-1,k-j+1}$. In the M-table, $N_{i+p-1,k-j+1}$ would lie just to the right of $N_{i+p,k-j}$. Knowing this, we can easily come up with the following rule for looking up the knot difference we need, when we want to compute the a-coefficients. The rule is as follows:

1. Get the transpose position of the corresponding N-value.

2. Add one to the row index.

If we compute the derivatives in succeeding order starting at 0, then $1, 2, .., j-1, j$, and we observe that when we compute the j'th derivative, we only need the a-coefficient values, which we found in the computation of the $j-1$'th derivatives (and the knot differences of course). This means that we only have to remember the a-coefficient from the previous iteration. Using a cyclic memory buffer makes it possible to implement a very efficient way of computing the a-coefficients.

Looking closely at (24.29), we see that some of the terms involved in the summation could potentially have a zero N-value. In an implementation, we could take advantage of this knowledge as follows: first we split the summation into three parts, each part corresponding to the three different ways of computing the a-coefficients (equations (24.30b)–(24.30d)). That is, we are going to use the following index values for the N-values:

$$i - k + 1 + r \text{ for } a_{j,0} \tag{24.45a}$$

$$i - k + 1 + r + 1 \text{ to } i - k + 1 + r + j - 1 \text{ for } a_{j,1} \text{ to } a_{j,j-1} \tag{24.45b}$$

$$i - k + 1 + r + j \text{ for } a_{j,j}. \tag{24.45c}$$

Now, since all these N-values are of order $k - j$ we know that there are at most $k - j$ nonzero N-values and we also know that their index range is

$$i - k + j + 1 \text{ to } i. \tag{24.46}$$

In other words, if

$$i - k + 1 + r \geq i - k + j + 1, \tag{24.47a}$$

$$\Downarrow$$

$$r \geq j, \tag{24.47b}$$

then the $a_{j,0}$ term have a nonzero N-value and should therefore be included in the summation. Similarly, we see that if

$$i - k + 1 + r + j \leq i, \tag{24.48a}$$

$$\Downarrow$$

$$r \leq k - 1 - j. \tag{24.48b}$$

Then the $a_{j,j}$ term should be included as well. The $a_{j,p}$ terms (for $p = 1$ to $j-1$) are handled a little differently. In this case, we want to derive the range of p-values, $p_{min}, \ldots, p_{max}$, which results in nonzero values. First, we look for a lower limit. If

$$i - k + 1 + r + 1 \geq i - k + j + 1, \tag{24.49a}$$

$$\Downarrow$$

$$r + 1 \geq j, \tag{24.49b}$$

then p_{min} should be set to 1. If not, we have to solve for p_{min}, such that we find the lowest value of p_{min} where:

$$i - k + 1 + r + p_{min} \geq i - k + j + 1, \tag{24.50a}$$

$$\Downarrow$$

$$p_{min} \geq j - r, \tag{24.50b}$$

$$\Downarrow$$

$$p_{min} = j - r. \tag{24.50c}$$

In a similar way we find p_{max}. If

$$i - k + 1 + r + j - 1 \leq i, \tag{24.51a}$$

$$\Downarrow$$

$$r \leq k - j, \tag{24.51b}$$

then $p_{max} = j - 1$. If not, then we need the biggest value of p_{max}, such that

$$i - k + 1 + r + p_{max} \leq i, \tag{24.52}$$

which is $p_{max} = k - 1 - r$.

This concludes our walk-through of implementation details, and we can now show the pseudocode of the entire algorithm. In Figure 24.2 pseudocode is shown for initializing the M-table; this initialization is used by the algorithm for computing the derivatives shown in Figure 24.3.

24.2 The B-Spline

Having taken care of the basis functions, we are now ready for the actual B-spline.

Definition 24.2

A nonperiodic, nonuniform, k-order B-spline *is defined by*

$$\boldsymbol{C}(u) = \sum_{i=0}^{n} N_{i,k}\boldsymbol{P}_i \tag{24.53}$$

```
algorithm initializeM(i,u,K,T)
  left = array(K+1)
  right = array(K+1)
  M = array(K,K)
  left[0]  = u - T[i+1]
  right[0] = T[i] - u

  left[1]  = u - T[i]
  right[1] = T[i+1] - u
  M[0][0] = 1

  For k = 2 to K do
    left[k] = u - T[i+1-k]
    right[k] = T[i+k] - u

    saved = 0

    For r=0 to k-2
      M[k-1][r] = (right[r+1]+left[k-r-1])
      tmp = M[r][k-2]/M[k-1][r]

      M[r][k-1] = saved + right[r+1]*tmp
      saved = left[k-r-1]*tmp;
    Next r
    M[k-1][k-1] = saved
  Next k
  return M
end algorithm
```

Figure 24.2: Initialization of M-table.

where

$$a \leq u \leq b \tag{24.54}$$

The $n+1$ *points* $\{\boldsymbol{P}_i | i = 0, \ldots, n\}$ *are called the* control points *and the functions* $\{N_{i,k} | i = 0, \ldots, n\}$ *are the* k*'th order normalized basis functions, which were treated in the previous sections.*

These are defined on a knot vector T, such that

$$T = [\underbrace{a, \ldots, a}_{k}, t_k, \ldots, t_n, \underbrace{b, \ldots, b}_{k}]^T. \tag{24.55}$$

Notice that the knot vector has a total of $n + k + 1$ elements and the first k-elements all have the same value and the last k elements also have the same value. Succeeding values in the knot vector should be nondecreasing.

```
algorithm derivatives(i,u,K,T,J)
  D =  array(J+1,K)  // D[j][r] = j'th derivative of N_{i-k+1+r,k}
  a = array(2,K)
  M = initializeM(i,u,K,T)

  For r=0 to K-1
    D[0][r] = M[r][K-1]
  Next r

  For r=0 to K-1
    s1 = 0, s2 = 1, a[0][0] = 1
    For j=1 to J
      djN = 0
      If r >= j then
        a[s2][0] = a[s1][0]/M[K-j][r-j]
        djN +=  a[s2][0] * M[r-j][K-j-1]
      End if
      If r + 1 >= j then pMin = 1
      Else pMin = j-r End if
      If r <= K -j  then pMax = j - 1
      Else pMax = K - 1 -r End if
      For p=pMin to pMax
        a[s2][p]=(a[s1][p]-a[s1][p-1])/M[K-j][r+p-j]
        djN+=a[s2][p]*M[r+p-j][K-j-1]
      Next p
      If r <= (K-1-j) then
        a[s2][j] = -a[s1][K-1]/M[K-j][r]
        djN +=  a[s2][j] * M[r][K-j-1]
      End if
      D[j][r] = djN
      swap(s1,s2)
    Next j
  Next r

  factor = K-1;
  For j=1 to J
    For r=0 to K-1
      D[j][r] = factor * D[j][r]
    Next r
    factor = factor * (K-1-j)
  next J
  return D
end algorithm
```

Figure 24.3: Pseudocode for computing derivatives of the B-spline basis functions.

```
algorithm curvePoint(u,K,T,P)
  i = knot index, such that t_i ≤ u < t_{i+1}
  N = BasisFuncs(i,u,K,T)
  C = 0
  For r=0 to K-1
    C = C + N[r]*P[i-K+1+r]
  Next r
  return C
end algorithm
```

Figure 24.4: Pseudocode for computing a point on a B-spline.

To obtain the derivative of a B-spline, we differentiate (24.53) with respect to u. By the product rule we get

$$\boldsymbol{C}'(u) = \sum_{i=0}^{n} N'_{i,k}\boldsymbol{P}_i + N_{i,k}\boldsymbol{P}'_i. \tag{24.56}$$

Since $\{\boldsymbol{P}_i\}$ are all constants and independent of u, this reduces to

$$\boldsymbol{C}'(u) = \sum_{i=0}^{n} N'_{i,k}\boldsymbol{P}_i. \tag{24.57}$$

From this, it is easily seen that

$$\boldsymbol{C}^{(j)}(u) = \sum_{i=0}^{n} N^{(j)}(i,k)\boldsymbol{P}_i. \tag{24.58}$$

Recalling our very first algorithm for computing the basis functions discussed in Section 24.1.1, we can easily derive an algorithm for computing a single point on a B-spline. This is shown in Figure 24.4. From (24.58) it is not hard to see how we can put our previous algorithm for computing the derivatives of the basis functions (see Section 24.1.3) to practical use. This is shown in Figure 24.5.

24.3 Global Interpolation

In this section, we will look at the inverse problem of computing points on a B-spline. Instead, we will try to compute the B-spline passing through a set of points on it. The approach we will take is called *global interpolation*. We call the initial given set of points for *break points* or *data points* and introduce the notation $\{\boldsymbol{X}_i\}$ for them. The indices have the meaning that if $j < i$, then we should encounter $\boldsymbol{X}_j$ before $\boldsymbol{X}_i$ if we walk along the resulting spline as the parameter u increases.

With the introduced formalism, we can state our task at hand quite simply: given a set of break points and a knot vector, we need to find the control points $\{\boldsymbol{P}_i\}$ of the nonuniform B-spline, which passes through all the break points. Assume that we have a knot vector consisting of the following knot values

$$t_0, t_1, t_2, \ldots, t_{k-1}, t_k, \ldots, t_n, t_{n+1}, t_{n+2}, \ldots, t_{n+k}, \tag{24.59}$$

```
algorithm curveDerivatives(u,K,T,P,J)
  i = knot index, such that t_i ≤ u < t_{i+1}
  J = Min(J,K-1)
  dC = array(J+1)
  dN = derivatives(i,u,K,T,J)
  For j=0 to J
    dC[j] = 0
    For r=0 to K-1
      dC[j] = dC[j] + N[j][r]*P[i-K+1+r]
    Next r
  Next j
  return dC
end algorithm
```

Figure 24.5: Pseudocode for computing the derivative of a B-spline.

where

$$t_0 = \cdots . = t_{k-1}, \tag{24.60}$$

and

$$t_{n+1} = \cdots = t_{n+k}. \tag{24.61}$$

Given such a knot vector, we know that

$$C(t_{k-1}) = P_0, \tag{24.62a}$$
$$C(t_{n+1}) = P_n. \tag{24.62b}$$

Each (unique) knot value will correspond to a single break point. From this we see that we must have a total of $n - k + 3$ break points:

$$X_0, X_1, X_2, \ldots, X_{n-k+1}, X_{n-k+2}. \tag{24.63}$$

For each of these break points we will require that

$$C(t_{i+k-1}) = X_i \qquad \text{for} \qquad 0 \le i \le n - k + 2. \tag{24.64}$$

That is, we have a total of $n - k + 3$ equations, but we have $n + 1$ unknowns, and a spline with $n + k + 1$ knot values must have $n + 1$ control points. In short, we might need a few more equations in order to solve our problem. Typically $k = 4$; this results in a fairly inexpensive spline computation with acceptable flexibility. When $k = 4$ two more equations are needed to solve for the control points. We could simply pick

$$P_0 = P_1, \qquad \text{and} \qquad P_n = P_{n-1}. \tag{24.65}$$

as the two extra equations. Now we can solve the system of linear equations given by (24.64). This strategy could be applied for an arbitrary value of k. However, we choose to work with $k = 4$; the reader

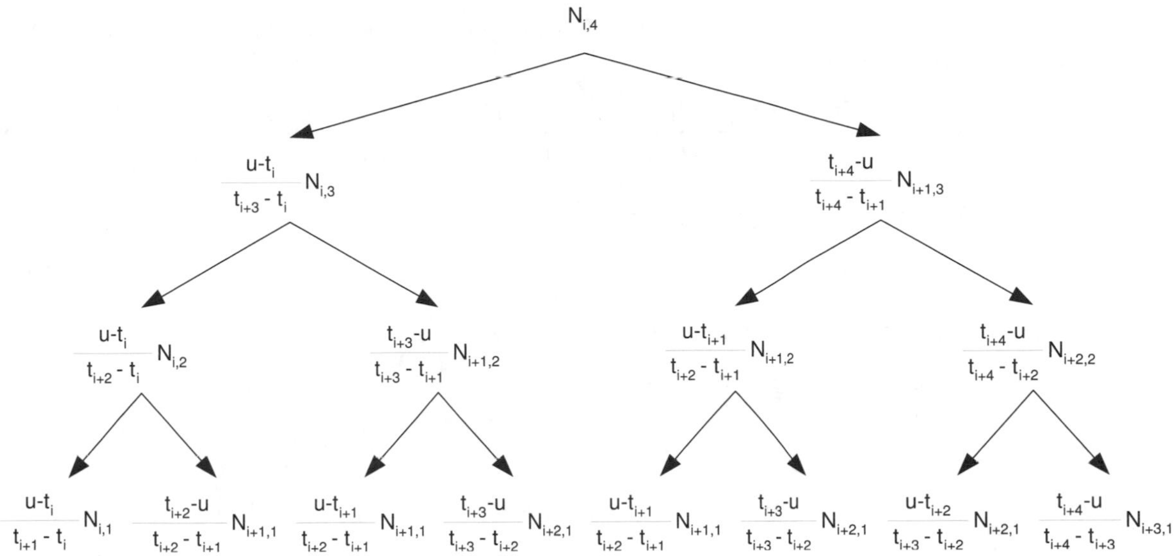

Figure 24.6: The computation of the basis function.

should be able to generalize from our derivations. Let us set the value of k to 4 and see if we can derive an efficient way of solving (24.41). We start out by writing up $\boldsymbol{C}(t_{i+3})$ as

$$\boldsymbol{C}(t_{i+3}) = \sum_{i=0}^{n} \boldsymbol{P}_i N_{i,4}. \tag{24.66}$$

Only $k = 4$ of the basis functions are potentially nonzero, since they have a support that overlaps with t_{i+3}. That is,

$$\boldsymbol{C}(t_{i+3}) = \sum_{i=0}^{n} \boldsymbol{P}_i N_{i,4} = \boldsymbol{P}_i N_{i,4} + \boldsymbol{P}_{i+1} N_{i+1,4} + \boldsymbol{P}_{i+2} N_{i+2,4} + \boldsymbol{P}_{i+3} N_{i+3,4}. \tag{24.67}$$

Now let us examine each of the 4 N-terms. We start by looking at $N_{i,4}$. By our definition of a basis function (see (24.1)) we can construct the tree shown in Figure 24.6, which shows how $N_{i,4}$ is computed. Since we know that $N_{i,4}$ should be evaluated at t_{i+3}, we can easily write up an explicit expression for $N_{i,4}$. From the tree in Figure 24.6 we see that it would be the terms along the path from the rightmost leaf up to the root of the tree, because $N_{i+3,1} = 1$ is the only nonzero leaf of the tree.

$$N_{i,4} = \left(\frac{t_{i+4} - t_{i+3}}{t_{i+4} - t_{i+1}}\right) \left(\frac{t_{i+4} - t_{i+3}}{t_{i+4} - t_{i+2}}\right) \left(\frac{(t_{i+4} - t_{i+3})}{(t_{i+4} - t_{i+3})} N_{i+3,1}\right) \tag{24.68a}$$

$$= \frac{(t_{i+4} - t_{i+3})^2}{(t_{i+4} - t_{i+1})(t_{i+4} - t_{i+2})}. \tag{24.68b}$$

If we draw similar trees for $N_{i+1,4}, N_{i+2,4}$, and $N_{i+3,4}$ and evaluate them at t_{i+3}, we can derive the remaining expressions we need,

$$N_{i+1,4} = \frac{(t_{i+5} - t_{i+3})(t_{i+3} - t_{i+2})}{(t_{i+5} - t_{i+2})(t_{i+4} - t_{i+2})} + \frac{(t_{i+3} - t_{i+1})(t_{i+4} - t_{i+3})}{(t_{i+4} - t_{i+1})(t_{i+4} - t_{i+2})}, \tag{24.69a}$$

$$N_{i+2,4} = \frac{(t_{i+3} - t_{i+2})^2}{(t_{i+5} - t_{i+2})(t_{i+4} - t_{i+2})}, \tag{24.69b}$$

$$N_{i+3,4} = 0. \tag{24.69c}$$

Now let us write up all the equations that determine the break points.

$$\begin{array}{llll} i = 0 & : \ \boldsymbol{C}(t_3) & = \boldsymbol{P}_1 & = \boldsymbol{X}_0, \\ i = 1 & : \ \boldsymbol{C}(t_4) & = \alpha_1 \boldsymbol{P}_1 + \beta_1 \boldsymbol{P}_2 + \gamma_1 \boldsymbol{P}_3 & = \boldsymbol{X}_1, \\ \vdots & & & \\ i = i & : \ \boldsymbol{C}(t_{i+3}) & = \alpha_i \boldsymbol{P}_i + \beta_i \boldsymbol{P}_{i+1} + \gamma_i \boldsymbol{P}_{i+2} & = \boldsymbol{X}_i, \\ \vdots & & & \\ i = n-2 & : \ \boldsymbol{C}(t_{n+1}) & = \boldsymbol{P}_{n-1} & = \boldsymbol{X}_{n-2}, \end{array} \tag{24.70}$$

where

$$\alpha_i = \frac{(t_{i+4} - t_{i+3})^2}{(t_{i+4} - t_{i+1})(t_{i+4} - t_{i+2})}, \tag{24.71a}$$

$$\beta_i = \frac{(t_{i+5} - t_{i+3})(t_{i+3} - t_{i+2})}{(t_{i+5} - t_{i+2})(t_{i+4} - t_{i+2})} + \frac{(t_{i+3} - t_{i+1})(t_{i+4} - t_{i+3})}{(t_{i+4} - t_{i+1})(t_{i+4} - t_{i+2})}, \tag{24.71b}$$

$$\gamma_i = \frac{(t_{i+3} - t_{i+2})^2}{(t_{i+5} - t_{i+2})(t_{i+4} - t_{i+2})}. \tag{24.71c}$$

All these $n - 1$ equations can be expressed in matrix form, as shown here:

$$\begin{bmatrix} 1 & & & & & & \\ \alpha_1 & \beta_1 & \gamma_1 & & & & \\ & & & \cdots & & & \\ & & & \cdots & \alpha_{n-3} & \beta_{n-3} & \gamma_{n-3} \\ & & & & & & 1 \end{bmatrix} \begin{bmatrix} \boldsymbol{P}_1 \\ \\ \\ \\ \boldsymbol{P}_{n-1} \end{bmatrix} = \begin{bmatrix} \boldsymbol{X}_0 \\ \\ \\ \\ \boldsymbol{X}_{n-2} \end{bmatrix}. \tag{24.72}$$

Looking at this matrix equation, we observe that it has a particularly appealing shape. Such shape is called tridiagonal, and it is particularly easy to solve a system of tridiagonal linear equations [Press et al., 1999b] and by doing so we can compute all the control points.

However, we have omitted a small detail: how should the knot vector be constructed if we are only given the break points? A good approach to this problem is to use a heuristic, which is known as the chord length heuristic (see [Watt et al., 1992]). We will require that the following condition is always fulfilled:

$$\frac{t_{i+4} - t_{i+3}}{t_{i+5} - t_{i+4}} = \frac{\|\boldsymbol{X}_{i+1} - \boldsymbol{X}_i\|}{\|\boldsymbol{X}_{i+2} - \boldsymbol{X}_{i+1}\|}. \tag{24.73}$$

24.4 Cubic Curve Decomposition

B-splines are attractive due to two properties. They have *local support* and they guarantee *continuity* across adjacent curve segments. These properties are not mutually present when having a composition of Bezier curve segments. Changing a control point on one curve segment means that one has to change the control points on all other curve segments to ensure continuity. However, a *Bezier curve composition* is far better to work with for rendering and evaluation. In our opinion it pays off in terms of performance to convert a B-spline to a composition of Bezier curve segments when one is finished with modeling the final shape of the spline.

Nonuniform B-splines are easily converted into a composition of corresponding Bezier curve segments [Hoschek et al., 1993] by performing an operation on them, which is called knot insertion. We have devoted this section to treat all the details about how one takes a nonuniform B-spline and ends up with a composition of cubic Bezier curve segments.

24.4.1 The Cubic Bezier Curve and the B-Spline Connection

The best way to see how a cubic nonuniform B-spline corresponds to a cubic Bezier curve is by direct computation. Assume that we have the nonuniform B-spline

$$\boldsymbol{C}(u) = \sum_{i=0}^{3} \boldsymbol{P}_i N_{i,4}, \tag{24.74}$$

defined on the knot vector

$$T = \left[0, 0, 0, 0, 1, 1, 1, 1\right]^T. \tag{24.75}$$

We say that such a knot vector has no internal knots and that the *multiplicity* of all its knots is $k = 4$. We immediately see that only four basis functions are involved. These are:

$$N_{0,4}, N_{1,4}, N_{2,4}, N_{3,4}. \tag{24.76}$$

Looking at Figure 24.6 it is fairly easy to evaluate these four basis functions. We can see that only those paths with leaves where the numerator $t_{j+1} - t_j$ are nonzero contributes to the value of the N-function. By direct substitution, we derive:

$$N_{0,4} = (1-u)^3, \tag{24.77a}$$
$$N_{1,4} = 3u\,(1-u)^2, \tag{24.77b}$$
$$N_{2,4} = 3u^2\,(1-u), \tag{24.77c}$$
$$N_{3,4} = u^3. \tag{24.77d}$$

Expansion of terms yield:

$$N_{0,4} = -u^3 + 3u^2 - 3u + 1, \tag{24.78a}$$
$$N_{1,4} = 3u^3 - 6u^2 + 3u, \tag{24.78b}$$
$$N_{2,4} = -3u^3 + 3u^2, \tag{24.78c}$$
$$N_{3,4} = u^3. \tag{24.78d}$$

Plugging our results into the original summation for the B-spline and using matrix notation we derive

$$\boldsymbol{C}(u) = \left[u^3, u^2, u, 1\right] \begin{bmatrix} -1 & 3 & -3 & 1 \\ 3 & -6 & 3 & 0 \\ -3 & 3 & 0 & 0 \\ 1 & 0 & 0 & 0 \end{bmatrix} \begin{bmatrix} \boldsymbol{P}_0 \\ \boldsymbol{P}_1 \\ \boldsymbol{P}_2 \\ \boldsymbol{P}_3 \end{bmatrix}. \tag{24.79}$$

But this is actually the matrix definition of a cubic Bezier curve. There is no doubt by now that there definitely is a connection between the spline and Bezier curve representations. However, there is a small complication: not all nonuniform B-splines have the particularly nice looking knot vector as we used to show the connection with Bezier curves. What should we do about a general looking B-spline? For now, we assume that every knot value in the general B-spline has multiplicity k (in the next section we will start on attacking the problem of twisting the spline into this form). The general cubic nonuniform B-spline can then be seen as a sequence of separate nonuniform B-splines, because at each unique knot value the first $k-1$ derivative vanishes (see Section 24.6.1). Each sequence of this special looking spline looks almost like the one we used in our derivation above. The only difference is that the knot values are not zeroes and ones. Instead, the knot vector looks like this:

$$T = \left[t_i, t_i, t_i, t_i, t_{i+1}, t_{i+1}, t_{i+1}, t_{i+1}\right]^T. \tag{24.80}$$

The indices are the ones from the original spline with multiplicity 1. We can easily get the zeroes by subtracting the left knot value from all the knot values. This is perfectly legal because we are looking at a local segment of the spline. We end up with a knot vector like the following:

$$T = \left[0, 0, 0, 0, s, s, s, s\right]^T, \tag{24.81}$$

where

$$s = t_{i+1} - t_i. \tag{24.82}$$

This knot vector almost looks like the one we want except for the s-value, which is not necessarily 1. If we repeat the above computation, we will derive at a cubic Bezier curve with similar parameter scaled by s. We can conclude that we still have the connection between cubic Bezier curves and nonuniform B-splines.

Let us try to get rid of this scaling problem. We introduce the terminology of global and local parameters. The *global parameter* is denoted by U and it is the parameter that was used to define the original nonuniform B-spline with (see (24.1)). We now use u for the *local parameter* of the i'th curve segment $\boldsymbol{B}(u)$ of the original spline. We want

$$\boldsymbol{B}(u) = \boldsymbol{C}(U). \tag{24.83}$$

If we compute u as follows:

$$u = f(U), \tag{24.84}$$

where

$$f(U) = \frac{U - t_i}{t_{i+1} - t_i}, \tag{24.85}$$

then our property is fulfilled. Another nice property is that u runs from 0 to 1.

24.4.2 Global and Local Parameter Conversion of Derivatives

Given a local Bezier segment $\boldsymbol{B}_i(u)$ of $\boldsymbol{C}(U)$ where we know that

$$\boldsymbol{C}(U) = \boldsymbol{B}_i(u). \tag{24.86}$$

We want to derive a conversion rule for the derivatives of the curve segments.

By straightforward differentiation we get

$$\frac{d}{dU}\boldsymbol{C}(U) = \frac{d}{dU}\boldsymbol{B}_i(f(U)) = \boldsymbol{B}_i'(f(U))f'(U), \tag{24.87}$$

where

$$f'(U) = \frac{1}{t_{i+1} - t_i}. \tag{24.88}$$

Putting it together we get the conversion rule for the first-order derivative we we're looking for.

$$\boldsymbol{C}'(U) = \frac{1}{t_{i+1} - t_i}\boldsymbol{B}_i'(f(U)) = \frac{1}{t_{i+1} - t_i}\boldsymbol{B}_i'(u). \tag{24.89}$$

If we continue our differentiation, we get

$$\frac{d^2}{dU^2}\boldsymbol{C}(U) = \frac{d}{dU}\boldsymbol{B}_i'(f(U))f'(U) = \boldsymbol{B}_i''(f(U))f'(U)^2 + \boldsymbol{B}_i'(f(U))f''(U), \tag{24.90}$$

and we can easily compute

$$f''(U) = \frac{d}{dU}\left(\frac{1}{t_{i+1} - t_i}\right) = 0. \tag{24.91}$$

Substituting back into our computation, we get the conversion rule we were looking for.

$$\boldsymbol{C}''(U) = \left(\frac{1}{t_{i+1} - t_i}\right)^2 \boldsymbol{B}_i''(f(U)) = \left(\frac{1}{t_{i+1} - t_i}\right)^2 \boldsymbol{B}_i''(u). \tag{24.92}$$

By now the pattern should be obvious and we can conclude

$$\boldsymbol{C}^{(j)}(U) = \left(\frac{1}{t_{i+1} - t_i}\right)^j \boldsymbol{B}_i^{(j)}(f(U)) = \left(\frac{1}{t_{i+1} - t_i}\right)^j \boldsymbol{B}_i^{(j)}(u). \tag{24.93}$$

24.4.3 Knot Insertion

We are now ready to tackle the task of *knot insertion*. Even though the resulting algorithm is quite simple and resembles the de Boor algorithm discussed in Section 24.7, we will need a number of preliminary definitions and theorems.

Definition 24.3 (Divided Differences)
Assume we have a function $g(t)$ and a knot vector

$$T = \left[\ldots, t_i, t_{i+1}, \ldots, t_{i+k}, \ldots^T\right], \tag{24.94}$$

where

$$\forall i : \; t_i \leq t_{i+1} < t_{i+k}. \tag{24.95}$$

We define the divided difference on g recursively[1] *in the following manner. The zero'th divided difference is given by*

$$\Delta_i g = g(t_i), \tag{24.96}$$

and for $k = 1$

$$\Delta_{i,i+1} g = \frac{\Delta_{i+1} g(t_i + 1) - \Delta_i g(t_i)}{t_{i+1} - t_i}. \tag{24.97}$$

The general k'th divided difference[2] *is defined by*

$$\Delta_{i,\ldots,i+k} g = \frac{\Delta_{i,\ldots,t_{r-1},t_{r+1},\ldots,i+k} g - \Delta_{i,\ldots,t_{s-1},t_{s+1},\ldots,i+k} g}{t_s - t_r}. \tag{24.98}$$

An important property of the divided difference, which we are going to use, is that it is symmetric. This is easily shown. It follows trivially in the case of $k = 0$. Using operator notation and assuming the $k-1$'th divided difference is symmetric for all $k > 2$, we notice that

$$\Delta_{i,\ldots,v,\ldots,w,\ldots,i+k} = \frac{\Delta_{i+1,\ldots,v,\ldots,w,\ldots,i+k} - \Delta_{i,\ldots,v,\ldots,w,\ldots,i+k-1}}{t_{i+k} - t_i} \tag{24.99a}$$

$$= \frac{\Delta_{i+1,\ldots,w,\ldots,v,\ldots,i+k} - \Delta_{i,\ldots,w,\ldots,v,\ldots,i+k-1}}{t_{i+k} - t_i} \tag{24.99b}$$

$$= \Delta_{i,\ldots,w,\ldots,v,\ldots,i+k}. \tag{24.99c}$$

This clearly shows that the divided difference is symmetric.

Theorem 24.3 (Leibniz' Formula)
If we have $f(t) = g(t)h(t)$ then Leibniz' formula states

$$\Delta_{i,\ldots,i+k} f = \sum_{r=i}^{i+k} \Delta_{i,\ldots,r} g \Delta_{r,\ldots,i+k} h. \tag{24.100}$$

[1] There are other ways to define the divided difference (see [Boor, 1978]).

[2] We have ignored the case $t_i = \cdots = t_{i+k}$ (see [Boor, 1978] for details).

The proof requires another definition of the divided difference The interested reader should refer to [Boor, 1978] for a proof.

Lemma 24.4 (Divided Difference Relation)
Given divided differences $\Delta_{i,\ldots,i+k}$, $\Delta_{i,\ldots,i+k-1,j}$, and $\Delta_{j,i+1,\ldots,i+k}$ the following holds:

$$0 = (t_i - t_{i+k})\Delta_{i,\ldots,i+k} + (t_j - t_i)\Delta_{i,\ldots,i+k-1,j} + (t_{i+k} - t_j)\Delta_{j,i+1,\ldots,i+k}. \tag{24.101}$$

Proof of Lemma 24.4:
For now, we will try to show that this funny equation is in fact true. We'll start out by using the definition of the divided differences on the funny (24.101):

$$\begin{aligned} 0 = (t_i - t_{i+k})\Delta_{i,\ldots,i+k} + (t_j - t_i)\frac{\Delta_{i+1,\ldots,i+k-1,j} - \Delta_{i,\ldots,i+k-1}}{t_j - t_i} \\ + (t_{i+k} - t_j)\frac{\Delta_{i+1,\ldots,i+k} - \Delta_{j,i+1,\ldots,i+k-1}}{t_{i+k} - t_j}. \end{aligned} \tag{24.102}$$

Cleaning up gives us

$$0 = \Delta_{i,\ldots,i+k} + \frac{\Delta_{i+1,\ldots,i+k-1,j} - \Delta_{j,i+1,\ldots,i+k-1}}{t_i - t_{i+k}} - \frac{\Delta_{i+1,\ldots,i+k} - \Delta_{i,\ldots,i+k-1}}{t_{i+k} - t_i}. \tag{24.103}$$

By symmetry of the divided difference we have:

$$\Delta_{i+1,\ldots,i+k-1,j} = \Delta_{j,i+1,\ldots,i+k-1} \tag{24.104}$$

so our second term vanishes from our equation. Now looking at the third term we recognize the definition of the divided difference, that is,

$$\Delta_{i,\ldots,i+k} = \frac{\Delta_{i+1,\ldots,i+k} \quad \Delta_{i,\ldots,i+k-1}}{t_{i+k} - t_i}. \tag{24.105}$$

So the first and third terms cancel each other out, and we immediately see that (24.101) is true. □

Definition 24.4 (The Ordinary B-Spline Basis Function)
The unnormalized k'th order B-spline basis function $M_{i,k}$, also called the ordinary B-spline basis function, *is defined recursively. This is very similar to* (24.1). *We have, for $k > 1$:*

$$M_{i,k} = \frac{u - t_i}{t_{i+k} - t_i} M_{i,k-1} + \frac{t_{i+k} - u}{t_{i+k} - t_i} M_{i+1,k-1}, \tag{24.106}$$

and for $k = 1$:

$$M_{i,1} = \begin{cases} \frac{1}{t_{i+1} - t_i} & \text{if } t_i \le u < t_{i+1}, \\ 0 & \text{otherwise.} \end{cases} \tag{24.107}$$

The ordinary B-spline basis function can be turned into the normalized B-spline basis function using:

Theorem 24.5 (Relation between Ordinary and Normalized B-Spline Bases)
An ordinary B-Spline basis M may be converted into a normalized B-spline N using

$$N_{i,k} = (t_{i+k} - t_i)M_{i,k}. \tag{24.108}$$

This is all easily verified by straightforward computation and comparison with the definition of the normalized B-spline basis function (see (24.1)).

We will now show how to obtain an Ordinary B-spline using divided differences.

Theorem 24.6 (Ordinary B-Spline from Divided Differences)
Given a known function[3] g,

$$g(t) = \begin{cases} 0 & \text{if } t \leq u, \\ (t-u)^{k-1} & \text{if } t > u, \end{cases} \tag{24.109}$$

then the k'th divided difference corresponds to the ordinary k'th order B-spline basis function as

$$M_{i,k} = \Delta_{i,\ldots,i+k}\left((t-u)^{k-1}\right)_{>u}. \tag{24.110}$$

We have adopted the notation $\left((t-u)^{k-1}\right)_{>u}$ to mean $(t-u)^{k-1}$ if $t > u$ and 0 otherwise. We will now show this by induction[4] on k.

Proof of Theorem 24.6:
First we observe that for $k = 1$ we have

$$M_{i,1} = \Delta_{i,i+1}\left((t-u)^0\right)_{>u} \tag{24.111a}$$

$$= \frac{\Delta_{i+1}\left((t-u)^0\right)_{>u} - \Delta_i\left((t-u)^0\right)_{>u}}{t_{i+1} - t_i} \tag{24.111b}$$

$$= \frac{\left((t_{i+1}-u)^0\right)_{>u} - \left((t_i-u)^0\right)_{>u}}{t_{i+1} - t_i}, \tag{24.111c}$$

Now if $u < t_i$ then

$$M_{i,1} = \frac{(t_{i+1}-u)^0 - (t_i-u)^0}{t_{i+1} - t_i} = \frac{1-1}{t_{i+1} - t_i} = 0. \tag{24.112}$$

If $t_i \leq u < t_{i+1}$ then

$$M_{i,1} = \frac{(t_{i+1}-u)^0 - 0}{t_{i+1} - t_i} = \frac{1-0}{t_{i+1} - t_i} = \frac{1}{t_{i+1} - t_i}. \tag{24.113}$$

And finally, if $u \geq t_{i+1}$ then

$$M_{i,1} = \frac{0-0}{t_{i+1} - t_i} = 0. \tag{24.114}$$

---

[3] Notice we have defined g differently than in [Boor, 1978, Boehm, 1980].

[4] Note that if we use the definition of g in [Boor, 1978, Boehm, 1980], then the base case will always fail.

So we can conclude that (24.110) is true when $k = 1$. Now let us assume that (24.110) is true for $k = k-1$ and examine

$$\left((t-u)^{k-1}\right)_{>u} = (t-u)\left((t-u)^{k-2}\right)_{>u}. \tag{24.115}$$

We can think of this as the product of two functions, so let's try to use Leibniz' formula (24.100) on it.

$$\begin{aligned}\Delta_{i,\ldots,i+k}\left((t-u)^{k-1}\right)_{>u} &= \Delta_i(t-u)\Delta_{i,\ldots,i+k}\left((t-u)^{k-2}\right)_{>u} \\ &+ \Delta_{i,i+1}(t-u)\Delta_{i+1,\ldots,i+k}\left((t-u)^{k-2}\right)_{>u} \\ &+ \Delta_{i,\ldots,i+2}(t-u)\Delta_{i+2,\ldots,i+k}\left((t-u)^{k-2}\right)_{>u} \\ &\ldots \\ &+ \Delta_{i,\ldots,i+k}(t-u)\Delta_{i+k}\left((t-u)^{k-2}\right)_{>u}.\end{aligned} \tag{24.116}$$

Now, by straightforward computation we have

$$\Delta_i(t-u) = (t_i - u) \tag{24.117a}$$

$$\Downarrow$$

$$\Delta_{i,i+1}(t-u) = \frac{(t_{i+1}-u)-(t_i-u)}{t_{i+1}-t_i} = 1 \tag{24.117b}$$

$$\Downarrow$$

$$\Delta_{i,\ldots,i+2}(t-u) = \frac{\Delta_{i+1,i+2}(t-u)-\Delta_{i,i+1}(t-u)}{t_{i+2}-t_i} = \frac{1-1}{t_{i+2}-l_i} = 0 \tag{24.117c}$$

$$\Downarrow$$

$$\vdots$$

$$\Downarrow$$

$$\Delta_{i,\ldots,i+k}(t-u) = 0. \tag{24.117d}$$

Using these results (24.116) reduces to

$$\Delta_{i,\ldots,i+k}\left((t-u)^{k-1}\right)_{>u} = (t_i-u)\Delta_{i,\ldots,i+k}\left((t-u)^{k-2}\right)_{>u} + \Delta_{i+1,\ldots,i+k}\left((t-u)^{k-2}\right)_{>u}. \tag{24.118}$$

By the definition of the k'th divided difference we have

$$\Delta_{i,\ldots,i+k} = \frac{\Delta_{i+1,\ldots,i+k} - \Delta_{i,\ldots,i+k-1}}{t_{i+k}-t_i}. \tag{24.119}$$

Multiplying by $(t_i - u)$ gives

$$(t_i-u)\Delta_{i,\ldots,i+k} = \frac{(t_i-u)}{(t_{i+k}-t_i)}\left(\Delta_{i+1,\ldots,i+k} - \Delta_{i,\ldots,i+k-1}\right). \tag{24.120}$$

Substituting this into (24.118) yields

$$\Delta_{i,\ldots,i+k}\left((t-u)^{k-1}\right)_{>u} = \frac{(t_i-u)}{(t_{i+k}-t_i)}\left(\Delta_{i+1,\ldots,i+k}\left((t-u)^{k-2}\right)_{>u} - \Delta_{i,\ldots,i+k-1}\left((t-u)^{k-2}\right)_{>u}\right) + \Delta_{i+1,\ldots,i+k}\left((t-u)^{k-2}\right)_{>u}. \tag{24.121}$$

Now, by induction, this means that we have

$$M_{i,k} = \frac{(t_i-u)}{(t_{i+k}-t_i)}\left(M_{i+1,k-1} - M_{i,k-1}\right) + M_{i+1,k-1}. \tag{24.122}$$

Rearranging the terms, this equation can be rewritten to

$$M_{i,k} = \frac{u-t_i}{t_{i+k}-t_i}M_{1,k-1} + \frac{t_{i+k}-u}{t_{i+k}-t_i}M_{i+1,k-1}. \tag{24.123}$$

But this is the definition of $M_{i,k}$, which means that we have proven the correspondence of $M_{i,k}$ and the k'th divided difference. □

Finally, we are ready to make the *knot insertion algorithm*. Imagine that we insert a new knot value, t^*, into the knot vector, T, where

$$t_r \leq t^* < t_{r+1}. \tag{24.124}$$

Then we get a new knot vector

$$\hat{T} = \left[\ldots, t_r, t^*, t_{r+1}, \ldots, t_{r+k}, \ldots\right]^T. \tag{24.125}$$

Observe that

$$\hat{t}_i = \begin{cases} t_i & \text{if } i \leq r, \\ t^* & \text{if } i = r+1, \\ t_{i-1} & \text{if } i > r+1. \end{cases} \tag{24.126}$$

Given a nonuniform B-spline, $\boldsymbol{C}(u)$, defined on T, we want to find a new nonuniform B-spline, $\hat{\boldsymbol{C}}(u)$, defined on $\hat{T}$, such that

$$\boldsymbol{C}(u) = \hat{\boldsymbol{C}}(u) \tag{24.127}$$

for all values of u. If we look at the definition of the nonuniform B-spline, this means that we have to find all $\hat{\boldsymbol{P}}_i$s such that

$$\sum_{i=0}^{n} N_{i,k}\boldsymbol{P}_i = \sum_{i=0}^{n+1} \hat{N}_{i,k}\hat{\boldsymbol{P}}_i, \tag{24.128}$$

where the hat-notation means that the quantity is defined with respect to $\hat{T}$. Recall that $N_{i,k}$ has support on the knot values $t_i, \ldots, t_{i+k}$. This means that t^* only affects the basis functions

$$N_{r-k+1,k}, \ldots, N_{r,k}. \tag{24.129}$$

Since $\boldsymbol{C}(u)$ and $\hat{\boldsymbol{C}}(u)$ should have the same shape we can conclude that

$$\hat{N}_i = \begin{cases} N_i & \text{if } i < r-k+1, \\ N_{i-1} & \text{if } i > r+1, \end{cases} \tag{24.130}$$

from which it follows that we must have

$$\hat{\boldsymbol{P}}_i = \begin{cases} \boldsymbol{P}_i & \text{if } i < r-k+1, \\ \boldsymbol{P}_{i-1} & \text{if } i > r+1. \end{cases} \tag{24.131}$$

This leaves us with the problem of determining the $\hat{\boldsymbol{P}}_i$s such that

$$\sum_{i=r-k+1}^{r} N_{i,k} \boldsymbol{P}_i = \sum_{i=r-k+1}^{r+1} \hat{N}_{i,k} \hat{\boldsymbol{P}}_i. \tag{24.132}$$

To solve this problem we will try to write N in terms of $\hat{N}$. To accomplish this we will turn back to the funny (24.101). Let's set $t_j = t^*$ and rearrange the equation. Then we have

$$(t_{i+k} - t_i)\Delta_{i,\ldots,i+k} = (t^* - t_i)\Delta_{i,\ldots,i+k-1,*} + (t_{i+k} - t^*)\Delta_{*,i+1,\ldots,i+k}. \tag{24.133}$$

Using (24.110) we get, for all values of $i = r-k+1$ to r:

$$(t_{i+k} - t_i)M_{i,k} = (t^* - t_i)\hat{M}_{i,k} + (t_{i+k} - t^*)\hat{M}_{i+1,k}. \tag{24.134}$$

We'll convert the M-terms into N-terms by using (24.108)

$$N_{i,k} = \frac{t^* - t_i}{\hat{t}_{i+k} - \hat{t}_i}\hat{N}_{i,k} + \frac{t_{i+k} - t^*}{\hat{t}_{i+k+1} - \hat{t}_{i+1}}\hat{N}_{i+1,k}. \tag{24.135}$$

Now we want to change notation from old knot values into new knot values. We can do this by observing that for any value of $i = r-k+1$ to r, we have:

$$t_i = \hat{t}_i \quad \text{and} \quad t_{i+k} = \hat{t}_{i+k+1}. \tag{24.136}$$

So we end up with

$$N_{i,k} = \frac{t^* - \hat{t}_i}{\hat{t}_{i+k} - \hat{t}_i}\hat{N}_{i,k} + \frac{\hat{t}_{i+k+1} - t^*}{\hat{t}_{i+k+1} - \hat{t}_{i+1}}\hat{N}_{i+1,k}. \tag{24.137}$$

We use this to rewrite the terms in the summation of $\boldsymbol{C}(u)$, that is,

$$\sum_{i=r-k+1}^{r} N_{i,k}\boldsymbol{P}_i = \sum_{i=r-k+1}^{r} \left(\frac{t^* - \hat{t}_i}{\hat{t}_{i+k} - \hat{t}_i} \hat{N}_{i,k} + \frac{\hat{t}_{i+k+1} - t^*}{\hat{t}_{i+k+1} - \hat{t}_{i+1}} \hat{N}_{i+1,k} \right) \boldsymbol{P}_i. \tag{24.138}$$

Expanding the summation gives

$$\begin{aligned}
\sum_{i=r-k+1}^{r} N_{i,k}\boldsymbol{P}_i = & \left(\frac{t^* - \hat{t}_{r-k+1}}{\hat{t}_{r+1} - \hat{t}_{r-k+1}} \hat{N}_{r-k+1,k} + \frac{\hat{t}_{r+2} - t^*}{\hat{t}_{r+2} - \hat{t}_{r-k+2}} \hat{N}_{r-k+2,k} \right) \boldsymbol{P}_{r-k+1} \\
& + \left(\frac{t^* - \hat{t}_{r-k+2}}{\hat{t}_{r+2} - \hat{t}_{r-k+2}} \hat{N}_{r-k+2,k} + \frac{\hat{t}_{r+3} - t^*}{\hat{t}_{r+3} - \hat{t}_{r-k+3}} \hat{N}_{r-k+3,k} \right) \boldsymbol{P}_{r-k+2} \\
& \vdots \\
& + \left(\frac{t^* - \hat{t}_r}{\hat{t}_{r+k} - \hat{t}_r} \hat{N}_{r,k} + \frac{\hat{t}_{r+k+1} - t^*}{\hat{t}_{r+k+1} - \hat{t}_{r+1}} \hat{N}_{r+1,k} \right) \boldsymbol{P}_r.
\end{aligned} \tag{24.139}$$

With the knowledge that $t^* = \hat{t}_{r+1}$, we immediately see that some of the fractions in the summation become 1. This reduction results in

$$\begin{aligned}
\sum_{i=r-k+1}^{r} N_{i,k}\boldsymbol{P}_i = & \left(\hat{N}_{r-k+1,k} + \frac{\hat{t}_{r+2} - t^*}{\hat{t}_{r+2} - \hat{t}_{r-k+2}} \hat{N}_{r-k+2,k} \right) \boldsymbol{P}_{r-k+1} \\
& + \left(\frac{t^* - \hat{t}_{r-k+2}}{\hat{t}_{r+2} - \hat{t}_{r-k+2}} \hat{N}_{r-k+2,k} + \frac{\hat{t}_{r+3} - t^*}{\hat{t}_{r+3} - \hat{t}_{r-k+3}} \hat{N}_{r-k+3,k} \right) \boldsymbol{P}_{r-k+2} \\
& \vdots \\
& + \left(\frac{t^* - \hat{t}_r}{\hat{t}_{r+k} - \hat{t}_r} \hat{N}_{r,k} + \hat{N}_{r+1,k} \right) \boldsymbol{P}_r.
\end{aligned} \tag{24.140}$$

We then collect terms of equal $\hat{N}$, to get

$$\begin{aligned}
\sum_{i=r-k+1}^{r} N_{i,k}\boldsymbol{P}_i = & \hat{N}_{r-k+1,k}\boldsymbol{P}_{r-k+1} \\
& + \hat{N}_{r-k+2,k} \left(\frac{\hat{t}_{r+2} - t^*}{\hat{t}_{r+2} - \hat{t}_{r-k+2}} \boldsymbol{P}_{r-k+1} + \frac{t^* - \hat{t}_{r-k+2}}{\hat{t}_{r+2} - \hat{t}_{r-k+2}} \boldsymbol{P}_{r-k+2} \right) \\
& \vdots \\
& + \hat{N}_{r,k} \left(\frac{\hat{t}_{r+k} - t^*}{\hat{t}_{r+k} - \hat{t}_r} \boldsymbol{P}_{r-1} + \frac{t^* - \hat{t}_r}{\hat{t}_{r+k} - \hat{t}_r} \boldsymbol{P}_r \right) \\
& + \hat{N}_{r+1,k}\boldsymbol{P}_r.
\end{aligned} \tag{24.141}$$

Observe that we now have a summation over $\hat{N}_i$ just like we wanted for (24.132). All we need now is to make the formulas look nicer. We do this by first expressing the fractions in terms of T and not $\hat{T}$.

$$\begin{aligned}\sum_{i=r-k+1}^{r} N_{i,k}\boldsymbol{P}_i = {} & \hat{N}_{r-k+1,k}\boldsymbol{P}_{r-k+1} \\ & + \hat{N}_{r-k+2,k}\left(\frac{t_{r+1}-t^*}{t_{r+1}-t_{r-k+2}}\boldsymbol{P}_{r-k+1} + \frac{t^*-t_{r-k+2}}{t_{r+1}-t_{r-k+2}}\boldsymbol{P}_{r-k+2}\right) \\ & \vdots \\ & + \hat{N}_{r,k}\left(\frac{t_{r+k-1}-t^*}{t_{r+k-1}-t_r}\boldsymbol{P}_{r-1} + \frac{t^*-t_r}{t_{r+k-1}-t_r}\boldsymbol{P}_r\right) \\ & + \hat{N}_{r+1,k}\boldsymbol{P}_r. \end{aligned} \tag{24.142}$$

Finally, we will introduce the notation

$$\alpha_i = \frac{t^*-t_i}{t_{i+k-1}-t_i}, \tag{24.143}$$

from which we observe that

$$(1-\alpha_i) = \frac{t_{i+k-1}-t^*}{t_{i+k-1}-t_i}. \tag{24.144}$$

With the new notation at hand, we have

$$\begin{aligned}\sum_{i=r-k+1}^{r} N_{i,k}\boldsymbol{P}_i = {} & \hat{N}_{r-k+1,k}\boldsymbol{P}_{r-k+1} \\ & + \hat{N}_{r-k+2,k}\left((1-\alpha_{r-k+2})\,\boldsymbol{P}_{r-k+1} + \alpha_{r-k+2}\boldsymbol{P}_{r-k+2}\right) \\ & \vdots \\ & + \hat{N}_{r,k}\left((1-\alpha_r)\,\boldsymbol{P}_{r-1} + \alpha_r\boldsymbol{P}_r\right) \\ & + \hat{N}_{r+1,k}\boldsymbol{P}_r. \end{aligned} \tag{24.145}$$

From this we conclude that the solution to (24.132) is

$$\hat{\boldsymbol{P}}_i = \begin{cases} \boldsymbol{P}_i & \text{if } i = r-k+1, \\ (1-\alpha_i)\,\boldsymbol{P}_{i-1} + \alpha_i\boldsymbol{P}_i & \text{if } r-k+2 \le i \le r, \\ \boldsymbol{P}_{i-1} & \text{if } i = r+1. \end{cases} \tag{24.146}$$

Putting it all together, we can now state the knot insertion algorithm. We have

$$\hat{\boldsymbol{C}}(u) = \sum_{i=0}^{n+1} \hat{N}_{i,k}\hat{\boldsymbol{P}}_i, \tag{24.147}$$

```
algorithm lookupSegment(s)
  int i=0;
  do{
    i++;
  }while(ArcLengthTable[i]<s);
  i--;
  return i;
end algorithm
```

Figure 24.7: Pseudocode for linear search of segment corresponding to a given arc length value.

with

$$\hat{\boldsymbol{P}}_i = (1 - \alpha_i)\,\boldsymbol{P}_{i-1} + \alpha_i \boldsymbol{P}_i, \tag{24.148}$$

where

$$\alpha_i = \begin{cases} 1 & \text{if } i \leq r - k + 1, \\ \frac{t^* - t_i}{t_{i+k-1} - t_i} & \text{if } r - k + 2 \leq i \leq r, \\ 0 & \text{if } i \geq r + 1. \end{cases} \tag{24.149}$$

If we compare the algorithm with the de Boor algorithm (see Section 24.7), then we will discover that the newly computed control points correspond to the de Boor points $\boldsymbol{P}^1_r, \boldsymbol{P}^1_{r-1}, \ldots, \boldsymbol{P}^1_{r-k+2}$.

24.5 Accumulated Arc Length Table

In the previous section we explained how the spline could be decomposed into a sequence of Bezier curves. Sometimes we are interested in quickly finding the Bezier curve segment that corresponds to a given arc length value along the spline $\boldsymbol{C}(u)$; for instance, if we do spline driven animation.

Stated mathematically, we are given an arc length value s and we are now looking for the Bezier curve segment $\boldsymbol{B}_i$, such that

$$S(t_i) \leq s < S(t_{i+1}). \tag{24.150}$$

One way to quickly determine the curve segment is by using an *accumulated arc length table*. After having found the decomposition of the spline into Bezier curve segments, $\boldsymbol{B}_0, \ldots, \boldsymbol{B}_{n-1}$, this table is easily constructed by computing the total arc length of each Bezier curve segment $S_{\boldsymbol{B}_i}$ and letting entry i store the value $\sum_{j=0}^{i-1} S_{\boldsymbol{B}_j}$. We can now perform a linear search through the table to find the segment we are looking for, or even better we can do a binary search. In Figure 24.7 pseudocode for a linear search of a segment is shown. This sort of strategy is also known under the name *accumulated chord length* and it comes in different flavors, but the basic idea still remains the same. For more details about the other flavors see [Watt et al., 1992].

24.6 The Regular Cubic Nonuniform B-Spline

In this section, we will look at a subclass of the B-splines, which is known as *regular B-splines*. A regular B-spline is defined by having nonzero first-order derivatives everywhere. Regular B-splines are useful for describing a physical meaningful motion. That is the center of mass trajectory of a real-world object (see, for instance, [Erleben et al., 2003a]).

In this section, we will formulate different conditions on how one should define a B-spline such that it would be a regular B-spline. We will only consider cubic B-splines.

24.6.1 First-Order Derivatives at Knot Values

Let us derive an equation for the derivative at the knot value t_i

$$\boldsymbol{C}'(t_i) = N'_{i-3,4}\boldsymbol{P}_{i-3} + N'_{i-2,4}\boldsymbol{P}_{i-2} + N'_{i-1,4}\boldsymbol{P}_{i-1} + N'_{i,4}\boldsymbol{P}_i \tag{24.151a}$$

$$\begin{aligned} &= \left(\frac{3}{t_i - t_{i-3}}N_{i-3,3} - \frac{3}{t_{i+1} - t_{i-2}}N_{i-2,3}\right)\boldsymbol{P}_{i-3} \\ &+ \left(\frac{3}{t_{i+1} - t_{i-2}}N_{i-2,3} - \frac{3}{t_{i+2} - t_{i-1}}N_{i-1,3}\right)\boldsymbol{P}_{i-2} \\ &+ \left(\frac{3}{t_{i+2} - t_{i-1}}N_{i-1,3} - \frac{3}{t_{i+3} - t_i}N_{i,3}\right)\boldsymbol{P}_{i-1} \\ &+ \left(\frac{3}{t_{i+3} - t_i}N_{i,3} - \frac{3}{t_{i+4} - t_{i+1}}N_{i+1,3}\right)\boldsymbol{P}_i. \end{aligned} \tag{24.151b}$$

Recall that $N_{i-3,3} = 0$ and $N_{i+1,3} = 0$ since we are looking at the i'th knot value of a third-order B-spline. Using this knowledge we can rewrite our equation into the following sum of differences

$$\begin{aligned} \boldsymbol{C}'(t_i) = &\frac{3N_{i-2,3}}{t_{i+1} - t_{i-2}}\left(\boldsymbol{P}_{i-2} - \boldsymbol{P}_{i-3}\right) \\ &+ \frac{3N_{i-1,3}}{t_{i+2} - t_{i-1}}\left(\boldsymbol{P}_{i-1} - \boldsymbol{P}_{i-2}\right) \\ &+ \frac{3N_{i,3}}{t_{i+3} - t_i}\left(\boldsymbol{P}_i - \boldsymbol{P}_{i-1}\right). \end{aligned} \tag{24.152}$$

We'll evaluate the basis functions by using de Cox's definition(24.1); we start by looking at $N_{i,3}$.

$N_{i,3}$
- ↙ $\frac{u-t_i}{t_{i+2}-t_i}N_{i,2}$
  - ↙ $\frac{u-t_i}{t_{i+1}-t_i}N_{i,1}$
  - ↖ $\frac{t_{i+2}-u}{t_{i+2}-t_{i+1}}N_{i+1,1}$
- ↖ $\frac{t_{i+3}-u}{t_{i+3}-t_{i+1}}N_{i+1,2}$
  - ↙ $\frac{u-t_{i+1}}{t_{i+2}-t_{i+1}}N_{i+1,1}$
  - ↖ $\frac{t_{i+3}-u}{t_{i+3}-t_{i+2}}N_{i+2,1}$

Recall that only $N_{i,1}$ is nonzero for $u = t_i$. From this we see that $N_{i,3}$ is always zero. Now let us look at $N_{i-1,3}$

$$
\begin{array}{ccccc}
 & & & \swarrow & \frac{u-t_{i-1}}{t_i-t_{i-1}}N_{i-1,1} \\
 & & \frac{u-t_{i-1}}{t_{i+1}-t_{i-1}}N_{i-1,2} & & \\
 & \swarrow & & \nwarrow & \frac{t_{i+1}-u}{t_{i+1}-t_i}N_{i,1} \\
N_{i-1,3} & & & & \\
 & \nwarrow & & \swarrow & \frac{u-t_i}{t_{i+1}-t_i}N_{i,1} \\
 & & \frac{t_{i+2}-u}{t_{i+2}-t_i}N_{i,2} & & \\
 & & & \nwarrow & \frac{t_{i+2}-u}{t_{i+2}-t_{i+1}}N_{i+1,1}
\end{array}
$$

Setting $u = t_i$, we see that

$$N_{i-1,3} = \frac{t_i - t_{i-1}}{t_{i+1} - t_{i-1}} \geq 0. \tag{24.153}$$

Finally, we only have to evaluate $N_{i-2,3}$

$$
\begin{array}{ccccc}
 & & & \swarrow & \frac{u-t_{i-2}}{t_{i-1}-t_{i-2}}N_{i-2,1} \\
 & & \frac{u-t_{i-2}}{t_i-t_{i-2}}N_{i-2,2} & & \\
 & \swarrow & & \nwarrow & \frac{t_i-u}{t_i-t_{i-1}}N_{i-1,1} \\
N_{i-2,3} & & & & \\
 & \nwarrow & & \swarrow & \frac{u-t_{i-1}}{t_i-t_{i-1}}N_{i-1,1} \\
 & & \frac{t_{i+1}-u}{t_{i+1}-t_{i-1}}N_{i-1,2} & & \\
 & & & \nwarrow & \frac{t_{i+1}-u}{t_{i+1}-t_i}N_{i,1}
\end{array}
$$

Again we have $u = t_i$, and from this we conclude that

$$N_{i-2,3} = \frac{t_{i+1} - t_i}{t_{i+1} - t_{i-1}} \geq 0. \tag{24.154}$$

Substituting the basis functions we just found into our equation for the first-order derivative, we obtain

$$\boldsymbol{C}'(t_i) = \frac{3}{t_{i+1} - t_{i-1}} \left(\frac{t_{i+1} - t_i}{t_{i+1} - t_{i-2}} (\boldsymbol{P}_{i-2} - \boldsymbol{P}_{i-3}) + \frac{t_i - t_{i-1}}{t_{i+2} - t_{i-1}} (\boldsymbol{P}_{i-1} - \boldsymbol{P}_{i-2}) \right). \tag{24.155}$$

If we wanted to make $\boldsymbol{C}'(t_i)$ equal to zero how could we then go about this? From our equation, we can by straightforward inspection derive the following complete list of conditions, which will make $\boldsymbol{C}'(t_i)$ equal to zero,

- $\boldsymbol{P}_{i-1} = \boldsymbol{P}_{i-2} = \boldsymbol{P}_{i-3}$,
- $\boldsymbol{P}_{i-1} = \boldsymbol{P}_{i-2}$ and $t_{i+1} = t_i$,
- $\boldsymbol{P}_{i-2} = \boldsymbol{P}_{i-3}$ and $t_i = t_{i-1}$,

- $t_{i+1} = t_i = t_{i-1}$,
- The final condition is a bit more difficult to derive

$$0 = \frac{t_{i+1} - t_i}{t_{i+1} - t_{i-2}} (\boldsymbol{P}_{i-2} - \boldsymbol{P}_{i-3}) + \frac{t_i - t_{i-1}}{t_{i+2} - t_{i-1}} (\boldsymbol{P}_{i-1} - \boldsymbol{P}_{i-2}). \tag{24.156}$$

From which we get

$$-\frac{(t_{i+1} - t_i)(t_{i+2} - t_{i-1})}{(t_{i+1} - t_{i-2})(t_i - t_{i-1})} (\boldsymbol{P}_{i-2} - \boldsymbol{P}_{i-3}) = (\boldsymbol{P}_{i-1} - \boldsymbol{P}_{i-2}). \tag{24.157}$$

This tells us that the three succeeding control points $\boldsymbol{P}_{i-3}$, $\boldsymbol{P}_{i-2}$, and $\boldsymbol{P}_{i-1}$ all have to lie on the same line and the magnitude of $(\boldsymbol{P}_{i-2} - \boldsymbol{P}_{i-3})$ must be a scalar multiple of the magnitude of $(\boldsymbol{P}_{i-1} - \boldsymbol{P}_{i-2})$.

With all this theory at our disposal we surely know how to avoid that $\boldsymbol{C}'(t_i)$ ever becomes zero for any knot value. $\boldsymbol{C}'(t_i)$ is always nonzero for any knot value t_i if the following three criteria is fulfilled.

1. No knot value has multiplicity greater than one.
2. All control points are unique.
3. We never have three (or more) succeeding control points lying on the same line.

Note that if we put this theory to practical use then it is slightly more restrictive than it needs to be; that is, it does exclude some splines having nonzero first-order derivatives.

24.6.2 First-Order Derivatives between Knot Values

By now we have complete knowledge about how we can control $\boldsymbol{C}'(u)$ at any knot value, t_i, but what happens between the knot values? That is, how do we ensure that

$$\boldsymbol{C}'(u) \neq 0 \tag{24.158}$$

for an u-value in between two knot values? That is,

$$t_i < u < t_{i+1}. \tag{24.159}$$

Let us start writing up the equation for $\boldsymbol{C}'(u)$ again

$$\begin{aligned}\boldsymbol{C}'(t_i) &= \frac{3N_{i-2,3}}{t_{i+1} - t_{i-2}} (\boldsymbol{P}_{i-2} - \boldsymbol{P}_{i-3}) \\ &\quad + \frac{3N_{i-1,3}}{t_{i+2} - t_{i-1}} (\boldsymbol{P}_{i-1} - \boldsymbol{P}_{i-2}) \\ &\quad + \frac{3N_{i,3}}{t_{i+3} - t_i} (\boldsymbol{P}_i - \boldsymbol{P}_{i-1}).\end{aligned} \tag{24.160}$$

And like previously, we will now evaluate the basis functions.

$$N_{i-2,3} = \frac{(t_{i+1} - u)^2}{(t_{i+1} - t_i)\,(t_{i+1} - t_{i-1})}, \tag{24.161a}$$

$$N_{i-1,3} = \frac{(t_{i+1} - u)}{(t_{i+1} - t_i)}\frac{(u - t_{i-1})}{(t_{i+1} - t_{i-1})} + \frac{(u - t_i)}{(t_{i+1} - t_i)}\frac{(t_{i+2} - u)}{(t_{i+2} - t_i)}, \tag{24.161b}$$

$$N_{i,3} = \frac{(u - t_i)^2}{(t_{i+1} - t_i)\,(t_{i+2} - t_i)}. \tag{24.161c}$$

From our knowledge of the knot vector

$$t_{i-1} < t_i < u < t_{i+1} < t_{i+2}. \tag{24.162}$$

We can conclude that $N_{i,3}$, $N_{i-1,3}$, and $N_{i-2,3}$ are always positive and never zero. So our equation for the first-order derivative reduces to the equation

$$\begin{aligned} \boldsymbol{C}'(t_i) = a\,(&\boldsymbol{P}_{i-2} - \boldsymbol{P}_{i-3}) \\ &+ b\,(\boldsymbol{P}_{i-1} - \boldsymbol{P}_{i-2}) \\ &+ c\,(\boldsymbol{P}_i - \boldsymbol{P}_{i-1}) \end{aligned} \tag{24.163}$$

where

$$a = \frac{3\,(t_{i+1} - u)^2}{(t_{i+1} - t_{i-2})\,(t_{i+1} - t_i)\,(t_{i+1} - t_{i-1})} > 0, \tag{24.164a}$$

$$b = \frac{3}{(t_{i+2} - t_{i-1})}\left(\frac{(t_{i+1} - u)\,(u - t_{i-1})}{(t_{i+1} - t_i)\,(t_{i+1} - t_{i-1})} + \frac{(u - t_i)\,(t_{i+2} - u)}{(t_{i+1} - t_i)\,(t_{i+2} - t_i)}\right) > 0, \tag{24.164b}$$

$$c = \frac{3\,(u - t_i)^2}{(t_{i+3} - t_i)\,(t_{i+1} - t_i)\,(t_{i+2} - t_i)} > 0. \tag{24.164c}$$

All we have left to do is to solve the linear system

$$a\boldsymbol{\Delta}_{i-2} + b\boldsymbol{\Delta}_{i-1} + c\boldsymbol{\Delta}_i = 0, \tag{24.165}$$

where $\boldsymbol{\Delta}_i = \boldsymbol{P}_i - \boldsymbol{P}_{i-1}$ and since we already have decided that none of the control points coincide we know that all $\boldsymbol{\Delta}_i$ are nonzero. In other words, we can only find a solution if the $\boldsymbol{\Delta}_i$s are linear dependent. In three dimensions and higher it is quite easy to come up with a condition, which always ensures that $\boldsymbol{C}'(u)$ is nonzero. Simply make sure that no four succeeding control points lie in the same plane. However, in two or one dimensions it is unavoidable to have linear dependent $\boldsymbol{\Delta}$s, and the problem still persists in 3D space (or higher) if one wants the spline (or a subpart of it) to lie in a plane. So let us try to handle the linear dependence.

Two Linear Dependent $\boldsymbol{\Delta}$s Recall that each a, b, and c is a function of u; actually they are all second-order polynomials. So assuming we have two linear independent $\boldsymbol{\Delta}$s at our disposal, then we have three possibilities.

$$s\boldsymbol{\Delta}_i + t\boldsymbol{\Delta}_{i-1} = \boldsymbol{\Delta}_{i-2}, \tag{24.166a}$$

$$v\boldsymbol{\Delta}_{i-2} + w\boldsymbol{\Delta}_i = \boldsymbol{\Delta}_{i-1}, \tag{24.166b}$$

$$x\boldsymbol{\Delta}_{i-1} + y\boldsymbol{\Delta}_{i-2} = \boldsymbol{\Delta}_i, \tag{24.166c}$$

for some nonzero scalar values s, t, v, w, x, and y. Now let us look closely at the first possibility.

$$a(u)\underbrace{(s\boldsymbol{\Delta}_i + t\boldsymbol{\Delta}_{i-1})}_{\boldsymbol{\Delta}_{i-2}} + b(u)\boldsymbol{\Delta}_{i-1} + c(u)\boldsymbol{\Delta}_i = 0, \tag{24.167a}$$

$$\Downarrow$$

$$(a(u)s + c(u))\boldsymbol{\Delta}_i + (a(u)t + b(u))\boldsymbol{\Delta}_{i-1} = 0. \tag{24.167b}$$

Since $\boldsymbol{\Delta}_i$ and $\boldsymbol{\Delta}_{i-1}$ are linear independent and different from zero, this can only occur if

$$a(u)s + c(u) = 0, \tag{24.168a}$$

$$a(u)t + b(u) = 0. \tag{24.168b}$$

Similarly, the other two possibilities give rise to

$$b(u)v + a(u) = 0, \tag{24.169a}$$

$$b(u)w + c(u) = 0, \tag{24.169b}$$

and

$$c(u)x + b(u) = 0, \tag{24.170a}$$

$$c(u)y + a(u) = 0. \tag{24.170b}$$

In other words, our problem has been reduced to determine if two parabola intersect and if they do then to determine the u-values where they intersect.

Three Linear Dependent $\boldsymbol{\Delta}$'s Following our derivation from the previous section, we have

$$a(u)x\boldsymbol{\Delta}_i + b(u)y\boldsymbol{\Delta}_i + c(u)z\boldsymbol{\Delta}_i = 0 \tag{24.171}$$

for some nonzero scalar values x, y, and z (all nonzero). All this boils down to a single equation.

$$a(u)x + b(u)y + c(u)z = 0. \tag{24.172}$$

By now we are tempted to repeat our earlier idea and look at the linear dependency of the three polynomials $a(u)$, $b(u)$, and $c(u)$. If they all are linear independent then no solutions exist and we are guaranteed that

$\boldsymbol{C}'(u)$ is always nonzero. If, on the other hand, we have some polynomials that are linear dependent, then we are once again left with determining if and where two parabola intersect. To see this, imagine we have

$$a(u) = vb(u) + wc(u), \tag{24.173}$$

then (24.172) becomes

$$a(u)x + b(u)y + c(u)z = 0, \tag{24.174a}$$
$$\Downarrow$$
$$(vb(u) + wc(u))x + b(u)y + c(u)z = 0, \tag{24.174b}$$
$$\Downarrow$$
$$(vx + y)b(u) + (wx + z)c(u) = 0, \tag{24.174c}$$
$$\Downarrow$$
$$\frac{(vx + y)}{(wx + z)}b(u) + c(u) = 0 \tag{24.174d}$$

just like we have seen previously.

We can conclude that we can only have $\boldsymbol{C}'(u) = 0$ between t_i and t_{i+1} when two second-order polynomials in u have an intersection in the interval $[t_i..t_{i+1}]$. In other words, the first derivative can only vanish at isolated values of u, that is, $\boldsymbol{C}'(u) = 0$ between knot values can only occur at *cusps*.

24.7 The de Boor Algorithm

In this section, we will state the *de Boor algorithm* and prove it.

Theorem 24.7 (The de Boor algorithm)
The de Boor algorithm can be stated as follows:

$$\boldsymbol{C}(u) = \sum_{i=0}^{n+j} N_{i,k-j}\boldsymbol{P}_i^j \qquad \textit{for} \quad 0 \le j \le k-1, \tag{24.175}$$

where

$$\boldsymbol{P}_i^j = (1 - a_{i,j})\boldsymbol{P}_{i-1}^{j-1} + a_{i,j}\boldsymbol{P}_i^{j-1} \qquad \textit{for} \quad j > 0, \tag{24.176}$$

and

$$a_{i,j} = \frac{t - t_i}{t_{i+k-j} - t_i}, \qquad \textit{and} \quad \boldsymbol{P}_i^0 = \boldsymbol{P}_i. \tag{24.177}$$

The points $\boldsymbol{P}_i^j$ are called the de Boor points.

Proof of Theorem 24.7:
Now we will prove the de Boor algorithm. First, let us write up the definition of a nonuniform B-spline.

$$\boldsymbol{C}(u) = \sum_{i=0}^{n} N_{i,k}\boldsymbol{P}_i. \tag{24.178}$$

If we now apply de Cox's definition for $N_{i,k}$ then we get

$$C(u) = \sum_{i=0}^{n} \frac{u - t_i}{t_{i+k-1} - t_i} N_{i,k-1} \boldsymbol{P}_i + \sum_{i=0}^{n} \frac{t_{i+k} - u}{t_{i+k} - t_{i+1}} N_{i+1,k-1} \boldsymbol{P}_i. \tag{24.179}$$

This looks a bit nasty, but by applying a little mathematical trick of shifting the index of the second term by $i = i - 1$, we get

$$C(u) = \sum_{i=0}^{n} \frac{u - t_i}{t_{i+k-1} - t_i} N_{i,k-1} \boldsymbol{P}_i + \sum_{i=1}^{n+1} \frac{t_{i+k-1} - u}{t_{i+k-1} - t_i} N_{i,k-1} \boldsymbol{P}_{i-1}. \tag{24.180}$$

Finally, if we define $\boldsymbol{P}_{-1} = 0$ and $\boldsymbol{P}_{n+1} = 0$, then we are allowed to rewrite the two summations into a single summation

$$C(u) = \sum_{i=0}^{n+1} \frac{\boldsymbol{P}_i (u - t_i) + \boldsymbol{P}_{i-1} (t_{i+k-1} - u)}{t_{i+k-1} - t_i} N_{i,k-1}. \tag{24.181}$$

Again, we apply a little mathematical trick of adding and subtracting t_i from the second term in the denominator. That is,

$$\begin{aligned} C(u) &= \sum_{i=0}^{n+1} \frac{\boldsymbol{P}_i (u - t_i) + \boldsymbol{P}_{i-1} (t_{i+k-1} - t_i + t_i - u)}{t_{i+k-1} - t_i} N_{i,k-1} \\ &= \sum_{i=0}^{n+1} \frac{\boldsymbol{P}_i (u - t_i) + \boldsymbol{P}_{i-1} (t_{i+k-1} - t_i - (u - t_i))}{t_{i+k-1} - t_i} N_{i,k-1} \\ &= \sum_{i=0}^{n+1} \left(\boldsymbol{P}_i \alpha_i^1 + \boldsymbol{P}_{i-1} \left(1 - \alpha_i^1\right) \right) N_{i,k-1}, \end{aligned} \tag{24.182}$$

where α_i^1 is defined as in the definition of the de Boor algorithm. The final equation is derived by introducing the notation

$$\boldsymbol{P}_i^1 = \left(1 - \alpha_i^1\right) \boldsymbol{P}_{i-1} + \alpha_i^1 \boldsymbol{P}_i. \tag{24.183}$$

So we get

$$C(u) = \sum_{i=0}^{n+1} \boldsymbol{P}_i^1 N_{i,k-1}. \tag{24.184}$$

From all this we can conclude that we have proven the de Boor algorithm in the case where $j = 1$. It is not hard to see that if we apply the same index shifting and definitions recursively we will end up with the de Boor algorithm in the general j'th case. □

24.8 Repeated Knot Insertion

If our spline, $\boldsymbol{C}(U)$, does not have any sequences of identical control points or knot values, then the local Bezier segment $\boldsymbol{B}_i(u)$ corresponding to the segment t_i to t_{i+1} will have *geometry vectors*, $\boldsymbol{G}_0$, $\boldsymbol{G}_1$, $\boldsymbol{G}_2$ and $\boldsymbol{G}_3$, which are unique and distinct. This postulate follows rather easily from direct computation.

Let us assume that we have a multiplicity of $k = 4$ for all knot values to the left of t_r and that all knot values to the right of t_r and t_r itself have a multiplicity of 1. Now imagine we have

$$t_r \le t^* < t_{r+1}. \tag{24.185}$$

This means that for a cubic spline (i.e., $k = 4$) we have $N_{r-3,4}, \ldots, N_{r,4} \neq 0$. From this we also know that it is the control points $\boldsymbol{P}_{r-3}$, $\boldsymbol{P}_{r-2}$, $\boldsymbol{P}_{r-1}$, and $\boldsymbol{P}_r$, which have to be recomputed in the new spline. The new de Boor points are generated as in the table below

$$\begin{array}{ccccc}
\boldsymbol{P}^0_{r-3} & & & & \\
 & \searrow & & & \\
 & & (1-a_{r-2}) & & \\
 & & & \searrow & \\
\boldsymbol{P}^0_{r-2} & \rightarrow & a_{r-2} & \rightarrow & \boldsymbol{P}^1_{r-2} \\
 & \searrow & & & \\
 & & (1-a_{r-1}) & & \\
 & & & \searrow & \\
\boldsymbol{P}^0_{r-1} & \rightarrow & a_{r-1} & \rightarrow & \boldsymbol{P}^1_{r-1} \\
 & \searrow & & & \\
 & & (1-a_{r}) & & \\
 & & & \searrow & \\
\boldsymbol{P}^0_{r} & \rightarrow & a_{r} & \rightarrow & \boldsymbol{P}^1_{r}
\end{array}$$

where

$$a_{r-2} = \frac{(t_r - t_{r-2})}{(t_{r+1} - t_{r-2})} > 0, \tag{24.186a}$$

$$a_{r-1} = \frac{(t_r - t_{r-1})}{(t_{r+2} - t_{r-1})} > 0, \tag{24.186b}$$

$$a_{r} = \frac{(t_r - t_{r})}{(t_{r+3} - t_{r})} = 0. \tag{24.186c}$$

Now we can construct the new control points $\hat{\boldsymbol{P}}$

$\boldsymbol{P}_0$	$\boldsymbol{P}_1$	$\boldsymbol{P}_2$	$\ldots$	$\boldsymbol{P}_{r-3}$	$\boldsymbol{P}^1_{r-2}$	$\boldsymbol{P}^1_{r-1}$	$\boldsymbol{P}^1_{r}$	$\boldsymbol{P}_r$	$\boldsymbol{P}_{r+1}$	$\ldots$	$\boldsymbol{P}_n$
$\boldsymbol{P}_0$	$\boldsymbol{P}_1$	$\boldsymbol{P}_2$	$\ldots$	$\boldsymbol{P}_{r-3}$	$\boldsymbol{P}^1_{r-2}$	$\boldsymbol{P}^1_{r-1}$	$\boldsymbol{P}_{r-1}$	$\boldsymbol{P}_r$	$\boldsymbol{P}_{r+1}$	$\ldots$	$\boldsymbol{P}_n$
$\hat{\boldsymbol{P}}_0$	$\hat{\boldsymbol{P}}_1$	$\hat{\boldsymbol{P}}_2$	$\ldots$	$\hat{\boldsymbol{P}}_{r-3}$	$\hat{\boldsymbol{P}}_{r-2}$	$\hat{\boldsymbol{P}}_{r-1}$	$\hat{\boldsymbol{P}}_{r}$	$\hat{\boldsymbol{P}}_{r+1}$	$\hat{\boldsymbol{P}}_{r+2}$	$\ldots$	$\hat{\boldsymbol{P}}_{n+1}$

and the new knot vector $\hat{T}$.

t_0	t_1	$\dots$	t_r	t^*	t_{r+1}	$\dots$	t_{n+k}
t_0	t_1	$\dots$	t_r	t_r	t_{r+1}	$\dots$	t_{n+k}
$\hat{t}_0$	$\hat{t}_1$	$\dots$	$\hat{t}_r$	$\hat{t}_{r+1}$	$\hat{t}_{r+2}$	$\dots$	$\hat{t}_{n+k+1}$

We now have multiplicity of 2 for the knot value t_r. Let's try to insert $t^* = t_r$ once more. This time we will discover that

$$\hat{t}_{r+1} \leq t^* < \hat{t}_{r+2}, \tag{24.187}$$

from which we conclude that it is the control points $\hat{\boldsymbol{P}}_{r-2}$, $\hat{\boldsymbol{P}}_{r-1}$, $\hat{\boldsymbol{P}}_r$, and $\hat{\boldsymbol{P}}_{r+1}$, which have to be recomputed in the new spline.

$$\begin{array}{ccccccc}
\hat{\boldsymbol{P}}^0_{r-2} & & & & \\
& \searrow & & & \\
& & (1-a_{r-1}) & & \\
& & & \searrow & \\
\hat{\boldsymbol{P}}^0_{r-1} & \rightarrow & a_{r-1} & \rightarrow & \hat{\boldsymbol{P}}^1_{r-1} \\
& \searrow & & & \\
& & (1-a_r) & & \\
& & & \searrow & \\
\hat{\boldsymbol{P}}^0_{r} & \rightarrow & a_{r} & \rightarrow & \hat{\boldsymbol{P}}^1_{r} \\
& \searrow & & & \\
& & (1-a_{r+1}) & & \\
& & & \searrow & \\
\hat{\boldsymbol{P}}^0_{r+1} & \rightarrow & a_{r+1} & \rightarrow & \hat{\boldsymbol{P}}^1_{r+1}
\end{array}$$

where

$$a_{r-1} = \frac{(t_r - \hat{t}_{r-1})}{(\hat{t}_{r+2} - \hat{t}_{r-1})} = \frac{t_r - t_{r-1}}{t_{r+1} - t_{r-1}} > 0, \tag{24.188a}$$

$$a_r = \frac{(t_r - \hat{t}_r)}{(\hat{t}_{r+3} - \hat{t}_r)} = \frac{t_r - t_r}{t_{r+2} - t_r} = 0, \tag{24.188b}$$

$$a_{r+1} = \frac{(t_r - \hat{t}_{r+1})}{(\hat{t}_{r+4} - \hat{t}_{r+1})} = \frac{t_r - t_r}{t_{r+2} - t_r} = 0. \tag{24.188c}$$

With this information we can write up the new control points $\tilde{\boldsymbol{P}}$

$\hat{\boldsymbol{P}}_0$	$\dots$	$\hat{\boldsymbol{P}}_{r-3}$	$\hat{\boldsymbol{P}}_{r-2}$	$\hat{\boldsymbol{P}}^1_{r-1}$	$\hat{\boldsymbol{P}}^1_{r}$	$\hat{\boldsymbol{P}}^1_{r+1}$	$\hat{\boldsymbol{P}}_{r+1}$	$\dots$	$\hat{\boldsymbol{P}}_{n+1}$
$\boldsymbol{P}_0$	$\dots$	$\boldsymbol{P}_{r-3}$	$\boldsymbol{P}^1_{r-2}$	$\hat{\boldsymbol{P}}^1_{r-1}$	$\hat{\boldsymbol{P}}^0_{r-1}$	$\hat{\boldsymbol{P}}^0_{r}$	$\boldsymbol{P}_{r}$	$\dots$	$\boldsymbol{P}_{n}$
$\boldsymbol{P}_0$	$\dots$	$\boldsymbol{P}_{r-3}$	$\boldsymbol{P}^1_{r-2}$	$\hat{\boldsymbol{P}}^1_{r-1}$	$\boldsymbol{P}^1_{r-1}$	$\boldsymbol{P}_{r-1}$	$\boldsymbol{P}_{r}$	$\dots$	$\boldsymbol{P}_{n}$
$\tilde{\boldsymbol{P}}_0$	$\dots$	$\tilde{\boldsymbol{P}}_{r-3}$	$\tilde{\boldsymbol{P}}_{r-2}$	$\tilde{\boldsymbol{P}}_{r-1}$	$\tilde{\boldsymbol{P}}_{r}$	$\tilde{\boldsymbol{P}}_{r+1}$	$\tilde{\boldsymbol{P}}_{r+2}$	$\dots$	$\tilde{\boldsymbol{P}}_{n+2}$

and the new knot vector $\tilde{T}$

$\hat{t}_0$	$\hat{t}_1$	$\dots$	$\hat{t}_r$	$\hat{t}_{r+1}$	t^*	$\hat{t}_{r+2}$	$\dots$	$\hat{t}_{n+k+1}$
t_0	t_1	$\dots$	t_r	t_r	t_r	t_{r+1}	$\dots$	t_{n+k}
$\tilde{t}_0$	$\tilde{t}_1$	$\dots$	$\tilde{t}_r$	$\tilde{t}_{r+1}$	$\tilde{t}_{r+2}$	$\tilde{t}_{r+3}$	$\dots$	$\tilde{t}_{n+k+2}$

We now have a multiplicity of 3 for the knot value t_r. Let's see what happens upon the last knot insertion. First, we see that we have.

$$\tilde{t}_{r+2} \leq t^* < \tilde{t}_{r+3}, \tag{24.189}$$

from which we know that we have to recompute the following control points.

$$\begin{array}{ccccc}
\tilde{\boldsymbol{P}}^0_{r-1} & & & & \\
 & \searrow & & & \\
 & & (1-a_r) & & \\
 & & & \searrow & \\
\tilde{\boldsymbol{P}}^0_{r} & \rightarrow & a_r & \rightarrow & \tilde{\boldsymbol{P}}^1_{r} \\
 & \searrow & & & \\
 & & (1-a_{r+1}) & & \\
 & & & \searrow & \\
\tilde{\boldsymbol{P}}^0_{r+1} & \rightarrow & a_{r+1} & \rightarrow & \tilde{\boldsymbol{P}}^1_{r+1} \\
 & \searrow & & & \\
 & & (1-a_{r+2}) & & \\
 & & & \searrow & \\
\tilde{\boldsymbol{P}}^0_{r+2} & \rightarrow & a_{r+2} & \rightarrow & \tilde{\boldsymbol{P}}^1_{r+2}
\end{array}$$

where

$$a_r = \frac{(t_r - \tilde{t}_r)}{(\tilde{t}_{r+3} - \tilde{t}_r)} = \frac{t_r - t_r}{t_{r+1} - t_r} = 0, \tag{24.190a}$$

$$a_{r+1} = \frac{(t_r - \tilde{t}_{r+1})}{(\tilde{t}_{r+4} - \tilde{t}_{r+1})} = \frac{t_r - t_r}{t_{r+2} - t_r} = 0, \tag{24.190b}$$

$$a_{r+2} = \frac{(t_r - \tilde{t}_{r+2})}{(\tilde{t}_{r+5} - \tilde{t}_{r+2})} = \frac{t_r - t_r}{t_{r+3} - t_r} = 0. \tag{24.190c}$$

Finally, we write up the new control points $\boldsymbol{\rho}$.

$\tilde{\boldsymbol{P}}_0$	$\dots$	$\tilde{\boldsymbol{P}}_{r-3}$	$\tilde{\boldsymbol{P}}_{r-2}$	$\tilde{\boldsymbol{P}}_{r-1}$	$\tilde{\boldsymbol{P}}^1_r$	$\tilde{\boldsymbol{P}}^1_{r+1}$	$\tilde{\boldsymbol{P}}^1_{r+2}$	$\tilde{\boldsymbol{P}}_{r+2}$	$\dots$	$\tilde{\boldsymbol{P}}_{n+2}$
$\boldsymbol{P}_0$	$\dots$	$\boldsymbol{P}_{r-3}$	$\boldsymbol{P}^1_{r-2}$	$\hat{\boldsymbol{P}}^1_{r-1}$	$\tilde{\boldsymbol{P}}_{r-1}$	$\tilde{\boldsymbol{P}}_r$	$\tilde{\boldsymbol{P}}_{r+1}$	$\boldsymbol{P}_r$	$\dots$	$\boldsymbol{P}_n$
$\boldsymbol{P}_0$	$\dots$	$\boldsymbol{P}_{r-3}$	$\boldsymbol{P}^1_{r-2}$	$\hat{\boldsymbol{P}}^1_{r-1}$	$\hat{\boldsymbol{P}}^1_{r-1}$	$\boldsymbol{P}^1_{r-1}$	$\boldsymbol{P}_{r-1}$	$\boldsymbol{P}_r$	$\dots$	$\boldsymbol{P}_n$
ρ_0	$\dots$	ρ_{r-3}	ρ_{r-2}	ρ_{r-1}	ρ_r	ρ_{r+1}	ρ_{r+2}	ρ_{r+3}	$\dots$	ρ_{n+3}

And the new knot vector τ.

$\tilde{t}_0$	$\dots$	$\tilde{t}_r$	$\tilde{t}_{r+1}$	$\tilde{t}_{r+2}$	t^*	$\tilde{t}_{r+3}$	$\dots$	$\tilde{t}_{n+k+2}$
t_0	$\dots$	t_r	t_r	t_r	t_r	t_{r+1}	$\dots$	t_{n+k}
τ_0	$\dots$	τ_r	τ_{r+1}	τ_{r+2}	τ_{r+3}	τ_{r+4}	$\dots$	τ_{n+k+3}

Now let us examine our results a little closer. We have now discovered that only three new control points are actually computed: $\boldsymbol{P}^1_{r-2}$, $\hat{\boldsymbol{P}}^1_{r-1}$, and $\boldsymbol{P}^1_{r-1}$, which are all distinct.

Notice that $\hat{\boldsymbol{P}}^1_{r-1} = \boldsymbol{P}^2_{r-1}$. This means the new control points actually can be computed directly by using the de Boor algorithm (see Chapter 24.7) on $\boldsymbol{P}_{r-3}$, $\boldsymbol{P}_{r-2}$, and $\boldsymbol{P}_{r-1}$.

$$
\begin{array}{ccccc}
\boldsymbol{P}^0_{r-3} & & & & \\
 & \searrow & & & \\
\boldsymbol{P}^0_{r-2} & \rightarrow & \boldsymbol{P}^1_{r-2} & & \\
 & \searrow & & \searrow & \\
\boldsymbol{P}^0_{r-1} & \rightarrow & \boldsymbol{P}^1_{r-1} & \rightarrow & \hat{\boldsymbol{P}}^2_{r-1}
\end{array}
$$

25

Software: OpenTissue

OpenTissue is an open-source library for physics-based animation developed mainly by the Computer Graphics Group at the Department of Computer Science, University of Copenhagen.

25.1 Background History of OpenTissue

The history of OpenTissue goes back to November 2001, where a small group of people: K. Erleben, H. Dohlmann, J. Sporring, and K. Henriksen started to collect a toolbox of code-pieces of their own work in order to ease project collaboration and teaching efforts. We, as well as students, often reinvent the wheel during project work, limiting the time set aside for in-depth understanding and experimenting with specific simulation methods. Around August 2003, OpenTissue had proven to be a valuable tool for students and researchers at the Department, and it was released under the terms of the GNU Lesser General Public License. Today, OpenTissue works as a foundation for research and student projects in physics-based animation at the Department of Computer Science, University of Copenhagen and it is used as a research platform at several universities.

Due to the experimental nature of OpenTissue, it contains a wide variety of algorithms and data structures. Some code-pieces are merely wrappers of third-party software ensuring that the programmers can use these tools within the common framework of OpenTissue. Other code-pieces consist of tools extracted from our own research projects in soft tissue simulation and medical image data acquisition. An increasing number of students are beginning to contribute their own code and are helping greatly in maintaining and improving OpenTissue. The list of tools in OpenTissue is constantly growing, but a summary of methods and data structures at the time of writing includes:

- Rectilinear 3D Grid Data Structures
- Twofold Mesh Data Structure
- Tetra4 Mesh Data Structure
- Chan-Vese Segmentation Tools
- Signed Distance Map Computations
- OpenGL-Based Voxelizer
- Quasi Static Stress-Strain Simulation (FEM)
- Relaxation-Based Particle System Simulation (support for surface meshes, solids, cloth meshes, pressure soft models, self-intersection, and much more)

- CJK, SAT, VClip and other algorithms for Collision Detection
- Mesh Plane Clipper and Patcher
- QHull Convex Hull Wrapper
- Script files for Maya and 3DMax for generating Mesh data files
- Generic Bounding Volume Hierarchies with Custom Bottom-Up Construction, Single and Tandem Traversals, etc.
- Multibody Dynamics Velocity-Based Complementarity Formulation
- First-Order World Rigid Body Simulation
- Volume Visualization Using 3D Texture-Based View Aligned Slabbing with 12-bit Preintegration
- and much more

25.2 Obtaining OpenTissue

The newest version of OpenTissue, demonstrations, and download and installation instructions, etc. can be found at:

`www.opentissue.org`

The following is the download and installation procedure as of the time of writing:

The development of the OpenTissue software is revisioned using *Subversion* (*SVN*). To download any version of OpenTissue, you must have Subversion installed on your system. Subversion can be obtained from, `subversion.tigris.org`. Gentoo Linux users may write, `emerge -av subversion`, as root. New users will most likely want to read the Subversion book at `svnbook.org`. There are also gui-interfaces, TortoiseSVN, `tortoisesvn.tigris`, for Windows® and RapidSVN, `rapidsvn.tigris.org`, for Linux.

For anonymous checkout through http use:

```
svn co http://image.diku.dk/svn/OpenTissue/trunk OpenTissue
```

You may also browse with a Web browser in the repository using the url: `image.diku.dk/svn/OpenTissue`. When browsing, you will notice three top-level directories. Normally, you will be interested in the most resent version in `trunk/`.

We have collected a small subset of DataTissue, containing data for the demos only. For anonymous checkout of the small subset through http use:

```
svn co http://image.diku.dk/svn/DataTissue/trunk/demos
```

You may also browse with a Web browser in the repository using the url: `image.diku.dk/svn/OpenTissue`. See the different READMEs in OpenTissue for details about data demo dependencies.

The full DataTissue (more than 1.6 GB) is available from

```
svn co http://image.diku.dk/svn/DataTissue/trunk/
```

To set up the OpenTissue for development, make sure you have the prerequisites in place before trying to compile any of the code. These consist of:

1. Fetching OpenTissue/trunk.
2. Fetching DataTissue/trunk/demos.
3. Fetching `boost_1_32_0` from `www.boost.org`.
4. Fetching bindings from `www.opentissue.org`.
5. Set the environment variables `OPENTISSUE`, `DATATISSUE`, and `BOOST`.
6. On Linux, have a link from `/usr/local/include/boost` to `boost_1_32_0/boost`.

See the different READMEs in OpenTissue for details.

25.3 Using OpenTissue

OpenTissue is mainly aimed for the Windows platform, although a high-priority in its design has always been to use only strict standard C++ constructs. In practice, this means that all code is required also to be compilable under Linux with a recent g++ version.

OpenTissue is installed simply by copying it onto a selected location on the hard drive of your own choice. Then an environment variable must be defined named OPENTISSUE that points to the topmost OpenTissue folder of your chosen location.

25.3.1 Developer Information

The source code of OpenTissue is located in the folder:

```
$(OPENTISSUE)/OpenTissue
```

Microsoft Visual Studio C++ .NET 2003 ® (*MSVC*) solution file and project file are located at:

```
$(OPENTISSUE)/
```

Demo applications are in:

```
$(OPENTISSUE)/demos/opengl/
```

Script files for Maya® and 3DMax® are located in:

```
$(OPENTISSUE)/scripts/
```

Various bat-files and MSVC project files to help setting up external dependencies have been built into:

```
$(OPENTISSUE)/dependencies
```

When building OpenTissue with MSVC on Windows 2000® or Windows XP® the following folder structure will be generated:

```
$(OpenTissue)/Release
$(OpenTissue)/Debug
$(OpenTissue)/lib/windows
```

The first two folders are used by the compiler to hold object files and temporaries, while the last folder contains the actual lib-file. Currently, the default settings of OpenTissue are to only build a lib-file for static-linking.

All demo applications have been set up to statically link with OpenTissue. Their binaries and temporaries are generated in local Debug and Release folders in every demo application.

25.3.1.1 File Structure of Data Structures

The subfolder structure is rather flat and not very deep. Each top-level subfolder usually contains a single data structure, and the next level of subfolders contains I/O-routines and algorithms for the data structure:

`$(OPENTISSUE)/OpenTissue/bitmap`	2D Bitmap data structure
`$(OPENTISSUE)/OpenTissue/bvh`	Generic Bounding volume hierarchy data structure
`$(OPENTISSUE)/OpenTissue/geometry`	Geometric Primitives
`$(OPENTISSUE)/OpenTissue/math`	Vector, Matrices, Quaternions, CoordSys
`$(OPENTISSUE)/OpenTissue/map`	3D rectilinear grid data structure
`$(OPENTISSUE)/OpenTissue/mesh`	Twofold mesh data structure
`$(OPENTISSUE)/OpenTissue/spline`	Nonuniform B-Splines
`$(OPENTISSUE)/OpenTissue/tetra4`	Tetrahedral Mesh data structure

25.3.1.2 File Structure of Utilities

OpenTissue also contains various utilities for different tasks, such as visualization, interaction, and wrappers for third-party software. Each utility is contained in a subfolder of its own:

`$(OPENTISSUE)/OpenTissue/mc`	Isosurface extractor
`$(OPENTISSUE)/OpenTissue/RenderTexture`	RenderTexture Wrapper
`$(OPENTISSUE)/OpenTissue/trackball`	Virtual Trackball
`$(OPENTISSUE)/OpenTissue/utility`	Various utilities
`$(OPENTISSUE)/OpenTissue/xml`	PUG XML wrapper
`$(OPENTISSUE)/OpenTissue/volvis`	Direct Volume Visualization

25.3.1.3 File Structure of Simulation Methods

All simulation methods using dynamics have been collected in a single top-level subfolder:

```
$(OPENTISSUE)/OpenTissue/dynamics
```

Algorithms based on kinematics are intended to be placed in another single top-level subfolder named:

```
$(OPENTISSUE)/OpenTissue/kinematics
```

Beneath the simulation method subfolder, another folder structure is used, indicating a classification of the simulation method. For instance, particle systems are placed in a particle system subfolder, multibody dynamics in a multibody folder and so on:

`$(OPENTISSUE)/OpenTissue/dynamics/cfd`	Computational Fluid Dynamics
`$(OPENTISSUE)/OpenTissue/dynamics/multibody`	Multibody Dynamics
`$(OPENTISSUE)/OpenTissue/dynamics/particleSystem`	Particle System
`$(OPENTISSUE)/OpenTissue/dynamics/deformation/terzopoulos/`	Elastic Deformable Models

25.3.2 Dependencies

OpenTissue has dependencies on a great many deal of third-party software. These third-party software libraries are distributed as binaries with OpenTissue or incorporated directly in the source code of OpenTissue, *except for Boost, which you must download and install yourself.* The list of third-party software includes:

- Boost `www.boost.org`
- RenderTexture `www.markmark.net/misc/rendertexture.html`
- Atlas `math-atlas.sourceforge.net`
- PUG XML `www.codeproject.com/soap/pugxml.asp`
- Matlab® `www.mathworks.com/products/matlab`
- QHull `www.qhull.org`
- GLEW `glew.sourceforge.net`
- DeVIL `openil.sourceforge.net`
- Cg `developer.nvidia.com`
- MovieMaker® (from NVSDK®) `developer.nvidia.com`
- PATH from CPNET `www.cs.wisc.edu/cpnet/cpnetsoftware`

As of this writing the OpenTissue-specific code parts contain the following dependencies on external libraries:

`OpenTissue/map/util/cscgl`	→	RenderTexture, openGL
`OpenTissue/map/util/voxelizer`	→	RenderTexture, openGL
`OpenTissue/map/CgUtil/*`	→	RenderTexture, Cg
`OpenTissue/math/algebra/*`	→	Atlas
`OpenTissue/math/lcp/dantzigBruteUblasAtlasAdapter`	→	Atlas
`OpenTissue/math/lcp/path.*`	→	PATH
`OpenTissue/math/lcp/m2cLemke`	→	Matlab®
`OpenTissue/mesh/util/ConvexHull`	→	QHull
`OpenTissue/tetra4/util/qsss`	→	Atlas

If you do not need some or all of these parts of OpenTissue, you should just remove them from your project file.

25.3.3 Sample Data

In our DEMO applications we use an environment variable, DATATISSUE. This should point to the folder location, where the demo application will look for data files. Sample data can be downloaded from the OpenTissue Web page:

- `www.opentissue.org`

Or freely available volume data sets (CT-scans and more) can be downloaded from the Web pages:

- `www.osc.edu/~jbryan/VolSuite/downloads.shtml`
- `openqvis.sourceforge.net/index.html`

25.3.4 Guidelines for Developing in OpenTissue

For those with write access to the OpenTissue Subversion (*SVN*) Repository, we kindly ask to follow some simple guidelines:

- Every file should at least contain the Lesser GPL license header.
- All headers should have the `pragma once` lines added immediately after the license header.
- The included guarding should reflect the file structure and file name of the header file, as an example: `OpenTissue/map/map.h` uses `OPENTISSUE_MAP_MAP_H`.
- Everything should be encapsulated into the OpenTissue namespace.
- No two classes should have the same name, even if they are located in different folders.
- Please make your own local copy of project files and solution files so you do not overwrite the ones in the repository with your specific settings. If you use Makefiles, then please do not pollute the Makefiles in the repository, which will prevent others from building OpenTissue.

- Please try to follow our naming conventions and usage of uppercase and lowercase letters.
- No data files should be added directly to OpenTissue.
- Please separate your data structure from algorithms and input/output routines. A good example of this is the map part of OpenTissue. The actual map data structure is located in the folder

  ```
  $(OPENTISSUE)/OpenTissue/map/
  ```

  Various classes for reading and writing different map file formats are located in

  ```
  $(OPENTISSUE)/OpenTissue/map/io
  ```

  All algorithms working on the map data structure are located in

  ```
  $(OPENTISSUE)/OpenTissue/map/util
  ```

- Please always document your code as well as possible. We use Doxygen style (`www.doxygen.org`) throughout all our code. We stride toward documenting code on class level, method, and member level as well. For methods this should include full description of all arguments and return values. If part of an algorithm, the intended caller/callee relationship would be nice to have in the long description of the method.

26

Notation, Units, and Physical Constants

With such a large and diverse field as physics-based animation, notation is doomed to be creatively and inconsistently used. A good attempt at a unified notation is found in [Weisstein, 2005b, Weisstein, 2005a]. Below we summarize the notation used in this book.

The international system of units and the fundamental physical and chemical constants form a basis of the physics and chemistry as we know it. The following have been selected from [NIST, 2005, Kaye et al., 1995] for convenience.

$\boldsymbol{C}$	A set
$\mathbb{Z}, \mathbb{R}, \mathbb{C}$	The set of integers, the real line, and the complex plane
$a, b, c, \dots, \alpha, \beta, \gamma$	A scalars or scalar field, e.g. $a \in \mathbb{R}$ or $f \in \mathbb{R}^3 \to \mathbb{R}$
$\|a\|$	The absolute value of a
$\boldsymbol{x} = \begin{bmatrix} x_1 \\ x_2 \\ \vdots \\ x_n \end{bmatrix}$	A vector or vector field e.g. $\boldsymbol{x} \in \mathbb{R}^3$ or $\boldsymbol{y} : \mathbb{R}^3 \to \mathbb{R}^3$
$\\|\boldsymbol{x}\\|, \\|\boldsymbol{A}\\|$	A general norm
$\\|\boldsymbol{x}\\|_2 = \sqrt{\boldsymbol{x} \cdot \boldsymbol{x}} = \sqrt{\sum_i x_i^2}$	The Euclidean vector norm
$\|\boldsymbol{x}\| = [\|x_1\|, \|x_2\|, \dots, \|x_n\|]^T$	The vector of absolute elements
$\boldsymbol{x} \cdot \boldsymbol{y}$, $\boldsymbol{x} \times \boldsymbol{y}$	The dot and cross product between two vectors
$\boldsymbol{e}_x, \boldsymbol{e}_y, \boldsymbol{e}_z$	The unit vectors defining a coordinate axes
$\boldsymbol{A} = \{a_{ij}\}$, $\boldsymbol{A}^T = \{a_{ji}\}$	A general matrix and its transpose
$\boldsymbol{AB} = \{\sum_k a_{ik} b_{kj}\}$	The matrix product
$\boldsymbol{A}^{-1}$	The inverse of a matrix
$\boldsymbol{A}_{i*}$, $\boldsymbol{A}_{*j}$	The i'th row and j'th column of matrix $\boldsymbol{A}$
$\boldsymbol{A} = [\boldsymbol{A}_{*1} \mid \boldsymbol{A}_{*2} \mid \cdots \mid \boldsymbol{A}_{*n}]$	Matrix concatenation
$\det \boldsymbol{A} = \|\boldsymbol{A}\|$	The determinant of matrix $\boldsymbol{A}$
$\mathbf{1}$	The identity matrix, having 1 on the diagonal and 0 elsewhere
$\boldsymbol{a}^\times = \boldsymbol{A}$	A cross matrix, such that $\boldsymbol{a} \times \boldsymbol{b} = \boldsymbol{a}^\times \boldsymbol{b} = \boldsymbol{Ab}$
$\frac{\partial}{\partial x} = \partial_x$	The partial differential operator w.r.t. coordinate axis $\boldsymbol{e}_x$
$\dot{\boldsymbol{x}} = \frac{\partial \boldsymbol{x}}{\partial t}$	The time derivative of $\boldsymbol{x}$
$\boldsymbol{r}$, $\boldsymbol{v} = \dot{\boldsymbol{r}}$, $\boldsymbol{a} = \ddot{\boldsymbol{r}}$	Typically the position, velocity, and acceleration
$da, d\boldsymbol{x}, d\boldsymbol{A}$	The differential of a scalar, vector, and matrix
$\nabla = \begin{bmatrix} \partial_x \\ \partial_y \\ \partial_z \end{bmatrix}$	The gradient operator
$\nabla_{\boldsymbol{x}}$	The gradient operator restricted to the elements of $\boldsymbol{x}$
∇_f	The functional derivative
$\frac{\delta L}{\delta f}$	The variational derivative
$\boldsymbol{A} = \nabla \boldsymbol{r}$	The Jacobian matrix
$\text{div} = \nabla \cdot$	The divergence operator
$\text{curl} = \nabla \times$	The curl or rotation operator

Table 26.1: Often-used notation

Name	Domain	Implementation	
Spatial Nabla		$\nabla = \nabla_{[x,y,z]^T} = \begin{bmatrix} \partial_x \\ \partial_y \\ \partial_z \end{bmatrix}$	(26.1)
Gradient	$f : \mathbb{R}^3 \to \mathbb{R}$ $\nabla f : \mathbb{R}^3 \to \mathbb{R}^3$	$\nabla f = \begin{bmatrix} f_x \\ f_y \\ f_z \end{bmatrix}$	(26.2)
Jacobian	$\boldsymbol{u} = [u, v, w]^T : \mathbb{R}^3 \to \mathbb{R}^3$ $\nabla \boldsymbol{u} : \mathbb{R}^3 \to \mathbb{R}^{3\times 3}$	$\nabla \boldsymbol{u} = \begin{bmatrix} (\nabla u)^T \\ (\nabla v)^T \\ (\nabla w)^T \end{bmatrix} = \begin{bmatrix} u_x & u_y & u_z \\ v_x & v_y & v_z \\ w_x & w_y & w_z \end{bmatrix}$	(26.3)
Divergence	$\boldsymbol{u} = [u, v, w]^T : \mathbb{R}^3 \to \mathbb{R}^3$ $\operatorname{div} \boldsymbol{u} : \mathbb{R}^3 \to \mathbb{R}$	$\operatorname{div} \boldsymbol{u} = \nabla \cdot \boldsymbol{u} = u_x + v_y + w_z$	(26.4)
Rotation	$\boldsymbol{u} = [u, v, w]^T : \mathbb{R}^3 \to \mathbb{R}^3$ $\operatorname{curl} \boldsymbol{u} : \mathbb{R}^3 \to \mathbb{R}^3$	$\operatorname{curl} \boldsymbol{u} = \nabla \times \boldsymbol{u} = \begin{bmatrix} w_y - v_z \\ u_z - w_x \\ v_x - u_y \end{bmatrix}$	(26.5)
Laplace	$f : \mathbb{R}^3 \to \mathbb{R}$ $\Delta f : \mathbb{R}^3 \to \mathbb{R}$	$\Delta f = \nabla^2 f = \nabla \cdot \nabla f$ $= f_{xx} + f_{yy} + f_{zz}$	(26.6a) (26.6b)
Laplace	$\boldsymbol{u} = [u, v, w]^T : \mathbb{R}^3 \to \mathbb{R}^3$ $\Delta \boldsymbol{u} : \mathbb{R}^3 \to \mathbb{R}^3$	$\Delta \boldsymbol{u} = \nabla^2 \boldsymbol{u} = \left(\nabla^T (\nabla \boldsymbol{u})^T\right)^T$ $= \begin{bmatrix} u_{xx} + u_{yy} + u_{zz} \\ v_{xx} + v_{yy} + v_{zz} \\ w_{xx} + w_{yy} + w_{zz} \end{bmatrix}$	(26.7a) (26.7b)

Table 26.2: Common differential operators used on vector and scalar fields in three-dimensional space.

English Name	Case Lower	Case Upper	English Name	Case Lower	Case Upper	English Name	Case Lower	Case Upper
Alpha	α	A	Iota	ι	I	Rho	ρ	P
Beta	β	B	Kappa	κ	K	Sigma	σ	Σ
Gamma	γ	Γ	Lambda	λ	Λ	Tau	τ	T
Delta	δ	Δ	Mu	μ	M	Upsilon	υ	Υ
Epsilon	ϵ	E	Nu	ν	N	Phi	ϕ	Φ
Zeta	ζ	Z	Xi	ξ	Ξ	Chi	χ	X
Eta	η	H	Omicron	o	O	Psi	ψ	Ψ
Theta	θ	Θ	Pi	π	Π	Omega	ω	Ω

Table 26.3: The Greek alphabet.

Unit	Name	Measures
m	Meter	Length
g	Gram	Mass
s	Second	Time
A	Ampere	Electrical Current
K	Kelvin	Temperature
mol	Mole	Molecules
cd	Candela	Luminous Intensity

Table 26.4: International System of Units (SI).

Prefix	Exponential value	Modifier
Giga	10^9	G
Mega	10^6	M
Kilo	10^3	k
Hecto	10^2	-
Deka	10^1	-
Base	10^0	-
Deci	10^{-1}	d
Centi	10^{-2}	c
Milli	10^{-3}	m
Micro	10^{-6}	μ
Nano	10^{-9}	n

Table 26.5: Metric modifiers.

Unit	Name	Measures
$\mathrm{Hz} = \mathrm{s}^{-1}$	Hertz	Frequency
$\mathrm{N} = \mathrm{m\,kg\,s}^{-2}$	Newton	Force
$\mathrm{J} = \mathrm{m}^2\,\mathrm{kg\,s}^{-2}$	Joule	Energy
$\mathrm{Pa} = \mathrm{kg\,m}^{-1}\,\mathrm{s}^{-2}$	Pascal	Pressure and stress

Table 26.6: Some derived units.

Symbol	Description
$\mathrm{G} = 6.6742\,10^{-11}\mathrm{m}^3\,\mathrm{kg}^{-1}\,\mathrm{s}^{-1}$	Newtonian constant of gravity
$\mathrm{R} = 8.314472\mathrm{J\,mol}^{-1}\,\mathrm{K}^{-1}$	Molar gas constant
$\mathrm{c} = 299792458\mathrm{m\,s}^{-1}$	Speed of light in vacuum

Table 26.7: Some fundamental constants.

Material	Density ρ/(kg m^{-3})	Shear viscosity η/(Pa s)	Kinematic viscosity μ/(m^{2}s^{-1})	Young's modulus GPa	Poisson's ratio -
Air	1.18	1.82×10^{-5}	1.54×10^{-5}	-	-
Bone	200	-	-	14	0.43
Cork	180	-	-	0.032	0.25
Glass	2.5×10^3	10^{18}–10^{21}	10^{15}–10^{18}	65	0.23
Granite	260		-	66	0.25
Honey	1.4×10^3	14	1×10^{-2}	-	-
Ice	920	-	-	9.1	0.28
Olive oil	0.9×10^3	6.7×10^{-2}	7.4×10^{-5}	-	-
Steel	780	-	-	210	0.28
Water	1.00×10^3	1.00×10^{-3}	1.00×10^{-6}	-	-
Blood	1.06×10^3	2.7×10^{-3}	2.5×10^{-6}	-	-

Table 26.8: Some physical properties.

Materials	Static Frictions	Kinematic Frictions
Steel on Steel	0.74	0.57
Rubber on Concrete	1.0	0.8
Glass on Glass	0.94	0.4
Ice on Ice	0.1	0.03

Table 26.9: Some friction coefficients.

Bibliography

[Aanæs et al., 2003] Aanæs, H. and Bærentzen, J. A. (2003). Pseudo–normals for signed distance computation. In *Proceedings of Vision, Modeling, and Visualization*.

[Adams, 1995] Adams, R. A. (1995). *Calculus: A Complete Course*. Addison-Wesley Publishing Company, 3rd edition.

[Airy, 1845] Airy, G. B. (1845). Tides and waves. In *Encyclopedia Metropolitan*. London, England.

[Ames, 1969] Ames, W. F. (1969). *Numerical Methods for Parital Differential Equations*. Thomas Nelson and Sons Ltd.

[Anitescu et al., 1997] Anitescu, M. and Potra, F. (1997). Formulating dynamic multi-rigid-body contact problems with friction as solvable linear complementary problems. *Nonlinear Dynamics*, 14:231–247.

[Anitescu et al., 2002] Anitescu, M. and Potra, F. (2002). A time-stepping method for stiff multibody dynamics with contact and friction. *International J. Numer. Methods Engineering*, 55(7):753–784.

[Anitescu et al., 1996] Anitescu, M. and Potra, F. A. (1996). Formulating dynamic multi-rigid-body contact problems with friction as solvable linear complementary problems. Reports on Computational Mathematics No 93/1996, Department of Mathematics, The University of Iowa.

[Armstrong et al., 1985] Armstrong, W. W. and Green, M. W. (1985). The dynamics of articulated rigid bodies for purposes of animation. *The Visual Computer*, 1(4):231–240.

[Arnold, 1989] Arnold, V. I. (1989). *Mathematical Method of Classical Mechanics*. Springer-Verlag, 2nd edition.

[Baciu et al., 2002] Baciu, G. and Wong, W. S.-K. (2002). Hardware-assisted self-collision for deformable surfaces. In *Proceedings of the ACM symposium on Virtual Reality Software and Technology*, pages 129–136. ACM Press.

[Baraff, 1989] Baraff, D. (1989). Analytical methods for dynamic simulation of non-penetrating rigid bodies. *Computer Graphics*, 23(3):223–232.

[Baraff, 1991] Baraff, D. (1991). Coping with friction for non-penetrating rigid body simulation. *Computer Graphics*, 25(4):31–40.

[Baraff, 1994] Baraff, D. (1994). Fast contact force computation for nonpenetrating rigid bodies. *Computer Graphics*, 28(Annual Conference Series):23–34.

[Baraff, 1995] Baraff, D. (1995). Interactive simulation of solid rigid bodies. *IEEE Computer Graphics and Applications*, 15(3):63–75.

[Baraff, 1997a] Baraff, D. (1997a). Physical based modeling: Differential equation basics. SIGGRAPH 2001 course notes, Pixar Animation Studios. `www-2.cs.cmu.edu/~baraff/sigcourse/`.

[Baraff, 1997b] Baraff, D. (1997b). Physical based modeling: Implicit methods. SIGGRAPH 2001 course notes, Pixar Animation Studios. `www-2.cs.cmu.edu/~baraff/sigcourse/`.

[Baraff, 2001] Baraff, D. (2001). Physical based modeling: Rigid body simulation. SIGGRAPH 2001 course notes, Pixar Animation Studios. `www-2.cs.cmu.edu/~baraff/sigcourse/`.

[Baraff et al., 1998] Baraff, D. and Witkin, A. (1998). Large steps in cloth simulation. In *Proceedings of the 25th annual conference on Computer Graphics and Interactive Techniques*, pages 43–54. ACM Press.

[Baraff et al., 2003a] Baraff, D., Witkin, A., Anderson, J., and Kass, M. (2003a). Physically based modeling. SIGGRAPH course notes.

[Baraff et al., 2003b] Baraff, D., Witkin, A., and Kass, M. (2003b). Untangling cloth. *ACM Transactions on Graphics*, 22(3):862–870.

[Barsky et al., 1991] Barsky, B., Badler, N., and Zeltzer, D., editors (1991). *Making Them Move: Mechanics Control and Animation of Articulated Figures*. The Morgan Kaufmann Series in Computer Graphics and Geometric Modeling. Morgan Kaufman Publishers.

[Barzel et al., 1988] Barzel, R. and Barr, A. (1988). A modeling system based on dynamic constraints. In *Computer Graphics*, volume 22, pages 179–187.

[Barzel et al., 1996] Barzel, R., Hughes, J. F., and Wood, D. N. (1996). Plausible motion simulation for computer graphics animation. In *Proceedings of the Eurographics Workshop, Computer Animation and Simulation*, pages 183–197.

[Berg et al., 1997] Berg, M. d., van Kreveld, M., Overmars, M., and Schwarzkopf, O. (1997). *Computational Geometry, Algorithms and Applications*. Springer-Verlag.

[Bergen, 1997] Bergen, G. v. d. (1997). Efficient collision detection of complex deformable models using AABB trees. *Journal of Graphics Tools*, 2(4):1–13.

[Bergen, 1999] Bergen, G. v. d. (1999). A fast and robust GJK implementation for collision detection of convex objects. *Journal of Graphics Tools: JGT*, 4(2):7–25.

[Bergen, 2001] Bergen, G. v. d. (2001). Proximity queries and penetration depth computation on 3D game objects. *Game Developers Conference*.

[Bergen, 2003a] Bergen, G. v. d., editor (2003a). *Collision Detection in Interactive 3D Environments*. Interactive 3D Technology Series. Morgan Kaufmann.

[Bergen, 2003b] Bergen, G. v. d. (2003b). *Collision Detection in Interactive 3D Environments*. Series in Interactive 3D Technology. Morgan Kaufmann.

[Boas, 1983] Boas, M. L., editor (1983). *Mathematical Methods in the Physical Sciences*. John Wiley & Sons, 2nd edition.

[Boehm, 1980] Boehm, W. (1980). Inserting new knots into B-spline curves. *Computer Aided Design*, 12:199–201.

[Boldt et al., 2004] Boldt, N. and Meyer, J. (2004). Self-intersections with CULLIDE. Available as DIKU Project No. 04-02-19.

[Boor, 1978] Boor, C. d. (1978). *A Practical Guide to Splines*, volume 27 of *Applied Mathematical Sciences*. Springer-Verlag.

[Bouma et al., 1993] Bouma, W. J. and Vaněček, Jr., G. (1993). Modeling contacts in a physically based simulation. In *SMA '93: Proceedings of the Second Symposium on Solid Modeling and Applications*, pages 409–418.

[Bradshaw ct al., 2004] Bradshaw, G. and O'Sullivan, C. (2004). Adaptive medial-axis approximation for sphere-tree construction. *ACM Transactions on Graphics*, 23(1). `isg.cs.tcd.ie/spheretree/`.

[Bridson et al., 2002] Bridson, R., Fedkiw, R., and Anderson, J. (2002). Robust treatment of collisions, contact and friction for cloth animation. *Proceedings of ACM SIGGRAPH*, 21(3):594–603.

[Bridson et al., 2003] Bridson, R., Marino, S., and Fedkiw, R. (2003). Simulation of clothing with folds and wrinkles. In *Proceedings of the 2003 ACM SIGGRAPH/Eurographics Symposium on Computer Animation*, pages 28–36. Eurographics Association.

[Bronshtein et al., 1997] Bronshtein, I. and Semendyayev, K. (1997). *Handbook of Mathematics*. Springer-Verlag, 3rd edition.

[Burden et al., 1997] Burden, R. L. and Faires, J. D. (1997). *Numerical Analysis*. Brooks/Cole Publishing Company, 6th edition.

[Butcher, 1963] Butcher, J. (1963). Coefficients for the study of Runge-Kutta integration processes. *J. Austral. Math. Soc.*, 3:185–201.

[Butcher, 2003] Butcher, J. C. (2003). *Numerical Methods for Ordinary Differential Equations*. John Wiley & Sons, 2nd edition.

[Cameron, 1990] Cameron, S. (1990). Collision detection by four–dimensional intersectin testing. *IEEE Transaction on Robotics and Automation*, 6(3):291–302.

[Cameron, 1997] Cameron, S. (1997). Enhancing GJK: computing minimum and penetration distances between convex polyhedra. *Int. Conf. Robotics & Automation*.

[Carlson et al., 2004] Carlson, M., Mucha, P. J., and Turk, G. (2004). Rigid fluid: animating the interplay between rigid bodies and fluid. *ACM Transactions on Graphics*, 23(3):377–384.

[Chatterjee, 1999] Chatterjee, A. (1999). On the realism of complementarity conditions in rigid body collisions. *Nonlinear Dynamics*, 20(2):159–168.

[Chatterjee et al., 1998] Chatterjee, A. and Ruina, A. (1998). A new algebraic rigid body collision law based on impulse space considerations. *Journal of Applied Mechanics*. `www.tam.cornell.edu/Ruina.html`.

[Chen et al., 1992] Chen, D. T. and Zeltzer, D. (1992). Pump it up: computer animation of a biomechanically based model of muscle using the finite element method. In *Proceedings of the 19th annual conference on Computer Graphics and Interactive Techniques*, pages 89–98. ACM Press.

[Choi et al., 2005] Choi, M. G. and Ko, H.-S. (2005). Modal warping: Real-time simulation of large rotational deformation and manipulation. *IEEE Transactions on Visualization and Computer Graphics*, 11(1):91–101.

[Christensen et al., 2004] Christensen, M. and Fleron, A. (2004). Integrity improvements in classically deformable solids. In Olsen, S. I., editor, *DSAGM 2004*, pages 87–93, August.

[Collatz, 1986] Collatz, L. (1986). *Differential Equations*. John Wiley & Sons.

[Cook et al., 2002] Cook, R. D., Malkus, D. S., Plesha, M. E., and Witt, R. J. (2002). *Concepts and Applications of Finite Element Analysis*. John Wiley & Sons. Inc., fourth edition.

[Cormen et al., 1994] Cormen, T. H., Leiserson, C. E., and Riverst, R. L. (1994). *Introduction to Algorithms*. MIT press, 14 print edition.

[Cottle et al., 1992] Cottle, R., Pang, J.-S., and Stone, R. E. (1992). *The Linear Complementarity Problem*. Computer Science and Scientific Computing. Academic Press.

[Courant et al., 1928] Courant, R., Friedrichs, K., and Lewy, H. (1928). Ü die partiellen differenzengleichungen der mathematischen physik. *Math. Ann.*, 100(32).

[Craig, 1986] Craig, J. J. (1986). *Introduction to Robotics, Mechanics and Controls*. Addision-Wesley Publishing Company, Inc., 2nd edition.

[Craik, 2004] Craik, A. D. D. (2004). The origins of water wave theory. *Annual Review of Fluid Mechanics*, 36:1–28.

[Dam et al., 1998] Dam, E. B., Koch, M., and Lillholm, M. (1998). Quaternions, interplation, and animation. Technical Report DIKU 98/5, Department of Computer Science, University of Copenhagen.

[Denaro, 2003] Denaro, F. M. (2003). On the application of the helmholtz-hodge decomposition in projection methods for incompressible flows with general boundary conditions. *International journal for Numerical Methods in Fluids*, 43:43–69.

[Dingliana et al., 2000] Dingliana, J. and O'Sullivan, C. (2000). Graceful degradation of collision handling in physically based animation. *Computer Graphics Forum*, 19(3).

[Eberly, 2003a] Eberly, D. (2003a). Derivative approximation by finite differences. Online Paper. `www.geometrictools.com`.

[Eberly, 2005a] Eberly, D. (2005a). Centers of simplex. Online Paper. `www.geometrictools.com`.

[Eberly, 2005b] Eberly, D. (2005b). Dynamic collision detection using oriented bounding boxes. Online Paper. `www.geometrictools.com`.

[Eberly, 2005c] Eberly, D. (2005c). Intersection of objects with linear and angular velocities using oriented bounding boxes. Online Paper. `www.geometrictools.com`.

[Eberly, 2000] Eberly, D. H. (2000). *3D Game Engine Design : A Practical Approach to Real-Time Computer Graphics*. Morgan Kaufmann.

[Eberly, 2003b] Eberly, D. H. (2003b). *Game Physics*. Interactive 3D Technology Series. Morgan Kaufmann.

[Ehmann et al., 2000a] Ehmann, S. and Lin, M. (2000a). Accelerated proximity queries between convex polyhedra by multi-level voronoi marching.

[Ehmann et al., 2000b] Ehmann, S. A. and Lin, M. C. (2000b). Swift: Accelerated proximity queries between convex polyhedra by multi-level voronoi marching. Technical report, Computer Science Department, University of North Carolina at Chapel Hill. `www.cs.unc.edu/$\sim$geom/SWIFT/`.

[Ehmann et al., 2001] Ehmann, S. A. and Lin, M. C. (2001). Accurate and fast proximity queries between polyhedra using convex surface decomposition. In Chalmers, A. and Rhyne, T.-M., editors, *EG 2001 Proceedings*, volume 20(3), pages 500–510. Blackwell Publishing.

[Elbek, 1994] Elbek, B. (1994). *Elektromagnetisme*. Niels Bohr Institutet, University of Copenhagen.

[Enright et al., 2002] Enright, D., Marschner, S., and Fedkiw, R. (2002). Animation and rendering of complex water surfaces. In *Proceedings of the 29th annual conference on Computer Graphics and Interactive Techniques*, pages 736–744. ACM Press.

[Eriksson et al., 1996] Eriksson, K., Estep, D., Hansbo, P., and Johnson, C. (1996). *Computational Differential Equations*. Cambridge University Press.

[Erleben, 2005] Erleben, K. (2005). *Stable, Robust, and Versatile Multibody Dynamics Animation*. PhD thesis, Department of Computer Science, University of Copenhagen (DIKU), Universitetsparken 1, DK-2100 Copenhagen, Denmark. `www.diku.dk/~kenny/thesis.pdf`.

[Erleben et al., 2004] Erleben, K., Dohlmann, H., and Sporring, J. (2004). The adaptive thin shell tetrahedral mesh. (Submitted to Conference).

[Erleben et al., 2003a] Erleben, K. and Henriksen, K. (2003a). Scripted bodies and spline driven animation. In Lande, J., editor, *Graphics Programming Methods*. Charles River Media.

[Erleben et al., 2003b] Erleben, K. and Sporring, J. (2003b). Review of a general module based design for rigid body simulators. Unpublished, draft version can be obtained by email request.

[Etzmuss et al., 2003] Etzmuss, O., Keckeisen, M., and Strasser, W. (2003). A fast finite element solution for cloth modelling. In *PG '03: Proceedings of the 11th Pacific Conference on Computer Graphics and Applications*, page 244, Washington, DC, USA. IEEE Computer Society.

[Euler, 1744] Euler, L. (1744). *Methodus inveniendi lineas curvas maximi minimive proprietate gaudentes, sive solutio problematis isoperimetrici lattissimo sensu accepti (A method for finding curved lines enjoying properties of maximum or minimum, or solution of isoperimetric problems in the broadest accepted sense)*, volume 24 of *1*. Opera Omnia. See `www.eulerarchive.com/` for a brief description.

[Euler, 1755] Euler, L. (1755). Principes géneraux du mouvement des fluides. *Mém. Acad. Sci. Berlin*, 11:274–315.

[Euler, 1768] Euler, L. (1768). *Institutioners Calculi Integralis*. PhD thesis, St. Petersburg.

[Farin, 1993] Farin, G. (1993). *Curves and Surfaces for Computer Aided Geometric Design. A Practical Guide*. Computer Science and Scientific Computing. Academic Press, Inc., third edition.

[Fattal et al., 2004] Fattal, R. and Lischinski, D. (2004). Target-driven smoke animation. *ACM Transactions on Graphics*, 23(3):441–448.

[Featherstone, 1998] Featherstone, R. (1998). *Robot Dynamics Algorithms*. Kluwer Academic Publishers. Second Printing.

[Feldman et al., 2003] Feldman, B. E., O'Brien, J. F., and Arikan, O. (2003). Animating suspended particle explosions. *ACM Transactions on Graphics*, 22(3):708–715.

[Finch et al., 2004] Finch, M. and Worlds, C. (2004). Effective water simulation from physical models. In Fernando, R., editor, *GPU Gems, Programming Techniques, Tips and Tricks for Real-Time graphics*, chapter 1. Addison-Wesley.

[Fisher et al., 2001] Fisher, S. and Lin, M. C. (2001). Deformed distance fields for simulation of non-penetrating flexible bodies. In *Proceedings of the Eurographic workshop on Computer Animation and Simulation*, pages 99–111. Springer-Verlag New York, Inc.

[Florack, 1997] Florack, L. (1997). *Image Structure*. Computational Imaging and Vision. Kluwer Academic Publishers, Dordrecht.

[Foley et al., 1996] Foley, J. D., van Dam, A., Feiner, S. K., and Hughes, J. F. (1996). *Computer Graphics: Principles and Pratice; In C*. Addison-Wesley, 2nd edition.

[Foster et al., 1997] Foster, N. and Metaxas, D. (1997). Modeling the motion of a hot, turbulent gas. In *Proceedings of the 24th annual conference on Computer Graphics and Interactive Techniques*, pages 181–188. ACM Press/Addison-Wesley Publishing Co.

[Frank et al., 1995] Frank, O. and Thomas, J. (1995). *Illusion of Life: Disney Animation*. Hyperion Press.

[Frisken et al., 2000] Frisken, S. F., Perry, R. N., Rockwood, A. P., and Jones, T. R. (2000). Adaptively sampled distance fields: a general representation of shape for computer graphics. In *Proceedings of the 27th annual conference on Computer Graphics and Interactive Techniques*, pages 249–254. ACM Press/Addison-Wesley Publishing Co.

[Fuhrmann et al., 2003] Fuhrmann, A., Sobottka, G., and Groß, C. (2003). Distance fields for rapid collision detection in physically based modeling. In *Proceedings of GraphiCon*, pages 58–65.

[Ganovelli et al., 2000] Ganovelli, F., Dingliana, J., and O'Sullivan, C. (2000). Buckettree: Improving collision detection between deformable objects. In *Spring Conference in Computer Graphics (SCCG2000)*, pages 156–163, Bratislava.

[Gerstner, 1802] Gerstner, F. J. v. (1802). Theorie der Wellen. *Abhand. Kön. Bömischen Gesel. Wiss.*

[Gilbert et al., 1988] Gilbert, E., Johnson, D., and Keerthi, S. (1988). A fast procedure for computing the distance between complex objects in three-dimensional space. *IEEE Journal of Robotics and Automation*, 4:193–203.

[Goktekin et al., 2004] Goktekin, T. G., Bargteil, A. W., and O'Brien, J. F. (2004). A method for animating viscoelastic fluids. *ACM Transactions on Graphics*, 23(3):463–468.

[Goldsmith et al., 1987] Goldsmith, J. and Salmon, J. (1987). Automatic creation of object hierarchies for ray tracing. *IEEE Computer Graphics and Applications*, 7(5):14–20. see Scherson & Caspary article for related work.

[Goldstein, 1980] Goldstein, H. (1980). *Classical Mechanics*. Addison-Wesley, Reading, MA, U.S.A., 3rd edition. 638 pages.

[Goldstein et al., 2002] Goldstein, H., Poole, C. P., Poole, C. P. J., and Safko, J. L. (2002). *Classical Mechanics*. Prentice Hall, 3rd edition.

[Golub et al., 1996] Golub, G. H. and Loan, C. F. V. (1996). *Matrix Computations*. The Johns Hopkins University Press, 3rd edition.

[Gottschalk, 2000] Gottschalk, S. (2000). *Collision Queries using Oriented Bounding Boxes*. PhD thesis, Department of Computer Science, University of N. Carolina, Chapel Hill.

[Gottschalk et al., 1996] Gottschalk, S., Lin, M. C., and Manocha, D. (1996). OBB-Tree: A hierarchical structure for rapid interference detection. Technical Report TR96-013, Department of Computer Science, University of N. Carolina, Chapel Hill. `www.cs.unc.edu/$\sim$geom/OBB/OBBT.html`.

[Gourret et al., 1989] Gourret, J. P., Magnenat-Thalmann, N., and Thalmann, D. (1989). Simulation of object and human skin deformations in a grasping task. *Computer Graphics*, 23(3):21–31.

[Govindaraju et al., 2003] Govindaraju, N., Redon, S., Lin, M., and Manocha, D. (2003). CULLIDE: Interactive collision detection between complex models in large environments using graphics hardware. *ACM SIGGRAPH/Eurographics Graphics Hardware*.

[Guendelman et al., 2003] Guendelman, E., Bridson, R., and Fedkiw, R. (2003). Nonconvex rigid bodies with stacking. *ACM Transaction on Graphics, Proceedings of ACM SIGGRAPH*.

[Hahn, 1988] Hahn, J. K. (1988). Realistic animation of rigid bodies. In *Computer Graphics*, volume 22, pages 299–308.

[Hairer et al., 2002] Hairer, E., Lubich, C., and Wanner, G. (2002). *Geomeric Numerical Integration*. Springer-Verlag.

[Halsey et al., 1986] Halsey, T. C., Jensen, M. H., Kadanoff, L. P., Procaccia, I., and Shraiman, B. I. (1986). Fractal measures and their singularities: The characterization of strange sets. *Physical Review A*, 33:1141–1151.

[Haltiner et al., 1980] Haltiner, G. J. and Williams, R. T. (1980). *Numerical Prediction and Dynamic Meteorology*. John Wiley & Sons IUnc., New York, 2nd edition.

[Hansen, 1988] Hansen, E. B. (1988). *Variationsregning*. Polyteknisk Forlag.

[Harris, 2004] Harris, M. J. (2004). Fast fluid dynamics simulation on the GPU. In Fernando, R., editor, *GPU Gems, Programming Techniques, Tips and Tricks for Real-Time graphics*, chapter 38. Addison-Wesley.

[Hart et al., 2003] Hart, G. D. and Anitescu, M. (2003). A hard-constraint time-stepping approach for rigid multibody dynamics with joints, contact, and friction. In *Proceedings of the 2003 conference on Diversity in Computing*, pages 34–41. ACM Press.

[Hasegawa et al., 2003] Hasegawa, S., Fujii, N., Koike, Y., and Sato, M. (2003). Real-time rigid body simulation based on volumetric penalty method. In *Proceedings of the 11th Symposium on Haptic Interfaces for Virtual Environment and Teleoperator Systems (HAPTICS'03)*, page 326. IEEE Computer Society.

[Hauser et al., 2003] Hauser, K. K., Shen, C., and O'Brien, J. F. (2003). Interactive deformation using modal analysis with constraints. In *Graphics Interface*, pages 247–256. CIPS, Canadian Human-Computer Commnication Society, A. K. Peters. ISBN 1-56881-207-8, ISSN 0713-5424, `www.graphicsinterface.org/proceedings/2003/`.

[He, 1999] He, T. (1999). Fast collision detection using quospo trees. In *Proceedings of the 1999 symposium on Interactive 3D graphics*, pages 55–62. ACM Press.

[Heidelberger et al., 2003] Heidelberger, B., Teschner, M., and Gross, M. (2003). Volumetric collision detection for deformable objects. Technical report, Computer Science Department, ETH Zurich.

[Heidelberger et al., 2004] Heidelberger, B., Teschner, M., and Gross, M. (2004). Detection of collisions and self-collisions using image-space techniques. In *Proc. WSCG*, pages 145–152, Plzen, Czech Republic.

[Hirota, 2002] Hirota, G. (2002). *An Improved Finite Element Contact Model for Anatomical Simulations*. PhD thesis, University of N. Carolina, Chapel Hill.

[Hirota et al., 2000] Hirota, G., Fisher, S., and Lin, M. (2000). Simulation of non-penetrating elastic bodies using distance fields. Technical report, University of North Carolina at Chapel Hill.

[Hirota et al., 2001] Hirota, G., Fisher, S., State, A., Lee, C., and Fuchs, H. (2001). An implicit finite element method for elastic solids in contact. In *Computer Animation*, Seoul, South Korea.

[Hoff, III et al., 1999] Hoff, III, K. E., Keyser, J., Lin, M., Manocha, D., and Culver, T. (1999). Fast computation of generalized voronoi diagrams using graphics hardware. In *Proceedings of the 26th annual conference on Computer Graphics and Interactive Techniques*, pages 277–286. ACM Press/Addison-Wesley Publishing Co.

[Hoff III et al., 2001] Hoff III, K. E., Zaferakis, A., Lin, M., and Manocha, D. (2001). Fast and simple 2D geometric proximity queries using graphics hardware. In *Proc. of ACM Symposium on Interactive 3D Graphics*.

[Hongbin et al., 2005] Hongbin, J. and Xin, D. (2005). On criterions for smoothed particle hydrodynamics kernels in stable field. *Journal of Computational Physics*, 202(2):699–709.

[Hoschek et al., 1993] Hoschek, J. and Lasser, D. (1993). *Fundamentals of Computer Aided Geometric Design*. A. K. Peters. English translation 1993 by A. K. Peters, Ltd.

[House et al., 2000] House, D. H. and Breen, D., editors (2000). *Cloth Modeling and Animation*. A. K. Peters.

[Hubbard, 1993] Hubbard, P. M. (1993). Interactive collision detection. In *Proceedings of the IEEE Symposium on Research Frontiers in Virtual Reality*, pages 24–32.

[Hubbard, 1996] Hubbard, P. M. (1996). Approximating polyhedra with spheres for time-critical collision detection. *ACM Transactions on Graphics*, 15(3):179–210.

[III et al., 2002] III, K. E. H., Zaferakis, A., Lin, M., and Manocha, D. (2002). Fast 3D geometric proximity queries between rigid and deformable models using graphics hardware acceleration. *UNC-CS Technical Report*.

[IO Interactive A/S, 2005] IO Interactive A/S (2005). `www.ioi.dk`.

[Irving et al., 2004] Irving, G., Teran, J., and Fedkiw, R. (2004). Invertible finite elements for robust simulation of large deformation. *ACM SIGGRAPH/Eurographics Symposium on Computer Animation (SCA)*.

[Irving et al., 2005] Irving, G., Teran, J., and Fedkiw, R. (2005). Tetrahedral and hexahedral invertible finite elements. Graphical Models (in press).

[Jakobsen, 2001] Jakobsen, T. (2001). Advanced character physics. Presentation, Game Developer's Conference. `www.ioi.dk/Homepages/thomasj/publications/AdvancedPhysics_files/v3_document.htm`.

[Jakobsen, 2005] Jakobsen, T. (2005). Personal communication.

[James et al., 2002] James, D. L. and Pai, D. K. (2002). Dyrt: dynamic response textures for real time deformation simulation with graphics hardware. In *SIGGRAPH '02: Proceedings of the 29th annual conference on Computer Graphics and Interactive Techniques*, pages 582–585. ACM Press.

[Jansson et al., 2002a] Jansson, J. and Vergeest, J. S. M. (2002a). Combining deformable and rigid body mechanics simulation. *The Visual Computer Journal*. `www.math.chalmers.se/$\sim$johanjan/`.

[Jansson et al., 2002b] Jansson, J. and Vergeest, J. S. M. (2002b). A discrete mechanics model for deformable bodies. *Computer-Aided Design*, 34(12):913–928.

[Jensen, 2001] Jensen, L. (2001). Deep-water animation and rendering. Gamasutra, `www.gamasutra.com/gdce/jensen/jensen_01.htm`.

[Johansen, 2005] Johansen, J. (2005). Personal Communication.

[Joukhadar et al., 1998] Joukhadar, A., Deguet, A., and Laugier, C. (1998). A collision model for rigid and deformable bodies. In *IEEE Int. Conference on Robotics and Automation, Vol. 2*, pages 982–988, Leuven (BE).

[Joukhadar et al., 1999] Joukhadar, A., Scheuer, A., and Laugier, C. (1999). Fast contact detection between moving deformable polyhedra. In *IEEE-RSJ Int. Conference on Intelligent Robots and Systems, Vol. 3*, pages 1810–1815, Kyongju (KR).

[Joukhadar et al., 1996] Joukhadar, A., Wabbi, A., and Laugier, C. (1996). Fast contact localisation between deformable polyhedra in motion. In *IEEE Computer Animation Conference*, pages 126–135, Geneva (CH).

[Karma, 2005] Karma (2005). Middleware physics software provider. MathEngine Karma, `www.mathengine.com/karma/`.

[Kačić-Alesić et al., 2003] Kačić-Alesić, Z., Nordenstam, M., and Bullock, D. (2003). A practical dynamics system. In *SCA '03: Proceedings of the 2003 ACM SIGGRAPH/Eurographics Symposium on Computer Animation*, pages 7–16, Aire-la-Ville, Switzerland, Switzerland. Eurographics Association.

[Kaye et al., 1995] Kaye, G. W. C. and Laby, T. H. (1995). *Tables of Physical and Chemical Constants*. Longman Group Ltd., 16th edition.

[Kelager et al., 2005] Kelager, M., Fleron, A., and Erleben, K. (2005). Area and volume restoration in elastically deformable solids. *Electronic Letters on Compuer Vision and Image Analysis (ELCVIA)*, 5(3):32–43. Special Issue on Articulated Motion, `elcvia.cvc.uab.es`.

[Kim et al., 2002] Kim, Y. J., Otaduy, M. A., Lin, M. C., and Manocha, D. (2002). Fast penetration depth computation for physically-based animation. In *Proceedings of the 2002 ACM SIGGRAPH/Eurographics symposium on Computer Animation*, pages 23–31. ACM Press.

[Kleppner et al., 1978] Kleppner, D. and Kolenkow, R. J. (1978). *An Introduction to Mechanics*. McGraw-Hill Book Co., international edition.

[Klosowski, 1998] Klosowski, J. T. (1998). Efficient collision detection for interactive 3D graphics and virtual environments. `www.ams.sunysb.edu/$\sim$jklosow/publications`.

[Klosowski et al., 1998] Klosowski, J. T., Held, M., Mitchell, J. S. B., Sowizral, H., and Zikan, K. (1998). Efficient collision detection using bounding volume hierarchies of k-DOPs. *IEEE Transactions on Visualization and Computer Graphics*, 4(1):21–36.

[Koenderink, 1990] Koenderink, J. J. (1990). *Solid Shape*. MIT Press, Cambridge.

[Kraus et al., 1997] Kraus, P. R. and Kumar, V. (1997). Compliant contact models for rigid body collisions. In *IEEE International Conference on Robotics and Automation*, Albuquerque.

[Kreyszig, 1993] Kreyszig, E. (1993). *Advanced Engineering Mathematics*. John Wiley & Sons, Inc., 7 edition.

[Krishnan et al., 1998] Krishnan, S., Pattekar, A., Lin, M., and Manocha, D. (1998). Spherical shell: A higher order bounding volume for fast proximity queries. In *Proc. of Third International Workshop on Algorithmic Foundations of Robotics*, pages 122–136.

[Lacoursiere, 2003] Lacoursiere, C. (2003). Splitting methods for dry frictional contact problems in rigid multibody systems: Preliminary performance results. In Ollila, M., editor, *The Annual SIGRAD Conference*, number 10 in Linkøping Electronic Conference Proceedings.

[Lagrange, 1762] Lagrange, J.-L. (1762). Calculus of variation. *Mélanges de Turin*.

[Larsen et al., 1999] Larsen, E., Gottschalk, S., Lin, M. C., and Manocha, D. (1999). Fast proximity queries with swept sphere volumes. Technical Report TR99-018, Department of Computer Science, University of N. Carolina, Chapel Hill. `www.cs.unc.edu/$\sim$geom/SSV`.

[Larsson et al., 2001] Larsson, T. and Akenine-Möller, T. (2001). Collision detection for continuously deforming bodies. In *Eurographics*, pages 325–333.

[Larsson et al., 2003] Larsson, T. and Akenine-Möller, T. (2003). Efficient collision detection for models deformed by morphing. *The Visual Computer*, 19(2):164–174.

[Lassiter, 1987] Lassiter, J. (1987). Principles of traditional animation applied to 3D computer animation. In *Proceedings of the 14th annual conference on Computer Graphics and Interactive Techniques*, pages 35–44. ACM Press.

[Lautrup, 2005] Lautrup, B. (2005). *Physics of Continuous Matter*. IoP.

[Layton et al., 2002] Layton, A. T. and Panne, M. v. d. (2002). A numerically efficient and stable algorithm for animating water waves. *The Visual Computer*, 18:41–53.

[Lin et al., 1998] Lin, M. C. and Gottschalk, S. (1998). Collision detection between geometric models: a survey. In *Proc. of IMA Conference on Mathematics of Surfaces*, pages 37–56.

[Lin et al., 1994] Lin, M. C. and Manocha, D. (1994). Efficient contact determination between geometric models. Technical Report TR94-024, The University of North Carolina at Chapel Hill, Department of Computer Science.

[llerhøj, 2004] llerhøj, K. M. (2004). Simulering af rigid-body systemer med coulomb friktion ved brug af en implicit tidsskridts metode. Master's thesis, Department of Computer Science, University of Copenhagen (DIKU). NO. 03-04-17.

[Lorensen et al., 1987] Lorensen, W. E. and Cline, H. E. (1987). Marching cubes: A high resolution 3D surface construction algorithm. *ACM Computer Graphics*, pages 163–169.

[M.M̃üller, 2004a] M.M̃üller, M. G. (2004a). Interactive virtual materials. In *Proceedings of Graphics Interface (GI 2004)*, pages 239–246, London, Ontario, Canada.

[M.M̃üller, 2004b] M.M̃üller, M.T̃eschner, M. G. (2004b). Physically-based simulation of objects represented by surface meshes. In *Proc. Computer Graphics International*, pages 26–33, Crete, Greece.

[Magnus et al., 1988] Magnus, J. R. and Neudecker, H. (1988). *Matrix Differential Calculus with Applications in Statistics and Econometrics*. John Wiley & Sons.

[Mandelbrot, 2004] Mandelbrot, B. B. (2004). *Fractals and Chaos*. Springer.

[Matyka et al., 2003] Matyka, M. and Ollila, M. (2003). Pressure model of soft body simulation. In *SIGRAD2003, The Annual SIGRAD Conference. Special Theme – Real-Time Simulations*, Linkö ping Electronic Conference Proceedings, UmeåUniversity, Umeå, Sweden. `www.ep.liu.se/ecp/010/007/`.

[Mauch, 2000] Mauch, S. (2000). A fast algorithm for computing the closest point and distance transform. `www.acm.caltech.edu/~seanm/software/cpt/cpt.html`.

[McClellan et al., 1998] McClellan, J. H., Schafer, R. W., and Yoder, M. A. (1998). *DSP First: A Multimedia Approach*. Prentice Hall.

[McInerney et al., 2000] McInerney, T. and Terzopoulos, D. (2000). T-snakes: Topology adaptive snakes. *Medical Image Analysis*, 4:73–91.

[McKenna et al., 1990] McKenna, M. and Zeltzer, D. (1990). Dynamic simulation of autonomous legged locomotion. In *Proceedings of the 17th annual conference on Computer Graphics and Interactive Techniques*, pages 29–38. ACM Press.

[McNamara et al., 2003] McNamara, A., Treuille, A., Popovic, Z., and Stam, J. (2003). Keyframe control of smoke simulations. *Proceedings of SIGGRAPH 2003*.

[Melax, 2001] Melax, S. (2001). Bsp collision detection as used in mdk2 and neverwinter nights. *Gamasutra*. `www.gamasutra.com/features/20010324/melax_01.htm`.

[Messer, 1994] Messer, R. (1994). *Linear Algebra: Gateway to Mathematics*. HarperCollins College Publishers.

[Mezger et al., 2003] Mezger, J., Kimmerle, S., and Etzmuss, O. (2003). Hierarchical techniques in collision detection for cloth animation. *WSCG*, 11(1).

[Milenkovic et al., 2001] Milenkovic, V. J. and Schmidl, H. (2001). Optimization-based animation. *SIGGRAPH Conference*.

[Mirtich, 1995] Mirtich, B. (1995). Hybrid simulation: Combining constraints and impulses. *Proceedings of First Workshop on Simulation and Interaction in Virtual Environments*.

[Mirtich, 1996] Mirtich, B. (1996). *Impulse-based Dynamic Simulation of Rigid Body Systems*. PhD thesis, University of California, Berkeley.

[Mirtich, 1998a] Mirtich, B. (1998a). Rigid body contact: Collision detection to force computation. Technical Report TR-98-01, MERL.

[Mirtich, 1998b] Mirtich, B. (1998b). V-clip: Fast and robust polyhedral collision detection. *ACM Transactions on Graphics*, 17(3):177–208.

[Mirtich et al., 1994] Mirtich, B. and Canny, J. F. (1994). Impulse-based dynamic simulation. Technical Report CSD-94-815, University of Califonia, Berkley, CA, USA.

[Mirtich et al., 1995] Mirtich, B. and Canny, J. F. (1995). Impulse-based simulation of rigid bodies. In *Symposium on Interactive 3D Graphics*, pages 181–188, 217.

[Molino et al., 2004] Molino, N., Bao, Z., and Fedkiw, R. (2004). A virtual node algorithm for changing mesh topology during simulation. *ACM Transactions on Graphics*, 23(3):385–392.

[Monaghan, 1988] Monaghan, J. J. (1988). An introduction to sph. *Computer Physics Communications*, 48:89–96.

[Monaghan, 1992] Monaghan, J. J. (1992). Smoothed particle hydrodynamics. *Annual Review of Astronomy and Astrophysics*, 30(1):543–574.

[Moore et al., 1988] Moore, M. and Wilhelms, J. (1988). Collision detection and response for computer animation. In *Computer Graphics*, volume 22, pages 289–298.

[Morton et al., 1994] Morton, K. and Mayers, D. (1994). *Numerical Solution of Partial Differential Equations.* Cambridge University Press.

[Mosegaard, 2003] Mosegaard, J. (2003). Realtime cardiac surgical simulation. Master's thesis, Department of Computer Science at the Faculty of Science, University of Aarhus, Denmark.

[Mosterman, 2001] Mosterman, P. J. (2001). On the normal component of centralized frictionless collision sequences. submitted to ASME Journal of Applied Mechanics, in review.

[Müller et al., 2003] Müller, M., Charypar, D., and Gross, M. (2003). Particle-based fluid simulation for interactive applications. In *Proceedings of the 2003 ACM SIGGRAPH/Eurographics Symposium on Computer Animation*, pages 154–159. Eurographics Association.

[Müller et al., 2002] Müller, M., Dorsey, J., McMillan, L., Jagnow, R., and Cutler, B. (2002). Stable real-time deformations. In *SCA '02: Proceedings of the 2002 ACM SIGGRAPH/Eurographics symposium on Computer Animation*, pages 49–54. ACM Press.

[Müller et al., 2004a] Müller, M. and Gross, M. (2004a). Interactive virtual materials. In Balakrishnan, R. and Heidrich, W., editors, *Proceedings of Graphics Interface 2004*, pages 239–246, Waterloo, Canada. Canadian Human-Computer Communications Society.

[Müller et al., 2004b] Müller, M., Teschner, M., and Gross, M. (2004b). Physically-based simulation of objects represented by surface meshes. In *Proceedings of Computer Graphics International 2004*.

[Murty, 1988] Murty, K. G. (1988). *Linear Complementarity, Linear and Nonlinear Programming*. Helderman-Verlag. This book is now available for download. `ioe.engin.umich.edu/people/fac/books/murty/linear_complementarity_webbook/`.

[Navier, 1822] Navier, C. L. M. H. (1822). Mémoire sur les lois du mouvement des fluides. *Mém. Aca. Sci. Inst. France*, 6:389–440.

[NIST, 2005] NIST (2005). The nist reference on constants, units, and uncertainty. `physics.nist.gov/cuu/Units/units.html`.

[Nooruddin et al., 2003] Nooruddin, F. S. and Turk, G. (2003). Simplification and repair of polygonal models using volumetric techniques. *IEEE Transactions on Visualization and Computer Graphics*, 9(2):191–205.

[Nordlund, 2005] Nordlund, Å. (2005). Personal Communication.

[NovodeX, 2005] NovodeX (2005). Novodex physics sdk v2. `www.novodex.com/`.

[O'Brien et al., 2002a] O'Brien, J. F., Bargteil, A. W., and Hodgins, J. K. (2002a). Graphical modeling and animation of ductile fracture. In *SIGGRAPH '02: Proceedings of the 29th annual conference on Computer Graphics and Interactive Techniques*, pages 291–294, New York, NY, USA. ACM Press.

[O'Brien et al., 1999] O'Brien, J. F. and Hodgins, J. K. (1999). Graphical modeling and animation of brittle fracture. In *SIGGRAPH '99: Proceedings of the 26th annual conference on Computer Graphics and Interactive Techniques*, pages 137–146, New York, NY, USA. ACM Press/Addison-Wesley Publishing Co.

[O'Brien et al., 2002b] O'Brien, J. F., Shen, C., and Gatchalian, C. M. (2002b). Synthesizing sounds from rigid-body simulations. In *SCA '02: Proceedings of the 2002 ACM SIGGRAPH/Eurographics symposium on Computer Animation*, pages 175–181. ACM Press.

[ODE, 2005] ODE (2005). Open Dynamics Engine. Opensource Project, Multibody Dynamics Software. `q12.org/ode/`.

[OpenTissue, 2005] OpenTissue (2005). `www.opentissue.org`.

[O'Rourke, 1998] O'Rourke, J. (1998). *Computational Geometry in C*. Cambridge University Press, 2nd edition. `cs.smith.edu/~orourke/`.

[Osher et al., 2003] Osher, S. and Fedkiw, R. (2003). *Level-Set Methods and Dynamic Implicit Surfaces*, volume 153 of *Applied Mathematical Sciences*. Springer.

[Osher et al., 1988] Osher, S. and Sethian, S. (1988). Fronts propagating with curvature dependent speed: algorithms based on the Hamilton-Jacobi formalism. *J. Computational Physics*, 79:12–49.

[O'Sullivan et al., 1999] O'Sullivan, C. and Dingliana, J. (1999). Real-time collision detection and response using sphere-trees.

[Palmer, 1995] Palmer, I. (1995). Collision detection for animation: The use of the sphere-tree data structure. In *The Second Departmental Workshop on Computing Research*. University of Bradford.

[Palmer et al., 1995] Palmer, I. and Grimsdale, R. (1995). Collision detection for animation using sphere-trees. *Computer Graphics Forum*, 14(2):105–116.

[Parent, 2001] Parent, R. (2001). *Computer Animation: Algorithms and Techniques*. Morgan Kaufmann.

[Path, 2005] Path (2005). Path cpnet software. `www.cs.wisc.edu/cpnet/cpnetsoftware/`.

[Pedersen et al., 2004] Pedersen, C., Erleben, K., and Sporring, J. (2004). Ballet balance strategies. In Elmegaard, B., Sporring, J., Erleben, K., and Sørensen, K., editors, *SIMS 2004*, pages 323–330.

[Pentland et al., 1989] Pentland, A. and Williams, J. (1989). Good vibrations: model dynamics for graphics and animation. In *SIGGRAPH '89: Proceedings of the 16th annual conference on Computer Graphics and Interactive Techniques*, pages 215–222. ACM Press.

[Pfeiffer et al., 1996a] Pfeiffer, F. and Glocker, C. (1996a). *Multibody Dynamics with Unilateral Contacts*. Wiley series in nonlinear science. John Wiley & Sons, Inc.

[Pfeiffer et al., 1996b] Pfeiffer, F. and Wösle, M. (1996b). Dynamics of multibody systems containing dependent unilateral constraints with friction. *Journal of Vibration and Control*, 2:161–192.

[Piegl et al., 1995] Piegl, L. and Tiller, W. (1995). *The NURBS Book.* Springer-Verlag Berlin Heidelberg New York.

[Platt et al., 1988] Platt, J. and Barr, A. (1988). Constraint methods for flexible bodies. In *Computer Graphics*, volume 22, pages 279–288.

[Ponamgi et al., 1997] Ponamgi, M. K., Manocha, D., and Lin, M. C. (1997). Incremental algorithms for collision detection between polygonal models:. *IEEE Transactions on Visualization and Computer Graphics*, 3(1):51–64.

[Press et al., 1999a] Press, W. H., Teukolsky, S. A., Vetterling, W. T., and Flannery, B. P. (1999a). *Numerical Recipes in C.* Cambridge University Press, 2nd edition.

[Press et al., 1999b] Press, W. H., Teukolsky, S. A., Vetterling, W. T., and P.Flannery, B. (1999b). *Numerical Recipes in C: The Art of Scientific Computing.* Cambridge University Press, sixth edition. `www.nr.com`.

[Provot, 1995] Provot, X. (1995). Deformation constraints in a mass-spring model to describe rigid cloth behavior. *In Procedings of Graphics Interface*, pages 147–154.

[Rasmussen et al., 2003] Rasmussen, N., Nguyen, D., Geiger, W., and Fedkiw, R. (2003). Smoke simulation for large scale phenomena. *ACM SIGGRAPH Transactions on Graphics*, 22(3).

[Redon, 2004a] Redon, S. (2004a). Continuous collision detection for rigid and articulated bodies. To appear in ACM SIGGRAPH Course Notes, 2004.

[Redon, 2004b] Redon, S. (2004b). Fast continuous collision detection and handling for desktop virtual prototyping. *Virtual Reality Journal.* Accepted for publication.

[Redon et al., 2002] Redon, S., Kheddar, A., and Coquillart, S. (2002). Fast continuous collision detection between rigid bodies. *Computer Graphics Forum (Eurographics 2002 Proceedings)*, 21(3).

[Redon et al., 2003] Redon, S., Kheddar, A., and Coquillart, S. (2003). Gauss least constraints principle and rigid body simulations. In *In proceedings of IEEE International Conference on Robotics and Automation.* `www.cs.unc.edu/~redon/`.

[Redon et al., 2004a] Redon, S., Kim, Y. J., Lin, M. C., and Manocha, D. (2004a). Fast continuous collision detection for articulated models. *Proceedings of ACM Symposium on Solid Modeling and Applications.* To appear.

[Redon et al., 2004b] Redon, S., Kim, Y. J., Lin, M. C., Manocha, D., and Templeman, J. (2004b). Interactive and continuous collision detection for avatars in virtual environments. *IEEE International Conference on Virtual Reality Proceedings.*

[Rettrup, 2005] Rettrup, S. (2005). Personal Communication.

[Rissanen, 1989] Rissanen, J. (1989). *Stochastic Complexity in Statistical Inquiry*. World Scientific, Singapore.

[Roy, 1995] Roy, T. M. (1995). Physically-based fluid modeling using smoothed particle hydrodynamics. Master's thesis, University of Illinois at Chicago. `www.plunk.org/~trina/work.html`.

[Rusinkiewicz et al., 2000] Rusinkiewicz, S. and Levoy, M. (2000). QSplat: A multiresolution point rendering system for large meshes. In *Proceedings of the 27th annual conference on Computer Graphics and Interactive Techniques*, pages 343–352.

[Saint-Venant, 1871] Saint-Venant, A. J. C. d. (1871). Théorie du mouvement non-permanent des eaux, avec crues des rivières et à l'introduction des marées dans leur lit. *C. R. Acad. Sci. Paris*, pages 147–154. (in French).

[Sauer et al., 1998] Sauer, J. and Schömer, E. (1998). A constraint-based approach to rigid body dynamics for virtual reality applications. *ACM Symposium on Virtual Reality Software and Technology*, pages 153–161.

[Schmidl, 2002] Schmidl, H. (2002). *Optimization-based animation.* PhD thesis, Univeristy of Miami.

[Sederberg et al., 1986] Sederberg, T. W. and Parry, S. R. (1986). Free-form deformation of solid geometric models. In *SIGGRAPH '86: Proceedings of the 13th annual conference on Computer Graphics and Interactive Techniques*, pages 151–160. ACM Press.

[Sethian, 1999] Sethian, J. A. (1999). *Level Set Methods and Fast Marching Methods. Evolving Interfaces in Computational Geometry, Fluid Mechanics, Computer Vision, and Materials Science*. Cambridge University Press. Cambridge Monograph on Applied and Computational Mathematics.

[SGI, 2005] SGI (2005). Opengl extension registry: `arb_occlusion_query`. Online web site. `oss.sgi.com/projects/ogl-sample/registry/ARB/occlusion_query.txt`.

[Shannon et al., 1949] Shannon, C. E. and Weaver, W. (1949). *The Mathematical Theory of Communication*. The University of Illinois Press, Urbana.

[Shao et al., 2003] Shao, S. and Lo, E. Y. M. (2003). Incompressible sph method for simulating newtonian and non-newtonian flows with a free surface. *Advances in Water Resources*, 26:787–800.

[Shen et al., 2004] Shen, C., O'Brien, J. F., and Shewchuk, J. R. (2004). Interpolating and approximating implicit surfaces from polygon soup. *ACM Transactions on Graphics*, 23(3):896–904.

[Shewchuk, 1994] Shewchuk, J. R. (1994). An introduction to the conjugate gradient method without the agonizing pain. Technical report, Carnegie Mellon University.

[Shoemake et al., 1992] Shoemake, K. and Duff, T. (1992). Matrix animation and polar decomposition. In *Proceedings of the conference on Graphics interface '92*, pages 258–264, San Francisco, CA, USA. Morgan Kaufmann Publishers Inc.

[Sigg et al., 2003] Sigg, C., Peikert, R., and Gross, M. (2003). Signed distance transform using graphics hardware. In *Proceedings of IEEE Visualization*, pages 83–90, Seattle, WA, USA. IEEE Computer Society Press.

[Somchaipeng et al., 2004] Somchaipeng, K., Erleben, K., and Sporring, J. (2004). A multi-scale singularity bounding volume hierarchy. DIKU technical report 04/08, Department of Computer Science, University of Copenhagen.

[Song et al., 2003] Song, P., Pang, J.-S., and Kumar, V. (2003). A semi-implicit time-stepping model for frictional compliant contact problems. Submitted to International Journal of Numerical Methods for Engineering. Avaible at `www.mts.jhu.edu/~pang/dcm_kps.pdf`.

[Sørensen, 2005] Sørensen, A. M. K. (2005). Personal Communication.

[Spiegel, 1968] Spiegel, M. R. (1968). *Mathematical Handbook of Formulas and Tables*. Schaum's outline series. McGraw-Hill.

[Stewart et al., 1996] Stewart, D. and Trinkle, J. (1996). An implicit time-stepping scheme for rigid body dynamics with inelastic collisions and coulomb friction. *International Journal of Numerical Methods in Engineering*.

[Stewart et al., 2000] Stewart, D. and Trinkle, J. (2000). An implicit time-stepping scheme for rigid body dynamics with coulomb friction. *IEEE International Conference on Robotics and Automation*, pages 162–169.

[Stewart, 2000] Stewart, D. E. (2000). Rigid-body dynamics with friction and impact. *SIAM Review*, 42(1):3–39.

[Stokes, 1845] Stokes, G. G. (1845). On the theories of the internal friction of fluids in motion. *Trans. Cambridge Philos. Soc.*, 8.

[Sud et al., 2004] Sud, A., Otaduy, M. A., and Manocha, D. (2004). Difi: Fast 3D distance field computation using graphics hardware. *Computer Graphics Forum*, 23(3):557–566. `gamma.cs.unc.edu/DiFi/`.

[Sundaraj et al., 2000] Sundaraj, K. and Laugier, C. (2000). Fast contact localisation of moving deformable polyhedras. In *IEEE Int. Conference on Control, Automation, Robotics and Vision*, Singapore (SG).

[Teran et al., 2003] Teran, J., Blemker, S., Hing, V. N. T., and Fedkiw, R. (2003). Finite volume methods for the simulation of skeletal muscle. In Breen, D. and Lin, M., editors, *ACM SIGGRAPH/Eurographics Symposium on Computer Animation (SCA)*, pages 68–74.

[Teran et al., 2005] Teran, J., Sifakis, E., Blemker, S., Ng Thow Hing, V., Lau, C., and Fedkiw, R. (2005). Creating and simulating skeletal muscle from the visible human data set. *IEEE Transactions on Visualization and Computer Graphics*, 11:317–328.

[Terzopoulos et al., 1987] Terzopoulos, D., Platt, J., Barr, A., and Fleischer, K. (1987). Elastic deformable models. In *Computer Graphics*, volume 21, pages 205–214.

[Terzopoulos et al., 1994] Terzopoulos, D., Tu, X., and Grzeszczuk, R. (1994). Artificial fishes. *Artificial Life*, 1(4):327–351.

[Teschner et al., 2003] Teschner, M., B.H̃eidelberger, M. M., Pomeranets, D., and Gross, M. (2003). Optimized spatial hashing for collision detection of deformable objects. In *Proc. Vision, Modeling, Visualization*, pages 47–54, Munich, Germany.

[Teschner et al., 2004] Teschner, M., Heidelberger, B., Müller, M., and Gross, M. (2004). A versatile and robust model for geometrically complex deformable solids. In *Proc. of CGI*.

[Trinkle et al., 1995] Trinkle, J., Pang, J.-S., Sudarsky, S., and Lo, G. (1995). On dynamic multi-rigid-body contact problems with coulomb friction. Technical Report TR95-003, Texas A&M University, Department of Computer Science.

[Trinkle et al., 2001] Trinkle, J. C., Tzitzoutis, J., and Pang, J.-S. (2001). Dynamic multi-rigid-body systems with concurrent distributed contacts: Theory and examples. *Philosophical Trans. on Mathematical, Physical, and Engineering Sciences*, 359(1789):2575–2593.

[Tritton, 1988] Tritton, D. (1988). *Physical Fluid Dynamics*. Oxford University Press.

[Tzafestas et al., 1996] Tzafestas, C. and Coiffet, P. (1996). Real-time collision detection using spherical octrees : Vr application.

[Verlet, 1967] Verlet, L. (1967). Computer "experiments" on classical fluids. I. Thermodynamical properties of Lennard-Jones molecules. *Physical Review*, 159(1):98–103.

[Vinter, 2005] Vinter, B. (2005). Personal Communication.

[Volino et al., 1995] Volino, P. and Magnenat Thalmann, N. (1995). Collision and self-collision detection: Efficient and robust solutions for highly deformable surfaces. In Terzopoulos, D. and Thalmann, D., editors, *Computer Animation and Simulation '95*, pages 55–65. Springer-Verlag.

[Volino et al., 2000] Volino, P. and Magnenat-Thalmann, N. (2000). *Virtual Clothing, Theory and Practice*. Springer-Verlag Berlin Heidelbarg.

[Volino et al., 1998] Volino, P. and Thalmann, N. M. (1998). Collision and self-collision detection: Efficient and robust solutions for highly deformable surfaces. Technical report, MIRALab.

[Vortex, 2005] Vortex (2005). CMLabs Vortex. `www.cm-labs.com/products/vortex/`.

[Wagenaar, 2001] Wagenaar, J. (2001). *Physically Based Simulation and Visualization: A particle-base approach*. PhD thesis, the Mærsk Mc-Kinney Møller Institute for Production Technology.

[Watt et al., 1992] Watt, A. and Watt, M. (1992). *Advanced Animation and Rendering Techniques, Theory and Practice*. Addison-Wesley.

[Weickert et al., 1997] Weickert, J., Ishikawa, S., and Imiya, A. (1997). On the history of Gaussian scale-space axiomatics. In Sporring, J., Nielsen, M., Florack, L., and Johansen, P., editors, *Gaussian Scale-Space Theory*, chapter 4, pages 45–59. Kluwer Academic Publishers, Dordrecht, The Netherlands.

[Weisstein, 2005a] Weisstein, E. (2005a). World of physics. `scienceworld.wolfram.com/physics/`.

[Weisstein, 2004] Weisstein, E. W. (2004). Frobenius norm. *From MathWorld–A Wolfram Web Resource*. `mathworld.wolfram.com/FrobeniusNorm.html`.

[Weisstein, 2005b] Weisstein, E. W. (2005b). Mathworld–the web's most extensive mathematics resource. `www.mathworld.com`.

[Wellman, 1993] Wellman, C. (1993). Inverse kinematics and geometric constraints for articulated figure manipulation. Master's thesis, Simon Fraser University.

[Welzl, 1991] Welzl, E. (1991). Smallest enclosing disks (balls and ellipsoids). In Maurer, H., editor, *New Results and New Trends in Computer Science*, LNCS. Springer.

[Wilhelms et al., 2001] Wilhelms, J. and Gelder, A. V. (2001). Fast and easy reach-cone joint limits. *Journal of Graphics Tools*, 6(2):27–41.

[Witkin et al., 1994] Witkin, A. P. and Heckbert, P. S. (1994). Using particles to sample and control implicit surfaces. In *Proceedings of the 21st annual conference on Computer Graphics and Interactive Techniques*, pages 269–277. ACM Press.

[Zachmann, 1998] Zachmann, G. (1998). Rapid collision detection by dynamically aligned dop-trees.

[Zachmann et al., 2003a] Zachmann, G. and Knittel, G. (2003a). An architecture for hierarchical collision detection. *WSCG*, 11(1). `www.gabrielzachmann.org`.

[Zachmann et al., 2003b] Zachmann, G. and Langetepe, E. (2003b). Geometric data structures for computer graphics. SIGGRAPH 2003 course notes.

[Zienkiewicz et al., 2000] Zienkiewicz, O. and Taylor, R. (2000). *The Finite Element Method: The Basis*, volume 1. Butterworth-Heinemann, 5th edition.

Index